MILITARY AIRCRAFT MARKINGS 2020
Howard J Curtis

Crécy Publishing Ltd

This 41st edition published by Crécy Publishing Ltd 2020

ISBN 9781910809389

Printed in Bulgaria by Multiprint

Crecy Publishing Ltd
1a Ringway Trading Est
Shadowmoss Rd
Manchester
M22 5LH
Tel +44 (0)161 499 0024
www.crecy.co.uk

Front cover:
Bombardier Sentinel R1 ASTOR ZJ692
seen here July 16 2018 at Fairford,
United Kingdom.
Copyright: Matthieu Douhaire

Rear cover top to bottom:
Typhoon FGR4 ZJ920 wears the colour
scheme and markings worn by most of
the Typhoon fleet, with a white 'last
three' on the tail and no discernible
squadron markings.

Illustrating the practice of adding a
hyphen between the letter and the
digits of the registration, Tiger Moth I
NM-138/41 is registered as G-ANEW
and is one of several based at
Henstridge in Somerset.

Boeing KC-135R Stratotanker 58-0100
of the 351st Air Refuelling
Squadron/100th Air Refuelling Wing is
based at RAF Mildenhall and received
the extra code EP-A as part of the
commemorations for the 75th
Anniversary of D-Day.

CONTENTS

INTRODUCTION

This 41st annual edition of *abc Military Aircraft Markings*, follows the pattern of previous years and lists in alphabetical and numerical order the aircraft that carry a United Kingdom military registration and which are normally based, or might be seen, in the UK. It also includes airworthy and current RAF/RN/Army aircraft that are based permanently or temporarily overseas. Aircraft used as targets on MoD ranges to which access is restricted, and UK military aircraft that have been permanently grounded overseas and unlikely to return to Britain have generally been omitted.

Aircraft in UK military service which carry civil registrations are listed, as are historic aircraft wearing overseas markings which are based in the UK or likely to be seen in the UK. All aircraft carrying Irish military markings are listed in a separate section. Similarly, aircraft belonging to the armed forces or governments of foreign countries are listed, including American military aircraft based in the UK and Europe.

In the main, the registrations listed are those markings presently displayed on the aircraft. Where an aircraft carries a false registration, this is quoted in *italic type* and very often these registrations are carried by replicas, which are denoted by <R> after the type. The manufacturer and aircraft type are given, together with recent alternative, previous, secondary or civil identity (shown in round brackets). The operating unit and its based location, along with any known unit and code markings [in square brackets] are given as accurately as possible. Where aircraft carry special or commemorative markings, a $ indicates this. To help identification of RN bases and landing platforms on ships, a list of tail-letter codes with their appropriate name, helicopter code number, ship pennant number and type of vessel, is included, as is a helicopter code number/ship's tail-letter code grid cross-reference.

Up-to-date code changes, for example when aircraft move between units, might not be as printed here because of subsequent events, but code lists are regularly updated and uploaded to the 'Military Aircraft Markings' web site, www.militaryaircraftmarkings.co.uk, from which monthly UK updates can also be accessed. Airframes which will not appear in the next edition because of sale, accident, etc., have their fates, where known, shown in italic type in the *locations* column.

2019 saw further, significant retirements from the Royal Air Force inventory, with the final flight of the Tornado GR4 on 14 March 2019, while the Tucano T1 was retired on 25 October 2019. In the case of the latter, as this publication goes to press, many Tucanos are in the process of being dismantled ready for transport and export, with the closure of RAF Linton-on-Ouse to follow. Typhoon production for the RAF has now ended and Germany & Italy have also received their final examples within recent months; a handful of Typhoons remain at Warton, undelivered, but it remains to be seen if any of these will end up with the RAF. RAF Marham continues to receive F-35B Lightning IIs, with 17 Squadron, 207 Squadron and 617 Squadron all now operating the type. At Marham the machines are pooled between 207 and 617 Squadrons and the whole fleet is now receiving sequential codes a la Tornado GR4, along with lightning flashes on the tail. Portsmouth now has both carriers, HMS *Queen Elizabeth* and HMS *Prince of Wales* docked there currently. Turning to helicopters, the RAF's fleet of Chinooks continues to be upgraded to HC6A status at Boscombe Down, while the Navy is also receiving Merlin HC4s from the conversion line at Yeovil. Not to be outdone, the Army is due to receive at least 38 AH-64E Apaches and a considerable number of its Apache AH1 fleet is now with Boeing in the USA, to be consumed as part of this process. Turning to training aircraft, the planned fleets of Prefect, Texan II and Phenom along with Juno and Jupiter helicopters have all been reached and training on the new Texan T1 got fully under way at RAF Valley in late 2019, with the former Tucano squadron, 72 Squadron, now operating the type. 2019 saw the first flight of a RAF Poseidon MRA1 on 13 July, followed by the first handover in the USA on 29 October. Currently three aircraft have flown and the first delivery to RAF Lossiemouth is expected in 2020. For QinetiQ 2019 saw its whole fleet put on the UK civil register, using the G-ETP sequence.

Across Europe, types such as the F-16, Alpha Jet, Transall C-160, Tornado and Mirage 2000 continue to be retired, while the F-35 Lightning population is now substantial, albeit without Turkish examples. The NATO A400M and Airbus 330MRTT fleet will see its first deliveries shortly, with one of the former already wearing Luxembourg Armed Forces titles. The Airbus H145 and H160 lines look good for many years ahead as these types, along with the NH-90 and AW101 continue to enter service. Boeing has had a troubled year but KC-46A deliveries to 22 ARW at McConnell AFB have now reached 20, with other units also picking up examples of the type. US Navy P-8A Poseidons and C-130J Hercules IIs continue to replace the dwindling P-3 Orion and C-130T Hercules fleets.

As with 2018, 2019 was another year in which there were few notable accidents, which is pleasing to report.

You can find 'MAM' on Facebook at www.facebook.com/MilitaryAircraftMarkings, on Twitter (@HJCurtisMAM) as well as on the 'MAM' web site, www.militaryaircraftmarkings.co.uk.

ACKNOWLEDGEMENTS

The compiler wishes to thank the many people who have taken the trouble to send comments, additions, deletions and other useful information since the publication of the previous edition of Military Aircraft Markings. In particular the following individuals: David Charles, Martin Condon, Glyn Coney, Ben Dunnell, Graham Gaff, Ian Grinter, Kevin Herpe, Norman Hibberd, Doug MacDonald, Peter R March, Alan Mawman, Tony McCarthy, Mike Phipp, Mark Ray, Ben Sadler, Tony Sinclair, David Thompson, Ian Thompson and Mike Tighe.

The 2020 edition has also relied upon the printed publications and/or associated internet web-sites as follows: Aerodata Quantum+, 'Aeroplane' magazine, Airfields Google Group, 'Air Forces Monthly' magazine, Aviation Heritage UK/Lloyd P Robinson, CAA G-INFO Web Site, Coningsby Aviation Site, Delta Reflex, EGHH Google Group, Fighter Control, 'FlyPast' magazine, Humberside Air Review, Joe Baugher's Home Page, Mildenhall and Lakenheath Movements Group (SMAS), Brian Pickering/'Military Aviation Review', Mil Spotters' Forum, NAMAR Group, The Official RAF Leeming Spotters' Group (Facebook), Planebase NG, RAF Shawbury Group, Scotavnet Google Group, Scramble' magazine, Souairport group, South West of England Aviation Movements (Facebook), Tom McGhee/UK Serials Resource Centre, the late Mick Boulanger/Wolverhampton Aviation Group and 'Wrecks & Relics'.

Information shown is believed to be correct at 24 February 2020.

HJC February 2020

Note: The compiler will be pleased to receive comments, corrections and further information for inclusion in subsequent editions of Military Aircraft Markings and the monthly up-date of additions and amendments. Please send your information to Military Aircraft Markings, Crécy Publishing Ltd, 1a Ringway trading Estate, Shadowmoss Road, Manchester M22 5LH or by e-mail to admin@aviation-links.co.uk.

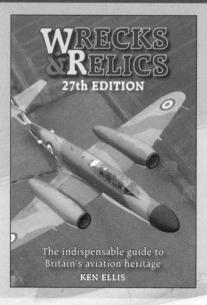

Wrecks & Relics 27th Edition

Ken Ellis

Wrecks & Relics is renowned as the go-to source charting the highlights, changes and trends in the preservation of the aviation heritage of the British Isles. With in-depth coverage of more than 700 locations across the UK and Ireland, it charts over 5,000 aircraft including their potted histories, build and arrival dates.

Wrecks & Relics is the only publication required to discover the incredible aeronautical treasures found across the United Kingdom and in Ireland. It provides a trusted, comprehensive rundown of museums and their exhibits – static or flying – workshops, military 'gate guardians', stored and instructional airframes. It also reveals redundant airframes being used for the most unlikely of purposes, including for 'glamping' and at paint-ball sites.

It is profusely illustrated and fully indexed. Whether it travels in the car or sits on the book shelf, *Wrecks & Relics* will prove to be a vital and faithful companion to the aviation heritage of the British Isles which will be referred to again and again.

ISBN: 9781910809396 **£18.95**   **Available May 2020**

Available at all good book shops, enthusiast shops and pilot shops
Crecy Publishing Ltd
1a Ringway Trading Est, Shadowmoss Rd, Manchester M22 5LH
Tel +44 (0)161 499 0024
www.crecy.co.uk

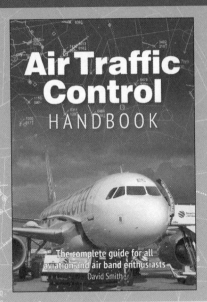

Air Traffic Control Handbook

David Smith

First published in 1986 as *Air Band Radio Guide,* air traffic controller David J Smith's *Air Traffic Control Handbook* is now in its 10th edition. The accessible and comprehensive guide to modern ATC incorporates recent changes in procedures, radio frequencies and call signs. The intricacies of air traffic control and its jargon are clearly explained alongside details of oceanic control, airfield visual aids, airport procedures and emergencies, enabling the reader to locate and interpret what is going on in the airways and airspace overhead. Covering many long-established ATC procedures and protocols, *Air Traffic Control Handbook* is a unique and invaluable insider's guide to Air Traffic Control which will appeal equally to civil and military aviation enthusiasts, pilots, aviation professionals and anyone considering a career in ATC.

ISBN: 9780859791830 **£17.95**

$	Aircraft in special markings
AAC	Army Air Corps
AACS	Airborne Air Control Squadron
AC	Air Cadets
ACCGS	Air Cadets Central Gliding School
ACS	Air Control Squadron
ACW	Air Control Wing
ADF	Air Defence Force
ADSU	Apache Depth Support Unit
AEF	Air Experience Flight
AESS	Air Engineering & Survival School
AEW	Airborne Early Warning
AFB	Air Force Base
AFD	Air Fleet Department
AFRC	Air Force Reserve Command
AG	Airlift Group
AGA	Academia General del Aire (General Air Academy)
AGS	Air Ground Surveillance
AK	Alaska
AL	Alabama
AMD-BA	Avions Marcel Dassault-Breguet Aviation
AMG	Aircraft Maintenance Group
AM&SU	Aircraft Maintenance & Storage Unit
AMRO	Aircraft Maintenance and Repair Organisation
AMW	Air Mobility Wing
ANG	Air National Guard
AR	Arkansas
ARS	Air Refueling Squadron
ARW	Air Refueling Wing
AS	Airlift Squadron/Air Squadron
ATC	Air Training Corps
ATCC	Air Traffic Control Centre
AVDEF	Aviation Defence Service
Avn	Aviation
AW	AgustaWestland/Airlift Wing/Armstrong Whitworth Aircraft
AWC	Air Warfare Centre
BAC	British Aircraft Corporation
BAe	British Aerospace
BAPC	British Aviation Preservation Council (now known as Aviation Heritage UK)
BATUK	British Army Training Unit Kenya
BATUS	British Army Training Unit Suffield
BBMF	Battle of Britain Memorial Flight
BDRF	Battle Damage Repair Flight
BDRT	Battle Damage Repair Training
Be	Beech
Bf	Bayerische Flugzeugwerke
BG	Bomber Group
BGA	British Gliding & Soaring Association
bk	black (squadron colours and markings)
bl	blue (squadron colours and markings)
Blt	Bojová letka (attack squadron)
BP	Boulton & Paul/Boulton Paul
br	brown (squadron colours and markings)
BS	Bomber Squadron
BUPERS SDC	Bureau of Personel Sea Duty Component
B-V	Boeing-Vertol
BW	Bomber Wing
CA	California
CAARP	Co-operative des Ateliers Air de la Région Parisienne
CAC	Commonwealth Aircraft Corporation
CACG	Command and Control Group
CAE	Centro Addastramento Equipaggi (Crew Training Centre)
CASA	Construcciones Aeronautics SA
CATS	Cassidian Aviation Training Services
CC	County Council
CC Air	Competence Centre Air
CCF	Combined Cadet Force/Canadian Car & Foundry Company
CEAM	Centre d'Expertise Aérienne Militaire (Centre of Military Air Expertise)

CEMAST	Centre of Excellence in Engineering & Manufacturing Advanced Skills Training
CEPA	Centre d'Expérimentation Pratique de l'Aéronautique Navale
CFAMI	Centre de Formation Aérienne Militaire Initiale de Salon
CFIA	Centre de Formation Interarmées NH.90
CFS	Central Flying School
CIEH	Centre d'Instruction des Equipages d'Hélicoptères
CHFMU	Commando Helicopter Force Maintenance Unit
CinC	Commander in Chief
CinCLANT	Commander in Chief Atlantic
CLV	Centrum Leteckeho Vycviku (Air Training Centre)
CMU	Central Maintenance Unit
Co	Company
CO	Colorado
COMALAT	Commandement de l'Aviation Légère de l'Armée de Terre
Comp	Composite with
CT	Connecticut
CV	Chance-Vought
D-BA	Daimler-Benz Aerospace
D-BD	Dassault-Breguet Dornier
D&G	Dumfries and Galloway
DCTT	Defence College of Technical Training
DE	Delaware
DE&S	Defence Equipment and Support
DEFTS	Defence Elementary Flying Training School
DEODS	Defence Explosives Ordnance Disposal School
Det	Detachment
DFTDC	Defence Fire Training and Development Centre
DGA	Délégation Générale de l'Armement
DH	de Havilland
DHC	de Havilland Canada
DHFS	Defence Helicopter Flying School
DMS	Defence Movements School
DS&TL	Defence Science & Technology Laboratory
DSAE	Defence School of Aeronautical Engineering
DSEME	Defence School of Electro-Mechanical Engineering
DSG	Defence Support Group
DSMarE	Defence School of Marine Engineering
Dvlt	Dopravná vrtul'niková letka (Helicopter Transport Squadron)
EA	Escadron Aérien (Air Squadron)
EAAT	Escadrille Avions de l'Armée de Terre
EAC	Ecole de l'Aviation de Chasse (Fighter Aviation School)
EALAT	Ecole de l'Aviation Légère de l'Armée de Terre
EAP	European Aircraft Project
EAT	Ecole de l'Aviation de Transport (Transport Aviation School)
EC	Escadre de Chasse (Fighter Wing)
E-CATS	EADS Cognac Aviation Training Services
ECG	Electronic Combat Group
ECM	Electronic Counter Measures
ECS	Electronic Countermeasures Squadron
EdC	Escadron de Convoyage
EDCA	Escadron de Détection et de Control Aéroportée (Airborne Detection & Control Sqn)
EE	English Electric/Escadrille Electronique
EEA	Escadron Electronique Aéroporté
EFA	Ecole Franco Allemande
EFTS	Elementary Flying Training School
EH	Escadron d'Helicoptères (Helicopter Squadron)
EHADT	Escadrille Helicoptères de l'Armée de Terre
EHI	European Helicopter Industries
EKW	Eidgenössiches Konstruktionswerkstätte
el	Eskadra Lotnicza (Air Sqn)
EL	Escadre de Liaison (Liaison Wing)
elt	Eskadra Lotnictwa Taktycznego (Tactical Air Squadron)
eltr	Eskadra Lotnictwa Transportowego (Air Transport Squadron)
EMA	East Midlands Airport
EMB	Ecoles Militaires de Bourges
EMVO	Elementaire Militaire Vlieg Opleiding (Elementary Flying Training)
EoN	Elliot's of Newbury
EPAA	Ecole de Pilotage Elementaire de l'Armée de l'Air (Air Force Elementary Flying School)

EPNER	Ecole du Personnel Navigant d'Essais et de Reception
ER	Escadre de Reconnaissance (Reconnaissance Wing)
ERV	Escadron de Ravitaillement en Vol (Aerial Refuelling Squadron)
ERVTS	Escadron de Ravitaillement en Vol et de Transport Stratégique (Air Refuelling and Strategic Transport Squadron]
ES	Escadrille de Servitude
ESAM	Ecole Supérieur d'Application du Matériel
Esc	Escuadron (Squadron)
ESHE	Ecole de Spécialisation sur Hélicoptères Embarqués (School of Specialisation on Embarked Helicopters)
Esk	Eskadrile/Eskadrille (Squadron)
Esq	Esquadra (Squadron)
ET	Escadre de Transport (Transport Wing)
ETED	Escadron de Transformation des Equipages Mirage 2000D
ETO	Escadron de Transition Operationnelle (Operational Transition Squadron)
ETPS	Empire Test Pilots' School
ETR	Escadron de Transformation Rafale
ETS	Engineering Training School/Escadron de Transport Stratégique
ETTL	Escadre de Transport Tactique et Logistique (Tactical and Logistics Transport Wing)
EVAA	Ecole de Voltige de l'Armée de l'Air (French Air Force Aerobatics School)
FAA	Fleet Air Arm (UK)/Federal Aviation Administration (USA)
FACO	Final Assembly & Check Out
FASGW	Future Anti-Surface Guided Weapon
FBS	Flugbereitschaftstaffel (Flight Readiness Squadron)
FBW	Fly-by-wire
FC	Forskokcentralen (Flight Centre)
FE	Further Education
FETC	Fire and Emergency Training Centre
ff	Front fuselage
FG	Fighter Group
FH	Fairchild-Hiller
FI	Falkland Islands
FJWOEU	Fast Jet & Weapons Operational Evaluation Unit
FL	Florida
FLO	Forsvarets Logistikk Organisasjon (Defence Logistics Organisation)
FlSt	Fliegerstaffel (Flight Squadron)
Flt	Flight
FMA	Fabrica Militar de Aviones
FMV	Forsvarets Materielwerk (Defence Material Works)
FS	Fighter Squadron
FTS	Flying Training School
FTW	Flying Training Wing
Fw	Focke Wulf
FW	Fighter Wing/FlugWerk/Foster Wickner
FY	Fiscal Year
GA	Georgia
GAF	Government Aircraft Factory
GAL	General Aircraft Ltd
GAM	Groupe Aerien Mixte (Composite Air Group)
GAM/STAT	Groupement Aéromobile/Section Technique de l'Armée de Terre
gd	gold (squadron colours and markings)
GD	General Dynamics
GEA	Gruppo Efficienza Aeromobili (Italian AF)/Gruppo Esplorazione Aeromarittima (GdiF)
GEM	Grupo de Escuelas de Matacán (Matacán Group of Schools)
GI	Ground Instruction/Groupement d'Instruction (Instructional Group)
GMS	Glider Maintenance Section
gn	green (squadron colours and markings)
GRD	Gruppe fur Rustunggdienste (Group for Service Preparation)
GT	Grupo de Transporte (Transport Wing)
GTT	Grupo de Transporte de Tropos (Troop Carrier Wing)
gy	grey (squadron colours and markings)
HAF	Historic Aircraft Flight
HAPS	High Altitude Pseudo-Satellite
HavLLv	Hävittäjälentolaivue
HC	Helicopter Combat Support Squadron
HekoP	Helikopteripataljoona (Helicopter Battalion)
HF	Historic Flying Ltd
HI	Hawaii

HK	Helikopterikomppannia (Helicopter Company)
Hkp.Bat	Helikopter Bataljon (Helicopter Battalion)
HMA	Helicopter Maritime Attack
HMS	Her Majesty's Ship
HP	Handley-Page
HQ	Headquarters
HS	Hawker Siddeley
HSG	Hubschraubergeschwader (Helicopter Squadron)
IA	Iowa
IAF	Israeli Air Force
IAP	International Airport
IL	Illinois
IlmaStk	IlmataiStelukeskus
IN	Indiana
IntHubschr-	Internationales Hubschrauberausbildungszentrum
AusbZ	(International Helicopter Training Centre)
IOW	Isle Of Wight
IWM	Imperial War Museums
JADTEU	Joint Air Delivery Test and Evaluation Unit
JARTS	Joint Aircraft Recovery & Transportation Sqn
JFACTSU	Joint Forward Air Control Training & Standards Unit
JHC	Joint Helicopter Command
JMRC	Joint Multinational Readiness Centre
KHR	Kampfhubschrauberregiment (Combat Helicopter Regiment)
Kridlo	Wing
KS	Kansas
LA	Louisiana
lbvr	letka Bitevnich Vrtulníků (Attack Helicopter Squadron)
Letka	Squadron
LTDB	Lufttransportdienst des Bundes (Federal Air Transport Services)
LTG	Lufttransportgeschwader (Air Transport Wing)
lTHSSta	leichte Transporthubschrauberstaffel
LTO	Letalska Transportni Oddelek (Air Transport Department)
LtSt	Lufttransport Staffel
LTV	Ling-Temco-Vought
LVG	Luftwaffen Versorgungs Geschwader (Air Force Maintenance Wing)/Luft Verkehrs Gesellschaft
LZO	Letecky Zku ební Odbor (Aviation Test Department)
m	multi-coloured (squadron colours and markings)
MA	Massachusetts
MADG	Marshall Aerospace & Defence Group
MAPK	Mira Anachestisis Pantos Kerou (All Weather Interception Sqn)
MBB	Messerschmitt Bolkow-Blohm
MCAS	Marine Corps Air Station
McD	McDonnell Douglas
MD	Maryland
MDMF	Merlin Depth Maintenance Facility
Med	Medical
MFG	Marine Flieger Geschwader (Naval Air Wing)
MFSU	Merlin Depth Forward Support Unit
MH	Max Holste
MI	Maritime Interdiction/Michigan
MIB	Military Intelligence Battalion
MiG	Mikoyan — Gurevich
MMF	(European) Multinational Multi-Role Tanker Transport Fleet
MN	Minnesota
MO	Missouri
Mod	Modified
MoD	Ministry of Defence
MPSU	Multi-Platform Support Unit
MR	Maritime Reconnaissance
MRH	Multi-role Helikopters
M&RU	Marketing & Recruitment Unit
MS	Mississippi/Morane-Saulnier
MT	Montana
MTHR	Mittlerer Transporthubschrauber Regiment (Medium Transport Helicopter Regiment)
MTM	Mira Taktikis Metaforon (Tactical Transport Sqn)
NA	North American

NACDS	Naval Air Command Driving School
NAEW&CF	NATO Airborne Early Warning & Control Force
NAF	Naval Air Facility
NAS	Naval Air Squadron (UK)/Naval Air Station (US)
NATO	North Atlantic Treaty Organisation
NAWC	Naval Air Warfare Center
NAWC-AD	Naval Air Warfare Center Aircraft Division
NBC	Nuclear, Biological and Chemical
ND	North Dakota
NDMA	Norwegian Defence Material Agency
NE	North-East/Nebraska
NFH	NATO Frigate Helicopter
NH	New Hampshire
NI	Northern Ireland
NJ	New Jersey
NM	New Mexico
NV	Nevada
NY	New York
NYARC	North Yorks Aircraft Restoration Centre
OEU	Operational Evaluation Unit
OFMC	Old Flying Machine Company
OGMA	Oficinas Gerais de Material Aeronautico
OH	Ohio
OK	Oklahoma
or	orange (squadron colours and markings)
OSAC	Operational Support Airlift Command
OSBL	Oddelek Sholskih Bojni Letal (Training & Combat School)
OT&E	Operational Test & Evaluation
P2MF	Puma 2 Maintenance Flight
PA	Pennsylvania
PAS	Presidential Airlift Squadron
PAT	Priority Air Transport Detachment
PBN	Pilatus Britten-Norman
PDSH	Puma Depth Support Hub
PLM	Pulk Lotnictwa Mysliwskiego (Fighter Regiment)
pr	purple (squadron colours and markings)
PR	Puerto Rico
r	red (squadron colours and markings)
R	Replica
RAeS	Royal Aeronautical Society
RAF	Royal Aircraft Factory/Royal Air Force
RAFC	Royal Air Force College
RAFM	Royal Air Force Museum
RAFGSA	Royal Air Force Gliding and Soaring Association
RE	Royal Engineers
Regt	Regiment
REME	Royal Electrical & Mechanical Engineers
rf	Rear fuselage
RFA	Royal Fleet Auxiliary
RHC	Régiment d'Helicoptères de Combat (Combat Helicopter Regiment)
RHFS	Régiment d'Helicoptères des Forces Spéciales (Special Forces Helicopter Regiment)
RI	Rhode Island
RJAF	Royal Jordanian Air Force
RM	Royal Marines
RMB	Royal Marines Base
RN	Royal Navy
RNAS	Royal Naval Air Station
RNGSA	Royal Navy Gliding and Soaring Association
RPAS	Remotely Piloted Air System
RQS	Rescue Squadron
R-R	Rolls-Royce
RS	Reid & Sigrist/Reconnaissance Squadron
RSV	Reparto Sperimentale Volo (Experimental Flight School)
RTP	Reduction To Produce
RW	Reconnaissance Wing
SA	Scottish Aviation
SAAB	Svenska Aeroplan Aktieboleg
SAAE	School of Army Aeronautical Engineering

SAC	Strategic Airlift Capability
SAL	Scottish Aviation Limited
SAR	Search and Rescue
Saro	Saunders-Roe
SARTU	Search and Rescue Training Unit
SC	South Carolina
SCW	Strategic Communications Wing
SD	South Dakota
SEPECAT	Société Européenne de Production de l'avion Ecole de Combat et d'Appui Tactique
SFB	Space Force Base
SFDO	School of Flight Deck Operations
SHAPE	Supreme Headquarters Allied Powers Europe
si	silver (squadron colours and markings)
SKAMG	Sea King Aircraft Maintenance Group
Skv	Skvadron (Squadron)
SLK	Stíhacie Letecké Kridlo (Fighter Air Wing)
slt	stíhací letka (Fighter Squadron)
SLV	School Licht Vliegwezen (Flying School)
Sm	Smaldeel (Squadron)
SNCAN	Société Nationale de Constructions Aéronautiques du Nord
SOG	Special Operations Group
SOS	Special Operations Squadron
SoTT	School of Technical Training
SOW	Special Operations Wing
SPAD	Société Pour les Appareils Deperdussin
SPP	Strojirny Prvni Petilesky
Sqn	Squadron
Sz.D.REB	'Szentgyörgyi Desző' Harcászati Repülö Bázis
TA	Territorial Army
TAP	Transporten Avio Polk (Air Transport Regiment)
TASF(N)	Tornado Aircraft Servicing Flight (North)
TAZLS	Technische Ausbildungs Zentrum Luftwaffe Süd (TAubZLwSüd, Technical Training Centre South)
TES	Test and Evaluation Squadron
TFC	The Fighter Collection
TGp	Test Groep
TH	Transporthelikopter
TIARA	Tornado Integrated Avionics Research Aircraft
tl	taktická letka (Tactical Squadron)
TLG	Taktisches Luftwaffegeschwader (Air Force Tactical Squadron)
TMU	Typhoon Maintenance Unit
TN	Tennessee
Tr AB	Transport Aviation Brigade
TS	Test Squadron
ts	transportnia speciální letka (special transport squadron)
TsAGI	Tsentral'ny Aerogidrodinamicheski Instut (Central Aero & Hydrodynamics Institute)
TSF	Tucano Servicing Flight
TsLw	Technische Schule der Luftwaffe (Luftwaffe Technical School)
TST	Tornado Support Team
TTH	Tactical Transport Helicopter
TukiLLv	Tukilentolaivue
TW	Test Wing
TX	Texas
UAS	University Air Squadron
UAV	Unmanned Air Vehicle
Überwg	Überwachungsgeschwader
UK	United Kingdom
US	United States
USAF	United States Air Force
USAFE	United States Air Forces in Europe
USAREUR	US Army Europe
USCGS	US Coast Guard Station
USEUCOM	United States European Command
USMC	United States Marine Corps
USN	United States Navy
USNWTSPM	United States Navy Test Pilots School
USW	University of South Wales
UT	Utah

VA	Virginia
VAAC	Vectored thrust Advanced Aircraft flight Control
VFW	Vereinigte Flugtechnische Werke
VGS	Volunteer Gliding Squadron
vlt	výcviková letka (training squadron)
VMGR	Marine Aerial Refuelling Squadron
VMGRT	Marine Aerial Refuelling/Transport Training Squadron
VQ	Fleet Air Reconnaissance Squadron
VR	Fleet Logistic Support Squadron
vrl	vrtulníková letka (helicopter squadron)
VS	Vickers-Supermarine
w	white (squadron colours and markings)
WA	Washington
WCM	Wildcat Contractor Maintenance
Wg	Wing
WHL	Westland Helicopters Ltd
WI	Wisconsin
WLT	Weapons Loading Training
WMF	Wildcat Maintenance Facility
WR-ALC	Warner Robins Air Logistics Complex
WRS	Weather Reconnaissance Squadron
WS	Westland
WSK	Wytwornia Sprzetu Kominikacyjnego
WST	Wildcat Support Team
WTD	Wehrtechnische Dienstelle (Technical Support Unit)
WV	West Virginia
WW2	World War II
WY	Wyoming
WZM	Wildcat Zonal Maintenance
y	yellow (squadron colours and markings)
zDL	základna Dopravního Letectva (Air Transport Base)
zL	základna Letectva (Air Force Base)
zSL	základna Speciálního Letectva (Training Air Base)
zTL	základna Taktického Letectva (Tactical Air Base)
zVrL	základna Vrtulníkového Letectva (Helicopter Air Base)

A Guide to the Location of Operational Military Bases in the UK

This section is to assist the reader to locate the places in the United Kingdom where operational military aircraft (including helicopters and gliders) are based.

The alphabetical order listing gives each location in relation to its county and to its nearest classified road(s) (*by* means adjoining; *of* means close to), together with its approximate direction and mileage from the centre of a nearby major town or city. Some civil airports are included where active military units are also based, but **excluded** are MoD sites with non-operational aircraft (e.g. *gate guardians*), the bases of privately-owned civil aircraft that wear military markings and museums. For GPS users, Latitude and Longitude are also listed.

User	Base name	County/Region	Location [Lat./long.]	Distance/direction from (town)
Army	Abingdon	Oxfordshire	W by B4017, W of A34 [N51°41'16" W001°18'58"]	5m SSW of Oxford
Army	Aldergrove/Belfast Airport	Co Antrim	W by A26 [N54°39'27" W006°12'578"]	13m W of Belfast
RAF	Barkston Heath	Lincolnshire	W by B6404, S of A153 [N52°57'46" W000°33'38"]	5m NNE of Grantham
RAF	Benson	Oxfordshire	E by A423 [N51°36'55" W001°05'45"]	1m NE of Wallingford
QinetiQ/ RAF	Boscombe Down	Wiltshire	S by A303, W of A338 [N51°09'12" W001°45'04"]	6m N of Salisbury
RAF	Brize Norton	Oxfordshire	W of A4095 [N51°45'00" W001°35'01"]	5m SW of Witney

User	Base name	County/Region	Location [Lat./long.]	Distance/direction from (town)
Marshall	Cambridge Airport/ Teversham	Cambridgeshire	S by A1303 [N52°12'18" E000°10'30"]	2m E of Cambridge
RAF	Coningsby	Lincolnshire	S of A153, W by B1192 [N53°05'35" W000°10'00"]	10m NW of Boston
DCAE	Cosford	Shropshire	W of A41, N of A464 [N52°38'25" W002°18'20"]	9m WNW of Wolverhampton
RAF	Cranwell	Lincolnshire	N by A17, S by B1429 [N53°01'49" W000°29'00"]	5m WNW of Sleaford
RN	Culdrose	Cornwall	E by A3083 [N50°05'08" W005°15'17"]	1m SE of Helston
USAF	Fairford	Gloucestershire	S of A417 [N51°41'01" W001°47'24"]	9m ESE of Cirencester
Standard-Aero	Fleetlands	Hampshire	E by A32 [N50°50'06" W001°10'07"]	2m SE of Fareham
RAF	Halton	Buckinghamshire	N of A4011, S of B4544 [N51°47'28" W000°44'11"]	4m ESE of Aylesbury
RAF	Kenley	Greater London	W of A22 [N51°18'20" W000°05'37"]	1m W of Warlingham
RAF	Kirknewton	Lothian	E by B7031, N by A70 [N55°52'32" W003°24'04"]	8m SW of Edinburgh
USAF	Lakenheath	Suffolk	W by A1065 [N52°24'33" E000°33'40"]	8m W of Thetford
RAF	Leeming	North Yorkshire	E by A1 [N54°17'33" W001°32'07"]	5m SW of Northallerton
RAF	Leuchars	Fife	E of A919 [N56°22'28" W002°51'50"]	7m SE of Dundee
RAF	Linton-on-Ouse	North Yorkshire	W of A19, E of A168 [N54°02'56" W001°15'10"]	9m NW of York
RAF	Lossiemouth	Grampian	W of B9135, S of B9040 [N57°42'22" W003°20'20"]	4m N of Elgin
RAF	Marham	Norfolk	N by A1122 [N52°38'54" E000°33'02"]	6m W of Swaffham
Army	Middle Wallop	Hampshire	S by A343 [N51°08'35" W001°34'14"]	6m SW of Andover
USAF	Mildenhall	Suffolk	S by A1101 [N52°21'42" E000°29'12"]	9m NNE of Newmarket
RAF	Northolt	Greater London	N by A40 [N51°33'11" W000°25'06"]	3m E of M40 jn 1
RAF	Odiham	Hampshire	E of A32 [N51°14'03" W000°56'34"]	2m S of M3 jn 5
RN	Predannack	Cornwall	W by A3083 [N50°00'07" W005°13'54"]	7m S of Helston
RAF	Scampton	Lincolnshire	W by A15 [N53°18'28" W000°33'04"]	6m N of Lincoln
RAF	Shawbury	Shropshire	W of B5063 [N52°47'53" W002°40'05"]	7m NNE of Shrewsbury
RAF	Syerston	Nottinghamshire	W by A46 [N53°01'22" W000°54'47"]	5m SW of Newark
RAF	Ternhill	Shropshire	SW by A41 [N52°52'24" W002°31'54"]	3m SW of Market Drayton
RAF/Army	Topcliffe	North Yorkshire	E of A167, W of A168 [N54°12'20" W001°22'55"]	3m SW of Thirsk
RAF	Valley	Gwynedd	S of A5 on Anglesey [N53°14'53" W004°32'06"]	5m SE of Holyhead
RAF	Waddington	Lincolnshire	E by A607, W by A15 [N53°09'58" W000°31'26"]	5m S of Lincoln
Army	Wattisham	Suffolk	N of B1078 [N52°07'38" E000°57'21"]	5m SSW of Stowmarket
RAF	Woodvale	Merseyside	W by A565 [N53°34'56" W003°03'24"]	5m SSW of Southport
RAF	Wittering	Cambridgeshire	W by A1, N of A47 [N52°36'52" W000°27'01"]	3m S of Stamford
RN	Yeovilton	Somerset	S by B3151, S of A303 [N51°00'30" W002°38'43"]	5m N of Yeovil

The Committee of Imperial Defence through its Air Committee introduced a standardised system of numbering aircraft in November 1912. The Air Department of the Admiralty was allocated the first batch 1-200 and used these to cover aircraft already in use and those on order. The Army was issued with the next block from 201-800, which included the number 304 which was given to the Cody Biplane now preserved in the Science Museum. By the outbreak of World War I, the Royal Navy was on its second batch of registrations 801-1600 and this system continued with alternating allocations between the Army and Navy until 1916 when number 10000, a Royal Flying Corps BE2C, was reached.

It was decided not to continue with five digit numbers but instead to start again from 1, prefixing RFC aircraft with the letter A and RNAS aircraft with the prefix N. The RFC allocations commenced with A1 an FE2D and before the end of the year had reached A9999 an Armstrong Whitworth FK8. The next group commenced with B1 and continued in logical sequence through the C, D, E and F prefixes. G was used on a limited basis to identify captured German aircraft, while H was the last block of wartime-ordered aircraft. To avoid confusion I was not used, so the new post-war machines were allocated registrations in the J range. A further minor change was made in the numbering system in August 1929 when it was decided to maintain four numerals after the prefix letter, thus omitting numbers 1 to 999. The new K series therefore commenced at K1000, which was allocated to an AW Atlas.

The Naval N prefix was not used in such a logical way. Blocks of numbers were allocated for specific types of aircraft such as seaplanes or flying-boats. By the late 1920s the sequence had largely been used up and a new series using the prefix S was commenced. In 1930 separate naval allocations were stopped and subsequent registrations were issued in the 'military' range which had by this time reached the K series. A further change in the pattern of allocations came in the L range. Commencing with L7272 numbers were issued in blocks with smaller blocks of registrations between not used. These were known as 'broken blocks'. As M had already been used as a suffix for Maintenance Command instructional airframes it was not used as a prefix. Although N had previously been used for naval aircraft it was used again for registrations allocated from 1937.

With the build-up to World War II, the rate of allocations quickly accelerated and the prefix R was being used when war was declared. The letters O and Q were not allotted, nor was S, which had been used up to S1865 for naval aircraft before integration into the RAF series. By 1940 the registration Z9999 had been reached, as part of a broken block, with the letters U and Y not used to avoid confusion.

The option to recommence registration allocation at A1000 was not taken up; instead it was decided to use an alphabetical two-letter prefix with three numerals running from 100 to 999. Thus, AA100 was allocated to a Blenheim IV and this two-letter, three-numeral registration system which started in 1940 continues today. The letters C, I, O, Q, U and Y were, with the exception of NC, not used. For various reasons the following letter combinations were not issued: DA, DB, DH, EA, GA to GZ, HA, HT, JE, JH, JJ, KR to KT, MR, NW, NZ, SA to SK, SV, TN, TR and VE. The first post-war registrations issued were in the VP range while the end of the WZs had been reached by the Korean War.

In January 1952 a civil servant at the then Air Ministry penned a memo to his superiors alerting them to the fact that a new military aircraft registration system would soon have to be devised. With allocations accelerating to accommodate a NATO response to the Korean War and a perceived Soviet threat building, he estimated that the end of the ZZs would quickly be reached. However, more than six decades later the allocations are only in the ZKs and at the present rate are unlikely to reach ZZ999 until the end of this century!

Military aircraft registrations are allocated by MoD Head Office and Corporate Services, where the Military Aircraft Register is maintained by the Military Aviation Authority. It should be pointed out that strictly the register places a space before the last three digits of the registration and, contrary to popular opinion, refers to them as 'registrations', not serials.

A change in policy in 2003 resulted in the use of the first 99 digits in the ZK sequence (ZK001 to ZK099), following on from ZJ999. The first of these, ZK001 to ZK004, were allocated to AgustaWestland Merlins. There is also a growing trend for 'out-of-sequence' registration numbers to be issued. At first this was to a manufacturer's prototype or development aircraft. However, following the Boeing C-17 Globemasters leased and subsequently purchased from Boeing (ZZ171-ZZ178), more allocations have been noted.

Since 2002 there has also been a new official policy concerning the use of military registration numbers on some types of UAV. 'Where a UAV is of modular construction the nationality and registration mark shall be applied to the fuselage of the vehicle or on the assembly forming the main part of the fuselage. To prevent the high usage of numbers for target drones which are eventually destroyed, a single registration mark (prefix) should be issued relating to the UAV type. The agency or service operating the target drone will be responsible for the identification of each individual UAV covered by that registration mark by adding a suffix.' This has resulted in the use of the same registration on a number of UAVs (or RPASs as they are now referred to) and drones with numbers following it - hence the appearance of ZZ420/001 etc. on Banshee drones. Aircraft using this system are denoted in the text by an asterisk (*).

A serial in *italics* denotes that it is not the genuine marking for that airframe.

Serial	Type (code/other identity)	Owner/operator, location or fate	Notes
168	Sopwith Tabloid Scout <R> (G-BFDE)	RAF Museum Reserve Collection, Stafford	
304	Cody Biplane (BAPC.62)	Science Museum, South Kensington	
471	RAF BE2a <R> (BAPC.321)	Montrose Air Station Heritage Centre	
687	RAF BE2c <R> (G-AWYI/*471*)	Privately owned, Sywell	
687	RAF BE2b <R> (BAPC.181)	RAF Museum, Hendon	
1264	Bristol Scout C <R> (G-FDHB)	Privately owned, Old Warden	
2345	Vickers FB5 Gunbus <R> (G-ATVP)	RAF Museum, Hendon	
2699	RAF BE2c	IWM Duxford	
2783	RAF BE2b <R> (BAPC.332)	Boscombe Down Aviation Collection, Old Sarum	
3066	Caudron GIII (G-AETA/9203M)	RAF Museum, Hendon	
5191	Morane-Saulnier Type N <R> (BAPC.472)	North-East Land, Sea & Air Museums, Usworth	
5964	DH2 <R> (BAPC.112)	Privately owned, Stretton on Dunsmore	
5964	DH2 <R> (G-BFVH)	Privately owned, Wickenby	
8359	Short 184 <ff>	FAA Museum, RNAS Yeovilton	
9828	Avro 504K <R> (*H1968*/BAPC.42)	Yorkshire Air Museum, stored Elvington	
9917	Sopwith Pup (G-EBKY/N5180)	The Shuttleworth Collection, Old Warden	
9970	RAF BE2c <R> (*6232*/BAPC.41)	Yorkshire Air Museum, Elvington	
A126	Nieuport 11 <R> (G-CILI)	Privately owned,	
A301	Morane BB (frame)	RAF Museum Reserve Collection, Stafford	
A653	Sopwith Pup <R> (*A7317*/BAPC.179)	Privately owned, Stow Maries, Essex	
A1452	Vickers FB5 Gunbus <R>	Spitfire Spares, Taunton, Somerset	
A1742	Bristol Scout D <R> (BAPC.38)	Aerospace Bristol, Filton	
A2767	RAF BE2e-1 <R> (G-CJZP)	WW1 Aviation Heritage Trust, Stow Maries	
A2943	RAF BE2e-1 <R> (G-CJZO)	WW1 Aviation Heritage Trust, Bicester	
A3930	RAF RE8 <R> (ZK-TVC)	RAF Museum, Hendon	
A4850	RAF SE5a <R> (BAPC.176)	Bygone Times Antique Warehouse, Eccleston, Lancs	
A6526	RAF FE2b <R> (BAPC.400)	RAF Museum, Hendon	
A7288	Bristol F2b Fighter <R> (BAPC.386)	Aerospace Bristol, Filton	
A8226	Sopwith 1½ Strutter <R> (G-BIDW)	RAF Museum, Cosford	
A8274	Sopwith 1½ Strutter <R> (BAPC.413)	WW1 Aviation Heritage Trust, Stow Maries	
B595	RAF SE5a <R> (G-BUOD) [W]	Privately owned, Defford	
B619	Sopwith 1½ Strutter <R> (BAPC.468)	RAF Manston History Museum	
B1474	Henry Farman F.20 <R>	WW1 Aviation Heritage Trust, Stow Maries	
B5539	Sopwith F.1 Camel <R>	Privately owned, Booker	
B5577	Sopwith F.1 Camel <R> (*D3419*/BAPC.59) [W]	*Repainted as B7320*	
B6401	Sopwith F.1 Camel <R> (G-AWYY/C1701)	FAA Museum, stored Cobham Hall, RNAS Yeovilton	
B7270	Sopwith F.1 Camel <R> (G-BFCZ)	Brooklands Museum, Weybridge	
B7320	Sopwith F.1 Camel <R> (*D3419/B5577*/BAPC.59) [P]	Montrose Air Station Heritage Centre	
C1096	Replica Plans SE5a <R> (G-ERFC)	Privately owned, Old Warden	
C1904	RAF SE5a <R> (G-PFAP) [Z]	Privately owned, Castle Bytham, Lincs	
C3009	Currie Wot (G-BFWD) [B]	Privately owned, Dunkeswell	
C3011	Phoenix Currie Super Wot (G-SWOT) [S]	Privately owned, Otherton, Staffs	
C3988	Sopwith 5F.1 Dolphin (BAPC.353) (comp D5329)	RAF Museum, Hendon	
C4451	Avro 504J <R> (BAPC.210)	Solent Sky, Southampton	
C4918	Bristol M1C <R> (G-BWJM)	The Shuttleworth Collection, Old Warden	
C4994	Bristol M1C <R> (G-BLWM)	RAF Museum, Cosford	
C5430	RAF SE5a <R> (G-CCXG) [V]	Privately owned, Wrexham	
C8996	RAF SE5a (G-ECAE/A2-25)	Privately owned, Milden	
C9533	RAF SE5a <R> (G-BUWE) [M]	Privately owned, Coventry	
D276	RAF SE5a <R> (BAPC.208) [A]	Prince's Mead Shopping Centre, Farnborough	
D1851	Sopwith F.1 Camel <R> (G-BZSC) [X]	The Shuttleworth Collection, Old Warden	
D3540	RAF SE5a <R> (N125QB) [K]	WW1 Aviation Heritage Trust, Old Warden	
D5649	Airco DH9	IWM Duxford	
D6447	Sopwith F.1 Camel <R> (BAPC.385)	Privately owned, Knutsford, Cheshire	

Notes	Serial	Type (code/other identity)	Owner/operator, location or fate
	D7560	Avro 504K	Science Museum, South Kensington
	D8096	Bristol F2b Fighter (G-AEPH) [D]	The Shuttleworth Collection, Old Warden
E449	Avro 504K (G-EBJE/9205M)	RAF Museum, Hendon
E2466	Bristol F2b Fighter (BAPC.165) [I]	RAF Museum, Hendon
E2581	Bristol F2b Fighter [13]	IWM Duxford
E2977	Avro 504K (G-EBHB)	Privately owned, Henlow
E3273	Avro 504K (H5199/BK892/ G-ACNB/G-ADEV/3118M)	The Shuttleworth Collection, Old Warden
E6655	Sopwith 7F.1 Snipe <R> (BAPC.348) [B]	RAF Museum, Hendon
E8894	Airco DH9 (G-CDLI)	Aero Vintage, Duxford
F141	RAF SE5a <R> (G-SEVA) [G]	Privately owned, Boscombe Down
F235	RAF SE5a <R> (G-BMDB) [B]	Privately owned, Stow Maries, Essex
F904	RAF SE5a (G-EBIA)	The Shuttleworth Collection, Old Warden
F904	RAF SE5a <R>	South Yorkshire Aircraft Museum, Doncaster
F938	RAF SE5a (G-EBIC/9208M)	RAF Museum, Hendon
F943	RAF SE5a <R> (G-BIHF) [S]	Privately owned, White Waltham
F943	RAF SE5a <R> (G-BKDT) [S]	Yorkshire Air Museum, Elvington
F1010	Airco DH9A [C]	RAF Museum, Hendon
F2211	Sopwith 1½ Strutter <R>	Privately owned, East Fortune
F2367	Sopwith 7F.1 Snipe <R> (ZK-SNI)	WW1 Aviation Heritage Trust, Stow Maries
F3556	RAF RE8	IWM Duxford
F5447	RAF SE5a <R> (G-BKER) [N]	Privately owned, Bridge of Weir
F5459	RAF SE5a <R> (G-INNY) [Y]	Privately owned, Sywell
F5475	RAF SE5a <R> (BAPC.250)	Brooklands Museum, Weybridge
F6314	Sopwith F.1 Camel (9206M) [B]	RAF Museum, Hendon
F8010	RAF SE5a <R> (G-BDWJ) [Z]	Privately owned, Langport, Somerset
F8614	Vickers FB27A Vimy IV <R> (G-AWAU)	RAF Museum, Hendon
J7326	DH53 Humming Bird (G-EBQP)	de Havilland Aircraft Museum, London Colney
J7904	Gloster Gamecock (BAPC.259) <R>	Jet Age Museum, Gloucester
J8067	Westland Pterodactyl 1a	Science Museum, South Kensington
J9941	Hawker Hart 2 (G-ABMR)	RAF Museum, Hendon
K1786	Hawker Tomtit (G-AFTA)	The Shuttleworth Collection, Old Warden
K1928	Hawker Fury I	Cambs Fighter & Bomber Society, Little Gransden
K2048	Isaacs Fury II (G-BZNW)	Privately owned, Fishburn
K2050	Isaacs Fury II (G-ASCM)	Privately owned, Enstone
K2059	Isaacs Fury II (G-PFAR)	Privately owned, Netherthorpe
K2060	Isaacs Fury II (G-BKZM)	Privately owned stored, Limetree, Ireland
K2065	Isaacs Fury II (G-AYJY/K2046)	Privately owned, Henstridge
K2075	Isaacs Fury II (G-BEER)	Privately owned, Combrook, Warks
K2227	Bristol 105 Bulldog IIA (G-ABBB)	RAF Museum, Hendon
K2567	DH82A Tiger Moth (DE306/G-MOTH/7035M)	Privately owned, Tadlow
K2572	DH82A Tiger Moth (NM129/G-AOZH)	Privately owned, Frensham, Surrey
K2585	DH82A Tiger Moth II (T6818/G-ANKT)	The Shuttleworth Collection, Old Warden
K2587	DH82A Tiger Moth <R> (G-BJAP)	Privately owned, Shobdon
K3241	Avro 621 Tutor (K3215/G-AHSA)	The Shuttleworth Collection, Old Warden
K3661	Hawker Nimrod II (G-BURZ) [562]	Aero Vintage, Duxford
K3731	Isaacs Fury (G-RODI)	Privately owned, RAF Waddington
K4232	Avro 671 Rota I (SE-AZB)	RAF Museum, Hendon
K4259	DH82A Tiger Moth (G-ANMO) [71]	Privately owned, Headcorn
K4556	Boulton & Paul Overstrand <R> (BAPC.358) [F-101]	Norfolk & Suffolk Avn Museum, Flixton
K4972	Hawker Hart Trainer IIA (1764M)	RAF Museum, Cosford
K5054	Supermarine Spitfire <R> (*EN398*/BAPC.190)	Privately owned, Hawkinge
K5054	Supermarine Spitfire <R> (BAPC.214)	Tangmere Military Aviation Museum
K5054	Supermarine Spitfire <R> (G-BRDV)	Privately owned, Kent
K5054	Supermarine Spitfire <R> (BAPC.297)	Kent Battle of Britain Museum, Hawkinge
K5054	Supermarine Spitfire <R>	Southampton Airport, on display
K5409	Hawker Hind	*Currently not known*
K5414	Hawker Hind (G-AENP/BAPC.78) [XV]	The Shuttleworth Collection, Old Warden
K5462	Hawker Hind	*Currently not known*

Serial	Type (code/other identity)	Owner/operator, location or fate	Notes
K5554	Hawker Hind	*Currently not known*	
K5600	Hawker Audax (G-BVVI/2015M)	Aero Vintage, Westfield, Sussex	
K5671	Isaacs Fury II (G-EMHF)	Privately owned, Prestwick	
K5673	Isaacs Fury II (G-BZAS)	Privately owned, Morpeth	
K5673	Hawker Fury I <R> (BAPC.249)	Brooklands Museum, Weybridge	
K5674	Hawker Fury I (G-CBZP)	Historic Aircraft Collection Ltd, Duxford	
K5682	Isaacs Fury II (S1579/G-BBVO) [6]	Privately owned, Felthorpe (wreck)	
K6035	Westland Wallace II (2361M)	RAF Museum Reserve Collection, Stafford	
K6618	Hawker Hind	*Currently not known*	
K6833	Hawker Hind	*Currently not known*	
K7271	Hawker Fury II <R> (BAPC.148)	Shropshire Wartime Aircraft Recovery Grp Mus, Sleap	
K7271	Isaacs Fury II <R> (G-CCKV)	Privately owned, Westonzoyland	
K7985	Gloster Gladiator I (L8032/G-AMRK)	The Shuttleworth Collection, Old Warden	
K8042	Gloster Gladiator II (8372M)	RAF Museum, Cosford	
K8203	Hawker Demon I (G-BTVE/2292M)	Demon Displays, Old Warden	
K8303	Isaacs Fury II (G-BWWN) [D]	Privately owned, RAF Henlow	
K9926	VS300 Spitfire I <R> (BAPC.217) [JH-C]	Privately owned, Newquay	
K9942	VS300 Spitfire I (8383M) [SD-D]	RAF Museum, Cosford	
K9998	VS300 Spitfire I (BAPC.431) <R> [QJ-K]	RAF Biggin Hill, on display	
L1019	VS300 Spitfire I <R> (BAPC.308) [LO-S]	Privately owned, Currie, Lothian	
L1035	VS300 Spitfire I <R> (BAPC.500) [SH-D]	Battle of Britain Bunker, Uxbridge	
L1067	VS300 Spitfire I <R> (BAPC.227) [XT-D]	Edinburgh Airport, on display	
L1592	Hawker Hurricane I [KW-Z]	Science Museum, South Kensington	
L1639	Hawker Hurricane I (BAPC.362)	Cambridge Fighter & Bomber Society, Little Gransden	
L1679	Hawker Hurricane I <R> (BAPC.241) [JX-G]	Tangmere Military Aviation Museum	
L1684	Hawker Hurricane I <R> (BAPC.219)	RAF Northolt, on display	
L2005	Hawker Hurricane I	Hawker Restorations, Elmsett	
L2301	VS Walrus I (G-AIZG)	FAA Museum, RNAS Yeovilton	
L2940	Blackburn Skua I	FAA Museum, RNAS Yeovilton	
L5343	Fairey Battle I	RAF Museum, Hendon	
L6739	Bristol 149 Bolingbroke IVT (G-BPIV/R3821f) [YP-Q]	Blenheim(Duxford) Ltd, Duxford	
L6906	Miles M14A Magister I (G-AKKY/T9841/BAPC.44)	Museum of Berkshire Aviation, Woodley	
L7005	Boulton Paul P82 Defiant I <R> [PS-B]	Kent Battle of Britain Museum, Hawkinge	
L7181	Hawker Hind (G-CBLK)	Aero Vintage, Duxford	
L7191	Hawker Hind	*Currently not known*	
L7775	Vickers Wellington B Ic <ff>	Lincolnshire Avn Heritage Centre, E Kirkby	
L8756	Bristol 149 Bolingbroke IVT (RCAF 10001) [XD-E]	RAF Museum, Hendon	
N248	Supermarine S6A (S1596)	Solent Sky, Southampton	
N500	Sopwith LC-1T Triplane <R> (G-PENY/G-BWRA)	Privately owned, Yarcombe, Devon/RNAS Yeovilton	
N540	Port Victoria PV8 Eastchurch Kitten <R>	Yorkshire Air Museum, Elvington	
N546	Wright Quadruplane 1 <R> (BAPC.164)	Solent Sky, Southampton	
N1671	Boulton Paul P82 Defiant I (8370M) [EW-D]	RAF Museum, Cosford	
N1854	Fairey Fulmar II (G-AIBE)	FAA Museum, RNAS Yeovilton	
N2078	Sopwith Baby (8214/8215/BAPC.442)	FAA Museum, RNAS Yeovilton	
N2532	Hawker Hurricane I <R> (BAPC.272) [GZ-H]	Kent Battle of Britain Museum, Hawkinge	
N2980	Vickers Wellington Ia [R]	Brooklands Museum, Weybridge	
N3200	VS300 Spitfire IA (G-CFGJ) [QV]	IWM Duxford	
N3289	VS300 Spitfire I <R> (BAPC.65) [DW-K]	Kent Battle of Britain Museum, Hawkinge	
N3290	VS300 Spitfire I <R> [AI-H]	Privately owned, St Mawgan	
N3310	VS361 Spitfire IX <R> (BAPC.393) [A]	Privately owned, Abingdon	
N3313	VS300 Spitfire I <R> (MH314/BAPC.69) [KL-B]	Repainted as P9398	
N3317	VS329 Spitfire II <R> (P8140/BAPC.71) [BO-U]	Norfolk & Suffolk Avn Museum, Flixton	
N3378	Boulton Paul P82 Defiant I (wreck)	RAF Museum, Cosford	
N3549	DH82A Tiger Moth II (PG645/N3549)	Privately owned, Netherthorpe	
N3788	Miles M14A Magister I (V1075/G-AKPF)	Privately owned, Old Warden	
N3827	Miles M14A Magister I (LV-X246/G-CLHY)	Privately owned, Henstridge	
N4389	Fairey Albacore (N4172) [4M]	FAA Museum, stored Cobham Hall, RNAS Yeovilton	
N4877	Avro 652A Anson I (G-AMDA) [MK-V]	IWM Duxford	
N5137	DH82A Tiger Moth (N6638/G-BNDW)	Caernarfon Air World	
N5177	Sopwith 1½ Strutter <R> (BAPC.452)	Privately owned, stored Mersham, Surrey	

Notes	Serial	Type (code/other identity)	Owner/operator, location or fate
	N5182	Sopwith Pup <R> (G-APUP/9213M)	RAF Museum, Cosford
	N5195	Sopwith Pup (G-ABOX)	Army Flying Museum, Middle Wallop
	N5199	Sopwith Pup <R> (G-BZND)	Privately owned, Yarcombe, Devon
	N5459	Sopwith Triplane <R> (BAPC.111)	FAA Museum, stored Cobham Hall, RNAS Yeovilton
	N5518	Gloster Sea Gladiator (N5579)	FAA Museum, stored Cobham Hall, RNAS Yeovilton
	N5628	Gloster Gladiator II	RAF Museum, Cosford
	N5719	Gloster Gladiator II (G-CBHO)	Privately owned, Dursley, Glos
	N5903	Gloster Gladiator II (N2276/G-GLAD)	The Fighter Collection, Duxford
	N5912	Sopwith Triplane (8385M)	RAF Museum, Hendon
	N5914	Gloster Gladiator II (frame)	Jet Age Museum, Gloucester
	N6161	Sopwith Pup (G-ELRT)	Privately owned, Turweston
	N6290	Sopwith Triplane <R> (G-BOCK)	The Shuttleworth Collection, Old Warden
	N6377	Sopwith F.1 Camel <R> (G-BPOB/B2458)	Privately owned, Stow Maries
	N6452	Sopwith Pup <R> (G-BIAU)	FAA Museum, stored Cobham Hall, RNAS Yeovilton
	N6466	DH82A Tiger Moth (G-ANKZ)	Privately owned, Compton Abbas
	N6473	DH82A Tiger Moth (F-GTBO)	Privately owned, Orbigny, France
	N6537	DH82A Tiger Moth (G-AOHY)	Privately owned, Wickenby
	N6635	DH82A Tiger Moth (comp G-APAO & G-APAP) [25]	IWM Duxford
	N6720	DH82A Tiger Moth (G-BYTN/7014M) [VX]	Privately owned, stored Darley Moor, Derbyshire
	N6797	DH82A Tiger Moth (G-ANEH)	Privately owned, Swyncombe
	N6812	Sopwith 2F.1 Camel	IWM London, Lambeth
	N6847	DH82A Tiger Moth (G-APAL)	Privately owned, Braceborough, Lincs
	N6965	DH82A Tiger Moth (G-AJTW) [FL-J]	Privately owned, Tibenham
	N7033	Noorduyn AT-16 Harvard IIb (FX442)	Kent Battle of Britain Museum, Hawkinge
	N9181	DH82A Tiger Moth (composite) [5]	Kent Battle of Britain Museum, Hawkinge
	N9191	DH82A Tiger Moth (G-ALND)	Privately owned, Pontypool
	N9192	DH82A Tiger Moth (G-DHZF) [RCO-N]	Privately owned, Sywell
	N9328	DH82A Tiger Moth (G-ALWS) [69]	Privately owned, Henstridge
	N9372	DH82A Tiger Moth (G-ANHK)	Privately owned, Sturgate
	N9389	DH82A Tiger Moth (G-ANJA)	Privately owned, stored Seething
	N9503	DH82A Tiger Moth II (G-ANFP) [39]	Privately owned, Podhořany, Czech Republic
	N9899	Supermarine Southampton I (fuselage)	RAF Museum, Hendon
	P1344	HP52 Hampden I (9175M) [PL-K]	Michael Beetham Conservation Centre, RAFM Cosford
	P2617	Hawker Hurricane I (8373M) [AF-F]	RAF Museum, Hendon
	P2725	Hawker Hurricane I (wreck)	IWM London, Lambeth
	P2725	Hawker Hurricane I <R> (BAPC.68) [TM-B]	Privately owned, Delabole, Cornwall
	P2725	Hawker Hurricane I <R> (Z3427/BAPC.205) [TM-B]	RAF Museum, Hendon
	P2793	Hawker Hurricane I <R> (BAPC.236) [SD-M]	Eden Camp Theme Park, stored Malton, North Yorkshire
	P2793	Hawker Hurricane I <R> (BAPC.399) [SD-M]	Eden Camp Theme Park, Malton, North Yorkshire
	P2902	Hawker Hurricane I (G-ROBT) [DX-R]	Privately owned, Duxford
	P2921	Hawker Hurricane I <R> (BAPC.273) [GZ-L]	Kent Battle of Britain Museum, Hawkinge
	P2921	Hawker Hurricane I <R> (BAPC.477) [GZ-L]	RAF Biggin Hill, on display
	P2921	Hawker Sea Hurricane X (AE977/G-CHTK) [GZ-L]	Privately owned, Biggin Hill
	P2970	Hawker Hurricane I <R> (BAPC.291) [US-X]	Battle of Britain Memorial, Capel le Ferne, Kent
	P3059	Hawker Hurricane I <R> (BAPC.64) [SD-N]	Kent Battle of Britain Museum, Hawkinge
	P3175	Hawker Hurricane I (wreck)	RAF Museum Reserve Collection, Stafford
	P3179	Hawker Hurricane I <ff>	Tangmere Military Aviation Museum
	P3208	Hawker Hurricane I <R> (BAPC.63/L1592) [SD-T]	Kent Battle of Britain Museum, Hawkinge
	P3351	Hawker Hurricane IIa (DR393/F-AZXR) [K]	Privately owned, Cannes, France
	P3386	Hawker Hurricane I <R> (BAPC.218) [FT-A]	RAF Bentley Priory, on display
	P3395	Hawker Hurricane IV (KX829)[JX-B]	Thinktank, Birmingham
	P3554	Hawker Hurricane I (composite)	The Air Defence Collection, Salisbury
	P3679	Hawker Hurricane I <R> (BAPC.278) [GZ-K]	Kent Battle of Britain Museum, Hawkinge
	P3700	Hawker Hurricane XIIa (Z5140/G-HURI) [RF-E]	Historic Aircraft Collection, Duxford
	P3708	Hawker Hurricane I	Norfolk & Suffolk Avn Museum, Flixton (on rebuild)
	P3717	Hawker Hurricane I (composite) (DR348/G-HITT) [SW-P]	Privately owned, Old Warden
	P3873	Hawker Hurricane I <R> (BAPC.265) [YO-H]	Yorkshire Air Museum, Elvington
	P3873	Hawker Hurricane I <R> (BAPC.499) [YO-H]	Battle of Britain Bunker, Uxbridge
	P3901	Hawker Hurricane I <R> (BAPC.475) [RF-E]	Battle of Britain Bunker, Uxbridge
	P4139	Fairey Swordfish II (HS618) [5H]	FAA Museum, RNAS Yeovilton

Serial	Type (code/other identity)	Owner/operator, location or fate	Notes
P6382	Miles M14A Hawk Trainer 3 (G-AJRS) [C]	The Shuttleworth Collection, Old Warden	
P7308	VS300 Spitfire IA (AR213/R9632/G-AIST) [XR-D]	Privately owned, Duxford	
P7350	VS329 Spitfire IIa (G-AWIJ) [KL-B]	RAF BBMF, Coningsby	
P7370	VS329 Spitfire II <R> (BAPC.410) [ZP-A]	Battle of Britain Experience, Canterbury	
P7540	VS329 Spitfire IIa [DU-W]	Dumfries & Galloway Avn Mus, Dumfries	
P7666	VS329 Spitfire II <R> (BAPC.335) [EB-Z]	RAF High Wycombe, on display	
P7819	VS329 Spitfire IIa (G-TCHZ)	Privately owned, Exeter	
P7823	VS329 Spitfire IIa <R> (BAPC.369) [TM-F]	Ulster Aviation Society, Long Kesh	
P7966	VS329 Spitfire II <R> [D-B]	Manx Aviation & Military Museum, Ronaldsway	
P8088	VS329 Spitfire IIa (G-CGRM) [NK-K]	Privately owned, Knutsford, Cheshire	
P8208	VS329 Spitfire IIb (G-RRFF)	Privately owned, Durley, Glos	
P8448	VS329 Spitfire II <R> (BAPC.225) [UM-D]	RAF Cranwell, on display	
P9398	Supermarine Aircraft Spitfire 26 (G-CEPL) [KL-B]	Privately owned, Rochester	
P9398	VS300 Spitfire I <R> (N3313/BAPC.69) [KL-B]	Kent Battle of Britain Museum, Hawkinge	
P9444	VS300 Spitfire Ia [RN-D]	Science Museum, South Kensington	
P9637	Supermarine Aircraft Spitfire 26 (G-RORB) [GR-B]	Privately owned, Perth	
R1914	Miles M14A Magister (G-AHUJ)	Privately owned, Gloucester	
R4118	Hawker Hurricane I (G-HUPW) [UP-W]	Privately owned, North Moreton, Oxon	
R4229	Hawker Hurricane I <R> (BAPC.334) [GN-J]	Alexandra Park, Windsor	
R4922	DH82A Tiger Moth II (G-APAO)	Privately owned, Henlow	
R4959	DH82A Tiger Moth II (G-ARAZ) [59]	Privately owned, Duxford	
R5136	DH82A Tiger Moth II (G-APAP)	Privately owned, Darley Moor, Derbyshire	
R5172	DH82A Tiger Moth II (G-AOIS) [FIJE]	Privately owned, Sywell	
R5246	DH82A Tiger Moth II (G-AMIV) [40]	Privately owned, Podhořany, Czech Republic	
R5868	Avro 683 Lancaster I (7325M) [PO-S]	RAF Museum, Hendon	
R5868	Avro 683 Lancaster I <R> (BAPC.471) [PO-S] <ff>	Avro Heritage Museum, Woodford	
R6599	VS300 Spitfire I <R> (BAPC.539) [DW-J]	Romney Marsh Wartime Collection	
R6690	VS300 Spitfire I <R> (BAPC.254) [PR-A]	Yorkshire Air Museum, Elvington	
R6775	VS300 Spitfire I <R> (BAPC.299) [YT-J]	Battle of Britain Memorial, Capel le Ferne, Kent	
R6904	VS300 Spitfire I <R> [BT-K]	Privately owned, Cornwall	
R6915	VS300 Spitfire I	IWM London, Lambeth	
R9125	Westland Lysander III (8377M)[JR-M]	Michael Beetham Conservation Centre, RAFM Cosford	
R9612	VS300 Spitfire I <R> [LC]	Privately owned, Duxford	
S1287	Fairey Flycatcher <R> (G-BEYB) [5]	FAA Museum, stored Cobham Hall, RNAS Yeovilton	
S1581	Hawker Nimrod I (G-BWWK) [573]	The Fighter Collection, Duxford	
S1595	Supermarine S6B [1]	Science Museum, South Kensington	
S1615	Isaacs Fury II (G-BMEU)	Privately owned, Tatenhill	
T5298	Bristol 156 Beaufighter I (4552M) <ff>	Midland Air Museum, Coventry	
T5424	DH82A Tiger Moth II (G-AJOA)	Privately owned, Swindon	
T5854	DH82A Tiger Moth II (G-ANKK)	Privately owned, Baxterley	
T5879	DH82A Tiger Moth II (G-AXBW) [RUC-W]	Privately owned, Frensham	
T6296	DH82A Tiger Moth II (8387M)	RAF Museum, Cosford	
T6953	DH82A Tiger Moth II (G-ANNI)	Privately owned, Tisted, Hants	
T6991	DH82A Tiger Moth II (DE694/HB-UPY)	Privately owned, Lausanne, Switzerland	
T7109	DH82A Tiger Moth II (G-AOIM)	Privately owned, Bicester	
T7230	DH82A Tiger Moth II (G-AFVE)	Privately owned, Mazowieckie, Poland	
T7281	DH82A Tiger Moth II (G-ARTL)	Privately owned, Egton, nr Whitby	
T7290	DH82A Tiger Moth II (G-ANNK) [14]	Privately owned, Podington, Beds	
T7793	DH82A Tiger Moth II (G-ANKV)	Privately owned, Wickenby	
T7794	DH82A Tiger Moth II (G-ASPV)	Privately owned, Bagby	
T7842	DH82A Tiger Moth II (G-AMTF)	Privately owned, Westfield, Surrey	
T7909	DH82A Tiger Moth II (G-ANON)	Privately owned, Sherburn-in-Elmet	
T7997	DH82A Tiger Moth II (NL750/G-AHUF)	Privately owned, Breighton	
T8191	DH82A Tiger Moth II (G-BWMK)	Privately owned, Henstridge	
T9707	Miles M14A Magister I (G-AKKR/8378M/T9708)	RAF Museum Reserve Collection, Stafford	
T9738	Miles M14A Magister I (G-AKAT)	Privately owned, Breighton	
V3388	Airspeed AS10 Oxford I (G-AHTW)	IWM Duxford	
V6028	Bristol 149 Bolingbroke IVT (G-MKIV) [GB-D] <rf>	The Aircraft Restoration Co, stored Duxford	

23

Notes	Serial	Type (code/other identity)	Owner/operator, location or fate
	V6555	Hawker Hurricane I (BAPC.411/P3144) <R> [DT-A]	Battle of Britain Experience, Canterbury
	V6799	Hawker Hurricane I <R> (BAPC.72/V7767) [SD-X]	Jet Age Museum, Gloucester
	V7313	Hawker Hurricane I <R> (BAPC.346) [US-F]	Privately owned, North Weald, on display
	V7350	Hawker Hurricane I <ff>	Romney Marsh Wartime Collection
	V7467	Hawker Hurricane I <R> (BAPC.223) [ZJ-L]	Repainted as V7752
	V7467	Hawker Hurricane I <R> (P2954/BAPC.267) [LE-D]	IWM Duxford
	V7467	Hawker Hurricane I <R> (BAPC.288) [LE-D]	Wonderland Pleasure Park, Farnsfield, Notts
	V7467	Hawker Hurricane I <R> (BAPC.378) [LE-D]	RAF High Wycombe, on display
	V7497	Hawker Hurricane I (G-HRLI) [SD-X]	Privately owned, Elmsett
	V7752	Hawker Hurricane I <R> (V7467/BAPC.223) [ZJ-L]	Hangar 42 Visitors Centre, Blackpool
	V9312	Westland Lysander IIIa (G-CCOM) [LX-E]	The Aircraft Restoration Co, Duxford
	V9367	Westland Lysander IIIa (G-AZWT) [MA-B]	The Shuttleworth Collection, Old Warden
	V9673	Westland Lysander IIIa (V9300/G-LIZY) [MA-J]	IWM Duxford
	V9723	Westland Lysander IIIa (V9546/OO-SOT) [MA-D]	SABENA Old Timers, Brussels, Belgium
	V9875	Westland Lysander IIIa <R> (BAPC.371) [MA-J]	Tangmere Military Aviation Museum
	W1048	HP59 Halifax II (8465M) [TL-S]	RAF Museum, Hendon
	W2068	Avro 652A Anson I (9261M/VH-ASM) [68]	RAF Museum, Hendon
	W2718	VS Walrus I (G-RNLI)	Privately owned, Duxford
	W3644	VS349 Spitfire V <R> (BAPC.323) [QV-J]	Privately owned, Lake Fairhaven, Lancs
	W3850	VS349 Spitfire V <R> (BAPC.304) [PR-A]	Privately owned, Knutsford, Cheshire
	W4041	Gloster E28/39	Science Museum, South Kensington
	W4041	Gloster E28/39 <R> (BAPC.331)	Jet Age Museum, Gloucester
	W4050	DH98 Mosquito	de Havilland Aircraft Museum, London Colney
	W5856	Fairey Swordfish I (G-BMGC) [4A]	RN, Yeovilton
	W9385	DH87B Hornet Moth (G-ADND) [YG-L,3]	Privately owned, Oaksey Park
	X4009	VS300 Spitfire I (G-EMET)	Privately owned,
	X4253	VS300 Spitfire I <R> (BAPC.326) [FY-N]	Hangar 42 Visitors Centre, Blackpool
	X4276	VS300 Spitfire I (G-CDGU)	Privately owned, Sandown
	X4474	VS300 Spitfire I <R> (X4178/BAPC.394) [QV-I]	IWM Duxford
	X4590	VS300 Spitfire I (8384M) [PR-F]	RAF Museum, Hendon
	X4650	VS300 Spitfire I (R9612/G-CGUK) [KL-A]	Privately owned, Duxford
	X4683	Jurca MJ10 Spitfire (G-MUTS) [EB-N]	Privately owned, Fishburn
	X4859	VS300 Spitfire I <R> (BAPC.319) [PQ-N]	Grangemouth Spitfire Memorial Trust
	X9407	Percival P.16A Q6 (G-AFFD)	Privately owned, Seething (on rebuild)
	Z1206	Vickers Wellington IV (fuselage)	Privately owned, Kenilworth
	Z2033	Fairey Firefly I (G-ASTL) [275/N]	FAA Museum, stored Cobham Hall, RNAS Yeovilton
	Z2315	Hawker Hurricane IIa [JU-E]	IWM Duxford
	Z2389	Hawker Hurricane IIa [XR-T]	Brooklands Museum, Weybridge
	Z5207	Hawker Hurricane IIb (G-BYDL)	Privately owned, Germany (on rebuild)
	Z7015	Hawker Sea Hurricane Ib (G-BKTH) [7-L]	The Shuttleworth Collection, Old Warden
	Z7197	Percival P30 Proctor III (G-AKZN/8380M)	RAF Museum Reserve Collection, Stafford
	Z7258	DH89A Dragon Rapide (NR786/G-AHGD)	Privately owned, Membury (wreck)
	AA810	VS353 Spitfire F IV (G-PRID)	Airframe Assemblies, Sandown (rebuild)
	AB196	Supermarine Aircraft Spitfire 26 (G-CCGH)	Privately owned, Hawarden
	AB910	VS349 Spitfire Vb (G-AISU) [SH-F]	RAF BBMF, Coningsby
	AD189	VS349 Spitfire Vb (G-CHVJ)	Privately owned, Raglan, Monmouthshire
	AD370	Jurca Spitfire (G-CHBW) [PJ-C]	Privately owned, Perranporth
	AD540	VS349 Spitfire Vb (wreck)	Privately owned, Launceston (on rebuild)
	AE436	HP52 Hampden I [PL-J] (parts)	Lincolnshire Avn Heritage Centre, E Kirkby
	AG244	Hawker Hurricane XII (RCAF 5487/G-CBOE)	Privately owned, Aalen, Germany
	AJ841	CCF T-6J Texan (MM53795/G-BJST/KF729)	Privately owned, Duxford
	AL246	Grumman Martlet I	FAA Museum, RNAS Yeovilton
	AP506	Cierva C30A (G-ACWM) (wreck)	The Helicopter Museum, Weston-super-Mare
	AP507	Cierva C30A (G-ACWP) [KX-P]	Science Museum, South Kensington
	AR501	VS349 Spitfire LF Vc (G-AWII/AR4474) [DU-E]	The Shuttleworth Collection, Old Warden
	AV511	EHI-101 Merlin <R> [511]	SFDO, RNAS Culdrose
	AW101	AgustaWestland AW101 Mk.510 (G-17-510)	AgustaWestland, Yeovil

Serial	Type (code/other identity)	Owner/operator, location or fate	Notes
BA377	VS361 Spitfire F IX <R> (EN398/BAPC.377)	Privately owned, Belper, Derbyshire	
BB803	DH82A Tiger Moth (G-ADWJ) [75]	Privately owned, Henstridge	
BB807	DH82A Tiger Moth (G-ADWO)	Solent Sky, Southampton	
BD713	Hawker Hurricane IIb	Currently not known	
BE505	Hawker Hurricane IIb (RCAF 5403/G-HHII) [XP-L]	Privately owned, Elmsett	
BH238	Hawker Hurricane IIb	Airframe Assemblies, stored Sandown	
BL614	VS349 Spitfire Vb (4354M) [ZD-F]	RAF Museum, Hendon	
BL655	VS349 Spitfire Vb (wreck)	Lincolnshire Avn Heritage Centre, East Kirkby	
BL688	VS349 Spitfire LF Vb (G-CJWO)	Privately owned, Launceston	
BL735	Supermarine Aircraft Spitfire 26 (G-HABT) [BT-A]	Privately owned, Hohenems, Austria	
BL924	VS349 Spitfire Vb <R> (BAPC.242) [AZ-G]	Beale Park, Pangbourne, Berks	
BL927	Supermarine Aircraft Spitfire 26 (G-CGWI) [JH-I]	Privately owned, Perth	
BM361	VS349 Spitfire Vb <R> (BAPC.269) [XR-C]	RAF Lakenheath, on display	
BM481	VS349 Spitfire Vb <R> (BAPC.301) [YO-T]	Thornaby Aerodrome Memorial	
	(also wears PK651/RAO-B)		
BM539	VS349 Spitfire LF Vb (G-SSVB)	Privately owned, Hastings	
BM597	VS349 Spitfire LF Vb (G-MKVB/5718M) [JH-C]	Historic Aircraft Collection, Duxford	
BN230	Hawker Hurricane IIc (LF751/5466M) [FT-A]	RAF Manston, Memorial Pavilion	
BP926	VS353 Spitfire PR IV (G-PRIV)	Privately owned, Newport Pagnell	
BR954	VS353 Spitfire PR IV <R> (N3194/BAPC.220) [JP-A]	Merlin ERD, Perth	
BS239	VS361 Spitfire IX <R> (BAPC.222) [5R-E]	Battle of Britain Bunker, Uxbridge	
BS410	VS509 Spitfire T9 (G-TCHI) [PK-A]	Privately owned, Postling, Kent	
BS435	VS361 Spitfire IX <R> (BAPC.324) [FY-F]	Hangar 42 Visitors Centre, Blackpool	
BW853	Hawker Hurricane XIIa (G-BRKE) (fuselage)	Currently not known	
DD931	Bristol 152 Beaufort VIII (9131M/BAPC.436) [L]	RAF Museum, Hendon	
DE208	DH82A Tiger Moth II (G-AGYU)	Privately owned, Treswell, Notts	
DE470	DH82A Tiger Moth II (G-ANMY) [16]	Privately owned, Garford, Oxon (rebuild)	
DE623	DH82A Tiger Moth II (G-ANFI)	Privately owned, Cardiff	
DE673	DH82A Tiger Moth II (G-ADNZ/6948M)	Privately owned, Tibenham	
DE971	DH82A Tiger Moth II (G-OOSY)	Privately owned, Bicester	
DE974	DH82A Tiger Moth II (G-ANZZ)	Privately owned, Clacton/Duxford	
DE992	DH82A Tiger Moth II (G-AXXV)	Privately owned, Membury, Berks	
DF112	DH82A Tiger Moth II (G-ANRM)	Privately owned, Clacton (on rebuild)	
DF128	DH82A Tiger Moth II (G-AOJJ) [RCO-U]	Privately owned, White Waltham	
DF198	DH82A Tiger Moth II (G-BBRB)	Privately owned, stored West Wickham, Kent	
DG202	Gloster F9/40 (5758M)	RAF Museum, stored Cosford	
DG590	Miles M2H Hawk Major (G-ADMW/8379M)	Montrose Air Station Heritage Centre	
DP872	Fairey Barracuda II <ff>	FAA Museum, stored Cobham Hall, RNAS Yeovilton	
DP872	Fairey Barracuda II <rf>	FAA Museum, RNAS Yeovilton	
DV372	Avro 683 Lancaster I <ff>	IWM London, Lambeth	
DZ313	DH98 Mosquito B IV <R>	Privately owned, Little Rissington	
EB518	Airspeed AS10 Oxford V	Hangar 42 Visitors Centre, Blackpool	
EE416	Gloster Meteor F3 <ff>	Martin Baker Aircraft, Chalgrove, fire section	
EE425	Gloster Meteor F3 <ff>	Jet Age Museum, Gloucester	
EE531	Gloster Meteor F4 (7090M)	Midland Air Museum, Coventry	
EE549	Gloster Meteor F4 (7008M) [A]	Tangmere Military Aviation Museum	
EE602	VS349 Spitfire LF Vc (G-IBSY) [DV-V]	Privately owned, Biggin Hill	
EF545	VS349 Spitfire LF Vc (G-CDGY)	Aero Vintage, Rye	
EJ922	Hawker Typhoon Ib <ff>	Privately owned, Booker	
EM720	DH82A Tiger Moth II (G-AXAN)	Privately owned, Duxford	
EM726	DH82A Tiger Moth II (G-ANDE) [FY]	Privately owned, Sywell	
EM840	DH82A Tiger Moth II (G-ANBY)	Privately owned, Middle Wallop	
EM973	DH82A Tiger Moth II (T6774/G-ALNA) [OY]	Privately owned, Darley Moor, Derbys	
EN130	Supermarine Aircraft Spitfire 26B (G-ENAA) [FN-A]	Privately owned, Enstone	
EN179	VS361 Spitfire F IX (G-TCHO)	Privately owned, Exeter	
EN224	VS366 Spitfire F XII (G-FXII)	Privately owned, Sywell	
EN398	VS361 Spitfire F IX <R> [JE-J]	AMSS, Pyle, Bridgend	
EN398	VS361 Spitfire F IX <R> (BAPC.541) [JE-J]	RAF Coningsby, on display	
EN398	VS361 Spitfire F IX <R> (BAPC.184) [JE-J]	Repainted as MK392	
EN398	VS361 Spitfire F IX <R> [JE-J]	Spitfire Spares, Taunton, Somerset	

Notes	Serial	Type (code/other identity)	Owner/operator, location or fate
	EN570	VS361 Spitfire F IX (G-CISP/LN-AOA)	Airframe Assemblies, Sandown
	EN961	Isaacs Spitfire <R> (G-CGIK) [SD-X]	Privately owned, Stoulton, Worcs
	EP120	VS349 Spitfire LF Vb (G-LFVB/5377M/8070M) [AE-A]	The Fighter Collection, Duxford
	EP121	VS349 Spitfire LF Vb <R> (BAPC.320) [LO-D]	Montrose Air Station Heritage Centre
	EV771	Fairchild UC-61 Argus <R> (BAPC.294)	Thorpe Camp Preservation Group, Lincs
	EX490	NA T-6H Texan (F-AZQK/G-CLCJ) [78]	Privately owned, Enstone
	EX976	NA AT-6D Harvard III (FAP 1657)	FAA Museum, RNAS Yeovilton
	FE511	Noorduyn AT-16 Harvard IIb (G-CIUW)	Privately owned, White Waltham
	FE695	Noorduyn AT-16 Harvard IIb (G-BTXI) [94]	The Fighter Collection, Duxford
	FE788	CCF Harvard IV (MM54137/G-CTKL)	Privately owned, Biggin Hill
	FE905	Noorduyn AT-16 Harvard IIb (LN-BNM)	RAF Museum, Hendon
	FJ801	Boeing-Stearman PT-27 Kaydet (N62842/BAPC.375)	Norfolk & Suffolk Avn Museum, Flixton
	FJ992	Boeing-Stearman PT-17 Kaydet (OO-JEH) [44]	Privately owned, Wevelgem, Belgium
	FK338	Fairchild 24W-41 Argus I (G-AJOZ)	Yorkshire Air Museum, Elvington
	FL586	Douglas C-47B Dakota (OO-SMA) [AI-N] (fuselage)	WWII Remembrance Museum, Handcross, W Sussex
	FR886	Piper L-4J Grasshopper (G-BDMS)	Privately owned, Old Sarum
	FS628	Fairchild Argus 2 (43-14601/G-AIZE)	RAF Museum, Cosford
	FS728	Noorduyn AT-16 Harvard IIb (D-FRCP)	Privately owned, Gelnhausen, Germany
	FT118	Noorduyn AT-16 Harvard IIb (G-BZHL) [TM-13]	Privately owned, Hibaldstow
	FT323	NA AT-6D Harvard III (FAP 1513/G-CCOY)	Privately owned, France
	FT391	Noorduyn AT-16 Harvard IIb (G-AZBN)	Privately owned, White Waltham
	FX322	Noorduyn AT-16 Harvard IIb <ff>	Privately owned, Doncaster
	FX760	Curtiss P-40N Kittyhawk IV (A29-556/9150M) [GA-?]	RAF Museum, Hendon
	FZ626	Douglas Dakota III (KN566/G-AMPO) [YS-DH]	RAF Brize Norton, for display
	GZ100	AgustaWestland AW109SP Grand New (G-ZIOO)	RAF No 32(The Royal) Sqn, Northolt
	HB612	Fairchild Argus II (G-AJSN)	Ulster Aviation Society, Long Kesh
	HB737	Fairchild Argus III (G-BCBH)	Privately owned, Spanhoe
	HB751	Fairchild Argus III (G-BCBL)	Privately owned, Woolsery, Devon
	HG691	DH89A Dragon Rapide (G-AIYR)	Privately owned, Clacton/Duxford
	HH268	GAL48 Hotspur II (HH379/BAPC.261) [H]	Army Flying Museum, Middle Wallop
	HJ711	DH98 Mosquito NF II (BAPC.434) [VI-C]	Lincolnshire Avn Heritage Centre, E Kirkby
	HM580	Cierva C-30A (G-ACUU) [KX-K]	IWM Duxford
	HS503	Fairey Swordfish IV (BAPC.108)	RAF Museum Reserve Collection, Stafford
	HS554	Fairey Swordfish III (G-RNMZ)	Privately owned, White Waltham
	IR206	Eurofighter Typhoon <R> (BAPC.360) [IR]	RAF M&RU, Bottesford
	IR808	B-V Chinook <R> (BAPC.361)	RAF M&RU, Bottesford
	JG241	Supermarine Aircraft Spitfire 26B (G-SMSP) [ZX-J]	Privately owned, Blackbushe
	JG668	VS502 Spitfire T8 (A58-441/G-CFGA)	Privately owned, Haverfordwest
	JG891	VS349 Spitfire F Vc (N5TF/G-LFVC) [T-B]	Privately owned, Duxford
	JN768	Hawker Tempest V (4887M/G-TMPV)	Privately owned, Sywell
	JP843	Hawker Typhoon Ib [Y]	Privately owned, Shrewsbury
	JR505	Hawker Typhoon Ib <ff>	Currently not known
	JV482	Grumman Wildcat V	Ulster Aviation Society, Long Kesh
	JV579	Grumman FM-2 Wildcat (N4845V/G-RUMW) [F]	The Fighter Collection, Duxford
	KB889	Avro 683 Lancaster B X (G-LANC) [NA-I]	IWM Duxford
	KB976	Avro 683 Lancaster B X <ff>	Lincolnshire Avn Heritage Centre, E Kirkby
	KB976	Avro 683 Lancaster B X (G-BCOH) <rf>	South Yorkshire Aircraft Museum, Doncaster
	KD345	Goodyear FG-1D Corsair (88297/G-FGID) [130-A]	The Fighter Collection, Duxford
	KD431	CV Corsair IV [E2-M]	FAA Museum, RNAS Yeovilton
	KE209	Grumman Hellcat II	FAA Museum, RNAS Yeovilton
	KE418	Hawker Tempest <rf>	Currently not known
	KF183	Noorduyn AT-16 Harvard IIb (G-CORS) [3]	Privately owned, Duxford
	KF388	Noorduyn AT-16 Harvard IIb (composite)	Bournemouth Aviation Museum
	KF402	NA T-6G Texan (49-3072/G-TEXN) [HT-Y]	Boultbee Flight Academy, Goodwood
	KF532	Noorduyn AT-16 Harvard IIb <ff>	Privately owned, Bruntingthorpe
	KF650	Noorduyn AT-16 Harvard IIb <ff>	Sywell Aviation Museum

Serial	Type (code/other identity)	Owner/operator, location or fate	Notes
KF741	Noorduyn AT-16 Harvard IIb <ff>	Privately owned, Kenilworth	
KG374	Douglas Dakota IV (KP208) [YS-DM]	Merville Barracks, Colchester, on display	
KG651	Douglas Dakota III (G-AMHJ)	Metheringham Airfield Visitor Centre, Lincs	
KH774	NA P-51D Mustang IV (44-73877/G-SHWN) [GA-S]	Privately owned, Goodwood	
KJ351	Airspeed AS58 Horsa II (TL659/BAPC.80) [23]	Army Flying Museum, Middle Wallop	
KJ994	Douglas Dakota III (F-AZTE)	Dakota et Cie, La Ferté Alais, France	
KK116	Douglas Dakota IV (G-AMPY)	Privately owned, Coventry	
KK527	Fairchild 24R Argus III (44-83184/G-RGUS)	Privately owned, Sibson	
KK995	Sikorsky Hoverfly I [E]	RAF Museum, Hendon	
KL216	Republic P-47D Thunderbolt (45-49295/9212M) [RS-L]	RAF Museum, Hendon	
KN353	Douglas Dakota IV (G-AMYJ)	Yorkshire Air Museum, Elvington	
KN645	Douglas Dakota IV (KG374/8355M)	RAF Museum, Cosford	
KN751	Consolidated Liberator C VI (IAF HE807) [F]	RAF Museum, Hendon	
KP220	Douglas Dakota IV (G-ANAF)	Privately owned, Coventry	
KZ191	Hawker Hurricane IV (frame only)	Privately owned, East Garston, Bucks	
KZ321	Hawker Hurricane IV (G-HURY/OO-HUR)	Privately owned, Brasschaat, Belgium	
LA198	VS356 Spitfire F21 (7118M) [RAI-G]	Kelvingrove Art Gallery & Museum, Glasgow	
LA226	VS356 Spitfire F21 (7119M)	RAF Museum Reserve Collection, Stafford	
LA255	VS356 Spitfire F21 (6490M)	RAF Lossiemouth, preserved	
LA543	VS474 Seafire F46 <ff>	The Air Defence Collection, Salisbury	
LA546	VS474 Seafire F46 (G-CFZJ)	Privately owned, Colchester	
LA564	VS474 Seafire F46 (G-FRSX)	Kennet Aviation, Old Warden	
LB264	Taylorcraft Plus D (G-AIXA)	RAF Museum, Hendon	
LB294	Taylorcraft Plus D (G-AHWJ)	Saywell Heritage Centre, Worthing	
LB312	Taylorcraft Plus D (HH982/G-AHXE)	Privately owned, Netheravon	
LB314	Taylorcraft Plus D (OY-DSZ)	South Yorkshire Aircraft Museum, Doncaster	
LB323	Taylorcraft Plus D (G-AHSD)	Privately owned, Spanhoe	
LB352	Taylorcraft Plus D (G-AHCR)	Privately owned, Dunkeswell	
LB367	Taylorcraft Plus D (G-AHGZ)	Privately owned, Melksham, Wilts	
LB375	Taylorcraft Plus D (G-AHGW)	Privately owned, Spanhoe	
LF363	Hawker Hurricane IIc [JX-B]	RAF BBMF, Coningsby	
LF738	Hawker Hurricane IIc (5405M) [UH-A]	RAF Museum, Cosford	
LF789	DH82 Queen Bee (K3584/BAPC.186) [R2-K]	de Havilland Aircraft Museum, London Colney	
LF858	DH82 Queen Bee (G-BLUZ)	Privately owned, Henlow	
LH291	Airspeed AS51 Horsa I <R> (BAPC.279)	RAF Museum, stored Cosford	
LS326	Fairey Swordfish II (G-AJVH) [L2]	RN, Yeovilton	
LV907	HP59 Halifax III (HR792/BAPC.449) [NP-F]	Yorkshire Air Museum, Elvington	
	(marked NP763 [H7-N] on port side)		
LZ551	DH100 Vampire	FAA Museum, RNAS Yeovilton	
LZ766	Percival P34 Proctor III (G-ALCK)	IWM Duxford	
LZ842	VS361 Spitfire F IX (G-CGZU) [EF-F]	Privately owned, Biggin Hill	
LZ844	VS349 Spitfire F Vc [UP-X]	Currently not known	
MA764	VS361 Spitfire F IX (G-MCDB)	Privately owned, Sway, Hants	
MD338	VS359 Spitfire LF VIII	Privately owned, Sandown	
MF628	Vickers Wellington T10 (9210M)	Michael Beetham Conservation Centre, RAFM Cosford	
MH314	VS361 Spitfire IX <R> (EN526/BAPC.221) [SZ-G]	RAF Northolt, on display	
MH415	VS361 Spitfire IX <R> (MJ751/BAPC.209) [DU-V]	The Aircraft Restoration Co, Duxford	
MH434	VS361 Spitfire LF IXb (G-ASJV) [ZD-B]	The Old Flying Machine Company, Duxford	
MH526	Supermarine Aircraft Spitfire 26 (G-CJWW) [LO-D]	Privately owned, Wethersfield, Essex	
MJ627	VS509 Spitfire T9 (G-BMSB) [9G-P]	Privately owned, Biggin Hill	
MJ755	VS361 Spitfire LF IXe (G-CLGS) [F-H]	Repainted in Greek markings, 2019	
MJ772	VS509 Spitfire T9 (G-AVAV) [GW-A]	Privately owned, Biggin Hill	
MJ832	VS361 Spitfire IX <R> (L1096/BAPC.229) [DN-Y]	RAF Digby, on display	
MK356	VS361 Spitfire LF IXe (5690M) [QJ-3]	RAF BBMF, Coningsby	
MK356	VS361 Spitfire LF IXc <R> [2I-V]	Kent Battle of Britain Museum, Hawkinge	
MK356	VS361 Spitfire LF IXc <R> (BAPC.298)	RAF Cosford, on display	
MK392	VS361 Spitfire LF IXc <R> (EN398/BAPC.184) [JE-J]	Boultbee Flight Academy, Goodwood	
MK805	VS361 Spitfire IX (BAPC.426) <R> [SH-B]	Simply Spitfire, Oulton Broad, Suffolk	
MK912	VS361 Spitfire LF IXc (G-BRRA) [SH-L]	Privately owned, Biggin Hill	
ML135	VS361 Spitfire IX <R> (BAPC.513)	Essex Memorial Spitfire Monument	

Notes	Serial	Type (code/other identity)	Owner/operator, location or fate
	ML295	VS361 Spitfire LF IXe (NH341/G-CICK)	Privately owned, Duxford
	ML407	VS509 Spitfire T9 (G-LFIX) [OU-V]	Privately owned, Sywell
	ML411	VS361 Spitfire LF IXe (G-CBNU)	Privately owned, Ashford, Kent
	ML427	VS361 Spitfire IX (6457M) [HK-A]	Thinktank, Birmingham
	ML796	Short S25 Sunderland V [NS-F]	IWM Duxford
	ML824	Short S25 Sunderland V [NS-Z]	RAF Museum, Hendon
	MN235	Hawker Typhoon Ib [I8-T]	RAF Museum, Hendon
	MP425	Airspeed AS10 Oxford I (G-AITB) [G]	RAF Museum, Hendon
	MS902	Miles M25 Martinet TT1 (TF-SHC)	Museum of Berkshire Aviation, Woodley
	MS968	Auster AOP5 (G-ALYG)	Privately owned, Old Sarum
	MT166	Auster AOP5 (G-BICD)	Privately owned, South Scarle, Notts
	MT182	Auster J/1 Autocrat (G-AJDY)	Privately owned, Spanhoe
	MT197	Auster IV (G-ANHS)	Privately owned, Spanhoe
	MT438	Auster III (G-AREI)	Privately owned, Eggesford
	MT818	VS502 Spitfire T8 (G-AIDN)	Privately owned, Biggin Hill
	MT928	VS359 Spitfire HF VIIIc (G-BKMI/MV154/AR654) [ZX-M]	Privately owned, Duxford
	MV268	VS379 Spitfire FR XIVe (MV293/G-SPIT) [JE-J]	Privately owned, Duxford
	MW401	Hawker Tempest II (IAF HA604/G-PEST)	Privately owned, Sywell
	MW763	Hawker Tempest II (IAF HA586/G-TEMT) [HF-A]	Repainted as PR533, 2019
	MW810	Hawker Tempest II (IAF HA591) <ff>	Privately owned, Bentwaters
	NF314	GEC Phoenix (BAPC.408)	Army, Larkhill, on display
	NF370	Fairey Swordfish III [NH-L]	IWM Duxford
	NF389	Fairey Swordfish III	RN, Yeovilton
	NH238	VS361 Spitfire LF IXe (G-MKIX) [D-A]	Privately owned, stored Greenham Common
	NH341	VS509 Spitfire T9 (G-CICK) [DB-E]	Privately owned, Headcorn
	NJ633	Auster 5D (G-AKXP)	Privately owned, Old Sarum
	NJ673	Auster 5D (G-AOCR)	Privately owned, Shenington, Oxon
	NJ689	Auster AOP5 (G-ALXZ)	Privately owned, Breighton
	NJ695	Auster AOP5 (G-AJXV)	Privately owned, Newark
	NJ703	Auster AOP5 (TJ207/G-AKPI) [P]	Privately owned, Wickenby
	NJ719	Auster AOP5 (TW385/G-ANFU)	South Yorkshire Aircraft Museum, Doncaster
	NJ728	Auster AOP5 (G-AIKE)	Privately owned, Little Gransden
	NJ889	Auster AOP3 (G-AHLK)	Privately owned, Ledbury, Herefordshire
	NL750	DH82A Tiger Moth II (T7997/G-AOBH)	Privately owned, Eaglescott
	NL985	DH82A Tiger Moth I (G-BWIK/7015M)	Privately owned, Oaksey Park
	NM138	DH82A Tiger Moth I (G-ANEW) [41]	Privately owned, Henstridge
	NM181	DH82A Tiger Moth I (G-AZGZ)	Privately owned, Rush Green
	NP294	Percival P31 Proctor IV [TB-M]	Lincolnshire Avn Heritage Centre, E Kirkby
	NV778	Hawker Tempest TT5 (8386M)	RAF Museum, Hendon
	NS710	DH98 Mosquito TT35 (TJ118) <ff>	Victoria and Albert Museum, Knightsbridge, London
	NX534	Auster III (G-BUDL)	Privately owned, Spanhoe
	NX611	Avro 683 Lancaster B VII (G-ASXX/8375M) [DX-F,LE-H]	Lincolnshire Avn Heritage Centre, E Kirkby
	PA474	Avro 683 Lancaster B I [AR-L,VN-T]	RAF BBMF, Coningsby
	PD685	Slingsby T7 Cadet TX1 (BAPC.355)	Tettenhall Transport Heritage Centre
	PF179	HS Gnat T1 (XR541/8602M)	Privately owned, North Weald
	PG657	DH82A Tiger Moth II (G-AGPK)	Privately owned, Clacton/Duxford
	PG712	DH82A Tiger Moth II (PH-CSL) [2]	Privately owned, Hilversum, The Netherlands
	PK519	VS356 Spitfire F22 [G-SPXX]	Privately owned, Newport Pagnell
	PK624	VS356 Spitfire F22 (8072M)	The Fighter Collection, Duxford
	PK664	VS356 Spitfire F22 (7759M) [V6-B]	Kennet Aviation, Old Warden
	PK683	VS356 Spitfire F24 (7150M)	Solent Sky, Southampton
	PK724	VS356 Spitfire F24 (7288M)	RAF Museum, Hendon
	PL256	VS361 Spitfire IX <R> (BAPC.325) [AI-L]	Privately owned, Leicester
	PL258	VS361 Spitfire IX (G-NSFS)	Norwegian Spitfire Foundation, Duxford (restoration)
	PL279	VS361 Spitfire IX <R> (N3317/BAPC.268) [ZF-Z]	Privately owned, St Mawgan
	PL344	VS361 Spitfire LF IXc (G-IXCC) [TL-B]	Privately owned, Sywell
	PL788	Supermarine Aircraft Spitfire 26 (G-CIEN)	Privately owned, Perth
	PL793	Supermarine Aircraft Spitfire 26 (G-CIXM)	Privately owned, Enstone

Serial	Type (code/other identity)	Owner/operator, location or fate	Notes
PL904	VS365 Spitfire PR XI <R> (EN343/BAPC.226)	RAF Benson, on display	
PL965	VS365 Spitfire PR XI (G-MKXI) [R]	Hangar 11 Collection, North Weald	
PL983	VS365 Spitfire PR XI (G-PRXI)	Privately owned, Duxford	
PM631	VS390 Spitfire PR XIX	RAF BBMF, Coningsby	
PM651	VS390 Spitfire PR XIX (7758M) [X]	RAF Museum, Cosford	
PN323	HP Halifax VII <ff>	IWM Duxford	
PP566	Fairey Firefly I <rf>	Privately owned, Newton Abbott, Devon	
PP972	VS358 Seafire LF IIIc (G-BUAR) [11-5/N]	Privately owned, Sywell	
PR478	Supermarine Aircraft Spitfire 26 [S]	Privately owned, Dunkeswell	
PR533	Hawker Tempest II (MW763/IAF HA586/G-TEMT) [5R-V]	Anglia Aircraft Restorations Ltd, Sywell	
PR536	Hawker Tempest II (IAF HA457)[OQ-H]	RAF Museum, Hendon	
PS004	Airbus Zephyr 8B	For MoD	
PS853	VS390 Spitfire PR XIX (G-RRGN) [C]	Rolls-Royce, East Midlands	
PS890	VS390 Spitfire PR XIX (F-AZJS) [UM-E]	Privately owned, Dijon, France	
PS915	VS390 Spitfire PR XIX (7548M/7711M)	RAF BBMF, Coningsby	
PT462	VS509 Spitfire T9 (G-CTIX/N462JC) [SW-A]	Privately owned, Caernarfon/Duxford	
PT462	VS361 Spitfire IX <R> (BAPC.318) [SW-A]	Privately owned, Moffat, Dumfries & Galloway	
PT879	VS361 Spitfire F IX (G-BYDE/G-PTIX)	Hangar 11 Collection, Biggin Hill (dismantled)	
PV202	VS509 Spitfire T9 (H-98/W3632/G-CCCA) [5R-H]	Historic Flying Ltd, Duxford	
PV303	Supermarine Aircraft Spitfire 26 (G-CCJL) [ON-B]	Privately owned, Enstone	
PZ460	BBC Mosquito (F-PMOZ) [NE-K]	Privately owned, Fontenay-le-Comte, France	
PZ865	Hawker Hurricane IIc (G-AMAU) [EG-S]	RAF BBMF, Biggin Hill (servicing)	
QQ100	Agusta A109E Power Elite (G-CFVB)	Registered as G-ETPI, 20 June 2019	
RA848	Slingsby T7 Cadet TX1 <ff>	Privately owned, Hooton Park	
RA854	Slingsby T7 Cadet TX1	Yorkshire Air Museum, Elvington	
RA897	Slingsby T7 Cadet TX1	Newark Air Museum, Winthorpe	
RA905	Slingsby T7 Cadet TX1 (BGA1143)	Trenchard Museum, RAF Halton	
RB142	Supermarine Aircraft Spitfire 26 (G-CEFC) [DW-B]	Privately owned, Lee-on-Solent	
RB159	VS379 Spitfire F XIV <R> [DW-D]	Privately owned, Delabole, Cornwall	
RB396	Hawker Typhoon IB (G-TIFY) [XP-W] (fuselage)	Hawker Typhoon Restoration Group, Sandown	
RD220	Bristol 156 Beaufighter TF X	National Museum of Flight, stored E Fortune	
RD253	Bristol 156 Beaufighter TF X (7931M)	RAF Museum, Hendon	
RF398	Avro 694 Lincoln B II (8376M) [398]	RAF Museum, Cosford	
RG333	Miles M38 Messenger IIA (G-AIEK)	Privately owned, North Coates	
RG904	VS Spitfire <R> (BAPC.333) [BT-K]	RAF Museum, Cosford	
RG907	Miles M25 Martinet <ff> (BAPC.514)	Tettenhall Transport Heritage Centre	
RH746	Bristol 164 Brigand TF1 (fuselage)	RAF Museum, stored Cosford	
RK838	VS349 Spitfire Vb <R> (BAPC.230/AB550) [GE-P]	Eden Camp Theme Park, Malton, North Yorkshire	
RK855	Supermarine Aircraft Spitfire 26 (G-PIXY) [FT-C]	Privately owned, Henstridge	
RK912	VS361 Spitfire LF IX (G-CLCS)	Privately owned, Duxford	
RL962	DH89A Dominie II (G-AHED)	RAF Museum Reserve Collection, Stafford	
RM169	Percival P31 Proctor IV (G-ANVY) [4-47]	Privately owned, Great Oakley, Essex	
RM221	Percival P31 Proctor IV (G-ANXR)	Privately owned, Headcorn	
RM689	VS379 Spitfire F XIV (G-ALGT)	Rolls-Royce, stored East Midlands Airport	
RM694	VS379 Spitfire F XIV (G-DBKL/6640M)	Privately owned, Booker	
RM927	VS379 Spitfire F XIV (G-JNMA)	Privately owned, Biggin Hill	
RN201	VS379 Spitfire F XIVe (G-BSKP)	Privately owned, Sywell	
RN203	VS379 Spitfire F XIV (G-CLCT)	Privately owned, Duxford	
RN218	Isaacs Spitfire <R> (G-BBJI) [N]	Privately owned, Builth Wells	
RP001*	AeroVironment RQ-20 Puma AE Micro UAV	Royal Navy	
RP002*	AeroVironment RQ-12 Wasp AE Micro UAV	Royal Navy	
RP003*	AeroVironment Shrike Mk1 Micro UAV	MoD	
RR232	VS361 Spitfire HF IXc (PV181/G-BRSF)	Privately owned, Goodwood	
RT486	Auster 5 (G-AJGJ)	RAF Manston History Museum	
RT520	Auster 5 (G-ALYB)	Thorpe Camp Visitors Centre, Lincs	
RT610	Auster 5A-160 (G-AKWS)	Privately owned, Woonton, Herefordshire	
RW382	VS361 Spitfire LF XVIe (G-PBIX/7245M/8075M) [3W-P]	Privately owned, Biggin Hill	
RW386	VS361 Spitfire LF XVIe (SE-BIR/6944M) [NG-D]	Privately owned, Angelholm, Sweden	

Notes	Serial	Type (code/other identity)	Owner/operator, location or fate
	RW388	VS361 Spitfire LF XVIe (6946M) [U4-U]	Stoke-on-Trent City Museum, Rochester (restoration)
	RX168	VS358 Seafire L IIIc (IAC 157/G-BWEM)	Privately owned, Launceston
	SL611	VS361 Spitfire LF XVIe (G-SAEA)	Supermarine Aero Engineering, Stoke-on-Trent
	SL674	VS361 Spitfire LF IX (8392M) [RAS-H]	RAF Museum Reserve Collection, Stafford
	SL721	VS361 Spitfire LF XVIe (OO-XVI) [AU-J]	Privately owned, Brasschaat, Belgium
	SM520	VS509 Spitfire T9 (H-99/G-ILDA) [KJ-I]	Boultbee Flight Academy, Goodwood
	SM639	VS361 Spitfire LF IXe (G-CKYM)	Privately owned, Godalming
	SM845	VS394 Spitfire FR XVIII (G-BUOS) [R]	Spitfire Ltd, Humberside
	SN280	Hawker Tempest V <ff>	South Yorkshire Aircraft Museum, Doncaster
	SR462	VS377 Seafire F XV (UB415/G-TGVP)	Airframe Assemblies, Sandown
	SR661	Hawker Fury ISS (G-CBEL)	Privately owned, Sywell
	SX137	VS384 Seafire F XVII	FAA Museum, RNAS Yeovilton
	SX300	VS384 Seafire F XVII (G-RIPH)	Kennet Aviation, Old Warden
	SX336	VS384 Seafire F XVII (G-KASX) [105/VL]	Kennet Aviation, Old Warden
	TA122	DH98 Mosquito FB VI [UP-G]	de Havilland Aircraft Museum, London Colney
	TA634	DH98 Mosquito TT35 (G-AWJV) [8K-K]	de Havilland Aircraft Museum, London Colney
	TA639	DH98 Mosquito TT35 (7806M) [AZ-E]	RAF Museum, Cosford
	TA719	DH98 Mosquito TT35 (G-ASKC) [56]	IWM Duxford
	TA805	VS361 Spitfire HF IX (G-PMNF) [FX-M]	Privately owned, Biggin Hill
	TB288	VS361 Spitfire LF IX <R> (MH486/46/BAPC.206) [HT-H]	RAF Museum, Hendon
	TB382	VS361 Spitfire LF XVIe (X4277/MK673)	Airframe Assemblies, Sandown
	TB675	VS361 Spitfire LF XVIe (RW393/7293M) [4D-V]	RAF Museum, Hendon
	TB752	VS361 Spitfire LF XVIe (8086M) [KH-Z]	RAF Manston, Memorial Pavilion
	TB885	VS361 Spitfire LF XVIe (G-CKUE) [3W-V]	Privately owned, Leeuwarden, The Netherlands
	TD248	VS361 Spitfire LF XVIe (G-OXVI/7246M) [CR-S]	Spitfire Ltd, Humberside
	TD248	VS361 Spitfire LF XVIe (BAPC.368) [8Q-T] (fuselage)	Norfolk & Suffolk Avn Mus'm, Flixton
	TD314	VS361 Spitfire LF IX (G-CGYJ) [FX-P]	Privately owned, Duxford
	TE184	VS361 Spitfire LF XVIe (G-MXVI/6850M) [9N-B]	Privately owned, Biggin Hill/Bremgarten, Germany
	TE308	VS509 Spitfire T9 (G-AWGB)	Privately owned, Biggin Hill
	TE311	VS361 Spitfire LF XVIe (MK178/7241M) [SZ-G]	RAF BBMF, Biggin Hill
	TE356	VS361 Spitfire LF XVIe (N356TE) [DD-E]	Privately owned, Biggin Hill
	TE462	VS361 Spitfire LF XVIe (7243M)	National Museum of Flight, E Fortune
	TE517	VS361 Spitfire LF IXe (G-JGCA) [HL-K]	Privately owned, Biggin Hill
	TE566	VS509 Spitfire T9 (VH-IXT)	Vintage Flyers, Cotswold Airport (rebuild)
	TG263	Saro SR A1 (G-12-1)	Solent Sky, Southampton
	TG511	HP67 Hastings T5 (8554M) [511]	RAF Museum, Cosford
	TG517	HP67 Hastings T5 [517]	Newark Air Museum, Winthorpe
	TG528	HP67 Hastings C1A [528,T]	IWM Duxford
	TJ138	DH98 Mosquito B35 (7607M) [VO-L]	RAF Museum, Hendon
	TJ343	Auster AOP5 (G-AJXC)	Privately owned, White Waltham
	TJ518	Auster J/1 Autocrat (G-AJIH)	Privately owned, Gloucester
	TJ534	Auster AOP5 (G-AKSY)	Privately owned, Dunsfold
	TJ569	Auster AOP5 (G-AKOW)	Army Flying Museum, Middle Wallop
	TJ652	Auster AOP5 (TJ565/G-AMVD)	Privately owned, Hardwick, Norfolk
	TJ672	Auster 5D (G-ANIJ) [TS-D]	Privately owned, Netheravon
	TK718	GAL59 Hamilcar I (fuselage)	The Tank Museum, Bovington
	TK777	GAL59 Hamilcar I (fuselage)	Army Flying Museum, Middle Wallop
	TP280	VS394 Spitfire FR XVIIIe (D-FSPT)	Hangar 10 Collection, Heringsdorf, Germany
	TP298	VS394 Spitfire FR XVIII (UM-T)	Airframe Assemblies, Sandown
	TS291	Slingsby T7 Cadet TX1 (BGA852)	Royal Scottish Mus'm of Flight, stored Granton
	TS798	Avro 685 York C1 (G-AGNV/MW100)	RAF Museum, Cosford
	TW439	Auster AOP5 (G-ANRP)	Privately owned, Breighton
	TW467	Auster AOP5 (G-ANIE)	Privately owned, Hardwick
	TW477	Auster AOP5 (OY-EFI)	Privately operated, Ringsted, Denmark
	TW501	Auster AOP5 (G-ALBJ)	Privately owned, Dunkeswell
	TW511	Auster AOP5 (G-APAF)	Privately owned, Chiseldon, Wilts
	TW519	Auster AOP5 (G-ANHX) [ROA-V]	Privately owned, RNAS Yeovilton
	TW536	Auster AOP6 (G-BNGE/7704M)	Privately owned, Popham
	TW591	Auster 6A (G-ARIH) [N]	Sold to the Czech Republic, 11 February 2020

Serial	Type (code/other identity)	Owner/operator, location or fate	Notes
TW641	Beagle A61 Terrier 2 (G-ATDN)	Privately owned, Biggin Hill	
TX176	Avro XIX Anson Series 2 (G-AHKX)	BAE Systems, Old Warden	
TX213	Avro 652A Anson C19 (G-AWRS)	North-East Land, Sea & Air Museums, Usworth	
TX214	Avro 652A Anson C19 (7817M)	RAF Museum, Cosford	
TX226	Avro 652A Anson C19 (7865M)	Montrose Air Station Heritage Centre	
TX235	Avro 652A Anson C19	Privately owned, stored Compton Verney	
TX310	DH89A Dragon Rapide 6 (G-AIDL)	Privately owned, Clacton/Duxford	
TZ164	Isaacs Spitfire (G-ISAC) [01-A]	Privately owned, Hampstead Norreys, Berks	
VF301	DH100 Vampire F1 (7060M) [RAL-G]	Midland Air Museum, Coventry	
VF512	Auster 6A (G-ARRX) [PF-M]	Privately owned, Popham	
VF516	Beagle A61 Terrier 2 (G-ASMZ)	Privately owned, Eshott	
VF519	Auster AOP6 (G-ASYN)	Privately owned, Doncaster	
VF526	Auster 6A (G-ARXU) [T]	Privately owned, Strubby	
VF557	Auster 6A (G-ARHM) [H]	Privately owned, Headcorn	
VF560	Auster 6A (frame)	South Yorkshire Aircraft Museum, stored Doncaster	
VF581	Beagle A61 Terrier 1 (G-ARSL) [G]	National Museum of Scotland, Edinburgh	
VF631	Auster AOP6 (G-ASDK)	Privately owned, Hibaldstow	
VH127	Fairey Firefly TT4 [200/R]	FAA Museum, stored Cobham Hall, RNAS Yeovilton	
VL348	Avro 652A Anson C19 (G-AVVO)	Newark Air Museum, Winthorpe	
VL349	Avro 652A Anson C19 (N5054/G-AWSA) [V7-Q]	Norfolk & Suffolk Avn Museum, Flixton	
VM325	Avro 652A Anson C19	Privately owned, Carew Cheriton, Pembrokeshire	
VM360	Avro 652A Anson C19 (G-APHV)	National Museum of Flight, E Fortune	
VM657	Slingsby T8 Tutor TX2 (IGA-6)	Privately owned, stored Ashbourne, Eire	
VM684	Slingsby T8 Tutor TX2 (BGA791)	Privately owned, Knutsford, Cheshire	
VM687	Slingsby T8 Tutor (BGA794)	Privately owned, Lee-on-Solent	
VM791	Slingsby Cadet TX3 (XA312/8876M)	RAF Manston History Museum	
VN485	VS356 Spitfire F24 (7326M)	IWM Duxford	
VN799	EE Canberra T4 (WJ874/G-CDSX)	Cornwall Aviation Heritage Centre, Newquay	
VP293	Avro 696 Shackleton T4 [X] <ff>	Shackleton Preservation Trust, Coventry	
VP519	Avro 652A Anson C19 (G-AVVR) <ff>	South Yorkshire Aircraft Museum, Doncaster	
VP952	DH104 Devon C2 (8820M)	RAF Museum, Cosford	
VP955	DH104 Devon C2 (G-DVON)	Privately owned, stored Cricklade, Wilts	
VP957	DH104 Devon C2 (8822M) <ff>	No 1137 Sqn ATC, Long Kesh	
VP967	DH104 Devon C2 (G-KOOL)	Yorkshire Air Museum, Elvington	
VP975	DH104 Devon C2 [M]	Science Museum, stored Wroughton	
VP981	DH104 Devon C2 (G-DHDV)	Aero Legends, Headcorn/Duxford	
VR137	Westland Wyvern TF1	FAA Museum, stored Cobham Hall, RNAS Yeovilton	
VR192	Percival P40 Prentice T1 (G-APIT)	Romney Marsh Wartime Collection	
VR249	Percival P40 Prentice T1 (G-APIY) [FA-EL]	Newark Air Museum, Winthorpe	
VR259	Percival P40 Prentice T1 (G-APJB) [M]	Privately owned, Postling, Kent	
VR930	Hawker Sea Fury FB11 (8382M) [110/Q]	RN, Yeovilton	
VS356	Percival P40 Prentice T1 (G-AOLU)	Privately owned, Fordoun, Aberdeenshire	
VS562	Avro 652A Anson T21 (8012M) <ff>	Shannon Aviation Museum, Eire	
VS610	Percival P40 Prentice T1 (G-AOKL)[K-L]	Privately owned, Fordoun, Aberdeenshire	
VS618	Percival P40 Prentice T1 (G-AOLK)	RAF Museum Reserve Collection, Stafford	
VS623	Percival P40 Prentice T1 (G-AOKZ)[KQ-F]	Midland Air Museum, Coventry	
VT812	DH100 Vampire F3 (7200M) [N]	RAF Museum, Hendon	
VT935	Boulton Paul P111A (VT769)	Midland Air Museum, Coventry	
VT987	Auster AOP6 (G-BKXP)	Privately owned, Thruxton	
VV106	Supermarine 510 (7175M)	FAA Museum, stored Cobham Hall, RNAS Yeovilton	
VV217	DH100 Vampire FB5 (7323M)	de Havilland Aircraft Museum, stored London Colney	
VV400	EoN Olympia 2 (BGA1697) [97]	Privately owned, Aston Down	
VV401	EoN Olympia 2 (BGA1125) [99]	Privately owned, Ringmer, E Sussex	
VV901	Avro 652A Anson T21	Yorkshire Air Museum, Elvington	
VW453	Gloster Meteor T7 (8703M)	Jet Age Museum, Gloucester	
VW957	DH103 Sea Hornet NF21 <rf>	Privately owned, Chelmsford	
VW993	Beagle A61 Terrier 2 (G-ASCD)	Yorkshire Air Museum, Elvington	
VX113	Auster AOP6 (G-ARNO) [36]	Privately owned, Stow Maries, Essex	
VX185	EE Canberra B(I)8 (7631M) <ff>	National Museum of Flight, E Fortune	
VX250	DH103 Sea Hornet NF21 [48] <rf>	de Havilland Aircraft Museum, London Colney	
VX272	Hawker P.1052 (7174M)	FAA Museum, stored RNAS Yeovilton	

Notes	Serial	Type (code/other identity)	Owner/operator, location or fate
	VX275	Slingsby T21B Sedbergh TX1 (BGA572/8884M)	RAF Museum Reserve Collection, Stafford
	VX281	Hawker Sea Fury T20S (G-RNHF) [120/VL]	Naval Aviation Ltd, RNAS Yeovilton
	VX573	Vickers Valetta C2 (8389M)	RAF Museum, stored Cosford
	VX580	Vickers Valetta C2 [580]	Norfolk & Suffolk Avn Museum, Flixton
	VX595	WS51 Dragonfly HR1	FAA Museum, RNAS Yeovilton
	VX665	Hawker Sea Fury FB11 <rf>	RN Historic Flight, at BAE Systems Brough
	VX924	Beagle A61 Terrier 2 (G-NTVE)	Privately owned, Fenland
	VX926	Auster T7 (G-ASKJ)	Privately owned, Gamlingay, Cambs
	VX927	Auster T7 (G-ASYG)	Privately owned, Dubová, Slovakia
	VZ193	DH100 Vampire FB5 <ff>	Privately owned, Warrington
	VZ305	DH100 Vampire FB6 (J-1196/PX-K/LN-DHY) [N]	Repainted in Norwegian markings as PX-K, May 2019
	VZ440	Gloster Meteor F8 (WA984) [X]	Tangmere Military Aviation Museum
	VZ477	Gloster Meteor F8 (7741M) <ff>	Midland Air Museum, Coventry
	VZ568	Gloster Meteor F8 (7261M) <ff>	RAF Halton
	VZ608	Gloster Meteor FR9	Newark Air Museum, Winthorpe
	VZ634	Gloster Meteor T7 (8657M)	Newark Air Museum, Winthorpe
	VZ638	Gloster Meteor T7 (G-JETM) [HF]	Gatwick Aviation Museum, Charlwood, Surrey
	VZ728	RS4 Desford Trainer (G-AGOS)	Privately owned, Spanhoe
	WA346	DH100 Vampire FB5	RAF Museum, stored Cosford
	WA473	VS Attacker F1 [102/J]	FAA Museum, RNAS Yeovilton
	WA576	Bristol 171 Sycamore 3 (G-ALSS/7900M)	Dumfries & Galloway Avn Mus, Dumfries
	WA577	Bristol 171 Sycamore 3 (G-ALST/7718M)	North-East Land, Sea & Air Museums, Usworth
	WA630	Gloster Meteor T7 [69] <ff>	Robertsbridge Aviation Society, Newhaven
	WA634	Gloster Meteor T7/8	RAF Museum, Cosford
	WA638	Gloster Meteor T7(mod) (G-JWMA)	Martin-Baker Aircraft, Chalgrove
	WA662	Gloster Meteor T7	South Yorkshire Aircraft Museum, Doncaster
	WB188	Hawker Hunter F3 (7154M)	Tangmere Military Aviation Museum
	WB188	Hawker Hunter GA11 (XF300/G-BZPC)	Privately owned, Kent
	WB440	Fairey Firefly AS6 <ff>	Privately owned, Newton Abbott, Devon
	WB491	Avro 706 Ashton 2 (TS897/G-AJJW) <ff>	Newark Air Museum, Winthorpe
	WB549	DHC1 Chipmunk 22A (G-BAPB)	Privately owned, Old Buckenham
	WB555	DHC1 Chipmunk 22 (G-CLKX)	Privately owned, Turweston
	WB560	DHC1 Chipmunk T10 (comp WG403) <ff>	Privately owned, Norwich
	WB565	DHC1 Chipmunk 22 (G-PVET) [X]	Privately owned, Rendcomb
	WB569	DHC1 Chipmunk 22 (G-BYSJ)	Privately owned, Duxford
	WB571	DHC1 Chipmunk 22 (D-EOSF) [34]	Privately owned, Porta Westfalica, Germany
	WB584	DHC1 Chipmunk T10 (comp WG303/7706M)	Solway Aviation Society, stored Carlisle
	WB585	DHC1 Chipmunk 22 (G-AOSY) [28]	Privately owned, Audley End
	WB588	DHC1 Chipmunk 22 (G-AOTD) [D]	Privately owned, Henstridge
	WB615	DHC1 Chipmunk 22 (G-BXIA) [E]	Privately owned, Blackpool
	WB624	DHC1 Chipmunk T10	Newark Air Museum, Winthorpe
	WB626	DHC1 Chipmunk T10 [19] <ff>	Trenchard Museum, RAF Halton
	WB627	DHC1 Chipmunk T10 (9248M) (fuselage) [N]	Dulwich College CCF
	WB645	DHC1 Chipmunk T10 (8218M) <rf>	Privately owned, Norwich
	WB652	DHC1 Chipmunk 22 (G-CHPY) [V]	Privately owned, stored Cricklade, Wilts
	WB654	DHC1 Chipmunk 22 (G-BXGO) [U]	Privately owned, Finmere
	WB657	DHC1 Chipmunk T10 [908]	RN Historic Flight, Yeovilton
	WB670	DHC1 Chipmunk T10 (comp WG303)(8361M)	Privately owned, Carlisle
	WB671	DHC1 Chipmunk 22 (G-BWTG) [910]	Privately owned, Teuge, The Netherlands
	WB685	DHC1 Chipmunk T10 (comp WP969/G-ATHC)	North-East Land, Sea & Air Museums, stored Usworth
	WB697	DHC1 Chipmunk 22 (G-BXCT) [95]	Privately owned, Wickenby
	WB702	DHC1 Chipmunk 22A (G-AOFE)	Privately owned, Audley End
	WB703	DHC1 Chipmunk 22A (G-ARMC)	Privately owned, Booker
	WB711	DHC1 Chipmunk 22 (G-APPM)	Privately owned, Jersey
	WB726	DHC1 Chipmunk 22A (G-AOSK) [E]	Privately owned, Turweston
	WB733	DHC1 Chipmunk T10 (comp WG422)	South Yorkshire Aircraft Museum, Doncaster
	WB758	DHC1 Chipmunk T10 (7729M) [P]	Privately owned, Torquay
	WB763	DHC1 Chipmunk 22 (G-BBMR) [K]	Privately owned, Turweston
	WB922	Slingsby T21B Sedbergh TX1 (BGA4366)	Privately owned, Shrivenham
	WB924	Slingsby T21B Sedbergh TX1 (BGA3901)	Privately owned, Dunstable

Serial	Type (code/other identity)	Owner/operator, location or fate	Notes
WB944	Slingsby T21B Sedbergh TX1 (BGA3160)	Privately owned, Bicester	
WB945	Slingsby T21B Sedbergh TX1 (BGA1254)	Privately owned, stored RAF Halton	
WB971	Slingsby T21B Sedbergh TX1 (BGA3324)	Privately owned, Eaglescott	
WB975	Slingsby T21B Sedbergh TX1 (BGA3288) [FJB]	Privately owned, Shipdham	
WB980	Slingsby T21B Sedbergh TX1 (BGA3290)	Privately owned, Husbands Bosworth	
WB981	Slingsby T21B Sedbergh TX1 (BGA3238)	Privately owned, Eaglescott	
WD286	DHC1 Chipmunk 22 (G-BBND)	Privately owned, Old Warden	
WD292	DHC1 Chipmunk 22 (G-BCRX)	Privately owned, White Waltham	
WD293	DHC1 Chipmunk T10 (7645M) <ff>	South Wales Aviation Museum, St Athan	
WD310	DHC1 Chipmunk 22 (G-BWUN) [B]	Privately owned, Jersey	
WD319	DHC1 Chipmunk 22 (OY-ATF)	Privately owned, France	
WD321	DHC1 Chipmunk 22 (G-BDCC)	Boscombe Down Aviation Collection, Old Sarum	
WD325	DHC1 Chipmunk T10 [N]	AAC, stored Middle Wallop	
WD331	DHC1 Chipmunk 22 (G-BXDH)	Privately owned, Farnborough	
WD355	DHC1 Chipmunk T10 (WD335/G-CBAJ)	Privately owned, Eastleigh	
WD363	DHC1 Chipmunk 22 (G-BCIH) [5]	Privately owned, Netheravon	
WD370	DHC1 Chipmunk T10 <ff>	No 225 Sqn ATC, Brighton	
WD373	DHC1 Chipmunk 22 (G-BXDI) [12]	Privately owned, Turweston	
WD377	DHC1 Chipmunk T10 <ff>	Wings Museum, Balcombe, W Sussex	
WD386	DHC1 Chipmunk T10 (comp WD377)	Ulster Aviation Soc, stored Upper Ballinderry, NI	
WD388	DHC1 Chipmunk 22 (D-EPAK) [68]	Quax Flieger, Hamm, Germany	
WD390	DHC1 Chipmunk 22 (G-BWNK) [68]	Privately owned, Compton Abbas	
WD413	Avro 652A Anson T21 (7881M/G-VROE)	Privately owned, Sleap	
WD615	Gloster Meteor TT20 (WD646/8189M) [R]	RAF Manston History Museum	
WD686	Gloster Meteor NF11	RAF Defford Museum, Croome Park	
WD790	Gloster Meteor NF11 (8743M) <ff>	Boscombe Down Aviation Collection, Old Sarum	
WD889	Fairey Firefly AS5 (comp VT809)	Privately owned, Newton Abbot, Devon	
WD935	EE Canberra B2 (8440M) <ff>	South Yorkshire Aircraft Museum, Doncaster	
WD954	EE Canberra B2 <ff>	Privately owned, St Mawgan	
WD956	EE Canberra B2 <ff>	RAF Defford Museum, Croome Park	
WE113	EE Canberra B2 <ff>	Privately owned, Tangmere	
WE122	EE Canberra TT18 [845] <ff>	Blyth Valley Aviation Collection, Walpole, Suffolk	
WE139	EE Canberra PR3 (8369M)	RAF Museum, Hendon	
WE168	EE Canberra PR3 (8049M) <ff>	Norfolk & Suffolk Avn Museum, Flixton	
WE173	EE Canberra PR3 (8740M) <ff>	Robertsbridge Aviation Society, Mayfield	
WE188	EE Canberra T4	Solway Aviation Society, Carlisle	
WE192	EE Canberra T4 <ff>	Blyth Valley Aviation Collection, Walpole, Suffolk	
WE275	DH112 Venom FB50 (J-1601/G-VIDI)	BAE Systems Hawarden, Fire Section	
WE558	Auster T7 (frame)	East Midlands Airport Aeropark	
WE569	Auster T7 (G-ASAJ)	Privately owned, Defford	
WE570	Auster T7 (G-ASBU)	Privately owned, Stonehaven	
WE591	Auster T7 (F-AZTJ)	Privately owned, Toussus-le-Noble, France	
WE600	Auster T7 Antarctic (7602M)	RAF Museum, Cosford	
WE724	Hawker Sea Fury FB11 (VX653/G-BUCM) [062]	The Fighter Collection, Duxford	
WE982	Slingsby T30B Prefect TX1 (8781M)	RAF Museum, stored Cosford	
WE987	Slingsby T30B Prefect TX1 (BGA2517)	South Yorkshire Aircraft Museum, Doncaster	
WE990	Slingsby T30B Prefect TX1 (BGA2583)	Privately owned, Tibenham	
WE992	Slingsby T30B Prefect TX1 (BGA2692)	Privately owned, Little Rissington	
WF118	Percival P57 Sea Prince T1 (G-DACA) [569/CU]	Privately owned, St Athan	
WF122	Percival P57 Sea Prince T1 [575/CU]	Ulster Aviation Society, Long Kesh	
WF128	Percival P57 Sea Prince T1 (8611M)	Norfolk & Suffolk Avn Museum, Flixton	
WF145	Hawker Sea Hawk F1 <ff>	Privately owned, Newton Abbot, Devon	
WF219	Hawker Sea Hawk F1 <rf>	FAA Museum, stored Cobham Hall, RNAS Yeovilton	
WF225	Hawker Sea Hawk F1 [CU]	RNAS Culdrose, at main gate	
WF259	Hawker Sea Hawk F2 [171/A]	National Museum of Flight, E Fortune	
WF369	Vickers Varsity T1 [F]	Newark Air Museum, Winthorpe	
WF372	Vickers Varsity T1	Brooklands Museum, Weybridge	
WF408	Vickers Varsity T1 (8395M) <ff>	Privately owned, Ashford, Kent	
WF643	Gloster Meteor F8 [F]	Norfolk & Suffolk Avn Museum, Flixton	

Notes	Serial	Type (code/other identity)	Owner/operator, location or fate
	WF784	Gloster Meteor T7 (7895M)	Jet Age Museum, Gloucester
	WF825	Gloster Meteor T7 (8359M) [A]	Montrose Air Station Heritage Centre
	WF911	EE Canberra B2 [CO] <ff>	Ulster Aviation Society, Long Kesh
	WF922	EE Canberra PR3	Midland Air Museum, Coventry
	WG303	DHC1 Chipmunk T10 (8208M) <ff> [83]	Privately owned, Hooton Park
	WG308	DHC1 Chipmunk 22 (G-BYHL) [8]	Privately owned, Averham, Notts
	WG316	DHC1 Chipmunk 22 (G-BCAH)	Privately owned, Gamston
	WG319	DHC1 Chipmunk T10 <ff>	Privately owned, Blandford Forum, Dorset
	WG321	DHC1 Chipmunk 22 (G-DHCC)	Privately owned, Wevelgem, Belgium
	WG322	DHC1 Chipmunk 22A (G-ARMF) [H]	Privately owned, Spanhoe
	WG348	DHC1 Chipmunk 22 (G-BBMV)	Boultbee Flight Academy, Goodwood
	WG350	DHC1 Chipmunk 22 (G-BPAL)	Privately owned, Popham
	WG362	DHC1 Chipmunk T10 (8437M/8630M/*WX643*) <ff>	No 1094 Sqn ATC, Ely
	WG407	DHC1 Chipmunk 22 (G-BWMX) [67]	Privately owned, Fen End Farm, Cambs
	WG418	DHC1 Chipmunk T10 (8209M/G-ATDY) <ff>	No 1940 Sqn ATC, Levenshulme, Gr Manchester
	WG419	DHC1 Chipmunk T10 (8206M) <ff>	Sywell Aviation Museum
	WG422	DHC1 Chipmunk 22 (8394M/G-BFAX) [16]	Privately owned, Egginton, Derbys
	WG432	DHC1 Chipmunk T10 [L]	Army Flying Museum, Middle Wallop
	WG458	DHC1 Chipmunk 22 (N458BG/G-CLLI) [2]	Privately owned, Wickenby
	WG465	DHC1 Chipmunk 22 (G-BCEY)	Privately owned, White Waltham
	WG471	DHC1 Chipmunk T10 (8210M) <ff>	*Currently not known*
	WG472	DHC1 Chipmunk 22A (G-AOTY)	Privately owned, Bryngwyn Bach, Clwyd
	WG477	DHC1 Chipmunk T10 (8362M/G-ATDP) <ff>	RAF Scampton Heritage Centre
	WG486	DHC1 Chipmunk T10 [E]	RAF BBMF, Coningsby
	WG498	Slingsby T21B Sedbergh TX1 (BGA3245)	Privately owned, Aston Down
	WG511	Avro 696 Shackleton T4 (fuselage)	Flambards Village Theme Park, Helston
	WG599	Hawker Sea Fury FB11 (G-SEAF) [161/R]	The Fighter Collection, Reno, Nevada, USA
	WG655	Hawker Sea Fury T20 (G-INVN) [910/GN]	Privately owned, Duxford
	WG719	WS51 Dragonfly HR5 (G-BRMA)	The Helicopter Museum, Weston-super-Mare
	WG724	WS51 Dragonfly HR5 [932/LM]	North-East Land, Sea & Air Museums, Usworth
	WG751	WS51 Dragonfly HR5 [710/GJ]	World Naval Base, Chatham
	WG760	EE P1A (7755M)	RAF Museum, Cosford
	WG763	EE P1A (7816M)	Museum of Science & Industry, Manchester
	WG768	Short SB5 (8005M)	RAF Museum, Cosford
	WG774	BAC 221	Science Museum, at FAA Museum, RNAS Yeovilton
	WG777	Fairey FD2 (7986M)	RAF Museum, Cosford
	WG789	EE Canberra B2/6 <ff>	Norfolk & Suffolk Avn Museum, Flixton
	WH132	Gloster Meteor T7 (7906M) [J]	Privately owned, Hooton Park
	WH166	Gloster Meteor T7 (8052M) [A]	Privately owned, Birlingham, Worcs
	WH291	Gloster Meteor F8	Privately owned, Liverpool Airport
	WH301	Gloster Meteor F8 (7930M) [T]	RAF Museum, Hendon
	WH364	Gloster Meteor F8 (8169M)	Jet Age Museum, Gloucester
	WH453	Gloster Meteor F8	Bentwaters Cold War Air Museum
	WH646	EE Canberra T17A <ff>	Midland Air Museum, Coventry
	WH657	EE Canberra B2 <ff>	Romney Marsh Wartime Collection
	WH725	EE Canberra B2	IWM Duxford
	WH734	EE Canberra B2(mod) <ff>	Privately owned, Pershore
	WH739	EE Canberra B2 <ff>	No 2475 Sqn ATC, Ammanford, Dyfed
	WH740	EE Canberra T17 (8762M) [K]	East Midlands Airport Aeropark
	WH775	EE Canberra PR7 (8128M/8868M) <ff>	Privately owned, Welshpool
	WH779	EE Canberra PR7 <ff>	South Yorkshire Aircraft Museum, Doncaster
	WH779	EE Canberra PR7 [BP] <rf>	RAF AM&SU, stored Shawbury
	WH792	EE Canberra PR7 (WH791/8165M/8176M/8187M)	Newark Air Museum, Winthorpe
	WH798	EE Canberra PR7 (8130M) <ff>	Suffolk Aviation Heritage Centre, Foxhall Heath
	WH840	EE Canberra T4 (8350M)	Privately owned, Flixton
	WH846	EE Canberra T4	Yorkshire Air Museum, Elvington
	WH850	EE Canberra T4 <ff>	RAF Marham Aviation Heritage Centre
	WH863	EE Canberra T17 (8693M) <ff>	Newark Air Museum, Winthorpe
	WH876	EE Canberra B2(mod) <ff>	Boscombe Down Aviation Collection, Old Sarum
	WH887	EE Canberra TT18 [847] <ff>	Sywell Aviation Museum

Serial	Type (code/other identity)	Owner/operator, location or fate	Notes
WH903	EE Canberra B2 <ff>	Yorkshire Air Museum, Elvington	
WH904	EE Canberra T19	Newark Air Museum, Winthorpe	
WH953	EE Canberra B6(mod) <ff>	Blyth Valley Aviation Collection, Walpole, Suffolk	
WH957	EE Canberra E15 (8869M) <ff>	Lincolnshire Avn Heritage Centre, East Kirkby	
WH960	EE Canberra B15 (8344M) <ff>	Rolls-Royce Heritage Trust, Derby	
WH964	EE Canberra E15 (8870M) <ff>	Privately owned, Lewes	
WH984	EE Canberra B15 (8101M) <ff>	City of Norwich Aviation Museum	
WH991	WS51 Dragonfly HR3	Yorkshire Helicopter Preservation Group, Elvington	
WJ231	Hawker Sea Fury FB11 (*WE726*) [115/O]	FAA Museum, RNAS Yeovilton	
WJ306	Slingsby T21B Sedbergh TX1 (BGA3240)	Privately owned, Weston-on-the-Green	
WJ306	Slingsby T21B Sedbergh TX1 (WB957/BGA2720)	Privately owned, Parham Park, Sussex	
WJ358	Auster AOP6 (G-ARYD)	Army Flying Museum, Middle Wallop	
WJ368	Auster AOP6 (G-ASZX)	Privately owned, Eggesford	
WJ404	Auster AOP6 (G-ASOI)	Privately owned, Bidford-on-Avon, Warks	
WJ476	Vickers Valetta T3 <ff>	South Yorkshire Aircraft Museum, Doncaster	
WJ565	EE Canberra T17 (8871M) <ff>	South Yorkshire Aircraft Museum, Doncaster	
WJ567	EE Canberra B2 <ff>	Privately owned, Houghton, Cambs	
WJ576	EE Canberra T17 <ff>	Tettenhall Transport Heritage Centre	
WJ633	EE Canberra T17 <ff>	City of Norwich Aviation Museum	
WJ639	EE Canberra TT18 [39]	North-East Land, Sea & Air Museums, Usworth	
WJ677	EE Canberra B2 <ff>	Privately owned, Redruth	
WJ717	EE Canberra TT18 (9052M) <ff>	*Currently not known*	
WJ721	EE Canberra TT18 [21] <ff>	Morayvia, Kinloss	
WJ731	EE Canberra B2T [BK] <ff>	Privately owned, Golders Green	
WJ775	EE Canberra B6 (8581M) <ff>	Privately owned, stored Farnborough	
WJ865	EE Canberra T4 <ff>	Boscombe Down Aviation Collection, Old Sarum	
WJ880	EE Canberra T4 (8491M) <ff>	Dumfries & Galloway Avn Mus, Dumfries	
WJ903	Vickers Varsity T1 <ff>	South Yorkshire Aircraft Museum, Doncaster	
WJ945	Vickers Varsity T1 (G-BEDV)	Cornwall Aviation Heritage Centre, Newquay	
WJ975	EE Canberra T19 <ff>	South Yorkshire Aircraft Museum, Doncaster	
WJ992	EE Canberra T4	Bournemouth Airport (derelict)	
WK001	Thales Watchkeeper 450 RPAS (4X-USC)	Army 47 Regt Royal Artillery, Boscombe Down	
WK002	Thales Watchkeeper 450 RPAS (4X-USD)	Army 47 Regt Royal Artillery, Boscombe Down	
WK003	Thales Watchkeeper 450 RPAS	Army 47 Regt Royal Artillery, Boscombe Down	
WK004	Thales Watchkeeper 450 RPAS	Army 47 Regt Royal Artillery, Boscombe Down	
WK005	Thales Watchkeeper 450 RPAS	Army 47 Regt Royal Artillery, Boscombe Down	
WK007	Thales Watchkeeper 450 RPAS	Army 47 Regt Royal Artillery, Boscombe Down	
WK008	Thales Watchkeeper 450 RPAS	Army 47 Regt Royal Artillery, Boscombe Down	
WK009	Thales Watchkeeper 450 RPAS	Army 47 Regt Royal Artillery, Boscombe Down	
WK010	Thales Watchkeeper 450 RPAS	Army 47 Regt Royal Artillery, Boscombe Down	
WK011	Thales Watchkeeper 450 RPAS	Army 47 Regt Royal Artillery, Boscombe Down	
WK012	Thales Watchkeeper 450 RPAS	Army 47 Regt Royal Artillery, Boscombe Down	
WK013	Thales Watchkeeper 450 RPAS	Army 47 Regt Royal Artillery, Boscombe Down	
WK014	Thales Watchkeeper 450 RPAS	Army 47 Regt Royal Artillery, Boscombe Down	
WK015	Thales Watchkeeper 450 RPAS	Army 47 Regt Royal Artillery, Boscombe Down	
WK016	Thales Watchkeeper 450 RPAS	Army 47 Regt Royal Artillery, Boscombe Down	
WK017	Thales Watchkeeper 450 RPAS	Army 47 Regt Royal Artillery, Boscombe Down	
WK018	Thales Watchkeeper 450 RPAS	Army 47 Regt Royal Artillery, Boscombe Down	
WK019	Thales Watchkeeper 450 RPAS	Army 47 Regt Royal Artillery, Boscombe Down	
WK020	Thales Watchkeeper 450 RPAS	Army 47 Regt Royal Artillery, Boscombe Down	
WK021	Thales Watchkeeper 450 RPAS	Army 47 Regt Royal Artillery, Boscombe Down	
WK022	Thales Watchkeeper 450 RPAS	Army 47 Regt Royal Artillery, Boscombe Down	
WK023	Thales Watchkeeper 450 RPAS	Army 47 Regt Royal Artillery, Boscombe Down	
WK024	Thales Watchkeeper 450 RPAS	Army 47 Regt Royal Artillery, Boscombe Down	
WK025	Thales Watchkeeper 450 RPAS	Army 47 Regt Royal Artillery, Boscombe Down	
WK026	Thales Watchkeeper 450 RPAS	Army 47 Regt Royal Artillery, Boscombe Down	
WK027	Thales Watchkeeper 450 RPAS	Army 47 Regt Royal Artillery, Boscombe Down	
WK028	Thales Watchkeeper 450 RPAS	Army 47 Regt Royal Artillery, Boscombe Down	
WK029	Thales Watchkeeper 450 RPAS	Army 47 Regt Royal Artillery, Boscombe Down	
WK030	Thales Watchkeeper 450 RPAS	Army 47 Regt Royal Artillery, Boscombe Down	

Notes	Serial	Type (code/other identity)	Owner/operator, location or fate
	WK032	Thales Watchkeeper 450 RPAS	Army 47 Regt Royal Artillery, Boscombe Down
	WK033	Thales Watchkeeper 450 RPAS	Army 47 Regt Royal Artillery, Boscombe Down
	WK034	Thales Watchkeeper 450 RPAS	Army 47 Regt Royal Artillery, Boscombe Down
	WK035	Thales Watchkeeper 450 RPAS	Army 47 Regt Royal Artillery, Boscombe Down
	WK036	Thales Watchkeeper 450 RPAS	Army 47 Regt Royal Artillery, Boscombe Down
	WK037	Thales Watchkeeper 450 RPAS	Army 47 Regt Royal Artillery, Boscombe Down
	WK038	Thales Watchkeeper 450 RPAS	Army 47 Regt Royal Artillery, Boscombe Down
	WK039	Thales Watchkeeper 450 RPAS	Army 47 Regt Royal Artillery, Boscombe Down
	WK040	Thales Watchkeeper 450 RPAS	Army 47 Regt Royal Artillery, Boscombe Down
	WK041	Thales Watchkeeper 450 RPAS	Army 47 Regt Royal Artillery, Boscombe Down
	WK044	Thales Watchkeeper 450 RPAS	Army 47 Regt Royal Artillery, Boscombe Down
	WK045	Thales Watchkeeper 450 RPAS	Army 47 Regt Royal Artillery, Boscombe Down
	WK046	Thales Watchkeeper 450 RPAS	Army 47 Regt Royal Artillery, Boscombe Down
	WK047	Thales Watchkeeper 450 RPAS	Army 47 Regt Royal Artillery, Boscombe Down
	WK048	Thales Watchkeeper 450 RPAS	Army 47 Regt Royal Artillery, Boscombe Down
	WK049	Thales Watchkeeper 450 RPAS	Army 47 Regt Royal Artillery, Boscombe Down
	WK050	Thales Watchkeeper 450 RPAS	*Crashed 13 June 2018, Aberporth*
	WK051	Thales Watchkeeper 450 RPAS	Army 47 Regt Royal Artillery, Boscombe Down
	WK052	Thales Watchkeeper 450 RPAS	Army 47 Regt Royal Artillery, Boscombe Down
	WK053	Thales Watchkeeper 450 RPAS	Army 47 Regt Royal Artillery, Boscombe Down
	WK054	Thales Watchkeeper 450 RPAS	Army 47 Regt Royal Artillery, Boscombe Down
	WK060	Thales Watchkeeper 450 RPAS	MoD/Thales, Aberporth
	WK102	EE Canberra T17 (8780M) <ff>	Privately owned, Welshpool
	WK118	EE Canberra TT18 [CQ] <ff>	Avro Heritage Museum, Woodford
	WK122	EE Canberra TT18 <ff>	Privately owned, Wesham, Lancs
	WK124	EE Canberra TT18 (9093M) [CR]	Privately owned, Gilberdyke, E Yorks
	WK126	EE Canberra TT18 (N2138J) [843]	Jet Age Museum, stored Gloucester
	WK127	EE Canberra TT18 (8985M) <ff>	Privately owned, stored Handcross, W Sussex
	WK128	EE Canberra B2 <ff>	South Wales Aviation Museum, St Athan
	WK146	EE Canberra B2 <ff>	Gatwick Aviation Museum, Charlwood, Surrey
	WK163	EE Canberra B2/6 (G-BVWC/G-CTTS)	Vulcan To The Sky Trust, Doncaster Sheffield Airport
	WK198	VS Swift F4 (7428M) (fuselage)	Brooklands Museum, Weybridge
	WK275	VS Swift F4	Privately owned,
	WK277	VS Swift FR5 (7719M) [N]	Newark Air Museum, Winthorpe
	WK281	VS Swift FR5 (7712M) [S]	Tangmere Military Aviation Museum
	WK393	DH112 Venom FB1 <ff>	Privately owned, Lavendon, Bucks
	WK512	DHC1 Chipmunk 22 (G-BXIM) [A]	Privately owned, RAF Halton
	WK514	DHC1 Chipmunk 22 (G-BBMO)	Privately owned, Wellesbourne Mountford
	WK517	DHC1 Chipmunk 22 (G-ULAS)	Privately owned, Goodwood
	WK518	DHC1 Chipmunk T10 [C]	RAF BBMF, Coningsby
	WK522	DHC1 Chipmunk 22 (G-BCOU)	Privately owned, Duxford
	WK549	DHC1 Chipmunk 22 (G-BTWF)	*Sold to France, June 2019*
	WK558	DHC1 Chipmunk 22A (G-ARMG) [DH]	Privately owned, Shenington, Oxon
	WK562	DHC1 Chipmunk 22 (F-AZUR) [91]	Privately owned, La Baule, France
	WK570	DHC1 Chipmunk T10 (8211M) <ff>	No 424 Sqn ATC, Solent Sky, Southampton
	WK576	DHC1 Chipmunk T10 (8357M) <ff>	Tettenhall Transport Heritage Centre
	WK577	DHC1 Chipmunk 22 (G-BCYM)	Privately owned, Oaksey Park
	WK584	DHC1 Chipmunk T10 (7556M) <ff>	No 511 Sqn ATC, Ramsey, Cambs
	WK585	DHC1 Chipmunk 22 (9265M/G-BZGA)	Privately owned, Compton Abbas
	WK586	DHC1 Chipmunk 22 (G-BXGX) [V]	Privately owned, Shoreham
	WK590	DHC1 Chipmunk 22 (G-BWVZ) [69]	Privately owned, Grimbergen, Belgium
	WK608	DHC1 Chipmunk T10 [906]	RN, Yeovilton
	WK609	DHC1 Chipmunk 22 (G-BXDN) [93]	Privately owned, Booker
	WK611	DHC1 Chipmunk 22 (G-ARWB)	Privately owned, Thruxton
	WK620	DHC1 Chipmunk T10 [T] (fuselage)	Privately owned, Hawarden
	WK622	DHC1 Chipmunk 22 (G-BCZH)	Privately owned, Wickenby
	WK624	DHC1 Chipmunk 22A (G-BWHI)	Privately owned, Blackpool
	WK626	DHC1 Chipmunk T10 (8213M) <ff>	South Yorkshire Aircraft Museum, Doncaster
	WK628	DHC1 Chipmunk 22 (G-BBMW)	Privately owned, Goodwood
	WK630	DHC1 Chipmunk 22 (G-BXDG)	Privately owned, Felthorpe
	WK633	DHC1 Chipmunk 22 (G-BXEC) [A]	Privately owned, Duxford
	WK634	DHC1 Chipmunk T10 (G-CIGE) [902]	Privately owned, Dunkeswell

Serial	Type (code/other identity)	Owner/operator, location or fate	Notes
WK635	DHC1 Chipmunk 22 (G-HFRH)	Privately owned, Hawarden	
WK638	DHC1 Chipmunk 22 (G-BWJZ) (fuselage)	Privately owned, South Marston, Swindon	
WK640	DHC1 Chipmunk 22A (G-BWUV) [C]	Privately owned, Hooton Park (wreck)	
WK640	OGMA/DHC1 Chipmunk T20 (G-CERD)	Privately owned, Spanhoe	
WK642	DHC1 Chipmunk 22 (EI-AFZ) [94]	Privately owned, Kilrush, Eire	
WK654	Gloster Meteor F8 (8092M)	City of Norwich Aviation Museum	
WK800	Gloster Meteor F8 [Z]	Boscombe Down Aviation Collection, Old Sarum	
WK864	Gloster Meteor F8 (WL168/7750M) [C]	Yorkshire Air Museum, Elvington	
WK935	Gloster Meteor Prone Pilot (7869M)	RAF Museum, Cosford	
WK991	Gloster Meteor F8 (7825M)	IWM Duxford	
WL131	Gloster Meteor F8 (7751M) <ff>	South Yorkshire Aircraft Museum, Doncaster	
WL181	Gloster Meteor F8 [X]	North-East Land, Sea & Air Museums, Usworth	
WL332	Gloster Meteor T7 [888]	Privately owned, Long Marston	
WL345	Gloster Meteor T7 (comp WL360)	*Repainted as WZ584, January 2020*	
WL349	Gloster Meteor T7	Jet Age Museum, Gloucester	
WL375	Gloster Meteor T7(mod)	Dumfries & Galloway Avn Mus, Dumfries	
WL405	Gloster Meteor T7 <ff>	South Wales Aviation Museum, St Athan	
WL419	Gloster Meteor T7(mod) (G-JSMA)	Martin-Baker Aircraft, Chalgrove	
WL505	DH100 Vampire FB9 (7705M/G-FBIX)	Privately owned, Mendlesham	
WL626	Vickers Varsity T1 (G-BHDD) [P]	East Midlands Airport Aeropark	
WL627	Vickers Varsity T1 (8488M) [D] <ff>	Privately owned, Preston, E Yorkshire	
WL679	Vickers Varsity T1 (9155M)	RAF Museum, Cosford	
WL732	BP P108 Sea Balliol T21	RAF Museum, Cosford	
WL795	Avro 696 Shackleton MR2C (8753M) [T]	Privately owned, Newquay	
WL798	Avro 696 Shackleton MR2C (8114M) <ff>	Privately owned, Elgin	
WM145	AW Meteor NF11 <ff>	Morayvia, Kinloss	
WM167	AW Meteor NF11 (G-LOSM)	Privately owned, Bruntingthorpe	
WM224	AW Meteor TT20 (*WM311*/8177M) [X]	East Midlands Airport Aeropark	
WM267	AW Meteor NF11 <ff>	City of Norwich Aviation Museum	
WM292	AW Meteor TT20 [841]	FAA Museum, stored Cobham Hall, RNAS Yeovilton	
WM366	AW Meteor NF13 (4X-FNA) (comp VZ462)	Jet Age Museum, Gloucester	
WM367	AW Meteor NF13 <ff>	East Midlands Airport Aeropark	
WM571	DH112 Sea Venom FAW21 [VL]	Solent Sky, stored Romsey	
WM729	DH113 Vampire NF10 <ff>	de Havilland Aircraft Mus'm, stored London Colney	
WM913	Hawker Sea Hawk FB5 (8162M) [456/J]	Newark Air Museum, Winthorpe	
WM961	Hawker Sea Hawk FB5 [J]	Caernarfon Air World	
WM969	Hawker Sea Hawk FB5 [10/Z]	IWM Duxford	
WN105	Hawker Sea Hawk FB3 (WF299/8164M)	Privately owned, Birlingham, Worcs	
WN108	Hawker Sea Hawk F2 [033]	Ulster Aviation Society, Long Kesh	
WN149	BP P108 Balliol T2 [AT]	RAF Museum, stored Cosford	
WN411	Fairey Gannet AS1 (fuselage)	Privately owned, Sholing, Hants	
WN493	WS51 Dragonfly HR5	FAA Museum, RNAS Yeovilton	
WN499	WS51 Dragonfly HR5	South Yorkshire Aircraft Museum, stored Doncaster	
WN516	BP P108 Balliol T2 <ff>	Tettenhall Transport Heritage Centre	
WN534	BP P108 Balliol T2 <ff>	Tettenhall Transport Heritage Centre	
WN890	Hawker Hunter F2 <ff>	Boscombe Down Aviation Collection, Old Sarum	
WN904	Hawker Hunter F2 (7544M) [Q]	Sywell Aviation Museum	
	(wears WN921 [S] on starboard side)		
WN907	Hawker Hunter F2 (7416M) <ff>	Robertsbridge Aviation Society, Newhaven	
WN957	Hawker Hunter F5 <ff>	Morayvia, Kinloss	
WP185	Hawker Hunter F5 (7583M)	Privately owned, Great Dunmow, Essex	
WP190	Hawker Hunter F5 (7582M/8473M/*WP180*) [K]	Tangmere Military Aviation Museum	
WP255	DH113 Vampire NF10 <ff>	South Yorkshire Aircraft Museum, stored Doncaster	
WP266	EoN AP.5 Primary (BAPC.423)	Privately owned, Fishburn	
WP269	EoN Eton TX1 (BGA3214)	Privately owned, Little Rissington	
WP270	EoN Eton TX1 (8598M)	Gliding Heritage Centre, Lasham	
WP308	Percival P57 Sea Prince T1 (G-GACA) [572/CU]	Gatwick Aviation Museum, Charlwood, Surrey	
WP313	Percival P57 Sea Prince T1 [568/CU]	FAA Museum, stored Cobham Hall, RNAS Yeovilton	

Notes	Serial	Type (code/other identity)	Owner/operator, location or fate
	WP314	Percival P57 Sea Prince T1 (8634M) [573/CU]	Privately owned, Carlisle Airport
	WP321	Percival P57 Sea Prince T1 (G-BRFC) [750/CU]	South Wales Aviation Museum, St Athan
	WP495	WS51 Dragonfly HR5 (G-AJOV) [915/LM]	Morayvia, Kinloss
	WP772	DHC1 Chipmunk T10 (WK518) [4]	RAF Manston History Museum
	WP784	DHC1 Chipmunk T10 (comp WZ876) [RCY-E]	East Midlands Airport Aeropark
	WP788	DHC1 Chipmunk 22A (G-BCHL)	Privately owned, Sleap
	WP790	DHC1 Chipmunk T10 (G-BBNC) [T]	de Havilland Aircraft Museum, London Colney
	WP795	DHC1 Chipmunk 22 (G-BVZZ) [901]	Privately owned, Lasham
	WP800	DHC1 Chipmunk 22 (G-BCXN) [2]	Privately owned, RAF Halton
	WP803	DHC1 Chipmunk 22 (G-HAPY) [G]	Privately owned, Booker
	WP805	DHC1 Chipmunk 22 (G-MAJR) [D]	Privately owned, Lee-on-Solent
	WP809	DHC1 Chipmunk 22A (G-BVTX) [78]	Privately owned, Husbands Bosworth
	WP811	DHC1 Chipmunk 22 (G-BCKN)	Privately owned, Husbands Bosworth
	WP835	DHC1 Chipmunk 22 (D-ERTY)	Privately owned, Rinteln, Germany
	WP840	DHC1 Chipmunk 22 (F-AZQM) [9]	Privately owned, Reims, France
	WP844	DHC1 Chipmunk 22 (G-BWOX) [85]	Privately owned, Adriers, France
	WP848	DHC1 Chipmunk 22 (8342M/G-BFAW)	Privately owned, Old Buckenham
	WP859	DHC1 Chipmunk 22 (G-BXCP) [E] (wreck)	Privately owned, Fishburn
	WP860	DHC1 Chipmunk 22 (G-BXDA) [6]	Privately owned, Kirknewton
	WP863	DHC1 Chipmunk T10 (8360M/G-ATJI) <ff>	No 2385 Sqn ATC, Melksham, Wilts
	WP869	DHC1 Chipmunk T10 (8215M) <ff>	de Havilland Aircraft Museum, London Colney
	WP870	DHC1 Chipmunk 22 (G-BCOI) [12]	Privately owned, Rayne Hall Farm, Essex
	WP896	DHC1 Chipmunk 22 (G-BWVY)	Privately owned, RAF Halton
	WP901	DHC1 Chipmunk 22 (G-BWNT) [B]	Privately owned, Biggin Hill
	WP903	DHC1 Chipmunk 22 (G-BCGC)	Privately owned, Henlow
	WP912	DHC1 Chipmunk T10 (8467M)	RAF Museum, Cosford
	WP921	DHC1 Chipmunk T10 (G-ATJJ) <ff>	Privately owned, Brooklands
	WP925	DHC1 Chipmunk 22 (G-BXHA/G-HVII) [C]	Privately owned, Old Warden
	WP927	DHC1 Chipmunk T10 (8216M/G-ATJK) <ff>	Privately owned, Wyton
	WP928	DHC1 Chipmunk 22 (G-BXGM) [D]	Privately owned, Goodwood
	WP929	DHC1 Chipmunk 22 (G-BXCV) [F]	Privately owned, Duxford
	WP930	DHC1 Chipmunk 22 (G-BXHF) [J]	Privately owned, Goodwood
	WP962	DHC1 Chipmunk T10 (9287M) [C]	RAF Museum, Hendon
	WP964	DHC1 Chipmunk T20 (G-HDAE)	Privately owned, Wellesbourne Mountford
	WP971	DHC1 Chipmunk 22 (G-ATHD)	Privately owned, Denham
	WP973	DHC1 Chipmunk 22 (G-BCPU)	Privately owned, Turweston
	WP977	DHC1 Chipmunk 22 (G-BHRD) <ff>	Privately owned, South Molton, Devon
	WP983	DHC1 Chipmunk 22 (G-BXNN) [B]	Privately owned, Eggesford
	WP984	DHC1 Chipmunk 22 (G-BWTO) [H]	Privately owned, Little Gransden
	WR360	DH112 Venom FB50 (J-1626/G-DHSS) <ff>	Privately owned, Maddenstown, Co Kildare, Eire
	WR410	DH112 Venom FB50 (J-1539/G-DHUU)	Shannon Aviation Museum, Eire
	WR470	DH112 Venom FB50 (J-1542/G-DHVM)	Privately owned, Bruntingthorpe
	WR539	DH112 Venom FB4 (8399M) <ff>	Privately owned, Cantley, Norfolk
	WR960	Avro 696 Shackleton AEW2 (8772M)	Museum of Science & Industry, Manchester
	WR963	Avro 696 Shackleton AEW2 (G-SKTN) [B-M]	Shackleton Preservation Trust, Coventry
	WR971	Avro 696 Shackleton MR3/3 (8119M) [Q] (fuselage)	Fenland & W Norfolk Aviation Museum, Wisbech
	WR974	Avro 696 Shackleton MR3/3 (8117M) [K]	Privately owned, Bruntingthorpe
	WR977	Avro 696 Shackleton MR3/3 (8186M) [B]	Newark Air Museum, Winthorpe
	WR982	Avro 696 Shackleton MR3/3 (8106M) [J]	Gatwick Aviation Museum, Charlwood, Surrey
	WR985	Avro 696 Shackleton MR3/3 (8103M) [H]	Privately owned, Long Marston
	WS103	Gloster Meteor T7 [709]	FAA Museum, stored Cobham Hall, RNAS Yeovilton
	WS692	Gloster Meteor NF12 (7605M) [C]	Newark Air Museum, Winthorpe
	WS726	Gloster Meteor NF14 (7960M) [H]	No 1855 Sqn ATC, Royton, Gr Manchester
	WS739	Gloster Meteor NF14 (7961M)	Newark Air Museum, Winthorpe
	WS760	Gloster Meteor NF14 (7964M)	East Midlands Airport Aeropark, stored
	WS776	Gloster Meteor NF14 (7716M) [K]	Bournemouth Aviation Museum
	WS788	Gloster Meteor NF14 (7967M) [Z]	Yorkshire Air Museum, Elvington
	WS792	Gloster Meteor NF14 (7965M) [K]	Brighouse Bay Caravan Park, Borgue, D&G
	WS807	Gloster Meteor NF14 (7973M) [N]	Jet Age Museum, Gloucester
	WS832	Gloster Meteor NF14 [W]	Solway Aviation Society, Carlisle

Serial	Type (code/other identity)	Owner/operator, location or fate	Notes
WS838	Gloster Meteor NF14 [D]	Midland Air Museum, Coventry	
WS840	Gloster Meteor NF14 (7969M) [N] <rf>	Privately owned, Upper Ballinderry, NI	
WS843	Gloster Meteor NF14 (7937M) [J]	RAF Museum, Cosford	
WT121	Douglas Skyraider AEW1 (WT983) [415/CU]	FAA Museum, stored Cobham Hall, RNAS Yeovilton	
WT205	EE Canberra B15 <ff>	RAF Manston History Museum	
WT308	EE Canberra B(I)6	RN, Predannack Fire School	
WT309	EE Canberra B(I)6 <ff>	Farnborough Air Sciences Trust, Farnborough	
WT319	EE Canberra B(I)6 <ff>	South Yorkshire Aircraft Museum, Doncaster	
WT333	EE Canberra B6(mod) (G-BVXC)	Privately owned, Bruntingthorpe	
WT339	EE Canberra B(I)8 (8198M)	RAF Barkston Heath Fire Section	
WT482	EE Canberra T4 <ff>	Privately owned, Marske by the Sea, Durham	
WT486	EE Canberra T4 (8102M) <ff>	Privately owned, Westbury	
WT507	EE Canberra PR7 (8131M/8548M) [44] <ff>	No 384 Sqn ATC, Mansfield	
WT520	EE Canberra PR7 (8094M/8184M) <ff>	Privately owned, Hooton Park	
WT525	EE Canberra T22 [855] <ff>	Cornwall College, Newquay Airport	
WT532	EE Canberra PR7 (8728M/8890M) <ff>	Bournemouth Aviation Museum	
WT534	EE Canberra PR7 (8549M) [43] <ff>	South Yorkshire Aircraft Museum, Doncaster	
WT536	EE Canberra PR7 (8063M) <ff>	South Yorkshire Aircraft Museum, Doncaster	
WT555	Hawker Hunter F1 (7499M)	Vanguard Haulage, Greenford, London	
WT569	Hawker Hunter F1 (7491M)	No 2117 Sqn ATC, Kenfig Hill, Mid-Glamorgan	
WT612	Hawker Hunter F1 (7496M)	RAF Henlow, on display	
WT619	Hawker Hunter F1 (7525M)	Montrose Air Station Heritage Centre	
WT648	Hawker Hunter F1 (7530M) <ff>	Boscombe Down Aviation Collection, Old Sarum	
WT651	Hawker Hunter F1 (7532M) [C]	Newark Air Museum, Winthorpe	
WT660	Hawker Hunter F1 (7421M) [C]	Highland Aviation Museum, Inverness	
WT680	Hawker Hunter F1 (7533M) [J]	Privately owned, Holbeach, Lincs	
WT684	Hawker Hunter F1 (7422M) <ff>	Privately owned, Lavendon, Bucks	
WT694	Hawker Hunter F1 (7510M)	Caernarfon Air World	
WT711	Hawker Hunter GA11 [833/DD]	Lakes Lightnings, Spark Bridge, Cumbria	
WT720	Hawker Hunter F51 (RDAF E-408/8565M) [B]	Repainted in Iraqi markings as 349, May 2019	
WT722	Hawker Hunter T8C (G-BWGN) [873]	Cornwall Aviation Heritage Centre, Newquay	
WT723	Hawker Hunter PR11 (XG194/G-PRII) [692/LM]	Hunter Flight Academy, St Athan	
WT741	Hawker Hunter GA11 [791] <ff>	Privately owned, South Yorks Air Mus'm, Doncaster	
WT744	Hawker Hunter GA11 [868/VL]	Privately owned, Braunton, Devon	
WT746	Hawker Hunter F4 (XF506/7770M) [A]	Dumfries & Galloway Avn Mus, Dumfries	
WT799	Hawker Hunter T8C [879]	Blue Lagoon Diving Centre, Womersley, N Yorks	
WT804	Hawker Hunter GA11 [831/DD]	Privately owned, Todenham, Glos	
WT806	Hawker Hunter GA11	Privately owned, Bruntingthorpe	
WT859	Supermarine 544 <ff>	Boscombe Down Aviation Collection, Old Sarum	
WT867	Slingsby T31B Cadet TX3	Privately owned, Eaglescott	
WT874	Slingsby T31B Cadet TX3 (BGA1255)	Privately owned,	
WT877	Slingsby T31B Cadet TX3	Tettenhall Transport Heritage Centre	
WT900	Slingsby T31B Cadet TX3 (BGA3272) [FHK]	Privately owned, Saltby, Leics	
WT905	Slingsby T31B Cadet TX3	Privately owned, Keevil	
WT908	Slingsby T31B Cadet TX3 (BGA3487)	Privately owned, Dunstable	
WT910	Slingsby T31B Cadet TX3 (BGA3953)	Privately owned, Llandegla, Denbighshire	
WT914	Slingsby T31B Cadet TX3 (BGA3194) (fuselage)	East Midlands Airport Aeropark	
WT933	Bristol 171 Sycamore 3 (G-ALSW/7709M)	Newark Air Museum, Winthorpe	
WV106	Douglas Skyraider AEW1 [427/C]	FAA Museum, stored Cobham Hall, RNAS Yeovilton	
WV198	Sikorsky S55 Whirlwind HAR21 (G-BJWY) [K]	Solway Aviation Society, Carlisle	
WV256	Hawker Hunter GA11 (WB188/G-BZPB) [D]	Cornwall Aviation Heritage Centre, Newquay	
WV314	Hawker Hunter F51 (G-9-445/E-424) [B]	South Yorkshire Aircraft Museum, Doncaster	
WV322	Hawker Hunter T8C (G-BZSE/9096M) [22/VL]	Privately owned, North Weald	
WV332	Hawker Hunter F4 (7673M) <ff>	Tangmere Military Aircraft Museum	
WV381	Hawker Hunter GA11 [732] <ff>	Hovercraft Museum, Lee-on-Solent	
WV382	Hawker Hunter GA11 [830/VL]	East Midlands Airport Aeropark	
WV383	Hawker Hunter T7	Farnborough Air Sciences Trust, Farnborough	
WV396	Hawker Hunter T8C (9249M) [91]	Tacla Taid Museum, Newborough, Anglesey	
WV493	Percival P56 Provost T1 (G-BDYG/7696M) [29]	National Museum of Flight, stored E Fortune	
WV499	Percival P56 Provost T1 (G-BZRF/7698M) [P3]	Privately owned, Westonzoyland, Somerset	

Notes	Serial	Type (code/other identity)	Owner/operator, location or fate
	WV514	Percival P56 Provost T51 (G-BLIW) [N-C]	Privately owned, Shoreham
	WV562	Percival P56 Provost T1 (XF688/7606M) [P-C]	RAF Museum, Cosford
	WV605	Percival P56 Provost T1 [T-B]	Norfolk & Suffolk Avn Museum, Flixton
	WV606	Percival P56 Provost T1 (7622M)[P-B]	Newark Air Museum, Winthorpe
	WV679	Percival P56 Provost T1 (7615M) [O-J]	Wellesbourne Wartime Museum
	WV705	Percival P66 Pembroke C1 <ff>	Privately owned, Awbridge, Hants
	WV740	Percival P66 Pembroke C1 (G-BNPH)	Privately owned, St Athan
	WV746	Percival P66 Pembroke C1 (8938M)	RAF Museum, Cosford
	WV781	Bristol 171 Sycamore HR12 (G-ALTD/7839M) <ff>	Caernarfon Air World
	WV783	Bristol 171 Sycamore HR12 (G-ALSP/7841M)	RAF Museum, Hendon
	WV787	EE Canberra B2/8 (8799M)	Newark Air Museum, Winthorpe
	WV795	Hawker Sea Hawk FGA6 (8151M)	Privately owned, Dunsfold
	WV797	Hawker Sea Hawk FGA6 (8155M) [491/J]	Midland Air Museum, Coventry
	WV798	Hawker Sea Hawk FGA6 [147/E]	Cornwall Aviation Heritage Centre, Newquay
	WV838	Hawker Sea Hawk FGA4 [182] <ff>	Norfolk & Suffolk Avn Museum, Flixton
	WV856	Hawker Sea Hawk FGA6 [163]	FAA Museum, RNAS Yeovilton
	WV903	Hawker Sea Hawk FGA6 (8153M) [128] <ff>	Privately owned, Stoneykirk, D&G
	WV908	Hawker Sea Hawk FGA6 (8154M) [188/A]	RN, stored Shawbury
	WV910	Hawker Sea Hawk FGA6 <ff>	Boscombe Down Aviation Collection, Old Sarum
	WV911	Hawker Sea Hawk FGA4 [115/C]	RNAS Yeovilton, Fire Section
	WW138	DH112 Sea Venom FAW22 [227/Z]	FAA Museum, RNAS Yeovilton
	WW145	DH112 Sea Venom FAW22 [680/LM]	National Museum of Flight, E Fortune
	WW217	DH112 Sea Venom FAW22 [351]	Newark Air Museum, Winthorpe
	WW388	Percival P56 Provost T1 (7616M) [O-F]	Provost Preservation, Cambridge
	WW421	Percival P56 Provost T1 (WW450/G-BZRE/7689M)	Repainted as WW450, 2019
	WW442	Percival P56 Provost T1 (7618M) [N]	East Midlands Airport Aeropark
	WW444	Percival P56 Provost T1 [D]	Privately owned, Brownhills, Staffs
	WW447	Percival P56 Provost T1 [F]	Privately owned, Shoreham
	WW450	Percival P56 Provost T1 (WW421/G-BZRE/7689M)	Bournemouth Aviation Museum
	WW453	Percival P56 Provost T1 (G-TMKI) [W-S]	Privately owned, Westonzoyland, Somerset
	WW654	Hawker Hunter GA11 [834/DD]	Privately owned, Ford, W Sussex
	WW664	Hawker Hunter F4 <ff>	Privately owned, Norfolk
	WX788	DH112 Venom NF3 <ff>	South Yorkshire Aircraft Museum, stored Doncaster
	WX853	DH112 Venom NF3 (7443M)	de Havilland Aircraft Mus'm, stored London Colney
	WX905	DH112 Venom NF3 (7458M)	Newark Air Museum, Winthorpe
	WZ425	DH115 Vampire T11	Privately owned, Birlingham, Worcs
	WZ447	DH115 Vampire T55 (U-1230/PX-M/LN-DHZ) [M]	Repainted in Norwegian markings as PX-M, May 2019
	WZ450	DH115 Vampire T11 <ff>	Privately owned, Corscombe, Dorset
	WZ507	DH115 Vampire T11 (G-VTII) [74]	Privately owned, North Weald
	WZ515	DH115 Vampire T11 [60]	Solway Aviation Society, Carlisle
	WZ518	DH115 Vampire T11 [B]	North-East Land, Sea & Air Museums, Usworth
	WZ549	DH115 Vampire T11 (8118M) [F]	Ulster Aviation Society, Long Kesh
	WZ553	DH115 Vampire T11 (G-DHYY) <ff>	Privately owned, Stockton, Warks
	WZ557	DH115 Vampire T11	Morayvia, Kinloss
	WZ572	DH115 Vampire T11 (8124M) [65] <ff>	Privately owned, Sholing, Hants
	WZ581	DH115 Vampire T11 <ff>	The Vampire Collection, Hemel Hempstead
	WZ584	DH115 Vampire T11 (G-BZRC) [K]	Sold to Canada, 2014
	WZ589	DH115 Vampire T11 [19]	Privately owned, Wigmore, Kent
	WZ590	DH115 Vampire T11 [49]	IWM Duxford
	WZ662	Auster AOP9 (G-BKVK)	Privately owned, Liverpool
	WZ679	Auster AOP9 (7863M/XP248/G-CIUX)	Privately owned, Whittlesford, Cambs
	WZ706	Auster AOP9 (7851M/G-BURR)	Privately owned, Darley Moor, Derbys
	WZ711	Auster AOP9/Beagle E3 (G-AVHT)	South Yorkshire Aircraft Museum, stored Doncaster
	WZ721	Auster AOP9	Army Flying Museum, Middle Wallop
	WZ724	Auster AOP9 (7432M) (frame)	Army Flying Museum, Middle Wallop
	WZ736	Avro 707A (7868M)	Museum of Science & Industry, Manchester
	WZ744	Avro 707C (7932M)	RAF Museum, stored Cosford
	WZ753	Slingsby T38 Grasshopper TX1	Boscombe Down Aviation Collection, Old Sarum
	WZ755	Slingsby T38 Grasshopper TX1 (BGA3481)	Tettenhall Transport Heritage Centre

Serial	Type (code/other identity)	Owner/operator, location or fate	Notes
WZ757	Slingsby T38 Grasshopper TX1 (comp XK820)	Privately owned, Saltby, Lincs	
WZ767	Slingsby T38 Grasshopper TX1	North-East Land, Sea & Air Museums, Usworth	
WZ772	Slingsby T38 Grasshopper TX1	Trenchard Museum, RAF Halton	
WZ773	Slingsby T38 Grasshopper TX1	Edinburgh Academy	
WZ784	Slingsby T38 Grasshopper TX1 (comp WZ824)	Solway Aviation Society, stored Carlisle	
WZ784	Slingsby T38 Grasshopper TX1	Privately owned, stored Felixstowe	
WZ791	Slingsby T38 Grasshopper TX1 (8944M)	RAF Museum, Hendon	
WZ793	Slingsby T38 Grasshopper TX1	Privately owned, Keevil	
WZ796	Slingsby T38 Grasshopper TX1	Privately owned, stored Aston Down	
WZ798	Slingsby T38 Grasshopper TX1	Privately owned, Eaglescott	
WZ816	Slingsby T38 Grasshopper TX1 (BGA3979)	*To Malta, 2018*	
WZ818	Slingsby T38 Grasshopper TX1 (BGA4361)	Privately owned, Nympsfield	
WZ819	Slingsby T38 Grasshopper TX1 (BGA3498)	Privately owned, Halton	
WZ820	Slingsby T38 Grasshopper TX1 <ff>	Sywell Aviation Museum, stored	
WZ822	Slingsby T38 Grasshopper TX1	South Yorkshire Aircraft Museum, stored Doncaster	
WZ824	Slingsby T38 Grasshopper TX1	Privately owned, Bridge of Weir, Renfrewshire	
WZ826	Vickers Valiant B(K)1 (XD826/7872M) <ff>	Privately owned, Rayleigh, Essex	
WZ828	Slingsby T38 Grasshopper TX1 (BGA4421)	Privately owned, Little Rissington	
WZ831	Slingsby T38 Grasshopper TX1	Privately owned, stored Nympsfield, Glos	
WZ846	DHC1 Chipmunk 22 (G-BCSC/8439M)	No 2427 Sqn ATC, Biggin Hill	
WZ847	DHC1 Chipmunk 22 (G-CPMK) [F]	Privately owned, Sleap	
WZ869	DHC1 Chipmunk T10 (8019M) <ff> [6]	South Wales Aviation Museum, stored St Athan	
WZ872	DHC1 Chipmunk 22 (G-BZGB) [E]	Privately owned, Blackpool	
WZ876	DHC1 Chipmunk 22 (G-BBWN) <ff>	Tangmere Military Aviation Museum	
WZ879	DHC1 Chipmunk 22 (G-BWUT) [X]	Privately owned, Audley End	
WZ882	DHC1 Chipmunk 22 (G-BXGP) [K]	Privately owned, Hurstbourne Tarrant	
XA109	DH115 Sea Vampire T22	Montrose Air Station Heritage Centre	
XA127	DH115 Sea Vampire T22 <ff>	FAA Museum, RNAS Yeovilton	
XA129	DH115 Sea Vampire T22	FAA Museum, stored Cobham Hall, RNAS Yeovilton	
XA225	Slingsby T38 Grasshopper TX1	Gliding Heritage Centre, Lasham	
XA226	Slingsby T38 Grasshopper TX1	Norfolk & Suffolk Avn Museum, Flixton	
XA228	Slingsby T38 Grasshopper TX1	National Museum of Flight, East Fortune	
XA230	Slingsby T38 Grasshopper TX1 (BGA4098)	Privately owned, Henlow	
XA231	Slingsby T38 Grasshopper TX1 (8888M)	RAF Manston History Museum	
XA240	Slingsby T38 Grasshopper TX1 (BGA4556)	Privately owned, Portmoak, Perth & Kinross	
XA241	Slingsby T38 Grasshopper TX1	Shuttleworth Collection, stored Old Warden	
XA243	Slingsby T38 Grasshopper TX1 (8886M)	Privately owned, Gransden Lodge, Cambs	
XA244	Slingsby T38 Grasshopper TX1	Privately owned, Brent Tor, Devon	
XA282	Slingsby T31B Cadet TX3	Caernarfon Air World	
XA290	Slingsby T31B Cadet TX3	Privately owned, Portmoak, Perth & Kinross	
XA293	Slingsby T31B Cadet TX3 <ff>	Privately owned, Hooton Park	
XA295	Slingsby T31B Cadet TX3 (BGA3336)	Privately owned, Eaglescott	
XA302	Slingsby T31B Cadet TX3 (BGA3786)	RAF Museum, Hendon	
XA310	Slingsby T31B Cadet TX3 (BGA4963)	Privately owned, Shrivenham	
XA459	Fairey Gannet ECM6 [E]	Solway Aviation Society, Carlisle	
XA460	Fairey Gannet ECM6 [768/BY]	Ulster Aviation Society, Long Kesh	
XA466	Fairey Gannet COD4 [777/LM]	FAA Museum, RNAS Yeovilton	
XA508	Fairey Gannet T2 [627/GN]	FAA Museum, at Midland Air Museum, Coventry	
XA564	Gloster Javelin FAW1 (7464M)	RAF Museum, Cosford	
XA634	Gloster Javelin FAW4 (7641M)	Jet Age Museum, stored Gloucester	
XA699	Gloster Javelin FAW5 (7809M)	Midland Air Museum, Coventry	
XA847	EE P1B (8371M)	Privately owned, Stowmarket, Suffolk	
XA862	WS55 Whirlwind HAR1 (G-AMJT) [704] <ff>	South Yorkshire Aircraft Museum, Doncaster	
XA864	WS55 Whirlwind HAR1	FAA Museum, stored Cobham Hall, RNAS Yeovilton	
XA870	WS55 Whirlwind HAR1 [911]	South Yorkshire Aircraft Museum, Doncaster	
XA880	DH104 Devon C2 (G-BVXR) <ff>	Privately owned, Elstree Studios	
XA893	Avro 698 Vulcan B1 (8591M) <ff>	RAF Museum, stored Cosford	
XA903	Avro 698 Vulcan B1 <ff>	Privately owned, Stoneykirk, D&G	
XA917	HP80 Victor B1 (7827M) <ff>	Privately owned, Cupar, Fife	
XB259	Blackburn B101 Beverley C1 (G-AOAI)	Fort Paull Armoury	

Notes	Serial	Type (code/other identity)	Owner/operator, location or fate
	XB261	Blackburn B101 Beverley C1 <ff>	Newark Air Museum, Winthorpe
	XB446	Grumman TBM-3 Avenger ECM6B	FAA Museum, Yeovilton
	XB480	Hiller HT1 [537]	FAA Museum, stored Cobham Hall, RNAS Yeovilton
	XB812	Canadair CL-13 Sabre F4 (9227M) [U]	RAF Museum, Cosford
	XD145	Saro SR53	RAF Museum, Cosford
	XD163	WS55 Whirlwind HAR10 (8645M) [X]	The Helicopter Museum, Weston-super-Mare
	XD165	WS55 Whirlwind HAR10 (8673M)	Caernarfon Airfield Fire Section
	XD215	VS Scimitar F1 <ff>	Privately owned, Cheltenham
	XD235	VS Scimitar F1 [148] <ff>	Privately owned, Lavendon, Bucks
	XD317	VS Scimitar F1 [112/R]	FAA Museum, RNAS Yeovilton
	XD332	VS Scimitar F1 [194/C]	Solent Sky, stored Romsey
	XD375	DH115 Vampire T11 (7887M)	Privately owned, Elland, W Yorks
	XD377	DH115 Vampire T11 (8203M) <ff>	South Yorkshire Aircraft Museum, stored Doncaster
	XD382	DH115 Vampire T11 (comp XD534) [41]	East Midlands Airport Aeropark
	XD425	DH115 Vampire T11 <ff>	Morayvia, Kinloss
	XD434	DH115 Vampire T11 [25]	Fenland & W Norfolk Aviation Museum, Wisbech
	XD445	DH115 Vampire T11 [51]	Tettenhall Transport Heritage Centre
	XD447	DH115 Vampire T11 [50]	East Midlands Airport Aeropark
	XD452	DH115 Vampire T11 (7990M) [66] <ff>	Privately owned, Dursley, Glos
	XD506	DH115 Vampire T11 (7983M)	Suffolk Aviation Heritage Centre, Foxhall Heath
	XD515	DH115 Vampire T11 (7998M/*XM515*)	RAF Museum, stored Cosford
	XD525	DH115 Vampire T11 (7882M) <ff>	Privately owned, Templepatrick, NI
	XD542	DH115 Vampire T11 (7604M) [N]	Privately owned, Patrington, E Yorks
	XD547	DH115 Vampire T11 (composite) [Z]	Privately owned, Cantley, Norfolk
	XD593	DH115 Vampire T11	Newark Air Museum, Winthorpe
	XD595	DH115 Vampire T11 <ff>	Privately owned, Glentham, Lincs
	XD596	DH115 Vampire T11 (7939M)	Solent Sky, stored Timsbury, Hants
	XD599	DH115 Vampire T11 [A] <ff>	Sywell Aviation Museum
	XD616	DH115 Vampire T11 [56]	Suffolk Aviation Heritage Centre, Foxhall Heath
	XD624	DH115 Vampire T11	Privately owned, Hooton Park
	XD626	DH115 Vampire T11 [Q]	Midland Air Museum, stored Coventry
	XD674	Hunting Jet Provost T1 (7570M)	RAF Museum, Cosford
	XD693	Hunting Jet Provost T1 (XM129/G-AOBU) [Z-Q]	Kennet Aviation, North Weald
	XD816	Vickers Valiant B(K)1 <ff>	Brooklands Museum, Weybridge
	XD818	Vickers Valiant B(K)1 (7894M)	RAF Museum, Cosford
	XD857	Vickers Valiant B(K)1 <ff>	RAF Marham Aviation Heritage Centre
	XD875	Vickers Valiant B(K)1 <ff>	Morayvia, Kinloss
	XE317	Bristol 171 Sycamore HR14 (G-AMWO)	South Yorkshire Aircraft Museum, Doncaster
	XE339	Hawker Sea Hawk FGA6 (8156M) [149] <ff>	Privately owned, Glos
	XE339	Hawker Sea Hawk FGA6 (8156M) [E] <rf>	Privately owned, Booker
	XE340	Hawker Sea Hawk FGA6 [131/Z]	FAA Museum, stored Cobham Hall, RNAS Yeovilton
	XE364	Hawker Sea Hawk FGA6 (G-JETH) (comp WM983) [485/J]	Gatwick Aviation Museum, Charlwood, Surrey
	XE368	Hawker Sea Hawk FGA6 [200/J]	Privately owned, Barrow-in-Furness
	XE521	Fairey Rotodyne Y (parts)	The Helicopter Museum, Weston-super-Mare
	XE584	Hawker Hunter FGA9 <ff>	Privately owned, Hooton Park
	XE597	Hawker Hunter FGA9 (8874M) <ff>	Privately owned, Bromsgrove
	XE620	Hawker Hunter F6A (XE606/8841M) [B]	RAF Waddington, on display
	XE624	Hawker Hunter FGA9 (8875M) [G]	Privately owned, Wickenby
	XE627	Hawker Hunter F6A [T]	IWM Duxford
	XE643	Hawker Hunter FGA9 (8586M) <ff>	No 1137 Sqn ATC, Aldergrove
	XE650	Hawker Hunter FGA9 (G-9-449) <ff>	*Scrapped*
	XE664	Hawker Hunter F4 <ff>	Jet Age Museum, Gloucester
	XE665	Hawker Hunter T8C (G-BWGM)	Privately owned, stored Cotswold Airport
	XE668	Hawker Hunter GA11 [832/DD]	Hamburger Hill Paintball, Marksbury, Somerset
	XE670	Hawker Hunter F4 (7762M/8585M) <ff>	RAF Museum, Cosford
	XE683	Hawker Hunter F51 (RDAF E-409) [G]	City of Norwich Aviation Museum
	XE685	Hawker Hunter GA11 (G-GAII) [861/VL]	RAF Scampton Heritage Centre
	XE688	Hawker Hunter T72 (XE704/PP-XHH)	Hawker Hunter Aviation, Scampton
	XE689	Hawker Hunter GA11 (G-BWGK) <ff>	Privately owned, Cotswold Airport

Serial	Type (code/other identity)	Owner/operator, location or fate	Notes
XE707	Hawker Hunter GA11 (N707XE) [865]	Bentwaters Cold War Museum	
XE762	Slingsby T8 Cadet TX2 (VM594)	Gliding Heritage Centre, Lasham	
XE786	Slingsby T31B Cadet TX3 (BGA4033)	Privately owned, Arbroath	
XE793	Slingsby T31B Cadet TX3 (8666M)	Privately owned, Tamworth	
XE797	Slingsby T31B Cadet TX3	South Yorkshire Aviation Museum, Doncaster	
XE799	Slingsby T31B Cadet TX3 (8943M) [R]	Privately owned, stored Riseley, Berks	
XE802	Slingsby T31B Cadet TX3 (BGA5283)	Privately owned, North Hill, Devon	
XE852	DH115 Vampire T11 [58]	No 2247 Sqn ATC, Hawarden	
XE855	DH115 Vampire T11 <ff>	Midland Air Museum, stored Coventry (wreck)	
XE856	DH115 Vampire T11 (G-DUSK) [V]	Bournemouth Aviation Museum	
XE864	DH115 Vampire T11(comp XD435) <ff>	Privately owned, Ingatstone, Essex	
XE872	DH115 Vampire T11 [62]	*Scrapped*	
XE874	DH115 Vampire T11 (8582M)	Paintball Commando, Birkin, W Yorks	
XE897	DH115 Vampire T11 (XD403)	Privately owned, Errol, Tayside	
XE921	DH115 Vampire T11 [VR] <ff>	Privately owned, Stoneykirk, D&G	
XE935	DH115 Vampire T11	South Yorkshire Aircraft Museum, Doncaster	
XE946	DH115 Vampire T11 (7473M) <ff>	RAF Cranwell Aviation Heritage Centre	
XE956	DH115 Vampire T11 (G-OBLN)	South Wales Aviation Museum, St Athan	
XE979	DH115 Vampire T11 [54] <ff>	Privately owned, Cantley, Norfolk	
XE979	DH115 Vampire T11 (fuselage)	Privately owned, Birlingham, Worcs	
XE982	DH115 Vampire T11 (7564M) (fuselage)	Privately owned, Tetbury, Glos	
XE985	DH115 Vampire T11 (*WZ476*)	Privately owned, New Inn, Torfaen	
XF113	VS Swift F7 [19] <ff>	Boscombe Down Aviation Collection, Old Sarum	
XF114	VS Swift F7 (G-SWIF)	Solent Sky, Southampton	
XF321	Hawker Hunter T7 <rf>	Phoenix Aviation, Bruntingthorpe	
XF368	Hawker Hunter F51 (RDAF E-412/*XF314*)	Brooklands Museum, Weybridge	
XF375	Hawker Hunter F6A (8736M/G-BUEZ) [6]	Boscombe Down Aviation Collection, Old Sarum	
XF382	Hawker Hunter F6A [15]	Midland Air Museum, Coventry	
XF383	Hawker Hunter F6 (8706M) <ff>	Gloster Aviation Club, Gloucester	
XF418	Hawker Hunter F51 (RDAF E-430)	Gatwick Aviation Museum, Charlwood, Surrey	
XF509	Hawker Hunter F6 (8708M)	Fort Paull Armoury	
XF522	Hawker Hunter F6 <ff>	Herts & Bucks ATC Wing, RAF Halton	
XF526	Hawker Hunter F6 (8679M) [78/E]	Privately owned, Birlingham, Worcs	
XF527	Hawker Hunter F6 (8680M)	RAF Halton, on display	
XF545	Percival P56 Provost T1 (7957M) [O-K]	Privately owned, Bucklebury, Berks	
XF597	Percival P56 Provost T1 (G-BKFW) [AH]	Privately owned, Audley End	
XF603	Percival P56 Provost T1 (G-KAPW)	Shuttleworth Collection, Old Warden	
XF690	Percival P56 Provost T1 (8041M/G-MOOS)	Kennet Aviation, Yeovilton	
XF708	Avro 716 Shackleton MR3/3 [C]	IWM Duxford	
XF785	Bristol 173 (7648M/G-ALBN)	Aerospace Bristol, Filton	
XF836	Percival P56 Provost T1 (8043M/G-AWRY) [JG]	Provost Preservation, stored Cambridge	
XF840	Percival P56 Provost T1 <ff>	Tangmere Military Aviation Museum	
XF926	Bristol 188 (8368M)	RAF Museum, Cosford	
XF940	Hawker Hunter F4 <ff>	Privately owned, Bournemouth	
XF994	Hawker Hunter T8C (G-CGHU) [873/VL]	Hawker Hunter Aviation, Scampton	
XF995	Hawker Hunter T8B (G-BZSF/9237M) [K]	Hawker Hunter Aviation, Scampton	
XG154	Hawker Hunter FGA9 (8863M)	RAF Museum, Hendon	
XG160	Hawker Hunter FGA9 (8831M/G-BWAF) [U]	Bournemouth Aviation Museum	
XG164	Hawker Hunter F6 (8681M)	Davidstow Airfield & Cornwall At War Museum	
XG168	Hawker Hunter F6A (XG172/8832M) [10]	City of Norwich Aviation Museum	
XG190	Hawker Hunter F51 (RDAF E-425) [C]	Solway Aviation Society, Carlisle	
XG193	Hawker Hunter FGA9 (XG297) (comp with WT741) <ff>	South Yorkshire Aircraft Museum, Doncaster	
XG194	Hawker Hunter FGA9 (8839M)	Wattisham Station Heritage Museum	
XG195	Hawker Hunter FGA9 <ff>	Privately owned, Lewes	
XG196	Hawker Hunter F6A (8702M) [31]	Privately owned, Bentwaters	
XG209	Hawker Hunter F6 (8709M) <ff>	Privately owned, Kingston-on-Thames	
XG210	Hawker Hunter F6	Privately owned, Beck Row, Suffolk	
XG225	Hawker Hunter F6A (8713M)	DSAE Cosford, at main gate	
XG226	Hawker Hunter F6A (8800M) <ff>	RAF Manston History Museum	

Notes	Serial	Type (code/other identity)	Owner/operator, location or fate
	XG254	Hawker Hunter FGA9 (8881M) [A]	Norfolk & Suffolk Avn Museum, Flixton
	XG274	Hawker Hunter F6 (8710M) [71]	Privately owned, Newmarket
	XG290	Hawker Hunter F6 (8711M) <ff>	Boscombe Down Aviation Collection, Old Sarum
	XG297	Hawker Hunter FGA9 [Y] <ff>	South Yorkshire Aircraft Museum, Doncaster
	XG325	EE Lightning F1 <ff>	Privately owned, Norfolk
	XG329	EE Lightning F1 (8050M)	Privately owned, Flixton
	XG331	EE Lightning F1 <ff>	Privately owned, Glos
	XG337	EE Lightning F1 (8056M) [M]	RAF Museum, Cosford
	XG452	Bristol 192 Belvedere HC1 (7997M/G-BRMB)	The Helicopter Museum, Weston-super-Mare
	XG454	Bristol 192 Belvedere HC1 (8366M)	Museum of Science & Industry, Manchester
	XG462	Bristol 192 Belvedere HC1 <ff>	The Helicopter Museum, Weston-super-Mare
	XG474	Bristol 192 Belvedere HC1 (8367M) [O]	RAF Museum, Hendon
	XG502	Bristol 171 Sycamore HR14	Army Flying Museum, Middle Wallop
	XG518	Bristol 171 Sycamore HR14 (8009M) [S-E]	Norfolk & Suffolk Avn Museum, Flixton
	XG523	Bristol 171 Sycamore HR14 <ff> [V]	Norfolk & Suffolk Avn Museum, Flixton
	XG545	Bristol 171 Sycamore HR52 (OE-XSY)	Flying Bulls, Salzburg, Austria
	XG574	WS55 Whirlwind HAR3 [752/PO]	FAA Museum, stored Cobham Hall, RNAS Yeovilton
	XG588	WS55 Whirlwind HAR3 (G-BAMH/VR-BEP)	East Midlands Airport Aeropark
	XG592	WS55 Whirlwind HAS7 [54]	Task Force Adventure Park, Cowbridge, S Glam
	XG594	WS55 Whirlwind HAS7 [517]	FAA Museum, stored Cobham Hall, RNAS Yeovilton
	XG596	WS55 Whirlwind HAS7 [66]	The Helicopter Museum, stored Weston-super-Mare
	XG629	DH112 Sea Venom FAW22	Privately owned, Stone, Staffs
	XG680	DH112 Sea Venom FAW22 [438]	North-East Aircraft Museum, Usworth
	XG692	DH112 Sea Venom FAW22 [668/LM]	Privately owned, Stockport
	XG730	DH112 Sea Venom FAW22	de Havilland Aircraft Museum, London Colney
	XG736	DH112 Sea Venom FAW22	Privately owned, East Midlands
	XG737	DH112 Sea Venom FAW22 [220/Z]	East Midlands Airport Aeropark
	XG743	DH115 Sea Vampire T22 [798/BY]	Historic Aviation Centre, Fishburn
	XG797	Fairey Gannet ECM6 [277]	IWM Duxford
	XG831	Fairey Gannet ECM6 [396]	Davidstow Airfield & Cornwall At War Museum
	XG882	Fairey Gannet T5 (8754M) [771/LM]	Privately owned, Errol, Tayside
	XG883	Fairey Gannet T5 [773/BY]	FAA Museum, at Museum of Berkshire Aviation, Woodley
	XG900	Short SC1	Science Museum, South Kensington
	XG905	Short SC1	Ulster Folk & Transport Mus, Holywood, Co Down
	XH131	EE Canberra PR9	Ulster Aviation Society, Long Kesh
	XH134	EE Canberra PR9 (G-OMHD)	Privately owned, stored Cotswold Airport
	XH135	EE Canberra PR9	Privately owned, Cotswold Airport
	XH136	EE Canberra PR9 (8782M) [W] <ff>	Romney Marsh Wartime Collection
	XH165	EE Canberra PR9 <ff>	Blyth Valley Aviation Collection, Walpole
	XH169	EE Canberra PR9	RAF Marham, on display
	XH170	EE Canberra PR9 (8739M)	RAF Wyton, on display
	XH171	EE Canberra PR9 (8746M) [U]	RAF Museum, Cosford
	XH174	EE Canberra PR9 <ff>	Privately owned, Cannock, Staffs
	XH175	EE Canberra PR9 <ff>	Privately owned, Bewdley, Worcs
	XH177	EE Canberra PR9 <ff>	Newark Air Museum, Winthorpe
	XH278	DH115 Vampire T11 (8595M/7866M) [42]	Yorkshire Air Museum, Elvington
	XH312	DH115 Vampire T11	Privately owned, Dodleston, Cheshire
	XH313	DH115 Vampire T11 (G-BZRD) [E]	Tangmere Military Aviation Museum
	XH318	DH115 Vampire T11 (7761M) [64]	Privately owned, Sholing, Hants
	XH328	DH115 Vampire T11 <ff>	Privately owned, Cantley, Norfolk
	XH330	DH115 Vampire T11 [73]	Privately owned, Milton Keynes
	XH537	Avro 698 Vulcan B2MRR (8749M) <ff>	Bournemouth Aviation Museum
	XH558	Avro 698 Vulcan B2 (G-VLCN)	Vulcan To The Sky Trust, Doncaster Sheffield Airport
	XH560	Avro 698 Vulcan K2 <ff>	Privately owned, Foulness
	XH563	Avro 698 Vulcan B2MRR <ff>	Morayvia, Kinloss
	XH584	EE Canberra T4 (G-27-374) <ff>	South Yorkshire Aircraft Museum, Doncaster
	XH592	HP80 Victor B1A (8429M) <ff>	Midland Air Museum, Coventry
	XH648	HP80 Victor K1A	IWM Duxford
	XH669	HP80 Victor K2 (9092M) <ff>	Privately owned, Foulness
	XH670	HP80 Victor SR2 <ff>	Privately owned, Foulness
	XH672	HP80 Victor K2 (9242M)	RAF Museum, Cosford

Serial	Type (code/other identity)	Owner/operator, location or fate	Notes
XH673	HP80 Victor K2 (8911M)	RAF Marham, for disposal	
XH767	Gloster Javelin FAW9 (7955M) [L]	Yorkshire Air Museum, Elvington	
XH783	Gloster Javelin FAW7 (7798M) <ff>	Privately owned, Catford	
XH837	Gloster Javelin FAW7 (8032M) <ff>	Caernarfon Air World	
XH892	Gloster Javelin FAW9R (7982M) [J]	Norfolk & Suffolk Avn Museum, Flixton	
XH897	Gloster Javelin FAW9	IWM Duxford	
XH903	Gloster Javelin FAW9 (7938M) [G]	Jet Age Museum, Gloucester	
XH992	Gloster Javelin FAW8 (7829M) [P]	Newark Air Museum, Winthorpe	
XJ314	RR Thrust Measuring Rig	Science Museum, South Kensington	
XJ380	Bristol 171 Sycamore HR14 (8628M)	Boscombe Down Aviation Collection, Old Sarum	
XJ389	Fairey Jet Gyrodyne (XD759/G-AJJP)	Museum of Berkshire Aviation, Woodley	
XJ398	WS55 Whirlwind HAR10 (XD768/G-BDBZ)	South Yorkshire Aircraft Museum, Doncaster	
XJ407	WS55 Whirlwind HAR10 (N7013H)	Privately owned, Tattershall Thorpe	
XJ435	WS55 Whirlwind HAR10 (XD804/8671M) [V]	*Scrapped*	
XJ476	DH110 Sea Vixen FAW1 <ff>	Boscombe Down Aviation Collection, Old Sarum	
XJ481	DH110 Sea Vixen FAW1 [VL]	FAA Museum, stored Cobham Hall, RNAS Yeovilton	
XJ482	DH110 Sea Vixen FAW1 [713/VL]	Norfolk & Suffolk Avn Museum, Flixton	
XJ488	DH110 Sea Vixen FAW1 <ff>	Robertsbridge Aviation Society, Mayfield	
XJ494	DH110 Sea Vixen FAW2 [121/E]	Privately owned, Bruntingthorpe	
XJ560	DH110 Sea Vixen FAW2 (8142M) [302]	Newark Air Museum, Winthorpe	
XJ565	DH110 Sea Vixen FAW2 [127/E]	de Havilland Aircraft Museum, London Colney	
XJ571	DH110 Sea Vixen FAW2 (8140M) [242]	Solent Sky, Southampton	
XJ575	DH110 Sea Vixen FAW2 <ff> [SAH-13]	Wellesbourne Wartime Museum	
XJ579	DH110 Sea Vixen FAW2 <ff>	Midland Air Museum, stored Coventry	
XJ580	DH110 Sea Vixen FAW2 [131/E]	Tangmere Military Aviation Museum	
XJ714	Hawker Hunter FR10 (comp XG226)	East Midlands Airport Aeropark	
XJ723	WS55 Whirlwind HAR10	Morayvia, Kinloss	
XJ726	WS55 Whirlwind HAR10	Caernarfon Air World	
XJ727	WS55 Whirlwind HAR10 (8661M)	Combat Paintball Park, Thetford	
XJ729	WS55 Whirlwind HAR10 (8732M/G-BVGE)	Privately owned, Chard, Somerset	
XJ758	WS55 Whirlwind HAR10 (8464M) <ff>	Privately owned, Welshpool	
XJ772	DH115 Vampire T11 [H]	de Havilland Aircraft Museum, London Colney	
XJ823	Avro 698 Vulcan B2A	Solway Aviation Society, Carlisle	
XJ824	Avro 698 Vulcan B2A	IWM Duxford	
XJ917	Bristol 171 Sycamore HR14 [H-S]	Aerospace Bristol, stored Filton	
XJ918	Bristol 171 Sycamore HR14 (8190M)	RAF Museum, Cosford	
XK416	Auster AOP9 (7855M/G-AYUA)	Privately owned, Widmerpool	
XK417	Auster AOP9 (G-AVXY)	Privately owned, Messingham, Lincs	
XK418	Auster AOP9 (7976M)	No 1894 Sqn ATC, Swaffham	
XK421	Auster AOP9 (8365M) (frame)	South Yorkshire Aircraft Museum, stored Doncaster	
XK488	Blackburn NA39 Buccaneer S1	FAA Museum, stored Cobham Hall, RNAS Yeovilton	
XK526	Blackburn NA39 Buccaneer S2 (8648M)	RAF Honington, at main gate	
XK527	Blackburn NA39 Buccaneer S2D (8818M) <ff>	Privately owned, North Wales	
XK532	Blackburn NA39 Buccaneer S1 (8867M) [632/LM]	Highland Aviation Museum, Inverness	
XK533	Blackburn NA39 Buccaneer S1 <ff>	Royal Scottish Mus'm of Flight, stored Granton	
XK590	DH115 Vampire T11 [V]	Wellesbourne Wartime Museum	
XK623	DH115 Vampire T11 (G-VAMP) [56]	Caernarfon Air World	
XK624	DH115 Vampire T11 [32]	Norfolk & Suffolk Avn Museum, Flixton	
XK625	DH115 Vampire T11 [14]	Romney Marsh Wartime Collection	
XK627	DH115 Vampire T11 <ff>	Davidstow Airfield & Cornwall At War Museum	
XK632	DH115 Vampire T11 <ff>	Privately owned, Greenford, London	
XK637	DH115 Vampire T11 [56]	Top Gun Flight Simulation Centre, Stalybridge	
XK695	DH106 Comet C2(RC) (G-AMXH/9164M) <ff>	de Havilland Aircraft Museum, London Colney	
XK699	DH106 Comet C2 (7971M) <ff>	Boscombe Down Aviation Collection, Old Sarum	
XK724	Folland Gnat F1 (7715M)	RAF Museum, stored Cosford	
XK740	Folland Gnat F1 (8396M)	Solent Sky, Southampton	
XK776	ML Utility 1	Army Flying Museum, Middle Wallop	
XK789	Slingsby T38 Grasshopper TX1	Midland Air Museum, Coventry	
XK790	Slingsby T38 Grasshopper TX1	Privately owned, stored Husbands Bosworth	
XK819	Slingsby T38 Grasshopper TX1	Privately owned, stored Rufforth	

Notes	Serial	Type (code/other identity)	Owner/operator, location or fate
	XK820	Slingsby T38 Grasshopper TX1 (comp WZ754/WZ778)	Privately owned, Bridge of Weir, Renfrewshire
	XK885	Percival P66 Pembroke C1 (8452M/N46EA)	Cornwall Aviation Heritage Centre, Newquay
	XK895	DH104 Sea Devon C20 (G-SDEV) [19/CU]	South Wales Aviation Museum, St Athan
	XK907	WS55 Whirlwind HAS7	Midland Air Museum, stored Coventry
	XK911	WS55 Whirlwind HAS7(mod)	Privately owned, Dagenham
	XK936	WS55 Whirlwind HAS7 [62]	IWM Duxford
	XK940	WS55 Whirlwind HAS7 (G-AYXT) [911]	The Helicopter Museum, Weston-super-Mare
	XK970	WS55 Whirlwind HAR10 (8789M)	Army, Bramley, Hants (for disposal)
	XL149	Blackburn B101 Beverley C1 (7988M) <ff>	South Yorkshire Aircraft Museum, Doncaster
	XL160	HP80 Victor K2 (8910M) <ff>	RAF Marham Aviation Heritage Centre
	XL164	HP80 Victor K2 (9215M) <ff>	Bournemouth Aviation Museum
	XL190	HP80 Victor K2 (9216M) <ff>	RAF Manston History Museum
	XL231	HP80 Victor K2	Yorkshire Air Museum, Elvington
	XL318	Avro 698 Vulcan B2 (8733M)	RAF Museum, Hendon
	XL319	Avro 698 Vulcan B2	North-East Aircraft Museum, Usworth
	XL360	Avro 698 Vulcan B2A	Midland Air Museum, Coventry
	XL388	Avro 698 Vulcan B2 <ff>	South Yorkshire Aircraft Museum, Doncaster
	XL426	Avro 698 Vulcan B2 (G-VJET)	Vulcan Restoration Trust, Southend
	XL445	Avro 698 Vulcan K2 (8811M) <ff>	RAF Scampton Heritage Centre
	XL449	Fairey Gannet AEW3 <ff>	Privately owned, Booker
	XL472	Fairey Gannet AEW3 [044/R]	South Wales Aviation Museum, stored St Athan
	XL497	Fairey Gannet AEW3 [041/R]	Dumfries & Galloway Avn Mus, Dumfries
	XL500	Fairey Gannet AEW3 (G-KAEW) [CU]	South Wales Aviation Museum, St Athan
	XL502	Fairey Gannet AEW3 (8610M/G-BMYP)	Yorkshire Air Museum, Elvington
	XL503	Fairey Gannet AEW3 [070/E]	FAA Museum, stored Cobham Hall, RNAS Yeovilton
	XL563	Hawker Hunter T7 (9218M)	Farnborough Air Sciences Trust, stored Farnborough
	XL564	Hawker Hunter T7 <ff>	City of Norwich Aviation Museum
	XL565	Hawker Hunter T7 (parts of WT745) [Y]	Privately owned, Bruntingthorpe
	XL568	Hawker Hunter T7A (9224M) [X]	RAF Museum, Cosford
	XL569	Hawker Hunter T7 (8833M)	East Midlands Airport Aeropark
	XL571	Hawker Hunter T7 (8834M/XL572/G-HNTR) [V]	Yorkshire Air Museum, Elvington
	XL573	Hawker Hunter T7 (G-BVGH)	South Wales Aviation Museum, St Athan
	XL580	Hawker Hunter T8M [723]	FAA Museum, stored Cobham Hall, RNAS Yeovilton
	XL586	Hawker Hunter T7 (comp XL578)	Action Park, Wickford, Essex
	XL587	Hawker Hunter T7 (8807M/G-HPUX)	Hawker Hunter Aviation, stored Scampton
	XL591	Hawker Hunter T7	Gatwick Aviation Museum, Charlwood, Surrey
	XL592	Hawker Hunter T7 (8836M) [Y]	Maidenhead Heritage Centre
	XL602	Hawker Hunter T8M (G-BWFT)	Hunter Flying Ltd, St Athan
	XL609	Hawker Hunter T7 <ff>	Privately owned, South Molton, Devon
	XL621	Hawker Hunter T7 (G-BNCX)	Privately owned, Dunsfold
	XL623	Hawker Hunter T7 (8770M)	Privately owned, Dunsfold
	XL629	EE Lightning T4	MoD/QinetiQ Boscombe Down, at main gate
	XL714	DH82A Tiger Moth II (T6099/G-AOGR)	Privately owned, Boughton, Lincs
	XL736	Saro Skeeter AOP12	The Helicopter Museum stored, Weston-super-Mare
	XL738	Saro Skeeter AOP12 (XM565/7861M)	Privately owned, Storwood, Yorkshire
	XL739	Saro Skeeter AOP12	Norfolk Tank Museum, Forncett St Peter
	XL762	Saro Skeeter AOP12 (8017M)	National Museum of Flight, stored E Fortune
	XL763	Saro Skeeter AOP12	Privately owned, Storwood, Yorkshire
	XL764	Saro Skeeter AOP12 (7940M) [J]	Newark Air Museum, Winthorpe
	XL765	Saro Skeeter AOP12	Privately owned, Melksham, Wilts
	XL770	Saro Skeeter AOP12 (8046M)	Solent Sky, Southampton
	XL809	Saro Skeeter AOP12 (G-BLIX)	Privately owned, Wilden, Beds
	XL811	Saro Skeeter AOP12	The Helicopter Museum, Weston-super-Mare
	XL812	Saro Skeeter AOP12 (G-SARO)	Historic Army Aircraft Flight, stored Middle Wallop
	XL813	Saro Skeeter AOP12	Army Flying Museum, Middle Wallop
	XL814	Saro Skeeter AOP12	Army Flying Museum, stored Middle Wallop
	XL824	Bristol 171 Sycamore HR14 (8021M)	Aerospace Bristol, Filton
	XL829	Bristol 171 Sycamore HR14	The Helicopter Museum, Weston-super-Mare
	XL840	WS55 Whirlwind HAS7	Privately owned, Bawtry
	XL853	WS55 Whirlwind HAS7 [PO]	FAA Museum, stored Cobham Hall, RNAS Yeovilton

Serial	Type (code/other identity)	Owner/operator, location or fate	Notes
XL875	WS55 Whirlwind HAR9	Perth Technical College	
XL929	Percival P66 Pembroke C1 (G-BNPU)	Privately owned, stored Compton Verney	
XL954	Percival P66 Pembroke C1 (9042M/N4234C/G-BXES)	Privately owned, Weston, Ireland	
XL993	SAL Twin Pioneer CC2 (8388M)	RAF Museum, Cosford	
XM135	BAC Lightning F1 [B]	IWM Duxford	
XM144	BAC Lightning F1 (8417M) <ff>	Shannon Aviation Museum, Eire (stored)	
XM169	BAC Lightning F1A (8422M) <ff>	Morayvia, Kinloss	
XM172	BAC Lightning F1A (8427M)	Lakes Lightnings, Spark Bridge, Cumbria	
XM173	BAC Lightning F1A (8414M) [A]	Privately owned, Malmesbury, Glos	
XM191	BAC Lightning F1A (7854M/8590M) <ff>	Privately owned, Thorpe Wood, N Yorks	
XM192	BAC Lightning F1A (8413M) [K]	Thorpe Camp Preservation Group, Lincs	
XM223	DH104 Devon C2 (G-BWWC) [J]	Privately owned, stored Compton Verney	
XM279	EE Canberra B(I)8 <ff>	South Yorkshire Aircraft Museum, Doncaster	
XM300	WS58 Wessex HAS1	Privately owned, Nantgarw, Rhondda	
XM328	WS58 Wessex HAS3 [653/PO]	The Helicopter Museum, Weston-super-Mare	
XM330	WS58 Wessex HAS1	The Helicopter Museum, Weston-super-Mare	
XM350	Hunting Jet Provost T3A (9036M)	South Yorkshire Aircraft Museum, Doncaster	
XM351	Hunting Jet Provost T3 (8078M) [Y]	RAF Museum, Cosford	
XM355	Hunting Jet Provost T3 (8229M)	Newcastle Aviation Academy	
XM358	Hunting Jet Provost T3A (8987M) [53]	Privately owned, Newbridge, Powys	
XM362	Hunting Jet Provost T3 (8230M)	DSAE No 1 SoTT, Cosford	
XM365	Hunting Jet Provost T3A (G-BXBH)	Privately owned, Bruntingthorpe	
XM373	Hunting Jet Provost T3 (7726M) [2] <ff>	Yorkshire Air Museum, Elvington	
XM383	Hunting Jet Provost T3A [90]	Newark Air Museum, Winthorpe	
XM402	Hunting Jet Provost T3 (8055AM) [18]	Fenland & W Norfolk Aviation Museum, Wisbech	
XM404	Hunting Jet Provost T3 (8055BM) <ff>	Bournemouth Aviation Museum	
XM409	Hunting Jet Provost T3 (8082M) <ff>	Air Scouts, Guernsey Airport	
XM410	Hunting Jet Provost T3 (8054AM) [B]	Privately owned, Gillingham, Kent	
XM411	Hunting Jet Provost T3 (8434M) <ff>	South Yorkshire Aircraft Museum, Doncaster	
XM412	Hunting Jet Provost T3A (9011M) [41]	Privately owned, Balado Bridge, Scotland	
XM414	Hunting Jet Provost T3 (8996M) [101]	Ulster Aviation Society, Long Kesh	
XM417	Hunting Jet Provost T3 (8054BM) [D] <ff>	Privately owned, Bracknell	
XM419	Hunting Jet Provost T3A (8990M) [102]	Newcastle Aviation Academy	
XM424	Hunting Jet Provost T3 (G-BWDS)	Privately owned, Coventry	
XM425	Hunting Jet Provost T3A (8995M) [88]	Privately owned, Longton, Staffs	
XM463	Hunting Jet Provost T3A [38] (fuselage)	RAF Museum, Hendon	
XM468	Hunting Jet Provost T3 (8081M) <ff>	Wings Museum, Balcombe, W Sussex	
XM473	Hunting Jet Provost T3A (8974M/G-TINY)	Privately owned, Wethersfield	
XM474	Hunting Jet Provost T3 (8121M) <ff>	No 247 Sqn ATC, Ashton-under-Lyne, Gr Manchester	
XM479	Hunting Jet Provost T3A (G-BVEZ) [U]	Privately owned, Newcastle	
XM480	Hunting Jet Provost T3 (8080M)	4x4 Car Centre, Chesterfield	
XM496	Bristol 253 Britannia C1 (EL-WXA) [496]	Britannia Preservation Society, Cotswold Airport	
XM497	Bristol 175 Britannia 312F (G-AOVF) [497]	RAF Museum, Cosford	
XM529	Saro Skeeter AOP12 (7979M/G-BDNS)	Privately owned, Handforth	
XM553	Saro Skeeter AOP12 (G-AWSV)	Yorkshire Air Museum, Elvington	
XM555	Saro Skeeter AOP12 (8027M)	North-East Aircraft Museum, Usworth	
XM557	Saro Skeeter AOP12 <ff>	The Helicopter Museum, stored Weston-super-Mare	
XM564	Saro Skeeter AOP12	The Tank Museum, stored Bovington	
XM569	Avro 698 Vulcan B2 <ff>	Jet Age Museum, Gloucester	
XM575	Avro 698 Vulcan B2A (G-BLMC)	East Midlands Airport Aeropark	
XM594	Avro 698 Vulcan B2	Newark Air Museum, Winthorpe	
XM597	Avro 698 Vulcan B2	National Museum of Flight, E Fortune	
XM598	Avro 698 Vulcan B2 (8778M)	RAF Museum, Cosford	
XM602	Avro 698 Vulcan B2 (8771M) <ff>	Avro Heritage Museum, Woodford	
XM603	Avro 698 Vulcan B2	Avro Heritage Museum, Woodford	
XM607	Avro 698 Vulcan B2 (8779M)	RAF Waddington, on display	
XM612	Avro 698 Vulcan B2	City of Norwich Aviation Museum	
XM651	Saro Skeeter AOP12 (XM561/7980M)	South Yorkshire Aircraft Museum, Doncaster	
XM652	Avro 698 Vulcan B2 <ff>	Privately owned, Welshpool	
XM655	Avro 698 Vulcan B2 (G-VULC)	Privately owned, Wellesbourne Mountford	
XM685	WS55 Whirlwind HAS7 (G-AYZJ) [513/PO]	Newark Air Museum, Winthorpe	

Notes	Serial	Type (code/other identity)	Owner/operator, location or fate
	XM692	HS Gnat T1 <ff>	Privately owned, Dunkeswell
	XM693	HS Gnat T1 (7891M)	GE Aviation Hamble, on display
	XM697	HS Gnat T1 (G-NAAT)	Privately owned, Blantyre, S Lanarkshire
	XM708	HS Gnat T1 (8573M)	Privately owned, Lytham St Annes
	XM715	HP80 Victor K2	Cold War Jets Collection, Bruntingthorpe
	XM717	HP80 Victor K2 <ff>	RAF Museum, Hendon
	XM819	Lancashire EP9 Prospector (G-APXW)	Army Flying Museum, stored Middle Wallop
	XM833	WS58 Wessex HAS3	South Wales Aviation Museum, stored St Athan
	XN126	WS55 Whirlwind HAR10 (8655M) [S]	*Scrapped*
	XN137	Hunting Jet Provost T3 <ff>	Privately owned, Little Addington, Northants
	XN149	Slingsby T21B (BGA1085/9G-ABD)	Boscombe Down Aviation Collection, Old Sarum
	XN156	Slingsby T21B Sedbergh TX1 (BGA3250)	Privately owned, Portmoak, Perth & Kinross
	XN157	Slingsby T21B Sedbergh TX1 (BGA3255)	Privately owned, Long Mynd
	XN185	Slingsby T21B Sedbergh TX1 (8942M/BGA4077)	Privately owned, Scampton
	XN186	Slingsby T21B Sedbergh TX1 (BGA3905) [HFG]	Privately owned, Wethersfield
	XN187	Slingsby T21B Sedbergh TX1 (BGA3903)	Privately owned, RAF Halton
	XN198	Slingsby T31B Cadet TX3	*Sold to Estonia, 2010*
	XN238	Slingsby T31B Cadet TX3 <ff>	South Yorkshire Aircraft Museum, Doncaster
	XN239	Slingsby T31B Cadet TX3 (8889M) [G]	IWM Duxford, stored
	XN246	Slingsby T31B Cadet TX3	Solent Sky, stored Southampton
	XN258	WS55 Whirlwind HAR9 [589/CU]	North-East Aircraft Museum, Usworth
	XN297	WS55 Whirlwind HAR9 (XN311) [12]	*Scrapped*
	XN298	WS55 Whirlwind HAR9 [810/LS]	*Scrapped*
	XN304	WS55 Whirlwind HAS7 [WW/B]	Norfolk & Suffolk Avn Museum, Flixton
	XN332	Saro P531 (G-APNV) [759]	FAA Museum, stored Cobham Hall, RNAS Yeovilton
	XN334	Saro P531	FAA Museum, stored Cobham Hall, RNAS Yeovilton
	XN344	Saro Skeeter AOP12 (8018M)	Science Museum, South Kensington
	XN345	Saro Skeeter AOP12 <ff>	The Helicopter Museum, stored Weston-super-Mare
	XN351	Saro Skeeter AOP12 (G-BKSC)	Morayvia, Kinloss
	XN380	WS55 Whirlwind HAS7	RAF Manston History Museum
	XN385	WS55 Whirlwind HAS7	Battlezone Paintball, Yarm, N Yorks
	XN386	WS55 Whirlwind HAR9 [435/ED]	South Yorkshire Aircraft Museum, Doncaster
	XN412	Auster AOP9	Auster 9 Group, Melton Mowbray
	XN437	Auster AOP9 (G-AXWA)	Privately owned, Rush Green
	XN441	Auster AOP9 (G-BGKT)	Privately owned, Exeter
	XN458	Hunting Jet Provost T3 (8234M/*XN594*) [19]	Privately owned, Northallerton
	XN459	Hunting Jet Provost T3A (G-BWOT) [59]	Privately owned, Hawarden
	XN462	Hunting Jet Provost T3A [17]	FAA Museum, stored Cobham Hall, RNAS Yeovilton
	XN466	Hunting Jet Provost T3A [29] <ff>	No 247 Sqn ATC, Ashton-under-Lyne, Gr Manchester
	XN492	Hunting Jet Provost T3 (8079M) <ff>	East Midlands Airport Aeropark
	XN494	Hunting Jet Provost T3A (9012M) [43]	Cornwall College, Newquay
	XN500	Hunting Jet Provost T3A	Norfolk & Suffolk Avn Museum, Flixton
	XN503	Hunting Jet Provost T3 <ff>	North-East Aircraft Museum, Usworth
	XN511	Hunting Jet Provost T3 [12] <ff>	South Yorkshire Aircraft Museum, Doncaster
	XN549	Hunting Jet Provost T3 (8235M) <ff>	Privately owned, Warrington
	XN551	Hunting Jet Provost T3A (8984M)	Privately owned, Felton Common, Bristol
	XN554	Hunting Jet Provost T3 (8436M) [K]	Gunsmoke Paintball, Colchester, Essex
	XN573	Hunting Jet Provost T3 [E] <ff>	Newark Air Museum, Winthorpe
	XN579	Hunting Jet Provost T3A (9137M) [14]	Gunsmoke Paintball, Colchester, Essex
	XN582	Hunting Jet Provost T3A (8957M) [95,H]	Privately owned, Bruntingthorpe
	XN584	Hunting Jet Provost T3A (9014M) [E]	USW Aerospace Centre, Treforest, Glamorgan
	XN586	Hunting Jet Provost T3A (9039M) [91]	Privately owned, Sproughton
	XN589	Hunting Jet Provost T3A (9143M) [46]	Yorkshire Air Museum, Elvington
	XN597	Hunting Jet Provost T3 (7984M) <ff>	Privately owned, Market Drayton, Shrops
	XN607	Hunting Jet Provost T3 <ff>	Morayvia, Kinloss
	XN623	Hunting Jet Provost T3 (XN632/8352M)	Privately owned, Birlingham, Worcs
	XN629	Hunting Jet Provost T3A (G-BVEG/G-KNOT) [49]	Suffolk Aviation Heritage Centre, Foxhall Heath
	XN634	Hunting Jet Provost T3A <ff>	Privately owned, Blackpool
	XN634	Hunting Jet Provost T3A [53] <rf>	BAE Systems Warton Fire Section
	XN637	Hunting Jet Provost T3 (G-BKOU) [03]	Privately owned, North Weald
	XN647	DH110 Sea Vixen FAW2 <ff>	Privately owned, Steventon, Oxon

Serial	Type (code/other identity)	Owner/operator, location or fate	Notes
XN650	DH110 Sea Vixen FAW2 [456] <ff>	Privately owned, Norfolk	
XN651	DH110 Sea Vixen FAW2 <ff>	Privately owned, Lavendon, Bucks	
XN685	DH110 Sea Vixen FAW2 (8173M) [703/VL]	Midland Air Museum, Coventry	
XN696	DH110 Sea Vixen FAW2 [751] <ff>	North-East Aircraft Museum, Usworth	
XN714	Hunting H126	RAF Museum, Cosford	
XN726	EE Lightning F2A (8545M) <ff>	Boscombe Down Aviation Collection, Old Sarum	
XN728	EE Lightning F2A (8546M) <ff>	Privately owned, Binbrook	
XN774	EE Lightning F2A (8551M) <ff>	Privately owned, Boston	
XN776	EE Lightning F2A (8535M) [C]	National Museum of Flight, E Fortune	
XN795	EE Lightning F2A <ff>	RAF Air Defence Radar Museum, Neatishead	
XN819	AW660 Argosy C1 (8205M) <ff>	Newark Air Museum, Winthorpe	
XN923	HS Buccaneer S1 [13]	Gatwick Aviation Museum, Charlwood, Surrey	
XN928	HS Buccaneer S1 (8179M) <ff>	Privately owned, Gravesend	
XN957	HS Buccaneer S1 [630/LM]	FAA Museum, RNAS Yeovilton	
XN964	HS Buccaneer S1 [630/LM]	Newark Air Museum, Winthorpe	
XN967	HS Buccaneer S1 [233] <ff>	City of Norwich Aviation Museum	
XN972	HS Buccaneer S1 (8183M/XN962) <ff>	RAF Museum, Cosford	
XN974	HS Buccaneer S2A	Yorkshire Air Museum, Elvington	
XN981	HS Buccaneer S2B (fuselage)	Privately owned, Errol	
XN983	HS Buccaneer S2B <ff>	Fenland & W Norfolk Aviation Museum, Wisbech	
XP110	WS58 Wessex HAS3 (A2636)	DSAE RNAESS, *HMS Sultan*, Gosport	
XP137	WS58 Wessex HAS3 [11/DD]	*Currently not known*	
XP142	WS58 Wessex HAS3	FAA Museum, stored Cobham Hall, RNAS Yeovilton	
XP150	WS58 Wessex HAS3 [LS]	South Wales Aviation Museum, stored St Athan	
XP165	WS Scout AH1	The Helicopter Museum, Weston-super-Mare	
XP190	WS Scout AH1	South Yorkshire Aircraft Museum, Doncaster	
XP191	WS Scout AH1	Privately owned, Prenton, The Wirral	
XP226	Fairey Gannet AEW3	Newark Air Museum, Winthorpe	
XP241	Auster AOP9 (G-CEHR)	Privately owned, Spanhoe	
XP242	Auster AOP9 (G-BUCI)	Historic Army Aircraft Flight, Middle Wallop	
XP244	Auster AOP9 (7864M/M7922)	Privately owned, Stretton on Dunsmore	
XP254	Auster AOP11 (G-ASCC)	Privately owned, Whittlesford, Cambs	
XP279	Auster AOP9 (G-BWKK)	Privately owned, stored Winchester	
XP280	Auster AOP9	Privately owned, stored Leics	
XP281	Auster AOP9	IWM, stored Duxford	
XP282	Auster AOP9 (G-BGTC)	Privately owned, Scampton	
XP286	Auster AOP9	Privately owned, South Molton, Devon	
XP299	WS55 Whirlwind HAR10 (8726M)	RAF Museum, Hendon	
XP328	WS55 Whirlwind HAR10 (G-BKHC)	Privately owned, Tattershall Thorpe (wreck)	
XP329	WS55 Whirlwind HAR10 (8791M) [V]	Privately owned, Tattershall Thorpe (wreck)	
XP330	WS55 Whirlwind HAR10	CAA Fire School, Teesside International	
XP344	WS55 Whirlwind HAR10 (8764M) [H723]	RAF North Luffenham Training Area	
XP345	WS55 Whirlwind HAR10 (8792M) [UN]	Yorkshire Helicopter Preservation Group, Doncaster	
XP346	WS55 Whirlwind HAR10 (8793M)	Privately owned, Honeybourne, Worcs	
XP350	WS55 Whirlwind HAR10	Privately owned, Bassetts Pole, Staffs	
XP351	WS55 Whirlwind HAR10 (8672M) [Z]	*Currently not known*	
XP354	WS55 Whirlwind HAR10 (8721M)	Privately owned, Mullingar, Eire	
XP355	WS55 Whirlwind HAR10 (8463M/G-BEBC)	City of Norwich Aviation Museum	
XP360	WS55 Whirlwind HAR10 [V]	Privately owned, Bicton, nr Leominster	
XP398	WS55 Whirlwind HAR10 (8794M)	*Currently not known*	
XP404	WS55 Whirlwind HAR10 (8682M)	The Helicopter Museum, stored Weston-super-Mare	
XP411	AW660 Argosy C1 (8442M) [C]	RAF Museum, Cosford	
XP454	Slingsby T38 Grasshopper TX1	Privately owned, Sywell	
XP459	Slingsby T38 Grasshopper TX1	Privately owned, Wattisham	
XP463	Slingsby T38 Grasshopper TX1 (frame)	Privately owned, Rufforth	
XP463	Slingsby T38 Grasshopper TX1 (BGA4372)	Privately owned, Lasham	
XP488	Slingsby T38 Grasshopper TX1	Privately owned, stored Rufforth	
XP490	Slingsby T38 Grasshopper TX1 (BGA4552)	Privately owned, stored Watton	
XP492	Slingsby T38 Grasshopper TX1 (BGA3480)	*Currently not known*	
XP493	Slingsby T38 Grasshopper TX1	Privately owned, stored Aston Down	
XP494	Slingsby T38 Grasshopper TX1	Privately owned, stored Baxterley	

Notes	Serial	Type (code/other identity)	Owner/operator, location or fate
	XP505	HS Gnat T1	Science Museum, stored Wroughton
	XP513	HS Gnat T1 (N513X)	Privately owned, North Weald
	XP516	HS Gnat T1 (8580M) [16]	Farnborough Air Sciences Trust, Farnborough
	XP540	HS Gnat T1 (8608M) [62]	Privately owned, Bruntingthorpe
	XP542	HS Gnat T1 (8575M)	No 424 Sqn ATC, Southampton
	XP556	Hunting Jet Provost T4 (9027M) [B]	RAF Cranwell Aviation Heritage Centre
	XP557	Hunting Jet Provost T4 (8494M) [72]	Dumfries & Galloway Avn Mus, Dumfries
	XP558	Hunting Jet Provost T4 (8627M) <ff>	Privately owned, Stoneykirk, D&G
	XP558	Hunting Jet Provost T4 (8627M)[20] <rf>	Privately owned, Sproughton
	XP568	Hunting Jet Provost T4	East Midlands Airport Aeropark
	XP573	Hunting Jet Provost T4 (8236M) [19]	Jersey Airport Fire Section
	XP585	Hunting Jet Provost T4 (8407M) [24]	NE Wales Institute, Wrexham
	XP627	Hunting Jet Provost T4	North-East Land, Sea & Air Museums, stored Usworth
	XP629	Hunting Jet Provost T4 (9026M) [P]	Privately owned, Market Rasen, Lincs
	XP640	Hunting Jet Provost T4 (8501M) [M]	Yorkshire Air Museum, Elvington
	XP642	Hunting Jet Provost T4 <ff>	Cornwall Aviation Heritage Centre, Newquay
	XP672	Hunting Jet Provost T4 (8458M/G-RAFI) [03]	South Wales Aviation Museum, St Athan
	XP680	Hunting Jet Provost T4 (8460M)	FETC, Moreton-in-Marsh, Glos
	XP686	Hunting Jet Provost T4 (8401M/8502M) [G]	Gunsmoke Paintball, Colchester, Essex
	XP701	BAC Lightning F3 (8924M) <ff>	Robertsbridge Aviation Society, Mayfield
	XP703	BAC Lightning F3 <ff>	Lightning Preservation Group, Bruntingthorpe
	XP706	BAC Lightning F3 (8925M)	South Yorkshire Aircraft Museum, Doncaster
	XP743	BAC Lightning F3 <ff>	Wattisham Station Heritage Museum
	XP745	BAC Lightning F3 (8453M) [H]	Vanguard Self Storage, Bristol
	XP757	BAC Lightning F3 <ff>	Privately owned, Boston, Lincs
	XP765	BAC Lightning F6 (XS897) [A]	Lakes Lightnings, RAF Coningsby
	XP820	DHC2 Beaver AL1 (G-CICP)	Historic Army Aircraft Flight, Middle Wallop
	XP821	DHC2 Beaver AL1 [MCO]	Army Flying Museum, Middle Wallop
	XP822	DHC2 Beaver AL1	Army Flying Museum, Middle Wallop
	XP831	Hawker P.1127 (8406M)	Science Museum, South Kensington
	XP841	Handley-Page HP115	FAA Museum, RNAS Yeovilton
	XP847	WS Scout AH1	Army Flying Museum, Middle Wallop
	XP848	WS Scout AH1	Farnborough Air Sciences Trust, Farnborough
	XP849	WS Scout AH1 (XP895)	Museum of Berkshire Aviation, Woodley, Berks
	XP853	WS Scout AH1	Privately owned, Sutton, Surrey
	XP854	WS Scout AH1 (7898M/TAD 043)	Mayhem Paintball, Abridge, Essex
	XP855	WS Scout AH1	Privately owned, Arncott, Oxon
	XP883	WS Scout AH1	Currently not known
	XP883	WS Scout AH1 (XW281/G-BYNZ) [T]	Privately owned, Dungannon, NI
	XP884	WS Scout AH1	AAC, stored Middle Wallop
	XP885	WS Scout AH1	AAC Wattisham, instructional use
	XP886	WS Scout AH1	The Helicopter Museum, stored Weston-super-Mare
	XP888	WS Scout AH1	Privately owned, Sproughton
	XP890	WS Scout AH1 [G] (fuselage)	Privately owned, Ipswich
	XP899	WS Scout AH1	Boscombe Down Aviation Collection, Old Sarum
	XP900	WS Scout AH1	AAC Wattisham, instructional use
	XP902	WS Scout AH1 <ff>	South Yorkshire Aircraft Museum, Doncaster
	XP905	WS Scout AH1	Privately owned, stored Sproughton
	XP907	WS Scout AH1 (G-SROE)	Privately owned, Wattisham
	XP910	WS Scout AH1	Army Flying Museum, Middle Wallop
	XP924	DH110 Sea Vixen D3 (G-CVIX) [134/E]	Naval Aviation Ltd, Yeovilton
	XP925	DH110 Sea Vixen FAW2 [752] <ff>	Privately owned, Stoneykirk, D&G
	XP980	Hawker P.1127	FAA Museum, RNAS Yeovilton
	XP984	Hawker P.1127	Brooklands Museum, Weybridge
	XR220	BAC TSR2 (7933M)	RAF Museum, Cosford
	XR222	BAC TSR2	IWM Duxford
	XR232	Sud Alouette AH2 (F-WEIP)	Army Flying Museum, Middle Wallop
	XR239	Auster AOP9	Privately owned, Stretton on Dunsmore
	XR240	Auster AOP9 (G-BDFH)	Privately owned, Eggesford
	XR241	Auster AOP9 (G-AXRR)	Privately owned, Eggesford
	XR244	Auster AOP9 (G-CICR)	Historic Army Aircraft Flight, Middle Wallop

Serial	Type (code/other identity)	Owner/operator, location or fate	Notes
XR246	Auster AOP9 (7862M/G-AZBU)	Privately owned, Scunthorpe	
XR267	Auster AOP9 (G-BJXR)	Privately owned, Hucknall	
XR271	Auster AOP9	Privately owned, stored Wroughton	
XR346	Northrop Shelduck D1 (comp XW578)	Bournemouth Aviation Museum	
XR371	SC5 Belfast C1	RAF Museum, Cosford	
XR447	Northrop Shelduck D1 (wreck)	Morayvia, Kinloss	
XR453	WS55 Whirlwind HAR10 (8873M) [A]	RAF Odiham, on gate	
XR485	WS55 Whirlwind HAR10 [Q]	Norfolk & Suffolk Avn Museum, Flixton	
XR486	WS55 Whirlwind HCC12 (8727M/G-RWWW)	The Helicopter Museum, Weston-super-Mare	
XR498	WS58 Wessex HC2 (9342M)	DSAE Cosford, on display	
XR502	WS58 Wessex HC2 (G-CCUP/N486KA) [Z]	Privately owned, Stonegate, E Sussex	
XR503	WS58 Wessex HC2	MoD DFTDC, Manston	
XR506	WS58 Wessex HC2 (9343M) [V]	Privately owned, Corley Moor, Warks	
XR516	WS58 Wessex HC2 (9319M) [V]	RAF Shawbury, on display	
XR517	WS58 Wessex HC2 [N]	Ulster Aviation Society, Long Kesh	
XR523	WS58 Wessex HC2 [M]	MoD Pembrey Sands Air Weapons Range, GI use	
XR525	WS58 Wessex HC2 [G]	RAF Museum, Cosford	
XR526	WS58 Wessex HC2 (8147M)	The Helicopter Museum, stored Weston-super-Mare	
XR528	WS58 Wessex HC2	Morayvia, Kinloss	
XR529	WS58 Wessex HC2 (9268M) [E]	Ulster Aviation Society, Long Kesh	
XR534	HS Gnat T1 (8578M) [65]	Newark Air Museum, Winthorpe	
XR537	HS Gnat T1 (8642M/G-NATY)	Privately owned, North Weald	
XR538	HS Gnat T1 (8621M/G-RORI) [01]	Heritage Aircraft Trust, North Weald	
XR540	HS Gnat T1 (XP502/8576M) [2]	Privately owned, Cotswold Airport	
XR571	HS Gnat T1 (8493M)	RAF Scampton Heritage Centre	
XR574	HS Gnat T1 (8631M) [72]	Trenchard Museum, Halton	
XR595	WS Scout AH1 (G-BWHU) [M]	Privately owned, North Weald	
XR601	WS Scout AH1	Privately owned, Sproughton	
XR627	WS Scout AH1 [X]	Privately owned, Storwood, Yorkshire	
XR628	WS Scout AH1	Privately owned, Ipswich	
XR629	WS Scout AH1 (fuselage)	Privately owned, Ipswich	
XR635	WS Scout AH1	Midland Air Museum, Coventry	
XR650	Hunting Jet Provost T4 (8459M) [28]	Boscombe Down Aviation Collection, Old Sarum	
XR654	Hunting Jet Provost T4 <ff>	Privately owned, Chester	
XR658	Hunting Jet Provost T4 (8192M)	RAF Manston History Museum	
XR662	Hunting Jet Provost T4 (8410M) [25]	Privately owned, Gilberdyke, E Yorks	
XR673	Hunting Jet Provost T4 (G-BXLO/9032M) [L]	Privately owned, Gamston	
XR681	Hunting Jet Provost T4 (8588M) <ff>	Robertsbridge Aviation Society, Mayfield	
XR700	Hunting Jet Provost T4 (8589M) <ff>	No 1137 Sqn ATC, Aldergrove	
XR713	BAC Lightning F3 (8935M) [C]	Lightning Preservation Grp, Bruntingthorpe	
	(wears XR718 on starboard side)		
XR718	BAC Lightning F6 (8932M) [DA]	Privately owned, Over Dinsdale, N Yorks	
XR724	BAC Lightning F6 (G-BTSY)	The Lightning Association, Binbrook	
XR725	BAC Lightning F6	Privately owned, Binbrook	
XR726	BAC Lightning F6 <ff>	Privately owned, Harrogate	
XR728	BAC Lightning F6 [JS]	Lightning Preservation Grp, Bruntingthorpe	
XR747	BAC Lightning F6 <ff>	No 20 Sqn ATC, Bideford, Devon	
XR749	BAC Lightning F3 (8934M) [DA]	Privately owned, Peterhead	
XR751	BAC Lightning F3 <ff>	Privately owned, Thorpe Wood, N Yorks	
XR753	BAC Lightning F6 (8969M) [XI]	RAF Coningsby on display	
XR753	BAC Lightning F53 (ZF578) [A]	Tangmere Military Aviation Museum	
XR754	BAC Lightning F6 (8972M) <ff>	Privately owned, Upwood, Cambs	
XR755	BAC Lightning F6	Privately owned, Callington, Cornwall	
XR757	BAC Lightning F6 <ff>	Newark Air Museum, Winthorpe	
XR759	BAC Lightning F6 <ff>	Privately owned, Haxey, Lincs	
XR768	BAC Lightning F53 (53-672/204/ZF580) [A]	Cornwall Aviation Heritage Centre, Newquay	
XR770	BAC Lightning F6 [AA]	RAF Manston History Museum	
XR771	BAC Lightning F6 [BF]	Midland Air Museum, Coventry	
XR806	BAC VC10 C1K (9285M) <ff>	RAF Brize Norton, BDRT	
XR808	BAC VC10 C1K [R] $	RAF Museum, Cosford	
XR810	BAC VC10 C1K <ff>	Privately owned, Crondall, Hants	
XR898	Northrop Shelduck D1 (XT005/BAPC.365)	Boscombe Down Aviation Collection, Old Sarum	

Notes	Serial	Type (code/other identity)	Owner/operator, location or fate
	XR944	Wallis WA116 (G-ATTB)	Privately owned, Old Buckenham
	XR977	HS Gnat T1 (8640M)	RAF Museum, Hendon
	XR992	HS Gnat T1 (8624M/XS102/G-MOUR)	Heritage Aircraft Trust, North Weald
	XR993	HS Gnat T1 (8620M/XP534/G-BVPP)	South Wales Aviation Museum, St Athan
	XS100	HS Gnat T1 (8561M) <ff>	Privately owned, stored Wimbledon
	XS100	HS Gnat T1 (8561M) <rf>	Privately owned, North Weald
	XS104	HS Gnat T1 (8604M/G-FRCE)	Privately owned, North Weald
	XS149	WS58 Wessex HAS3 [661/GL]	The Helicopter Museum, Weston-super-Mare
	XS176	Hunting Jet Provost T4 (8514M) <ff>	Morayvia, Kinloss
	XS177	Hunting Jet Provost T4 (9044M) [N]	Privately owned, Gilberdyke, E Yorks
	XS179	Hunting Jet Provost T4 (8237M) [20]	Secret Nuclear Bunker, Hack Green, Cheshire
	XS180	Hunting Jet Provost T4 (8238M/8338M) [21]	MoD JARTS, Boscombe Down
	XS181	Hunting Jet Provost T4 (9033M) <ff>	Lakes Lightnings, Spark Bridge, Cumbria
	XS183	Hunting Jet Provost T4 <ff>	Privately owned, Plymouth
	XS186	Hunting Jet Provost T4 (8408M) [M]	Metheringham Airfield Visitors Centre
	XS209	Hunting Jet Provost T4 (8409M)	Solway Aviation Society, Carlisle
	XS216	Hunting Jet Provost T4 <ff>	South Yorkshire Aircraft Museum, Doncaster
	XS218	Hunting Jet Provost T4 (8508M) <ff>	No 447 Sqn ATC, Henley-on-Thames, Berks
	XS231	BAC Jet Provost T5 (G-ATAJ)	Boscombe Down Aviation Collection, Old Sarum
	XS235	DH106 Comet 4C (G-CPDA)	Cold War Jets Collection, Bruntingthorpe
	XS238	Auster AOP9 (TAD 200)	Newark Air Museum, Winthorpe
	XS416	BAC Lightning T5	Privately owned, New York, Lincs
	XS417	BAC Lightning T5 [DZ]	Newark Air Museum, Winthorpe
	XS420	BAC Lightning T5	Privately owned, FAST, Farnborough
	XS421	BAC Lightning T5 <ff>	RAF Air Defence Radar Museum, Neatishead
	XS456	BAC Lightning T5 [DX]	Skegness Water Leisure Park
	XS457	BAC Lightning T5 <ff>	Privately owned, Binbrook
	XS458	BAC Lightning T5 [T]	T5 Projects, Cranfield
	XS459	BAC Lightning T5 [AW]	Fenland & W Norfolk Aviation Museum, Wisbech
	XS481	WS58 Wessex HU5	South Yorkshire Aircraft Museum, Doncaster
	XS482	WS58 Wessex HU5	RAF Manston History Museum
	XS486	WS58 Wessex HU5 (9272M) [524/CU,F]	The Helicopter Museum, Weston-super-Mare
	XS488	WS58 Wessex HU5 (9056M) [F]	Privately owned, Tiptree, Essex
	XS489	WS58 Wessex HU5 [R]	Privately owned, Westerham, Kent
	XS493	WS58 Wessex HU5	StandardAero, stored Fleetlands
	XS507	WS58 Wessex HU5	Privately owned, stored Chard, Somerset
	XS508	WS58 Wessex HU5	FAA Museum, RNAS Yeovilton
	XS510	WS58 Wessex HU5 [626/PO]	Morayvia, Kinloss
	XS511	WS58 Wessex HU5 [M]	Tangmere Military Aircraft Museum
	XS513	WS58 Wessex HU5	RNAS Yeovilton Fire Section
	XS515	WS58 Wessex HU5 [N]	Army, Keogh Barracks, Aldershot, instructional use
	XS516	WS58 Wessex HU5 [Q]	Privately owned, Redruth, Cornwall
	XS520	WS58 Wessex HU5 [F]	Currently not known
	XS522	WS58 Wessex HU5 [ZL]	Blackball Paintball, Truro, Cornwall
	XS527	WS Wasp HAS1	FAA Museum, stored Cobham Hall, RNAS Yeovilton
	XS529	WS Wasp HAS1	Privately owned, Redruth, Cornwall
	XS539	WS Wasp HAS1 [435]	StandardAero Fleetlands Apprentice School
	XS567	WS Wasp HAS1 [434/E]	IWM Duxford
	XS568	WS Wasp HAS1 (A2715) [441]	DSAE RNAESS, HMS Sultan, Gosport
	XS574	Northrop Shelduck D1 <R>	FAA Museum, stored Cobham Hall, RNAS Yeovilton
	XS576	DH110 Sea Vixen FAW2 [125/E]	IWM Duxford
	XS587	DH110 Sea Vixen FAW(TT)2 (8828M/G-VIXN)	Gatwick Aviation Museum, Charlwood, Surrey
	XS590	DH110 Sea Vixen FAW2 [131/E]	FAA Museum, RNAS Yeovilton
	XS639	HS Andover E3A (9241M)	RAF Museum, Cosford
	XS641	HS Andover C1PR (9198M) (fuselage)	Privately owned, Sandbach, Cheshire
	XS643	HS Andover E3A (9278M) <ff>	Privately owned, Dudley, W Mids
	XS646	HS Andover C1(mod) (fuselage)	MoD JARTS, Boscombe Down
	XS651	Slingsby T45 Swallow TX1 (BGA1211) [BYB]	Privately owned, Lasham
	XS652	Slingsby T45 Swallow TX1 (BGA1107)	Privately owned, Chipping, Lancs
	XS674	WS58 Wessex HC2 [R]	Privately owned, Biggin Hill
	XS695	HS Kestrel FGA1 [5]	RAF Museum, Cosford

Serial	Type (code/other identity)	Owner/operator, location or fate	Notes
XS709	HS125 Dominie T1 [M]	RAF Museum, Cosford	
XS710	HS125 Dominie T1 (9259M) [O]	RAF Cranwell Fire Section	
XS713	HS125 Dominie T1 [C]	RAF Shawbury Fire Section	
XS714	HS125 Dominie T1 (9246M) [P]	MoD DFTDC, Manston	
XS726	HS125 Dominie T1 (9273M) [T]	Newark Air Museum, Winthorpe	
XS727	HS125 Dominie T1 [D]	RAF Cranwell, on display	
XS731	HS125 Dominie T1 (N19XY) (fuselage)	Privately owned, Marlborough, Wilts	
XS734	HS125 Dominie T1 (9260M) [N]	Privately owned, Sproughton	
XS735	HS125 Dominie T1 (9264M) [R]	South Yorkshire Aircraft Museum, Doncaster	
XS736	HS125 Dominie T1 [S]	MoD Winterbourne Gunner, Wilts	
XS738	HS125 Dominie T1 (9274M) [U]	RN, Predannack Fire School	
XS743	Beagle B206Z	QinetiQ Apprentice Training School, Boscombe Down	
XS765	Beagle B206 Basset CC1 (G-BSET)	QinetiQ Apprentice Training School, Boscombe Down	
XS770	Beagle B206 Basset CC1 (G-HRHI)	*Currently not known*	
XS790	HS748 Andover CC2 <ff>	Boscombe Down Aviation Collection, Old Sarum	
XS791	HS748 Andover CC2 (fuselage)	Privately owned, Stock, Essex	
XS859	Slingsby T45 Swallow TX1 (BGA1136) [859]	Privately owned, stored Felthorpe	
XS863	WS58 Wessex HAS1 [304/R]	IWM Duxford	
XS865	WS58 Wessex HAS1 (A2694)	Privately owned, Ballygowan, NI	
XS885	WS58 Wessex HAS1 [512/DD]	Delta Force Paintball, Burnley	
XS886	WS58 Wessex HAS1 [527/CU]	Privately owned, Ditchling, E Sussex	
XS887	WS58 Wessex HAS1 [403/FI]	South Yorkshire Aircraft Museum, Doncaster	
XS898	BAC Lightning F6 <ff>	Privately owned, Lavendon, Bucks	
XS899	BAC Lightning F6 <ff>	Privately owned, Binbrook	
XS903	BAC Lightning F6 [BA]	Yorkshire Air Museum, Elvington	
XS904	BAC Lightning F6 [BQ]	Lightning Preservation Grp, Bruntingthorpe	
XS919	BAC Lightning F6	Privately owned,	
XS921	BAC Lightning F6 <R> [BA]	BAE Systems, Samlesbury, on display	
XS922	BAC Lightning F6 (8973M) <ff>	Lakes Lightnings, Spark Bridge, Cumbria	
XS923	BAC Lightning F6 <ff>	Privately owned, Welshpool	
XS925	BAC Lightning F6 (8961M) [BA]	RAF Museum, Hendon	
XS928	BAC Lightning F6 [AD]	BAE Systems Warton, on display	
XS932	BAC Lightning F6 <ff>	Privately owned, Walcott, Lincs	
XS933	BAC Lightning F6 <ff>	Privately owned, Farnham	
XS933	BAC Lightning F53 (ZF594) [BE]	North-East Land, Sea & Air Museums, Usworth	
XS936	BAC Lightning F6	Castle Motors, Liskeard, Cornwall	
XT108	Agusta-Bell 47G-3 Sioux AH1 [U]	Army Flying Museum, Middle Wallop	
XT123	WS Sioux AH1 (XT827) [D]	AAC Middle Wallop, at main gate	
XT131	Agusta-Bell 47G-3 Sioux AH1 (G-CICN) [B]	Historic Army Aircraft Flight, Middle Wallop	
XT140	Agusta-Bell 47G-3 Sioux AH1	Privately owned, Malmesbury	
XT148	Agusta-Bell 47G-3 Sioux AH1	North-East Land, Sea & Air Museums, Usworth	
XT150	Agusta-Bell 47G-3 Sioux AH1 (7883M) [R]	South Yorkshire Aircraft Museum, stored Doncaster	
XT151	WS Sioux AH1	Army Flying Museum, stored Middle Wallop	
XT176	WS Sioux AH1 [U]	FAA Museum, stored Cobham Hall, RNAS Yeovilton	
XT190	WS Sioux AH1	The Helicopter Museum, Weston-super-Mare	
XT200	WS Sioux AH1 [F]	Newark Air Museum, Winthorpe	
XT208	WS Sioux AH1 (wreck)	Privately owned, Fivemiletown, Co Tyrone, NI	
XT236	WS Sioux AH1 (frame only)	Privately owned, Cheshire	
XT242	WS Sioux AH1 (composite) [12]	South Yorkshire Aircraft Museum, Doncaster	
XT257	WS58 Wessex HAS3 (8719M)	Bournemouth Aviation Museum	
XT277	HS Buccaneer S2A (8853M) <ff>	Privately owned, Welshpool	
XT280	HS Buccaneer S2A <ff>	Dumfries & Galloway Avn Mus, Dumfries	
XT284	HS Buccaneer S2A (8855M) <ff>	Privately owned, Felixstowe	
XT288	HS Buccaneer S2B (9134M)	National Museum of Flight, E Fortune	
XT420	WS Wasp HAS1 (G-CBUI) [606]	Privately owned, North Weald	
XT427	WS Wasp HAS1 [606]	FAA Museum, stored Cobham Hall, RNAS Yeovilton	
XT431	WS Wasp HAS1 (comp XS463) [462]	Bournemouth Aviation Museum	
XT434	WS Wasp HAS1 (G-CGGK) [455]	Privately owned, Breighton	
XT435	WS Wasp HAS1 (NZ3907/G-RIMM) [430]	Privately owned, North Weald	
XT437	WS Wasp HAS1 [423]	Boscombe Down Aviation Collection, Old Sarum	
XT439	WS Wasp HAS1 [605]	Privately owned, Hemel Hempstead	

Notes	Serial	Type (code/other identity)	Owner/operator, location or fate
	XT443	WS Wasp HAS1 [422/AU]	The Helicopter Museum, Weston-super-Mare
	XT453	WS58 Wessex HU5 (A2756) [B/PO]	DSAE, stored HMS Sultan, Gosport
	XT455	WS58 Wessex HU5 (A2654) [U]	Mayhem Paintball, Abridge, Essex
	XT456	WS58 Wessex HU5 (8941M) [XZ]	Belfast Airport Fire Section
	XT466	WS58 Wessex HU5 (A2617/8921M) [528/CU]	Morayvia, Kinloss
	XT467	WS58 Wessex HU5 (8922M) [BF]	Gunsmoke Paintball, Hadleigh, Suffolk
	XT469	WS58 Wessex HU5 (8920M)	Privately owned, Clatterford, Isle of Wight
	XT472	WS58 Wessex HU5 [XC]	The Helicopter Museum, stored Weston-super-Mare
	XT480	WS58 Wessex HU5 [468/RG]	Rednal Paintball, Shropshire
	XT482	WS58 Wessex HU5 [ZM/VL]	FAA Museum, RNAS Yeovilton
	XT486	WS58 Wessex HU5 (8919M)	Dumfries & Galloway Avn Mus, Dumfries
	XT550	WS Sioux AH1 [D]	Currently not known
	XT575	Vickers Viscount 837 <ff>	Brooklands Museum, Weybridge
	XT581	Northrop Shelduck D1	Muckleburgh Collection, Weybourne, Norfolk
	XT583	Northrop Shelduck D1	Privately owned, Wroughton
	XT596	McD F-4K Phantom FG1	FAA Museum, RNAS Yeovilton
	XT597	McD F-4K Phantom FG1	Privately owned, stored Wymeswold, Leics
	XT601	WS58 Wessex HC2 (9277M) (composite)	RAF Odiham, BDRT
	XT604	WS58 Wessex HC2	East Midlands Airport Aeropark
	XT617	WS Scout AH1	Wattisham Station Heritage Museum
	XT621	WS Scout AH1	Defence Academy of the UK, Shrivenham
	XT623	WS Scout AH1	DSAE SAAE, Lyneham
	XT626	WS Scout AH1 (G-CIBW) [Q]	Army Historic Aircraft Flt, Middle Wallop
	XT630	WS Scout AH1 (G-BXRL) [X]	Privately owned, Rough Close, Staffs
	XT631	WS Scout AH1 [D]	Privately owned, Ipswich
	XT633	WS Scout AH1	Privately owned, Barton Ashes, Hants
	XT634	WS Scout AH1 (G-BYRX) [T]	Privately owned, North Weald
	XT638	WS Scout AH1 [N]	AAC Middle Wallop, at main gate
	XT640	WS Scout AH1	Privately owned, Westbury
	XT643	WS Scout AH1	Army, Thorpe Camp, East Wretham (wreck)
	XT653	Slingsby T45 Swallow TX1 (BGA3469)	Privately owned, Keevil, Wilts
	XT672	WS58 Wessex HC2 [WE]	RAF Stafford, on display
	XT681	WS58 Wessex HC2 (9279M) [U] <ff>	Privately owned, Wallingford, Oxon
	XT761	WS58 Wessex HU5 (G-WSEX)	Privately owned, Chard, Somerset
	XT762	WS58 Wessex HU5	Hamburger Hill Paintball, Marksbury, Somerset
	XT765	WS58 Wessex HU5 [J]	FAA Museum, stored Cobham Hall, RNAS Yeovilton
	XT765	WS58 Wessex HU5 (XT458/A2768) [P/VL]	RNAS Yeovilton, on display
	XT769	WS58 Wessex HU5 [823]	FAA Museum, RNAS Yeovilton
	XT771	WS58 Wessex HU5 [620/PO]	Privately owned, stored Chard, Somerset
	XT773	WS58 Wessex HU5 (9123M)	RAF Shawbury Fire Section
	XT778	WS Wasp HAS1 [430]	FAA Museum, stored Cobham Hall, RNAS Yeovilton
	XT780	WS Wasp HAS1 [636]	CEMAST, Fareham College, Lee-on-Solent
	XT787	WS Wasp HAS1 (NZ3905/G-KAXT)	Westland Wasp Historic Flt, Barton Ashes, Hants
	XT788	WS Wasp HAS1 (G-BMIR) [474]	Privately owned, Storwood, Yorkshire
	XT793	WS Wasp HAS1 (G-BZPP) <ff>	South Yorkshire Aircraft Museum, Doncaster
	XT863	McD F-4K Phantom FG1 <ff>	Privately owned, Cowes, IOW
	XT864	McD F-4K Phantom FG1 (8998M/XT684) [007/R]	Ulster Aviation Society, Long Kesh
	XT891	McD F-4M Phantom FGR2 (9136M)	RAF Coningsby, at main gate
	XT903	McD F-4M Phantom FGR2 <ff>	RAF Museum, stored Cosford
	XT905	McD F-4M Phantom FGR2 (9286M) [P]	Privately owned, stored Wymeswold, Leics
	XT907	McD F-4M Phantom FGR2 (9151M) [W]	Privately owned, Bentwaters
	XT914	McD F-4M Phantom FGR2 (9269M) [Z]	Wattisham Station Heritage Museum
	XV104	BAC VC10 C1K <ff>	South Wales Aviation Museum, stored St Athan
	XV106	BAC VC10 C1K <ff>	Avro Heritage Museum, Woodford
	XV108	BAC VC10 C1K <ff>	East Midlands Airport Aeropark
	XV109	BAC VC10 C1K <ff>	South Wales Aviation Museum, stored St Athan
	XV118	WS Scout AH1 (9141M) <ff>	Kennet Aviation, North Weald
	XV122	WS Scout AH1 [D]	Defence Academy of the UK, Shrivenham
	XV123	WS Scout AH1 [V]	Vanguard Self Storage, Greenford
	XV124	WS Scout AH1 [W]	Privately owned, Godstone, Surrey
	XV127	WS Scout AH1	Army Flying Museum, Middle Wallop

Serial	Type (code/other identity)	Owner/operator, location or fate	Notes
XV130	WS Scout AH1 (G-BWJW) [R]	Privately owned, North Weald	
XV136	WS Scout AH1 [X]	Ulster Aviation Society, Long Kesh	
XV137	WS Scout AH1 (G-CRUM)	Privately owned, Chiseldon, Wilts	
XV138	WS Scout AH1 (G-SASM) [S]	Privately owned, North Weald	
XV139	WS Scout AH1 (comp XP886)	South Yorkshire Aircraft Museum, Doncaster	
XV141	WS Scout AH1	REME Museum, Lyneham	
XV148	HS Nimrod MR1(mod) <ff>	Privately owned, Malmesbury	
XV161	HS Buccaneer S2B (9117M) <ff>	Dundonald Aviation Centre	
XV165	HS Buccaneer S2B <ff>	Privately owned, Ashford, Kent	
XV168	HS Buccaneer S2B [AF]	Yorkshire Air Museum, Elvington	
XV177	Lockheed C-130K Hercules C3A [177]	*Scrapped*	
XV188	Lockheed C-130K Hercules C3A [188]	*Scrapped*	
XV200	Lockheed C-130K Hercules C1 [200]	*Scrapped*	
XV201	Lockheed C-130K Hercules C1K <ff>	Marshalls, Cambridge	
XV202	Lockheed C-130K Hercules C3 [202]	RAF Museum, Cosford	
XV208	Lockheed C-130K Hercules W2 <ff>	Marshalls, Cambridge	
XV209	Lockheed C-130K Hercules C3A [209]	*Scrapped*	
XV221	Lockheed C-130K Hercules C3 <ff>	Privately owned, White Waltham	
XV226	HS Nimrod MR2 $	Cold War Jets Collection, Bruntingthorpe	
XV229	HS Nimrod MR2 [29]	MoD DFTDC, Manston	
XV231	HS Nimrod MR2 [31]	Aviation Viewing Park, Manchester	
XV232	HS Nimrod MR2 [32]	Privately owned, Coventry	
XV235	HS Nimrod MR2 [35] <ff>	Avro Heritage Museum, Woodford	
XV240	HS Nimrod MR2 [40] <ff>	Morayvia, Kinloss	
XV241	HS Nimrod MR2 [41] <ff>	National Museum of Flight, E Fortune	
XV244	HS Nimrod MR2 [44]	Morayvia, RAF Kinloss	
XV249	HS Nimrod R1 $	RAF Museum, Cosford	
XV250	HS Nimrod MR2 [50]	Yorkshire Air Museum, Elvington	
XV252	HS Nimrod MR2 [52] <ff>	Privately owned, Cullen, Moray	
XV254	HS Nimrod MR2 [54] <ff>	Highland Aviation Museum, Inverness	
XV255	HS Nimrod MR2 [55]	City of Norwich Aviation Museum	
XV259	BAe Nimrod AEW3 <ff>	Privately owned, Wales	
XV263	BAe Nimrod AEW3P (8967M) <ff>	BAE Systems, Brough	
XV263	BAe Nimrod AEW3P (8967M) <rf>	MoD/BAE Systems, Woodford	
XV268	DHC2 Beaver AL1 (G-BVER)	Privately owned, Cumbernauld	
XV277	HS P.1127(RAF)	National Museum of Flight, E Fortune	
XV279	HS P.1127(RAF) (8566M)	Harrier Heritage Centre, RAF Wittering	
XV280	HS P.1127(RAF) <ff>	South Yorkshire Aviation Museum, Doncaster	
XV281	HS P.1127(RAF) (BAPC 484)	South Yorkshire Aviation Museum, Doncaster	
XV302	Lockheed C-130K Hercules C3 [302]	Marshalls, Cambridge, fatigue test airframe	
XV304	Lockheed C-130K Hercules C3A	RAF JADTEU, Brize Norton, instructional use	
XV328	BAC Lightning T5 <ff>	Lightning Preservation Group, Bruntingthorpe	
XV333	HS Buccaneer S2B [234/H]	FAA Museum, RNAS Yeovilton	
XV344	HS Buccaneer S2C	QinetiQ Farnborough, on display	
XV350	HS Buccaneer S2B	East Midlands Airport Aeropark	
XV352	HS Buccaneer S2B <ff>	RAF Manston History Museum	
XV359	HS Buccaneer S2B [035/R]	Privately owned, Topsham, Devon	
XV361	HS Buccaneer S2B	Ulster Aviation Society, Long Kesh	
XV370	Sikorsky SH-3D (A2682) [260]	DSAE RNAESS, *HMS Sultan*, Gosport	
XV371	WS61 Sea King HAS1(DB) [61/DD]	RN, Predannack Fire School	
XV372	WS61 Sea King HAS1	MoD Pembrey Sands Air Weapons Range, GI use	
XV383	Northrop MQM-57A/3 (fuselage)	Privately owned, Wimborne, Dorset	
XV401	McD F-4M Phantom FGR2 [I]	Privately owned, Bentwaters	
XV402	McD F-4M Phantom FGR2 <ff>	Privately owned, Kent	
XV406	McD F-4M Phantom FGR2 (9098M)	Solway Aviation Society, Carlisle	
XV408	McD F-4M Phantom FGR2 (9165M) [Z]	Tangmere Military Aviation Museum	
XV411	McD F-4M Phantom FGR2 (9103M) [L]	MoD DFTDC, Manston	
XV415	McD F-4M Phantom FGR2 (9163M) [E]	RAF Boulmer, on display	
XV424	McD F-4M Phantom FGR2 (9152M) [I]	RAF Museum, Hendon	
XV426	McD F-4M Phantom FGR2 <ff>	City of Norwich Aviation Museum	
XV426	McD F-4M Phantom FGR2 [P] <rf>	RAF Coningsby, BDRT	
XV460	McD F-4M Phantom FGR2 <ff>	Privately owned, Bentwaters	

Notes	Serial	Type (code/other identity)	Owner/operator, location or fate
	XV474	McD F-4M Phantom FGR2 [T]	The Old Flying Machine Company, Duxford
	XV490	McD F-4M Phantom FGR2 [R] <ff>	Newark Air Museum, Winthorpe
	XV497	McD F-4M Phantom FGR2 (9295M) [D]	Privately owned, Bentwaters
	XV499	McD F-4M Phantom FGR2 <ff>	South Wales Aviation Museum, St Athan
	XV581	McD F-4K Phantom FG1 (9070M) <ff>	Staffordshire Wing ATC Aerospace & Technology Centre
	XV582	McD F-4K Phantom FG1 (9066M) [M]	South Wales Aviation Museum, St Athan
	XV586	McD F-4K Phantom FG1 (9067M) [010-R]	Privately owned, RNAS Yeovilton
	XV591	McD F-4K Phantom FG1 [013] <ff>	RAF Museum, Cosford
	XV631	WS Wasp HAS1 (fuselage)	Farnborough Air Sciences Trust, stored Farnborough
	XV642	WS61 Sea King HAS2A (A2614) [259]	DSAE RNAESS, HMS Sultan, Gosport
	XV643	WS61 Sea King HAS6 [262]	DSAE, stored HMS Sultan, Gosport
	XV647	WS61 Sea King HU5 [28]	DSAE RNAESS, HMS Sultan, Gosport
	XV648	WS61 Sea King HU5 [18/CU]	Privately owned, Acharacle, Argyll
	XV649	WS61 Sea King ASaC7 [180]	DSAE, stored HMS Sultan, Gosport
	XV651	WS61 Sea King HU5	Holmside Park, Edmondsley, Durham
	XV653	WS61 Sea King HAS6 (9326M) [63/CU]	DSAE No 1 SoTT, Cosford
	XV654	WS61 Sea King HAS6 [705/DD] (wreck)	RN, Predannack Fire School
	XV655	WS61 Sea King HAS6 [270/N]	DSAE RNAESS, HMS Sultan, Gosport
	XV656	WS61 Sea King ASaC7 [185]	DSAE, stored HMS Sultan, Gosport
	XV657	WS61 Sea King HAS5 (ZA135) [32/DD]	RN, Predannack Fire School
	XV659	WS61 Sea King HAS6 (9324M) [62/CU]	DSAE No 1 SoTT, Cosford
	XV660	WS61 Sea King HAS6 [269/N]	DSAE RNAESS, HMS Sultan, Gosport
	XV661	WS61 Sea King HU5 [26]	Currently not known
	XV663	WS61 Sea King HAS6 [18]	FAA Museum, RNAS Yeovilton
	XV664	WS61 Sea King ASaC7 [190]	DSAE, stored HMS Sultan, Gosport
	XV665	WS61 Sea King HAS6 [507/CU]	DSAE RNAESS, HMS Sultan, Gosport
	XV666	WS61 Sea King HU5	HeliOperations Ltd, Portland
	XV670	WS61 Sea King HU5 [17]	DSAE, stored HMS Sultan, Gosport
	XV671	WS61 Sea King ASaC7 [183/CU]	DSAE, stored HMS Sultan, Gosport
	XV672	WS61 Sea King ASaC7 [187]	DSAE, stored HMS Sultan, Gosport
	XV673	WS61 Sea King HU5 [827/CU]	RN Culdrose, on display
	XV674	WS61 Sea King HAS6	Privately owned, Horsham
	XV675	WS61 Sea King HAS6 [701/PW]	DSAE RNAESS, HMS Sultan, Gosport
	XV676	WS61 Sea King HC6 [ZE]	DSAE RNAESS, HMS Sultan, Gosport
	XV677	WS61 Sea King HAS6 [269]	South Yorkshire Aircraft Museum, Doncaster
	XV696	WS61 Sea King HAS6 [267/L]	SFDO, RNAS Culdrose
	XV697	WS61 Sea King ASaC7 [181/CU]	DSAE, stored HMS Sultan, Gosport
	XV699	WS61 Sea King HU5 [823/PW]	DSAE RNAESS, HMS Sultan, Gosport
	XV700	WS61 Sea King HC6 [ZC]	RAF St Mawgan, instructional use
	XV701	WS61 Sea King HAS6 [268/N,64]	DSAE RNAESS, HMS Sultan, Gosport
	XV703	WS61 Sea King HC6 [ZD]	DSAE RNAESS, HMS Sultan, Gosport
	XV705	WS61 Sea King HU5 [29]	Privately owned, Woodmancote, W Sussex
	XV706	WS61 Sea King HAS6 (9344M) [017/L]	DSAE RNAESS, HMS Sultan, Gosport
	XV707	WS61 Sea King ASaC7 [184]	DSAE, stored HMS Sultan, Gosport
	XV708	WS61 Sea King HAS6 [501/CU]	DSAE RNAESS, HMS Sultan, Gosport
	XV709	WS61 Sea King HAS6 (9303M)	MoD/QinetiQ, Boscombe Down
	XV711	WS61 Sea King HAS6 [15/CW]	DSAE, stored HMS Sultan, Gosport
	XV712	WS61 Sea King HAS6 [66]	IWM Duxford
	XV713	WS61 Sea King HAS6 (A2646) [018/L]	DSAE RNAESS, HMS Sultan, Gosport
	XV714	WS61 Sea King ASaC7 [188]	DSAE, stored HMS Sultan, Gosport
	XV720	WS58 Wessex HC2 (A2701)	Privately owned, Culham, Oxon
	XV722	WS58 Wessex HC2 (8805M) [WH]	Privately owned, Badgers Mount, Kent
	XV724	WS58 Wessex HC2	DSAE RNAESS, HMS Sultan, Gosport
	XV725	WS58 Wessex HC2 [C]	MoD DFTDC, Manston
	XV726	WS58 Wessex HC2 [J]	Privately owned, Biggin Hill
	XV728	WS58 Wessex HC2 [A]	Newark Air Museum, Winthorpe
	XV731	WS58 Wessex HC2 [Y]	Privately owned, Badgers Mount, Kent
	XV732	WS58 Wessex HCC4	RAF Museum, Hendon
	XV733	WS58 Wessex HCC4	The Helicopter Museum, Weston-super-Mare
	XV741	HS Harrier GR3 (A2608)	Brooklands Museum, Weybridge
	XV744	HS Harrier GR3 (9167M) [3K]	Tangmere Military Aviation Museum
	XV748	HS Harrier GR3 [B]	Yorkshire Air Museum, Elvington

Serial	Type (code/other identity)	Owner/operator, location or fate	Notes
XV751	HS Harrier GR3 [AU]	Gatwick Aviation Museum, Charlwood, Surrey	
XV752	HS Harrier GR3 (9075M) [B]	South Yorkshire Aircraft Museum, Doncaster	
XV753	HS Harrier GR3 (9078M) [53/DD]	Cornwall Aviation Heritage Centre, Newquay	
XV759	HS Harrier GR3 [O] <ff>	Privately owned, Hitchin, Herts	
XV760	HS Harrier GR3 <ff>	Solent Sky, Southampton	
XV779	HS Harrier GR3 (8931M)	Harrier Heritage Centre, RAF Wittering	
XV783	HS Harrier GR3 [83/DD]	Privately owned, Corley Moor, Warks	
XV784	HS Harrier GR3 (8909M) <ff>	Boscombe Down Aviation Collection, Old Sarum	
XV786	HS Harrier GR3 [123] <ff>	RNAS Culdrose Fire Section	
XV786	HS Harrier GR3 [S] <rf>	RN, Predannack Fire School	
XV798	HS Harrier GR1(mod) (BAPC 450)	Rolls Royce Heritage Trust, Hucknall	
XV806	HS Harrier GR3 <ff>	Privately owned, Worksop, Notts	
XV808	HS Harrier GR3 (9076M/A2687) [08/DD]	Privately owned, Chetton, Shrops	
XV810	HS Harrier GR3 (9038M) [K]	Privately owned, Walcott, Lincs	
XV814	DH106 Comet 4 (G-APDF) <ff>	Privately owned, Chipping Campden	
XV863	HS Buccaneer S2B (9115M/9139M/9145M) [S]	Privately owned, Weston, Eire	
XV864	HS Buccaneer S2B (9234M)	MoD DFTDC, Manston	
XV865	HS Buccaneer S2B (9226M)	IWM Duxford	
XV867	HS Buccaneer S2B <ff>	Morayvia, Kinloss	
XW175	HS Harrier T4(VAAC)	Privately owned, Selby, N Yorks	
XW198	WS Puma HC1	RAF AM&SU, stored Shawbury	
XW199	WS Puma HC2	RAF, stored Benson	
XW202	WS Puma HC1	Army, Stensall Barracks, York	
XW204	WS Puma HC2	RAF No 28 Sqn/No 33 Sqn/No 230 Sqn, Benson	
XW208	WS Puma HC1	Newark Air Museum, Winthorpe	
XW209	WS Puma HC2	RAF No 28 Sqn/No 33 Sqn/No 230 Sqn, Benson	
XW210	WS Puma HC1 (comp XW215)	RAF AM&SU, stored Shawbury	
XW212	WS Puma HC2	RAF No 28 Sqn/No 33 Sqn/No 230 Sqn, Benson	
XW213	WS Puma HC2	RAF No 28 Sqn/No 33 Sqn/No 230 Sqn, Benson	
XW214	WS Puma HC2	RAF No 28 Sqn/No 33 Sqn/No 230 Sqn, Benson	
XW216	WS Puma HC2 (F-ZWDD) [G]	RAF No 28 Sqn/No 33 Sqn/No 230 Sqn, Benson	
XW217	WS Puma HC2 [H]	RAF No 28 Sqn/No 33 Sqn/No 230 Sqn, Benson	
XW219	WS Puma HC2	RAF No 28 Sqn/No 33 Sqn/No 230 Sqn, Benson	
XW220	WS Puma HC2 [K]	RAF No 28 Sqn/No 33 Sqn/No 230 Sqn, Benson	
XW222	WS Puma HC1	Ulster Aviation Society, Long Kesh	
XW223	WS Puma HC1	RAF AM&SU, stored Shawbury	
XW224	WS Puma HC2 $	RAF No 28 Sqn/No 33 Sqn/No 230 Sqn, Benson	
XW225	WS Puma HC1	Newark Air Museum, Winthorpe (spares use)	
XW226	WS Puma HC1	RAF AM&SU, stored Shawbury	
XW231	WS Puma HC2 [N]	RAF No 28 Sqn/No 33 Sqn/No 230 Sqn, Benson	
XW232	WS Puma HC2 (F-ZWDE) [P]	RAF No 28 Sqn/No 33 Sqn/No 230 Sqn, Benson	
XW235	WS Puma HC2 (F-ZWBI)	RAF, stored Benson	
XW236	WS Puma HC1	RAF Defence Movements School, Brize Norton	
XW237	WS Puma HC2	RAF, stored Benson	
XW241	Sud SA330E Puma	Farnborough Air Sciences Trust, Farnborough	
XW264	HS Harrier T2 <ff>	Jet Age Museum, Gloucester	
XW265	HS Harrier T4A (9258M) <ff>	No 2345 Sqn ATC, RAF Leuchars	
XW267	HS Harrier T4 (9263M)	Privately owned, Bentwaters	
XW268	HS Harrier T4N	City of Norwich Aviation Museum	
XW269	HS Harrier T4 [TB]	Caernarfon Air World	
XW270	HS Harrier T4 [T]	Coventry University, instructional use	
XW276	Aérospatiale SA341 Gazelle (F-ZWRI)	Newark Air Museum, Winthorpe	
XW283	WS Scout AH1 (G-CIMX) [U]	Kennet Aviation, North Weald	
XW289	BAC Jet Provost T5A (G-BVXT/G-JPVA) [73]	RAF St Athan, on display	
XW290	BAC Jet Provost T5A (9199M) [41,MA]	Privately owned, Bruntingthorpe	
XW293	BAC Jet Provost T5 (G-BWCS) [Z]	Privately owned, Bournemouth	
XW299	BAC Jet Provost T5A (G-CLJW/9146M) [60,MB]	Privately owned, Hawarden (for export to Australia)	
XW303	BAC Jet Provost T5A (9119M) [127]	RAF Halton	
XW304	BAC Jet Provost T5 (9172M) [MD]	Privately owned, Eye, Suffolk	
XW309	BAC Jet Provost T5 (9179M) [V,ME]	Hartlepool College of Further Education	
XW311	BAC Jet Provost T5 (9180M) [W,MF]	Privately owned, North Weald	

Notes	Serial	Type (code/other identity)	Owner/operator, location or fate
	XW315	BAC Jet Provost T5A <ff>	Privately owned, Preston
	XW320	BAC Jet Provost T5A (9015M) [71]	DSAE No 1 SoTT, Cosford
	XW321	BAC Jet Provost T5A (9154M) [62,MH]	Privately owned, Bentwaters
	XW323	BAC Jet Provost T5A (9166M) [86]	RAF Museum, Hendon
	XW324	BAC Jet Provost T5 (G-BWSG) [U]	Privately owned, East Midlands
	XW325	BAC Jet Provost T5B (G-BWGF) [E]	Privately owned, Coventry
	XW327	BAC Jet Provost T5A (9130M) [62]	DSAE No 1 SoTT, Cosford
	XW330	BAC Jet Provost T5A (9195M) [82,MJ]	Privately owned, Knutsford, Cheshire
	XW333	BAC Jet Provost T5A (G-BVTC)	Global Aviation, Humberside
	XW353	BAC Jet Provost T5A (9090M) [3]	RAF Cranwell, on display
	XW358	BAC Jet Provost T5A (9181M) [59,MK]	CEMAST, Fareham College, Lee-on-Solent
	XW360	BAC Jet Provost T5A (9153M) [61,ML]	Privately owned, Thorpe Wood, N Yorks
	XW363	BAC Jet Provost T5A [36]	Dumfries & Galloway Avn Mus, stored Dumfries
	XW364	BAC Jet Provost T5A (9188M) [35,MN]	RAF Halton, GI use
	XW370	BAC Jet Provost T5A (9196M) [72,MP]	Privately owned, Sproughton
	XW375	BAC Jet Provost T5A (9149M) [52]	DSAE No 1 SoTT, Cosford
	XW404	BAC Jet Provost T5A (9049M) [77]	Hartlepool FE College
	XW405	BAC Jet Provost T5A (9187M)	Hartlepool FE College, on display
	XW409	BAC Jet Provost T5A (9047M)	Privately owned, Hawarden
	XW410	BAC Jet Provost T5A (9125M) [80] <ff>	Privately owned, Conington
	XW418	BAC Jet Provost T5A (9173M) [MT]	RAF Museum, Cosford
	XW419	BAC Jet Provost T5A (9120M) [125]	Privately owned, Tore, Highland
	XW420	BAC Jet Provost T5A (9194M) [83,MU]	South Wales Aviation Museum, St Athan
	XW422	BAC Jet Provost T5A (G-BWEB) [3]	Privately owned, Cotswold Airport
	XW423	BAC Jet Provost T5A (G-BWUW) [14]	Deeside College, Connah's Quay, Clwyd
	XW430	BAC Jet Provost T5A (9176M) [77,MW]	Privately owned, Arncott, Oxon
	XW432	BAC Jet Provost T5A (9127M) [76,MX]	Privately owned, Thame
	XW433	BAC Jet Provost T5A (G-JPRO)	Privately owned, Inverness Airport
	XW434	BAC Jet Provost T5A (9091M) [78,MY]	Halfpenny Green Airport, on display
	XW436	BAC Jet Provost T5A (9148M) [68]	DSAE No 1 SoTT, Cosford
	XW530	HS Buccaneer S2B [530]	Buccaneer Service Station, Elgin
	XW541	HS Buccaneer S2B (8858M) <ff>	Privately owned, Lavendon, Bucks
	XW544	HS Buccaneer S2B (8857M) [O]	The Buccaneer Aviation Group, Bruntingthorpe
	XW547	HS Buccaneer S2B (9095M/9169M) [R]	RAF Museum, Hendon
	XW550	HS Buccaneer S2B <ff>	Privately owned, Bruntingthorpe
	XW560	SEPECAT Jaguar S <ff>	Boscombe Down Aviation Collection, Old Sarum
	XW563	SEPECAT Jaguar S (XX822/8563M)	County Hall, Norwich, on display
	XW566	SEPECAT Jaguar B	Farnborough Air Sciences Trust, Farnborough
	XW612	WS Scout AH1 (G-KAXW)	Privately owned, North Weald
	XW613	WS Scout AH1 (G-BXRS)	Privately owned, North Weald
	XW616	WS Scout AH1	AAC Dishforth, instructional use
	XW630	HS Harrier GR3	RNAS Yeovilton, Fire Section
	XW635	Beagle D5/180 (G-AWSW)	Privately owned, Spanhoe
	XW664	HS Nimrod R1	East Midlands Airport Aeropark
	XW666	HS Nimrod R1 <ff>	South Yorkshire Aircraft Museum, Doncaster
	XW763	HS Harrier GR3 (9002M/9041M) <ff>	Privately owned, Wigston, Leics
	XW768	HS Harrier GR3 (9072M) [N]	MoD DFTDC, Manston
	XW784	Mitchell-Procter Kittiwake I (G-BBRN) [VL]	Privately owned, RNAS Yeovilton
	XW795	WS Scout AH1	Privately owned, Fivemiletown, Co Tyrone, NI
	XW796	WS Scout AH1	Gunsmoke Paintball, Colchester, Essex
	XW838	WS Lynx (TAD009)	DSAE SAAE, Lyneham
	XW839	WS Lynx	The Helicopter Museum, Weston-super-Mare
	XW844	WS Gazelle AH1	StandardAero Fleetlands, preserved
	XW846	WS Gazelle AH1	MoD/StandardAero, Fleetlands
	XW847	WS Gazelle AH1	MoD/StandardAero, Fleetlands
	XW848	WS Gazelle AH1 [D]	Privately owned, Stapleford Tawney
	XW849	WS Gazelle AH1	Privately owned, Hurstbourne Tarrant, Hants
	XW852	WS Gazelle HCC4 (9331M)	DSAE, stored HMS Sultan, Gosport
	XW855	WS Gazelle HCC4	RAF Museum, Hendon
	XW858	WS Gazelle HT3 (G-ONNE) [C]	Privately owned, Steeple Bumstead, Cambs
	XW860	WS Gazelle HT2 (TAD 021)	DSAE SAAE, Lyneham
	XW863	WS Gazelle HT2 (TAD 022)	Sold to Bulgaria, January 2020

Serial	Type (code/other identity)	Owner/operator, location or fate	Notes
XW864	WS Gazelle HT2 [54/CU]	FAA Museum, stored Cobham Hall, RNAS Yeovilton	
XW865	WS Gazelle AH1	AAC No 29 Flt, BATUS, Suffield, Canada	
XW870	WS Gazelle HT3 (9299M) [F]	MoD DFTDC, Manston	
XW888	WS Gazelle AH1 (TAD 017)	DSAE SAAE, Lyneham	
XW889	WS Gazelle AH1 (TAD 018)	DSAE No 1 SoTT, Cosford	
XW890	WS Gazelle HT2	RNAS Yeovilton, on display	
XW892	WS Gazelle AH1 (G-CGJX/9292M)	Privately owned, Hurstbourne Tarrant, Hants	
XW897	WS Gazelle AH1	Privately owned, Colsterworth, Lincs	
XW899	WS Gazelle AH1 [Z]	Privately owned, stored Deighton, N Yorks	
XW900	WS Gazelle AH1 (TAD 900)	Army, Bramley, Hants	
XW904	WS Gazelle AH1 [H]	AAC, stored Middle Wallop	
XW906	WS Gazelle HT3 [J]	QinetiQ Apprentice Training School, Boscombe Down	
XW908	WS Gazelle AH1 [A]	QinetiQ, Boscombe Down (spares use)	
XW909	WS Gazelle AH1 (G-HSDL)	Privately owned, Hapton, Lancs	
XW912	WS Gazelle AH1 (TAD 019)	DSAE SAAE, Lyneham	
XW913	WS Gazelle AH1	*Currently not known*	
XW917	HS Harrier GR3 (8975M)	NATS Air Traffic Control Centre, Swanwick	
XW922	HS Harrier GR3 (8885M)	MoD DFTDC, Manston	
XW923	HS Harrier GR3 (8724M) <ff>	Harrier Heritage Centre, RAF Wittering	
XW924	HS Harrier GR3 (9073M) [G]	RAF Coningsby, preserved	
XW927	HS Harrier T4 <ff>	Privately owned, South Molton, Devon	
XW934	HS Harrier T4 [Y]	Farnborough Air Sciences Trust, Farnborough	
XW994	Northrop Chukar D1	FAA Museum, stored Cobham Hall, RNAS Yeovilton	
XW999	Northrop Chukar D1	Davidstow Airfield & Cornwall At War Museum	
XX108	SEPECAT Jaguar GR1(mod)	IWM Duxford	
XX109	SEPECAT Jaguar GR1 (8918M) [GH]	City of Norwich Aviation Museum	
XX110	SEPECAT Jaguar GR1 (8955M) [EP]	RAF Cosford, on display	
XX110	SEPECAT Jaguar GR1 <R> (BAPC 169)	DSAE No 1 SoTT, Cosford	
XX112	SEPECAT Jaguar GR3A [EA]	DSAE No 1 SoTT, Cosford	
XX115	SEPECAT Jaguar GR1 (8821M) (fuselage)	*Scrapped*	
XX116	SEPECAT Jaguar GR3A [EO]	MoD DFTDC, Manston	
XX117	SEPECAT Jaguar GR3A [ES]	DSAE No 1 SoTT, Cosford	
XX119	SEPECAT Jaguar GR3A (8898M) [AI]$	DSAE No 1 SoTT, Cosford	
XX121	SEPECAT Jaguar GR1 [EQ]	Privately owned, Selby, N Yorks	
XX139	SEPECAT Jaguar T4 [PT]	Privately owned, Sproughton	
XX140	SEPECAT Jaguar T2 (9008M) <ff>	Privately owned, Selby, N Yorks	
XX141	SEPECAT Jaguar T2A (9297M) [T]	DSAE No 1 SoTT, Cosford	
XX144	SEPECAT Jaguar T2A [U]	Privately owned, Sproughton	
XX145	SEPECAT Jaguar T2A	Privately owned, Bruntingthorpe	
XX146	SEPECAT Jaguar T4 [GT]	Bradwell Bay Military & Science Museum, Essex	
XX153	WS Lynx AH1 (9320M)	Army Flying Museum, Middle Wallop	
XX154	HS Hawk T1	Boscombe Down Aviation Collection, Old Sarum	
XX156	HS Hawk T1 [156]	RAF Valley, on display	
XX157	HS Hawk T1A [CU]	RAF AM&SU, stored Shawbury	
XX158	HS Hawk T1A [158]	RAF AM&SU, stored Shawbury	
XX159	HS Hawk T1A [159]	RAF AM&SU, stored Shawbury	
XX160	HS Hawk T1 [160]	RAF AM&SU, stored Shawbury	
XX161	HS Hawk T1 [161]	RN No 736 NAS, Culdrose	
XX162	HS Hawk T1	RAF Centre of Aviation Medicine, Boscombe Down	
XX165	HS Hawk T1 [165] (fuselage)	QinetiQ, Boscombe Down, spares use	
XX167	HS Hawk T1 [167]	RAF AM&SU, stored Shawbury	
XX168	HS Hawk T1 [168]	RAF AM&SU, stored Shawbury	
XX169	HS Hawk T1W [169]	RAF AM&SU, stored Shawbury	
XX170	HS Hawk T1 [CH]	RAF AM&SU, stored Shawbury	
XX171	HS Hawk T1 [171]	RAF AM&SU, stored Shawbury	
XX172	HS Hawk T1 [172] (fuselage)	QinetiQ Boscombe Down, GI use	
XX173	HS Hawk T1	RAF AM&SU, stored Shawbury	
XX174	HS Hawk T1 [174]	RAF AM&SU, stored Shawbury	
XX175	HS Hawk T1 [175]	Privately owned, St Athan	
XX176	HS Hawk T1W [176]	RAF AM&SU, stored Shawbury	
XX177	HS Hawk T1	RAF AMRO, Valley	

Notes	Serial	Type (code/other identity)	Owner/operator, location or fate
	XX178	HS Hawk T1W [178]	DSAE No 1 SoTT, Cosford
	XX181	HS Hawk T1 [181]	RAF AM&SU, stored Shawbury
	XX184	HS Hawk T1 [CQ]	Sheffield University, GI use
	XX185	HS Hawk T1 [185]	RAF AM&SU, stored Shawbury
	XX187	HS Hawk T1A [CN]	RAF AMRO, Valley
	XX188	HS Hawk T1A	RAF *Red Arrows*, Scampton
	XX189	HS Hawk T1A [CR]	RAF AMRO, stored Valley
	XX190	HS Hawk T1A [CN]	RAF AM&SU, stored Shawbury
	XX191	HS Hawk T1A [CC]	RAF No 100 Sqn, Leeming
	XX194	HS Hawk T1A [CP]	RAF AM&SU, stored Shawbury
	XX195	HS Hawk T1W [195]	RAF AM&SU, stored Shawbury
	XX198	HS Hawk T1A [CH]	RAF AMRO, Valley
	XX199	HS Hawk T1A [199]	RAF AM&SU, stored Shawbury
	XX200	HS Hawk T1A [CO]	RN No 736 NAS, Culdrose
	XX201	HS Hawk T1A [CQ]	RAF AM&SU, Shawbury
	XX202	HS Hawk T1A [CS]	RAF Leeming (damaged)
	XX203	HS Hawk T1A [CF]	RAF No 100 Sqn, Leeming
	XX205	HS Hawk T1A [CK]	RAF No 100 Sqn, Leeming
	XX217	HS Hawk T1A [217]	RAF AM&SU, stored Shawbury
	XX218	HS Hawk T1A [218]	RAF AM&SU, stored Shawbury
	XX219	HS Hawk T1A	RAF *Red Arrows*, Scampton
	XX220	HS Hawk T1A [220]	RAF AM&SU, stored Shawbury
	XX221	HS Hawk T1A [CO]	RAF AMRO, Valley
	XX222	HS Hawk T1A [CI]	RAF AM&SU, stored Shawbury
	XX224	HS Hawk T1 [224]	RAF AM&SU, stored Shawbury
	XX225	HS Hawk T1 [322]	RAF AM&SU, stored Shawbury
	XX226	HS Hawk T1 [226]	Privately owned, St Athan
XX227	HS Hawk T1 <R> (*XX226*/BAPC 152)	RAF Scampton Heritage Centre
	XX227	HS Hawk T1A	DSAE No 1 SoTT, Cosford
	XX228	HS Hawk T1 [CG]	RAF AM&SU, stored Shawbury
	XX230	HS Hawk T1A [CM]	RAF AM&SU, stored Shawbury
	XX231	HS Hawk T1W [213]	RAF AM&SU, stored Shawbury
	XX232	HS Hawk T1	RAF *Red Arrows*, Scampton
	XX234	HS Hawk T1 [234]	RAF AM&SU, stored Shawbury
	XX235	HS Hawk T1 [235]	RAF AM&SU, stored Shawbury
	XX236	HS Hawk T1W [236]	DSAE No 1 SoTT, Cosford
	XX237	HS Hawk T1	Privately owned, St Athan
	XX238	HS Hawk T1 [238]	RAF AM&SU, stored Shawbury
	XX239	HS Hawk T1W [842/CU]	RAF AMRO, Valley
	XX240	HS Hawk T1 [840/CU]	MoD, Cornwall Aviation Heritage Centre, Newquay
	XX242	HS Hawk T1	RAF *Red Arrows*, Scampton
	XX244	HS Hawk T1	RAF *Red Arrows*, Scampton
	XX245	HS Hawk T1	RAF *Red Arrows*, Scampton
	XX246	HS Hawk T1A [CA]	RAF No 100 Sqn, Leeming
	XX247	HS Hawk T1A [247]	RAF Woodvale, at main gate
	XX248	HS Hawk T1A [CJ]	RAF AM&SU, stored Shawbury
	XX250	HS Hawk T1W [250]	RAF AM&SU, stored Shawbury
	XX253	HS Hawk T1A	RAF Scampton, on display
XX254	HS Hawk T1A <R>	Privately owned, Marlow, Bucks
	XX255	HS Hawk T1A [CB]	RAF No 100 Sqn, Leeming
	XX256	HS Hawk T1A [846/CU]	RN No 736 NAS, Culdrose
	XX258	HS Hawk T1A [CE]	RAF AMRO, Valley
	XX260	HS Hawk T1A	RAF AM&SU, stored Shawbury
	XX261	HS Hawk T1A [CJ]	RAF No 100 Sqn, Leeming
	XX263	HS Hawk T1A	Cardiff University, GI use
	XX264	HS Hawk T1A $	RAF AM&SU, stored Shawbury
	XX265	HS Hawk T1A [CP]	RAF AM&SU, stored Shawbury
	XX266	HS Hawk T1A	RAF Scampton, instructional use
	XX278	HS Hawk T1A	RAF *Red Arrows*, Scampton
	XX280	HS Hawk T1A [280]	RN No 736 NAS, Culdrose
	XX281	HS Hawk T1A	RN No 736 NAS, Culdrose
	XX283	HS Hawk T1W [283]	RAF AM&SU, stored Shawbury

Serial	Type (code/other identity)	Owner/operator, location or fate	Notes
XX284	HS Hawk T1A [CN]	RAF AM&SU, stored Shawbury	
XX285	HS Hawk T1A [CK] $	RN No 736 NAS, Culdrose	
XX286	HS Hawk T1A [286]	RAF AM&SU, stored Shawbury	
XX287	HS Hawk T1A [287]	RAF AM&SU, stored Shawbury	
XX289	HS Hawk T1A [CO]	RAF AM&SU, stored Shawbury	
XX290	HS Hawk T1W	Privately owned, St Athan	
XX292	HS Hawk T1	Privately owned, Bentwaters	
XX294	HS Hawk T1	RAF AM&SU, stored Shawbury	
XX295	HS Hawk T1 [295]	RAF AM&SU, stored Shawbury	
XX296	HS Hawk T1 [296]	RAF AM&SU, stored Shawbury	
XX299	HS Hawk T1W [299]	RAF AM&SU, stored Shawbury	
XX301	HS Hawk T1A $	RAF AM&SU, stored Shawbury	
XX303	HS Hawk T1A [CR]	RAF No 100 Sqn, Leeming	
XX306	HS Hawk T1A	RAF Scampton, on display	
XX307	HS Hawk T1 [307]	RAF AM&SU, stored Shawbury	
XX308	HS Hawk T1	National Museum of Flight, E Fortune	
XX308	HS Hawk T1 <R> (XX263/BAPC 171)	RAF M&RU, Bottesford	
XX309	HS Hawk T1	RAF AM&SU, stored Shawbury	
XX310	HS Hawk T1	RAF Red Arrows, Scampton	
XX311	HS Hawk T1	RAF Red Arrows, Scampton	
XX312	HS Hawk T1W [312]	Norwich Airport, on display	
XX313	HS Hawk T1W [313]	RAF AM&SU, stored Shawbury	
XX314	HS Hawk T1W [314]	RAF AM&SU, stored Shawbury	
XX315	HS Hawk T1A [315]	RAF AM&SU, stored Shawbury	
XX316	HS Hawk T1A [849/CU]	RAF AMRO, Valley	
XX317	HS Hawk T1A [849/CU]	RAF No 100 Sqn, Leeming	
XX318	HS Hawk T1A [CG]	RAF No 100 Sqn, Leeming	
XX319	HS Hawk T1A	RAF Red Arrows, Scampton	
XX320	HS Hawk T1A <ff>	RAF Scampton Heritage Centre	
XX321	HS Hawk T1A [CI]	RAF No 100 Sqn, Leeming	
XX322	HS Hawk T1A	RAF Red Arrows, Scampton	
XX323	HS Hawk T1A	RAF Red Arrows, Scampton	
XX324	HS Hawk T1A [324]	RN No 736 NAS, Culdrose	
XX325	HS Hawk T1	RAF Red Arrows, Scampton	
XX327	HS Hawk T1A	RAF Centre of Aviation Medicine, Boscombe Down	
XX329	HS Hawk T1A [844/CU]	RN No 736 NAS, Culdrose	
XX330	HS Hawk T1A [330]	RAF AM&SU, stored Shawbury	
XX331	HS Hawk T1A [331]	RAF AM&SU, stored Shawbury	
XX332	HS Hawk T1A [CD]	RAF No 100 Sqn, Leeming	
XX335	HS Hawk T1A [335]	DSAE No 1 SoTT, Cosford	
XX337	HS Hawk T1A [CM]	RAF No 100 Sqn, Leeming	
XX338	HS Hawk T1W	RAF AM&SU, stored Shawbury	
XX339	HS Hawk T1A [CL]	RAF No 100 Sqn, Leeming	
XX341	HS Hawk T1 ASTRA	Privately owned, Thorpe Wood, N Yorks	
XX342	HS Hawk T1 [2]	Privately owned, St Athan	
XX343	HS Hawk T1 [3] (fuselage)	Boscombe Down Aviation Collection, Old Sarum	
XX345	HS Hawk T1A [CB]	RAF AM&SU, stored Shawbury	
XX346	HS Hawk T1A [CP]	RAF No 100 Sqn, Leeming	
XX348	HS Hawk T1A [CQ]	RAF No 100 Sqn, Leeming	
XX349	HS Hawk T1W <ff>	RAF Scampton Fire Section	
XX350	HS Hawk T1A [D] $	RAF AM&SU, stored Shawbury	
XX351	HS Hawk T1A	RAF No 71(IR) Sqn, Wittering, GI use	
XX372	WS Gazelle AH1 <ff>	Privately owned, Hurstbourne Tarrant, Hants	
XX375	WS Gazelle AH1	Privately owned,	
XX378	WS Gazelle AH1 [Q]	Privately owned, Colsterworth, Lincs	
XX379	WS Gazelle AH1 [Y]	MoD Boscombe Down, GI use	
XX380	WS Gazelle AH1 [A]	AAC Wattisham, on display	
XX381	WS Gazelle AH1	Privately owned, Welbeck	
XX386	WS Gazelle AH1 (G-KEMH)	Privately owned, Stapleford Tawney	
XX387	WS Gazelle AH1 (TAD 014)	Privately owned, stored Cranfield	
XX392	WS Gazelle AH1	Army, Middle Wallop, preserved	
XX394	WS Gazelle AH1 [X]	Privately owned, Stapleford Tawney	

Notes	Serial	Type (code/other identity)	Owner/operator, location or fate
	XX396	WS Gazelle HT3 (8718M) [N]	Privately owned, Arncott, Oxon
	XX398	WS Gazelle AH1	*Currently not known*
	XX399	WS Gazelle AH1 <ff>	Privately owned, Hurstbourne Tarrant, Hants
	XX403	WS Gazelle AH1 [U]	Privately owned, Colsterworth, Lincs
	XX405	WS Gazelle AH1	MoD/StandardAero, Fleetlands
	XX406	WS Gazelle HT3 (G-CBSH) [P]	Privately owned, Hurstbourne Tarrant, Hants
	XX411	WS Gazelle AH1 [X]	South Yorkshire Aircraft Museum, Doncaster
	XX411	WS Gazelle AH1 <rf>	FAA Museum, RNAS Yeovilton
	XX412	WS Gazelle AH1 [B]	DSAE, stored *HMS Sultan*, Gosport
	XX414	WS Gazelle AH1 [V]	Privately owned, Biggin Hill
	XX416	WS Gazelle AH1	Privately owned, Stapleford Tawney
	XX418	WS Gazelle AH1 <ff>	Privately owned, Hurstbourne Tarrant, Hants
	XX419	WS Gazelle AH1	*Scrapped*
	XX431	WS Gazelle HT2 (9300M) [43/CU]	DSAE RNAESS, *HMS Sultan*, Gosport
	XX433	WS Gazelle AH1 <ff>	Privately owned, Hurstbourne Tarrant, Hants
	XX435	WS Gazelle AH1 (fuselage)	QinetiQ, Boscombe Down (spares use)
	XX436	WS Gazelle HT2 (G-ZZLE) [39/CU]	Privately owned, Hurstbourne Tarrant, Hants
	XX437	WS Gazelle AH1	Privately owned, Stapleford Tawney
	XX438	WS Gazelle AH1 [F]	Privately owned, Stapleford Tawney
	XX442	WS Gazelle AH1 [E]	Privately owned, Colsterworth, Lincs
	XX443	WS Gazelle AH1 [Y]	Army, Aldergrove, on display
	XX444	WS Gazelle AH1	Wattisham Station Heritage Museum
	XX445	WS Gazelle AH1 [T]	Privately owned, Stapleford Tawney
	XX447	WS Gazelle AH1 [D1]	Privately owned, Colsterworth, Lincs
	XX449	WS Gazelle AH1	MoD/StandardAero, stored Fleetlands
	XX450	WS Gazelle AH1 [D]	Privately owned, Hurstbourne Tarrant, Hants
	XX452	WS Gazelle AH1 (wreck)	AAC Middle Wallop Fire Section
	XX453	WS Gazelle AH1	MoD/StandardAero, stored Fleetlands
	XX453	WS Gazelle AH1 (XZ331) [D]	Privately owned, stored Hurstbourne Tarrant, Hants
	XX454	WS Gazelle AH1 (TAD 023)	DSAE SAAE, Lyneham
	XX455	WS Gazelle AH1	Privately owned, Stapleford Tawney
	XX456	WS Gazelle AH1	Privately owned, Stapleford Tawney
	XX457	WS Gazelle AH1 (TAD 001)	East Midlands Airport Aeropark
	XX460	WS Gazelle AH1	AAC AM&SU, stored Shawbury
	XX462	WS Gazelle AH1 [W]	*Currently not known*
	XX466	HS Hunter T66B/T7 [830] <ff>	Privately owned, Glos
	XX467	HS Hunter T66B/T7 (XL605/G-TVII) [86]	Newark Air Museum, Winthorpe
	XX477	HP137 Jetstream T1 (G-AXXS/8462M) <ff>	Solway Aviation Society, Carlisle
	XX478	HP137 Jetstream T2 (G-AXXT) [564/CU]	Solihull College, Woodlands Campus
	XX479	HP137 Jetstream T2 (G-AXUR)	RN, Predannack Fire School
	XX483	SA Jetstream T2 [562] <ff>	Dumfries & Galloway Avn Mus, Dumfries
	XX487	SA Jetstream T2 [568/CU]	Int'l Centre for Aerospace Training, Cardiff Airport
	XX491	SA Jetstream T1 [K]	Northbrook College, Shoreham, instructional use
	XX492	SA Jetstream T1 [A]	Newark Air Museum, Winthorpe
	XX494	SA Jetstream T1 [B]	East Midlands Airport Aeropark
	XX495	SA Jetstream T1 [C]	South Yorkshire Aircraft Museum, Doncaster
	XX496	SA Jetstream T1 [D]	RAF Museum, Cosford
	XX499	SA Jetstream T1 [G]	Privately owned, Wainfleet, Lincs
	XX510	WS Lynx HAS2 [69/DD]	SFDO, RNAS Culdrose
	XX513	SA Bulldog T1 (G-KKKK) [10]	Privately owned, Bagby
	XX515	SA Bulldog T1 (G-CBBC) [4]	Privately owned, Blackbushe
	XX518	SA Bulldog T1 (G-UDOG) [S]	Privately owned, Ursel, Belgium
	XX520	SA Bulldog T1 (9288M) [A]	No 172 Sqn ATC, Haywards Heath
	XX521	SA Bulldog T1 (G-CBEH) [H]	Privately owned, North Moreton, Oxon
	XX522	SA Bulldog T1 (G-DAWG) [06]	Privately owned, Blackpool
	XX524	SA Bulldog T1 (G-DDOG) [04]	Privately owned, Malaga, Spain
	XX528	SA Bulldog T1 (G-BZON) [D]	Privately owned, Earls Colne
	XX530	SA Bulldog T1 (XX637/9197M) [F]	Ulster Aviation Society, Long Kesh
	XX534	SA Bulldog T1 (G-EDAV) [B]	Privately owned, Tollerton
	XX537	SA Bulldog T1 (G-CBCB) [C]	Privately owned, RAF Halton
	XX538	SA Bulldog T1 (G-TDOG) [O]	Privately owned, Shobdon
	XX539	SA Bulldog T1 [L]	Privately owned, Derbyshire

Serial	Type (code/other identity)	Owner/operator, location or fate	Notes
XX546	SA Bulldog T1 (G-WINI) [03]	Privately owned, Conington	
XX549	SA Bulldog T1 (G-CBID) [6]	Privately owned, White Waltham	
XX550	SA Bulldog T1 (G-CBBL) [Z]	Privately owned, Abbeyshrule, Eire	
XX551	SA Bulldog T1 (G-BZDP) [E]	Privately owned, Boscombe Down	
XX554	SA Bulldog T1 (G-BZMD) [09]	Privately owned, stored Thruxton	
XX557	SA Bulldog T1	Privately owned, stored Fort Paull, Yorks	
XX561	SA Bulldog T1 (G-BZEP) [7]	Privately owned, Eggesford	
XX611	SA Bulldog T1 (G-CBDK) [7]	Privately owned, Coventry	
XX612	SA Bulldog T1 (G-BZXC) [A,03]	Ayr College, instructional use	
XX614	SA Bulldog T1 (G-GGRR) [1]	Privately owned, Cotswold Airport	
XX619	SA Bulldog T1 (G-CBBW) [T]	Privately owned, Coventry	
XX621	SA Bulldog T1 (G-CBEF) [H]	Privately owned, Little Gransden	
XX622	SA Bulldog T1 (G-CBGX) [B]	Privately owned, Shoreham	
XX623	SA Bulldog T1 [M]	*Scrapped at Hurstbourne Tarrant, Hants*	
XX624	SA Bulldog T1 (G-KDOG) [E]	Privately owned, Hurstbourne Tarrant, Hants	
XX625	SA Bulldog T1 (XX543/G-UWAS) [U]	Privately owned, Dornoch, Highland	
XX626	SA Bulldog T1 (G-CDVV/9290M) [W,02]	Privately owned, Abbots Bromley, Staffs	
XX628	SA Bulldog T1 (G-CBFU) [9]	Privately owned, Faversham	
XX629	SA Bulldog T1 (G-BZXZ)	Privately owned, Wellesbourne Mountford	
XX630	SA Bulldog T1 (G-SIJW) [5]	Privately owned, Audley End	
XX631	SA Bulldog T1 (G-BZXS) [W]	Privately owned, Sligo, Eire	
XX634	SA Bulldog T1 [T]	Newark Air Museum, Winthorpe	
XX636	SA Bulldog T1 (G-CBFP) [Y]	Privately owned, Netherthorpe	
XX638	SA Bulldog T1 (G-DOGG)	Privately owned, Hurstbourne Tarrant, Hants	
XX639	SA Bulldog T1 (F-AZTF) [D]	Privately owned, La Baule, France	
XX654	SA Bulldog T1 [3]	RAF Museum, Cosford	
XX655	SA Bulldog T1 (9294M) [V] <ff>	Privately owned, Stockport	
XX656	SA Bulldog T1 [C]	Privately owned, Derbyshire	
XX658	SA Bulldog T1 (G-BZPS) [07]	Privately owned, Cambs	
XX659	SA Bulldog T1 [E]	Privately owned, Derbyshire	
XX664	SA Bulldog T1 (F-AZTV) [04]	Privately owned, Pontoise, France	
XX665	SA Bulldog T1 (9289M) [V]	Privately owned, Evesham, Worcs	
XX667	SA Bulldog T1 (G-BZFN) [16]	Privately owned, Ronaldsway, IoM	
XX668	SA Bulldog T1 (G-CBAN) [1]	Privately owned, St Athan	
XX669	SA Bulldog T1 (8997M) [B]	South Yorkshire Aircraft Museum, Doncaster	
XX687	SA Bulldog T1 [F]	Int'l Centre for Aerospace Training, Cardiff Airport	
XX690	SA Bulldog T1 [A]	Privately owned, Strathaven, S Lanarks	
XX692	SA Bulldog T1 (G-BZMH) [A]	Privately owned, Wellesbourne Mountford	
XX693	SA Bulldog T1 (G-BZML) [07]	Privately owned, Elmsett	
XX694	SA Bulldog T1 (G-CBBS) [E]	Privately owned, Turweston	
XX695	SA Bulldog T1 (G-CBBT)	Privately owned, Perth	
XX698	SA Bulldog T1 (G-BZME) [9]	Privately owned, Sleap	
XX700	SA Bulldog T1 (G-CBEK) [17]	Privately owned, Thruxton	
XX702	SA Bulldog T1 (G-CBCR) [π]	Privately owned, Egginton	
XX704	SA122 Bulldog (G-BCUV/G-112)	Privately owned, Bournemouth	
XX705	SA Bulldog T1 [5]	Privately owned, Norfolk	
XX707	SA Bulldog T1 (G-CBDS) [4]	Privately owned, stored Caernarfon	
XX711	SA Bulldog T1 (G-CBBU) [X]	Privately owned, stored Perth	
XX720	SEPECAT Jaguar GR3A [FL]	Privately owned, Sproughton	
XX722	SEPECAT Jaguar GR1 (9252M) <ff>	*Currently not known*	
XX723	SEPECAT Jaguar GR3A [EU]	DSAE No 1 SoTT, Cosford	
XX724	SEPECAT Jaguar GR3A [C]	DSAE No 1 SoTT, Cosford	
XX725	SEPECAT Jaguar GR3A [KC-F,T]	DSAE No 1 SoTT, Cosford	
XX726	SEPECAT Jaguar GR1 (8947M) [EB]	DSAE No 1 SoTT, Cosford	
XX727	SEPECAT Jaguar GR1 (8951M) [ER]	DSAE No 1 SoTT, Cosford	
XX729	SEPECAT Jaguar GR1 [EL]	DSAE No 1 SoTT, Cosford	
XX734	SEPECAT Jaguar GR1 (8816M)	Boscombe Down Aviation Collection, Old Sarum	
XX736	SEPECAT Jaguar GR1 (9110M) <ff>	South Yorkshire Aircraft Museum, Doncaster	
XX738	SEPECAT Jaguar GR3A [ED]	DSAE No 1 SoTT, Cosford	
XX739	SEPECAT Jaguar GR1 (8902M) [I]	Delta Force Paintball, Birmingham	
XX741	SEPECAT Jaguar GR1A [EJ]	Bentwaters Cold War Museum	
XX743	SEPECAT Jaguar GR1 (8949M) [EG]	DSAE No 1 SoTT, Cosford	

Notes	Serial	Type (code/other identity)	Owner/operator, location or fate
	XX744	SEPECAT Jaguar GR1 (9251M)	Mayhem Paintball, Abridge, Essex
	XX745	SEPECAT Jaguar GR1A <ff>	No 1350 Sqn ATC, Fareham
	XX746	SEPECAT Jaguar GR1 (8895M) [S]	DSAE No 1 SoTT, Cosford
	XX747	SEPECAT Jaguar GR1 (8903M)	Privately owned, Thorpe Wood, N Yorks
	XX748	SEPECAT Jaguar GR3A [L]	DSAE No 1 SoTT, Cosford
	XX751	SEPECAT Jaguar GR1 (8937M) [10]	Iron Curtain Museum, Alton, Hants
	XX752	SEPECAT Jaguar GR3A [EK]	DSAE No 1 SoTT, Cosford
	XX753	SEPECAT Jaguar GR1 (9087M) <ff>	Newark Air Museum, Winthorpe
	XX756	SEPECAT Jaguar GR1 (8899M) [W]	DSAE No 1 SoTT, Cosford
	XX761	SEPECAT Jaguar GR1 (8600M) <ff>	Boscombe Down Aviation Collection, Old Sarum
	XX763	SEPECAT Jaguar GR1 (9009M) [24]	Bournemouth Aviation Museum
	XX764	SEPECAT Jaguar GR1 (9010M)	Privately owned, Enstone
	XX765	SEPECAT Jaguar ACT	RAF Museum, Cosford
	XX766	SEPECAT Jaguar GR3A [EF]	DSAE No 1 SoTT, Cosford
	XX767	SEPECAT Jaguar GR3A [Z]	DSAE No 1 SoTT, Cosford
	XX818	SEPECAT Jaguar GR1 (8945M) [DE]	RAF Waddington Fire Section
	XX819	SEPECAT Jaguar GR1 (8923M) [CE]	DSAE No 1 SoTT, Cosford
	XX821	SEPECAT Jaguar GR1 (8896M) [P]	DSAE No 1 SoTT, Cosford
	XX824	SEPECAT Jaguar GR1 (9019M) [AD]	RAF Museum, Hendon
	XX825	SEPECAT Jaguar GR1 (9020M) [BN]	DSAE No 1 SoTT, Cosford
	XX826	SEPECAT Jaguar GR1 (9021M) [34] <ff>	Shannon Aviation Museum, Eire (stored)
	XX829	SEPECAT Jaguar T2A [GZ]	Newark Air Museum, Winthorpe
	XX830	SEPECAT Jaguar T2 <ff>	City of Norwich Aviation Museum
	XX833	SEPECAT Jaguar T2B	DSAE No 1 SoTT, Cosford
	XX835	SEPECAT Jaguar T4 [P]	DSAE No 1 SoTT, Cosford
	XX836	SEPECAT Jaguar T2A [X]	Privately owned, Sproughton
	XX837	SEPECAT Jaguar T2 (8978M) [Z]	DSAE No 1 SoTT, Cosford
	XX838	SEPECAT Jaguar T4 [FZ]	Privately owned, Bentwaters
	XX840	SEPECAT Jaguar T4 [T]	DSAE No 1 SoTT, Cosford
	XX841	SEPECAT Jaguar T4	Privately owned, North Weald
	XX842	SEPECAT Jaguar T2A [FX]	Privately owned, Bentwaters
	XX845	SEPECAT Jaguar T4 [EV]	RN, Predannack Fire School
	XX847	SEPECAT Jaguar T4 [EZ]	DSAE No 1 SoTT, Cosford
	XX885	HS Buccaneer S2B (9225M/G-HHAA)	Hawker Hunter Aviation, Scampton
	XX888	HS Buccaneer S2B <ff>	Privately owned, Barnstaple
	XX889	HS Buccaneer S2B [T]	Privately owned, Cosford
	XX892	HS Buccaneer S2B <ff>	Blue Sky Experiences, Methven, Perth & Kinross
	XX894	HS Buccaneer S2B [020/R]	The Buccaneer Aviation Group, Bruntingthorpe
	XX895	HS Buccaneer S2B <ff>	Privately owned, Tattershall Thorpe
	XX897	HS Buccaneer S2B(mod)	Shannon Aviation Museum, Eire
	XX899	HS Buccaneer S2B <ff>	Newark Air Museum, Winthorpe
	XX900	HS Buccaneer S2B [900]	Cold War Jets Collection, Bruntingthorpe
	XX901	HS Buccaneer S2B [N]	Yorkshire Air Museum, Elvington
	XX910	WS Lynx HAS2	The Helicopter Museum, Weston-super-Mare
	XX919	BAC 1-11/402AP (PI-C1121) <ff>	Boscombe Down Aviation Collection, Old Sarum
	XX946	Panavia Tornado (P02) (8883M)	RAF Museum, stored Cosford
	XX956	SEPECAT Jaguar GR1 (8950M) [BE]	Privately owned
	XX958	SEPECAT Jaguar GR1 (9022M) [BK]	*To Pembrey ranges, June 2019*
	XX959	SEPECAT Jaguar GR1 (8953M) [CJ]	DSAE No 1 SoTT, Cosford
	XX962	SEPECAT Jaguar GR1B (9257M) <ff>	RAF Coningsby
	XX965	SEPECAT Jaguar GR1A (9254M) [C]	DSAE No 1 SoTT, Cosford
	XX967	SEPECAT Jaguar GR1 (9006M) [AC]	DSAE No 1 SoTT, Cosford
	XX968	SEPECAT Jaguar GR1 (9007M) [AJ]	DSAE No 1 SoTT, Cosford
	XX969	SEPECAT Jaguar GR1 (8897M) [01]	DSAE No 1 SoTT, Cosford
	XX970	SEPECAT Jaguar GR3A [EH]	DSAE No 1 SoTT, Cosford
	XX975	SEPECAT Jaguar GR1 (8905M) [07]	DSAE No 1 SoTT, Cosford
	XX976	SEPECAT Jaguar GR1 (8906M) [BD]	DSAE No 1 SoTT, Cosford
	XX977	SEPECAT Jaguar GR1 (9132M) [DL,05] <rf>	Privately owned, Sproughton
	XX979	SEPECAT Jaguar GR1A (9306M) <ff>	RAF Air Defence Radar Museum, Neatishead
	XZ103	SEPECAT Jaguar GR3A [EF]	DSAE No 1 SoTT, Cosford
	XZ104	SEPECAT Jaguar GR3A [FM]	DSAE No 1 SoTT, Cosford

Serial	Type (code/other identity)	Owner/operator, location or fate	Notes
XZ106	SEPECAT Jaguar GR3A [FR]	RAF Manston History Museum	
XZ107	SEPECAT Jaguar GR3A [FH]	Privately owned, Selby, N Yorks	
XZ109	SEPECAT Jaguar GR3A [EN]	DSAE No 1 SoTT, Cosford	
XZ112	SEPECAT Jaguar GR3A [GW]	DSAE No 1 SoTT, Cosford	
XZ113	SEPECAT Jaguar GR3 [A,30]	Morayvia, Kinloss	
XZ114	SEPECAT Jaguar GR3 [EO]	DSAE No 1 SoTT, Cosford	
XZ115	SEPECAT Jaguar GR3 [ER]	DSAE No 1 SoTT, Cosford	
XZ117	SEPECAT Jaguar GR3 [ES]	DSAE No 1 SoTT, Cosford	
XZ119	SEPECAT Jaguar GR1A (9266M) [FG]	National Museum of Flight, E Fortune	
XZ130	HS Harrier GR3 (9079M) [A]	Privately owned, Thorpe Wood, N Yorks	
XZ131	HS Harrier GR3 (9174M) <ff>	Privately owned, Spark Bridge, Cumbria	
XZ132	HS Harrier GR3 (9168M) [C]	Privately owned, Gloucestershire Airport	
XZ133	HS Harrier GR3 [10]	IWM Duxford	
XZ138	HS Harrier GR3 (9040M) <ff>	RAFC Cranwell, Trenchard Hall	
XZ146	HS Harrier T4 (9281M) [S]	Harrier Heritage Centre, RAF Wittering	
XZ166	WS Lynx HAS2 <ff>	Farnborough Air Sciences Trust, stored Farnborough	
XZ170	WS Lynx AH9	DSAE SAAE, Lyneham	
XZ171	WS Lynx AH7	Army, Salisbury Plain	
XZ172	WS Lynx AH7	DSAE SAAE, Lyneham	
XZ173	WS Lynx AH7 [6] <ff>	Privately owned, Weeton, Lancs	
XZ174	WS Lynx AH7 <ff>	Defence Coll of Policing, Gosport, instructional use	
XZ175	WS Lynx AH7	Privately owned, Barby, Northants	
XZ177	Aérospatiale SA341G Gazelle (G-SFTA/XZ345) [T]	North-East Land, Sea & Air Museums, Usworth	
XZ177	WS Lynx AH7	Delta Force, Kegworth	
XZ178	WS Lynx AH7 <ff>	Bilsthorpe Paintball Park, Notts	
XZ179	WS Lynx AH7 (G-NCKS) [W]	Privately owned, North Weald	
XZ180	WS Lynx AH7 [C]	DSAE SAAE, Lyneham	
XZ181	WS Lynx AH1	AAC Middle Wallop Fire Section	
XZ183	WS Lynx AH7 <ff>	MoD JARTS, Boscombe Down	
XZ184	WS Lynx AH7 [B]	AAC Middle Wallop, at main gate	
XZ187	WS Lynx AH7	DSAE SAAE, Lyneham	
XZ188	WS Lynx AH7	DSAE SAAE, Lyneham	
XZ190	WS Lynx AH7 <ff>	Army, Longmoor Camp, Hants, GI use	
XZ191	WS Lynx AH7 [R]	DSAE SAAE, Lyneham	
XZ192	WS Lynx AH7 [H]	AAC, stored St Athan	
XZ193	WS Lynx AH7 [4] <ff>	Kidderminster Paintball	
XZ194	WS Lynx AH7 [V]	IWM Duxford	
XZ195	WS Lynx AH7 <ff>	Privately owned, Mildenhall	
XZ203	WS Lynx AH7 [F]	Army, Salisbury Plain	
XZ206	WS Lynx AH7 <ff>	Privately owned, Hixon, Staffs	
XZ207	WS Lynx AH7 <rf>	DSAE SAAE, Lyneham	
XZ208	WS Lynx AH7	Privately owned, Sproughton	
XZ209	WS Lynx AH7 <ff>	MoD JARTS, Boscombe Down	
XZ211	WS Lynx AH7	Bawtry Paintball Park, S Yorks	
XZ212	WS Lynx AH7 [X]	AAC Middle Wallop Fire Section	
XZ213	WS Lynx AH1 (TAD 213)	Privately owned, Sproughton	
XZ214	WS Lynx AH7	DSAE SAAE, Lyneham	
XZ216	WS Lynx AH7 <ff>	MoD DFTDC, Manston	
XZ217	WS Lynx AH7	Privately owned, Guildford	
XZ218	WS Lynx AH7	Privately owned, Shrewsbury	
XZ219	WS Lynx AH7 <ff>	Army, Bramley, Hants	
XZ220	WS Lynx AH7 <ff>	Privately owned, South Clifton, Notts	
XZ222	WS Lynx AH7	DSAE SAAE, Lyneham	
XZ228	WS Lynx HAS3GMS [313]	AAC, stored Middle Wallop	
XZ229	WS Lynx HAS3GMS [360/MC]	Privately owned, Hixon, Staffs	
XZ232	WS Lynx HAS3GMS	Falck Nutec UK, Aberdeen, GI use	
XZ233	WS Lynx HAS3S [635] $	RN, stored St Athan	
XZ234	WS Lynx HAS3S	Privately owned, Sproughton	
XZ235	WS Lynx HAS3S(ICE) [630]	Wild Park Derbyshire, Brailsford	
XZ236	WS Lynx HMA8 [LST-1]	Currently not known	
XZ237	WS Lynx HAS3S [631]	Privately owned, Wild Park, Derbyshire	
XZ239	WS Lynx HAS3GMS [633]	Privately owned, Hixon, Staffs	

Notes	Serial	Type (code/other identity)	Owner/operator, location or fate
	XZ246	WS Lynx HAS3S(ICE) [434/EE]	South Yorkshire Aircraft Museum, Doncaster
	XZ248	WS Lynx HAS3S	SFDO, RNAS Culdrose
	XZ250	WS Lynx HAS3S [426/PO] $	RN, Portland, on display
	XZ252	WS Lynx HAS3S	Privately owned, Hixon, Staffs
	XZ254	WS Lynx HAS3S	Privately owned, Hixon, Staffs
	XZ255	WS Lynx HMA8SRU [454/DF]	DSAE SAAE, Lyneham
	XZ257	WS Lynx HAS3S	RN Yeovilton, GI use (Wildcat ground trainer)
	XZ287	BAe Nimrod AEW3 (9140M) (fuselage)	RAF TSW, Stafford
	XZ290	WS Gazelle AH1	AAC No 665 Sqn/5 Regt, Aldergrove
	XZ292	WS Gazelle AH1	*Currently not known*
	XZ294	WS Gazelle AH1 [X]	AAC AM&SU, stored Shawbury
	XZ295	WS Gazelle AH1	Privately owned, Hurstbourne Tarrant, Hants
	XZ298	WS Gazelle AH1 <ff>	AAC Middle Wallop, GI use
	XZ300	WS Gazelle AH1	Army, Bramley, Hants
	XZ303	WS Gazelle AH1	Privately owned, Colsterworth, Lincs
	XZ304	WS Gazelle AH1	Privately owned, Stapleford Tawney
	XZ305	WS Gazelle AH1 (TAD 020)	DSAE, stored *HMS Sultan*, Gosport
	XZ308	WS Gazelle AH1	QinetiQ, Boscombe Down (spares use)
	XZ311	WS Gazelle AH1 [U]	Privately owned, Colsterworth, Lincs
	XZ312	WS Gazelle AH1	RAF Henlow, instructional use
	XZ313	WS Gazelle AH1 <ff>	*Rebuilt as ZA731*
	XZ314	WS Gazelle AH1 [A]	*Currently not known*
	XZ315	WS Gazelle AH1 <ff>	Privately owned, Babcary, Somerset
	XZ316	WS Gazelle AH1 [B]	DSAE SAAE, Lyneham
	XZ318	WS Gazelle AH1 (fuselage)	Tong Paintball Park, Shropshire
	XZ320	WS Gazelle AH1	AAC No 665 Sqn/5 Regt, Aldergrove
	XZ321	WS Gazelle AH1 (G-CDNS) [D]	Privately owned, Hurstbourne Tarrant, Hants
	XZ322	WS Gazelle AH1 (9283M) [N]	DSAE SAAE, Lyneham
	XZ323	WS Gazelle AH1 [J]	Privately owned, stored Hurstbourne Tarrant, Hants
	XZ324	WS Gazelle AH1	Privately owned, Stapleford Tawney
	XZ325	WS Gazelle AH1	DSAE SAAE, Lyneham
	XZ326	WS Gazelle AH1	AAC No 665 Sqn/5 Regt, Aldergrove
	XZ327	WS Gazelle AH1	AAC Middle Wallop (recruiting aid)
	XZ328	WS Gazelle AH1 [C]	AAC AM&SU, stored Shawbury
	XZ329	WS Gazelle AH1 (G-BZYD) [J]	Privately owned, Lewes, Sussex
	XZ330	WS Gazelle AH1 [Y]	AAC Wattisham, instructional use
	XZ332	WS Gazelle AH1	DSAE SAAE, Lyneham
	XZ333	WS Gazelle AH1	DSAE SAAE, Lyneham
	XZ334	WS Gazelle AH1	MoD/StandardAero, stored Fleetlands
	XZ335	WS Gazelle AH1 <ff>	Boscombe Down Aviation Collection, Old Sarum
	XZ337	WS Gazelle AH1 [Z]	Privately owned, Colsterworth, Lincs
	XZ340	WS Gazelle AH1	AAC No 29 Flt, BATUS, Suffield, Canada
	XZ341	WS Gazelle AH1	AAC AM&SU, stored Shawbury
	XZ342	WS Gazelle AH1	*Currently not known*
	XZ343	WS Gazelle AH1	AAC AM&SU, stored Shawbury
	XZ344	WS Gazelle AH1 [Y]	Privately owned, Stapleford Tawney
	XZ345	WS Gazelle AH1 [M]	AAC, stored Middle Wallop
	XZ346	WS Gazelle AH1	AAC Middle Wallop, at main gate
	XZ356	SEPECAT Jaguar GR3A [FU]	Privately owned, Welshpool
	XZ358	SEPECAT Jaguar GR1A (9262M) [L]	DSAE No 1 SoTT, Cosford
	XZ360	SEPECAT Jaguar GR3 [FN]	Teesside International Airport Fire Section
	XZ361	SEPECAT Jaguar GR3 [FT]	*Sold to Estonia, October 2019*
	XZ363	SEPECAT Jaguar GR1A <R> (XX824/BAPC 151) [A]	RAF M&RU, Bottesford
	XZ364	SEPECAT Jaguar GR3A <ff>	Privately owned, Thorpe Wood, N Yorks
	XZ366	SEPECAT Jaguar GR3A [FC]	Privately owned, Bentwaters
	XZ367	SEPECAT Jaguar GR3 [EE]	DSAE No 1 SoTT, Cosford
	XZ368	SEPECAT Jaguar GR1 [8900M] [E]	DSAE No 1 SoTT, Cosford
	XZ369	SEPECAT Jaguar GR3A [EU]	Delta Force Paintball, Rugby
	XZ370	SEPECAT Jaguar GR1 (9004M) [JB]	DSAE No 1 SoTT, Cosford
	XZ371	SEPECAT Jaguar GR1 (8907M) [AP]	DSAE No 1 SoTT, Cosford
	XZ372	SEPECAT Jaguar GR3 [FV]	Aberdeen Airport Fire Section
	XZ374	SEPECAT Jaguar GR1 (9005M) [JC]	DSAE, stored Cosford

Serial	Type (code/other identity)	Owner/operator, location or fate	Notes
XZ375	SEPECAT Jaguar GR1A (9255M) <ff>	City of Norwich Aviation Museum	
XZ377	SEPECAT Jaguar GR3A [P]	DSAE No 1 SoTT, Cosford	
XZ378	SEPECAT Jaguar GR1A [EP]	Privately owned, Topsham, Devon	
XZ382	SEPECAT Jaguar GR1 (8908M)	Cold War Jets Collection, Bruntingthorpe	
XZ383	SEPECAT Jaguar GR1 (8901M) [AF]	DSAE No 1 SoTT, Cosford	
XZ384	SEPECAT Jaguar GR1 (8954M) [BC]	DSAE No 1 SoTT, Cosford	
XZ385	SEPECAT Jaguar GR1 [FT]	Privately owned, Selby, N Yorks	
XZ389	SEPECAT Jaguar GR1 (8946M) [BL]	DSAE No 1 SoTT, Cosford	
XZ390	SEPECAT Jaguar GR1 (9003M) [DM]	DSAE No 1 SoTT, Cosford	
XZ391	SEPECAT Jaguar GR3A [ET]	DSAE No 1 SoTT, Cosford	
XZ392	SEPECAT Jaguar GR3A [EM]	DSAE No 1 SoTT, Cosford	
XZ394	SEPECAT Jaguar GR3	Privately owned, Tattersett, Norfolk	
XZ398	SEPECAT Jaguar GR3A [EQ]	DSAE No 1 SoTT, Cosford	
XZ399	SEPECAT Jaguar GR3A [EJ]	DSAE No 1 SoTT, Cosford	
XZ400	SEPECAT Jaguar GR3A [FQ]	Privately owned, Selby, N Yorks	
XZ431	HS Buccaneer S2B (9233M) <ff>	South Yorkshire Aviation Museum, stored Doncaster	
XZ440	BAe Sea Harrier FA2 [40/DD]	SFDO, RNAS Culdrose	
XZ455	BAe Sea Harrier FA2 [001] (wreck)	Privately owned, Thorpe Wood, N Yorks	
XZ457	BAe Sea Harrier FA2 [104/VL]	Boscombe Down Aviation Collection, Old Sarum	
XZ459	BAe Sea Harrier FA2 [126]	Privately owned, Sussex	
XZ493	BAe Sea Harrier FRS1 (comp XV760) [001/N]	FAA Museum, RNAS Yeovilton	
XZ493	BAe Sea Harrier FRS1 <ff>	RN Yeovilton, Fire Section	
XZ494	BAe Sea Harrier FA2 [128]	Privately owned, Wedmore, Somerset	
XZ497	BAe Sea Harrier FA2 [126]	Privately owned, Charlwood	
XZ499	BAe Sea Harrier FA2 [003]	FAA Museum, stored Cobham Hall, RNAS Yeovilton	
XZ559	Slingsby T61F Venture T2 (G-BUEK)	Privately owned, Tibenham	
XZ570	WS61 Sea King HAS5(mod)	RN, Predannack Fire School	
XZ574	WS61 Sea King HAS6	FAA Museum, stored Cobham Hall, RNAS Yeovilton	
XZ575	WS61 Sea King HU5	Privately owned, Charlwood	
XZ576	WS61 Sea King HAS6	DSAE RNAESS, *HMS Sultan*, Gosport	
XZ578	WS61 Sea King HU5 [30]	*Sold to Slovakia, 2019*	
XZ579	WS61 Sea King HAS6 [707/PW]	DSAE RNAESS, *HMS Sultan*, Gosport	
XZ580	WS61 Sea King HC6 [ZB]	DSAE RNAESS, *HMS Sultan*, Gosport	
XZ581	WS61 Sea King HAS6 [69/CU]	DSAE RNAESS, *HMS Sultan*, Gosport	
XZ585	WS61 Sea King HAR3 [A]	RAF Museum, Hendon	
XZ586	WS61 Sea King HAR3 [B]	DSAE, stored *HMS Sultan*, Gosport	
XZ587	WS61 Sea King HAR3 [C]	RAF St Mawgan, on display	
XZ588	WS61 Sea King HAR3 [D]	Privately owned, stored Chard, Somerset	
XZ589	WS61 Sea King HAR3 [E] $	DSAE RNAESS, *HMS Sultan*, Gosport	
XZ590	WS61 Sea King HAR3 [F]	DSAE, stored *HMS Sultan*, Gosport	
XZ592	WS61 Sea King HAR3 [H]	Morayvia, Kinloss	
XZ594	WS61 Sea King HAR3	DSAE, stored *HMS Sultan*, Gosport	
XZ595	WS61 Sea King HAR3 [K]	Privately owned, Charlwood	
XZ596	WS61 Sea King HAR3 [L]	DSAE, stored *HMS Sultan*, Gosport	
XZ597	WS61 Sea King HAR3 (G-SKNG) [M]	Privately owned, Chard, Somerset	
XZ598	WS61 Sea King HAR3 [N]	*Sold to Slovakia, 2019*	
XZ605	WS Lynx AH7	Wattisham Station Heritage Museum	
XZ606	WS Lynx AH7 [O]	Delta Force Paintball, Billericay, Essex	
XZ607	WS Lynx AH7 <ff>	MoD, Cornwall Aviation Heritage Centre, Newquay	
XZ607	WS Lynx AH7 (comp XZ215)	MoD DFTDC, Manston	
XZ608	WS Lynx AH7 (fuselage)	Army Bury St Edmunds, GI use	
XZ608	WS Lynx AH7 (comp XZ680) [N]	Privately owned, East Grinstead	
XZ609	WS Lynx AH7	Army Bury St Edmunds, GI use	
XZ611	WS Lynx AH7 <ff>	Bilsthorpe Paintball Park, Notts	
XZ612	WS Lynx AH7	Delta Force Paintball, Bovingdon	
XZ613	WS Lynx AH7 [F]	Privately owned, Belstead, Suffolk	
XZ615	WS Lynx AH7 <ff>	*Currently not known*	
XZ616	WS Lynx AH7	Privately owned, stored Chard, Somerset	
XZ617	WS Lynx AH7 <ff>	DSAE SAAE, Lyneham	
XZ630	Panavia Tornado (P12) (8976M)	RAF Halton, on display	
XZ631	Panavia Tornado (P15)	Yorkshire Air Museum, Elvington	
XZ642	WS Lynx AH7	DSAE SAAE, Lyneham	

Notes	Serial	Type (code/other identity)	Owner/operator, location or fate
	XZ643	WS Lynx AH7 [C]	Privately owned, Culham, Oxon
	XZ645	WS Lynx AH7	Delta Force Paintball, Romsey, Hants
	XZ646	WS Lynx AH7 <ff>	MoD JARTS, Boscombe Down
XZ646	WS Lynx AH7 (really XZ649)	Bristol University, instructional use
	XZ647	WS Lynx AH7 <ff>	Aberdeen Airport Fire Section
	XZ648	WS Lynx AH7 <ff>	Privately owned, Weeton, Lancs
	XZ651	WS Lynx AH7 [O]	AAC Middle Wallop (for disposal)
	XZ652	WS Lynx AH7	IFTC, Teesside International
	XZ653	WS Lynx AH7	DSAE SAAE, Lyneham
	XZ654	WS Lynx AH7	Shannon Aviation Museum, Eire (stored)
	XZ655	WS Lynx AH7 [3] <ff>	Privately owned, Weeton, Lancs
	XZ661	WS Lynx AH7 [V]	Army, Bramley, Hants
	XZ663	WS Lynx AH7 <ff>	Privately owned, Hixon, Staffs
	XZ664	WS Lynx AH7	Warfighters R6 Centre, Barby, Northants
	XZ665	WS Lynx AH7	Privately owned, Barby, Northants
	XZ666	WS Lynx AH7	DSAE SAAE, Lyneham
	XZ668	WS Lynx AH7 [UN] <ff>	Privately owned, stored Cranfield
	XZ670	WS Lynx AH7 [A]	RNAS Yeovilton, on display
	XZ671	WS Lynx AH7 <ff>	Leonardo MW, Yeovil, instructional use
	XZ672	WS Lynx AH7 <ff>	AAC Middle Wallop Fire Section
	XZ673	WS Lynx AH7 [5]	Privately owned, Weeton, Lancs
	XZ674	WS Lynx AH7 [T]	RNAS Yeovilton Fire Section
	XZ675	WS Lynx AH7 [H]	Army Flying Museum, Middle Wallop
	XZ676	WS Lynx AH7 [N]	Privately owned, Weeton, Lancs
	XZ677	WS Lynx AH7 <ff>	Army, Longmoor Camp, Hants, GI use
	XZ678	WS Lynx AH7 <ff>	Privately owned, Sproughton
	XZ679	WS Lynx AH7 [W]	DSAE SAAE, Lyneham
	XZ680	WS Lynx AH7 <ff>	*Rebuilt with the tail of XZ608, 2019*
	XZ689	WS Lynx HMA8SRU [314]	*Currently not known*
	XZ690	WS Lynx HMA8SRU [640]	Delta Force Paintball, West Glasgow
	XZ691	WS Lynx HMA8SRU [310]	FAA Museum, stored Cobham Hall, RNAS Yeovilton
	XZ692	WS Lynx HMA8SRU [764/SN] $	DSAE *HMS Sultan*, Gosport, on display
	XZ693	WS Lynx HAS3S [311]	Wild Park Derbyshire, Brailsford
	XZ694	WS Lynx HAS3GMS [434]	Privately owned, South Clifton, Notts
	XZ696	WS Lynx HAS3GMS [633]	Privately owned, Hixon, Staffs
	XZ697	WS Lynx HMA8SRU [313]	MoD/StandardAero, Fleetlands
XZ698	WS Lynx HMA8SRU (ZD258) [365]	Privately owned, Bentwaters
	XZ699	WS Lynx HAS2	FAA Museum, RNAS Yeovilton
	XZ719	WS Lynx HMA8SRU [64]	RNAS Yeovilton Fire Section
	XZ720	WS Lynx HAS3GMS [410/GC]	FAA Museum, RNAS Yeovilton
	XZ721	WS Lynx HAS3GMS [322]	East Midlands Airport Aeropark
	XZ723	WS Lynx HMA8SRU [672]	Delta Force Paintball, Thornbury, Glos
	XZ725	WS Lynx HMA8SRU [415/MM]	FAA Museum, stored Cobham Hall, RNAS Yeovilton
	XZ726	WS Lynx HMA8SRU [316]	School of Maritime Survival *HMS Raleigh*, Plymouth
	XZ727	WS Lynx HAS3S [634]	Delta Force Paintball, Romsey, Hants
	XZ728	WS Lynx HMA8 [326/AW]	RNAS Yeovilton, on display
	XZ729	WS Lynx HMA8SRU [425/DT]	Privately owned
	XZ730	WS Lynx HAS3S	Privately owned, Hixon, Staffs
	XZ731	WS Lynx HMA8SRU [311/VL]	Privately owned
	XZ732	WS Lynx HMA8SRU [315/VL]	DSAE SAAE, Lyneham
	XZ735	WS Lynx HAS3GMS <ff>	Privately owned, Sproughton
	XZ736	WS Lynx HMA8SRU [815]	RN Yeovilton, GI use
	XZ791	Northrop Shelduck D1	Davidstow Airfield & Cornwall at War Museum
	XZ795	Northrop Shelduck D1	Army Flying Museum, Middle Wallop
	XZ920	WS61 Sea King HU5 [24]	HeliOperations Ltd, Portland
	XZ921	WS61 Sea King HAS6 [269/N]	Holmside Park, Edmondsley, Durham
	XZ922	WS61 Sea King HC6 [ZA]	DSAE RNAESS, *HMS Sultan*, Gosport
	XZ930	WS Gazelle HT3 (A2713) [SN]	DSAE, *HMS Sultan*, Gosport, on display
	XZ933	WS Gazelle HT3 (*XZ936*/G-CGJZ)	Privately owned, Hurstbourne Tarrant, Hants
	XZ934	WS Gazelle HT3 (G-CBSI)	Privately owned, Hurstbourne Tarrant, Hants
	XZ935	WS Gazelle HCC4 (9332M)	DSAE SAAE, Lyneham
	XZ936	WS Gazelle HT3 (G-CLHO) [6]	Privately owned, stored Hurstbourne Tarrant, Hants

Serial	Type (code/other identity)	Owner/operator, location or fate	Notes
XZ939	WS Gazelle HT3 (G-CLGO)	Privately owned, Hurstbourne Tarrant, Hants	
XZ941	WS Gazelle HT3 (9301M) [B]	*Currently not known*	
XZ964	BAe Harrier GR3 [D]	Royal Engineers Museum, Chatham	
XZ966	BAe Harrier GR3 (9221M) [G]	MoD DFTDC, Manston	
XZ968	BAe Harrier GR3 (9222M) [3G]	Muckleborough Collection, Weybourne	
XZ969	BAe Harrier GR3 [69/DD]	RN, Predannack Fire School	
XZ971	BAe Harrier GR3 (9219M)	HQ DSDA, Donnington, Shropshire, on display	
XZ987	BAe Harrier GR3 (9185M) [C]	RAF Stafford, at main gate	
XZ990	BAe Harrier GR3 <ff>	*Currently not known*	
XZ990	BAe Harrier GR3 <rf>	RAF Wittering, derelict	
XZ991	BAe Harrier GR3 (9162M)	DSAE Cosford, on display	
XZ993	BAe Harrier GR3 (9240M) <ff>	Privately owned, Upwood, Cambs	
XZ995	BAe Harrier GR3 (9220M/G-CBGK) [3G]	Privately owned, Dolly's Grove, Co Dublin, Eire	
XZ996	BAe Harrier GR3 [96/DD]	Privately owned, Bentwaters	
XZ997	BAe Harrier GR3 (9122M) [V]	RAF Museum, Cosford	
ZA101	BAe Hawk 100 (G-HAWK)	Brooklands Museum, Weybridge	
ZA105	WS61 Sea King HAR3 [Q]	DSAE, stored *HMS Sultan*, Gosport	
ZA110	BAe Jetstream T2 (F-BTMI) [563/CU]	Aberdeen Airport Fire Section	
ZA111	BAe Jetstream T2 (9Q-CTC) [565/CU]	RN, Predannack Fire School	
ZA126	WS61 Sea King ASaC7 [91]	DSAE, stored *HMS Sultan*, Gosport	
ZA127	WS61 Sea King HAS6 [509/CU]	Privately owned, Thornhill, Stirlingshire	
ZA128	WS61 Sea King HAS6 [010]	DSAE No 1 SoTT, Cosford	
ZA130	WS61 Sea King HU5 [19]	Privately owned, Charlwood	
ZA131	WS61 Sea King HAS6 [271/N]	DSAE RNAESS, *HMS Sultan*, Gosport	
ZA133	WS61 Sea King HAS6 [831/CU]	DSAE RNAESS, *HMS Sultan*, Gosport	
ZA134	WS61 Sea King HU5 [25]	DSAE, stored *HMS Sultan*, Gosport	
ZA135	WS61 Sea King HAS6	Privately owned, Woodperry, Oxon	
ZA136	WS61 Sea King HAS6 [018]	Mayhem Paintball, Abridge, Essex	
ZA137	WS61 Sea King HU5 [20]	DSAE, stored *HMS Sultan*, Gosport	
ZA147	BAe VC10 K3 (5H-MMT) [F]	Privately owned, Bruntingthorpe	
ZA148	BAe VC10 K3 (5Y-ADA) [G]	Cornwall Aviation Heritage Centre, Newquay	
ZA150	BAe VC10 K3 (5H-MOG) [J]	Brooklands Museum, Dunsfold	
ZA166	WS61 Sea King HU5	HeliOperations Ltd, Portland	
ZA167	WS61 Sea King HU5 [22/CU]	DSAE RNAESS, *HMS Sultan*, Gosport	
ZA168	WS61 Sea King HAS6 [830/CU]	DSAE RNAESS, *HMS Sultan*, Gosport	
ZA169	WS61 Sea King HAS6 [515/CW]	DSAE No 1 SoTT, Cosford	
ZA170	WS61 Sea King HAS5	*Currently not known*	
ZA175	BAe Sea Harrier FA2	Norfolk & Suffolk Avn Museum, Flixton	
ZA176	BAe Sea Harrier FA2 [126/R]	Newark Air Museum, Winthorpe	
ZA195	BAe Sea Harrier FA2 [710]	South Wales Aviation Museum, St Athan	
ZA209	Short MATS-B	Army Flying Museum, Middle Wallop	
ZA220	Short MATS-B (ZA242)	Boscombe Down Aviation Collection, Old Sarum	
ZA250	BAe Harrier T52 (G-VTOL)	Brooklands Museum, Weybridge	
ZA267	Panavia Tornado F2 (9284M) [FA]	Privately owned, RAF Syerston	
ZA291	WS61 Sea King HC4 [N]	Holmside Park, Edmondsley, Durham	
ZA298	WS61 Sea King HC4 (G-BJNM) [Y]	FAA Museum, RNAS Yeovilton	
ZA312	WS61 Sea King HC4 [E]	Privately owned, Charlwood	
ZA313	WS61 Sea King HC4 [M]	Holmside Park, Edmondsley, Durham	
ZA314	WS61 Sea King HC4 (G-CMDO) [WT]	Privately owned, stored Chard, Somerset	
ZA319	Panavia Tornado GR1 (9315M)	DSDA, Arncott, Oxon, on display	
ZA320	Panavia Tornado GR1 (9314M) [CA]	RAF Cosford, on display	
ZA323	Panavia Tornado GR1 [TAZ]	DSAE RNAESS, *HMS Sultan*, Gosport	
ZA325	Panavia Tornado GR1 <ff>	RAF Manston History Museum	
ZA325	Panavia Tornado GR1 [TAX] <rf>	RAF AM&SU, stored Shawbury	
ZA326	Panavia Tornado GR1P	South Wales Aviation Museum, St Athan	
ZA327	Panavia Tornado GR1 <ff>	Privately owned, Spark Bridge, Cumbria	
ZA328	Panavia Tornado GR1	BAE Systems, Samlesbury	
ZA353	Panavia Tornado GR1 [B-53]	Privately owned, Thorpe Wood, N Yorks	
ZA354	Panavia Tornado GR1	Yorkshire Air Museum, Elvington	
ZA355	Panavia Tornado GR1 (9310M) [TAA]	Privately owned, White Waltham	
ZA356	Panavia Tornado GR1 <ff>	DSAE No 1 SoTT, Cosford	

Notes	Serial	Type (code/other identity)	Owner/operator, location or fate
	ZA357	Panavia Tornado GR1 [TTV]	DSAE No 1 SoTT, Cosford
	ZA359	Panavia Tornado GR1	Privately owned, Thorpe Wood, N Yorks
	ZA360	Panavia Tornado GR1 (9318M) <ff>	*Currently not known*
	ZA362	Panavia Tornado GR1 [TR]	Highland Aviation Museum, Inverness
	ZA398	Panavia Tornado GR4A [087]	MoD, Cornwall Aviation Heritage Centre, Newquay
	ZA399	Panavia Tornado GR1 (9316M) [AJ-C]	Privately owned, Knutsford, Cheshire
	ZA407	Panavia Tornado GR1 (9336M) [AJ-N]	RAF Marham, on display
	ZA447	Panavia Tornado GR4 [019]	DSAE No 1 SoTT, Cosford
	ZA449	Panavia Tornado GR4 [020]	*Scrapped at Marham*
	ZA450	Panavia Tornado GR1 (9317M) [TH]	DSAE No 1 SoTT, Cosford
	ZA452	Panavia Tornado GR4 [021]	Midland Air Museum, Coventry
	ZA457	Panavia Tornado GR1 [AJ-J]	RAF Museum, Hendon
	ZA459	Panavia Tornado GR4 [025]	DSAE No 1 SoTT, Cosford
	ZA463	Panavia Tornado GR4 [028]	RAF Lossiemouth, for display
	ZA465	Panavia Tornado GR1 [FF]	IWM Duxford
	ZA469	Panavia Tornado GR4 [029]	IWM Duxford
	ZA472	Panavia Tornado GR4 [031]	RAF Marham (wfu)
	ZA475	Panavia Tornado GR1 (9311M) [AJ-G]	RAF Lossiemouth, on display
	ZA542	Panavia Tornado GR4 [035]	RAF Marham (wfu)
	ZA549	Panavia Tornado GR4 [041]	BAE Systems Aircraft Maintenance Academy, Humberside
	ZA553	Panavia Tornado GR4 [045]	RAF Honington, GI use
	ZA554	Panavia Tornado GR4 [046]	*Scrapped at Lossiemouth, 2019*
	ZA556	Panavia Tornado GR4 [047]	Defence Academy of the UK, Shrivenham
	ZA556	Panavia Tornado GR1 <R> (ZA368/BAPC.155) [Z]	RAF M&RU, Bottesford
	ZA559	Panavia Tornado GR4 [049]	RAF Leeming, RTP
	ZA560	Panavia Tornado GR4 [EB-Q]	RAF Wittering, GI use
	ZA585	Panavia Tornado GR4 [054]	DSAE No 1 SoTT, Cosford
	ZA587	Panavia Tornado GR4 [055]	RAF Honington, GI use
	ZA588	Panavia Tornado GR4 [056]	RAF TST, Marham
	ZA597	Panavia Tornado GR4 [063]	RAF Marham (wfu)
	ZA601	Panavia Tornado GR4 [066]	*Scrapped, May 2019*
	ZA604	Panavia Tornado GR4 <ff>	MoD JARTS, Boscombe Down
	ZA607	Panavia Tornado GR4 [EB-X]	RAF Sealand, on display
	ZA611	Panavia Tornado GR4 [073]	*Scrapped at Marham, February 2018*
	ZA612	Panavia Tornado GR4 [074]	MoD Porton Down, GI use
	ZA613	Panavia Tornado GR4 [075]	RAF Honington, GI use
	ZA614	Panavia Tornado GR4 [076]	RAF Marham, for display
	ZA630	Slingsby T61F Venture T2 (G-BUGL)	Privately owned, Tibenham
	ZA634	Slingsby T61F Venture T2 (G-BUHA) [C]	Privately owned, Saltby, Leics
	ZA652	Slingsby T61F Venture T2 (G-BUDC)	Privately owned, Enstone
	ZA656	Slingsby T61F Venture T2 (G-BTWC)	Privately owned, Nympsfield
	ZA665	Slingsby T61F Venture T2 (G-BVKK)	Privately owned, Saltby, Leics
	ZA670	B-V Chinook HC6A (N37010)	MoD/Boeing/QinetiQ, Boscombe Down (conversion)
	ZA671	B-V Chinook HC6A (N37011)	MoD/Boeing/QinetiQ, Boscombe Down (conversion)
	ZA674	B-V Chinook HC6A (N37019)	MoD/StandardAero, Fleetlands
	ZA675	B-V Chinook HC6A (N37020)	MoD/StandardAero, Fleetlands
	ZA677	B-V Chinook HC6A (N37022)	MoD/StandardAero, Fleetlands
	ZA678	B-V Chinook HC1 (N37023/9229M) [EZ] (wreck)	RAF Odiham, BDRT
	ZA679	B-V Chinook HC6A (N37025)	RAF No 28 Sqn, Benson
	ZA680	B-V Chinook HC6A (N37026)	MoD/Boeing/QinetiQ, Boscombe Down (conversion)
	ZA681	B-V Chinook HC6A (N37027)	RAF No 18 Sqn, Odiham
	ZA682	B-V Chinook HC6A (N37029)	RAF No 1310 Flt, Mali
	ZA683	B-V Chinook HC6A (N37030)	RAF No 18 Sqn, Odiham
	ZA684	B-V Chinook HC6A (N37031)	RAF No 7 Sqn, Odiham
	ZA704	B-V Chinook HC6A (N37033)	RAF No 27 Sqn, Odiham
	ZA705	B-V Chinook HC6A (N37035)	MoD/Boeing/QinetiQ, Boscombe Down (conversion)
	ZA707	B-V Chinook HC6A (N37040)	RAF No 18 Sqn, Odiham
	ZA708	B-V Chinook HC6A (N37042)	RAF No 18 Sqn, Odiham
	ZA710	B-V Chinook HC6A (N37044)	RAF No 28 Sqn, Benson
	ZA711	B-V Chinook HC6A (N37046)	MoD/Boeing/QinetiQ, Boscombe Down (conversion)
	ZA712	B-V Chinook HC6A (N37047)	RAF No 28 Sqn, Benson
	ZA713	B-V Chinook HC6A (N37048)	MoD/Boeing/QinetiQ, Boscombe Down (conversion)

Serial	Type (code/other identity)	Owner/operator, location or fate	Notes
ZA714	B-V Chinook HC6A (N37051)	RAF No 28 Sqn, Benson	
ZA717	B-V Chinook HC1 (N37056/9238M) (wreck)	Newark Air Museum, Winthorpe	
ZA718	B-V Chinook HC6A (N37058)	MoD/Boeing/QinetiQ, Boscombe Down (conversion)	
ZA720	B-V Chinook HC6A (N37060)	RAF No 18 Sqn, Odiham	
ZA726	WS Gazelle AH1 [F1]	Privately owned, Stapleford Tawney	
ZA726	WS Gazelle AH1 (XW851/G-CIEY)	Privately owned, Escrick, N Yorks	
ZA728	WS Gazelle AH1 [E]	Privately owned, Stapleford Tawney	
ZA729	WS Gazelle AH1	AAC Wattisham, BDRT	
ZA730	WS Gazelle AH1 (G-FUKM) <ff>	Privately owned, Hurstbourne Tarrant, Hants	
ZA731	WS Gazelle AH1	AAC No 29 Flt, BATUS, Suffield, Canada	
ZA731	WS Gazelle AH1 (comp XZ313)	Privately owned, Durham	
ZA735	WS Gazelle AH1	DSAE SAAE, Lyneham	
ZA736	WS Gazelle AH1	AAC No 29 Flt, BATUS, Suffield, Canada	
ZA737	WS Gazelle AH1	Army Flying Museum, Middle Wallop	
ZA766	WS Gazelle AH1	AAC 7 Regiment Conversion Flt, Middle Wallop	
ZA769	WS Gazelle AH1 [K]	DSAE SAAE, Lyneham	
ZA771	WS Gazelle AH1	Privately owned, Colsterworth, Lincs	
ZA772	WS Gazelle AH1	MoD/StandardAero, stored Fleetlands	
ZA773	WS Gazelle AH1 [F]	AAC AM&SU, stored Shawbury	
ZA774	WS Gazelle AH1	Privately owned, Babcary, Somerset	
ZA775	WS Gazelle AH1	AAC No 665 Sqn/5 Regt, Aldergrove	
ZA776	WS Gazelle AH1 [F]	Privately owned, Stapleford Tawney	
ZA804	WS Gazelle HT3	Privately owned, Solstice Park, Amesbury, Wilts	
ZA935	WS Puma HC2	RAF, stored Benson	
ZA936	WS Puma HC2	RAF, stored Benson	
ZA937	WS Puma HC1	RAF Benson (wfu)	
ZA939	WS Puma HC2	RAF, stored Benson	
ZA940	WS Puma HC2 (F-ZWBZ) [V]	MoD/QinetiQ, Boscombe Down	
ZA947	Douglas Dakota C3	RAF BBMF, Coningsby	
ZB500	WS Lynx 800 (G-LYNX/ZA500)	The Helicopter Museum, Weston-super-Mare	
ZB506	WS61 Sea King Mk 4X	Privately owned, Charlwood	
ZB507	WS61 Sea King HC4 [F]	*Currently not known*	
ZB601	BAe Harrier T4 (fuselage)	Privately owned, Selby, N Yorks	
ZB603	BAe Harrier T8 [T03/DD]	SFDO, RNAS Culdrose	
ZB604	BAe Harrier T8 [722]	FAA Museum, stored Cobham Hall, RNAS Yeovilton	
ZB615	SEPECAT Jaguar T2A	DSAE No 1 SoTT, Cosford	
ZB625	WS Gazelle HT3 (G-TSTR)	Privately owned, Hurstbourne Tarrant, Hants	
ZB627	WS Gazelle HT3 (G-CBSK) [A]	Privately owned, Hurstbourne Tarrant, Hants	
ZB646	WS Gazelle HT2 (G-CBGZ) [59/CU]	Privately owned, Knebworth	
ZB647	WS Gazelle HT2 (G-CBSF) [40]	Privately owned, Hurstbourne Tarrant, Hants	
ZB665	WS Gazelle AH1	AAC No 665 Sqn/5 Regt, Aldergrove	
ZB667	WS Gazelle AH1	AAC AM&SU, stored Shawbury	
ZB668	WS Gazelle AH1 (TAD 015)	DSAE SAAE, Lyneham	
ZB669	WS Gazelle AH1	AAC No 665 Sqn/5 Regt, Aldergrove	
ZB670	WS Gazelle AH1	Territorial Army Centre, Taunton, on display	
ZB671	WS Gazelle AH1	AAC 7 Regiment Conversion Flt, Middle Wallop	
ZB672	WS Gazelle AH1	Army Training Regiment, Winchester	
ZB673	WS Gazelle AH1 [P]	Privately owned, Stapleford Tawney	
ZB674	WS Gazelle AH1	AAC 7 Regiment Conversion Flt, Middle Wallop	
ZB677	WS Gazelle AH1 [5B]	AAC, stored Suffield, Canada	
ZB678	WS Gazelle AH1	AAC No 665 Sqn/5 Regt, Aldergrove	
ZB679	WS Gazelle AH1	AAC No 665 Sqn/5 Regt, Aldergrove	
ZB683	WS Gazelle AH1	AAC No 667 Sqn/7 Regt, Middle Wallop	
ZB684	WS Gazelle AH1	RAF JADTEU, Brize Norton, instructional use	
ZB686	WS Gazelle AH1 <ff>	The Helicopter Museum, Weston-super-Mare	
ZB689	WS Gazelle AH1	AAC No 665 Sqn/5 Regt, Aldergrove	
ZB690	WS Gazelle AH1	MoD/StandardAero, Fleetlands	
ZB691	WS Gazelle AH1 [S]	AAC 7 Regiment Conversion Flt, Middle Wallop	
ZB692	WS Gazelle AH1 [Y]	MoD/StandardAero, Fleetlands	
ZB693	WS Gazelle AH1	AAC No 665 Sqn/5 Regt, Aldergrove	

BRITISH MILITARY AIRCRAFT MARKINGS

Notes	Serial	Type (code/other identity)	Owner/operator, location or fate
	ZD230	BAC Super VC10 K4 (G-ASGA) <ff>	Privately owned, Crondall, Hants
	ZD240	BAC Super VC10 K4 (G-ASGL) <ff>	Privately owned, Crondall, Hants
	ZD241	BAC Super VC10 K4 (G-ASGM) [N]	Privately owned, Bruntingthorpe
	ZD242	BAC Super VC10 K4 (G-ASGP) <ff>	JARTS, Boscombe Down
	ZD249	WS Lynx HMA8SRU (XZ698) (comp ZD249) [316]	Delta Force Paintball, Edinburgh
	ZD250	WS Lynx HAS3S [636]	RAF Henlow, instructional use
	ZD251	WS Lynx HAS3S	Privately owned, Hixon, Staffs
	ZD252	WS Lynx HMA8SRU [312/VL]	RN Yeovilton, GI use
	ZD254	WS Lynx HAS3S [305]	DSAE AESS, *HMS Sultan*, Gosport
	ZD255	WS Lynx HAS3GMS [635]	Bawtry Paintball Park, S Yorks
	ZD257	WS Lynx HMA8SRU [302/VL]	Privately owned
	ZD258	WS Lynx HMA8SRU [365]	*Rebuilt as XZ698, 2019*
	ZD259	WS Lynx HMA8SRU [474/RM]	RN, stored St Athan
	ZD260	WS Lynx HMA8SRU [313/VL]	AAC, stored Middle Wallop
	ZD261	WS Lynx HMA8SRU [314]	Privately owned
	ZD262	WS Lynx HMA8SRU [316]	Privately owned
	ZD263	WS Lynx HAS3S [632]	Bawtry Paintball Park, S Yorks
	ZD264	WS Lynx HAS3GMS [407] (fuselage)	Air Defence Collection, Wilts
	ZD265	WS Lynx HMA8SRU [302]	AAC Middle Wallop (for disposal)
	ZD266	WS Lynx HMA8SRU [673]	Bradwell Bay Military & Science Museum, Essex
	ZD267	WS Lynx HMA8 (comp XZ672) [LST-2]	RN, stored St Athan
	ZD268	WS Lynx HMA8SRU [366/YB]	Privately owned
	ZD274	WS Lynx AH7 [M]	Privately owned, Sproughton
	ZD276	WS Lynx AH7	Mayhem Paintball, Abridge, Essex
	ZD278	WS Lynx AH7 [F]	Delta Force, Liverpool
	ZD279	WS Lynx AH7 <ff>	Privately owned, Hixon, Staffs
	ZD280	WS Lynx AH7	Farnborough Air Sciences Trust, Farnborough
	ZD281	WS Lynx AH7 [K]	Privately owned, Willenhall, Staffs
	ZD283	WS Lynx AH7 <ff>	Privately owned, Stoke-on-Trent
	ZD284	WS Lynx AH7 [K]	Privately owned, Corley Moor, Warks
	ZD285	WS Lynx AH7	MoD JARTS, Boscombe Down
	ZD318	BAe Harrier GR7A	Harrier Heritage Centre, RAF Wittering
	ZD433	BAe Harrier GR9A [45A]	FAA Museum, RNAS Yeovilton
	ZD461	BAe Harrier GR9A [51A]	IWM London, Lambeth
	ZD462	BAe Harrier GR7 (9302M) [52]	Privately owned, Malmesbury, Glos
	ZD465	BAe Harrier GR9 [55]	RAF Cosford
	ZD469	BAe Harrier GR7A [59A]	RAF Wittering, on display
	ZD476	WS61 Sea King HC4 [WZ]	Privately owned, Charlwood
	ZD477	WS61 Sea King HC4 [E]	East Midlands Airport Aeropark
	ZD478	WS61 Sea King HC4 [J]	Privately owned, Hixon, Staffs
	ZD479	WS61 Sea King HC4 [WQ]	DSAE, stored *HMS Sultan*, Gosport
	ZD480	WS61 Sea King HC4 [J]	StandardAero, Fleetlands, on display
	ZD559	WS Lynx AH5X	QinetiQ Apprentice Training School, Boscombe Down
	ZD560	WS Lynx AH7	Privately owned,
	ZD565	WS Lynx HMA8SRU [404/IR]	Delta Force Paintball, Cardiff
	ZD566	WS Lynx HMA8SRU [305]	Privately owned, Sproughton
	ZD574	B-V Chinook HC6A (N37077)	MoD/StandardAero, Fleetlands
	ZD575	B-V Chinook HC6A (N37078)	RAF No 7 Sqn, Odiham
	ZD578	BAe Sea Harrier FA2 [000,122]	RNAS Yeovilton, at main gate
	ZD579	BAe Sea Harrier FA2 [79/DD]	SFDO, RNAS Culdrose
	ZD581	BAe Sea Harrier FA2 [124]	RN, Predannack Fire School
	ZD582	BAe Sea Harrier FA2 [002/N]	Privately owned, Banbury, Oxon
	ZD607	BAe Sea Harrier FA2	DSDA, Arncott, Oxon, preserved
	ZD610	BAe Sea Harrier FA2 [714,002/N]	Aerospace Bristol, Filton
	ZD611	BAe Sea Harrier FA2 [001]	RN, Portsmouth, preserved
	ZD612	BAe Sea Harrier FA2 [724]	Privately owned, Topsham, Devon
	ZD613	BAe Sea Harrier FA2 [127/R]	Privately owned, Cross Green, Leeds
	ZD614	BAe Sea Harrier FA2	Privately owned, Walcott, Lincs
	ZD620	BAe 125 CC3	Bournemouth Aviation Museum
	ZD621	BAe 125 CC3	RAF Northolt, on display
	ZD625	WS61 Sea King HC4 [P]	Holmside Park, Edmondsley, Durham
	ZD627	WS61 Sea King HC4 <ff>	South Wales Aviation Museum, stored St Athan

Serial	Type (code/other identity)	Owner/operator, location or fate	Notes
ZD630	WS61 Sea King HAS6 [012/L]	DSAE RNAESS, *HMS Sultan*, Gosport	
ZD631	WS61 Sea King HAS6 [66] (fuselage)	Privately owned, St Agnes, Cornwall	
ZD634	WS61 Sea King HAS6 [503]	SFDO, RNAS Culdrose	
ZD636	WS61 Sea King ASaC7 [182/CU]	DSAE, stored *HMS Sultan*, Gosport	
ZD637	WS61 Sea King HAS6 [700/PW]	DSAE RNAESS, *HMS Sultan*, Gosport	
ZD667	BAe Harrier GR3 (9201M) [U]	Bentwaters Cold War Museum	
ZD703	BAe 125 CC3	Privately owned, Shepton Mallet	
ZD704	BAe 125 CC3	MoD, Cornwall Aviation Heritage Centre, Newquay	
ZD710	Panavia Tornado GR1 <ff>	Privately owned, Hawarden	
ZD711	Panavia Tornado GR4 [079]	RAF Honington, GI use	
ZD713	Panavia Tornado GR4 [081]	RAF Leeming, RTP	
ZD715	Panavia Tornado GR4 [083]	RAF Cosford, GI use	
ZD716	Panavia Tornado GR4 [DH] $	RAF Marham (wfu)	
ZD744	Panavia Tornado GR4 [092]	RAF Honington, GI use	
ZD793	Panavia Tornado GR4	DSAE No 1 SoTT, Cosford	
ZD848	Panavia Tornado GR4 [109]	RAF Marham (wfu)	
ZD849	Panavia Tornado GR4 [110]	DSAE No 1 SoTT, Cosford	
ZD899	Panavia Tornado F2	Privately owned, Thorpe Wood, N Yorks	
ZD902	Panavia Tornado F2A(TIARA)	Privately owned, Church Fenton	
ZD932	Panavia Tornado F2 (comp ZE255) (9308M) (fuselage)	Privately owned, Thorpe Wood, N Yorks	
ZD936	Panavia Tornado F2 (comp ZE251) <ff>	Boscombe Down Aviation Collection, Old Sarum	
ZD938	Panavia Tornado F2 (comp ZE295) <ff>	South Yorkshire Aircraft Museum, Doncaster	
ZD939	Panavia Tornado F2 (comp ZE292) <ff>	DSAE No 1 SoTT, Cosford, instructional use	
ZD948	Lockheed TriStar KC1 (G-BFCA/N304CS)	Privately owned, Bruntingthorpe	
ZD951	Lockheed TriStar K1 (G-BFCD/N309CS) $	Privately owned, Bruntingthorpe	
ZD980	B-V Chinook HC6A (N37082)	MoD/Boeing/QinetiQ, Boscombe Down (conversion)	
ZD981	B-V Chinook HC6A (N37083)	RAF No 27 Sqn, Odiham	
ZD982	B-V Chinook HC6A (N37085)	RAF No 18 Sqn, Odiham	
ZD983	B-V Chinook HC6A (N37086)	MoD/Boeing/QinetiQ, Boscombe Down	
ZD984	B-V Chinook HC6A (N37088)	MoD/Boeing/QinetiQ, Boscombe Down (conversion)	
ZD990	BAe Harrier T8 (G-RNTB) [T90/DD]	Privately owned, St Athan	
ZD992	BAe Harrier T8 [724]	Privately owned, Knutsford, Cheshire	
ZE114	Panavia Tornado IDS (RSAF 703)	*Returned to Saudi Arabia, March 2019*	
ZE119	Panavia Tornado IDS (RSAF 760)	*Returned to Saudi Arabia, 10 April 2019*	
ZE165	Panavia Tornado F3 [GE]	MoD DFTDC, Manston	
ZE168	Panavia Tornado F3 <ff>	Privately owned, Thorpe Wood, N Yorks	
ZE204	Panavia Tornado F3 [FC]	MoD DFTDC, Manston	
ZE256	Panavia Tornado F3 [DZ] (wears ZE343 on port side)	*Sold to Estonia, March 2019*	
ZE340	Panavia Tornado F3 (ZE758/9298M) [GO]	DSAE No 1 SoTT, Cosford	
ZE342	Panavia Tornado F3 [HP]	Rolls Royce, RAF Leeming	
ZE352	McD F-4J(UK) Phantom (9086M) <ff>	*Currently not known*	
ZE360	McD F-4J(UK) Phantom (9059M) [O]	MoD DFTDC, Manston	
ZE368	WS61 Sea King HAR3 [R]	Holmside Park, stored Edmondsley, Durham	
ZE369	WS61 Sea King HAR3 [S]	Privately owned, Charlwood	
ZE370	WS61 Sea King HAR3 [T]	*Currently not known*	
ZE375	WS Lynx AH9A	Privately owned, Bentwaters	
ZE376	WS Lynx AH9A	Sheffield University, GI use	
ZE378	WS Lynx AH7	AAC, Middle Wallop (for disposal)	
ZE379	WS Lynx AH7 <ff>	QinetiQ, Boscombe Down	
ZE380	WS Lynx AH9A	Army, Pirbright, Surrey, GI use	
ZE381	WS Lynx AH7 [X]	DSAE SAAE, Lyneham	
ZE395	BAe 125 CC3	Privately owned, Dunsfold	
ZE410	Agusta A109A (AE-334)	Army Flying Museum, Middle Wallop	
ZE412	Agusta A109A	Army, Credenhill	
ZE413	Agusta A109A	Perth Technical College	
ZE416	Agusta A109E Power Elite (G-ESLH)	*To G-ETPJ, 20 June 2019*	
ZE418	WS61 Sea King ASaC7 [186]	DSAE, stored *HMS Sultan*, Gosport	
ZE420	WS61 Sea King ASaC7 [189]	HeliOperations Ltd, Portland, GI use	
ZE422	WS61 Sea King ASaC7 [192]	DSAE, stored *HMS Sultan*, Gosport	
ZE425	WS61 Sea King HC4 [WR]	Holmside Park, Edmondsley, Durham	

Notes	Serial	Type (code/other identity)	Owner/operator, location or fate
	ZE426	WS61 Sea King HC4 [WX]	DSAE RNAESS, *HMS Sultan*, Gosport
	ZE428	WS61 Sea King HC4 [H]	Holmside Park, Edmondsley, Durham (damaged)
	ZE432	BAC 1-11/479FU (DQ-FBV) <ff>	Bournemouth Aviation Museum
	ZE499	Grob G103 Viking T1 (BGA3004) [VD]	RAF ACCGS/No 644 VGS, Syerston
	ZE477	WS Lynx 3	The Helicopter Museum, Weston-super-Mare
	ZE495	Grob G103 Viking T1 (BGA3000) [VA]	RAF No 621 VGS/No 637 VGS, Little Rissington
	ZE496	Grob G103 Viking T1 (BGA3001) [VB]	RAF/Serco GMS, Syerston
	ZE498	Grob G103 Viking T1 (BGA3003) [VC]	RAF, stored Little Rissington
	ZE499	Grob G103 Viking T1 (BGA3004) [VD]	RAF/Serco GMS, Syerston
	ZE500	Grob G103 Viking T1 (BGA3005) <ff>	Privately owned, Gransden Lodge
	ZE502	Grob G103 Viking T1 (BGA3007) [VF]	RAF/Serco, stored Syerston
	ZE503	Grob G103 Viking T1 (BGA3008) [VG]	MoD/MADG, Cambridge (spares use)
	ZE504	Grob G103 Viking T1 (BGA3009) [VH]	RAF/Serco, stored Syerston
	ZE520	Grob G103 Viking T1 (BGA3010) [VJ]	RAF/Serco GMS, Syerston
	ZE521	Grob G103 Viking T1 (BGA3011) [VK]	RAF No 622 VGS, Upavon
	ZE522	Grob G103 Viking T1 (BGA3012) [VL]	RAF ACCGS/No 644 VGS, Syerston
	ZE524	Grob G103 Viking T1 (BGA3014) [VM]	RAF No 637 VGS, Little Rissington, GI use
	ZE526	Grob G103 Viking T1 (BGA3016) [VN]	RAF No 622 VGS, Upavon
	ZE527	Grob G103 Viking T1 (BGA3017) [VP]	RAF No 622 VGS, Upavon
	ZE528	Grob G103 Viking T1 (BGA3018) [VQ]	RAF No 632 VGS, Ternhill
	ZE529	Grob G103 Viking T1 (BGA3019) (comp ZE655) [VR]	RAF ACCGS/No 644 VGS, Syerston
	ZE530	Grob G103 Viking T1 (BGA3020) [VS]	RAF, stored Little Rissington
	ZE531	Grob G103 Viking T1 (BGA3021) [VT]	RAF, stored Little Rissington
	ZE532	Grob G103 Viking T1 (BGA3022) [VU]	RAF/Serco GMS, Syerston
	ZE533	Grob G103 Viking T1 (BGA3023) [VV]	RAF/Serco GMS, Syerston
	ZE550	Grob G103 Viking T1 (BGA3025) [VX]	MoD/MADG, Cambridge (spares use)
	ZE551	Grob G103 Viking T1 (BGA3026) [VY]	RAF ACCGS/No 644 VGS, Syerston
	ZE552	Grob G103 Viking T1 (BGA3027) [VZ]	RAF, stored Little Rissington
	ZE553	Grob G103 Viking T1 (BGA3028) [WA]	RAF No 622 VGS, Upavon
	ZE554	Grob G103 Viking T1 (BGA3029) [WB]	RAF, stored Little Rissington
	ZE555	Grob G103 Viking T1 (BGA3030) [WC]	RAF No 626 VGS, Predannack
	ZE556	Grob G103 Viking T1 (BGA3031) <ff>	No 308 Sqn ATC, Colchester
	ZE557	Grob G103 Viking T1 (BGA3032) [WE]	RAF/Serco GMS, Syerston
	ZE558	Grob G103 Viking T1 (BGA3033) [WF]	RAF, stored Little Rissington
	ZE559	Grob G103 Viking T1 (BGA3034) [WG]	RAF/Serco GMS, Syerston
	ZE560	Grob G103 Viking T1 (BGA3035) [WH]	RAF/Serco GMS, Syerston
	ZE561	Grob G103 Viking T1 (BGA3036) [WJ]	RAF/Southern Sailplanes, Membury
	ZE562	Grob G103 Viking T1 (BGA3037) [WK]	RAF/Serco, stored Syerston
	ZE563	Grob G103 Viking T1 (BGA3038) [WL]	RAF/Serco GMS, Syerston
	ZE564	Grob G103 Viking T1 (BGA3039) [WN]	RAF No 661 VGS, Kirknewton
	ZE584	Grob G103 Viking T1 (BGA3040) [WP]	RAF No 626 VGS, Predannack
	ZE585	Grob G103 Viking T1 (BGA3041) [WQ]	RAF/Serco GMS, Syerston
	ZE586	Grob G103 Viking T1 (BGA3042) [WR]	RAF ACCGS/No 644 VGS, Syerston
	ZE587	Grob G103 Viking T1 (BGA3043) [WS]	RAF No 626 VGS, Predannack
	ZE590	Grob G103 Viking T1 (BGA3046) [WT]	RAF/Serco GMS, Syerston
	ZE591	Grob G103 Viking T1 (BGA3047) [WU]	RAF, stored Little Rissington
	ZE592	Grob G103 Viking T1 (BGA3048) <ff>	RAF, Upavon, GI use
	ZE593	Grob G103 Viking T1 (BGA3049) [WW]	RAF, stored Little Rissington
	ZE594	Grob G103 Viking T1 (BGA3050) [WX]	RAF No 621 VGS/No 637 VGS, Little Rissington
	ZE595	Grob G103 Viking T1 (BGA3051) [WY]	RAF No 645 VGS, Topcliffe
	ZE600	Grob G103 Viking T1 (BGA3052) [WZ]	RAF ACCGS/No 644 VGS, Syerston
	ZE601	Grob G103 Viking T1 (BGA3053) [XA]	RAF No 621 VGS/No 637 VGS, Little Rissington
	ZE602	Grob G103 Viking T1 (BGA3054) [XB]	RAF No 632 VGS, Ternhill
	ZE603	Grob G103 Viking T1 (BGA3055) [XC]	RAF, stored Little Rissington
	ZE604	Grob G103 Viking T1 (BGA3056) [XD]	RAF, stored Little Rissington
	ZE605	Grob G103 Viking T1 (BGA3057) [XE]	RAF/Serco GMS, Syerston
	ZE606	Grob G103 Viking T1 (BGA3058) [XF]	RAF/Serco GMS, Syerston
	ZE607	Grob G103 Viking T1 (BGA3059) [XG]	RAF, stored Little Rissington
	ZE608	Grob G103 Viking T1 (BGA3060) [XH]	RAF/Serco, stored Syerston
	ZE609	Grob G103 Viking T1 (BGA3061) [XJ]	RAF ACCGS/No 644 VGS, Syerston
	ZE610	Grob G103 Viking T1 (BGA3062) [XK]	RAF, stored Little Rissington
	ZE611	Grob G103 Viking T1 (BGA3063) [XL]	RAF, stored Little Rissington

Serial	Type (code/other identity)	Owner/operator, location or fate	Notes
ZE613	Grob G103 Viking T1 (BGA3065) [XM]	RAF ACCGS/No 644 VGS, Syerston	
ZE614	Grob G103 Viking T1 (BGA3066) [XN]	RAF No 632 VGS, Ternhill	
ZE625	Grob G103 Viking T1 (BGA3067) [XP]	RAF No 621 VGS/No 637 VGS, Little Rissington	
ZE626	Grob G103 Viking T1 (BGA3068) [XQ]	RAF/Serco GMS, Syerston	
ZE627	Grob G103 Viking T1 (BGA3069) [XR]	RAF, stored Little Rissington	
ZE628	Grob G103 Viking T1 (BGA3070) [XS]	RAF No 632 VGS, Ternhill	
ZE629	Grob G103 Viking T1 (BGA3071) [XT]	RAF/Serco GMS, Syerston	
ZE630	Grob G103 Viking T1 (BGA3072) [XU]	RAF/Serco GMS, Syerston	
ZE631	Grob G103 Viking T1 (BGA3073) [XV]	RAF/Serco GMS, Syerston	
ZE632	Grob G103 Viking T1 (BGA3074) [XW]	RAF ACCGS/No 644 VGS, Syerston	
ZE633	Grob G103 Viking T1 (BGA3075) [XX]	RAF/Serco GMS, Syerston	
ZE636	Grob G103 Viking T1 (BGA3078) [XZ]	RAF/Serco GMS, Syerston	
ZE637	Grob G103 Viking T1 (BGA3079) [YA]	RAF No 661 VGS, Kirknewton	
ZE650	Grob G103 Viking T1 (BGA3080) [YB]	RAF/Serco GMS, Syerston	
ZE651	Grob G103 Viking T1 (BGA3081) [YC]	RAF/Serco GMS, Syerston	
ZE652	Grob G103 Viking T1 (BGA3082) [YD]	RAF/Serco, stored Syerston	
ZE653	Grob G103 Viking T1 (BGA3083) [YE]	RAF/Serco GMS, Syerston	
ZE656	Grob G103 Viking T1 (BGA3086) [YH]	RAF, stored Little Rissington	
ZE657	Grob G103 Viking T1 (BGA3087) [YJ]	RAF, stored Little Rissington	
ZE658	Grob G103 Viking T1 (BGA3088) [YK]	RAF/Serco, stored Syerston	
ZE677	Grob G103 Viking T1 (BGA3090) [YM]	RAF, stored Little Rissington	
ZE678	Grob G103 Viking T1 (BGA3091) [YN]	RAF/Serco, stored Syerston	
ZE679	Grob G103 Viking T1 (BGA3092) [YP]	RAF, stored Little Rissington	
ZE680	Grob G103 Viking T1 (BGA3093) [YQ]	RAF/Serco GMS, Syerston	
ZE681	Grob G103 Viking T1 (BGA3094) <ff>	Privately owned, Frampton Cotterell, Glos, GI use	
ZE682	Grob G103 Viking T1 (BGA3095) [YS]	RAF/Serco GMS, Syerston	
ZE683	Grob G103 Viking T1 (BGA3096) [YT]	RAF, stored Little Rissington	
ZE684	Grob G103 Viking T1 (BGA3097) [YU]	RAF, stored Little Rissington	
ZE685	Grob G103 Viking T1 (BGA3098) [YV]	RAF No 661 VGS, Kirknewton	
ZE686	Grob G103 Viking T1 (BGA3099) <ff>	Privately owned, Stow Maries, Essex	
ZE690	BAe Sea Harrier FA2 [90/DD]	SFDO, RNAS Culdrose	
ZE691	BAe Sea Harrier FA2 [710]	Classic Autos, Winsford, Cheshire	
ZE692	BAe Sea Harrier FA2 [92/DD]	SFDO, RNAS Culdrose	
ZE694	BAe Sea Harrier FA2 [004]	Midland Air Museum, Coventry	
ZE697	BAe Sea Harrier FA2 [006]	Privately owned, Binbrook	
ZE698	BAe Sea Harrier FA2 [001]	Privately owned, Charlwood	
ZE700	BAe 146 CC2 (G-6-021)	RAF No 32(The Royal) Sqn, Northolt	
ZE701	BAe 146 CC2 (G-6-029)	RAF No 32(The Royal) Sqn, Northolt	
ZE704	Lockheed TriStar C2 (N508PA/N507CS)	Privately owned, Bruntingthorpe	
ZE705	Lockheed TriStar C2 (N509PA/N703CS)	Privately owned, Bruntingthorpe	
ZE707	BAe 146 C3 (OO-TAZ)	RAF No 32(The Royal) Sqn, Northolt	
ZE708	BAe 146 C3 (OO-TAY)	RAF No 32(The Royal) Sqn, Northolt	
ZE760	Panavia Tornado F3 (MM7206) [AP]	RAF Coningsby, on display	
ZE887	Panavia Tornado F3 [GF] $	RAF Museum, Hendon	
ZE934	Panavia Tornado F3 [TA]	National Museum of Flight, E Fortune	
ZE936	Panavia Tornado F3 <ff>	RAF Air Defence Radar Museum, Neatishead	
ZE965	Panavia Tornado F3 <ff>	Privately owned,	
ZE966	Panavia Tornado F3 [VT]	Tornado Heritage Centre, Hawarden	
ZE967	Panavia Tornado F3 [UT]	RAF Leuchars, at main gate	
ZF115	WS61 Sea King HC4 [R,WV]	DSAE, stored HMS Sultan, Gosport	
ZF116	WS61 Sea King HC4 [WP]	Privately owned,	
ZF118	WS61 Sea King HC4 [O]	School of Maritime Survival HMS Raleigh, Plymouth	
ZF119	WS61 Sea King HC4 [WY]	DSAE RNAESS, HMS Sultan, Gosport	
ZF120	WS61 Sea King HC4 [Z]	Currently not known	
ZF121	WS61 Sea King HC4 [T]	Holmside Park, Edmondsley, Durham	
ZF122	WS61 Sea King HC4 [V]	Privately owned, stored Chard, Somerset	
ZF135	Shorts Tucano T1 [135]	RAF Linton-on-Ouse (dismantled)	
ZF137	Shorts Tucano T1 [137]	RAF Linton-on-Ouse (dismantled)	
ZF139	Shorts Tucano T1 [139]	RAF Linton-on-Ouse (dismantled)	
ZF140	Shorts Tucano T1 [140] $	RAF Linton-on-Ouse (dismantled)	
ZF142	Shorts Tucano T1 [142]	RAF Linton-on-Ouse (dismantled)	

BRITISH MILITARY AIRCRAFT MARKINGS

Notes	Serial	Type (code/other identity)	Owner/operator, location or fate
	ZF143	Shorts Tucano T1 [143]	RAF Linton-on-Ouse (dismantled)
	ZF144	Shorts Tucano T1 [144]	RAF Linton-on-Ouse (dismantled)
	ZF145	Shorts Tucano T1 [145]	RAF Linton-on-Ouse (dismantled)
	ZF160	Shorts Tucano T1 [160]	Privately owned, Bentwaters
	ZF163	Shorts Tucano T1 [163]	RAF AM&SU, stored Shawbury
	ZF166	Shorts Tucano T1 [166]	Privately owned, Bentwaters
	ZF167	Shorts Tucano T1 (fuselage)	Ulster Aviation Society, Long Kesh
	ZF169	Shorts Tucano T1 [169]	RAF Linton-on-Ouse (dismantled)
	ZF170	Shorts Tucano T1 [MP-A]	RAF Linton-on-Ouse (dismantled)
	ZF171	Shorts Tucano T1 [171]	RAF Linton-on-Ouse (dismantled)
	ZF172	Shorts Tucano T1 [172]	RAF Linton-on-Ouse (dismantled)
	ZF202	Shorts Tucano T1 [202]	RAF Linton-on-Ouse, on display (for RAF Syerston)
	ZF204	Shorts Tucano T1 [204]	RAF Linton-on-Ouse (dismantled)
	ZF205	Shorts Tucano T1 [205]	RAF Linton-on-Ouse (dismantled)
	ZF210	Shorts Tucano T1 [210]	RAF Linton-on-Ouse (dismantled)
	ZF211	Shorts Tucano T1 [211]	Privately owned, Bentwaters
	ZF239	Shorts Tucano T1 [239]	RAF Linton-on-Ouse (dismantled)
	ZF240	Shorts Tucano T1 [240]	RAF Linton-on-Ouse (dismantled)
	ZF243	Shorts Tucano T1 [243]	RAF Linton-on-Ouse (dismantled)
	ZF244	Shorts Tucano T1 [244]	RAF Linton-on-Ouse (dismantled)
	ZF263	Shorts Tucano T1 [263]	RAF AM&SU, stored Shawbury
	ZF264	Shorts Tucano T1 [264]	RAF Linton-on-Ouse (dismantled)
	ZF268	Shorts Tucano T1 [268]	RAF AM&SU, stored Shawbury
	ZF269	Shorts Tucano T1 [269]	RAF Linton-on-Ouse (dismantled)
	ZF286	Shorts Tucano T1 [286]	RAF AM&SU, stored Shawbury
	ZF287	Shorts Tucano T1 [287]	RAF Linton-on-Ouse (dismantled)
	ZF288	Shorts Tucano T1 [288]	RAF AM&SU, stored Shawbury
	ZF289	Shorts Tucano T1 [289]	Bombardier, Belfast
	ZF290	Shorts Tucano T1 [290] $	RAF Linton-on-Ouse (dismantled)
	ZF291	Shorts Tucano T1 [291]	RAF Linton-on-Ouse (dismantled)
	ZF292	Shorts Tucano T1 [292]	RAF Linton-on-Ouse (dismantled)
	ZF293	Shorts Tucano T1 [293] $	RAF Linton-on-Ouse (dismantled)
	ZF294	Shorts Tucano T1 [294]	RAF Linton-on-Ouse (dismantled)
	ZF295	Shorts Tucano T1 [295] $	Bombardier, Belfast
	ZF315	Shorts Tucano T1 [315]	RAF AM&SU, stored Shawbury
	ZF317	Shorts Tucano T1 [317]	RAF Linton-on-Ouse (dismantled)
	ZF318	Shorts Tucano T1 [318] $	RAF AM&SU, stored Shawbury
	ZF319	Shorts Tucano T1 [319]	RAF Linton-on-Ouse (dismantled)
	ZF338	Shorts Tucano T1 [338]	RAF Linton-on-Ouse (dismantled)
	ZF341	Shorts Tucano T1 [341]	RAF Linton-on-Ouse (dismantled)
	ZF342	Shorts Tucano T1 [342]	RAF Linton-on-Ouse (dismantled)
	ZF343	Shorts Tucano T1 [343]	RAF Linton-on-Ouse (dismantled)
	ZF347	Shorts Tucano T1 [347]	RAF Linton-on-Ouse (dismantled)
	ZF348	Shorts Tucano T1 [348]	RAF Linton-on-Ouse (dismantled)
	ZF349	Shorts Tucano T1 [349] (fuselage)	*Scrapped at Linton-on-Ouse, 2019*
	ZF350	Shorts Tucano T1 [350]	RAF AM&SU, stored Shawbury
	ZF355	WS Lynx HAS3S(ICE) (XZ238) [633]	Privately owned, White Waltham
	ZF372	Shorts Tucano T1 [372]	RAF AM&SU, stored Shawbury
	ZF374	Shorts Tucano T1 [374]	RAF Linton-on-Ouse (dismantled)
	ZF376	Shorts Tucano T1 [376]	RAF AM&SU, stored Shawbury
	ZF377	Shorts Tucano T1 [377]	RAF Linton-on-Ouse (dismantled)
	ZF378	Shorts Tucano T1 [RN-S] $	RAF Linton-on-Ouse (dismantled)
	ZF379	Shorts Tucano T1 [379]	RAF Linton-on-Ouse (dismantled)
	ZF380	Shorts Tucano T1 [380]	Privately owned, Bentwaters
	ZF405	Shorts Tucano T1 [405]	RAF AM&SU, stored Shawbury
	ZF406	Shorts Tucano T1 [406]	RAF Linton-on-Ouse (dismantled)
	ZF407	Shorts Tucano T1 [407]	RAF Linton-on-Ouse (dismantled)
	ZF408	Shorts Tucano T1 [408]	RAF AM&SU, stored Shawbury
	ZF412	Shorts Tucano T1 [412]	Privately owned, Bentwaters
	ZF414	Shorts Tucano T1 [414]	RAF AM&SU, stored Shawbury
	ZF416	Shorts Tucano T1 [416]	RAF AM&SU, stored Shawbury
	ZF417	Shorts Tucano T1 [417]	RAF Linton-on-Ouse (dismantled)

Serial	Type (code/other identity)	Owner/operator, location or fate	Notes
ZF418	Shorts Tucano T1 [418]	RAF AM&SU, stored Shawbury	
ZF446	Shorts Tucano T1 [446]	RAF AM&SU, stored Shawbury	
ZF448	Shorts Tucano T1 [448] $	RAF Linton-on-Ouse (dismantled)	
ZF449	Shorts Tucano T1 [449]	RAF AM&SU, stored Shawbury	
ZF485	Shorts Tucano T1 (G-BULU) [485]	RAF Linton-on-Ouse (dismantled)	
ZF486	Shorts Tucano T1 [486]	RAF AM&SU, stored Shawbury	
ZF487	Shorts Tucano T1 [487]	RAF AM&SU, stored Shawbury	
ZF488	Shorts Tucano T1 [488]	RAF AM&SU, stored Shawbury	
ZF489	Shorts Tucano T1 [489]	RAF Linton-on-Ouse (dismantled)	
ZF490	Shorts Tucano T1 [490]	RAF AM&SU, stored Shawbury	
ZF491	Shorts Tucano T1 [491]	RAF Linton-on-Ouse (dismantled)	
ZF492	Shorts Tucano T1 [492]	RAF AM&SU, stored Shawbury	
ZF510	Shorts Tucano T1 [510]	QinetiQ, Boscombe Down (wfu)	
ZF511	Shorts Tucano T1 [511]	QinetiQ, Boscombe Down (wfu)	
ZF512	Shorts Tucano T1 [512]	RAF Linton-on-Ouse (dismantled)	
ZF513	Shorts Tucano T1 [513]	RAF AM&SU, stored Shawbury	
ZF515	Shorts Tucano T1 [515]	RAF Linton-on-Ouse (dismantled)	
ZF516	Shorts Tucano T1 [516]	Privately owned, Bentwaters	
ZF534	BAe EAP	RAF Museum, Cosford	
ZF537	WS Lynx AH9A	AAC, stored Middle Wallop	
ZF538	WS Lynx AH9A	AAC, stored Middle Wallop	
ZF539	WS Lynx AH9A	Privately owned, Southend	
ZF557	WS Lynx HMA8SRU [426/PD]	South Wales Aviation Museum, St Athan	
ZF558	WS Lynx HMA8SRU [336/WK]	Privately owned	
ZF560	WS Lynx HMA8SRU [456]	Privately owned	
ZF562	WS Lynx HMA8SRU [353/MB]	Privately owned	
ZF563	WS Lynx HMA8SRU [312/VL]	Privately owned, Goodwood	
ZF581	BAC Lightning F53 (53-675/206)	Bentwaters Cold War Museum	
ZF582	BAC Lightning F53 (53-676/210/207) <ff>	Bournemouth Aviation Museum	
ZF583	BAC Lightning F53 (53-681/306/210)	Solway Aviation Society, Carlisle	
ZF584	BAC Lightning F53 (53-682/307/211)	Dumfries & Galloway Avn Mus, Dumfries	
ZF587	BAC Lightning F53 (53-691/215) <ff>	Lashenden Air Warfare Museum, Headcorn	
ZF587	BAC Lightning F53 (53-691/215) <rf>	Privately owned, Stowmarket, Suffolk	
ZF588	BAC Lightning F53 (53-693/216) [L]	East Midlands Airport Aeropark	
ZF589	BAC Lightning F53 (53-700/218) <ff>	Gatwick Aviation Museum, stored Charlwood	
ZF590	BAC Lightning F53 (53-679/206/1302/220) <ff>	Privately owned, stored Bruntingthorpe	
ZF595	BAC Lightning T55 (55-714/212/1317/231) <ff>	Lightning Preservation Grp, Bruntingthorpe	
ZF595	BAC Lightning T55 (55-714/212/1317/231) <rf>	Privately owned, Binbrook	
ZF596	BAC Lightning T55 (55-715/305/205/220/233) <ff>	Lakes Lightnings, Spark Bridge, Cumbria	
ZF622	Piper PA-31 Navajo Chieftain 350 (N3548Y)	MoD JARTS, Boscombe Down	
ZF641	EHI-101 [PP1]	SFDO, RNAS Culdrose	
ZF649	EHI-101 Merlin (A2714) [PP5]	DSAE AESS, HMS Sultan, Gosport	
ZG347	Northrop Chukar D2	Davidstow Airfield & Cornwall At War Museum	
ZG477	BAe Harrier GR9 $	RAF Museum, Hendon	
ZG478	BAe Harrier GR9 (fuselage)	Privately owned, Sproughton	
ZG509	BAe Harrier GR7 [80]	Privately owned, Petersfield, Hants	
ZG631	Northrop Chukar D2	Farnborough Air Sciences Trust, Farnborough	
ZG751	Panavia Tornado F3 (fuselage)	MoD JARTS, Boscombe Down	
ZG752	Panavia Tornado GR4 $	RAF Honington, GI use	
ZG771	Panavia Tornado GR4 $	RAF Marham (wfu)	
ZG773	Panavia Tornado GR4	QinetiQ, stored Boscombe Down	
ZG775	Panavia Tornado GR4 [AF] $	RAF Marham (wfu)	
ZG791	Panavia Tornado GR4 [137]	RAF Marham (wfu)	
ZG816	WS61 Sea King HAS6 [014/L]	DSAE, stored HMS Sultan, Gosport	
ZG817	WS61 Sea King HAS6 [702/PW]	DSAE RNAESS, HMS Sultan, Gosport	
ZG818	WS61 Sea King HAS6 [707/PW]	DSAE RNAESS, HMS Sultan, Gosport	
ZG819	WS61 Sea King HAS6 [265/N]	DSAE RNAESS, HMS Sultan, Gosport	
ZG822	WS61 Sea King HC4 [WS]	South Wales Aviation Museum, St Athan	
ZG844	PBN 2T Islander R1 (G-BLNE)	RAF AM&SU, stored Shawbury	
ZG845	PBN 2T Islander R1 (G-BLNT)	RAF No 651 Sqn/5 Regt, Aldergrove	
ZG846	PBN 2T Islander R1 (G-BLNU)	MoD/Britten-Norman, Lee-on-Solent	

Notes	Serial	Type (code/other identity)	Owner/operator, location or fate
	ZG847	PBN 2T Islander R1 (G-BLNV)	RAF AM&SU, stored Shawbury
	ZG848	PBN 2T Islander R1 (G-BLNY)	MoD/Britten-Norman, Lee-on-Solent
	ZG875	WS61 Sea King HAS6 [013] <ff>	Privately owned, Crewe
	ZG875	WS61 Sea King HAS6 <rf>	Mayhem Paintball, Aybridge, Essex
	ZG884	WS Lynx AH9A	Privately owned, Bentwaters
	ZG885	WS Lynx AH9A	Privately owned, Sproughton
	ZG886	WS Lynx AH9A	Privately owned, Bentwaters
	ZG887	WS Lynx AH9A	Privately owned, Sproughton
	ZG888	WS Lynx AH9A	Privately owned, Sproughton
	ZG889	WS Lynx AH9A	Privately owned, Bentwaters
	ZG914	WS Lynx AH9A	Privately owned, Wainfleet, Lincs
	ZG915	WS Lynx AH9A	RN, Predannack Fire School
	ZG916	WS Lynx AH9A	Privately owned, Sproughton
	ZG917	WS Lynx AH9A $	AAC, stored Middle Wallop
	ZG918	WS Lynx AH9A	AAC Middle Wallop, RTP
	ZG919	WS Lynx AH9A	RN, Predannack Fire School
	ZG920	WS Lynx AH9A	AAC, stored Middle Wallop
	ZG921	WS Lynx AH9A	AAC, Middle Wallop (for disposal)
	ZG922	WS Lynx AH9	Privately owned, Staverton, instructional use
	ZG923	WS Lynx AH9A	AAC Middle Wallop, RTP
	ZG969	Pilatus PC-9 (HB-HQE)	BAE Systems, Warton, GI use
	ZG993	PBN 2T Islander AL1 (G-BOMD)	Army Flying Museum, Middle Wallop
	ZG994	PBN 2T Islander AL1 (G-BPLN) (fuselage)	*Scrapped at Bembridge*
	ZG995	PBN 2T Defender R2 (G-SURV)	RAF No 651 Sqn/5 Regt, Aldergrove
	ZG996	PBN 2T Defender R2 (G-BWPR)	RAF No 651 Sqn/5 Regt, Aldergrove
	ZG997	PBN 2T Defender R2 (G-BWPV)	RAF No 651 Sqn/5 Regt, Aldergrove
	ZG998	PBN 2T Defender R2 (G-BWPX)	RAF No 651 Sqn/5 Regt, Aldergrove
	ZH001	PBN 2T Defender R2 (G-CEIO)	RAF No 651 Sqn/5 Regt, Aldergrove
	ZH002	PBN 2T Defender R2 (G-CEIP)	MoD/Britten-Norman, Lee-on-Solent
	ZH003	PBN 2T Defender R2 (G-CEIR)	RAF No 651 Sqn/5 Regt, Aldergrove
	ZH004	PBN 2T Defender T3 (G-BWPO)	MoD/Britten-Norman, Lee-on-Solent
	ZH005	PBN 2T Defender R2 (G-CGVB)	RAF No 651 Sqn/5 Regt, Aldergrove
	ZH101	Boeing E-3D Sentry AEW1 [01]	RAF No 8 Sqn/No 54 Sqn, Waddington
	ZH102	Boeing E-3D Sentry AEW1 [02]	RAF, stored Waddington
	ZH103	Boeing E-3D Sentry AEW1 [03]	RAF No 8 Sqn/No 54 Sqn, Waddington
	ZH104	Boeing E-3D Sentry AEW1 [04]	RAF, stored Lake Charles Airport, USA
	ZH105	Boeing E-3D Sentry AEW1 [05]	RAF, stored Waddington
	ZH106	Boeing E-3D Sentry AEW1 [06]	RAF No 8 Sqn/No 54 Sqn, Waddington
	ZH107	Boeing E-3D Sentry AEW1 [07] $	RAF, stored Waddington
	ZH115	Grob G109B Vigilant T1 [TA]	RAF, stored Little Rissington
	ZH116	Grob G109B Vigilant T1 [TB]	RAF, stored Watton
	ZH117	Grob G109B Vigilant T1 [TC]	RAF, stored Little Rissington
	ZH118	Grob G109B Vigilant T1 [TD]	RAF, stored Watton
	ZH119	Grob G109B Vigilant T1 (fuselage)	RAF, stored Little Rissington
	ZH120	Grob G109B Vigilant T1 [TF]	RAF, stored Little Rissington
	ZH121	Grob G109B Vigilant T1 [TG]	RAF, stored Little Rissington
	ZH122	Grob G109B Vigilant T1 [TH]	RAF, stored Little Rissington
	ZH123	Grob G109B Vigilant T1 [TJ]	RAF, stored Little Rissington
	ZH124	Grob G109B Vigilant T1 [TK]	RAF, stored Little Rissington
	ZH125	Grob G109B Vigilant T1 [TL]	RAF, stored Little Rissington
	ZH126	Grob G109B Vigilant T1 (D-KGRA) [TM]	RAF, stored Little Rissington
	ZH127	Grob G109B Vigilant T1 (D-KEEC) [TN]	RAF/Serco, stored Syerston
	ZH128	Grob G109B Vigilant T1 [TP]	RAF/Serco, stored Syerston
	ZH129	Grob G109B Vigilant T1 [TQ]	RAF/Serco, stored Syerston
	ZH139	BAe Harrier GR7 <R> (BAPC.191/ZD472)	*Currently not known*
	ZH144	Grob G109B Vigilant T1 [TR]	Grob Aircraft, Tussenhausen, Germany (for disposal)
	ZH145	Grob G109B Vigilant T1 [TS]	RAF, stored Little Rissington
	ZH146	Grob G109B Vigilant T1 [TT]	RAF, stored Linton-on-Ouse
	ZH147	Grob G109B Vigilant T1 [TU]	RAF, stored Little Rissington
	ZH148	Grob G109B Vigilant T1 [TV]	RAF, stored Little Rissington
	ZH184	Grob G109B Vigilant T1 [TW]	RAF, stored Little Rissington

Serial	Type (code/other identity)	Owner/operator, location or fate	Notes
ZH185	Grob G109B Vigilant T1 [TX]	RAF/Serco, stored Syerston	
ZH186	Grob G109B Vigilant T1 [TY]	RAF, stored Little Rissington	
ZH187	Grob G109B Vigilant T1 [TZ]	RAF, stored Little Rissington	
ZH188	Grob G109B Vigilant T1 [UA]	RAF, stored Little Rissington	
ZH189	Grob G109B Vigilant T1 [UB]	RAF, stored Little Rissington	
ZH190	Grob G109B Vigilant T1 [UC]	RAF, stored Little Rissington	
ZH191	Grob G109B Vigilant T1 [UD]	RAF, stored Abingdon	
ZH192	Grob G109B Vigilant T1 [UE]	RAF, stored Little Rissington	
ZH193	Grob G109B Vigilant T1 [UF]	RAF, stored Little Rissington	
ZH194	Grob G109B Vigilant T1 [UG]	RAF, stored Little Rissington	
ZH195	Grob G109B Vigilant T1 [UH]	RAF, stored Little Rissington	
ZH196	Grob G109B Vigilant T1 [UJ]	RAF, stored Little Rissington	
ZH197	Grob G109B Vigilant T1 [UK]	RAF, stored Little Rissington	
ZH200	BAe Hawk 200	Loughborough University ·	
ZH205	Grob G109B Vigilant T1 [UL]	RAF, stored Linton-on-Ouse	
ZH206	Grob G109B Vigilant T1 [UM]	RAF/Serco, stored Syerston	
ZH207	Grob G109B Vigilant T1 [UN]	RAF, stored Little Rissington	
ZH208	Grob G109B Vigilant T1 [UP]	RAF, stored Little Rissington	
ZH209	Grob G109B Vigilant T1 [UQ]	RAF, stored Little Rissington	
ZH211	Grob G109B Vigilant T1 [UR]	RAF, stored Little Rissington	
ZH247	Grob G109B Vigilant T1 [US]	RAF, stored Little Rissington	
ZH248	Grob G109B Vigilant T1 [UT]	RAF, stored Little Rissington	
ZH249	Grob G109B Vigilant T1 [UU]	RAF/Serco, stored Syerston	
ZH257	B-V CH-47C Chinook (9217M) (fuselage)	RAF Odiham, BDRT	
ZH263	Grob G109B Vigilant T1 [UV]	RAF, stored Little Rissington	
ZH264	Grob G109B Vigilant T1 [UW]	RAF, stored Little Rissington	
ZH265	Grob G109B Vigilant T1 [UX]	RAF, stored Little Rissington	
ZH266	Grob G109B Vigilant T1 [UY]	RAF, stored Abingdon	
ZH267	Grob G109B Vigilant T1 [UZ]	RAF, stored Little Rissington	
ZH268	Grob G109B Vigilant T1 [SA]	RAF, stored Little Rissington	
ZH269	Grob G109B Vigilant T1 [SB]	RAF, stored Little Rissington	
ZH270	Grob G109B Vigilant T1 [SC]	RAF, stored Little Rissington	
ZH271	Grob G109B Vigilant T1 [SD]	RAF Topcliffe, GI use	
ZH278	Grob G109B Vigilant T1 (D-KAIS) [SF]	RAF, stored Little Rissington	
ZH279	Grob G109B Vigilant T1 (D-KNPS) [SG]	RAF, stored Little Rissington	
ZH552	Panavia Tornado F3	RAF Leeming, at main gate	
ZH553	Panavia Tornado F3 [RT]	MoD, Cornwall Aviation Heritage Centre, Newquay	
ZH588	Eurofighter Typhoon (DA2)	RAF Museum, Hendon	
ZH590	Eurofighter Typhoon (DA4)	IWM Duxford	
ZH654	BAe Harrier T10 <ff>	Currently not known	
ZH655	BAe Harrier T10 <ff>	Privately owned, Worksop, Notts	
ZH658	BAe Harrier T10 (fuselage)	Privately owned, Sproughton	
ZH763	BAC 1-11/539GL (G-BGKE)	Aerohub, Newquay	
ZH775	B-V Chinook HC6A (N7424J)	RAF No 27 Sqn, Odiham	
ZH776	B-V Chinook HC6A (N7424L)	MoD/StandardAero, Fleetlands	
ZH777	B-V Chinook HC6A (N7424M)	RAF No 18 Sqn, Odiham	
ZH796	BAe Sea Harrier FA2 [001/L]	DSAE No 1 SoTT, stored Cosford	
ZH797	BAe Sea Harrier FA2 [97/DD]	SFDO, RNAS Culdrose	
ZH798	BAe Sea Harrier FA2 [98/DD]	SFDO, RNAS Culdrose	
ZH800	BAe Sea Harrier FA2 (ZH801) [123]	RNAS Yeovilton, stored	
ZH801	BAe Sea Harrier FA2 (ZH800) [001]	RNAS Yeovilton, stored	
ZH802	BAe Sea Harrier FA2 [02/DD]	SFDO, RNAS Culdrose	
ZH803	BAe Sea Harrier FA2 (G-RNFA) [03/DD]	Privately owned, St Athan	
ZH804	BAe Sea Harrier FA2 [003/L]	RN, stored Culdrose	
ZH806	BAe Sea Harrier FA2 [007]	Privately owned, Bentwaters	
ZH807	BAe Sea Harrier FA2 <ff>	Privately owned, Thorpe Wood, N Yorks	
ZH811	BAe Sea Harrier FA2 [002/L]	RN, stored Culdrose	
ZH812	BAe Sea Harrier FA2 [005/L]	Privately owned, Bentwaters	
ZH813	BAe Sea Harrier FA2 [13/DD]	SFDO, RNAS Culdrose	
ZH814	Bell 212HP AH1 (G-BGMH) [X]	AAC No 7 Flt, Brunei	
ZH815	Bell 212HP AH1 (G-BGCZ) [Y]	AAC No 7 Flt, Brunei	
ZH816	Bell 212HP AH1 (G-BGMG)	AAC No 7 Flt, Brunei	

Notes	Serial	Type (code/other identity)	Owner/operator, location or fate
	ZH821	EHI-101 Merlin HM1	Morayvia, Kinloss
	ZH822	EHI-101 Merlin HM1	MoD/Leonardo MW, Yeovil
	ZH823	EHI-101 Merlin HM1	*To Karup, Denmark for GI use, 2019*
	ZH824	EHI-101 Merlin HM2	RN MDMF, Culdrose
	ZH825	EHI-101 Merlin HM2 [583]	RN
	ZH826	EHI-101 Merlin HM2 [11]	RN No 820 NAS, Culdrose
	ZH827	EHI-101 Merlin HM2 [10]	RN No 820 NAS, Culdrose
	ZH828	EHI-101 Merlin HM2 [88/CU]	RN No 814 NAS, Culdrose
	ZH829	EHI-101 Merlin HM2 (Crowsnest)	MoD/Leonardo MW, Yeovil
	ZH830	EHI-101 Merlin HM1 [88]	QinetiQ, stored Boscombe Down
	ZH831	EHI-101 Merlin HM2 (Crowsnest)	MoD/Leonardo MW, Yeovil
	ZH832	EHI-101 Merlin HM2 [81]	MoD/AFD/QinetiQ, Boscombe Down
	ZH833	EHI-101 Merlin HM2 (Crowsnest)	MoD/Leonardo MW, Yeovil (conversion)
	ZH834	EHI-101 Merlin HM2 [87]	RN No 824 NAS, Culdrose
	ZH835	EHI-101 Merlin HM2	RN MDMF, Culdrose
	ZH836	EHI-101 Merlin HM2 [80]	RN No 824 NAS, Culdrose
	ZH837	EHI-101 Merlin HM2 [14]	RN No 820 NAS, Culdrose
	ZH838	EHI-101 Merlin HM1 [70]	QinetiQ, stored Boscombe Down
	ZH839	EHI-101 Merlin HM2 [69]	RN No 814 NAS, Culdrose
	ZH840	EHI-101 Merlin HM2 [81]	RN No 824 NAS, Culdrose
	ZH841	EHI-101 Merlin HM2 [84]	RN No 824 NAS, Culdrose
	ZH842	EHI-101 Merlin HM2 [82]	RN No 814 NAS, Culdrose
	ZH843	EHI-101 Merlin HM2	RN MDMF, Culdrose
	ZH845	EHI-101 Merlin HM2	RN No 814 NAS, Culdrose
	ZH846	EHI-101 Merlin HM2 [12/CU]	RN MDMF, Culdrose
	ZH847	EHI-101 Merlin HM2 [66/CU]	RN No 814 NAS, Culdrose
	ZH848	EHI-101 Merlin HM1	QinetiQ, stored Boscombe Down
	ZH849	EHI-101 Merlin HM1 [67]	QinetiQ, stored Boscombe Down
	ZH850	EHI-101 Merlin HM2 [83]	RN No 824 NAS, Culdrose
	ZH851	EHI-101 Merlin HM2 [88]	RN No 824 NAS, Culdrose
	ZH852	EHI-101 Merlin HM1(mod)	QinetiQ, stored Boscombe Down
	ZH853	EHI-101 Merlin HM2 [68]	RN No 814 NAS, Culdrose
	ZH854	EHI-101 Merlin HM2	RN MDMF, Culdrose
	ZH855	EHI-101 Merlin HM1 [68]	QinetiQ, stored Boscombe Down
	ZH856	EHI-101 Merlin HM2 [11]	RN No 820 NAS, Culdrose
	ZH857	EHI-101 Merlin HM2	RN No 820 NAS, Culdrose
	ZH858	EHI-101 Merlin HM1 [17]	QinetiQ, stored Boscombe Down
	ZH860	EHI-101 Merlin HM2	RN No 814 NAS, Culdrose
	ZH861	EHI-101 Merlin HM2 [85]	RN MDMF, Culdrose
	ZH862	EHI-101 Merlin HM2 [86]	RN No 824 NAS, Culdrose
	ZH863	EHI-101 Merlin HM1 [80]	RN stored, QinetiQ Boscombe Down
	ZH864	EHI-101 Merlin HM2 (Crowsnest) [85]	MoD/AFD/QinetiQ, Boscombe Down
	ZH865	Lockheed C-130J-30 Hercules C4 (N130JA) [865]	RAF No 24 Sqn/No 30 Sqn/No 47 Sqn, Brize Norton
	ZH866	Lockheed C-130J-30 Hercules C4 (N130JE) [866] $	MoD/MADG, stored Cambridge
	ZH867	Lockheed C-130J-30 Hercules C4 (N130JJ) [867]	MoD/MADG, Cambridge
	ZH868	Lockheed C-130J-30 Hercules C4 (N130JN) [868]	MoD/MADG, Cambridge
	ZH869	Lockheed C-130J-30 Hercules C4 (N130JV) [869]	RAF No 24 Sqn/No 30 Sqn/No 47 Sqn, Brize Norton
	ZH870	Lockheed C-130J-30 Hercules C4 (N78235) [870]	MoD/MADG, Cambridge
	ZH871	Lockheed C-130J-30 Hercules C4 (N73238) [871]	RAF No 24 Sqn/No 30 Sqn/No 47 Sqn, Brize Norton
	ZH872	Lockheed C-130J-30 Hercules C4 (N4249Y) [872]	RAF No 24 Sqn/No 30 Sqn/No 47 Sqn, Brize Norton
	ZH874	Lockheed C-130J-30 Hercules C4 (N41030) [874]	MoD/MADG, Cambridge
	ZH875	Lockheed C-130J-30 Hercules C4 (N4099R) [875]	RAF No 24 Sqn/No 30 Sqn/No 47 Sqn, Brize Norton
	ZH877	Lockheed C-130J-30 Hercules C4 (N4081M) [877]	RAF No 24 Sqn/No 30 Sqn/No 47 Sqn, Brize Norton
	ZH878	Lockheed C-130J-30 Hercules C4 (N73232) [878]	RAF No 24 Sqn/No 30 Sqn/No 47 Sqn, Brize Norton
	ZH879	Lockheed C-130J-30 Hercules C4 (N4080M) [879]	RAF No 24 Sqn/No 30 Sqn/No 47 Sqn, Brize Norton
	ZH880	Lockheed C-130J Hercules C5 (N73238) [880]	MADG, Cambridge, for R Bahraini AF as 701
	ZH881	Lockheed C-130J Hercules C5 (N4081M) [881]	*To Bangladesh AF as 99-5479/S3-AGE, 23 August 2019*
	ZH882	Lockheed C-130J Hercules C5 (N4099R) [882]	MADG, Cambridge, for Bangladesh AF as 99-5480
	ZH883	Lockheed C-130J Hercules C5 (N4242N) [883] $	MADG, Cambridge, for Bangladesh AF as 99-5481
	ZH884	Lockheed C-130J Hercules C5 (N4249Y) [884]	MADG, Cambridge, for Bangladesh AF as 99-5482/S3-AGF
	ZH885	Lockheed C-130J Hercules C5 (N41030) [885]	MADG, Cambridge, for the US Navy

Serial	Type (code/other identity)	Owner/operator, location or fate	Notes
ZH887	Lockheed C-130J Hercules C5 (N4187W) [887] $	MADG, Cambridge, for Bangladesh AF as 99-5485	
ZH888	Lockheed C-130J Hercules C5 (N4187) [888]	RAF No 24 Sqn/No 30 Sqn/No 47 Sqn, Brize Norton	
ZH889	Lockheed C-130J Hercules C5 (N4099R) [889]	RAF No 24 Sqn/No 30 Sqn/No 47 Sqn, Brize Norton	
ZH890	Grob G109B Vigilant T1 [SE]	RAF, stored Little Rissington	
ZH891	B-V Chinook HC6A (N20075)	RAF No 27 Sqn, Odiham	
ZH892	B-V Chinook HC6A (N2019V)	MoD/StandardAero, Fleetlands	
ZH893	B-V Chinook HC6A (N2025L)	RAF No 28 Sqn, Benson	
ZH894	B-V Chinook HC6A (N2026E)	RAF No 27 Sqn, Odiham	
ZH895	B-V Chinook HC6A (N2034K)	RAF No 28 Sqn, Benson	
ZH896	B-V Chinook HC6A (N2038G)	MoD/StandardAero, Fleetlands	
ZH897	B-V Chinook HC5 (N2045G)	RAF No 27 Sqn, Odiham	
ZH898	B-V Chinook HC5 (N2057Q)	RAF No 1310 Flt, Mali	
ZH899	B-V Chinook HC5 (N2057R)	MoD/StandardAero, Fleetlands	
ZH900	B-V Chinook HC5 (N2060H)	RAF No 27 Sqn, Odiham	
ZH901	B-V Chinook HC5 (N2060M)	MoD/Boeing, Boscombe Down (update)	
ZH902	B-V Chinook HC5 (N2064W)	RAF No 27 Sqn, Odiham	
ZH903	B-V Chinook HC5 (N20671)	MoD/Boeing, Boscombe Down (update)	
ZH904	B-V Chinook HC5 (N2083K)	RAF No 1310 Flt, Mali	
ZH966	Westland Lynx Mk.21A (AH-11B) (N-4005)	*To the Brazilian Navy as N-4005, January 2020*	
ZJ100	BAe Hawk 102D	BAE Systems National Training Academy, Humberside	
ZJ117	EHI-101 Merlin HC3 [A]	QinetiQ, stored Boscombe Down	
ZJ118	EHI-101 Merlin HC4 [B]	MoD/Leonardo MW, Yeovil	
ZJ119	EHI-101 Merlin HC4 [C]	RN No 846 NAS, Yeovilton	
ZJ120	EHI-101 Merlin HC4 [D]	RN No 845 NAS, Yeovilton	
ZJ121	EHI-101 Merlin HC4 [E]	RN No 845 NAS, Yeovilton	
ZJ122	EHI-101 Merlin HC4 [F]	RN No 845 NAS, Yeovilton	
ZJ123	EHI-101 Merlin HC4 [G]	RN No 846 NAS, Yeovilton	
ZJ124	EHI-101 Merlin HC4 [H]	RN No 846 NAS, Yeovilton	
ZJ125	EHI-101 Merlin HC4 [J]	RN No 846 NAS, Yeovilton	
ZJ126	EHI-101 Merlin HC3i [K]	RN No 846 NAS, Yeovilton	
ZJ127	EHI-101 Merlin HC4 [L]	RN No 845 NAS, Yeovilton	
ZJ128	EHI-101 Merlin HC4 [M]	RN No 846 NAS, Yeovilton	
ZJ129	EHI-101 Merlin HC4 [N]	RN No 845 NAS, Yeovilton	
ZJ130	EHI-101 Merlin HC3i [O]	RN No 846 NAS, Yeovilton	
ZJ131	EHI-101 Merlin HC4 [P]	RN No 845 NAS, Yeovilton	
ZJ132	EHI-101 Merlin HC3i [Q]	RN No 846 NAS, Yeovilton	
ZJ133	EHI-101 Merlin HC3 [R]	QinetiQ, stored Boscombe Down	
ZJ134	EHI-101 Merlin HC4 [S]	RN No 845 NAS, Yeovilton	
ZJ135	EHI-101 Merlin HC3i [T]	RN No 846 NAS, Yeovilton	
ZJ136	EHI-101 Merlin HC3i [U]	RN MDMF, Culdrose	
ZJ137	EHI-101 Merlin HC3i [W]	RN MDMF, Culdrose	
ZJ138	EHI-101 Merlin HC3 [X]	RN, Yeovilton, GI use	
ZJ164	AS365N-2 Dauphin 2 (G-BTLC)	RN/Bond Helicopters, Newquay	
ZJ165	AS365N-2 Dauphin 2 (G-NTOO)	RN/Bond Helicopters, Newquay	
ZJ166	WAH-64 Apache AH1 (N9219G)	MoD/Boeing, Mesa, USA	
ZJ167	WAH-64 Apache AH1 (N3266B)	MoD/Boeing, Mesa, USA	
ZJ168	WAH-64 Apache AH1 (N3123T)	MoD/Boeing, Mesa, USA	
ZJ169	WAH-64 Apache AH1 (N3114H)	MoD/Boeing, Mesa, USA	
ZJ170	WAH-64 Apache AH1 (N3065U)	MoD/Boeing, Mesa, USA	
ZJ171	WAH-64 Apache AH1 (N3266T)	AAC ADSU, stored Wattisham	
ZJ172	WAH-64 Apache AH1	MoD/Boeing, Mesa, USA	
ZJ173	WAH-64 Apache AH1 (N3266W)	MoD/Boeing, Mesa, USA	
ZJ174	WAH-64 Apache AH1	MoD/Boeing, Mesa, USA	
ZJ175	WAH-64 Apache AH1 (N3218V)	MoD/Boeing, Mesa, USA	
ZJ176	WAH-64 Apache AH1	MoD/Boeing, Mesa, USA	
ZJ177	WAH-64 Apache AH1	RN No 1710 NAS, Portsmouth	
ZJ178	WAH-64 Apache AH1	AAC No 673 Sqn/7 Regt, Middle Wallop	
ZJ179	WAH-64 Apache AH1	AAC No 3 Regt, Wattisham	
ZJ180	WAH-64 Apache AH1	MoD/Boeing, Mesa, USA	
ZJ181	WAH-64 Apache AH1	AAC No 3 Regt, Wattisham	
ZJ182	WAH-64 Apache AH1	AAC No 4 Regt, Wattisham	

Notes	Serial	Type (code/other identity)	Owner/operator, location or fate
	ZJ183	WAH-64 Apache AH1	AAC No 4 Regt, Wattisham
	ZJ184	WAH-64 Apache AH1	MoD/Boeing, Mesa, USA
	ZJ185	WAH-64 Apache AH1	MoD/Boeing, Mesa, USA
	ZJ186	WAH-64 Apache AH1	AAC No 3 Regt, Wattisham
	ZJ187	WAH-64 Apache AH1	AAC No 4 Regt, Wattisham
	ZJ188	WAH-64 Apache AH1	AAC No 3 Regt, Wattisham
	ZJ189	WAH-64 Apache AH1	AAC No 4 Regt, Wattisham
	ZJ190	WAH-64 Apache AH1	AAC No 4 Regt, Wattisham
	ZJ191	WAH-64 Apache AH1	AAC No 3 Regt, Wattisham
	ZJ192	WAH-64 Apache AH1	AAC No 3 Regt, Wattisham
	ZJ193	WAH-64 Apache AH1	AAC No 3 Regt, Wattisham
	ZJ194	WAH-64 Apache AH1	AAC No 3 Regt, Wattisham
	ZJ195	WAH-64 Apache AH1	AAC No 4 Regt, Wattisham
	ZJ196	WAH-64 Apache AH1	AAC No 673 Sqn/7 Regt, Middle Wallop
	ZJ197	WAH-64 Apache AH1	AAC No 4 Regt, Wattisham
	ZJ198	WAH-64 Apache AH1	AAC No 4 Regt, Wattisham
	ZJ199	WAH-64 Apache AH1	AAC No 3 Regt, Wattisham
	ZJ200	WAH-64 Apache AH1	AAC No 3 Regt, Wattisham
	ZJ202	WAH-64 Apache AH1	MoD/Boeing, Mesa, USA
	ZJ203	WAH-64 Apache AH1	AAC No 673 Sqn/7 Regt, Middle Wallop
	ZJ204	WAH-64 Apache AH1	AAC No 673 Sqn/7 Regt, Middle Wallop
	ZJ205	WAH-64 Apache AH1	AAC No 3 Regt, Wattisham
	ZJ206	WAH-64 Apache AH1	MoD/Boeing, Mesa, USA
	ZJ207	WAH-64 Apache AH1	AAC No 673 Sqn/7 Regt, Middle Wallop
	ZJ208	WAH-64 Apache AH1	AAC No 3 Regt, Wattisham
	ZJ209	WAH-64 Apache AH1	AAC No 673 Sqn/7 Regt, Middle Wallop
	ZJ210	WAH-64 Apache AH1	AAC No 4 Regt, Wattisham
	ZJ211	WAH-64 Apache AH1	AAC No 3 Regt, Wattisham
	ZJ212	WAH-64 Apache AH1	MoD/Boeing, Mesa, USA
	ZJ213	WAH-64 Apache AH1	AAC No 4 Regt, Wattisham
	ZJ214	WAH-64 Apache AH1	MoD/Boeing, Mesa, USA
	ZJ215	WAH-64 Apache AH1	AAC No 4 Regt, Wattisham
	ZJ216	WAH-64 Apache AH1	AAC No 673 Sqn/7 Regt, Middle Wallop
	ZJ217	WAH-64 Apache AH1	AAC No 3 Regt, Wattisham
	ZJ218	WAH-64 Apache AH1	AAC No 4 Regt, Wattisham
	ZJ219	WAH-64 Apache AH1	MoD/Boeing, Mesa, USA
	ZJ220	WAH-64 Apache AH1	MoD/Boeing, Mesa, USA
	ZJ221	WAH-64 Apache AH1	AAC No 4 Regt, Wattisham
	ZJ222	WAH-64 Apache AH1	AAC No 3 Regt, Wattisham
	ZJ223	WAH-64 Apache AH1	AAC No 4 Regt, Wattisham
	ZJ224	WAH-64 Apache AH1	AAC No 4 Regt, Wattisham
	ZJ225	WAH-64 Apache AH1	AAC No 4 Regt, Wattisham
	ZJ226	WAH-64 Apache AH1	AAC No 4 Regt, Wattisham
	ZJ227	WAH-64 Apache AH1	AAC No 673 Sqn/7 Regt, Middle Wallop
	ZJ228	WAH-64 Apache AH1	AAC No 3 Regt, Wattisham
	ZJ229	WAH-64 Apache AH1	MoD/Boeing, Mesa, USA
	ZJ230	WAH-64 Apache AH1	AAC Wattisham (damaged)
	ZJ231	WAH-64 Apache AH1	AAC No 3 Regt, Wattisham
	ZJ232	WAH-64 Apache AH1	MoD/Boeing, Mesa, USA
	ZJ233	WAH-64 Apache AH1	AAC No 673 Sqn/7 Regt, Middle Wallop
	ZJ240	Bell 412EP Griffin HT1 (G-BXIR) [U]	MoD/Cobham Helicopter Academy, Newquay
	ZJ242	Bell 412EP Griffin HT1 (G-BXDK) [E]	MoD/Cobham Helicopter Academy, Newquay
	ZJ243	AS350BB Squirrel HT2 (G-BWZS) [43]	MoD/Cobham Helicopter Academy, Newquay
	ZJ244	AS350BB Squirrel HT2 (G-BXMD) [44]	MoD/Cobham Helicopter Academy, Newquay
	ZJ246	AS350BB Squirrel HT2 (G-BXMJ) [46]	MoD/Cobham Helicopter Academy, Newquay
	ZJ248	AS350BB Squirrel HT2 (G-BXNE) [48]	MoD/Cobham Helicopter Academy, Newquay
	ZJ249	AS350BB Squirrel HT2 (G-BXNJ) [49]	MoD/Cobham, Bournemouth
	ZJ250	AS350BB Squirrel HT2 (G-BXNY) [50]	MoD/Cobham, Bournemouth
	ZJ251	AS350BB Squirrel HT2 (G-BXOG) [51]	MoD/Cobham, Bournemouth
	ZJ252	AS350BB Squirrel HT2 (G-BXOK) [52]	MoD/Cobham Helicopter Academy, Newquay
	ZJ253	AS350BB Squirrel HT2 (G-BXPG) [53]	MoD/Cobham, Bournemouth
	ZJ254	AS350BB Squirrel HT2 (G-BXPJ) [54]	MoD/Cobham, Bournemouth

Serial	Type (code/other identity)	Owner/operator, location or fate	Notes
ZJ264	AS350BB Squirrel HT1 (G-BXHW) [64]	MoD/Cobham, Bournemouth	
ZJ267	AS350BB Squirrel HT1 (G-BXIP) [67]	MoD/Cobham, Bournemouth	
ZJ268	AS350BB Squirrel HT1 (G-BXJE) [68]	MoD/Cobham, Bournemouth	
ZJ271	AS350BB Squirrel HT1 (G-BXKE) [71]	MoD/Cobham, Bournemouth	
ZJ272	AS350BB Squirrel HT1 (G-BXKN) [72]	MoD/Cobham, Bournemouth	
ZJ273	AS350BB Squirrel HT1 (G-BXKP) [73]	MoD/Cobham, Bournemouth	
ZJ277	AS350BB Squirrel HT1 (G-BXLH) [77]	MoD/Cobham, Bournemouth	
ZJ279	AS350BB Squirrel HT1 (G-BXMC) [79]	MoD/Cobham, Bournemouth	
ZJ369	GEC Phoenix RPAS	Defence Academy of the UK, Shrivenham	
ZJ385	GEC Phoenix RPAS	Muckleburgh Collection, Weybourne, Norfolk	
ZJ392	GEC Phoenix RPAS	*Sold to Belgium*	
ZJ449	GEC Phoenix RPAS	REME Museum, Lyneham	
ZJ452	GEC Phoenix RPAS	Science Museum, stored Wroughton	
ZJ469	GEC Phoenix RPAS	Army, Larkhill, on display	
ZJ481	Northrop MQM-74C Chukar D2	RNAS Culdrose, preserved	
ZJ493	GAF Jindivik 104AL (A92-814)	RAF Museum Reserve Collection, Stafford	
ZJ496	GAF Jindivik 104AL (A92-901)	Farnborough Air Sciences Trust, Farnborough	
ZJ515	BAE Systems Nimrod MRA4 (XV258) <ff>	Cranfield University, instructional use	
ZJ620	AgustaWestland Merlin Simulator	RN No 824 NAS, Culdrose	
ZJ621	AgustaWestland Merlin Simulator	RN No 824 NAS, Culdrose	
ZJ622	AgustaWestland Merlin Simulator	RN No 824 NAS, Culdrose	
ZJ623	AgustaWestland Merlin Simulator	RN No 824 NAS, Culdrose	
ZJ624	AgustaWestland Merlin Simulator	RN No 824 NAS, Culdrose	
ZJ625	AgustaWestland Merlin Simulator	RN No 824 NAS, Culdrose	
ZJ626	AgustaWestland Merlin Simulator	RN No 824 NAS, Culdrose	
ZJ645	D-BD Alpha Jet (98+62) [45]	*Sold to Canada, February 2020*	
ZJ646	D-BD Alpha Jet (98+55) [46]	*Sold as C-FTOK, June 2019*	
ZJ647	D-BD Alpha Jet (98+71) [47]	*Sold as C-GTOJ, June 2019*	
ZJ648	D-BD Alpha Jet (98+09) [48]	*Sold as C-GVTA, June 2019*	
ZJ649	D-BD Alpha Jet (98+73) [49]	*Sold to Canada, February 2020*	
ZJ650	D-BD Alpha Jet (98+35)	*Sold to Canada, February 2020*	
ZJ651	D-BD Alpha Jet (41+42) [51]	*Sold to Canada, February 2020*	
ZJ652	D-BD Alpha Jet (41+09)	*Sold to Canada, February 2020*	
ZJ653	D-BD Alpha Jet (40+22)	*Sold to Canada, February 2020*	
ZJ654	D-BD Alpha Jet (41+02)	*Sold to Canada, February 2020*	
ZJ655	D-BD Alpha Jet (41+19)	*Sold to Canada, February 2020*	
ZJ656	D-BD Alpha Jet (41+40)	*Sold to Canada, February 2020*	
ZJ690	Bombardier Sentinel R1 (C-GJRG)	MoD/Raytheon, Hawarden	
ZJ691	Bombardier Sentinel R1 (C-FZVM)	RAF No 5 Sqn, Waddington	
ZJ692	Bombardier Sentinel R1 (C-FZWW)	RAF No 5 Sqn, Waddington	
ZJ693	Bombardier Sentinel R1 (C-FZXC)	MoD/Raytheon, Hawarden	
ZJ694	Bombardier Sentinel R1 (C-FZYL)	RAF No 5 Sqn, Waddington	
ZJ699	Eurofighter Typhoon (PT001)	MoD/BAE Systems, Warton	
ZJ700	Eurofighter Typhoon (PS002)	MoD/BAE Systems, Warton	
ZJ703	Bell 412EP Griffin HAR2 (G-CBST) [Spades,3]	RAF No 84 Sqn, Akrotiri	
ZJ704	Bell 412EP Griffin HAR2 (G-CBWT) [Clubs,4]	RAF No 84 Sqn, Akrotiri	
ZJ705	Bell 412EP Griffin HAR2 (G-CBXL) [Hearts,5]	MoD/ETPS, Boscombe Down	
ZJ706	Bell 412EP Griffin HAR2 (G-CBYR) [Diamonds,6]	RAF No 84 Sqn, Akrotiri	
ZJ707	Bell 412EP Griffin HT1 (G-CBUB)	MoD/Cobham Helicopter Academy, Newquay	
ZJ765	Meteor Mirach 100/5	QinetiQ Apprentice Training School, Boscombe Down	
ZJ780	AS365N-3 Dauphin AH1 (G-CEXT)	AAC No 658 Sqn, Credenhill	
ZJ781	AS365N-3 Dauphin AH1 (G-CEXU)	AAC No 658 Sqn, Credenhill	
ZJ782	AS365N-3 Dauphin AH1 (G-CEXV)	AAC No 658 Sqn, Credenhill	
ZJ783	AS365N-3 Dauphin AH1 (G-CEXW)	AAC No 658 Sqn, Credenhill	
ZJ785	AS365N-3 Dauphin AH1 (G-CFFW)	AAC No 658 Sqn, Credenhill	
ZJ787	AS365N-3 Dauphin AH1 (G-CHNJ)	AAC No 658 Sqn, Credenhill	
ZJ800	Eurofighter Typhoon T3 [BC]	BAE Systems Aircraft Maintenance Academy, Humberside	
ZJ801	Eurofighter Typhoon T3 [BJ]	BAE Systems, Warton (stress testing)	
ZJ802	Eurofighter Typhoon T3 [802]	*Scrapped, February 2019*	
ZJ803	Eurofighter Typhoon T3 (fuselage)	*Scrapped, 2018*	
ZJ804	Eurofighter Typhoon T3 (fuselage)	*Scrapped, 2018*	
ZJ805	Eurofighter Typhoon T3 [BD]	*Scrapped, March 2019*	

Notes	Serial	Type (code/other identity)	Owner/operator, location or fate
	ZJ806	Eurofighter Typhoon T3 (fuselage)	*Scrapped, 2018*
	ZJ807	Eurofighter Typhoon T3 (fuselage)	MoD JARTS, Boscombe Down
	ZJ808	Eurofighter Typhoon T3 (fuselage)	*Scrapped, 2018*
	ZJ809	Eurofighter Typhoon T3 (fuselage)	*Scrapped, 2018*
	ZJ810	Eurofighter Typhoon T3 (fuselage)	RAF, stored Coningsby
	ZJ811	Eurofighter Typhoon T3 (fuselage)	*Scrapped, 2018*
	ZJ812	Eurofighter Typhoon T3 (fuselage)	*Scrapped, January 2019*
	ZJ813	Eurofighter Typhoon T3 (fuselage)	*Scrapped, May 2019*
	ZJ814	Eurofighter Typhoon T3 (fuselage)	*Scrapped, 2018*
	ZJ815	Eurofighter Typhoon T3 (fuselage)	*Scrapped, 2018*
	ZJ910	Eurofighter Typhoon FGR4 [DO]	RAF AM&SU, stored Shawbury
	ZJ911	Eurofighter Typhoon FGR4 [QO-Z]	RAF AM&SU, stored Shawbury
	ZJ912	Eurofighter Typhoon FGR4 [912]	RAF AM&SU, stored Shawbury
	ZJ913	Eurofighter Typhoon FGR4 [913,WS-Y]	RAF No 9 Sqn, Lossiemouth
	ZJ914	Eurofighter Typhoon FGR4 [914]	RAF TMF, Coningsby
	ZJ915	Eurofighter Typhoon FGR4 [F]	RAF No 1435 Flt, Mount Pleasant, FI
	ZJ916	Eurofighter Typhoon FGR4 [916]	RAF No 29 Sqn, Coningsby
	ZJ917	Eurofighter Typhoon FGR4 [917,WS-R]	RAF No 9 Sqn, Lossiemouth
	ZJ918	Eurofighter Typhoon FGR4	RAF AM&SU, stored Shawbury
	ZJ919	Eurofighter Typhoon FGR4 [919]	RAF No 6 Sqn, Lossiemouth
	ZJ920	Eurofighter Typhoon FGR4 [920]	RAF No 29 Sqn, Coningsby
	ZJ921	Eurofighter Typhoon FGR4 [921]	RAF No 9 Sqn, Lossiemouth
	ZJ922	Eurofighter Typhoon FGR4 [QO-C]	MoD/BAE Systems, Warton
	ZJ923	Eurofighter Typhoon FGR4 [923]	RAF No 1 Sqn, Lossiemouth
	ZJ924	Eurofighter Typhoon FGR4 [924,WS-J]	RAF No 9 Sqn, Lossiemouth
	ZJ925	Eurofighter Typhoon FGR4 [DXI] $	RAF AM&SU, stored Shawbury
	ZJ926	Eurofighter Typhoon FGR4 [H]	RAF No 1435 Flt, Mount Pleasant, FI
	ZJ927	Eurofighter Typhoon FGR4 [927]	RAF AM&SU, stored Shawbury
	ZJ928	Eurofighter Typhoon FGR4 [928]	RAF No 29 Sqn, Coningsby
	ZJ929	Eurofighter Typhoon FGR4 [929]	RAF No 12 Sqn, Coningsby
	ZJ930	Eurofighter Typhoon FGR4 [930]	RAF AM&SU, stored Shawbury
	ZJ931	Eurofighter Typhoon FGR4 [931]	RAF No 29 Sqn, Coningsby
	ZJ932	Eurofighter Typhoon FGR4 [DB]	RAF AM&SU, stored Shawbury
	ZJ933	Eurofighter Typhoon FGR4 [C]	RAF No 1435 Flt, Mount Pleasant, FI
	ZJ934	Eurofighter Typhoon FGR4 [934]	RAF AM&SU, stored Shawbury
	ZJ935	Eurofighter Typhoon FGR4 [935]	RAF No 9 Sqn, Lossiemouth
	ZJ936	Eurofighter Typhoon FGR4 [QO-C]	RAF AM&SU, stored Shawbury
	ZJ937	Eurofighter Typhoon FGR4 [937]	RAF No 29 Sqn, Coningsby
	ZJ938	Eurofighter Typhoon FGR4	MoD/BAE Systems, Warton
	ZJ939	Eurofighter Typhoon FGR4 [939]	RAF TMF, Coningsby
	ZJ940	Eurofighter Typhoon FGR4 [DJ666]	RAF, stored Coningsby
	ZJ941	Eurofighter Typhoon FGR4 [D]	RAF No 1435 Flt, Mount Pleasant, FI
	ZJ942	Eurofighter Typhoon FGR4 [942]	RAF TMF, Coningsby
	ZJ943	Eurofighter Typhoon FGR4 (fuselage)	RAF AM&SU, stored Shawbury (wreck)
	ZJ944	Eurofighter Typhoon FGR4	RAF, stored Coningsby
	ZJ945	Eurofighter Typhoon FGR4	RAF, stored Coningsby
	ZJ946	Eurofighter Typhoon FGR4 [946]	RAF No 6 Sqn, Lossiemouth
	ZJ947	Eurofighter Typhoon FGR4 [947]	RAF No 9 Sqn, Lossiemouth
	ZJ948	Eurofighter Typhoon FGR4	RAF, stored Coningsby
	ZJ949	Eurofighter Typhoon FGR4 [949]	RAF TMF, Coningsby
	ZJ950	Eurofighter Typhoon FGR4 [950]	RAF No 6 Sqn, Lossiemouth
	ZJ951	BAE Systems Advanced Hawk 120D	MoD/BAE Systems, Warton (wfu)
	ZJ954	SA330H Puma HC2 (SAAF 144) [W]	RAF No 28 Sqn/No 33 Sqn/No 230 Sqn, Benson
	ZJ955	SA330H Puma HC2 (SAAF 148) [X]	RAF No 28 Sqn/No 33 Sqn/No 230 Sqn, Benson
	ZJ956	SA330H Puma HC2 (SAAF 172/F-ZWCC) [Y]	RAF No 28 Sqn/No 33 Sqn/No 230 Sqn, Benson
	ZJ957	SA330H Puma HC2 (SAAF 169) [Z]	RAF No 28 Sqn/No 33 Sqn/No 230 Sqn, Benson
	ZJ960	Grob G109B Vigilant T1 (D-KSMU) [SH]	RAF, stored Little Rissington
	ZJ961	Grob G109B Vigilant T1 (D-KLCW) [SJ]	RAF, stored Little Rissington
	ZJ962	Grob G109B Vigilant T1 (D-KBEU) [SK]	RAF, stored Little Rissington
	ZJ963	Grob G109B Vigilant T1 (D-KMSN) [SL]	RAF, stored Little Rissington
	ZJ967	Grob G109B Vigilant T1 (G-DEWS) [SM]	RAF, stored Little Rissington
	ZJ968	Grob G109B Vigilant T1 (N109BT) [SN]	RAF, stored Little Rissington

Serial	Type (code/other identity)	Owner/operator, location or fate	Notes
ZJ969	Bell 212HP AH1 (G-BGLJ) [K]	AAC JHC/No 7 Regt, Middle Wallop	
ZJ990	EHI-101 Merlin HC4A (M-501) [AA]	MoD/Leonardo MW, Yeovil (conversion)	
ZJ992	EHI-101 Merlin HC4A (M-503) [AB]	MoD/Leonardo MW, Yeovil (conversion)	
ZJ994	EHI-101 Merlin HC4A (M-505) [AC]	MoD/Leonardo MW, Yeovil (conversion)	
ZJ995	EHI-101 Merlin HC4A (M-506) [AD]	MoD/Leonardo MW, Yeovil	
ZJ998	EHI-101 Merlin HC4A (M-509) [AE]	MoD/Leonardo MW, Yeovil (conversion)	
ZK001	EHI-101 Merlin HC3A (M-511) [AF]	MoD/Leonardo MW, Yeovil (conversion)	
ZK005	Grob G109B Vigilant T1 (OH-797) [SP]	RAF, stored Little Rissington	
ZK010	BAE Systems Hawk T2 [FN]	RAF No 4 FTS/25 Sqn, Valley	
ZK011	BAE Systems Hawk T2 [B]	RAF No 4 FTS/4 Sqn, Valley	
ZK012	BAE Systems Hawk T2 [C]	RAF No 4 FTS/4 Sqn, Valley	
ZK013	BAE Systems Hawk T2 [D]	RAF No 4 FTS/4 Sqn, Valley	
ZK014	BAE Systems Hawk T2 [E]	RAF No 4 FTS/4 Sqn, Valley	
ZK015	BAE Systems Hawk T2 [F]	RAF No 4 FTS/4 Sqn, Valley	
ZK016	BAE Systems Hawk T2 [G]	RAF No 4 FTS/4 Sqn, Valley	
ZK017	BAE Systems Hawk T2 [H]	RAF No 4 FTS/4 Sqn, Valley	
ZK018	BAE Systems Hawk T2 [I]	RAF No 4 FTS/4 Sqn, Valley	
ZK019	BAE Systems Hawk T2 [J]	RAF No 4 FTS/4 Sqn, Valley	
ZK020	BAE Systems Hawk T2 [K] $	RAF No 4 FTS/4 Sqn, Valley	
ZK021	BAE Systems Hawk T2 [L]	RAF No 4 FTS/4 Sqn, Valley	
ZK022	BAE Systems Hawk T2 [M]	RAF No 4 FTS/4 Sqn, Valley	
ZK023	BAE Systems Hawk T2 [N]	RAF No 4 FTS/4 Sqn, Valley	
ZK024	BAE Systems Hawk T2 [O]	RAF, stored Valley	
ZK025	BAE Systems Hawk T2 [FA]	RAF No 4 FTS/25 Sqn, Valley	
ZK026	BAE Systems Hawk T2 [FB]	RAF No 4 FTS/25 Sqn, Valley	
ZK027	BAE Systems Hawk T2 [FC]	RAF No 4 FTS/25 Sqn, Valley	
ZK028	BAE Systems Hawk T2 [FD]	RAF No 4 FTS/25 Sqn, Valley	
ZK029	BAE Systems Hawk T2 [FE]	RAF No 4 FTS/25 Sqn, Valley	
ZK030	BAE Systems Hawk T2 [FF]	RAF No 4 FTS/25 Sqn, Valley	
ZK031	BAE Systems Hawk T2 [FG]	RAF No 4 FTS/25 Sqn, Valley	
ZK032	BAE Systems Hawk T2 [FH]	RAF No 4 FTS/25 Sqn, Valley	
ZK033	BAE Systems Hawk T2 [FI]	RAF No 4 FTS/25 Sqn, Valley	
ZK034	BAE Systems Hawk T2 [FJ]	RAF No 4 FTS/25 Sqn, Valley	
ZK035	BAE Systems Hawk T2 [FK]	RAF No 4 FTS/25 Sqn, Valley	
ZK036	BAE Systems Hawk T2 [FL]	RAF No 4 FTS/25 Sqn, Valley	
ZK037	BAE Systems Hawk T2 [FM]	RAF No 4 FTS/25 Sqn, Valley	
ZK067	Bell 212HP AH3 (G-BFER) [B]	AAC, Middle Wallop	
ZK114	M2370 RPAS	QinetiQ	
ZK150*	Lockheed Martin Desert Hawk 3 RPAS	Army 47 Regt Royal Artillery, Thorney Island	
ZK150	Lockheed Martin Desert Hawk 3 RPAS (ZK150/617)	Imperial War Museum, Lambeth	
ZK155*	Honeywell T-Hawk RPAS	Army 32 Regt Royal Artillery, Larkhill	
ZK205	Grob G109B Vigilant T1 (D-KBRU) [SS]	RAF/Serco, stored Syerston	
ZK210	BAE Systems Mantis RPAS	MoD/BAE Systems, Warton	
ZK300	Eurofighter Typhoon FGR4 [300]	RAF No 29 Sqn, Coningsby	
ZK301	Eurofighter Typhoon FGR4 [301]	RAF No 29 Sqn, Coningsby	
ZK302	Eurofighter Typhoon FGR4 [302]	RAF No 6 Sqn, Lossiemouth	
ZK303	Eurofighter Typhoon T3 [AX]	MoD/BAE Systems, Warton	
ZK304	Eurofighter Typhoon FGR4 [304]	RAF No 3 Sqn, Coningsby	
ZK305	Eurofighter Typhoon FGR4 [305]	RAF, stored Coningsby	
ZK306	Eurofighter Typhoon FGR4 [306]	RAF No 1 Sqn, Lossiemouth	
ZK307	Eurofighter Typhoon FGR4 [307]	RAF No 12 Sqn, Coningsby	
ZK308	Eurofighter Typhoon FGR4 [308]	RAF No 11 Sqn, Coningsby	
ZK309	Eurofighter Typhoon FGR4 [309]	RAF No 3 Sqn, Coningsby	
ZK310	Eurofighter Typhoon FGR4 [310]	RAF No 1 Sqn, Lossiemouth	
ZK311	Eurofighter Typhoon FGR4 [311]	RAF No 6 Sqn, Lossiemouth	
ZK312	Eurofighter Typhoon FGR4 [312]	RAF No 3 Sqn, Coningsby	
ZK313	Eurofighter Typhoon FGR4 [313]	RAF No 11 Sqn, Coningsby	
ZK314	Eurofighter Typhoon FGR4 [314]	RAF Lossiemouth, WLT	
ZK315	Eurofighter Typhoon FGR4 [315]	RAF AWC/FJWOEU/No 41 Sqn, Coningsby	
ZK316	Eurofighter Typhoon FGR4 [316]	RAF No 3 Sqn, Coningsby	
ZK317	Eurofighter Typhoon FGR4 [317]	RAF No 3 Sqn, Coningsby	

Notes	Serial	Type (code/other identity)	Owner/operator, location or fate
	ZK318	Eurofighter Typhoon FGR4 [318]	RAF No 29 Sqn, Coningsby
	ZK319	Eurofighter Typhoon FGR4 [319]	RAF No 11 Sqn, Coningsby
	ZK320	Eurofighter Typhoon FGR4 [320]	RAF No 1 Sqn, Lossiemouth
	ZK321	Eurofighter Typhoon FGR4 [321]	RAF TMF, Coningsby
	ZK322	Eurofighter Typhoon FGR4 [322]	RAF No 3 Sqn, Coningsby
	ZK323	Eurofighter Typhoon FGR4 [323]	RAF No 1 Sqn, Lossiemouth
	ZK324	Eurofighter Typhoon FGR4 [324]	RAF No 1 Sqn, Lossiemouth
	ZK325	Eurofighter Typhoon FGR4 [325]	RAF TMF, Coningsby
	ZK326	Eurofighter Typhoon FGR4 [FB]	RAF, stored Coningsby
	ZK327	Eurofighter Typhoon FGR4 [327]	RAF TMF, Coningsby
	ZK328	Eurofighter Typhoon FGR4 [328]	RAF TMF, Coningsby
	ZK329	Eurofighter Typhoon FGR4 [329]	RAF No 12 Sqn, Coningsby
	ZK330	Eurofighter Typhoon FGR4 [330]	RAF No 6 Sqn, Lossiemouth
	ZK331	Eurofighter Typhoon FGR4 [331]	RAF No 11 Sqn, Coningsby
	ZK332	Eurofighter Typhoon FGR4 [332]	RAF No 1 Sqn, Lossiemouth
	ZK333	Eurofighter Typhoon FGR4 [333]	RAF No 1 Sqn, Lossiemouth
	ZK334	Eurofighter Typhoon FGR4 [334]	RAF No 6 Sqn, Lossiemouth
	ZK335	Eurofighter Typhoon FGR4 [335]	RAF AWC/FJWOEU/No 41 Sqn, Coningsby
	ZK336	Eurofighter Typhoon FGR4 [336]	RAF No 1 Sqn, Lossiemouth
	ZK337	Eurofighter Typhoon FGR4 [337]	RAF No 2 Sqn, Lossiemouth
	ZK338	Eurofighter Typhoon FGR4 [338]	RAF TMF, Coningsby
	ZK339	Eurofighter Typhoon FGR4 [339]	RAF AWC/FJWOEU/No 41 Sqn, Coningsby
	ZK340	Eurofighter Typhoon FGR4 [340]	RAF Coningsby, WLT
	ZK341	Eurofighter Typhoon FGR4 [341]	RAF No 2 Sqn, Lossiemouth
	ZK342	Eurofighter Typhoon FGR4 [342]	RAF No 11 Sqn, Coningsby
	ZK343	Eurofighter Typhoon FGR4 [343]	RAF No 11 Sqn, Coningsby
	ZK344	Eurofighter Typhoon FGR4 [344]	RAF No 2 Sqn, Lossiemouth
	ZK345	Eurofighter Typhoon FGR4 [345]	RAF No 3 Sqn, Coningsby
	ZK346	Eurofighter Typhoon FGR4 [346]	RAF No 11 Sqn, Coningsby
	ZK347	Eurofighter Typhoon FGR4 [347]	RAF TMF, Coningsby
	ZK348	Eurofighter Typhoon FGR4 [348]	RAF No 29 Sqn, Coningsby
	ZK349	Eurofighter Typhoon FGR4 [349]	RAF No 2 Sqn, Lossiemouth
	ZK350	Eurofighter Typhoon FGR4	RAF TMF, Coningsby
	ZK351	Eurofighter Typhoon FGR4 [351]	RAF No 3 Sqn, Coningsby
	ZK352	Eurofighter Typhoon FGR4 [352]	RAF No 11 Sqn, Coningsby
	ZK353	Eurofighter Typhoon FGR4 [353]	RAF No 2 Sqn, Lossiemouth
	ZK354	Eurofighter Typhoon FGR4 [354]	RAF No 11 Sqn, Coningsby
	ZK355	Eurofighter Typhoon FGR4	MoD/BAE Systems, Warton
	ZK356	Eurofighter Typhoon FGR4	MoD/BAE Systems, Warton
	ZK357	Eurofighter Typhoon FGR4 [357]	RAF No 3 Sqn, Coningsby
	ZK358	Eurofighter Typhoon FGR4 [358]	RAF No 12 Sqn, Coningsby
	ZK359	Eurofighter Typhoon FGR4 [359]	RAF No 11 Sqn, Coningsby
	ZK360	Eurofighter Typhoon FGR4 [360]	RAF No 1 Sqn, Lossiemouth
	ZK361	Eurofighter Typhoon FGR4 [361]	RAF No 11 Sqn, Coningsby
	ZK362	Eurofighter Typhoon FGR4 [362]	RAF No 12 Sqn, Coningsby
	ZK363	Eurofighter Typhoon FGR4 [363]	RAF No 29 Sqn, Coningsby
	ZK364	Eurofighter Typhoon FGR4 [364]	RAF No 6 Sqn, Lossiemouth
	ZK365	Eurofighter Typhoon FGR4 [365]	RAF AWC/FJWOEU/No 41 Sqn, Coningsby
	ZK366	Eurofighter Typhoon FGR4 [366]	RAF No 11 Sqn, Coningsby
	ZK367	Eurofighter Typhoon FGR4 [EB-R]	RAF AWC/FJWOEU/No 41 Sqn, Coningsby
	ZK368	Eurofighter Typhoon FGR4 [368]	RAF No 1 Sqn, Lossiemouth
	ZK369	Eurofighter Typhoon FGR4 [369]	RAF No 11 Sqn, Coningsby
	ZK370	Eurofighter Typhoon FGR4	MoD/BAE Systems, Warton
	ZK371	Eurofighter Typhoon FGR4	RAF TMF, Coningsby
	ZK372	Eurofighter Typhoon FGR4 [372]	RAF No 12 Sqn, Coningsby
	ZK373	Eurofighter Typhoon FGR4 [373]	RAF No 12 Sqn, Coningsby
	ZK374	Eurofighter Typhoon FGR4 [374]	RAF No 3 Sqn, Coningsby
	ZK375	Eurofighter Typhoon FGR4 [375]	RAF AWC/FJWOEU/No 41 Sqn, Coningsby
	ZK376	Eurofighter Typhoon FGR4 [376]	RAF AWC/FJWOEU/No 41 Sqn, Coningsby
	ZK377	Eurofighter Typhoon FGR4 [377]	MoD/BAE Systems, stored Warton
	ZK378	Eurofighter Typhoon FGR4 [378]	RAF No 6 Sqn, Lossiemouth
	ZK379	Eurofighter Typhoon T3 [379]	RAF AWC/FJWOEU/No 41 Sqn, Coningsby

Serial	Type (code/other identity)	Owner/operator, location or fate	Notes
ZK380	Eurofighter Typhoon T3 [380]	RAF No 29 Sqn, Coningsby	
ZK381	Eurofighter Typhoon T3 [381]	RAF No 29 Sqn, Coningsby	
ZK382	Eurofighter Typhoon T3 [382]	RAF No 29 Sqn, Coningsby	
ZK383	Eurofighter Typhoon T3 [383]	RAF No 12 Sqn, Coningsby	
ZK424	Eurofighter Typhoon FGR4 [424]	RAF No 2 Sqn, Lossiemouth	
ZK425	Eurofighter Typhoon FGR4 [425]	RAF No 6 Sqn, Lossiemouth	
ZK426	Eurofighter Typhoon FGR4 [426]	RAF No 6 Sqn, Lossiemouth	
ZK427	Eurofighter Typhoon FGR4 [427]	MoD/BAE Systems, stored Warton	
ZK428	Eurofighter Typhoon FGR4 [428]	RAF No 29 Sqn, Coningsby	
ZK429	Eurofighter Typhoon FGR4 [429]	RAF No 29 Sqn, Coningsby	
ZK430	Eurofighter Typhoon FGR4 [430]	RAF No 3 Sqn, Coningsby	
ZK431	Eurofighter Typhoon FGR4 [431]	RAF No 11 Sqn, Coningsby	
ZK432	Eurofighter Typhoon FGR4 [432]	RAF No 29 Sqn, Coningsby	
ZK433	Eurofighter Typhoon FGR4 [433]	RAF AWC/FJWOEU/No 41 Sqn, Coningsby	
ZK434	Eurofighter Typhoon FGR4 [434]	RAF No 6 Sqn, Lossiemouth	
ZK435	Eurofighter Typhoon FGR4 [435]	RAF No 12 Sqn, Coningsby	
ZK436	Eurofighter Typhoon FGR4 [436]	RAF No 29 Sqn, Coningsby	
ZK437	Eurofighter Typhoon FGR4 [437]	RAF No 29 Sqn, Coningsby	
ZK438	Eurofighter Typhoon FGR4 [438]	RAF No 29 Sqn, Coningsby	
ZK439	Eurofighter Typhoon FGR4 [439]	RAF No 29 Sqn, Coningsby	
ZK531	BAe Hawk T53 (LL-5306)	Humberside Airport, on display	
ZK532	BAe Hawk T53 (LL-5315)	MoD/BAE Systems, Warton	
ZK533	BAe Hawk T53 (LL-5317)	MoD/BAE Systems, Samlesbury, GI use	
ZK534	BAe Hawk T53 (LL-5319)	Horizon Aircraft Services, St Athan	
ZK535	BAe Hawk T53 (LL-5320)	BAE Systems Aircraft Maintenance Academy, Humberside	
ZK550	Boeing Chinook HC6 (N701UK)	MoD/StandardAero, Fleetlands	
ZK551	Boeing Chinook HC6 (N702UK)	RAF No 7 Sqn, Odiham	
ZK552	Boeing Chinook HC6 (N703UK)	RAF No 7 Sqn, Odiham	
ZK553	Boeing Chinook HC6 (N700UK)	RAF No 7 Sqn, Odiham	
ZK554	Boeing Chinook HC6 (N705UK)	RAF No 7 Sqn, Odiham	
ZK555	Boeing Chinook HC6 (N706UK)	RAF No 7 Sqn, Odiham	
ZK556	Boeing Chinook HC6 (N707UK)	RAF No 7 Sqn, Odiham	
ZK557	Boeing Chinook HC6 (N708UK)	RAF No 7 Sqn, Odiham	
ZK558	Boeing Chinook HC6 (N709UK)	RAF No 7 Sqn, Odiham	
ZK559	Boeing Chinook HC6 (N710UK)	RAF No 7 Sqn, Odiham	
ZK560	Boeing Chinook HC6 (N711UK)	RAF No 7 Sqn, Odiham	
ZK561	Boeing Chinook HC6 (N712UK)	RAF No 7 Sqn, Odiham	
ZK562	Boeing Chinook HC6 (N713UK)	MoD/StandardAero, Fleetlands	
ZK563	Boeing Chinook HC6 (N714UK)	MoD/Boeing, Boscombe Down (update)	
ZK848	McD F-4F Phantom II (38+48)	For Hawker Hunter Aviation	
ZM135	Lockheed Martin F-35B Lightning II (168315) [001]	RAF No 17 Sqn, Edwards AFB, California	
ZM136	Lockheed Martin F-35B Lightning II (168316) [002]	RAF No 17 Sqn, Edwards AFB, California	
ZM137	Lockheed Martin F-35B Lightning II (168737) [137]	RAF No 207 Sqn/No 617 Sqn, Marham	
ZM138	Lockheed Martin F-35B Lightning II (169170) [004]	RAF No 17 Sqn, Edwards AFB, California	
ZM139	Lockheed Martin F-35B Lightning II (169298) [005]	RAF No 207 Sqn/No 617 Sqn, Marham	
ZM140	Lockheed Martin F-35B Lightning II (169299)	RAF No 207 Sqn/No 617 Sqn, Marham	
ZM141	Lockheed Martin F-35B Lightning II (169300) [007]	RAF No 207 Sqn/No 617 Sqn, Marham	
ZM142	Lockheed Martin F-35B Lightning II (169301) [008]	RAF No 207 Sqn/No 617 Sqn, Marham	
ZM143	Lockheed Martin F-35B Lightning II (169417)	RAF No 207 Sqn/No 617 Sqn, Marham	
ZM144	Lockheed Martin F-35B Lightning II (169418) [010]	RAF No 207 Sqn/No 617 Sqn, Marham	
ZM145	Lockheed Martin F-35B Lightning II (169419) [011]	RAF No 207 Sqn/No 617 Sqn, Marham	
ZM146	Lockheed Martin F-35B Lightning II (169420) [012]	RAF No 207 Sqn/No 617 Sqn, Marham	
ZM147	Lockheed Martin F-35B Lightning II (169421) [013]	RAF No 207 Sqn/No 617 Sqn, Marham	
ZM148	Lockheed Martin F-35B Lightning II (169422) [014]	RAF No 207 Sqn/No 617 Sqn, Marham	
ZM149	Lockheed Martin F-35B Lightning II (169596) [015]	RAF No 207 Sqn/No 617 Sqn, Marham	
ZM150	Lockheed Martin F-35B Lightning II (169597) [016]	RAF No 207 Sqn/No 617 Sqn, Marham	
ZM151	Lockheed Martin F-35B Lightning II (169598) [017]	RAF No 207 Sqn/No 617 Sqn, Marham	
ZM152	Lockheed Martin F-35B Lightning II (169629) [018]	RAF No 207 Sqn/No 617 Sqn, Marham	
ZM153	Lockheed Martin F-35B Lightning II (169630)	LMTAS, Fort Worth, Texas, for RAF/RN	
ZM154	Lockheed Martin F-35B Lightning II	Reservation for RAF/RN	
ZM155	Lockheed Martin F-35B Lightning II	Reservation for RAF/RN	

Notes	Serial	Type (code/other identity)	Owner/operator, location or fate
	ZM156	Lockheed Martin F-35B Lightning II	Reservation for RAF/RN
	ZM157	Lockheed Martin F-35B Lightning II	Reservation for RAF/RN
	ZM158	Lockheed Martin F-35B Lightning II	Reservation for RAF/RN
	ZM159	Lockheed Martin F-35B Lightning II	Reservation for RAF/RN
	ZM160	Lockheed Martin F-35B Lightning II	Reservation for RAF/RN
	ZM161	Lockheed Martin F-35B Lightning II	Reservation for RAF/RN
	ZM162	Lockheed Martin F-35B Lightning II	Reservation for RAF/RN
	ZM163	Lockheed Martin F-35B Lightning II	Reservation for RAF/RN
	ZM164	Lockheed Martin F-35B Lightning II	Reservation for RAF/RN
	ZM165	Lockheed Martin F-35B Lightning II	Reservation for RAF/RN
	ZM166	Lockheed Martin F-35B Lightning II	Reservation for RAF/RN
	ZM167	Lockheed Martin F-35B Lightning II	Reservation for RAF/RN
	ZM168	Lockheed Martin F-35B Lightning II	Reservation for RAF/RN
	ZM169	Lockheed Martin F-35B Lightning II	Reservation for RAF/RN
	ZM170	Lockheed Martin F-35B Lightning II	Reservation for RAF/RN
	ZM171	Lockheed Martin F-35B Lightning II	Reservation for RAF/RN
	ZM172	Lockheed Martin F-35B Lightning II	Reservation for RAF/RN
	ZM173	Lockheed Martin F-35B Lightning II	Reservation for RAF/RN
	ZM174	Lockheed Martin F-35B Lightning II	Reservation for RAF/RN
	ZM175	Lockheed Martin F-35B Lightning II	Reservation for RAF/RN
	ZM176	Lockheed Martin F-35B Lightning II	Reservation for RAF/RN
	ZM177	Lockheed Martin F-35B Lightning II	Reservation for RAF/RN
	ZM178	Lockheed Martin F-35B Lightning II	Reservation for RAF/RN
	ZM179	Lockheed Martin F-35B Lightning II	Reservation for RAF/RN
	ZM180	Lockheed Martin F-35B Lightning II	Reservation for RAF/RN
	ZM181	Lockheed Martin F-35B Lightning II	Reservation for RAF/RN
	ZM182	Lockheed Martin F-35B Lightning II	Reservation for RAF/RN
	ZM183	Lockheed Martin F-35 Lightning II	Reservation for RAF/RN
	ZM184	Lockheed Martin F-35 Lightning II	Reservation for RAF/RN
	ZM185	Lockheed Martin F-35 Lightning II	Reservation for RAF/RN
	ZM186	Lockheed Martin F-35 Lightning II	Reservation for RAF/RN
	ZM187	Lockheed Martin F-35 Lightning II	Reservation for RAF/RN
	ZM188	Lockheed Martin F-35 Lightning II	Reservation for RAF/RN
	ZM189	Lockheed Martin F-35 Lightning II	Reservation for RAF/RN
	ZM190	Lockheed Martin F-35 Lightning II	Reservation for RAF/RN
	ZM191	Lockheed Martin F-35 Lightning II	Reservation for RAF/RN
	ZM192	Lockheed Martin F-35 Lightning II	Reservation for RAF/RN
	ZM193	Lockheed Martin F-35 Lightning II	Reservation for RAF/RN
	ZM194	Lockheed Martin F-35 Lightning II	Reservation for RAF/RN
	ZM195	Lockheed Martin F-35 Lightning II	Reservation for RAF/RN
	ZM196	Lockheed Martin F-35 Lightning II	Reservation for RAF/RN
	ZM197	Lockheed Martin F-35 Lightning II	Reservation for RAF/RN
	ZM198	Lockheed Martin F-35 Lightning II	Reservation for RAF/RN
	ZM199	Lockheed Martin F-35 Lightning II	Reservation for RAF/RN
	ZM200	Lockheed Martin F-35 Lightning II	Reservation for RAF/RN
	ZM300	Grob G120TP-A Prefect T1 (D-ETPJ/G-MFTS)	Affinity/RAF No 3 FTS/No 57 Sqn, Barkston Heath
	ZM301	Grob G120TP-A Prefect T1 (D-EGUX/G-MEFT)	Affinity/RAF No 3 FTS/No 57 Sqn, Barkston Heath
	ZM302	Grob G120TP-A Prefect T1 (D-ETPT/G-CJYB)	Affinity/RAF No 3 FTS/No 57 Sqn, Cranwell
	ZM303	Grob G120TP-A Prefect T1 (G-CJYG)	Affinity/RAF No 3 FTS/No 57 Sqn, Cranwell
	ZM304	Grob G120TP-A Prefect T1 (G-CJYH)	Affinity/RAF No 3 FTS/No 57 Sqn, Barkston Heath
	ZM305	Grob G120TP-A Prefect T1 (G-CJZR)	Affinity/RAF No 3 FTS/No 57 Sqn, Cranwell
	ZM306	Grob G120TP-A Prefect T1 (G-CJZJ)	Affinity/RAF No 3 FTS/No 57 Sqn, Barkston Heath
	ZM307	Grob G120TP-A Prefect T1 (G-CJZI)	Affinity/RAF No 3 FTS/No 57 Sqn, Barkston Heath
	ZM308	Grob G120TP-A Prefect T1 (G-CJZF)	Affinity/RAF No 3 FTS/No 57 Sqn, Barkston Heath
	ZM309	Grob G120TP-A Prefect T1 (G-CKCO)	Affinity/RAF No 3 FTS/No 57 Sqn, Barkston Heath
	ZM310	Grob G120TP-A Prefect T1 (G-CKCS)	Affinity/RAF No 3 FTS/No 57 Sqn, Cranwell
	ZM311	Grob G120TP-A Prefect T1 (G-CKIA)	Affinity/RAF No 3 FTS/No 57 Sqn, Cranwell
	ZM312	Grob G120TP-A Prefect T1 (G-CKIB)	Affinity/RAF No 3 FTS/No 57 Sqn, Cranwell
	ZM313	Grob G120TP-A Prefect T1 (G-CKIC)	Affinity/RAF No 3 FTS/No 57 Sqn, Barkston Heath
	ZM314	Grob G120TP-A Prefect T1 (G-CKID)	Affinity/RAF No 3 FTS/No 57 Sqn, Cranwell
	ZM315	Grob G120TP-A Prefect T1 (G-CKIV)	Affinity/RAF No 3 FTS/No 57 Sqn, Cranwell
	ZM316	Grob G120TP-A Prefect T1 (G-CKIW)	Affinity/RAF No 3 FTS/No 57 Sqn, Barkston Heath

Serial	Type (code/other identity)	Owner/operator, location or fate	Notes
ZM317	Grob G120TP-A Prefect T1 (G-CKLJ)	Affinity/RAF No 3 FTS/No 57 Sqn, Barkston Heath	•
ZM318	Grob G120TP-A Prefect T1 (G-CKLO)	Affinity/RAF No 3 FTS/No 57 Sqn, Cranwell	
ZM319	Grob G120TP-A Prefect T1 (G-CKRY)	Affinity/RAF No 3 FTS/No 57 Sqn, Barkston Heath	
ZM320	Grob G120TP-A Prefect T1 (G-CKRP)	Affinity/RAF No 3 FTS/No 57 Sqn, Cranwell	
ZM321	Grob G120TP-A Prefect T1 (G-CKSJ)	Affinity/RAF No 3 FTS/No 57 Sqn, Cranwell	
ZM322	Grob G120TP-A Prefect T1 (G-CKSI)	Affinity/RAF No 3 FTS/No 57 Sqn, Cranwell	
ZM323	Beechcraft T-6C Texan T1 (N2824B/G-TBFT) [323]	Affinity/RAF No 4 FTS/No 72 Sqn, Valley	
ZM324	Beechcraft T-6C Texan T1 (N2826B/G-CKGO) [324]	Affinity/RAF No 4 FTS/No 72 Sqn, Valley	
ZM325	Beechcraft T-6C Texan T1 (N2843B/G-CKGP) [325]	Affinity/RAF No 4 FTS/No 72 Sqn, Valley	
ZM326	Beechcraft T-6C Texan T1 (N2770B/G-CKGW) [326]	Affinity/RAF No 4 FTS/No 72 Sqn, Valley	
ZM327	Beechcraft T-6C Texan T1 (N2856B/G-CKVL) [327]	Affinity/RAF No 4 FTS/No 72 Sqn, Valley	
ZM328	Beechcraft T-6C Texan T1 (N2857B/G-CKVN) [328]	Affinity/RAF No 4 FTS/No 72 Sqn, Valley	
ZM329	Beechcraft T-6C Texan T1 (N2858B/G-CKVO) [329]	Affinity/RAF No 4 FTS/No 72 Sqn, Valley	
ZM330	Beechcraft T-6C Texan T1 (N2859B/G-CKVR) [330]	Affinity/RAF No 4 FTS/No 72 Sqn, Valley	
ZM331	Beechcraft T-6C Texan T1 (N2860B/G-CKVS) [331]	Affinity/RAF No 4 FTS/No 72 Sqn, Valley	
ZM332	Beechcraft T-6C Texan T1 (N2872B/G-CKVU) [332]	Affinity/RAF No 4 FTS/No 72 Sqn, Valley	
ZM333	Embraer EMB-500 Phenom T1 (PR-PHK/G-MEPT)	Affinity/RAF No 3 FTS/No 45 Sqn, Cranwell	
ZM334	Embraer EMB-500 Phenom T1 (PR-ING/G-MEPS)	Affinity/RAF No 3 FTS/No 45 Sqn, Cranwell	
ZM335	Embraer EMB-500 Phenom T1 (PR-LTE/G-CJXH)	Affinity/RAF No 3 FTS/No 45 Sqn, Cranwell	
ZM336	Embraer EMB-500 Phenom T1 (PR-LTF/G-CKCU)	Affinity/RAF No 3 FTS/No 45 Sqn, Cranwell	
ZM337	Embraer EMB-500 Phenom T1 (PR-LTJ/G-CKEF)	Affinity/RAF No 3 FTS/No 45 Sqn, Cranwell	
ZM398	Airbus A400M Atlas Full Flight Simulator	RAF Brize Norton	
ZM399	Airbus A400M Atlas Full Flight Simulator	RAF Brize Norton	
ZM400	Airbus A400M Atlas C1 (A4M015/EC-405)	RAF No 24 Sqn/No 70 Sqn, Brize Norton	
ZM401	Airbus A400M Atlas C1 (A4M016/EC-406)	RAF No 24 Sqn/No 70 Sqn, Brize Norton	
ZM402	Airbus A400M Atlas C1 (A4M017/EC-407)	RAF No 24 Sqn/No 70 Sqn, Brize Norton	
ZM403	Airbus A400M Atlas C1 (A4M020)	RAF No 24 Sqn/No 70 Sqn, Brize Norton	
ZM404	Airbus A400M Atlas C1 (A4M021/EC-401)	RAF No 24 Sqn/No 70 Sqn, Brize Norton	
ZM405	Airbus A400M Atlas C1 (A4M024)	RAF No 24 Sqn/No 70 Sqn, Brize Norton	
ZM406	Airbus A400M Atlas C1 (A4M025/EC-405)	RAF No 24 Sqn/No 70 Sqn, Brize Norton	
ZM407	Airbus A400M Atlas C1 (A4M026)	RAF No 24 Sqn/No 70 Sqn, Brize Norton	
ZM408	Airbus A400M Atlas C1 (A4M027)	RAF No 24 Sqn/No 70 Sqn, Brize Norton	
ZM409	Airbus A400M Atlas C1 (A4M034) $	MoD/Airbus Defence & Space, Getafe	
ZM410	Airbus A400M Atlas C1 (A4M038)	MoD/Airbus Defence & Space, Getafe	
ZM411	Airbus A400M Atlas C1 (A4M039)	MoD/Airbus Defence & Space, Getafe	
ZM412	Airbus A400M Atlas C1 (A4M042)	MoD/Airbus Defence & Space, Getafe	
ZM413	Airbus A400M Atlas C1 (A4M045)	RAF No 24 Sqn/No 70 Sqn, Brize Norton	
ZM414	Airbus A400M Atlas C1 (A4M047)	RAF No 1312 Flt, Mount Pleasant, FI	
ZM415	Airbus A400M Atlas C1 (A4M052)	RAF No 24 Sqn/No 70 Sqn, Brize Norton	
ZM416	Airbus A400M Atlas C1 (A4M058)	RAF No 24 Sqn/No 70 Sqn, Brize Norton	
ZM417	Airbus A400M Atlas C1 (A4M060)	RAF No 24 Sqn/No 70 Sqn, Brize Norton	
ZM418	Airbus A400M Atlas C1 (A4M072)	MoD/Airbus Defence & Space, Getafe	
ZM419	Airbus A400M Atlas C1 (A4M077)	RAF No 24 Sqn/No 70 Sqn, Brize Norton	
ZM420	Airbus A400M Atlas C1 (A4M095)	Airbus Defence & Space, Seville, for RAF	
ZM421	Airbus A400M Atlas C1 (A4M056/EC-400)	Airbus Defence & Space, Seville, for RAF	
ZM500	Airbus H145 Jupiter HT1 (D-HADT/G-CJIV) [00]	DHFS, RAF Shawbury	
ZM501	Airbus H145 Jupiter HT1 (D-HADM/G-CJIZ/G-CKGE) [01]	DHFS, RAF Shawbury	
ZM502	Airbus H145 Jupiter HT1 (D-HADQ/G-CJRW) [02]	DHFS No 202 Sqn, RAF Valley	
ZM503	Airbus H145 Jupiter HT1	Reservation for MoD	
ZM504	Airbus H135 Juno HT1 (D-HECZ/G-CJJG) [04]	DHFS, RAF Shawbury	
ZM505	Airbus H135 Juno HT1 (D-HECV/G-CJIW) [05]	DHFS, RAF Shawbury	
ZM506	Airbus H135 Juno HT1 (D-HECW/G-CJIY) [06]	DHFS, RAF Shawbury	
ZM507	Airbus H135 Juno HT1 (D-HECX/G-CJRP) [07]	DHFS, RAF Shawbury	
ZM508	Airbus H135 Juno HT1 (D-HECD/G-CJRY) [08]	DHFS, RAF Shawbury	
ZM509	Airbus H135 Juno HT1 (D-HECB/G-CJTZ) [09]	DHFS, RAF Shawbury	
ZM510	Airbus H135 Juno HT1 (D-HECG/G-CJUA) [10]	DHFS, RAF Shawbury	
ZM511	Airbus H135 Juno HT1 (D-HECJ/G-CJUC) [11]	DHFS, RAF Shawbury	
ZM512	Airbus H135 Juno HT1 (D-HECQ/G-CJXS) [12]	DHFS, RAF Shawbury	
ZM513	Airbus H135 Juno HT1 (D-HECP/G-CJXU) [13]	DHFS No 202 Sqn, RAF Valley	
ZM514	Airbus H135 Juno HT1 (D-HECV/G-CJXV) [14]	DHFS, RAF Shawbury	
ZM515	Airbus H135 Juno HT1 (D-HECT/G-CJSO) [15]	DHFS, RAF Shawbury	

Notes	Serial	Type (code/other identity)	Owner/operator, location or fate
	ZM516	Airbus H135 Juno HT1 (D-HECY/G-CJZS) [16]	DHFS, RAF Shawbury
	ZM517	Airbus H135 Juno HT1 (D-HECL/G-CJZT) [17]	DHFS, RAF Shawbury
	ZM518	Airbus H135 Juno HT1 (D-HCBA/G-CKEO) [18]	DHFS, RAF Shawbury
	ZM519	Airbus H135 Juno HT1 (D-HCBC/G-CKEU) [19]	DHFS, RAF Shawbury
	ZM520	Airbus H135 Juno HT1 (D-HCBD/G-CKEW) [20]	DHFS, RAF Shawbury
	ZM521	Airbus H135 Juno HT1 (D-HECJ/G-CKIK) [21]	DHFS, RAF Shawbury
	ZM522	Airbus H135 Juno HT1 (D-HCBB/G-CKIM) [22]	DHFS, RAF Shawbury
	ZM523	Airbus H135 Juno HT1 (G-CKJW) [23]	DHFS, RAF Shawbury
	ZM524	Airbus H135 Juno HT1 (D-HECK/G-CKJU) [24]	DHFS, RAF Shawbury
	ZM525	Airbus H135 Juno HT1 (D-HECQ/G-CKJX) [25]	DHFS, RAF Shawbury
	ZM526	Airbus H135 Juno HT1 (D-HECU/G-CKOC) [26]	DHFS, RAF Shawbury
	ZM527	Airbus H135 Juno HT1 (D-HECX/G-CKOB) [27]	DHFS, RAF Shawbury
	ZM528	Airbus H135 Juno HT1 (G-CKOA) [28] $	DHFS, RAF Shawbury
	ZM529	Airbus H135 Juno HT1 (D-HECW/G-CKPT) [29]	DHFS, RAF Shawbury
	ZM530	Airbus H135 Juno HT1 (D-HECD/G-CKRA) [30]	DHFS, RAF Shawbury
	ZM531	Airbus H135 Juno HT1 (D-HECA/G-CKSB) [31]	DHFS, RAF Shawbury
	ZM532	Airbus H135 Juno HT1 (D-HECY/G-CKSA) [32]	DHFS No 202 Sqn, RAF Valley
	ZM533	Airbus H135 Juno HT1	Reservation for MoD
	ZM534	Airbus H135 Juno HT1	Reservation for MoD
	ZM700	Boeing AH-64E Apache	For AAC
	ZM701	Boeing AH-64E Apache	For AAC
	ZM702	Boeing AH-64E Apache	For AAC
	ZM703	Boeing AH-64E Apache	For AAC
	ZM704	Boeing AH-64E Apache	For AAC
	ZM705	Boeing AH-64E Apache	For AAC
	ZM706	Boeing AH-64E Apache	For AAC
	ZM707	Boeing AH-64E Apache	For AAC
	ZM708	Boeing AH-64E Apache	For AAC
	ZM709	Boeing AH-64E Apache	For AAC
	ZM710	Boeing AH-64E Apache	For AAC
	ZM711	Boeing AH-64E Apache	For AAC
	ZM712	Boeing AH-64E Apache	For AAC
	ZM713	Boeing AH-64E Apache	For AAC
	ZM714	Boeing AH-64E Apache	For AAC
	ZM715	Boeing AH-64E Apache	For AAC
	ZM716	Boeing AH-64E Apache	For AAC
	ZM717	Boeing AH-64E Apache	For AAC
	ZM718	Boeing AH-64E Apache	For AAC
	ZM719	Boeing AH-64E Apache	For AAC
	ZM720	Boeing AH-64E Apache	For AAC
	ZM721	Boeing AH-64E Apache	For AAC
	ZM722	Boeing AH-64E Apache	For AAC
	ZM723	Boeing AH-64E Apache	For AAC
	ZM724	Boeing AH-64E Apache	For AAC
	ZM725	Boeing AH-64E Apache	For AAC
	ZM726	Boeing AH-64E Apache	For AAC
	ZM727	Boeing AH-64E Apache	For AAC
	ZM728	Boeing AH-64E Apache	For AAC
	ZM729	Boeing AH-64E Apache	For AAC
	ZM730	Boeing AH-64E Apache	For AAC
	ZM731	Boeing AH-64E Apache	For AAC
	ZM732	Boeing AH-64E Apache	For AAC
	ZM733	Boeing AH-64E Apache	For AAC
	ZM734	Boeing AH-64E Apache	For AAC
	ZM735	Boeing AH-64E Apache	For AAC
	ZM736	Boeing AH-64E Apache	For AAC
	ZM737	Boeing AH-64E Apache	For AAC
	ZM738	Boeing AH-64E Apache	For AAC
	ZM739	Boeing AH-64E Apache	For AAC
	ZM740	Boeing AH-64E Apache	For AAC
	ZM741	Boeing AH-64E Apache	For AAC
	ZM742	Boeing AH-64E Apache	For AAC

Serial	Type (code/other identity)	Owner/operator, location or fate	Notes
ZM743	Boeing AH-64E Apache	For AAC	
ZM744	Boeing AH-64E Apache	For AAC	
ZM745	Boeing AH-64E Apache	For AAC	
ZM746	Boeing AH-64E Apache	For AAC	
ZM747	Boeing AH-64E Apache	For AAC	
ZM748	Boeing AH-64E Apache	For AAC	
ZM749	Boeing AH-64E Apache	For AAC	
ZP801	Boeing P-8A Poseidon MRA1 (169573/N456DS) [01]	RAF No 120 Sqn, Kinloss	
ZP802	Boeing P-8A Poseidon MRA1 (N469DS) [02]	RAF No 120 Sqn, NAS Jacksonville, FL, USA	
ZP803	Boeing P-8A Poseidon MRA1 (N480DS) [03]	Boeing, Seattle, USA, for RAF	
ZP804	Boeing P-8A Poseidon MRA1	For RAF	
ZP805	Boeing P-8A Poseidon MRA1	For RAF	
ZP806	Boeing P-8A Poseidon MRA1	For RAF	
ZP807	Boeing P-8A Poseidon MRA1	For RAF	
ZP808	Boeing P-8A Poseidon MRA1	For RAF	
ZP809	Boeing P-8A Poseidon MRA1	For RAF	
ZP810	Boeing P-8A Poseidon MRA1	Reservation for RAF	
ZP811	Boeing P-8A Poseidon MRA1	Reservation for RAF	
ZP812	Boeing P-8A Poseidon MRA1	Reservation for RAF	
ZP813	Boeing P-8A Poseidon MRA1	Reservation for RAF	
ZP814	Boeing P-8A Poseidon MRA1	Reservation for RAF	
ZP815	Boeing P-8A Poseidon MRA1	Reservation for RAF	
ZR283	AgustaWestland AW139 (G-FBHA)	*Sold as G-FBHA, 18 February 2020*	
ZR324	Agusta A109E Power (G-EMHB)	*Sold as G-EMHB, 18 February 2020*	
ZR325	Agusta A109E Power (G-BZEI)	*Sold as G-BZEI, 18 February 2020*	
ZR339	AgustaWestland AW101 Mk.641 (ZW-4302)	Leonardo MW, stored Yeovil	
ZR342	AgustaWestland AW101 Mk.641 (ZW-4305)	Leonardo MW, stored Yeovil	
ZR346	AgustaWestland AW101 Mk.641 (ZW-4309)	Leonardo MW, stored Yeovil	
ZR347	AgustaWestland AW101 Mk.641 (ZW-4310)	Leonardo MW, Yeovil, for Azerbaijan as 4K-Ai010	
ZR348	AgustaWestland AW101 Mk.641 (ZW-4311)	Leonardo MW, stored Yeovil	
ZR349	AgustaWestland AW101 Mk.641 (ZW-4312)	Leonardo MW, stored Yeovil	
ZR358	AgustaWestland AW101 Mk.611 [15-07]	*To Italian AF as MM81870, 8 April 2019*	
ZR359	AgustaWestland AW101 Mk.611 [15-10]	*To Italian AF as MM81871, 30 July 2019*	
ZR360	AgustaWestland AW101 Mk.611 [15-11]	*To Italian AF as MM81872, 26 September 2019*	
ZR361	AgustaWestland AW101 Mk.611 [15-12]	*To Italian AF as MM81873, 28 January 2020*	
ZR362	AgustaWestland AW101 Mk.611 [15-13]	*To Italian AF as MM81874, 18 February 2020*	
ZR363	AgustaWestland AW101 Mk.611 [15-14]	Leonardo MW, Yeovil, for Italian AF as MM81875	
ZS782	WS WG25 Sharpeye (BAPC.451)	The Helicopter Museum, Weston-super-Mare	
ZT800	WS Super Lynx Mk 300	Yeovil College, instructional use	
ZZ100	AgustaWestland AW101 Mk.612 (0262)	Leonardo MW, Yeovil, for Norway as 0262	
ZZ102	AgustaWestland AW101 Mk.612 (0265)	Leonardo MW, Yeovil	
ZZ103	AgustaWestland AW101 Mk.612	Leonardo MW, Yeovil, for Norway as 0268	
ZZ105	AgustaWestland AW101 Mk.612	*To Norway as 0273, 20 March 2019*	
ZZ106	AgustaWestland AW101 Mk.612	*To Norway as 0275, 21 June 2019*	
ZZ107	AgustaWestland AW101 Mk.612	Leonardo MW, Yeovil, for Norway as 0276	
ZZ108	AgustaWestland AW101 Mk.612	Leonardo MW, Yeovil, for Norway as 0277	
ZZ109	AgustaWestland AW101 Mk.612	Leonardo MW, Yeovil, for Norway as 0278	
ZZ110	AgustaWestland AW101 Mk.612	Leonardo MW, Yeovil, for Norway as 0279	
ZZ111	AgustaWestland AW101 Mk.612	Leonardo MW, Yeovil, for Norway as 0280	
ZZ112	AgustaWestland AW101 Mk.612	Leonardo MW, Yeovil, for Norway as 0281	
ZZ113	AgustaWestland AW101 Mk.612	Leonardo MW, Yeovil, for Norway as 0282	
ZZ114	AgustaWestland AW101 Mk.612	Leonardo MW, Yeovil, for Norway as 0283	
ZZ115	AgustaWestland AW101 Mk.612	Leonardo MW, Yeovil, for Norway as 0284	
ZZ171	Boeing C-17A Globemaster III (00-201/N171UK)	RAF No 99 Sqn, Brize Norton	
ZZ172	Boeing C-17A Globemaster III (00-202/N172UK)	RAF No 99 Sqn, Brize Norton	
ZZ173	Boeing C-17A Globemaster III (00-203/N173UK)	RAF No 99 Sqn, Brize Norton	
ZZ174	Boeing C-17A Globemaster III (00-204/N174UK)	RAF No 99 Sqn, Brize Norton	

Notes	Serial	Type (code/other identity)	Owner/operator, location or fate
	ZZ175	Boeing C-17A Globemaster III (06-0205/N9500Z)	RAF No 99 Sqn, Brize Norton
	ZZ176	Boeing C-17A Globemaster III (08-0206/N9500B)	RAF/Boeing, San Antonio, Texas, USA
	ZZ177	Boeing C-17A Globemaster III (09-8207/N9500B)	RAF No 99 Sqn, Brize Norton
	ZZ178	Boeing C-17A Globemaster III (12-0208/N9500N)	RAF No 99 Sqn, Brize Norton
	ZZ190	Hawker Hunter F58 (J-4066/G-HHAE)	Hawker Hunter Aviation, Scampton
	ZZ191	Hawker Hunter F58 (J-4058/G-HHAD)	Hawker Hunter Aviation, Scampton
	ZZ192	Grob G109B Vigilant T1 (D-KLVI) [SQ]	RAF, stored Little Rissington
	ZZ193	Grob G109B Vigilant T1 (D-KBLO) [SR]	RAF, stored Little Rissington
	ZZ194	Hawker Hunter F58 (J-4021/G-HHAC)	Hawker Hunter Aviation, Scampton
	ZZ201	General Atomics Reaper RPAS (07-0111)	Crashed, 17 October 2015
	ZZ202	General Atomics Reaper RPAS (07-0117)	RAF No 13 Sqn/No 39 Sqn, Creech AFB, Nevada, USA
	ZZ203	General Atomics Reaper RPAS (08-0113)	RAF No 13 Sqn/No 39 Sqn, Creech AFB, Nevada, USA
	ZZ204	General Atomics Reaper RPAS (10-0157)	RAF No 13 Sqn/No 39 Sqn, Creech AFB, Nevada, USA
	ZZ205	General Atomics Reaper RPAS (10-0157)	RAF No 13 Sqn/No 39 Sqn, Creech AFB, Nevada, USA
	ZZ206	General Atomics Reaper RPAS (12-0707)	RAF No 13 Sqn/No 39 Sqn, Creech AFB, Nevada, USA
	ZZ207	General Atomics Reaper RPAS (12-0708)	RAF No 13 Sqn/No 39 Sqn, Creech AFB, Nevada, USA
	ZZ208	General Atomics Reaper RPAS (12-0709)	RAF No 13 Sqn/No 39 Sqn, Creech AFB, Nevada, USA
	ZZ209	General Atomics Reaper RPAS (12-0710)	RAF No 13 Sqn/No 39 Sqn, Creech AFB, Nevada, USA
	ZZ210	General Atomics Reaper RPAS (12-0711)	RAF No 13 Sqn/No 39 Sqn, Creech AFB, Nevada, USA
	ZZ211	General Atomics Reaper RPAS	General Atomics, for RAF
	ZZ212	General Atomics Reaper RPAS	General Atomics, for RAF
	ZZ213	General Atomics Reaper RPAS	General Atomics, for RAF
	ZZ250	BAE Systems Taranis RPAS	BAE Systems, Warton
	ZZ251	BAE Systems HERTI RPAS	BAE Systems, Warton
	ZZ252	BAE Systems HERTI RPAS	BAE Systems, Woomera, Australia
	ZZ253	BAE Systems HERTI RPAS	BAE Systems, Woomera, Australia
	ZZ254	BAE Systems HERTI RPAS	BAE Systems, Woomera, Australia
	ZZ330	Airbus A330 Voyager KC2 (MRTT017/EC-337/G-VYGA)	RAF No 10 Sqn/No 101 Sqn, Brize Norton
	ZZ331	Airbus A330 Voyager KC2 (MRTT018/EC-331/G-VYGB)	RAF No 10 Sqn/No 101 Sqn, Brize Norton
	ZZ332	Airbus A330 Voyager KC3 (MRTT019/EC-330/G-VYGC)	RAF No 1312 Flt, Mount Pleasant, FI
	ZZ333	Airbus A330 Voyager KC3 (MRTT020/EC-337/G-VYGD)	RAF No 10 Sqn/No 101 Sqn, Brize Norton
	ZZ334	Airbus A330 Voyager KC3 (MRTT016/EC-335/G-VYGE)	RAF No 10 Sqn/No 101 Sqn, Brize Norton
	ZZ335	Airbus A330 Voyager KC3 (MRTT021/EC-338/G-VYGF)	RAF No 10 Sqn/No 101 Sqn, Brize Norton
	ZZ336	Airbus A330 Voyager KC3 (MRTT022/EC-333/G-VYGG)	RAF No 10 Sqn/No 101 Sqn, Brize Norton
	ZZ337	Airbus A330 Voyager KC3 (MRTT023/EC-336/G-VYGH)	RAF No 10 Sqn/No 101 Sqn, Brize Norton
	ZZ338	Airbus A330 Voyager KC3 (MRTT024/EC-331/G-VYGI)	RAF No 10 Sqn/No 101 Sqn, Brize Norton
	ZZ339	Airbus A330-243 (MRTT025/EC-333/G-VYGJ)	Airtanker Ltd, Brize Norton [flies as G-VYGJ]
	ZZ340	Airbus A330-243 (MRTT026/EC-330/G-VYGK)	Airtanker Ltd/Condor, Frankfurt, Germany [flies as G-VYGK]
	ZZ341	Airbus A330-243 (MRTT027/EC-336/G-VYGL)	Airtanker Ltd/Jet2, Manchester [flies as G-VYGL]
	ZZ342	Airbus A330-243 (MRTT028/EC-332/G-VYGM)	Airtanker Ltd, Brize Norton [flies as G-VYGM]
	ZZ343	Airbus A330 Voyager KC2 (MRTT029/EC-331/G-VYGN)	RAF No 10 Sqn/No 101 Sqn, Brize Norton
	ZZ375	AgustaWestland AW159 Wildcat HMA2	RN No 815 NAS, Yeovilton
	ZZ376	AgustaWestland AW159 Wildcat HMA2	RN No 825 NAS, Yeovilton
	ZZ377	AgustaWestland AW159 Wildcat HMA2	RN No 825 NAS, Yeovilton
	ZZ378	AgustaWestland AW159 Wildcat HMA2	MoD/Leonardo MW, Yeovil (FASGW trials)
	ZZ379	AgustaWestland AW159 Wildcat HMA2	MoD/Leonardo MW, Yeovil
	ZZ380	AgustaWestland AW159 Wildcat HMA2	MoD/Leonardo MW, Yeovil
	ZZ381	AgustaWestland AW159 Wildcat HMA2	RN No 815 NAS, Yeovilton
	ZZ382	AgustaWestland AW159 Wildcat AH1	AAC WCM, Yeovilton
	ZZ383	AgustaWestland AW159 Wildcat AH1	AAC No 1 Regiment, Yeovilton
	ZZ384	AgustaWestland AW159 Wildcat AH1	RN No 847 NAS, Yeovilton

Serial	Type (code/other identity)	Owner/operator, location or fate	Notes
ZZ385	AgustaWestland AW159 Wildcat AH1	AAC No 1 Regiment, Yeovilton	
ZZ386	AgustaWestland AW159 Wildcat AH1	RN No 847 NAS, Yeovilton	
ZZ387	AgustaWestland AW159 Wildcat AH1	AAC WCM, Yeovilton	
ZZ388	AgustaWestland AW159 Wildcat AH1	AAC No 1 Regiment, Yeovilton	
ZZ389	AgustaWestland AW159 Wildcat AH1	MoD/Leonardo MW, Yeovil	
ZZ390	AgustaWestland AW159 Wildcat AH1	AAC No 1 Regiment, Yeovilton	
ZZ391	AgustaWestland AW159 Wildcat AH1	AAC WST, stored Yeovilton	
ZZ392	AgustaWestland AW159 Wildcat AH1	AAC No 1 Regiment, Yeovilton	
ZZ393	AgustaWestland AW159 Wildcat AH1	AAC No 1 Regiment, Yeovilton	
ZZ394	AgustaWestland AW159 Wildcat AH1	AAC WCM, Yeovilton	
ZZ395	AgustaWestland AW159 Wildcat AH1	MoD/Leonardo MW, Yeovil	
ZZ396	AgustaWestland AW159 Wildcat HMA2	RN WST, Yeovilton	
ZZ397	AgustaWestland AW159 Wildcat HMA2	RN No 815 NAS, Yeovilton	
ZZ398	AgustaWestland AW159 Wildcat AH1	AAC WST, stored Yeovilton	
ZZ399	AgustaWestland AW159 Wildcat AH1	RN No 847 NAS, Yeovilton	
ZZ400	AgustaWestland AW159 Wildcat (TI01)	RNAS Yeovilton, GI use	
ZZ401	AgustaWestland AW159 Wildcat (TI02)	Privately owned, Gloucestershire Airport, GI use	
ZZ402	AgustaWestland AW159 Wildcat (TI03)	DSAE RNAESS, *HMS Sultan*, Gosport	
ZZ403	AgustaWestland AW159 Wildcat AH1	AAC WST, stored Yeovilton	
ZZ404	AgustaWestland AW159 Wildcat AH1	MoD/Leonardo MW, Yeovil	
ZZ405	AgustaWestland AW159 Wildcat AH1	AAC No 1 Regiment, Yeovilton	
ZZ406	AgustaWestland AW159 Wildcat AH1	AAC WST/WZM, Yeovilton	
ZZ407	AgustaWestland AW159 Wildcat AH1	AAC WST, Yeovilton	
ZZ408	AgustaWestland AW159 Wildcat AH1	AAC No 1 Regiment, Yeovilton	
ZZ409	AgustaWestland AW159 Wildcat AH1	AAC WCM, Yeovilton	
ZZ410	AgustaWestland AW159 Wildcat AH1	AAC WCM, Yeovilton	
ZZ413	AgustaWestland AW159 Wildcat HMA2	RN No 825 NAS, Yeovilton	
ZZ414	AgustaWestland AW159 Wildcat HMA2	RN No 815 NAS, Yeovilton	
ZZ415	AgustaWestland AW159 Wildcat HMA2	MoD/Leonardo MW, Yeovil (FASGW trials)	
ZZ416	Hawker Beechcraft Shadow R1 (G-JENC)	RAF No 14 Sqn, Waddington	
ZZ417	Hawker Beechcraft Shadow R1+ (G-NICY)	RAF No 14 Sqn, Waddington	
ZZ418	Hawker Beechcraft Shadow R1 (G-JIMG)	RAF No 14 Sqn, Waddington	
ZZ419	Hawker Beechcraft Shadow R1+ (G-OTCS)	RAF No 14 Sqn, Waddington	
ZZ500	Hawker Beechcraft Avenger T1 (G-MFTA)	RN No 750 NAS, Culdrose	
ZZ501	Hawker Beechcraft Avenger T1 (G-MFTB)	RN No 750 NAS, Culdrose	
ZZ502	Hawker Beechcraft Avenger T1 (G-MFTC)	RN No 750 NAS, Culdrose	
ZZ503	Hawker Beechcraft Avenger T1 (G-MFTD)	RN No 750 NAS, Culdrose	
ZZ504	Hawker Beechcraft Shadow R1 (G-CGUM)	RAF No 14 Sqn, Waddington	
ZZ505	Hawker Beechcraft Shadow R2 (G-DAYP)	RAF, on order	
ZZ506	Hawker Beechcraft Shadow R2 (G-GMAD)	RAF, on order	
ZZ507	Hawker Beechcraft Shadow R1+ (G-LBSB)	RAF No 14 Sqn, Waddington	
ZZ510	AgustaWestland AW159 Wildcat AH1	AAC WCM, Yeovilton	
ZZ511	AgustaWestland AW159 Wildcat AH1	AAC No 1 Regiment, Yeovilton	
ZZ512	AgustaWestland AW159 Wildcat AH1	RN No 847 NAS, Yeovilton	
ZZ513	AgustaWestland AW159 Wildcat HMA2	MoD/Leonardo MW, Yeovil (FASGW trials)	
ZZ514	AgustaWestland AW159 Wildcat HMA2	RN No 825 NAS, Yeovilton	
ZZ515	AgustaWestland AW159 Wildcat HMA2	RN No 815 NAS, Yeovilton	
ZZ516	AgustaWestland AW159 Wildcat HMA2	RN No 815 NAS, Yeovilton	
ZZ517	AgustaWestland AW159 Wildcat HMA2	RN No 825 NAS, Yeovilton	
ZZ518	AgustaWestland AW159 Wildcat HMA2	RN No 815 NAS, Yeovilton	
ZZ519	AgustaWestland AW159 Wildcat HMA2	RN No 825 NAS, Yeovilton	
ZZ520	AgustaWestland AW159 Wildcat AH1	AAC WCM, Yeovilton	
ZZ521	AgustaWestland AW159 Wildcat AH1	RN No 847 NAS, Yeovilton	
ZZ522	AgustaWestland AW159 Wildcat HMA2	RN No 815 NAS, Yeovilton	
ZZ523	AgustaWestland AW159 Wildcat AH1	AAC No 1 Regiment, Yeovilton	
ZZ524	AgustaWestland AW159 Wildcat AH1	AAC No 1 Regiment, Yeovilton	
ZZ525	AgustaWestland AW159 Wildcat AH1	AAC No 1 Regiment, Yeovilton	
ZZ526	AgustaWestland AW159 Wildcat AH1	MoD/Leonardo MW, Yeovil	
ZZ527	AgustaWestland AW159 Wildcat AH1	RN No 847 NAS, Yeovilton	
ZZ528	AgustaWestland AW159 Wildcat HMA2	RN No 825 NAS, Yeovilton	
ZZ529	AgustaWestland AW159 Wildcat HMA2	RN No 815 NAS, Yeovilton	
ZZ530	AgustaWestland AW159 Wildcat HMA2	RN No 815 NAS, Yeovilton	

Notes	Serial	Type (code/other identity)	Owner/operator, location or fate
	ZZ531	AgustaWestland AW159 Wildcat HMA2	RN WST/WZM, Yeovilton
	ZZ532	AgustaWestland AW159 Wildcat HMA2	RN WST/WZM, Yeovilton
	ZZ533	AgustaWestland AW159 Wildcat HMA2	RN No 815 NAS, Yeovilton
	ZZ534	AgustaWestland AW159 Wildcat HMA2	RN WST, stored Yeovilton
	ZZ535	AgustaWestland AW159 Wildcat HMA2	RN No 825 NAS, Yeovilton
	ZZ549	AgustaWestland AW159 Mk.220	*To the Philippine Navy as 440, 30 April 2019*
	ZZ550	AgustaWestland AW159 Mk.220	*To the Philippine Navy as 441, 30 April 2019*
	ZZ664	Boeing RC-135W (64-14833) $	RAF No 51 Sqn, Waddington
	ZZ665	Boeing RC-135W (64-14838)	RAF/Northrop Grumman, Greenville, SC, USA
	ZZ666	Boeing RC-135W (64-14830)	RAF No 51 Sqn, Waddington
	Z....	Airbus H145 Jupiter HT1	MoD (on order)
	Z....	Airbus H145 Jupiter HT1	MoD (on order)
	Z....	Airbus H145 Jupiter HT1	MoD (on order)
	Z....	Airbus H145 Jupiter HT1	MoD (on order)

Typhoon FGR4 ZK367/EB-R of No 41 (Test and Evaluation) Squadron at RAF Coningsby was the last of the type to wear full 41 Squadron markings and codes.

A line up of six Typhoon FGR4s at RAF Coningsby.

Serial	Type (code/other identity)	Owner/operator, location or fate	Notes
G-BYUB	Grob G.115E Tutor T1	Babcock/Cambridge UAS/East Midlands Universities AS/ University of London AS/No 115 Sqn, Wittering	
G-BYUC	Grob G.115E Tutor T1	Babcock/No 3 FTS/No 16 Sqn, Cranwell	
G-BYUD	Grob G.115E Tutor T1	Babcock/Yorkshire Universities AS, Linton-on-Ouse	
G-BYUE	Grob G.115E Tutor T1	Babcock/Cambridge UAS/East Midlands Universities AS/ University of London AS/No 115 Sqn, Wittering	
G-BYUF	Grob G.115E Tutor T1	Babcock/Northumbrian Universities AS, Leeming	
G-BYUH	Grob G.115E Tutor T1	Babcock/Bristol UAS/Southampton UAS, Boscombe Down	
G-BYUI	Grob G.115E Tutor T1	Babcock/Liverpool UAS/Manchester and Salford Universities AS, Woodvale	
G-BYUJ	Grob G.115E Tutor T1	Babcock/East of Scotland UAS, Leuchars	
G-BYUK	Grob G.115E Tutor T1	Babcock/Cambridge UAS/East Midlands Universities AS/ University of London AS/No 115 Sqn, Wittering	
G-BYUL	Grob G.115E Tutor T1	Babcock/Cambridge UAS/East Midlands Universities AS/ University of London AS/No 115 Sqn, Wittering	
G-BYUM	Grob G.115E Tutor T1	Babcock/Cambridge UAS/East Midlands Universities AS/ University of London AS/No 115 Sqn, Wittering	
G-BYUN	Grob G.115E Tutor T1	Babcock/No 3 FTS/No 16 Sqn, Cranwell	
G-BYUO	Grob G.115E Tutor T1	Babcock/No 3 FTS/No 16 Sqn, Cranwell	
G-BYUR	Grob G.115E Tutor T1	Babcock/East of Scotland UAS, Leuchars	
G-BYUS	Grob G.115E Tutor T1	Babcock/East of Scotland UAS, Leuchars	
G-BYUU	Grob G.115E Tutor T1	Babcock/Cambridge UAS/East Midlands Universities AS/ University of London AS/No 115 Sqn, Wittering	
G-BYUV	Grob G.115E Tutor T1	Babcock/No 1 EFTS/676 Sqn, Middle Wallop	
G-BYUW	Grob G.115E Tutor T1	Babcock/No 3 FTS/No 16 Sqn, Cranwell	
G-BYUX	Grob G.115E Tutor T1	Babcock/No 3 FTS/No 16 Sqn, Cranwell	
G-BYUY	Grob G.115E Tutor T1	Babcock/Liverpool UAS/Manchester and Salford Universities AS, Woodvale	
G-BYUZ	Grob G.115E Tutor T1	Babcock/No 3 FTS/No 16 Sqn, Cranwell	
G-BYVA	Grob G.115E Tutor T1	Babcock/Bristol UAS/Southampton UAS, Boscombe Down	
G-BYVB	Grob G.115E Tutor T1	Babcock/University of Wales AS, St Athan	
G-BYVC	Grob G.115E Tutor T1	Babcock/Cambridge UAS/East Midlands Universities AS/ University of London AS/No 115 Sqn, Wittering	
G-BYVD	Grob G.115E Tutor T1	Babcock/Bristol UAS/Southampton UAS, Boscombe Down	
G-BYVE	Grob G.115E Tutor T1	Babcock/Cambridge UAS/East Midlands Universities AS/ University of London AS/No 115 Sqn, Wittering	
G-BYVF	Grob G.115E Tutor T1	Babcock/RN No 727 NAS, Yeovilton	
G-BYVG	Grob G.115E Tutor T1	Babcock/Cambridge UAS/East Midlands Universities AS/ University of London AS/No 115 Sqn, Wittering	
G-BYVH	Grob G.115E Tutor T1	Babcock/Cambridge UAS/East Midlands Universities AS/ University of London AS/No 115 Sqn, Wittering	
G-BYVI	Grob G.115E Tutor T1	Babcock/Liverpool UAS/Manchester and Salford Universities AS, Woodvale	
G-BYVK	Grob G.115E Tutor T1	Babcock/RN No 727 NAS, Yeovilton	
G-BYVL	Grob G.115E Tutor T1	Babcock/University of Birmingham AS, Cosford	
G-BYVM	Grob G.115E Tutor T1	Babcock/Bristol UAS/Southampton UAS, Boscombe Down	
G-BYVO	Grob G.115E Tutor T1	Babcock/University of Wales AS, St Athan	
G-BYVP	Grob G.115E Tutor T1	Babcock/Liverpool UAS/Manchester and Salford Universities AS, Woodvale	
G-BYVR	Grob G.115E Tutor T1	Babcock/Cambridge UAS/East Midlands Universities AS/ University of London AS/No 115 Sqn, Wittering	
G-BYVU	Grob G.115E Tutor T1	Babcock/No 1 EFTS/676 Sqn, Middle Wallop	
G-BYVW	Grob G.115E Tutor T1	Babcock/University of Wales AS, St Athan	
G-BYVY	Grob G.115E Tutor T1	Babcock/Bristol UAS/Southampton UAS, Boscombe Down	
G-BYVZ	Grob G.115E Tutor T1	Babcock/University of Birmingham AS, Cosford	
G-BYWA	Grob G.115E Tutor T1	Babcock/Yorkshire Universities AS, Linton-on-Ouse	
G-BYWB	Grob G.115E Tutor T1	Babcock/Bristol UAS/Southampton UAS, Boscombe Down	
G-BYWD	Grob G.115E Tutor T1	Babcock/University of Birmingham AS, Cosford	

Notes	Serial	Type (code/other identity)	Owner/operator, location or fate
	G-BYWF	Grob G.115E Tutor T1	Babcock/RN No 727 NAS, Yeovilton
	G-BYWG	Grob G.115E Tutor T1	Babcock/University of Birmingham AS, Cosford
	G-BYWH	Grob G.115E Tutor T1	Babcock/Cambridge UAS/East Midlands Universities AS/ University of London AS/No 115 Sqn, Wittering
	G-BYWI	Grob G.115E Tutor T1	Babcock/Northern Ireland Universities AS, Aldergrove
	G-BYWK	Grob G.115E Tutor T1	Babcock/Northumbrian Universities AS, Leeming
	G-BYWL	Grob G.115E Tutor T1	Babcock/Bristol UAS/Southampton UAS, Boscombe Down
	G-BYWM	Grob G.115E Tutor T1	Babcock/Cambridge UAS/East Midlands Universities AS/ University of London AS/No 115 Sqn, Wittering
	G-BYWO	Grob G.115E Tutor T1	Babcock/Cambridge UAS/East Midlands Universities AS/ University of London AS/No 115 Sqn, Wittering
	G-BYWR	Grob G.115E Tutor T1	Babcock/University of Birmingham AS, Cosford
	G-BYWS	Grob G.115E Tutor T1	Babcock/Northern Ireland Universities AS, Aldergrove
	G-BYWU	Grob G.115E Tutor T1	Babcock/University of Birmingham AS, Cosford
	G-BYWV	Grob G.115E Tutor T1	Babcock/Cambridge UAS/East Midlands Universities AS/ University of London AS/No 115 Sqn, Wittering
	G-BYWW	Grob G.115E Tutor T1	Babcock/Bristol UAS/Southampton UAS, Boscombe Down
	G-BYWX	Grob G.115E Tutor T1	Babcock/Cambridge UAS/East Midlands Universities AS/ University of London AS/No 115 Sqn, Wittering
	G-BYWY	Grob G.115E Tutor T1	Babcock/University of Birmingham AS, Cosford
	G-BYWZ	Grob G.115E Tutor T1	Babcock/Cambridge UAS/East Midlands Universities AS/ University of London AS/No 115 Sqn, Wittering
	G-BYXA	Grob G.115E Tutor T1	Babcock/Northern Ireland Universities AS, Aldergrove
	G-BYXC	Grob G.115E Tutor T1	Babcock/Cambridge UAS/East Midlands Universities AS/ University of London AS/No 115 Sqn, Wittering
	G-BYXD	Grob G.115E Tutor T1	Babcock/University of Wales AS, St Athan
	G-BYXE	Grob G.115E Tutor T1	Babcock/Cambridge UAS/East Midlands Universities AS/ University of London AS/No 115 Sqn, Wittering
	G-BYXF	Grob G.115E Tutor T1	Babcock/No 1 EFTS/676 Sqn, Middle Wallop
	G-BYXG	Grob G.115E Tutor T1	Babcock/Bristol UAS/Southampton UAS, Boscombe Down
	G-BYXH	Grob G.115E Tutor T1	Babcock/Cambridge UAS/East Midlands Universities AS/ University of London AS/No 115 Sqn, Wittering
	G-BYXI	Grob G.115E Tutor T1	Babcock/No 1 EFTS/676 Sqn, Middle Wallop
	G-BYXJ	Grob G.115E Tutor T1	Babcock/Northumbrian Universities AS, Leeming
	G-BYXK	Grob G.115E Tutor T1	Babcock/RN No 727 NAS, Yeovilton
	G-BYXL	Grob G.115E Tutor T1	Babcock/Liverpool UAS/Manchester and Salford Universities AS, Woodvale
	G-BYXM	Grob G.115E Tutor T1 $	Babcock/Cambridge UAS/East Midlands Universities AS/ University of London AS/No 115 Sqn, Wittering
	G-BYXO	Grob G.115E Tutor T1	Babcock/East of Scotland UAS, Leuchars
	G-BYXP	Grob G.115E Tutor T1	Babcock/Cambridge UAS/East Midlands Universities AS/ University of London AS/No 115 Sqn, Wittering
	G-BYXS	Grob G.115E Tutor T1	Babcock/RN No 727 NAS, Yeovilton
	G-BYXT	Grob G.115E Tutor T1	Babcock/Yorkshire Universities AS, Linton-on-Ouse
	G-BYXX	Grob G.115E Tutor T1	Babcock/East of Scotland UAS, Leuchars
	G-BYXZ	Grob G.115E Tutor T1 $	Babcock/Cambridge UAS/East Midlands Universities AS/ University of London AS/No 115 Sqn, Wittering
	G-BYYA	Grob G.115E Tutor T1	Babcock/Northumbrian Universities AS, Leeming
	G-BYYB	Grob G.115E Tutor T1	Babcock/Yorkshire Universities AS, Linton-on-Ouse
	G-CGKD	Grob G.115E Tutor T1EA	Babcock/Oxford UAS, Benson
	G-CGKE	Grob G.115E Tutor T1EA	Babcock/Universities of Glasgow & Strathclyde AS, Glasgow
	G-CGKG	Grob G.115E Tutor T1EA	Babcock/Oxford UAS, Benson
	G-CGKH	Grob G.115E Tutor T1EA	Babcock/Oxford UAS, Benson
	G-CGKK	Grob G.115E Tutor T1EA	Babcock/Oxford UAS, Benson
	G-CGKL	Grob G.115E Tutor T1EA	Babcock/Cambridge UAS/East Midlands Universities AS/ University of London AS/No 115 Sqn, Wittering
	G-CGKN	Grob G.115E Tutor T1EA	Babcock/Oxford UAS, Benson
	G-CGKP	Grob G.115E Tutor T1EA	Babcock/Oxford UAS, Benson

Serial	Type (code/other identity)	Owner/operator, location or fate	Notes
G-CGKR	Grob G.115E Tutor T1EA	Babcock/Universities of Glasgow & Strathclyde AS, Glasgow	
G-CGKS	Grob G.115E Tutor T1EA	Babcock/Oxford UAS, Benson	
G-CGKU	Grob G.115E Tutor T1EA	Babcock/Universities of Glasgow & Strathclyde AS, Glasgow	
G-CGKW	Grob G.115E Tutor T1EA	Babcock/Oxford UAS, Benson	
G-DAYP	Hawker Beechcraft Super King Air 350C	MoD/Raytheon, Hawarden (for conversion to Shadow R2 ZZ505)	
G-ETPA	Pilatus PC-21 (HB-HYX)	QinetiQ/ETPS, MoD Boscombe Down	
G-ETPB	Pilatus PC-21 (HB-HYY)	QinetiQ/ETPS, MoD Boscombe Down	
G-ETPC	Grob G.120TP-A (D-ETQI)	QinetiQ/ETPS, MoD Boscombe Down	
G-ETPD	Grob G.120TP-A (D-ETIQ)	QinetiQ/ETPS, MoD Boscombe Down	
G-ETPE	Airbus Helicopters H.125	QinetiQ/ETPS, MoD Boscombe Down	
G-ETPF	Airbus Helicopters H.125	QinetiQ/ETPS, MoD Boscombe Down	
G-ETPG	Airbus Helicopters H.125	QinetiQ/ETPS, MoD Boscombe Down	
G-ETPH	Airbus Helicopters H.125	QinetiQ/ETPS, MoD Boscombe Down	
G-ETPI	Agusta A109E Power Elite (G-CFVB/QQ100)	QinetiQ/ETPS, MoD Boscombe Down	
G-ETPJ	Agusta A109E Power Elite (G-ESLH/ZE416)	QinetiQ/ETPS, MoD Boscombe Down	
G-ETPK	BAe RJ.70ER (G-BVRJ/QQ102)	QinetiQ/ETPS, MoD Boscombe Down	
G-ETPL	BAe RJ.100 (G-BZAY/QQ101)	QinetiQ/ETPS, MoD Boscombe Down	
G-ETPM	Diamond DA.42M-NG Twin Star (G-LTPA/QQ103)	QinetiQ/ETPS, MoD Boscombe Down	
G-FFRA	Dassault Falcon 20DC (N902FR)	Cobham Leasing Ltd, Bournemouth	
G-FRAD	Dassault Falcon 20E (9M-BDK)	Cobham Leasing Ltd, Teesside International	
G-FRAF	Dassault Falcon 20E (N911FR)	Cobham Leasing Ltd, Teesside International	
G-FRAH	Dassault Falcon 20DC (N900FR)	Cobham Leasing Ltd, Teesside International	
G-FRAI	Dassault Falcon 20E (N901FR)	Cobham Leasing Ltd, Bournemouth	
G-FRAJ	Dassault Falcon 20E (N903FR)	Cobham Leasing Ltd, Teesside International	
G-FRAK	Dassault Falcon 20DC (N905FR)	Cobham Leasing Ltd, Bournemouth	
G-FRAL	Dassault Falcon 20DC (N904FR)	Cobham Leasing Ltd, Bournemouth	
G-FRAP	Dassault Falcon 20DC (N908FR)	Cobham Leasing Ltd, Bournemouth	
G-FRAR	Dassault Falcon 20DC (N909FR)	Cobham Leasing Ltd, Teesside International	
G-FRAS	Dassault Falcon 20C (117501)	Cobham Leasing Ltd, Teesside International	
G-FRAT	Dassault Falcon 20C (117502)	Cobham Leasing Ltd, Bournemouth	
G-FRAU	Dassault Falcon 20C (117504)	Cobham Leasing Ltd, Bournemouth	
G-FRAW	Dassault Falcon 20ECM (117507)	Cobham Leasing Ltd, Bournemouth	
G-GMAD	Hawker Beechcraft Super King Air 350C	MoD/Raytheon, Hawarden (for conversion to Shadow R2 ZZ506)	

G-FRAL is a Dassault Falcon 20DC, operated by Cobham Leasing. This fleet of Falcon 20s are spread between bases at Bournemouth and Durham/Tees Valley and this is very much a type which has disappeared from UK skies with even some of the Cobham fleet now being retired with no obvious replacement in sight.

1764M/K4972	7473M/XE946	7827M/XA917	8017M/XL762
2015M/K5600	7491M/WT569	7829M/XH992	8018M/XN344
2292M/K8203	7496M/WT612	7839M/WV781	8019M/WZ869
2361M/K6035	7499M/WT555	7841M/WV783	8021M/XL824
3118M/H5199/(BK892)	7510M/WT694	7851M/WZ706	8027M/XM555
3858M/X7688	7525M/WT619	7854M/XM191	8032M/XH837
4354M/BL614	7530M/WT648	7855M/XK416	8034M/*XL554*/ (XL703)
4552M/T5298	7532M/WT651	7859M/XP283	8041M/XF690
4887M/JN768	7533M/WT680	7861M/*XL738*/(XM565)	8043M/XF836
5377M/EP120	7544M/WN904	7862M/XR246	8046M/XL770
5405M/LF738	7548M/PS915	7863M/*XP248*	8049M/WE168
5466M/*BN230*/(LF751)	7556M/WK584	7864M/XP244	8050M/XG329
5690M/MK356	7564M/XE982	7865M/TX226	8052M/WH166
5718M/BM597	7570M/XD674	7866M/XH278	8054AM/XM410
5758M/DG202	7582M/WP190	7868M/WZ736	8054BM/XM417
6457M/ML427	7583M/WP185	7869M/WK935	8055AM/XM402
6490M/LA255	7602M/WE600	7872M/*WZ826*/(XD826)	8055BM/XM404
6640M/RM694	7605M/WS692	7881M/WD413	8056M/XG337
6850M/TE184	7606M/*XF688*/ (WV562)	7882M/XD525	8057M/XR243
6946M/RW388	7607M/TJ138	7883M/XT150	8063M/WT536
6948M/DE673	7615M/WV679	7887M/XD375	8070M/EP120
6960M/MT847	7616M/WW388	7891M/XM693	8072M/PK624
7008M/EE549	7618M/WW442	7894M/XD818	8073M/TB252
7014M/N6720	7622M/WV606	7895M/WF784	8075M/RW382
7015M/NL985	7631M/VX185	7898M/XP854	8078M/XM351
7035M/*K2567*/(DE306)	7641M/XA634	7900M/WA576	8080M/XM480
7060M/VF301	7645M/WD293	7906M/WH132	8081M/XM468
7090M/EE531	7648M/XF785	7917M/WA591	8082M/XM409
7118M/LA198	7673M/WV332	7930M/WH301	8086M/TB752
7119M/LA226	7689M/WW450	7931M/RD253	8092M/WK654
7150M/PK683	7696M/WV493	7932M/WZ744	8094M/WT520
7154M/WB188	7698M/WV499	7933M/XR220	8097M/XN492
7174M/VX272	7704M/TW536	7937M/WS843	8101M/WH984
7175M/VV106	7705M/WL505	7938M/XH903	8102M/WT486
7200M/VT812	7706M/WB584	7939M/XD596	8103M/WR985
7241M/TE311/*(MK178)*	7709M/WT933	7940M/XL764	8106M/WR982
7243M/TE462	7711M/PS915	7955M/XH767	8114M/WL798
7245M/RW382	7712M/WK281	7957M/XF545	8117M/WR974
7246M/TD248	7715M/XK724	7960M/WS726	8118M/WZ549
7256M/TB752	7716M/WS776	7961M/WS739	8119M/WR971
7257M/TB252	7718M/WA577	7964M/WS760	8121M/XM474
7261M/VZ568	7719M/WK277	7965M/WS792	8124M/WZ572
7279M/TB752	7726M/XM373	7967M/WS788	8128M/WH775
7281M/TB252	7729M/WB758	7969M/WS840	8130M/WH798
7288M/PK724	7741M/VZ477	7971M/XK699	8131M/WT507
7293M/*TB675*/(RW393)	7750M/*WK864*/(WL168)	7973M/WS807	8140M/XJ571
7323M/VV217	7751M/WL131	7979M/XM529	8142M/XJ560
7325M/R5868	7755M/WG760	7980M/XM561	8147M/XR526
7326M/VN485	7759M/PK664	7982M/XH892	8151M/WV795
7362M/475081/(VP546)	7761M/XH318	7983M/XD506	8153M/WV903
7416M/WN907	7762M/XE670	7984M/XN597	8154M/WV908
7421M/WT660	7764M/XH318	7986M/WG777	8155M/WV797
7422M/WT684	7770M/*XF506*/(WT746)	7988M/XL149	8156M/XE339
7428M/WK198	7793M/XG523	7990M/XD452	8158M/XE369
7432M/WZ724	7798M/XH783	7997M/XG452	8162M/WM913
7438M/*18671*/(WP905)	7806M/TA639	7998M/*XM515*/(XD515)	8164M/*WN105*/(WF299)
7443M/WX853	7809M/XA699	8005M/WG768	8165M/WH791
7458M/WX905	7816M/WG763	8009M/XG518	8169M/WH364
7464M/XA564	7817M/TX214	8010M/XG547	8173M/XN685
7470M/XA553	7825M/WK991	8012M/VS562	8176M/WH791

8177M/WM224	8390M/SL542	8514M/XS176	8706M/XF383
8179M/XN928	8392M/SL674	8535M/XN776	8708M/XF509
8183M/*XN972*/(XN962)	8394M/WG422	8538M/XN781	8709M/XG209
8184M/WT520	8395M/WF408	8545M/XN726	8710M/XG274
8186M/WR977	8396M/XK740	8546M/XN728	8711M/XG290
8187M/WH791	8399M/WR539	8548M/WT507	8713M/XG225
8189M/*WD615* (WD646)	8401M/XP686	8549M/WT534	8718M/XX396
8190M/XJ918	8406M/XP831	8554M/TG511	8719M/XT257
8192M/XR658	8407M/XP585	8561M/XS100	8721M/XP354
8198M/WT339	8408M/XS186	8563M/*XX822*/(XW563)	8724M/XW923
8203M/XD377	8409M/XS209	8565M/*349*/(E-408)	8726M/XP299
8205M/XN819	8410M/XR662	8566M/XV279	8727M/XR486
8206M/WG419	8413M/XM192	8573M/XM708	8728M/WT532
8208M/WG303	8414M/XM173	8575M/XP542	8729M/WJ815
8209M/WG418	8417M/XM144	8576M/XP502	8732M/XJ729
8210M/WG471	8422M/XM169	8578M/XR534	8733M/XL318
8211M/WK570	8427M/XM172	8581M/WJ775	8736M/XF375
8213M/WK626	8429M/XH592	8582M/XE874	8739M/XH170
8215M/WP869	8434M/XM411	8583M/BAPC 94	8740M/WE173
8216M/WP927	8436M/XN554	8585M/XE670	8741M/XW329
8218M/WB645	8437M/WG362	8586M/XE643	8743M/WD790
8229M/XM355	8439M/WZ846	8588M/XR681	8746M/XH171
8230M/XM362	8440M/WD935	8589M/XR700	8749M/XH537
8234M/XN458	8442M/XP411	8590M/XM191	8751M/XT255
8235M/XN549	8452M/XK885	8591M/XA813	8753M/WL795
8236M/XP573	8453M/XP745	8595M/XH278	8762M/WH740
8237M/XS179	8458M/XP672	8598M/WP270	8764M/XP344
8238M/XS180	8459M/XR650	8600M/XX761	8768M/A-522
8338M/XS180	8460M/XP680	8602M/*PF179*/(XR541)	8769M/A-426
8342M/WP848	8462M/XX477	8604M/XS104	8770M/XL623
8344M/WH960	8463M/XP355	8606M/XP530	8771M/XM602
8350M/WH840	8464M/XJ758	8608M/XP540	8772M/WR960
8352M/XN632	8465M/W1048	8610M/XL502	8778M/XM598
8355M/KN645	8466M/L-866	8611M/WF128	8779M/XM607
8357M/WK576	8467M/WP912	8620M/XP534	8780M/WK102
8359M/WF825	8468M/MM5701/(BT474)	8621M/XR538	8781M/WE982
8361M/WB670	8469M/100503	8624M/*XR991*/(XS102)	8782M/XH136
8362M/WG477	8470M/584219	8627M/XP558	8785M/XS642
8364M/WG464	8471M/701152	8628M/XJ380	8789M/XK970
8365M/XK421	8472M/120227/(VN679)	8630M/WG362	8791M/XP329
8366M/XG454	8473M/WP190	8631M/XR574	8792M/XP345
8367M/XG474	8474M/494083	8633M/3W-17/MK732	8793M/XP346
8368M/XF926	8475M/360043/(PJ876)	8634M/WP314	8794M/XP398
8369M/WE139	8476M/24	8640M/XR977	8796M/XK943
8370M/N1671	8477M/4101/(DG200)	8642M/XR537	8799M/WV787
8371M/XA847	8478M/10639	8645M/XD163	8800M/XG226
8372M/K8042	8479M/730301	8648M/XK526	8805M/XV722
8373M/P2617	8481M/191614	8653M/XS120	8807M/XL587
8375M/NX611	8482M/112372/(VK893)	8656M/XP405	8810M/XJ825
8376M/RF398	8483M/420430	8657M/VZ634	8816M/XX734
8377M/R9125	8484M/5439	8661M/XJ727	8818M/XK527
8378M/*T9707*	8485M/997	8666M/XE793	8820M/VP952
8379M/DG590	8486M/BAPC 99	8672M/XP351	8822M/VP957
8380M/Z7197	8487M/J-1172	8673M/XD165	8828M/XS587
8382M/VR930	8488M/WL627	8676M/XL577	8830M/*N-294*/(XF515)
8383M/K9942	8491M/WJ880	8679M/XF526	8831M/XG160
8384M/X4590	8493M/XR571	8680M/XF527	8832M/*XG168*/(XG172)
8385M/N5912	8494M/XP557	8681M/XG164	8833M/XL569
8386M/NV778	8501M/XP640	8682M/XP404	8834M/XL572
8387M/T6296	8502M/XP686	8693M/WH863	8836M/XL592
8388M/XL993	8508M/XS218	8702M/XG196	8838M/*34037*/(429356)
8389M/VX573	8509M/XT141	8703M/VW453	8839M/XG194

8841M/XE606	8950M/XX956	9073M/XW924	9185M/XZ987
8853M/XT277	8951M/XX727	9075M/XV752	9187M/XW405
8855M/XT284	8953M/XX959	9076M/XV808	9188M/XW364
8857M/XW544	8954M/XZ384	9078M/XV753	9194M/XW420
8858M/XW541	8955M/XX110	9079M/XZ130	9195M/XW330
8863M/XG154	8957M/XN582	9080M/ZE350	9196M/XW370
8867M/XK532	8961M/XS925	9086M/ZE352	9197M/*XX530*/(XX637)
8868M/WH775	8967M/XV263	9087M/XX753	9198M/XS641
8869M/WH957	8969M/XR753	9090M/XW353	9199M/XW290
8870M/WH964	8972M/XR754	9091M/XW434	9201M/ZD667
8871M/WJ565	8973M/XS922	9092M/XH669	9203M/*3066*
8873M/XR453	8974M/XM473	9093M/WK124	9205M/*E449*
8874M/XE597	8975M/XW917	9095M/XW547	9206M/F6314
8875M/XE624	8976M/XZ630	9096M/WV322	9207M/8417/18
8876M/*VM791*/(XA312)	8978M/XX837	9098M/XV406	9208M/F938
8880M/XF435	8984M/XN551	9103M/XV411	9210M/MF628
8881M/XG254	8985M/WK127	9110M/XX736	9211M/733682
8883M/XX946	8986M/XV261	9111M/XW421	9212M/*KL216*/(45-49295)
8884M/VX275	8987M/XM358	9115M/XV863	9213M/N5182
8885M/XW922	8990M/XM419	9117M/XV161	9215M/XL164
8886M/XA243	8995M/XM425	9119M/XW303	9216M/XL190
8888M/XA231	8996M/XM414	9120M/XW419	9217M/ZH257
8889M/XN239	8997M/XX669	9122M/XZ997	9218M/XL563
8890M/WT532	8998M/XT864	9123M/XT773	9219M/XZ971
8895M/XX746	9002M/XW763	9125M/XW410	9221M/XZ966
8896M/XX821	9003M/XZ390	9127M/XW432	9222M/XZ968
8897M/XX969	9004M/XZ370	9130M/XW327	9224M/XL568
8898M/XX119	9005M/XZ374	9131M/*DD931*	9225M/XX885
8899M/XX756	9006M/XX967	9132M/XX977	9226M/XV865
8900M/XZ368	9007M/XX968	9133M/*413573*	9227M/XB812
8901M/XZ383	9008M/XX140	9134M/XT288	9229M/ZA678
8902M/XV739	9009M/XX763	9136M/XT891	9233M/XZ431
8903M/XX747	9010M/XX764	9137M/XN579	9234M/XV864
8905M/XX975	9011M/XM412	9139M/XV863	9236M/WV318
8906M/XX976	9012M/XN494	9140M/XZ287	9237M/XF445
8907M/XZ371	9014M/XN584	9141M/XV118	9238M/ZA717
8908M/XZ382	9015M/XW320	9143M/XN589	9239M/7198/18
8909M/XV784	9017M/ZE449	9145M/XV863	9241M/XS639
8910M/XL160	9019M/XX824	9146M/XW299	9242M/XH672
8911M/XH673	9020M/XX825	9148M/XW436	9246M/XS714
8918M/XX109	9021M/XX826	9149M/XW375	9248M/WB627
8919M/XT486	9026M/XP629	9150M/*FX760*	9249M/WV396
8920M/XT469	9027M/XP556	9151M/XT907	9251M/XX744
8921M/XT466	9032M/XR673	9152M/XV424	9252M/XX722
8922M/XT467	9033M/XS181	9153M/XW360	9254M/XX965
8923M/XX819	9036M/XM350	9154M/XW321	9255M/XZ375
8924M/XP701	9038M/XV810	9155M/WL679	9257M/XX962
8925M/XP706	9039M/XN586	9162M/XZ991	9258M/XW265
8931M/XV779	9040M/XZ138	9163M/XV415	9259M/XS710
8932M/XR718	9041M/XW763	9166M/XW323	9260M/XS734
8934M/XR749	9042M/XL954	9167M/XV744	9261M/*W2068*
8935M/XR713	9044M/XS177	9168M/XZ132	9262M/XZ358
8937M/XX751	9047M/XW409	9169M/XW547	9263M/XW267
8938M/WV746	9048M/XM403	9170M/XZ994	9264M/XS735
8941M/XT456	9049M/XW404	9172M/XW304	9265M/WK585
8942M/XN185	9052M/WJ717	9173M/XW418	9266M/XZ119
8943M/XE799	9056M/XS488	9174M/XZ131	9267M/XW269
8944M/WZ791	9059M/ZE360	9175M/P1344	9268M/XR529
8945M/XX818	9066M/XV582	9176M/XW430	9269M/XT914
8946M/XZ389	9067M/XV586	9179M/XW309	9270M/XZ145
8947M/XX726	9070M/XV581	9180M/XW311	9272M/XS486
8949M/XX743	9072M/XW768	9181M/XW358	9273M/XS726

9274M/XS738	9292M/XW892	9314M/ZA320	9330M/ZB684
9275M/XS729	9293M/XX830	9315M/ZA319	9331M/XW852
9277M/XT601	9294M/XX655	9316M/ZA399	9332M/XZ935
9278M/XS643	9295M/XV497	9317M/ZA450	9336M/ZA407
9279M/XT681	9298M/ZE340	9318M/ZA360	9337M/ZA774
9281M/XZ146	9299M/XW870	9319M/XR516	9338M/ZA325
9283M/XZ322	9300M/XX483	9320M/XX153	9339M/ZA323
9284M/ZA267	9301M/XZ941	9321M/XZ367	9340M/XX745
9285M/XR806	9302M/ZD462	9322M/ZB686	9341M/ZA357
9286M/XT905	9303M/XV709	9323M/XV643	9342M/XR498
9287M/WP962	9306M/XX979	9324M/XV659	9343M/XR506
9288M/XX520	9308M/ZD932	9326M/XV653	9344M/XV706
9289M/XX665	9310M/ZA355	9328M/ZD607	
9290M/XX626	9311M/ZA475	9329M/ZD578	

The retirement of the RAF's Tornado GR4 fleet was commemorated in a number of ways, including a series of fly pasts over the UK. Here three Tornado GR4s overfly Boscombe Down on 20 February 2019 for one last time, just three weeks before the final flight.

RN LANDING PLATFORM AND SHORE STATION CODE-LETTERS

Deck Letters	Vessel Name and Pennant No.	Vessel Type and Unit
AB	HMS *Albion* (L14)	Assault
AS	RFA *Argus* (A135)	Aviation Training ship
AY	HMS *Argyll* (F231)	Type 23
BK	HMS *Bulwark* (L15)	Assault
BV	RFA *Black Rover* (A273)	Fleet tanker
CB	RFA *Cardigan Bay* (L3009)	Landing ship
CU	RNAS Culdrose (HMS *Seahawk*)	
DA	HMS *Daring* (D32)	Type 45
DF	HMS *Defender* (D36)	Type 45
DG	RFA *Diligence* (A132)	Maintenance
DM	HMS *Diamond* (D34)	Type 45
DN	HMS *Dragon* (D35)	Type 45
DT	HMS *Dauntless* (D33)	Type 45
DU	HMS *Duncan* (D37)	Type 45
FA	RFA *Fort Austin* (A386)	Support ship
FE	RFA *Fort Rosalie* (A385)	Support ship
FV	RFA *Fort Victoria* (A387)	Auxiliary Oiler
IR	HMS *Iron Duke* (F234)	Type 23
KT	HMS *Kent* (F78)	Type 23
LA	HMS *Lancaster* (F229)	Type 23
MB	RFA *Mounts Bay* (L3008)	Landing ship
MM	HMS *Monmouth* (F235)	Type 23
MR	HMS *Montrose* (F236)	Type 23
NL	HMS *Northumberland* (F238)	Type 23
O	HMS *Ocean* (L12)	Helicopter carrier
P	HMS *Prince of Wales* (R09)	Aircraft carrier
Q	HMS *Queen Elizabeth* (R08)	Aircraft carrier
PD	HMS *Portland* (F79)	Type 23
RM	HMS *Richmond* (F239)	Type 23
SB	HMS *St Albans* (F83)	Type 23
SM	HMS *Somerset* (F82)	Type 23
SU	HMS *Sutherland* (F81)	Type 23
VL	RNAS Yeovilton (HMS *Heron*)	
WK	RFA *Wave Knight* (A389)	Fleet tanker
WM	HMS *Westminster* (F237)	Type 23
YB	RFA *Lyme Bay* (L3007)	Landing ship
–	HMS *Protector* (A173)	Ice patrol
–	RFA *Wave Ruler* (A390)	Fleet tanker

RN CODE – SQUADRON – BASE – AIRCRAFT CROSS-CHECK

Deck/Base Code Numbers	Letters	Unit	Location	Aircraft Type(s)
010 — 015	CU	820 NAS	Culdrose	Merlin HM2
264 — 274	CU	814 NAS	Culdrose	Merlin HM2
500 — 515	CU	829 NAS	Culdrose	Merlin HM2
580 — 588	CU	824 NAS	Culdrose	Merlin HM2

Note that only the 'last two' digits of the Code are worn by some aircraft types, especially helicopters.

ROYAL AIR FORCE SQUADRON MARKINGS

This table gives brief details of the markings worn by aircraft of RAF squadrons. While this may help to identify the operator of a particular machine, it may not always give the true picture. For example, from time to time aircraft are loaned to other units while others wear squadron marks but are actually operated on a pool basis. Squadron badges are usually located on the front fuselage.

Squadron	Type(s) operated	Base(s)	Distinguishing marks & other comments
No 1(F) Sqn	Typhoon T3/FGR4	RAF Lossiemouth	Badge (on tail): A red 1 with yellow wings on a white background, flanked in red. Roundel is flanked by two white chevrons, edged in red.
No 2(AC) Sqn/ II(AC) Sqn	Typhoon T3/FGR4	RAF Lossiemouth	Badge: A wake knot on a white circular background flanked on either side by black and white triangles. Tail fin has a black stripe with white triangles and the badge repeated on it.
No 3(F) Sqn	Typhoon T3/FGR4	RAF Coningsby	Badge: A blue cockatrice on a white circular background flanked by two green bars edged with yellow. Tail fin as a green stripe edged with yellow.
No 4 Sqn/ IV Sqn	Hawk T2	RAF Valley	Badge (on nose): A yellow lightning flash on a red background with IV superimposed. Aircraft carry a yellow lightning flash on a red and black background on the tail and this is repeated in bars either side of the roundel on the fuselage. Part of No 4 FTS.
No 5(AC) Sqn/ V(AC) Sqn	Sentinel R1	RAF Waddington	Badge (on tail): A green maple leaf on a white circle over a red horizontal band.
No 6 Sqn	Typhoon T3/FGR4	RAF Lossiemouth	Badge (on tail): A red, winged can opener on a blue shield, edged in red. The roundel is flanked by a red zigzag on a blue background.
No 7 Sqn	Chinook HC6	RAF Odiham	Badge (on tail): A blue badge containing the seven stars of Ursa Major ('The Plough') in yellow.
No 8 Sqn	Sentry AEW1	RAF Waddington	Badge (on tail): A grey, sheathed, Arabian dagger. Aircraft pooled with No 54 Sqn. [To convert to the E-7 Wedgetail when the Sentry retires.]
No 9 Sqn/	Typhoon T3/FGR4	RAF Lossiemouth	Badge: A green bat on a black circular background, IX Sqn flanked by yellow and green horizontal stripes. The green bat also appears on the tail, edged in yellow.
No 10 Sqn	Voyager KC2/KC3	RAF Brize Norton	No markings worn.
No 11 Sqn	Typhoon T3/FGR4	RAF Coningsby	Badge (on tail): Two eagles in flight on a white shield. The roundel is flanked by yellow and black triangles.
No 12 Sqn	Typhoon T3/FGR4	RAF Coningsby	No markings worn.
No 13 Sqn	Reaper	RAF Waddington	No markings worn.
No 14 Sqn	Shadow R1/R1+/R2	RAF Waddington	No markings worn.
No 16 Sqn	Tutor T1	RAF Cranwell	No markings carried. Part of No 1 EFTS.
No 17 Test & Evaluation Sqn	Lightning II	Edwards AFB, USA	No markings worn
No 18(B) Sqn	Chinook HC4/HC5/HC6/ HC6A	RAF Odiham	Badge (on tail): A red winged horse on a black circle. Aircraft pooled with No 27 Sqn.

Squadron	Type(s) operated	Base(s)	Distinguishing marks & other comments
No 24 Sqn/ XXIV Sqn	Hercules C4/C5/ Atlas C1	RAF Brize Norton	No squadron markings carried. Aircraft pooled with No 30 Sqn, No 47 Sqn and No 70 Sqn.
No 25 Sqn/ XXV Sqn	Hawk T2	RAF Valley	Badge (on tail): A hawk on a gauntlet. Aircraft have XXV on the tail and silver and grey bars either side of the roundel on the fuselage. Part of No 4 FTS. Aircraft are coded F*.
No 27 Sqn	Chinook HC4/ HC5/HC6	RAF Odiham	Badge (on tail): A dark green elephant on a green circle, flanked by green and dark green stripes. Aircraft pooled with No 18 Sqn.
No 28 Sqn	Chinook HC4/ Puma HC2	RAF Benson	Badge: A winged horse above two white crosses on a red shield.
No 29 Sqn	Typhoon T3/FGR4	RAF Coningsby	Badge (on tail): An eagle in flight, preying on a buzzard, with three red Xs across the top. The roundel is flanked by two white bars outlined by a red line, each containing three red Xs.
No 30 Sqn	Hercules C4/C5	RAF Brize Norton	No squadron markings carried. Aircraft pooled with No 24 Sqn and No 47 Sqn.
No 32(The Royal) Sqn	BAe 146 CC2/146 C3/ Agusta 109	RAF Northolt	No squadron markings carried but aircraft carry a distinctive livery with a red stripe, edged in blue along the middle of the fuselage and a red tail.
No 33 Sqn	Puma HC2	RAF Benson	Badge: A stag's head.
No 39 Sqn	Predator/ Reaper	Nellis AFB Creech AFB	No markings worn.
No 41 Test & Evaluation Sqn [FJWOEU]	Typhoon T3/FGR4	RAF Coningsby	Badge: A red, double armed cross on the tail with a gold crown above. White and red horizontal bars flanking the roundel on the fuselage. Aircraft are coded EB-*.
No 45 Sqn	Phenom/Tutor T1EA	RAF Cranwell	The Phenoms carry a dark blue stripe on the tail superimposed with red diamonds. Part of No 3 FTS.
No 47 Sqn	Hercules C4/C5	RAF Brize Norton	No squadron markings usually carried. Aircraft pooled with No 24 Sqn and No 30 Sqn.
No 51 Sqn	RC-135W	RAF Waddington	Badge (on tail): A red goose in flight.
No 54 Sqn [ISTAR OCU]	Shadow R1/ Sentry AEW1/ Sentinel R1	RAF Waddington	Based aircraft as required.
No 56 Sqn [ISTAR Test & Evaluation Sqn]	Shadow R1/ Sentry AEW1/ Sentinel R1	RAF Waddington	Based aircraft as required.
No 57 Sqn	Prefect T1	RAF Barkston Heath/ RAF Cranwell	No markings carried. Part of No 1 EFTS.
No 60 Sqn	Juno HT1	RAF Shawbury [DHFS]	No squadron markings usually carried.
No 70 Sqn Fixed Wing Air Mobility OCU/LXX Sqn	Atlas C1	RAF Brize Norton	No squadron markings usually carried. Aircraft pooled with No 24 Sqn.

Squadron	Type(s) operated	Base(s)	Distinguishing marks & other comments
No 72 Sqn	Texan T1	RAF Valley	Badge: A black swift in flight on a red disk, flanked with blue bars edged with red. Part of No 4 FTS.
No 84 Sqn	Griffin HAR2	RAF Akrotiri	Badge (on tail): A scorpion on a playing card symbol (diamonds, clubs etc.). Aircraft carry a vertical light blue stripe through the roundel on the fuselage.
No 99 Sqn	Globemaster III	RAF Brize Norton	Badge (on tail): A black puma leaping.
No 100 Sqn	Hawk T1A	RAF Leeming	Badge (on tail): A skull in front of two bones crossed. Aircraft are usually coded C*. Incorporates the Joint Forward Air Control Training and Standards Unit (JFACTSU)
No 101 Sqn	Voyager KC2/KC3	RAF Brize Norton	No markings worn.
No 115 Sqn	Tutor T1	Wittering	No markings carried. Part of the CFS.
No 202 Sqn	Jupiter HT1	RAF Valley	Badge: A mallard alighting on a white circle.
No 206 Sqn [HAT&ES]	Hercules C4/C5	RAF Brize Norton/ Boscombe Down	No squadron markings usually carried.
No 207 Sqn	Lightning II	RAF Marham	No markings worn
No 230 Sqn	Puma HC2	RAF Benson	Badge: A tiger in front of a palm tree on a black pentagon.
No 617 Sqn	Lightning II	RAF Marham	No markings worn
No 1310 Flt	Chinook HC4	Mount Pleasant, FI	No markings worn
No 1312 Flt	Hercules C5/ Voyager KC2/KC3	Mount Pleasant, FI	Badge (on tail): A red Maltese cross on a white circle, flanked by red and white horizontal bars.
No 1435 Flt	Typhoon FGR4	Mount Pleasant, FI	Badge (on tail): A red Maltese cross on a white circle, flanked by red and white horizontal bars.

Hawk T2 ZK027 is one of 14 that have been painted in 25 Squadron markings colours and in this case coded FC. It is seen here at the Royal International Air Tattoo, wearing its previous code, R, and markings of No 4 Squadron, part of No 4 FTS at RAF Valley, a few months prior to the change.

UNIVERSITY AIR SQUADRONS/AIR EXPERIENCE FLIGHTS*

As from 7 September 2015 all UAS flights and AEFs are commanded and managed by No 6 FTS RAF. Some UAS aircraft carry squadron badges and markings, usually on the tail. Squadron crests all consist of a white circle surrounded by a blue circle, topped with a red crown and having a yellow scroll beneath. Each differs by the motto on the scroll, the UAS name running around the blue circle & by the contents at the centre and it is the latter which are described below.

* All AEFs come under the administration of local UASs and these are listed here.

UAS	Base	Marks
Bristol UAS/ No 3 AEF	Boscombe Down	A sailing ship on water.
Cambridge UAS/ No 5 AEF	Wittering	A heraldic lion in front of a red badge. Aircraft pooled with University of London AS.
East Midlands Universities AS/ No 7 AEF	Wittering	A yellow quiver, full of arrows.
East of Scotland UAS/ No 12 AEF	RAF Leuchars	An open book in front of a white diagonal cross edged in blue.
Liverpool UAS	RAF Woodvale	A bird atop an open book, holding a branch in its beak. Aircraft pooled with Manchester and Salford Universities AS
Manchester and Salford Universities AS/ No 10 AEF	RAF Woodvale	A bird of prey with a green snake in its beak. Aircraft pooled with Liverpool UAS
Northern Ireland Universities AS/ No 14 AEF	JHFS Aldergrove	(Currently not known)
Northumbrian Universities AS/ No 11 AEF	RAF Leeming	A white cross on a blue background.
Oxford UAS/ No 6 AEF	RAF Benson	An open book in front of crossed swords.
Southampton UAS/ No 2 AEF	Boscombe Down	A red stag in front of a stone pillar.
Universities of Glasgow and Strathclyde AS/ No 4 AEF	Glasgow	A bird of prey in flight, holding a branch in its beak, in front of an upright sword.
University of Birmingham AS/ No 8 AEF	DCAE Cosford	A blue griffon with two heads.
University of London AS	Wittering	A globe superimposed over an open book. Aircraft pooled with Cambridge UAS.
University of Wales AS/ No 1 AEF	MoD St Athan	A red Welsh dragon in front of an open book, clasping a sword. Some aircraft have the dragon in front of white and green squares.
Yorkshire Universities AS/ No 9 AEF	RAF Linton-on-Ouse	An open book in front of a Yorkshire rose with leaves.

This table gives brief details of the markings worn by aircraft of FAA squadrons. Squadron badges, when worn, are usually located on the front fuselage. All FAA squadron badges comprise a crown atop a circle edged in gold braid and so the badge details below list only what appears in the circular part.

Squadron	Type(s) operated	Base(s)	Distinguishing marks & other comments
No 700X NAS	RQ-12 Wasp/ RQ-20 Puma/Scan Eagle RM1	RNAS Culdrose	Badge: No markings carried.
No 727 NAS	Tutor T1	RNAS Yeovilton	Badge: The head of Britannia wearing a gold helmet on a background of blue and white waves.
No 736 NAS	Hawk T1A	RNAS Culdrose & RNAS Yeovilton	A white lightning bolt on the tail.
No 744 NAS	Chinook HC6A/ Merlin (Crowsnest)	MoD Boscombe Down	Badge: No details
No 750 NAS	Avenger T1	RNAS Culdrose	Badge: A Greek runner bearing a torch & sword on a background of blue and white waves.
No 814 NAS	Merlin HM2	RNAS Culdrose	Badge: A winged tiger mask on a background of dark blue and white waves.
No 815 NAS	Wildcat HMA2	RNAS Yeovilton	Badge: A winged, gold harpoon on a background of blue and white waves.
No 820 NAS	Merlin HM2	RNAS Culdrose	Badge: A flying fish on a background of blue and white waves.
No 824 NAS	Merlin HM2	RNAS Culdrose	Badge: A heron on a background of blue and white waves.
No 825 NAS	Wildcat HMA2	RNAS Yeovilton	Badge: An eagle over a Maltese cross.
No 845 NAS	Merlin HC3A/HC3i/HC4	RNAS Yeovilton	Badge: A dragonfly on a background of blue and white waves.
No 846 NAS	Merlin HC3i/HC4	RNAS Yeovilton	Badge: A swordsman riding a winged horse whilst a serpent on a background of blue and white waves.
No 847 NAS	Wildcat AH1	RNAS Yeovilton	Badge (not currently worn): A gold sea lion on a blue background. Aircraft wear ARMY titles.

ZH857 is a Merlin HM2, based at RNAS Culdrose. These machines are hard worked and often deployed on ships and clearly the weather is beginning to take its toll as this isn't the only one in the fleet where the white letter of its owner and identity have begun to peel off.

This section lists the codes worn by some UK military aircraft and, alongside, the Registration of the aircraft currently wearing this code. It should be pointed out that in some cases more than one aircraft wears the same code but the aircraft listed is the one believed to be in service with the unit concerned at the time of going to press. This list will be updated regularly and those with Internet access can download the latest version via the 'Military Aircraft Markings' Web Site, www.militaryaircraftmarkings.co.uk.

ROYAL AIR FORCE
BAE Hawk T1/T2

Code	Registration
B	ZK011
C	ZK012
D	ZK013
E	ZK014
F	ZK015
G	ZK016
H	ZK017
I	ZK018
J	ZK019
K	ZK020
L	ZK021
M	ZK022
N	ZK023
O	ZK024
CA	XX246
CB	XX255
CC	XX191
CD	XX332
CF	XX203
CG	XX318
CH	XX198
CI	XX321
CJ	XX261
CK	XX205 & XX285
CL	XX339
CM	XX337
CN	XX187
CP	XX346
CQ	XX348
CR	XX189 & XX303
CS	XX202
CU	XX329
FA	ZK025
FB	ZK026
FC	ZK027
FD	ZK028
FE	ZK029
FF	ZK030
FG	ZK031
FH	ZK032
FI	ZK033
FJ	ZK034
FK	ZK035
FL	ZK036
FM	ZK037
FN	ZK010

Eurofighter Typhoon

Code	Registration
C	ZJ935
D	ZJ941
F	ZJ915
H	ZJ926
AX	ZK303
EB-R	ZK367
WS-J	ZJ924
WS-R	ZJ917
WS-Y	ZJ913

Lockheed Martin F-35B
Lightning II

Code	Registration
001	ZM135
002	ZM136
004	ZM138
005	ZM139
007	ZM141
008	ZM142
010	ZM144
011	ZM145
012	ZM146
013	ZM147
014	ZM148
015	ZM149
016	ZM150
017	ZM151
018	ZM152

WS Puma HC2

Code	Registration
G	XW216
H	XW217
K	XW220
N	XW231
P	XW232
V	ZA940
W	ZJ954
X	ZJ955
Y	ZJ956
Z	ZJ957

ROYAL NAVY
BAE Hawk T1

Code	Registration
842	XX239
844	XX329
846	XX256
849	XX316 & XX317

EHI-101 Merlin

Code	Registration
10	ZH827
11	ZH826
12	ZH846
13	ZH835
14	ZH837
61	ZH841
66	ZH847
68	ZH853
69	ZH839
70	ZH847
80	ZH836
81	ZH840
82	ZH842
83	ZH850
84	ZH841
85	ZH861 & ZH864
86	ZH862
87	ZH834
88	ZH828 & ZH851
A	ZJ117
B	ZJ118
C	ZJ119
D	ZJ120
E	ZJ121
F	ZJ122
G	ZJ123
H	ZJ124
J	ZJ125
K	ZJ126
L	ZJ127
M	ZJ128
N	ZJ129
O	ZJ130
P	ZJ131
Q	ZJ132
R	ZJ133
S	ZJ134
T	ZJ135
U	ZJ136
W	ZJ137
X	ZJ138
AA	ZJ990
AB	ZJ992
AC	ZJ994
AD	ZJ995
AE	ZJ998
AF	ZK001

ARMY AIR CORPS
Bell 212

Code	Registration
B	ZK067
K	ZJ969
X	ZH814
Y	ZH815

WS Gazelle AH1

Code	Registration
S	ZB691

Some *historic, classic and warbird* aircraft carry the markings of overseas air arms and can be seen in the UK, mainly preserved in museums and collections or taking part in air shows.

Serial	Type (code/other identity)	Owner/operator, location or fate	Notes
AFGHANISTAN			
-	Hawker Afghan Hind (K4672/BAPC 82)	RAF Museum Reserve Collection, Stafford	
ARGENTINA			
-	Bell UH-1H Iroquois (AE-406/*998-8888*) [Z]	South Yorkshire Aircraft Museum, Doncaster	
0729	Beech T-34C Turbo Mentor	FAA Museum, stored Cobham Hall, RNAS Yeovilton	
0767	Aermacchi MB339AA	South Yorkshire Aircraft Museum, Doncaster	
A-515	FMA IA58 Pucará (ZD485)	RAF Museum, stored Cosford	
A-517	FMA IA58 Pucará (G-BLRP)	Privately owned, Channel Islands	
A-522	FMA IA58 Pucará (8768M)	FAA Museum, at NE Aircraft Museum, Usworth	
A-528	FMA IA58 Pucará (8769M)	Norfolk & Suffolk Avn Museum, Flixton	
A-533	FMA IA58 Pucará (ZD486) <ff>	Privately owned, Chelmsford	
A-549	FMA IA58 Pucará (ZD487)	IWM Duxford	
AE-331	Agusta A109A (ZE411)	FAA Museum, stored Cobham Hall, RNAS Yeovilton	
AE-409	Bell UH-1H Iroquois [656]	Army Flying Museum, Middle Wallop	
AE-422	Bell UH-1H Iroquois	FAA Museum, stored Cobham Hall, RNAS Yeovilton	
AUSTRALIA			
369	Hawker Fury ISS (F-AZXL) [D]	Privately owned, Cannes, France	
A2-4	Supermarine Seagull V (VH-ALB)	RAF Museum Reserve Collection, Stafford	
A11-301	Auster J/5G (G-ARKG) [931-NW]	Privately owned, Spanhoe	
A16-199	Lockheed Hudson IIIA (G-BEOX) [SF-R]	RAF Museum, Hendon	
A17-48	DH82A Tiger Moth (G-BPHR)	Privately owned, Wanborough, Wilts	
A17-376	DH82A Tiger Moth (T6830/G-ANJI) [376]	Privately owned, Gloucester	
A19-144	Bristol 156 Beaufighter XIc (JM135/A8-324)	The Fighter Collection, Duxford	
A92-255	GAF Jindivik 102	QinetiQ Apprentice Training School, Boscombe Down	
A92-466	GAF Jindivik 103A (BAPC.485)	Boscombe Down Aviation Collection, Old Sarum	
A92-708	GAF Jindivik 103BL	Aerospace Bristol, stored Filton	
A92-908	GAF Jindivik 104AL (ZJ503)	Privately owned, Llanbedr	
N16-114	WS61 Sea King Mk.50A [05]	Privately owned, Horsham	
N16-125	WS61 Sea King Mk.50A [10]	Privately owned, Horsham	
N16-238	WS61 Sea King Mk.50A [20]	Privately owned, Horsham	
N16-239	WS61 Sea King Mk.50A [21]	Privately owned, Horsham	
N16-918	WS61 Sea King Mk.50B (XZ918) [22]	Privately owned, Horsham	
WH589	Hawker Fury ISS (F-AZXJ) [115-NW]	Privately owned, Dijon, France	
AUSTRIA			
5S-TC	Short SC.7 Skyvan 3 Variant 100 (G-BEOL)	*Sold to Guyana, June 2019*	
BELGIUM			
A-41	SA318C Alouette II	The Helicopter Museum, Weston-super-Mare	
FT-36	Lockheed T-33A Shooting Star	Dumfries & Galloway Avn Mus, Dumfries	
H-02	Agusta A109HO (N504TS)	Privately owned, Cotswold Airport	
H-05	Agusta A109HO (N504WG)	*Currently not known*	
H-50	Noorduyn AT-16 Harvard IIb (OO-DAF)	Privately owned, Brasschaat, Belgium	
IF-68	Hawker Hunter F6 <ff>	Privately owned, Kings Lynn	
L-44	Piper L-18C Super Cub (OO-SPQ)	Royal Aéro Para Club de Spa, Belgium	
L-47	Piper L-18C Super Cub (OO-SPG)	Aeroclub Brasschaat VZW, Brasschaat, Belgium	
OL-L49	Piper L-18C Super Cub (L-156/OO-LGB)	Aeroclub Brasschaat VZW, Brasschaat, Belgium	
V-4	SNCAN Stampe SV-4B (OO-EIR)	Antwerp Stampe Centre, Antwerp-Deurne, Belgium	
V-18	SNCAN Stampe SV-4B (OO-GWD)	Antwerp Stampe Centre, Antwerp-Deurne, Belgium	

Notes	Serial	Type (code/other identity)	Owner/operator, location or fate
	V-29	SNCAN Stampe SV-4B (OO-GWB)	Antwerp Stampe Centre, Antwerp-Deurne, Belgium
	V-66	SNCAN Stampe SV-4C (OO-GWA)	Antwerp Stampe Centre, Antwerp-Deurne, Belgium
	BOLIVIA		
	FAB-108	BAe RJ.70	Privately owned, Southend
	BRAZIL		
	1317	Embraer T-27 Tucano	Shorts, Belfast (engine test bed)
	BURKINA FASO		
	BF8431	SIAI-Marchetti SF.260 (G-NRRA) [31]	Privately owned, Lydd
	CANADA		
	622	Piasecki HUP-3 Retriever (51-16622/N6699D)	The Helicopter Museum, Weston-super-Mare
	920	VS Stranraer (CF-BXO) [Q-N]	RAF Museum, Hendon
	3091	NA81 Harvard II (3019/G-CPPM)	Beech Restorations, Bruntingthorpe
	3349	NA64 Yale (G-BYNF)	Privately owned, Duxford
	5084	DH82C Tiger Moth (G-FCTK)	Privately owned, Hailsham
	9041	Bristol 149 Bolingbroke IV <ff>	Manx Aviation Museum, Ronaldsway
	9048	Bristol 149 Bolingbroke IV	Aerospace Bristol, Filton
	9893	Bristol 149 Bolingbroke IVT <ff>	Kent Battle of Britain Museum, Hawkinge
	9893	Bristol 149 Bolingbroke IVT <rf>	IWM, stored Duxford
	9940	Bristol 149 Bolingbroke IVT	National Museum of Flight, E Fortune
	15252	Fairchild PT-19A Cornell (comp 15195)	RAF Museum Reserve Collection, Stafford
	16693	Auster J/1N Alpha (G-BLPG) [693]	Privately owned, Dunkeswell
	17447	McD F-101F Voodoo (56-0312)	Midland Air Museum, Coventry
	18393	Avro Canada CF-100 Canuck 4B (G-BCYK)	IWM Duxford
	18871	DHC1 Chipmunk 22 (WP905/7438M/G-BNZC) [671]	The Shuttleworth Collection, Old Warden
	20249	Noorduyn AT-16 Harvard IIb (PH-KLU) [XS-249]	Privately owned, Texel, The Netherlands
	21417	Canadair CT-133 Silver Star	Yorkshire Air Museum, Elvington
	23140	Canadair CL-13A Sabre 5 [AX] <rf>	Midland Air Museum, Coventry
	23380	Canadair CL-13B Sabre 6 <rf>	Privately owned, Haverigg
	FE992	Noorduyn AT-16 Harvard IIb (G-BDAM) [ER-992]	Privately owned, Duxford
	FJ662	Fairchild PT-26 Cornell (G-CRNL) [662]	Privately owned, Wickenby
	KN448	Douglas Dakota IV <ff>	Science Museum, South Kensington
	CHILE		
	H-255	Aérospatiale SA330H Puma	Ultimate Activity, Faygate
	CHINA		
	68 r	Nanchang CJ-6A Chujiao (2751219/G-BVVG)	Privately owned, stored Strubby
	61367	Nanchang CJ-6A Chujiao (4532009/G-CGHB) [37]	Privately owned, Redhill
	CZECH REPUBLIC		
	3677	Letov S-103 (MiG-15bisSB) (613677)	National Museum of Flight, E Fortune
	3794	Letov S-102 (MiG-15) (623794)	Norfolk & Suffolk Avn Museum, Flixton
		(starboard side only, painted in Polish marks as 1972 on port side)	
	9147	Mil Mi-4	The Helicopter Museum, Weston-super-Mare
	DENMARK		
	A-011	SAAB A-35XD Draken	Privately owned, Westhoughton, Lancs
	AR-107	SAAB S-35XD Draken	Newark Air Museum, Winthorpe
	E-419	Hawker Hunter F51 (G-9-441)	North-East Land, Sea & Air Museums, Usworth
	E-420	Hawker Hunter F51 (G-9-442) <ff>	Privately owned, Walton-on-Thames
	E-421	Hawker Hunter F51 (G-9-443)	Brooklands Museum, Weybridge
	ET-272	Hawker Hunter T53 <ff>	Norfolk & Suffolk Avn Museum, Flixton
	K-682	Douglas C-47A Skytrain (OY-BPB)	*Withdrawn from use, 2019*
	L-866	Consolidated PBY-6A Catalina (8466M)	RAF Museum, Cosford
	P-129	DHC-1 Chipmunk 22 (OY-ATO)	Privately owned, Tonder, Denmark

Serial	Type (code/other identity)	Owner/operator, location or fate	Notes
P-139	DHC-1 Chipmunk 22 (OY-AVF)	Privately owned, Vaerløse, Denmark	
R-756	Lockheed F-104G Starfighter	Midland Air Museum, Coventry	
S-881	Sikorsky S-55C	The Helicopter Museum, Weston-super-Mare	
S-882	Sikorsky S-55C	Skirmish Paintball, Portishead	
S-886	Sikorsky S-55C	Hamburger Hill Paintball, Marksbury, Somerset	
S-887	Sikorsky S-55C	The Helicopter Museum, Weston-super-Mare	
EGYPT			
356	Heliopolis Gomhouria Mk 6	Privately owned, stored Ellerton, E Yorks	
764	Mikoyan MiG-21SPS <ff>	Privately owned, Northampton	
771	WS61 Sea King Mk.47 (WA.826)	DSTO Shoeburyness, Essex, GI use	
773	WS61 Sea King Mk.47 (WA.823)	RNAS Yeovilton Fire Section	
776	WS61 Sea King Mk.47 (WA.825) <ff>	Mayhem Paintball, Aybridge, Essex	
0446	Mikoyan MiG-21UM <ff>	*Currently not known*	
7907	Sukhoi Su-7 <ff>	Robertsbridge Aviation Society, Mayfield	
FINLAND			
GA-43	Gloster Gamecock II (G-CGYF)	Privately owned, Dursley, Glos	
GN-101	Folland Gnat F1 (XK741)	Midland Air Museum, Coventry	
SZ-12	Focke-Wulf Fw44J Stieglitz (D-EXWO)	Privately owned, Bienenfarm, Germany	
VI-3	Valtion Viima 2 (OO-EBL)	Privately owned, Brasschaat, Belgium	
FRANCE			
1/4513	Spad XIII <R> (G-BFYO/S3398)	American Air Museum, Duxford	
5	MH1521C Broussard (C-GRBL/G-CLLK) [30-QA]	Privately owned, Oaksey Park	
7	Nord NC854 (G-NORD)	Privately owned, English Bicknor, Glos	
28	Fouga CM175 Zéphyr [F-AZPF]	Association Zéphyr 28, Nîmes, France	
32	Morane-Saulnier MS760 Paris (F-AZLT)	Armor Aéro Passion, Morlaix, France	
37	Nord 3400 (G-ZARA) [MAB]	Privately owned, stored Swaffham, Norfolk	
45	Dassault Mirage IVP [BR]	Yorkshire Air Museum, Elvington	
54	SNCAN NC856A Norvigie (G-CGWR) [AOM]	Privately owned, Spanhoe	
59	Breguet Br1050 Alizé (F-AZYI)	Alizé Marine, Nîmes/Garons, France	
67	SNCAN 1101 Noralpha (F-GMCY) [CY]	Privately owned, la Ferté-Alais, France	
70	Dassault Mystère IVA [8-NV]	Midland Air Museum, Coventry	
78	Nord 3202B-1 (G-BIZK)	Privately owned, Swaffham, Norfolk	
79	Dassault Mystère IVA [2-EG]	Norfolk & Suffolk Avn Museum, Flixton	
82	Curtiss H75-C1 Hawk (G-CCVH) [X-881]	The Fighter Collection, Duxford	
82	NA T-28D Fennec (F-AZKG)	Privately owned, Strasbourg, France	
83	Dassault Mystère IVA [8-MS]	Newark Air Museum, Winthorpe	
83	Morane-Saulnier MS733 Alcyon (F-AZKS)	Privately owned, Montlucon, France	
85	Dassault Mystère IVA [8-MV]	Cold War Jets Collection, Bruntingthorpe	
104	MH1521M Broussard (F-GHFG) [307-FG]	Privately owned, Montceau-les-Mines, France	
105	Nord N2501F Noratlas (F-AZVM) [62-SI]	Le Noratlas de Provence, Marseilles, France	
106	MH1521M Broussard (F-GKJT) [33-JT]	Privately owned, Montceau-les-Mines, France	
108	MH1521M Broussard (F-BNEX) [50S9]	Privately owned, Lelystad, The Netherlands	
108	SO1221 Djinn (FR108) [CDL]	The Helicopter Museum, Weston-super-Mare	
121	Dassault Mystère IVA [8-MY]	City of Norwich Aviation Museum	
128	Morane-Saulnier MS733 Alcyon (F-BMMY)	Privately owned, St Cyr, France	
143	Morane-Saulnier MS733 Alcyon (G-MSAL)	Privately owned, Spanhoe	
146	Dassault Mystère IVA [8-MC]	*Sold to Poland, January 2020*	
154	MH1521M Broussard (F-GKRO) [315-SM]	Privately owned, Damyns Hall, Essex	
156	SNCAN Stampe SV-4B (G-NIFE)	Privately owned, Headcorn	
158	Dassault MD312 Flamant (F-AZGE) [12-XA]	Privately owned, Albert, France	
160	Dassault MD312 Flamant (F-AZDR) [V]	Privately owned, Alençon, France	
189	Dassault MD312 Flamant (F-AZVG) [G]	Ailes Anciennes de Corbas, Lyon, France	
208	MH1521C1 Broussard (G-YYYY) [IR]	Privately owned, Eggesford	
226	Dassault MD312 Flamant (F-AZES) [319-CG]	Privately owned, Montbeliard, France	
237	Dassault MD312 Flamant (F-AZFE) [319-DM]	Privately owned, Alençon, France	
255	MH1521M Broussard (G-CIGH) [5-ML]	Privately owned, Breighton	
260	Dassault MD311 Flamant (F-AZKT) [316-KT]	Privately owned, Albert, France	
261	MH1521M Broussard (F-GIBN) [30-QA]	Privately owned, Walldürn, Germany	
276	Dassault MD311 Flamant (F-AZER)	Privately owned, Alençon, France	

Notes	Serial	Type (code/other identity)	Owner/operator, location or fate
	290	Dewoitine D27 (F-AZJD)	Les Casques de Cuir, la Ferté-Alais, France
	316	MH1521M Broussard (F-GGKR) [315-SN]	Privately owned, Lognes, France
	318	Dassault Mystère IVA [8-NY]	Dumfries & Galloway Avn Mus, Dumfries
	319	Dassault Mystère IVA [8-ND]	Rebel Air Museum, Andrewsfield
	351	Morane-Saulnier MS317 (G-MOSA) [HY22]	*Sold to France, August 2019*
	354	Morane-Saulnier MS315E-D2 (G-BZNK)	Privately owned, Wickenby
	538	Dassault Mirage IIIE [3-QH]	Yorkshire Air Museum, Elvington
	569	Fouga CM170R Magister [F-AZZP]	Privately owned, Le Havre, France
	3615	Aérospatiale SA.342M Gazelle (HA-HSG)	Privately owned, Breighton
	24541	Cessna L-19E Bird Dog (G-JDOG) [BMG]	Privately owned, Cotswold Airport
	24545	Cessna L-19E Bird Dog (F-AZTA) [BYA]	Privately owned, Chavenay, France
	42157	NA F-100D Super Sabre [11-ER]	North-East Land, Sea & Air Museums, Usworth
	54439	Lockheed T-33A Shooting Star (55-4439) [WI]	South Wales Aviation Museum, St Athan
	125716	Douglas AD-4N Skyraider (F-AZFN) [22-DG]	Privately owned, Mélun, France
	127002	Douglas AD-4NA Skyraider (F-AZHK) [20-LN]	Privately owned, Avignon, France
	18-5395	Piper L-18C Super Cub (52-2436/G-CUBJ) [CDG]	Privately owned, Old Warden
	C850	Salmson 2A2 <R>	Barton Aviation Heritage Society, Barton
	FR41	Piasecki H-21C	The Helicopter Museum, Weston-super-Mare
	MS824	Morane-Saulnier Type N <R> (G-AWBU)	Privately owned, Stow Maries
	N856	SNCAN NC856 (G-CDWE)	Privately owned, Wickenby
	N1977	Nieuport Scout 17/23 <R> (N1723/G-BWMJ) [8]	Privately owned, Stow Maries
	XC	Piper L-4J Grasshopper (44-80513/G-BSYO)	Privately owned, Postling, Kent
	GERMANY		
	-	Fieseler Fi103R-IV (V-1) (BAPC 91)	Lashenden Air Warfare Museum, Headcorn
	-	Fokker Dr1 Dreidekker <R> (BAPC 88)	FAA Museum, stored Cobham Hall, RNAS Yeovilton
	-	Messerschmitt Bf109 <R> (6357/BAPC 74) [6]	Kent Battle of Britain Museum, Hawkinge
	-	Messerschmitt Bf109 <R> [<-]	Battle of Britain Experience, Canterbury
	White 1	Focke-Wulf Fw190 <R> (G-WULF)	Privately owned, Halfpenny Green
	3	SNCAN 1101 Noralpha (G-BAYV) (fuselage)	Privately owned, Newquay
	Yellow 3	Hispano HA 1.112M1L Buchón (C.4K-40/D-FDME)	Messerschmitt Stiftung, Manching, Germany
	White 5	Hispano HA 1.112M1L Buchón (C.4K-152/G-AWHR)	Privately owned, Sywell
	Red 7	Hispano HA 1.112M1L Buchón (C.4K-75/D-FWME)	Messerschmitt Stiftung, Manching, Germany
	Yellow 7	Hispano HA 1.112M1L Buchón (C.4K-99/G-AWHM)	Privately owned, Sywell
	Black 8	Hispano HA 1.112M1L Buchón (C.4K-102/G-AWHK)	Historic Flying Ltd, Duxford
	White 9	Focke-Wulf Fw190 <R> (G-CCFW)	Privately owned, Oaksey Park
	White 9	Hispano HA 1.112M1L Buchón (C.4K-105/G-AWHH)	Privately owned, Sywell
	Red 11	Hispano HA 1.112K1L Buchón (C.4K-112/G-AWHC)	Privately owned, Sywell
	White 14	Messerschmitt Bf109 <R> (BAPC 67)	Kent Battle of Britain Museum, Hawkinge
	Yellow 14	Nord 1002 (G-ETME)	Privately owned, White Waltham
	Yellow 27	Hispano HA 1.112K1L Buchón (D-FMGZ)	Air Fighter Academy, Heringsdorf, Germany
	33/15	Fokker EIII <R> (G-CHAW)	Privately owned, Membury
	87	Heinkel He111 <R> <ff>	Privately owned, East Kirkby
	105/15	Fokker EIII <R> (G-UDET)	Privately owned, Horsham
	152/17	Fokker Dr1 Dreidekker <R> (F-AZPQ)	Les Casques de Cuir, la Ferté-Alais, France
	152/17	Fokker Dr1 Dreidekker <R> (G-BVGZ)	Privately owned, Breighton
	157/18	Fokker D.VIII <R> (BAPC 239)	Norfolk & Suffolk Air Museum, Flixton
	210/16	Fokker EIII (BAPC 56)	Science Museum, South Kensington
	403/17	Fokker Dr1 Dreidekker <R> (G-CDXR)	Privately owned, Popham
	416/15	Fokker EIII <R> (G-GSAL)	Privately owned, Aston Down
	422/15	Fokker EIII <R> (G-AVJO)	Privately owned, Stow Maries
	422/15	Fokker EIII <R> (G-FOKR)	Privately owned, Eshott
	425/17	Fokker Dr1 Dreidekker <R> (BAPC 133)	Kent Battle of Britain Museum, Hawkinge
	425/17	Fokker Dr1 Dreidekker <R> (G-DREI)	Privately owned, Felthorpe
	477/17	Fokker Dr1 Dreidekker <R> (G-FOKK)	Privately owned, Sywell
	556/17	Fokker Dr1 Dreidekker <R> (G-CFHY)	Privately owned, Tibenham
	626/8	Fokker DVII <R> (N6268)	Privately owned, Booker
	764	Mikoyan MiG-21SPS <ff>	Privately owned, Norfolk
	959	Mikoyan MiG-21SPS	Midland Air Museum, Coventry
	1160	Dornier Do17Z-2	Michael Beetham Conservation Centre, Cosford
	1190	Messerschmitt Bf109E-3 [White 4]	IWM Duxford

Serial	Type (code/other identity)	Owner/operator, location or fate	Notes
1480	Messerschmitt Bf109 <R> (BAPC 66) [6]	Kent Battle of Britain Museum, Hawkinge	
1801/18	Bowers Fly Baby 1A (G-BNPV)	Privately owned, Chessington	
1803/18	Bowers Fly Baby 1A (G-BUYU)	Privately owned, Chessington	
1983	Messerschmitt Bf109E-3 (G-EMIL)	Privately owned, Colchester	
3579	Messerschmitt Bf109E-7 (G-CIPB) [White 14]	Privately owned, Biggin Hill	
4101	Messerschmitt Bf109E-3 (DG200/8477M) [Black 12]	RAF Museum, Hendon	
4477	CASA 1.131E Jungmann (G-RETA) [GD+EG]	The Shuttleworth Collection, Old Warden	
7198/18	LVG CVI (G-AANJ/9239M)	Michael Beetham Conservation Centre, Cosford	
8417/18	Fokker DVII (9207M)	RAF Museum, Hendon	
10639	Messerschmitt Bf109G-2/Trop (8478M/G-USTV) [Black 6]	RAF Museum, Cosford	
12802	Antonov An-2T (D-FOFM)	Historische Flugzeuge, Grossenhain, Germany	
13605	Messerschmitt Bf109G-2(G-JIMP) [Yellow 12]	Privately owned, Knutsford	
15919	Messerschmitt Bf109 <R> (BAPC 240) [Green 1]	Yorkshire Air Museum, Elvington	
100143	Focke-Achgelis Fa330A-1 Bachstelze	IWM Duxford	
100502	Focke-Achgelis Fa330A-1 Bachstelze	Privately owned, Millom	
100503	Focke-Achgelis Fa330A-1 Bachstelze (8469M)	RAF Museum, Cosford	
100509	Focke-Achgelis Fa330A-1 Bachstelze	Science Museum, stored Wroughton	
100545	Focke-Achgelis Fa330A-1 Bachstelze	FAA Museum, RNAS Yeovilton	
100549	Focke-Achgelis Fa330A-1 Bachstelze	Lashenden Air Warfare Museum, Headcorn	
112372	Messerschmitt Me262A-2a (VK893/8482M) [Yellow 4]	RAF Museum, Cosford	
120227	Heinkel He162A-2 Salamander (VN679/8472M) [Red 2]	RAF Museum, Hendon	
120235	Heinkel He162A-1 Salamander (AM.68) [Yellow 6]	IWM Duxford	
191316	Messerschmitt Me163B Komet	Science Museum, South Kensington	
191454	Messerschmitt Me163B Komet <R> (BAPC 271)	The Shuttleworth Collection, Old Warden	
191461	Messerschmitt Me163B Komet (191614/8481M) [Yellow 14]	RAF Museum, Cosford	
191659	Messerschmitt Me163B Komet (8480M) [Yellow 15]	National Museum of Flight, E Fortune	
280020	Flettner Fl282/B-V20 Kolibri (frame only)	Midland Air Museum, Coventry	
360043	Junkers Ju88R-1 (PJ876/8475M) [D5+EV]	RAF Museum, Cosford	
420430	Messerschmitt Me410A-1/U2 (AM.72/8483M) [3U+CC]	Michael Beetham Conservation Centre, Cosford	
475081	Fieseler Fi156C-7 Storch (VP546/AM.101/7362M) [GM+AK]	RAF Museum, Cosford	
494083	Junkers Ju87D-3 (8474M) [RI+JK]	RAF Museum, Hendon	
502074	Heliopolis Gomhouria Mk 6 (158/G-CGEV) [CG+EV]	Privately owned, Dunkeswell	
584219	Focke-Wulf Fw190F-8/U1 (AM.29/8470M) [Black 38]	RAF Museum, Hendon	
701152	Heinkel He111H-23 (8471M) [NT+SL]	RAF Museum, Hendon	
730301	Messerschmitt Bf110G-4 (AM.34/8479M) [D5+RL]	RAF Museum, Hendon	
733682	Focke-Wulf Fw190A-8/R7 (AM.75/9211M)	RAF Museum, Cosford	
980554	Flug Werk Fw190A-8/N (D-FWMW)	Meier Motors, Bremgarten, Germany	
2+1	Focke-Wulf Fw190 <R> (G-SYFW) [7334]	Privately owned, Empingham, Rutland	
20+45	Mikoyan MiG-23BN	Privately owned, Danbury, Essex	
22+35	Lockheed F-104G Starfighter	Privately owned, Bruntingthorpe	
28+08	Aero L-39ZO Albatros (142/28+04)	Pinewood Studios, Bucks	
2E+RA	Fieseler Fi-156C-3 Storch (F-AZRA)	Amicale J-B Salis, la Ferté-Alais, France	
4+1	Focke-Wulf Fw190 <R> (G-BSLX)	Privately owned, Norwich	
6G+ED	Slepcev Storch (G-BZOB) [5447]	Privately owned, Breighton	
37+86	McD F-4F Phantom II <ff>	Privately owned,	
37+89	McD F-4F Phantom II	Hawker Hunter Aviation Ltd, Scampton (spares)	
58+89	Dornier Do28D-2 Skyservant (D-ICDY)	Privately owned, Uetersen, Germany	
72+59	Dornier UH-1D Iroquois (comp 73+01)	Privately owned, Dunsfold	
80+55	MBB Bo.105M	Lufthansa Resource Technical Training, Cotswold Airport	
80+77	MBB Bo.105M	Lufthansa Resource Technical Training, Cotswold Airport	
81+00	MBB Bo.105M (D-HZYR)	The Helicopter Museum, Weston-super-Mare	
96+26	Mil Mi-24D (421)	The Helicopter Museum, Weston-super-Mare	
98+14	Sukhoi Su-22M-4	Hawker Hunter Aviation Ltd, stored Scampton	
99+18	NA OV-10B Bronco (G-ONAA)	Bronco Demo Team, Wevelgem, Belgium	
99+26	NA OV-10B Bronco (G-BZGL)	Bronco Demo Team, Wevelgem, Belgium	
AZ+JU	CASA 3.52L (F-AZJU)	Amicale J-B Salis, la Ferté-Alais, France	
BB+103	Canadair CL-13B Sabre 6 (1730/JB+114)	Privately owned,	
BF+070	CCF T-6J Texan (G-CHYN)	Privately owned, Dunkeswell	

Notes	Serial	Type (code/other identity)	Owner/operator, location or fate
	BG+KM	Nord 1002 Pingouin (G-ASTG)	Privately owned, Peterborough
	BU+CC	CASA 1.131E Jungmann (G-BUCC)	Privately owned, Deanland
	CX+HI	CASA 1.131E Jungmann (E.3B-379/G-CDJU)	Privately owned, Sleap
	D2263	Albatros DVA-1 <R> (ZK-ALB/G-WAHT)	Privately owned, Stow Maries
	D7343/17	Albatros DVA <R> (ZK-TVD)	RAF Museum, Hendon
	DG+BE	CASA 1.131E Jungmann (E.3B-350/G-BHPL)	Privately owned, Henstridge
	DM+BK	Morane-Saulnier MS505 (G-BPHZ)	Aero Vintage, Westfield, E Sussex
	E37/15	Fokker EIII <R> (G-CGJF)	Privately owned, Herts
	ES+BH	Messerschmitt Bf108B-2 (D-ESBH)	Messerschmitt Stiftung, Manching, Germany
	FI+S	Morane-Saulnier MS505 (G-BIRW)	National Museum of Flight, stored E Fortune
	FM+BB	Messerschmitt Bf109G-6 (D-FMBB)	Messerschmitt Stiftung, Manching, Germany
	KG+GB	CASA 1.131E Jungmann (G-BHSL)	Privately owned, Old Warden
	LG+01	CASA 1.133L Jungmeister (ES.1-16/G-CIJV)	Privately owned, Sleap
	LG+03	Bücker Bü133C Jungmeister (G-AEZX)	Privately owned, Milden
	NJ+C11	Nord 1002 (G-ATBG)	Privately owned, Duxford
	NM+AA	CASA 1.131E Jungmann 1000 (G-BZJV)	Privately owned, Sleap
	NQ+NR	Klemm KI35D (D-EQXD)	Quax Flieger, Paderborn, Germany
	NV+KG	Focke-Wulf Fw44J Stieglitz (D-ENAY)	Quax Flieger, Paderborn, Germany
	S4-A07	CASA 1.131E Jungmann (G-BWHP)	Privately owned, Yarcombe, Devon
	TP+WX	Heliopolis Gomhouria Mk 6 (G-TPWX)	Privately owned, Swanborough
	GHANA		
	G360	PBN 2T Islander (G-BRSR)	Privately owned, Biggin Hill
	G361	PBN 2T Islander (G-BRPB)	Privately owned, Biggin Hill
	G362	PBN 2T Islander (G-BRPC)	Privately owned, Biggin Hill
	G363	PBN 2T Islander (G-BRSV)	Privately owned, Biggin Hill
	GREECE		
	26541	Republic F-84F Thunderflash (52-6541) [541]	North-East Land, Sea & Air Museums, Usworth
	MJ755	VS361 Spitfire LF IXe (G-CLGS) [F-H]	Privately owned, Biggin Hill
	HONG KONG		
	HKG-5	SA128 Bulldog (G-BULL)	Privately owned, Cotswold Airport
	HKG-6	SA128 Bulldog (G-BPCL)	Privately owned, North Weald
	HKG-11	Slingsby T.67M Firefly 200 (G-BYRY)	Privately owned, Wellesbourne Mountford
	HKG-13	Slingsby T.67M Firefly 200 (G-BXKW)	Privately owned, St Ghislain, Belgium
	HUNGARY		
	125	Aero L-39ZO Albatros (831125/G-JMGP)	Privately owned, France
	335	Mil Mi-24D (3532461715415)	Privately owned, Dunsfold
	501	Mikoyan MiG-21PF	IWM Duxford
	503	Mikoyan MiG-21SMT (G-BRAM)	RAF Museum, Cosford
	INDIA		
	E296	Hindustan Gnat F1 (G-SLYR)	Privately owned, North Weald
	Q497	EE Canberra T4 (WE191) <ff>	Privately owned, Stoneykirk, D&G
	HA561	Hawker Tempest II (MW743)	Privately owned, stored Wickenby
	INDONESIA		
	LL-5313	BAe Hawk T53	BAE Systems, Brough, on display
	IRAQ		
	249	Hawker Fury ISS (OO-ISS)	Privately owned, Brasschaat, Belgium
	333	DH115 Vampire T55 <ff>	South Yorkshire Aircraft Mus'm, stored Doncaster
	349	Hawker Hunter F51 (E-408/G-9-436/WT720/8565M)	Centreprise International, Chineham, Hants
	ITALY		
	MM5701	Fiat CR42 (BT474/8468M) [13-95]	RAF Museum, Hendon
	MM6976	Fiat CR42 (2542/G-CBLS) [85-16]	The Fighter Collection, Duxford
	MM53211	Fiat G46-1B (MM52799) [ZI-4]	Privately owned, Shipdham
	MM53692	CCF T-6G Texan	RAeS Medway Branch, Rochester
	MM53774	Fiat G59-4B (I-MRSV) [181]	Privately owned, Parma, Italy

Serial	Type (code/other identity)	Owner/operator, location or fate	Notes
MM54099	NA T-6G Texan (G-BRBC) [RR-56]	Privately owned, Chigwell	
MM54532	SIAI-Marchetti SF.260AM (G-ITAF) [70-42]	Privately owned, Leicester	
MM80927	Agusta-Bell AB206A-1 JetRanger [CC-49]	The Helicopter Museum, Weston-super-Mare	
MM81205	Agusta A109A-2 SEM [GF-128]	The Helicopter Museum, Weston-super-Mare	
MM52-2392	Piper L-21B Super Cub (G-HELN) [E.I.69]	Privately owned, White Waltham	
MM54-2372	Piper L-21B Super Cub	Privately owned, Foxhall Heath, Suffolk	
JAPAN			
-	Kawasaki Ki100-1B (16336/8476M/BAPC 83)	RAF Museum, Cosford	
-	Mitsubishi A6M5-52 Zero (196) [BI-05] <ff>	IWM Duxford	
-	Yokosuka MXY 7 Ohka II (BAPC 159)	IWM Duxford, stored	
997	Yokosuka MXY 7 Ohka II (8485M/BAPC 98)	Museum of Science & Industry, Manchester	
3443	NA T-6 Texan Zero (F-AZRO)	Privately owned, St Rambert d'Albon, France	
5439	Mitsubishi Ki46-III (8484M/BAPC 84)	RAF Museum, Cosford	
15-1585	Yokosuka MXY 7 Ohka II (BAPC 58)	Science Museum, stored Cobham Hall, RNAS Yeovilton	
I-13	Yokosuka MXY 7 Ohka II (8486M/BAPC 99)	RAF Museum, Cosford	
Y2-176	Mitsubishi A6M3-2 Zero (3685) [76]	IWM London, Lambeth	
JORDAN			
408	SA125 Bulldog (G-BDIN)	*Currently not known*	
KENYA			
115	Dornier Do28D-2 Skyservant	Privately owned, stored Hibaldstow	
117	Dornier Do28D-2 Skyservant	Privately owned, stored Hibaldstow	
MALAYSIA			
M25-04	SA102 Bulldog (FM1224) (fuselage)	South Wales Aviation Museum, stored St Athan	
MALTA			
AS0022	SA Bulldog T1 (XX709/G-CLJC)	Privately owned, Oxon	
AS0023	SA Bulldog T1 (XX714/G-CLJD)	Privately owned, Oxon	
MYANMAR			
UB441	VS361 Spitfire IX (ML119/G-SDNI)	Privately owned, stored West Wycombe, Bucks	
THE NETHERLANDS			
16-218	Consolidated PBY-5A Catalina (2459/PH-PBY)	*Sold as N459CF, May 2019*	
174	Fokker S-11 Instructor (E-31/G-BEPV) [K]	Privately owned, Spanhoe	
179	Fokker S-11 Instructor (PH-ACG) [K]	Privately owned, Lelystad, The Netherlands	
197	Fokker S-11 Instructor (PH-GRY) [K]	KLu Historic Flt, Gilze-Rijen, The Netherlands	
204	Lockheed SP-2H Neptune [V]	RAF Museum, Cosford	
272	Westland SH-14D Lynx	Privately owned, Woodmancote, W Sussex	
A-57	DH82A Tiger Moth (PH-TYG)	KLu Historic Flt, Gilze-Rijen, The Netherlands	
B-64	Noorduyn AT-16 Harvard IIb (PH-LSK)	KLu Historic Flt, Gilze-Rijen, The Netherlands	
B-71	Noorduyn AT-16 Harvard IIb (PH-MLM)	KLu Historic Flt, Gilze-Rijen, The Netherlands	
B-118	Noorduyn AT-16 Harvard IIb (PH-IIB)	KLu Historic Flt, Gilze-Rijen, The Netherlands	
B-182	Noorduyn AT-16 Harvard IIb (PH-TBR)	KLu Historic Flt, Gilze-Rijen, The Netherlands	
E-14	Fokker S-11 Instructor (PH-AFS)	Privately owned, Lelystad, The Netherlands	
E-15	Fokker S-11 Instructor (G-BIYU)	Privately owned, Bagby	
E-20	Fokker S-11 Instructor (PH-GRB)	Privately owned, Gilze-Rijen, The Netherlands	
E-27	Fokker S-11 Instructor (PH-HOL)	Privately owned, Lelystad, The Netherlands	
E-29	Fokker S-11 Instructor (PH-HOK)	Privately owned, Lelystad, The Netherlands	
E-32	Fokker S-11 Instructor (PH-HOl)	Privately owned, Gilze-Rijen, The Netherlands	
E-39	Fokker S-11 Instructor (PH-HOG)	Privately owned, Lelystad, The Netherlands	
G-29	Beech D18S (PH-KHV)	KLu Historic Flt, Gilze-Rijen, The Netherlands	
MK732	VS361 Spitfire LF IXc (8633M/PH-OUQ) [3W-17]	KLu Historic Flt, Gilze-Rijen, The Netherlands	
N-202	Hawker Hunter F6 [10] <ff>	Privately owned, Stockport	
N-250	Hawker Hunter F6 (G-9-185) <ff>	IWM Duxford	
N-294	Hawker Hunter F6A (XF515/G-KAXF)	Stichting Hawker Hunter Foundation, Leeuwarden, The Netherlands	
N-302	Hawker Hunter T7 (ET-273/G-9-431) <ff>	South Yorkshire Aircraft Museum, Doncaster	

Notes	Serial	Type (code/other identity)	Owner/operator, location or fate
	N-315	Hawker Hunter T7 (comp XM121)	Privately owned, Netherley, Aberdeenshire
	N-321	Hawker Hunter T8C (G-BWGL)	Stichting Hawker Hunter Foundation, Leeuwarden, The Netherlands
	N5-149	NA B-25J Mitchell (44-29507/HD346/PH-XXV) [232511]	KLu Historic Flt, Gilze-Rijen, The Netherlands
	R-18	Auster III (PH-NGK)	KLu Historic Flt, Gilze-Rijen, The Netherlands
	R-55	Piper L-18C Super Cub (52-2466/G-BLMI)	Privately owned, Antwerp-Deurne, Belgium
	R-109	Piper L-21B Super Cub (54-2337/PH-GAZ)	KLu Historic Flt, Gilze-Rijen, The Netherlands
	R-122	Piper L-21B Super Cub (54-2412/PH-PPW)	KLu Historic Flt, Gilze-Rijen, The Netherlands
	R-124	Piper L-21B Super Cub (54-2414/PH-APA)	Privately owned, Eindhoven, The Netherlands
	R-137	Piper L-21B Super Cub (54-2427/PH-PSC)	Privately owned, Gilze-Rijen, The Netherlands
	R-151	Piper L-21B Super Cub (54-2441/G-BIYR)	Privately owned, Yarcombe, Devon
	R-156	Piper L-21B Super Cub (54-2446/G-ROVE)	Privately owned, Damyn's Hall
	R-167	Piper L-21B Super Cub (54-2457/G-LION)	Privately owned,
	R-170	Piper L-21B Super Cub (52-6222/PH-ENJ)	Privately owned, Seppe, The Netherlands
	R-177	Piper L-21B Super Cub (54-2467/PH-KNR)	KLu Historic Flt, Gilze-Rijen, The Netherlands
	R-181	Piper L-21B Super Cub (54-2471/PH-GAU)	Privately owned, Gilze-Rijen, The Netherlands
	R-213	Piper L-21A Super Cub (51-15682/PH-RED)	Privately owned, Seppe, The Netherlands
	R-345	Piper L-4J Grasshopper (PH-UCS)	Privately owned, Hilversum, The Netherlands
	S-9	DHC2 L-20A Beaver (55-4585/PH-DHC)	KLu Historic Flt, Gilze-Rijen, The Netherlands

NEW ZEALAND

Notes	Serial	Type (code/other identity)	Owner/operator, location or fate
	NZ3909	WS Wasp HAS1 (XT782/G-KANZ)	Privately owned, Thruxton
	NZ5911	Bristol 170 Freighter 31M (ZK-EPG)	Aerospace Bristol, stored Filton

NORTH KOREA

Notes	Serial	Type (code/other identity)	Owner/operator, location or fate
	-	WSK Lim-2 (MiG-15) (01420/G-BMZF)	FAA Museum, RNAS Yeovilton

NORTH VIETNAM

Notes	Serial	Type (code/other identity)	Owner/operator, location or fate
	1211	WSK Lim-5 (MiG-17F) (G-MIGG)	Privately owned, North Weald

NORWAY

Notes	Serial	Type (code/other identity)	Owner/operator, location or fate
	145	DH82A Tiger Moth II (DE248/LN-BDM)	Privately owned, Kjeller, Norway
	163	Fairchild PT-19A Cornell (42-83641/LN-BIF)	Privately owned, Kjeller, Norway
	171	DH82A Tiger Moth II (T6168/LN-KAY)	Privately owned, Kjeller, Norway
	599	Canadair CT-133AUP Silver Star Mk.3 (133599/LN-DPS)	Norwegian AF Historical Sqn, Ørland, Norway
	848	Piper L-18C Super Cub (LN-ACL) [FA-N]	Privately owned, Norway
	56321	SAAB S91B Safir (G-BKPY)	Newark Air Museum, Winthorpe
	PX-K	DH100 Vampire FB6 (J-1196/VZ305/LN-DHY)	Norwegian AF Historical Sqn, Rygge, Norway
	PX-M	DH115 Vampire T55 (U-1230/WZ447/LN-DHZ)	Norwegian AF Historical Sqn, Rygge, Norway

OMAN

Notes	Serial	Type (code/other identity)	Owner/operator, location or fate
	417	BAC Strikemaster Mk.80A (G-RSAF)	Privately owned, Hawarden
	425	BAC Strikemaster Mk.82A (G-SOAF)	Privately owned, Hawarden
	801	Hawker Hunter T66B <ff>	Privately owned, St Athan
	801	Hawker Hunter T66B <rf>	Privately owned, Hawarden
	853	Hawker Hunter FR10 (XF426)	RAF Museum, stored Cosford
	XL554	SAL Pioneer CC1 (XL703/8034M)	Michael Beetham Conservation Centre, Cosford

POLAND

Notes	Serial	Type (code/other identity)	Owner/operator, location or fate
	05	WSK SM-2 (Mi-2) (S2-03006)	The Helicopter Museum, Weston-super-Mare
	309	WSK SBLim-2A (MiG-15UTI) <ff>	R Scottish Mus'm of Flight, stored Granton
	458	Mikoyan MiG-23ML (04 red/024003607)	Newark Air Museum, Winthorpe
	618	Mil Mi-8P (10618)	Painted in Soviet markings as 07 r, 2019
	1018	WSK-PZL Mielec TS-11 Iskra (1H-1018/G-ISKA)	Cold War Jets Collection, Bruntingthorpe
	1120	WSK Lim-2 (MiG-15bis)	RAF Museum, Cosford
	1706	WSK-PZL Mielec TS-11 Iskra (1H-0408)	Midland Air Museum, Coventry
	1972	Letov S-102 (MiG-15) (623794) (port side only, painted in Czech marks as 3794 on starboard side)	Norfolk & Suffolk Avn Museum, Flixton
	7811	Mikoyan MiG-21MF (96N7811)	Iron Curtain Museum, Alton, Hants

Serial	Type (code/other identity)	Owner/operator, location or fate	Notes
PORTUGAL			
1350	OGMA/DHC1 Chipmunk T20 (G-CGAO)	Privately owned, Duxford	
1365	OGMA/DHC1 Chipmunk T20 (G-DHPM)	Privately owned, Sleap	
1367	OGMA/DHC1 Chipmunk T20 (G-UANO)	Privately owned, Sherburn-in-Elmet	
1372	OGMA/DHC1 Chipmunk T20 (HB-TUM)	Privately owned, Switzerland	
1373	OGMA/DHC1 Chipmunk T20 (G-CBJG)	Privately owned, Winwick, Cambs	
1375	OGMA/DHC1 Chipmunk T20 (F-AZJV)	Privately owned, Valenciennes, France	
1377	DHC1 Chipmunk 22 (WK520/G-BARS)	Privately owned, Yeovilton	
1741	CCF T-6J Texan (G-HRVD)	Privately owned, Bruntingthorpe	
1747	CCF T-6J Texan (20385/G-BGPB)	Privately owned, Gloucestershire Airport	
3303	MH1521M Broussard (G-CBGL)	Privately owned, Rochester	
QATAR			
QA10	Hawker Hunter FGA78	Yorkshire Air Museum, Elvington	
QA12	Hawker Hunter FGA78 <ff>	Privately owned, New Inn, Torfaen	
QP30	WS Lynx Mk.28 (G-BFDV/TAD013)	DSAE SAAE, Lyneham	
QP31	WS Lynx Mk.28	Newark Air Museum, Winthorpe	
QP32	WS Lynx Mk.28 (TD 016) [A]	DSAE SAAE, Lyneham, on display	
ROMANIA			
29	LET L-29 Delfin	Privately owned, Pocklington	
42	LET L-29 Delfin <ff>	Privately owned, Catshill, Worcs	
42	LET L-29 Delfin <rf>	Privately owned, Hinstock, Shrops	
47	LET L-29 Delfin <ff>	Top Gun Flight Simulator Centre, Stalybridge	
53	LET L-29 Delfin [66654]	Privately owned, Bruntingthorpe	
RUSSIA (& FORMER SOVIET UNION)			
-	Mil Mi-24D (3532464505029)	Midland Air Museum, Coventry	
00 w	Yakovlev Yak-3M (0470202/G-OLEG)	Privately owned, Sywell	
1 w	SPP Yak C-11 (171314/G-BZMY)	Privately owned, Alscot Park, Warks	
01 y	Yakovlev Yak-52 (9311709/G-YKSZ)	Privately owned, White Waltham	
03 bl	Yakovlev Yak-55M (910103/RA-01274)	Privately owned, Halfpenny Green	
03 w	Yakovlev Yak-18A (1160004/G-CEIB)	Privately owned, Breighton	
5 w	Yakovlev Yak-3UA (0470204/D-FYGJ)	Privately owned, Bremgarten, Germany	
06 y	Yakovlev Yak-9UM (HB-RYA)	Flying Fighter Association, Bex, Switzerland	
07 r	Mil Mi-8P (10618)	The Helicopter Museum, Weston-super-Mare	
07 y	WSK SM-1 (Mi-1) (Polish AF 2007)	The Helicopter Museum, Weston-super-Mare	
07 y	Yakovlev Yak-18M (G-BMJY)	Privately owned, Membury, Bucks	
9 w	SPP Yak C-11 (1701139/G-OYAK)	Privately owned, Little Gransden	
10 r	Yakovlev Yak-52 (877610/G-YAKE)	Privately owned, Henstridge	
14 r	WSK-PZL An-2R (HA-MKE)	Morayvia, Kinloss	
15 w	SPP Yak C-11 (170103/D-FYAK)	Classic Aviation Company, Hannover, Germany	
17 w	Bell P-63C Kingcobra (44-4315)	Wings Museum, Balcombe, W Sussex	
18 r	LET L-29 Delfin (591771/YL-PAF)	Privately owned, Hawarden	
18 r	WSK SBLim-2 (MiG-15UTI) (1A01004/N104CJ)	Norwegian AF Historical Sqn, Rygge, Norway	
18 r	Yakovlev Yak-50 (801810/G-BTZB)	Privately owned, Henstridge	
20 r	Yakovlev Yak-50 (812003/G-YAAK)	Privately owned, Henstridge	
20 w	Lavochkin La-11	The Fighter Collection, Duxford	
21 w	Yakovlev Yak-3UA (0470203/G-CDBJ)	Privately owned, Folkestone	
21 w	Yakovlev Yak-9UM (0470403/D-FENK)	Privately owned, Magdeburg, Germany	
23 y	Bell P-39Q Airacobra (44-2911)	Privately owned, Sussex	
23 r	Mikoyan MiG-27D (83712515040)	Privately owned, Hawarden	
26 bl	Yakovlev Yak-52 (9111306/G-BVXK)	Privately owned, White Waltham	
27 w	Yakovlev Yak-3UTI-PW (9/04623/F-AZIM)	Privately owned, la Ferté-Alais, France	
27 r	Yakovlev Yak-52 (9111307/G-YAKX)	Privately owned, Popham	
28 w	Polikarpov Po-2 (0094/G-BSSY)	The Shuttleworth Collection, Old Warden	
33 r	Yakovlev Yak-50 (853206/G-YAKZ)	Privately owned, Henstridge	
33 w	Yakovlev Yak-52 (899915/G-YAKH)	Privately owned, White Waltham	
35 r	Sukhoi Su-17M-3 (25102)	Privately owned, Hawarden	
36 w	LET/Yak C-11 (171101/G-KYAK)	Privately owned, North Weald	
36 r	Yakovlev Yak-52 (9111604/G-IUII)	Privately owned, St Athan	
43 bl	Yakovlev Yak-52 (877601/G-BWSV)	Privately owned, Elstree	

Notes	Serial	Type (code/other identity)	Owner/operator, location or fate
	48 w	Yakovlev Yak-3UPW <R> (F-AZZK)	Privately owned, Lelystad, The Netherlands
	49 r	Yakovlev Yak-50 (822305/G-YAKU)	Privately owned, Henstridge
	50 gy	Yakovlev Yak-52 (9111415/G-CBRW)	Meier Motors, Bremgarten, Germany
	50 y	Yakovlev Yak-50 (801804/G-EYAK)	Privately owned, Leicester
	51 r	LET L-29S Delfin (491273/YL-PAG)	Privately owned, Breighton
	51 y	Yakovlev Yak-50 (812004/G-BWYK)	Sold to Italy, November 2017
	52 bk	Yakovlev Yak-52 (877409/G-FLSH)	Privately owned, St Athan
	52 w	Yakovlev Yak-52 (9612001/G-CCJK)	Privately owned, White Waltham
	52 y	Yakovlev Yak-52 (878202/G-BWVR)	Privately owned, Eshott
	54 r	Sukhoi Su-17M (69004)	Privately owned, Hawarden
	61 r	Yakovlev Yak-50 (842710/G-YAKM)	Privately owned, Henstridge
	66 r	Yakovlev Yak-52 (855905/G-YAKN)	Privately owned, Henstridge
	71 r	Mikoyan MiG-27K (61912507006)	Newark Air Museum, Winthorpe
	74 w	Yakovlev Yak-52 (877404/G-OUGH) [JA-74, IV-62]	Privately owned, Swansea
	86 r	Yakovlev Yak-52 (867212/G-YAKC)	Privately owned, Henstridge
	100 bl	Yakovlev Yak-52 (866904/G-YAKI)	Privately owned, Popham
	100 w	Yakovlev Yak-3M (0470107/G-CGXG)	Sold to the USA, July 2019
	139 y	Yakovlev Yak-52 (833810/G-BWOD)	Sold as G-STNR, 2010
	526 bk	Mikoyan MiG-29 (2960725887) <ff>	South Wales Aviation Museum, St Athan
	1342	Yakovlev Yak-1 (G-BTZD)	Privately owned, Westfield, Sussex
	1870710	Ilyushin Il-2 (G-BZVW)	Privately owned, Wickenby
	1878576	Ilyushin Il-2 (G-BZVX)	Privately owned, Wickenby
	(RK858)	VS361 Spitfire LF IX (G-CGJE)	The Fighter Collection, Duxford

SAUDI ARABIA

Notes	Serial	Type (code/other identity)	Owner/operator, location or fate
	1115	BAC Strikemaster Mk.80A	Global Aviation, Humberside
	1129	BAC Strikemaster Mk.80A	Humberside Airport, on display
	1133	BAC Strikemaster Mk.80A (G-BESY)	IWM Duxford
	53-671	BAC Lightning F53 (203/ZF579)	Gatwick Aviation Museum, Charlwood
	53-686	BAC Lightning F53 (G-AWON/201/1305/223/ZF592)	City of Norwich Aviation Museum
	55-713	BAC Lightning T55 (206/1316/235/ZF598) [C]	Midland Air Museum, Coventry

SIERRA LEONE

Notes	Serial	Type (code/other identity)	Owner/operator, location or fate
	SL-01	Westland Commando Mk.2C	Privately owned, Dunsfold

SINGAPORE

Notes	Serial	Type (code/other identity)	Owner/operator, location or fate
	311	BAC Strikemaster Mk.84 (G-MXPH)	Privately owned, stored Hawarden
	323	BAC Strikemaster Mk.81 (N21419)	Privately owned, stored Hawarden

SOUTH AFRICA

Notes	Serial	Type (code/other identity)	Owner/operator, location or fate
	91	Westland Wasp HAS1 (pod)	Privately owned, Oaksey Park
	92	Westland Wasp HAS1 (G-BYCX)	Privately owned, Thruxton
	6130	Lockheed Ventura II (AJ469)	RAF Museum, stored Cosford
	7429	NA AT-6D Harvard III (D-FASS)	Privately owned, Aachen, Germany

SOUTH ARABIA

Notes	Serial	Type (code/other identity)	Owner/operator, location or fate
	104	BAC Jet Provost T52A (G-PROV)	Privately owned, North Weald

SOUTH VIETNAM

Notes	Serial	Type (code/other identity)	Owner/operator, location or fate
	24550	Cessna L-19E Bird Dog (G-PDOG) [GP]	Privately owned, Fenland

SPAIN

Notes	Serial	Type (code/other identity)	Owner/operator, location or fate
	B.2I-27	CASA 2.111B (He111H-16) (B.2I-103)	Kent Battle of Britain Museum, Hawkinge
	C.4K-30	Hispano HA 1.112M1L Buchón [471-26]	Privately owned, Sywell
	C.4K-111	Hispano HA 1.112M1L Buchón (G-HISP) [471-15]	Privately owned, Sywell
	C.4K-152	Hispano HA 1.112M1L Buchón (G-AWHR/N4109G)	Repainted as White 5, April 2019
	E.3B-143	CASA 1.131E Jungmann (G-JUNG)	Privately owned, White Waltham
	E.3B-153	CASA 1.131E Jungmann (G-BPTS) [781-75]	Privately owned, Egginton
	E.3B-494	CASA 1.131E Jungmann (G-CDLC) [81-47]	Privately owned, Chiseldon
	E.3B-521	CASA 1.131E Jungmann [781-3]	RAF Museum Reserve Collection, Stafford
	E.3B-599	CASA 1.131E Jungmann (G-CGTX) [31]	Privately owned, Archerfield, Lothian
	E.18-2	Piper PA-31P Navajo 425 [42-71]	High Harthay Outdoor Pursuits, Huntingdon

Serial	Type (code/other identity)	Owner/operator, location or fate	Notes
SRI LANKA			
CT130	Nanchang CJ-6A Chujiao (3151215/G-CJSA)	Privately owned, White Waltham	
CT180	Nanchang CJ-6A Chujiao (2632016/G-BXZB)	Privately owned, White Waltham	
SWEDEN			
-	Thulin A/Bleriot XI (SE-XMC)	Privately owned, Loberod, Sweden	
087	CFM 01 Tummelisa <R> (SE-XIL)	Privately owned, Loberod, Sweden	
5033	Klemm Kl35D (SE-BPT) [78]	Privately owned, Barkaby, Sweden	
5060	Klemm Kl35D (SE-BPU) [174]	Privately owned, Barkaby, Sweden	
05108	DH60 Moth	Privately owned, Langham	
17239	SAAB B 17A (SE-BYH) [7-J]	Flygvapenmuseum, Linköping, Sweden	
29640	SAAB J 29F [20-08]	Midland Air Museum, Coventry	
29670	SAAB J 29F (SE-DXB) [10-R]	Swedish Air Force Historic Flt, Såtenäs, Sweden	
32028	SAAB 32A Lansen (G-BMSG) <ff>	Privately owned, Willenhall, Staffs	
32542	SAAB J 32B Lansen (SE-RMD) [23]	Swedish Air Force Historic Flt, Såtenäs, Sweden	
35075	SAAB J 35A Draken [40]	Dumfries & Galloway Aviation Museum	
35515	SAAB J 35F Draken [49]	Airborne Systems, Llangeinor	
35556	SAAB J 35J Draken (SE-DXR) [10-56]	Swedish Air Force Historic Flt, Såtenäs, Sweden	
35810	SAAB Sk 35C Draken (SE-DXP) [79]	Swedish Air Force Historic Flt, Såtenäs, Sweden	
37098	SAAB AJSF 37 Viggen (SE-DXN) [52]	Swedish Air Force Historic Flt, Såtenäs, Sweden	
37809	SAAB Sk 37E Viggen (SE-DXO) [61]	Swedish Air Force Historic Flt, Såtenäs, Sweden	
37918	SAAB AJSH 37 Viggen [57]	Newark Air Museum, Winthorpe	
60140	SAAB Sk 60E (SE-DXG) [140-5]	Swedish Air Force Historic Flt, Såtenäs, Sweden	
91130	SAAB S91A Safir (SE-BNN) [10-30]	Privately owned, Barkaby, Sweden	
SWITZERLAND			
-	DH112 Venom FB54 (J-1758/N203DM)	Grove Technology Park, Wantage, Oxon	
A-10	CASA 1.131E Jungmann (G-BECW)	Privately owned, Postling, Kent	
A-44	CASA 1.131E Jungmann 2000 (G-CIUE)	Privately owned, Breighton	
A-57	CASA 1.131E Jungmann (G-BECT)	Privately owned, Goodwood	
A-125	Pilatus P2-05 (G-BLKZ) (fuselage)	Privately owned, Newquay	
A-806	Pilatus P3-03 (G-BTLL)	Privately owned, Guist, Norfolk	
A-815	Pilatus P3-03 (HB-RCQ)	Privately owned, Locarno, Switzerland	
A-818	Pilatus P3-03 (HB-RCH)	Privately owned, Ambri, Switzerland	
A-829	Pilatus P3-03 (HB-RCJ)	Privately owned, Altenrhein, Switzerland	
A-873	Pilatus P3-03 (HB-RCL)	Privately owned, Locarno, Switzerland	
C-509	EKW C-3605 (HB-RDH)	46 Aviation, Sion, Switzerland	
C-552	EKW C-3605 (G-DORN)	Privately owned, Little Gransden (dismantled)	
C-558	EKW C-3605 (G-CCYZ)	Privately owned, Wickenby	
J-143	F+W D-3801 (MS406) (HB-RCF)	Privately owned, Bex, Switzerland	
J-1008	DH100 Vampire FB6	de Havilland Aircraft Museum, London Colney	
J-1169	DH100 Vampire FB6	Privately owned, Henley-on-Thames	
J-1172	DH100 Vampire FB6 (8487M)	RAF Museum Reserve Collection, Stafford	
J-1573	DH112 Venom FB50 (G-VICI) <ff>	Privately owned, Tetbury, Glos	
J-1605	DH112 Venom FB50 (G-BLID)	Gatwick Aviation Museum, Charlwood, Surrey	
J-1629	DH112 Venom FB50	Privately owned, Shropshire	
J-1632	DH112 Venom FB50 (G-VNOM) <ff>	Privately owned, Lavendon, Bucks	
J-1649	DH112 Venom FB50 <ff>	Cornwall Aviation Heritage Centre, Newquay	
J-1704	DH112 Venom FB54	RAF Museum, stored Cosford	
J-1790	DH112 Venom FB54 (G-BLKA/WR410)	Historic Aviation Centre, Fishburn	
J-4015	Hawker Hunter F58 (J-4040/HB-RVS)	Privately owned, St Stephan, Switzerland	
J-4064	Hawker Hunter F58 (HB-RVQ)	Fliegermuseum Altenrhein, Switzerland	
J-4086	Hawker Hunter F58 (HB-RVU)	Privately owned, Altenrhein, Switzerland	
J-4110	Hawker Hunter F58A (XF318/G-CJWL)	Hawker Hunter Aviation Ltd, Scampton	
J-4201	Hawker Hunter T68 (HB-RVR)	Amici dell'Hunter, Sion, Switzerland	
J-4205	Hawker Hunter T68 (HB-RVP)	Fliegermuseum Altenrhein, Switzerland	
J-4206	Hawker Hunter T68 (HB-RVV)	Fliegermuseum Altenrhein, Switzerland	
U-80	Bücker Bü133D Jungmeister (G-BUKK)	Privately owned, Coventry	
U-95	Bücker Bü133C Jungmeister (G-BVGP)	Privately owned, Turweston	
U-99	Bücker Bü133C Jungmeister (G-AXMT)	Privately owned, Breighton	
U-1215	DH115 Vampire T11 (XE998)	Solent Sky, Southampton	
V-54	SE3130 Alouette II (2-BVSD)	Privately owned, Glos	

Notes	Serial	Type (code/other identity)	Owner/operator, location or fate
	UNITED ARAB EMIRATES		
	DU-103	Bell 206B JetRanger II	Privately owned, Coney Park, Leeds
	USA		
	-	Noorduyn AT-16 Harvard IIB (KLu B-168)	American Air Museum, Duxford
	001	Ryan ST-3KR Recruit (G-BYPY)	*Sold to the USA, July 2019*
	07	Boeing-Stearman PT-17 Kaydet (N62658)	Privately owned, Hurstbourne Tarrant, Hants
	14	Boeing-Stearman A75N-1 Kaydet (3486/G-ISDN)	Privately owned, Oaksey Park
	18	Agusta-Bell AB204B (MM80279/*MM80270*)	MAG36-UK, Manston, Kent
	23	Fairchild PT-23 (N49272)	Privately owned, Sleap
	26	Boeing-Stearman A75N-1 Kaydet (G-BAVO)	Privately owned, Enstone
	27	Boeing-Stearman N2S-3 Kaydet (4304/G-CJYK)	Privately owned, Enstone
	27	NA SNJ-7 Texan (90678/G-BRVG)	*Repainted as G-BRVG, May 2019*
	28	Boeing-Stearman PT-27 Kaydet (42-15666/G-CKSR)	Privately owned, Enstone
	31	Boeing-Stearman A75N-1 Kaydet (42-16338/G-KAYD)	Privately owned, Gamston
	43	Noorduyn AT-16 Harvard IIB (43-13064/G-AZSC) [SC]	Privately owned, Goodwood
	44	Boeing-Stearman D75N-1 Kaydet (42-15852/G-DINS)	Privately owned, Duxford
	72	NA SNJ-5 Texan (42-85897/*431917*/G-DHHF) [JF]	DH Heritage Flights Ltd, Compton Abbas
	85	WAR P-47 Thunderbolt <R> (G-BTBI)	Privately owned, Perth
	104	Boeing-Stearman PT-13D Kaydet (42-16931/N4712V) [W]	Privately owned, Hardwick, Norfolk
	107	Boeing-Stearman PT-17 Kaydet (42-16107/N62658)	Privately owned, Hurstbourne Tarrant, Hants
	112	Boeing-Stearman PT-13D Kaydet (42-17397/G-BSWC)	Privately owned, Gloucester
	131	Boeing-Stearman PT-17 Kaydet (38254/N74677)	Privately owned, Enstone
	164	Boeing-Stearman PT-13B Kaydet (41-0823/N60320)	Privately owned, Fenland
	286	Boeing-Stearman N2S-4 Kaydet (55749/N10053)	Privately owned, Breighton
	317	Boeing-Stearman PT-18 Kaydet (41-61042/G-CIJN)	Privately owned, Goodwood
	379	Boeing-Stearman PT-13D Kaydet (42-14865/G-ILLE)	Privately owned, Hohenems, Austria
	399	Boeing-Stearman N2S-5 Kaydet (38495/N67193)	Privately owned, Gelnhausen, Germany
	441	Boeing-Stearman N2S-4 Kaydet (30010/G-BTFG)	Privately owned, Postling, Kent
	443	Boeing-Stearman E75 Kaydet (N43YP) [6018]	Privately owned, Bicester
	466	Boeing-Stearman PT-13A Kaydet (37-0089/G-PTBA)	Privately owned, Gloucester
	540	Piper L-4H Grasshopper (43-29877/G-BCNX)	Privately owned, Monewden
	560	Bell UH-1H Iroquois (73-22077/G-HUEY)	Privately owned, North Weald
	578	Boeing-Stearman N2S-5 Kaydet (N1364V)	Privately owned, North Weald
	586	Boeing-Stearman N2S-3 Kaydet (07874/N74650)	Privately owned, Seppe, The Netherlands
	628	Beech D17S (44-67761/N18V)	Privately owned, stored East Garston, Bucks
	669	Boeing-Stearman A75N-1 Kaydet (37869/G-CCXA)	Privately owned, Old Buckenham
	671	Boeing-Stearman PT-13D Kaydet (61181/G-CGPY)	Privately owned, Dunkeswell
	699	Boeing-Stearman N2S-3 Kaydet (38233/G-CCXB)	Privately owned, Goodwood
	716	Boeing-Stearman PT-13D Kaydet (42-17553/N1731B)	Privately owned, Compton Abbas
	718	Boeing-Stearman PT-13D Kaydet (42-17555/N5345N)	Privately owned, Tibenham
	744	Boeing-Stearman A75N-1 Kaydet (42-16532/OO-USN)	Privately owned, Wevelgem, Belgium
	805	Boeing-Stearman PT-17 Kaydet (42-17642/N3922B)	Privately owned, Tibenham
	854	Ryan PT-22 Recruit (41-20854/G-BTBH)	Privately owned, Goodwood
	855	Ryan PT-22 Recruit (41-15510/N56421)	Privately owned, Sleap
	897	Aeronca 11AC Chief (G-BJEV) [E]	Privately owned, English Bicknor, Glos
	985	Boeing-Stearman PT-13D Kaydet (42-16930/OO-OPS)	Privately owned, Brasschaat, Belgium
	1102	Boeing-Stearman N2S-5 Kaydet (43449/G-AZLE) [102]	DH Heritage Flights Ltd, Compton Abbas
	1164	Beech D18S (G-BKGL)	*Sold to Saudi Arabia, November 2019*
	2610	Boeing-Stearman A75 Kaydet (4280/G-FRDM) [408]	Privately owned, Enstone
	3072	NA T-6G Texan (49-3072/G-TEXN) [72]	*Repainted as KF402, May 2018*
	3397	Boeing-Stearman N2S-3 Kaydet (G-OBEE) [174]	Privately owned, Inverness
	3403	Boeing-Stearman N2S-3 Kaydet (N75TQ) [180]	Privately owned, Tibenham
	3583	Piper L-4B Grasshopper (43-0583/G-FINT) [44-D]	Privately owned, Eggesford
	3681	Piper L-4J Grasshopper (44-80248/G-AXGP)	Privately owned, Bentwaters
	3914	Piper L-4B Grasshopper (43-0914/G-BHZU)	Privately owned, Fishburn
	4406	Naval Aircraft Factory N3N-3 (G-ONAF) [12]	Privately owned, Sandown
	4826	Boeing-Stearman PT-17 Kaydet (42-16663/G-CJIN) [582]	Privately owned, Enstone
	6136	Boeing-Stearman A75N-1 Kaydet(42-16136/G-BRUJ) [205]	Privately owned, Liverpool
	6771	Republic F-84F Thunderstreak (BAF FU-6)	Bentwaters Cold War Museum
	7797	Aeronca L-16A Grasshopper (47-0797/G-BFAF)	Privately owned, Finmere
	8242	NA F-86A Sabre (48-0242) [FU-242]	Midland Air Museum, Coventry

Serial	Type (code/other identity)	Owner/operator, location or fate	Notes
01532	Northrop F-5E Tiger II <R> (BAPC 336)	RAF Alconbury on display	
02538	Fairchild PT-19B (N33870)	Privately owned, Mendlesham, Suffolk	
07539	Boeing-Stearman N2S-3 Kaydet (N63590) [143]	Privately owned, North Weald	
14286	Lockheed T-33A Shooting Star (51-4286)	IWM, stored Duxford	
O-14419	Lockheed T-33A Shooting Star (51-4419)	Midland Air Museum, Coventry	
14863	NA AT-6D Harvard III (41-33908/G-BGOR)	Privately owned, Sywell	
15372	Piper L-18C Super Cub (51-15372/N123SA) [372-A]	Privately owned, Crowfield	
15979	Hughes OH-6A Cayuse (69-15979)	RAF Mildenhall, instructional use	
15990	Bell AH-1F Hueycobra (70-15990)	Army Flying Museum, Middle Wallop	
16011	Hughes OH-6A Cayuse (69-16011/G-OHGA)	Privately owned, Wesham, Lancs	
16037	Piper J-3C-65 Cub (G-BSFD)	Privately owned, Sleap	
16171	NA F-86D Sabre (51-6171)	North-East Land, Sea & Air Museums, Usworth	
16445	Bell AH-1F Hueycobra (69-16445)	Defence Academy of the UK, Shrivenham	
16506	Hughes OH-6A Cayuse (67-16506)	The Helicopter Museum, Weston-super-Mare	
16544	NA AT-6A Texan (41-16544/N13FY) [FY]	Privately owned, Hilversum, The Netherlands	
16579	Bell UH-1H Iroquois (66-16579)	The Helicopter Museum, Weston-super-Mare	
16718	Lockheed T-33A Shooting Star (51-6718) [TR-999]	City of Norwich Aviation Museum	
O-16957	Cessna L-19A Bird Dog (N51-16957/N5308G)	Privately owned, Sleap	
17692	NA T-28S Fennec (51-7692/G-TROY) [TL-692]	Privately owned, Sywell	
17962	Lockheed SR-71A Blackbird (61-7962)	American Air Museum, Duxford	
18263	Boeing-Stearman PT-17 Kaydet (41-8263/N38940) [822]	Privately owned, Tibenham	
19252	Lockheed T-33A Shooting Star (51-9252)	Bentwaters Cold War Museum	
21300	Cessna O-2A Super Skymaster (67-21300/N590D)	Privately owned, Lelystad, The Netherlands	
21509	Bell UH-1H Iroquois (72-21509/G-UHIH)	Privately owned, Wesham, Lancs	
21605	Bell UH-1H Iroquois (72-21605)	American Air Museum, Duxford	
23648	Breda-Nardi NH-500MC (MM81000)	Privately owned, Bristol	
24538	Kaman HH-43F Huskie (62-4535)	Midland Air Museum, Coventry	
24568	Cessna L-19E Bird Dog (LN-WNO)	Army Aviation Norway, Kjeller, Norway	
24582	Cessna L-19E Bird Dog (G-VDOG)	Privately owned, Dundee	
28521	CCF T-6J Texan(52-8521/G-TVIJ) [TA-521]	Sold to Saudi Arabia, November 2019	
28562	CCF T-6J Texan (52-8562/20310/G-BSBG) [TA-562]	Privately owned, Liverpool	
30274	Piper AE-1 Cub Cruiser (N203SA)	Privately owned, Nangis, France	
30861	NA TB-25J Mitchell (44-30861/N9089Z)	Privately owned,	
31145	Piper L-4B Grasshopper (43-1145/G-BBLH) [26-G]	Privately owned, Biggin Hill	
31430	Piper L-4B Grasshopper (43-1430/G-BHVV)	Privately owned, Perranporth	
31952	Aeronca O-58B Defender (G-BRPR)	Privately owned, Lee-on-Solent	
34037	NA TB-25N Mitchell (44-29366/N9115Z/8838M)	RAF Museum, Hendon	
34064	NA B-25J Mitchell (44-31171/N7614C) [8U]	American Air Museum, Duxford	
36922	Titan T-51 Mustang (G-CMPC) [WD-Y]	Privately owned, Benwick, Cambs	
37414	McD F-4C Phantom II (63-7414)	Midland Air Museum, stored Coventry	
39624	Wag Aero Sport Trainer (EI-GMH) [39-D]	Privately owned, Abbeyshrule, Eire	
41386	Thomas-Morse S4 Scout <R> (G-MJTD)	Privately owned, Lutterworth	
42165	NA F-100D Super Sabre (54-2165) [VM]	IWM, stored Duxford	
42196	NA F-100D Super Sabre (54-2196)	Norfolk & Suffolk Avn Museum, Flixton	
43517	Boeing-Stearman N2S-5 Kaydet (G-NZSS) [227]	Privately owned, Woodchurch, Kent	
46214	Grumman TBM-3E Avenger (69327/CF-KCG) [X-3]	IWM, Duxford	
51970	NA AT-6D Texan (41-33888/G-TXAN) [V-970]	Privately owned, Aalen, Germany	
53319	Grumman TBM-3E Avenger (HB-RDG) [19]	Privately owned, Lausanne, Switzerland	
54433	Lockheed T-33A Shooting Star (55-4433) [TR-433]	Norfolk & Suffolk Avn Museum, Flixton	
54884	Piper L-4J Grasshopper (45-4884/N61787) [57-D]	Privately owned, Sywell	
55771	Boeing-Stearman N2S-4 Kaydet (N68427) [427]	Privately owned, Bodmin	
56498	Douglas C-54Q Skymaster (N44914)	Privately owned, stored North Weald	
60344	Ryan Navion (N4956C)	Privately owned, Earls Colne	
60689	Boeing B-52D Stratofortress (56-0689)	American Air Museum, Duxford	
63319	NA F-100D Super Sabre (54-2269) [FW-319]	RAF Lakenheath, on display	
66692	Lockheed U-2CT (56-6692)	American Air Museum, Duxford	
70270	McD F-101B Voodoo (57-270) (fuselage)	Midland Air Museum, stored Coventry	
80105	Replica SE5a <R> (PH-WWI/G-CCBN) [19]	Privately owned, White Waltham	
82062	DHC U-6A Beaver (58-2062)	Midland Air Museum, Coventry	
82127	Cessna 310 (G-APNJ)	Newark Air Museum, Winthorpe	
85061	NA SNJ-5 Texan (G-CHIA) [7F]	Privately owned, Kidlington	
86690	Grumman FM-2 Wildcat (G-KINL) [F-2]	Privately owned, Duxford	

Notes	Serial	Type (code/other identity)	Owner/operator, location or fate
	96995	CV F4U-4 Corsair (OE-EAS) [BR-37]	Flying Bulls, Salzburg, Austria
	111836	NA AT-6C Harvard IIa (41-33262/G-TSIX) [JZ-6]	Privately owned, Earls Colne
	111989	Cessna L-19A Bird Dog (51-11989/N33600)	Army Flying Museum, Middle Wallop
	114700	NA T-6G Texan (51-14700/G-TOMC)	Privately owned, Netherthorpe
	115042	NA T-6G Texan (51-15042/G-BGHU) [TA-042]	Privately owned, Postling, Kent
	115227	NA T-6G Texan (51-15227/G-BKRA)	Privately owned, Shoreham
	115302	Piper L-18C Super Cub (51-15302/G-BJTP) [TP]	Privately owned, Defford
	115373	Piper L-18C Super Cub (51-15373/G-AYPM) [A-373]	Privately owned, Leicester
	115684	Piper L-21A Super Cub (51-15684/G-BKVM) [849-DC]	Privately owned, Dunkeswell
	117415	Canadair CT-133 Silver Star (G-BYOY) [TR-415]	RAF Manston History Museum
	117529	Lockheed T-33A Shooting Star (17473) [TR-529]	Midland Air Museum, Coventry
	121714	Grumman F8F-2P Bearcat (G-RUMM) [201-B]	The Fighter Collection, Duxford
	123716	CV F4U-5NL Corsair (124541/D-FCOR) [19-WF]	Meier Motors, Bremgarten, Germany
	124143	Douglas AD-4NA Skyraider (F-AZDP) [205-RM]	Amicale J-B Salis, la Ferté-Alais, France
	124485	Boeing B-17G Flying Fortress (44-85784/G-BEDF)[DF-A]	B-17 Preservation Ltd, Duxford
	124724	CV F4U-5NL Corsair (F-AZEG) [22-NP]	Les Casques de Cuir, la Ferté-Alais, France
	126922	Douglas AD-4NA Skyraider (G-RADR) [503-H]	Kennet Aviation, North Weald
	134076	NA AT-6D Texan (41-34671/F-AZSC) [TA076]	Privately owned, Yvetot, France
	138179	NA T-28A Trojan (OE-ESA) [BA]	The Flying Bulls, Salzburg, Austria
	138266	NA T-28B Trojan (HB-RCT) [266-CT]	Jet Alpine Fighter, Sion, Switzerland
	138343	NA T-28B Trojan (N343NA) [212]	Privately owned, Siegerland, Germany
	140547	NA T-28C Trojan (F-AZHN) [IF-28]	Privately owned, Toussus le Noble, France
	140566	NA T-28C Trojan (N556EB) [252]	Privately owned, la Ferté-Alais, France
	146289	NA T-28C Trojan (N99153) [2W]	Norfolk & Suffolk Avn Museum, Flixton
	150225	WS58 Wessex 60 (G-AWOX) [123]	Privately owned, Lulsgate
	155454	NA OV-10B Bronco (158300/99+24/F-AZKM) [26]	Privately owned, Montelimar, France
	155529	McD F-4J(UK) Phantom II (ZE359) [AJ-114]	American Air Museum, Duxford
	155848	McD F-4S Phantom II [WT-11]	National Museum of Flight, E Fortune
	159233	HS AV-8A Harrier [CG-33]	IWM North, Salford Quays
	162068	McD AV-8B Harrier II <ff>	*Sold to Canada, 2019*
	162071	McD AV-8B Harrier II (fuselage)	Rolls-Royce, Filton
	162074	McD AV-8B Harrier II <ff>	Privately owned, South Molton, Devon
	162730	McD AV-8B Harrier II <ff>	Privately owned, Liverpool
	162737	McD AV-8B Harrier II (fuselage) [38]	MoD/JARTS, Boscombe Down
	162958	McD AV-8B Harrier II <ff>	QinetiQ, Farnborough
	162964	McD AV-8B Harrier II <ff>	Harrier Heritage Centre, RAF Wittering
	162964	McD AV-8B Harrier II <rf>	Privately owned, Charlwood, Surrey
	163205	McD AV-8B Harrier II (fuselage)	Privately owned, Thorpe Wood, N Yorks
	163423	McD AV-8B Harrier II <ff>	QinetiQ, Boscombe Down
	163423	McD AV-8B Harrier II <rf>	Privately owned, Sproughton
	210766	Douglas C-47B Skytrain (composite) (K-1) [4U]	Wings Museum, Balcombe, W Sussex
	217786	Boeing-Stearman PT-17 Kaydet (41-8169/CF-EQS) [25]	American Air Museum, Duxford
	224319	Douglas C-47B Skytrain (44-77047/G-AMSN) <ff>	Privately owned, Sussex
	226413	Republic P-47D Thunderbolt (45-49192/N47DD) [UN-Z]	American Air Museum, Duxford
	234539	Fairchild PT-19B Cornell (42-34539/N50429) [63]	Privately owned, Dunkeswell
	236657	Piper L-4A Grasshopper (42-36657/G-BGSJ) [72-D]	Privately owned, Langport, Somerset
	237123	Waco CG-4A Hadrian <R> (fuselage)	Yorkshire Air Museum, Elvington
	238133	Boeing B-17G Flying Fortress (44-83735/F-BDRS) [C]	American Air Museum, Duxford
	238410	Piper L-4A Grasshopper (42-38410/G-BHPK) [44-A]	Privately owned, Tibenham
	241079	Waco CG-4A Hadrian <R> (BAPC 370)	RAF Museum, stored Cosford
	243809	Waco CG-4A Hadrian (BAPC 185)	Army Flying Museum, Middle Wallop
	252983	Schweizer TG-3A (42-52983/N66630)	IWM Duxford, stored
	285068	NA AT-6D Texan (42-85068/G-KAMY)	Kennet Aviation, North Weald/Yeovilton
	298177	Stinson L-5A Sentinel (42-98177/N6438C) [8-R]	Privately owned, Tibenham
	313048	NA AT-6D Texan (44-81506/G-TDJN)	*Sold to Belgium, November 2019*
	314887	Fairchild Argus III (43-14887/G-AJPI)	Privately owned, Eelde, The Netherlands
	315509	Douglas C-47A Skytrain (43-15509/G-BHUB) [W7-S]	American Air Museum, Duxford
	319764	Waco CG-4A Hadrian (237123/BAPC 157) (fuselage)	Yorkshire Air Museum, Elvington
	329282	Piper J-3C-65 Cub (N46779)	Privately owned, Abbots Bromley
	329405	Piper L-4H Grasshopper (43-29405/G-BCOB) [23-A]	Privately owned, Bicester
	329417	Piper L-4A Grasshopper (42-38400/G-BDHK)	Privately owned, English Bicknor, Glos
	329471	Piper L-4H Grasshopper (43-29471/G-BGXA) [44-F]	Privately owned, Martley, Worcs

Serial	Type (code/other identity)	Owner/operator, location or fate	Notes
329594	Piper L-4H Grasshopper (43-29594/G-BROR)	Privately owned, East Winch, Norfolk	
329601	Piper L-4H Grasshopper (43-29601/G-AXHR) [44-D]	Privately owned, Nayland	
329707	Piper L-4H Grasshopper (43-29707/G-BFBY) [44-S]	Privately owned, Old Buckenham	
329854	Piper L-4H Grasshopper (43-29854/G-BMKC) [44-R]	Privately owned, Biggin Hill	
329934	Piper L-4H Grasshopper (43-29934/G-BCPH) [72-B]	Privately owned, Garford, Oxon	
330238	Piper L-4H Grasshopper (43-30238/G-LIVH) [24-A]	Privately owned, Yarcombe, Devon	
330244	Piper L-4H Grasshopper (43-30244/G-CGIY) [46-C]	Privately owned, Church Fenton	
330314	Piper L-4H Grasshopper (43-30314/G-BAET)	Privately owned, Winwick, Cambs	
330372	Piper L-4H Grasshopper (43-30372/G-AISX)	Privately owned, Booker	
330426	Piper L-4J Grasshopper (45-4884/N61787) [53-K]	Privately owned, Podington, Beds	
330485	Piper L-4H Grasshopper (43-30485/G-AJES) [44-C]	Privately owned, Shifnal	
379994	Piper J-3L-65 Cub (G-BPUR) [52-J]	Privately owned, Popham	
411622	NA P-51D Mustang (44-74427/F-AZSB) [G4-C]	Privately owned, Melun, France	
411631	NA P-51D Mustang (44-73979/472218) [MX-V]	American Air Museum, Duxford	
413317	NA P-51D Mustang (44-74409/N51RT) [VF-B]	RAF Museum, Hendon	
413357	NA P-51D Mustang <R> [B7-R]	Privately owned, Byfleet, Surrey	
413573	NA P-51D Mustang (44-73415/9133M/N6526D) [B6-V]	RAF Museum, stored Cosford	
413578	NA P-51D Mustang (44-74923/PH-JAT) [C5-W]	Privately owned, Lelystad, The Netherlands	
413926	Stewart S-51 Mustang (G-CGOI) [E2-S]	Privately owned, Benwick, Cambs	
414251	NA TF-51D Mustang (44-84847/G-TFSI) [WZ-I]	Privately owned, Sywell	
414673	Bonsall Replica Mustang (G-BDWM) [LH-I]	Privately owned, Sherburn-in-Elmet	
414907	Titan T-51 Mustang (G-DHYS) [CY-S]	Privately owned, Pershore	
431212	Douglas C-47A Skytrain (42-100884/N147DC) [D]	*Repainted as 2100884, 2019*	
433915	Consolidated PBV-1A Canso A (RCAF 11005/G-PBYA)	Privately owned, Duxford	
434602	Douglas A-26B Invader (44-34602/LN-IVA) [B]	Nordic Warbirds, Västerås, Sweden	
436021	Piper J-3C-65 Cub (G-BWEZ)	Privately owned, Archerfield, Lothian	
436784	Beech G18S (N45CF)	Privately owned, Bressaucourt, Switzerland	
441968	Titan T-51 Mustang (G-FION) [VF-E]	Privately owned, Netherthorpe	
442268	Noorduyn AT-16 Harvard IIb (KF568/LN-TEX) [TA-268]	Privately owned, Kjeller, Norway	
454467	Piper L-4J Grasshopper (45-4467/G-BILI) [44-J]	Privately owned, RAF Halton	
454471	Piper L-4J Grasshopper (45-4471/G-AKTH)	Privately owned, Goodwood	
454537	Piper L-4J Grasshopper (45-4537/G-BFDL) [04-J]	Privately owned, Shempston Farm, Lossiemouth	
454630	Piper L-4J Grasshopper (45-4446/G-BDOL) [LI-7]	Privately owned, Bidford, Warks	
461748	Boeing B-29A Superfortress (44-61748/G-BHDK) [Y]	American Air Museum, Duxford	
463209	NA P-51D Mustang <R> (BAPC 255) [WZ-S]	IWM Duxford	
464005	NA P-51D Mustang (44-64005/N51CK) [E9-Z]	Privately owned, Sywell	
472216	NA P-51D Mustang (44-72216/G-BIXL) [HO-M]	Privately owned, Goodwood	
472218	Titan T-51 Mustang (G-MUZY) [WZ-I]	Privately owned, Tibenham	
472773	NA P-51D Mustang (44-72773/D-FPSI) [QP-M]	Meier Motors, Bremgarten, Germany	
472922	NA TF-51D Mustang (44-72922/OO-RYL) [L2-W]	Privately owned, Brasschaat, Belgium	
473871	NA TF-51D Mustang (44-73871/D-FTSI) [TF-871]	Meier Motors, Bremgarten, Germany	
474008	Jurca MJ77 Gnatsum (G-PSIR) [VF-R]	Privately owned, Fishburn	
474425	NA P-51D Mustang (44-74425/PH-PSI) [OC-G]	Privately owned, Lelystad, The Netherlands	
479712	Piper L-4H Grasshopper (44-79826/G-AHIP) [8-R]	Privately owned, Coleford	
479744	Piper L-4H Grasshopper (44-79744/G-BGPD) [49-M]	Privately owned, Marsh, Bucks	
479766	Piper L-4H Grasshopper (44-79766/G-BKHG) [63-D]	Privately owned, Holmbeck Farm, Beds	
479781	Piper L-4H Grasshopper (44-79781/G-AISS)	Privately owned, Insch (under restoration)	
479878	Piper L-4H Grasshopper (44-79878/G-BEUI) [MF-D]	Privately owned, Yarcombe, Devon	
479897	Piper L-4H Grasshopper (44-79897/G-BOXJ) [JD]	Privately owned, Rochester	
480015	Piper L-4H Grasshopper (44-80015/G-AKIB) [44-M]	Privately owned, Perranporth	
480133	Piper L-4J Grasshopper (44-80133/G-BDCD) [44-B]	Privately owned, Slinfold	
480173	Piper L-4J Grasshopper (44-80609/G-RRSR) [57-H]	Privately owned, Shotteswell	
480321	Piper L-4J Grasshopper (44-80321/G-FRAN) [44-H]	Privately owned, Rayne, Essex	
480480	Piper L-4J Grasshopper (44-80480/G-BECN) [44-E]	Privately owned, Rayne, Essex	
480636	Piper L-4J Grasshopper (44-80636/G-AXHP) [58-A]	Privately owned, Great Ponton, Lincs	
480723	Piper L-4J Grasshopper (44-80723/G-BFZB) [E5-J]	Privately owned, Egginton	
480752	Piper L-4J Grasshopper (44-80752/G-BCXJ) [39-E]	Privately owned, Melksham	
481273	CCF T-6J Harvard IV (20306/G-CJWE) [NG]	Privately owned, Leicester	
483868	Boeing B-17G Flying Fortress (44-83868/N5237V) [A-N]	RAF Museum, Hendon	
484786	NA F-6D Mustang (44-84786/N51BS) [5M-K]	Privately owned, Duxford (damaged)	
493209	NA T-6G Texan (49-3209/G-DDMV/*41*)	Privately owned, Headcorn	
542454	Piper L-21B Super Cub (54-2454/D-ESMV)	Privately owned, Membury	

Notes	Serial	Type (code/other identity)	Owner/operator, location or fate
	549192	Republic P-47D Thunderbolt (45-49192/G-THUN) [F4-J]	Privately owned, Duxford/Sywell
	779465	Hiller UH-12C (N5315V)	Privately owned, Lower Upham, Hants
	2106638	Titan T-51 Mustang (G-CIFD) [E9-R]	Privately owned, Shobdon
	2100882	Douglas C-47A Skytrain (42-100882/N473DC) [3X-P]	Privately owned, North Weald
	2100884	Douglas C-47A Skytrain (42-100884/N147DC) [S6-A]	Privately owned, Dunsfold
	2105915	Curtiss P-40N Kittyhawk (42-105915/F-AZKU)	France's Flying Warbirds, Melun, France
	03-08003	B-V CH-47F Chinook [DT]	RAF Odiham, at main gate
	03-33119	General Atomics MQ-1B Predator [CH]	RAF Museum, Hendon
	03-33120	General Atomics MQ-1B Predator [CH]	American Air Museum, Duxford
	3-1923	Aeronca O-58B Defender (43-1923/G-BRHP)	Privately owned, Chiseldon
	18-2001	Piper L-18C Super Cub (52-2401/G-BIZV)	Privately owned, Wicklow, Ireland
	22-296	Eberhardt SE5E Replica (G-BLXT)	Privately owned
	39-139	Beech YC-43 Traveler (N295BS)	Duke of Brabant AF, Eindhoven, The Netherlands
	39-0285	Curtiss P-40B Warhawk	The Fighter Collection, stored Duxford (wreck)
	39-0287	Curtiss P-40B Warhawk	The Fighter Collection, stored Duxford (wreck)
	40-2538	Fairchild PT-19A Cornell (N33870)	Privately owned, Mendlesham
	41-8689	Boeing-Stearman PT-17D Kaydet (G-BIXN) (frame)	Privately owned, Rendcomb
	41-13357	Curtiss P-40C Warhawk (G-CIIO) [160,10AB]	The Fighter Collection, Duxford
	41-19393	Douglas A-20C Havoc (wreck)	Wings Museum, Balcombe, W Sussex
	41-33275	NA AT-6C Texan (G-BICE) [CE]	Privately owned, Great Oakley, Essex
	41-35253	Martin B-26C Marauder <rf>	Boxted Airfield Museum
	42-66841	Lockheed P-38H Lightning [153]	Privately owned, Bentwaters
	42-12417	Noorduyn AT-16 Harvard IIb (KLu. B-163)	Newark Air Museum, Winthorpe
	42-35870	Taylorcraft DCO-65 (G-BWLJ) [129]	Privately owned, Nayland
	42-46703	Stinson AT-19 Reliant (FK877/N69745)	Privately owned, RNAS Yeovilton
	42-58678	Taylorcraft DF-65 (G-BRIY) [IY]	Privately owned, Carlisle
	42-78044	Aeronca 11AC Chief (G-BRXL)	Privately owned, Andrewsfield
	42-84555	NA AT-6D Harvard III (FAP.1662/G-ELMH) [EP-H]	Privately owned, Hardwick, Norfolk
	42-93510	Douglas C-47A Skytrain [CM] <ff>	Privately owned, Kew
	43-9628	Douglas A-20G Havoc <ff>	Privately owned, Hinckley, Leics
	43-11137	Bell P-63C Kingcobra (wreck)	Wings Museum, Balcombe, W Sussex
	43-21664	Douglas A-20G Havoc (wreck)	Wings Museum, Balcombe, W Sussex
	43-35943	Beech 3N (G-BKRN) [943]	Beech Restorations, Bruntingthorpe
	43-36140	NA B-25J Mitchell <ff>	Wings Museum, Balcombe, W Sussex
	44-4368	Bell P-63C Kingcobra	Privately owned, Surrey
	44-13954	NA P-51D Mustang (G-UAKE)	Mustang Restoration Co Ltd, Coventry
	44-14574	NA P-51D Mustang (fuselage)	East Essex Aviation Museum, Clacton
	44-42914	Douglas DC-4 (N31356) <ff>	Privately owned, Burtonwood
	44-51228	Consolidated B-24M Liberator [EC-493]	American Air Museum, Duxford
	44-79609	Piper L-4H Grasshopper (G-BHXY) [PR]	Privately owned, Bealbury, Cornwall
	44-79649	Piper L-4H Grasshopper (G-AIIH)	Privately owned, Stonesfield, Oxon
	44-80594	Piper L-4J Grasshopper (G-BEDJ)	Privately owned, White Waltham
	44-80647	Piper L-4J Grasshopper (D-EGAF)	Privately owned, Donauwörth, Germany
	45-5772	Piper J-5A Cub Cruiser (G-BSXT)	Privately owned, Norwich
	51-9036	Lockheed T-33A Shooting Star	Newark Air Museum, Winthorpe
	51-15319	Piper L-18C Super Cub (G-FUZZ) [A-319]	Privately owned, Elvington
	51-15555	Piper L-18C Super Cub (G-OSPS) [A-555]	Privately owned, Enstone
	54-005	NA F-100D Super Sabre (54-2163) [HA]	Dumfries & Galloway Avn Mus, Dumfries
	54-174	NA F-100D Super Sabre (54-2174) [SM]	Midland Air Museum, Coventry
	54-2223	NA F-100D Super Sabre	Newark Air Museum, Winthorpe
	54-2445	Piper L-21B Super Cub (G-OTAN) [A-445]	Privately owned, Hawarden
	54-2447	Piper L-21B Super Cub (G-SCUB)	Privately owned, Anwick
	55-138354	NA T-28B Trojan (138354/N1328B) [TL-354]	Privately owned, Zwartberg, Belgium
	63-699	McD F-4C Phantom II (63-7699) [CG]	Midland Air Museum, Coventry
	64-0553	Lockheed WC-130E Hercules <ff>	RAF Museum, Hendon
	64-17657	Douglas B-26K Counter Invader (N99218) <ff>	WWII Remembrance Museum, Handcross, W Sussex
	65-777	McD F-4C Phantom II (63-7419) [SA]	RAF Lakenheath, on display
	66-374	Helio H.295 Super Courier (G-BAGT) [EO]	Privately owned, Spanhoe
	67-120	GD F-111E Aardvark (67-0120) [UH]	American Air Museum, Duxford
	68-0060	GD F-111E Aardvark <ff>	Dumfries & Galloway Avn Mus, Dumfries
	68-8284	Sikorsky MH-53M Pave Low IV	RAF Museum, Cosford

Serial	Type (code/other identity)	Owner/operator, location or fate	Notes
70-0389	GD F-111E Aardvark (68-0011) [LN]	RAF Lakenheath, on display	
72-1447	GD F-111F Aardvark <ff>	American Air Museum, Duxford	
74-0177	GD F-111F Aardvark [FN]	RAF Museum, Cosford	
76-020	McD F-15A Eagle (76-0020) [BT]	American Air Museum, Duxford	
76-124	McD F-15B Eagle (76-0124) [LN]	RAF Lakenheath, instructional use	
77-259	Fairchild A-10A Thunderbolt (77-0259) [AR]	American Air Museum, Duxford	
80-219	Fairchild GA-10A Thunderbolt (80-0219) [WR]	Bentwaters Cold War Museum	
82-23762	B-V CH-47D Chinook <ff>	RAF Odiham, instructional use	
83-24104	B-V CH-47D Chinook [BN] <ff>	RAF Museum, Hendon	
86-180	McD F-15A Eagle (74-0131) [LN]	RAF Lakenheath, on display	
	(starboard side only, painted as 86-169 on port side)		
86-01677	B-V CH-47D Chinook	RAF, stored Odiham	
89-00159	B-V CH-47D Chinook	RAF, stored Odiham	
108-1601	Stinson 108-1 Voyager (G-CFGE) [H]	Privately owned, Spanhoe	
146-11042	Wolf W-11 Boredom Fighter (G-BMZX) [7]	Privately owned, Popham	
146-11083	Wolf W-11 Boredom Fighter (G-BNAI) [5]	Privately owned, Haverfordwest	
A3-3	NA P-51D Mustang (44-72035/G-SIJJ)	Hangar 11 Collection, North Weald	
S666	Noorduyn AT-16 Harvard IIb (KF435) [BS]	Maidenhead Heritage Centre	
X-17	Curtiss P-40F Warhawk (41-19841/G-CGZP)	The Fighter Collection, Duxford	
CY-G	Titan T-51 Mustang (G-TSIM)	Privately owned, Shobdon	
PA50	Curtiss P-36C Hawk (38-0210/G-CIXJ)	The Fighter Collection, Duxford	

YUGOSLAVIA

30131	Soko P-2 Kraguj [131]	*Sold to France, 2019*	
30140	Soko P-2 Kraguj (G-RADA) [140]	Privately owned, Fishburn	
30146	Soko P-2 Kraguj (G-BSXD) [146]	Privately owned, Fishburn	
30149	Soko P-2 Kraguj (G-SOKO) [149]	Privately owned, Fenland	
51109	UTVA-66 (G-CLJX)	Privately owned, Eshott	

Painted as *671*, PT-13D Kaydet G-CGPY is based at Gloucester and used for wing walking. It began life as PT-13D 42-17140 with the US Army Air Force before serving with the US Navy as N2S-5 61181. When it was put on the American civil register as N75671 it (and several others) were painted as 'VN2S-5s' to avoid any confusion between the designation and the registration, after the FAA took issue.

Notes	Serial	Type (code/other identity)	Owner/operator, location or fate
	C7	Avro 631 Cadet (EI-AGO)	IAC Museum, Baldonnel
	34	Miles M14A Magister I (N5392)	National Museum of Ireland, Dublin
	141	Avro 652A Anson C19	IAC Museum, Baldonnel
	164	DHC1 Chipmunk T20	IAC Museum, Baldonnel
	168	DHC1 Chipmunk T20 (EI-HFA)	Irish Historic Flight, Ballyboy
	169	DHC1 Chipmunk 22 (WD305/EI-HFB)	Irish Historic Flight, Ballyboy
	170	DHC1 Chipmunk 22 (WP857/EI-HFC)	Irish Historic Flight, Ballyboy
	172	DHC1 Chipmunk T20	IAC, stored Baldonnel
	173	DHC1 Chipmunk T20	South East Aviation Enthusiasts, Dromod
	176	DH104 Dove 4 (VP-YKF)	South East Aviation Enthusiasts, Waterford
	183	Percival P56 Provost T51	IAC Museum, Baldonnel
	184	Percival P56 Provost T51	South East Aviation Enthusiasts, Dromod
	187	DH115 Vampire T55 <ff>	South East Aviation Enthusiasts, Dromod
	191	DH115 Vampire T55	IAC Museum, Baldonnel
	192	DH115 Vampire T55 <ff>	South East Aviation Enthusiasts, Dromod
	195	Sud SA316 Alouette III (F-WJDH)	IAC Museum, stored Baldonnel
	198	DH115 Vampire T11 (XE977)	National Museum of Ireland, Dublin
	199	DHC1 Chipmunk T20	IAC, stored Baldonnel
	202	Sud SA316 Alouette III	Ulster Aviation Society, Long Kesh
	203	Reims-Cessna FR172H	IAC Baldonnel (wfu)
	205	Reims-Cessna FR172H	IAC Baldonnel (wfu)
	206	Reims-Cessna FR172H	IAC Baldonnel (wfu)
	207	Reims-Cessna FR172H	IAC, stored Waterford
	208	Reims-Cessna FR172H	IAC Baldonnel (wfu)
	210	Reims-Cessna FR172H	IAC Baldonnel (wfu)
	215	Fouga CM170R Super Magister	IAC Baldonnel, GI use
	216	Fouga CM170R Super Magister	IAC Museum, Baldonnel
	218	Fouga CM170R Super Magister	IAC, stored Baldonnel
	219	Fouga CM170R Super Magister	IAC Museum, Baldonnel
	220	Fouga CM170R Super Magister	Cork University, instructional use
	221	Fouga CM170R Super Magister [3-KE]	IAC Museum, stored Baldonnel
	231	SIAI SF-260WE Warrior	IAC Museum, Baldonnel
	240	Beech Super King Air 200MR	IAC No 102 Sqn/1 Operations Wing, Baldonnel
	251	Grumman G1159C Gulfstream IV (N17584)	*Sold as N297PJ, November 2013*
	252	Airtech CN.235 MPA Persuader	IAC No 101 Sqn/1 Operations Wing, Baldonnel
	253	Airtech CN.235 MPA Persuader	IAC No 101 Sqn/1 Operations Wing, Baldonnel
	254	PBN-2T Defender 4000 (G-BWPN)	IAC No 106 Sqn/1 Operations Wing, Baldonnel
	256	Eurocopter EC135T-1 (G-BZRM)	IAC No 106 Sqn/1 Operations Wing, Baldonnel
	258	Gates Learjet 45 (N5009T)	IAC No 102 Sqn/1 Operations Wing, Baldonnel
	260	Pilatus PC-9M (HB-HQS)	IAC Flying Training School, Baldonnel
	261	Pilatus PC-9M (HB-HQT)	IAC Flying Training School, Baldonnel
	262	Pilatus PC-9M (HB-HQU)	IAC Flying Training School, Baldonnel
	263	Pilatus PC-9M (HB-HQV)	IAC Flying Training School, Baldonnel
	264	Pilatus PC-9M (HB-HQW)	IAC Flying Training School, Baldonnel
	266	Pilatus PC-9M (HB-HQY)	IAC Flying Training School, Baldonnel
	267	Pilatus PC-9M (HB-HQZ)	IAC Flying Training School, Baldonnel
	269	Pilatus PC-9M (HB-HXI)	IAC Flying Training School, Baldonnel
	270	Eurocopter EC135P-2 (D-HECF)	IAC No 302 Sqn/3 Operations Wing, Baldonnel
	271	Eurocopter EC135P-2 (D-HECB)	IAC No 302 Sqn/3 Operations Wing, Baldonnel
	272	Eurocopter EC135T-2 (G-CECT)	IAC No 106 Sqn/1 Operations Wing, Baldonnel
	274	AgustaWestland AW139	IAC No 301 Sqn/3 Operations Wing, Baldonnel
	275	AgustaWestland AW139	IAC No 301 Sqn/3 Operations Wing, Baldonnel
	276	AgustaWestland AW139	IAC No 301 Sqn/3 Operations Wing, Baldonnel
	277	AgustaWestland AW139	IAC No 301 Sqn/3 Operations Wing, Baldonnel
	278	AgustaWestland AW139	IAC No 301 Sqn/3 Operations Wing, Baldonnel
	279	AgustaWestland AW139	IAC No 301 Sqn/3 Operations Wing, Baldonnel
	2..	Pilatus PC.XII/47E (HB-FSF/N280NG)	IAC (on order)
	2..	Pilatus PC.XII/47E	IAC (on order)
	2..	Pilatus PC.XII/47E	IAC (on order)
	2..	CASA C-295W	IAC (on order)
	2..	CASA C-295W	IAC (on order)

Serial	Type (code/other identity)	Owner/operator, location or fate	Notes

Aircraft included in this section include those likely to be seen visiting UK civil and military airfields on transport flights, exchange visits, exercises and for air shows. It is not a comprehensive list of *all* aircraft operated by the air arms concerned.

ALBANIA

Serial	Type (code/other identity)	Owner/operator, location or fate	Notes
TC-ANA	Airbus A.319CJ-115X	Albanian Government, Tirana	

ALGERIA
Ministry of Defence

Serial	Type	Owner/operator	Notes
7T-VPC	Grumman G.1159C Gulfstream IVSP (1418)	Ministry of Defence, Boufarik	
7T-VPG	Gulfstream Aerospace Gulfstream V (617)	Ministry of Defence, Boufarik	
7T-VPM	Grumman G.1159C Gulfstream IVSP (1421)	Ministry of Defence, Boufarik	
7T-VPP	Airbus A.340-541	Ministry of Defence, Boufarik	
7T-VPR	Grumman G.1159C Gulfstream IVSP (1288)	Ministry of Defence, Boufarik	
7T-VPS	Grumman G.1159C Gulfstream IVSP (1291)	Ministry of Defence, Boufarik	

Force Aérienne Algérienne (FAA)/Al Quwwat al Jawwiya al Jaza'eriya

Serial	Type	Owner/operator	Notes
7T-WHA	Lockheed C-130H-30 Hercules (4997)	FAA 2 ETTL, Boufarik	
7T-WHB	Lockheed C-130H-30 Hercules (5224)	FAA 2 ETTL, Boufarik	
7T-WHD	Lockheed C-130H-30 Hercules (4987)	FAA 2 ETTL, Boufarik	
7T-WHE	Lockheed C-130H Hercules (4935)	FAA 2 ETTL, Boufarik	
7T-WHF	Lockheed C-130H Hercules (4934)	FAA 2 ETTL, Boufarik	
7T-WHI	Lockheed C-130H Hercules (4930)	FAA 2 ETTL, Boufarik	
7T-WHJ	Lockheed C-130H Hercules (4928)	FAA 2 ETTL, Boufarik	
7T-WHL	Lockheed C-130H-30 Hercules (4989)	FAA 2 ETTL, Boufarik	
7T-WHN	Lockheed C-130H-30 Hercules (4894)	FAA 2 ETTL, Boufarik	
7T-WHO	Lockheed C-130H-30 Hercules (4897)	FAA 2 ETTL, Boufarik	
7T-WHP	Lockheed C-130H-30 Hercules (4921)	FAA 2 ETTL, Boufarik	
7T-WHQ	Lockheed C-130H Hercules (4926)	FAA 2 ETTL, Boufarik	
7T-WHR	Lockheed C-130H Hercules (4924)	FAA 2 ETTL, Boufarik	
7T-WHS	Lockheed C-130H Hercules (4912)	FAA 2 ETTL, Boufarik	
7T-WHY	Lockheed C-130H Hercules (4913)	FAA 2 ETTL, Boufarik	
7T-WHZ	Lockheed C-130H Hercules (4914)	FAA 2 ETTL, Boufarik	
7T-WIA	Ilyushin Il-76MD	FAA 347 ETS, Boufarik	
7T-WIB	Ilyushin Il-76MD	FAA 347 ETS, Boufarik	
7T-WIC	Ilyushin Il-76MD	FAA 347 ETS, Boufarik	
7T-WID	Ilyushin Il-76TD	FAA 347 ETS, Boufarik	
7T-WIE	Ilyushin Il-76TD	FAA 347 ETS, Boufarik	
7T-WIF	Ilyushin Il-78	FAA 357 ERV, Boufarik	
7T-WIG	Ilyushin Il-76TD	FAA 347 ETS, Boufarik	
7T-WIL	Ilyushin Il-78	FAA 357 ERV, Boufarik	
7T-WIM	Ilyushin Il-76TD	FAA 347 ETS, Boufarik	
7T-WIN	Ilyushin Il-78	FAA 357 ERV, Boufarik	
7T-WIP	Ilyushin Il-76TD	FAA 347 ETS, Boufarik	
7T-WIQ	Ilyushin Il-78	FAA 357 ERV, Boufarik	
7T-WIR	Ilyushin Il-76TD	FAA 347 ETS, Boufarik	
7T-WIS	Ilyushin Il-78	FAA 357 ERV, Boufarik	
7T-WIT	Ilyushin Il-76TD	FAA 347 ETS, Boufarik	
7T-WIU	Ilyushin Il-76TD	FAA 347 ETS, Boufarik	

ANGOLA

Serial	Type	Owner/operator	Notes
D2-ANG	Bombardier Global Express XRS	Angola Government, Luanda	
D2-ANH	Bombardier Global Express	Angola Government, Luanda	

ARMENIA

Serial	Type	Owner/operator	Notes
701	Airbus A.319CJ-132	Armenian Government, Yerevan	

AUSTRALIA
Royal Australian Air Force (RAAF)

Serial	Type	Owner/operator	Notes
A9-657	Lockheed EAP-3C Orion	RAAF 10 Sqn/42 Wing, Edinburgh, South Australia	
A9-659	Lockheed AP-3C Orion	*Withdrawn from use, 2019*	
A9-660	Lockheed EAP-3C Orion	RAAF 10 Sqn/42 Wing, Edinburgh, South Australia	
A9-752	Lockheed AP-3C Orion	*Withdrawn from use, March 2019*	
A9-759	Lockheed AP-3C Orion	*Withdrawn from use, 2019*	

Notes	Serial	Type (code/other identity)	Owner/operator, location or fate
	A9-760	Lockheed AP-3C Orion	*Withdrawn from use, 2019*
	A30-001	Boeing E-7A Wedgetail (737-7ES)	RAAF 2 Sqn/41 Wing, Canberra, ACT
	A30-002	Boeing E-7A Wedgetail (737-7ES)	RAAF 2 Sqn/41 Wing, Canberra, ACT
	A30-003	Boeing E-7A Wedgetail (737-7ES)	RAAF 2 Sqn/41 Wing, Canberra, ACT
	A30-004	Boeing E-7A Wedgetail (737-7ES)	RAAF 2 Sqn/41 Wing, Canberra, ACT
	A30-005	Boeing E-7A Wedgetail (737-7ES)	RAAF 2 Sqn/41 Wing, Canberra, ACT
	A30-006	Boeing E-7A Wedgetail (737-7ES)	RAAF 2 Sqn/41 Wing, Canberra, ACT
	A36-001	Boeing 737-7DT	RAAF 34 Sqn/84 Wing, Canberra, ACT
	A36-002	Boeing 737-7DF	RAAF 34 Sqn/84 Wing, Canberra, ACT
	A37-001	Canadair CL.604 Challenger	*Sold as VH-OFA, June 2019*
	A37-002	Canadair CL.604 Challenger	RAAF 34 Sqn/84 Wing, Canberra, ACT
	A37-003	Canadair CL.604 Challenger	RAAF 34 Sqn/84 Wing, Canberra, ACT
	A39-001	Airbus KC-30A (A.330-203 MRTT)	RAAF 33 Sqn/84 Wing, Amberley, Queensland
	A39-002	Airbus KC-30A (A.330-203 MRTT)	RAAF 33 Sqn/84 Wing, Amberley, Queensland
	A39-003	Airbus KC-30A (A.330-203 MRTT)	RAAF 33 Sqn/84 Wing, Amberley, Queensland
	A39-004	Airbus KC-30A (A.330-203 MRTT)	RAAF 33 Sqn/84 Wing, Amberley, Queensland
	A39-005	Airbus KC-30A (A.330-203 MRTT)	RAAF 33 Sqn/84 Wing, Amberley, Queensland
	A39-006	Airbus KC-30A (A.330-203 MRTT) (VH-EBH)	RAAF 33 Sqn/84 Wing, Amberley, Queensland
	A39-007	Airbus KC-30A (A.330-203 MRTT) (VH-EBI)	RAAF 33 Sqn/84 Wing, Amberley, Queensland
	A41-206	Boeing C-17A Globemaster III (06-0206)	RAAF 36 Sqn/86 Wing, Amberley, Queensland
	A41-207	Boeing C-17A Globemaster III (06-0207)	RAAF 36 Sqn/86 Wing, Amberley, Queensland
	A41-208	Boeing C-17A Globemaster III (06-0208)	RAAF 36 Sqn/86 Wing, Amberley, Queensland
	A41-209	Boeing C-17A Globemaster III (06-0209)	RAAF 36 Sqn/86 Wing, Amberley, Queensland
	A41-210	Boeing C-17A Globemaster III (11-0210)	RAAF 36 Sqn/86 Wing, Amberley, Queensland
	A41-211	Boeing C-17A Globemaster III (12-0211)	RAAF 36 Sqn/86 Wing, Amberley, Queensland
	A41-212	Boeing C-17A Globemaster III (14-0001)	RAAF 36 Sqn/86 Wing, Amberley, Queensland
	A41-213	Boeing C-17A Globemaster III (14-0002)	RAAF 36 Sqn/86 Wing, Amberley, Queensland
	A47-001	Boeing P-8A Poseidon (N940DS)	RAAF 11 Sqn/92 Wing, Edinburgh, South Australia
	A47-002	Boeing P-8A Poseidon (N956DS)	RAAF 11 Sqn/92 Wing, Edinburgh, South Australia
	A47-003	Boeing P-8A Poseidon (N959DS)	RAAF 11 Sqn/92 Wing, Edinburgh, South Australia
	A47-004	Boeing P-8A Poseidon (N974DS)	RAAF 11 Sqn/92 Wing, Edinburgh, South Australia
	A47-005	Boeing P-8A Poseidon (N832DS)	RAAF 11 Sqn/92 Wing, Edinburgh, South Australia
	A47-006	Boeing P-8A Poseidon (N849DS)	RAAF 11 Sqn/92 Wing, Edinburgh, South Australia
	A47-007	Boeing P-8A Poseidon (N862DS)	RAAF 11 Sqn/92 Wing, Edinburgh, South Australia
	A47-008	Boeing P-8A Poseidon (N872DS)	RAAF 11 Sqn/92 Wing, Edinburgh, South Australia
	A47-009	Boeing P-8A Poseidon (N391DS)	RAAF 11 Sqn/92 Wing, Edinburgh, South Australia
	A47-010	Boeing P-8A Poseidon (N397DS)	RAAF 11 Sqn/92 Wing, Edinburgh, South Australia
	A47-011	Boeing P-8A Poseidon (N398DS)	RAAF 11 Sqn/92 Wing, Edinburgh, South Australia
	A47-012	Boeing P-8A Poseidon (N468DS)	RAAF 11 Sqn/92 Wing, Edinburgh, South Australia
	A47-013	Boeing P-8A Poseidon	RAAF (on order)
	A47-014	Boeing P-8A Poseidon	RAAF (on order)
	A47-015	Boeing P-8A Poseidon	RAAF (on order)
	A56-001	Dassault Falcon 7X (F-WWHE)	RAAF 34 Sqn/84 Wing, Canberra, ACT
	A56-002	Dassault Falcon 7X (F-WWHF)	RAAF 34 Sqn/84 Wing, Canberra, ACT
	A56-003	Dassault Falcon 7X (F-WWHK)	RAAF 34 Sqn/84 Wing, Canberra, ACT
	A97-440	Lockheed C-130J-30 Hercules II	RAAF 37 Sqn/86 Wing, Richmond, NSW
	A97-441	Lockheed C-130J-30 Hercules II	RAAF 37 Sqn/86 Wing, Richmond, NSW
	A97-442	Lockheed C-130J-30 Hercules II	RAAF 37 Sqn/86 Wing, Richmond, NSW
	A97-447	Lockheed C-130J-30 Hercules II	RAAF 37 Sqn/86 Wing, Richmond, NSW
	A97-448	Lockheed C-130J-30 Hercules II	RAAF 37 Sqn/86 Wing, Richmond, NSW
	A97-449	Lockheed C-130J-30 Hercules II	RAAF 37 Sqn/86 Wing, Richmond, NSW
	A97-450	Lockheed C-130J-30 Hercules II	RAAF 37 Sqn/86 Wing, Richmond, NSW
	A97-464	Lockheed C-130J-30 Hercules II	RAAF 37 Sqn/86 Wing, Richmond, NSW
	A97-465	Lockheed C-130J-30 Hercules II	RAAF 37 Sqn/86 Wing, Richmond, NSW
	A97-466	Lockheed C-130J-30 Hercules II	RAAF 37 Sqn/86 Wing, Richmond, NSW
	A97-467	Lockheed C-130J-30 Hercules II	RAAF 37 Sqn/86 Wing, Richmond, NSW
	A97-468	Lockheed C-130J-30 Hercules II	RAAF 37 Sqn/86 Wing, Richmond, NSW
	AUSTRIA		
	Öesterreichische Luftstreitkräfte (OL)		
	3C-OA	Bell OH-58B Kiowa	OL Mehrzweckhubschrauberstaffel, Tulln
	3C-OB	Bell OH-58B Kiowa	OL Mehrzweckhubschrauberstaffel, Tulln

Serial	Type (code/other identity)	Owner/operator, location or fate	Notes
3C-OC	Bell OH-58B Kiowa	OL Mehrzweckhubschrauberstaffel, Tulln	
3C-OD	Bell OH-58B Kiowa	OL Mehrzweckhubschrauberstaffel, Tulln	
3C-OE	Bell OH-58B Kiowa	OL Mehrzweckhubschrauberstaffel, Tulln	
3C-OH	Bell OH-58B Kiowa $	OL Mehrzweckhubschrauberstaffel, Tulln	
3C-OI	Bell OH-58B Kiowa	OL Mehrzweckhubschrauberstaffel, Tulln	
3C-OJ	Bell OH-58B Kiowa	OL Mehrzweckhubschrauberstaffel, Tulln	
3C-OK	Bell OH-58B Kiowa $	OL Mehrzweckhubschrauberstaffel, Tulln	
3C-OL	Bell OH-58B Kiowa	OL Mehrzweckhubschrauberstaffel, Tulln	
3G-EB	Pilatus PC-6B/B2-H2 Turbo Porter	OL leichte Lufttransportstaffel, Tulln	
3G-ED	Pilatus PC-6B/B2-H2 Turbo Porter	OL leichte Lufttransportstaffel, Tulln	
3G-EE	Pilatus PC-6B/B2-H2 Turbo Porter	OL leichte Lufttransportstaffel, Tulln	
3G-EF	Pilatus PC-6B/B2-H2 Turbo Porter	OL leichte Lufttransportstaffel, Tulln	
3G-EG	Pilatus PC-6B/B2-H2 Turbo Porter	OL leichte Lufttransportstaffel, Tulln	
3G-EH	Pilatus PC-6B/B2-H2 Turbo Porter	OL leichte Lufttransportstaffel, Tulln	
3G-EL	Pilatus PC-6B/B2-H2 Turbo Porter	OL leichte Lufttransportstaffel, Tulln	
3G-EN	Pilatus PC-6B/B2-H4 Turbo Porter $	OL leichte Lufttransportstaffel, Tulln	
3H-FA	Pilatus PC-7 Turbo Trainer	OL Lehrabteilung Fläche, Zeltweg	
3H-FB	Pilatus PC-7 Turbo Trainer	OL Lehrabteilung Fläche, Zeltweg	
3H-FC	Pilatus PC-7 Turbo Trainer $	OL Lehrabteilung Fläche, Zeltweg	
3H-FD	Pilatus PC-7 Turbo Trainer	OL Lehrabteilung Fläche, Zeltweg	
3H-FE	Pilatus PC-7 Turbo Trainer	OL Lehrabteilung Fläche, Zeltweg	
3H-FF	Pilatus PC-7 Turbo Trainer	OL Lehrabteilung Fläche, Zeltweg	
3H-FG	Pilatus PC-7 Turbo Trainer $	OL Lehrabteilung Fläche, Zeltweg	
3H-FH	Pilatus PC-7 Turbo Trainer	OL Lehrabteilung Fläche, Zeltweg	
3H-FJ	Pilatus PC-7 Turbo Trainer	OL Lehrabteilung Fläche, Zeltweg	
3H-FK	Pilatus PC-7 Turbo Trainer	OL Lehrabteilung Fläche, Zeltweg	
3H-FL	Pilatus PC-7 Turbo Trainer	OL Lehrabteilung Fläche, Zeltweg	
3H-FM	Pilatus PC-7 Turbo Trainer	OL Lehrabteilung Fläche, Zeltweg	
3H-FO	Pilatus PC-7 Turbo Trainer	OL Lehrabteilung Fläche, Zeltweg	
5D-HB	Agusta-Bell AB.212	OL 1 Staffel/2 Staffel ITHSSta, Linz	
5D-HC	Agusta-Bell AB.212	OL 1 Staffel/2 Staffel ITHSSta, Linz	
5D-HD	Agusta-Bell AB.212	OL 1 Staffel/2 Staffel ITHSSta, Linz	
5D-HF	Agusta-Bell AB.212	OL 1 Staffel/2 Staffel ITHSSta, Linz	
5D-HG	Agusta-Bell AB.212	OL 1 Staffel/2 Staffel ITHSSta, Linz	
5D-HH	Agusta-Bell AB.212	OL 1 Staffel/2 Staffel ITHSSta, Linz	
5D-HI	Agusta-Bell AB.212	OL 1 Staffel/2 Staffel ITHSSta, Linz	
5D-HJ	Agusta-Bell AB.212	OL 1 Staffel/2 Staffel ITHSSta, Linz	
5D-HK	Agusta-Bell AB.212	OL 1 Staffel/2 Staffel ITHSSta, Linz	
5D-HL	Agusta-Bell AB.212	OL 1 Staffel/2 Staffel ITHSSta, Linz	
5D-HN	Agusta-Bell AB.212	OL 1 Staffel/2 Staffel ITHSSta, Linz	
5D-HO	Agusta-Bell AB.212	OL 1 Staffel/2 Staffel ITHSSta, Linz	
5D-HP	Agusta-Bell AB.212	OL 1 Staffel/2 Staffel ITHSSta, Linz	
5D-HQ	Agusta-Bell AB.212	OL 1 Staffel/2 Staffel ITHSSta, Linz	
5D-HR	Agusta-Bell AB.212	OL 1 Staffel/2 Staffel ITHSSta, Linz	
5D-HS	Agusta-Bell AB.212	OL 1 Staffel/2 Staffel ITHSSta, Linz	
5D-HT	Agusta-Bell AB.212	OL 1 Staffel/2 Staffel ITHSSta, Linz	
5D-HU	Agusta-Bell AB.212	OL 1 Staffel/2 Staffel ITHSSta, Linz	
5D-HV	Agusta-Bell AB.212	OL 1 Staffel/2 Staffel ITHSSta, Linz	
5D-HW	Agusta-Bell AB.212	OL 1 Staffel/2 Staffel ITHSSta, Linz	
5D-HX	Agusta-Bell AB.212	OL 1 Staffel/2 Staffel ITHSSta, Linz	
5D-HY	Bell 212	OL 1 Staffel/2 Staffel ITHSSta, Linz	
5D-HZ	Agusta-Bell AB.212 $	OL 1 Staffel/2 Staffel ITHSSta, Linz	
6M-BA	Sikorsky S-70A	OL mittlere Transporthubschrauberstaffel, Tulln	
6M-BB	Sikorsky S-70A	OL mittlere Transporthubschrauberstaffel, Tulln	
6M-BC	Sikorsky S-70A	OL mittlere Transporthubschrauberstaffel, Tulln	
6M-BD	Sikorsky S-70A	OL mittlere Transporthubschrauberstaffel, Tulln	
6M-BE	Sikorsky S-70A	OL mittlere Transporthubschrauberstaffel, Tulln	
6M-BF	Sikorsky S-70A	OL mittlere Transporthubschrauberstaffel, Tulln	
6M-BG	Sikorsky S-70A	OL mittlere Transporthubschrauberstaffel, Tulln	
6M-BH	Sikorsky S-70A	OL mittlere Transporthubschrauberstaffel, Tulln	
6M-BI	Sikorsky S-70A	OL mittlere Transporthubschrauberstaffel, Tulln	
7L-WA	Eurofighter EF.2000	OL 1 Staffel/2 Staffel Überwg, Zeltweg	

Notes	Serial	Type (code/other identity)	Owner/operator, location or fate
	7L-WB	Eurofighter EF.2000 $	OL 1 Staffel/2 Staffel Überwg, Zeltweg
	7L-WC	Eurofighter EF.2000 $	OL 1 Staffel/2 Staffel Überwg, Zeltweg
	7L-WD	Eurofighter EF.2000	OL 1 Staffel/2 Staffel Überwg, Zeltweg
	7L-WE	Eurofighter EF.2000	OL 1 Staffel/2 Staffel Überwg, Zeltweg
	7L-WF	Eurofighter EF.2000	OL 1 Staffel/2 Staffel Überwg, Zeltweg
	7L-WG	Eurofighter EF.2000	OL 1 Staffel/2 Staffel Überwg, Zeltweg
	7L-WH	Eurofighter EF.2000	OL 1 Staffel/2 Staffel Überwg, Zeltweg
	7L-WI	Eurofighter EF.2000	OL 1 Staffel/2 Staffel Überwg, Zeltweg
	7L-WJ	Eurofighter EF.2000	OL 1 Staffel/2 Staffel Überwg, Zeltweg
	7L-WK	Eurofighter EF.2000	OL 1 Staffel/2 Staffel Überwg, Zeltweg
	7L-WL	Eurofighter EF.2000	OL 1 Staffel/2 Staffel Überwg, Zeltweg
	7L-WM	Eurofighter EF.2000	OL 1 Staffel/2 Staffel Überwg, Zeltweg
	7L-WN	Eurofighter EF.2000	OL 1 Staffel/2 Staffel Überwg, Zeltweg
	7L-WO	Eurofighter EF.2000	OL 1 Staffel/2 Staffel Überwg, Zeltweg
	8T-CA	Lockheed C-130K Hercules (XV181)	OL Lufttransportstaffel, Linz
	8T-CB	Lockheed C-130K Hercules (XV291)	OL Lufttransportstaffel, Linz
	8T-CC	Lockheed C-130K Hercules (XV292)	OL Lufttransportstaffel, Linz
	BA-31	SAAB 105ÖE [blue A]	OL Düsentrainerstaffel Überwg, Linz
	BE-35	SAAB 105ÖE [blue E]	OL Düsentrainerstaffel Überwg, Linz
	BF-36	SAAB 105ÖE [blue F]	OL Düsentrainerstaffel Überwg, Linz
	BG-37	SAAB 105ÖE [blue G]	OL Düsentrainerstaffel Überwg, Linz
	BI-39	SAAB 105ÖE [blue I]	OL, stored Linz
	BJ-40	SAAB 105ÖE [blue J]	OL Düsentrainerstaffel Überwg, Linz
	GD-14	SAAB 105ÖE [green D] $	OL Düsentrainerstaffel Überwg, Linz
	GG-17	SAAB 105ÖE [green G]	OL Düsentrainerstaffel Überwg, Linz
	RB-22	SAAB 105ÖE [red B]	OL Düsentrainerstaffel Überwg, Linz
	RC-23	SAAB 105ÖE [red C]	OL Düsentrainerstaffel Überwg, Linz
	RD-24	SAAB 105ÖE [red D]	OL Düsentrainerstaffel Überwg, Linz
	RE-25	SAAB 105ÖE [red E] $	OL Düsentrainerstaffel Überwg, Linz
	RF-26	SAAB 105ÖE [red F] $	OL Düsentrainerstaffel Überwg, Linz
	RG-27	SAAB 105ÖE [red G]	OL Düsentrainerstaffel Überwg, Linz
	RH-28	SAAB 105ÖE [red H]	OL Düsentrainerstaffel Überwg, Linz
	RI-29	SAAB 105ÖE [red I]	OL Düsentrainerstaffel Überwg, Linz
	RJ-30	SAAB 105ÖE [red J]	OL Düsentrainerstaffel Überwg, Linz
	YI-09	SAAB 105ÖE [yellow I]	OL Düsentrainerstaffel Überwg, Linz
	YJ-10	SAAB 105ÖE [yellow J]	OL Düsentrainerstaffel Überwg, Linz

AZERBAIJAN

	4K-AI01	Boeing 767-32LER	Azerbaijan Government, Baku
	4K-AI02	Airbus A.319-115LR	Azerbaijan Government, Baku
	4K-AI88	Gulfstream Aerospace G.650	Azerbaijan Government, Baku

BAHRAIN

	A9C-AWL	BAE RJ.100	Royal Bahraini Air Force
	A9C-BAH	Gulfstream Aerospace G.650	Bahrain Royal Flight
	A9C-BDF	BAE RJ.100	Royal Bahraini Air Force
	A9C-BG	Grumman G.1159 Gulfstream IITT	Bahrain Royal Flight
	A9C-BHR	Gulfstream Aerospace G.450	Bahrain Royal Flight
	A9C-BRF	Grumman G.1159C Gulfstream IV-SP	Bahrain Royal Flight
	A9C-BRN	Gulfstream Aerospace G.550	Bahrain Royal Flight
	A9C-HAK	Boeing 747-4F6	Bahrain Royal Flight
	A9C-HAK	Boeing 747SP-Z5	*Withdrawn from use*
	A9C-HMH	Boeing 767-4FSER	Bahrain Royal Flight
	A9C-HMK	Boeing 747-4P8	Bahrain Royal Flight
	A9C-HWR	BAE RJ.85	Royal Bahraini Air Force
	A9C-ISA	Boeing 737-86J	Bahrain Royal Flight

BELGIUM

Force Aérienne Belge (FAB)/Belgische Luchtmacht: Composante Aérienne Belge/Belgische Luchtcomponent

	AT-01	D-BD Alpha Jet 1B+	*Withdrawn from use at Beauvechain, 2019*
	AT-02	D-BD Alpha Jet 1B+	*Withdrawn from use at Beauvechain, January 2020*
	AT-03	D-BD Alpha Jet 1B+	*Withdrawn from use at Beauvechain, 2019*

Serial	Type (code/other identity)	Owner/operator, location or fate	Notes
AT-05	D-BD Alpha Jet 1B+	*Withdrawn from use at Beauvechain, 2019*	
AT-06	D-BD Alpha Jet 1B+	*Withdrawn from use at Beauvechain, January 2020*	
AT-08	D-BD Alpha Jet 1B+	*Withdrawn from use at Beauvechain, 2019*	
AT-10	D-BD Alpha Jet 1B+	*Withdrawn from use at Beauvechain, 2019*	
AT-11	D-BD Alpha Jet 1B+	*Withdrawn from use at Beauvechain, 2019*	
AT-12	D-BD Alpha Jet 1B+	*Withdrawn from use at Beauvechain, 2019*	
AT-13	D-BD Alpha Jet 1B+	*Withdrawn from use at Beauvechain, January 2020*	
AT-14	D-BD Alpha Jet 1B+	*Withdrawn from use at Beauvechain, 2019*	
AT-15	D-BD Alpha Jet 1B+	*Withdrawn from use at Beauvechain, January 2020*	
AT-17	D-BD Alpha Jet 1B+	*Withdrawn from use at Beauvechain, January 2020*	
AT-18	D-BD Alpha Jet 1B+	*Withdrawn from use at Beauvechain, January 2020*	
AT-19	D-BD Alpha Jet 1B+	*Withdrawn from use at Beauvechain, January 2020*	
AT-20	D-BD Alpha Jet 1B+	*Preserved at Cazaux, 2019*	
AT-22	D-BD Alpha Jet 1B+	*Withdrawn from use at Beauvechain, 2019*	
AT-23	D-BD Alpha Jet 1B+	*Withdrawn from use at Beauvechain, 2019*	
AT-24	D-BD Alpha Jet 1B+ $	*Withdrawn from use at Beauvechain, January 2020*	
AT-25	D-BD Alpha Jet 1B+	*Withdrawn from use at Beauvechain, January 2020*	
AT-26	D-BD Alpha Jet 1B+	*Withdrawn from use at Beauvechain, January 2020*	
AT-27	D-BD Alpha Jet 1B+	*Withdrawn from use at Beauvechain, January 2020*	
AT-28	D-BD Alpha Jet 1B+	*Withdrawn from use at Beauvechain, 2019*	
AT-29	D-BD Alpha Jet 1B+ $	*Withdrawn from use at Beauvechain, 2019*	
AT-30	D-BD Alpha Jet 1B+	*Withdrawn from use at Beauvechain, 2019*	
AT-32	D-BD Alpha Jet 1B+ $	*Preserved at Beauvechain, 2019*	
AT-33	D-BD Alpha Jet 1B+ $	*Withdrawn from use at Beauvechain, 2019*	
CD-01	Dassault Falcon 900B	*Withdrawn from use, 2019*	
CE-01	Embraer ERJ.135LR	FAB 21 Smaldeel (15 Wg), Brussels/Melsbroek	
CE-02	Embraer ERJ.135LR $	FAB 21 Smaldeel (15 Wg), Brussels/Melsbroek	
CE-03	Embraer ERJ.145LR $	FAB 21 Smaldeel (15 Wg), Brussels/Melsbroek	
CH-01	Lockheed C-130H Hercules	FAB 20 Smaldeel (15 Wg), Brussels/Melsbroek	
CH-03	Lockheed C-130H Hercules	*Withdrawn from use, October 2019*	
CH-04	Lockheed C-130H Hercules	FAB 20 Smaldeel (15 Wg), Brussels/Melsbroek	
CH-05	Lockheed C-130H Hercules	FAB 20 Smaldeel (15 Wg), Brussels/Melsbroek	
CH-07	Lockheed C-130H Hercules $	FAB 20 Smaldeel (15 Wg), Brussels/Melsbroek	
CH-09	Lockheed C-130H Hercules	FAB 20 Smaldeel (15 Wg), Brussels/Melsbroek	
CH-11	Lockheed C-130H Hercules $	FAB 20 Smaldeel (15 Wg), Brussels/Melsbroek	
CH-12	Lockheed C-130H Hercules	FAB 20 Smaldeel (15 Wg), Brussels/Melsbroek	
CH-13	Lockheed C-130H Hercules $	FAB 20 Smaldeel (15 Wg), Brussels/Melsbroek	
CT-01	Airbus Military A.400M	NATO (on order) [to be operated by FAB 20 Smaldeel (15 Wg), Brussels/Melsbroek for Luxembourg Armed Forces]	
CT-02	Airbus Military A.400M	FAB/NATO (on order)	
CT-03	Airbus Military A.400M	FAB/NATO (on order)	
CT-04	Airbus Military A.400M	FAB/NATO (on order)	
CT-05	Airbus Military A.400M	FAB/NATO (on order)	
CT-06	Airbus Military A.400M	FAB/NATO (on order)	
CT-07	Airbus Military A.400M	FAB/NATO (on order)	
CT-08	Airbus Military A.400M	FAB/NATO (on order)	
FA-56	SABCA (GD) F-16A MLU Fighting Falcon	FAB 31 Sm/349 Sm/OCU (10 Wg), Kleine-Brogel	
FA-57	SABCA (GD) F-16A MLU Fighting Falcon [MN-L] $	FAB 1 Sm/350 Sm (2 Wg), Florennes	
FA-67	SABCA (GD) F-16A MLU Fighting Falcon	FAB 1 Sm/350 Sm (2 Wg), Florennes	
FA-68	SABCA (GD) F-16A MLU Fighting Falcon $	FAB 1 Sm/350 Sm (2 Wg), Florennes	
FA-69	SABCA (GD) F-16A MLU Fighting Falcon	FAB 1 Sm/350 Sm (2 Wg), Florennes	
FA-70	SABCA (GD) F-16A MLU Fighting Falcon	FAB 31 Sm/349 Sm/OCU (10 Wg), Kleine-Brogel	
FA-71	SABCA (GD) F-16A MLU Fighting Falcon	FAB 1 Sm/350 Sm (2 Wg), Florennes	
FA-72	SABCA (GD) F-16A MLU Fighting Falcon	FAB 1 Sm/350 Sm (2 Wg), Florennes	
FA-77	SABCA (GD) F-16A MLU Fighting Falcon $	FAB 31 Sm/349 Sm/OCU (10 Wg), Kleine-Brogel	
FA-81	SABCA (GD) F-16A MLU Fighting Falcon	FAB 31 Sm/349 Sm/OCU (10 Wg), Kleine-Brogel	
FA-82	SABCA (GD) F-16A MLU Fighting Falcon	FAB 31 Sm/349 Sm/OCU (10 Wg), Kleine-Brogel	
FA-83	SABCA (GD) F-16A MLU Fighting Falcon	FAB 1 Sm/350 Sm (2 Wg), Florennes	
FA-84	SABCA (GD) F-16A MLU Fighting Falcon $	FAB 1 Sm/350 Sm (2 Wg), Florennes	
FA-86	SABCA (GD) F-16A MLU Fighting Falcon	FAB 31 Sm/349 Sm/OCU (10 Wg), Kleine-Brogel	
FA-87	SABCA (GD) F-16A MLU Fighting Falcon	FAB 31 Sm/349 Sm/OCU (10 Wg), Kleine-Brogel	

Notes	Serial	Type (code/other identity)	Owner/operator, location or fate
	FA-89	SABCA (GD) F-16A MLU Fighting Falcon	FAB 1 Sm/350 Sm (2 Wg), Florennes
	FA-91	SABCA (GD) F-16A MLU Fighting Falcon	FAB 1 Sm/350 Sm (2 Wg), Florennes
	FA-92	SABCA (GD) F-16A MLU Fighting Falcon	FAB 1 Sm/350 Sm (2 Wg), Florennes
	FA-94	SABCA (GD) F-16A MLU Fighting Falcon	FAB 31 Sm/349 Sm/OCU (10 Wg), Kleine-Brogel
	FA-95	SABCA (GD) F-16A MLU Fighting Falcon	FAB 31 Sm/349 Sm/OCU (10 Wg), Kleine-Brogel
	FA-97	SABCA (GD) F-16A MLU Fighting Falcon	FAB 31 Sm/349 Sm/OCU (10 Wg), Kleine-Brogel
	FA-98	SABCA (GD) F-16A MLU Fighting Falcon	FAB 1 Sm/350 Sm (2 Wg), Florennes
	FA-101	SABCA (GD) F-16A MLU Fighting Falcon $	FAB 31 Sm/349 Sm/OCU (10 Wg), Kleine-Brogel
	FA-102	SABCA (GD) F-16A MLU Fighting Falcon	FAB 31 Sm/349 Sm/OCU (10 Wg), Kleine-Brogel
	FA-103	SABCA (GD) F-16A MLU Fighting Falcon	FAB 31 Sm/349 Sm/OCU (10 Wg), Kleine-Brogel
	FA-104	SABCA (GD) F-16A MLU Fighting Falcon	FAB 31 Sm/349 Sm/OCU (10 Wg), Kleine-Brogel
	FA-106	SABCA (GD) F-16A MLU Fighting Falcon	FAB 31 Sm/349 Sm/OCU (10 Wg), Kleine-Brogel
	FA-107	SABCA (GD) F-16A MLU Fighting Falcon	FAB 31 Sm/349 Sm/OCU (10 Wg), Kleine-Brogel
	FA-109	SABCA (GD) F-16A MLU Fighting Falcon	FAB 1 Sm/350 Sm (2 Wg), Florennes
	FA-110	SABCA (GD) F-16A MLU Fighting Falcon	FAB 31 Sm/349 Sm/OCU (10 Wg), Kleine-Brogel
	FA-114	SABCA (GD) F-16A MLU Fighting Falcon	FAB 31 Sm/349 Sm/OCU (10 Wg), Kleine-Brogel
	FA-116	SABCA (GD) F-16A MLU Fighting Falcon $	FAB 31 Sm/349 Sm/OCU (10 Wg), Kleine-Brogel
	FA-117	SABCA (GD) F-16A MLU Fighting Falcon	FAB 1 Sm/350 Sm (2 Wg), Florennes
	FA-118	SABCA (GD) F-16A MLU Fighting Falcon	FAB 31 Sm/349 Sm/OCU (10 Wg), Kleine-Brogel
	FA-119	SABCA (GD) F-16A MLU Fighting Falcon	FAB 31 Sm/349 Sm/OCU (10 Wg), Kleine-Brogel
	FA-121	SABCA (GD) F-16A MLU Fighting Falcon	FAB 1 Sm/350 Sm (2 Wg), Florennes
	FA-123	SABCA (GD) F-16A MLU Fighting Falcon	FAB 31 Sm/349 Sm/OCU (10 Wg), Kleine-Brogel
	FA-124	SABCA (GD) F-16A MLU Fighting Falcon [GE-S] $	FAB 31 Sm/349 Sm/OCU (10 Wg), Kleine-Brogel
	FA-126	SABCA (GD) F-16A MLU Fighting Falcon	FAB 1 Sm/350 Sm (2 Wg), Florennes
	FA-127	SABCA (GD) F-16A MLU Fighting Falcon	FAB 31 Sm/349 Sm/OCU (10 Wg), Kleine-Brogel
	FA-129	SABCA (GD) F-16A MLU Fighting Falcon	FAB 1 Sm/350 Sm (2 Wg), Florennes
	FA-130	SABCA (GD) F-16A MLU Fighting Falcon	FAB 1 Sm/350 Sm (2 Wg), Florennes
	FA-131	SABCA (GD) F-16A MLU Fighting Falcon	FAB 31 Sm/349 Sm/OCU (10 Wg), Kleine-Brogel
	FA-132	SABCA (GD) F-16A MLU Fighting Falcon $	FAB 1 Sm/350 Sm (2 Wg), Florennes
	FA-133	SABCA (GD) F-16A MLU Fighting Falcon	FAB 1 Sm/350 Sm (2 Wg), Florennes
	FA-134	SABCA (GD) F-16A MLU Fighting Falcon	FAB 31 Sm/349 Sm/OCU (10 Wg), Kleine-Brogel
	FA-135	SABCA (GD) F-16A MLU Fighting Falcon $	FAB 1 Sm/350 Sm (2 Wg), Florennes
	FA-136	SABCA (GD) F-16A MLU Fighting Falcon	FAB 31 Sm/349 Sm/OCU (10 Wg), Kleine-Brogel
	FB-12	SABCA (GD) F-16B MLU Fighting Falcon	FAB 1 Sm/350 Sm (2 Wg), Florennes
	FB-14	SABCA (GD) F-16B MLU Fighting Falcon	FAB 31 Sm/349 Sm/OCU (10 Wg), Kleine-Brogel
	FB-15	SABCA (GD) F-16B MLU Fighting Falcon	FAB 31 Sm/349 Sm/OCU (10 Wg), Kleine-Brogel
	FB-17	SABCA (GD) F-16B MLU Fighting Falcon	FAB 31 Sm/349 Sm/OCU (10 Wg), Kleine-Brogel
	FB-18	SABCA (GD) F-16B MLU Fighting Falcon	*Crashed 19 September 2019, Pluvigner, France*
	FB-20	SABCA (GD) F-16B MLU Fighting Falcon	FAB 31 Sm/349 Sm/OCU (10 Wg), Kleine-Brogel
	FB-21	SABCA (GD) F-16B MLU Fighting Falcon	FAB 1 Sm/350 Sm (2 Wg), Florennes
	FB-22	SABCA (GD) F-16B MLU Fighting Falcon	FAB 1 Sm/350 Sm (2 Wg), Florennes
	FB-23	SABCA (GD) F-16B MLU Fighting Falcon	FAB 31 Sm/349 Sm/OCU (10 Wg), Kleine-Brogel
	FB-24	SABCA (GD) F-16B MLU Fighting Falcon $	FAB 31 Sm/349 Sm/OCU (10 Wg), Kleine-Brogel
	G-01	Cessna 182Q Skylane	FAB Federal Police, Brussels/Melsbroek
	G-04	Cessna 182R Skylane	FAB Federal Police, Brussels/Melsbroek
	G-10	MDH MD.902 Explorer	FAB Federal Police, Brussels/Melsbroek
	G-11	MDH MD.902 Explorer	FAB Federal Police, Brussels/Melsbroek
	G-12	MDH MD.902 Explorer	FAB Federal Police, Brussels/Melsbroek
	G-14	MDH MD.520N	FAB Federal Police, Brussels/Melsbroek
	G-15	MDH MD.520N	FAB Federal Police, Brussels/Melsbroek
	G-16	MDH MD.902 Explorer	FAB Federal Police, Brussels/Melsbroek
	G-17	MDH MD.902 Explorer	FAB Federal Police (on order)
	H-20	Agusta A109HA	FAB, stored Beauvechain
	H-21	Agusta A109HA	FAB 17 Smaldeel MRH (1 Wg), Beauvechain
	H-22	Agusta A109HA	FAB 17 Smaldeel MRH (1 Wg), Beauvechain
	H-24	Agusta A109HA $	FAB 17 Smaldeel MRH (1 Wg), Beauvechain
	H-25	Agusta A109HA	FAB, stored Beauvechain
	H-26	Agusta A109HA	FAB 17 Smaldeel MRH (1 Wg), Beauvechain
	H-27	Agusta A109HA	FAB 17 Smaldeel MRH (1 Wg), Beauvechain
	H-28	Agusta A109HA	FAB 17 Smaldeel MRH (1 Wg), Beauvechain
	H-29	Agusta A109HA $	FAB 17 Smaldeel MRH (1 Wg), Beauvechain
	H-30	Agusta A109HA	FAB, stored Beauvechain

Serial	Type (code/other identity)	Owner/operator, location or fate	Notes
H-31	Agusta A109HA	FAB 17 Smaldeel MRH (1 Wg), Beauvechain	
H-33	Agusta A109HA	FAB, stored Beauvechain	
H-35	Agusta A109HA	FAB 17 Smaldeel MRH (1 Wg), Beauvechain	
H-36	Agusta A109HA	FAB 17 Smaldeel MRH (1 Wg), Beauvechain	
H-38	Agusta A109HA	FAB 17 Smaldeel MRH (1 Wg), Beauvechain	
H-40	Agusta A109HA	FAB, stored Beauvechain	
H-41	Agusta A109HA	FAB, stored Beauvechain	
H-42	Agusta A109HA	FAB SLV (1 Wg), Beauvechain	
H-44	Agusta A109HA	FAB 17 Smaldeel MRH (1 Wg), Beauvechain	
H-45	Agusta A109HA	FAB 17 Smaldeel MRH (1 Wg), Beauvechain	
H-46	Agusta A109HA	FAB 17 Smaldeel MRH (1 Wg), Beauvechain	
LB-01	Piper L-21B Super Cub	FAB Air Cadets, Florennes/Goetsenhoeven/Zoersel	
LB-02	Piper L-21B Super Cub	FAB Air Cadets, Florennes/Goetsenhoeven/Zoersel	
LB-03	Piper L-21B Super Cub	FAB Air Cadets, Florennes/Goetsenhoeven/Zoersel	
LB-05	Piper L-21B Super Cub	FAB Air Cadets, Florennes/Goetsenhoeven/Zoersel	
M-1	Sud SA.316B Alouette III	FAB 40 Smaldeel, Koksijde	
M-2	Sud SA.316B Alouette III	FAB 40 Smaldeel, Koksijde	
M-3	Sud SA.316B Alouette III	FAB 40 Smaldeel, Koksijde	
RN-01	NH Industries NH.90-NFH	FAB 40 Smaldeel (1 Wg), Koksijde	
RN-02	NH Industries NH.90-NFH	FAB 40 Smaldeel (1 Wg), Koksijde	
RN-03	NH Industries NH.90-NFH	FAB 40 Smaldeel (1 Wg), Koksijde	
RN-04	NH Industries NH.90-NFH	FAB 40 Smaldeel (1 Wg), Koksijde	
RN-05	NH Industries NH.90-TTH	FAB 18 Smaldeel MRH (1 Wg), Beauvechain	
RN-06	NH Industries NH.90-TTH	FAB 18 Smaldeel MRH (1 Wg), Beauvechain	
RN-07	NH Industries NH.90-TTH	FAB 18 Smaldeel MRH (1 Wg), Beauvechain	
RN-08	NH Industries NH.90-TTH	FAB 18 Smaldeel MRH (1 Wg), Beauvechain	
RS-05	Westland Sea King Mk.48 $	*Withdrawn from use, 20 March 2019*	
ST-02	SIAI Marchetti SF260M+	FAB *Red Devils*, CC Air, Beauvechain	
ST-03	SIAI Marchetti SF260M+	FAB 5 Smaldeel/9 Smaldeel, CC Air, Beauvechain	
ST-04	SIAI Marchetti SF260M+	FAB 5 Smaldeel/9 Smaldeel, CC Air, Beauvechain	
ST-06	SIAI Marchetti SF260M+	FAB *Red Devils*, CC Air, Beauvechain	
ST-12	SIAI Marchetti SF260M+	FAB 5 Smaldeel/9 Smaldeel, CC Air, Beauvechain	
ST-15	SIAI Marchetti SF260M+	FAB *Red Devils*, CC Air, Beauvechain	
ST-16	SIAI Marchetti SF260M+	FAB *Red Devils*, CC Air, Beauvechain	
ST-17	SIAI Marchetti SF260M+	FAB 5 Smaldeel/9 Smaldeel, CC Air, Beauvechain	
ST-18	SIAI Marchetti SF260M+	FAB 5 Smaldeel/9 Smaldeel, CC Air, Beauvechain	
ST-19	SIAI Marchetti SF260M+	FAB 5 Smaldeel/9 Smaldeel, CC Air, Beauvechain	
ST-20	SIAI Marchetti SF260M+	FAB 5 Smaldeel/9 Smaldeel, CC Air, Beauvechain	
ST-22	SIAI Marchetti SF260M+ $	FAB *Red Devils*, CC Air, Beauvechain	
ST-23	SIAI Marchetti SF260M+	FAB *Red Devils*, CC Air, Beauvechain	
ST-24	SIAI Marchetti SF260M+	FAB 5 Smaldeel/9 Smaldeel, CC Air, Beauvechain	
ST-25	SIAI Marchetti SF260M+	FAB 5 Smaldeel/9 Smaldeel, CC Air, Beauvechain	
ST-26	SIAI Marchetti SF260M+	FAB 5 Smaldeel/9 Smaldeel, CC Air, Beauvechain	
ST-27	SIAI Marchetti SF260M+	FAB *Red Devils*, CC Air, Beauvechain	
ST-30	SIAI Marchetti SF260M+ $	FAB 5 Smaldeel/9 Smaldeel, CC Air, Beauvechain	
ST-31	SIAI Marchetti SF260M+	FAB *Red Devils*, CC Air, Beauvechain	
ST-32	SIAI Marchetti SF260M+	FAB 5 Smaldeel/9 Smaldeel, CC Air, Beauvechain	
ST-34	SIAI Marchetti SF260M+	FAB *Red Devils*, CC Air, Beauvechain	
ST-35	SIAI Marchetti SF260M+	FAB *Red Devils*, CC Air, Beauvechain	
ST-36	SIAI Marchetti SF260M+	FAB *Red Devils*, CC Air, Beauvechain	
ST-40	SIAI Marchetti SF260D	FAB 5 Smaldeel/9 Smaldeel, CC Air, Beauvechain	
ST-41	SIAI Marchetti SF260D	FAB 5 Smaldeel/9 Smaldeel, CC Air, Beauvechain	
ST-42	SIAI Marchetti SF260D	FAB 5 Smaldeel/9 Smaldeel, CC Air, Beauvechain	
ST-43	SIAI Marchetti SF260D	FAB 5 Smaldeel/9 Smaldeel, CC Air, Beauvechain	
ST-44	SIAI Marchetti SF260D	FAB 5 Smaldeel/9 Smaldeel, CC Air, Beauvechain	
ST-45	SIAI Marchetti SF260D	FAB 5 Smaldeel/9 Smaldeel, CC Air, Beauvechain	
ST-46	SIAI Marchetti SF260D	FAB 5 Smaldeel/9 Smaldeel, CC Air, Beauvechain	
ST-47	SIAI Marchetti SF260D	FAB 5 Smaldeel/9 Smaldeel, CC Air, Beauvechain	
ST-48	SIAI Marchetti SF260D	FAB 5 Smaldeel/9 Smaldeel, CC Air, Beauvechain	
..-01	Dassault Falcon 7X	On order	
..-02	Dassault Falcon 7X	On order	
CS-TRJ	Airbus A.321-231	FAB 21 Smaldeel (15 Wg), Brussels/Melsbroek	

133

Notes	Serial	Type (code/other identity)	Owner/operator, location or fate
	BOTSWANA		
	Botswana Defence Force (BDF)		
	OK1	Bombardier Global Express	BDF VIP Sqn, Sir Seretse Kharma IAP, Gaborone
	OM-1	Lockheed C-130B Hercules	BDF Z10 Sqn, Thebephatshwa
	OM-2	Lockheed C-130B Hercules	BDF Z10 Sqn, Thebephatshwa
	OM-3	Lockheed C-130B Hercules	BDF Z10 Sqn, Thebephatshwa
	BRAZIL		
	Força Aérea Brasileira (FAB)		
	2101	Airbus A.319-133CJ (VC-1A)	FAB 1° GT Especial, 1° Esq, Brasilia
	2461	Lockheed KC-130M Hercules	FAB 1° GT, 1° Esq, Galeão
	2462	Lockheed KC-130H Hercules	FAB 1° GT, 1° Esq, Galeão
	2466	Lockheed C-130M Hercules	FAB 1° GT, 1° Esq, Galeão
	2467	Lockheed C-130M Hercules	FAB 1° GT, 1° Esq, Galeão
	2471	Lockheed C-130H Hercules	FAB 1° GT, 1° Esq, Galeão
	2472	Lockheed C-130H Hercules	FAB 1° GT, 1° Esq, Galeão
	2473	Lockheed C-130M Hercules	FAB 1° GT, 1° Esq, Galeão
	2474	Lockheed C-130M Hercules	FAB 1° GT, 1° Esq, Galeão
	2475	Lockheed C-130H Hercules	FAB 1° GT, 1° Esq, Galeão
	2476	Lockheed C-130M Hercules	FAB 1° GTT, 1° Esq, Afonsos
	2477	Lockheed C-130H Hercules	FAB 1° GT, 1° Esq, Galeão
	2479	Lockheed C-130M Hercules	FAB 1° GT, 1° Esq, Galeão
	2550	Embraer VC-99A Legacy	FAB 2° GT Especial, 1° Esq, Brasilia
	2560	Embraer VC-99C Legacy	FAB 2° GT Especial, 1° Esq, Brasilia
	2561	Embraer VC-99C Legacy	FAB 2° GT Especial, 1° Esq, Brasilia
	2580	Embraer VC-99B Legacy	FAB 2° GT Especial, 1° Esq, Brasilia
	2581	Embraer VC-99B Legacy	FAB 2° GT Especial, 1° Esq, Brasilia
	2582	Embraer VC-99B Legacy	FAB 2° GT Especial, 1° Esq, Brasilia
	2583	Embraer VC-99B Legacy	FAB 2° GT Especial, 1° Esq, Brasilia
	2584	Embraer VC-99B Legacy	FAB 2° GT Especial, 1° Esq, Brasilia
	2585	Embraer VC-99B Legacy	FAB 2° GT Especial, 1° Esq, Brasilia
	2586	Embraer VC-99B Legacy	FAB 2° GT Especial, 1° Esq, Brasilia
	2590	Embraer EMB.190-190IGW (VC-2)	FAB 1° GT Especial, 1° Esq, Brasilia
	2591	Embraer EMB.190-190IGW (VC-2)	FAB 1° GT Especial, 1° Esq, Brasilia
	2900	Boeing 767-31AER (C-767)	*Sold as N328MP, July 2019*
	6700	Embraer E-99	FAB 2° Esq, 6° GAv, Anapolis
	6701	Embraer R-99A	FAB 2° Esq, 6° GAv, Anapolis
	6702	Embraer R-99A	FAB 2° Esq, 6° GAv, Anapolis
	6703	Embraer E-99	FAB 2° Esq, 6° GAv, Anapolis
	6704	Embraer R-99A	FAB 2° Esq, 6° GAv, Anapolis
	6750	Embraer R-99B	FAB 2° Esq, 6° GAv, Anapolis
	6751	Embraer R-99B	FAB 2° Esq, 6° GAv, Anapolis
	6752	Embraer R-99B	FAB 2° Esq, 6° GAv, Anapolis
	BRUNEI		
	V8-001	Airbus A.340-212 (V8-BKH)	*Withdrawn from use, 2019*
	V8-BKH	Boeing 747-8LQ	Brunei Government, Bandar Seri Bergawan
	V8-MHB	Boeing 767-27GER	Brunei Government, Bandar Seri Bergawan
	V8-OAS	Boeing 787-8 (N508BJ)	Brunei Government, Bandar Seri Bergawan
	BULGARIA		
	Bulgarsky Voenno-Vazdushni Sily (BVVS)		
	020	Pilatus PC.XII/45	BVVS 16 TAP, Sofia/Dobroslavtzi
	055	Antonov An-30	*Withdrawn from use*
	071	Aeritalia C-27J Spartan	BVVS 16 TAB, Sofia/Vrazhdebna
	072	Aeritalia C-27J Spartan	BVVS 16 TAB, Sofia/Vrazhdebna
	073	Aeritalia C-27J Spartan	BVVS 16 TAB, Sofia/Vrazhdebna
	Bulgarian Government		
	LZ-AOB	Airbus A.319-112	Bulgarian Government/BH Air, Sofia
	LZ-OOI	Dassault Falcon 2000	Bulgarian Government, Sofia

Serial	Type (code/other identity)	Owner/operator, location or fate	Notes
BURKINA FASO			
XT-BFA	Boeing 727-282	Government of Burkina Faso, Ouagadougou	
CAMEROON			
TJ-AAW	Grumman G.1159A Gulfstream III	Government of Cameroon, Yaounde	
CANADA			
Royal Canadian Air Force (RCAF)			
15001	Airbus CC-150 Polaris (A.310-304) [991]	RCAF 437 Sqn (8 Wing), Trenton	
15002	Airbus CC-150 Polaris (A.310-304F) [992]	RCAF 437 Sqn (8 Wing), Trenton	
15003	Airbus CC-150 Polaris (A.310-304F) [993] $	RCAF 437 Sqn (8 Wing), Trenton	
15004	Airbus CC-150 Polaris (A.310-304F) [994]	RCAF 437 Sqn (8 Wing), Trenton	
15005	Airbus CC-150 Polaris (A.310-304F) [995]	RCAF 437 Sqn (8 Wing), Trenton	
130332	Lockheed CC-130H(SAR) Hercules	RCAF 413 Sqn (14 Wing), Greenwood	
130334	Lockheed CC-130H(SAR) Hercules	RCAF 413 Sqn (14 Wing), Greenwood	
130335	Lockheed CC-130H Hercules	RCAF 426 Sqn (8 Wing), Trenton	
130336	Lockheed CC-130H Hercules	RCAF 426 Sqn (8 Wing), Trenton	
130337	Lockheed CC-130H Hercules	RCAF 426 Sqn (8 Wing), Trenton	
130338	Lockheed CC-130H(T) Hercules	RCAF 435 Sqn (17 Wing), Winnipeg	
130339	Lockheed CC-130H(T) Hercules	RCAF 435 Sqn (17 Wing), Winnipeg	
130340	Lockheed CC-130H(T) Hercules	RCAF 435 Sqn (17 Wing), Winnipeg	
130341	Lockheed CC-130H(T) Hercules	RCAF 435 Sqn (17 Wing), Winnipeg	
130343	Lockheed CC-130H-30 Hercules	RCAF 426 Sqn (8 Wing), Trenton	
130344	Lockheed CC-130H-30 Hercules	RCAF 426 Sqn (8 Wing), Trenton	
130601	Lockheed CC-130J Hercules II	RCAF 436 Sqn (8 Wing), Trenton	
130602	Lockheed CC-130J Hercules II	RCAF 436 Sqn (8 Wing), Trenton	
130603	Lockheed CC-130J Hercules II	RCAF 436 Sqn (8 Wing), Trenton	
130604	Lockheed CC-130J Hercules II	RCAF 436 Sqn (8 Wing), Trenton	
130605	Lockheed CC-130J Hercules II	RCAF 436 Sqn (8 Wing), Trenton	
130606	Lockheed CC-130J Hercules II	RCAF 436 Sqn (8 Wing), Trenton	
130607	Lockheed CC-130J Hercules II	RCAF 436 Sqn (8 Wing), Trenton	
130608	Lockheed CC-130J Hercules II	RCAF 436 Sqn (8 Wing), Trenton	
130609	Lockheed CC-130J Hercules II	RCAF 436 Sqn (8 Wing), Trenton	
130610	Lockheed CC-130J Hercules II	RCAF 436 Sqn (8 Wing), Trenton	
130611	Lockheed CC-130J Hercules II	RCAF 436 Sqn (8 Wing), Trenton	
130612	Lockheed CC-130J Hercules II	RCAF 436 Sqn (8 Wing), Trenton	
130613	Lockheed CC-130J Hercules II	RCAF 436 Sqn (8 Wing), Trenton	
130614	Lockheed CC-130J Hercules II $	RCAF 436 Sqn (8 Wing), Trenton	
130615	Lockheed CC-130J Hercules II	RCAF 436 Sqn (8 Wing), Trenton	
130616	Lockheed CC-130J Hercules II	RCAF 436 Sqn (8 Wing), Trenton	
130617	Lockheed CC-130J Hercules II	RCAF 436 Sqn (8 Wing), Trenton	
140101	Lockheed CP-140M Aurora	RCAF 404 Sqn/405 Sqn (14 Wing), Greenwood	
140103	Lockheed CP-140M Aurora	RCAF 404 Sqn/405 Sqn (14 Wing), Greenwood	
140104	Lockheed CP-140M Aurora	RCAF 404 Sqn/405 Sqn (14 Wing), Greenwood	
140105	Lockheed CP-140M Aurora	RCAF 407 Sqn (19 Wing), Comox	
140106	Lockheed CP-140 Aurora	RCAF 404 Sqn/405 Sqn (14 Wing), Greenwood	
140108	Lockheed CP-140M Aurora	RCAF 404 Sqn/405 Sqn (14 Wing), Greenwood	
140109	Lockheed CP-140 Aurora	RCAF 404 Sqn/405 Sqn (14 Wing), Greenwood	
140110	Lockheed CP-140 Aurora	RCAF 407 Sqn (19 Wing), Comox	
140111	Lockheed CP-140M Aurora	RCAF 404 Sqn/405 Sqn (14 Wing), Greenwood	
140112	Lockheed CP-140M Aurora	RCAF 404 Sqn/405 Sqn (14 Wing), Greenwood	
140113	Lockheed CP-140 Aurora	RCAF 407 Sqn (19 Wing), Comox	
140114	Lockheed CP-140M Aurora	RCAF 404 Sqn/405 Sqn (14 Wing), Greenwood	
140115	Lockheed CP-140M Aurora	RCAF 407 Sqn (19 Wing), Comox	
140116	Lockheed CP-140M Aurora	RCAF 407 Sqn (19 Wing), Comox	
140117	Lockheed CP-140M Aurora	RCAF 407 Sqn (19 Wing), Comox	
140118	Lockheed CP-140M Aurora	RCAF 407 Sqn (19 Wing), Comox	
142803	De Havilland Canada CT-142	RCAF 402 Sqn (17 Wing), Winnipeg	
142804	De Havilland Canada CT-142	RCAF 402 Sqn (17 Wing), Winnipeg	
142805	De Havilland Canada CT-142	RCAF 402 Sqn (17 Wing), Winnipeg	
142806	De Havilland Canada CT-142	RCAF 402 Sqn (17 Wing), Winnipeg	
144614	Canadair CC-144B Challenger (C-GCUP)	RCAF 412 Sqn (8 Wing), Ottawa	

Notes	Serial	Type (code/other identity)	Owner/operator, location or fate
	144615	Canadair CC-144B Challenger (C-GCUR)	RCAF 412 Sqn (8 Wing), Ottawa
	144617	Canadair CC-144C Challenger (C-GKGR)	RCAF 412 Sqn (8 Wing), Ottawa
	144618	Canadair CC-144C Challenger (C-GKGS)	RCAF 412 Sqn (8 Wing), Ottawa
	177701	Boeing CC-177 Globemaster III (07-7701/N9500B)	RCAF 429 Sqn (8 Wing), Trenton
	177702	Boeing CC-177 Globemaster III (07-7702/N9500H)	RCAF 429 Sqn (8 Wing), Trenton
	177703	Boeing CC-177 Globemaster III (07-7703/N9500N)	RCAF 429 Sqn (8 Wing), Trenton
	177704	Boeing CC-177 Globemaster III (07-7704/N9500R) $	RCAF 429 Sqn (8 Wing), Trenton
	177705	Boeing CC-177 Globemaster III (14-0004/N273ZD)	RCAF 429 Sqn (8 Wing), Trenton

CHAD
| | TT-ABD | Boeing 737-74Q | Chad Government, N'djamena |

CHILE
Fuerza Aérea de Chile (FACh)

Note: One of the GameBirds below was lost in a crash at El Bosque on 7 September 2019 – possibly 0005/N259GC.

	0005	Game Composites GB1 GameBird (N259GC)	FACh *Los Halcones*, Santiago
	0006	Game Composites GB1 GameBird (N963GC)	FACh *Los Halcones*, Santiago
	0007	Game Composites GB1 GameBird (N898GC)	FACh *Los Halcones*, Santiago
	....	Game Composites GB1 GameBird	FACh *Los Halcones* (on order)
	....	Game Composites GB1 GameBird	FACh *Los Halcones* (on order)
	....	Game Composites GB1 GameBird	FACh *Los Halcones* (on order)
	....	Game Composites GB1 GameBird	FACh *Los Halcones* (on order)
	145	Extra EA-300L [5]	FACh *Los Halcones*, Santiago
	146	Extra EA-300L [4]	FACh *Los Halcones*, Santiago
	147	Extra EA-300L [2]	FACh *Los Halcones*, Santiago
	902	Boeing 707-351C	FACh, Grupo de Aviación 10, Santiago
	904	Boeing 707-358C	FACh, Grupo de Aviación 10, Santiago
	911	Grumman G.1159C Gulfstream IV	FACh, Grupo de Aviación 10, Santiago
	912	Grumman G.1159C Gulfstream IV	FACh, Grupo de Aviación 10, Santiago
	921	Boeing 737-58N	FACh, Grupo de Aviación 10, Santiago
	922	Boeing 737-330	FACh, Grupo de Aviación 10, Santiago
	982	Boeing KC-135E Stratotanker	FACh, Grupo de Aviación 10, Santiago
	983	Boeing KC-135E Stratotanker	FACh, Grupo de Aviación 10, Santiago
	985	Boeing 767-3Y0ER	FACh, Grupo de Aviación 10, Santiago
	990	Lockheed KC-130R Hercules	*Crashed 9 December 2019, Drake Passage, Antarctica*
	991	Lockheed C-130H Hercules	FACh, Grupo de Aviación 10, Santiago
	992	Lockheed KC-130R Hercules	FACh, Grupo de Aviación 10, Santiago
	995	Lockheed C-130H Hercules	FACh, Grupo de Aviación 10, Santiago
	996	Lockheed C-130H Hercules	FACh, Grupo de Aviación 10, Santiago
	999	Lockheed KC-130R Hercules	FACh, Grupo de Aviación 10, Santiago
	1304	Extra EA-300L [3]	FACh *Los Halcones*, Santiago
	1325	Extra EA-300L [1]	FACh *Los Halcones*, Santiago

COLOMBIA
Fuerza Aérea Colombiana (FAC)

| | FAC-0001 | Boeing 737-74V | FAC Escuadrón de Transporte Especial, Bogotà |

CROATIA
Hrvatske Zračne Snage (HZS)

	054	Pilatus PC-9M	HZS 93 Zakroplova Baza, Zadar
	055	Pilatus PC-9M	HZS 93 Zakroplova Baza, Zadar
	056	Pilatus PC-9M	HZS 93 Zakroplova Baza, Zadar
	057	Pilatus PC-9M	HZS 93 Zakroplova Baza, Zadar
	059	Pilatus PC-9M $	HZS 93 Zakroplova Baza, Zadar
	061	Pilatus PC-9M	HZS 93 Zakroplova Baza, Zadar
	062	Pilatus PC-9M	HZS 93 Zakroplova Baza, Zadar
	063	Pilatus PC-9M	HZS 93 Zakroplova Baza, Zadar
	064	Pilatus PC-9M	HZS 93 Zakroplova Baza, Zadar
	066	Pilatus PC-9M	HZS 93 Zakroplova Baza, Zadar
	067	Pilatus PC-9M	HZS 93 Zakroplova Baza, Zadar
	068	Pilatus PC-9M	HZS 93 Zakroplova Baza, Zadar

Serial	Type (code/other identity)	Owner/operator, location or fate	Notes
069	Pilatus PC-9M	HZS 93 Zakroplova Baza, Zadar	
070	Pilatus PC-9M	HZS 93 Zakroplova Baza, Zadar	
Croatian Government			
9A-CRO	Canadair CL.601 Challenger	Croatian Government, Zagreb	
9A-CRT	Canadair CL.601 Challenger	Croatian Government, Zagreb	
CZECH REPUBLIC			
Vzdušné Síly Armády (Czech Air Force)			
0107	Aero L-39C Albatros	*Withdrawn from use*	
0108	Aero L-39C Albatros	*Preserved at Cáslav*	
0113	Aero L-39C Albatros	Czech AF CLV, Pardubice	
0115	Aero L-39C Albatros	Czech AF CLV, Pardubice	
0260	Yakovlev Yak-40	Czech AF 241.dlt/24.zDL, Praha/Kbely	
0441	Aero L-39C Albatros	Czech AF CLV, Pardubice	
0444	Aero L-39C Albatros	Czech AF CLV, Pardubice	
0445	Aero L-39C Albatros	Czech AF CLV, Pardubice	
0448	Aero L-39C Albatros	Czech AF CLV, Pardubice	
0452	CASA C-295M	Czech AF 242.tsl/24.zDL, Praha/Kbely	
0453	CASA C-295M	Czech AF 242.tsl/24.zDL, Praha/Kbely	
0454	CASA C-295M	Czech AF 242.tsl/24.zDL, Praha/Kbely	
0455	CASA C-295M	Czech AF 242.tsl/24.zDL, Praha/Kbely	
0457	Mil Mi-17V-11	Czech AF CLV, Pardubice	
0475	Aero L-39NG Albatros (7001)	Aero, Vodochody	
0476	Aero L-39NG Albatros (7004)	Aero, Vodochody	
0731	LET L-410UVP-E Turbolet	Czech AF CLV, Pardubice	
0825	Mil Mi-17	Czech AF CLV, Pardubice	
0828	Mil Mi-17	Czech AF CLV, Pardubice	
0832	Mil Mi-17	Czech AF CLV, Pardubice	
0834	Mil Mi-17	Czech AF 243.vrl/24.zDL, Praha/Kbely	
0835	Mil Mi-17	Czech AF CLV, Pardubice	
0836	Mil Mi-17	Czech AF CLV, Pardubice	
0837	Mil Mi-17	Czech AF CLV, Pardubice	
0839	Mil Mi-17	Czech AF 243.vrl/24.zDL, Praha/Kbely	
0848	Mil Mi-17	Czech AF 243.vrl/24.zDL, Praha/Kbely	
0849	Mil Mi-17	Czech AF 243.vrl/24.zDL, Praha/Kbely	
0850	Mil Mi-17	Czech AF 243.vrl/24.zDL, Praha/Kbely	
0928	LET L-410UVP-T Turbolet	Czech AF CLV, Pardubice	
0981	Mil Mi-24V2	Czech AF 221.lbvr/22.zL, Náměšt	
1257	Yakovlev Yak-40K	Czech AF 241.dlt/24.zDL, Praha/Kbely	
1525	LET L-410FG Turbolet	Czech AF 242.tsl/24.zDL, Praha/Kbely	
1526	LET L-410FG Turbolet	Czech AF 242.tsl/24.zDL, Praha/Kbely	
2312	LET L-410UVP-E Turbolet	Czech AF 242.tsl/24.zDL, Praha/Kbely	
2415	Aero L-39ZA Albatros	Czech AF 213.vlt/21.zTL, Cáslav	
2421	Aero L-39ZA Albatros	Czech AF 213.vlt/21.zTL, Cáslav	
2601	LET L-410UVP-E Turbolet	Czech AF 242.tsl/24.zDL, Praha/Kbely	
2602	LET L-410UVP-E Turbolet	Czech AF 242.tsl/24.zDL, Praha/Kbely	
2626	Aero L-39CW Albatros	Aero, Vodochody	
2710	LET L-410UVP-E Turbolet	Czech AF 242.tsl/24.zDL, Praha/Kbely	
2801	Airbus A.319CJ-115X	Czech AF 241.dlt/24.zDL, Praha/Kbely	
3085	Airbus A.319CJ-115X	Czech AF 241.dlt/24.zDL, Praha/Kbely	
3361	Mil Mi-35	Czech AF 221.lbvr/22.zL, Náměšt	
3362	Mil Mi-35	Czech AF 221.lbvr/22.zL, Náměšt	
3365	Mil Mi-35	Czech AF 221.lbvr/22.zL, Náměšt	
3366	Mil Mi-35 $	Czech AF 221.lbvr/22.zL, Náměšt	
3367	Mil Mi-35	Czech AF 221.lbvr/22.zL, Náměšt	
3368	Mil Mi-35	Czech AF 221.lbvr/22.zL, Náměšt	
3369	Mil Mi-35	Czech AF 221.lbvr/22.zL, Náměšt	
3370	Mil Mi-35 $	Czech AF 221.lbvr/22.zL, Náměšt	
3371	Mil Mi-35	Czech AF 221.lbvr/22.zL, Náměšt	
3903	Aero L-39ZA Albatros	*Withdrawn from use*	
5015	Aero L-39ZA Albatros	*Withdrawn from use, May 2019*	
5017	Aero L-39ZA Albatros	*Withdrawn from use, June 2019*	

Notes	Serial	Type (code/other identity)	Owner/operator, location or fate
	5019	Aero L-39ZA Albatros $	*Withdrawn from use, June 2019*
	5105	Canadair CL.601-3A Challenger	Czech AF 241.dlt/24.zDL, Praha/Kbely
	5832	Aero L-159B ALCA	*Withdrawn from use*
	6028	Aero L-159T-2 ALCA	Czech AF 213.vlt/21.zTL, Cáslav
	6031	Aero L-159T-2 ALCA	Czech AF 213.vlt/21.zTL, Cáslav
	6038	Aero L-159T-2 ALCA	Czech AF 213.vlt/21.zTL, Cáslav
	6046	Aero L-159T-1 ALCA	Czech AF 213.vlt/21.zTL, Cáslav
	6047	Aero L-159T-1 ALCA	Czech AF 213.vlt/21.zTL, Cáslav
	6048	Aero L-159A ALCA	Czech AF 212.tl/21.zTL, Cáslav
	6050	Aero L-159A ALCA	Czech AF 212.tl/21.zTL, Cáslav
	6051	Aero L-159A ALCA	Czech AF 212.tl/21.zTL, Cáslav
	6052	Aero L-159A ALCA	Czech AF 212.tl/21.zTL, Cáslav
	6053	Aero L-159A ALCA (*AD572/DU-C*) $	Czech AF 212.tl/21.zTL, Cáslav
	6054	Aero L-159A ALCA	Czech AF 212.tl/21.zTL, Cáslav
	6057	Aero L-159A ALCA	Czech AF 212.tl/21.zTL, Cáslav
	6058	Aero L-159A ALCA	Czech AF 212.tl/21.zTL, Cáslav
	6059	Aero L-159A ALCA	Czech AF 212.tl/21.zTL, Cáslav
	6060	Aero L-159A ALCA	Czech AF 212.tl/21.zTL, Cáslav
	6062	Aero L-159A ALCA	Czech AF 212.tl/21.zTL, Cáslav
	6063	Aero L-159A ALCA	Czech AF 212.tl/21.zTL, Cáslav
	6064	Aero L-159A ALCA	Czech AF 212.tl/21.zTL, Cáslav
	6066	Aero L-159A ALCA $	Czech AF 212.tl/21.zTL, Cáslav
	6067	Aero L-159T-1 ALCA	Czech AF 213.vlt/21.zTL, Cáslav
	6070	Aero L-159A ALCA	Czech AF 212.tl/21.zTL, Cáslav
	6073	Aero L-159T-2X ALCA	Aero, Vodochody
	6077	Aero L-159T-1 ALCA	Czech AF 213.vlt/21.zTL, Cáslav
	6078	Aero L-159T-1 ALCA	Czech AF 213.vlt/21.zTL, Cáslav
	7353	Mil Mi-24V $	Czech AF 221.lbvr/22.zL, Náměšt
	7354	Mil Mi-24V	Czech AF 221.lbvr/22.zL, Náměšt
	7355	Mil Mi-24V	Czech AF 221.lbvr/22.zL, Náměšt
	7356	Mil Mi-24V	Czech AF 221.lbvr/22.zL, Náměšt
	7357	Mil Mi-24V	Czech AF 221.lbvr/22.zL, Náměšt
	7360	Mil Mi-24V	Czech AF 221.lbvr/22.zL, Náměšt
	9234	SAAB JAS 39C Gripen $	Czech AF 211.tl/21.zTL, Cáslav
	9235	SAAB JAS 39C Gripen $	Czech AF 211.tl/21.zTL, Cáslav
	9236	SAAB JAS 39C Gripen $	Czech AF 211.tl/21.zTL, Cáslav
	9237	SAAB JAS 39C Gripen	Czech AF 211.tl/21.zTL, Cáslav
	9238	SAAB JAS 39C Gripen	Czech AF 211.tl/21.zTL, Cáslav
	9239	SAAB JAS 39C Gripen	Czech AF 211.tl/21.zTL, Cáslav
	9240	SAAB JAS 39C Gripen	Czech AF 211.tl/21.zTL, Cáslav
	9241	SAAB JAS 39C Gripen	Czech AF 211.tl/21.zTL, Cáslav
	9242	SAAB JAS 39C Gripen	Czech AF 211.tl/21.zTL, Cáslav
	9243	SAAB JAS 39C Gripen	Czech AF 211.tl/21.zTL, Cáslav
	9244	SAAB JAS 39C Gripen	Czech AF 211.tl/21.zTL, Cáslav
	9245	SAAB JAS 39C Gripen	Czech AF 211.tl/21.zTL, Cáslav
	9767	Mil Mi-171Sh	Czech AF 221.lbvr & 222.vrlt/22.zVrL, Náměšt
	9774	Mil Mi-171Sh	Czech AF 221.lbvr & 222.vrlt/22.zVrL, Náměšt
	9781	Mil Mi-171Sh	Czech AF 221.lbvr & 222.vrlt/22.zVrL, Náměšt
	9799	Mil Mi-171Sh	Czech AF 221.lbvr & 222.vrlt/22.zVrL, Náměšt
	9806	Mil Mi-171Sh	Czech AF 221.lbvr & 222.vrlt/22.zVrL, Náměšt
	9813	Mil Mi-171Sh	Czech AF 221.lbvr & 222.vrlt/22.zVrL, Náměšt
	9819	SAAB JAS 39D Gripen $	Czech AF 211.tl/21.zTL, Cáslav
	9820	SAAB JAS 39D Gripen	Czech AF 211.tl/21.zTL, Cáslav
	9825	Mil Mi-171Sh	Czech AF 221.lbvr & 222.vrlt/22.zVrL, Náměšt
	9837	Mil Mi-171Sh	Czech AF 221.lbvr & 222.vrlt/22.zVrL, Náměšt
	9844	Mil Mi-171Sh	Czech AF 221.lbvr & 222.vrlt/22.zVrL, Náměšt
	9868	Mil Mi-171Sh	Czech AF 221.lbvr & 222.vrlt/22.zVrL, Náměšt
	9873	Mil Mi-171Sh	Czech AF 221.lbvr & 222.vrlt/22.zVrL, Náměšt
	9887	Mil Mi-171Sh	Czech AF 221.lbvr & 222.vrlt/22.zVrL, Náměšt
	9892	Mil Mi-171Sh	Czech AF 221.lbvr & 222.vrlt/22.zVrL, Náměšt
	9904	Mil Mi-171Sh	Czech AF 221.lbvr & 222.vrlt/22.zVrL, Náměšt
	9915	Mil Mi-171Sh	Czech AF 221.lbvr & 222.vrlt/22.zVrL, Náměšt

Serial	Type (code/other identity)	Owner/operator, location or fate	Notes
9926	Mil Mi-171Sh	Czech AF 221.lbvr & 222.vrlt/22.zVrL, Náměšt	
....	Aero L-39NG Albatros (7002)	Aero, Vodochody	
....	Aero L-39NG Albatros (7003)	Aero, Vodochody	
....	CASA C-295W	Czech AF (on order)	
....	CASA C-295W	Czech AF (on order)	
....	CASA C-295W	Czech AF (on order)	
....	CASA C-295W	Czech AF (on order)	

DENMARK
Kongelige Danske Flyvevåben (KDF)

Serial	Type (code/other identity)	Owner/operator, location or fate	Notes
B-536	Lockheed C-130J-30 Hercules II	KDF Eskadrille 721, Aalborg	
B-537	Lockheed C-130J-30 Hercules II	KDF Eskadrille 721, Aalborg	
B-538	Lockheed C-130J-30 Hercules II	KDF Eskadrille 721, Aalborg	
B-583	Lockheed C-130J-30 Hercules II	KDF Eskadrille 721, Aalborg	
C-080	Canadair CL.604 Challenger	KDF Eskadrille 721, Aalborg	
C-168	Canadair CL.604 Challenger $	KDF Eskadrille 721, Aalborg	
C-172	Canadair CL.604 Challenger	KDF Eskadrille 721, Aalborg	
C-215	Canadair CL.604 Challenger	KDF Eskadrille 721, Aalborg	
E-004	SABCA (GD) F-16A MLU Fighting Falcon	KDF Eskadrille 727, Skrydstrup	
E-005	SABCA (GD) F-16A MLU Fighting Falcon	KDF Eskadrille 727, Skrydstrup	
E-006	SABCA (GD) F-16A MLU Fighting Falcon	KDF Eskadrille 730, Skrydstrup	
E-007	SABCA (GD) F-16A MLU Fighting Falcon	KDF Eskadrille 727, Skrydstrup	
E-008	SABCA (GD) F-16A MLU Fighting Falcon $	KDF, stored Skrydstrup	
E-011	GD F-16A MLU Fighting Falcon	KDF Eskadrille 727, Skrydstrup	
E-016	SABCA (GD) F-16A MLU Fighting Falcon	KDF Eskadrille 730, Skrydstrup	
E-017	SABCA (GD) F-16A MLU Fighting Falcon	KDF, stored Skrydstrup	
E-018	SABCA (GD) F-16A MLU Fighting Falcon	KDF Eskadrille 730, Skrydstrup	
E-024	GD F-16A MLU Fighting Falcon	KDF, stored Skrydstrup	
E-074	GD F-16A MLU Fighting Falcon	KDF Eskadrille 730, Skrydstrup	
E-075	GD F-16A MLU Fighting Falcon	KDF Eskadrille 727, Skrydstrup	
E-107	GD F-16A MLU Fighting Falcon	KDF, stored Skrydstrup	
E-189	SABCA (GD) F-16A MLU Fighting Falcon	KDF Eskadrille 730, Skrydstrup	
E-190	SABCA (GD) F-16A MLU Fighting Falcon	KDF Eskadrille 730, Skrydstrup	
E-191	SABCA (GD) F-16A MLU Fighting Falcon $	KDF Eskadrille 730, Skrydstrup	
E-194	SABCA (GD) F-16A MLU Fighting Falcon $	KDF Eskadrille 730, Skrydstrup	
E-596	SABCA (GD) F-16A MLU Fighting Falcon	KDF, stored Skrydstrup	
E-597	SABCA (GD) F-16A MLU Fighting Falcon	KDF Eskadrille 730, Skrydstrup	
E-598	SABCA (GD) F-16A MLU Fighting Falcon	KDF Eskadrille 730, Skrydstrup	
E-599	SABCA (GD) F-16A MLU Fighting Falcon	KDF Eskadrille 727, Skrydstrup	
E-600	SABCA (GD) F-16A MLU Fighting Falcon	KDF Eskadrille 730, Skrydstrup	
E-601	SABCA (GD) F-16A MLU Fighting Falcon $	KDF Eskadrille 730, Skrydstrup	
E-602	SABCA (GD) F-16A MLU Fighting Falcon	KDF Eskadrille 730, Skrydstrup	
E-603	SABCA (GD) F-16A MLU Fighting Falcon	KDF Eskadrille 730, Skrydstrup	
E-604	SABCA (GD) F-16A MLU Fighting Falcon	KDF Eskadrille 730, Skrydstrup	
E-605	SABCA (GD) F-16A MLU Fighting Falcon	KDF Eskadrille 730, Skrydstrup	
E-606	SABCA (GD) F-16A MLU Fighting Falcon	KDF Eskadrille 730, Skrydstrup	
E-607	SABCA (GD) F-16A MLU Fighting Falcon $	KDF Eskadrille 727, Skrydstrup	
E-608	SABCA (GD) F-16A MLU Fighting Falcon	KDF Eskadrille 730, Skrydstrup	
E-609	SABCA (GD) F-16A MLU Fighting Falcon	KDF Eskadrille 727, Skrydstrup	
E-610	SABCA (GD) F-16A MLU Fighting Falcon	KDF, stored Skrydstrup	
E-611	SABCA (GD) F-16A MLU Fighting Falcon	KDF, stored Skrydstrup	
ET-022	Fokker (GD) F-16B MLU Fighting Falcon	KDF Eskadrille 730, Skrydstrup	
ET-197	Fokker (GD) F-16B MLU Fighting Falcon	KDF Eskadrille 727, Skrydstrup	
ET-198	Fokker (GD) F-16B MLU Fighting Falcon	KDF Eskadrille 727, Skrydstrup	
ET-199	Fokker (GD) F-16B MLU Fighting Falcon	KDF Eskadrille 730, Skrydstrup	
ET-207	SABCA (GD) F-16B MLU Fighting Falcon	KDF Eskadrille 727, Skrydstrup	
ET-208	SABCA (GD) F-16B MLU Fighting Falcon	KDF Eskadrille 730, Skrydstrup	
ET-210	SABCA (GD) F-16B MLU Fighting Falcon	*Withdrawn from use at Skrydstrup, 2019*	
ET-612	SABCA (GD) F-16B MLU Fighting Falcon	KDF Eskadrille 727, Skrydstrup	
ET-613	SABCA (GD) F-16B MLU Fighting Falcon	KDF Eskadrille 727, Skrydstrup	
ET-614	SABCA (GD) F-16B MLU Fighting Falcon	KDF Eskadrille 727, Skrydstrup	
ET-615	SABCA (GD) F-16B MLU Fighting Falcon	KDF Eskadrille 730, Skrydstrup	

Notes	Serial	Type (code/other identity)	Owner/operator, location or fate
	M-502	AgustaWestland EH.101 Mk.512 (ZJ991)	KDF Eskadrille 722, Karup
	M-504	AgustaWestland EH.101 Mk.512 (ZJ993)	KDF Eskadrille 722, Karup
	M-507	AgustaWestland EH.101 Mk.512 (ZJ996)	KDF Eskadrille 722, Karup
	M-508	AgustaWestland EH.101 Mk.512 (ZJ997)	KDF Eskadrille 722, Karup
	M-510	AgustaWestland EH.101 Mk.512 (ZJ999)	KDF Eskadrille 722, Karup
	M-512	AgustaWestland EH.101 Mk.512 (ZK002)	KDF Eskadrille 722, Karup
	M-513	AgustaWestland EH.101 Mk.512 (ZK003)	KDF Eskadrille 722, Karup
	M-514	AgustaWestland EH.101 Mk.512 (ZK004)	KDF Eskadrille 722, Karup
	M-515	AgustaWestland EH.101 Mk.512 (ZK160)	KDF Eskadrille 722, Karup
	M-516	AgustaWestland EH.101 Mk.512 (ZK161)	KDF Eskadrille 722, Karup
	M-517	AgustaWestland EH.101 Mk.512 (ZK162)	KDF Eskadrille 722, Karup
	M-518	AgustaWestland EH.101 Mk.512 (ZK163)	KDF Eskadrille 722, Karup
	M-519	AgustaWestland EH.101 Mk.512 (ZK164)	KDF Eskadrille 722, Karup
	M-520	AgustaWestland EH.101 Mk.512	KDF Eskadrille 722, Karup
	N-971	Sikorsky MH-60R Sea Hawk	KDF Eskadrille 723, Karup
	N-972	Sikorsky MH-60R Sea Hawk	KDF Eskadrille 723, Karup
	N-973	Sikorsky MH-60R Sea Hawk	KDF Eskadrille 723, Karup
	N-974	Sikorsky MH-60R Sea Hawk	KDF Eskadrille 723, Karup
	N-975	Sikorsky MH-60R Sea Hawk	KDF Eskadrille 723, Karup
	N-976	Sikorsky MH-60R Sea Hawk	KDF Eskadrille 723, Karup
	N-977	Sikorsky MH-60R Sea Hawk	KDF Eskadrille 723, Karup
	N-978	Sikorsky MH-60R Sea Hawk	KDF Eskadrille 723, Karup
	N-979	Sikorsky MH-60R Sea Hawk	KDF Eskadrille 723, Karup
	P-090	Aérospatiale AS.550C-2 Fennec	KDF Eskadrille 724, Karup
	P-234	Aérospatiale AS.550C-2 Fennec	KDF Eskadrille 724, Karup
	P-254	Aérospatiale AS.550C-2 Fennec	KDF Eskadrille 724, Karup
	P-275	Aérospatiale AS.550C-2 Fennec	KDF Eskadrille 724, Karup
	P-276	Aérospatiale AS.550C-2 Fennec	KDF Eskadrille 724, Karup
	P-287	Aérospatiale AS.550C-2 Fennec	KDF Eskadrille 724, Karup
	P-288	Aérospatiale AS.550C-2 Fennec	KDF Eskadrille 724, Karup
	P-319	Aérospatiale AS.550C-2 Fennec	KDF Eskadrille 724, Karup
	P-320	Aérospatiale AS.550C-2 Fennec	KDF Eskadrille 724, Karup
	P-339	Aérospatiale AS.550C-2 Fennec	KDF Eskadrille 724, Karup
	P-352	Aérospatiale AS.550C-2 Fennec	KDF Eskadrille 724, Karup
	P-369	Aérospatiale AS.550C-2 Fennec	KDF Eskadrille 724, Karup
	T-401	SAAB T-17 Supporter	KDF Flyveskolen, Karup
	T-402	SAAB T-17 Supporter	KDF Flyveskolen, Karup
	T-403	SAAB T-17 Supporter	KDF Flyveskolen, Karup
	T-404	SAAB T-17 Supporter	KDF Flyveskolen, Karup
	T-405	SAAB T-17 Supporter	KDF Skrydstrup Station Flight
	T-407	SAAB T-17 Supporter	KDF Eskadrille 721, Aalborg
	T-409	SAAB T-17 Supporter	KDF Flyveskolen, Karup
	T-410	SAAB T-17 Supporter	KDF Flyveskolen, Karup
	T-411	SAAB T-17 Supporter	KDF Skrydstrup Station Flight
	T-412	SAAB T-17 Supporter	KDF Flyveskolen, Karup
	T-413	SAAB T-17 Supporter	KDF Flyveskolen, Karup
	T-414	SAAB T-17 Supporter	KDF Eskadrille 721, Aalborg
	T-415	SAAB T-17 Supporter	KDF Flyveskolen, Karup
	T-417	SAAB T-17 Supporter	KDF Flyveskolen, Karup
	T-418	SAAB T-17 Supporter	KDF Skrydstrup Station Flight
	T-419	SAAB T-17 Supporter	KDF Flyveskolen, Karup
	T-420	SAAB T-17 Supporter	KDF Skrydstrup Station Flight
	T-421	SAAB T-17 Supporter	KDF Flyveskolen, Karup
	T-423	SAAB T-17 Supporter	KDF Flyveskolen, Karup
	T-425	SAAB T-17 Supporter	KDF Flyveskolen, Karup
	T-426	SAAB T-17 Supporter	KDF Flyveskolen, Karup
	T-427	SAAB T-17 Supporter	KDF Flyveskolen, Karup
	T-428	SAAB T-17 Supporter	KDF Flyveskolen, Karup
	T-429	SAAB T-17 Supporter	KDF Flyveskolen, Karup
	T-430	SAAB T-17 Supporter	KDF Flyveskolen, Karup
	T-431	SAAB T-17 Supporter	KDF Eskadrille 721, Aalborg
	T-432	SAAB T-17 Supporter	KDF Flyveskolen, Karup

Serial	Type (code/other identity)	Owner/operator, location or fate	Notes

ECUADOR
Fuerza Aérea Ecuatoriana (FAE)

Serial	Type (code/other identity)	Owner/operator, location or fate	Notes
FAE-051	Embraer ERJ.135 Legacy 600	FAE Escuadrón de Transporte 1114, Quito	
FAE-052	Dassault Falcon 7X	FAE Escuadrón de Transporte 1114, Quito	

EGYPT
Al Quwwat al-Jawwiya il Misriya (Egyptian Air Force)

1331	Ilyushin Il-76MF (SU-BTX)	Egyptian AF 16 Sqn, Cairo West	
1332	Ilyushin Il-76MF (SU-BTY)	Egyptian AF 16 Sqn, Cairo West	
1271	Lockheed C-130H Hercules (SU-BAB)	Egyptian AF 16 Sqn, Cairo West	
1273	Lockheed C-130H Hercules (SU-BAD)	Egyptian AF 16 Sqn, Cairo West	
1274	Lockheed C-130H Hercules (SU-BAE)	Egyptian AF 16 Sqn, Cairo West	
1275	Lockheed C-130H Hercules (SU-BAF)	Egyptian AF 16 Sqn, Cairo West	
1277	Lockheed C-130H Hercules (SU-BAI)	Egyptian AF 16 Sqn, Cairo West	
1278	Lockheed C-130H Hercules (SU-BAJ)	Egyptian AF 16 Sqn, Cairo West	
1279	Lockheed C-130H Hercules (SU-BAK)	Egyptian AF 16 Sqn, Cairo West	
1280	Lockheed C-130H Hercules (SU-BAL)	Egyptian AF 16 Sqn, Cairo West	
1281	Lockheed C-130H Hercules (SU-BAM)	Egyptian AF 16 Sqn, Cairo West	
1282	Lockheed C-130H Hercules (SU-BAN)	Egyptian AF 16 Sqn, Cairo West	
1283	Lockheed C-130H Hercules (SU-BAP)	Egyptian AF 16 Sqn, Cairo West	
1284	Lockheed C-130H Hercules (SU-BAQ)	Egyptian AF 16 Sqn, Cairo West	
1285	Lockheed C-130H Hercules (SU-BAR)	Egyptian AF 16 Sqn, Cairo West	
1286	Lockheed C-130H Hercules (SU-BAS)	Egyptian AF 16 Sqn, Cairo West	
1287	Lockheed C-130H Hercules (SU-BAT)	Egyptian AF 16 Sqn, Cairo West	
1288	Lockheed C-130H Hercules (SU-BAU)	Egyptian AF 16 Sqn, Cairo West	
1289	Lockheed C-130H Hercules (SU-BAV)	Egyptian AF 16 Sqn, Cairo West	
1290	Lockheed C-130H Hercules (SU-BEW)	Egyptian AF 16 Sqn, Cairo West	
1291	Lockheed C-130H Hercules (SU-BEX)	Egyptian AF 16 Sqn, Cairo West	
1292	Lockheed C-130H Hercules (SU-BEY)	Egyptian AF 16 Sqn, Cairo West	
1293	Lockheed C-130H-30 Hercules (SU-BKS)	Egyptian AF 16 Sqn, Cairo West	
1294	Lockheed C-130H-30 Hercules (SU-BKT)	Egyptian AF 16 Sqn, Cairo West	
1295	Lockheed C-130H-30 Hercules (SU-BKU)	Egyptian AF 16 Sqn, Cairo West	
1296	Lockheed C-130H Hercules (SU-BPJ)	Egyptian AF 16 Sqn, Cairo West	
1297	Lockheed C-130H Hercules (SU-BPK)	Egyptian AF 16 Sqn, Cairo West	
1298	Lockheed C-130H Hercules (SU-BPL)	Egyptian AF 16 Sqn, Cairo West	
....	Lockheed C-130J Hercules II	Egyptian AF (on order)	
....	Lockheed C-130J Hercules II	Egyptian AF (on order)	

Egyptian Government

SU-BGV	Grumman G.1159A Gulfstream III	Egyptian AF/Government, Cairo	
SU-BNC	Grumman G.1159C Gulfstream IV	Egyptian AF/Government, Cairo	
SU-BND	Grumman G.1159C Gulfstream IV	Egyptian AF/Government, Cairo	
SU-BNO	Grumman G.1159C Gulfstream IV-SP	Egyptian AF/Government, Cairo	
SU-BNP	Grumman G.1159C Gulfstream IV-SP	Egyptian AF/Government, Cairo	
SU-BPE	Gulfstream Aerospace G.400	Egyptian AF/Government, Cairo	
SU-BPF	Gulfstream Aerospace G.400	Egyptian AF/Government, Cairo	
SU-BRF	Cessna 680 Citation Sovereign	Egyptian Government, Cairo	
SU-BRG	Cessna 680 Citation Sovereign	Egyptian Government, Cairo	
SU-BTT	Dassault Falcon 7X (F-WWHP)	Egyptian AF/Government, Cairo	
SU-BTU	Dassault Falcon 7X (F-WWUR)	Egyptian AF/Government, Cairo	
SU-BTV	Dassault Falcon 7X (F-WWUQ)	Egyptian AF/Government, Cairo	
SU-BTW	Dassault Falcon 8X (F-WWVL)	Egyptian AF/Government, Cairo	
SU-GGG	Airbus A.340-211	Egyptian Government, Cairo	

ESTONIA
Estonian Air Force

10	Aero L-39C Albatros (ES-RAZ)	Estonian AF 2.Eskadrill/Lennugrupp, Ämari	
11	Aero L-39C Albatros (ES-TLH)	Estonian AF 2.Eskadrill/Lennugrupp, Ämari	
14	Aero L-39C Albatros (ES-TLU)	Estonian AF 2.Eskadrill/Lennugrupp, Ämari	
15	Aero L-39C Albatros (ES-TLV)	Estonian AF 2.Eskadrill/Lennugrupp, Ämari	
40 y	WSK-PZL An-2T	Estonian AF 1.Eskadrill/Lennugrupp, Ämari	
41 y	Antonov An-2	Estonian AF 1.Eskadrill/Lennugrupp, Ämari	
44 bk	PZL-Mielec M28-05 Skytruck (09-0317)	Estonian AF 1.Eskadrill/Lennugrupp, Ämari	

Notes	Serial	Type (code/other identity)	Owner/operator, location or fate
	45 bk	PZL-Mielec M28-05 Skytruck	Estonian AF (on order)

FINLAND

Suomen Ilmavoimat (Finnish Air Force) & Suomen Maavoimat (Finnish Army)

Notes	Serial	Type (code/other identity)	Owner/operator, location or fate
	CC-1	CASA C-295M	Ilmavoimat TukiLLv, Tampere/Pirkkala
	CC-2	CASA C-295M	Ilmavoimat TukiLLv, Tampere/Pirkkala
	CC-3	CASA C-295M	Ilmavoimat TukiLLv, Tampere/Pirkkala
	HN-401	McDonnell Douglas F-18C Hornet	Ilmavoimat HävLLv 31, Kuopio/Rissala
	HN-402	McDonnell Douglas F-18C Hornet	Ilmavoimat HävLLv 11, Roveniemi
	HN-403	McDonnell Douglas F-18C Hornet	Ilmavoimat HävLLv 31, Kuopio/Rissala
	HN-404	McDonnell Douglas F-18C Hornet	Ilmavoimat HävLLv 31, Kuopio/Rissala
	HN-405	McDonnell Douglas F-18C Hornet	Ilmavoimat HävLLv 31, Kuopio/Rissala
	HN-406	McDonnell Douglas F-18C Hornet	Ilmavoimat HävLLv 11, Roveniemi
	HN-407	McDonnell Douglas F-18C Hornet	Ilmavoimat HävLLv 31, Kuopio/Rissala
	HN-408	McDonnell Douglas F-18C Hornet	Ilmavoimat HävLLv 31, Kuopio/Rissala
	HN-409	McDonnell Douglas F-18C Hornet	Ilmavoimat HävLLv 11, Roveniemi
	HN-410	McDonnell Douglas F-18C Hornet	Ilmavoimat HävLLv 11, Roveniemi
	HN-411	McDonnell Douglas F-18C Hornet	Ilmavoimat HävLLv 11, Roveniemi
	HN-412	McDonnell Douglas F-18C Hornet	Ilmavoimat HävLLv 11, Roveniemi
	HN-414	McDonnell Douglas F-18C Hornet	Ilmavoimat HävLLv 31, Kuopio/Rissala
	HN-415	McDonnell Douglas F-18C Hornet	Ilmavoimat HävLLv 31, Kuopio/Rissala
	HN-416	McDonnell Douglas F-18C Hornet	Ilmavoimat HävLLv 11, Roveniemi
	HN-417	McDonnell Douglas F-18C Hornet	Ilmavoimat HävLLv 31, Kuopio/Rissala
	HN-418	McDonnell Douglas F-18C Hornet	Ilmavoimat HävLLv 11, Roveniemi
	HN-419	McDonnell Douglas F-18C Hornet	Ilmavoimat HävLLv 11, Roveniemi
	HN-420	McDonnell Douglas F-18C Hornet	Ilmavoimat HävLLv 31, Kuopio/Rissala
	HN-421	McDonnell Douglas F-18C Hornet	Ilmavoimat HävLLv 31, Kuopio/Rissala
	HN-422	McDonnell Douglas F-18C Hornet	Ilmavoimat HävLLv 11, Roveniemi
	HN-423	McDonnell Douglas F-18C Hornet	Ilmavoimat HävLLv 31, Kuopio/Rissala
	HN-424	McDonnell Douglas F-18C Hornet	Ilmavoimat HävLLv 31, Kuopio/Rissala
	HN-425	McDonnell Douglas F-18C Hornet	Ilmavoimat HävLLv 31, Kuopio/Rissala
	HN-426	McDonnell Douglas F-18C Hornet	Ilmavoimat HävLLv 31, Kuopio/Rissala
	HN-427	McDonnell Douglas F-18C Hornet	Ilmavoimat HävLLv 11, Roveniemi
	HN-428	McDonnell Douglas F-18C Hornet	Ilmavoimat HävLLv 11, Roveniemi
	HN-429	McDonnell Douglas F-18C Hornet	Ilmavoimat HävLLv 11, Roveniemi
	HN-431	McDonnell Douglas F-18C Hornet	Ilmavoimat HävLLv 31, Kuopio/Rissala
	HN-432	McDonnell Douglas F-18C Hornet	Ilmavoimat HävLLv 31, Kuopio/Rissala
	HN-433	McDonnell Douglas F-18C Hornet	Ilmavoimat HävLLv 31, Kuopio/Rissala
	HN-434	McDonnell Douglas F-18C Hornet	Ilmavoimat HävLLv 11, Roveniemi
	HN-435	McDonnell Douglas F-18C Hornet	Ilmavoimat HävLLv 11, Roveniemi
	HN-436	McDonnell Douglas F-18C Hornet	Ilmavoimat HävLLv 31, Kuopio/Rissala
	HN-437	McDonnell Douglas F-18C Hornet	Ilmavoimat HävLLv 31, Kuopio/Rissala
	HN-438	McDonnell Douglas F-18C Hornet	Ilmavoimat HävLLv 11, Roveniemi
	HN-439	McDonnell Douglas F-18C Hornet	Ilmavoimat HävLLv 31, Kuopio/Rissala
	HN-440	McDonnell Douglas F-18C Hornet	Ilmavoimat HävLLv 11, Roveniemi
	HN-441	McDonnell Douglas F-18C Hornet	Ilmavoimat HävLLv 11, Roveniemi
	HN-442	McDonnell Douglas F-18C Hornet	Ilmavoimat HävLLv 11, Roveniemi
	HN-443	McDonnell Douglas F-18C Hornet	Ilmavoimat HävLLv 31, Kuopio/Rissala
	HN-444	McDonnell Douglas F-18C Hornet	Ilmavoimat HävLLv 11, Roveniemi
	HN-445	McDonnell Douglas F-18C Hornet	Ilmavoimat HävLLv 11, Roveniemi
	HN-446	McDonnell Douglas F-18C Hornet	Ilmavoimat HävLLv 11, Roveniemi
	HN-447	McDonnell Douglas F-18C Hornet	Ilmavoimat HävLLv 31, Kuopio/Rissala
	HN-448	McDonnell Douglas F-18C Hornet	Ilmavoimat HävLLv 31, Kuopio/Rissala
	HN-449	McDonnell Douglas F-18C Hornet	Ilmavoimat HävLLv 11, Roveniemi
	HN-450	McDonnell Douglas F-18C Hornet	Ilmavoimat HävLLv 11, Roveniemi
	HN-451	McDonnell Douglas F-18C Hornet	Ilmavoimat HävLLv 31, Kuopio/Rissala
	HN-452	McDonnell Douglas F-18C Hornet	Ilmavoimat HävLLv 11, Roveniemi
	HN-453	McDonnell Douglas F-18C Hornet	Ilmavoimat HävLLv 31, Kuopio/Rissala
	HN-454	McDonnell Douglas F-18C Hornet	Ilmavoimat HävLLv 31, Kuopio/Rissala
	HN-455	McDonnell Douglas F-18C Hornet	Ilmavoimat HävLLv 31, Kuopio/Rissala
	HN-456	McDonnell Douglas F-18C Hornet	Ilmavoimat HävLLv 31, Kuopio/Rissala
	HN-457	McDonnell Douglas F-18C Hornet	Ilmavoimat HävLLv 11, Roveniemi

Serial	Type (code/other identity)	Owner/operator, location or fate	Notes
HN-461	McDonnell Douglas F-18D Hornet	Ilmavoimat HävLLv 31, Kuopio/Rissala	
HN-462	McDonnell Douglas F-18D Hornet	Ilmavoimat HävLLv 11, Roveniemi	
HN-463	McDonnell Douglas F-18D Hornet	Ilmavoimat HävLLv 11, Roveniemi	
HN-464	McDonnell Douglas F-18D Hornet	Ilmavoimat HävLLv 11, Roveniemi	
HN-465	McDonnell Douglas F-18D Hornet	Ilmavoimat HävLLv 31, Kuopio/Rissala	
HN-466	McDonnell Douglas F-18D Hornet	Ilmavoimat HävLLv 31, Kuopio/Rissala	
HN-467	McDonnell Douglas F-18D Hornet	Ilmavoimat HävLLv 11, Roveniemi	
HW-307	BAe Hawk 51	Ilmavoimat HävLLv 41, Jyväskylä/Tikkakoski	
HW-320	BAe Hawk 51	Ilmavoimat HävLLv 41, Jyväskylä/Tikkakoski	
HW-321	BAe Hawk 51	Ilmavoimat HävLLv 41, Jyväskylä/Tikkakoski	
HW-327	BAe Hawk 51	Ilmavoimat HävLLv 41, Jyväskylä/Tikkakoski	
HW-330	BAe Hawk 51	Ilmavoimat, stored Halli (for upgrade)	
HW-334	BAe Hawk 51	Ilmavoimat HävLLv 41, Jyväskylä/Tikkakoski	
HW-336	BAe Hawk 51	Ilmavoimat, stored Halli (for upgrade)	
HW-338	BAe Hawk 51	Ilmavoimat HävLLv 41, Jyväskylä/Tikkakoski	
HW-339	BAe Hawk 51	Ilmavoimat HävLLv 41, Jyväskylä/Tikkakoski	
HW-340	BAe Hawk 51	Ilmavoimat HävLLv 41, Jyväskylä/Tikkakoski	
HW-341	BAe Hawk 51 [1]	Ilmavoimat HävLLv 41, Jyväskylä/Tikkakoski	
HW-343	BAe Hawk 51 [3]	Ilmavoimat HävLLv 41, Jyväskylä/Tikkakoski	
HW-344	BAe Hawk 51	Ilmavoimat HävLLv 41, Jyväskylä/Tikkakoski	
HW-345	BAe Hawk 51	Ilmavoimat HävLLv 41, Jyväskylä/Tikkakoski	
HW-348	BAe Hawk 51	Ilmavoimat HävLLv 41, Jyväskylä/Tikkakoski	
HW-349	BAe Hawk 51	Ilmavoimat HävLLv 41, Jyväskylä/Tikkakoski	
HW-350	BAe Hawk 51 [4]	Ilmavoimat HävLLv 41, Jyväskylä/Tikkakoski	
HW-351	BAe Hawk 51A	Ilmavoimat HävLLv 41, Jyväskylä/Tikkakoski	
HW-352	BAe Hawk 51A [7]	Ilmavoimat HävLLv 41, Jyväskylä/Tikkakoski	
HW-353	BAe Hawk 51A	Ilmavoimat HävLLv 41, Jyväskylä/Tikkakoski	
HW-354	BAe Hawk 51A	Ilmavoimat HävLLv 41, Jyväskylä/Tikkakoski	
HW-355	BAe Hawk 51A	Ilmavoimat HävLLv 41, Jyväskylä/Tikkakoski	
HW-356	BAe Hawk 51A	Ilmavoimat HävLLv 41, Jyväskylä/Tikkakoski	
HW-357	BAe Hawk 51A [2]	Ilmavoimat HävLLv 41, Jyväskylä/Tikkakoski	
HW-360	BAe Hawk 66	Ilmavoimat HävLLv 41, Jyväskylä/Tikkakoski	
HW-361	BAe Hawk 66	Ilmavoimat HävLLv 41, Jyväskylä/Tikkakoski	
HW-362	BAe Hawk 66	Ilmavoimat HävLLv 41, Jyväskylä/Tikkakoski	
HW-363	BAe Hawk 66	Ilmavoimat HävLLv 41, Jyväskylä/Tikkakoski	
HW-364	BAe Hawk 66	Ilmavoimat HävLLv 41, Jyväskylä/Tikkakoski	
HW-365	BAe Hawk 66	Ilmavoimat HävLLv 41, Jyväskylä/Tikkakoski	
HW-366	BAe Hawk 66	Ilmavoimat HävLLv 41, Jyväskylä/Tikkakoski	
HW-367	BAe Hawk 66	Ilmavoimat HävLLv 41, Jyväskylä/Tikkakoski	
HW-368	BAe Hawk 66	Ilmavoimat HävLLv 41, Jyväskylä/Tikkakoski	
HW-370	BAe Hawk 66	Ilmavoimat HävLLv 41, Jyväskylä/Tikkakoski	
HW-371	BAe Hawk 66	Ilmavoimat HävLLv 41, Jyväskylä/Tikkakoski	
HW-373	BAe Hawk 66	Ilmavoimat HävLLv 41, Jyväskylä/Tikkakoski	
HW-374	BAe Hawk 66	Ilmavoimat HävLLv 41, Jyväskylä/Tikkakoski	
HW-375	BAe Hawk 66	Ilmavoimat HävLLv 41, Jyväskylä/Tikkakoski	
HW-376	BAe Hawk 66	Ilmavoimat HävLLv 41, Jyväskylä/Tikkakoski	
HW-377	BAe Hawk 66	Ilmavoimat HävLLv 41, Jyväskylä/Tikkakoski	
LJ-1	Gates Learjet 35A	Ilmavoimat TukiLLv (Det.), Kuopio/Rissala	
LJ-2	Gates Learjet 35A	Ilmavoimat TukiLLv, Tampere/Pirkkala	
LJ-3	Gates Learjet 35A	Ilmavoimat TukiLLv, Tampere/Pirkkala	
NH-202	NH Industries NH.90-TTH	Maavoimat 1.HK/HekoP, Utti	
NH-203	NH Industries NH.90-TTH	Maavoimat 1.HK/HekoP, Utti	
NH-204	NH Industries NH.90-TTH	Maavoimat 1.HK/HekoP, Utti	
NH-205	NH Industries NH.90-TTH	Maavoimat 1.HK/HekoP, Utti	
NH-206	NH Industries NH.90-TTH	Maavoimat 1.HK/HekoP, Utti	
NH-207	NH Industries NH.90-TTH	Maavoimat 1.HK/HekoP, Utti	
NH-208	NH Industries NH.90-TTH	Maavoimat 1.HK/HekoP, Utti	
NH-209	NH Industries NH.90-TTH	Maavoimat 1.HK/HekoP, Utti	
NH-210	NH Industries NH.90-TTH	Maavoimat 1.HK/HekoP, Utti	
NH-211	NH Industries NH.90-TTH	Maavoimat 1.HK/HekoP, Utti	
NH-212	NH Industries NH.90-TTH	Maavoimat 1.HK/HekoP, Utti	
NH-213	NH Industries NH.90-TTH	Maavoimat 1.HK/HekoP, Utti	

Notes	Serial	Type (code/other identity)	Owner/operator, location or fate
	NH-214	NH Industries NH.90-TTH	Maavoimat 1.HK/HekoP, Utti
	NH-215	NH Industries NH.90-TTH	Maavoimat 1.HK/HekoP, Utti
	NH-216	NH Industries NH.90-TTH	Maavoimat 1.HK/HekoP, Utti
	NH-217	NH Industries NH.90-TTH	Maavoimat 1.HK/HekoP, Utti
	NH-218	NH Industries NH.90-TTH	Maavoimat 1.HK/HekoP, Utti
	NH-219	NH Industries NH.90-TTH	Maavoimat 1.HK/HekoP, Utti
	NH-220	NH Industries NH.90-TTH	Maavoimat 1.HK/HekoP, Utti
	NH-221	NH Industries NH.90-TTH	Maavoimat 1.HK/HekoP, Utti
	PI-01	Pilatus PC-12/47E	Ilmavoimat TukiLLv, Tampere/Pirkkala
	PI-02	Pilatus PC-12/47E	Ilmavoimat TukiLLv, Tampere/Pirkkala
	PI-03	Pilatus PC-12/47E	Ilmavoimat TukiLLv, Tampere/Pirkkala
	PI-04	Pilatus PC-12/47E	Ilmavoimat TukiLLv, Tampere/Pirkkala
	PI-05	Pilatus PC-12/47E	Ilmavoimat TukiLLv, Tampere/Pirkkala
	PI-06	Pilatus PC-12/47E	Ilmavoimat TukiLLv, Tampere/Pirkkala

FRANCE

NB: Due to the way in which French military aircraft serials are issued, this section is sorted by type

Armée de l'Air (AA)

Notes	Serial	Type (code/other identity)	Owner/operator, location or fate
	418	Airbus A.310-304 (F-RADC)	AA ET 03.060 *Esterel*, Paris/Charles de Gaulle
	421	Airbus A.310-304 (F-RADA)	*Withdrawn from use, September 2019*
	422	Airbus A.310-304 (F-RADB)	AA ET 03.060 *Esterel*, Paris/Charles de Gaulle
	240	Airbus A.330-223 (F-RARF)	AA ET 00.060, Evreux
	041	Airbus A.330-243 MRTT Phénix (MRTT041) [F-UJCG]	AA ERVTS 01.031 *Bretagne*, Istres
	042	Airbus A.330-243 MRTT Phénix (MRTT042) [F-UJCH]	AA ERVTS 01.031 *Bretagne*, Istres
	043	Airbus A.330-243 MRTT Phénix (MRTT043) [F-UJCI]	AA ERVTS 01.031 *Bretagne*, Istres (on order)
	...	Airbus A.330-243 MRTT Phénix [F-UJCJ]	AA ERVTS 01.031 *Bretagne*, Istres (on order)
	...	Airbus A.330-243 MRTT Phénix [F-UJCK]	AA ERVTS 01.031 *Bretagne*, Istres (on order)
	...	Airbus A.330-243 MRTT Phénix [F-UJCL]	AA ERVTS 01.031 *Bretagne*, Istres (on order)
	...	Airbus A.330-243 MRTT Phénix	AA ERVTS 01.031 *Bretagne*, Istres (on order)
	...	Airbus A.330-243 MRTT Phénix	AA ERVTS 01.031 *Bretagne*, Istres (on order)
	...	Airbus A.330-243 MRTT Phénix	AA ERVTS 01.031 *Bretagne*, Istres (on order)
	...	Airbus A.330-243 MRTT Phénix	AA ERVTS 01.031 *Bretagne*, Istres (on order)
	...	Airbus A.330-243 MRTT Phénix	AA ERVTS 01.031 *Bretagne*, Istres (on order)
	...	Airbus A.330-243 MRTT Phénix	AA ERVTS 01.031 *Bretagne*, Istres (on order)
	...	Airbus A.330-243 MRTT Phénix	AA ERVTS 01.031 *Bretagne*, Istres (on order)
	...	Airbus A.330-243 MRTT Phénix	AA ERVTS 01.031 *Bretagne*, Istres (on order)
	075	Airbus A.340-212 (F-RAJA)	AA ET 03.060 *Esterel*, Paris/Charles de Gaulle
	081	Airbus A.340-212 (F-RAJB)	AA ET 03.060 *Esterel*, Paris/Charles de Gaulle
	0007	Airbus Military A.400M [F-RBAA] $	AA ET 01.061 *Touraine*, Orléans
	0008	Airbus Military A.400M [F-RBAB]	AA ET 01.061 *Touraine*, Orléans
	0010	Airbus Military A.400M [F-RBAC]	AA ET 01.061 *Touraine*, Orléans
	0011	Airbus Military A.400M [F-RBAD]	AA ET 01.061 *Touraine*, Orléans
	0012	Airbus Military A.400M [F-RBAE]	AA ET 01.061 *Touraine*, Orléans
	0014	Airbus Military A.400M [F-RBAF]	AA ET 01.061 *Touraine*, Orléans
	0019	Airbus Military A.400M [F-RBAG]	AA ET 01.061 *Touraine*, Orléans
	0031	Airbus Military A.400M [F-RBAH]	AA ET 01.061 *Touraine*, Orléans
	0033	Airbus Military A.400M [F-RBAI]	AA ET 01.061 *Touraine*, Orléans
	0037	Airbus Military A.400M [F-RBAJ]	AA ET 01.061 *Touraine*, Orléans
	0053	Airbus Military A.400M [F-RBAK]	AA ET 01.061 *Touraine*, Orléans
	0062	Airbus Military A.400M [F-RBAL] $	AA ET 01.061 *Touraine*, Orléans
	0065	Airbus Military A.400M [F-RBAM]	AA ET 01.061 *Touraine*, Orléans
	0073	Airbus Military A.400M [F-RBAN]	AA ET 01.061 *Touraine*, Orléans
	0089	Airbus Military A.400M [F-RBAO]	AA ET 01.061 *Touraine*, Orléans
	0095	Airbus Military A.400M [F-RBAP]	AA ET 01.061 *Touraine*, Orléans
	0102	Airbus Military A.400M [F-RBAQ]	Airbus Defence & Space, Getafe
	0117	Airbus Military A.400M [F-RBAR]	AA (on order)
	0124	Airbus Military A.400M [F-RBAS]	AA (on order)
	0125	Airbus Military A.400M [F-RBAT]	AA (on order)
	0132	Airbus Military A.400M [F-RBAU]	AA (on order)
	0137	Airbus Military A.400M [F-RBAV]	AA (on order)
	0146	Airbus Military A.400M [F-RBAW]	AA (on order)

Serial	Type (code/other identity)	Owner/operator, location or fate	Notes
0153	Airbus Military A.400M [F-RBAX]	AA (on order)	
0154	Airbus Military A.400M [F-RBAY]	AA (on order)	
045	Airtech CN-235M-200 [64-IB]	AA ET 01.062 *Vercours*, Evreux	
065	Airtech CN-235M-200 [52-IC]	AA ET 00.052 *La Tontouta*, Nouméa	
066	Airtech CN-235M-200 [52-ID]	AA ET 00.052 *La Tontouta*, Nouméa	
071	Airtech CN-235M-200 [62-IE]	AA ET 01.062 *Vercours*, Evreux	
072	Airtech CN-235M-200 [62-IF]	AA ET 01.062 *Vercours*, Evreux	
105	Airtech CN-235M-200 [52-IG]	AA ET 00.052 *La Tontouta*, Nouméa	
107	Airtech CN-235M-200 [52-IH]	AA ET 00.052 *La Tontouta*, Nouméa	
111	Airtech CN-235M-200 [64-II]	AA ET 01.062 *Vercours*, Evreux	
114	Airtech CN-235M-200 [62-IJ]	AA ET 01.062 *Vercours*, Evreux	
123	Airtech CN-235M-200 [62-IM]	AA ET 01.062 *Vercours*, Evreux	
128	Airtech CN-235M-200 [64-IK]	AA ET 01.062 *Vercours*, Evreux	
129	Airtech CN-235M-200 [62-IL]	AA ET 01.062 *Vercours*, Evreux	
137	Airtech CN-235M-200 [62-IN]	AA ET 01.062 *Vercours*, Evreux	
141	Airtech CN-235M-200 [62-IO]	AA ET 00.058 *Antilles*, Fort-de-France	
152	Airtech CN-235M-200 [62-IP]	AA ET 01.062 *Vercours*, Evreux	
156	Airtech CN-235M-200 [62-IQ]	AA ET 01.062 *Vercours*, Evreux	
158	Airtech CN-235M-200 [62-IR]	AA ET 01.062 *Vercours*, Evreux	
160	Airtech CN-235M-200 [64-IS]	AA ET 01.062 *Vercours*, Evreux	
165	Airtech CN-235M-200 [62-IT]	AA ET 01.062 *Vercours*, Evreux	
193	Airtech CN-235M-300 [64-HA]	AA ET 03.062 *Ventoux*, Evreux	
194	Airtech CN-235M-300 [62-HB]	AA EE 03.062 *Ventoux*, Evreux	
195	Airtech CN-235M-300 [64-HC]	AA ET 03.062 *Ventoux*, Evreux	
196	Airtech CN-235M-300 [62-HD]	AA ET 03.062 *Ventoux*, Evreux	
197	Airtech CN-235M-300 [62-HE]	AA ET 03.062 *Ventoux*, Evreux	
198	Airtech CN-235M-300 [62-HF]	AA ET 03.062 *Ventoux*, Evreux	
199	Airtech CN-235M-300 [62-HG]	AA ET 03.062 *Ventoux*, Evreux	
200	Airtech CN-235M-300 [62-HH]	AA ET 03.062 *Ventoux*, Evreux	
1018	Beechcraft King Air 350 (F-WTAO) [F-ZACG]	AA DGA EV, Istres	
1030	Beechcraft King Air 350 (F-WTAP) [F-ZACH]	AA DGA EV, Istres	
470	Boeing C-135FR Stratotanker [31-CA]	AA ERV 04.031 *Sologne*, Istres	
471	Boeing C-135FR Stratotanker [31-CB]	AA ERV 04.031 *Sologne*, Istres	
472	Boeing C-135FR Stratotanker [31-CC]	AA ERV 04.031 *Sologne*, Istres	
474	Boeing C-135FR Stratotanker [31-CE]	AA ERV 04.031 *Sologne*, Istres	
475	Boeing C-135FR Stratotanker [31-CF]	AA ERV 04.031 *Sologne*, Istres	
497	Boeing KC-135RG Stratotanker [31-CM] $	AA ERV 04.031 *Sologne*, Istres	
525	Boeing KC-135RG Stratotanker [31-CN]	AA ERV 04.031 *Sologne*, Istres	
574	Boeing KC-135RG Stratotanker [31-CP]	AA ERV 04.031 *Sologne*, Istres	
735	Boeing C-135FR Stratotanker [31-CG]	AA ERV 04.031 *Sologne*, Istres	
736	Boeing C-135FR Stratotanker [31-CH]	AA ERV 04.031 *Sologne*, Istres	
737	Boeing C-135FR Stratotanker [31-CI]	AA ERV 04.031 *Sologne*, Istres	
738	Boeing C-135FR Stratotanker [31-CJ]	AA ERV 04.031 *Sologne*, Istres	
739	Boeing C-135FR Stratotanker [31-CK]	AA ERV 04.031 *Sologne*, Istres	
740	Boeing C-135FR Stratotanker [31-CL]	AA ERV 04.031 *Sologne*, Istres	
201	Boeing E-3F Sentry [36-CA]	AA EDCA 00.036, Avord	
202	Boeing E-3F Sentry [36-CB]	AA EDCA 00.036, Avord	
203	Boeing E-3F Sentry [36-CC]	AA EDCA 00.036, Avord	
204	Boeing E-3F Sentry [36-CD] $	AA EDCA 00.036, Avord	
377	CASA 212-300 Aviocar [F-ZAEA]	AA DGA EV, Cazaux & Istres	
378	CASA 212-300 Aviocar [MP]	AA DGA EV, Cazaux & Istres	
386	CASA 212-300 Aviocar [MQ]	AA DGA EV, Cazaux & Istres	
820	Cessna 310Q [CL]	*Withdrawn from use*	
981	Cessna 310Q [BF]	*Withdrawn from use*	
E4	D-BD Alpha Jet E	AA DGA EV, Cazaux & Istres	
E7	D-BD Alpha Jet E [705-TU]	AA EAC 00.314, Tours	
E8	D-BD Alpha Jet E	AA DGA EV, Cazaux & Istres	
E11	D-BD Alpha Jet E [8-UB]	AA EE 03.008 *Côte d'Or*, Cazaux	
E12	D-BD Alpha Jet E	AA DGA EV, Cazaux & Istres	
E13	D-BD Alpha Jet E [8-MM]	AA, stored Châteaudun	
E17	D-BD Alpha Jet E [705-AA]	AA, stored Châteaudun	
E18	D-BD Alpha Jet E	*Preserved at Cazaux, 2019*	

Notes	Serial	Type (code/other identity)	Owner/operator, location or fate
	E20	D-BD Alpha Jet E [F-TEMS,4]	AA *Patrouille de France*, Salon de Provence
	E22	D-BD Alpha Jet E [8-LS] $	AA EE 03.008 *Côte d'Or*, Cazaux
	E25	D-BD Alpha Jet E [8-TJ]	AA EE 03.008 *Côte d'Or*, Cazaux
	E26	D-BD Alpha Jet E [705-ND] $	AA EAC 00.314, Tours
	E28	D-BD Alpha Jet E [705-AB]	AA EAC 00.314, Tours
	E29	D-BD Alpha Jet E [102-NB]	AA EE 03.008 *Côte d'Or*, Cazaux
	E30	D-BD Alpha Jet E [705-MD]	AA, stored Châteaudun
	E31	D-BD Alpha Jet E [705-RK]	AA EAC 00.314, Tours
	E32	D-BD Alpha Jet E [102-FI]	AA EE 03.008 *Côte d'Or*, Cazaux
	E33	D-BD Alpha Jet E [705-FJ] $	AA EAC 00.314, Tours
	E35	D-BD Alpha Jet E	AA
	E37	D-BD Alpha Jet E [705-NL]	AA EAC 00.314, Tours
	E38	D-BD Alpha Jet E [8-LH]	AA ETO 01.008 *Saintonge*, Cazaux
	E42	D-BD Alpha Jet E [705-TA] $	AA EAC 00.314, Tours
	E44	D-BD Alpha Jet E [F-UHRE,1]	AA *Patrouille de France*, Salon de Provence
	E45	D-BD Alpha Jet E [F-TETF]	AA *Patrouille de France*, Salon de Provence
	E46	D-BD Alpha Jet E [F-UHRF,7]	AA *Patrouille de France*, Salon de Provence
	E48	D-BD Alpha Jet E [8-MH]	AA EE 03.008 *Côte d'Or*, Cazaux
	E51	D-BD Alpha Jet E [705-AD]	AA EAC 00.314, Tours
	E53	D-BD Alpha Jet E [102-LI]	AA EE 03.008 *Côte d'Or*, Cazaux
	E58	D-BD Alpha Jet E [705-TK]	AA, stored Châteaudun
	E60	D-BD Alpha Jet E	AA EPNER, Istres
	E67	D-BD Alpha Jet E [705-TB]	AA EAC 00.314, Tours
	E68	D-BD Alpha Jet E [F-TEMO,0]	AA *Patrouille de France*, Salon de Provence
	E72	D-BD Alpha Jet E [705-LA]	AA, stored Châteaudun
	E73	D-BD Alpha Jet E [F-TENE]	AA *Patrouille de France*, Salon de Provence
	E74	D-BD Alpha Jet E	AA
	E75	D-BD Alpha Jet E [8-AE]	AA EE 03.008 *Côte d'Or*, Cazaux
	E76	D-BD Alpha Jet E [102-RJ]	AA EE 03.008 *Côte d'Or*, Cazaux
	E79	D-BD Alpha Jet E [8-NA]	AA EE 03.008 *Côte d'Or*, Cazaux
	E80	D-BD Alpha Jet E	AA DGA EV, Cazaux & Istres
	E81	D-BD Alpha Jet E [8-FO]	AA ETO 01.008 *Saintonge*, Cazaux
	E82	D-BD Alpha Jet E [8-LW]	AA ETO 01.008 *Saintonge*, Cazaux
	E83	D-BD Alpha Jet E [705-TZ]	AA EAC 00.314, Tours
	E85	D-BD Alpha Jet E [F-UGFF]	AA *Patrouille de France*, Salon de Provence
	E86	D-BD Alpha Jet E [102-FB]	*Withdrawn from use*
	E87	D-BD Alpha Jet E [F-TELC,9]	AA *Patrouille de France*, Salon de Provence
	E88	D-BD Alpha Jet E [F-TELL]	AA, stored Châteaudun
	E89	D-BD Alpha Jet E [120-LX]	*Withdrawn from use at Rochefort, 2019*
	E90	D-BD Alpha Jet E [8-TH]	AA ETO 01.008 *Saintonge*, Cazaux
	E93	D-BD Alpha Jet E [8-TX]	AA ETO 01.008 *Saintonge*, Cazaux
	E94	D-BD Alpha Jet E [705-RH]	AA EAC 00.314, Tours
	E95	D-BD Alpha Jet E [F-TERQ]	AA, stored Châteaudun
	E97	D-BD Alpha Jet E [102-MB]	AA, stored Châteaudun
	E98	D-BD Alpha Jet E [F-TEMF]	AA *Patrouille de France*, Salon de Provence
	E99	D-BD Alpha Jet E [120-AH]	*Withdrawn from use at Rochefort, 2019*
	E100	D-BD Alpha Jet E $	AA EPNER, Istres
	E101	D-BD Alpha Jet E [120-TT]	AA ETO 01.008 *Saintonge*, Cazaux
	E102	D-BD Alpha Jet E [120-LM]	AA, stored Châteaudun
	E104	D-BD Alpha Jet E [8-TG]	AA ETO 01.008 *Saintonge*, Cazaux
	E105	D-BD Alpha Jet E [8-FM]	AA EE 03.008 *Côte d'Or*, Cazaux
	E107	D-BD Alpha Jet E [705-UD]	AA EAC 00.314, Tours
	E108	D-BD Alpha Jet E [8-AF]	AA ETO 01.008 *Saintonge*, Cazaux
	E109	D-BD Alpha Jet E [8-AG]	AA ETO 01.008 *Saintonge*, Cazaux
	E110	D-BD Alpha Jet E [705-AH]	AA EAC 00.314, Tours
	E112	D-BD Alpha Jet E [705-AO]	AA EAC 00.314, Tours
	E113	D-BD Alpha Jet E [F-TETD,8]	AA *Patrouille de France*, Salon de Provence
	E114	D-BD Alpha Jet E [705-RR] $	AA EAC 00.314, Tours
	E115	D-BD Alpha Jet E [705-MR]	AA EAC 00.314, Tours
	E116	D-BD Alpha Jet E [8-FN]	AA ETO 01.008 *Saintonge*, Cazaux
	E117	D-BD Alpha Jet E [705-RI]	AA EAC 00.314, Tours
	E118	D-BD Alpha Jet E [8-LN]	AA ETO 01.008 *Saintonge*, Cazaux

Serial	Type (code/other identity)	Owner/operator, location or fate	Notes
E119	D-BD Alpha Jet E [F-UGFE]	AA *Patrouille de France*, Salon de Provence	
E120	D-BD Alpha Jet E [705-LG]	AA EAC 00.314, Tours	
E123	D-BD Alpha Jet E [8-RM]	AA EE 03.008 *Côte d'Or*, Cazaux	
E124	D-BD Alpha Jet E [8-RN]	AA ETO 01.008 *Saintonge*, Cazaux	
E125	D-BD Alpha Jet E [705-LK]	AA EAC 00.314, Tours	
E127	D-BD Alpha Jet E [F-UGFK,5]	AA *Patrouille de France*, Salon de Provence	
E128	D-BD Alpha Jet E [705-TM]	AA EAC 00.314, Tours	
E129	D-BD Alpha Jet E [F-TELP,6]	AA *Patrouille de France*, Salon de Provence	
E130	D-BD Alpha Jet E [8-RP]	AA EE 03.008 *Côte d'Or*, Cazaux	
E131	D-BD Alpha Jet E [8-RO]	AA ETO 01.008 *Saintonge*, Cazaux	
E134	D-BD Alpha Jet E [705-RM]	AA EAC 00.314, Tours	
E135	D-BD Alpha Jet E [8-RX]	AA EE 03.008 *Côte d'Or*, Cazaux	
E136	D-BD Alpha Jet E [8-RP]	AA, stored Châteaudun	
E137	D-BD Alpha Jet E [705-LJ]	AA EAC 00.314, Tours	
E138	D-BD Alpha Jet E [8-RQ]	AA EE 03.008 *Côte d'Or*, Cazaux	
E139	D-BD Alpha Jet E [F-UGFC,3]	AA *Patrouille de France*, Salon de Provence	
E140	D-BD Alpha Jet E [102-FA]	AA, stored Châteaudun	
E141	D-BD Alpha Jet E [8-NF]	AA EE 03.008 *Côte d'Or*, Cazaux	
E142	D-BD Alpha Jet E [8-LO]	AA ETO 01.008 *Saintonge*, Cazaux	
E143	D-BD Alpha Jet E	AA	
E144	D-BD Alpha Jet E [8-AK]	AA ETO 01.008 *Saintonge*, Cazaux	
E145	D-BD Alpha Jet E	*Preserved at Lyon/Corbas*	
E146	D-BD Alpha Jet E [F-UHRR,2]	*Crashed 25 July 2019, Perpignan*	
E147	D-BD Alpha Jet E [8-LT]	AA ETO 01.008 *Saintonge*, Cazaux	
E148	D-BD Alpha Jet E [705-LU]	AA EAC 00.314, Tours	
E149	D-BD Alpha Jet E [8-RS]	AA EE 03.008 *Côte d'Or*, Cazaux	
E151	D-BD Alpha Jet E [8-FD]	AA EE 03.008 *Côte d'Or*, Cazaux	
E152	D-BD Alpha Jet E [F-UHRT]	AA *Patrouille de France*, Salon de Provence	
E153	D-BD Alpha Jet E [705-RU]	AA EAC 00.314, Tours	
E154	D-BD Alpha Jet E [8-AL]	AA ETO 01.008 *Saintonge*, Cazaux	
E156	D-BD Alpha Jet E [30-TI]	AA, stored Châteaudun	
E157	D-BD Alpha Jet E [8-UC]	AA ETO 01.008 *Saintonge*, Cazaux	
E158	D-BD Alpha Jet E [705-RF]	AA EAC 00.314, Tours	
E160	D-BD Alpha Jet E [8-UH]	AA ETO 01.008 *Saintonge*, Cazaux	
E162	D-BD Alpha Jet E [8-RJ]	AA EE 03.008 *Côte d'Or*, Cazaux	
E163	D-BD Alpha Jet E [705-RB]	AA EAC 00.314, Tours	
E164	D-BD Alpha Jet E [120-RV]	AA ETO 01.008 *Saintonge*, Cazaux	
E165	D-BD Alpha Jet E [8-RE]	AA, stored Châteaudun	
E166	D-BD Alpha Jet E [705-RW]	AA EAC 00.314, Tours	
E167	D-BD Alpha Jet E [705-MN]	*Withdrawn from use at Rochefort, 2019*	
E168	D-BD Alpha Jet E [8-FP]	AA EE 03.008 *Côte d'Or*, Cazaux	
E169	D-BD Alpha Jet E [30-RX]	AA, stored Châteaudun	
E170	D-BD Alpha Jet E [705-RY]	AA EAC 00.314, Tours	
E171	D-BD Alpha Jet E [705-RZ]	AA EAC 00.314, Tours	
E173	D-BD Alpha Jet E [705-MA]	AA EAC 00.314, Tours	
E176	D-BD Alpha Jet E [8-MB]	AA ETO 01.008 *Saintonge*, Cazaux	
68	Dassault Falcon 7X (F-RAFA)	AA ET 00.060, Villacoublay	
86	Dassault Falcon 7X (F-RAFB)	AA ET 00.060, Villacoublay	
79	Dassault Falcon 20C [CT]	AA DGA EV, Cazaux & Istres	
104	Dassault Falcon 20C [CW]	AA DGA EV, Cazaux & Istres	
138	Dassault Falcon 20C [CR]	AA, stored Cazaux	
252	Dassault Falcon 20E [CA]	*Withdrawn from use*	
288	Dassault Falcon 20E [CV]	AA DGA EV, Cazaux & Istres	
342	Dassault Falcon 20F [CU]	AA DGA EV, Cazaux & Istres	
375	Dassault Falcon 20F [CZ]	AA DGA EV, Cazaux & Istres	
02	Dassault Falcon 900 (F-RAFP)	AA ET 00.060, Villacoublay	
004	Dassault Falcon 900 (F-RAFQ)	AA ET 00.060, Villacoublay	
231	Dassault Falcon 2000LX (F-RAFC)	AA ET 00.060, Villacoublay	
237	Dassault Falcon 2000LX (F-RAFD)	AA ET 00.060, Villacoublay	
501	Dassault Mirage 2000B (BX1)	AA DGA EV, Cazaux & Istres	
523	Dassault Mirage 2000B [115-KJ]	AA EC 02.005 *Ile de France*, Orange	
524	Dassault Mirage 2000B [115-OA]	AA EC 02.005 *Ile de France*, Orange	

Notes	Serial	Type (code/other identity)	Owner/operator, location or fate
	525	Dassault Mirage 2000B [115-AM]	AA EC 02.005 *Ile de France*, Orange
	527	Dassault Mirage 2000B [115-OR]	AA EC 02.005 *Ile de France*, Orange
	528	Dassault Mirage 2000B [115-KS]	AA EC 02.005 *Ile de France*, Orange
	529	Dassault Mirage 2000B [115-OC]	AA EC 02.005 *Ile de France*, Orange
	530	Dassault Mirage 2000B [115-OL]	AA EC 02.005 *Ile de France*, Orange
	01	Dassault Mirage 2000-5F	AA DGA EV, Istres
	2	Dassault Mirage 2000C	AA, stored Châteaudun
	38	Dassault Mirage 2000-5F	AA GC 01.002 *Cigognes*, Luxeuil
	40	Dassault Mirage 2000-5F [2-EX]	AA GC 01.002 *Cigognes*, Luxeuil
	41	Dassault Mirage 2000-5F [2-FZ]	AA GC 01.002 *Cigognes*, Luxeuil
	42	Dassault Mirage 2000-5F [2-EY]	AA GC 01.002 *Cigognes*, Luxeuil
	43	Dassault Mirage 2000-5F $	AA GC 01.002 *Cigognes*, Luxeuil
	44	Dassault Mirage 2000-5F [2-EQ]	AA GC 01.002 *Cigognes*, Luxeuil
	45	Dassault Mirage 2000-5F [2-EF]	AA GC 01.002 *Cigognes*, Luxeuil
	46	Dassault Mirage 2000-5F [2-EN]	AA GC 01.002 *Cigognes*, Luxeuil
	47	Dassault Mirage 2000-5F [2-EP]	AA GC 01.002 *Cigognes*, Luxeuil
	48	Dassault Mirage 2000-5F [2-EW]	AA GC 01.002 *Cigognes*, Luxeuil
	49	Dassault Mirage 2000-5F [2-EA] $	AA GC 01.002 *Cigognes*, Luxeuil
	51	Dassault Mirage 2000-5F	AA DGA EV, Istres
	52	Dassault Mirage 2000-5F [2-EH]	AA GC 01.002 *Cigognes*, Luxeuil
	54	Dassault Mirage 2000-5F [2-EZ]	AA GC 01.002 *Cigognes*, Luxeuil
	55	Dassault Mirage 2000-5F [2-EU]	AA GC 01.002 *Cigognes*, Luxeuil
	56	Dassault Mirage 2000-5F [2-EG]	AA GC 01.002 *Cigognes*, Luxeuil
	57	Dassault Mirage 2000-5F [2-ET]	AA GC 01.002 *Cigognes*, Luxeuil
	58	Dassault Mirage 2000-5F [2-EL]	AA GC 01.002 *Cigognes*, Luxeuil
	59	Dassault Mirage 2000-5F [2-EV]	AA GC 01.002 *Cigognes*, Luxeuil
	61	Dassault Mirage 2000-5F [2-ME]	AA GC 01.002 *Cigognes*, Luxeuil
	62	Dassault Mirage 2000-5F [2-ED]	AA GC 01.002 *Cigognes*, Luxeuil
	63	Dassault Mirage 2000-5F [2-EM]	AA GC 01.002 *Cigognes*, Luxeuil
	64	Dassault Mirage 2000C	AA DGA EV, Istres
	65	Dassault Mirage 2000-5F [2-MG]	AA GC 01.002 *Cigognes*, Luxeuil
	66	Dassault Mirage 2000-5F [2-EO]	AA GC 01.002 *Cigognes*, Luxeuil
	67	Dassault Mirage 2000-5F [2-MH]	AA GC 01.002 *Cigognes*, Luxeuil
	71	Dassault Mirage 2000-5F	AA GC 01.002 *Cigognes*, Luxeuil
	74	Dassault Mirage 2000-5F [2-MK]	AA GC 01.002 *Cigognes*, Luxeuil
	77	Dassault Mirage 2000-5F [2-AX]	AA GC 01.002 *Cigognes*, Luxeuil
	78	Dassault Mirage 2000-5F [2-EC]	AA GC 01.002 *Cigognes*, Luxeuil
	82	Dassault Mirage 2000C [115-YL]	AA EC 02.005 *Ile de France*, Orange
	83	Dassault Mirage 2000C [115-YC]	AA EC 02.005 *Ile de France*, Orange
	85	Dassault Mirage 2000C [115-LK]	*Withdrawn from use at Rochefort, 2019*
	88	Dassault Mirage 2000C [115-KV]	*Withdrawn from use, 2019*
	93	Dassault Mirage 2000C [115-YA]	AA EC 02.005 *Ile de France*, Orange
	94	Dassault Mirage 2000C [115-KB]	AA, stored Châteaudun
	96	Dassault Mirage 2000C [115-KI]	AA EC 02.005 *Ile de France*, Orange
	99	Dassault Mirage 2000C [115-YB]	AA EC 02.005 *Ile de France*, Orange
	100	Dassault Mirage 2000C [115-YF]	AA EC 02.005 *Ile de France*, Orange
	101	Dassault Mirage 2000C [115-KE] $	AA EC 02.005 *Ile de France*, Orange
	102	Dassault Mirage 2000C [115-KR]	AA EC 02.005 *Ile de France*, Orange
	104	Dassault Mirage 2000C [115-KG]	*Preserved at Mont-de-Marsan, 2019*
	105	Dassault Mirage 2000C [115-LJ]	AA EC 02.005 *Ile de France*, Orange
	106	Dassault Mirage 2000C [115-KL]	AA EC 02.005 *Ile de France*, Orange
	107	Dassault Mirage 2000C [115-YD]	AA EC 02.005 *Ile de France*, Orange
	108	Dassault Mirage 2000C [115-LC]	AA EC 02.005 *Ile de France*, Orange
	109	Dassault Mirage 2000C [115-YH]	AA EC 02.005 *Ile de France*, Orange
	111	Dassault Mirage 2000C [115-KF]	AA EC 02.005 *Ile de France*, Orange
	113	Dassault Mirage 2000C [115-YO]	AA EC 02.005 *Ile de France*, Orange
	115	Dassault Mirage 2000C [115-YM]	AA, stored Châteaudun
	117	Dassault Mirage 2000C [115-LD]	AA, stored Châteaudun
	118	Dassault Mirage 2000C [115-YG]	AA EC 02.005 *Ile de France*, Orange
	120	Dassault Mirage 2000C [115-KC] $	AA EC 02.005 *Ile de France*, Orange
	121	Dassault Mirage 2000C [115-KN]	AA EC 02.005 *Ile de France*, Orange
	122	Dassault Mirage 2000C [115-YE]	AA EC 02.005 *Ile de France*, Orange

Serial	Type (code/other identity)	Owner/operator, location or fate	Notes
123	Dassault Mirage 2000C [115-KD]	AA EC 02.005 *Ile de France*, Orange	
124	Dassault Mirage 2000C [115-YT]	AA EC 02.005 *Ile de France*, Orange	
601	Dassault Mirage 2000D [3-JG]	AA EC 01.003 *Navarre*, Nancy	
602	Dassault Mirage 2000D [3-XJ] $	AA EC 03.003 *Ardennes*, Nancy	
603	Dassault Mirage 2000D [3-XL]	AA EC 03.003 *Ardennes*, Nancy	
604	Dassault Mirage 2000D [3-IP]	AA EC 03.003 *Ardennes*, Nancy	
605	Dassault Mirage 2000D [133-LF]	AA EC 02.003 *Champagne*, Nancy	
606	Dassault Mirage 2000D [3-JC]	AA EC 02.003 *Champagne*, Nancy	
607	Dassault Mirage 2000D	AA DGA EV, Istres	
609	Dassault Mirage 2000D [3-IF]	AA EC 03.003 *Ardennes*, Nancy	
610	Dassault Mirage 2000D [133-XX]	AA EC 03.003 *Ardennes*, Nancy	
611	Dassault Mirage 2000D [3-JP]	AA EC 02.003 *Champagne*, Nancy	
613	Dassault Mirage 2000D [3-MO]	AA EC 03.003 *Ardennes*, Nancy	
614	Dassault Mirage 2000D [3-JU]	AA EC 02.003 *Champagne*, Nancy	
615	Dassault Mirage 2000D [3-JY]	AA EC 02.003 *Champagne*, Nancy	
616	Dassault Mirage 2000D	AA CEAM/ECE 01.030 *Côte d'Argent*, Mont-de-Marsan	
617	Dassault Mirage 2000D [30-IS]	AA CEAM/ECE 01.030 *Côte d'Argent*, Mont-de-Marsan	
618	Dassault Mirage 2000D [3-XC] $	AA EC 03.003 *Ardennes*, Nancy	
620	Dassault Mirage 2000D [3-IU] $	AA EC 01.003 *Navarre*, Nancy	
622	Dassault Mirage 2000D [3-IL]	AA EC 01.003 *Navarre*, Nancy	
623	Dassault Mirage 2000D [133-MP]	AA EC 02.003 *Champagne*, Nancy	
624	Dassault Mirage 2000D [3-IT] $	AA EC 01.003 *Navarre*, Nancy	
625	Dassault Mirage 2000D [30-XG]	AA CEAM/ECE 01.030 *Côte d'Argent*, Mont-de-Marsan	
626	Dassault Mirage 2000D [3-IC]	AA EC 01.003 *Navarre*, Nancy	
627	Dassault Mirage 2000D [30-JO]	AA CEAM/ECE 01.030 *Côte d'Argent*, Mont-de-Marsan	
628	Dassault Mirage 2000D [133-JL]	AA EC 02.003 *Champagne*, Nancy	
629	Dassault Mirage 2000D [3-XO]	AA EC 03.003 *Ardennes*, Nancy	
630	Dassault Mirage 2000D [3-XD] $	AA EC 03.003 *Ardennes*, Nancy	
631	Dassault Mirage 2000D [3-IH]	AA EC 01.003 *Navarre*, Nancy	
632	Dassault Mirage 2000D [133-XE]	AA EC 01.003 *Navarre*, Nancy	
634	Dassault Mirage 2000D [133-JE]	AA EC 01.003 *Navarre*, Nancy	
635	Dassault Mirage 2000D [3-AS]	AA EC 01.003 *Navarre*, Nancy	
636	Dassault Mirage 2000D [133-JV]	AA EC 02.003 *Champagne*, Nancy	
637	Dassault Mirage 2000D [30-XQ]	AA CEAM/ECE 01.030 *Côte d'Argent*, Mont-de-Marsan	
638	Dassault Mirage 2000D [3-IJ]	AA EC 03.003 *Ardennes*, Nancy	
639	Dassault Mirage 2000D [3-JJ]	AA EC 02.003 *Champagne*, Nancy	
640	Dassault Mirage 2000D [3-IN]	AA EC 01.003 *Navarre*, Nancy	
641	Dassault Mirage 2000D [3-JW]	AA EC 02.003 *Champagne*, Nancy	
642	Dassault Mirage 2000D [3-IE]	AA EC 01.003 *Navarre*, Nancy	
643	Dassault Mirage 2000D [3-JD]	AA EC 02.003 *Champagne*, Nancy	
644	Dassault Mirage 2000D $	AA DGA EV, Istres	
645	Dassault Mirage 2000D [3-XP]	AA EC 03.003 *Ardennes*, Nancy	
646	Dassault Mirage 2000D [3-MQ]	AA EC 01.003 *Navarre*, Nancy	
647	Dassault Mirage 2000D [3-IO]	AA EC 01.003 *Navarre*, Nancy	
648	Dassault Mirage 2000D [3-XT] $	AA EC 03.003 *Ardennes*, Nancy	
649	Dassault Mirage 2000D [3-XY]	AA EC 03.003 *Ardennes*, Nancy	
650	Dassault Mirage 2000D [3-IA]	AA EC 01.003 *Navarre*, Nancy	
652	Dassault Mirage 2000D [3-XN] $	AA EC 03.003 *Ardennes*, Nancy	
653	Dassault Mirage 2000D [3-AU]	AA ETD 04.003 *Argonne*, Nancy	
654	Dassault Mirage 2000D [30-ID]	AA CEAM/ECE 01.030 *Côte d'Argent*, Mont-de-Marsan	
655	Dassault Mirage 2000D [3-LH]	AA EC 01.003 *Navarre*, Nancy	
657	Dassault Mirage 2000D [3-JM]	AA EC 03.003 *Ardennes*, Nancy	
658	Dassault Mirage 2000D [3-JN]	AA EC 02.003 *Champagne*, Nancy	
659	Dassault Mirage 2000D [30-XR]	AA CEAM/ECE 01.030 *Côte d'Argent*, Mont-de-Marsan	
660	Dassault Mirage 2000D [3-JF]	AA ETD 04.003 *Argonne*, Nancy	

Notes	Serial	Type (code/other identity)	Owner/operator, location or fate
	661	Dassault Mirage 2000D [133-XI]	AA EC 03.003 *Ardennes*, Nancy
	662	Dassault Mirage 2000D [3-XA]	AA EC 03.003 *Ardennes*, Nancy
	664	Dassault Mirage 2000D [133-IW]	AA EC 01.003 *Navarre*, Nancy
	666	Dassault Mirage 2000D [133-IQ]	AA EC 01.003 *Navarre*, Nancy
	668	Dassault Mirage 2000D [3-IG]	AA EC 03.003 *Ardennes*, Nancy
	669	Dassault Mirage 2000D [133-AL]	AA ETD 04.003 *Argonne*, Nancy
	670	Dassault Mirage 2000D [3-XF]	AA EC 03.003 *Ardennes*, Nancy
	671	Dassault Mirage 2000D [3-XK]	AA EC 03.003 *Ardennes*, Nancy
	672	Dassault Mirage 2000D [3-XV]	AA EC 03.003 *Ardennes*, Nancy
	673	Dassault Mirage 2000D	AA DGA EV, Istres
	674	Dassault Mirage 2000D [30-IR]	AA CEAM/ECE 01.030 *Côte d'Argent*, Mont-de-Marsan
	675	Dassault Mirage 2000D [3-JI] $	AA EC 01.003 *Navarre*, Nancy
	676	Dassault Mirage 2000D $	AA DGA EV, Istres
	677	Dassault Mirage 2000D [3-JT]	AA EC 02.003 *Champagne*, Nancy
	678	Dassault Mirage 2000D [133-JB]	AA EC 02.003 *Champagne*, Nancy
	679	Dassault Mirage 2000D [3-JX]	AA EC 01.003 *Navarre*, Nancy
	680	Dassault Mirage 2000D [3-XM]	AA EC 03.003 *Ardennes*, Nancy
	681	Dassault Mirage 2000D [3-AG]	AA EC 01.003 *Navarre*, Nancy
	682	Dassault Mirage 2000D [3-JR]	AA EC 02.003 *Champagne*, Nancy
	683	Dassault Mirage 2000D [3-IV]	AA EC 01.003 *Navarre*, Nancy
	684	Dassault Mirage 2000D	AA
	685	Dassault Mirage 2000D [3-XZ]	AA EC 01.003 *Navarre*, Nancy
	686	Dassault Mirage 2000D [133-JH]	AA EC 02.003 *Champagne*, Nancy
	D02	Dassault Mirage 2000D	AA DGA EV, Istres
	301	Dassault Mirage 2000N	AA DGA EV, Istres
	334	Dassault Mirage 2000N	AA DGA EV, Istres
	369	Dassault Mirage 2000N [125-AG]	AA DGA EV, Istres
	301	Dassault Rafale B	AA DGA EV, Istres
	302	Dassault Rafale B	AA DGA EV, Istres
	303	Dassault Rafale B [4-EA]	AA ETR 03.004 *Aquitaine*, St Dizier
	304	Dassault Rafale B [30-EB]	AA CEAM/ECE 01.030 *Côte d'Argent*, Mont-de-Marsan
	305	Dassault Rafale B [4-EC]	AA ETR 03.004 *Aquitaine*, St Dizier
	306	Dassault Rafale B [30-IB]	AA EC 03.030 *Lorraine*, St Dizier
	307	Dassault Rafale B [4-IA]	AA ETR 03.004 *Aquitaine*, St Dizier
	308	Dassault Rafale B [4-HA]	AA EC 01.004 *Gascogne*, St Dizier
	309	Dassault Rafale B [4-HB]	AA EC 02.004 *La Fayette*, St Dizier
	310	Dassault Rafale B [4-HC]	AA ETR 03.004 *Aquitaine*, St Dizier
	311	Dassault Rafale B [4-HD]	AA EC 01.004 *Gascogne*, St Dizier
	312	Dassault Rafale B [4-HF]	AA EC 01.004 *Gascogne*, St Dizier
	313	Dassault Rafale B [4-HI]	AA ETR 03.004 *Aquitaine*, St Dizier
	314	Dassault Rafale B [4-HP]	AA EC 01.004 *Gascogne*, St Dizier
	315	Dassault Rafale B [30-HK]	AA CEAM/ECE 01.030 *Côte d'Argent*, Mont-de-Marsan
	317	Dassault Rafale B [30-HO]	AA EC 02.030 *Normandie-Niémen*, Mont-de-Marsan
	318	Dassault Rafale B [4-HM]	AA EC 01.004 *Gascogne*, St Dizier
	319	Dassault Rafale B [4-HN]	AA EC 01.004 *Gascogne*, St Dizier
	320	Dassault Rafale B [4-HV]	AA EC 01.004 *Gascogne*, St Dizier
	321	Dassault Rafale B [4-HQ]	AA EC 03.030 *Lorraine*, St Dizier
	322	Dassault Rafale B [4-HU]	AA EC 01.004 *Gascogne*, St Dizier
	323	Dassault Rafale B [4-HT]	AA EC 01.004 *Gascogne*, St Dizier
	324	Dassault Rafale B [30-HW]	AA EC 03.030 *Lorraine*, St Dizier
	325	Dassault Rafale B [4-HX]	AA ETR 03.004 *Aquitaine*, St Dizier
	326	Dassault Rafale B [113-HY]	AA EC 01.004 *Gascogne*, St Dizier
	327	Dassault Rafale B [4-HZ]	AA EC 01.004 *Gascogne*, St Dizier
	328	Dassault Rafale B [4-IC]	AA EC 01.004 *Gascogne*, St Dizier
	329	Dassault Rafale B [30-ID]	AA CEAM/ECE 01.030 *Côte d'Argent*, Mont-de-Marsan
	330	Dassault Rafale B [4-IE]	AA EC 01.004 *Gascogne*, St Dizier

Serial	Type (code/other identity)	Owner/operator, location or fate	Notes
331	Dassault Rafale B [30-IF]	AA CEAM/ECE 01.030 *Côte d'Argent*, Mont-de-Marsan	
332	Dassault Rafale B [4-IG]	AA EC 01.004 *Gascogne*, St Dizier	
333	Dassault Rafale B [4-IH]	AA ETR 03.004 *Aquitaine*, St Dizier	
334	Dassault Rafale B [4-II]	AA ETR 03.004 *Aquitaine*, St Dizier	
335	Dassault Rafale B [4-IJ]	AA EC 01.004 *Gascogne*, St Dizier	
336	Dassault Rafale B [4-IK] $	AA EC 01.004 *Gascogne*, St Dizier	
337	Dassault Rafale B [4-IL]	AA EC 01.004 *Gascogne*, St Dizier	
338	Dassault Rafale B [4-IO]	AA EC 01.004 *Gascogne*, St Dizier	
339	Dassault Rafale B [4-FF]	AA ETR 03.004 *Aquitaine*, St Dizier	
340	Dassault Rafale B [4-FG]	AA EC 01.004 *Gascogne*, St Dizier	
341	Dassault Rafale B [4-FH]	AA EC 01.004 *Gascogne*, St Dizier	
342	Dassault Rafale B [4-FI]	AA EC 01.004 *Gascogne*, St Dizier	
343	Dassault Rafale B [4-FJ]	AA EC 01.004 *Gascogne*, St Dizier	
344	Dassault Rafale B [4-FK]	AA EC 01.004 *Gascogne*, St Dizier	
345	Dassault Rafale B [4-FL]	AA EC 01.004 *Gascogne*, St Dizier	
346	Dassault Rafale B [4-FM]	AA ETR 03.004 *Aquitaine*, St Dizier	
347	Dassault Rafale B [4-FN]	AA ETR 03.004 *Aquitaine*, St Dizier	
348	Dassault Rafale B [4-FO]	AA ETR 03.004 *Aquitaine*, St Dizier	
349	Dassault Rafale B [4-FP] $	AA ETR 03.004 *Aquitaine*, St Dizier	
350	Dassault Rafale B [113-FQ]	AA ETR 03.004 *Aquitaine*, St Dizier	
351	Dassault Rafale B [4-FR]	AA EC 02.004 *La Fayette*, St Dizier	
352	Dassault Rafale B [4-FS]	AA EC 01.004 *Gascogne*, St Dizier	
353	Dassault Rafale B [4-FT]	AA EC 02.004 *La Fayette*, St Dizier	
354	Dassault Rafale B [4-FU]	AA EC 02.004 *La Fayette*, St Dizier	
355	Dassault Rafale B [4-FV]	AA EC 02.004 *La Fayette*, St Dizier	
356	Dassault Rafale B [4-FW]	AA EC 02.004 *La Fayette*, St Dizier	
357	Dassault Rafale B [4-FX]	AA EC 02.004 *La Fayette*, St Dizier	
358	Dassault Rafale B [4-FY]	AA EC 02.004 *La Fayette*, St Dizier	
101	Dassault Rafale C	AA DGA EV, Istres	
102	Dassault Rafale C [30-EF]	AA CEAM/ECE 01.030 *Côte d'Argent*, Mont-de-Marsan	
103	Dassault Rafale C [30-HR]	AA EC 03.030 *Lorraine*, St Dizier	
104	Dassault Rafale C [30-HH]	AA EC 03.030 *Lorraine*, St Dizier	
105	Dassault Rafale C [30-HE]	AA CEAM/ECE 01.030 *Côte d'Argent*, Mont-de-Marsan	
106	Dassault Rafale C [113-HG]	AA EC 03.030 *Lorraine*, St Dizier	
107	Dassault Rafale C [113-HJ] $	AA EC 03.030 *Lorraine*, St Dizier	
108	Dassault Rafale C [30-HS]	AA EC 03.030 *Lorraine*, St Dizier	
109	Dassault Rafale C [4-IM] $	AA ETR 03.004 *Aquitaine*, St Dizier	
110	Dassault Rafale C [30-IN]	AA EC 03.030 *Lorraine*, St Dizier	
111	Dassault Rafale C [30-IP]	AA EC 02.030 *Normandie-Niémen*, Mont-de-Marsan	
112	Dassault Rafale C [30-IQ]	AA EC 02.030 *Normandie-Niémen*, Mont-de-Marsan	
113	Dassault Rafale C [30-IR]	AA EC 02.030 *Normandie-Niémen*, Mont-de-Marsan	
114	Dassault Rafale C [30-IS]	AA EC 02.030 *Normandie-Niémen*, Mont-de-Marsan	
115	Dassault Rafale C [30-IT]	AA EC 03.030 *Lorraine*, St Dizier	
116	Dassault Rafale C [30-IU]	AA EC 02.030 *Normandie-Niémen*, Mont-de-Marsan	
117	Dassault Rafale C [30-IV]	AA EC 01.007 *Provence*, Al Dhafra, UAE	
118	Dassault Rafale C [30-IW]	AA EC 02.030 *Normandie-Niémen*, Mont-de-Marsan	
119	Dassault Rafale C [30-IX]	AA EC 03.030 *Lorraine*, St Dizier	
120	Dassault Rafale C [30-IY] $	AA EC 03.030 *Lorraine*, St Dizier	
121	Dassault Rafale C [113-IZ]	AA EC 01.004 *Gascogne*, St Dizier	
122	Dassault Rafale C [4-GA]	AA ETR 03.004 *Aquitaine*, St Dizier	
123	Dassault Rafale C [30-GB]	AA EC 02.030 *Normandie-Niémen*, Mont-de-Marsan	

Notes	Serial	Type (code/other identity)	Owner/operator, location or fate
	124	Dassault Rafale C [30-GC]	AA CEAM/ECE 01.030 Côte d'Argent, Mont-de-Marsan
	125	Dassault Rafale C [7-GD]	AA EC 01.007 Provence, Al Dhafra, UAE
	126	Dassault Rafale C [30-GE]	AA EC 02.030 Normandie-Niémen, Mont-de-Marsan
	127	Dassault Rafale C [30-GF]	AA EC 02.030 Normandie-Niémen, Mont-de-Marsan
	128	Dassault Rafale C [30-GG]	AA EC 02.030 Normandie-Niémen, Mont-de-Marsan
	129	Dassault Rafale C [4-GH]	AA ETR 03.004 Aquitaine, St Dizier
	130	Dassault Rafale C [7-GI]	AA EC 01.007 Provence, Al Dhafra, UAE
	131	Dassault Rafale C [4-GJ]	AA ETR 03.004 Aquitaine, St Dizier
	132	Dassault Rafale C [30-GK]	AA EC 02.030 Normandie-Niémen, Mont-de-Marsan
	133	Dassault Rafale C [4-GL] $	AA ETR 03.004 Aquitaine, St Dizier
	134	Dassault Rafale C [30-GM]	AA EC 02.030 Normandie-Niémen, Mont-de-Marsan
	135	Dassault Rafale C [30-GN] $	AA EC 03.030 Lorraine, St Dizier
	136	Dassault Rafale C [104-GO]	AA EC 01.007 Provence, Al Dhafra, UAE
	137	Dassault Rafale C [30-GP]	AA EC 02.030 Normandie-Niémen, Mont-de-Marsan
	138	Dassault Rafale C [30-GQ]	AA EC 02.030 Normandie-Niémen, Mont-de-Marsan
	139	Dassault Rafale C [30-GR]	AA EC 02.030 Normandie-Niémen, Mont-de-Marsan
	140	Dassault Rafale C [30-GS]	AA EC 02.030 Normandie-Niémen, Mont-de-Marsan
	141	Dassault Rafale C [7-GT]	AA EC 01.007 Provence, Al Dhafra, UAE
	142	Dassault Rafale C [30-GU] $	AA EC 03.030 Lorraine, St Dizier
	143	Dassault Rafale C [30-GV] $	AA EC 03.030 Lorraine, St Dizier
	144	Dassault Rafale C [30-GW]	AA EC 03.030 Lorraine, St Dizier
	145	Dassault Rafale C [30-GX]	AA EC 03.030 Lorraine, St Dizier
	146	Dassault Rafale C [7-GY]	AA EC 01.007 Provence, Al Dhafra, UAE
	147	Dassault Rafale C [30-GZ]	AA EC 02.030 Normandie-Niémen, Mont-de-Marsan
	148	Dassault Rafale C [30-VA] $	AA EC 02.030 Normandie-Niémen, Mont-de-Marsan
	149	Dassault Rafale C	AA (on order)
	150	Dassault Rafale C	AA (on order)
	151	Dassault Rafale C	AA (on order)
	152	Dassault Rafale C	AA (on order)
	153	Dassault Rafale C	AA (on order)
	154	Dassault Rafale C	AA (on order)
	155	Dassault Rafale C	AA (on order)
	156	Dassault Rafale C	AA (on order)
	157	Dassault Rafale C	AA (on order)
	158	Dassault Rafale C	AA (on order)
	159	Dassault Rafale C	AA (on order)
	160	Dassault Rafale C	AA (on order)
	292	DHC-6 Twin Otter 200 [F-RACC]	AA GAM 00.056 Vaucluse, Evreux
	298	DHC-6 Twin Otter 200 [F-RACD]	AA GAM 00.056 Vaucluse, Evreux
	300	DHC-6 Twin Otter 200 [F-RACE]	AA GAM 00.056 Vaucluse, Evreux
	730	DHC-6 Twin Otter 300 [F-RACA]	AA ET 03.061 Poitou, Orléans
	745	DHC-6 Twin Otter 300 [CV]	AA ET 03.061 Poitou, Orléans
	054	Embraer EMB.121AA Xingu [YX]	AA EAT 00.319 Capitaine Dartigues, Avord
	064	Embraer EMB.121AA Xingu [YY]	AA EAT 00.319 Capitaine Dartigues, Avord
	066	Embraer EMB.121AN Xingu [ZA]	AA EAT 00.319 Capitaine Dartigues, Avord
	072	Embraer EMB.121AA Xingu [YA]	AA EAT 00.319 Capitaine Dartigues, Avord
	075	Embraer EMB.121AA Xingu [YC]	AA EAT 00.319 Capitaine Dartigues, Avord
	078	Embraer EMB.121AA Xingu [YE]	AA EAT 00.319 Capitaine Dartigues, Avord
	082	Embraer EMB.121AA Xingu [YG] $	AA EAT 00.319 Capitaine Dartigues, Avord
	083	Embraer EMB.121AN Xingu [ZE]	AA EAT 00.319 Capitaine Dartigues, Avord

Serial	Type (code/other identity)	Owner/operator, location or fate	Notes
084	Embraer EMB.121AA Xingu [YH]	AA EAT 00.319 *Capitaine Dartigues*, Avord	
086	Embraer EMB.121AA Xingu [YI]	AA EAT 00.319 *Capitaine Dartigues*, Avord	
089	Embraer EMB.121AA Xingu [YJ]	AA EAT 00.319 *Capitaine Dartigues*, Avord	
090	Embraer EMB.121AN Xingu [ZF]	AA EAT 00.319 *Capitaine Dartigues*, Avord	
091	Embraer EMB.121AA Xingu [YK]	AA EAT 00.319 *Capitaine Dartigues*, Avord	
092	Embraer EMB.121AA Xingu [YL]	AA EAT 00.319 *Capitaine Dartigues*, Avord	
096	Embraer EMB.121AA Xingu [YN]	AA EAT 00.319 *Capitaine Dartigues*, Avord	
098	Embraer EMB.121AA Xingu [YO]	AA EAT 00.319 *Capitaine Dartigues*, Avord	
099	Embraer EMB.121AA Xingu [YP]	AA EAT 00.319 *Capitaine Dartigues*, Avord	
102	Embraer EMB.121AA Xingu [YS]	AA EAT 00.319 *Capitaine Dartigues*, Avord	
103	Embraer EMB.121AA Xingu [YT]	AA EAT 00.319 *Capitaine Dartigues*, Avord	
105	Embraer EMB.121AA Xingu [YU]	AA EAT 00.319 *Capitaine Dartigues*, Avord	
107	Embraer EMB.121AA Xingu [YV]	AA EAT 00.319 *Capitaine Dartigues*, Avord	
108	Embraer EMB.121AA Xingu [YW]	AA EAT 00.319 *Capitaine Dartigues*, Avord	
2233	Eurocopter AS.332L-1 Super Puma [FY]	AA GAM 00.056 *Vaucluse*, Evreux	
2235	Eurocopter AS.332L-1 Super Puma [FZ]	AA EH 03.067 *Parisis*, Villacoublay	
2377	Eurocopter AS.332L-1 Super Puma [FU]	AA EH 03.067 *Parisis*, Villacoublay	
2461	Eurocopter EC.725AP Caracal [SA]	AA EH 01.067 *Pyrénées*, Cazaux	
2549	Eurocopter EC.725AP Caracal [SB]	AA EH 01.067 *Pyrénées*, Cazaux	
2552	Eurocopter EC.725AP Caracal [SE]	AA EH 01.067 *Pyrénées*, Cazaux	
2619	Eurocopter EC.725AP Caracal [SC]	AA EH 05.067 *Alpilles*, Aix-en-Provence	
2626	Eurocopter EC.725AP Caracal [SD]	AA EH 01.067 *Pyrénées*, Cazaux	
2741	Eurocopter EC.225LP Caracal [SY]	AA GAM 00.056 *Vaucluse*, Evreux	
2752	Eurocopter EC.225LP Caracal [SZ]	AA GAM 00.056 *Vaucluse*, Evreux	
2770	Eurocopter EC.725R-2 Caracal [SG]	AA EH 01.067 *Pyrénées*, Cazaux	
2772	Eurocopter EC.725R-2 Caracal [SH]	AA EH 01.067 *Pyrénées*, Cazaux	
2778	Eurocopter EC.725R-2 Caracal [SI]	AA EH 01.067 *Pyrénées*, Cazaux	
2789	Eurocopter EC.725R-2 Caracal [SJ]	AA EH 01.067 *Pyrénées*, Cazaux	
2802	Eurocopter EC.725R-2 Caracal [SK]	AA EH 01.067 *Pyrénées*, Cazaux	
5361	Eurocopter AS.555AN Fennec [UT]	AA EH 05.067 *Alpilles*, Orange	
5382	Eurocopter AS.555AN Fennec [UV]	AA EH 05.067 *Alpilles*, Orange	
5386	Eurocopter AS.555AN Fennec [UX]	AA EH 05.067 *Alpilles*, Orange	
5387	Eurocopter AS.555AN Fennec [UY]	AA EH 05.067 *Alpilles*, Orange	
5390	Eurocopter AS.555AN Fennec [UZ]	AA EH 03.067 *Parisis*, Villacoublay	
5391	Eurocopter AS.555AN Fennec [VA]	AA EH 05.067 *Alpilles*, Orange	
5392	Eurocopter AS.555AN Fennec [VB]	AA EH 05.067 *Alpilles*, Orange	
5393	Eurocopter AS.555AN Fennec [VC]	AA EH 05.067 *Alpilles*, Orange	
5396	Eurocopter AS.555AN Fennec [VD]	AA EH 05.067 *Alpilles*, Orange	
5397	Eurocopter AS.555AN Fennec [VE]	AA ET 00.068 *Antilles-Guyane*, Cayenne	
5398	Eurocopter AS.555AN Fennec [VF]	AA EH 03.067 *Parisis*, Villacoublay	
5399	Eurocopter AS.555AN Fennec [VG] $	AA	
5400	Eurocopter AS.555AN Fennec [VH]	AA EH 05.067 *Alpilles*, Orange	
5412	Eurocopter AS.555AN Fennec [VI]	AA EH 05.067 *Alpilles*, Orange	
5427	Eurocopter AS.555AN Fennec [VJ]	AA EH 03.067 *Parisis*, Villacoublay	
5430	Eurocopter AS.555AN Fennec [VL]	AA EH 03.067 *Parisis*, Villacoublay	
5431	Eurocopter AS.555AN Fennec [VM] $	AA EH 05.067 *Alpilles*, Orange	
5440	Eurocopter AS.555AN Fennec [VN]	AA, stored Creil	
5441	Eurocopter AS.555AN Fennec [VO]	AA EH 03.067 *Parisis*, Villacoublay	
5444	Eurocopter AS.555AN Fennec [VP]	AA EH 03.067 *Parisis*, Villacoublay	
5445	Eurocopter AS.555AN Fennec [VQ] $	AA EH 05.067 *Alpilles*, Orange	
5448	Eurocopter AS.555AN Fennec [VR]	AA EH 03.067 *Parisis*, Villacoublay	
5452	Eurocopter AS.555AN Fennec [VS]	AA EH 05.067 *Alpilles*, Orange	
5455	Eurocopter AS.555AN Fennec [VT]	AA EH 03.067 *Parisis*, Villacoublay	
5457	Eurocopter AS.555AN Fennec [VU]	AA ET 00.068 *Antilles-Guyane*, Cayenne	
5458	Eurocopter AS.555AN Fennec [VV]	AA EH 05.067 *Alpilles*, Orange	
5466	Eurocopter AS.555AN Fennec [VW]	AA ET 00.068 *Antilles-Guyane*, Cayenne	
5468	Eurocopter AS.555AN Fennec [VX]	AA EH 03.067 *Parisis*, Villacoublay	
5490	Eurocopter AS.555AN Fennec [VY]	AA EH 05.067 *Alpilles*, Orange	
5506	Eurocopter AS.555AN Fennec [WA]	AA EH 05.067 *Alpilles*, Orange	
5509	Eurocopter AS.555AN Fennec [WB]	AA EH 05.067 *Alpilles*, Orange	
5511	Eurocopter AS.555AN Fennec [WC] $	AA EH 03.067 *Parisis*, Villacoublay	
5516	Eurocopter AS.555AN Fennec [WD]	AA EH 03.067 *Parisis*, Villacoublay	

Notes	Serial	Type (code/other identity)	Owner/operator, location or fate
	5520	Eurocopter AS.555AN Fennec [WE]	AA EH 03.067 *Parisis*, Villacoublay
	5523	Eurocopter AS.555AN Fennec [WF]	AA EH 05.067 *Alpilles*, Orange
	5526	Eurocopter AS.555AN Fennec [WG]	AA EH 03.067 *Parisis*, Villacoublay
	5530	Eurocopter AS.555AN Fennec [WH]	AA EH 05.067 *Alpilles*, Orange
	5532	Eurocopter AS.555AN Fennec [WI]	AA EH 05.067 *Alpilles*, Orange
	5534	Eurocopter AS.555AN Fennec [WJ]	AA EH 05.067 *Alpilles*, Orange
	5536	Eurocopter AS.555AN Fennec [WK]	AA EH 03.067 *Parisis*, Villacoublay
	5559	Eurocopter AS.555AN Fennec [WL]	AA EH 05.067 *Alpilles*, Orange
	03	Extra EA-330LC [F-TGCH]	AA EVAA, Salon de Provence
	04	Extra EA-330SC [F-TGCI]	AA EVAA, Salon de Provence
	05	Extra EA-330SC [F-TGCJ]	AA EVAA, Salon de Provence
	290	Fokker 100 [F-ZAFT]	AA DGA EV, Istres
	...	Fokker 100	AA DGA EV, Istres (on order)
	4588	Lockheed C-130H Hercules [61-PM] $	AA ET 02.061 *Franche-Comté*, Orléans
	4589	Lockheed C-130H Hercules [61-PN]	AA ET 02.061 *Franche-Comté*, Orléans
	5114	Lockheed C-130H Hercules [61-PA]	AA ET 02.061 *Franche-Comté*, Orléans
	5116	Lockheed C-130H Hercules [61-PB]	AA ET 02.061 *Franche-Comté*, Orléans
	5119	Lockheed C-130H Hercules [61-PC]	AA ET 02.061 *Franche-Comté*, Orléans
	5140	Lockheed C-130H Hercules [61-PD]	AA ET 02.061 *Franche-Comté*, Orléans
	5142	Lockheed C-130H-30 Hercules [61-PE]	AA ET 02.061 *Franche-Comté*, Orléans
	5144	Lockheed C-130H-30 Hercules [61-PF] $	AA ET 02.061 *Franche-Comté*, Orléans
	5150	Lockheed C-130H-30 Hercules [61-PG]	AA ET 02.061 *Franche-Comté*, Orléans
	5151	Lockheed C-130H-30 Hercules [61-PH]	AA ET 02.061 *Franche-Comté*, Orléans
	5152	Lockheed C-130H-30 Hercules [61-PI]	AA ET 02.061 *Franche-Comté*, Orléans
	5153	Lockheed C-130H-30 Hercules [61-PJ]	AA ET 02.061 *Franche-Comté*, Orléans
	5226	Lockheed C-130H-30 Hercules [61-PK]	AA ET 02.061 *Franche-Comté*, Orléans
	5227	Lockheed C-130H-30 Hercules [61-PL]	AA ET 02.061 *Franche-Comté*, Orléans
	5836	Lockheed C-130J Hercules II [61-PO]	AA ET 02.061 *Franche-Comté*, Orléans
	5847	Lockheed C-130J Hercules II [61-PP]	AA ET 02.061 *Franche-Comté*, Orléans
	5874	Lockheed KC-130J Hercules II [61-PQ]	AA ET 02.061 *Franche-Comté*, Orléans
	5890	Lockheed KC-130J Hercules II [61-PR]	AA ET 02.061 *Franche-Comté*, Orléans
	01	Pilatus PC-21 (HB-HVA) [709-FC]	AA EPAA 00.315, Cognac
	02	Pilatus PC-21 (HB-HVB) [709-FD]	AA EPAA 00.315, Cognac
	03	Pilatus PC-21 (HB-HVC/F-ZXAC) [709-FE]	AA EPAA 00.315, Cognac
	04	Pilatus PC-21 (HB-HVD) [709-FF]	AA EPAA 00.315, Cognac
	05	Pilatus PC-21 (HB-HVE) [709-FG]	AA EPAA 00.315, Cognac
	06	Pilatus PC-21 (HB-HVF) [709-FH]	AA EPAA 00.315, Cognac
	07	Pilatus PC-21 (HB-HVG) [709-FI]	AA EPAA 00.315, Cognac
	08	Pilatus PC-21 (HB-HVH) [709-FJ]	AA EPAA 00.315, Cognac
	09	Pilatus PC-21 (HB-HVI) [709-FK]	AA EPAA 00.315, Cognac
	10	Pilatus PC-21 (HB-HVJ) [709-FL]	AA EPAA 00.315, Cognac
	11	Pilatus PC-21 (HB-HVK) [709-FM]	AA EPAA 00.315, Cognac
	12	Pilatus PC-21 (HB-HVL) [709-FN]	AA EPAA 00.315, Cognac
	13	Pilatus PC-21 (HB-HVM) [709-FO]	AA EPAA 00.315, Cognac
	14	Pilatus PC-21 (HB-HVN) [709-FP]	AA EPAA 00.315, Cognac
	15	Pilatus PC-21 (HB-HVO) [709-FQ]	AA EPAA 00.315, Cognac
	16	Pilatus PC-21 (HB-HVP) [709-FR]	AA EPAA 00.315, Cognac
	17	Pilatus PC-21 (HB-HVQ) [709-FS]	AA EPAA 00.315, Cognac
	7	SOCATA TB-30 Epsilon [315-UF]	*Withdrawn from use at Cognac, May 2019*
	26	SOCATA TB-30 Epsilon [315-UY]	*Preserved at Angers, June 2017*
	27	SOCATA TB-30 Epsilon [315-UZ]	*Withdrawn from use*
	30	SOCATA TB-30 Epsilon [315-VC]	*Withdrawn from use*
	64	SOCATA TB-30 Epsilon [315-WG]	*Withdrawn from use*
	65	SOCATA TB-30 Epsilon [315-WH]	*To the Senegalese Air Force as 6W-ZEE, May 2019*
	66	SOCATA TB-30 Epsilon [315-WI]	*Withdrawn from use at Cognac, 2019*
	67	SOCATA TB-30 Epsilon [315-WJ] $	*Withdrawn from use at Cognac, September 2019*
	69	SOCATA TB-30 Epsilon [F-SEWL]	AA Cartouche Dorée (EPAA 00.315), Cognac
	73	SOCATA TB-30 Epsilon [315-WP]	*Withdrawn from use*
	78	SOCATA TB-30 Epsilon [315-WU]	*Withdrawn from use*
	82	SOCATA TB-30 Epsilon [315-WY]	*Withdrawn from use at Cognac, September 2019*
	83	SOCATA TB-30 Epsilon [315-WZ]	*Withdrawn from use at Cognac, September 2019*
	84	SOCATA TB-30 Epsilon [315-XA]	*To the Senegalese Air Force as 6W-ZEF, May 2019*

Serial	Type (code/other identity)	Owner/operator, location or fate	Notes
90	SOCATA TB-30 Epsilon [F-SEXG]	*Sold as F-AYXG, April 2019*	
91	SOCATA TB-30 Epsilon [315-XH]	*Withdrawn from use at Cognac, September 2019*	
92	SOCATA TB-30 Epsilon [315-XI]	*Withdrawn from use*	
95	SOCATA TB-30 Epsilon [315-XL]	*Withdrawn from use*	
96	SOCATA TB-30 Epsilon [315-XM]	*Withdrawn from use at Cognac, September 2019*	
97	SOCATA TB-30 Epsilon [315-XN]	*Withdrawn from use at Cognac, September 2019*	
99	SOCATA TB-30 Epsilon [F-SEXP]	*Withdrawn from use*	
101	SOCATA TB-30 Epsilon [315-XR] $	*Withdrawn from use at Cognac, September 2019*	
102	SOCATA TB-30 Epsilon [F-SEXS,2]	*Withdrawn from use*	
103	SOCATA TB-30 Epsilon [315-XT]	*Withdrawn from use*	
104	SOCATA TB-30 Epsilon [315-XU] $	*Withdrawn from use at Cognac, September 2019*	
113	SOCATA TB-30 Epsilon [F-SEYD]	*Withdrawn from use*	
116	SOCATA TB-30 Epsilon [F-SEYG]	*Withdrawn from use*	
117	SOCATA TB-30 Epsilon [315-YH]	*Withdrawn from use*	
118	SOCATA TB-30 Epsilon [315-YI] $	*Withdrawn from use at Cognac, September 2019*	
121	SOCATA TB-30 Epsilon [315-YL]	*Sold as F-AYYL, April 2019*	
127	SOCATA TB-30 Epsilon [315-YR]	*Withdrawn from use*	
131	SOCATA TB-30 Epsilon [315-YV] $	*Withdrawn from use at Cognac, September 2019*	
133	SOCATA TB-30 Epsilon [315-YX]	*Withdrawn from use at Cognac, September 2019*	
136	SOCATA TB-30 Epsilon [315-ZA]	*Withdrawn from use*	
141	SOCATA TB-30 Epsilon [F-SEZF]	*Withdrawn from use at Cognac, September 2019*	
142	SOCATA TB-30 Epsilon [315-ZG]	*Withdrawn from use*	
144	SOCATA TB-30 Epsilon [315-ZI]	*Withdrawn from use at Cognac, September 2019*	
146	SOCATA TB-30 Epsilon [315-ZK]	*Withdrawn from use at Cognac, September 2019*	
149	SOCATA TB-30 Epsilon [315-ZM] $	*Withdrawn from use at Cognac, September 2019*	
150	SOCATA TB-30 Epsilon [315-ZN] $	*Withdrawn from use at Cognac, September 2019*	
33	SOCATA TBM 700A [XA]	AA ET 00.043 *Médoc*, Bordeaux	
35	SOCATA TBM 700A [BW]	AA DGA EV, Cazaux & Istres	
77	SOCATA TBM 700A [XD]	AA ET 00.043 *Médoc*, Bordeaux	
78	SOCATA TBM 700A [XE]	AA CEAM, Mont-de-Marsan	
80	SOCATA TBM 700A [BY]	AA DGA EV, Cazaux & Istres	
93	SOCATA TBM 700A [XL]	AA ET 00.041 *Verdun*, Villacoublay	
94	SOCATA TBM 700A [BZ]	AA DGA EV, Cazaux & Istres	
95	SOCATA TBM 700A [XH]	AA CEAM, Mont-de-Marsan	
103	SOCATA TBM 700A [XI]	AA ET 00.041 *Verdun*, Villacoublay	
104	SOCATA TBM 700A [XJ]	AA ET 00.043 *Médoc*, Bordeaux	
105	SOCATA TBM 700A [XK] $	AA ET 00.043 *Médoc*, Bordeaux	
106	SOCATA TBM 700A [BX]	*Withdrawn from use, September 2018*	
110	SOCATA TBM 700A [XP]	AA ET 00.041 *Verdun*, Villacoublay	
111	SOCATA TBM 700A [XM]	AA ET 00.041 *Verdun*, Villacoublay	
115	SOCATA TBM 700A [BQ]	AA DGA EV, Cazaux & Istres	
117	SOCATA TBM 700A [XN]	AA ET 00.043 *Médoc*, Bordeaux	
125	SOCATA TBM 700A [XO]	AA ET 00.043 *Médoc*, Bordeaux	
131	SOCATA TBM 700A [XQ]	AA ET 00.041 *Verdun*, Villacoublay	
146	SOCATA TBM 700A [XR]	AA ET 00.041 *Verdun*, Villacoublay	
147	SOCATA TBM 700A [XS]	AA ET 00.041 *Verdun*, Villacoublay	
R201	Transall C-160R [64-GA]	*Withdrawn from use, 2019*	
R202	Transall C-160R [64-GB]	AA ET 02.064 *Anjou*, Evreux	
R203	Transall C-160R [64-GC] $	AA ET 02.064 *Anjou*, Evreux	
R204	Transall C-160R [64-GD]	AA ET 02.064 *Anjou*, Evreux	
R206	Transall C-160R [64-GF]	AA ET 02.064 *Anjou*, Evreux	
R208	Transall C-160R [64-GH] $	*Withdrawn from use, 2019*	
R210	Transall C-160R [64-GJ]	AA ET 02.064 *Anjou*, Evreux	
R212	Transall C-160R [64-GL]	AA ET 02.064 *Anjou*, Evreux	
R213	Transall C-160R [64-GM]	AA ET 02.064 *Anjou*, Evreux	
R214	Transall C-160R [64-GN]	AA ET 02.064 *Anjou*, Evreux	
F216	Transall C-160NG GABRIEL [GT]	AA EEA 00.054 *Dunkerque*, Evreux	
R217	Transall C-160R [64-GQ]	AA ET 02.064 *Anjou*, Evreux	
R218	Transall C-160R [64-GR]	AA ET 02.064 *Anjou*, Evreux	
F221	Transall C-160NG GABRIEL [GS] $	AA EEA 00.054 *Dunkerque*, Evreux	
R223	Transall C-160R [64-GW]	*Withdrawn from use, 2019*	
R224	Transall C-160R [64-GX]	*Withdrawn from use, 2019*	

Notes	Serial	Type (code/other identity)	Owner/operator, location or fate
	R225	Transall C-160R [64-GY]	AA ET 02.064 *Anjou*, Evreux
	R226	Transall C-160R [64-GZ]	AA ET 02.064 *Anjou*, Evreux
Aéronautique Navale/Marine (AN)			
	2	Dassault-Breguet Atlantique 2	AN 21 Flottille, Lorient/Lann Bihoué
	3	Dassault-Breguet Atlantique 2	AN 23 Flottille, Lorient/Lann Bihoué
	4	Dassault-Breguet Atlantique 2	AN 23 Flottille, Lorient/Lann Bihoué
	5	Dassault-Breguet Atlantique 2	AN 21 Flottille, Lorient/Lann Bihoué
	9	Dassault-Breguet Atlantique 2	AN 23 Flottille, Lorient/Lann Bihoué
	11	Dassault-Breguet Atlantique 2	AN 23 Flottille, Lorient/Lann Bihoué
	12	Dassault-Breguet Atlantique 2	AN 21 Flottille, Lorient/Lann Bihoué
	13	Dassault-Breguet Atlantique 2	AN 21 Flottille, Lorient/Lann Bihoué
	14	Dassault-Breguet Atlantique 2	*Withdrawn from use at Cuers*
	15	Dassault-Breguet Atlantique 2	AN 21 Flottille, Lorient/Lann Bihoué
	16	Dassault-Breguet Atlantique 2	AN 21 Flottille, Lorient/Lann Bihoué
	17	Dassault-Breguet Atlantique 2 $	AN 21 Flottille, Lorient/Lann Bihoué
	18	Dassault-Breguet Atlantique 2	AN 21 Flottille, Lorient/Lann Bihoué
	19	Dassault-Breguet Atlantique 2	AN 23 Flottille, Lorient/Lann Bihoué
	20	Dassault-Breguet Atlantique 2	AN 23 Flottille, Lorient/Lann Bihoué
	21	Dassault-Breguet Atlantique 2	AN 21 Flottille, Lorient/Lann Bihoué
	22	Dassault-Breguet Atlantique 2	AN 21 Flottille, Lorient/Lann Bihoué
	23	Dassault-Breguet Atlantique 2	AN 21 Flottille, Lorient/Lann Bihoué
	24	Dassault-Breguet Atlantique 2	AN 21 Flottille, Lorient/Lann Bihoué
	26	Dassault-Breguet Atlantique 2	AN 21 Flottille, Lorient/Lann Bihoué
	27	Dassault-Breguet Atlantique 2	AN 21 Flottille, Lorient/Lann Bihoué
	28	Dassault-Breguet Atlantique 2	AN 23 Flottille, Lorient/Lann Bihoué
	32	Dassault Falcon 10(MER)	AN 57 Escadrille, Landivisiau
	101	Dassault Falcon 10(MER)	AN 57 Escadrille, Landivisiau
	129	Dassault Falcon 10(MER)	AN 57 Escadrille, Landivisiau
	133	Dassault Falcon 10(MER)	AN 57 Escadrille, Landivisiau
	143	Dassault Falcon 10(MER)	AN 57 Escadrille, Landivisiau
	185	Dassault Falcon 10(MER) $	AN 57 Escadrille, Landivisiau
	48	Dassault Falcon 20G Guardian	AN 25 Flottille, Papeete & Tontouta
	65	Dassault Falcon 20G Guardian	AN 25 Flottille, Papeete & Tontouta
	72	Dassault Falcon 20G Guardian	AN 25 Flottille, Papeete & Tontouta
	77	Dassault Falcon 20G Guardian	AN 25 Flottille, Papeete & Tontouta
	80	Dassault Falcon 20G Guardian	AN 25 Flottille, Papeete & Tontouta
	5	Dassault Falcon 50MS SURMAR	AN 24 Flottille, Lorient/Lann Bihoué
	7	Dassault Falcon 50MI SURMAR	AN 24 Flottille, Lorient/Lann Bihoué
	27	Dassault Falcon 50MS SURMAR	AN 24 Flottille, Lorient/Lann Bihoué
	30	Dassault Falcon 50MI SURMAR	AN 24 Flottille, Lorient/Lann Bihoué
	34	Dassault Falcon 50MS SURMAR	AN 24 Flottille, Lorient/Lann Bihoué
	36	Dassault Falcon 50MI SURMAR	AN 24 Flottille, Lorient/Lann Bihoué
	78	Dassault Falcon 50MS SURMAR	AN 24 Flottille, Lorient/Lann Bihoué
	132	Dassault Falcon 50MI SURMAR	AN 24 Flottille, Lorient/Lann Bihoué
	2	Dassault Rafale M	AN 17 Flottille, Landivisiau
	3	Dassault Rafale M	AN ETR 03.004 *Aquitaine*, St Dizier
	5	Dassault Rafale M $	AN 12 Flottille, Landivisiau
	6	Dassault Rafale M	AN ETR 03.004 *Aquitaine*, St Dizier
	7	Dassault Rafale M	AN 11 Flottille, Landivisiau
	8	Dassault Rafale M	AN 12 Flottille, Landivisiau
	9	Dassault Rafale M	AN 12 Flottille, Landivisiau
	10	Dassault Rafale M	AN 12 Flottille, Landivisiau
	11	Dassault Rafale M $	AN 11 Flottille, Landivisiau
	12	Dassault Rafale M	AN ETR 03.004 *Aquitaine*, St Dizier
	13	Dassault Rafale M	AN 11 Flottille, Landivisiau
	14	Dassault Rafale M	AN 11 Flottille, Landivisiau
	15	Dassault Rafale M	AN 12 Flottille, Landivisiau
	16	Dassault Rafale M	AN 12 Flottille, Landivisiau
	17	Dassault Rafale M	AN 12 Flottille, Landivisiau
	19	Dassault Rafale M	AN 11 Flottille, Landivisiau
	20	Dassault Rafale M	AN 17 Flottille, Landivisiau
	21	Dassault Rafale M	AN 12 Flottille, Landivisiau

Serial	Type (code/other identity)	Owner/operator, location or fate	Notes
23	Dassault Rafale M	AN 12 Flottille, Landivisiau	
26	Dassault Rafale M	AN 12 Flottille, Landivisiau	
27	Dassault Rafale M $	AN ETR 03.004 *Aquitaine*, St Dizier	
28	Dassault Rafale M	AN ETR 03.004 *Aquitaine*, St Dizier	
29	Dassault Rafale M	AN 12 Flottille, Landivisiau	
30	Dassault Rafale M	AN CEPA/10 Escadrille, Landivisiau	
31	Dassault Rafale M	AN 11 Flottille, Landivisiau	
32	Dassault Rafale M	AN 11 Flottille, Landivisiau	
33	Dassault Rafale M	AN ETR 03.004 *Aquitaine*, St Dizier	
34	Dassault Rafale M	AN 11 Flottille, Landivisiau	
35	Dassault Rafale M	AN 12 Flottille, Landivisiau	
36	Dassault Rafale M $	AN 11 Flottille, Landivisiau	
37	Dassault Rafale M	AN ETR 03.004 *Aquitaine*, St Dizier	
38	Dassault Rafale M	AN 12 Flottille, Landivisiau	
39	Dassault Rafale M	AN 11 Flottille, Landivisiau	
40	Dassault Rafale M	AN 11 Flottille, Landivisiau	
41	Dassault Rafale M	AN	
42	Dassault Rafale M	AN 11 Flottille, Landivisiau	
43	Dassault Rafale M	AN 11 Flottille, Landivisiau	
44	Dassault Rafale M $	AN 11 Flottille, Landivisiau	*
45	Dassault Rafale M	AN 11 Flottille, Landivisiau	
46	Dassault Rafale M	AN 17 Flottille, Landivisiau	
47	Dassault Rafale M	AN (on order)	
48	Dassault Rafale M	AN (on order)	
49	Dassault Rafale M	AN (on order)	
50	Dassault Rafale M	AN (on order)	
M02	Dassault Rafale M	AN DGA EV, Istres	
65	Embraer EMB.121AN Xingu	AN 28 Flottille, Hyères	
67	Embraer EMB.121AN Xingu $	AN 28 Flottille, Hyères	
68	Embraer EMB.121AN Xingu	AN 28 Flottille, Hyères	
69	Embraer EMB.121AN Xingu	AN 28 Flottille, Hyères	
71	Embraer EMB.121AN Xingu	AN 28 Flottille, Hyères	
74	Embraer EMB.121AN Xingu $	AN 28 Flottille, Hyères	
77	Embraer EMB.121AN Xingu	AN 28 Flottille, Hyères	
81	Embraer EMB.121AN Xingu	AN 24 Flottille, Lorient/Lann Bihoué	
85	Embraer EMB.121AN Xingu	AN 24 Flottille, Lorient/Lann Bihoué	
87	Embraer EMB.121AN Xingu	AN 28 Flottille, Hyères	
17	Eurocopter AS.365N Dauphin	AN 35 Flottille, Le Touquet	
19	Eurocopter AS.365N Dauphin	AN 35 Flottille, Hyères	
24	Eurocopter AS.365N Dauphin	AN 35 Flottille, Hyères	
57	Eurocopter AS.365N Dauphin	AN 35 Flottille, Hyères	
81	Eurocopter AS.365N Dauphin $	AN 35 Flottille, Hyères	
91	Eurocopter AS.365N Dauphin	AN 35 Flottille, Hyères	
157	Eurocopter AS.365N Dauphin	AN 35 Flottille, Hyères	
313	Eurocopter SA.365F-1 Dauphin II	AN 35 Flottille, Hyères	
318	Eurocopter SA.365F-1 Dauphin II $	AN 35 Flottille, Hyères	
322	Eurocopter SA.365F-1 Dauphin II	AN 35 Flottille, Hyères	
355	Eurocopter AS.565MA Panther	AN 36 Flottille, Hyères	
362	Eurocopter AS.565MA Panther	AN 36 Flottille, Hyères	
403	Eurocopter AS.565MA Panther	AN 36 Flottille, Hyères	
436	Eurocopter AS.565MA Panther	AN 36 Flottille, Hyères	
452	Eurocopter AS.565MA Panther	AN 36 Flottille, Hyères	
453	Eurocopter AS.565MA Panther	AN 36 Flottille, Hyères	
466	Eurocopter AS.565MA Panther	AN 36 Flottille, Hyères	
482	Eurocopter AS.565MA Panther	AN 36 Flottille, Hyères	
486	Eurocopter AS.565MA Panther	AN 36 Flottille, Hyères	
488	Eurocopter AS.565MA Panther	AN 36 Flottille, Hyères	
503	Eurocopter AS.565MA Panther	AN 36 Flottille, Hyères	
505	Eurocopter AS.565MA Panther	AN 36 Flottille, Hyères	
506	Eurocopter AS.565MA Panther	AN 36 Flottille, Hyères	
507	Eurocopter AS.565MA Panther $	AN 36 Flottille, Hyères	
511	Eurocopter AS.565MA Panther	AN 36 Flottille, Hyères	

Notes	Serial	Type (code/other identity)	Owner/operator, location or fate
	519	Eurocopter AS.565MA Panther	AN 36 Flottille, Hyères
	522	Eurocopter AS.565MA Panther	AN 36 Flottille, Hyères
	524	Eurocopter AS.565MA Panther	AN 36 Flottille, Hyères
	542	Eurocopter AS.565MA Panther	AN 36 Flottille, Hyères
	6872	Eurocopter AS.365N-3 Dauphin	AN 35 Flottille, Tahiti
	6928	Eurocopter AS.365N-3 Dauphin	AN 35 Flottille, Tahiti
	1	NH Industries NH.90-NFH Caïman (F-ZWTO)	AN 33 Flottille, Lanvéoc/Poulmic
	2	NH Industries NH.90-NFH Caïman	AN CEPA/10 Escadrille, Hyères
	3	NH Industries NH.90-NFH Caïman	AN 31 Flottille, Hyères
	4	NH Industries NH.90-NFH Caïman	AN 33 Flottille, Lanvéoc/Poulmic
	5	NH Industries NH.90-NFH Caïman	AN 33 Flottille, Lanvéoc/Poulmic
	6	NH Industries NH.90-NFH Caïman	AN 33 Flottille, Lanvéoc/Poulmic
	7	NH Industries NH.90-NFH Caïman	AN 33 Flottille, Lanvéoc/Poulmic
	8	NH Industries NH.90-NFH Caïman	AN 31 Flottille, Hyères
	9	NH Industries NH.90-NFH Caïman	AN 31 Flottille, Hyères
	10	NH Industries NH.90-NFH Caïman	AN 31 Flottille, Hyères
	11	NH Industries NH.90-NFH Caïman	AN 33 Flottille, Lanvéoc/Poulmic
	12	NH Industries NH.90-NFH Caïman	AN 31 Flottille, Hyères
	13	NH Industries NH.90-NFH Caïman	AN 31 Flottille, Hyères
	14	NH Industries NH.90-NFH Caïman	AN 33 Flottille, Lanvéoc/Poulmic
	15	NH Industries NH.90-NFH Caïman	AN CEPA/10 Escadrille, Hyères
	16	NH Industries NH.90-NFH Caïman	AN 31 Flottille, Hyères
	17	NH Industries NH.90-NFH Caïman	AN
	18	NH Industries NH.90-NFH Caïman	AN 31 Flottille, Hyères
	19	NH Industries NH.90-NFH Caïman	AN
	20	NH Industries NH.90-NFH Caïman	AN 33 Flottille, Lanvéoc/Poulmic
	21	NH Industries NH.90-NFH Caïman	AN
	22	NH Industries NH.90-NFH Caïman	AN 31 Flottille, Hyères
	23	NH Industries NH.90-NFH Caïman	AN (on order)
	24	NH Industries NH.90-NFH Caïman	AN (on order)
	25	NH Industries NH.90-NFH Caïman	AN (on order)
	26	NH Industries NH.90-NFH Caïman	AN (on order)
	27	NH Industries NH.90-NFH Caïman	AN (on order)
	1	Northrop Grumman E-2C Hawkeye (165455)	AN 4 Flottille, Lorient/Lann Bihoué
	2	Northrop Grumman E-2C Hawkeye (165456)	AN 4 Flottille, Lorient/Lann Bihoué
	3	Northrop Grumman E-2C Hawkeye (166417)	AN 4 Flottille, Lorient/Lann Bihoué
	13	Sud Aviation SE.3160 Alouette III	AN 35 Flottille, Hyères
	14	Sud Aviation SE.3160 Alouette III	AN 22 Escadrille/ESHE, Lanvéoc/Poulmic
	41	Sud Aviation SE.3160 Alouette III	AN 35 Flottille, Hyères
	100	Sud Aviation SA.319B Alouette III	AN 22 Escadrille/ESHE, Lanvéoc/Poulmic
	106	Sud Aviation SA.319B Alouette III	AN 22 Escadrille/ESHE, Lanvéoc/Poulmic
	114	Sud Aviation SA.319B Alouette III	AN 22 Escadrille/ESHE, Lanvéoc/Poulmic
	160	Sud Aviation SA.319B Alouette III	AN 22 Escadrille/ESHE, Lanvéoc/Poulmic
	161	Sud Aviation SA.319B Alouette III	AN 22 Escadrille/ESHE, Lanvéoc/Poulmic
	219	Sud Aviation SE.3160 Alouette III	AN 35 Flottille, Hyères
	237	Sud Aviation SA.319B Alouette III	AN 35 Flottille, Hyères
	244	Sud Aviation SE.3160 Alouette III	AN 22 Escadrille/ESHE, Lanvéoc/Poulmic
	245	Sud Aviation SE.3160 Alouette III	AN 22 Escadrille/ESHE, Lanvéoc/Poulmic
	262	Sud Aviation SA.319B Alouette III	AN 22 Escadrille/ESHE, Lanvéoc/Poulmic
	268	Sud Aviation SA.319B Alouette III	AN 22 Escadrille/ESHE, Lanvéoc/Poulmic
	279	Sud Aviation SE.3160 Alouette III	AN 22 Escadrille/ESHE, Lanvéoc/Poulmic
	302	Sud Aviation SA.319B Alouette III	AN 22 Escadrille/ESHE, Lanvéoc/Poulmic
	303	Sud Aviation SA.319B Alouette III	AN 22 Escadrille/ESHE, Lanvéoc/Poulmic
	309	Sud Aviation SA.319B Alouette III	AN 22 Escadrille/ESHE, Lanvéoc/Poulmic
	347	Sud Aviation SA.319B Alouette III	AN 22 Escadrille/ESHE, Lanvéoc/Poulmic
	358	Sud Aviation SA.319B Alouette III	AN 22 Escadrille/ESHE, Lanvéoc/Poulmic
	444	Sud Aviation SE.3160 Alouette III	AN 22 Escadrille/ESHE, Lanvéoc/Poulmic
	731	Sud Aviation SA.316B Alouette III	AN 22 Escadrille/ESHE, Lanvéoc/Poulmic
	806	Sud Aviation SA.316B Alouette III	AN 22 Escadrille/ESHE, Lanvéoc/Poulmic
	809	Sud Aviation SA.316B Alouette III	AN 22 Escadrille/ESHE, Lanvéoc/Poulmic
	997	Sud Aviation SA.319B Alouette III	AN 22 Escadrille/ESHE, Lanvéoc/Poulmic
	263	Westland Lynx HAS2(FN) (XZ263)	AN 34 Flottille, Lanvéoc/Poulmic

Serial	Type (code/other identity)	Owner/operator, location or fate	Notes
264	Westland Lynx HAS2(FN) (XZ264)	AN 34 Flottille, Lanvéoc/Poulmic	
265	Westland Lynx HAS2(FN) (XZ265)	AN 34 Flottille, Lanvéoc/Poulmic	
267	Westland Lynx HAS2(FN) (XZ267)	AN 34 Flottille, Lanvéoc/Poulmic	
270	Westland Lynx HAS2(FN) (XZ270)	AN 34 Flottille, Lanvéoc/Poulmic	
272	Westland Lynx HAS2(FN) (XZ272) $	AN 34 Flottille, Lanvéoc/Poulmic	
273	Westland Lynx HAS2(FN) (XZ273)	AN 34 Flottille, Lanvéoc/Poulmic	
276	Westland Lynx HAS2(FN) (XZ276)	AN 34 Flottille, Lanvéoc/Poulmic	
621	Westland Lynx HAS2(FN) (XZ621)	AN 34 Flottille, Lanvéoc/Poulmic	
622	Westland Lynx HAS2(FN) (XZ622)	AN 34 Flottille, Lanvéoc/Poulmic	
624	Westland Lynx HAS2(FN) (XZ624)	AN 34 Flottille, Lanvéoc/Poulmic	
802	Westland Lynx HAS4(FN)	AN 34 Flottille, Lanvéoc/Poulmic	
804	Westland Lynx HAS4(FN)	AN 34 Flottille, Lanvéoc/Poulmic	
806	Westland Lynx HAS4(FN)	AN 34 Flottille, Lanvéoc/Poulmic	
807	Westland Lynx HAS4(FN)	AN 34 Flottille, Lanvéoc/Poulmic	
808	Westland Lynx HAS4(FN)	AN 34 Flottille, Lanvéoc/Poulmic	
810	Westland Lynx HAS4(FN)	AN 34 Flottille, Lanvéoc/Poulmic	
811	Westland Lynx HAS4(FN)	AN 34 Flottille, Lanvéoc/Poulmic	
814	Westland Lynx HAS4(FN)	AN 34 Flottille, Lanvéoc/Poulmic	
Aviation Legére de l'Armée de Terre (ALAT)			
1005	Aérospatiale SA.330Ba Puma [DCA]	ALAT ESAM, Bourges	
1006	Aérospatiale SA.330Ba Puma [DAA]	ALAT	
1020	Aérospatiale SA.330Ba Puma [DAB]	ALAT	
1036	Aérospatiale SA.330Ba Puma [DAC]	ALAT 3 RHC, Etain	
1037	Aérospatiale SA.330Ba Puma [DAD]	ALAT	
1049	Aérospatiale SA.330Ba Puma [DAE]	ALAT	
1052	Aérospatiale SA.330Ba Puma [DCB]	ALAT EALAT, Le Luc	
1055	Aérospatiale SA.330Ba Puma [DAF]	ALAT GIH, Cazaux	
1056	Aérospatiale SA.330Ba Puma [DCC]	ALAT GAM/STAT, Valence	
1057	Aérospatiale SA.330Ba Puma [DCD]	ALAT EALAT, Le Luc	
1069	Aérospatiale SA.330Ba Puma [DAG]	ALAT	
1071	Aérospatiale SA.330Ba Puma [DCE]	ALAT EALAT, Le Luc	
1073	Aérospatiale SA.330Ba Puma [DCF]	ALAT EALAT, Le Luc	
1078	Aérospatiale SA.330Ba Puma [DAH]	ALAT 3 RHC, Etain	
1092	Aérospatiale SA.330Ba Puma [DAI]	ALAT	
1093	Aérospatiale SA.330Ba Puma [DCG]	ALAT, stored Montauban	
1100	Aérospatiale SA.330Ba Puma [DAJ]	ALAT 3 RHC, Etain	
1102	Aérospatiale SA.330Ba Puma [DAK]	ALAT	
1107	Aérospatiale SA.330Ba Puma [DAL]	ALAT	
1109	Aérospatiale SA.330Ba Puma [DAM]	ALAT	
1114	Aérospatiale SA.330Ba Puma [DCH]	ALAT, stored Montauban	
1122	Aérospatiale SA.330Ba Puma [DCI]	ALAT	
1123	Aérospatiale SA.330Ba Puma [DCJ]	ALAT, stored Montauban	
1128	Aérospatiale SA.330Ba Puma [DAN]	ALAT 3 RHC, Etain	
1130	Aérospatiale SA.330Ba Puma [DCK]	ALAT 3 RHC, Etain	
1135	Aérospatiale SA.330Ba Puma [DCL]	ALAT, stored Montauban	
1136	Aérospatiale SA.330Ba Puma [DCM]	ALAT	
1142	Aérospatiale SA.330Ba Puma [DCN]	ALAT, stored Montauban	
1143	Aérospatiale SA.330Ba Puma [DAO]	ALAT	
1145	Aérospatiale SA.330Ba Puma [DCO]	ALAT, stored Montauban	
1149	Aérospatiale SA.330Ba Puma [DAP]	ALAT 3 RHC, Etain	
1150	Aérospatiale SA.330Ba Puma [DCP]	ALAT, stored Montauban	
1155	Aérospatiale SA.330Ba Puma [DCQ]	ALAT	
1156	Aérospatiale SA.330Ba Puma [DAQ]	ALAT 3 RHC, Etain	
1163	Aérospatiale SA.330Ba Puma [DCR]	ALAT, stored Montauban	
1164	Aérospatiale SA.330Ba Puma [DCS]	ALAT, stored Montauban	
1165	Aérospatiale SA.330Ba Puma [DCT]	ALAT, stored Montauban	
1171	Aérospatiale SA.330Ba Puma [DCU]	ALAT, stored Montauban	
1172	Aérospatiale SA.330Ba Puma [DCV]	ALAT, stored Montauban	
1173	Aérospatiale SA.330Ba Puma [DAR]	ALAT 3 RHC, Etain	
1176	Aérospatiale SA.330Ba Puma [DAS]	ALAT 3 RHC, Etain	
1177	Aérospatiale SA.330Ba Puma [DCW]	ALAT, stored Montauban	
1179	Aérospatiale SA.330Ba Puma [DCX]	ALAT	

Notes	Serial	Type (code/other identity)	Owner/operator, location or fate
	1182	Aérospatiale SA.330Ba Puma [DCY]	ALAT
	1186	Aérospatiale SA.330Ba Puma [DCZ]	ALAT
	1190	Aérospatiale SA.330Ba Puma [DDA]	ALAT
	1192	Aérospatiale SA.330Ba Puma [DDB]	ALAT, stored Montauban
	1196	Aérospatiale SA.330Ba Puma [DDC]	ALAT EALAT, Le Luc
	1197	Aérospatiale SA.330Ba Puma [DAU]	ALAT
	1198	Aérospatiale SA.330Ba Puma [DDD]	ALAT
	1204	Aérospatiale SA.330Ba Puma [DAV]	ALAT 3 RHC, Etain
	1206	Aérospatiale SA.330Ba Puma [DDE]	*Withdrawn from use, 2019*
	1211	Aérospatiale SA.330Ba Puma [DAW]	ALAT
	1213	Aérospatiale SA.330Ba Puma [DDF]	ALAT
	1214	Aérospatiale SA.330Ba Puma [DAX]	ALAT 3 RHC, Etain
	1217	Aérospatiale SA.330Ba Puma [DAY]	ALAT 3 RHC, Etain
	1219	Aérospatiale SA.330Ba Puma [DAZ]	ALAT 3 RHC, Etain
	1222	Aérospatiale SA.330Ba Puma [DDG]	ALAT 3 RHC, Etain
	1223	Aérospatiale SA.330Ba Puma [DDH]	ALAT, stored Montauban
	1229	Aérospatiale SA.330Ba Puma [DDJ]	*Preserved at Villacoublay, 2019*
	1231	Aérospatiale SA.330Ba Puma [DDK]	ALAT 3 RHC, Etain
	1232	Aérospatiale SA.330Ba Puma [DBA]	ALAT
	1235	Aérospatiale SA.330Ba Puma [DDL]	ALAT, stored Montauban
	1236	Aérospatiale SA.330Ba Puma [DDM]	ALAT EALAT, Le Luc
	1239	Aérospatiale SA.330Ba Puma [DDN]	ALAT
	1243	Aérospatiale SA.330Ba Puma [DBB]	ALAT 3 RHC, Etain
	1244	Aérospatiale SA.330Ba Puma [DDO]	ALAT 3 RHC, Etain
	1248	Aérospatiale SA.330Ba Puma [DBC]	ALAT 3 RHC, Etain
	1252	Aérospatiale SA.330Ba Puma [DDP]	ALAT EALAT, Le Luc
	1255	Aérospatiale SA.330Ba Puma [DDQ]	ALAT
	1256	Aérospatiale SA.330Ba Puma [DDR]	ALAT GAM/STAT, Valence
	1260	Aérospatiale SA.330Ba Puma [DDS]	ALAT EALAT, Le Luc
	1262	Aérospatiale SA.330Ba Puma [DBD]	ALAT 3 RHC, Etain
	1269	Aérospatiale SA.330Ba Puma [DDT]	ALAT 3 RHC, Etain
	1277	Aérospatiale SA.330Ba Puma [DBE]	ALAT 3 RHC, Etain
	1411	Aérospatiale SA.330Ba Puma [DDU]	ALAT, stored Montauban
	1417	Aérospatiale SA.330Ba Puma [DBF]	ALAT 3 RHC, Etain
	1419	Aérospatiale SA.330Ba Puma [DDV]	*Withdrawn from use at Rochefort, 2019*
	1438	Aérospatiale SA.330Ba Puma [DBG]	ALAT GAM/STAT, Valence
	1447	Aérospatiale SA.330Ba Puma [DDW]	ALAT 3 RHC, Etain
	1451	Aérospatiale SA.330Ba Puma [DBH]	ALAT
	1507	Aérospatiale SA.330Ba Puma [DBI]	ALAT EALAT, Le Luc
	1510	Aérospatiale SA.330Ba Puma [DBJ]	ALAT 3 RHC, Etain
	1512	Aérospatiale SA.330Ba Puma [DBK]	ALAT 3 RHC, Etain
	1519	Aérospatiale SA.330Ba Puma [DBL]	ALAT 3 RHC, Etain
	1617	Aérospatiale SA.330Ba Puma [DBM]	ALAT
	1632	Aérospatiale SA.330Ba Puma [DBN]	ALAT
	1634	Aérospatiale SA.330Ba Puma [DBO]	ALAT 3 RHC, Etain
	1654	Aérospatiale SA.330Ba Puma [DBP]	ALAT 3 RHC, Etain
	1662	Aérospatiale SA.330Ba Puma [DDX]	ALAT EALAT, Le Luc
	1663	Aérospatiale SA.330Ba Puma [DBQ]	ALAT 3 RHC, Etain
	5682	Aérospatiale SA.330Ba Puma [DBR]	ALAT
	1732	Aérospatiale SA.342M Gazelle [GJA]	ALAT EALAT, Le Luc
	3458	Aérospatiale SA.342M Gazelle [GNA]	ALAT EALAT, Le Luc
	3459	Aérospatiale SA.342M Gazelle [GAA]	ALAT 1 RHC, Phalsbourg
	3476	Aérospatiale SA.342M Gazelle [GAB] $	*Withdrawn from use at Etain*
	3511	Aérospatiale SA.342M Gazelle [GJC]	ALAT EALAT, Le Luc
	3512	Aérospatiale SA.342M Gazelle [GAC]	ALAT 1 RHC, Phalsbourg
	3513	Aérospatiale SA.342M Gazelle [GNB]	ALAT 1 RHC, Phalsbourg
	3529	Aérospatiale SA.342M Gazelle [GJD]	*Withdrawn from use at Etain*
	3530	Aérospatiale SA.342M Gazelle [GAD]	ALAT
	3546	Aérospatiale SA.342M Gazelle [GJF]	ALAT EALAT, Le Luc
	3548	Aérospatiale SA.342M Gazelle [GAE]	ALAT 1 RHC, Phalsbourg
	3549	Aérospatiale SA.342M Gazelle [GNC]	ALAT EALAT, Le Luc
	3567	Aérospatiale SA.342M Gazelle [GMA]	ALAT EALAT, Le Luc

5191 is a Morane-Saulnier Type N replica. It has been allocated the number BAPC.472 by Aviation Heritage UK (formerly the British Aviation Preservation Council). Displayed incomplete at the RAF100 air show at Cosford in 2018, it is now back on display at the North-East Land, Sea & Air Museums at Usworth.

AT-16 Harvard IIb G-CORS is based at Duxford and still wears the markings that it bore when in service as KF183 with the A&AEE (later QinetiQ) at Boscombe Down.

Spitfire LF XVIe TD248 is registered as G-OXVI and wears the code 'CR-S' for Air Vice Marshall Cliff Spink, former Commanding Officer of No 74 Squadron RAF. The badge of the latter is worn on the nose.

WD363/5 is a DHC-1 Chipmunk 22, registered as G-BCIH and based at the Army airfield at Netheravon in Wiltshire.

WK039 is a Thales Watchkeeper 450, itself based on the Elbit Hermes 450. Operated by 47 Regiment, Royal Artillery based at Boscombe Down, it is seen in front of a purpose-built trailer used to transport these around … and close inspection reveals a second example still dismantled inside.

Armstrong-Whitworth-built Gloster Meteor NF14 WS776/K is on display at the delightful Bournemouth Aviation Museum, where visitors can even sit in its cockpit. It wears the colours it bore when in service with No 25 Squadron RAF in 1954.

The annual air day at Yeovilton is an event when visitors can also see rare outings of Fleet Air Arm Museum aircraft. The 2019 event was no exception, when Sea Hawk FGA6 WV856/163 came outside. It is painted in the colours of 806 Naval Air Squadron.

It is not often that new aviation museums are set up, so the opening of the South Wales Aviation Museum at St Athan in Easter 2019 was an exciting event, not least because of the wide range of exhibits it has already collected together, including Sea Devon C20 XK895 (G-SDEV) seen here.

Following the crash at Shoreham several years ago, many two-seat Hawker Hunters in civilian hands have been grounded or sold abroad. In the case of Hunter T7 G-BVGH, it is painted in this silver scheme and in the tender care of the South Wales Aviation Museum at St Athan.

If this familiar airframe looks unusual that may be because this is the sole Auster AOP11 built, converted from an Auster AOP9 by the addition of a more powerful Continental IO-470-D engine. XP254 is on the UK civil register as G-ASCC and now lives in Cambridgeshire.

'XS933' is a Lightning F53, preserved at the North-East Land, Sea & Air Museums at Usworth. It was one of a number built for the Royal Saudi Air Force which were returned to the UK and put back on the military register, in this case as ZF594.

Wessex HU5 XT761 (G-WSEX) took to the air again after 32 years on 15 February 2019. Currently the sole flying example of the type, it fittingly opened the flying display at the 2019 Yeovilton International Air Day. One of a number of helicopters in the care of Historic Helicopters, based near Chard in Somerset.

XV582/M is a Phantom FG1, formerly the gate guard at RAF Leuchars. Painted in 111 Squadron markings, 'Black Mike' is now on display at the South Wales Aviation Museum at St Athan.

45 years to the day of its first flight, Hawk T1 XX154, the first aircraft built, made the short hop from Boscombe Down to Old Sarum on 21 August 2019 for preservation with the Boscombe Down Aviation Museum.

Sea Harrier FA2 ZA195/710 made the journey from the Tangmere Military Aviation Museum to its new home at the South Wales Aviation Museum at St Athan during 2019.

ZA326 is the sole Panavia Tornado GR1P and is now on display at the excellent South Wales Aviation Museum at St Athan.

Although painted as ZH801, this Sea Harrier FA2 is actually ZH800. Painted as 001 of 801 Naval Air Squadron, it is preserved at RNAS Yeovilton.

Deliveries of the Merlin HC4 to the Royal Navy at Yeovilton are now well under way, following conversion at nearby Yeovil. Several of the six Merlin HC3As have now begun the transformation also. ZJ125/J of 846 Naval Air Squadron was delivered during 2019 and displays the new grey scheme worn by the type.

Apache AH1 ZJ231 is based at Wattisham with 3 Regiment Army Air Corps. More than 50 of the Army's Apaches are now included in the process to upgrade the fleet to AH-64E standard, with registrations ZM700 to ZM749 allocated.

Typhoon FGR4 ZJ913 wears the markings of No 9 Squadron RAF, based at RAF Lossiemouth and is one of a handful to also carry wartime codes, in this case WS-Y. This code was worn by No 9 Squadron Lancaster LM220, credited with dropping the bomb that sank the German battleship *Tirpitz* in 1944.

2019 saw the final deliveries of the Typhoon FGR4 to the RAF and this one, ZK436, based at RAF Coningsby, is number 152 of the 155 built. The bulges on the rear fuselage identify this as a Tranche 3 airframe, as are ZK355 et seq.

Deliveries of the Lockheed Martin F-35B Lightning II continue at a slow rate, with 18 delivered by December 2019. The whole fleet is now receiving sequential codes, in a similar way to the Tornado GR4 that it replaced, along with a toned-down lightning flash on the tail. By the end of 2019 ZM146, operated in a pool by both no 207 Squadron and No 617 Squadron at RAF Marham, was coded 012.

ZM324 is a Beechcraft T-6C Texan T1, one of ten which have replaced the Shorts Tucano T1 fleet and which are based at RAF Valley.

Just five Embraer Phenom T1s are operated by the RAF and for much of 2019 only four were available as the fifth, ZM336, was being repaired. ZM333 is operated by No 45 Squadron, part of No 3 FTS at RAF Cranwell.

ZM519/19 is an Airbus H135 Juno T1, operated by the Defence Helicopter Flying School at RAF Shawbury.

ZZ520 is an AgustaWestland Wildcat AH1 which, like the HMA2, is based at RNAS Yeovilton in Somerset. ZZ520 was operated by No 652 Squadron, part of No 1 Regiment, Army Air Corps when this photo was taken but unusually the 847 Naval Air Squadron AH1s based here also wear Army titles.

G-ETPB is one of two Pilatus PC-21s operated by QinetiQ from Boscombe Down.

BAe RJ.70-ER G-ETPK is sistership to RJ.100 G-ETPL, both of which now wear the striking colours depicted here. During 2019 the last of the military-registered QinetiQ assets, based at Boscombe Down, were moved to the UK civil register, all now in the G-ETP. Series.

A welcome visitor to the UK in 2019 was the sole flying Breguet Br1050 Alizé, 59 (F-AZYI), operated by Alizé Marine and based at Nîmes/Garons in France.

417 is a BAC Strikemaster Mk80A and one of a pair flown on the air show circuit from Hawarden. Its civil registration, G-RSAF, gives away the fact that this is in fact not an ex Omani machine but one that saw operation with the Royal Saudi Air Force (as 1120).

J-35J Draken SE-DXR is ex 35556/10-56 of the Swedish Air Force. Operated by the Swedish Air Force Historic Flight from Såtenäs, this magnificent machine has now been repainted since this photo was taken at the end of August 2019.

270 is one of a pair of Eurocopter EC135P-2s operated by No 302 squadron of 3 Operations Wing of the Irish Air Corps at Baldonnel. The serial is hard to see – in black on the dark green of the tail.

M-2 is one of three Sud SA.316B Alouette IIIs operated by the Belgian Air Force's 40 Smaldeel, Koksijde. Delivered in 1971, these are nearly fifty years old.

E-191 is a SABCA-built F-16A MLU Fighting Falcon of Eskadrille 730 of the Royal Danish Air Force, based at Skrydstrup. In 2019 it wore special markings to commemorate the 800th anniversary of the Danish flag.

GALLERY

The *Patrouille de France* is the French Air Force aerobatic team, operating the Alpha Jet E from Salon de Provence. Close inspection of the rear fuselage of this example, coded 9, reveals the radio call sign FTELC, which identifies this as E87.

Eurofighter EF.2000GS 30+25 is operated by the Luftwaffe's TLG 71 *Richthofen*, based at Wittmund. This aircraft celebrates 60 years of the unit, with suitable artwork for the *Red Baron* on the tail.

RJF 01 is one of five new Extra EA-330LX aircraft now operated by the *Royal Jordanian Falcons* aerobatic team, based in Aqaba. The team is based in Europe in the Summer and a welcome and popular act at air shows.

The Lithuanian Air Force's Transporto Eskadrile, based at Siauliai/Zokniai operates three Aeritalia C-27J Spartans, including this one, 06 blue.

691 is a Fokker-built F-16B MLU Fighting Falcon, belonging to 331 Skv of the Norwegian Air Force and based at Bodø. To celebrate its 75th anniversary, the air force painted this Fighting Falcon in the colours worn by Spitfire IX, PL258 FN-K, of 331 (Norwegian) Squadron.

The Cessna 550 Citation II is rarely seen in military markings, at least in Europe, but the Spanish Navy has three, belonging to 4 Escadrilla, based at Rota, including this one, U20-2.

2019 saw the return of the Harrier to the Royal International Air Tattoo and the Spanish Navy painted the pair that it sent in special markings for the event, including this one, McDonnell Douglas EAV-8B+ Matador VA.1B-37/01-925 from 9 Escadrilla, based at Rota.

J-5011 is a McDonnell Douglas F/A-18C Hornet of the Swiss Air Force, which operates them from bases at Meiringen and Payerne. This one is painted in special tiger markings associated with Fliegerstaffel 11 at Meiringen, which is a special member of the NATO Tiger Association, even though Switzerland is, of course, not a NATO member.

(08-)0051 is a Bell-Boeing CV-22B Osprey, one of nine operated by the 7th Special Operations Squadron, part of the 352nd Special Operations Wing based at RAF Mildenhall in Suffolk.

F-15C Eagle 84-0010/LN is operated by the 493rd Fighter Squadron of the 48th Fighter Wing at RAF Lakenheath. In connection with the 75th Anniversary of D-Day, it received these special markings with blue rudders and red and white checks on the nose.

In the event of an emergency, the F-15 Eagle is equipped with a tail hook, which can be used with an airfield's Rotary Hydraulic Arrestor Gear to bring it to a halt. Here F-15E Strike Eagle 91-0310/LN of the 494th Fighter Squadron of the 48th Fighter Wing at RAF Lakenheath comes in for an approach with its hook deployed. Fortunately, a safe landing was made, and no-one was hurt.

F-15E Strike Eagle 91-0603/LN is operated by the 494th Fighter Squadron of the 48th Fighter Wing at RAF Lakenheath. In connection with the 75th Anniversary of D-Day, it received these special markings with yellow rudders and red and white checks on the nose and the name *Madeline II*.

F-16CM-50 Fighting Falcon 96-0080/SP is operated by the 480th Fighter Squadron of the 52nd Fighter Wing at Spangdahlem in Germany and wears special 480 FS markings. In July 2019 it was performing at the Royal international Air Tattoo when the pilot noticed a severe vibration. Close inspection of the photo reveals the issue with the rear of the starboard tail plane having broken away. A safe emergency landing ensued.

To commemorate the final year of service with the Tucano T1, ZF448 was used by the Tucano Display team with the badges of every RAF Tucano operator on the fuselage. Here it is seen on approach with spare ZF264 on approach to Bournemouth for its penultimate display in late August 2019.

Serial	Type (code/other identity)	Owner/operator, location or fate	Notes
3617	Aérospatiale SA.342M Gazelle [GND]	ALAT GAM/STAT, Valence	
3664	Aérospatiale SA.342M Gazelle [GAF]	ALAT 1 RHC, Phalsbourg	
3848	Aérospatiale SA.342M Gazelle [GAG]	ALAT 5 RHC, Pau	
3849	Aérospatiale SA.342M Gazelle [GAH]	ALAT 5 RHC, Pau	
3850	Aérospatiale SA.342M Gazelle [GAI]	ALAT 1 RHC, Phalsbourg	
3851	Aérospatiale SA.342M Gazelle [GJI]	ALAT EALAT, Le Luc	
3852	Aérospatiale SA.342M Gazelle [GNE]	ALAT 1 RHC, Phalsbourg	
3853	Aérospatiale SA.342M Gazelle [GNF]	ALAT EALAT, Le Luc	
3855	Aérospatiale SA.342M Gazelle [GJJ]	ALAT EALAT, Le Luc	
3856	Aérospatiale SA.342M Gazelle [GAJ]	ALAT 5 RHC, Pau	
3857	Aérospatiale SA.342M Gazelle [GJK]	ALAT EALAT, Le Luc	
3858	Aérospatiale SA.342M Gazelle [GNG]	*Sold to Togo as 5V-MCQ, 2019*	
3859	Aérospatiale SA.342M Gazelle [GAK]	ALAT 5 RHC, Pau	
3862	Aérospatiale SA.342M Gazelle [GAL] $	ALAT 1 RHC, Phalsbourg	
3863	Aérospatiale SA.342M Gazelle [GAM]	ALAT 3 RHC, Etain	
3864	Aérospatiale SA.342M Gazelle [GJL]	ALAT EALAT, Le Luc	
3865	Aérospatiale SA.342M Gazelle [GAN]	ALAT EALAT, Le Luc	
3867	Aérospatiale SA.342M Gazelle [GJM]	ALAT EALAT, Le Luc	
3868	Aérospatiale SA.342M Gazelle [GAO]	ALAT EALAT, Le Luc	
3870	Aérospatiale SA.342M Gazelle [GME]	ALAT	
3896	Aérospatiale SA.342M Gazelle [GNJ]	ALAT	
3911	Aérospatiale SA.342M Gazelle [GAP]	ALAT 1 RHC, Phalsbourg	
3921	Aérospatiale SA.342M Gazelle [GAQ]	ALAT EALAT, Le Luc	
3929	Aérospatiale SA.342M Gazelle [GJN]	ALAT EALAT, Le Luc	
3930	Aérospatiale SA.342M Gazelle [GMF]	*Sold to Iraq as YI-295*	
3938	Aérospatiale SA.342M Gazelle [GAR]	ALAT EALAT, Le Luc	
3939	Aérospatiale SA.342M Gazelle [GMG]	*Sold to Iraq as YI-296*	
3947	Aérospatiale SA.342M Gazelle [GAS]	ALAT 5 RHC, Pau	
3948	Aérospatiale SA.342M Gazelle [GAT]	ALAT 1 RHC, Phalsbourg	
3956	Aérospatiale SA.342M Gazelle [GNK]	ALAT	
3957	Aérospatiale SA.342M Gazelle [GAU]	ALAT 5 RHC, Pau	
3964	Aérospatiale SA.342M Gazelle [GAV]	ALAT 3 RHC, Etain	
3965	Aérospatiale SA.342M Gazelle [GJO]	ALAT EALAT, Le Luc	
3992	Aérospatiale SA.342M Gazelle [GNM]	ALAT EALAT, Le Luc	
3996	Aérospatiale SA.342M Gazelle [GAW]	ALAT EALAT, Le Luc	
4008	Aérospatiale SA.342M Gazelle [GNN]	*Sold to Iraq as YI-299*	
4014	Aérospatiale SA.342M Gazelle [GJP]	ALAT GAM/STAT, Valence	
4018	Aérospatiale SA.342M Gazelle [GAX]	ALAT 3 RHC, Etain	
4020	Aérospatiale SA.342M Gazelle [GAZ]	ALAT 1 RHC, Phalsbourg	
4022	Aérospatiale SA.342M Gazelle [GJQ]	ALAT EALAT, Le Luc	
4023	Aérospatiale SA.342M Gazelle [GMH]	ALAT ESAM, Bourges	
4026	Aérospatiale SA.342M Gazelle [GBA]	ALAT 1 RHC, Phalsbourg	
4032	Aérospatiale SA.342M Gazelle [GNO]	ALAT EALAT, Le Luc	
4034	Aérospatiale SA.342M Gazelle [GBB]	ALAT 1 RHC, Phalsbourg	
4038	Aérospatiale SA.342M Gazelle [GJR]	ALAT EALAT, Le Luc	
4039	Aérospatiale SA.342M Gazelle [GBC]	ALAT 1 RHC, Phalsbourg	
4042	Aérospatiale SA.342M Gazelle [GMB]	ALAT EALAT, Le Luc	
4047	Aérospatiale SA.342M Gazelle [GJS]	ALAT EALAT, Le Luc	
4048	Aérospatiale SA.342M Gazelle [GBD]	ALAT EALAT, Le Luc	
4049	Aérospatiale SA.342M Gazelle [GNP]	ALAT EALAT, Le Luc	
4053	Aérospatiale SA.342M Gazelle [GBE]	ALAT 3 RHC, Etain	
4059	Aérospatiale SA.342M Gazelle [GBF]	ALAT 1 RHC, Phalsbourg	
4060	Aérospatiale SA.342M Gazelle [GNQ]	ALAT EALAT, Le Luc	
4061	Aérospatiale SA.342M Gazelle [GBG]	ALAT GAM/STAT, Valence	
4065	Aérospatiale SA.342M Gazelle [GNR]	ALAT EALAT, Le Luc	
4066	Aérospatiale SA.342M Gazelle [GBH]	ALAT 3 RHC, Etain	
4067	Aérospatiale SA.342M Gazelle [GJU]	ALAT EALAT, Le Luc	
4071	Aérospatiale SA.342M Gazelle [GNS]	ALAT EHADT, Etain	
4072	Aérospatiale SA.342M Gazelle [GBI]	ALAT 3 RHC, Etain	
4078	Aérospatiale SA.342M Gazelle [GJV]	ALAT EALAT, Le Luc	
4079	Aérospatiale SA.342M Gazelle [GMC]	ALAT EALAT, Le Luc	
4083	Aérospatiale SA.342M Gazelle [GNT]	ALAT EALAT, Le Luc	

Notes	Serial	Type (code/other identity)	Owner/operator, location or fate
	4084	Aérospatiale SA.342M Gazelle [GBJ] $	ALAT 3 RHC, Etain
	4095	Aérospatiale SA.342M Gazelle [GBL]	ALAT 5 RHC, Pau
	4096	Aérospatiale SA.342M Gazelle [GNU]	ALAT EALAT, Le Luc
	4102	Aérospatiale SA.342M Gazelle [GJW]	ALAT EALAT, Le Luc
	4103	Aérospatiale SA.342M Gazelle [GJX]	ALAT EALAT, Le Luc
	4108	Aérospatiale SA.342M Gazelle [GBM]	ALAT GAM/STAT, Valence
	4109	Aérospatiale SA.342M Gazelle [GBN]	ALAT 5 RHC, Pau
	4114	Aérospatiale SA.342M Gazelle [GBO]	ALAT EALAT, Le Luc
	4115	Aérospatiale SA.342M Gazelle [GBP]	ALAT 5 RHC, Pau
	4118	Aérospatiale SA.342M Gazelle [GNV]	ALAT EALAT, Le Luc
	4119	Aérospatiale SA.342M Gazelle [GBQ]	ALAT 5 RHC, Pau
	4120	Aérospatiale SA.342M Gazelle [GBR]	ALAT EALAT, Le Luc
	4123	Aérospatiale SA.342M Gazelle [GJY]	ALAT EALAT, Le Luc
	4124	Aérospatiale SA.342M Gazelle [GBS]	ALAT 1 RHC, Phalsbourg
	4135	Aérospatiale SA.342M Gazelle [GNW]	ALAT
	4136	Aérospatiale SA.342M Gazelle [GBT]	ALAT 1 RHC, Phalsbourg
	4140	Aérospatiale SA.342M Gazelle [GBU]	ALAT 1 RHC, Phalsbourg
	4141	Aérospatiale SA.342M Gazelle [GBV]	ALAT 1 RHC, Phalsbourg
	4142	Aérospatiale SA.342M Gazelle [GBW]	ALAT 5 RHC, Pau
	4143	Aérospatiale SA.342M Gazelle [GNX]	ALAT EALAT, Le Luc
	4144	Aérospatiale SA.342M Gazelle [GBX]	ALAT 3 RHC, Etain
	4145	Aérospatiale SA.342M Gazelle [GBY] $	ALAT 3 RHC, Etain
	4146	Aérospatiale SA.342M Gazelle [GNY]	ALAT EALAT, Le Luc
	4151	Aérospatiale SA.342M Gazelle [GBZ]	ALAT 3 RHC, Etain
	4159	Aérospatiale SA.342M Gazelle [GNZ]	ALAT EALAT, Le Luc
	4160	Aérospatiale SA.342M Gazelle [GCC]	ALAT 1 RHC, Phalsbourg
	4161	Aérospatiale SA.342M Gazelle [GCD]	ALAT 1 RHC, Phalsbourg
	4162	Aérospatiale SA.342M Gazelle [GCE]	ALAT 5 RHC, Pau
	4164	Aérospatiale SA.342M Gazelle [GCF]	ALAT 3 RHC, Etain
	4166	Aérospatiale SA.342M Gazelle [GJZ]	ALAT EALAT, Le Luc
	4168	Aérospatiale SA.342M Gazelle [GCG]	ALAT 5 RHC, Pau
	4171	Aérospatiale SA.342M Gazelle [GMI]	ALAT EALAT, Le Luc
	4175	Aérospatiale SA.342M Gazelle [GCI]	ALAT 1 RHC, Phalsbourg
	4176	Aérospatiale SA.342M Gazelle [GKA]	ALAT EALAT, Le Luc
	4177	Aérospatiale SA.342M Gazelle [GKB]	ALAT 1 RHC, Phalsbourg
	4178	Aérospatiale SA.342M Gazelle [GOA]	ALAT EALAT, Le Luc
	4179	Aérospatiale SA.342M Gazelle [GCJ]	ALAT 3 RHC, Etain
	4180	Aérospatiale SA.342M Gazelle [GCK]	ALAT GAM/STAT, Valence
	4181	Aérospatiale SA.342M Gazelle [GCL]	ALAT 3 RHC, Etain
	4182	Aérospatiale SA.342M Gazelle [GKC]	ALAT EALAT, Le Luc
	4183	Aérospatiale SA.342M Gazelle [GOB]	ALAT EALAT, Le Luc
	4184	Aérospatiale SA.342M Gazelle [GOC]	ALAT 1 RHC, Phalsbourg
	4185	Aérospatiale SA.342M Gazelle [GKD]	ALAT 3 RHC, Etain
	4186	Aérospatiale SA.342M Gazelle [GCM]	ALAT 1 RHC, Phalsbourg
	4187	Aérospatiale SA.342M Gazelle [GKE]	*To the Togo Air Force, May 2019*
	4189	Aérospatiale SA.342M Gazelle [GCN]	ALAT 5 RHC, Pau
	4190	Aérospatiale SA.342M Gazelle [GMJ]	ALAT EALAT, Le Luc
	4191	Aérospatiale SA.342M Gazelle [GCO]	ALAT 5 RHC, Pau
	4192	Aérospatiale SA.342M Gazelle [GOD]	ALAT EALAT, Le Luc
	4194	Aérospatiale SA.342M Gazelle [GMD]	ALAT EALAT, Le Luc
	4195	Aérospatiale SA.342M Gazelle [GCP]	ALAT 3 RHC, Etain
	4198	Aérospatiale SA.342M Gazelle [GCQ]	ALAT 3 RHC, Etain
	4201	Aérospatiale SA.342M Gazelle [GMK]	ALAT EALAT, Le Luc
	4205	Aérospatiale SA.342L-1 Gazelle [GEA]	ALAT 1 RHC, Phalsbourg
	4206	Aérospatiale SA.342L-1 Gazelle [GEB]	ALAT EALAT, Le Luc
	4207	Aérospatiale SA.342L-1 Gazelle [GEC]	ALAT 3 RHC, Etain
	4208	Aérospatiale SA.342L-1 Gazelle [GED]	ALAT GAM/STAT, Valence
	4210	Aérospatiale SA.342L-1 Gazelle [GEF]	ALAT 1 RHC, Phalsbourg
	4211	Aérospatiale SA.342L-1 Gazelle [GEG]	ALAT 5 RHC, Pau
	4214	Aérospatiale SA.342L-1 Gazelle [GEI]	ALAT EALAT, Le Luc
	4215	Aérospatiale SA.342L-1 Gazelle [GEJ]	ALAT 5 RHC, Pau
	4216	Aérospatiale SA.342L-1 Gazelle [GEK]	ALAT GAM/STAT, Valence

Serial	Type (code/other identity)	Owner/operator, location or fate	Notes
4217	Aérospatiale SA.342L-1 Gazelle [GEL]	ALAT 3 RHC, Etain	
4218	Aérospatiale SA.342L-1 Gazelle [GEM]	ALAT 1 RHC, Phalsbourg	
4219	Aérospatiale SA.342L-1 Gazelle [GEN]	ALAT	
4220	Aérospatiale SA.342L-1 Gazelle [GEO]	ALAT 3 RHC, Etain	
4221	Aérospatiale SA.342L-1 Gazelle [GEP]	ALAT EALAT, Le Luc	
4222	Aérospatiale SA.342L-1 Gazelle [GEQ]	ALAT EALAT, Le Luc	
4223	Aérospatiale SA.342L-1 Gazelle [GER]	ALAT GAM/STAT, Valence	
4224	Aérospatiale SA.342L-1 Gazelle [GES]	ALAT 1 RHC, Phalsbourg	
4225	Aérospatiale SA.342L-1 Gazelle [GET]	ALAT GAM/STAT, Valence	
4226	Aérospatiale SA.342L-1 Gazelle [GEU]	ALAT GAM/STAT, Valence	
4227	Aérospatiale SA.342L-1 Gazelle [GEV]	ALAT 1 RHC, Phalsbourg	
4228	Aérospatiale SA.342L-1 Gazelle [GEW]	ALAT 1 RHC, Phalsbourg	
4229	Aérospatiale SA.342L-1 Gazelle [GEX]	ALAT 3 RHC, Etain	
4230	Aérospatiale SA.342L-1 Gazelle [GEY]	ALAT GAM/STAT, Valence	
4231	Aérospatiale SA.342L-1 Gazelle [GEZ]	ALAT 5 RHC, Pau	
4232	Aérospatiale SA.342L-1 Gazelle [GFA]	ALAT EALAT, Le Luc	
4233	Aérospatiale SA.342L-1 Gazelle [GFB]	ALAT 3 RHC, Etain	
4234	Aérospatiale SA.342L-1 Gazelle [GFC]	*Written off*	
2252	Aérospatiale AS.532UL Cougar [CGA]	ALAT GAM/STAT, Valence	
2266	Aérospatiale AS.532UL Cougar [CGB]	ALAT 5 RHC, Pau	
2267	Aérospatiale AS.532UL Cougar [CGC]	ALAT 4 RHFS, Pau	
2271	Aérospatiale AS.532UL Cougar [CGD]	ALAT 4 RHFS, Pau	
2272	Aérospatiale AS.532UL Cougar [CGE]	ALAT GAM/STAT, Valence	
2273	Aérospatiale AS.532UL Cougar [CGF]	ALAT 1 RHC, Phalsbourg	
2282	Aérospatiale AS.532UL Cougar [CGG]	ALAT	
2285	Aérospatiale AS.532UL Cougar [CGH]	ALAT	
2290	Aérospatiale AS.532UL Cougar [CGI]	ALAT 4 RHFS, Pau	
2293	Aérospatiale AS.532UL Cougar [CGJ]	ALAT 4 RHFS, Pau	
2299	Aérospatiale AS.532UL Cougar [CGK]	ALAT 4 RHFS, Pau	
2300	Aérospatiale AS.532UL Cougar [CGL]	ALAT 1 RHC, Phalsbourg	
2301	Aérospatiale AS.532UL Cougar [CGM]	ALAT 1 RHC, Phalsbourg	
2303	Aérospatiale AS.532UL Cougar [CGN]	ALAT 1 RHC, Phalsbourg	
2316	Aérospatiale AS.532UL Cougar [CGO]	ALAT 4 RHFS, Pau	
2323	Aérospatiale AS.532UL Cougar [CGQ]	ALAT 4 RHFS, Pau	
2324	Aérospatiale AS.532UL Cougar [CGR]	ALAT 4 RHFS, Pau	
2325	Aérospatiale AS.532UL Cougar [CGS]	ALAT	
2327	Aérospatiale AS.532UL Cougar [CGT]	ALAT	
2331	Aérospatiale AS.532UL Cougar [CGU]	ALAT GAM/STAT, Valence	
2336	Aérospatiale AS.532UL Cougar [CGV]	ALAT 4 RHFS, Pau	
2342	Aérospatiale AS.532UL Cougar [CHA]	ALAT	
2369	Aérospatiale AS.532UL Cougar [CHB]	ALAT	
2375	Aérospatiale AS.532UL Cougar [CHC]	ALAT	
2443	Aérospatiale AS.532UL Cougar [CGW]	ALAT	
2446	Aérospatiale AS.532UL Cougar [CGX]	ALAT 1 RHC, Phalsbourg	
2001	Eurocopter EC.665 Tigre HAP [BHH]	ALAT EFA, Le Luc	
2002	Eurocopter EC.665 Tigre HAP [BHI]	ALAT EFA, Le Luc	
2003	Eurocopter EC.665 Tigre HAP [BHJ]	ALAT 5 RHC, Pau	
2004	Eurocopter EC.665 Tigre HAP [BHK]	ALAT EFA, Le Luc	
2006	Eurocopter EC.665 Tigre HAP [BHL]	ALAT EFA, Le Luc	
2009	Eurocopter EC.665 Tigre HAP [BHB]	ALAT EFA, Le Luc	
2010	Eurocopter EC.665 Tigre HAP [BHA]	ALAT EFA, Le Luc	
2011	Eurocopter EC.665 Tigre HAP [BHM]	ALAT 5 RHC, Pau	
2012	Eurocopter EC.665 Tigre HAP [BHT]	ALAT GAM/STAT, Valence	
2013	Eurocopter EC.665 Tigre HAP [BHC]	ALAT GAM/STAT, Valence	
2015	Eurocopter EC.665 Tigre HAP [BHD]	ALAT 5 RHC, Pau	
2016	Eurocopter EC.665 Tigre HAP [BIA]	Airbus Helicopters, Marseille	
2018	Eurocopter EC.665 Tigre HAP [BHE]	ALAT 5 RHC, Pau	
2019	Eurocopter EC.665 Tigre HAP [BHF]	ALAT 5 RHC, Pau	
2021	Eurocopter EC.665 Tigre HAP [BHN] $	ALAT EFA, Le Luc	
2022	Eurocopter EC.665 Tigre HAP [BHG]	ALAT 5 RHC, Pau	
2023	Eurocopter EC.665 Tigre HAP [BHP]	ALAT 5 RHC, Pau	
2024	Eurocopter EC.665 Tigre HAP [BHO]	ALAT 3 RHC, Etain	

Notes	Serial	Type (code/other identity)	Owner/operator, location or fate
	2025	Eurocopter EC.665 Tigre HAP [BHQ]	ALAT 5 RHC, Pau
	2026	Eurocopter EC.665 Tigre HAP [BHR]	ALAT GAM/STAT, Valence
	2027	Eurocopter EC.665 Tigre HAP [BHS]	ALAT 5 RHC, Pau
	2028	Eurocopter EC.665 Tigre HAP [BHU]	ALAT TsLw 3, Fassberg, Germany
	2029	Eurocopter EC.665 Tigre HAP [BHV]	ALAT 5 RHC, Pau
	2030	Eurocopter EC.665 Tigre HAP [BHW]	ALAT 5 RHC, Pau
	2031	Eurocopter EC.665 Tigre HAP [BHX]	ALAT EFA, Le Luc
	2033	Eurocopter EC.665 Tigre HAP [BHZ]	ALAT 5 RHC, Pau
	2034	Eurocopter EC.665 Tigre HAP [BIB]	ALAT EFA, Le Luc
	2035	Eurocopter EC.665 Tigre HAP [BIC]	ALAT 4 RHFS, Pau
	2037	Eurocopter EC.665 Tigre HAP [BIE]	ALAT 5 RHC, Pau
	2038	Eurocopter EC.665 Tigre HAP [BIF]	ALAT 5 RHC, Pau
	2039	Eurocopter EC.665 Tigre HAP [BIG]	ALAT EALAT, Le Luc
	2040	Eurocopter EC.665 Tigre HAP [BIH]	ALAT 5 RHC, Pau
	2041	Eurocopter EC.665 Tigre HAP [BII]	ALAT 5 RHC, Pau
	2042	Eurocopter EC.665 Tigre HAP [BIJ]	ALAT 5 RHC, Pau
	2043	Eurocopter EC.665 Tigre HAP [BIK]	ALAT 5 RHC, Pau
	2044	Eurocopter EC.665 Tigre HAP [BIL]	ALAT GAM/STAT, Valence
	2045	Eurocopter EC.665 Tigre HAP [BIM]	ALAT EFA, Le Luc
	2046	Eurocopter EC.665 Tigre HAP [BIN]	ALAT EFA, Le Luc
	2047	Eurocopter EC.665 Tigre HAP [BIO]	ALAT (on order)
	2048	Eurocopter EC.665 Tigre HAP [BIP]	ALAT (on order)
	2049	Eurocopter EC.665 Tigre HAP [BIQ]	ALAT (on order)
	2050	Eurocopter EC.665 Tigre HAP [BIR]	ALAT (on order)
	2051	Eurocopter EC.665 Tigre HAP [BIS]	ALAT (on order)
	2052	Eurocopter EC.665 Tigre HAP [BIT]	ALAT (on order)
	6001	Eurocopter EC.665 Tigre HAD [BJA]	ALAT 1 RHC, Phalsbourg
	6002	Eurocopter EC.665 Tigre HAD [BJB]	ALAT EFA, Le Luc
	6003	Eurocopter EC.665 Tigre HAD [BJC]	ALAT EFA, Le Luc
	6004	Eurocopter EC.665 Tigre HAD [BJD]	ALAT EFA, Le Luc
	6005	Eurocopter EC.665 Tigre HAD [BJE]	ALAT EFA, Le Luc
	6006	Eurocopter EC.665 Tigre HAD [BJF]	ALAT 1 RHC, Phalsbourg
	6007	Eurocopter EC.665 Tigre HAD [BJG]	ALAT EFA, Le Luc
	6008	Eurocopter EC.665 Tigre HAD [BJH]	ALAT
	6009	Eurocopter EC.665 Tigre HAD [BJI]	ALAT 1 RHC, Phalsbourg
	6010	Eurocopter EC.665 Tigre HAD [BJJ]	ALAT GAM/STAT, Valence
	6011	Eurocopter EC.665 Tigre HAD [BJK]	ALAT
	6012	Eurocopter EC.665 Tigre HAD [BJL]	ALAT 1 RHC, Phalsbourg
	6013	Eurocopter EC.665 Tigre HAD [BJM]	ALAT 1 RHC, Phalsbourg
	6014	Eurocopter EC.665 Tigre HAD [BJN]	ALAT EALAT, Le Luc
	6015	Eurocopter EC.665 Tigre HAD [BJO]	ALAT 1 RHC, Phalsbourg
	6016	Eurocopter EC.665 Tigre HAD [BJP]	ALAT 1 RHC, Phalsbourg
	6017	Eurocopter EC.665 Tigre HAD [BJQ]	ALAT 1 RHC, Phalsbourg
	6018	Eurocopter EC.665 Tigre HAD [BJR]	ALAT 1 RHC, Phalsbourg
	6019	Eurocopter EC.665 Tigre HAD [BJS]	ALAT
	6020	Eurocopter EC.665 Tigre HAD [BJT]	ALAT 1 RHC, Phalsbourg
	6021	Eurocopter EC.665 Tigre HAD [BJU]	ALAT EALAT, Le Luc
	6022	Eurocopter EC.665 Tigre HAD [BJV]	ALAT
	6023	Eurocopter EC.665 Tigre HAD [BJW]	ALAT
	6024	Eurocopter EC.665 Tigre HAD [BJX]	ALAT
	6025	Eurocopter EC.665 Tigre HAD [BJY]	ALAT
	6026	Eurocopter EC.665 Tigre HAD [BJZ]	ALAT
	6027	Eurocopter EC.665 Tigre HAD [BKA]	ALAT (on order)
	6028	Eurocopter EC.665 Tigre HAD [BKB]	ALAT (on order)
	6029	Eurocopter EC.665 Tigre HAD [BKC]	ALAT (on order)
	6030	Eurocopter EC.665 Tigre HAD [BKD]	ALAT (on order)
	6031	Eurocopter EC.665 Tigre HAD [BKE]	ALAT (on order)
	2611	Eurocopter EC.725AP Caracal [CAA]	ALAT 4 RHFS, Pau
	2628	Eurocopter EC.725AP Caracal [CAB]	ALAT GIH, Cazaux
	2630	Eurocopter EC.725AP Caracal [CAC]	ALAT 4 RHFS, Pau
	2631	Eurocopter EC.725AP Caracal [CAD]	ALAT 4 RHFS, Pau
	2633	Eurocopter EC.725AP Caracal [CAE]	ALAT 4 RHFS, Pau

Serial	Type (code/other identity)	Owner/operator, location or fate	Notes
2638	Eurocopter EC.725AP Caracal [CAF]	ALAT GIH, Cazaux	
2640	Eurocopter EC.725AP Caracal [CAG]	ALAT GIH, Cazaux	
2642	Eurocopter EC.725AP Caracal [CAH]	ALAT GIH, Cazaux	
1239	NH Industries NH.90-TTH Caïman [EAA]	ALAT CFIA NH.90, Le Luc	
1256	NH Industries NH.90-TTH Caïman [EAB]	ALAT GAM/STAT, Valence	
1271	NH Industries NH.90-TTH Caïman [EAC]	ALAT CFIA NH.90, Le Luc	
1273	NH Industries NH.90-TTH Caïman [EAD]	ALAT 1 RHC, Phalsbourg	
1290	NH Industries NH.90-TTH Caïman [EAE]	ALAT CFIA NH.90, Le Luc	
1291	NH Industries NH.90-TTH Caïman [EAF]	ALAT CFIA NH.90, Le Luc	
1292	NH Industries NH.90-TTH Caïman [EAG]	ALAT 1 RHC, Phalsbourg	
1293	NH Industries NH.90-TTH Caïman [EAH]	ALAT CFIA NH.90, Le Luc	
1294	NH Industries NH.90-TTH Caïman [EAI]	ALAT 1 RHC, Phalsbourg	
1295	NH Industries NH.90-TTH Caïman [EAJ]	ALAT 1 RHC, Phalsbourg	
1306	NH Industries NH.90-TTH Caïman [EAK]	ALAT	
1307	NH Industries NH.90-TTH Caïman [EAL]	ALAT 1 RHC, Phalsbourg	
1308	NH Industries NH.90-TTH Caïman [EAM]	ALAT	
1309	NH Industries NH.90-TTH Caïman [EAN]	ALAT	
1310	NH Industries NH.90-TTH Caïman [EAO]	ALAT 1 RHC, Phalsbourg	
1311	NH Industries NH.90-TTH Caïman [EAP]	ALAT 1 RHC, Phalsbourg	
1312	NH Industries NH.90-TTH Caïman [EAQ]	ALAT 1 RHC, Phalsbourg	
1313	NH Industries NH.90-TTH Caïman [EAR]	ALAT 1 RHC, Phalsbourg	
1332	NH Industries NH.90-TTH Caïman [EAS]	ALAT 1 RHC, Phalsbourg (damaged)	
1333	NH Industries NH.90-TTH Caïman [EAT]	ALAT	
1334	NH Industries NH.90-TTH Caïman [EAU]	ALAT 1 RHC, Phalsbourg	
1335	NH Industries NH.90-TTH Caïman [EAV]	ALAT 1 RHC, Phalsbourg	
1336	NH Industries NH.90-TTH Caïman [EAW]	ALAT 1 RHC, Phalsbourg	
1337	NH Industries NH.90-TTH Caïman [EAX]	ALAT 1 RHC, Phalsbourg	
1338	NH Industries NH.90-TTH Caïman [EAY]	ALAT 1 RHC, Phalsbourg	
1386	NH Industries NH.90-TTH Caïman [EAZ]	ALAT 1 RHC, Phalsbourg	
1390	NH Industries NH.90-TTH Caïman [EBA]	ALAT 1 RHC, Phalsbourg	
1391	NH Industries NH.90-TTH Caïman [EBB]	ALAT 1 RHC, Phalsbourg	
1387	NH Industries NH.90-TTH Caïman [EBC]	ALAT 1 RHC, Phalsbourg	
1392	NH Industries NH.90-TTH Caïman [EBD]	ALAT 1 RHC, Phalsbourg	
1401	NH Industries NH.90-TTH Caïman [EBE]	ALAT 5 RHC, Pau	
1402	NH Industries NH.90-TTH Caïman [EBF]	ALAT 1 RHC, Phalsbourg	
1403	NH Industries NH.90-TTH Caïman [EBG]	ALAT 5 RHC, Pau	
1404	NH Industries NH.90-TTH Caïman [EBH]	ALAT 1 RHC, Phalsbourg	
1405	NH Industries NH.90-TTH Caïman [EBI]	ALAT 5 RHC, Pau	
1427	NH Industries NH.90-TTH Caïman [EBK]	ALAT 5 RHC, Pau	
1428	NH Industries NH.90-TTH Caïman [EBL]	ALAT (on order)	
1429	NH Industries NH.90-TTH Caïman [EBM]	ALAT (on order)	
1430	NH Industries NH.90-TTH Caïman [EBO]	ALAT (on order)	
1431	NH Industries NH.90-TTH Caïman [EBP]	ALAT (on order)	
1432	NH Industries NH.90-TTH Caïman [EBJ]	ALAT (on order)	
1433	NH Industries NH.90-TTH Caïman [EBN]	ALAT (on order)	
1441	NH Industries NH.90-TTH Caïman [EBR]	ALAT (on order)	
14..	NH Industries NH.90-TTH Caïman [EBQ]	ALAT (on order)	
14..	NH Industries NH.90-TTH Caïman [EBS]	ALAT (on order)	
14..	NH Industries NH.90-TTH Caïman [EBT]	ALAT (on order)	
14..	NH Industries NH.90-TTH Caïman [EBU]	ALAT (on order)	
887	Pilatus PC-6B/B2-H4 Turbo Porter [MCA]	ALAT 1 GSALAT, Montauban	
888	Pilatus PC-6B/B2-H4 Turbo Porter [MCB]	ALAT 1 GSALAT, Montauban	
889	Pilatus PC-6B/B2-H4 Turbo Porter [MCC]	ALAT 1 GSALAT, Montauban	
890	Pilatus PC-6B/B2-H4 Turbo Porter [MCD]	ALAT 1 GSALAT, Montauban	
891	Pilatus PC-6B/B2-H4 Turbo Porter [MCE]	ALAT 1 GSALAT, Montauban	
99	SOCATA TBM 700A [ABO]	ALAT EAAT, Rennes	
100	SOCATA TBM 700A [ABP]	ALAT EAAT, Rennes	
136	SOCATA TBM 700A [ABR]	ALAT EAAT, Rennes	
139	SOCATA TBM 700A [ABS]	ALAT EAAT, Rennes	
156	SOCATA TBM 700B [ABT]	ALAT EAAT, Rennes	
159	SOCATA TBM 700B [ABU]	ALAT EAAT, Rennes	
160	SOCATA TBM 700B [ABV]	ALAT EAAT, Rennes	

Notes	Serial	Type (code/other identity)	Owner/operator, location or fate
	French Government		
	JBA	Eurocopter EC.145C-1 (9008)	Gendarmerie
	JBC	Eurocopter EC.145C-1 (9018)	Gendarmerie
	JBD	Eurocopter EC.145C-1 (9019)	Gendarmerie
	JBE	Eurocopter EC.145C-1 (9025)	Gendarmerie
	JBF	Eurocopter EC.145C-2 (9035)	Gendarmerie
	JBG	Eurocopter EC.145C-2 (9036)	Gendarmerie
	JBH	Eurocopter EC.145C-2 (9037)	Gendarmerie
	JBI	Eurocopter EC.145C-2 (9127)	Gendarmerie
	JBJ	Eurocopter EC.145C-2 (9140)	Gendarmerie, Briançon
	JBK	Eurocopter EC.145C-2 (9162)	Gendarmerie
	JBM	Eurocopter EC.145C-2 (9113)	Gendarmerie
	JBN	Eurocopter EC.145C-2 (9173)	Gendarmerie
	JBO	Eurocopter EC.145C-2 (9124)	Gendarmerie
	JBR	Eurocopter EC.145C-2 (9169)	Gendarmerie
	JBT	Eurocopter EC.145C-2 (9173)	Gendarmerie
	JBU	Eurocopter EC.145C-2 (9700)	Gendarmerie, Villacoublay
	JCA	Aérospatiale AS.350BA Ecureuil (1028)	Gendarmerie, St Nazaire
	JCB	Aérospatiale AS.350BA Ecureuil (1574)	Gendarmerie, Bayonne
	JCD	Aérospatiale AS.350BA Ecureuil (1576)	Gendarmerie, Hyères
	JCE	Aérospatiale AS.350B-2 Ecureuil (1812)	Gendarmerie, Saint-Denis, Réunion
	JCF	Aérospatiale AS.350B-2 Ecureuil (1691)	Gendarmerie, Mayotte
	JCI	Aérospatiale AS.350B-2 Ecureuil (2222)	Gendarmerie, Pointe-à-Pitre
	JCK	Aérospatiale AS.350BA Ecureuil (1953)	Gendarmerie, Egletons
	JCL	Aérospatiale AS.350B-2 Ecureuil (1811)	Gendarmerie, Fort-de-France
	JCM	Aérospatiale AS.350BA Ecureuil (1952)	Gendarmerie, Rennes
	JCN	Aérospatiale AS.350BA Ecureuil (2044)	Gendarmerie, Bordeaux
	JCO	Aérospatiale AS.350BA Ecureuil (1917)	Gendarmerie, Metz
	JCP	Aérospatiale AS.350BA Ecureuil (2045)	Gendarmerie, stored Orléans
	JCQ	Aérospatiale AS.350BA Ecureuil (2057)	Gendarmerie, Dijon
	JCR	Aérospatiale AS.350BA Ecureuil (2088)	Gendarmerie, stored Orléans
	JCS	Aérospatiale AS.350B-2 Ecureuil (1575)	Gendarmerie, Cayenne
	JCT	Aérospatiale AS.350BA Ecureuil (2104)	Gendarmerie, Amiens
	JCU	Aérospatiale AS.350BA Ecureuil (2117)	Gendarmerie, Orléans
	JCV	Aérospatiale AS.350BA Ecureuil (2118)	Gendarmerie, Orléans
	JCW	Aérospatiale AS.350BA Ecureuil (2218)	Gendarmerie, Cazaux
	JCX	Aérospatiale AS.350BA Ecureuil (2219)	Gendarmerie, Tours
	JCY	Aérospatiale AS.350BA Ecureuil (2221)	Gendarmerie, Limoges
	JCZ	Aérospatiale AS.350BA Ecureuil (1467) $	Gendarmerie, Lyon
	JDA	Eurocopter EC.135T-2 (0642)	Gendarmerie
	JDB	Eurocopter EC.135T-2 (0654)	Gendarmerie, Toulouse/Francazal
	JDC	Eurocopter EC.135T-2 (0717)	Gendarmerie, Lyon
	JDD	Eurocopter EC.135T-2 (0727)	Gendarmerie, Lille/Lesquin
	JDE	Eurocopter EC.135T-2 (0747)	Gendarmerie
	JDF	Eurocopter EC.135T-2 (0757)	Gendarmerie, Brest/Guipavas
	JDG	Eurocopter EC.135T-2 (0772)	Gendarmerie
	JDH	Eurocopter EC.135T-2 (0787)	Gendarmerie
	JDI	Eurocopter EC.135T-2 (0797)	Gendarmerie
	JDJ	Eurocopter EC.135T-2 (0806)	Gendarmerie
	JDK	Eurocopter EC.135T-2 (0857)	Gendarmerie, Toulouse/Francazal
	JDL	Eurocopter EC.135T-2 (0867)	Gendarmerie
	JDM	Eurocopter EC.135T-2 (1055)	Gendarmerie
	JDN	Eurocopter EC.135T-2 (1058)	Gendarmerie
	JDO	Eurocopter EC.135T-2 (1086)	Gendarmerie, Bordeaux/Merignac
	JED	Aérospatiale AS.350B-2 Ecureuil (2096)	Gendarmerie, St Nazaire
	JEE	Aérospatiale AS.350B-2 Ecureuil (2423)	Gendarmerie, Nouméa
	JEF	Aérospatiale AS.350B-2 Ecureuil (2225)	Gendarmerie, Nouméa
	F-ZBAA	Conair Turbo Firecat [22]	*Crashed 2 August 2019, Générac, Gard*
	F-ZBAB	Cessna F.406 Caravan II (0025)	*Sold to the USA, 2019*
	F-ZBAD	Aérospatiale AS.355F-2 Twin Ecureuil	Douanes Françaises
	F-ZBAP	Conair Turbo Firecat [12]	*Withdrawn from use, February 2020*
	F-ZBAZ	Conair Turbo Firecat [01]	*Withdrawn from use, February 2020*

Serial	Type (code/other identity)	Owner/operator, location or fate	Notes
F-ZBBN	Aérospatiale AS.350B-2 Ecureuil	*Withdrawn from use*	
F-ZBCE	Cessna F.406 Caravan II (0042)	Douanes Françaises	
F-ZBCF	Cessna F.406 Caravan II (0077)	*Sold as F-WTAV, July 2019*	
F-ZBCG	Cessna F.406 Caravan II (0066)	Douanes Françaises	
F-ZBCH	Cessna F.406 Caravan II (0075)	*Withdrawn from use 2018*	
F-ZBCI	Cessna F.406 Caravan II (0070)	*Sold as F-WTAW, July 2019*	
F-ZBCJ	Cessna F.406 Caravan II (0074)	Douanes Françaises	
F-ZBCZ	Conair Turbo Firecat [23]	*Withdrawn from use, February 2020*	
F-ZBEA	Aérospatiale AS.350B-2 Ecureuil	*Withdrawn from use*	
F-ZBEF	Aérospatiale AS.355F-1 Twin Ecureuil	Douanes Françaises	
F-ZBEG	Canadair CL-415 [39]	Sécurité Civile, Nîmes/Garons	
F-ZBEH	Conair Turbo Firecat [20]	*Withdrawn from use, February 2020*	
F-ZBEK	Aérospatiale AS.355F-1 Twin Ecureuil	Douanes Françaises	
F-ZBEL	Aérospatiale AS.355F-1 Twin Ecureuil	Douanes Françaises	
F-ZBES	Cessna F.406 Caravan II (0017)	Douanes Françaises	
F-ZBET	Conair Turbo Firecat [15]	*Withdrawn from use, February 2020*	
F-ZBEU	Canadair CL-415 [42]	Sécurité Civile, Nîmes/Garons	
F-ZBEW	Conair Turbo Firecat [11] $	*Withdrawn from use, February 2020*	
F-ZBEY	Conair Turbo Firecat [07]	*Withdrawn from use, February 2020*	
F-ZBFC	Aérospatiale AS.350B-2 Ecureuil	*Withdrawn from use*	
F-ZBFD	Aérospatiale AS.350B-2 Ecureuil	*Withdrawn from use*	
F-ZBFJ	Beech Super King Air B200 [98]	Sécurité Civile, Nîmes/Garons	
F-ZBFK	Beech Super King Air B200 [96]	Sécurité Civile, Nîmes/Garons	
F-ZBFN	Canadair CL-415 [33]	Sécurité Civile, Nîmes/Garons	
F-ZBFP	Canadair CL-415 [31]	Sécurité Civile, Nîmes/Garons	
F-ZBFS	Canadair CL-415 [32] $	Sécurité Civile, Nîmes/Garons	
F-ZBFV	Canadair CL-415 [37]	Sécurité Civile, Nîmes/Garons	
F-ZBFW	Canadair CL-415 [38]	Sécurité Civile, Nîmes/Garons	
F-ZBFX	Canadair CL-415 [34]	Sécurité Civile, Nîmes/Garons	
F-ZBFY	Canadair CL-415 [35]	Sécurité Civile, Nîmes/Garons	
F-ZBGA	Cessna F.406 Caravan II (0086)	Douanes Françaises	
F-ZBGD	Cessna F.406 Caravan II (0090)	Douanes Françaises	
F-ZBGE	Cessna F.406 Caravan II (0061)	*Sold as OO-SLX, 2014*	
F-ZBGF	Eurocopter EC.135T-2	Douanes Françaises	
F-ZBGG	Eurocopter EC.135T-2	Douanes Françaises, Calais	
F-ZBGH	Eurocopter EC.135T-2	Douanes Françaises	
F-ZBGI	Eurocopter EC.135T-2	Douanes Françaises	
F-ZBGJ	Eurocopter EC.135T-2	Douanes Françaises	
F-ZBGK	Hawker Beechcraft King Air B350ER (FL-682)	Douanes Françaises	
F-ZBGL	Hawker Beechcraft King Air B350ER (FL-746)	Douanes Francaises, Lorient/Lann Bihoué	
F-ZBGM	Hawker Beechcraft King Air B350ER (FL-752)	Douanes Francaises	
F-ZBGN	Hawker Beechcraft King Air B350ER (FL-781)	Douanes Francaises, Le Lamentin, Guadeloupe	
F-ZBGO	Hawker Beechcraft King Air B350ER (FL-800)	Douanes Françaises	
F-ZBGP	Hawker Beechcraft King Air B350ER (FL-802)	Douanes Françaises	
F-ZBGQ	Hawker Beechcraft King Air B350ER (FL-777)	Douanes Françaises	
F-ZBGR	Hawker Beechcraft King Air B350ER	Douanes Francaises (on order)	
F-ZBMA	Conair Turbo Firecat [24]	Sécurité Civile, Nîmes/Garons	
F-ZBMB	Beech Super King Air B200 [97]	Sécurité Civile, Nîmes/Garons	
F-ZBMC	De Havilland Canada DHC-8Q-402MR [73] $	Sécurité Civile, Nîmes/Garons	
F-ZBMD	De Havilland Canada DHC-8Q-402MR [74]	Sécurité Civile, Nîmes/Garons	
F-ZBME	Canadair CL-415 [44]	Sécurité Civile, Nîmes/Garons	
F-ZBMF	Canadair CL-415 [45]	Sécurité Civile, Nîmes/Garons	
F-ZBMG	Canadair CL-415 [48]	Sécurité Civile, Nîmes/Garons	
F-ZBMH	De Havilland Canada DHC-8Q-402MR [75]	Sécurité Civile, Nîmes/Garons	
F-ZBMI	De Havilland Canada DHC-8Q-402MR [76]	Sécurité Civile, Nîmes/Garons	
F-ZBM.	De Havilland Canada DHC-8Q-402MR [77]	Sécurité Civile (on order)	
F-ZBM.	De Havilland Canada DHC-8Q-402MR [78]	Sécurité Civile (on order)	
F-ZBM.	De Havilland Canada DHC-8Q-402MR [79]	Sécurité Civile (on order)	
F-ZBM.	De Havilland Canada DHC-8Q-402MR [80]	Sécurité Civile (on order)	
F-ZBPA	Eurocopter EC.145C-1	Sécurité Civile, Perpignan	
F-ZBPD	Eurocopter EC.145C-1	Sécurité Civile, Granville	
F-ZBPE	Eurocopter EC.145C-1	*Crashed 2 December 2019, Rove, France*	

Notes	Serial	Type (code/other identity)	Owner/operator, location or fate
	F-ZBPF	Eurocopter EC.145C-1	Sécurité Civile, Lorient/Lann Bihoué
	F-ZBPG	Eurocopter EC.145C-1	Sécurité Civile, Strasbourg/Entzheim
	F-ZBPH	Eurocopter EC.145C-1	Sécurité Civile, Le Luc
	F-ZBPI	Eurocopter EC.145C-1	Sécurité Civile, Quimper
	F-ZBPJ	Eurocopter EC.145C-1	Sécurité Civile, La Rochelle
	F-ZBPK	Eurocopter EC.145C-1	Sécurité Civile, Ajaccio
	F-ZBPL	Eurocopter EC.145C-1	Sécurité Civile, Le Havre/Octeville
	F-ZBPM	Eurocopter EC.145C-1	Sécurité Civile, Bordeaux/Merignac
	F-ZBPN	Eurocopter EC.145C-1	Sécurité Civile, Courchevel
	F-ZBPO	Eurocopter EC.145C-1	Sécurité Civile, Paris/Issy-les-Molineaux
	F-ZBPP	Eurocopter EC.145C-2	Sécurité Civile, La Rochelle
	F-ZBPQ	Eurocopter EC.145C-2	Sécurité Civile, Chamonix
	F-ZBPS	Eurocopter EC.145C-2	Sécurité Civile, Nîmes/Garons
	F-ZBPT	Eurocopter EC.145C-2	Sécurité Civile, L'Alpe de Huez
	F-ZBPU	Eurocopter EC.145C-2	Sécurité Civile, Lorient
	F-ZBPV	Eurocopter EC.145C-2	Sécurité Civile, Besançon/La Veze
	F-ZBPW	Eurocopter EC.145C-2	Sécurité Civile, Annecy
	F-ZBPX	Eurocopter EC.145C-2	Sécurité Civile, Paris/Issy-les-Molineaux
	F-ZBPY	Eurocopter EC.145C-2	Sécurité Civile, Montpellier
	F-ZBPZ	Eurocopter EC.145C-2	Sécurité Civile, Mende-Brenoux
	F-ZBQA	Eurocopter EC.145C-2	Sécurité Civile, Perpignan
	F-ZBQB	Eurocopter EC.145C-2	Sécurité Civile, Nîmes/Garons
	F-ZBQC	Eurocopter EC.145C-2	Sécurité Civile, Strasbourg/Entzheim
	F-ZBQD	Eurocopter EC.145C-2	Sécurité Civile, Le Raizet, Guadeloupe
	F-ZBQE	Eurocopter EC.145C-2	Sécurité Civile, Guyane
	F-ZBQF	Eurocopter EC.145C-2	Sécurité Civile, Marseille/Provence
	F-ZBQG	Eurocopter EC.145C-2	Sécurité Civile, Nîmes/Garons
	F-ZBQH	Eurocopter EC.145C-2	Sécurité Civile, Nîmes/Garons
	F-ZBQI	Eurocopter EC.145C-2	Sécurité Civile, Grenoble/Le Versoud
	F-ZBQJ	Eurocopter EC.145C-2	Sécurité Civile, Bastia
	F-ZBQK	Eurocopter EC.145C-2	Sécurité Civile, Pau
	F-ZBQL	Eurocopter EC.145C-2	Sécurité Civile, Bordeaux/Merignac
	Civil operated aircraft in military use		
	F-GJDB	Dassault Falcon 20C	AVDEF, Nîmes/Garons
	F-GKCI	Cirrus SR.22	CATS/CFAMI 05.312, Salon de Provence
	F-GPAA	Dassault Falcon 20ECM	AVDEF, Nîmes/Garons
	F-GPAD	Dassault Falcon 20E	AVDEF, Nîmes/Garons
	F-GUKA	Grob G120A-F	CATS/EPAA 00.315, Cognac
	F-GUKB	Grob G120A-F	CATS/EPAA 00.315, Cognac
	F-GUKC	Grob G120A-F	CATS/EPAA 00.315, Cognac
	F-GUKD	Grob G120A-F	CATS/EPAA 00.315, Cognac
	F-GUKE	Grob G120A-F	CATS/EPAA 00.315, Cognac
	F-GUKF	Grob G120A-F	CATS/EPAA 00.315, Cognac
	F-GUKG	Grob G120A-F	CATS/EPAA 00.315, Cognac
	F-GUKH	Grob G120A-F	CATS/EPAA 00.315, Cognac
	F-GUKI	Grob G120A-F	CATS/EPAA 00.315, Cognac
	F-GUKJ	Grob G120A-F	CATS/EPAA 00.315, Cognac
	F-GUKK	Grob G120A-F	CATS/EPAA 00.315, Cognac
	F-GUKL	Grob G120A-F	CATS/EPAA 00.315, Cognac
	F-GUKM	Grob G120A-F	CATS/EPAA 00.315, Cognac
	F-GUKN	Grob G120A-F	CATS/EPAA 00.315, Cognac
	F-GUKO	Grob G120A-F	CATS/EPAA 00.315, Cognac
	F-GUKP	Grob G120A-F	CATS/EPAA 00.315, Cognac
	F-GUKR	Grob G120A-F	CATS/EPAA 00.315, Cognac
	F-GUKS	Grob G120A-F	CATS/EPAA 00.315, Cognac
	F-HAVD	BAE Jetstream 41	AVDEF, Nîmes/Garons
	F-HAVF	BAE Jetstream 41	AVDEF, Nîmes/Garons
	F-HDHN	Eurocopter AS.365N-3 Dauphin	AN 22 Escadrille/ESHE, Lanvéoc/Poulmic
	F-HGDU	Cirrus SR.20	CATS/CFAMI 05.312, Salon de Provence
	F-HKCA	Cirrus SR.22	CATS/CFAMI 05.312, Salon de Provence
	F-HKCB	Cirrus SR.20	CATS/CFAMI 05.312, Salon de Provence
	F-HKCC	Cirrus SR.22	CATS/CFAMI 05.312, Salon de Provence

Serial	Type (code/other identity)	Owner/operator, location or fate	Notes
F-HKCD	Cirrus SR.20	CATS/CFAMI 05.312, Salon de Provence	
F-HKCE	Cirrus SR.20	CATS/CFAMI 05.312, Salon de Provence	
F-HKCF	Cirrus SR.22	CATS/CFAMI 05.312, Salon de Provence	
F-HKCG	Cirrus SR.20	CATS/CFAMI 05.312, Salon de Provence	
F-HKCH	Cirrus SR.20	CATS/CFAMI 05.312, Salon de Provence	
F-HKCI	Cirrus SR.22	CATS/CFAMI 05.312, Salon de Provence	
F-HKCJ	Cirrus SR.20	CATS/CFAMI 05.312, Salon de Provence	
F-HKCK	Cirrus SR.20	CATS/CFAMI 05.312, Salon de Provence	
F-HKCL	Cirrus SR.22	CATS/CFAMI 05.312, Salon de Provence	
F-HKCN	Cirrus SR.20	CATS/CFAMI 05.312, Salon de Provence	
F-HKCO	Cirrus SR.22	CATS/CFAMI 05.312, Salon de Provence	
F-HKCP	Cirrus SR.20	CATS/CFAMI 05.312, Salon de Provence	
F-HKCQ	Cirrus SR.20	CATS/CFAMI 05.312, Salon de Provence	
F-HKCR	Cirrus SR.22	*Crashed 7 April 2015, Salon de Provence*	
F-HKCS	Cirrus SR.22	CATS/CFAMI 05.312, Salon de Provence	
F-HKCT	Cirrus SR.20	CATS/CFAMI 05.312, Salon de Provence	
F-HKCU	Cirrus SR.20	CATS/CFAMI 05.312, Salon de Provence	
F-HKCV	Cirrus SR.20	CATS/CFAMI 05.312, Salon de Provence	
F-HKCX	Cirrus SR.20	CATS/CFAMI 05.312, Salon de Provence	
F-HKCY	Cirrus SR.22	CATS/CFAMI 05.312, Salon de Provence	
F-HKCZ	Cirrus SR.22	CATS/CFAMI 05.312, Salon de Provence	
F-HNHN	Eurocopter AS.365N-3 Dauphin	AN 22 Escadrille/ESHE, Lanvéoc/Poulmic	
F-HOHN	Eurocopter AS.365N-3 Dauphin	AN 22 Escadrille/ESHE, Lanvéoc/Poulmic	
F-HYHN	Eurocopter AS.365N-3 Dauphin	AN 22 Escadrille/ESHE, Lanvéoc/Poulmic	

GABON

Serial	Type (code/other identity)	Owner/operator, location or fate	Notes
TR-KGM	Gulfstream Aerospace G.650ER	Gabonese Government, Libreville	
TR-KPR	Boeing 777-236	Gabonese Government, Libreville	
TR-KSP	Grumman G.1159C Gulfstream IVSP	Gabonese Government, Libreville	
TR-LEX	Dassault Falcon 900EX	Gabonese Government, Libreville	

GERMANY

Please note that German serials do not officially include the '+' part in them but aircraft wearing German markings are often painted with a cross in the middle, which is why it is included here.

Luftwaffe, Marineflieger & Heeresfliegertruppe (Heer)

Serial	Type (code/other identity)	Owner/operator, location or fate	Notes
10+23	Airbus A.310-304	Luftwaffe 1/FBS, Köln-Bonn	
10+24	Airbus A.310-304/MRTT	Luftwaffe 1/FBS, Köln-Bonn	
10+25	Airbus A.310-304/MRTT	Luftwaffe 1/FBS, Köln-Bonn	
10+26	Airbus A.310-304/MRTT	Luftwaffe 1/FBS, Köln-Bonn	
10+27	Airbus A.310-304/MRTT	Luftwaffe 1/FBS, Köln-Bonn	
14+01	Bombardier Global 5000	*Damaged beyond repair, 16 April 2019, Berlin*	
14+02	Bombardier Global 5000	Luftwaffe 3/FBS, Köln-Bonn	
14+03	Bombardier Global 5000	Luftwaffe 3/FBS, Köln-Bonn	
14+04	Bombardier Global 5000	Luftwaffe 3/FBS, Köln-Bonn	
14+05	Bombardier Global 6000 (C-GDRL)	Luftwaffe 3/FBS, Köln-Bonn	
14+06	Bombardier Global 6000 (C-GEVP)	Luftwaffe 3/FBS, Köln-Bonn	
14+07	Bombardier Global 6000 (C-GEVX)	Luftwaffe 3/FBS, Köln-Bonn	
15+01	Airbus A.319CJ-115X	Luftwaffe 3/FBS, Köln-Bonn	
15+02	Airbus A.319CJ-115X	Luftwaffe 3/FBS, Köln-Bonn	
15+03	Airbus A.319CJ-133X (98+11)	Luftwaffe 3/FBS, Köln-Bonn	
15+04	Airbus A.321-231 (D-AISE/98+10)	Luftwaffe 3/FBS, Köln-Bonn	
16+01	Airbus A.340-313X	Luftwaffe 3/FBS, Köln-Bonn	
16+02	Airbus A.340-313X	Luftwaffe 3/FBS, Köln-Bonn	
..+..	Airbus A350-900 (F-WZFF/D-AKAY)	Luftwaffe (on order)	
..+..	Airbus A350-900	Luftwaffe (on order)	
..+..	Airbus A350-900	Luftwaffe (on order)	
30+01	Eurofighter EF.2000GT	Luftwaffe TLG 73 *Steinhoff*, Laage	
30+02	Eurofighter EF.2000GT	Luftwaffe TLG 71 *Richthofen*, Wittmund	
30+03	Eurofighter EF.2000GT	Luftwaffe TLG 74 *Molders*, Neuburg/Donau	
30+04	Eurofighter EF.2000GT	Luftwaffe TLG 71 *Richthofen*, Wittmund	
30+05	Eurofighter EF.2000GT	Luftwaffe TLG 31 *Boelcke*, Nörvenich	
30+06	Eurofighter EF.2000GS	Luftwaffe TLG 71 *Richthofen*, Wittmund	

Notes	Serial	Type (code/other identity)	Owner/operator, location or fate
	30+07	Eurofighter EF.2000GS	Luftwaffe TLG 74 *Molders*, Neuburg/Donau
	30+09	Eurofighter EF.2000GS	Luftwaffe TAubZLwSüd, Kaufbeuren
	30+10	Eurofighter EF.2000GT	Luftwaffe TLG 74 *Molders*, Neuburg/Donau
	30+11	Eurofighter EF.2000GS	Luftwaffe TLG 74 *Molders*, Neuburg/Donau
	30+12	Eurofighter EF.2000GS	Luftwaffe TLG 71 *Richthofen*, Wittmund
	30+14	Eurofighter EF.2000GT	Luftwaffe TLG 71 *Richthofen*, Wittmund
	30+15	Eurofighter EF.2000GS	Luftwaffe TLG 74 *Molders*, Neuburg/Donau
	30+17	Eurofighter EF.2000GT	Luftwaffe TLG 73 *Steinhoff*, Laage
	30+20	Eurofighter EF.2000GT	Luftwaffe TLG 73 *Steinhoff*, Laage
	30+22	Eurofighter EF.2000GS	Luftwaffe TLG 74 *Molders*, Neuburg/Donau
	30+23	Eurofighter EF.2000GS	Luftwaffe TLG 71 *Richthofen*, Wittmund
	30+24	Eurofighter EF.2000GT	Luftwaffe TLG 73 *Steinhoff*, Laage
	30+25	Eurofighter EF.2000GS $	Luftwaffe TLG 71 *Richthofen*, Wittmund
	30+26	Eurofighter EF.2000GS $	Luftwaffe TLG 74 *Molders*, Neuburg/Donau
	30+27	Eurofighter EF.2000GT	Luftwaffe TLG 73 *Steinhoff*, Laage
	30+28	Eurofighter EF.2000GS	Luftwaffe TLG 71 *Richthofen*, Wittmund
	30+29	Eurofighter EF.2000GS $	Luftwaffe TLG 74 *Molders*, Neuburg/Donau
	30+30	Eurofighter EF.2000GS	Luftwaffe TLG 74 *Molders*, Neuburg/Donau
	30+31	Eurofighter EF.2000GT	Luftwaffe TLG 31 *Boelcke*, Nörvenich
	30+32	Eurofighter EF.2000GS	Luftwaffe TLG 71 *Richthofen*, Wittmund
	30+33	Eurofighter EF.2000GS	Luftwaffe TLG 71 *Richthofen*, Wittmund
	30+35	Eurofighter EF.2000GT	Luftwaffe TLG 73 *Steinhoff*, Laage
	30+38	Eurofighter EF.2000GT	Luftwaffe TLG 73 *Steinhoff*, Laage
	30+39	Eurofighter EF.2000GS	Luftwaffe TLG 74 *Molders*, Neuburg/Donau
	30+40	Eurofighter EF.2000GS	Luftwaffe TLG 71 *Richthofen*, Wittmund
	30+42	Eurofighter EF.2000GT	Luftwaffe TLG 74 *Molders*, Neuburg/Donau
	30+45	Eurofighter EF.2000GS	Luftwaffe TLG 74 *Molders*, Neuburg/Donau
	30+46	Eurofighter EF.2000GS	Luftwaffe TLG 73 *Steinhoff*, Laage
	30+47	Eurofighter EF.2000GS	Luftwaffe TLG 71 *Richthofen*, Wittmund
	30+48	Eurofighter EF.2000GS $	*Crashed 24 June 2019, Mecklenburg-Vorpemmen*
	30+49	Eurofighter EF.2000GS	Luftwaffe TLG 31 *Boelcke*, Nörvenich
	30+50	Eurofighter EF.2000GS	Luftwaffe TLG 73 *Steinhoff*, Laage
	30+51	Eurofighter EF.2000GS	Luftwaffe TLG 73 *Steinhoff*, Laage
	30+52	Eurofighter EF.2000GS	Luftwaffe TLG 31 *Boelcke*, Nörvenich
	30+53	Eurofighter EF.2000GS	Luftwaffe TLG 74 *Molders*, Neuburg/Donau
	30+54	Eurofighter EF.2000GT	Luftwaffe TLG 31 *Boelcke*, Nörvenich
	30+55	Eurofighter EF.2000GS	*Crashed 24 June 2019, Mecklenburg-Vorpemmen*
	30+56	Eurofighter EF.2000GS	Luftwaffe TLG 73 *Steinhoff*, Laage
	30+57	Eurofighter EF.2000GS	Luftwaffe TLG 71 *Richthofen*, Wittmund
	30+58	Eurofighter EF.2000GS	Luftwaffe TLG 71 *Richthofen*, Wittmund
	30+59	Eurofighter EF.2000GT	Luftwaffe TLG 73 *Steinhoff*, Laage
	30+60	Eurofighter EF.2000GS	Luftwaffe TLG 73 *Steinhoff*, Laage
	30+61	Eurofighter EF.2000GS	Luftwaffe TLG 73 *Steinhoff*, Laage
	30+62	Eurofighter EF.2000GS	Luftwaffe TLG 73 *Steinhoff*, Laage
	30+63	Eurofighter EF.2000GS	Luftwaffe TLG 74 *Molders*, Neuburg/Donau
	30+64	Eurofighter EF.2000GS	Luftwaffe TLG 73 *Steinhoff*, Laage
	30+65	Eurofighter EF.2000GS	Luftwaffe TLG 73 *Steinhoff*, Laage
	30+66	Eurofighter EF.2000GS	Luftwaffe TLG 71 *Richthofen*, Wittmund
	30+67	Eurofighter EF.2000GT	Luftwaffe TLG 73 *Steinhoff*, Laage
	30+68	Eurofighter EF.2000GS $	Luftwaffe TLG 74 *Molders*, Neuburg/Donau
	30+69	Eurofighter EF.2000GS	Luftwaffe TLG 74 *Molders*, Neuburg/Donau
	30+70	Eurofighter EF.2000GS	Luftwaffe TLG 74 *Molders*, Neuburg/Donau
	30+71	Eurofighter EF.2000GT	Luftwaffe TLG 71 *Richthofen*, Wittmund
	30+72	Eurofighter EF.2000GS	Luftwaffe TLG 74 *Molders*, Neuburg/Donau
	30+73	Eurofighter EF.2000GS $	Luftwaffe TLG 73 *Steinhoff*, Laage
	30+74	Eurofighter EF.2000GS	Luftwaffe TLG 74 *Molders*, Neuburg/Donau
	30+75	Eurofighter EF.2000GS $	Luftwaffe TLG 74 *Molders*, Neuburg/Donau
	30+76	Eurofighter EF.2000GS	Luftwaffe TLG 74 *Molders*, Neuburg/Donau
	30+77	Eurofighter EF.2000GT	Luftwaffe TLG 73 *Steinhoff*, Laage
	30+78	Eurofighter EF.2000GS	Luftwaffe TLG 71 *Richthofen*, Wittmund
	30+79	Eurofighter EF.2000GS	Luftwaffe TLG 73 *Steinhoff*, Laage
	30+80	Eurofighter EF.2000GS	Luftwaffe TLG 74 *Molders*, Neuburg/Donau

Serial	Type (code/other identity)	Owner/operator, location or fate	Notes
30+81	Eurofighter EF.2000GS	Luftwaffe TLG 73 *Steinhoff*, Laage	
30+82	Eurofighter EF.2000GS	Luftwaffe TLG 71 *Richthofen*, Wittmund	
30+83	Eurofighter EF.2000GS	Luftwaffe TLG 71 *Richthofen*, Wittmund	
30+84	Eurofighter EF.2000GT	Luftwaffe TLG 31 *Boelcke*, Nörvenich	
30+85	Eurofighter EF.2000GS	Luftwaffe TLG 71 *Richthofen*, Wittmund	
30+86	Eurofighter EF.2000GS	Luftwaffe TLG 71 *Richthofen*, Wittmund	
30+87	Eurofighter EF.2000GS $	Luftwaffe TLG 71 *Richthofen*, Wittmund	
30+88	Eurofighter EF.2000GS	Luftwaffe TLG 74 *Molders*, Neuburg/Donau	
30+89	Eurofighter EF.2000GS	Luftwaffe TLG 71 *Richthofen*, Wittmund	
30+90	Eurofighter EF.2000GS $	Luftwaffe TLG 71 *Richthofen*, Wittmund	
30+91	Eurofighter EF.2000GS	Luftwaffe TLG 31 *Boelcke*, Nörvenich	
30+92	Eurofighter EF.2000GS	Luftwaffe TLG 71 *Richthofen*, Wittmund	
30+93	Eurofighter EF.2000GS	Luftwaffe TLG 74 *Molders*, Neuburg/Donau	
30+94	Eurofighter EF.2000GS	Luftwaffe TLG 74 *Molders*, Neuburg/Donau	
30+95	Eurofighter EF.2000GT	Luftwaffe TLG 74 *Molders*, Neuburg/Donau	
30+96	Eurofighter EF.2000GS	Luftwaffe TLG 31 *Boelcke*, Nörvenich	
30+97	Eurofighter EF.2000GS	Luftwaffe TLG 31 *Boelcke*, Nörvenich	
30+98	Eurofighter EF.2000GS	Luftwaffe TLG 31 *Boelcke*, Nörvenich	
30+99	Eurofighter EF.2000GT	Luftwaffe TLG 31 *Boelcke*, Nörvenich	
31+00	Eurofighter EF.2000GS	Luftwaffe TLG 74 *Molders*, Neuburg/Donau	
31+01	Eurofighter EF.2000GS	Luftwaffe TLG 71 *Richthofen*, Wittmund	
31+02	Eurofighter EF.2000GS	Luftwaffe TLG 74 *Molders*, Neuburg/Donau	
31+03	Eurofighter EF.2000GT	Airbus Defence & Space, Manching	
31+04	Eurofighter EF.2000GS	Luftwaffe TLG 31 *Boelcke*, Nörvenich	
31+05	Eurofighter EF.2000GS	Luftwaffe TLG 31 *Boelcke*, Nörvenich	
31+06	Eurofighter EF.2000GS	Luftwaffe TLG 74 *Molders*, Neuburg/Donau	
31+07	Eurofighter EF.2000GS	Luftwaffe TLG 71 *Richthofen*, Wittmund	
31+08	Eurofighter EF.2000GS	Luftwaffe TLG 71 *Richthofen*, Wittmund	
31+09	Eurofighter EF.2000GS	Luftwaffe TLG 31 *Boelcke*, Nörvenich	
31+10	Eurofighter EF.2000GS	Luftwaffe TLG 31 *Boelcke*, Nörvenich	
31+11	Eurofighter EF.2000GS	Luftwaffe TLG 74 *Molders*, Neuburg/Donau	
31+12	Eurofighter EF.2000GS	Luftwaffe TLG 71 *Richthofen*, Wittmund	
31+13	Eurofighter EF.2000GT	Luftwaffe TLG 73 *Steinhoff*, Laage	
31+14	Eurofighter EF.2000GS	Luftwaffe TLG 31 *Boelcke*, Nörvenich	
31+15	Eurofighter EF.2000GS	Luftwaffe TLG 73 *Steinhoff*, Laage	
31+16	Eurofighter EF.2000GS	Luftwaffe TLG 31 *Boelcke*, Nörvenich	
31+17	Eurofighter EF.2000GS	Luftwaffe TLG 31 *Boelcke*, Nörvenich	
31+18	Eurofighter EF.2000GS $	Luftwaffe TLG 73 *Steinhoff*, Laage	
31+19	Eurofighter EF.2000GS	Luftwaffe TLG 74 *Molders*, Neuburg/Donau	
31+20	Eurofighter EF.2000GS	Luftwaffe TLG 73 *Steinhoff*, Laage	
31+21	Eurofighter EF.2000GS	Luftwaffe TLG 73 *Steinhoff*, Laage	
31+22	Eurofighter EF.2000GS	Luftwaffe TLG 73 *Steinhoff*, Laage	
31+24	Eurofighter EF.2000GT	Luftwaffe TLG 73 *Steinhoff*, Laage	
31+25	Eurofighter EF.2000GT	Luftwaffe TLG 74 *Molders*, Neuburg/Donau	
31+26	Eurofighter EF.2000GT	Luftwaffe TLG 73 *Steinhoff*, Laage	
31+27	Eurofighter EF.2000GT	Airbus Defence & Space, Manching	
31+28	Eurofighter EF.2000GT	Luftwaffe TLG 31 *Boelcke*, Nörvenich	
31+29	Eurofighter EF.2000GS	Luftwaffe TLG 31 *Boelcke*, Nörvenich	
31+30	Eurofighter EF.2000GS	Luftwaffe TLG 31 *Boelcke*, Nörvenich	
31+31	Eurofighter EF.2000GS $	Luftwaffe TLG 31 *Boelcke*, Nörvenich	
31+32	Eurofighter EF.2000GS $	Luftwaffe TLG 31 *Boelcke*, Nörvenich	
31+33	Eurofighter EF.2000GS	Luftwaffe TLG 31 *Boelcke*, Nörvenich	
31+34	Eurofighter EF.2000GS	Luftwaffe TLG 31 *Boelcke*, Nörvenich	
31+35	Eurofighter EF.2000GS	Luftwaffe TLG 31 *Boelcke*, Nörvenich	
31+36	Eurofighter EF.2000GS	Luftwaffe TLG 31 *Boelcke*, Nörvenich	
31+37	Eurofighter EF.2000GS	Luftwaffe TLG 31 *Boelcke*, Nörvenich	
31+38	Eurofighter EF.2000GS	Luftwaffe TLG 31 *Boelcke*, Nörvenich	
31+39	Eurofighter EF.2000GS	Luftwaffe TLG 31 *Boelcke*, Nörvenich	
31+40	Eurofighter EF.2000GS	Luftwaffe TLG 31 *Boelcke*, Nörvenich	
31+41	Eurofighter EF.2000GS	Luftwaffe TLG 31 *Boelcke*, Nörvenich	
31+42	Eurofighter EF.2000GS	Airbus Defence & Space, Manching	
31+43	Eurofighter EF.2000GS	Airbus Defence & Space, Manching	

Notes	Serial	Type (code/other identity)	Owner/operator, location or fate
	31+44	Eurofighter EF.2000GS	Luftwaffe TLG 71 *Richthofen*, Wittmund
	31+45	Eurofighter EF.2000GS	Luftwaffe TLG 31 *Boelcke*, Nörvenich
	31+46	Eurofighter EF.2000GS	Luftwaffe TLG 31 *Boelcke*, Nörvenich
	31+47	Eurofighter EF.2000GS	Luftwaffe TLG 31 *Boelcke*, Nörvenich
	31+48	Eurofighter EF.2000GS	Luftwaffe TLG 31 *Boelcke*, Nörvenich
	31+49	Eurofighter EF.2000GS	Luftwaffe TLG 31 *Boelcke*, Nörvenich
	31+50	Eurofighter EF.2000GS	Luftwaffe TLG 31 *Boelcke*, Nörvenich
	31+51	Eurofighter EF.2000GS	Luftwaffe TLG 31 *Boelcke*, Nörvenich
	31+52	Eurofighter EF.2000GS	Luftwaffe TLG 31 *Boelcke*, Nörvenich
	31+53	Eurofighter EF.2000GS	Luftwaffe TLG 31 *Boelcke*, Nörvenich
	43+01	Panavia Tornado IDS(T) $	Luftwaffe TLG 33, Büchel
	43+07	Panavia Tornado IDS(T)	Luftwaffe TLG 51 *Immelmann*, Schleswig/Jagel
	43+10	Panavia Tornado IDS(T)	Luftwaffe TLG 33, Büchel
	43+25	Panavia Tornado IDS $	Luftwaffe TLG 51 *Immelmann*, Schleswig/Jagel
	43+29	Panavia Tornado IDS(T)	Luftwaffe TLG 51 *Immelmann*, Schleswig/Jagel
	43+34	Panavia Tornado IDS	*Withdrawn from use at Kaufbeuren*
	43+38	Panavia Tornado IDS	Luftwaffe TLG 33, Büchel
	43+42	Panavia Tornado IDS(T)	*Withdrawn from use*
	43+45	Panavia Tornado IDS(T)	Luftwaffe TLG 51 *Immelmann*, Schleswig/Jagel
	43+46	Panavia Tornado IDS	Luftwaffe TLG 33, Büchel
	43+48	Panavia Tornado IDS	Luftwaffe TLG 33, Büchel
	43+50	Panavia Tornado IDS	Luftwaffe TLG 33, Büchel
	43+52	Panavia Tornado IDS	Luftwaffe TLG 33, Büchel
	43+54	Panavia Tornado IDS	Luftwaffe TAubZLwSüd, Kaufbeuren
	43+59	Panavia Tornado IDS	Luftwaffe TAubZLwSüd, Kaufbeuren
	43+92	Panavia Tornado IDS(T)	Luftwaffe TLG 33, Büchel
	43+97	Panavia Tornado IDS(T)	Luftwaffe TLG 51 *Immelmann*, Schleswig/Jagel
	43+98	Panavia Tornado IDS	Luftwaffe TLG 33, Büchel
	44+16	Panavia Tornado IDS(T)	Luftwaffe TLG 33, Büchel
	44+17	Panavia Tornado IDS	Luftwaffe TLG 51 *Immelmann*, Schleswig/Jagel
	44+21	Panavia Tornado IDS	Luftwaffe TLG 51 *Immelmann*, Schleswig/Jagel
	44+23	Panavia Tornado IDS	Luftwaffe TLG 33, Büchel
	44+29	Panavia Tornado IDS	Luftwaffe TLG 33, Büchel
	44+30	Panavia Tornado IDS	Luftwaffe TLG 51 *Immelmann*, Schleswig/Jagel
	44+33	Panavia Tornado IDS	Luftwaffe TLG 33, Büchel
	44+34	Panavia Tornado IDS	Luftwaffe TLG 33, Büchel
	44+58	Panavia Tornado IDS	Luftwaffe TLG 33, Büchel
	44+61	Panavia Tornado IDS $	Luftwaffe TLG 33, Büchel
	44+64	Panavia Tornado IDS	Luftwaffe TLG 33, Büchel
	44+65	Panavia Tornado IDS	Luftwaffe TLG 51 *Immelmann*, Schleswig/Jagel
	44+69	Panavia Tornado IDS	Luftwaffe TLG 51 *Immelmann*, Schleswig/Jagel
	44+70	Panavia Tornado IDS	Luftwaffe TLG 33, Büchel
	44+72	Panavia Tornado IDS(T)	Luftwaffe TLG 33, Büchel
	44+73	Panavia Tornado IDS(T)	Luftwaffe WTD 61, Ingolstadt
	44+75	Panavia Tornado IDS(T)	Luftwaffe TLG 51 *Immelmann*, Schleswig/Jagel
	44+78	Panavia Tornado IDS	Luftwaffe TLG 33, Büchel
	44+79	Panavia Tornado IDS	Luftwaffe TLG 33, Büchel
	44+90	Panavia Tornado IDS	Luftwaffe TLG 33, Büchel
	45+00	Panavia Tornado IDS	Luftwaffe TLG 33, Büchel
	45+09	Panavia Tornado IDS	Luftwaffe TLG 33, Büchel
	45+13	Panavia Tornado IDS(T)	Luftwaffe TLG 51 *Immelmann*, Schleswig/Jagel
	45+14	Panavia Tornado IDS(T)	*Withdrawn from use*
	45+16	Panavia Tornado IDS(T)	Luftwaffe TLG 51 *Immelmann*, Schleswig/Jagel
	45+19	Panavia Tornado IDS	Luftwaffe TLG 33, Büchel
	45+20	Panavia Tornado IDS	Luftwaffe TLG 33, Büchel
	45+22	Panavia Tornado IDS	Luftwaffe TLG 51 *Immelmann*, Schleswig/Jagel
	45+23	Panavia Tornado IDS	Luftwaffe TLG 33, Büchel
	45+28	Panavia Tornado IDS	Luftwaffe TLG 33, Büchel
	45+35	Panavia Tornado IDS	Luftwaffe TLG 33, Büchel
	45+39	Panavia Tornado IDS	Luftwaffe TLG 51 *Immelmann*, Schleswig/Jagel
	45+50	Panavia Tornado IDS	Luftwaffe TLG 51 *Immelmann*, Schleswig/Jagel
	45+53	Panavia Tornado IDS	Luftwaffe TAubZLwSüd, Kaufbeuren

Serial	Type (code/other identity)	Owner/operator, location or fate	Notes
45+57	Panavia Tornado IDS	Luftwaffe TLG 33, Büchel	
45+59	Panavia Tornado IDS	Luftwaffe TLG 51 *Immelmann*, Schleswig/Jagel	
45+61	Panavia Tornado IDS(T)	Luftwaffe TLG 51 *Immelmann*, Schleswig/Jagel	
45+64	Panavia Tornado IDS	Luftwaffe TLG 33, Büchel	
45+66	Panavia Tornado IDS	Luftwaffe TLG 33, Büchel	
45+67	Panavia Tornado IDS	Luftwaffe TLG 33, Büchel	
45+68	Panavia Tornado IDS	Luftwaffe TLG 33, Büchel	
45+69	Panavia Tornado IDS	Luftwaffe TLG 33, Büchel	
45+70	Panavia Tornado IDS(T)	Luftwaffe TLG 51 *Immelmann*, Schleswig/Jagel	
45+71	Panavia Tornado IDS	Luftwaffe TLG 33, Büchel	
45+74	Panavia Tornado IDS	Luftwaffe TAubZLwSüd, Kaufbeuren	
45+76	Panavia Tornado IDS	Luftwaffe TLG 33, Büchel	
45+77	Panavia Tornado IDS(T)	Luftwaffe TLG 51 *Immelmann*, Schleswig/Jagel	
45+84	Panavia Tornado IDS	Luftwaffe TLG 33, Büchel	
45+85	Panavia Tornado IDS	Luftwaffe TLG 33, Büchel	
45+88	Panavia Tornado IDS	Luftwaffe TLG 33, Büchel	
45+90	Panavia Tornado IDS	Luftwaffe TLG 33, Büchel	
45+92	Panavia Tornado IDS	Luftwaffe TLG 33, Büchel	
45+93	Panavia Tornado IDS	Luftwaffe TLG 33, Büchel	
45+94	Panavia Tornado IDS	Luftwaffe TLG 33, Büchel	
46+02	Panavia Tornado IDS	Luftwaffe TLG 51 *Immelmann*, Schleswig/Jagel	
46+05	Panavia Tornado IDS(T)	Luftwaffe TLG 33, Büchel	
46+07	Panavia Tornado IDS(T)	Luftwaffe TLG 33, Büchel	
46+10	Panavia Tornado IDS	Luftwaffe TLG 33, Büchel	
46+11	Panavia Tornado IDS	Luftwaffe TLG 33, Büchel	
46+15	Panavia Tornado IDS	Luftwaffe TLG 33, Büchel	
46+18	Panavia Tornado IDS	Luftwaffe TLG 33, Büchel	
46+20	Panavia Tornado IDS	Luftwaffe TLG 51 *Immelmann*, Schleswig/Jagel	
46+21	Panavia Tornado IDS	Luftwaffe TLG 33, Büchel	
46+22	Panavia Tornado IDS	Luftwaffe TLG 33, Büchel	
46+23	Panavia Tornado ECR $	Luftwaffe TLG 51 *Immelmann*, Schleswig/Jagel	
46+24	Panavia Tornado ECR	Luftwaffe TLG 51 *Immelmann*, Schleswig/Jagel	
46+25	Panavia Tornado ECR	Luftwaffe TLG 51 *Immelmann*, Schleswig/Jagel	
46+28	Panavia Tornado ECR $	Luftwaffe TLG 51 *Immelmann*, Schleswig/Jagel	
46+32	Panavia Tornado ECR	Luftwaffe TLG 51 *Immelmann*, Schleswig/Jagel	
46+35	Panavia Tornado ECR	Luftwaffe TLG 51 *Immelmann*, Schleswig/Jagel	
46+36	Panavia Tornado ECR	Luftwaffe TLG 51 *Immelmann*, Schleswig/Jagel	
46+38	Panavia Tornado ECR	Luftwaffe TLG 51 *Immelmann*, Schleswig/Jagel	
46+39	Panavia Tornado ECR	Luftwaffe TAubZLwSüd, Kaufbeuren	
46+40	Panavia Tornado ECR	Luftwaffe TLG 51 *Immelmann*, Schleswig/Jagel	
46+44	Panavia Tornado ECR	Luftwaffe TLG 51 *Immelmann*, Schleswig/Jagel	
46+45	Panavia Tornado ECR	Luftwaffe TLG 51 *Immelmann*, Schleswig/Jagel	
46+46	Panavia Tornado ECR	Luftwaffe TLG 51 *Immelmann*, Schleswig/Jagel	
46+48	Panavia Tornado ECR	Luftwaffe TLG 51 *Immelmann*, Schleswig/Jagel	
46+49	Panavia Tornado ECR	Luftwaffe TLG 51 *Immelmann*, Schleswig/Jagel	
46+50	Panavia Tornado ECR	Luftwaffe TLG 51 *Immelmann*, Schleswig/Jagel	
46+51	Panavia Tornado ECR	Luftwaffe TLG 51 *Immelmann*, Schleswig/Jagel	
46+52	Panavia Tornado ECR	Luftwaffe TLG 51 *Immelmann*, Schleswig/Jagel	
46+54	Panavia Tornado ECR $	Luftwaffe TLG 51 *Immelmann*, Schleswig/Jagel	
46+55	Panavia Tornado ECR	Luftwaffe TLG 51 *Immelmann*, Schleswig/Jagel	
46+56	Panavia Tornado ECR	Luftwaffe TLG 51 *Immelmann*, Schleswig/Jagel	
46+57	Panavia Tornado ECR $	Luftwaffe TLG 51 *Immelmann*, Schleswig/Jagel	
50+17	Transall C-160D	Luftwaffe LTG 63 (4.LwDiv), Hohn	
50+29	Transall C-160D	*Withdrawn from use*	
50+33	Transall C-160D	Luftwaffe LTG 63 (4.LwDiv), Hohn	
50+36	Transall C-160D	Luftwaffe LTG 63 (4.LwDiv), Hohn	
50+38	Transall C-160D	Luftwaffe LTG 63 (4.LwDiv), Hohn	
50+40	Transall C-160D	Luftwaffe LTG 63 (4.LwDiv), Hohn	
50+44	Transall C-160D	Luftwaffe	
50+45	Transall C-160D	*Withdrawn from use at Landsberg*	
50+48	Transall C-160D $	Luftwaffe	
50+49	Transall C-160D	Luftwaffe LTG 63 (4.LwDiv), Hohn	

Notes	Serial	Type (code/other identity)	Owner/operator, location or fate
	50+51	Transall C-160D	Luftwaffe LTG 63 (4.LwDiv), Hohn
	50+53	Transall C-160D	Luftwaffe LTG 63 (4.LwDiv), Hohn
	50+54	Transall C-160D	*Withdrawn from use at Hannover, 2019*
	50+55	Transall C-160D	Luftwaffe LTG 63 (4.LwDiv), Hohn
	50+57	Transall C-160D	Luftwaffe LTG 63 (4.LwDiv), Hohn
	50+58	Transall C-160D	Luftwaffe LTG 63 (4.LwDiv), Hohn
	50+59	Transall C-160D	Luftwaffe LTG 63 (4.LwDiv), Hohn
	50+61	Transall C-160D	*Withdrawn from use at Hohn, May 2019*
	50+65	Transall C-160D $	Luftwaffe LTG 63 (4.LwDiv), Hohn
	50+66	Transall C-160D	Luftwaffe LTG 63 (4.LwDiv), Hohn
	50+67	Transall C-160D	Luftwaffe LTG 63 (4.LwDiv), Hohn
	50+69	Transall C-160D	Luftwaffe LTG 63 (4.LwDiv), Hohn
	50+71	Transall C-160D	Luftwaffe LTG 63 (4.LwDiv), Hohn
	50+72	Transall C-160D $	Luftwaffe LTG 63 (4.LwDiv), Hohn
	50+73	Transall C-160D	Luftwaffe LTG 63 (4.LwDiv), Hohn
	50+74	Transall C-160D	Luftwaffe
	50+75	Transall C-160D	Luftwaffe LTG 63 (4.LwDiv), Hohn
	50+76	Transall C-160D	Luftwaffe LTG 63 (4.LwDiv), Hohn
	50+77	Transall C-160D	Luftwaffe LTG 63 (4.LwDiv), Hohn
	50+78	Transall C-160D	Luftwaffe LTG 63 (4.LwDiv), Hohn
	50+79	Transall C-160D	Luftwaffe LTG 63 (4.LwDiv), Hohn
	50+81	Transall C-160D	*Withdrawn from use at Celle, 2019*
	50+82	Transall C-160D $	Luftwaffe LTG 63 (4.LwDiv), Hohn
	50+83	Transall C-160D	Luftwaffe LTG 63 (4.LwDiv), Hohn
	50+86	Transall C-160D	Luftwaffe WTD 61, Ingolstadt
	50+87	Transall C-160D	Luftwaffe LTG 63 (4.LwDiv), Hohn
	50+88	Transall C-160D	Luftwaffe LTG 63 (4.LwDiv), Hohn
	50+91	Transall C-160D	Luftwaffe LTG 63 (4.LwDiv), Hohn
	50+92	Transall C-160D	Luftwaffe
	50+93	Transall C-160D $	Luftwaffe LTG 63 (4.LwDiv), Hohn
	50+96	Transall C-160D	*Withdrawn from use*
	50+97	Transall C-160D	*Withdrawn from use at Wunsdorf, 2019*
	51+03	Transall C-160D	Luftwaffe LTG 63 (4.LwDiv), Hohn
	51+04	Transall C-160D	Luftwaffe LTG 63 (4.LwDiv), Hohn
	51+05	Transall C-160D	Luftwaffe LTG 63 (4.LwDiv), Hohn
	51+08	Transall C-160D	Luftwaffe WTD 61, Ingolstadt
	51+10	Transall C-160D	Luftwaffe
	51+12	Transall C-160D	Luftwaffe LTG 63 (4.LwDiv), Hohn
	51+14	Transall C-160D	Luftwaffe LTG 63 (4.LwDiv), Hohn
	54+01	Airbus Military A.400M	Luftwaffe LTG 62, Wunstorf
	54+02	Airbus Military A.400M	Luftwaffe LTG 62, Wunstorf
	54+03	Airbus Military A.400M $	Luftwaffe LTG 62, Wunstorf
	54+04	Airbus Military A.400M	Luftwaffe LTG 62, Wunstorf
	54+05	Airbus Military A.400M	Luftwaffe LTG 62, Wunstorf
	54+06	Airbus Military A.400M	Luftwaffe LTG 62, Wunstorf
	54+07	Airbus Military A.400M	Luftwaffe LTG 62, Wunstorf
	54+08	Airbus Military A.400M	Luftwaffe LTG 62, Wunstorf
	54+09	Airbus Military A.400M	Luftwaffe LTG 62, Wunstorf
	54+10	Airbus Military A.400M	Luftwaffe LTG 62, Wunstorf
	54+11	Airbus Military A.400M	Luftwaffe LTG 62, Wunstorf
	54+12	Airbus Military A.400M	Luftwaffe LTG 62, Wunstorf
	54+13	Airbus Military A.400M	Luftwaffe LTG 62, Wunstorf
	54+14	Airbus Military A.400M	Luftwaffe LTG 62, Wunstorf
	54+15	Airbus Military A.400M	Luftwaffe LTG 62, Wunstorf
	54+16	Airbus Military A.400M	Luftwaffe LTG 62, Wunstorf
	54+17	Airbus Military A.400M	Luftwaffe LTG 62, Wunstorf
	54+18	Airbus Military A.400M	Luftwaffe LTG 62, Wunstorf
	54+19	Airbus Military A.400M	Luftwaffe LTG 62, Wunstorf
	54+20	Airbus Military A.400M	Luftwaffe LTG 62, Wunstorf
	54+21	Airbus Military A.400M	Luftwaffe LTG 62, Wunstorf
	54+22	Airbus Military A.400M	Luftwaffe LTG 62, Wunstorf
	54+23	Airbus Military A.400M	Luftwaffe LTG 62, Wunstorf

Serial	Type (code/other identity)	Owner/operator, location or fate	Notes
54+24	Airbus Military A.400M	Luftwaffe LTG 62, Wunstorf	
54+25	Airbus Military A.400M	Luftwaffe LTG 62, Wunstorf	
54+26	Airbus Military A.400M	Luftwaffe LTG 62, Wunstorf	
54+27	Airbus Military A.400M	Luftwaffe LTG 62, Wunstorf	
54+28	Airbus Military A.400M	Luftwaffe LTG 62, Wunstorf	
54+29	Airbus Military A.400M	Luftwaffe LTG 62, Wunstorf	
54+30	Airbus Military A.400M	Luftwaffe LTG 62, Wunstorf	
54+31	Airbus Military A.400M	Luftwaffe LTG 62, Wunstorf	
54+32	Airbus Military A.400M	Airbus Military, Sevilla/Morón	
54+33	Airbus Military A.400M	Airbus Military, Sevilla/Morón	
54+34	Airbus Military A.400M	Airbus Military, Sevilla/Morón	
54+35	Airbus Military A.400M	Airbus Military, Sevilla/Morón	
54+36	Airbus Military A.400M	Airbus Military, Sevilla/Morón	
54+37	Airbus Military A.400M	Luftwaffe (on order)	
54+38	Airbus Military A.400M	Luftwaffe (on order)	
54+39	Airbus Military A.400M	Luftwaffe (on order)	
54+40	Airbus Military A.400M	Luftwaffe (on order)	
54+41	Airbus Military A.400M	Luftwaffe (on order)	
54+42	Airbus Military A.400M	Luftwaffe (on order)	
54+43	Airbus Military A.400M	Luftwaffe (on order)	
54+44	Airbus Military A.400M	Luftwaffe (on order)	
54+45	Airbus Military A.400M	Luftwaffe (on order)	
54+46	Airbus Military A.400M	Luftwaffe (on order)	
54+47	Airbus Military A.400M	Luftwaffe (on order)	
54+48	Airbus Military A.400M	Luftwaffe (on order)	
54+49	Airbus Military A.400M	Luftwaffe (on order)	
54+50	Airbus Military A.400M	Luftwaffe (on order)	
54+51	Airbus Military A.400M	Luftwaffe (on order)	
54+52	Airbus Military A.400M	Luftwaffe (on order)	
54+53	Airbus Military A.400M	Luftwaffe (on order)	
57+04	Dornier Do.228LM	Marineflieger MFG 3, Nordholz	
57+05	Dornier Do.228NG	Marineflieger MFG 3, Nordholz	
5.+..	Lockheed C-130J Hercules II	Luftwaffe (on order)	
5.+..	Lockheed C-130J Hercules II	Luftwaffe (on order)	
5.+..	Lockheed C-130J Hercules II	Luftwaffe (on order)	
5.+..	Lockheed C-130J Hercules II	Luftwaffe (on order)	
5.+..	Lockheed C-130J Hercules II	Luftwaffe (on order)	
5.+..	Lockheed C-130J Hercules II	Luftwaffe (on order)	
60+01	Lockheed P-3C CUP Orion $	Marineflieger MFG 3, Nordholz	
60+02	Lockheed P-3C CUP Orion	Marineflieger MFG 3, Nordholz	
60+03	Lockheed P-3C CUP Orion	Marineflieger MFG 3, Nordholz	
60+04	Lockheed P-3C CUP Orion	Marineflieger MFG 3, Nordholz	
60+05	Lockheed P-3C CUP Orion $	Marineflieger MFG 3, Nordholz	
60+06	Lockheed P-3C CUP Orion	Marineflieger MFG 3, Nordholz	
60+07	Lockheed P-3C CUP Orion	Marineflieger MFG 3, Nordholz	
60+08	Lockheed P-3C CUP Orion	Marineflieger MFG 3, Nordholz	
74+01	Eurocopter EC.665 Tiger UHT	Luftwaffe WTD 61, Ingolstadt	
74+02	Eurocopter EC.665 Tiger UHT	Heer KHR 36, Fritzlar	
74+03	Eurocopter EC.665 Tiger UHT	Luftwaffe TsLw 3, Fassberg	
74+05	Eurocopter EC.665 Tiger UHT	Heer IntHubschrAusbZ, Le Luc, France	
74+06	Eurocopter EC.665 Tiger UHT	Heer KHR 36, Fritzlar	
74+07	Eurocopter EC.665 Tiger UHT	Luftwaffe TsLw 3, Fassberg	
74+08	Eurocopter EC.665 Tiger UHT	Heer	
74+09	Eurocopter EC.665 Tiger UHT	Heer IntHubschrAusbZ, Le Luc, France	
74+10	Eurocopter EC.665 Tiger UHT	Luftwaffe TsLw 3, Fassberg	
74+11	Eurocopter EC.665 Tiger UHT	Heer IntHubschrAusbZ, Le Luc, France	
74+13	Eurocopter EC.665 Tiger UHT	Luftwaffe TsLw 3, Fassberg	
74+14	Eurocopter EC.665 Tiger UHT	Luftwaffe TsLw 3, Fassberg	
74+15	Eurocopter EC.665 Tiger UHT	Heer IntHubschrAusbZ, Le Luc, France	
74+16	Eurocopter EC.665 Tiger UHT	Heer KHR 36, Fritzlar	
74+17	Eurocopter EC.665 Tiger UHT	Heer KHR 36, Fritzlar	
74+18	Eurocopter EC.665 Tiger UHT	Heer KHR 36, Fritzlar	

Notes	Serial	Type (code/other identity)	Owner/operator, location or fate
	74+19	Eurocopter EC.665 Tiger UHT	Heer KHR 36, Fritzlar
	74+20	Eurocopter EC.665 Tiger UHT	Heer KHR 36, Fritzlar
	74+21	Eurocopter EC.665 Tiger UHT	Heer KHR 36, Fritzlar
	74+22	Eurocopter EC.665 Tiger UHT	Heer KHR 36, Fritzlar
	74+23	Eurocopter EC.665 Tiger UHT	Heer KHR 36, Fritzlar
	74+24	Eurocopter EC.665 Tiger UHT	Heer KHR 36, Fritzlar
	74+25	Eurocopter EC.665 Tiger UHT	Heer KHR 36, Fritzlar
	74+26	Eurocopter EC.665 Tiger UHT	Heer KHR 36, Fritzlar
	74+28	Eurocopter EC.665 Tiger UHT	Heer KHR 36, Fritzlar
	74+29	Eurocopter EC.665 Tiger UHT	Heer KHR 36, Fritzlar
	74+30	Eurocopter EC.665 Tiger UHT	Heer KHR 36, Fritzlar
	74+31	Eurocopter EC.665 Tiger UHT	Heer KHR 36, Fritzlar
	74+32	Eurocopter EC.665 Tiger UHT	Heer KHR 36, Fritzlar
	74+34	Eurocopter EC.665 Tiger UHT	Heer KHR 36, Fritzlar
	74+35	Eurocopter EC.665 Tiger UHT	Heer KHR 36, Fritzlar
	74+36	Eurocopter EC.665 Tiger UHT	Heer KHR 36, Fritzlar
	74+37	Eurocopter EC.665 Tiger UHT	Heer IntHubschrAusbZ, Le Luc, France
	74+38	Eurocopter EC.665 Tiger UHT	Heer KHR 36, Fritzlar
	74+39	Eurocopter EC.665 Tiger UHT	Heer
	74+40	Eurocopter EC.665 Tiger UHT	Heer KHR 36, Fritzlar
	74+41	Eurocopter EC.665 Tiger UHT	Heer
	74+42	Eurocopter EC.665 Tiger UHT	Heer KHR 36, Fritzlar
	74+43	Eurocopter EC.665 Tiger UHT	Heer
	74+44	Eurocopter EC.665 Tiger UHT	Heer
	74+45	Eurocopter EC.665 Tiger UHT	Heer KHR 36, Fritzlar
	74+46	Eurocopter EC.665 Tiger UHT	Heer KHR 36, Fritzlar
	74+47	Eurocopter EC.665 Tiger UHT	Luftwaffe WTD 61, Ingolstadt
	74+48	Eurocopter EC.665 Tiger UHT	Heer KHR 26, Roth
	74+50	Eurocopter EC.665 Tiger UHT	Heer KHR 36, Fritzlar
	74+51	Eurocopter EC.665 Tiger UHT	Heer IntHubschrAusbZ, Le Luc, France
	74+52	Eurocopter EC.665 Tiger UHT	Airbus Helicopters, stored Donauwörth
	74+53	Eurocopter EC.665 Tiger UHT	Heer KHR 36, Fritzlar
	74+54	Eurocopter EC.665 Tiger UHT	Heer KHR 36, Fritzlar
	74+55	Eurocopter EC.665 Tiger UHT	Heer
	74+56	Eurocopter EC.665 Tiger UHT	Heer KHR 36, Fritzlar
	74+57	Eurocopter EC.665 Tiger UHT	Heer KHR 36, Fritzlar
	74+58	Eurocopter EC.665 Tiger UHT	Heer
	74+59	Eurocopter EC.665 Tiger UHT	Heer
	74+61	Eurocopter EC.665 Tiger UHT	Heer KHR 36, Fritzlar
	74+62	Eurocopter EC.665 Tiger UHT	Airbus Helicopters, Donauwörth
	74+63	Eurocopter EC.665 Tiger UHT	Heer KHR 36, Fritzlar
	74+64	Eurocopter EC.665 Tiger UHT	Heer (on order)
	74+65	Eurocopter EC.665 Tiger UHT	Heer (on order)
	74+66	Eurocopter EC.665 Tiger UHT	Airbus Helicopters, Donauwörth
	74+67	Eurocopter EC.665 Tiger UHT	Heer KHR 36, Fritzlar
	74+68	Eurocopter EC.665 Tiger UHT	Airbus Helicopters, Donauwörth
	74+69	Eurocopter EC.665 Tiger UHT	Heer
	74+70	Eurocopter EC.665 Tiger UHT	Heer KHR 36, Fritzlar
	76+01	Airbus Helicopters H.145M	Luftwaffe HSG 64, Laupheim
	76+02	Airbus Helicopters H.145M	Luftwaffe HSG 64, Laupheim
	76+03	Airbus Helicopters H.145M	Luftwaffe HSG 64, Laupheim
	76+04	Airbus Helicopters H.145M	Luftwaffe HSG 64, Laupheim
	76+05	Airbus Helicopters H.145M	Luftwaffe HSG 64, Laupheim
	76+06	Airbus Helicopters H.145M	Luftwaffe HSG 64, Laupheim
	76+07	Airbus Helicopters H.145M	Luftwaffe HSG 64, Laupheim
	76+08	Airbus Helicopters H.145M	Luftwaffe HSG 64, Laupheim
	76+09	Airbus Helicopters H.145M	Luftwaffe HSG 64, Laupheim
	76+10	Airbus Helicopters H.145M	Luftwaffe HSG 64, Laupheim
	76+11	Airbus Helicopters H.145M	Luftwaffe HSG 64, Laupheim
	76+12	Airbus Helicopters H.145M	Luftwaffe HSG 64, Laupheim
	76+13	Airbus Helicopters H.145M	Luftwaffe HSG 64, Laupheim
	76+14	Airbus Helicopters H.145M	Luftwaffe HSG 64, Laupheim

Serial	Type (code/other identity)	Owner/operator, location or fate	Notes
76+15	Airbus Helicopters H.145M	Luftwaffe HSG 64, Laupheim	
78+01	NH Industries NH.90-TTH (98+91)	Heer IntHubschrAusbZ, Bückeburg	
78+02	NH Industries NH.90-TTH (98+92)	Heer IntHubschrAusbZ, Bückeburg	
78+03	NH Industries NH.90-TTH (98+93)	Heer IntHubschrAusbZ, Bückeburg	
78+04	NH Industries NH.90-TTH (98+94)	Heer	
78+05	NH Industries NH.90-TTH	Luftwaffe TsLw 3, Fassberg	
78+06	NH Industries NH.90-TTH	Heer IntHubschrAusbZ, Bückeburg	
78+07	NH Industries NH.90-TTH	Heer IntHubschrAusbZ, Bückeburg	
78+08	NH Industries NH.90-TTH	Heer IntHubschrAusbZ, Bückeburg	
78+09	NH Industries NH.90-TTH (98+92)	Heer THR 30, Niederstetten	
78+10	NH Industries NH.90-TTH (98+94)	Heer THR 10, Fassberg	
78+11	NH Industries NH.90-TTH (98+95)	Heer THR 10, Fassberg	
78+12	NH Industries NH.90-TTH (98+96)	Heer THR 30, Niederstetten	
78+13	NH Industries NH.90-TTH	Heer IntHubschrAusbZ, Bückeburg	
78+14	NH Industries NH.90-TTH	Heer THR 10, Fassberg	
78+15	NH Industries NH.90-TTH	Heer THR 10, Fassberg	
78+16	NH Industries NH.90-TTH	Heer THR 10, Fassberg	
78+17	NH Industries NH.90-TTH	Heer THR 10, Fassberg	
78+18	NH Industries NH.90-TTH	Heer THR 10, Fassberg	
78+19	NH Industries NH.90-TTH (98+49)	Heer IntHubschrAusbZ, Bückeburg	
78+20	NH Industries NH.90-TTH (98+52)	Heer IntHubschrAusbZ, Bückeburg	
78+21	NH Industries NH.90-TTH (98+56)	Heer THR 10, Fassberg	
78+22	NH Industries NH.90-TTH (98+57)	Heer IntHubschrAusbZ, Bückeburg	
78+23	NH Industries NH.90-TTH	Heer THR 10, Fassberg	
78+24	NH Industries NH.90-TTH	Heer THR 10, Fassberg	
78+25	NH Industries NH.90-TTH	Luftwaffe TsLw 3, Fassberg	
78+26	NH Industries NH.90-TTH	Heer IntHubschrAusbZ, Bückeburg	
78+27	NH Industries NH.90-TTH	Heer THR 10, Fassberg	
78+28	NH Industries NH.90-TTH	Heer THR 10, Fassberg	
78+29	NH Industries NH.90-TTH	Heer IntHubschrAusbZ, Bückeburg	
78+30	NH Industries NH.90-TTH	Heer THR 10, Fassberg	
78+31	NH Industries NH.90-TTH	Heer THR 10, Fassberg	
78+32	NH Industries NH.90-TTH	Heer THR 10, Fassberg	
78+33	NH Industries NH.90-TTH	Heer THR 10, Fassberg	
78+34	NH Industries NH.90-TTH	Heer THR 10, Fassberg	
78+35	NH Industries NH.90-TTH	Heer THR 30, Niederstetten	
78+36	NH Industries NH.90-TTH	Heer THR 30, Niederstetten	
78+37	NH Industries NH.90-TTH	Heer THR 30, Niederstetten	
78+38	NH Industries NH.90-TTH	Heer IntHubschrAusbZ, Bückeburg	
78+39	NH Industries NH.90-TTH	Heer THR 30, Niederstetten	
78+40	NH Industries NH.90-TTH	Heer THR 30, Niederstetten	
78+41	NH Industries NH.90-TTH	Heer (on order)	
78+42	NH Industries NH.90-TTH	Heer (on order)	
78+43	NH Industries NH.90-TTH	Heer (on order)	
78+44	NH Industries NH.90-TTH	Heer (on order)	
78+45	NH Industries NH.90-TTH	Heer (on order)	
78+46	NH Industries NH.90-TTH	Heer (on order)	
78+47	NH Industries NH.90-TTH	Heer (on order)	
78+48	NH Industries NH.90-TTH	Heer (on order)	
78+49	NH Industries NH.90-TTH	Heer (on order)	
78+50	NH Industries NH.90-TTH	Heer (on order)	
79+01	NH Industries NH.90-TTH (98+91)	Heer IntHubschrAusbZ, Bückeburg	
79+02	NH Industries NH.90-TTH	Heer THR 30, Niederstetten	
79+03	NH Industries NH.90-TTH	Heer THR 10, Fassberg	
79+04	NH Industries NH.90-TTH	Heer THR 10, Fassberg	
79+05	NH Industries NH.90-TTH	Heer THR 10, Fassberg	
79+06	NH Industries NH.90-TTH	Heer THR 10, Fassberg	
79+07	NH Industries NH.90-TTH	Heer THR 10, Fassberg	
79+08	NH Industries NH.90-TTH (98+50)	Luftwaffe TsLw 3, Fassberg	
79+09	NH Industries NH.90-TTH	Heer THR 10, Fassberg	
79+10	NH Industries NH.90-TTH	Heer THR 10, Fassberg	
79+11	NH Industries NH.90-TTH	Heer THR 30, Niederstetten	

Notes	Serial	Type (code/other identity)	Owner/operator, location or fate
	79+12	NH Industries NH.90-TTH	Heer THR 10, Fassberg
	79+13	NH Industries NH.90-TTH	Heer THR 30, Niederstetten
	79+14	NH Industries NH.90-TTH	Heer THR 30, Niederstetten
	79+15	NH Industries NH.90-TTH	Heer THR 30, Niederstetten
	79+16	NH Industries NH.90-TTH	Heer THR 30, Niederstetten
	79+17	NH Industries NH.90-TTH	Heer IntHubschrAusbZ, Bückeburg
	79+18	NH Industries NH.90-TTH	Heer IntHubschrAusbZ, Bückeburg
	79+19	NH Industries NH.90-TTH	Heer IntHubschrAusbZ, Bückeburg
	79+20	NH Industries NH.90-TTH	Heer IntHubschrAusbZ, Bückeburg
	79+21	NH Industries NH.90-TTH	Heer IntHubschrAusbZ, Bückeburg
	79+23	NH Industries NH.90-TTH	Heer IntHubschrAusbZ, Bückeburg
	79+24	NH Industries NH.90-TTH (98+93)	Heer THR 30, Niederstetten
	79+25	NH Industries NH.90-TTH (98+97)	Heer IntHubschrAusbZ, Bückeburg
	79+26	NH Industries NH.90-TTH (98+99)	Heer THR 10, Fassberg
	79+27	NH Industries NH.90-TTH	Heer THR 30, Niederstetten
	79+28	NH Industries NH.90-TTH	Heer IntHubschrAusbZ, Bückeburg
	79+29	NH Industries NH.90-TTH	Heer (on order)
	79+30	NH Industries NH.90-TTH	Heer (on order)
	79+31	NH Industries NH.90-TTH	Airbus Helicopters, Donauwörth
	79+32	NH Industries NH.90-TTH	Heer THR 10, Fassberg
	79+33	NH Industries NH.90-TTH	Heer (on order)
	79+34	NH Industries NH.90-TTH	Heer (on order)
	79+35	NH Industries NH.90-TTH	Heer (on order)
	79+36	NH Industries NH.90-TTH	Heer (on order)
	79+37	NH Industries NH.90-TTH	Heer (on order)
	79+38	NH Industries NH.90-TTH	Heer (on order)
	79+39	NH Industries NH.90-TTH	Heer (on order)
	79+40	NH Industries NH.90-TTH	Heer (on order)
	79+51	NH Industries NH.90-NFH Sea Lion (98+51)	Marineflieger/Heer THR 10, Fassberg
	79+52	NH Industries NH.90-NFH Sea Lion (98+56)	Airbus Helicopters, Donauwörth
	79+53	NH Industries NH.90-NFH Sea Lion (98+40)	Airbus Helicopters, Donauwörth
	79+54	NH Industries NH.90-NFH Sea Lion	Marineflieger MFG 5, Nordholz
	79+55	NH Industries NH.90-NFH Sea Lion	Marineflieger (on order)
	79+56	NH Industries NH.90-NFH Sea Lion	Marineflieger (on order)
	79+57	NH Industries NH.90-NFH Sea Lion	Marineflieger (on order)
	79+58	NH Industries NH.90-NFH Sea Lion	Marineflieger (on order)
	79+59	NH Industries NH.90-NFH Sea Lion	Marineflieger (on order)
	79+60	NH Industries NH.90-NFH Sea Lion	Marineflieger (on order)
	79+61	NH Industries NH.90-NFH Sea Lion	Marineflieger (on order)
	79+62	NH Industries NH.90-NFH Sea Lion	Marineflieger (on order)
	79+63	NH Industries NH.90-NFH Sea Lion	Marineflieger (on order)
	79+64	NH Industries NH.90-NFH Sea Lion	Marineflieger (on order)
	79+65	NH Industries NH.90-NFH Sea Lion	Marineflieger (on order)
	79+66	NH Industries NH.90-NFH Sea Lion	Marineflieger (on order)
	79+67	NH Industries NH.90-NFH Sea Lion	Marineflieger (on order)
	79+68	NH Industries NH.90-NFH Sea Lion	Marineflieger (on order)
	82+01	Eurocopter AS.532U-2 Cougar	Luftwaffe 3/FBS, Berlin-Tegel
	82+02	Eurocopter AS.532U-2 Cougar	Luftwaffe 3/FBS, Berlin-Tegel
	82+03	Eurocopter AS.532U-2 Cougar	Luftwaffe 3/FBS, Berlin-Tegel
	82+51	Eurocopter EC.135P-1	Heer IntHubschrAusbZ, Bückeburg
	82+52	Eurocopter EC.135P-1	Heer IntHubschrAusbZ, Bückeburg
	82+53	Eurocopter EC.135P-1	Heer IntHubschrAusbZ, Bückeburg
	82+54	Eurocopter EC.135P-1	Heer IntHubschrAusbZ, Bückeburg
	82+55	Eurocopter EC.135P-1	Heer IntHubschrAusbZ, Bückeburg
	82+56	Eurocopter EC.135P-1	Heer IntHubschrAusbZ, Bückeburg
	82+57	Eurocopter EC.135P-1	Heer IntHubschrAusbZ, Bückeburg
	82+59	Eurocopter EC.135P-1	Heer IntHubschrAusbZ, Bückeburg
	82+60	Eurocopter EC.135P-1	Heer IntHubschrAusbZ, Bückeburg
	82+61	Eurocopter EC.135P-1	Heer IntHubschrAusbZ, Bückeburg
	82+62	Eurocopter EC.135P-1	Heer IntHubschrAusbZ, Bückeburg
	82+63	Eurocopter EC.135P-1	Heer IntHubschrAusbZ, Bückeburg
	82+64	Eurocopter EC.135P-1	Heer IntHubschrAusbZ, Bückeburg

Serial	Type (code/other identity)	Owner/operator, location or fate	Notes
82+65	Eurocopter EC.135P-1	Heer IntHubschrAusbZ, Bückeburg	
83+02	Westland Sea Lynx Mk88A	Marineflieger MFG 5, Nordholz	
83+03	Westland Sea Lynx Mk88A	Marineflieger MFG 5, Nordholz	
83+04	Westland Sea Lynx Mk88A	Marineflieger MFG 5, Nordholz	
83+05	Westland Sea Lynx Mk88A	Marineflieger MFG 5, Nordholz	
83+06	Westland Sea Lynx Mk88A	Marineflieger MFG 5, Nordholz	
83+07	Westland Sea Lynx Mk88A	Luftwaffe WTD 61, Ingolstadt	
83+09	Westland Sea Lynx Mk88A	Marineflieger MFG 5, Nordholz	
83+10	Westland Sea Lynx Mk88A	Marineflieger MFG 5, Nordholz	
83+11	Westland Sea Lynx Mk88A $	Marineflieger MFG 5, Nordholz	
83+12	Westland Sea Lynx Mk88A	Marineflieger MFG 5, Nordholz	
83+13	Westland Sea Lynx Mk88A	Marineflieger MFG 5, Nordholz	
83+15	Westland Sea Lynx Mk88A	Marineflieger MFG 5, Nordholz	
83+17	Westland Sea Lynx Mk88A	Marineflieger MFG 5, Nordholz	
83+18	Westland Sea Lynx Mk88A	Marineflieger MFG 5, Nordholz	
83+19	Westland Sea Lynx Mk88A	Marineflieger MFG 5, Nordholz	
83+20	Westland Sea Lynx Mk88A $	Marineflieger MFG 5, Nordholz	
83+21	Westland Sea Lynx Mk88A	Marineflieger MFG 5, Nordholz	
83+22	Westland Sea Lynx Mk88A	Marineflieger MFG 5, Nordholz	
83+23	Westland Sea Lynx Mk88A	Marineflieger MFG 5, Nordholz	
83+24	Westland Sea Lynx Mk88A	Marineflieger MFG 5, Nordholz	
83+25	Westland Sea Lynx Mk88A	Marineflieger MFG 5, Nordholz	
84+05	Sikorsky/VFW CH-53G	Luftwaffe HSG 64, Laupheim & Rheine-Bentlage	
84+09	Sikorsky/VFW CH-53G	Luftwaffe TsLw 3, Fassberg	
84+10	Sikorsky/VFW CH-53G	*Withdrawn from use, 2019*	
84+12	Sikorsky/VFW CH-53G	Luftwaffe HSG 64, Laupheim & Rheine-Bentlage	
84+13	Sikorsky/VFW CH-53GA	Luftwaffe HSG 64, Laupheim & Rheine-Bentlage	
84+14	Sikorsky/VFW CH-53GE	Luftwaffe HSG 64, Laupheim & Rheine-Bentlage	
84+15	Sikorsky/VFW CH-53GS	Luftwaffe HSG 64, Laupheim & Rheine-Bentlage	
84+16	Sikorsky/VFW CH-53G	*Withdrawn from use at Haldensleben, 2019*	
84+18	Sikorsky/VFW CH-53G	Luftwaffe HSG 64, Laupheim & Rheine-Bentlage	
84+19	Sikorsky/VFW CH-53G	Luftwaffe TsLw 3, Fassberg	
84+24	Sikorsky/VFW CH-53GA	Luftwaffe HSG 64, Laupheim & Rheine-Bentlage	
84+25	Sikorsky/VFW CH-53GS	Luftwaffe HSG 64, Laupheim & Rheine-Bentlage	
84+26	Sikorsky/VFW CH-53GE	Luftwaffe WTD 61, Ingolstadt	
84+27	Sikorsky/VFW CH-53G	Luftwaffe	
84+28	Sikorsky/VFW CH-53GA	Luftwaffe HSG 64, Laupheim & Rheine-Bentlage	
84+29	Sikorsky/VFW CH-53G	Luftwaffe HSG 64, Laupheim & Rheine-Bentlage	
84+30	Sikorsky/VFW CH-53GS	Luftwaffe HSG 64, Laupheim & Rheine-Bentlage	
84+31	Sikorsky/VFW CH-53GA	Luftwaffe HSG 64, Laupheim & Rheine-Bentlage	
84+32	Sikorsky/VFW CH-53G	Luftwaffe HSG 64, Laupheim & Rheine-Bentlage	
84+33	Sikorsky/VFW CH-53GA	Luftwaffe HSG 64, Laupheim & Rheine-Bentlage	
84+34	Sikorsky/VFW CH-53G	Luftwaffe HSG 64, Laupheim & Rheine-Bentlage	
84+35	Sikorsky/VFW CH-53GA	Luftwaffe HSG 64, Laupheim & Rheine-Bentlage	
84+37	Sikorsky/VFW CH-53GA	Luftwaffe HSG 64, Laupheim & Rheine-Bentlage	
84+38	Sikorsky/VFW CH-53G	Luftwaffe HSG 64, Laupheim & Rheine-Bentlage	
84+39	Sikorsky/VFW CH-53GA	Luftwaffe HSG 64, Laupheim & Rheine-Bentlage	
84+40	Sikorsky/VFW CH-53G	Luftwaffe HSG 64, Laupheim & Rheine-Bentlage	
84+42	Sikorsky/VFW CH-53GS	Luftwaffe HSG 64, Laupheim & Rheine-Bentlage	
84+43	Sikorsky/VFW CH-53G	Luftwaffe HSG 64, Laupheim & Rheine-Bentlage	
84+44	Sikorsky/VFW CH-53G	Luftwaffe HSG 64, Laupheim & Rheine-Bentlage	
84+45	Sikorsky/VFW CH-53GS	Luftwaffe HSG 64, Laupheim & Rheine-Bentlage	
84+46	Sikorsky/VFW CH-53G	Luftwaffe HSG 64, Laupheim & Rheine-Bentlage	
84+47	Sikorsky/VFW CH-53GA	Luftwaffe HSG 64, Laupheim & Rheine-Bentlage	
84+48	Sikorsky/VFW CH-53G	Luftwaffe HSG 64, Laupheim & Rheine-Bentlage	
84+49	Sikorsky/VFW CH-53GA	Luftwaffe HSG 64, Laupheim & Rheine-Bentlage	
84+50	Sikorsky/VFW CH-53GA	Luftwaffe HSG 64, Laupheim & Rheine-Bentlage	
84+51	Sikorsky/VFW CH-53GS	Luftwaffe HSG 64, Laupheim & Rheine-Bentlage	
84+52	Sikorsky/VFW CH-53GS	Luftwaffe HSG 64, Laupheim & Rheine-Bentlage	
84+53	Sikorsky/VFW CH-53GE	Luftwaffe HSG 64, Laupheim & Rheine-Bentlage	
84+54	Sikorsky/VFW CH-53G	Luftwaffe HSG 64, Laupheim & Rheine-Bentlage	
84+55	Sikorsky/VFW CH-53G	Airbus Helicopters, Donauwörth	

Notes	Serial	Type (code/other identity)	Owner/operator, location or fate
	84+57	Sikorsky/VFW CH-53G	Luftwaffe HSG 64, Laupheim & Rheine-Bentlage
	84+58	Sikorsky/VFW CH-53G	Luftwaffe HSG 64, Laupheim & Rheine-Bentlage
	84+59	Sikorsky/VFW CH-53GS	Luftwaffe HSG 64, Laupheim & Rheine-Bentlage
	84+60	Sikorsky/VFW CH-53G	Luftwaffe HSG 64, Laupheim & Rheine-Bentlage
	84+62	Sikorsky/VFW CH-53GS	Luftwaffe HSG 64, Laupheim & Rheine-Bentlage
	84+63	Sikorsky/VFW CH-53G	Luftwaffe HSG 64, Laupheim & Rheine-Bentlage
	84+64	Sikorsky/VFW CH-53GS	Luftwaffe HSG 64, Laupheim & Rheine-Bentlage
	84+65	Sikorsky/VFW CH-53GA	Luftwaffe HSG 64, Laupheim & Rheine-Bentlage
	84+66	Sikorsky/VFW CH-53GS	Luftwaffe HSG 64, Laupheim & Rheine-Bentlage
	84+67	Sikorsky/VFW CH-53GS	Luftwaffe HSG 64, Laupheim & Rheine-Bentlage
	84+68	Sikorsky/VFW CH-53GS	Luftwaffe HSG 64, Laupheim & Rheine-Bentlage
	84+70	Sikorsky/VFW CH-53GA	Luftwaffe TsLw 3, Fassberg
	84+71	Sikorsky/VFW CH-53G	Luftwaffe HSG 64, Laupheim & Rheine-Bentlage
	84+72	Sikorsky/VFW CH-53G	Luftwaffe HSG 64, Laupheim & Rheine-Bentlage
	84+73	Sikorsky/VFW CH-53GS	Luftwaffe HSG 64, Laupheim & Rheine-Bentlage
	84+74	Sikorsky/VFW CH-53G	Luftwaffe HSG 64, Laupheim & Rheine-Bentlage
	84+75	Sikorsky/VFW CH-53G	Luftwaffe HSG 64, Laupheim & Rheine-Bentlage
	84+76	Sikorsky/VFW CH-53G	Luftwaffe HSG 64, Laupheim & Rheine-Bentlage
	84+77	Sikorsky/VFW CH-53G	*Withdrawn from use at Hammelburg, 2019*
	84+78	Sikorsky/VFW CH-53GS	Luftwaffe TsLw 3, Fassberg
	84+79	Sikorsky/VFW CH-53GS	Luftwaffe HSG 64, Laupheim & Rheine-Bentlage
	84+80	Sikorsky/VFW CH-53G	Luftwaffe HSG 64, Laupheim & Rheine-Bentlage
	84+82	Sikorsky/VFW CH-53GE	Luftwaffe HSG 64, Laupheim & Rheine-Bentlage
	84+83	Sikorsky/VFW CH-53G	Luftwaffe TsLw 3, Fassberg
	84+84	Sikorsky/VFW CH-53G	Luftwaffe HSG 64, Laupheim & Rheine-Bentlage
	84+85	Sikorsky/VFW CH-53GS	Luftwaffe HSG 64, Laupheim & Rheine-Bentlage
	84+86	Sikorsky/VFW CH-53GA	Luftwaffe HSG 64, Laupheim & Rheine-Bentlage
	84+87	Sikorsky/VFW CH-53GS	Luftwaffe HSG 64, Laupheim & Rheine-Bentlage
	84+88	Sikorsky/VFW CH-53G	Luftwaffe HSG 64, Laupheim & Rheine-Bentlage
	84+89	Sikorsky/VFW CH-53GA	Luftwaffe HSG 64, Laupheim & Rheine-Bentlage
	84+90	Sikorsky/VFW CH-53G	Luftwaffe HSG 64, Laupheim & Rheine-Bentlage
	84+91	Sikorsky/VFW CH-53GS	Luftwaffe HSG 64, Laupheim & Rheine-Bentlage
	84+92	Sikorsky/VFW CH-53GS	Luftwaffe HSG 64, Laupheim & Rheine-Bentlage
	84+94	Sikorsky/VFW CH-53G	Luftwaffe WTD 61, Ingolstadt
	84+95	Sikorsky/VFW CH-53GA	*Withdrawn from use, 2019*
	84+96	Sikorsky/VFW CH-53GE	Luftwaffe HSG 64, Laupheim & Rheine-Bentlage
	84+97	Sikorsky/VFW CH-53G	Luftwaffe HSG 64, Laupheim & Rheine-Bentlage
	84+98	Sikorsky/VFW CH-53GS	Luftwaffe HSG 64, Laupheim & Rheine-Bentlage
	84+99	Sikorsky/VFW CH-53GA	Luftwaffe HSG 64, Laupheim & Rheine-Bentlage
	85+00	Sikorsky/VFW CH-53GS	Luftwaffe HSG 64, Laupheim & Rheine-Bentlage
	85+01	Sikorsky/VFW CH-53GS	Luftwaffe HSG 64, Laupheim & Rheine-Bentlage
	85+02	Sikorsky/VFW CH-53G	*Withdrawn from use at Jever, 2019*
	85+03	Sikorsky/VFW CH-53G	Luftwaffe HSG 64, Laupheim & Rheine-Bentlage
	85+04	Sikorsky/VFW CH-53GA	Luftwaffe HSG 64, Laupheim & Rheine-Bentlage
	85+05	Sikorsky/VFW CH-53GS	Luftwaffe HSG 64, Laupheim & Rheine-Bentlage
	85+06	Sikorsky/VFW CH-53GA	Luftwaffe HSG 64, Laupheim & Rheine-Bentlage
	85+07	Sikorsky/VFW CH-53GS	Luftwaffe HSG 64, Laupheim & Rheine-Bentlage
	85+08	Sikorsky/VFW CH-53G	Luftwaffe HSG 64, Laupheim & Rheine-Bentlage
	85+10	Sikorsky/VFW CH-53GS	Luftwaffe HSG 64, Laupheim & Rheine-Bentlage
	85+11	Sikorsky/VFW CH-53G	Luftwaffe HSG 64, Laupheim & Rheine-Bentlage
	85+12	Sikorsky/VFW CH-53GS	Luftwaffe HSG 64, Laupheim & Rheine-Bentlage
	89+50	Westland Sea King Mk.41	Marineflieger MFG 5, Nordholz
	89+51	Westland Sea King Mk.41	Marineflieger MFG 5, Nordholz
	89+52	Westland Sea King Mk.41	Marineflieger MFG 5, Nordholz
	89+53	Westland Sea King Mk.41	Marineflieger MFG 5, Nordholz
	89+54	Westland Sea King Mk.41	Marineflieger MFG 5, Nordholz
	89+55	Westland Sea King Mk.41 $	Marineflieger MFG 5, Nordholz
	89+56	Westland Sea King Mk.41	Marineflieger MFG 5, Nordholz
	89+57	Westland Sea King Mk.41	Marineflieger MFG 5, Nordholz
	89+58	Westland Sea King Mk.41 $	Marineflieger MFG 5, Nordholz
	89+60	Westland Sea King Mk.41	Marineflieger MFG 5, Nordholz
	89+61	Westland Sea King Mk.41	Marineflieger MFG 5, Nordholz

Serial	Type (code/other identity)	Owner/operator, location or fate	Notes
89+62	Westland Sea King Mk.41	Marineflieger MFG 5, Nordholz	
89+63	Westland Sea King Mk.41	Marineflieger MFG 5, Nordholz	
89+64	Westland Sea King Mk.41 $	Marineflieger MFG 5, Nordholz	
89+65	Westland Sea King Mk.41	Marineflieger MFG 5, Nordholz	
89+66	Westland Sea King Mk.41	Marineflieger MFG 5, Nordholz	
89+67	Westland Sea King Mk.41	*Withdrawn from use at Jever, 2019*	
89+68	Westland Sea King Mk.41	Marineflieger MFG 5, Nordholz	
89+69	Westland Sea King Mk.41	Marineflieger MFG 5, Nordholz	
89+70	Westland Sea King Mk.41	Marineflieger MFG 5, Nordholz	
89+71	Westland Sea King Mk.41	Marineflieger MFG 5, Nordholz	
98+03	Eurofighter EF.2000(T) (IPA3)	Luftwaffe WTD 61, Ingolstadt	
98+07	Eurofighter EF.2000 (IPA7)	Luftwaffe WTD 61, Ingolstadt	
98+08	Eurofighter EF.2000GT (IPA8)	Airbus Defence & Space, Manching	
98+16	Eurocopter EC.665 Tiger UHT	Luftwaffe TsLw 3, Fassberg	
98+18	Eurocopter EC.665 Tiger UHT	Airbus Helicopters, Donauwörth	
98+40	NH Industries NH.90-NFH Sea Lion (79+53)	*To 79+53, 2019*	
98+49	Eurocopter EC.665 Tiger UHT (74+49)	Airbus Helicopters, Donauwörth	
98+59	Panavia Tornado IDS(T) (43+21)	Luftwaffe WTD 61, Ingolstadt	
98+60	Panavia Tornado IDS (43+89)	Luftwaffe WTD 61, Ingolstadt	
98+77	Panavia Tornado IDS (45+29) $	Luftwaffe WTD 61, Ingolstadt	
98+79	Panavia Tornado ECR (45+75)	Luftwaffe WTD 61, Ingolstadt	
98+90	NH Industries NH.90-TTH	Airbus Helicopters, Donauwörth	
99+01	Northrop Grumman RQ-4E Euro Hawk	Luftwaffe WTD 61, Manching	
Civil operated aircraft in military use			
D-HCDL	Eurocopter EC.135P-2+	Marineflieger MFG 5, Nordholz	
D-HDDL	Eurocopter EC.135P-2+	Marineflieger MFG 5, Nordholz	

GHANA

Serial	Type (code/other identity)	Owner/operator, location or fate	Notes
9G-EXE	Dassault Falcon 900EASy	Ghana Air Force VIP Flight, Accra	

GREECE

Ellinikí Polemikí Aeroporía/Hellenic Air Force (HAF)

Serial	Type (code/other identity)	Owner/operator, location or fate	Notes
001	Lockheed Martin F-16C-52 Fighting Falcon	HAF 335 Mira/116 PM, Áraxos	
002	Lockheed Martin F-16C-52 Fighting Falcon	HAF 335 Mira/116 PM, Áraxos	
003	Lockheed Martin F-16C-52 Fighting Falcon	HAF 335 Mira/116 PM, Áraxos	
004	Lockheed Martin F-16C-52 Fighting Falcon	HAF 335 Mira/116 PM, Áraxos	
005	Lockheed Martin F-16C-52+ Fighting Falcon $	HAF 335 Mira/116 PM, Áraxos	
006	Lockheed Martin F-16C-52 Fighting Falcon	HAF 335 Mira/116 PM, Áraxos	
007	Lockheed Martin F-16C-52 Fighting Falcon	HAF 335 Mira/116 PM, Áraxos	
008	Lockheed Martin F-16C-52 Fighting Falcon	HAF 335 Mira/116 PM, Áraxos	
009	Lockheed Martin F-16C-52 Fighting Falcon	HAF 335 Mira/116 PM, Áraxos	
010	Lockheed Martin F-16C-52 Fighting Falcon	HAF 335 Mira/116 PM, Áraxos	
011	Lockheed Martin F-16C-52 Fighting Falcon	HAF 335 Mira/116 PM, Áraxos	
012	Lockheed Martin F-16C-52 Fighting Falcon	HAF 335 Mira/116 PM, Áraxos	
013	Lockheed Martin F-16C-52 Fighting Falcon	HAF 335 Mira/116 PM, Áraxos	
014	Lockheed Martin F-16C-52 Fighting Falcon	HAF 335 Mira/116 PM, Áraxos	
015	Lockheed Martin F-16C-52 Fighting Falcon	HAF 335 Mira/116 PM, Áraxos	
016	Lockheed Martin F-16C-52 Fighting Falcon	HAF 335 Mira/116 PM, Áraxos	
017	Lockheed Martin F-16C-52 Fighting Falcon	HAF 335 Mira/116 PM, Áraxos	
018	Lockheed Martin F-16C-52 Fighting Falcon	HAF 335 Mira/116 PM, Áraxos	
019	Lockheed Martin F-16C-52 Fighting Falcon	HAF 335 Mira/116 PM, Áraxos	
020	Lockheed Martin F-16C-52 Fighting Falcon	HAF 335 Mira/116 PM, Áraxos	
021	Lockheed Martin F-16D-52 Fighting Falcon	HAF 335 Mira/116 PM, Áraxos	
022	Lockheed Martin F-16D-52 Fighting Falcon	HAF 335 Mira/116 PM, Áraxos	
023	Lockheed Martin F-16D-52 Fighting Falcon $	HAF 335 Mira/116 PM, Áraxos	
024	Lockheed Martin F-16D-52 Fighting Falcon	HAF 335 Mira/116 PM, Áraxos	
025	Lockheed Martin F-16D-52 Fighting Falcon	HAF 335 Mira/116 PM, Áraxos	
026	Lockheed Martin F-16D-52 Fighting Falcon	HAF 335 Mira/116 PM, Áraxos	
027	Lockheed Martin F-16D-52 Fighting Falcon	HAF 335 Mira/116 PM, Áraxos	
028	Lockheed Martin F-16D-52 Fighting Falcon	HAF 335 Mira/116 PM, Áraxos	
029	Lockheed Martin F-16D-52 Fighting Falcon	HAF 335 Mira/116 PM, Áraxos	
030	Lockheed Martin F-16D-52 Fighting Falcon	HAF 335 Mira/116 PM, Áraxos	

Notes	Serial	Type (code/other identity)	Owner/operator, location or fate
	045	Lockheed Martin F-16C-50 Fighting Falcon	HAF 347 Mira/111 PM, Nea Ankhialos
	046	Lockheed Martin F-16C-50 Fighting Falcon	HAF 341 Mira/111 PM, Nea Ankhialos
	047	Lockheed Martin F-16C-50 Fighting Falcon	HAF 347 Mira/111 PM, Nea Ankhialos
	048	Lockheed Martin F-16C-50 Fighting Falcon	HAF 341 Mira/111 PM, Nea Ankhialos
	049	Lockheed Martin F-16C-50 Fighting Falcon	HAF 347 Mira/111 PM, Nea Ankhialos
	050	Lockheed Martin F-16C-50 Fighting Falcon	HAF 341 Mira/111 PM, Nea Ankhialos
	051	Lockheed Martin F-16C-50 Fighting Falcon	HAF 347 Mira/111 PM, Nea Ankhialos
	052	Lockheed Martin F-16C-50 Fighting Falcon	HAF 341 Mira/111 PM, Nea Ankhialos
	053	Lockheed Martin F-16C-50 Fighting Falcon	HAF 347 Mira/111 PM, Nea Ankhialos
	054	Lockheed Martin F-16C-50 Fighting Falcon	HAF 341 Mira/111 PM, Nea Ankhialos
	055	Lockheed Martin F-16C-50 Fighting Falcon	HAF 347 Mira/111 PM, Nea Ankhialos
	056	Lockheed Martin F-16C-50 Fighting Falcon	HAF 341 Mira/111 PM, Nea Ankhialos
	057	Lockheed Martin F-16C-50 Fighting Falcon	HAF 347 Mira/111 PM, Nea Ankhialos
	058	Lockheed Martin F-16C-50 Fighting Falcon	HAF 341 Mira/111 PM, Nea Ankhialos
	060	Lockheed Martin F-16C-50 Fighting Falcon	HAF 347 Mira/111 PM, Nea Ankhialos
	061	Lockheed Martin F-16C-50 Fighting Falcon	HAF 347 Mira/111 PM, Nea Ankhialos
	062	Lockheed Martin F-16C-50 Fighting Falcon $	HAF 341 Mira/111 PM, Nea Ankhialos
	063	Lockheed Martin F-16C-50 Fighting Falcon	HAF 347 Mira/111 PM, Nea Ankhialos
	064	Lockheed Martin F-16C-50 Fighting Falcon	HAF 341 Mira/111 PM, Nea Ankhialos
	065	Lockheed Martin F-16C-50 Fighting Falcon	HAF 347 Mira/111 PM, Nea Ankhialos
	066	Lockheed Martin F-16C-50 Fighting Falcon	HAF 341 Mira/111 PM, Nea Ankhialos
	067	Lockheed Martin F-16C-50 Fighting Falcon	HAF 347 Mira/111 PM, Nea Ankhialos
	068	Lockheed Martin F-16C-50 Fighting Falcon	HAF 341 Mira/111 PM, Nea Ankhialos
	069	Lockheed Martin F-16C-50 Fighting Falcon	HAF 347 Mira/111 PM, Nea Ankhialos
	070	Lockheed Martin F-16C-50 Fighting Falcon	HAF 341 Mira/111 PM, Nea Ankhialos
	071	Lockheed Martin F-16C-50 Fighting Falcon	HAF 347 Mira/111 PM, Nea Ankhialos
	072	Lockheed Martin F-16C-50 Fighting Falcon	HAF 341 Mira/111 PM, Nea Ankhialos
	073	Lockheed Martin F-16C-50 Fighting Falcon	HAF 347 Mira/111 PM, Nea Ankhialos
	074	Lockheed Martin F-16C-50 Fighting Falcon	HAF 341 Mira/111 PM, Nea Ankhialos
	075	Lockheed Martin F-16C-50 Fighting Falcon	HAF 347 Mira/111 PM, Nea Ankhialos
	076	Lockheed Martin F-16C-50 Fighting Falcon $	HAF 341 Mira/111 PM, Nea Ankhialos
	077	Lockheed Martin F-16D-50 Fighting Falcon	HAF 341 Mira/111 PM, Nea Ankhialos
	078	Lockheed Martin F-16D-50 Fighting Falcon	HAF 347 Mira/111 PM, Nea Ankhialos
	079	Lockheed Martin F-16D-50 Fighting Falcon	HAF 347 Mira/111 PM, Nea Ankhialos
	080	Lockheed Martin F-16D-50 Fighting Falcon	HAF 341 Mira/111 PM, Nea Ankhialos
	081	Lockheed Martin F-16D-50 Fighting Falcon	HAF 347 Mira/111 PM, Nea Ankhialos
	082	Lockheed Martin F-16D-50 Fighting Falcon	HAF 341 Mira/111 PM, Nea Ankhialos
	083	Lockheed Martin F-16D-50 Fighting Falcon	HAF 347 Mira/111 PM, Nea Ankhialos
	110	Lockheed Martin F-16C-30 Fighting Falcon	HAF 330 Mira/111 PM, Nea Ankhialos
	111	Lockheed Martin F-16C-30 Fighting Falcon	HAF 330 Mira/111 PM, Nea Ankhialos
	112	Lockheed Martin F-16C-30 Fighting Falcon	HAF 330 Mira/111 PM, Nea Ankhialos
	113	Lockheed Martin F-16C-30 Fighting Falcon	HAF 330 Mira/111 PM, Nea Ankhialos
	114	Lockheed Martin F-16C-30 Fighting Falcon	HAF 330 Mira/111 PM, Nea Ankhialos
	115	Lockheed Martin F-16C-30 Fighting Falcon	HAF 330 Mira/111 PM, Nea Ankhialos
	116	Lockheed Martin F-16C-30 Fighting Falcon	HAF 330 Mira/111 PM, Nea Ankhialos
	117	Lockheed Martin F-16C-30 Fighting Falcon	HAF 330 Mira/111 PM, Nea Ankhialos
	118	Lockheed Martin F-16C-30 Fighting Falcon	HAF 330 Mira/111 PM, Nea Ankhialos
	119	Lockheed Martin F-16C-30 Fighting Falcon	HAF 330 Mira/111 PM, Nea Ankhialos
	120	Lockheed Martin F-16C-30 Fighting Falcon	HAF 330 Mira/111 PM, Nea Ankhialos
	121	Lockheed Martin F-16C-30 Fighting Falcon	HAF 341 Mira/111 PM, Nea Ankhialos
	122	Lockheed Martin F-16C-30 Fighting Falcon	HAF 330 Mira/111 PM, Nea Ankhialos
	124	Lockheed Martin F-16C-30 Fighting Falcon	HAF 330 Mira/111 PM, Nea Ankhialos
	125	Lockheed Martin F-16C-30 Fighting Falcon	HAF 330 Mira/111 PM, Nea Ankhialos
	126	Lockheed Martin F-16C-30 Fighting Falcon	HAF 330 Mira/111 PM, Nea Ankhialos
	127	Lockheed Martin F-16C-30 Fighting Falcon	HAF 330 Mira/111 PM, Nea Ankhialos
	128	Lockheed Martin F-16C-30 Fighting Falcon	HAF 330 Mira/111 PM, Nea Ankhialos
	129	Lockheed Martin F-16C-30 Fighting Falcon	HAF 330 Mira/111 PM, Nea Ankhialos
	130	Lockheed Martin F-16C-30 Fighting Falcon	HAF 330 Mira/111 PM, Nea Ankhialos
	132	Lockheed Martin F-16C-30 Fighting Falcon	HAF 330 Mira/111 PM, Nea Ankhialos
	133	Lockheed Martin F-16C-30 Fighting Falcon	HAF 330 Mira/111 PM, Nea Ankhialos
	134	Lockheed Martin F-16C-30 Fighting Falcon	HAF 330 Mira/111 PM, Nea Ankhialos
	136	Lockheed Martin F-16C-30 Fighting Falcon	HAF 330 Mira/111 PM, Nea Ankhialos

Serial	Type (code/other identity)	Owner/operator, location or fate	Notes
138	Lockheed Martin F-16C-30 Fighting Falcon	HAF 330 Mira/111 PM, Nea Ankhialos	
139	Lockheed Martin F-16C-30 Fighting Falcon	HAF 330 Mira/111 PM, Nea Ankhialos	
140	Lockheed Martin F-16C-30 Fighting Falcon	HAF 330 Mira/111 PM, Nea Ankhialos	
141	Lockheed Martin F-16C-30 Fighting Falcon	HAF 330 Mira/111 PM, Nea Ankhialos	
143	Lockheed Martin F-16C-30 Fighting Falcon	HAF 330 Mira/111 PM, Nea Ankhialos	
144	Lockheed Martin F-16C-30 Fighting Falcon	HAF 330 Mira/111 PM, Nea Ankhialos	
145	Lockheed Martin F-16D-30 Fighting Falcon	HAF 330 Mira/111 PM, Nea Ankhialos	
146	Lockheed Martin F-16D-30 Fighting Falcon	*Crashed 14 October 2014, Mount Pilio*	
147	Lockheed Martin F-16D-30 Fighting Falcon	*Crashed 14 October 2014, Mount Pilio*	
148	Lockheed Martin F-16D-30 Fighting Falcon	HAF 330 Mira/111 PM, Nea Ankhialos	
149	Lockheed Martin F-16D-30 Fighting Falcon	HAF 330 Mira/111 PM, Nea Ankhialos	
201	Dassault Mirage 2000-BG	HAF 332 MAPK/114 PM, Tanagra	
202	Dassault Mirage 2000-BG	HAF 332 MAPK/114 PM, Tanagra	
210	Dassault Mirage 2000-EG	HAF 332 MAPK/114 PM, Tanagra	
212	Dassault Mirage 2000-EG	HAF 332 MAPK/114 PM, Tanagra	
213	Dassault Mirage 2000-EG	HAF 332 MAPK/114 PM, Tanagra	
215	Dassault Mirage 2000-EG	HAF 332 MAPK/114 PM, Tanagra	
216	Dassault Mirage 2000-EG	HAF 332 MAPK/114 PM, Tanagra	
217	Dassault Mirage 2000-EG	HAF 332 MAPK/114 PM, Tanagra	
218	Dassault Mirage 2000-EG	HAF 332 MAPK/114 PM, Tanagra	
219	Dassault Mirage 2000-EG	HAF 332 MAPK/114 PM, Tanagra	
220	Dassault Mirage 2000-EG	HAF 332 MAPK/114 PM, Tanagra	
221	Dassault Mirage 2000-EG	HAF 332 MAPK/114 PM, Tanagra	
226	Dassault Mirage 2000-EG	HAF 332 MAPK/114 PM, Tanagra	
231	Dassault Mirage 2000-EG	HAF 332 MAPK/114 PM, Tanagra	
232	Dassault Mirage 2000-EG	HAF 332 MAPK/114 PM, Tanagra	
233	Dassault Mirage 2000-EG	HAF 332 MAPK/114 PM, Tanagra	
237	Dassault Mirage 2000-EG	HAF 332 MAPK/114 PM, Tanagra	
241	Dassault Mirage 2000-EG	HAF 332 MAPK/114 PM, Tanagra	
242	Dassault Mirage 2000-EG	HAF 332 MAPK/114 PM, Tanagra	
374	Embraer ERJ.145H AEW&C	HAF 380 Mira/112 PM, Elefsís	
500	Lockheed Martin F-16C-52 Fighting Falcon	HAF 343 Mira/115 PM, Souda	
501	Lockheed Martin F-16C-52 Fighting Falcon	HAF 337 Mira/110 PM, Larissa	
502	Lockheed Martin F-16C-52 Fighting Falcon	HAF 337 Mira/110 PM, Larissa	
503	Lockheed Martin F-16C-52 Fighting Falcon	HAF 343 Mira/115 PM, Souda	
504	Lockheed Martin F-16C-52 Fighting Falcon	HAF 343 Mira/115 PM, Souda	
505	Dassault Mirage 2000-5BG	HAF 331 MAPK/114 PM, Tanagra	
505	Lockheed Martin F-16C-52 Fighting Falcon $	HAF 343 Mira/115 PM, Souda	
506	Dassault Mirage 2000-5BG	HAF 331 MAPK/114 PM, Tanagra	
506	Lockheed Martin F-16C-52 Fighting Falcon	HAF 340 Mira/115 PM, Souda	
507	Dassault Mirage 2000-5BG	HAF 331 MAPK/114 PM, Tanagra	
507	Lockheed Martin F-16C-52 Fighting Falcon	HAF 337 Mira/110 PM, Larissa	
508	Dassault Mirage 2000-5BG	HAF 331 MAPK/114 PM, Tanagra	
508	Lockheed Martin F-16C-52 Fighting Falcon	HAF 337 Mira/110 PM, Larissa	
509	Dassault Mirage 2000-5BG	HAF 331 MAPK/114 PM, Tanagra	
509	Lockheed Martin F-16C-52 Fighting Falcon	HAF 343 Mira/115 PM, Souda	
510	Lockheed Martin F-16C-52 Fighting Falcon	HAF 343 Mira/115 PM, Souda	
511	Dassault Mirage 2000-5BG	HAF 331 MAPK/114 PM, Tanagra	
511	Lockheed Martin F-16C-52 Fighting Falcon	HAF 343 Mira/115 PM, Souda	
513	Lockheed Martin F-16C-52 Fighting Falcon	HAF 343 Mira/115 PM, Souda	
514	Dassault Mirage 2000-5BG	HAF 331 MAPK/114 PM, Tanagra	
515	Lockheed Martin F-16C-52 Fighting Falcon	HAF 343 Mira/115 PM, Souda	
517	Lockheed Martin F-16C-52 Fighting Falcon	HAF 337 Mira/110 PM, Larissa	
518	Lockheed Martin F-16C-52 Fighting Falcon	HAF 340 Mira/115 PM, Souda	
519	Lockheed Martin F-16C-52 Fighting Falcon	HAF 340 Mira/115 PM, Souda	
520	Lockheed Martin F-16C-52 Fighting Falcon	HAF 343 Mira/115 PM, Souda	
521	Lockheed Martin F-16C-52 Fighting Falcon	HAF 340 Mira/115 PM, Souda	
523	Lockheed Martin F-16C-52 Fighting Falcon $	HAF 340 Mira/115 PM, Souda	
524	Lockheed Martin F-16C-52 Fighting Falcon	HAF 337 Mira/110 PM, Larissa	
525	Lockheed Martin F-16C-52 Fighting Falcon	HAF 340 Mira/115 PM, Souda	
526	Lockheed Martin F-16C-52 Fighting Falcon	HAF 343 Mira/115 PM, Souda	
527	Dassault Mirage 2000-5BG	HAF 331 MAPK/114 PM, Tanagra	

Notes	Serial	Type (code/other identity)	Owner/operator, location or fate
	527	Lockheed Martin F-16C-52 Fighting Falcon	HAF 343 Mira/115 PM, Souda
	528	Lockheed Martin F-16C-52 Fighting Falcon	HAF 337 Mira/110 PM, Larissa
	529	Lockheed Martin F-16C-52 Fighting Falcon	HAF 343 Mira/115 PM, Souda
	530	Dassault Mirage 2000-5BG	HAF 331 MAPK/114 PM, Tanagra
	530	Lockheed Martin F-16C-52 Fighting Falcon	HAF 337 Mira/110 PM, Larissa
	531	Lockheed Martin F-16C-52 Fighting Falcon $	HAF 337 Mira/110 PM, Larissa
	532	Lockheed Martin F-16C-52 Fighting Falcon	HAF 337 Mira/110 PM, Larissa
	533	Lockheed Martin F-16C-52 Fighting Falcon	HAF 340 Mira/115 PM, Souda
	534	Dassault Mirage 2000-5BG	HAF 331 MAPK/114 PM, Tanagra
	534	Lockheed Martin F-16C-52 Fighting Falcon	HAF 340 Mira/115 PM, Souda
	535	Dassault Mirage 2000-5BG	HAF 331 MAPK/114 PM, Tanagra
	535	Lockheed Martin F-16C-52 Fighting Falcon	HAF 340 Mira/115 PM, Souda
	536	Dassault Mirage 2000-5BG	HAF 331 MAPK/114 PM, Tanagra
	536	Lockheed Martin F-16C-52 Fighting Falcon	HAF 340 Mira/115 PM, Souda
	537	Lockheed Martin F-16C-52 Fighting Falcon	HAF 340 Mira/115 PM, Souda
	538	Lockheed Martin F-16C-52 Fighting Falcon	HAF 340 Mira/115 PM, Souda
	539	Lockheed Martin F-16C-52 Fighting Falcon	HAF 337 Mira/110 PM, Larissa
	540	Dassault Mirage 2000-5BG	HAF 331 MAPK/114 PM, Tanagra
	543	Dassault Mirage 2000-5BG	HAF 331 MAPK/114 PM, Tanagra
	545	Dassault Mirage 2000-5BG	HAF 331 MAPK/114 PM, Tanagra
	547	Dassault Mirage 2000-5BG	HAF 331 MAPK/114 PM, Tanagra
	548	Dassault Mirage 2000-5BG	HAF 331 MAPK/114 PM, Tanagra
	549	Dassault Mirage 2000-5BG	HAF 331 MAPK/114 PM, Tanagra
	550	Dassault Mirage 2000-5BG	HAF 331 MAPK/114 PM, Tanagra
	551	Dassault Mirage 2000-5BG	HAF 331 MAPK/114 PM, Tanagra
	552	Dassault Mirage 2000-5BG	HAF 331 MAPK/114 PM, Tanagra
	553	Dassault Mirage 2000-5BG	HAF 331 MAPK/114 PM, Tanagra
	554	Dassault Mirage 2000-5BG	HAF 331 MAPK/114 PM, Tanagra
	555	Dassault Mirage 2000-5BG	HAF 331 MAPK/114 PM, Tanagra
	600	Lockheed Martin F-16D-52 Fighting Falcon	HAF 337 Mira/110 PM, Larissa
	601	Lockheed Martin F-16D-52 Fighting Falcon	HAF 340 Mira/115 PM, Souda
	602	Lockheed Martin F-16D-52 Fighting Falcon	HAF 340 Mira/115 PM, Souda
	603	Lockheed Martin F-16D-52 Fighting Falcon	HAF 340 Mira/115 PM, Souda
	605	Lockheed Martin F-16D-52 Fighting Falcon	HAF 340 Mira/115 PM, Souda
	606	Lockheed Martin F-16D-52 Fighting Falcon	HAF 337 Mira/110 PM, Larissa
	607	Lockheed Martin F-16D-52 Fighting Falcon	HAF 343 Mira/115 PM, Souda
	608	Lockheed Martin F-16D-52 Fighting Falcon	HAF 340 Mira/115 PM, Souda
	609	Lockheed Martin F-16D-52 Fighting Falcon	HAF 337 Mira/110 PM, Larissa
	610	Lockheed Martin F-16D-52 Fighting Falcon	HAF 340 Mira/115 PM, Souda
	611	Lockheed Martin F-16D-52 Fighting Falcon	HAF 337 Mira/110 PM, Larissa
	612	Lockheed Martin F-16D-52 Fighting Falcon	HAF 337 Mira/110 PM, Larissa
	613	Lockheed Martin F-16D-52 Fighting Falcon	HAF 343 Mira/115 PM, Souda
	615	Lockheed Martin F-16D-52 Fighting Falcon	HAF 343 Mira/115 PM, Souda
	616	Lockheed Martin F-16D-52 Fighting Falcon	HAF 343 Mira/115 PM, Souda
	617	Lockheed Martin F-16D-52 Fighting Falcon	HAF 343 Mira/115 PM, Souda
	618	Lockheed Martin F-16D-52 Fighting Falcon	HAF 343 Mira/115 PM, Souda
	619	Lockheed Martin F-16D-52 Fighting Falcon $	HAF 337 Mira/110 PM, Larissa
	671	Embraer ERJ.145H AEW&C	HAF 380 Mira/112 PM, Elefsis
	678	Gulfstream Aerospace Gulfstream V	HAF 352 MMYP/112 PM, Elefsís
	729	Embraer ERJ.145H AEW&C	HAF 380 Mira/112 PM, Elefsis
	741	Lockheed C-130H Hercules (ECM)	HAF 356 MTM/112 PM, Elefsís
	742	Lockheed C-130H Hercules	HAF 356 MTM/112 PM, Elefsís
	743	Lockheed C-130H Hercules	HAF 356 MTM/112 PM, Elefsís
	744	Lockheed C-130H Hercules	HAF 356 MTM/112 PM, Elefsís
	745	Lockheed C-130H Hercules $	HAF 356 MTM/112 PM, Elefsís
	746	Lockheed C-130H Hercules	HAF 356 MTM/112 PM, Elefsís
	747	Lockheed C-130H Hercules (ECM)	HAF 356 MTM/112 PM, Elefsís
	749	Lockheed C-130H Hercules	HAF 356 MTM/112 PM, Elefsís
	751	Lockheed C-130H Hercules	HAF 356 MTM/112 PM, Elefsís
	752	Lockheed C-130H Hercules $	HAF 356 MTM/112 PM, Elefsís
	757	Embraer ERJ.145H AEW&C	HAF 380 Mira/112 PM, Elefsis
	4117	Aeritalia C-27J Spartan	HAF 354 Mira, Elefsis

Serial	Type (code/other identity)	Owner/operator, location or fate	Notes
4118	Aeritalia C-27J Spartan	HAF 354 Mira, Elefsís	
4120	Aeritalia C-27J Spartan	HAF 354 Mira, Elefsís	
4121	Aeritalia C-27J Spartan	HAF 354 Mira, Elefsís	
4122	Aeritalia C-27J Spartan	HAF 354 Mira, Elefsís	
4123	Aeritalia C-27J Spartan	HAF 354 Mira, Elefsís	
4124	Aeritalia C-27J Spartan	HAF 354 Mira, Elefsís	
4125	Aeritalia C-27J Spartan	HAF 354 Mira, Elefsís	
135L-484	Embraer ERJ.135BJ Legacy	HAF 352 MMYP/112 PM, Elefsís	
145-209	Embraer ERJ.135LR	HAF 352 MMYP/112 PM, Elefsís	

HONDURAS
Fuerza Aérea Hondureña (FAH)/Honduran Air Force

FAH-001	Embraer ERJ.135BJ Legacy 600	FAH, Tegucigalpa	

HUNGARY
Magyar Légierö/Hungarian Air Force

01	Boeing C-17A Globemaster III (08-0001)	NATO SAC, Heavy Airlift Wing, Pápa	
02	Boeing C-17A Globemaster III (08-0002)	NATO SAC, Heavy Airlift Wing, Pápa	
03	Boeing C-17A Globemaster III (08-0003)	NATO SAC, Heavy Airlift Wing, Pápa	
30	SAAB 39C Gripen	Hungarian AF 59 Sz.D.REB, Kecskemét	
31	SAAB 39C Gripen	Hungarian AF 59 Sz.D.REB, Kecskemét	
32	SAAB 39C Gripen	Hungarian AF 59 Sz.D.REB, Kecskemét	
33	SAAB 39C Gripen	Hungarian AF 59 Sz.D.REB, Kecskemét	
34	SAAB 39C Gripen	Hungarian AF 59 Sz.D.REB, Kecskemét	
35	SAAB 39C Gripen	Hungarian AF 59 Sz.D.REB, Kecskemét	
36	SAAB 39C Gripen	Hungarian AF 59 Sz.D.REB, Kecskemét	
37	SAAB 39C Gripen	Hungarian AF 59 Sz.D.REB, Kecskemét	
38	SAAB 39C Gripen	Hungarian AF 59 Sz.D.REB, Kecskemét	
39	SAAB 39C Gripen	Hungarian AF 59 Sz.D.REB, Kecskemét	
40	SAAB 39C Gripen $	Hungarian AF 59 Sz.D.REB, Kecskemét	
41	SAAB 39C Gripen	Hungarian AF 59 Sz.D.REB, Kecskemét	
43	SAAB 39D Gripen	Hungarian AF 59 Sz.D.REB, Kecskemét	
44	SAAB 39D Gripen (39842)	Hungarian AF 59 Sz.D.REB, Kecskemét	
110	Antonov An-26	Hungarian AF 59 Sz.D.REB, Kecskemét	
405	Antonov An-26	Hungarian AF 59 Sz.D.REB, Kecskemét	
406	Antonov An-26	Hungarian AF 59 Sz.D.REB, Kecskemét	
407	Antonov An-26	Hungarian AF 59 Sz.D.REB, Kecskemét	
603	Antonov An-26	Hungarian AF 59 Sz.D.REB, Kecskemét	
604	Airbus A.319-112 (9H-AGM)	Hungarian AF 59 Sz.D.REB, Kecskemét	
605	Airbus A.319-112 (9H-AGN)	Hungarian AF 59 Sz.D.REB, Kecskemét	
606	Dassault Falcon 7X (9H-AGO)	Hungarian AF 59 Sz.D.REB, Kecskemét	
607	Dassault Falcon 7X (HA-LKX)	Hungarian AF 59 Sz.D.REB, Kecskemét	

INDIA
Bharatiya Vayu Sena/Indian Air Force (IAF)

CB-8001	Boeing C-17A Globemaster III (11-0101)	IAF 81 Sqn, Hindon AB	
CB-8002	Boeing C-17A Globemaster III (11-0102)	IAF 81 Sqn, Hindon AB	
CB-8003	Boeing C-17A Globemaster III (11-0103)	IAF 81 Sqn, Hindon AB	
CB-8004	Boeing C-17A Globemaster III (11-0104)	IAF 81 Sqn, Hindon AB	
CB-8005	Boeing C-17A Globemaster III (11-0105)	IAF 81 Sqn, Hindon AB	
CB-8006	Boeing C-17A Globemaster III (11-0106)	IAF 81 Sqn, Hindon AB	
CB-8007	Boeing C-17A Globemaster III (11-0107)	IAF 81 Sqn, Hindon AB	
CB-8008	Boeing C-17A Globemaster III (11-0108)	IAF 81 Sqn, Hindon AB	
CB-8009	Boeing C-17A Globemaster III (11-0109)	IAF 81 Sqn, Hindon AB	
CB-8010	Boeing C-17A Globemaster III (11-0110)	IAF 81 Sqn, Hindon AB	
CB-8011	Boeing C-17A Globemaster III (14-0003)	IAF 81 Sqn, Hindon AB	
KC-3801	Lockheed C-130J-30 Hercules II	IAF 77 Sqn, Hindon AB	
KC-3802	Lockheed C-130J-30 Hercules II	IAF 77 Sqn, Hindon AB	
KC-3804	Lockheed C-130J-30 Hercules II	IAF 77 Sqn, Hindon AB	
KC-3805	Lockheed C-130J-30 Hercules II	IAF 77 Sqn, Hindon AB	
KC-3806	Lockheed C-130J-30 Hercules II	IAF 77 Sqn, Hindon AB	
KC-3807	Lockheed C-130J-30 Hercules II	IAF 87 Sqn, Arjan Singh AB	

Notes	Serial	Type (code/other identity)	Owner/operator, location or fate
	KC-3808	Lockheed C-130J-30 Hercules II	IAF 87 Sqn, Arjan Singh AB
	KC-3809	Lockheed C-130J-30 Hercules II	IAF 87 Sqn, Arjan Singh AB
	KC-3810	Lockheed C-130J-30 Hercules II	IAF 87 Sqn, Arjan Singh AB
	KC-3811	Lockheed C-130J-30 Hercules II	IAF 87 Sqn, Arjan Singh AB
	KC-3812	Lockheed C-130J-30 Hercules II	IAF 87 Sqn, Arjan Singh AB
	KC-3813	Lockheed C-130J-30 Hercules II	IAF 77 Sqn, Hindon AB
	INDONESIA		
	Indonesian Government		
	A-001	Boeing 737-8U3	Government of Indonesia, Jakarta
	ISRAEL		
	Heyl ha'Avir/Israeli Air Force		
	102	Lockheed C-130H Karnaf	Israeli AF 131 Sqn, Nevatim
	140	Boeing KC-707 Re'em	*Withdrawn from use, 18 March 2019*
	208	Lockheed C-130E Karnaf	*Withdrawn from use*
	248	Boeing KC-707 Re'em	*Withdrawn from use, 2018*
	250	Boeing KC-707 Re'em	Israeli AF 120 Sqn, Nevatim
	260	Boeing KC-707 Re'em	Israeli AF 120 Sqn, Nevatim
	264	Boeing KC-707 Re'em	Israeli AF 120 Sqn, Nevatim
	272	Boeing KC-707 Re'em	Israeli AF 120 Sqn, Nevatim
	275	Boeing KC-707 Re'em	Israeli AF 120 Sqn, Nevatim
	290	Boeing KC-707 Re'em	Israeli AF 120 Sqn, Nevatim
	295	Boeing KC-707 Re'em	Israeli AF 120 Sqn, Nevatim
	305	Lockheed C-130E Karnaf	Israeli AF 131 Sqn, Nevatim
	309	Lockheed C-130E Karnaf	*Withdrawn from use*
	310	Lockheed C-130E Karnaf	*Withdrawn from use*
	314	Lockheed C-130E Karnaf	*Withdrawn from use*
	318	Lockheed C-130E Karnaf	Israeli AF 131 Sqn, Nevatim
	420	Lockheed KC-130H Karnaf	Israeli AF 131 Sqn, Nevatim
	427	Lockheed C-130H Karnaf	Israeli AF 131 Sqn, Nevatim
	428	Lockheed C-130H Karnaf	Israeli AF 131 Sqn, Nevatim
	435	Lockheed C-130H Karnaf	Israeli AF 131 Sqn, Nevatim
	436	Lockheed KC-130H Karnaf	Israeli AF 131 Sqn, Nevatim
	522	Lockheed KC-130H Karnaf	Israeli AF 131 Sqn, Nevatim
	545	Lockheed KC-130H Karnaf	Israeli AF 131 Sqn, Nevatim
	661	Lockheed C-130J-30 Shimshon	Israeli AF 103 Sqn, Nevatim
	662	Lockheed C-130J-30 Shimshon	Israeli AF 103 Sqn, Nevatim
	663	Lockheed C-130J-30 Shimshon	Israeli AF 103 Sqn, Nevatim
	664	Lockheed C-130J-30 Shimshon	(on order)
	665	Lockheed C-130J-30 Shimshon	Israeli AF 103 Sqn, Nevatim
	667	Lockheed C-130J-30 Shimshon	Israeli AF 103 Sqn, Nevatim
	668	Lockheed C-130J-30 Shimshon	Israeli AF 103 Sqn, Nevatim
	669	Lockheed C-130J-30 Shimshon	Israeli AF 103 Sqn, Nevatim
	Israeli Government		
	4X-ISR	Boeing 767-338ER	Israeli AF/State of Israel, Tel Aviv
	ITALY:		
	Aeronautica Militare Italiana (AMI), Aviazione dell'Esercito, Guardia di Finanza (GdiF) &		
	Marina Militare Italiana (MMI)		
	MMX602	Eurofighter F-2000A Typhoon $	*Preserved at Torino/Caselle*
	MMX614	Eurofighter TF-2000A Typhoon	Alenia, Torino/Caselle
	CPX616	Aermacchi M-346 Master	Aermacchi, Venegono
	CPX622	Aermacchi M-346FA	Aermacchi, Venegono
	CPX624	Aermacchi T-345A	Aermacchi, Venegono
	MM7004	Panavia A-200C Tornado (IDS (MLU)) [6-55]	AMI GEA 6° Stormo, Ghedi
	MM7006	Panavia A-200C Tornado (IDS (MLU)) [6-31] $	AMI GEA 6° Stormo, Ghedi
	MM7007	Panavia A-200A Tornado (IDS) [6-01] $	AMI GEA 6° Stormo, Ghedi
	MM7008	Panavia A-200C Tornado (IDS (MLU)) [50-53]	AMI GEA 6° Stormo, Ghedi
	MM7013	Panavia A-200C Tornado (IDS (MLU)) [6-75]	AMI GEA 6° Stormo, Ghedi
	MM7014	Panavia A-200C Tornado (IDS (MLU)) [6-13]	AMI GEA 6° Stormo, Ghedi
	MM7015	Panavia A-200C Tornado (IDS (MLU)) [6-32]	AMI GEA 6° Stormo, Ghedi

Serial	Type (code/other identity)	Owner/operator, location or fate	Notes
MM7019	Panavia EA-200B Tornado (ECR) [6-02]	AMI GEA 6° Stormo, Ghedi	
MM7020	Panavia EA-200D Tornado (ECR (MLU)) [6-77]	AMI GEA 6° Stormo, Ghedi	
MM7021	Panavia EA-200B Tornado (ECR) [6-20]	AMI GEA 6° Stormo, Ghedi	
MM7023	Panavia A-200A Tornado (IDS) [6-63]	AMI GEA 6° Stormo, Ghedi	
MM7024	Panavia A-200C Tornado (IDS (MLU)) [6-50]	AMI GEA 6° Stormo, Ghedi	
MM7025	Panavia A-200A Tornado (IDS) [6-05]	AMI GEA 6° Stormo, Ghedi	
MM7026	Panavia A-200C Tornado (IDS (MLU)) [6-35]	AMI GEA 6° Stormo, Ghedi	
MM7029	Panavia A-200A Tornado (IDS) [6-22]	AMI GEA 6° Stormo, Ghedi	
MM7030	Panavia EA-200D Tornado (ECR (MLU)) [6-73]	AMI GEA 6° Stormo, Ghedi	
MM7034	Panavia EA-200B Tornado (ECR)	AMI, stored Gioia del Colle	
MM7035	Panavia A-200C Tornado (IDS (MLU)) [6-27]	AMI GEA 6° Stormo, Ghedi	
MM7036	Panavia EA-200B Tornado (ECR) [6-06]	AMI GEA 6° Stormo, Ghedi	
MM7037	Panavia A-200A Tornado (IDS) [6-16]	*Preserved at Pratica di Mare*	
MM7038	Panavia A-200C Tornado (IDS (MLU)) [6-37]	AMI GEA 6° Stormo, Ghedi	
MM7039	Panavia EA-200D Tornado (ECR (MLU)) [6-33]	AMI GEA 6° Stormo, Ghedi	
MM7040	Panavia A-200A Tornado (IDS) [6-21]	AMI GEA 6° Stormo, Ghedi	
CSX7041	Panavia A-200C Tornado (IDS (MLU)) [RS-01] $	AMI RSV, Pratica di Mare	
MM7043	Panavia A-200A Tornado (IDS) [6-25]	AMI GEA 6° Stormo, Ghedi	
MM7044	Panavia A-200C Tornado (IDS (MLU)) [6-76]	AMI GEA 6° Stormo, Ghedi	
MM7047	Panavia EA-200D Tornado (ECR (MLU)) [6-61]	AMI GEA 6° Stormo, Ghedi	
MM7051	Panavia EA-200B Tornado (ECR) [6-72]	AMI GEA 6° Stormo, Ghedi	
MM7052	Panavia EA-200D Tornado (ECR (MLU)) [6-64]	AMI GEA 6° Stormo, Ghedi	
MM7053	Panavia EA-200D Tornado (ECR (MLU)) [6-101]	AMI GEA 6° Stormo, Ghedi	
MM7054	Panavia EA-200D Tornado (ECR (MLU)) [6-100] $	AMI GEA 6° Stormo, Ghedi	
MM7055	Panavia EA-200D Tornado (ECR (MLU)) [6-65]	AMI GEA 6° Stormo, Ghedi	
MM7056	Panavia A-200A Tornado (IDS)	AMI GEA 6° Stormo, Ghedi	
MM7057	Panavia A-200A Tornado (IDS) [6-04]	AMI GEA 6° Stormo, Ghedi	
MM7058	Panavia A-200C Tornado (IDS (MLU)) [6-11]	AMI GEA 6° Stormo, Ghedi	
MM7059	Panavia A-200A Tornado (IDS) [6-66]	AMI GEA 6° Stormo, Ghedi	
MM7062	Panavia EA-200D Tornado (ECR (MLU)) [6-74]	AMI GEA 6° Stormo, Ghedi	
MM7063	Panavia A-200C Tornado (IDS (MLU)) [6-26]	AMI GEA 6° Stormo, Ghedi	
MM7066	Panavia EA-200D Tornado (ECR (MLU)) [6-43]	AMI GEA 6° Stormo, Ghedi	
MM7067	Panavia EA-200D Tornado (ECR (MLU)) [6-41]	AMI GEA 6° Stormo, Ghedi	
MM7068	Panavia EA-200B Tornado (ECR) [6-67]	AMI GEA 6° Stormo, Ghedi	
MM7070	Panavia EA-200D Tornado (ECR (MLU)) [6-71]	AMI GEA 6° Stormo, Ghedi	
MM7071	Panavia A-200C Tornado (IDS (MLU)) [6-12]	AMI GEA 6° Stormo, Ghedi	
MM7072	Panavia A-200C Tornado (IDS (MLU)) [6-30]	AMI GEA 6° Stormo, Ghedi	
MM7073	Panavia EA-200B Tornado (ECR) [6-34]	AMI GEA 6° Stormo, Ghedi	
MM7075	Panavia A-200A Tornado (IDS) [6-07]	AMI GEA 6° Stormo, Ghedi	
CMX7079	Panavia EA-200B Tornado (ECR)	Alenia, Torino/Caselle	
MM7081	Panavia EA-200D Tornado (ECR (MLU)) [6-57]	AMI GEA 6° Stormo, Ghedi	
MM7082	Panavia EA-200D Tornado (ECR (MLU)) [6-62]	AMI GEA 6° Stormo, Ghedi	
MM7083	Panavia A-200A Tornado (IDS)	AMI GEA 6° Stormo, Ghedi	
MM7084	Panavia EA-200D Tornado (ECR (MLU)) [6-03]	AMI GEA 6° Stormo, Ghedi	
CMX7085	Panavia A-200A Tornado (IDS) [36-50]	Alenia, Torino/Caselle	
MM7086	Panavia A-200A Tornado (IDS) [6-60]	AMI GEA 6° Stormo, Ghedi	
MM7088	Panavia A-200A Tornado (IDS) [6-10]	AMI GEA 6° Stormo, Ghedi	
MM7114	Aeritalia-EMB A-11B Ghibli (AMX-ACOL) [51-27] $	AMI GEA 51° Stormo, Istrana	
MM7126	Aeritalia-EMB A-11B Ghibli (AMX-ACOL) [51-61]	AMI, stored Istrana	
MM7129	Aeritalia-EMB A-11B Ghibli (AMX-ACOL) [32-15]	AMI, stored Amendola	
MM7148	Aeritalia-EMB A-11B Ghibli (AMX-ACOL)	AMI, stored Amendola	
MM7149	Aeritalia-EMB A-11B Ghibli (AMX-ACOL) [51-26]	AMI GEA 51° Stormo, Istrana	
MM7151	Aeritalia-EMB A-11B Ghibli (AMX-ACOL) [51-51]	AMI GEA 51° Stormo, Istrana	
MM7160	Aeritalia-EMB A-11B Ghibli (AMX-ACOL)	AMI, stored Amendola	
MM7161	Aeritalia-EMB A-11B Ghibli (AMX-ACOL) [51-31]	AMI, stored Istrana	
MM7162	Aeritalia-EMB A-11B Ghibli (AMX-ACOL) [51-33]	AMI GEA 51° Stormo, Istrana	
MM7163	Aeritalia-EMB A-11B Ghibli (AMX-ACOL) [51-72]	AMI GEA 51° Stormo, Istrana	
MM7164	Aeritalia-EMB A-11B Ghibli (AMX-ACOL) [51-40]	AMI GEA 51° Stormo, Istrana	
MM7165	Aeritalia-EMB A-11B Ghibli (AMX-ACOL) [32-16]	AMI, stored Amendola	
MM7166	Aeritalia-EMB A-11B Ghibli (AMX-ACOL) [51-32]	AMI GEA 51° Stormo, Istrana	
MM7167	Aeritalia-EMB A-11B Ghibli (AMX-ACOL) [51-56]	AMI GEA 51° Stormo, Istrana	
MM7168	Aeritalia-EMB A-11B Ghibli (AMX-ACOL) [51-55]	AMI GEA 51° Stormo, Istrana	

Notes	Serial	Type (code/other identity)	Owner/operator, location or fate
	MM7169	Aeritalia-EMB A-11B Ghibli (AMX-ACOL) [51-66]	AMI GEA 51° Stormo, Istrana
	MM7170	Aeritalia-EMB A-11B Ghibli (AMX-ACOL) [51-30]	AMI GEA 51° Stormo, Istrana
	MM7171	Aeritalia-EMB A-11B Ghibli (AMX-ACOL) [51-52]	AMI GEA 51° Stormo, Istrana
	MM7172	Aeritalia-EMB A-11B Ghibli (AMX-ACOL) [51-67]	AMI, stored Istrana
	MM7173	Aeritalia-EMB A-11B Ghibli (AMX-ACOL) [51-63]	AMI, stored Istrana
	MM7174	Aeritalia-EMB A-11B Ghibli (AMX-ACOL) [51-60]	AMI GEA 51° Stormo, Istrana
	MM7175	Aeritalia-EMB A-11B Ghibli (AMX-ACOL) [51-45]	AMI GEA 51° Stormo, Istrana
	MM7176	Aeritalia-EMB A-11B Ghibli (AMX-ACOL)	AMI GEA 51° Stormo, Istrana
	MM7177	Aeritalia-EMB A-11B Ghibli (AMX-ACOL) [51-42]	AMI GEA 51° Stormo, Istrana
	MM7178	Aeritalia-EMB A-11B Ghibli (AMX-ACOL) [51-43]	AMI GEA 51° Stormo, Istrana
	MM7179	Aeritalia-EMB A-11B Ghibli (AMX-ACOL) [51-64]	Preserved at Istrana, September 2019
	MM7180	Aeritalia-EMB A-11B Ghibli (AMX-ACOL) [51-53] $	AMI GEA 51° Stormo, Istrana
	MM7182	Aeritalia-EMB A-11B Ghibli (AMX-ACOL) [51-62]	AMI GEA 51° Stormo, Istrana
	MM7183	Aeritalia-EMB A-11B Ghibli (AMX-ACOL) [51-41]	AMI GEA 51° Stormo, Istrana
	MM7184	Aeritalia-EMB A-11B Ghibli (AMX-ACOL) [51-65]	AMI GEA 51° Stormo, Istrana
	MM7185	Aeritalia-EMB A-11B Ghibli (AMX-ACOL) [51-36]	AMI GEA 51° Stormo, Istrana
	MM7186	Aeritalia-EMB A-11B Ghibli (AMX-ACOL) [51-50]	AMI GEA 51° Stormo, Istrana
	MM7189	Aeritalia-EMB A-11B Ghibli (AMX-ACOL) [51-71]	AMI GEA 51° Stormo, Istrana
	MM7190	Aeritalia-EMB A-11B Ghibli (AMX-ACOL) [51-57]	AMI GEA 51° Stormo, Istrana
	MM7191	Aeritalia-EMB A-11B Ghibli (AMX-ACOL) [51-34]	AMI GEA 51° Stormo, Istrana
	MM7192	Aeritalia-EMB A-11B Ghibli (AMX-ACOL) [51-70]	AMI GEA 51° Stormo, Istrana
	MM7194	Aeritalia-EMB A-11B Ghibli (AMX-ACOL) $	AMI GEA 51° Stormo, Istrana
	MM7196	Aeritalia-EMB A-11B Ghibli (AMX-ACOL) [51-35]	AMI GEA 51° Stormo, Istrana
	MM7197	Aeritalia-EMB A-11B Ghibli (AMX-ACOL) [51-46]	AMI GEA 51° Stormo, Istrana
	MM7198	Aeritalia-EMB A-11B Ghibli (AMX-ACOL) [51-44] $	AMI GEA 51° Stormo, Istrana
	MM7199	McDonnell Douglas AV-8B Harrier II+ [1-03]	MMI Gruppo Aerei Imbarcati, Taranto/Grottaglie
	MM7200	McDonnell Douglas AV-8B Harrier II+ [1-04]	MMI Gruppo Aerei Imbarcati, Taranto/Grottaglie
	MM7201	McDonnell Douglas AV-8B Harrier II+ [1-05]	MMI Gruppo Aerei Imbarcati, Taranto/Grottaglie
	MM7212	McDonnell Douglas AV-8B Harrier II+ [1-06]	MMI Gruppo Aerei Imbarcati, Taranto/Grottaglie
	MM7213	McDonnell Douglas AV-8B Harrier II+ [1-07]	MMI Gruppo Aerei Imbarcati, Taranto/Grottaglie
	MM7214	McDonnell Douglas AV-8B Harrier II+ [1-08]	MMI Gruppo Aerei Imbarcati, Taranto/Grottaglie
	MM7215	McDonnell Douglas AV-8B Harrier II+ [1-09]	MMI Gruppo Aerei Imbarcati, Taranto/Grottaglie
	MM7217	McDonnell Douglas AV-8B Harrier II+ [1-11]	MMI Gruppo Aerei Imbarcati, Taranto/Grottaglie
	MM7218	McDonnell Douglas AV-8B Harrier II+ [1-12]	MMI Gruppo Aerei Imbarcati, Taranto/Grottaglie
	MM7219	McDonnell Douglas AV-8B Harrier II+ [1-13] $	MMI Gruppo Aerei Imbarcati, Taranto/Grottaglie
	MM7220	McDonnell Douglas AV-8B Harrier II+ [1-14]	MMI Gruppo Aerei Imbarcati, Taranto/Grottaglie
	MM7222	McDonnell Douglas AV-8B Harrier II+ [1-16]	MMI Gruppo Aerei Imbarcati, Taranto/Grottaglie
	MM7223	McDonnell Douglas AV-8B Harrier II+ [1-18]	MMI Gruppo Aerei Imbarcati, Taranto/Grottaglie
	MM7224	McDonnell Douglas AV-8B Harrier II+ [1-19] $	MMI Gruppo Aerei Imbarcati, Taranto/Grottaglie
	MM7235	Eurofighter F-2000A Typhoon [4-13]	AMI 904° GEA, Grosseto
	MM7270	Eurofighter F-2000A Typhoon [4-1]	AMI 904° GEA, Grosseto
	MM7271	Eurofighter F-2000A Typhoon [4-15]	AMI 904° GEA, Grosseto
	MM7272	Eurofighter F-2000A Typhoon [4-18]	AMI 904° GEA, Grosseto
	MM7273	Eurofighter F-2000A Typhoon [4-10]	AMI 904° GEA, Grosseto
	MM7274	Eurofighter F-2000A Typhoon [4-4]	AMI 904° GEA, Grosseto
	MM7275	Eurofighter F-2000A Typhoon [4-19]	AMI 904° GEA, Grosseto
	MM7276	Eurofighter F-2000A Typhoon [36-05]	AMI 936° GEA, Gioia del Colle
	MM7277	Eurofighter F-2000A Typhoon [36-14]	AMI 936° GEA, Gioia del Colle
	MM7279	Eurofighter F-2000A Typhoon [4-20]	AMI 904° GEA, Grosseto
	MM7280	Eurofighter F-2000A Typhoon [36-30]	AMI 936° GEA, Gioia del Colle
	MM7281	Eurofighter F-2000A Typhoon [36-03]	AMI 936° GEA, Gioia del Colle
	MM7282	Eurofighter F-2000A Typhoon [4-8]	AMI 904° GEA, Grosseto
	MM7284	Eurofighter F-2000A Typhoon [4-12]	AMI 904° GEA, Grosseto
	MM7285	Eurofighter F-2000A Typhoon	AMI 904° GEA, Grosseto
	MM7286	Eurofighter F-2000A Typhoon [36-02]	AMI 936° GEA, Gioia del Colle
	MM7287	Eurofighter F-2000A Typhoon [4-3]	AMI 904° GEA, Grosseto
	MM7288	Eurofighter F-2000A Typhoon [36-42]	AMI 936° GEA, Gioia del Colle
	MM7289	Eurofighter F-2000A Typhoon [4-5]	AMI 904° GEA, Grosseto
	MM7290	Eurofighter F-2000A Typhoon [4-7]	AMI 904° GEA, Grosseto
	MM7291	Eurofighter F-2000A Typhoon [4-11]	AMI 904° GEA, Grosseto
	MM7292	Eurofighter F-2000A Typhoon [36-21]	AMI 936° GEA, Gioia del Colle
	MM7293	Eurofighter F-2000A Typhoon [37-22]	AMI 18° Gruppo/37° Stormo, Trapani/Birgi

Serial	Type (code/other identity)	Owner/operator, location or fate	Notes
MM7294	Eurofighter F-2000A Typhoon [37-11]	AMI 18° Gruppo/37° Stormo, Trapani/Birgi	
MM7295	Eurofighter F-2000A Typhoon [4-51]	AMI 904° GEA, Grosseto	
MM7296	Eurofighter F-2000A Typhoon [36-22]	AMI 936° GEA, Gioia del Colle	
MM7297	Eurofighter F-2000A Typhoon [36-23] $	AMI 936° GEA, Gioia del Colle	
MM7298	Eurofighter F-2000A Typhoon [36-24]	AMI 936° GEA, Gioia del Colle	
MM7299	Eurofighter F-2000A Typhoon [4-41]	AMI 904° GEA, Grosseto	
MM7300	Eurofighter F-2000A Typhoon [4-44]	AMI 904° GEA, Grosseto	
MM7301	Eurofighter F-2000A Typhoon	AMI	
MM7302	Eurofighter F-2000A Typhoon [36-25]	AMI 936° GEA, Gioia del Colle	
MM7303	Eurofighter F-2000A Typhoon [4-2]	AMI 904° GEA, Grosseto	
MM7304	Eurofighter F-2000A Typhoon [4-21]	AMI 904° GEA, Grosseto	
CSX7305	Eurofighter F-2000A Typhoon	AMI RSV, Pratica di Mare	
MM7306	Eurofighter F-2000A Typhoon [4-50]	AMI 904° GEA, Grosseto	
MM7307	Eurofighter F-2000A Typhoon [37-01]	AMI 18° Gruppo/37° Stormo, Trapani/Birgi	
MM7308	Eurofighter F-2000A Typhoon [36-31]	AMI 936° GEA, Gioia del Colle	
MM7309	Eurofighter F-2000A Typhoon [4-22]	AMI 904° GEA, Grosseto	
MM7310	Eurofighter F-2000A Typhoon [36-32]	AMI 936° GEA, Gioia del Colle	
MM7311	Eurofighter F-2000A Typhoon [4-55]	AMI 904° GEA, Grosseto	
MM7312	Eurofighter F-2000A Typhoon [36-34] $	AMI 936° GEA, Gioia del Colle	
MM7313	Eurofighter F-2000A Typhoon [36-35]	AMI 936° GEA, Gioia del Colle	
MM7314	Eurofighter F-2000A Typhoon [51-03]	AMI 132° Gruppo/51° Stormo, Istrana	
MM7315	Eurofighter F-2000A Typhoon [36-46]	AMI 936° GEA, Gioia del Colle	
MM7316	Eurofighter F-2000A Typhoon [51-01]	AMI 132° Gruppo/51° Stormo, Istrana	
MM7317	Eurofighter F-2000A Typhoon [4-43]	AMI 904° GEA, Grosseto	
MM7318	Eurofighter F-2000A Typhoon [36-12] $	AMI 936° GEA, Gioia del Colle	
MM7319	Eurofighter F-2000A Typhoon [36-45]	AMI 936° GEA, Gioia del Colle	
MM7320	Eurofighter F-2000A Typhoon [51-02]	AMI 132° Gruppo/51° Stormo, Istrana	
MM7321	Eurofighter F-2000A Typhoon [37-12]	AMI 18° Gruppo/37° Stormo, Trapani/Birgi	
MM7322	Eurofighter F-2000A Typhoon [36-40] $	AMI 936° GEA, Gioia del Colle	
MM7323	Eurofighter F-2000A Typhoon [4-6]	AMI 904° GEA, Grosseto	
MM7324	Eurofighter F-2000A Typhoon [36-41]	AMI 936° GEA, Gioia del Colle	
MM7325	Eurofighter F-2000A Typhoon [36-44]	AMI 936° GEA, Gioia del Colle	
MM7326	Eurofighter F-2000A Typhoon [4-46] $	AMI 904° GEA, Grosseto	
MM7327	Eurofighter F-2000A Typhoon [4-47]	AMI 904° GEA, Grosseto	
MM7328	Eurofighter F-2000A Typhoon [4-57]	AMI 904° GEA, Grosseto	
MM7329	Eurofighter F-2000A Typhoon [37-15]	AMI 18° Gruppo/37° Stormo, Trapani/Birgi	
MM7330	Eurofighter F-2000A Typhoon [4-56]	AMI 904° GEA, Grosseto	
MM7331	Eurofighter F-2000A Typhoon [37-16]	AMI 18° Gruppo/37° Stormo, Trapani/Birgi	
MM7332	Lockheed Martin F-35A Lightning II [32-01]	AMI 62nd FS/56th FW, Luke AFB, AZ, USA	
MM7333	Lockheed Martin F-35A Lightning II [32-02]	AMI 62nd FS/56th FW, Luke AFB, AZ, USA	
MM7334	Lockheed Martin F-35A Lightning II [32-03]	AMI 13° Gruppo/32° Stormo, Amendola	
MM7335	Lockheed Martin F-35A Lightning II [32-04]	AMI 13° Gruppo/32° Stormo, Amendola	
MM7336	Lockheed Martin F-35A Lightning II [32-05]	AMI 13° Gruppo/32° Stormo, Amendola	
MM7337	Lockheed Martin F-35A Lightning II [32-13]	AMI 13° Gruppo/32° Stormo, Amendola	
MM7338	Eurofighter F-2000A Typhoon [4-60]	AMI 904° GEA, Grosseto	
MM7339	Eurofighter F-2000A Typhoon [4-61]	AMI 904° GEA, Grosseto	
MM7340	Eurofighter F-2000A Typhoon [4-64]	AMI 904° GEA, Grosseto	
MM7341	Eurofighter F-2000A Typhoon [36-10] $	AMI 936° GEA, Gioia del Colle	
MM7342	Eurofighter F-2000A Typhoon [36-51]	AMI 936° GEA, Gioia del Colle	
MM7343	Eurofighter F-2000A Typhoon [RS-11]	AMI RSV, Pratica di Mare	
MM7344	Eurofighter F-2000A Typhoon [4-62]	AMI 904° GEA, Grosseto	
MM7345	Eurofighter F-2000A Typhoon [37-45]	AMI 18° Gruppo/37° Stormo, Trapani/Birgi	
MM7346	Eurofighter F-2000A Typhoon [37-37]	AMI 18° Gruppo/37° Stormo, Trapani/Birgi	
MM7347	Eurofighter F-2000A Typhoon [36-53]	AMI 936° GEA, Gioia del Colle	
MM7348	Eurofighter F-2000A Typhoon [37-24]	AMI 18° Gruppo/37° Stormo, Trapani/Birgi	
MM7349	Eurofighter F-2000A Typhoon [36-54]	AMI 936° GEA, Gioia del Colle	
MM7350	Eurofighter F-2000A Typhoon [RS-22]	AMI RSV, Pratica di Mare	
MM7351	Eurofighter F-2000A Typhoon [4-9]	AMI 904° GEA, Grosseto	
MM7352	Eurofighter F-2000A Typhoon [36-55]	AMI 936° GEA, Gioia del Colle	
MM7353	Eurofighter F-2000A Typhoon [36-56]	AMI 936° GEA, Gioia del Colle	
MM7354	Eurofighter F-2000A Typhoon [37-54]	AMI 18° Gruppo/37° Stormo, Trapani/Birgi	
CSX7355	Eurofighter F-2000A Typhoon	Leonardo, Torino/Caselle	

Notes	Serial	Type (code/other identity)	Owner/operator, location or fate
	CSX7356	Eurofighter F-2000A Typhoon	Leonardo, Torino/Caselle
	MM7357	Lockheed Martin F-35A Lightning II [32-07] $	AMI 13° Gruppo/32° Stormo, Amendola
	MM7358	Lockheed Martin F-35A Lightning II [32-08]	AMI 13° Gruppo/32° Stormo, Amendola
	MM7359	Lockheed Martin F-35A Lightning II [32-09]	AMI 13° Gruppo/32° Stormo, Amendola
	MM7360	Lockheed Martin F-35A Lightning II [32-10]	AMI 13° Gruppo/32° Stormo, Amendola
	MM7361	Lockheed Martin F-35A Lightning II [32-11]	AMI 13° Gruppo/32° Stormo, Amendola
	MM7451	Lockheed Martin F-35B Lightning II [4-01]	MMI Beaufort MCAS, SC, USA
	MM7452	Lockheed Martin F-35B Lightning II [4-02]	MMI, Amendola
	MM7453	Lockheed Martin F-35B Lightning II [4-03]	AMI 13° Gruppo/32° Stormo, Amendola
	MM54456	Aermacchi T-339A (MB339A) [61-10]	AMI, stored Lecce
	MM54457	Aermacchi T-339A (MB339A(MLU)) [61-11]	AMI, stored Lecce
	MM54458	Aermacchi T-339A (MB339A(MLU)) [61-121]	AMI 61° Stormo, Lecce
	MM54465	Aermacchi T-339A (MB339A(MLU)) [61-21]	AMI 61° Stormo, Lecce
	MM54468	Aermacchi T-339A (MB339A(MLU)) [61-241]	AMI 61° Stormo, Lecce
	MM54473	Aermacchi AT-339A (MB339PAN)	AMI *Frecce Tricolori* (313° Gruppo), Rivolto
	MM54477	Aermacchi AT-339A (MB339PAN)	AMI *Frecce Tricolori* (313° Gruppo), Rivolto
	MM54479	Aermacchi AT-339A (MB339PAN)	AMI, stored Lecce
	MM54480	Aermacchi AT-339A (MB339PAN)	AMI *Frecce Tricolori* (313° Gruppo), Rivolto
	MM54482	Aermacchi AT-339A (MB339PAN)	AMI *Frecce Tricolori* (313° Gruppo), Rivolto
	MM54487	Aermacchi AT-339A (MB339PAN)	AMI *Frecce Tricolori* (313° Gruppo), Rivolto
	MM54488	Aermacchi T-339A (MB339(MLU)) [61-32]	AMI 61° Stormo, Lecce
	MM54492	Aermacchi T-339A (MB339A(MLU)) [61-36]	AMI 61° Stormo, Lecce
	MM54493	Aermacchi T-339A (MB339A(MLU)) [61-37]	AMI 61° Stormo, Lecce
	MM54496	Aermacchi T-339A (MB339A(MLU)) [61-42]	AMI 61° Stormo, Lecce
	MM54499	Aermacchi T-339A (MB339A(MLU)) [61-45]	AMI 61° Stormo, Lecce
	MM54500	Aermacchi AT-339A (MB339PAN)	AMI *Frecce Tricolori* (313° Gruppo), Rivolto
	MM54504	Aermacchi T-339A (MB339A(MLU)) [61-52]	AMI 61° Stormo, Lecce
	MM54505	Aermacchi AT-339A (MB339PAN) [9]	AMI *Frecce Tricolori* (313° Gruppo), Rivolto
	MM54507	Aermacchi T-339A (MB339A(MLU)) [61-55]	AMI 61° Stormo, Lecce
	MM54509	Aermacchi T-339A (MB339A(MLU)) [61-57]	AMI 61° Stormo, Lecce
	MM54510	Aermacchi AT-339A (MB339PAN) [7]	AMI *Frecce Tricolori* (313° Gruppo), Rivolto
	MM54511	Aermacchi T-339A (MB339A(MLU)) [61-61]	AMI 61° Stormo, Lecce
	MM54512	Aermacchi T-339A (MB339A(MLU)) [61-62]	AMI 61° Stormo, Lecce
	MM54514	Aermacchi AT-339A (MB339PAN)	AMI *Frecce Tricolori* (313° Gruppo), Rivolto
	MM54515	Aermacchi T-339A (MB339A(MLU)) [61-65]	AMI 61° Stormo, Lecce
	MM54516	Aermacchi T-339A (MB339A(MLU)) [61-66]	AMI 61° Stormo, Lecce
	MM54517	Aermacchi AT-339A (MB339PAN) [3]	AMI *Frecce Tricolori* (313° Gruppo), Rivolto
	MM54518	Aermacchi AT-339A (MB339PAN) [2]	AMI *Frecce Tricolori* (313° Gruppo), Rivolto
	MM54533	Aermacchi T-339A (MB339A(MLU)) [61-72]	AMI 61° Stormo, Lecce
	MM54534	Aermacchi AT-339A (MB339PAN) [4]	AMI *Frecce Tricolori* (313° Gruppo), Rivolto
	MM54535	Aermacchi T-339A (MB339A(MLU)) [61-74]	AMI 61° Stormo, Lecce
	MM54538	Aermacchi AT-339A (MB339PAN)	AMI *Frecce Tricolori* (313° Gruppo), Rivolto
	MM54539	Aermacchi AT-339A (MB339PAN) [8]	AMI *Frecce Tricolori* (313° Gruppo), Rivolto
	MM54547	Aermacchi AT-339A (MB339PAN)	AMI *Frecce Tricolori* (313° Gruppo), Rivolto
	MM54548	Aermacchi T-339A (MB339A(MLU)) [61-106]	AMI 61° Stormo, Lecce
	MM54549	Aermacchi T-339A (MB339A(MLU)) [61-107]	AMI 61° Stormo, Lecce
	MM54551	Aermacchi AT-339A (MB339PAN) [1]	AMI *Frecce Tricolori* (313° Gruppo), Rivolto
	MM55002	Panavia TA-200A Tornado (IDS Trainer) [6-52] $	AMI GEA 6° Stormo, Ghedi
	MM55003	Panavia TA-200A Tornado (IDS Trainer)	AMI
	MM55004	Panavia TA-200A Tornado (IDS Trainer) [6-53]	AMI GEA 6° Stormo, Ghedi
	MM55006	Panavia TA-200C Tornado (IDS Trainer (MLU)) [6-15]	AMI GEA 6° Stormo, Ghedi
	MM55007	Panavia TA-200A Tornado (IDS Trainer) [6-51]	AMI GEA 6° Stormo, Ghedi
	MM55008	Panavia TA-200A Tornado (IDS Trainer) [6-45]	AMI GEA 6° Stormo, Ghedi
	MM55009	Panavia TA-200A Tornado (IDS Trainer) [6-44]	AMI GEA 6° Stormo, Ghedi
	MM55010	Panavia TA-200A Tornado (IDS Trainer) [6-42]	AMI GEA 6° Stormo, Ghedi
	MM55032	McDonnell Douglas TAV-8B Harrier II+ [1-01]	MMI Gruppo Aerei Imbarcarti, Taranto/Grottaglie
	MM55033	McDonnell Douglas TAV-8B Harrier II+ [1-02]	MMI, stored Taranto/Grottaglie
	MM55034	Aeritalia-EMB TA-11B Ghibli (AMX-T-ACOL) [RS-20]	AMI RSV, Pratica di Mare
	MM55036	Aeritalia-EMB TA-11B Ghibli (AMX-T-ACOL) [32-51]	AMI, stored Amendola
	MM55037	Aeritalia-EMB TA-11B Ghibli (AMX-T-ACOL) [51-80]	AMI GEA 51° Stormo, Istrana
	MM55042	Aeritalia-EMB TA-11B Ghibli (AMX-T-ACOL) [32-56]	AMI, stored Amendola
	MM55043	Aeritalia-EMB TA-11B Ghibli (AMX-T-ACOL) [51-81]	AMI GEA 51° Stormo, Istrana

Serial	Type (code/other identity)	Owner/operator, location or fate	Notes
MM55044	Aeritalia-EMB TA-11B Ghibli (AMX-T-ACOL) [51-82] $	AMI GEA 51° Stormo, Istrana	
MM55046	Aeritalia-EMB TA-11B Ghibli (AMX-T-ACOL) [32-47]	AMI, stored Amendola	
MM55047	Aeritalia-EMB TA-11B Ghibli (AMX-T-ACOL) [32-53]	AMI, stored Amendola	
MM55049	Aeritalia-EMB TA-11B Ghibli (AMX-T-ACOL) [51-83]	AMI GEA 51° Stormo, Istrana	
MM55051	Aeritalia-EMB TA-11B Ghibli (AMX-T-ACOL) [51-84]	AMI GEA 51° Stormo, Istrana	
MM55052	Aermacchi AT-339A (MB339PAN) [6]	AMI *Frecce Tricolori* (313° Gruppo), Rivolto	
MM55053	Aermacchi AT-339A (MB339PAN) [0]	AMI *Frecce Tricolori* (313° Gruppo), Rivolto	
MM55054	Aermacchi AT-339A (MB339PAN)	AMI *Frecce Tricolori* (313° Gruppo), Rivolto	
MM55055	Aermacchi AT-339A (MB339PAN)	AMI *Frecce Tricolori* (313° Gruppo), Rivolto	
MM55058	Aermacchi AT-339A (MB339PAN) [11]	AMI *Frecce Tricolori* (313° Gruppo), Rivolto	
MM55059	Aermacchi AT-339A (MB339PAN) [5]	AMI *Frecce Tricolori* (313° Gruppo), Rivolto	
MM55062	Aermacchi FT-339 (MB339CD) [61-126]	AMI 61° Stormo, Lecce	
MM55063	Aermacchi FT-339 (MB339CD) [61-127]	AMI 61° Stormo, Lecce	
MM55064	Aermacchi FT-339 (MB339CD) [61-130]	AMI 61° Stormo, Lecce	
MM55065	Aermacchi FT-339 (MB339CD) [61-131]	AMI 61° Stormo, Lecce	
MM55066	Aermacchi FT-339 (MB339CD) [61-132]	AMI 632ª SC/32° Stormo, Amendola	
MM55067	Aermacchi FT-339 (MB339CD) [61-133]	AMI 61° Stormo, Lecce	
MM55068	Aermacchi FT-339 (MB339CD) [RS-33]	AMI RSV, Pratica di Mare	
MM55069	Aermacchi FT-339 (MB339CD) [61-135]	AMI 61° Stormo, Lecce	
MM55070	Aermacchi FT-339 (MB339CD) [61-136]	AMI 61° Stormo, Lecce	
MM55072	Aermacchi FT-339 (MB339CD) [61-140]	AMI 61° Stormo, Lecce	
MM55073	Aermacchi FT-339 (MB339CD) [61-141]	AMI 61° Stormo, Lecce	
MM55074	Aermacchi FT-339 (MB339CD) [36-06]	AMI 12° Gruppo/36° Stormo, Gioia del Colle	
MM55075	Aermacchi FT-339 (MB339CD) [61-143]	AMI 61° Stormo, Lecce	
MM55076	Aermacchi FT-339 (MB339CD) [61-144]	AMI 61° Stormo, Lecce	
MM55077	Aermacchi FT-339 (MB339CD) [61-145]	AMI 61° Stormo, Lecce	
MM55078	Aermacchi FT-339 (MB339CD) [61-146]	AMI 61° Stormo, Lecce	
MM55079	Aermacchi FT-339 (MB339CD) [61-147]	AMI 61° Stormo, Lecce	
MM55080	Aermacchi FT-339 (MB339CD) [61-150]	AMI 61° Stormo, Lecce	
MM55081	Aermacchi FT-339 (MB339CD) [61-151]	AMI 61° Stormo, Lecce	
MM55082	Aermacchi FT-339 (MB339CD) [61-152]	AMI 61° Stormo, Lecce	
MM55084	Aermacchi FT-339 (MB339CD) [61-154]	AMI 61° Stormo, Lecce	
MM55085	Aermacchi FT-339 (MB339CD) [61-155]	AMI 61° Stormo, Lecce	
MM55086	Aermacchi FT-339 (MB339CD) [61-156]	AMI 61° Stormo, Lecce	
MM55087	Aermacchi FT-339 (MB339CD) [61-167]	AMI 61° Stormo, Lecce	
MM55088	Aermacchi FT-339 (MB339CD) [61-160]	AMI 61° Stormo, Lecce	
MM55089	Aermacchi FT-339 (MB339CD) [32-161]	AMI 632ª SC/32° Stormo, Amendola	
MM55090	Aermacchi FT-339 (MB339CD) [61-162]	AMI 61° Stormo, Lecce	
MM55091	Aermacchi FT-339 (MB339CD) [RS-32]	AMI RSV, Pratica di Mare	
MM55092	Eurofighter TF-2000A Typhoon [36-62]	AMI 936° GEA, Gioia del Colle	
MM55093	Eurofighter TF-2000A Typhoon [4-31]	AMI 904° GEA, Grosseto	
MM55094	Eurofighter TF-2000A Typhoon [36-60]	AMI 936° GEA, Gioia del Colle	
MM55095	Eurofighter TF-2000A Typhoon [36-63]	AMI 936° GEA, Gioia del Colle	
MM55096	Eurofighter TF-2000A Typhoon [4-30]	AMI 904° GEA, Grosseto	
MM55097	Eurofighter TF-2000A Typhoon [4-27]	AMI 904° GEA, Grosseto	
MM55128	Eurofighter TF-2000A Typhoon [36-64]	AMI 936° GEA, Gioia del Colle	
MM55129	Eurofighter TF-2000A Typhoon [4-32]	AMI 904° GEA, Grosseto	
MM55130	Eurofighter TF-2000A Typhoon [4-33]	AMI 904° GEA, Grosseto	
MM55131	Eurofighter TF-2000A Typhoon [4-34]	AMI 904° GEA, Grosseto	
MM55132	Eurofighter TF-2000A Typhoon [4-35]	AMI 904° GEA, Grosseto	
MM55133	Eurofighter TF-2000A Typhoon [37-33]	AMI 18° Gruppo/37° Stormo, Trapani/Birgi	
MM55144	Aermacchi T-346A Master [61-02]	AMI 61° Stormo, Lecce	
CSX55145	Aermacchi T-346A Master	Leonardo, Turin	
MT55152	Aermacchi M-346FT [61-11]	Leonardo, Turin	
MM55153	Aermacchi T-346A Master [61-05]	AMI 61° Stormo, Lecce	
MM55154	Aermacchi T-346A Master [61-01]	AMI 61° Stormo, Lecce	
MM55155	Aermacchi T-346A Master [61-04]	AMI 61° Stormo, Lecce	
MM55168	Eurofighter TF-2000A Typhoon [4-37] $	AMI 904° GEA, Grosseto	
MM55169	Eurofighter TF-2000A Typhoon	Leonardo, Turin	
MM55213	Aermacchi T-346A Master [61-06]	AMI 61° Stormo, Lecce	
MM55214	Aermacchi T-346A Master [61-07]	AMI 61° Stormo, Lecce	
MM55215	Aermacchi T-346A Master [61-10]	AMI 61° Stormo, Lecce	

Notes	Serial	Type (code/other identity)	Owner/operator, location or fate
	MM55216	Aermacchi T-346A Master [61-12]	AMI 61° Stormo, Lecce
	MM55217	Aermacchi T-346A Master [61-13]	AMI 61° Stormo, Lecce
	MM55218	Aermacchi T-346A Master [61-14]	AMI 61° Stormo, Lecce
	MT55219	Aermacchi T-346A Master [61-20]	AMI 61° Stormo, Lecce
	MM55220	Aermacchi T-346A Master [61-16]	AMI 61° Stormo, Lecce
	MM55221	Aermacchi T-346A Master [61-15]	AMI 61° Stormo, Lecce
	MT55222	Aermacchi T-346A Master [61-21]	AMI 61° Stormo, Lecce
	MT55223	Aermacchi T-346A Master [61-22]	AMI 61° Stormo, Lecce
	MM55224	Aermacchi T-346A Master [61-23]	AMI 61° Stormo, Lecce
	MT55229	Aermacchi T-346FA	Leonardo, Turin
	MT55231	Aermacchi T-346A Master	AMI 61° Stormo, Lecce
	MT55232	Aermacchi T-346A Master	AMI 61° Stormo, Lecce
	CSX55233	Aermacchi T-345A	Leonardo, Venegono
	MM55234	Aermacchi T-345A	AMI (on order)
	MM55235	Aermacchi T-345A	AMI (on order)
	MM55236	Aermacchi T-345A	AMI (on order)
	MM55237	Aermacchi T-345A	AMI (on order)
	CSX55239	Aermacchi T-346A Master	AMI (on order)
	CSX55240	Aermacchi T-346A Master	AMI (on order)
	MM62026	Dassault VC-50A (Falcon 50)	AMI 93° Gruppo/31° Stormo, Roma-Ciampino
	MM62029	Dassault VC-50A (Falcon 50)	AMI 93° Gruppo/31° Stormo, Roma-Ciampino
	CSX62127	Aeritalia MC-27J Pretorian	Alenia, Turin
	MM62156	Dornier UC-228 (Do.228-212) [E.I.101]	Esercito 28° Gruppo Squadroni, Viterbo
	MM62157	Dornier UC-228 (Do.228-212) [E.I.102]	Esercito 28° Gruppo Squadroni, Viterbo
	MM62158	Dornier UC-228 (Do.228-212) [E.I.103]	Esercito 28° Gruppo Squadroni, Viterbo
	MM62159	Piaggio VC-180A (P-180AM) Avanti	AMI RSV, Pratica di Mare
	MM62160	Piaggio EC-180A (P-180RM) Avanti	AMI 71° Gruppo/14° Stormo, Pratica di Mare
	MM62161	Piaggio VC-180A (P-180AM) Avanti	AMI RSV, Pratica di Mare
	MM62162	Piaggio EC-180A (P-180RM) Avanti	AMI 71° Gruppo/14° Stormo, Pratica di Mare
	MM62163	Piaggio EC-180A (P-180RM) Avanti	AMI 71° Gruppo/14° Stormo, Pratica di Mare
	CSX62164	Piaggio EC-180A (P-180RM) Avanti	Piaggio Aerospace, stored Genoa
	MM62165	Aérospatiale P-42A (ATR.42-400MP) [GF-13]	GdiF GEA, Pratica di Mare
	MM62166	Aérospatiale P-42A (ATR.42-400MP) [GF-14]	GdiF GEA, Pratica di Mare
	MM62167	Piaggio VC-180A (P-180AM) Avanti	Esercito 28° Gruppo Sqd Det, Roma/Ciampino
	MM62168	Piaggio VC-180A (P-180AM) Avanti	Esercito 28° Gruppo Sqd Det, Roma/Ciampino
	MM62169	Piaggio VC-180A (P-180AM) Avanti	Esercito 28° Gruppo Sqd Det, Roma/Ciampino
	MM62170	Aérospatiale P-42A (ATR.42-400MP) [10-01]	Guardia Costiera 3° Nucleo, Pescara
	MM62171	Dassault VC-900A (Falcon 900EX) $	*Sold as I-OUNI, June 2017*
	MM62174	Airbus VC-319A (A.319CJ-115X)	AMI 306° Gruppo/31° Stormo, Roma-Ciampino
	MM62175	Lockheed C-130J Hercules II [46-40]	AMI, stored Pisa
	MM62177	Lockheed C-130J Hercules II [46-42]	AMI 46ª Brigata Aerea, Pisa
	MM62178	Lockheed C-130J Hercules II [46-43]	AMI 46ª Brigata Aerea, Pisa
	MM62179	Lockheed C-130J Hercules II [46-44]	AMI 46ª Brigata Aerea, Pisa
	MM62180	Lockheed C-130J Hercules II [46-45]	AMI 46ª Brigata Aerea, Pisa
	MM62181	Lockheed KC-130J Hercules II [46-46]	AMI 46ª Brigata Aerea, Pisa
	MM62182	Lockheed C-130J Hercules II [46-47]	AMI, stored Pisa
	MM62183	Lockheed KC-130J Hercules II [46-48]	AMI 46ª Brigata Aerea, Pisa
	MM62184	Lockheed KC-130J Hercules II [46-49]	AMI 46ª Brigata Aerea, Pisa
	MM62185	Lockheed C-130J Hercules II [46-50]	AMI 46ª Brigata Aerea, Pisa
	MM62186	Lockheed C-130J Hercules II [46-51]	AMI 46ª Brigata Aerea, Pisa
	MM62187	Lockheed C-130J-30 Hercules II [46-53]	AMI, stored Pisa
	MM62188	Lockheed C-130J-30 Hercules II [46-54]	AMI 46ª Brigata Aerea, Pisa
	MM62189	Lockheed C-130J-30 Hercules II [46-55]	AMI 46ª Brigata Aerea, Pisa
	MM62190	Lockheed C-130J-30 Hercules II [46-56]	AMI 46ª Brigata Aerea, Pisa
	MM62191	Lockheed C-130J-30 Hercules II [46-57]	AMI, stored Pisa
	MM62192	Lockheed C-130J-30 Hercules II [46-58]	AMI, stored Pisa
	MM62193	Lockheed C-130J-30 Hercules II [46-59]	AMI 46ª Brigata Aerea, Pisa
	MM62194	Lockheed C-130J-30 Hercules II [46-60]	AMI, stored Pisa
	MM62195	Lockheed C-130J-30 Hercules II [46-61]	AMI 46ª Brigata Aerea, Pisa
	MM62196	Lockheed C-130J-30 Hercules II [46-62]	AMI 46ª Brigata Aerea, Pisa
	MM62199	Piaggio VC-180A (P-180AM) Avanti	AMI CAE Multicrew, Pratica di Mare
	MM62200	Piaggio VC-180A (P-180AM) Avanti	AMI 71° Gruppo/14° Stormo, Pratica di Mare

Serial	Type (code/other identity)	Owner/operator, location or fate	Notes
MM62201	Piaggio VC-180A (P-180AM) Avanti	AMI CAE Multicrew, Pratica di Mare	
MM62202	Piaggio VC-180A (P-180AM) Avanti	AMI 71° Gruppo/14° Stormo, Pratica di Mare	
MM62203	Piaggio VC-180A (P-180AM) Avanti	AMI CAE Multicrew, Pratica di Mare	
MM62204	Piaggio VC-180A (P-180AM) Avanti	AMI 71° Gruppo/14° Stormo, Pratica di Mare	
MM62205	Piaggio VC-180A (P-180AM) Avanti	AMI CAE Multicrew, Pratica di Mare	
MM62206	Piaggio VC-180A (P-180AM) Avanti	Piaggio Aerospace, stored Genoa	
MM62207	Piaggio VC-180A (P-180AM) Avanti	AMI CAE Multicrew, Pratica di Mare	
MM62208	Aérospatiale P-42A (ATR.42-400MP) [10-02]	Guardia Costiera 2° Nucleo, Catania	
MM62209	Airbus VC-319A (A.319CJ-115X)	AMI 306° Gruppo/31° Stormo, Roma-Ciampino	
MM62210	Dassault VC-900A (Falcon 900EX)	AMI 93° Gruppo/31° Stormo, Roma-Ciampino	
MM62211	Piaggio VC-180A (P-180AM) Avanti [9-02]	MMI 9ª Brigata Aerea, Pratica di Mare	
MM62212	Piaggio VC-180A (P-180AM) Avanti [9-01]	MMI 9ª Brigata Aerea, Pratica di Mare	
MM62213	Piaggio VC-180A (P-180AM) Avanti [9-03]	MMI 9ª Brigata Aerea, Pratica di Mare	
MM62214	Aeritalia C-27J Spartan [46-84]	AMI 46ª Brigata Aerea, Pisa	
MM62215	Aeritalia C-27J Spartan [46-80]	AMI 98° Gruppo/46ª Brigata Aerea, Pisa	
MM62217	Aeritalia C-27J Spartan [46-81]	AMI, stored Pisa	
MM62218	Aeritalia C-27J Spartan [46-82]	AMI 98° Gruppo/46ª Brigata Aerea, Pisa	
CSX62219	Aeritalia C-27J Spartan [RS-50]	AMI RSV, Pratica di Mare	
MM62220	Aeritalia MC-27J Pretorian [46-83]	AMI 98° Gruppo/46ª Brigata Aerea, Pisa	
MM62221	Aeritalia EC-27J JEDI [46-85]	AMI 98° Gruppo/46ª Brigata Aerea, Pisa	
MM62222	Aeritalia C-27J Spartan [46-86]	AMI 98° Gruppo/46ª Brigata Aerea, Pisa	
MM62223	Aeritalia C-27J Spartan [46-88]	AMI 98° Gruppo/46ª Brigata Aerea, Pisa	
MM62224	Aeritalia EC-27J JEDI [46-89]	AMI 98° Gruppo/46ª Brigata Aerea, Pisa	
MM62225	Aeritalia C-27J Spartan [46-90]	AMI 98° Gruppo/46ª Brigata Aerea, Pisa	
MM62226	Boeing KC-767A (767-2EYER) [14-01] $	AMI 8° Gruppo/14° Stormo, Pratica di Mare	
MM62227	Boeing KC-767A (767-2EYER) [14-02]	AMI 8° Gruppo/14° Stormo, Pratica di Mare	
MM62228	Boeing KC-767A (767-2EYER) [14-03]	AMI 8° Gruppo/14° Stormo, Pratica di Mare	
MM62229	Boeing KC-767A (767-2EYER) [14-04]	AMI 8° Gruppo/14° Stormo, Pratica di Mare	
MM62230	Aérospatiale P-42A (ATR.42-400MP) [GF-15]	GdiF GEA, Pratica di Mare	
MM62243	Airbus VC-319A (A.319CJ-115X)	AMI 306° Gruppo/31° Stormo, Roma-Ciampino	
MM62244	Dassault VC-900B (Falcon 900EX EASy)	AMI 93° Gruppo/31° Stormo, Roma-Ciampino	
MM62245	Dassault VC-900B (Falcon 900EX EASy)	AMI 93° Gruppo/31° Stormo, Roma-Ciampino	
MM62248	Piaggio VC-180A (P-180AM) Avanti [GF-18]	GdiF GEA, Pratica di Mare	
MM62249	Piaggio VC-180B (P-180AM) Avanti II [GF-19]	GdiF GEA, Pratica di Mare	
MM62250	Aeritalia C-27J Spartan [46-91]	AMI 98° Gruppo/46ª Brigata Aerea, Pisa	
MM62251	Aérospatiale P-42A (ATR.42-400MP) [GF-16]	GdiF GEA, Pratica di Mare	
MM62270	Aérospatiale P-42B (ATR.42-500MP) [10-03]	Guardia Costiera 2° Nucleo, Catania	
MM62279	Aérospatiale P-72A Argo(ATR.72-600MP) [41-01]	AMI 88° Gruppo/41° Stormo, Catania	
CSX62280	Aérospatiale P-72A Argo (ATR.72-600MP) [41-02]	Alenia	
MM62281	Aérospatiale P-72A Argo (ATR.72-600MP) [41-04]	AMI 88° Gruppo/41° Stormo, Catania	
CSX62282	Aérospatiale P-72A Argo (ATR.72-600MP) [41-05]	(on order)	
MM62286	Piaggio VC-180B (P-180AM) Avanti II	AMI 93° Gruppo/31° Stormo, Roma-Ciampino	
MM62287	Piaggio VC-180B (P-180AM) Avanti II	AMI 93° Gruppo/31° Stormo, Roma-Ciampino	
MM62293	Gulfstream Aerospace E-550A (N849GA) [14-11]	AMI 71° Gruppo/14° Stormo, Pratica di Mare	
MM62298	Aérospatiale P-72A Argo (ATR.72-600MP) [41-03]	AMI 71° Gruppo/14° Stormo, Pratica di Mare	
MM62300	Beechcraft King Air 350ER	AMI 71° Gruppo/14° Stormo, Pratica di Mare	
MM62303	Gulfstream Aerospace E-550A (N554GA) [14-12]	AMI 71° Gruppo/14° Stormo, Pratica di Mare	
CSX62311	Aérospatiale P-72B (ATR.72-600MP) [GF-20]	GdiF GEA, Pratica di Mare	
CSX62315	Aérospatiale P-72B (ATR.72-600MP) [GF-21]	GdiF GEA, Pratica di Mare	
MM81480	AgustaWestland SH-101A (EH-101 Mk110 ASW) [2-01]	MMI 3° Grupelicot, Catania	
MM81481	AgustaWestland SH-101A (EH-101 Mk110 ASW) [2-02]	MMI 3° Grupelicot, Catania	
MM81482	AgustaWestland SH-101A (EH-101 Mk110 ASW) [2-03]	MMI 3° Grupelicot, Catania	
MM81483	AgustaWestland SH-101A (EH-101 Mk110 ASW) [2-04]	MMI 3° Grupelicot, Catania	
MM81484	AgustaWestland SH-101A (EH-101 Mk110 ASW) [2-05]	MMI 3° Grupelicot, Catania	
MM81485	AgustaWestland SH-101A (EH-101 Mk110 ASW) [2-06]	MMI 3° Grupelicot, Catania	
MM81486	AgustaWestland SH-101A (EH-101 Mk110 ASW) [2-07]	MMI 3° Grupelicot, Catania	
MM81487	AgustaWestland SH-101A (EH-101 Mk110 ASW) [2-08]	Crashed 6 November 2019, Mediterranean Sea	
MM81488	AgustaWestland EH-101A (EH-101 Mk112 AEW) [2-09]	MMI 1° Grupelicot, La Spezia/Luni	
MM81489	AgustaWestland EH-101A (EH-101 Mk112 AEW) [2-10]	MMI 3° Grupelicot, Catania	
MM81490	AgustaWestland EH-101A (EH-101 Mk112 AEW) [2-11]	MMI 3° Grupelicot, Catania	
MM81491	AgustaWestland EH-101A (EH-101 Mk112 AEW) [2-12]	MMI 1° Grupelicot, La Spezia/Luni	
MM81492	AgustaWestland MH-101A (EH-101 Mk410 UTY) [2-13]	MMI 1° Grupelicot, La Spezia/Luni	

Notes	Serial	Type (code/other identity)	Owner/operator, location or fate
	MM81493	AgustaWestland MH-101A (EH-101 Mk410 UTY) [2-14]	MMI 1º Grupelicot, La Spezia/Luni
	MM81494	AgustaWestland MH-101A (EH-101 Mk410 UTY) [2-15]	MMI 1º Grupelicot, La Spezia/Luni
	MM81495	AgustaWestland MH-101A (EH-101 Mk410 UTY) [2-16]	MMI 1º Grupelicot, La Spezia/Luni
	MM81633	AgustaWestland MH-101A (EH-101 Mk413 ASH) [2-18]	MMI 1º Grupelicot, La Spezia/Luni
	MM81634	AgustaWestland MH-101A (EH-101 Mk413 ASH) [2-19]	MMI 1º Grupelicot, La Spezia/Luni
	MM81635	AgustaWestland MH-101A (EH-101 Mk413 ASH) [2-20]	MMI 1º Grupelicot, La Spezia/Luni
	MM81636	AgustaWestland MH-101A (EH-101 Mk413 ASH) [2-21]	MMI 1º Grupelicot, La Spezia/Luni
	MM81719	AgustaWestland SH-101A (EH-101 Mk110 ASW) [2-22]	MMI 1º Grupelicot, La Spezia/Luni
	MM81726	AgustaWestland SH-101A (EH-101 Mk110 ASW) [2-23]	MMI 1º Grupelicot, La Spezia/Luni
	MM81796	AgustaWestland HH-139A [15-40]	AMI 83º Gruppo SAR/15º Stormo, Cervia
	MM81797	AgustaWestland HH-139A [15-41]	AMI 82º Centro SAR/15º Stormo, Trapani/Birgi
	MM81798	AgustaWestland HH-139A [15-42]	AMI 82º Centro SAR/15º Stormo, Trapani/Birgi
	MM81799	AgustaWestland HH-139A [15-43]	AMI 81º Centro/15º Stormo, Cervia
	MM81800	AgustaWestland HH-139A [15-44]	AMI 82º Centro SAR/15º Stormo, Trapani/Birgi
	MM81801	AgustaWestland HH-139A [15-45]	AMI 85º Centro SAR/15º Stormo, Gioia del Colle
	MM81802	AgustaWestland HH-139A [15-46]	AMI 85º Centro SAR/15º Stormo, Gioia del Colle
	MM81803	AgustaWestland HH-139A [15-47]	AMI 81º Centro/15º Stormo, Cervia
	MM81804	AgustaWestland HH-139A [15-48]	AMI 83º Gruppo SAR/15º Stormo, Cervia
	MM81805	AgustaWestland HH-139A [15-49]	AMI 82º Centro SAR/15º Stormo, Trapani/Birgi
	MM81806	AgustaWestland VH-139A	AMI 93º Gruppo/31º Stormo, Roma-Ciampino
	MM81807	AgustaWestland VH-139A	AMI 93º Gruppo/31º Stormo, Roma-Ciampino
	MM81811	AgustaWestland VH-139A	AMI 93º Gruppo/31º Stormo, Roma-Ciampino
	MM81812	AgustaWestland VH-139A	AMI 93º Gruppo/31º Stormo, Roma-Ciampino
	MM81822	AgustaWestland HH-139A [15-50]	AMI 85º Centro SAR/15º Stormo, Gioia del Colle
	MM81823	AgustaWestland HH-139A [15-51]	AMI 81º Centro/15º Stormo, Cervia
	MM81824	AgustaWestland HH-139A [15-52]	AMI 85º Centro SAR/15º Stormo, Gioia del Colle
	CSX81848	AgustaWestland AW149 [1-49]	Leonardo
	MM81864	AgustaWestland HH-101A Caesar (ZR352) [15-01]	AMI 81º Centro/15º Stormo, Cervia
	MM81865	AgustaWestland HH-101A Caesar (ZR353) [15-02]	AMI 81º Centro/15º Stormo, Cervia
	MM81866	AgustaWestland HH-101A Caesar (ZR354) [15-03]	AMI 85º Centro SAR/15º Stormo, Pratica di Mare
	MM81867	AgustaWestland HH-101A Caesar (ZR355) [15-04]	AMI 23º Gruppo/15º Stormo, Cervia
	MM81868	AgustaWestland HH-101A Caesar (ZR356) [15-05]	AMI 81º Centro/15º Stormo, Cervia
	MM81869	AgustaWestland HH-101A Caesar (ZR357) [15-06]	AMI 81º Centro/15º Stormo, Cervia
	MM81870	AgustaWestland HH-101A Caesar (ZR358) [15-07]	AMI 81º Centro/15º Stormo, Cervia
	MM81871	AgustaWestland HH-101A Caesar (ZR359) [15-10]	AMI 81º Centro/15º Stormo, Cervia
	MM81872	AgustaWestland HH-101A Caesar (ZR360) [15-11]	AMI 81º Centro/15º Stormo, Cervia
	MM81873	AgustaWestland HH-101A Caesar (ZR361) [15-12]	AMI 23º Gruppo/15º Stormo, Cervia
	MM81874	AgustaWestland HH-101A Caesar (ZR362) [15-13]	AMI 23º Gruppo/15º Stormo, Cervia
	MM81875	AgustaWestland HH-101A Caesar (ZR363) [15-14]	AMI (on order)
	CSX81890	AgustaWestland AW149	Leonardo

Italian Government

	I-NEMO	Dassault Falcon 900EX EASy	Italian Government/Soc. CAI, Roma/Ciampino
	I-OUNI	Dassault Falcon 900EX (MM62171)	Italian Government/Soc. CAI, Roma/Ciampino
	I-TARH	Dassault Falcon 900EX (MM62172)	Italian Government/Soc. CAI, Roma/Ciampino

IVORY COAST

	TU-VAD	Grumman G.1159C Gulfstream IV	Ivory Coast Government, Abidjan
	TU-VAE	Gulfstream Aerospace G.550	Ivory Coast Government, Abidjan
	TU-VAF	Grumman G.1159A Gulfstream III	*Withdrawn from use, January 2020*
	TU-VAS	Airbus A.319CJ-133	Ivory Coast Government, Abidjan

JAPAN
Japan Air Self Defence Force (JASDF)

	07-3604	Boeing KC-767J	JASDF 404th Hikotai, Nagoya
	14-3611	Boeing KC-46A	JASDF (on order)
	14-3612	Boeing KC-46A	JASDF (on order)
	14-3613	Boeing KC-46A	JASDF (on order)
	20-1101	Boeing 747-47C	*Sold as N7474C, June 2019*
	20-1102	Boeing 747-47C	*Sold as N7477C, June 2019*
	80-1111	Boeing 777-3SB(ER) (N509BJ)	JASDF 701st Hikotai, Chitose
	80-1112	Boeing 777-3SB(ER) (N511BJ)	JASDF 701st Hikotai, Chitose
	87-3601	Boeing KC-767J	JASDF 404th Hikotai, Nagoya

Serial	Type (code/other identity)	Owner/operator, location or fate	Notes
87-3602	Boeing KC-767J	JASDF 404th Hikotai, Nagoya	
97-3603	Boeing KC-767J	JASDF 404th Hikotai, Nagoya	
..-....	Boeing KC-46A	JASDF (on order)	
..-....	Boeing KC-46A	JASDF (on order)	
Japan Maritime Self Defence Force (JMSDF)			
5502	Kawasaki P-1	JMSDF 51st Kokutai, Atsugi	
5503	Kawasaki P-1	JMSDF 51st Kokutai, Atsugi	
5504	Kawasaki P-1	JMSDF 3rd Kokutai, Atsugi	
5505	Kawasaki P-1	JMSDF 3rd Kokutai, Atsugi	
5506	Kawasaki P-1	JMSDF 3rd Kokutai, Atsugi	
5507	Kawasaki P-1	JMSDF 3rd Kokutai, Atsugi	
5508	Kawasaki P-1	JMSDF 3rd Kokutai, Atsugi	
5509	Kawasaki P-1	JMSDF 3rd Kokutai, Atsugi	
5510	Kawasaki P-1	JMSDF 3rd Kokutai, Atsugi	
5511	Kawasaki P-1	JMSDF 51st Kokutai, Atsugi	
5512	Kawasaki P-1	JMSDF 3rd Kokutai, Atsugi	
5513	Kawasaki P-1	JMSDF 3rd Kokutai, Atsugi	
5514	Kawasaki P-1	JMSDF 3rd Kokutai, Atsugi	
5515	Kawasaki P-1	JMSDF 3rd Kokutai, Atsugi	
5516	Kawasaki P-1	JMSDF 51st Kokutai, Atsugi	
5517	Kawasaki P-1	JMSDF 1st Kokutai, Kanoya	
5518	Kawasaki P-1	JMSDF 3rd Kokutai, Atsugi	
5519	Kawasaki P-1	JMSDF 3rd Kokutai, Atsugi	
5520	Kawasaki P-1	JMSDF 1st Kokutai, Kanoya	
5521	Kawasaki P-1	JMSDF 3rd Kokutai, Atsugi	
5522	Kawasaki P-1	JMSDF 3rd Kokutai, Atsugi	
5523	Kawasaki P-1	JMSDF 3rd Kokutai, Atsugi	
5524	Kawasaki P-1	JMSDF (on order)	
5525	Kawasaki P-1	JMSDF (on order)	
JORDAN			
Al Quwwat al Jawwiya al Malakiya al Urduniya/Jordanian Air Force			
344	Lockheed C-130H Hercules	Jordanian AF 3 Sqn, Amman/Marka	
345	Lockheed C-130H Hercules $	Jordanian AF 3 Sqn, Amman/Marka	
346	Lockheed C-130H Hercules	Jordanian AF 3 Sqn, Amman/Marka	
347	Lockheed C-130H Hercules $	Jordanian AF 3 Sqn, Amman/Marka	
360	Ilyushin Il-76MF (JY-JIC)	*Sold to Egypt as 1331/SU-BTX, July 2019*	
361	Ilyushin Il-76MF (JY-JID)	*Sold to Egypt as 1332/SU-BTY, July 2019*	
RJF 01	Extra EA-330LX	Jordanian AF *Royal Jordanian Falcons*, Aqaba	
RJF 02	Extra EA-330LX	Jordanian AF *Royal Jordanian Falcons*, Aqaba	
RJF 03	Extra EA-330LX	Jordanian AF *Royal Jordanian Falcons*, Aqaba	
RJF 04	Extra EA-330LX	Jordanian AF *Royal Jordanian Falcons*, Aqaba	
RJF 05	Extra EA-330LX	Jordanian AF *Royal Jordanian Falcons*, Aqaba	
Jordanian Government			
VQ-BDD	Airbus A.318-112	*Sold as TC-ANK, 2018*	
VQ-BMZ	Gulfstream Aerospace G.650	Jordanian Government, Amman/Queen Alia Int'l	
VQ-BNZ	Gulfstream Aerospace G.650ER	Jordanian Government, Amman/Queen Alia Int'l	
KAZAKHSTAN			
01 r	CASA C-295M	Kazakstan ADF 18th Air Transport Sqn, Almaty	
02 r	CASA C-295M	Kazakstan ADF 18th Air Transport Sqn, Almaty	
03 r	CASA C-295M	Kazakstan ADF 18th Air Transport Sqn, Almaty	
04 r	CASA C-295M	Kazakstan ADF 18th Air Transport Sqn, Almaty	
05 r	CASA C-295M	Kazakstan ADF 18th Air Transport Sqn, Almaty	
06 r	CASA C-295M	Kazakstan ADF 18th Air Transport Sqn, Almaty	
07 r	Antonov An-72	Kazakstan ADF 18th Air Transport Sqn, Almaty	
07 r	CASA C-295M	Kazakstan ADF 18th Air Transport Sqn, Almaty	
08 r	Antonov An-72	Kazakstan ADF 18th Air Transport Sqn, Almaty	
08 r	CASA C-295M	Kazakstan ADF 18th Air Transport Sqn, Almaty	
UP-A3001	Airbus A.330-223	Government of Kazakhstan, Almaty	
UP-B5701	Boeing 757-2M6	Government of Kazakhstan, Almaty	
UP-T5401	Tupolev Tu-154M	Government of Kazakhstan, Almaty	

Notes	Serial	Type (code/other identity)	Owner/operator, location or fate
	KENYA		
	KAF 308	Fokker 70ER	Kenyan Government, Nairobi
	KUWAIT		
	Al Quwwat al Jawwiya al Kuwaitiya/Kuwaiti Air Force		
	KAF 323	Lockheed L100-30 Hercules	Kuwaiti AF, stored Kuwait International
	KAF 324	Lockheed L100-30 Hercules	Kuwaiti AF, stored Kuwait International
	KAF 325	Lockheed L100-30 Hercules	Kuwaiti AF, stored Kuwait International
	KAF 326	Lockheed KC-130J Hercules II	Kuwaiti AF 41 Sqn, Kuwait International
	KAF 327	Lockheed KC-130J Hercules II	Kuwaiti AF 41 Sqn, Kuwait International
	KAF 328	Lockheed KC-130J Hercules II	Kuwaiti AF 41 Sqn, Kuwait International
	KAF 342	Boeing C-17A Globemaster III (13-0001)	Kuwaiti AF 41 Sqn, Kuwait International
	KAF 343	Boeing C-17A Globemaster III (13-0002)	Kuwaiti AF 41 Sqn, Kuwait International
	Kuwaiti Government		
	9K-AKD	Airbus A.320-212	Kuwaiti Government, Safat
	9K-GAA	Boeing 747-8JK	Kuwaiti Government, Safat
	9K-GBA	Airbus A.340-542	Kuwaiti Government, Safat
	9K-GBB	Airbus A.340-542	Kuwaiti Government, Safat
	9K-GCC	Boeing 737-9BQER	Kuwaiti Government, Safat
	9K-GEA	Airbus A.319CJ-115X	Kuwaiti Government, Safat
	9K-GFA	Gulfstream Aerospace G.550	Kuwaiti Government, Safat
	9K-GGA	Gulfstream Aerospace G.650	Kuwaiti Government, Safat
	9K-GGB	Gulfstream Aerospace G.650	Kuwaiti Government, Safat
	9K-GGC	Gulfstream Aerospace G.650	Kuwaiti Government, Safat
	9K-GGD	Gulfstream Aerospace G.650	Kuwaiti Government, Safat
	KYRGYZSTAN		
	EX-00001	Tupolev Tu-154M	Government of Kyrgyzstan, Bishkek
	LITHUANIA		
	Karines Oro Pajegos (KOP)		
	01 bl	LET 410UVP Turbolet	KOP Transporto Esk, Siauliai/Zokniai
	06 bl	Aeritalia C-27J Spartan	KOP Transporto Esk, Siauliai/Zokniai
	07 bl	Aeritalia C-27J Spartan	KOP Transporto Esk, Siauliai/Zokniai
	08 bl	Aeritalia C-27J Spartan	KOP Transporto Esk, Siauliai/Zokniai
	21 bl	Mil Mi-8MTV-1	KOP Sraigtasparniu Esk, Siauliai/Zokniai
	23 bl	Mil Mi-8T	KOP Sraigtasparniu Esk, Siauliai/Zokniai
	25 bl	Mil Mi-8T (10 bl)	KOP Sraigtasparniu Esk, Siauliai/Zokniai
	26 bl	Mil Mi-8T (09 bl)	KOP Sraigtasparniu Esk, Siauliai/Zokniai
	28 bl	Mil Mi-8T	KOP Sraigtasparniu Esk, Siauliai/Zokniai
	LUXEMBOURG		
	Note: see also Belgium for A400M		
	NATO		
	LX-N90442	Boeing E-3A Sentry	NATO NAEW&CF, Geilenkirchen, Germany
	LX-N90443	Boeing E-3A Sentry $	NATO NAEW&CF, Geilenkirchen, Germany $
	LX-N90444	Boeing E-3A Sentry	NATO NAEW&CF, Geilenkirchen, Germany
	LX-N90445	Boeing E-3A Sentry	NATO NAEW&CF, Geilenkirchen, Germany
	LX-N90446	Boeing E-3A Sentry	NATO NAEW&CF, Geilenkirchen, Germany
	LX-N90447	Boeing E-3A Sentry	NATO NAEW&CF, Geilenkirchen, Germany
	LX-N90448	Boeing E-3A Sentry	NATO NAEW&CF, Geilenkirchen, Germany
	LX-N90450	Boeing E-3A Sentry $	NATO NAEW&CF, Geilenkirchen, Germany
	LX-N90451	Boeing E-3A Sentry	NATO NAEW&CF, Geilenkirchen, Germany
	LX-N90452	Boeing E-3A Sentry	NATO NAEW&CF, Geilenkirchen, Germany
	LX-N90453	Boeing E-3A Sentry	NATO NAEW&CF, Geilenkirchen, Germany
	LX-N90454	Boeing E-3A Sentry	Airbus, Manching, Germany (on upgrade)
	LX-N90456	Boeing E-3A Sentry	NATO NAEW&CF, Geilenkirchen, Germany
	LX-N90459	Boeing E-3A Sentry	NATO NAEW&CF, Geilenkirchen, Germany
	OO-TFA	Boeing 757-28A	NATO, Geilenkirchen, Germany
	MACEDONIA		
	Z3-MKD	Bombardier Lear 60	Macedonian Government, Skopje

Serial	Type (code/other identity)	Owner/operator, location or fate	Notes
MALAYSIA			
Tentera Udara Diraja Malaysia/Royal Malaysian Air Force (RMAF)			
M30-01	Lockheed C-130T Hercules	RMAF 20 Sqn, Subang	
M30-02	Lockheed C-130H Hercules	RMAF 20 Sqn, Subang	
M30-03	Lockheed C-130H Hercules	RMAF 14 Sqn, Labuan	
M30-04	Lockheed C-130H-30 Hercules	RMAF 20 Sqn, Subang	
M30-05	Lockheed C-130H-30 Hercules	RMAF 14 Sqn, Labuan	
M30-06	Lockheed C-130H-30 Hercules	RMAF 14 Sqn, Labuan	
M30-07	Lockheed C-130T Hercules	RMAF 20 Sqn, Subang	
M30-08	Lockheed C-130H(MP) Hercules	RMAF 20 Sqn, Subang	
M30-09	Lockheed C-130H(MP) Hercules	RMAF 20 Sqn, Subang	
M30-10	Lockheed C-130H-30 Hercules	RMAF 20 Sqn, Subang	
M30-11	Lockheed C-130H-30 Hercules	RMAF 20 Sqn, Subang	
M30-12	Lockheed C-130H-30 Hercules	RMAF 20 Sqn, Subang	
M30-14	Lockheed C-130H-30 Hercules	RMAF 14 Sqn, Labuan	
M30-15	Lockheed C-130H-30 Hercules	RMAF 20 Sqn, Subang	
M30-16	Lockheed C-130H-30 Hercules	RMAF 20 Sqn, Subang	
M37-01	Dassault Falcon 900	RMAF 2 Sqn, Simpang	
M48-02	Bombardier BD.700-1A10 Global Express	RMAF 2 Sqn, Simpang	
M53-01	Boeing 737-7H6	RMAF 2 Sqn, Simpang	
M54-01	Airbus Military A.400M	RMAF 22 Sqn, Subang	
M54-02	Airbus Military A.400M	RMAF 22 Sqn, Subang	
M54-03	Airbus Military A.400M	RMAF 22 Sqn, Subang	
M54-04	Airbus Military A.400M	RMAF 22 Sqn, Subang	
9M-NAA	Airbus A.319CJ-115X	RMAF, Subang	
9M-NAB	Airbus A.320CJ-214 (M37-07)	RMAF, Subang	
MALI			
TZ-PRM	Boeing 737-7DW	Government of Mali, Bamako	
MALTA			
Armed Forces of Malta			
AS1428	AgustaWestland AW139	AFM Air Wing, 2nd Regiment, Luqa	
AS1429	AgustaWestland AW139	AFM Air Wing, 2nd Regiment, Luqa	
AS1630	AgustaWestland AW139	AFM Air Wing, 2nd Regiment, Luqa	
Maltese Government			
9H-AFK	Bombardier Learjet 60	Government of Malta, Luqa	
MEXICO			
Fuerza Aérea Mexicana (FAM)/Mexican Air Force			
TP-02	Boeing 757-225 (XC-UJM)	*Withdrawn from use, April 2019*	
Armada de Mexico/Mexican Navy			
ANX-1201	Gulfstream Aerospace G.550	Armada PRIESCAERTRANS, Mexico City	
XC-LMF	Gulfstream Aerospace G.450	Armada PRIESCAERTRANS, Mexico City	
MOROCCO			
Al Quwwat al Jawwiya al Malakiya Marakishiya/Force Aérienne Royaume Marocaine/Royal Moroccan Air Force			
(RMAF) & Moroccan Government			
CN-ABP	CAP-232 (28) [6]	RMAF *Marche Verte*, Marrakech/Ménara	
CN-ABQ	CAP-232 (29) [7]	RMAF *Marche Verte*, Marrakech/Ménara	
CN-ABR	CAP-232 (31) [2]	RMAF *Marche Verte*, Marrakech/Ménara	
CN-ABS	CAP-232 (36) [3]	RMAF *Marche Verte*, Marrakech/Ménara	
CN-ABT	CAP-232 (37) [1]	RMAF *Marche Verte*, Marrakech/Ménara	
CN-ABU	CAP-232 (41) [5]	RMAF *Marche Verte*, Marrakech/Ménara	
CN-ABV	CAP-232 (42) [4]	RMAF *Marche Verte*, Marrakech/Ménara	
CN-ABW	CAP-232 (43) [8]	RMAF *Marche Verte*, Marrakech/Ménara	
CN-ABX	CAP-232 (44) [7]	RMAF *Marche Verte*, Marrakech/Ménara	
CN-AMA	Airtech CN.235M-100 (023)	RMAF Escadrille de Transport 3, Kenitra	
CN-AMB	Airtech CN.235M-100 (024)	RMAF Escadrille de Transport 3, Kenitra	
CN-AMC	Airtech CN.235M-100 (025)	RMAF Escadrille de Transport 3, Kenitra	
CN-AMD	Airtech CN.235M-100 (026)	RMAF Escadrille de Transport 3, Kenitra	

Notes	Serial	Type (code/other identity)	Owner/operator, location or fate
	CN-AMG	Airtech CN.235M-100 (031)	RMAF Escadrille de Transport 3, Kenitra
	CN-AMH	Gulfstream Aerospace G.650	*Repainted as CN-MMH, 2019*
	CN-AMJ	Cessna 560XLS+ Citation Excel	*Repainted as CN-MMJ, 2019*
	CN-AMK	Cessna 560XLS+ Citation Excel	RMAF VIP Flight, Rabat
	CN-AMN	Aeritalia C-27J Spartan	RMAF Escadrille de Transport 3, Kenitra
	CN-AMO	Aeritalia C-27J Spartan	RMAF Escadrille de Transport 3, Kenitra
	CN-AMP	Aeritalia C-27J Spartan	RMAF Escadrille de Transport 3, Kenitra
	CN-AMQ	Aeritalia C-27J Spartan	RMAF Escadrille de Transport 3, Kenitra
	CN-AMR	Gulfstream Aerospace G.550	*Repainted as CN-MMR, 2019*
	CN-AMS	Gulfstream Aerospace G.550	*Repainted as CN-MMT, 2019*
	CN-AMY	Cessna 560XLS+ Citation Excel	*Repainted as CN-MMY, 2019*
	CN-ANL	Grumman G.1159 Gulfstream IITT	RMAF VIP Flight, Rabat
	CN-ANO	Dassault Falcon 50	RMAF VIP Flight, Rabat
	CN-ANU	Grumman G.1159A Gulfstream III	RMAF VIP Flight, Rabat
	CNA-NV	Cessna 560 Citation V	RMAF VIP Flight, Rabat
	CNA-NW	Cessna 560 Citation V	RMAF VIP Flight, Rabat
	CN-AOA	Lockheed C-130H Hercules (4535)	RMAF Escadrille de Transport 3, Kenitra
	CNA-OC	Lockheed C-130H Hercules (4551)	RMAF Escadrille de Transport 3, Kenitra
	CN-AOD	Lockheed C-130H Hercules (4575)	RMAF Escadrille de Transport 3, Kenitra
	CN-AOE	Lockheed C-130H Hercules (4581)	RMAF Escadrille de Transport 3, Kenitra
	CN-AOF	Lockheed C-130H Hercules (4583)	RMAF, stored Perpignan, France
	CN-AOG	Lockheed C-130H Hercules (4713)	RMAF Escadrille de Transport 3, Kenitra
	CN-AOI	Lockheed C-130H Hercules (4733)	RMAF Escadrille de Transport 3, Kenitra
	CNA-OJ	Lockheed C-130H Hercules (4738)	RMAF Escadrille de Transport 3, Kenitra
	CN-AOK	Lockheed C-130H Hercules (4739)	RMAF Escadrille de Transport 3, Kenitra
	CN-AOL	Lockheed C-130H Hercules (4742)	RMAF Escadrille de Transport 3, Kenitra
	CN-AOM	Lockheed C-130H Hercules (4875)	RMAF Escadrille de Transport 3, Kenitra
	CN-AON	Lockheed C-130H Hercules (4876)	RMAF Escadrille de Transport 3, Kenitra
	CN-AOO	Lockheed EC-130H Hercules (4877)	RMAF Escadron Electronique, Kenitra
	CN-AOP	Lockheed C-130H Hercules (4888)	RMAF, stored Perpignan, France
	CN-AOR	Lockheed KC-130H Hercules (4907)	RMAF Escadrille de Transport 3, Kenitra
	CN-AOS	Lockheed KC-130H Hercules (4909)	RMAF Escadrille de Transport 3, Kenitra
Moroccan Government			
	CNA-SM	BAE RJ100	Government of Morocco, Rabat
	CN-MBH	Boeing 747-8Z5 (A6-PFA)	Government of Morocco, Rabat
	CN-MMH	Gulfstream Aerospace G.650 (CN-AMH)	Government of Morocco, Rabat
	CN-MMJ	Cessna 560XLS+ Citation Excel (CN-AMJ)	Government of Morocco, Rabat
	CN-MMR	Gulfstream Aerospace G.550 (CN-AMR)	Government of Morocco, Rabat
	CN-MMS	Gulfstream Aerospace G.550 (CN-AMS)	Government of Morocco, Rabat
	CN-MMY	Cessna 560XLS+ Citation Excel (CN-AMY)	Government of Morocco, Rabat
	CN-MVI	Boeing 737-8KB	Government of Morocco, Rabat
NAMIBIA			
	V5-GON	Dassault Falcon 7X	Government of Namibia, Eros
	V5-NAM	Dassault Falcon 900B	Government of Namibia, Eros
NETHERLANDS			
Koninklijke Luchtmacht (KLu)			
	D-101	Boeing-Vertol CH-47D Chinook	KLu 298 Sqn, Gilze-Rijen
	D-102	Boeing-Vertol CH-47D Chinook	KLu 298 Sqn, Gilze-Rijen
	D-103	Boeing-Vertol CH-47D Chinook	KLu 298 Sqn, Gilze-Rijen
	D-106	Boeing-Vertol CH-47D Chinook	KLu 298 Sqn, Gilze-Rijen
	D-661	Boeing-Vertol CH-47D Chinook	KLu 298 Sqn, Gilze-Rijen
	D-662	Boeing-Vertol CH-47D Chinook	KLu 298 Sqn, Gilze-Rijen
	D-663	Boeing-Vertol CH-47D Chinook	KLu 298 Sqn, Gilze-Rijen
	D-664	Boeing-Vertol CH-47D Chinook	KLu 298 Sqn, Gilze-Rijen
	D-665	Boeing-Vertol CH-47D Chinook	KLu 298 Sqn, Gilze-Rijen
	D-666	Boeing-Vertol CH-47D Chinook	KLu 298 Sqn, Gilze-Rijen
	D-667	Boeing-Vertol CH-47D Chinook	KLu 298 Sqn, Gilze-Rijen
	D-890	Boeing-Vertol CH-47F Chinook	KLu 298 Sqn, Gilze-Rijen
	D-891	Boeing-Vertol CH-47F Chinook	KLu 302 Sqn, Fort Hood, Texas, USA
	D-892	Boeing-Vertol CH-47F Chinook	KLu 298 Sqn, Gilze-Rijen

Serial	Type (code/other identity)	Owner/operator, location or fate	Notes
D-893	Boeing-Vertol CH-47F Chinook	KLu 302 Sqn, Fort Hood, Texas, USA	
D-894	Boeing-Vertol CH-47F Chinook	KLu 302 Sqn, Fort Hood, Texas, USA	
D-895	Boeing-Vertol CH-47F Chinook	KLu 302 Sqn, Fort Hood, Texas, USA	
F-001	Lockheed Martin F-35A Lightning II	KLu 323 TES, Edwards AFB, California, USA	
F-002	Lockheed Martin F-35A Lightning II [OT]	KLu 323 TES, Edwards AFB, California, USA	
F-003	Lockheed Martin F-35A Lightning II	KLu 308th FS/56th FW, Luke AFB, Arizona, USA	
F-004	Lockheed Martin F-35A Lightning II	KLu 308th FS/56th FW, Luke AFB, Arizona, USA	
F-005	Lockheed Martin F-35A Lightning II	KLu 308th FS/56th FW, Luke AFB, Arizona, USA	
F-006	Lockheed Martin F-35A Lightning II	KLu 308th FS/56th FW, Luke AFB, Arizona, USA	
F-007	Lockheed Martin F-35A Lightning II	KLu 308th FS/56th FW, Luke AFB, Arizona, USA	
F-008	Lockheed Martin F-35A Lightning II	KLu 308th FS/56th FW, Luke AFB, Arizona, USA	
F-009	Lockheed Martin F-35A Lightning II	KLu 322 Sqn, Leeuwarden	
F-010	Lockheed Martin F-35A Lightning II	KLu 322 Sqn, Leeuwarden	
F-011	Lockheed Martin F-35A Lightning II	KLu 322 Sqn, Leeuwarden	
F-012	Lockheed Martin F-35A Lightning II	KLu (on order)	
F-013	Lockheed Martin F-35A Lightning II	KLu (on order)	
F-014	Lockheed Martin F-35A Lightning II	KLu (on order)	
F-015	Lockheed Martin F-35A Lightning II	KLu (on order)	
F-016	Lockheed Martin F-35A Lightning II	KLu (on order)	
F-017	Lockheed Martin F-35A Lightning II	KLu (on order)	
F-018	Lockheed Martin F-35A Lightning II	KLu (on order)	
F-019	Lockheed Martin F-35A Lightning II	KLu (on order)	
F-020	Lockheed Martin F-35A Lightning II	KLu (on order)	
G-273	Lockheed C-130H-30 Hercules	KLu 336 Sqn, Eindhoven	
G-275	Lockheed C-130H-30 Hercules	KLu 336 Sqn, Eindhoven	
G-781	Lockheed C-130H Hercules $	KLu 336 Sqn, Eindhoven	
G-988	Lockheed C-130H Hercules	KLu 336 Sqn, Eindhoven	
J-001	Fokker (GD) F-16AM Fighting Falcon [AZ]	KLu 148th FS/162th FW, Tucson IAP, Arizona, USA	
J-002	Fokker (GD) F-16AM Fighting Falcon $	KLu 322 Sqn, Leeuwarden	
J-003	Fokker (GD) F-16AM Fighting Falcon	KLu 313 Sqn, Volkel	
J-004	Fokker (GD) F-16AM Fighting Falcon [AZ]	KLu 148th FS/162th FW, Tucson IAP, Arizona, USA	
J-005	Fokker (GD) F-16AM Fighting Falcon	KLu 313 Sqn, Volkel	
J-006	Fokker (GD) F-16AM Fighting Falcon	KLu 323 Sqn, Leeuwarden	
J-008	Fokker (GD) F-16AM Fighting Falcon $	KLu 313 Sqn, Volkel	
J-009	Fokker (GD) F-16AM Fighting Falcon	KLu 322 Sqn, Leeuwarden	
J-010	Fokker (GD) F-16AM Fighting Falcon [AZ] [148 FS]	KLu 148th FS/162th FW, Tucson IAP, Arizona, USA	
J-011	Fokker (GD) F-16AM Fighting Falcon	KLu 312 Sqn/313 Sqn, Volkel	
J-013	Fokker (GD) F-16AM Fighting Falcon	KLu 312 Sqn/313 Sqn, Volkel	
J-014	Fokker (GD) F-16AM Fighting Falcon	KLu 313 Sqn, Volkel	
J-015	Fokker (GD) F-16AM Fighting Falcon	KLu 312 Sqn/313 Sqn, Volkel	
J-016	Fokker (GD) F-16AM Fighting Falcon	KLu 313 Sqn, Volkel	
J-017	Fokker (GD) F-16AM Fighting Falcon	KLu 312 Sqn, Volkel	
J-018	Fokker (GD) F-16AM Fighting Falcon [AZ]	KLu 148th FS/162th FW, Tucson IAP, Arizona, USA	
J-019	Fokker (GD) F-16AM Fighting Falcon [AZ]	KLu 148th FS/162th FW, Tucson IAP, Arizona, USA	
J-020	Fokker (GD) F-16AM Fighting Falcon	KLu 312 Sqn, Volkel	
J-021	Fokker (GD) F-16AM Fighting Falcon	KLu 322 Sqn, Leeuwarden	
J-055	Fokker (GD) F-16AM Fighting Falcon	KLu 313 Sqn, Volkel	
J-060	Fokker (GD) F-16AM Fighting Falcon	KLu 322 Sqn, Leeuwarden	
J-061	Fokker (GD) F-16AM Fighting Falcon	KLu 322 Sqn, Leeuwarden	
J-062	Fokker (GD) F-16AM Fighting Falcon	KLu 313 Sqn, Volkel	
J-063	Fokker (GD) F-16AM Fighting Falcon	KLu 313 Sqn, Volkel	
J-064	Fokker (GD) F-16BM Fighting Falcon [AZ]	KLu 148th FS/162th FW, Tucson IAP, Arizona, USA	
J-065	Fokker (GD) F-16BM Fighting Falcon	KLu 322 Sqn, Leeuwarden	
J-066	Fokker (GD) F-16BM Fighting Falcon	KLu Test Flt, Leeuwarden	
J-067	Fokker (GD) F-16BM Fighting Falcon [AZ]	KLu 148th FS/162th FW, Tucson IAP, Arizona, USA	
J-135	Fokker (GD) F-16AM Fighting Falcon	KLu 322 Sqn, Leeuwarden	
J-136	Fokker (GD) F-16AM Fighting Falcon	KLu 312 Sqn/313 Sqn, Volkel	
J-142	Fokker (GD) F-16AM Fighting Falcon	KLu 322 Sqn, Leeuwarden	
J-144	Fokker (GD) F-16AM Fighting Falcon	KLu 312 Sqn/313 Sqn, Volkel	
J-146	Fokker (GD) F-16AM Fighting Falcon	KLu 323 Sqn, Leeuwarden	
J-196	Fokker (GD) F-16AM Fighting Falcon $	To Volkel for GI use	
J-197	Fokker (GD) F-16AM Fighting Falcon	KLu 312 Sqn/313 Sqn, Volkel	

Notes	Serial	Type (code/other identity)	Owner/operator, location or fate
	J-201	Fokker (GD) F-16AM Fighting Falcon	KLu 322 Sqn, Leeuwarden
	J-202	Fokker (GD) F-16AM Fighting Falcon	KLu, stored Volkel
	J-209	Fokker (GD) F-16BM Fighting Falcon [AZ]	KLu 148th FS/162th FW, Tucson IAP, Arizona, USA
	J-210	Fokker (GD) F-16BM Fighting Falcon [AZ]	KLu 148th FS/162th FW, Tucson IAP, Arizona, USA
	J-362	Fokker (GD) F-16AM Fighting Falcon	KLu 322 Sqn, Leeuwarden
	J-366	Fokker (GD) F-16AM Fighting Falcon [AZ]	KLu 148th FS/162th FW, Tucson IAP, Arizona, USA
	J-367	Fokker (GD) F-16AM Fighting Falcon	KLu 322 Sqn, Leeuwarden
	J-368	Fokker (GD) F-16BM Fighting Falcon	KLu 313 Sqn, Volkel
	J-369	Fokker (GD) F-16BM Fighting Falcon [AZ]	KLu 148th FS/162th FW, Tucson IAP, Arizona, USA
	J-508	Fokker (GD) F-16AM Fighting Falcon	KLu 313 Sqn, Volkel
	J-509	Fokker (GD) F-16AM Fighting Falcon	KLu 322 Sqn, Leeuwarden
	J-511	Fokker (GD) F-16AM Fighting Falcon	KLu 322 Sqn, Leeuwarden
	J-512	Fokker (GD) F-16AM Fighting Falcon	KLu 313 Sqn, Volkel
	J-513	Fokker (GD) F-16AM Fighting Falcon	KLu 323 Sqn, Volkel
	J-514	Fokker (GD) F-16AM Fighting Falcon	KLu 313 Sqn, Volkel
	J-515	Fokker (GD) F-16AM Fighting Falcon	KLu 312 Sqn/313 Sqn, Volkel
	J-516	Fokker (GD) F-16AM Fighting Falcon	KLu 322 Sqn, Leeuwarden
	J-616	Fokker (GD) F-16AM Fighting Falcon	KLu 322 Sqn, Leeuwarden
	J-624	Fokker (GD) F-16AM Fighting Falcon	KLu 322 Sqn, Leeuwarden
	J-628	Fokker (GD) F-16AM Fighting Falcon	KLu 322 Sqn, Leeuwarden
	J-630	Fokker (GD) F-16AM Fighting Falcon	KLu 322 Sqn, Leeuwarden
	J-631	Fokker (GD) F-16AM Fighting Falcon $	KLu 322 Sqn, Leeuwarden
	J-632	Fokker (GD) F-16AM Fighting Falcon	KLu 312 Sqn, Volkel
	J-641	Fokker (GD) F-16AM Fighting Falcon	KLu 312 Sqn, Volkel
	J-642	Fokker (GD) F-16AM Fighting Falcon	Withdrawn from use at Volkel, August 2019
	J-643	Fokker (GD) F-16AM Fighting Falcon	Withdrawn from use, 2019
	J-644	Fokker (GD) F-16AM Fighting Falcon	KLu 322 Sqn, Leeuwarden
	J-646	Fokker (GD) F-16AM Fighting Falcon $	KLu 312 Sqn, Volkel
	J-647	Fokker (GD) F-16AM Fighting Falcon	To Woensdrecht for GI use
	J-866	Fokker (GD) F-16AM Fighting Falcon	Withdrawn from use, 2019
	J-871	Fokker (GD) F-16AM Fighting Falcon	KLu 322 Sqn, Leeuwarden
	J-877	Fokker (GD) F-16AM Fighting Falcon	KLu 322 Sqn, Leeuwarden
	J-879	Fokker (GD) F-16AM Fighting Falcon $	KLu 322 Sqn, Leeuwarden
	J-881	Fokker (GD) F-16AM Fighting Falcon	KLu 322 Sqn, Leeuwarden
	J-882	Fokker (GD) F-16BM Fighting Falcon $	KLu 312 Sqn/313 Sqn, Volkel
	L-01	Pilatus PC-7 Turbo Trainer	KLu 131 EMVO Sqn, Woensdrecht
	L-02	Pilatus PC-7 Turbo Trainer $	KLu 131 EMVO Sqn, Woensdrecht
	L-03	Pilatus PC-7 Turbo Trainer	KLu 131 EMVO Sqn, Woensdrecht
	L-04	Pilatus PC-7 Turbo Trainer	KLu 131 EMVO Sqn, Woensdrecht
	L-05	Pilatus PC-7 Turbo Trainer	KLu 131 EMVO Sqn, Woensdrecht
	L-06	Pilatus PC-7 Turbo Trainer	KLu 131 EMVO Sqn, Woensdrecht
	L-07	Pilatus PC-7 Turbo Trainer	KLu 131 EMVO Sqn, Woensdrecht
	L-08	Pilatus PC-7 Turbo Trainer	KLu 131 EMVO Sqn, Woensdrecht
	L-09	Pilatus PC-7 Turbo Trainer	KLu 131 EMVO Sqn, Woensdrecht
	L-10	Pilatus PC-7 Turbo Trainer	KLu 131 EMVO Sqn, Woensdrecht
	L-11	Pilatus PC-7 Turbo Trainer	KLu 131 EMVO Sqn, Woensdrecht
	L-12	Pilatus PC-7 Turbo Trainer	KLu 131 EMVO Sqn, Woensdrecht
	L-13	Pilatus PC-7 Turbo Trainer $	KLu 131 EMVO Sqn, Woensdrecht
	N-088	NH Industries NH.90-NFH	KLu 860 Sqn, De Kooij
	N-102	NH Industries NH.90-NFH	KLu 860 Sqn, De Kooij
	N-110	NH Industries NH.90-NFH	KLu 860 Sqn, De Kooij
	N-164	NH Industries NH.90-NFH	KLu 860 Sqn, De Kooij
	N-175	NH Industries NH.90-NFH	KLu 860 Sqn, De Kooij
	N-195	NH Industries NH.90-NFH	KLu 860 Sqn, De Kooij
	N-227	NH Industries NH.90-NFH	KLu 860 Sqn, De Kooij
	N-228	NH Industries NH.90-NFH	KLu 860 Sqn, De Kooij
	N-233	NH Industries NH.90-NFH	KLu 860 Sqn, De Kooij
	N-234	NH Industries NH.90-NFH	KLu 860 Sqn, De Kooij
	N-258	NH Industries NH.90-NFH	KLu 860 Sqn, De Kooij
	N-277	NH Industries NH.90-NFH	KLu 860 Sqn, De Kooij
	N-316	NH Industries NH.90-NFH	KLu 860 Sqn, De Kooij
	N-317	NH Industries NH.90-NFH	KLu 860 Sqn, De Kooij

Serial	Type (code/other identity)	Owner/operator, location or fate	Notes
N-318	NH Industries NH.90-NFH	KLu 860 Sqn, De Kooij	
N-319	NH Industries NH.90-NFH	KLu 860 Sqn, De Kooij	
N-324	NH Industries NH.90-NFH	KLu 860 Sqn, De Kooij	
N-325	NH Industries NH.90-NFH	KLu 860 Sqn, De Kooij	
N-326	NH Industries NH.90-NFH	KLu 860 Sqn, De Kooij	
N-327	NH Industries NH.90-NFH	KLu 860 Sqn, De Kooij	
Q-01	MDH AH-64D Apache Longbow	KLu 301 Sqn, Gilze-Rijen	
Q-02	MDH AH-64D Apache Longbow	KLu 302 Sqn, Fort Hood, Texas, USA	
Q-03	MDH AH-64D Apache Longbow	KLu 302 Sqn, Fort Hood, Texas, USA	
Q-04	MDH AH-64D Apache Longbow	KLu 301 Sqn, Gilze-Rijen	
Q-05	MDH AH-64D Apache Longbow	KLu 301 Sqn, Gilze-Rijen	
Q-06	MDH AH-64D Apache Longbow	KLu 302 Sqn, Fort Hood, Texas, USA	
Q-07	MDH AH-64D Apache Longbow	KLu 302 Sqn, Fort Hood, Texas, USA	
Q-08	MDH AH-64D Apache Longbow	KLu 301 Sqn, Gilze-Rijen	
Q-09	MDH AH-64D Apache Longbow	KLu 301 Sqn, Gilze-Rijen	
Q-10	MDH AH-64D Apache Longbow	KLu 301 Sqn, Gilze-Rijen	
Q-11	MDH AH-64D Apache Longbow	KLu 302 Sqn, Fort Hood, Texas, USA	
Q-12	MDH AH-64D Apache Longbow	KLu 302 Sqn, Fort Hood, Texas, USA	
Q-13	MDH AH-64D Apache Longbow	KLu 301 Sqn, Gilze-Rijen	
Q-14	MDH AH-64D Apache Longbow	KLu 301 Sqn, Gilze-Rijen	
Q-16	MDH AH-64D Apache Longbow	KLu 301 Sqn, Gilze-Rijen	
Q-17	MDH AH-64D Apache Longbow	KLu 301 Sqn, Gilze-Rijen	
Q-18	MDH AH-64D Apache Longbow	KLu 301 Sqn, Gilze-Rijen	
Q-19	MDH AH-64D Apache Longbow	KLu 301 Sqn, Gilze-Rijen	
Q-21	MDH AH-64D Apache Longbow	KLu 301 Sqn, Gilze-Rijen	
Q-22	MDH AH-64D Apache Longbow	KLu 301 Sqn, Gilze-Rijen	
Q-23	MDH AH-64D Apache Longbow	KLu 301 Sqn, Gilze-Rijen	
Q-24	MDH AH-64D Apache Longbow	KLu 301 Sqn, Gilze-Rijen	
Q-25	MDH AH-64D Apache Longbow	KLu 301 Sqn, Gilze-Rijen	
Q-26	MDH AH-64D Apache Longbow	KLu 301 Sqn, Gilze-Rijen	
Q-27	MDH AH-64D Apache Longbow	KLu 302 Sqn, Fort Hood, Texas, USA	
Q-28	MDH AH-64D Apache Longbow	KLu 302 Sqn, Fort Hood, Texas, USA	
Q-29	MDH AH-64D Apache Longbow	KLu 301 Sqn, Gilze-Rijen	
Q-30	MDH AH-64D Apache Longbow	KLu 301 Sqn, Gilze-Rijen	
S-419	Eurocopter AS.532U-2 Cougar	KLu 300 Sqn, Gilze-Rijen	
S-440	Eurocopter AS.532U-2 Cougar	KLu 300 Sqn, Gilze-Rijen	
S-441	Eurocopter AS.532U-2 Cougar	KLu 300 Sqn, Gilze-Rijen	
S-442	Eurocopter AS.532U-2 Cougar	KLu 300 Sqn, Gilze-Rijen	
S-444	Eurocopter AS.532U-2 Cougar	KLu 300 Sqn, Gilze-Rijen	
S-445	Eurocopter AS.532U-2 Cougar	KLu 300 Sqn, Gilze-Rijen	
S-447	Eurocopter AS.532U-2 Cougar	KLu 300 Sqn, Gilze-Rijen	
S-453	Eurocopter AS.532U-2 Cougar	KLu 300 Sqn, Gilze-Rijen	
S-454	Eurocopter AS.532U-2 Cougar	KLu 300 Sqn, Gilze-Rijen	
S-456	Eurocopter AS.532U-2 Cougar	KLu 300 Sqn, Gilze-Rijen	
S-457	Eurocopter AS.532U-2 Cougar	KLu, Woensdrecht (wfu)	
S-458	Eurocopter AS.532U-2 Cougar	KLu 300 Sqn, Gilze-Rijen	
S-459	Eurocopter AS.532U-2 Cougar	KLu 300 Sqn, Gilze-Rijen	
T-054	Airbus A.330-243 MRTT (KC-30) (EC-340/MRTT054)	KLu/MMF (or order)	
T-055	Airbus A.330-243 MRTT (KC-30) (EC-336/MRTT056)	KLu/MMF (or order)	
T-056	Airbus A.330-243 MRTT (KC-30)	KLu/MMF (or order)	
T-057	Airbus A.330-243 MRTT (KC-30)	KLu/MMF (or order)	
T-058	Airbus A.330-243 MRTT (KC-30)	KLu/MMF (or order)	
T-059	Airbus A.330-243 MRTT (KC-30)	KLu/MMF (or order)	
T-060	Airbus A.330-243 MRTT (KC-30)	KLu/MMF (or order)	
T-061	Airbus A.330-243 MRTT (KC-30)	KLu/MMF (or order)	
T-235	McDonnell Douglas KDC-10 $	KLu 334 Sqn, Eindhoven	
T-264	McDonnell Douglas KDC-10	*Sold as N264DE, February 2020*	
V-11	Grumman G.1159C Gulfstream IV	KLu 334 Sqn, Eindhoven	
Kustwacht & Netherlands Government			
PH-CGC	Dornier Do.228-212	Kustwacht, Amsterdam/Schiphol	
PH-CGN	Dornier Do.228-212	Kustwacht, Amsterdam/Schiphol	
PH-GOV	Boeing 737-700(BBJ) (N513BJ)	Dutch Royal Flight, Amsterdam/Schiphol	

Notes	Serial	Type (code/other identity)	Owner/operator, location or fate
	PH-KBX	Fokker 70	*Sold to Australia as VH-KBX, 2017*

NEW ZEALAND
Royal New Zealand Air Force (RNZAF)

Notes	Serial	Type (code/other identity)	Owner/operator, location or fate
	NZ4201	Lockheed P-3K2 Orion	RNZAF 5 Sqn, Whenuapai
	NZ4202	Lockheed P-3K2 Orion	RNZAF 5 Sqn, Whenuapai
	NZ4203	Lockheed P-3K2 Orion	RNZAF 5 Sqn, Whenuapai
	NZ4204	Lockheed P-3K2 Orion	RNZAF 5 Sqn, Whenuapai
	NZ4205	Lockheed P-3K2 Orion	RNZAF 5 Sqn, Whenuapai
	NZ4206	Lockheed P-3K2 Orion	RNZAF 5 Sqn, Whenuapai
	NZ7001	Lockheed C-130H(NZ) Hercules $	RNZAF 40 Sqn, Whenuapai
	NZ7002	Lockheed C-130H(NZ) Hercules	RNZAF 40 Sqn, Whenuapai
	NZ7003	Lockheed C-130H(NZ) Hercules	RNZAF 40 Sqn, Whenuapai
	NZ7004	Lockheed C-130H(NZ) Hercules	RNZAF 40 Sqn, Whenuapai
	NZ7005	Lockheed C-130H(NZ) Hercules	RNZAF 40 Sqn, Whenuapai
	NZ7571	Boeing 757-2K2	RNZAF 40 Sqn, Whenuapai
	NZ7572	Boeing 757-2K2	RNZAF 40 Sqn, Whenuapai

NIGER

Notes	Serial	Type (code/other identity)	Owner/operator, location or fate
	5U-GRN	Boeing 737-75U	Government of Niger, Niamey

NIGERIA
Nigerian Air Force (NAF)

Notes	Serial	Type (code/other identity)	Owner/operator, location or fate
	NAF-913	Lockheed C-130H Hercules	NAF 301 HAG, Ikeja
	NAF-917	Lockheed C-130H-30 Hercules	NAF 301 HAG, Ikeja
	NAF-918	Lockheed C-130H-30 Hercules	NAF, stored Ikeja
	NAF-961	Dassault Falcon 900	NAF 307 HAG, Minna

Nigerian Government

Notes	Serial	Type (code/other identity)	Owner/operator, location or fate
	5N-FGS	Gulfstream Aerospace Gulfstream V	Federal Government of Nigeria, Abuja
	5N-FGT	Boeing 737-7N6 [001]	Federal Government of Nigeria, Abuja
	5N-FGU	Dassault Falcon 7X	Federal Government of Nigeria, Abuja
	5N-FGV	Dassault Falcon 7X	Federal Government of Nigeria, Abuja
	5N-FGW	Gulfstream Aerospace G.550	Federal Government of Nigeria, Abuja
	5N-FGX	Hawker 4000 Horizon	Federal Government of Nigeria, Abuja

NORWAY
Luftforsvaret/Royal Norwegian Air Force (RNoAF)

Notes	Serial	Type (code/other identity)	Owner/operator, location or fate
	013	NH Industries NH.90-NFH (CSX81691)	RNoAF (on order)
	027	NH Industries NH.90-NFH (CSX81752)	RNoAF (on order)
	041	Dassault Falcon 20 ECM	RNoAF 717 Skv, Gardermoen
	049	NH Industries NH.90-NFH	RNoAF 337 Skv, Bardufoss
	053	Dassault Falcon 20 ECM	RNoAF 717 Skv, Gardermoen
	057	NH Industries NH.90-NFH	RNoAF 337 Skv, Bardufoss
	058	NH Industries NH.90-NFH	RNoAF 337 Skv, Bardufoss
	060	Westland Sea King Mk.43B	RNoAF 330 Skv Bodø/Banak/Ørland & Sola
	062	Westland Sea King Mk.43B	RNoAF 330 Skv Bodø/Banak/Ørland & Sola
	066	Westland Sea King Mk.43B	RNoAF 330 Skv Bodø/Banak/Ørland & Sola
	069	Westland Sea King Mk.43B	RNoAF 330 Skv Bodø/Banak/Ørland & Sola
	070	Westland Sea King Mk.43B	RNoAF 330 Skv Bodø/Banak/Ørland & Sola
	071	Westland Sea King Mk.43B	RNoAF 330 Skv Bodø/Banak/Ørland & Sola
	073	Westland Sea King Mk.43B	RNoAF 330 Skv Bodø/Banak/Ørland & Sola
	074	Westland Sea King Mk.43B	RNoAF 330 Skv Bodø/Banak/Ørland & Sola
	087	NH Industries NH.90-NFH (CSX81745)	RNoAF 337 Skv, Bardufoss
	139	Bell 412HP	RNoAF 339 Skv, Bardufoss
	140	Bell 412HP	RNoAF 339 Skv, Bardufoss
	141	Bell 412HP	RNoAF 339 Skv, Bardufoss
	142	Bell 412HP	RNoAF 339 Skv, Bardufoss
	143	Bell 412HP	RNoAF 339 Skv, Bardufoss
	144	Bell 412HP	RNoAF 339 Skv, Bardufoss
	145	Bell 412HP	RNoAF 339 Skv, Bardufoss
	146	Bell 412HP	RNoAF 339 Skv, Bardufoss
	147	Bell 412HP	RNoAF 339 Skv, Bardufoss

Serial	Type (code/other identity)	Owner/operator, location or fate	Notes
148	Bell 412HP	RNoAF 339 Skv, Bardufoss	
149	Bell 412HP	RNoAF 339 Skv, Bardufoss	
161	Bell 412HP	RNoAF 339 Skv, Bardufoss	
162	Bell 412HP	RNoAF 339 Skv, Bardufoss	
163	Bell 412HP	RNoAF 339 Skv, Bardufoss	
164	Bell 412HP	RNoAF 339 Skv, Bardufoss	
165	Bell 412HP	RNoAF 339 Skv, Bardufoss	
166	Bell 412HP	RNoAF 339 Skv, Bardufoss	
167	Bell 412HP	RNoAF 339 Skv, Bardufoss	
171	NH Industries NH.90-NFH	RNoAF 337 Skv, Bardufoss	
189	Westland Sea King Mk.43B	RNoAF 330 Skv Bodø/Banak/Ørland & Sola	
194	Bell 412SP	RNoAF 339 Skv, Bardufoss	
217	NH Industries NH.90-ASW (CSX81843)	RNoAF (on order)	
0262	AgustaWestland AW101 Mk.612 (ZZ100)	RNoAF (on order)	
0264	AgustaWestland AW101 Mk.612 (ZZ101)	RNoAF OT&E, Sola	
0265	AgustaWestland AW101 Mk.612 (ZZ102)	*To ZZ102, June 2019*	
0268	AgustaWestland AW101 Mk.612 (ZZ103)	RNoAF/Leonardo MW, Yeovil (rebuild)	
0270	AgustaWestland AW101 Mk.612 (ZZ104)	RNoAF OT&E, Sola	
272	Fokker (GD) F-16A MLU Fighting Falcon $	RNoAF 331 Skv, Bodø	
273	Fokker (GD) F-16A MLU Fighting Falcon	RNoAF 331 Skv, Bodø	
0273	AgustaWestland AW101 Mk.612 (ZZ105)	RNoAF OT&E, Sola	
275	Fokker (GD) F-16A MLU Fighting Falcon	RNoAF 331 Skv, Bodø	
0275	AgustaWestland AW101 Mk.612 (ZZ106)	RNoAF OT&E, Sola	
276	Fokker (GD) F-16A MLU Fighting Falcon	RNoAF 331 Skv, Bodø	
0276	AgustaWestland AW101 Mk.612 (ZZ107)	RNoAF (on order)	
277	Fokker (GD) F-16A MLU Fighting Falcon $	RNoAF 331 Skv, Bodø	
0277	AgustaWestland AW101 Mk.612 (ZZ108)	RNoAF (on order)	
0278	AgustaWestland AW101 Mk.612 (ZZ109)	RNoAF (on order)	
279	Fokker (GD) F-16A MLU Fighting Falcon	RNoAF 331 Skv, Bodø	
0279	AgustaWestland AW101 Mk.612 (ZZ110)	RNoAF (on order)	
0280	AgustaWestland AW101 Mk.612 (ZZ111)	RNoAF (on order)	
281	Fokker (GD) F-16A MLU Fighting Falcon	RNoAF 331 Skv, Bodø	
0281	AgustaWestland AW101 Mk.612 (ZZ112)	RNoAF (on order)	
282	Fokker (GD) F-16A MLU Fighting Falcon	RNoAF 331 Skv, Bodø	
0282	AgustaWestland AW101 Mk.612 (ZZ113)	RNoAF (on order)	
0283	AgustaWestland AW101 Mk.612 (ZZ114)	RNoAF (on order)	
284	Fokker (GD) F-16A MLU Fighting Falcon	RNoAF 331 Skv, Bodø	
0284	AgustaWestland AW101 Mk.612 (ZZ115)	RNoAF (on order)	
285	Fokker (GD) F-16A MLU Fighting Falcon	RNoAF 331 Skv, Bodø	
286	Fokker (GD) F-16A MLU Fighting Falcon	RNoAF 331 Skv, Bodø	
288	Fokker (GD) F-16A MLU Fighting Falcon	RNoAF 331 Skv, Bodø	
289	Fokker (GD) F-16A MLU Fighting Falcon	RNoAF 331 Skv, Bodø	
291	Fokker (GD) F-16A MLU Fighting Falcon	RNoAF 331 Skv, Bodø	
292	Fokker (GD) F-16A MLU Fighting Falcon	RNoAF 331 Skv, Bodø	
293	Fokker (GD) F-16A MLU Fighting Falcon	RNoAF 331 Skv, Bodø	
295	Fokker (GD) F-16A MLU Fighting Falcon	RNoAF 331 Skv, Bodø	
297	Fokker (GD) F-16A MLU Fighting Falcon	RNoAF 331 Skv, Bodø	
298	Fokker (GD) F-16A MLU Fighting Falcon $	RNoAF 331 Skv, Bodø	
299	Fokker (GD) F-16A MLU Fighting Falcon	RNoAF 331 Skv, Bodø	
302	Fokker (GD) F-16B MLU Fighting Falcon	RNoAF 331 Skv, Bodø	
304	Fokker (GD) F-16B MLU Fighting Falcon	RNoAF 331 Skv, Bodø	
305	Fokker (GD) F-16B MLU Fighting Falcon	RNoAF 331 Skv, Bodø	
306	Fokker (GD) F-16B MLU Fighting Falcon	RNoAF 331 Skv, Bodø	
322	Westland Sea King Mk.43B (ZH566)	RNoAF 330 Skv Bodø/Banak/Ørland & Sola	
329	Westland Sea King Mk.43B (ZJ162)	RNoAF 330 Skv Bodø/Banak/Ørland & Sola	
330	Westland Sea King Mk.43B (ZJ163)	*Withdrawn from use, September 2019*	
352	NH Industries NH.90-ASW	RNoAF 334 Skv, Haakonsvern	
353	NH Industries NH.90-ASW	RNoAF 334 Skv, Haakonsvern	
354	NH Industries NH.90-ASW	RNoAF 334 Skv, Haakonsvern	
358	NH Industries NH.90-NFH	RNoAF 337 Skv, Bardufoss	
658	Fokker (GD) F-16A MLU Fighting Falcon	RNoAF 331 Skv, Bodø	
659	Fokker (GD) F-16A MLU Fighting Falcon	RNoAF 331 Skv, Bodø	

Notes	Serial	Type (code/other identity)	Owner/operator, location or fate
	660	Fokker (GD) F-16A MLU Fighting Falcon	RNoAF 331 Skv, Bodø
	661	Fokker (GD) F-16A MLU Fighting Falcon	RNoAF 331 Skv, Bodø
	662	Fokker (GD) F-16A MLU Fighting Falcon	RNoAF 331 Skv, Bodø
	663	Fokker (GD) F-16A MLU Fighting Falcon	RNoAF 331 Skv, Bodø
	664	Fokker (GD) F-16A MLU Fighting Falcon $	RNoAF 331 Skv, Bodø
	665	Fokker (GD) F-16A MLU Fighting Falcon	RNoAF 331 Skv, Bodø
	666	Fokker (GD) F-16A MLU Fighting Falcon	RNoAF/USAF 416th FTS/412th TW, Edwards AFB, USA
	667	Fokker (GD) F-16A MLU Fighting Falcon	RNoAF 331 Skv, Bodø
	668	Fokker (GD) F-16A MLU Fighting Falcon	RNoAF 331 Skv, Bodø
	670	Fokker (GD) F-16A MLU Fighting Falcon	RNoAF 331 Skv, Bodø
	671	Fokker (GD) F-16A MLU Fighting Falcon $	RNoAF 331 Skv, Bodø
	672	Fokker (GD) F-16A MLU Fighting Falcon	RNoAF 331 Skv, Bodø
	673	Fokker (GD) F-16A MLU Fighting Falcon	RNoAF 331 Skv, Bodø
	674	Fokker (GD) F-16A MLU Fighting Falcon	RNoAF 331 Skv, Bodø
	675	Fokker (GD) F-16A MLU Fighting Falcon	RNoAF 331 Skv, Bodø
	677	Fokker (GD) F-16A MLU Fighting Falcon	RNoAF 331 Skv, Bodø
	678	Fokker (GD) F-16A MLU Fighting Falcon	RNoAF 331 Skv, Bodø
	680	Fokker (GD) F-16A MLU Fighting Falcon	RNoAF 331 Skv, Bodø
	681	Fokker (GD) F-16A MLU Fighting Falcon	RNoAF 331 Skv, Bodø
	682	Fokker (GD) F-16A MLU Fighting Falcon	RNoAF 331 Skv, Bodø
	683	Fokker (GD) F-16A MLU Fighting Falcon	RNoAF 331 Skv, Bodø
	686	Fokker (GD) F-16A MLU Fighting Falcon $	RNoAF 331 Skv, Bodø
	687	Fokker (GD) F-16A MLU Fighting Falcon	RNoAF 331 Skv, Bodø
	688	Fokker (GD) F-16A MLU Fighting Falcon	RNoAF 331 Skv, Bodø
	689	Fokker (GD) F-16B MLU Fighting Falcon	RNoAF 331 Skv, Bodø
	691	Fokker (GD) F-16B MLU Fighting Falcon [FN-K] $	RNoAF 331 Skv, Bodø
	692	Fokker (GD) F-16B MLU Fighting Falcon $	RNoAF 331 Skv, Bodø
	693	Fokker (GD) F-16B MLU Fighting Falcon	RNoAF 331 Skv, Bodø
	711	GD F-16B MLU Fighting Falcon	RNoAF 331 Skv, Bodø
	1216	NH Industries NH.90-NFH (CSX81751)	RNoAF 337 Skv, Bardufoss
	3296	Lockheed P-3C UIP Orion	RNoAF 333 Skv, Andøya
	3297	Lockheed P-3C UIP Orion	RNoAF 333 Skv, Andøya
	3298	Lockheed P-3C UIP Orion	RNoAF 333 Skv, Andøya
	3299	Lockheed P-3C UIP Orion	RNoAF 333 Skv, Andøya
	4576	Lockheed P-3N Orion	RNoAF 333 Skv, Andøya
	5087	Lockheed Martin F-35A Lightning II	RNoAF 62nd FS/56th FW, Luke AFB, AZ, USA
	5088	Lockheed Martin F-35A Lightning II	RNoAF 62nd FS/56th FW, Luke AFB, AZ, USA
	5110	Lockheed Martin F-35A Lightning II	RNoAF 62nd FS/56th FW, Luke AFB, AZ, USA
	5111	Lockheed Martin F-35A Lightning II	RNoAF 62nd FS/56th FW, Luke AFB, AZ, USA
	5145	Lockheed Martin F-35A Lightning II	RNoAF 62nd FS/56th FW, Luke AFB, AZ, USA
	5146	Lockheed Martin F-35A Lightning II	RNoAF 62nd FS/56th FW, Luke AFB, AZ, USA
	5147	Lockheed Martin F-35A Lightning II	RNoAF 62nd FS/56th FW, Luke AFB, AZ, USA
	5148	Lockheed Martin F-35A Lightning II	RNoAF 332 Skv, Ørland
	5149	Lockheed Martin F-35A Lightning II	RNoAF 332 Skv, Ørland
	5150	Lockheed Martin F-35A Lightning II	RNoAF 332 Skv, Ørland
	5205	Lockheed Martin F-35A Lightning II	RNoAF 332 Skv, Ørland
	5206	Lockheed Martin F-35A Lightning II	RNoAF 332 Skv, Ørland
	5207	Lockheed Martin F-35A Lightning II	RNoAF 332 Skv, Ørland
	5208	Lockheed Martin F-35A Lightning II	RNoAF 332 Skv, Ørland
	5209	Lockheed Martin F-35A Lightning II	RNoAF 332 Skv, Ørland
	5210	Lockheed Martin F-35A Lightning II	RNoAF 332 Skv, Ørland
	5288	Lockheed Martin F-35A Lightning II	RNoAF 332 Skv, Ørland
	5289	Lockheed Martin F-35A Lightning II	RNoAF 332 Skv, Ørland
	5290	Lockheed Martin F-35A Lightning II	RNoAF 332 Skv, Ørland
	5291	Lockheed Martin F-35A Lightning II	RNoAF 332 Skv, Ørland
	5292	Lockheed Martin F-35A Lightning II	RNoAF 332 Skv, Ørland
	5293	Lockheed Martin F-35A Lightning II	RNoAF 332 Skv, Ørland
	5601	Lockheed C-130J-30 Hercules II	RNoAF 335 Skv, Gardermoen
	5607	Lockheed C-130J-30 Hercules II	RNoAF 335 Skv, Gardermoen
	5629	Lockheed C-130J-30 Hercules II	RNoAF 335 Skv, Gardermoen
	5699	Lockheed C-130J-30 Hercules II	RNoAF 335 Skv, Gardermoen

Serial	Type (code/other identity)	Owner/operator, location or fate	Notes
6603	Lockheed P-3N Orion	RNoAF 333 Skv, Andøya	
....	Lockheed Martin F-35A Lightning II	RNoAF (on order)	
....	Lockheed Martin F-35A Lightning II	RNoAF (on order)	
....	Lockheed Martin F-35A Lightning II	RNoAF (on order)	
....	Lockheed Martin F-35A Lightning II	RNoAF (on order)	
....	Lockheed Martin F-35A Lightning II	RNoAF (on order)	
...	NH Industries NH.90-NFH	RNoAF (on order)	
...	NH Industries NH.90-NFH	RNoAF (on order)	

OMAN
Royal Air Force of Oman (RAFO)

501	Lockheed C-130H Hercules	RAFO 16 Sqn, Al Musana	
502	Lockheed C-130H Hercules	RAFO 16 Sqn, Al Musana	
503	Lockheed C-130H Hercules	RAFO 16 Sqn, Al Musana	
505	Lockheed C-130J Hercules II	RAFO 16 Sqn, Al Musana	
506	Lockheed C-130J Hercules II	RAFO 16 Sqn, Al Musana	
507	Lockheed C-130J-30 Hercules II	RAFO (on order)	
508	Lockheed C-130J-30 Hercules II	RAFO (on order)	
525	Lockheed C-130J-30 Hercules II	RAFO Royal Flt, Seeb	
554	Airbus A.320-214X	RAFO 4 Sqn, Seeb	
555	Airbus A.320-214X	RAFO 4 Sqn, Seeb	
556	Airbus A.320-214X	RAFO 4 Sqn, Seeb	
557	Grumman G.1159C Gulfstream IV	RAFO 4 Sqn, Seeb	
558	Grumman G.1159C Gulfstream IV	RAFO 4 Sqn, Seeb	
901	CASA C-295M	RAFO 5 Sqn, Salalah	
902	CASA C-295M	RAFO 5 Sqn, Salalah	
903	CASA C-295M	RAFO 5 Sqn, Salalah	
904	CASA C-295M	RAFO 5 Sqn, Salalah	
905	CASA C-295M	RAFO (on order)	
906	CASA C-295M	RAFO (on order)	
907	CASA C-295M	RAFO (on order)	
908	CASA C-295M	RAFO (on order)	
909	CASA C-295M	RAFO (on order)	
910	CASA C-295MPA Persuader	RAFO 2 Sqn, Al Musana	
911	CASA C-295MPA Persuader	RAFO 2 Sqn, Al Musana	
912	CASA C-295MPA Persuader	RAFO 2 Sqn, Al Musana	
913	CASA C-295MPA Persuader	RAFO 2 Sqn, Al Musana	
914	CASA C-295MPA Persuader	RAFO (on order)	
915	CASA C-295MPA Persuader	RAFO (on order)	
916	CASA C-295MPA Persuader	RAFO (on order)	

Omani Government

A4O-AA	Airbus A.320-233	Government of Oman, Seeb	
A4O-AD	Gulfstream Aerospace G.550	Government of Oman, Seeb	
A4O-AE	Gulfstream Aerospace G.550	Government of Oman, Seeb	
A4O-AJ	Airbus A.319-115CJ	Government of Oman, Seeb	
A4O-SO	Boeing 747SP-27	Government of Oman, Seeb	
A4O-HMS	Boeing 747-8H0	Government of Oman, Seeb	
A4O-OMN	Boeing 747-430	Government of Oman, Seeb	

PAKISTAN
Pakistan Air Force (PAF)/Pakistani Army

4119	Lockheed C-130E Hercules [119]	PAF 21 Sqn, Karachi	
4144	Lockheed L.100 Hercules [144]	PAF 6 Sqn, Islamabad	
4148	Lockheed C-130E Hercules [148]	PAF 6 Sqn, Islamabad	
4153	Lockheed C-130E Hercules [153] $	PAF 21 Sqn, Karachi	
4159	Lockheed C-130E Hercules [159]	PAF 21 Sqn, Karachi	
4171	Lockheed C-130E Hercules [171]	PAF 6 Sqn, Islamabad	
4177	Lockheed C-130E Hercules [177]	PAF 6 Sqn, Islamabad	
4178	Lockheed C-130E Hercules [178]	PAF 21 Sqn, Karachi	
4189	Lockheed C-130E Hercules [189]	PAF 6 Sqn, Islamabad	
4270	Gulfstream Aerospace G.450	Pakistani Army, Rawalpindi	
4282	Lockheed C-130E Hercules [282]	PAF 6 Sqn, Islamabad	

Notes	Serial	Type (code/other identity)	Owner/operator, location or fate
	EYE77	Bombardier Challenger 605	Pakistani Army, Rawalpindi
	J-754	Cessna 560 Citation VI	PAF 12 VIP Communications Sqn, Islamabad
	J-755	Gulfstream Aerospace G.1159C Gulfstream IV-SP	PAF 12 VIP Communications Sqn, Islamabad
	J-756	Gulfstream Aerospace G.450	PAF 12 VIP Communications Sqn, Islamabad

POLAND

Sily Powietrzne (SP)/Polish Air Force & Lotnictwo Marynarki Wojennej (LMW)/Polish Navy

Notes	Serial	Type (code/other identity)	Owner/operator, location or fate
	0001	Gulfstream Aerospace G.550 (N547GA)	SP 1.BLTr, Warszawa
	0002	Gulfstream Aerospace G.550 (N554GD)	SP 1.BLTr, Warszawa
	011	CASA C-295M	SP 13.eltr/8.BLTr, Kraków/Balice
	012	CASA C-295M $	SP 13.eltr/8.BLTr, Kraków/Balice
	013	CASA C-295M	SP 13.eltr/8.BLTr, Kraków/Balice
	014	CASA C-295M	SP 13.eltr/8.BLTr, Kraków/Balice
	015	CASA C-295M	SP 13.eltr/8.BLTr, Kraków/Balice
	15	Mikoyan MiG-29UBM $	SP 1.elt/23.BLT, Minsk/Mazowiecki
	016	CASA C-295M	SP 13.eltr/8.BLTr, Kraków/Balice
	016	PZL 130TC-I Orlik	SP 2.OSzL/42.BLSz, Radom
	017	CASA C-295M	SP 13.eltr/8.BLTr, Kraków/Balice
	018	CASA C-295M	SP 13.eltr/8.BLTr, Kraków/Balice
	020	CASA C-295M	SP 13.eltr/8.BLTr, Kraków/Balice
	021	CASA C-295M	SP 13.eltr/8.BLTr, Kraków/Balice
	022	CASA C-295M	SP 13.eltr/8.BLTr, Kraków/Balice
	023	CASA C-295M	SP 13.eltr/8.BLTr, Kraków/Balice
	024	CASA C-295M	SP 13.eltr/8.BLTr, Kraków/Balice
	025	CASA C-295M	SP 13.eltr/8.BLTr, Kraków/Balice
	026	CASA C-295M	SP 13.eltr/8.BLTr, Kraków/Balice
	027	CASA C-295M	SP 13.eltr/8.BLTr, Kraków/Balice
	28	Mikoyan MiG-29UBM	SP 1.elt/23.BLT, Minsk/Mazowiecki
	029	PZL 130TC-II Orlik	SP 2.OSzL/42.BLSz, Radom
	030	PZL 130TC-II Orlik	SP 2.OSzL/42.BLSz, Radom
	031	PZL 130TC-II Orlik	SP 2.OSzL/42.BLSz, Radom
	032	PZL 130TC-II Orlik	SP 2.OSzL/42.BLSz, Radom
	037	PZL 130TC-II Orlik	SP 2.OSzL/42.BLSz, Radom
	38	Mikoyan MiG-29M	SP 1.elt/23.BLT, Minsk/Mazowiecki
	038	PZL 130TC-II Orlik	SP 2.OSzL/42.BLSz, Radom
	040	PZL 130TC-II Orlik	SP 2.OSzL/42.BLSz, Radom
	041	PZL 130TC-II Orlik	SP 2.OSzL/42.BLSz, Radom
	42	Mikoyan MiG-29UBM	SP 1.elt/23.BLT, Minsk/Mazowiecki
	042	PZL 130TC-II Orlik	SP 2.OSzL/42.BLSz, Radom
	043	PZL 130TC-II Orlik	SP 2.OSzL/42.BLSz, Radom
	045	PZL 130TC-I Orlik	SP 2.OSzL/42.BLSz, Radom
	047	PZL 130TC-II Orlik	SP 2.OSzL/42.BLSz, Radom
	048	PZL 130TC-II Orlik	SP 2.OSzL/42.BLSz, Radom
	049	PZL 130TC-II Orlik	SP 2.OSzL/42.BLSz, Radom
	050	PZL 130TC-II Orlik	SP 2.OSzL/42.BLSz, Radom
	051	PZL 130TC-II Orlik	SP 2.OSzL/42.BLSz, Radom
	052	PZL 130TC-II Orlik	SP 2.OSzL/42.BLSz, Radom
	54	Mikoyan MiG-29M	SP 1.elt/23.BLT, Minsk/Mazowiecki
	56	Mikoyan MiG-29M	SP 1.elt/23.BLT, Minsk/Mazowiecki
	59	Mikoyan MiG-29M	SP 1.elt/23.BLT, Minsk/Mazowiecki
	64	Mikoyan MiG-29UB	SP
	65	Mikoyan MiG-29A	SP 41.elt/22.BLT, Malbork
	66	Mikoyan MiG-29A	SP 41.elt/22.BLT, Malbork
	70	Mikoyan MiG-29A	SP 41.elt/22.BLT, Malbork
	83	Mikoyan MiG-29M	SP 1.elt/23.BLT, Minsk/Mazowiecki
	89	Mikoyan MiG-29M	SP 1.elt/23.BLT, Minsk/Mazowiecki
	92	Mikoyan MiG-29A	SP 41.elt/22.BLT, Malbork
	105	Mikoyan MiG-29M	SP 1.elt/23.BLT, Minsk/Mazowiecki
	108	Mikoyan MiG-29M	SP 1.elt/23.BLT, Minsk/Mazowiecki
	0110	Boeing 737-800 (N893BA)	SP 1.BLTr, Warszawa
	111	Mikoyan MiG-29M	SP 1.elt/23.BLT, Minsk/Mazowiecki
	0111	Boeing 737-800 (N784BJ)	SP (on order)

Serial	Type (code/other identity)	Owner/operator, location or fate	Notes
0112	Boeing 737-800 (N785BJ)	SP (on order)	
114	Mikoyan MiG-29M	SP 1.elt/23.BLT, Minsk/Mazowiecki	
115	Mikoyan MiG-29AM	SP 1.elt/23.BLT, Minsk/Mazowiecki	
0204	PZL M28B-TD Bryza	SP 1.OSzL/41.BLSz, Deblin	
0205	PZL M28B-TD Bryza	SP 1.OSzL/41.BLSz, Deblin	
0206	PZL M28B-TD Bryza	SP 14.eltr/33.BLTr, Powidz	
0207	PZL M28B-TD Bryza	SP 13.eltr/8.BLTr, Kraków/Balice	
0208	PZL M28B-TD Bryza	SP 14.eltr/33.BLTr, Powidz	
0209	PZL M28B-TD Bryza	SP 14.eltr/33.BLTr, Powidz	
0210	PZL M28B-TD Bryza	SP 14.eltr/33.BLTr, Powidz	
0211	PZL M28B-TD Bryza	SP 14.eltr/33.BLTr, Powidz	
0212	PZL M28B-TD Bryza	SP 13.eltr/8.BLTr, Kraków/Balice	
0213	PZL M28B/PT Bryza	SP 13.eltr/8.BLTr, Kraków/Balice	
0214	PZL M28B/PT Bryza	SP 13.eltr/8.BLTr, Kraków/Balice	
0215	PZL M28B/PT Bryza	SP 13.eltr/8.BLTr, Kraków/Balice	
0216	PZL M28B/PT Bryza	SP 13.eltr/8.BLTr, Kraków/Balice	
0217	PZL M28B/PT Bryza	SP 13.eltr/8.BLTr, Kraków/Balice	
0218	PZL M28B/PT Bryza	SP 13.eltr/8.BLTr, Kraków/Balice	
0219	PZL M28B/PT Bryza	SP 13.eltr/8.BLTr, Kraków/Balice	
0220	PZL M28B/PT Bryza	SP 13.eltr/8.BLTr, Kraków/Balice	
0221	PZL M28B/PT Bryza	SP 13.eltr/8.BLTr, Kraków/Balice	
0222	PZL M28B/PT Bryza	SP 13.eltr/8.BLTr, Kraków/Balice	
0223	PZL M28B/PT Bryza	SP 13.eltr/8.BLTr, Kraków/Balice	
0224	PZL M28B/PT Bryza	SP 13.eltr/8.BLTr, Kraków/Balice	
0225	PZL M28B/PT Bryza	SP 13.eltr/8.BLTr, Kraków/Balice	
305	Sukhoi Su-22UM-3K $	SP 8.elt/21.BLT, Swidwin	
308	Sukhoi Su-22UM-3K	SP 40.elt/21.BLT, Swidwin	
310	Sukhoi Su-22UM-3K	SP 40.elt/21.BLT, Swidwin	
0404	PZL M28B-1E Bryza	LMW 30.el/44.BLMW, Cewice/Siemirowice	
0405	PZL M28B-1E Bryza	LMW 30.el/44.BLMW, Cewice/Siemirowice	
508	Sukhoi Su-22UM-3K	SP 8.elt/21.BLT, Swidwin	
509	Sukhoi Su-22UM-3K	SP 40.elt/21.BLT, Swidwin	
707	Sukhoi Su-22UM-3K $	SP 8.elt/21.BLT, Swidwin	
0723	PZL M28B-TD Bryza	LMW 28.el/43.BLMW, Gdynia/Babie Doly	
0810	PZL M28B-1RM Bryza	LMW 30.el/44.BLMW, Cewice/Siemirowice	
1001	Mil Mi-14PL	LMW 29.el/44.BLMW, Darlowo	
1002	Mil Mi-14PL	LMW 29.el/44.BLMW, Darlowo	
1003	Mil Mi-14PL	LMW 29.el/44.BLMW, Darlowo	
1003	PZL M28B-TD Bryza	LMW 28.el/43.BLMW, Gdynia/Babie Doly	
1005	Mil Mi-14PL	LMW 29.el/44.BLMW, Darlowo	
1006	PZL M28B-1R Bryza	LMW 30.el/44.BLMW, Cewice/Siemirowice	
1007	Mil Mi-14PL	LMW 29.el/44.BLMW, Darlowo	
1008	Mil Mi-14PL	LMW 29.el/44.BLMW, Darlowo	
1008	PZL M28B-1R Bryza	LMW 30.el/44.BLMW, Cewice/Siemirowice	
1009	Mil Mi-14PL	LMW 29.el/44.BLMW, Darlowo	
1010	Mil Mi-14PL	LMW 29.el/44.BLMW, Darlowo	
1011	Mil Mi-14PL	LMW 29.el/44.BLMW, Darlowo	
1012	Mil Mi-14PL/R	LMW 29.el/44.BLMW, Darlowo	
1017	PZL M28B-1R Bryza $	LMW 30.el/44.BLMW, Cewice/Siemirowice	
1022	PZL M28B-1R Bryza	LMW 30.el/44.BLMW, Cewice/Siemirowice	
1114	PZL M28B-1R Bryza	LMW 30.el/44.BLMW, Cewice/Siemirowice	
1115	PZL M28B-1R Bryza	LMW 30.el/44.BLMW, Cewice/Siemirowice	
1116	PZL M28B-1R Bryza	LMW 30.el/44.BLMW, Cewice/Siemirowice	
1117	PZL M28B-1 Bryza	LMW 28.el/43.BLMW, Gdynia/Babie Doly	
1118	PZL M28B-1 Bryza	LMW 28.el/43.BLMW, Gdynia/Babie Doly	
1501	Lockheed C-130E Hercules	SP 14.eltr/33.BLTr, Powidz	
1502	Lockheed C-130E Hercules	SP 14.eltr/33.BLTr, Powidz	
1503	Lockheed C-130E Hercules	SP 14.eltr/33.BLTr, Powidz	
1504	Lockheed C-130E Hercules	SP 14.eltr/33.BLTr, Powidz	
1505	Lockheed C-130E Hercules $	SP 14.eltr/33.BLTr, Powidz	
3201	Sukhoi Su-22M-4	SP 8.elt/21.BLT, Swidwin	
3304	Sukhoi Su-22M-4	SP 8.elt/21.BLT, Swidwin	

Notes	Serial	Type (code/other identity)	Owner/operator, location or fate
	3612	Sukhoi Su-22M-4	SP 40.elt/21.BLT, Swidwin
	3713	Sukhoi Su-22M-4 $	SP 40.elt/21.BLT, Swidwin
	3715	Sukhoi Su-22M-4	SP 40.elt/21.BLT, Swidwin
	3816	Sukhoi Su-22M-4	SP 40.elt/21.BLT, Swidwin
	3817	Sukhoi Su-22M-4	SP 40.elt/21.BLT, Swidwin
	3819	Sukhoi Su-22M-4	SP 8.elt/21.BLT, Swidwin
	3920	Sukhoi Su-22M-4	SP 40.elt/21.BLT, Swidwin
	4040	Lockheed Martin F-16C-52 Fighting Falcon	SP/USAF 416th FTS/412th TW, Edwards AFB, USA
	4041	Lockheed Martin F-16C-52 Fighting Falcon	SP 6.elt/31.BLT, Poznan/Krzesiny
	4042	Lockheed Martin F-16C-52 Fighting Falcon	SP 3.elt/31.BLT, Poznan/Krzesiny
	4043	Lockheed Martin F-16C-52 Fighting Falcon	SP 3.elt/31.BLT, Poznan/Krzesiny
	4044	Lockheed Martin F-16C-52 Fighting Falcon	SP 3.elt/31.BLT, Poznan/Krzesiny
	4045	Lockheed Martin F-16C-52 Fighting Falcon	SP 3.elt/31.BLT, Poznan/Krzesiny
	4046	Lockheed Martin F-16C-52 Fighting Falcon	SP 3.elt/31.BLT, Poznan/Krzesiny
	4047	Lockheed Martin F-16C-52 Fighting Falcon	SP 3.elt/31.BLT, Poznan/Krzesiny
	4048	Lockheed Martin F-16C-52 Fighting Falcon	SP 3.elt/31.BLT, Poznan/Krzesiny
	4049	Lockheed Martin F-16C-52 Fighting Falcon	SP 3.elt/31.BLT, Poznan/Krzesiny
	4050	Lockheed Martin F-16C-52 Fighting Falcon	SP 3.elt/31.BLT, Poznan/Krzesiny
	4051	Lockheed Martin F-16C-52 Fighting Falcon	SP 3.elt/31.BLT, Poznan/Krzesiny
	4052	Lockheed Martin F-16C-52 Fighting Falcon $	SP 6.elt/31.BLT, Poznan/Krzesiny
	4053	Lockheed Martin F-16C-52 Fighting Falcon	SP 6.elt/31.BLT, Poznan/Krzesiny
	4054	Lockheed Martin F-16C-52 Fighting Falcon	SP 6.elt/31.BLT, Poznan/Krzesiny
	4055	Lockheed Martin F-16C-52 Fighting Falcon $	SP 6.elt/31.BLT, Poznan/Krzesiny
	4056	Lockheed Martin F-16C-52 Fighting Falcon	SP 6.elt/31.BLT, Poznan/Krzesiny
	4057	Lockheed Martin F-16C-52 Fighting Falcon	SP 6.elt/31.BLT, Poznan/Krzesiny
	4058	Lockheed Martin F-16C-52 Fighting Falcon $	SP 6.elt/31.BLT, Poznan/Krzesiny
	4059	Lockheed Martin F-16C-52 Fighting Falcon	SP 6.elt/31.BLT, Poznan/Krzesiny
	4060	Lockheed Martin F-16C-52 Fighting Falcon	SP 6.elt/31.BLT, Poznan/Krzesiny
	4061	Lockheed Martin F-16C-52 Fighting Falcon	SP 6.elt/31.BLT, Poznan/Krzesiny
	4062	Lockheed Martin F-16C-52 Fighting Falcon $	SP 6.elt/31.BLT, Poznan/Krzesiny
	4063	Lockheed Martin F-16C-52 Fighting Falcon	SP 10.elt/32.BLT, Lask
	4064	Lockheed Martin F-16C-52 Fighting Falcon	SP 10.elt/32.BLT, Lask
	4065	Lockheed Martin F-16C-52 Fighting Falcon	SP 10.elt/32.BLT, Lask
	4066	Lockheed Martin F-16C-52 Fighting Falcon	SP 10.elt/32.BLT, Lask
	4067	Lockheed Martin F-16C-52 Fighting Falcon	SP 10.elt/32.BLT, Lask
	4068	Lockheed Martin F-16C-52 Fighting Falcon	SP 10.elt/32.BLT, Lask
	4069	Lockheed Martin F-16C-52 Fighting Falcon	SP 10.elt/32.BLT, Lask
	4070	Lockheed Martin F-16C-52 Fighting Falcon	SP 10.elt/32.BLT, Lask
	4071	Lockheed Martin F-16C-52 Fighting Falcon	SP 10.elt/32.BLT, Lask
	4072	Lockheed Martin F-16C-52 Fighting Falcon	SP 10.elt/32.BLT, Lask
	4073	Lockheed Martin F-16C-52 Fighting Falcon	SP 10.elt/32.BLT, Lask
	4074	Lockheed Martin F-16C-52 Fighting Falcon	SP 10.elt/32.BLT, Lask
	4075	Lockheed Martin F-16C-52 Fighting Falcon	SP 10.elt/32.BLT, Lask
	4076	Lockheed Martin F-16D-52 Fighting Falcon	SP 3.elt/31.BLT, Poznan/Krzesiny
	4077	Lockheed Martin F-16D-52 Fighting Falcon	SP 3.elt/31.BLT, Poznan/Krzesiny
	4078	Lockheed Martin F-16D-52 Fighting Falcon	SP 3.elt/31.BLT, Poznan/Krzesiny
	4079	Lockheed Martin F-16D-52 Fighting Falcon	SP 3.elt/31.BLT, Poznan/Krzesiny
	4080	Lockheed Martin F-16D-52 Fighting Falcon	SP 3.elt/31.BLT, Poznan/Krzesiny
	4081	Lockheed Martin F-16D-52 Fighting Falcon	SP 3.elt/31.BLT, Poznan/Krzesiny
	4082	Lockheed Martin F-16D-52 Fighting Falcon $	SP 6.elt/31.BLT, Poznan/Krzesiny
	4083	Lockheed Martin F-16D-52 Fighting Falcon	SP 6.elt/31.BLT, Poznan/Krzesiny
	4084	Lockheed Martin F-16D-52 Fighting Falcon $	SP 6.elt/31.BLT, Poznan/Krzesiny
	4085	Lockheed Martin F-16D-52 Fighting Falcon	SP 10.elt/32.BLT, Lask
	4086	Lockheed Martin F-16D-52 Fighting Falcon	SP 10.elt/32.BLT, Lask
	4087	Lockheed Martin F-16D-52 Fighting Falcon	SP 10.elt/32.BLT, Lask
	4101	Mikoyan MiG-29A	SP 41.elt/22.BLT, Malbork
	4104	Mikoyan MiG-29A	SP 41.elt/22.BLT, Malbork
	4105	Mikoyan MiG-29A	SP 1.elt/23.BLT, Minsk/Mazowiecki
	4110	Mikoyan MiG-29UB	SP 41.elt/22.BLT, Malbork
	4113	Mikoyan MiG-29A	SP 41.elt/22.BLT, Malbork
	4116	Mikoyan MiG-29A	SP 41.elt/22.BLT, Malbork
	4120	Mikoyan MiG-29A	SP 41.elt/22.BLT, Malbork

Serial	Type (code/other identity)	Owner/operator, location or fate	Notes
4121	Mikoyan MiG-29A	SP 41.elt/22.BLT, Malbork	
4122	Mikoyan MiG-29A	SP 41.elt/22.BLT, Malbork	
4123	Mikoyan MiG-29UB	SP 41.elt/22.BLT, Malbork	
7701	Aermacchi M-346 Master (CSX55209)	SP 1.OSzL/41.BLSz, Deblin	
7702	Aermacchi M-346 Master (CSX55210)	SP 1.OSzL/41.BLSz, Deblin	
7703	Aermacchi M-346 Master (CSX55211)	SP 1.OSzL/41.BLSz, Deblin	
7704	Aermacchi M-346 Master (CSX55212)	SP 1.OSzL/41.BLSz, Deblin	
7705	Aermacchi M-346 Master (MM55225)	SP 1.OSzL/41.BLSz, Deblin	
7706	Aermacchi M-346 Master (MM55226)	SP 1.OSzL/41.BLSz, Deblin	
7707	Aermacchi M-346 Master (MT55227)	SP 1.OSzL/41.BLSz, Deblin	
7708	Aermacchi M-346 Master (CSX55228)	SP 1.OSzL/41.BLSz, Deblin	
7709	Aermacchi M-346 Master (CSX55238)	SP 1.OSzL/41.BLSz, Deblin	
7710	Aermacchi M-346 Master	SP (on order)	
7711	Aermacchi M-346 Master	SP (on order)	
7712	Aermacchi M-346 Master	SP (on order)	
8101	Sukhoi Su-22M-4	SP 40.elt/21.BLT, Swidwin	
8205	Sukhoi Su-22M-4	SP 40.elt/21.BLT, Swidwin	
8309	Sukhoi Su-22M-4	SP 40.elt/21.BLT, Swidwin	
....	AgustaWestland AW101	SP (on order)	
....	AgustaWestland AW101	SP (on order)	
....	AgustaWestland AW101	SP (on order)	
....	AgustaWestland AW101	SP (on order)	
Straz Graniczna (Polish Border Guard)			
SN-50YG	PZL M28-05 Skytruck	Straz Graniczna, Gdansk/Rebiechowo	
SN-60YG	PZL M28-05 Skytruck	Straz Graniczna, Gdansk/Rebiechowo	
Polish Government			
SP-LIG	Embraer EMB.175-200LR	Polish Government, Warszawa	
SP-LIH	Embraer EMB.175-200LR	Polish Government, Warszawa	
PORTUGAL			
Força Aérea Portuguesa (FAP)/Marinha			
11401	Aérospatiale TB-30 Epsilon	FAP Esq 101, Beja	
11402	Aérospatiale TB-30 Epsilon $	FAP Esq 101, Beja	
11403	Aérospatiale TB-30 Epsilon	FAP Esq 101, Beja	
11404	Aérospatiale TB-30 Epsilon	FAP Esq 101, Beja	
11405	Aérospatiale TB-30 Epsilon $	FAP Esq 101, Beja	
11406	Aérospatiale TB-30 Epsilon	FAP Esq 101, Beja	
11407	Aérospatiale TB-30 Epsilon	FAP Esq 101, Beja	
11410	Aérospatiale TB-30 Epsilon $	FAP Esq 101, Beja	
11411	Aérospatiale TB-30 Epsilon	FAP Esq 101, Beja	
11413	Aérospatiale TB-30 Epsilon	FAP Esq 101, Beja	
11414	Aérospatiale TB-30 Epsilon	FAP Esq 101, Beja	
11415	Aérospatiale TB-30 Epsilon	FAP Esq 101, Beja	
11416	Aérospatiale TB-30 Epsilon $	FAP, stored Beja	
11417	Aérospatiale TB-30 Epsilon	FAP Esq 101, Beja	
11418	Aérospatiale TB-30 Epsilon	FAP Esq 101, Beja	
14807	Lockheed P-3C CUP+ Orion	FAP Esq 601, Beja	
14808	Lockheed P-3C CUP+ Orion $	FAP Esq 601, Beja	
14809	Lockheed P-3C CUP+ Orion	FAP Esq 601, Beja	
14810	Lockheed P-3C CUP+ Orion	FAP, stored Beja	
14811	Lockheed P-3C CUP+ Orion	FAP Esq 601, Beja	
15101	Lockheed Martin F-16A MLU Fighting Falcon	FAP Esq 201/Esq 301, Monte Real	
15102	Lockheed Martin F-16A MLU Fighting Falcon	FAP Esq 201/Esq 301, Monte Real	
15103	Lockheed Martin F-16A MLU Fighting Falcon $	FAP Esq 201/Esq 301, Monte Real	
15104	Lockheed Martin F-16A MLU Fighting Falcon	FAP Esq 201/Esq 301, Monte Real	
15105	Lockheed Martin F-16A MLU Fighting Falcon	FAP Esq 201/Esq 301, Monte Real	
15106	Lockheed Martin F-16A MLU Fighting Falcon $	FAP Esq 201/Esq 301, Monte Real	
15107	Lockheed Martin F-16A MLU Fighting Falcon	FAP Esq 201/Esq 301, Monte Real	
15108	Lockheed Martin F-16A MLU Fighting Falcon	FAP Esq 201/Esq 301, Monte Real	
15109	Lockheed Martin F-16A MLU Fighting Falcon	FAP Esq 201/Esq 301, Monte Real	
15110	Lockheed Martin F-16A MLU Fighting Falcon	FAP Esq 201/Esq 301, Monte Real	
15112	Lockheed Martin F-16A MLU Fighting Falcon	FAP Esq 201/Esq 301, Monte Real	

Notes	Serial	Type (code/other identity)	Owner/operator, location or fate
	15113	Lockheed Martin F-16A MLU Fighting Falcon	FAP Esq 201/Esq 301, Monte Real
	15114	Lockheed Martin F-16A MLU Fighting Falcon	FAP Esq 201/Esq 301, Monte Real
	15115	Lockheed Martin F-16A MLU Fighting Falcon	FAP Esq 201/Esq 301, Monte Real
	15116	Lockheed Martin F-16A MLU Fighting Falcon	FAP Esq 201/Esq 301, Monte Real
	15117	Lockheed Martin F-16A MLU Fighting Falcon	FAP Esq 201/Esq 301, Monte Real
	15118	Lockheed Martin F-16B MLU Fighting Falcon	FAP Esq 201/Esq 301, Monte Real
	15119	Lockheed Martin F-16B MLU Fighting Falcon	FAP Esq 201/Esq 301, Monte Real
	15120	Lockheed Martin F-16B MLU Fighting Falcon	FAP Esq 201/Esq 301, Monte Real
	15122	Lockheed Martin F-16A MLU Fighting Falcon	*FAP, for Romania*
	15131	Lockheed Martin F-16A MLU Fighting Falcon	FAP Esq 201/Esq 301, Monte Real
	15132	Lockheed Martin F-16A MLU Fighting Falcon	*FAP, for Romania*
	15133	Lockheed Martin F-16A MLU Fighting Falcon	FAP Esq 201/Esq 301, Monte Real
	15134	Lockheed Martin F-16A MLU Fighting Falcon	*FAP, for Romania*
	15135	Lockheed Martin F-16A MLU Fighting Falcon	*FAP, for Romania*
	15136	Lockheed Martin F-16A MLU Fighting Falcon	FAP Esq 201/Esq 301, Monte Real
	15141	Lockheed Martin F-16A MLU Fighting Falcon	*FAP, for Romania*
	15142	Lockheed Martin F-16A MLU Fighting Falcon	FAP Esq 201/Esq 301, Monte Real
	15143	Lockheed Martin F-16A MLU Fighting Falcon	FAP (on order)
	15144	Lockheed Martin F-16B MLU Fighting Falcon	FAP (on order)
	16701	CASA C-295M	FAP Esq 502, Lisbon/Montijo & Lajes
	16702	CASA C-295M	FAP Esq 502, Lisbon/Montijo & Lajes
	16703	CASA C-295M	FAP Esq 502, Lisbon/Montijo & Lajes
	16704	CASA C-295M	FAP Esq 502, Lisbon/Montijo & Lajes
	16705	CASA C-295M	FAP Esq 502, Lisbon/Montijo & Lajes
	16706	CASA C-295M	FAP Esq 502, Lisbon/Montijo & Lajes
	16707	CASA C-295M	FAP Esq 502, Lisbon/Montijo & Lajes
	16708	CASA C-295MPA	FAP Esq 502, Lisbon/Montijo & Lajes
	16709	CASA C-295MPA	FAP Esq 502, Lisbon/Montijo & Lajes
	16710	CASA C-295MPA	FAP Esq 502, Lisbon/Montijo & Lajes
	16711	CASA C-295MPA	FAP Esq 502, Lisbon/Montijo & Lajes
	16712	CASA C-295MPA	FAP Esq 502, Lisbon/Montijo & Lajes
	16801	Lockheed C-130H-30 Hercules	FAP Esq 501, Lisbon/Montijo
	16802	Lockheed C-130H-30 Hercules	FAP, stored Lisbon/Montijo
	16803	Lockheed C-130H Hercules	FAP Esq 501, Lisbon/Montijo
	16805	Lockheed C-130H Hercules	FAP Esq 501, Lisbon/Montijo
	16806	Lockheed C-130H-30 Hercules $	FAP Esq 501, Lisbon/Montijo
	17401	Dassault Falcon 50	FAP Esq 504, Lisbon/Montijo
	17402	Dassault Falcon 50	FAP Esq 504, Lisbon/Montijo
	17403	Dassault Falcon 50	FAP Esq 504, Lisbon/Montijo
	19201	Westland Super Lynx Mk.95 (ZH580)	Marinha Esq de Helicopteros, Lisbon/Montijo
	19202	Westland Super Lynx Mk.95 (ZH581)	Marinha Esq de Helicopteros, Lisbon/Montijo
	19203	Westland Super Lynx Mk.95 (ZH582)	Marinha Esq de Helicopteros, Lisbon/Montijo
	19204	Westland Super Lynx Mk.95 (ZH583)	Leonardo MW, Yeovil, UK (update)
	19205	Westland Super Lynx Mk.95 (ZH584)	Marinha Esq de Helicopteros, Lisbon/Montijo
	19601	EHI EH-101 Mk.514	FAP Esq 751, Sintra
	19602	EHI EH-101 Mk.514	FAP Esq 751, Sintra
	19603	EHI EH-101 Mk.514	FAP Esq 751, Sintra
	19604	EHI EH-101 Mk.514	FAP Esq 751, Sintra
	19605	EHI EH-101 Mk.514	FAP Esq 751, Sintra
	19606	EHI EH-101 Mk.514	FAP Esq 751, Sintra
	19607	EHI EH-101 Mk.515	FAP Esq 751, Sintra
	19608	EHI EH-101 Mk.515	FAP Esq 751, Sintra
	19609	EHI EH-101 Mk.516	FAP Esq 751, Sintra
	19610	EHI EH-101 Mk.516	FAP Esq 751, Sintra
	19611	EHI EH-101 Mk.516	FAP Esq 751, Sintra
	19612	EHI EH-101 Mk.516	FAP Lisbon/Montijo (damaged)

QATAR
Qatar Emiri Air Force (QEAF)

	211	Lockheed C-130J-30 Hercules II (08-0211) [MAH]	QEAF 12 Transport Sqn, Al-Udeid
	212	Lockheed C-130J-30 Hercules II (08-0212) [MAI]	QEAF 12 Transport Sqn, Al-Udeid
	213	Lockheed C-130J-30 Hercules II (08-0213) [MAJ]	QEAF 12 Transport Sqn, Al-Udeid

Serial	Type (code/other identity)	Owner/operator, location or fate	Notes
214	Lockheed C-130J-30 Hercules II (08-0214) [MAK]	QEAF 12 Transport Sqn, Al-Udeid	
MAA	Boeing C-17A Globemaster III (08-0201)	QEAF 12 Transport Sqn, Al-Udeid	
MAB	Boeing C-17A Globemaster III (08-0202)	QEAF 12 Transport Sqn, Al-Udeid	
MAC	Boeing C-17A Globemaster III (12-0203)	QEAF 12 Transport Sqn, Al-Udeid	
MAE	Boeing C-17A Globemaster III (12-0204)	QEAF 12 Transport Sqn, Al-Udeid	
MAM	Boeing C-17A Globemaster III (14-0005)	QEAF 12 Transport Sqn, Al-Udeid	
MAN	Boeing C-17A Globemaster III (14-0006)	QEAF 12 Transport Sqn, Al-Udeid	
MAO	Boeing C-17A Globemaster III (14-0009)	QEAF 12 Transport Sqn, Al-Udeid	
MAP	Boeing C-17A Globemaster III (14-0010)	QEAF 12 Transport Sqn, Al-Udeid	

Qatari Government

A7-AAG	Airbus A.320-232	Qatari Amiri Flight, Doha	
A7-AAH	Airbus A.340-313X	Qatari Amiri Flight, Doha	
A7-AAM	Bombardier Global Express	Qatari Amiri Flight/Qatar Airways, Doha	
A7-AFE	Airbus A.310-308	Qatari Amiri Flight, Doha	
A7-HBJ	Boeing 747-8KB	Qatari Amiri Flight, Doha	
A7-HHE	Boeing 747-8KB	Qatari Amiri Flight, Doha	
A7-HHF	Boeing 747-8Z5	Qatari Amiri Flight, Doha	
A7-HHH	Airbus A.340-541	Qatari Amiri Flight, Doha	
A7-HHJ	Airbus A.319CJ-133	Qatari Amiri Flight, Doha	
A7-HHK	Airbus A.340-211	Qatari Amiri Flight, Doha	
A7-HHM	Airbus A.330-203	Qatari Amiri Flight, Doha	
A7-HJJ	Airbus A.330-202	Qatari Amiri Flight, Doha	
A7-HSJ	Airbus A.320-232	Qatari Amiri Flight, Doha	
A7-MBK	Airbus A.320-232CJ	Qatari Amiri Flight, Doha	
A7-MED	Airbus A.319CJ-133	Qatari Amiri Flight, Doha	
A7-MHH	Airbus A.319CJ-115	Qatari Amiri Flight, Doha	

ROMANIA
Fortele Aeriene Romania (FAR)

2701	Alenia C-27J Spartan	FAR Escadrilla 902, Bucharest/Otopeni	
2702	Alenia C-27J Spartan	FAR Escadrilla 902, Bucharest/Otopeni	
2703	Alenia C-27J Spartan	FAR Escadrilla 902, Bucharest/Otopeni	
2704	Alenia C-27J Spartan	FAR Escadrilla 902, Bucharest/Otopeni	
2705	Alenia C-27J Spartan	FAR Escadrilla 902, Bucharest/Otopeni	
2706	Alenia C-27J Spartan	FAR Escadrilla 902, Bucharest/Otopeni	
2707	Alenia C-27J Spartan	FAR Escadrilla 902, Bucharest/Otopeni	
5930	Lockheed C-130B Hercules	FAR Escadrilla 901, Bucharest/Otopeni	
6166	Lockheed C-130H Hercules	FAR Escadrilla 901, Bucharest/Otopeni	
6191	Lockheed C-130H Hercules	FAR Escadrilla 901, Bucharest/Otopeni	

RUSSIA
Voenno-Vozdushniye Sily Rossioki Federatsii (VVS) (Russian Air Force)/Russian Government

595 w	Sukhoi Su-27P(LL) (36911037511)	VVS, Gromov Research Institute, Zhukhovsky	
597 w	Sukhoi Su-30LL (79371010102)	VVS, Gromov Research Institute, Zhukhovsky	
598 w	Sukhoi Su-27P(LL) (36911037820)	VVS, Gromov Research Institute, Zhukhovsky	
RA-09007	Dassault Falcon 7X	Rossiya Special Flight Det, Moscow/Vnukovo	
RA-26226	Antonov An-30	VVS (Open Skies), Moscow/Kubinka	
RA-30078	Antonov An-30	VVS (Open Skies), Moscow/Kubinka	
RA-64053	Tupolev Tu-204-300	Rossiya Special Flight Det, Moscow/Vnukovo	
RA-64057	Tupolev Tu-204-300	Rossiya Special Flight Det, Moscow/Vnukovo	
RA-64058	Tupolev Tu-204-300	Rossiya Special Flight Det, Moscow/Vnukovo	
RA-64059	Tupolev Tu-204-300	Rossiya Special Flight Det, Moscow/Vnukovo	
RA-64504	Tupolev Tu-214	Rossiya Special Flight Det, Moscow/Vnukovo	
RA-64505	Tupolev Tu-214	Rossiya Special Flight Det, Moscow/Vnukovo	
RA-64506	Tupolev Tu-214	Rossiya Special Flight Det, Moscow/Vnukovo	
RA-64515	Tupolev Tu-214SR	Rossiya Special Flight Det, Moscow/Vnukovo	
RA-64516	Tupolev Tu-214SR	Rossiya Special Flight Det, Moscow/Vnukovo	
RA-64517	Tupolev Tu-214PU	Rossiya Special Flight Det, Moscow/Vnukovo	
RA-64520	Tupolev Tu-214PU	Rossiya Special Flight Det, Moscow/Vnukovo	
RA-64521	Tupolev Tu-214	Rossiya Special Flight Det, Ulyanovsk	
RA-64522	Tupolev Tu-214SUS	Rossiya Special Flight Det, Moscow/Vnukovo	
RA-64524	Tupolev Tu-214SUS	Rossiya Special Flight Det, Moscow/Vnukovo	

Notes	Serial	Type (code/other identity)	Owner/operator, location or fate
	RA-64526	Tupolev Tu-214SR	Rossiya Special Flight Det, Moscow/Vnukovo
	RA-64527	Tupolev Tu-214SR	Rossiya Special Flight Det, Moscow/Vnukovo
	RA-64528	Tupolev Tu-214SR	Rossiya Special Flight Det, Moscow/Vnukovo
	RA-64531	Tupolev Tu-214PU	Rossiya Special Flight Det (on order)
	RA-65904	Tupolev Tu-134AK-3	Rossiya Special Flight Det, Moscow/Vnukovo
	RA-65905	Tupolev Tu-134AK-3	Rossiya Special Flight Det, Moscow/Vnukovo
	RA-65911	Tupolev Tu-134AK-3	Rossiya Special Flight Det, Moscow/Vnukovo
	RA-73026	Airbus A.319-115CJ	Rossiya Special Flight Det, Moscow/Vnukovo
	RA-73026	Airbus A.319-115CJ	Rossiya Special Flight Det, Moscow/Vnukovo
	RA-82035	Antonov An-124-100	VVS 224th Transport Regiment, Seshcha/Bryansk
	RA-82038	Antonov An-124-100	VVS 224th Transport Regiment, Seshcha/Bryansk
	RA-82039	Antonov An-124-100	VVS 224th Transport Regiment, Seshcha/Bryansk
	RA-85041	Tupolev Tu-154M	VVS 6991 AvB, Chalovskiy
	RA-85155	Tupolev Tu-154M	VVS 8 oae, Chalovskiy
	RA-96012	Ilyushin Il-96-300PU	Rossiya Special Flight Det, Moscow/Vnukovo
	RA-96016	Ilyushin Il-96-300PU	Rossiya Special Flight Det, Moscow/Vnukovo
	RA-96017	Ilyushin Il-96-300S	Rossiya Special Flight Det, Moscow/Vnukovo
	RA-96018	Ilyushin Il-96-300	Rossiya Special Flight Det, Moscow/Vnukovo
	RA-96019	Ilyushin Il-96-300	Rossiya Special Flight Det, Moscow/Vnukovo
	RA-96020	Ilyushin Il-96-300PU	Rossiya Special Flight Det, Moscow/Vnukovo
	RA-96021	Ilyushin Il-96-300PU	Rossiya Special Flight Det, Moscow/Vnukovo
	RA-96022	Ilyushin Il-96-300PU	Rossiya Special Flight Det, Moscow/Vnukovo
	RA-96023	Ilyushin Il-96-300	Rossiya Special Flight Det, Moscow/Vnukovo
	RA-96102	Ilyushin Il-96-400T	Rossiya Special Flight Det, Moscow/Vnukovo
	RA-96104	Ilyushin Il-96-400T	Rossiya Special Flight Det, Moscow/Vnukovo
	RF-36052	Antonov An-30B (87 bk)	VVS (Open Skies), Moscow/Kubinka
	RF-64519	Tupolev Tu-214ON	VVS (Open Skies), Moscow/Kubinka
	RF-82011	Antonov An-124-100	VVS 224th Transport Regiment, Seshcha/Bryansk
	RF-82041	Antonov An-124-100	VVS 224th Transport Regiment, Seshcha/Bryansk
	RF-85655	Tupolev Tu-154M-LK1	VVS (Open Skies), Moscow/Kubinka

SAUDI ARABIA

Al Quwwat al Jawwiya as Sa'udiya/Royal Saudi Air Force (RSAF) & Saudi Government

Notes	Serial	Type (code/other identity)	Owner/operator, location or fate
	111	Lockheed VC-130H Hercules	RSAF 1 Sqn, Riyadh
	112	Lockheed VC-130H Hercules	RSAF 1 Sqn, Riyadh
	464	Lockheed C-130H Hercules	RSAF 4 Sqn, Jeddah
	465	Lockheed C-130H Hercules	RSAF 4 Sqn, Jeddah
	466	Lockheed C-130H Hercules	RSAF 4 Sqn, Jeddah
	467	Lockheed C-130H Hercules	RSAF 4 Sqn, Jeddah
	468	Lockheed C-130H Hercules	RSAF 4 Sqn, Jeddah
	472	Lockheed C-130H Hercules	RSAF 4 Sqn, Jeddah
	473	Lockheed C-130H Hercules	RSAF 4 Sqn, Jeddah
	474	Lockheed C-130H Hercules	RSAF 4 Sqn, Jeddah
	475	Lockheed C-130H Hercules	RSAF 4 Sqn, Jeddah
	477	Lockheed C-130H Hercules	RSAF 4 Sqn, Jeddah
	478	Lockheed C-130H Hercules	RSAF 4 Sqn, Jeddah
	482	Lockheed C-130H Hercules	RSAF 4 Sqn, Jeddah
	483	Lockheed C-130H Hercules	RSAF 4 Sqn, Jeddah
	484	Lockheed C-130H Hercules	RSAF 4 Sqn, Jeddah
	485	Lockheed C-130H Hercules	RSAF 4 Sqn, Jeddah
	486	Lockheed C-130H Hercules	RSAF 4 Sqn, Jeddah
	1601	Lockheed C-130H Hercules	RSAF 4 Sqn, Jeddah
	1602	Lockheed C-130H Hercules	RSAF 16 Sqn, Jeddah
	1604	Lockheed C-130H Hercules	RSAF 16 Sqn, Jeddah
	1605	Lockheed C-130H Hercules	RSAF 16 Sqn, Jeddah
	1615	Lockheed C-130H Hercules	RSAF 16 Sqn, Jeddah
	1622	Lockheed C-130H-30 Hercules	RSAF 16 Sqn, Jeddah
	1623	Lockheed C-130H Hercules	RSAF 16 Sqn, Jeddah
	1624	Lockheed C-130H Hercules	RSAF 16 Sqn, Jeddah
	1625	Lockheed C-130H Hercules	RSAF 16 Sqn, Jeddah
	1626	Lockheed C-130H Hercules	RSAF 16 Sqn, Jeddah
	1627	Lockheed C-130H Hercules	RSAF 16 Sqn, Jeddah

Serial	Type (code/other identity)	Owner/operator, location or fate	Notes
1628	Lockheed C-130H Hercules	RSAF 16 Sqn, Jeddah	
1629	Lockheed C-130H Hercules	RSAF 16 Sqn, Jeddah	
1630	Lockheed C-130H-30 Hercules	RSAF 16 Sqn, Jeddah	
1631	Lockheed C-130H-30 Hercules	RSAF 16 Sqn, Jeddah	
1632	Lockheed L.100-30 Hercules	RSAF 16 Sqn, Jeddah	
1801	Boeing E-3A Sentry	RSAF 18 Sqn, Al Kharj	
1802	Boeing E-3A Sentry	RSAF 18 Sqn, Al Kharj	
1803	Boeing E-3A Sentry	RSAF 18 Sqn, Al Kharj	
1804	Boeing E-3A Sentry	RSAF 18 Sqn, Al Kharj	
1805	Boeing E-3A Sentry	RSAF 18 Sqn, Al Kharj	
1901	Boeing RE-3A (1817)	RSAF 19 Sqn, Al Kharj	
1902	Boeing RE-3B	RSAF 19 Sqn, Al Kharj	
2301	Boeing KE-3A Sentry (1811)	RSAF 23 Sqn, Al Kharj	
2302	Boeing KE-3A Sentry (1812)	RSAF 23 Sqn, Al Kharj	
2303	Boeing KE-3A Sentry (1813)	RSAF 23 Sqn, Al Kharj	
2304	Boeing KE-3A Sentry (1814)	RSAF 23 Sqn, Al Kharj	
2305	Boeing KE-3A Sentry (1815)	RSAF 23 Sqn, Al Kharj	
2306	Boeing KE-3A Sentry (1816)	RSAF 23 Sqn, Al Kharj	
2307	Boeing KE-3A Sentry (1818)	RSAF 23 Sqn, Al Kharj	
2401	Airbus A.330-203 MRTT	RSAF 24 Sqn, Al Kharj	
2402	Airbus A.330-203 MRTT $	RSAF 24 Sqn, Al Kharj	
2403	Airbus A.330-203 MRTT $	RSAF 24 Sqn, Al Kharj	
2404	Airbus A.330-203 MRTT	RSAF 24 Sqn, Al Kharj	
2405	Airbus A.330-203 MRTT	RSAF 24 Sqn, Al Kharj	
2406	Airbus A.330-203 MRTT	RSAF 24 Sqn, Al Kharj	
3201	Lockheed KC-130H Hercules	RSAF 32 Sqn, Al Kharj	
3202	Lockheed KC-130H Hercules	RSAF 32 Sqn, Al Kharj	
3203	Lockheed KC-130H Hercules	RSAF 32 Sqn, Al Kharj	
3204	Lockheed KC-130H Hercules	RSAF 32 Sqn, Al Kharj	
3205	Lockheed KC-130H Hercules	RSAF 32 Sqn, Al Kharj	
3206	Lockheed KC-130H Hercules	RSAF 32 Sqn, Al Kharj	
3207	Lockheed KC-130H Hercules	RSAF 32 Sqn, Al Kharj	
3208	Lockheed KC-130J Hercules II	RSAF 32 Sqn, Al Kharj	
3209	Lockheed KC-130J Hercules II	RSAF 32 Sqn, Al Kharj	
8805	BAe Hawk 65A	RSAF 88 Sqn, *Saudi Hawks*, Tabuk	
8806	BAe Hawk 65A	RSAF 88 Sqn, *Saudi Hawks*, Tabuk	
8807	BAe Hawk 65	RSAF 88 Sqn, *Saudi Hawks*, Tabuk	
8808	BAe Hawk 65	RSAF 88 Sqn, *Saudi Hawks*, Tabuk	
8810	BAe Hawk 65	RSAF 88 Sqn, *Saudi Hawks*, Tabuk	
8811	BAe Hawk 65A	RSAF 88 Sqn, *Saudi Hawks*, Tabuk	
8812	BAe Hawk 65A	RSAF 88 Sqn, *Saudi Hawks*, Tabuk	
8813	BAe Hawk 65	RSAF 88 Sqn, *Saudi Hawks*, Tabuk	
8814	BAe Hawk 65	RSAF 88 Sqn, *Saudi Hawks*, Tabuk	
8816	BAe Hawk 65A	RSAF 88 Sqn, *Saudi Hawks*, Tabuk	
8817	BAe Hawk 65	RSAF 88 Sqn, *Saudi Hawks*, Tabuk	
8818	BAe Hawk 65A	RSAF 88 Sqn, *Saudi Hawks*, Tabuk	
8819	BAe Hawk 65	RSAF 88 Sqn, *Saudi Hawks*, Tabuk	
8820	BAe Hawk 65	RSAF 88 Sqn, *Saudi Hawks*, Tabuk	
8821	BAe Hawk 65	RSAF 88 Sqn, *Saudi Hawks*, Tabuk	
HZ-101	Boeing 737-7DP	RSAF 1 Sqn, Riyadh	
HZ-102	Boeing 737-8DP	RSAF 1 Sqn, Riyadh	
HZ-103	Grumman G.1159C Gulfstream IV	RSAF 1 Sqn, Riyadh	
HZ-105	BAe 125-800	RSAF 1 Sqn, Riyadh	
HZ-109	BAe 125-800B	RSAF 1 Sqn, Riyadh	
HZ-110	BAe 125-800B	RSAF 1 Sqn, Riyadh	
HZ-117	Lockheed L.100-30 Hercules	RSAF 1 Sqn, Riyadh	
HZ-124	Airbus A.340-211	*Withdrawn from use*	
HZ-128	Lockheed L.100-30 Hercules	RSAF 1 Sqn, Riyadh	
HZ-129	Lockheed L.100-30 Hercules	RSAF 1 Sqn, Riyadh	
HZ-130	BAe 125-800B	RSAF 1 Sqn, Riyadh	
HZ-132	Lockheed L.100-30 Hercules	RSAF 1 Sqn, Riyadh	
HZ-133	Cessna 550 Citation II	RSAF 1 Sqn, Riyadh	

Notes	Serial	Type (code/other identity)	Owner/operator, location or fate
	HZ-134	Cessna 550 Citation II	RSAF 1 Sqn, Riyadh
	HZ-135	Cessna 550 Citation II	RSAF 1 Sqn, Riyadh
	HZ-136	Cessna 550 Citation II	RSAF 1 Sqn, Riyadh
	HZ-AFN	Grumman G.1159A Gulfstream III	Saudi Special Flight Services, Jeddah
	HZ-AFR	Grumman G.1159A Gulfstream III	Saudi Special Flight Services, Jeddah
	HZ-AFT	Dassault Falcon 900	Saudi Special Flight Services, Jeddah
	HZ-AFZ	Dassault Falcon 900	Saudi Special Flight Services, Jeddah
	HZ-AS99	Airbus A.318-112CJ	Saudi Royal Flight, Jeddah
	HZ-HM1	Boeing 747-468	Saudi Royal Flight, Jeddah
	HZ-HM1A	Boeing 747-3G1	*Withdrawn from use*
	HZ-HM1B	Boeing 747SP-68	*Withdrawn from use*
	HZ-HM1C	Boeing 747SP-68	*Withdrawn from use*
	HZ-HMED	Boeing 757-23A	Saudi Royal Flight, Riyadh
	HZ-HMS2	Airbus A.340-213X	*Withdrawn from use*
	HZ-MS1A	Bombardier Lear 60	Saudi Armed Forces Medical Services, Riyadh
	HZ-MS1B	Bombardier Lear 60	Saudi Armed Forces Medical Services, Riyadh
	HZ-MS02	Lockheed C-130H Hercules	Saudi Armed Forces Medical Services, Riyadh
	HZ-MS4	Grumman G.1159C Gulfstream IV-SP	Saudi Armed Forces Medical Services, Riyadh
	HZ-MS4A	Gulfstream Aerospace G.450	Saudi Armed Forces Medical Services, Riyadh
	HZ-MS4B	Gulfstream Aerospace G.450	Saudi Armed Forces Medical Services, Riyadh
	HZ-MS4C	Gulfstream Aerospace G.450	Saudi Armed Forces Medical Services, Riyadh
	HZ-MS5A	Gulfstream Aerospace Gulfstream V	Saudi Armed Forces Medical Services, Riyadh
	HZ-MS5B	Gulfstream Aerospace Gulfstream V	Saudi Armed Forces Medical Services, Riyadh
	HZ-MS06	Lockheed L.100-30 Hercules	Saudi Armed Forces Medical Services, Riyadh
	HZ-MS07	Lockheed C-130H Hercules	Saudi Armed Forces Medical Services, Riyadh
	HZ-MS09	Lockheed L.100-30 Hercules	Saudi Armed Forces Medical Services, Riyadh

SENEGAL

	6V-ONE	Airbus A.319CJ-115X	Government of Senegal, Dakar

SERBIA

	YU-BNA	Dassault Falcon 50	Government of Serbia, Belgrade
	YU-SRB	Embraer ERJ.135BJ Legacy 600	Government of Serbia, Belgrade

SINGAPORE
Republic of Singapore Air Force (RSAF)

	720	Lockheed KC-130B Hercules	RSAF 122 Sqn, Paya Labar
	721	Lockheed KC-130B Hercules	RSAF 122 Sqn, Paya Labar
	724	Lockheed KC-130B Hercules	RSAF 122 Sqn, Paya Labar
	725	Lockheed KC-130B Hercules	RSAF 122 Sqn, Paya Labar
	730	Lockheed C-130H Hercules	RSAF 122 Sqn, Paya Labar
	731	Lockheed KC-130H Hercules	RSAF 122 Sqn, Paya Labar
	732	Lockheed C-130H Hercules	RSAF 122 Sqn, Paya Labar
	733	Lockheed C-130H Hercules	RSAF 122 Sqn, Paya Labar
	734	Lockheed KC-130H Hercules	RSAF 122 Sqn, Paya Labar
	735	Lockheed C-130H Hercules	RSAF 122 Sqn, Paya Labar
	750	Boeing KC-135R Stratotanker	*Withdrawn from use, 26 June 2019*
	751	Boeing KC-135R Stratotanker	*Withdrawn from use, 26 June 2019*
	752	Boeing KC-135R Stratotanker	*Withdrawn from use, 26 June 2019*
	753	Boeing KC-135R Stratotanker	*Withdrawn from use, 26 June 2019*
	760	Airbus A.330-203 MRTT (EC-333/MRTT033)	RSAF 112 Sqn, Changi
	761	Airbus A.330-203 MRTT (EC-332/MRTT034) $	RSAF 112 Sqn, Changi
	762	Airbus A.330-203 MRTT (EC-336/MRTT035)	RSAF (on order)
	763	Airbus A.330-203 MRTT (EC-337/MRTT036)	RSAF (on order)
	764	Airbus A.330-203 MRTT (EC-335/MRTT037)	RSAF (on order)
	765	Airbus A.330-203 MRTT (EC-332/MRTT038)	RSAF (on order)

SLOVAKIA
Slovenské Vojenske Letectvo (SVL)

	0619	Mikoyan MiG-29AS	SVL 1.Blt/Zmiešané Letecké Kridlo, Sliač
	0807	Mil Mi-17	SVL 2.Dvlt/Vrtulnikové Letecké Kridlo, Prešov
	0808	Mil Mi-17	SVL 2.Dvlt/Vrtulnikové Letecké Kridlo, Prešov

Serial	Type (code/other identity)	Owner/operator, location or fate	Notes
0820	Mil Mi-17	SVL 2.Dvlt/Vrtulníkové Letecké Kridlo, Prešov	
0821	Mil Mi-17	SVL, stored Prešov	
0823	Mil Mi-17M	SVL 2.Dvlt/Vrtulníkové Letecké Kridlo, Prešov	
0824	Mil Mi-17	SVL 2.Dvlt/Vrtulníkové Letecké Kridlo, Prešov	
0826	Mil Mi-17	SVL, stored Prešov	
0841	Mil Mi-17	SVL 2.Dvlt/Vrtulníkové Letecké Kridlo, Prešov	
0844	Mil Mi-17	SVL 2.Dvlt/Vrtulníkové Letecké Kridlo, Prešov	
0845	Mil Mi-17	SVL 2.Dvlt/Vrtulníkové Letecké Kridlo, Prešov	
0846	Mil Mi-17	SVL 2.Dvlt/Vrtulníkové Letecké Kridlo, Prešov	
0847	Mil Mi-17	SVL, stored Prešov	
0921	Mikoyan MiG-29AS	SVL 1.Blt/Zmiešané Letecké Kridlo, Sliač	
1133	LET L-410T Turbolet	SVL, stored Malacky	
1303	Mikoyan MiG-29UBS $	SVL 1.Blt/Zmiešané Letecké Kridlo, Sliač	
1521	LET L-410FG Turbolet	SVL 1.Dopravná Letka/Dopravné Kridlo, Malacky	
1931	Aeritalia C-27J Spartan (CSX62302)	SVL 1.Dopravná Letka/Dopravné Kridlo, Malacky	
1962	Aeritalia C-27J Spartan (CSX62306)	SVL 1.Dopravná Letka/Dopravné Kridlo, Malacky	
2123	Mikoyan MiG-29AS	SVL 1.Blt/Zmiešané Letecké Kridlo, Sliač	
2311	LET L-410UVP Turbolet	SVL 1.Dopravná Letka/Dopravné Kridlo, Malacky	
2421	LET L-410UVP Turbolet	SVL 1.Dopravná Letka/Dopravné Kridlo, Malacky	
2718	LET L-401UVP-E Turbolet	SVL 1.Dopravná Letka/Dopravné Kridlo, Malacky	
2721	LET L-401UVP-E Turbolet	SVL 1.Dopravná Letka/Dopravné Kridlo, Malacky	
2818	LET L-401UVP-20 Turbolet	SVL 1.Dopravná Letka/Dopravné Kridlo, Malacky	
2901	LET L-401UVP-20 Turbolet	SVL 1.Dopravná Letka/Dopravné Kridlo, Malacky	
3709	Mikoyan MiG-29AS	SVL, stored Sliač	
3911	Mikoyan MiG-29AS	SVL 1.Blt/Zmiešané Letecké Kridlo, Sliač	
4701	Aero L-39ZAM Albatros	SVL 2.vlt/Zmiešané Letecké Kridlo, Sliač	
4703	Aero L-39ZAM Albatros	SVL 2.vlt/Zmiešané Letecké Kridlo, Sliač	
4707	Aero L-39ZAM Albatros	SVL, stored Sliač	
5252	Aero L-39CM Albatros	SVL 2.vlt/Zmiešané Letecké Kridlo, Sliač	
5253	Aero L-39CM Albatros	SVL 2.vlt/Zmiešané Letecké Kridlo, Sliač	
5301	Aero L-39CM Albatros $	SVL 2.vlt/Zmiešané Letecké Kridlo, Sliač	
5302	Aero L-39CM Albatros	SVL 2.vlt/Zmiešané Letecké Kridlo, Sliač	
5304	Mikoyan MiG-29UBS $	SVL 1.Blt/Zmiešané Letecké Kridlo, Sliač	
6124	Mikoyan MiG-29AS	SVL 1.Blt/Zmiešané Letecké Kridlo, Sliač	
6526	Mikoyan MiG-29AS	*Crashed 28 September 2019, Nitra*	
6627	Mikoyan MiG-29AS	SVL 1.Blt/Zmiešané Letecké Kridlo, Sliač	
6728	Mikoyan MiG-29AS	SVL 1.Blt/Zmiešané Letecké Kridlo, Sliač	
7445	Sikorsky UH-60M Black Hawk	SVL 1.vlt/Vrtulníkové Letecké Kridlo, Prešov	
7446	Sikorsky UH-60M Black Hawk	SVL 1.vlt/Vrtulníkové Letecké Kridlo, Prešov	
7447	Sikorsky UH-60M Black Hawk	SVL 1.vlt/Vrtulníkové Letecké Kridlo, Prešov	
7448	Sikorsky UH-60M Black Hawk	SVL 1.vlt/Vrtulníkové Letecké Kridlo, Prešov	
7449	Sikorsky UH-60M Black Hawk	SVL 1.vlt/Vrtulníkové Letecké Kridlo, Prešov	
7639	Sikorsky UH-60M Black Hawk	SVL 1.vlt/Vrtulníkové Letecké Kridlo, Prešov	
7640	Sikorsky UH-60M Black Hawk	SVL 1.vlt/Vrtulníkové Letecké Kridlo, Prešov	
7641	Sikorsky UH-60M Black Hawk	SVL 1.vlt/Vrtulníkové Letecké Kridlo, Prešov	
7642	Sikorsky UH-60M Black Hawk	SVL 1.vlt/Vrtulníkové Letecké Kridlo, Prešov	
Slovak Government			
OM-BYA	Airbus A.319-115	Slovak Government, Bratislava/Ivanka	
OM-BYB	Fokker 100	Slovak Government, Bratislava/Ivanka	
OM-BYC	Fokker 100	Slovak Government, Bratislava/Ivanka	
OM-BYK	Airbus A.319-115XCJ	Slovak Government, Bratislava/Ivanka	
SLOVENIA			
Slovenska Vojska (SV)/Slovenian Armed Forces			
L1-01	Dassault Falcon 2000EX	Government of Slovenia, Ljubljana	
L4-01	LET 410UVP-E Turbolet	SV 107.Letalska Baza, Cerklje ob Krki	
L9-61	Pilatus PC-9M	SV Letalska Šola, Cerklje ob Krki	
L9-62	Pilatus PC-9M	SV Letalska Šola, Cerklje ob Krki	
L9-63	Pilatus PC-9M	SV Letalska Šola, Cerklje ob Krki	
L9-64	Pilatus PC-9M	SV Letalska Šola, Cerklje ob Krki	
L9-65	Pilatus PC-9M	SV Letalska Šola, Cerklje ob Krki	
L9-66	Pilatus PC-9M	SV Letalska Šola, Cerklje ob Krki	

Notes	Serial	Type (code/other identity)	Owner/operator, location or fate
	L9-67	Pilatus PC-9M	SV Letalska Šola, Cerklje ob Krki
	L9-68	Pilatus PC-9M	SV Letalska Šola, Cerklje ob Krki
	L9-69	Pilatus PC-9M	SV Letalska Šola, Cerklje ob Krki

SOUTH AFRICA
Suid Afrikaanse Lugmag/South African Air Force (SAAF)

	401	Lockheed C-130BZ Hercules	SAAF 28 Sqn, Waterkloof
	402	Lockheed C-130BZ Hercules	SAAF 28 Sqn, Waterkloof
	403	Lockheed C-130BZ Hercules	Crashed 9 January 2020, Goma
	404	Lockheed C-130BZ Hercules	SAAF 28 Sqn, Waterkloof
	405	Lockheed C-130BZ Hercules $	SAAF 28 Sqn, Waterkloof
	406	Lockheed C-130BZ Hercules	SAAF 28 Sqn, Waterkloof
	409	Lockheed C-130BZ Hercules	SAAF 28 Sqn, Waterkloof
	ZS-NAN	Dassault Falcon 900	SAAF 21 Sqn, Waterkloof
	ZS-RSA	Boeing 737-7ED	SAAF 21 Sqn, Waterkloof

SOUTH KOREA
Han Guk Gong Gun/Republic of Korea Air Force

	10001	Boeing 747-4B5	RoKAF 296 Sqn/35 Combined Group, Seoul AB
	18-001	Airbus KC-330 Cygnus (MRTT050)	RoKAF 261 Air Tanker Sqn/5 Tactical Air Transport Wing, Gimhae
	19-002	Airbus KC-330 Cygnus (MRTT051)	RoKAF 261 Air Tanker Sqn/5 Tactical Air Transport Wing, Gimhae
	19-003	Airbus KC-330 Cygnus (MRTT052)	RoKAF 261 Air Tanker Sqn/5 Tactical Air Transport Wing, Gimhae
	19-004	Airbus KC-330 Cygnus (MRTT053)	RoKAF 261 Air Tanker Sqn/5 Tactical Air Transport Wing, Gimhae

SPAIN
Arma Aérea de l'Armada Española, Ejército del Aire (EdA)/Spanish Air Force & Guardia Civil

	CE.15-01	McDonnell Douglas EF-18BM Hornet [15-70] $	EdA 151 Esc/152 Esc/153 Esc/Ala 15, Zaragoza
	CE.15-2	McDonnell Douglas EF-18BM Hornet [15-71]	EdA 151 Esc/152 Esc/153 Esc/Ala 15, Zaragoza
	CE.15-03	McDonnell Douglas EF-18BM Hornet [15-72]	EdA 151 Esc/152 Esc/153 Esc/Ala 15, Zaragoza
	CE.15-04	McDonnell Douglas EF-18BM Hornet [15-73]	EdA 151 Esc/152 Esc/153 Esc/Ala 15, Zaragoza
	CE.15-5	McDonnell Douglas EF-18BM Hornet [15-74]	EdA 151 Esc/152 Esc/153 Esc/Ala 15, Zaragoza
	CE.15-06	McDonnell Douglas EF-18BM Hornet [15-75]	EdA 151 Esc/152 Esc/153 Esc/Ala 15, Zaragoza
	CE.15-07	McDonnell Douglas EF-18BM Hornet [15-76]	EdA 151 Esc/152 Esc/153 Esc/Ala 15, Zaragoza
	CE.15-08	McDonnell Douglas EF-18BM Hornet [12-71]	EdA 121 Esc/122 Esc/Ala 12, Madrid/Torrejón
	CE.15-09	McDonnell Douglas EF-18BM Hornet [15-77]	EdA 151 Esc/152 Esc/153 Esc/Ala 15, Zaragoza
	CE.15-10	McDonnell Douglas EF-18BM Hornet [12-73] $	EdA 121 Esc/122 Esc/Ala 12, Madrid/Torrejón
	CE.15-11	McDonnell Douglas EF-18BM Hornet [12-74]	EdA 121 Esc/122 Esc/Ala 12, Madrid/Torrejón
	CE.15-12	McDonnell Douglas EF-18BM Hornet [12-75]	EdA 121 Esc/122 Esc/Ala 12, Madrid/Torrejón
	C.15-13	McDonnell Douglas EF-18M Hornet [12-01]	EdA 121 Esc/122 Esc/Ala 12, Madrid/Torrejón
	C.15-14	McDonnell Douglas EF-18M Hornet [15-01] $	EdA 151 Esc/152 Esc/153 Esc/Ala 15, Zaragoza
	C.15-15	McDonnell Douglas EF-18M Hornet [15-02]	EdA 151 Esc/152 Esc/153 Esc/Ala 15, Zaragoza
	C.15-16	McDonnell Douglas EF-18M Hornet [15-03]	EdA 151 Esc/152 Esc/153 Esc/Ala 15, Zaragoza
	C.15-18	McDonnell Douglas EF-18M Hornet [15-05]	EdA 151 Esc/152 Esc/153 Esc/Ala 15, Zaragoza
	C.15-20	McDonnell Douglas EF-18M Hornet [15-07]	EdA 151 Esc/152 Esc/153 Esc/Ala 15, Zaragoza
	C.15-21	McDonnell Douglas EF-18M Hornet [15-08]	EdA 151 Esc/152 Esc/153 Esc/Ala 15, Zaragoza
	C.15-22	McDonnell Douglas EF-18M Hornet [15-09]	EdA 151 Esc/152 Esc/153 Esc/Ala 15, Zaragoza
	C.15-23	McDonnell Douglas EF-18M Hornet [15-10]	EdA 151 Esc/152 Esc/153 Esc/Ala 15, Zaragoza
	C.15-24	McDonnell Douglas EF-18M Hornet [15-11]	EdA 151 Esc/152 Esc/153 Esc/Ala 15, Zaragoza
	C.15-25	McDonnell Douglas EF-18M Hornet [15-12]	EdA 151 Esc/152 Esc/153 Esc/Ala 15, Zaragoza
	C.15-26	McDonnell Douglas EF-18M Hornet [15-13] $	EdA 151 Esc/152 Esc/153 Esc/Ala 15, Zaragoza
	C.15-27	McDonnell Douglas EF-18M Hornet [15-14]	EdA 151 Esc/152 Esc/153 Esc/Ala 15, Zaragoza
	C.15-28	McDonnell Douglas EF-18M Hornet [15-15]	EdA 151 Esc/152 Esc/153 Esc/Ala 15, Zaragoza
	C.15-29	McDonnell Douglas EF-18M Hornet [15-16]	EdA 151 Esc/152 Esc/153 Esc/Ala 15, Zaragoza
	C.15-30	McDonnell Douglas EF-18M Hornet [15-17]	EdA 151 Esc/152 Esc/153 Esc/Ala 15, Zaragoza
	C.15-31	McDonnell Douglas EF-18M Hornet [15-18]	EdA 151 Esc/152 Esc/153 Esc/Ala 15, Zaragoza
	C.15-32	McDonnell Douglas EF-18M Hornet [15-19]	EdA 151 Esc/152 Esc/153 Esc/Ala 15, Zaragoza
	C.15-33	McDonnell Douglas EF-18M Hornet [15-20]	EdA 151 Esc/152 Esc/153 Esc/Ala 15, Zaragoza
	C.15-34	McDonnell Douglas EF-18M Hornet [12-50] $	EdA 121 Esc/122 Esc/Ala 12, Madrid/Torrejón

Serial	Type (code/other identity)	Owner/operator, location or fate	Notes
C.15-35	McDonnell Douglas EF-18M Hornet [15-22]	EdA 151 Esc/152 Esc/153 Esc/Ala 15, Zaragoza	
C.15-36	McDonnell Douglas EF-18M Hornet [15-23]	EdA 151 Esc/152 Esc/153 Esc/Ala 15, Zaragoza	
C.15-37	McDonnell Douglas EF-18M Hornet [15-24]	EdA 151 Esc/152 Esc/153 Esc/Ala 15, Zaragoza	
C.15-38	McDonnell Douglas EF-18M Hornet [15-25]	EdA, stored Zaragoza	
C.15-39	McDonnell Douglas EF-18M Hornet [15-26]	EdA 151 Esc/152 Esc/153 Esc/Ala 15, Zaragoza	
C.15-40	McDonnell Douglas EF-18M Hornet [15-27]	EdA 151 Esc/152 Esc/153 Esc/Ala 15, Zaragoza	
C.15-41	McDonnell Douglas EF-18M Hornet [15-28] $	EdA 151 Esc/152 Esc/153 Esc/Ala 15, Zaragoza	
C.15-43	McDonnell Douglas EF-18M Hornet [15-30]	EdA 151 Esc/152 Esc/153 Esc/Ala 15, Zaragoza	
C.15-44	McDonnell Douglas EF-18M Hornet [12-02]	EdA 121 Esc/122 Esc/Ala 12, Madrid/Torrejón	
C.15-45	McDonnell Douglas EF-18M Hornet [12-03]	EdA 121 Esc/122 Esc/Ala 12, Madrid/Torrejón	
C.15-46	McDonnell Douglas EF-18M Hornet [12-04]	EdA 121 Esc/122 Esc/Ala 12, Madrid/Torrejón	
C.15-47	McDonnell Douglas EF-18M Hornet [15-31]	EdA 151 Esc/152 Esc/153 Esc/Ala 15, Zaragoza	
C.15-48	McDonnell Douglas EF-18M Hornet [12-06]	EdA 121 Esc/122 Esc/Ala 12, Madrid/Torrejón	
C.15-49	McDonnell Douglas EF-18M Hornet [12-07]	EdA 121 Esc/122 Esc/Ala 12, Madrid/Torrejón	
C.15-50	McDonnell Douglas EF-18M Hornet [12-08]	EdA 121 Esc/122 Esc/Ala 12, Madrid/Torrejón	
C.15-51	McDonnell Douglas EF-18M Hornet [12-09]	EdA 121 Esc/122 Esc/Ala 12, Madrid/Torrejón	
C.15-53	McDonnell Douglas EF-18M Hornet [12-11]	EdA 121 Esc/122 Esc/Ala 12, Madrid/Torrejón	
C.15-54	McDonnell Douglas EF-18M Hornet [12-12]	EdA 121 Esc/122 Esc/Ala 12, Madrid/Torrejón	
C.15-55	McDonnell Douglas EF-18M Hornet [12-13]	EdA 121 Esc/122 Esc/Ala 12, Madrid/Torrejón	
C.15-56	McDonnell Douglas EF-18M Hornet [12-14]	EdA 121 Esc/122 Esc/Ala 12, Madrid/Torrejón	
C.15-57	McDonnell Douglas EF-18M Hornet [12-15]	EdA 121 Esc/122 Esc/Ala 12, Madrid/Torrejón	
C.15-59	McDonnell Douglas EF-18M Hornet [12-17]	EdA 121 Esc/122 Esc/Ala 12, Madrid/Torrejón	
C.15-60	McDonnell Douglas EF-18M Hornet [12-18]	EdA 121 Esc/122 Esc/Ala 12, Madrid/Torrejón	
C.15-61	McDonnell Douglas EF-18M Hornet [12-19]	EdA 121 Esc/122 Esc/Ala 12, Madrid/Torrejón	
C.15-62	McDonnell Douglas EF-18M Hornet [12-20]	EdA 121 Esc/122 Esc/Ala 12, Madrid/Torrejón	
C.15-64	McDonnell Douglas EF-18M Hornet [15-34]	EdA 151 Esc/152 Esc/153 Esc/Ala 15, Zaragoza	
C.15-65	McDonnell Douglas EF-18M Hornet [12-23]	EdA 121 Esc/122 Esc/Ala 12, Madrid/Torrejón	
C.15-66	McDonnell Douglas EF-18M Hornet [12-24]	EdA 121 Esc/122 Esc/Ala 12, Madrid/Torrejón	
C.15-67	McDonnell Douglas EF-18M Hornet [15-33]	EdA 151 Esc/152 Esc/153 Esc/Ala 15, Zaragoza	
C.15-68	McDonnell Douglas EF-18M Hornet [12-26] $	EdA 121 Esc/122 Esc/Ala 12, Madrid/Torrejón	
C.15-69	McDonnell Douglas EF-18M Hornet [12-27]	EdA 121 Esc/122 Esc/Ala 12, Madrid/Torrejón	
C.15-70	McDonnell Douglas EF-18M Hornet [12-28]	EdA 121 Esc/122 Esc/Ala 12, Madrid/Torrejón	
C.15-72	McDonnell Douglas EF-18M Hornet [12-30]	EdA 121 Esc/122 Esc/Ala 12, Madrid/Torrejón	
C.15-73	McDonnell Douglas F/A-18A+ Hornet [46-01] $	EdA 462 Esc/Ala 46, Gran Canaria	
C.15-75	McDonnell Douglas F/A-18A+ Hornet [46-03]	EdA 462 Esc/Ala 46, Gran Canaria	
C.15-77	McDonnell Douglas F/A-18A+ Hornet [46-05]	EdA 462 Esc/Ala 46, Gran Canaria	
C.15-79	McDonnell Douglas F/A-18A+ Hornet [46-07]	EdA 462 Esc/Ala 46, Gran Canaria	
C.15-80	McDonnell Douglas F/A-18A+ Hornet [46-08]	EdA 462 Esc/Ala 46, Gran Canaria	
C.15-81	McDonnell Douglas F/A-18A+ Hornet [46-09]	EdA 462 Esc/Ala 46, Gran Canaria	
C.15-82	McDonnell Douglas F/A-18A+ Hornet [46-10]	EdA 462 Esc/Ala 46, Gran Canaria	
C.15-83	McDonnell Douglas F/A-18A+ Hornet [46-11]	EdA 462 Esc/Ala 46, Gran Canaria	
C.15-84	McDonnell Douglas F/A-18A+ Hornet [46-12]	EdA 462 Esc/Ala 46, Gran Canaria	
C.15-85	McDonnell Douglas F/A-18A+ Hornet [46-13]	EdA 462 Esc/Ala 46, Gran Canaria	
C.15-86	McDonnell Douglas F/A-18A+ Hornet [46-14]	EdA 462 Esc/Ala 46, Gran Canaria	
C.15-87	McDonnell Douglas F/A-18A+ Hornet [46-15]	EdA, stored Albacete	
C.15-88	McDonnell Douglas F/A-18A+ Hornet [46-16] $	EdA 462 Esc/Ala 46, Gran Canaria	
C.15-89	McDonnell Douglas F/A-18A+ Hornet [46-17]	EdA 462 Esc/Ala 46, Gran Canaria	
C.15-90	McDonnell Douglas F/A-18A+ Hornet [46-18]	EdA 462 Esc/Ala 46, Gran Canaria	
C.15-92	McDonnell Douglas F/A-18A+ Hornet [46-20]	EdA 462 Esc/Ala 46, Gran Canaria	
C.15-93	McDonnell Douglas F/A-18A+ Hornet [46-21]	EdA 462 Esc/Ala 46, Gran Canaria	
C.15-94	McDonnell Douglas F/A-18A+ Hornet [46-22]	EdA 462 Esc/Ala 46, Gran Canaria	
C.15-95	McDonnell Douglas F/A-18A+ Hornet [46-23]	EdA 462 Esc/Ala 46, Gran Canaria	
C.15-96	McDonnell Douglas F/A-18A+ Hornet [46-24]	EdA 462 Esc/Ala 46, Gran Canaria	
CE.16-01	Eurofighter EF.2000(T) Tifón [11-70]	EdA 111 Esc/113 Esc/Ala 11, Sevilla/Morón	
CE.16-02	Eurofighter EF.2000(T) Tifón [11-71]	EdA 111 Esc/113 Esc/Ala 11, Sevilla/Morón	
CE.16-03	Eurofighter EF.2000(T) Tifón [11-72]	EdA 111 Esc/113 Esc/Ala 11, Sevilla/Morón	
CE.16-04	Eurofighter EF.2000(T) Tifón [11-73]	EdA 111 Esc/113 Esc/Ala 11, Sevilla/Morón	
CE.16-05	Eurofighter EF.2000(T) Tifón [11-74]	EdA 111 Esc/113 Esc/Ala 11, Sevilla/Morón	
CE.16-06	Eurofighter EF.2000(T) Tifón [11-06]	EdA 111 Esc/113 Esc/Ala 11, Sevilla/Morón	
CE.16-07	Eurofighter EF.2000(T) Tifón [11-76]	EdA 111 Esc/113 Esc/Ala 11, Sevilla/Morón	
CE.16-09	Eurofighter EF.2000(T) Tifón [11-78]	EdA 111 Esc/113 Esc/Ala 11, Sevilla/Morón	
CE.16-10	Eurofighter EF.2000(T) Tifón [11-79]	EdA 111 Esc/113 Esc/Ala 11, Sevilla/Morón	

Notes	Serial	Type (code/other identity)	Owner/operator, location or fate
	CE.16-11	Eurofighter EF.2000(T) Tifón [14-70]	EdA 142 Esc/Ala 14, Albacete/Los Llanos
	CE.16-12	Eurofighter EF.2000(T) Tifón (10000) [14-71]	EdA 142 Esc/Ala 14, Albacete/Los Llanos
	CE.16-13	Eurofighter EF.2000(T) Tifón (10005) [11-13]	EdA 111 Esc/113 Esc/Ala 11, Sevilla/Morón
	CE.16-14	Eurofighter EF.2000(T) Tifón (10015) [11-14]	EdA 111 Esc/113 Esc/Ala 11, Sevilla/Morón
	C.16-20	Eurofighter EF.2000 Tifón [11-91]	EdA 111 Esc/113 Esc/Ala 11, Sevilla/Morón
	C.16-21	Eurofighter EF.2000 Tifón [11-21]	EdA 111 Esc/113 Esc/Ala 11, Sevilla/Morón
	C.16-22	Eurofighter EF.2000 Tifón [11-02]	EdA 111 Esc/113 Esc/Ala 11, Sevilla/Morón
	C.16-23	Eurofighter EF.2000 Tifón [11-03]	EdA 541 Esc/CLAEX/Grupo 54, Madrid/Torrejón
	C.16-24	Eurofighter EF.2000 Tifón [11-04]	EdA 111 Esc/113 Esc/Ala 11, Sevilla/Morón
	C.16-25	Eurofighter EF.2000 Tifón [11-05]	EdA 111 Esc/113 Esc/Ala 11, Sevilla/Morón
	C.16-26	Eurofighter EF.2000 Tifón [11-26]	EdA 111 Esc/113 Esc/Ala 11, Sevilla/Morón
	C.16-27	Eurofighter EF.2000 Tifón [11-07]	EdA 111 Esc/113 Esc/Ala 11, Sevilla/Morón
	C.16-28	Eurofighter EF.2000 Tifón [11-08]	EdA 111 Esc/113 Esc/Ala 11, Sevilla/Morón
	C.16-29	Eurofighter EF.2000 Tifón [11-09]	EdA 111 Esc/113 Esc/Ala 11, Sevilla/Morón
	C.16-30	Eurofighter EF.2000 Tifón [11-10]	EdA 111 Esc/113 Esc/Ala 11, Sevilla/Morón
	C.16-31	Eurofighter EF.2000 Tifón [14-01]	EdA 142 Esc/Ala 14, Albacete/Los Llanos
	C.16-32	Eurofighter EF.2000 Tifón [11-11]	EdA 111 Esc/113 Esc/Ala 11, Sevilla/Morón
	C.16-33	Eurofighter EF.2000 Tifón [11-33]	EdA 111 Esc/113 Esc/Ala 11, Sevilla/Morón
	C.16-35	Eurofighter EF.2000 Tifón [11-35]	EdA 111 Esc/113 Esc/Ala 11, Sevilla/Morón
	C.16-36	Eurofighter EF.2000 Tifón [14-03]	EdA 142 Esc/Ala 14, Albacete/Los Llanos
	C.16-37	Eurofighter EF.2000 Tifón [14-04]	EdA 142 Esc/Ala 14, Albacete/Los Llanos
	C.16-38	Eurofighter EF.2000 Tifón [11-38]	EdA 111 Esc/113 Esc/Ala 11, Sevilla/Morón
	C.16-39	Eurofighter EF.2000 Tifón [14-06]	EdA 142 Esc/Ala 14, Albacete/Los Llanos
	C.16-40	Eurofighter EF.2000 Tifón [11-16]	EdA 111 Esc/113 Esc/Ala 11, Sevilla/Morón
	C.16-41	Eurofighter EF.2000 Tifón [11-17]	EdA 111 Esc/113 Esc/Ala 11, Sevilla/Morón
	C.16-42	Eurofighter EF.2000 Tifón [11-42]	EdA 111 Esc/113 Esc/Ala 11, Sevilla/Morón
	C.16-43	Eurofighter EF.2000 Tifón [11-43]	EdA 111 Esc/113 Esc/Ala 11, Sevilla/Morón
	C.16-44	Eurofighter EF.2000 Tifón [14-09]	EdA 142 Esc/Ala 14, Albacete/Los Llanos
	C.16-45	Eurofighter EF.2000 Tifón [14-10]	EdA 142 Esc/Ala 14, Albacete/Los Llanos
	C.16-46	Eurofighter EF.2000 Tifón [11-46]	EdA 111 Esc/113 Esc/Ala 11, Sevilla/Morón
	C.16-47	Eurofighter EF.2000 Tifón [14-11]	EdA 142 Esc/Ala 14, Albacete/Los Llanos
	C.16-48	Eurofighter EF.2000 Tifón [14-12]	EdA 142 Esc/Ala 14, Albacete/Los Llanos
	C.16-49	Eurofighter EF.2000 Tifón [14-13]	EdA 142 Esc/Ala 14, Albacete/Los Llanos
	C.16-50	Eurofighter EF.2000 Tifón [14-14]	EdA 142 Esc/Ala 14, Albacete/Los Llanos
	C.16-51	Eurofighter EF.2000 Tifón [11-51]	EdA 111 Esc/113 Esc/Ala 11, Sevilla/Morón
	C.16-52	Eurofighter EF.2000 Tifón (C.16-10001) [11-52]	EdA 111 Esc/113 Esc/Ala 11, Sevilla/Morón
	C.16-53	Eurofighter EF.2000 Tifón (C.16-10002) [11-53]	EdA 111 Esc/113 Esc/Ala 11, Sevilla/Morón
	C.16-54	Eurofighter EF.2000 Tifón (C.16-10003) [11-54]	EdA 111 Esc/113 Esc/Ala 11, Sevilla/Morón
	C.16-55	Eurofighter EF.2000 Tifón (C.16-10004) [11-55]	EdA 111 Esc/113 Esc/Ala 11, Sevilla/Morón
	C.16-56	Eurofighter EF.2000 Tifón (10007)	EdA 142 Esc/Ala 14, Albacete/Los Llanos
	C.16-57	Eurofighter EF.2000 Tifón (10012) [11-57]	EdA 111 Esc/113 Esc/Ala 11, Sevilla/Morón
	C.16-58	Eurofighter EF.2000 Tifón (10019) [14-17]	EdA 142 Esc/Ala 14, Albacete/Los Llanos
	C.16-59	Eurofighter EF.2000 Tifón (10020) [14-18]	EdA 142 Esc/Ala 14, Albacete/Los Llanos
	C.16-60	Eurofighter EF.2000 Tifón (10040) [14-19]	EdA 142 Esc/Ala 14, Albacete/Los Llanos
	C.16-61	Eurofighter EF.2000 Tifón (10046) [14-20]	EdA 142 Esc/Ala 14, Albacete/Los Llanos
	C.16-62	Eurofighter EF.2000 Tifón (10047) [14-21]	EdA 142 Esc/Ala 14, Albacete/Los Llanos
	C.16-63	Eurofighter EF.2000 Tifón (10048) [11-63]	EdA 111 Esc/113 Esc/Ala 11, Sevilla/Morón
	C.16-64	Eurofighter EF.2000 Tifón (10053) [14-22]	EdA 142 Esc/Ala 14, Albacete/Los Llanos
	C.16-65	Eurofighter EF.2000 Tifón (10054) [14-23]	EdA 142 Esc/Ala 14, Albacete/Los Llanos
	C.16-66	Eurofighter EF.2000 Tifón (10064) [14-24]	EdA 142 Esc/Ala 14, Albacete/Los Llanos
	C.16-67	Eurofighter EF.2000 Tifón (10090) [14-25]	EdA 142 Esc/Ala 14, Albacete/Los Llanos
	C.16-68	Eurofighter EF.2000 Tifón (10091) [14-26]	EdA 142 Esc/Ala 14, Albacete/Los Llanos
	C.16-70	Eurofighter EF.2000 Tifón (10145) [14-28]	EdA (on order)
	C.16-71	Eurofighter EF.2000 Tifón (10146) [14-29]	EdA 142 Esc/Ala 14, Albacete/Los Llanos
	C.16-72	Eurofighter EF.2000 Tifón (10147) [14-30]	EdA 142 Esc/Ala 14, Albacete/Los Llanos
	C.16-73	Eurofighter EF.2000 Tifón (10155) [14-31]	EdA 142 Esc/Ala 14, Albacete/Los Llanos
	C.16-74	Eurofighter EF.2000 Tifón (10202) [14-32]	EdA 142 Esc/Ala 14, Albacete/Los Llanos
	C.16-75	Eurofighter EF.2000 Tifón (10205) [14-33]	EdA 142 Esc/Ala 14, Albacete/Los Llanos
	C.16-76	Eurofighter EF.2000 Tifón (10215) [14-34]	EdA 142 Esc/Ala 14, Albacete/Los Llanos
	C.16-77	Eurofighter EF.2000 Tifón (10234) [14-35]	EdA 142 Esc/Ala 14, Albacete/Los Llanos
	C.16-78	Eurofighter EF.2000 Tifón (10235) [14-36] $	EdA 142 Esc/Ala 14, Albacete/Los Llanos
	D.4-01	Airtech CN.235M-100(MPA) (T.19B-12)	EdA 801 Esc/Ala 49, Palma/Son San Juan

Serial	Type (code/other identity)	Owner/operator, location or fate	Notes
D.4-02	Airtech CN.235M-100(MPA) (T.19B-09) [37-02]	EdA 801 Esc/Ala 49, Palma/Son San Juan	
D.4-03	Airtech CN.235M-100(MPA) (T.19B-10)	EdA 801 Esc/Ala 49, Palma/Son San Juan	
D.4-04	Airtech CN.235M-100(MPA) (T.19B-08)	EdA 802 Esc/Ala 46, Gran Canaria	
D.4-05	Airtech CN.235M-100(MPA) (T.19B-06)	EdA 801 Esc/Ala 49, Palma/Son San Juan	
D.4-06	Airtech CN.235M-100(MPA) (T.19B-05)	EdA 801 Esc/Ala 49, Palma/Son San Juan	
D.4-07	Airtech CN.235M-100(MPA) (T.19B-15)	EdA 803 Esc/Ala 48, Madrid/Getafe	
D.4-08	Airtech CN.235M-100(MPA) (T.19B-14)	EdA 802 Esc/Ala 46, Gran Canaria	
E.25-05	CASA 101EB Aviojet [79-05]	EdA 793 Esc/794 Esc/AGA, Murcia/San Javier	
E.25-06	CASA 101EB Aviojet [79-06]	EdA 793 Esc/794 Esc/AGA, Murcia/San Javier	
E.25-08	CASA 101EB Aviojet [79-08]	EdA 793 Esc/794 Esc/AGA, Murcia/San Javier	
E.25-09	CASA 101EB Aviojet [79-09]	EdA 793 Esc/794 Esc/AGA, Murcia/San Javier	
E.25-11	CASA 101EB Aviojet [79-11]	EdA 793 Esc/794 Esc/AGA, Murcia/San Javier	
E.25-12	CASA 101EB Aviojet [79-12]	EdA 793 Esc/794 Esc/AGA, Murcia/San Javier	
E.25-13	CASA 101EB Aviojet [79-13,5]	EdA Patrulla Aguila/AGA, Murcia/San Javier	
E.25-14	CASA 101EB Aviojet [79-14]	EdA 793 Esc/794 Esc/AGA, Murcia/San Javier	
E.25-15	CASA 101EB Aviojet [79-15]	EdA 793 Esc/794 Esc/AGA, Murcia/San Javier	
E.25-16	CASA 101EB Aviojet [79-16]	EdA 793 Esc/794 Esc/AGA, Murcia/San Javier	
E.25-17	CASA 101EB Aviojet [74-40]	EdA 741 Esc/GEM, Salamanca/Matacán	
E.25-18	CASA 101EB Aviojet [74-42] $	EdA 741 Esc/GEM, Salamanca/Matacán	
E.25-19	CASA 101EB Aviojet [79-19]	EdA 793 Esc/794 Esc/AGA, Murcia/San Javier	
E.25-20	CASA 101EB Aviojet [79-20]	Crashed 26 August 2019, Manga del Mar Menor	
E.25-21	CASA 101EB Aviojet [79-21]	EdA 793 Esc/794 Esc/AGA, Murcia/San Javier	
E.25-22	CASA 101EB Aviojet [79-22]	EdA 793 Esc/794 Esc/AGA, Murcia/San Javier	
E.25-23	CASA 101EB Aviojet [79-23]	Withdrawn from use, 2019	
E.25-24	CASA 101EB Aviojet [79-24]	EdA 793 Esc/794 Esc/AGA, Murcia/San Javier	
E.25-25	CASA 101EB Aviojet [79-25]	EdA 793 Esc/794 Esc/AGA, Murcia/San Javier	
E.25-26	CASA 101EB Aviojet [79-26]	EdA 793 Esc/794 Esc/AGA, Murcia/San Javier	
E.25-27	CASA 101EB Aviojet [79-27,7]	EdA Patrulla Aguila/AGA, Murcia/San Javier	
E.25-28	CASA 101EB Aviojet [79-28]	EdA 793 Esc/794 Esc/AGA, Murcia/San Javier	
E.25-29	CASA 101EB Aviojet [74-45]	EdA 741 Esc/GEM, Salamanca/Matacán	
E.25-31	CASA 101EB Aviojet [79-31,1]	EdA Patrulla Aguila/AGA, Murcia/San Javier	
E.25-33	CASA 101EB Aviojet [74-02]	EdA 741 Esc/GEM, Salamanca/Matacán	
E.25-34	CASA 101EB Aviojet [74-44]	EdA 741 Esc/GEM, Salamanca/Matacán	
E.25-35	CASA 101EB Aviojet [54-20] $	EdA 541 Esc/CLAEX/Grupo 54, Madrid/Torrejón	
E.25-37	CASA 101EB Aviojet [79-37]	EdA 793 Esc/794 Esc/AGA, Murcia/San Javier	
E.25-38	CASA 101EB Aviojet [79-38,2]	EdA Patrulla Aguila/AGA, Murcia/San Javier	
E.25-40	CASA 101EB Aviojet [79-40]	EdA 793 Esc/794 Esc/AGA, Murcia/San Javier	
E.25-41	CASA 101EB Aviojet [74-41]	EdA 741 Esc/GEM, Salamanca/Matacán	
E.25-43	CASA 101EB Aviojet [74-43]	EdA 741 Esc/GEM, Salamanca/Matacán	
E.25-44	CASA 101EB Aviojet [79-44]	EdA 793 Esc/794 Esc/AGA, Murcia/San Javier	
E.25-50	CASA 101EB Aviojet [79-33]	EdA 741 Esc/GEM, Salamanca/Matacán	
E.25-51	CASA 101EB Aviojet [74-07]	EdA 741 Esc/GEM, Salamanca/Matacán	
E.25-52	CASA 101EB Aviojet [79-34,3]	EdA Patrulla Aguila/AGA, Murcia/San Javier	
E.25-53	CASA 101EB Aviojet [74-09]	EdA 741 Esc/GEM, Salamanca/Matacán	
E.25-54	CASA 101EB Aviojet [79-35]	EdA 793 Esc/794 Esc/AGA, Murcia/San Javier	
E.25-55	CASA 101EB Aviojet [54-21]	EdA 541 Esc/CLAEX/Grupo 54, Madrid/Torrejón	
E.25-56	CASA 101EB Aviojet [74-11]	EdA 741 Esc/GEM, Salamanca/Matacán	
E.25-57	CASA 101EB Aviojet [793-57]	EdA 793 Esc/794 Esc/AGA, Murcia/San Javier	
E.25-59	CASA 101EB Aviojet [74-13]	EdA 741 Esc/GEM, Salamanca/Matacán	
E.25-61	CASA 101EB Aviojet [54-22]	EdA 741 Esc/GEM, Salamanca/Matacán	
E.25-62	CASA 101EB Aviojet [79-17]	EdA 793 Esc/794 Esc/AGA, Murcia/San Javier	
E.25-63	CASA 101EB Aviojet [74-17,5]	EdA Patrulla Aguila/AGA, Murcia/San Javier	
E.25-65	CASA 101EB Aviojet [79-95]	Crashed 27 February 2020, off San Javier	
E.25-66	CASA 101EB Aviojet [74-20]	EdA 741 Esc/GEM, Salamanca/Matacán	
E.25-67	CASA 101EB Aviojet [74-21]	EdA 741 Esc/GEM, Salamanca/Matacán	
E.25-68	CASA 101EB Aviojet [741-68]	EdA 741 Esc/GEM, Salamanca/Matacán	
E.25-69	CASA 101EB Aviojet [79-97,8]	EdA Patrulla Aguila/AGA, Murcia/San Javier	
E.25-71	CASA 101EB Aviojet [74-25]	EdA 741 Esc/GEM, Salamanca/Matacán	
E.25-72	CASA 101EB Aviojet [74-26]	EdA 741 Esc/GEM, Salamanca/Matacán	
E.25-73	CASA 101EB Aviojet [79-98]	EdA 793 Esc/794 Esc/AGA, Murcia/San Javier	
E.25-74	CASA 101EB Aviojet [74-28]	EdA 741 Esc/GEM, Salamanca/Matacán	
E.25-76	CASA 101EB Aviojet [74-30]	EdA 741 Esc/GEM, Salamanca/Matacán	

Notes	Serial	Type (code/other identity)	Owner/operator, location or fate
	E.25-78	CASA 101EB Aviojet [79-02,4]	EdA *Patrulla Aguila*/AGA, Murcia/San Javier
	E.25-79	CASA 101EB Aviojet [79-39]	EdA 793 Esc/794 Esc/AGA, Murcia/San Javier
	E.25-80	CASA 101EB Aviojet [79-03]	EdA 793 Esc/794 Esc/AGA, Murcia/San Javier
	E.25-81	CASA 101EB Aviojet [74-34]	EdA 741 Esc/GEM, Salamanca/Matacán
	E.25-83	CASA 101EB Aviojet [74-35]	EdA 741 Esc/GEM, Salamanca/Matacán
	E.25-84	CASA 101EB Aviojet [79-04]	EdA 793 Esc/794 Esc/AGA, Murcia/San Javier
	E.25-86	CASA 101EB Aviojet [79-32]	EdA 793 Esc/794 Esc/AGA, Murcia/San Javier
	E.25-87	CASA 101EB Aviojet [79-29]	EdA 793 Esc/794 Esc/AGA, Murcia/San Javier
	E.25-88	CASA 101EB Aviojet [74-39]	EdA 741 Esc/GEM, Salamanca/Matacán
	E.27-01	Pilatus PC-21	EdA (on order)
	E.27-02	Pilatus PC-21	EdA (on order)
	E.27-03	Pilatus PC-21	EdA (on order)
	E.27-04	Pilatus PC-21	EdA (on order)
	E.27-05	Pilatus PC-21	EdA (on order)
	E.27-06	Pilatus PC-21	EdA (on order)
	E.27-07	Pilatus PC-21	EdA (on order)
	E.27-08	Pilatus PC-21	EdA (on order)
	E.27-09	Pilatus PC-21	EdA (on order)
	E.27-10	Pilatus PC-21	EdA (on order)
	E.27-11	Pilatus PC-21	EdA (on order)
	E.27-12	Pilatus PC-21	EdA (on order)
	E.27-13	Pilatus PC-21	EdA (on order)
	E.27-14	Pilatus PC-21	EdA (on order)
	E.27-15	Pilatus PC-21	EdA (on order)
	E.27-16	Pilatus PC-21	EdA (on order)
	E.27-17	Pilatus PC-21	EdA (on order)
	E.27-18	Pilatus PC-21	EdA (on order)
	E.27-19	Pilatus PC-21	EdA (on order)
	E.27-20	Pilatus PC-21	EdA (on order)
	E.27-21	Pilatus PC-21	EdA (on order)
	E.27-22	Pilatus PC-21	EdA (on order)
	E.27-23	Pilatus PC-21	EdA (on order)
	E.27-24	Pilatus PC-21	EdA (on order)
	HS.23-01	Sikorsky SH-60B Seahawk [01-1001]	Armada 10 Esc, Rota
	HS.23-02	Sikorsky SH-60B Seahawk [01-1002]	Armada 10 Esc, Rota
	HS.23-03	Sikorsky SH-60B Seahawk [01-1003]	Armada 10 Esc, Rota
	HS.23-04	Sikorsky SH-60B Seahawk [01-1004]	Armada 10 Esc, Rota
	HS.23-05	Sikorsky SH-60B Seahawk [01-1005]	Armada 10 Esc, Rota
	HS.23-06	Sikorsky SH-60B Seahawk [01-1006]	Armada 10 Esc, Rota
	HS.23-07	Sikorsky SH-60B Seahawk [01-1007]	Armada 10 Esc, Rota
	HS.23-08	Sikorsky SH-60B Seahawk [01-1008]	Armada 10 Esc, Rota
	HS.23-09	Sikorsky SH-60B Seahawk [01-1009]	Armada 10 Esc, Rota
	HS.23-10	Sikorsky SH-60B Seahawk [01-1010]	Armada 10 Esc, Rota
	HS.23-11	Sikorsky SH-60B Seahawk [01-1011]	Armada 10 Esc, Rota
	HS.23-12	Sikorsky SH-60B Seahawk [01-1012]	Armada 10 Esc, Rota
	HT.23-13	Sikorsky SH-60F Seahawk (10013) [01-1014]	Armada 10 Esc, Rota
	HT.23-14	Sikorsky SH-60F Seahawk (10014) [01-1015]	Armada 10 Esc, Rota
	HT.23-15	Sikorsky SH-60F Seahawk	Armada (on order)
	HT.23-16	Sikorsky SH-60F Seahawk	Armada (on order)
	HT.23-17	Sikorsky SH-60F Seahawk	Armada (on order)
	HT.23-18	Sikorsky SH-60F Seahawk	Armada (on order)
	HE.25-1	Eurocopter EC.120B Colibri [78-20]	EdA *Patrulla Aspa*/Ala 78, Granada/Armilla
	HE.25-2	Eurocopter EC.120B Colibri [78-21]	EdA *Patrulla Aspa*/Ala 78, Granada/Armilla
	HE.25-3	Eurocopter EC.120B Colibri [78-22]	EdA *Patrulla Aspa*/Ala 78, Granada/Armilla
	HE.25-4	Eurocopter EC.120B Colibri [78-23]	EdA *Patrulla Aspa*/Ala 78, Granada/Armilla
	HE.25-5	Eurocopter EC.120B Colibri [78-24]	EdA *Patrulla Aspa*/Ala 78, Granada/Armilla
	HE.25-6	Eurocopter EC.120B Colibri [78-25]	EdA *Patrulla Aspa*/Ala 78, Granada/Armilla
	HE.25-7	Eurocopter EC.120B Colibri [78-26]	EdA *Patrulla Aspa*/Ala 78, Granada/Armilla
	HE.25-8	Eurocopter EC.120B Colibri [78-27]	EdA *Patrulla Aspa*/Ala 78, Granada/Armilla
	HE.25-9	Eurocopter EC.120B Colibri [78-28]	EdA *Patrulla Aspa*/Ala 78, Granada/Armilla
	HE.25-10	Eurocopter EC.120B Colibri [78-29]	EdA 782 Esc/Ala 78, Granada/Armilla
	HE.25-11	Eurocopter EC.120B Colibri [782-11]	EdA 782 Esc/Ala 78, Granada/Armilla

Serial	Type (code/other identity)	Owner/operator, location or fate	Notes
HE.25-12	Eurocopter EC.120B Colibri [78-31]	EdA *Patrulla Aspa*/Ala 78, Granada/Armilla	
HE.25-13	Eurocopter EC.120B Colibri [78-32]	EdA *Patrulla Aspa*/Ala 78, Granada/Armilla	
HE.25-14	Eurocopter EC.120B Colibri [78-33]	EdA *Patrulla Aspa*/Ala 78, Granada/Armilla	
HE.25-15	Eurocopter EC.120B Colibri [78-34]	EdA *Patrulla Aspa*/Ala 78, Granada/Armilla	
P.3M-08	Lockheed P-3M Orion [22-31]	EdA 221 Esc/Grupo 22, Sevilla/Morón	
P.3M-09	Lockheed P-3M Orion [22-32]	EdA 221 Esc/Grupo 22, Sevilla/Morón	
P.3M-12	Lockheed P-3M Orion [22-35]	EdA 221 Esc/Grupo 22, Sevilla/Morón	
TL.10-01	Lockheed C-130H-30 Hercules [31-01]	EdA 311 Esc/312 Esc/Ala 31, Zaragoza	
T.10-03	Lockheed C-130H Hercules [31-03]	EdA 311 Esc/312 Esc/Ala 31, Zaragoza	
T.10-04	Lockheed C-130H Hercules [31-04]	EdA, stored Sevilla/Morón	
TK.10-05	Lockheed KC-130H Hercules [31-50]	EdA 311 Esc/312 Esc/Ala 31, Zaragoza	
TK.10-06	Lockheed KC-130H Hercules [31-51]	EdA 311 Esc/312 Esc/Ala 31, Zaragoza	
TK.10-07	Lockheed KC-130H Hercules [31-52]	EdA 311 Esc/312 Esc/Ala 31, Zaragoza	
T.10-08	Lockheed C-130H Hercules [31-05]	EdA 311 Esc/312 Esc/Ala 31, Zaragoza	
T.10-09	Lockheed C-130H Hercules [31-06]	EdA 311 Esc/312 Esc/Ala 31, Zaragoza	
T.10-10	Lockheed C-130H Hercules [31-07]	EdA 311 Esc/312 Esc/Ala 31, Zaragoza	
TK.10-11	Lockheed KC-130H Hercules [31-53]	EdA 311 Esc/312 Esc/Ala 31, Zaragoza	
TK.10-12	Lockheed KC-130H Hercules [31-54]	EdA 311 Esc/312 Esc/Ala 31, Zaragoza	
TM.11-3	Dassault Falcon 20D [472-03]	EdA 472 Esc/Grupo Mixto 47, Madrid/Torrejón	
TM.11-4	Dassault Falcon 20E [472-04]	EdA 472 Esc/Grupo Mixto 47, Madrid/Torrejón	
T.12B-13	CASA 212A Aviocar [72-13]	EdA 721 Esc/Ala 72, Murcia/Alcantarilla	
T.12B-49	CASA 212A Aviocar [72-49]	EdA 721 Esc/Ala 72, Murcia/Alcantarilla	
T.12B-62	CASA 212A Aviocar (D.3A-2) [72-62]	EdA 721 Esc/Ala 72, Murcia/Alcantarilla	
T.12B-63	CASA 212A Aviocar [72-63]	EdA 721 Esc/Ala 72, Murcia/Alcantarilla	
T.12B-65	CASA 212A Aviocar [72-11]	EdA 721 Esc/Ala 72, Murcia/Alcantarilla	
T.12B-66	CASA 212A Aviocar [72-66]	EdA 721 Esc/Ala 72, Murcia/Alcantarilla	
T.12B-67	CASA 212A Aviocar [72-12]	EdA 721 Esc/Ala 72, Murcia/Alcantarilla	
T.12B-69	CASA 212A Aviocar [72-69]	EdA 721 Esc/Ala 72, Murcia/Alcantarilla	
T.12B-70	CASA 212A Aviocar [72-71]	EdA 721 Esc/Ala 72, Murcia/Alcantarilla	
T.12B-71	CASA 212A Aviocar [72-10] $	EdA 721 Esc/Ala 72, Murcia/Alcantarilla	
TM.12D-72	CASA 212-200ECM Aviocar [47-12]	EdA 472 Esc/Grupo Mixto 47, Madrid/Torrejón	
T.12D-74	CASA 212-200 Aviocar [54-11]	EdA 541 Esc/CLAEX/Grupo 54, Madrid/Torrejón	
T.12D-75	CASA 212-200 Aviocar [47-14]	EdA 472 Esc/Grupo Mixto 47, Madrid/Torrejón	
TR.12D-76	CASA 212-200 Aviocar [72-21]	EdA 721 Esc/Ala 72, Murcia/Alcantarilla	
TR.12D-77	CASA 212-200 Aviocar [72-22]	EdA 721 Esc/Ala 72, Murcia/Alcantarilla	
TR.12D-79	CASA 212-200 Aviocar [72-23]	*Withdrawn from use, December 2018*	
TR.12D-81	CASA 212-200 Aviocar [72-24]	EdA 721 Esc/Ala 72, Murcia/Alcantarilla	
T.18-1	Dassault Falcon 900 [45-40]	EdA 451 Esc/Grupo 45, Madrid/Torrejón	
T.18-2	Dassault Falcon 900 [45-41]	EdA 451 Esc/Grupo 45, Madrid/Torrejón	
T.18-3	Dassault Falcon 900B [45-42]	EdA 451 Esc/Grupo 45, Madrid/Torrejón	
T.18-4	Dassault Falcon 900B [45-04]	EdA 451 Esc/Grupo 45, Madrid/Torrejón	
T.18-5	Dassault Falcon 900B [45-44]	EdA 451 Esc/Grupo 45, Madrid/Torrejón	
T.19A-01	Airtech CN.235M-10 [403-01]	EdA 403 Esc, Madrid/Getafe	
T.19A-02	Airtech CN.235M-10 [403-02]	EdA 403 Esc, Madrid/Getafe	
T.19B-07	Airtech CN.235M-100 [74-07]	EdA 744 Esc/GEM, Salamanca/Matacán	
T.19B-11	Airtech CN.235M-100 [74-11]	EdA 744 Esc/GEM, Salamanca/Matacán	
T.19B-13	Airtech CN.235M-100 [74-13]	EdA 744 Esc/GEM, Salamanca/Matacán	
T.19B-16	Airtech CN.235M-100 [74-16]	EdA 744 Esc/GEM, Salamanca/Matacán	
T.19B-17	Airtech CN.235M-100 [74-17]	EdA 744 Esc/GEM, Salamanca/Matacán	
T.19B-18	Airtech CN.235M-100 [74-18]	EdA 744 Esc/GEM, Salamanca/Matacán	
T.19B-19	Airtech CN.235M-100 [74-19]	EdA 744 Esc/GEM, Salamanca/Matacán	
T.19B-20	Airtech CN.235M-100 [74-20]	EdA 744 Esc/GEM, Salamanca/Matacán	
T.19B-21	Airtech CN.235M VIGMA [09-501]	Guardia Civil Servicio Aéreo, Gran Canaria	
T.19B-22	Airtech CN.235M VIGMA [09-502]	Guardia Civil Servicio Aéreo, Gran Canaria	
TR.20-01	Cessna 560 Citation VI [403-11]	EdA 403 Esc, Madrid/Getafe	
TR.20-02	Cessna 560 Citation VI [403-12]	EdA 403 Esc, Madrid/Getafe	
TR.20-03	Cessna 560 Citation VI [403-21]	EdA 403 Esc, Madrid/Getafe	
T.21-01	CASA C-295M [35-39]	EdA 353 Esc/Ala 35, Madrid/Getafe	
T.21-02	CASA C-295M [35-40]	EdA 353 Esc/Ala 35, Madrid/Getafe	
T.21-03	CASA C-295M [35-41]	EdA 353 Esc/Ala 35, Madrid/Getafe	
T.21-04	CASA C-295M [35-42]	EdA 353 Esc/Ala 35, Madrid/Getafe	
T.21-05	CASA C-295M [35-43]	EdA 353 Esc/Ala 35, Madrid/Getafe	

Notes	Serial	Type (code/other identity)	Owner/operator, location or fate
	T.21-06	CASA C-295M [35-44]	EdA 353 Esc/Ala 35, Madrid/Getafe
	T.21-07	CASA C-295M [35-45]	EdA 353 Esc/Ala 35, Madrid/Getafe
	T.21-08	CASA C-295M [35-46]	EdA 353 Esc/Ala 35, Madrid/Getafe
	T.21-09	CASA C-295M [35-09]	EdA 353 Esc/Ala 35, Madrid/Getafe
	T.21-10	CASA C-295M [35-48]	*Crashed Santa Cilia, 3 April 2019*
	T.21-11	CASA C-295M [35-49]	EdA 353 Esc/Ala 35, Madrid/Getafe
	T.21-12	CASA C-295M [35-50]	EdA 353 Esc/Ala 35, Madrid/Getafe
	T.21-13	CASA C-295M [35-51]	EdA 353 Esc/Ala 35, Madrid/Getafe
	T.22-1	Airbus A.310-304 [45-50]	EdA 451 Esc/Grupo 45, Madrid/Torrejón
	T.22-2	Airbus A.310-304 [45-51]	EdA 451 Esc/Grupo 45, Madrid/Torrejón
	T.23-01	Airbus Military A.400M (10074) [31-21]	EdA 311 Esc/312 Esc/Ala 31, Zaragoza
	TK.23-02	Airbus Military A.400M (10075) [31-22]	EdA 311 Esc/312 Esc/Ala 31, Zaragoza
	TK.23-03	Airbus Military A.400M (10076) [31-23]	EdA 311 Esc/312 Esc/Ala 31, Zaragoza
	T.23-04	Airbus Military A.400M (10174) [31-24]	EdA (on order)
	T.23-05	Airbus Military A.400M (10206) [31-25]	EdA 311 Esc/312 Esc/Ala 31, Zaragoza
	T.23-06	Airbus Military A.400M [31-26]	EdA (on order)
	TK.23-07	Airbus Military A.400M [31-27]	EdA (on order)
	T.23-08	Airbus Military A.400M (10217) [31-28]	EdA (on order)
	T.23-09	Airbus Military A.400M (10217) [31-29]	EdA (on order)
	U.20-1	Cessna 550 Citation II [01-405]	Armada 4 Esc, Rota
	U.20-2	Cessna 550 Citation II [01-406]	Armada 4 Esc, Rota
	U.20-3	Cessna 550 Citation II [01-407]	Armada 4 Esc, Rota
	U.21-01	Cessna 650 Citation VII [01-408]	Armada 4 Esc, Rota
	VA.1B-24	McDonnell Douglas EAV-8B+ Matador [01-914]	Armada 9 Esc, Rota
	VA.1B-25	McDonnell Douglas EAV-8B+ Matador [01-915]	Armada, stored Rota
	VA.1B-26	McDonnell Douglas EAV-8B+ Matador [01-916]	Armada 9 Esc, Rota
	VA.1B-27	McDonnell Douglas EAV-8B+ Matador [01-917]	Armada 9 Esc, Rota
	VA.1B-28	McDonnell Douglas EAV-8B+ Matador [01-918]	Armada, stored Rota
	VA.1B-29	McDonnell Douglas EAV-8B+ Matador [01-919]	Armada 9 Esc, Rota
	VA.1B-30	McDonnell Douglas EAV-8B+ Matador [01-920]	Armada 9 Esc, Rota
	VA.1B-33	McDonnell Douglas TAV-8B Matador [01-922]	Armada 9 Esc, Rota
	VA.1B-35	McDonnell Douglas EAV-8B+ Matador [01-923]	Armada 9 Esc, Rota
	VA.1B-36	McDonnell Douglas EAV-8B+ Matador [01-924]	Armada 9 Esc, Rota
	VA.1B-37	McDonnell Douglas EAV-8B+ Matador [01-925]	Armada 9 Esc, Rota
	VA.1B-38	McDonnell Douglas EAV-8B+ Matador [01-926]	Armada 9 Esc, Rota
	VA.1B-39	McDonnell Douglas EAV-8B+ Matador [01-927]	Armada 9 Esc, Rota
	SUDAN		
	ST-PSA	Dassault Falcon 900B	Sudanese Government, Khartoum
	ST-PSR	Dassault Falcon 50	Sudanese Government, Khartoum
	SWAZILAND		
	3DC-SDF	Airbus A.340-213X	Government of Swaziland, Manzini/Sikhupe

SWEDEN

Försvarsmakten/Swedish Armed Forces: Försvarsmaktens Helikopterflottilj (Hkpflj)/Armed Forces Helicopter Wing & Svenska Flygvapnet/Swedish Air Force

Notes	Serial	Type (code/other identity)	Owner/operator, location or fate
	39-6	SAAB JAS 39C Gripen [6]	SAAB, Linköping/Malmen
	39-7	SAAB JAS 39NG Gripen	SAAB, Linköping/Malmen
	39-8	SAAB JAS 39E Gripen	SAAB, Linköping/Malmen
	39-9	SAAB JAS 39E Gripen	SAAB, Linköping/Malmen
	39-10	SAAB JAS 39E Gripen	SAAB, Linköping/Malmen
	39-6002	SAAB JAS 39E Gripen	SAAB, Linköping/Malmen
	39208	SAAB JAS 39C Gripen [208]	Flygvapnet Flottilj 17, Ronneby/Kallinge
	39209	SAAB JAS 39C Gripen [209]	Flygvapnet Flottiljer 7, Såtenäs
	39210	SAAB JAS 39C Gripen [210] $	Flygvapnet Flottilj 17, Ronneby/Kallinge
	39211	SAAB JAS 39C Gripen [211]	Flygvapnet Flottiljer 7, Såtenäs
	39212	SAAB JAS 39C Gripen [212]	Flygvapnet Flottilj 17, Ronneby/Kallinge
	39213	SAAB JAS 39C Gripen [213]	Flygvapnet Flottiljer 7, Såtenäs
	39214	SAAB JAS 39C Gripen [214]	Flygvapnet Flottiljer 7, Såtenäs
	39215	SAAB JAS 39C Gripen [215]	Flygvapnet Flottiljer 7, Såtenäs
	39216	SAAB JAS 39C Gripen [216]	Flygvapnet Flottilj 17, Ronneby/Kallinge

Serial	Type (code/other identity)	Owner/operator, location or fate	Notes
39217	SAAB JAS 39C Gripen [217]	Flygvapnet Flottiljer 7, Såtenäs	
39218	SAAB JAS 39C Gripen [218]	Flygvapnet Flottiljer 21, Luleå/Kallax	
39219	SAAB JAS 39C Gripen [219]	Flygvapnet Flottiljer 21, Luleå/Kallax	
39220	SAAB JAS 39C Gripen [220]	Flygvapnet Flottiljer 7, Såtenäs	
39221	SAAB JAS 39C Gripen [221]	Flygvapnet Flottiljer 17, Ronneby/Kallinge	
39222	SAAB JAS 39C Gripen [222]	Flygvapnet Flottiljer 17, Ronneby/Kallinge	
39223	SAAB JAS 39C Gripen [223]	Flygvapnet Flottiljer 21, Luleå/Kallax	
39224	SAAB JAS 39C Gripen [224]	Flygvapnet Flottiljer 17, Ronneby/Kallinge	
39225	SAAB JAS 39C Gripen [225]	Flygvapnet Flottiljer 7, Såtenäs	
39226	SAAB JAS 39C Gripen [226]	Flygvapnet Flottiljer 7, Såtenäs	
39227	SAAB JAS 39C Gripen [227]	Flygvapnet Flottiljer 7, Såtenäs	
39228	SAAB JAS 39C Gripen [228]	Flygvapnet Flottiljer 17, Ronneby/Kallinge	
39229	SAAB JAS 39C Gripen [229]	Flygvapnet Flottiljer 21, Luleå/Kallax	
39230	SAAB JAS 39C Gripen [230]	Flygvapnet Flottiljer 17, Ronneby/Kallinge	
39231	SAAB JAS 39C Gripen [231]	Flygvapnet Flottiljer 7, Såtenäs	
39232	SAAB JAS 39C Gripen [232]	Flygvapnet Flottiljer 21, Luleå/Kallax	
39233	SAAB JAS 39C Gripen [233]	Flygvapnet Flottiljer 17, Ronneby/Kallinge	
39246	SAAB JAS 39C Gripen [246]	Flygvapnet Flottiljer 17, Ronneby/Kallinge	
39247	SAAB JAS 39C Gripen [247]	Flygvapnet Flottiljer 17, Ronneby/Kallinge	
39248	SAAB JAS 39C Gripen [248]	Flygvapnet Flottiljer 21, Luleå/Kallax	
39249	SAAB JAS 39C Gripen [249]	Flygvapnet Flottiljer 21, Luleå/Kallax	
39250	SAAB JAS 39C Gripen [250]	Flygvapnet FC, Linköping/Malmen	
39251	SAAB JAS 39C Gripen [251]	Flygvapnet FC, Linköping/Malmen	
39252	SAAB JAS 39C Gripen [252]	Crashed 21 August 2018, Ronneby	
39253	SAAB JAS 39C Gripen [253]	Flygvapnet Flottiljer 7, Såtenäs	
39254	SAAB JAS 39C Gripen [254]	Flygvapnet Flottiljer 17, Ronneby/Kallinge	
39255	SAAB JAS 39C Gripen [255]	Flygvapnet Flottiljer 17, Ronneby/Kallinge	
39256	SAAB JAS 39C Gripen [256]	Flygvapnet Flottiljer 17, Ronneby/Kallinge	
39257	SAAB JAS 39C Gripen [257]	Flygvapnet Flottiljer 21, Luleå/Kallax	
39258	SAAB JAS 39C Gripen [258]	Flygvapnet Flottiljer 21, Luleå/Kallax	
39260	SAAB JAS 39C Gripen [260]	Flygvapnet Flottiljer 21, Luleå/Kallax	
39261	SAAB JAS 39C Gripen [261]	Flygvapnet Flottiljer 21, Luleå/Kallax	
39262	SAAB JAS 39C Gripen [262]	SAAB, Linköping/Malmen	
39263	SAAB JAS 39C Gripen [263]	Flygvapnet Flottiljer 21, Luleå/Kallax	
39264	SAAB JAS 39C Gripen [264]	Flygvapnet Flottiljer 17, Ronneby/Kallinge	
39265	SAAB JAS 39C Gripen [265]	Flygvapnet Flottiljer 21, Luleå/Kallax	
39266	SAAB JAS 39C Gripen [266]	Flygvapnet Flottiljer 7, Såtenäs	
39267	SAAB JAS 39C Gripen [267]	Flygvapnet Flottiljer 21, Luleå/Kallax	
39268	SAAB JAS 39C Gripen [268]	Flygvapnet Flottiljer 7, Såtenäs	
39269	SAAB JAS 39C Gripen [269]	Flygvapnet Flottiljer 17, Ronneby/Kallinge	
39270	SAAB JAS 39C Gripen [270]	Flygvapnet Flottiljer 17, Ronneby/Kallinge	
39271	SAAB JAS 39C Gripen [271]	Flygvapnet Flottiljer 21, Luleå/Kallax	
39272	SAAB JAS 39C Gripen [272]	Flygvapnet Flottiljer 7, Såtenäs	
39273	SAAB JAS 39C Gripen [273]	Flygvapnet Flottiljer 17, Ronneby/Kallinge	
39274	SAAB JAS 39C Gripen [274]	Flygvapnet Flottiljer 21, Luleå/Kallax	
39275	SAAB JAS 39C Gripen [275]	Flygvapnet Flottiljer 7, Såtenäs	
39276	SAAB JAS 39C Gripen [276]	Flygvapnet Flottiljer 21, Luleå/Kallax	
39277	SAAB JAS 39C Gripen [277]	Flygvapnet Flottiljer 7, Såtenäs	
39278	SAAB JAS 39C Gripen [278]	Flygvapnet Flottiljer 7, Såtenäs	
39279	SAAB JAS 39C Gripen [279]	Flygvapnet Flottiljer 21, Luleå/Kallax	
39280	SAAB JAS 39C Gripen [280]	Flygvapnet Flottiljer 21, Luleå/Kallax	
39281	SAAB JAS 39C Gripen [281]	Flygvapnet Flottiljer 17, Ronneby/Kallinge	
39282	SAAB JAS 39C Gripen [282]	Flygvapnet Flottiljer 7, Såtenäs	
39283	SAAB JAS 39C Gripen [283]	Flygvapnet Flottiljer 21, Luleå/Kallax	
39284	SAAB JAS 39C Gripen [284]	Flygvapnet Flottiljer 17, Ronneby/Kallinge	
39285	SAAB JAS 39C Gripen [285]	Flygvapnet Flottiljer 21, Luleå/Kallax	
39286	SAAB JAS 39C Gripen [286]	Flygvapnet Flottiljer 21, Luleå/Kallax	
39287	SAAB JAS 39C Gripen [287]	Flygvapnet Flottiljer 17, Ronneby/Kallinge	
39288	SAAB JAS 39C Gripen [288]	Flygvapnet Flottiljer 21, Luleå/Kallax	
39289	SAAB JAS 39C Gripen [289]	Flygvapnet Flottiljer 7, Såtenäs	
39290	SAAB JAS 39C Gripen [290]	Flygvapnet Flottiljer 21, Luleå/Kallax	
39291	SAAB JAS 39C Gripen [291]	Flygvapnet Flottiljer 7, Såtenäs	

Notes	Serial	Type (code/other identity)	Owner/operator, location or fate
	39292	SAAB JAS 39C Gripen [292]	Flygvapnet Flottiljer 17, Ronneby/Kallinge
	39293	SAAB JAS 39C Gripen [293]	Flygvapnet Flottiljer 7, Såtenäs
	39294	SAAB JAS 39C Gripen [294]	Flygvapnet Flottiljer 17, Ronneby/Kallinge
	39815	SAAB JAS 39D Gripen [815]	Flygvapnet Flottiljer 7, Såtenäs
	39816	SAAB JAS 39D Gripen [816]	Flygvapnet Flottiljer 7, Såtenäs
	39817	SAAB JAS 39D Gripen [817]	Flygvapnet Flottiljer 21, Luleå/Kallax
	39821	SAAB JAS 39D Gripen [821]	Flygvapnet Flottiljer 7, Såtenäs
	39822	SAAB JAS 39D Gripen [822]	Flygvapnet Flottiljer 21, Luleå/Kallax
	39823	SAAB JAS 39D Gripen [823]	Flygvapnet Flottiljer 21, Luleå/Kallax
	39824	SAAB JAS 39D Gripen [824]	Flygvapnet Flottiljer 21, Luleå/Kallax
	39825	SAAB JAS 39D Gripen [825]	Flygvapnet Flottiljer 7, Såtenäs
	39826	SAAB JAS 39D Gripen [826]	Flygvapnet Flottiljer 17, Ronneby/Kallinge
	39827	SAAB JAS 39D Gripen [827]	Flygvapnet Flottiljer 7, Såtenäs
	39829	SAAB JAS 39D Gripen [829]	Flygvapnet Flottiljer 17, Ronneby/Kallinge
	39830	SAAB JAS 39D Gripen [830]	SAAB, Linköping/Malmen
	39831	SAAB JAS 39D Gripen [831]	Flygvapnet Flottiljer 17, Ronneby/Kallinge
	39832	SAAB JAS 39D Gripen [832]	SAAB, Linköping/Malmen
	39833	SAAB JAS 39D Gripen [833]	Flygvapnet Flottiljer 21, Luleå/Kallax
	39834	SAAB JAS 39D Gripen [834]	Flygvapnet Flottiljer 7, Såtenäs
	39835	SAAB JAS 39D Gripen [835]	Flygvapnet Flottiljer 7, Såtenäs
	39836	SAAB JAS 39D Gripen [836]	Flygvapnet Flottiljer 17, Ronneby/Kallinge
	39837	SAAB JAS 39D Gripen [837]	SAAB, Linköping/Malmen
	39838	SAAB JAS 39D Gripen [838]	Flygvapnet Flottiljer 21, Luleå/Kallax
	39839	SAAB JAS 39D Gripen [839]	Flygvapnet Flottiljer 7, Såtenäs
	39840	SAAB JAS 39D Gripen [840]	Flygvapnet Flottiljer 21, Luleå/Kallax
	39841	SAAB JAS 39D Gripen [841]	Flygvapnet Flottiljer 7, Såtenäs
	84001	Lockheed C-130H Hercules (Tp.84) [841]	MADG, stored Cambridge
	84003	Lockheed C-130H Hercules (Tp.84) [843]	MADG, stored Cambridge
	84004	Lockheed C-130H Hercules (Tp.84) [844]	Flygvapnet TSFE, Såtenäs
	84005	Lockheed C-130H Hercules (Tp.84) [845]	Flygvapnet TSFE, Såtenäs
	84006	Lockheed C-130H Hercules (Tp.84) [846]	Flygvapnet TSFE, Såtenäs
	84007	Lockheed C-130H Hercules (Tp.84) [847]	Flygvapnet TSFE, Såtenäs
	84008	Lockheed C-130H Hercules (Tp.84) [848]	Flygvapnet TSFE, Såtenäs
	86001	Rockwell Sabreliner-40 (Tp.86) [861]	Flygvapnet FC, Linköping/Malmen
	100001	SAAB SF.340 (OS.100) [001]	Flygvapnet TSFE, Linköping/Malmen
	100003	SAAB SF.340AEW&C (S.100D Argus) [003]	Flygvapnet TSFE, Linköping/Malmen
	100004	SAAB SF.340AEW&C (S.100D Argus) [004]	Flygvapnet TSFE, Linköping/Malmen
	100008	SAAB SF.340 (Tp.100C) [008]	Flygvapnet TSFE, Linköping/Malmen
	102002	Grumman G.1159C Gulfstream IV (S.102B Korpen)[022]	Flygvapnet TSFE, Linköping/Malmen
	102003	Grumman G.1159C Gulfstream IV (S.102B Korpen)[023]	Flygvapnet TSFE, Linköping/Malmen
	102004	Grumman G.1159C Gulfstream IV-SP (Tp.102C) [024]	Flygvapnet TSFE, Linköping/Malmen
	102005	Gulfstream Aerospace G.550 (Tp.102D) [025]	Flygvapnet TSFE, Linköping/Malmen
	141041	NH Industries NH.90-TTH (Hkp.14A) [41]	Airbus Helicopters, Marignane, France
	141047	NH Industries NH.90-TTH (Hkp.14A) [47]	Hkpflj 1.HkpSkv, Luleå/Kallax
	142042	NH Industries NH.90-TTH (Hkp.14B) [42]	Hkpflj 3.HkpSkv, Ronneby/Kallinge
	142043	NH Industries NH.90-TTH (Hkp.14B) [43]	Hkpflj 3.HkpSkv, Ronneby/Kallinge
	142044	NH Industries NH.90-TTH (Hkp.14B) [44]	Hkpflj 3.HkpSkv, Ronneby/Kallinge
	142045	NH Industries NH.90-TTH (Hkp.14B) [45]	Hkpflj 1.HkpSkv, Luleå/Kallax
	144048	NH Industries NH.90-TTH (Hkp.14D) [48]	Hkpflj 1.HkpSkv, Luleå/Kallax
	144049	NH Industries NH.90-TTH (Hkp.14D) [49]	Hkpflj 1.HkpSkv, Luleå/Kallax
	144050	NH Industries NH.90-TTH (Hkp.14D) [50]	Hkpflj 1.HkpSkv, Luleå/Kallax
	144051	NH Industries NH.90-TTH (Hkp.14D) [51]	Hkpflj 1.HkpSkv, Luleå/Kallax
	144052	NH Industries NH.90-TTH (Hkp.14D) [52]	Hkpflj 1.HkpSkv, Luleå/Kallax
	144053	NH Industries NH.90-TTH (Hkp.14D) [53]	Hkpflj 1.HkpSkv, Luleå/Kallax
	144054	NH Industries NH.90-TTH (Hkp.14D) [54]	Hkpflj 3.HkpSkv, Ronneby/Kallinge
	142055	NH Industries NH.90-SAR (Hkp.14B) [55]	Hkpflj 3.HkpSkv, Ronneby/Kallinge
	145046	NH Industries NH.90-TTH (Hkp.14E) [46]	Hkpflj 1.HkpSkv, Luleå/Kallax
	146056	NH Industries NH.90-SAR (Hkp.14F) [56]	Hkpflj 3.HkpSkv, Ronneby/Kallinge
	146057	NH Industries NH.90-SAR (Hkp.14F) [57]	Hkpflj 3.HkpSkv, Ronneby/Kallinge
	146058	NH Industries NH.90-SAR (Hkp.14F) [58]	Hkpflj 3.HkpSkv, Ronneby/Kallinge
	146059	NH Industries NH.90-SAR (Hkp.14F) [59]	Hkpflj 3.HkpSkv, Ronneby/Kallinge
	151751	Agusta A109LUH Power (Hkp.15A) [21]	Hkpflj 2.HkpSkv, Linköping/Malmen

Serial	Type (code/other identity)	Owner/operator, location or fate	Notes
151752	Agusta A109LUH Power (Hkp.15A) [22]	Hkpflj 2.HkpSkv, Linköping/Malmen	
151753	Agusta A109LUH Power (Hkp.15A) [23]	Hkpflj 2.HkpSkv, Linköping/Malmen	
151754	Agusta A109LUH Power (Hkp.15A) [24]	Hkpflj 2.HkpSkv, Linköping/Malmen	
151755	Agusta A109LUH Power (Hkp.15A) [25]	Hkpflj 2.HkpSkv, Linköping/Malmen	
151756	Agusta A109LUH Power (Hkp.15A) [26]	Hkpflj 2.HkpSkv, Linköping/Malmen	
151757	Agusta A109LUH Power (Hkp.15A) [27]	Hkpflj 2.HkpSkv, Linköping/Malmen	
151758	Agusta A109LUH Power (Hkp.15A) [28]	Hkpflj 2.HkpSkv, Linköping/Malmen	
151759	Agusta A109LUH Power (Hkp.15A) [29]	Hkpflj 2.HkpSkv, Linköping/Malmen	
152760	Agusta A109LUH Power (Hkp.15B) [30]	Hkpflj 3.HkpSkv, Ronneby/Kallinge	
151761	Agusta A109LUH Power (Hkp.15A) [31]	Hkpflj 2.HkpSkv, Linköping/Malmen	
151762	Agusta A109LUH Power (Hkp.15A) [32]	Hkpflj 2.HkpSkv, Linköping/Malmen	
152763	Agusta A109LUH Power (Hkp.15B) [33]	Hkpflj 3.HkpSkv, Ronneby/Kallinge	
151764	Agusta A109LUH Power (Hkp.15A) [34]	Hkpflj 2.HkpSkv, Linköping/Malmen	
152765	Agusta A109LUH Power (Hkp.15B) [35]	Hkpflj 3.HkpSkv, Ronneby/Kallinge	
152766	Agusta A109LUH Power (Hkp.15B) [36]	Hkpflj 3.HkpSkv, Ronneby/Kallinge	
152767	Agusta A109LUH Power (Hkp.15B) [37]	Hkpflj 3.HkpSkv, Ronneby/Kallinge	
152768	Agusta A109LUH Power (Hkp.15B) [38]	Hkpflj 3.HkpSkv, Ronneby/Kallinge	
152769	Agusta A109LUH Power (Hkp.15B) [39]	Hkpflj 3.HkpSkv, Ronneby/Kallinge	
152770	Agusta A109LUH Power (Hkp.15B) [40]	Hkpflj 3.HkpSkv, Ronneby/Kallinge	
161226	Sikorsky UH-60M Black Hawk (Hkp.16A) [01]	Hkpflj 2.HkpSkv, Linköping/Malmen	
161227	Sikorsky UH-60M Black Hawk (Hkp.16A) [02]	Hkpflj 2.HkpSkv, Linköping/Malmen	
161228	Sikorsky UH-60M Black Hawk (Hkp.16A) [03]	Hkpflj 2.HkpSkv, Linköping/Malmen	
161229	Sikorsky UH-60M Black Hawk (Hkp.16A) [04]	Hkpflj 2.HkpSkv, Linköping/Malmen	
161230	Sikorsky UH-60M Black Hawk (Hkp.16A) [05]	Hkpflj 2.HkpSkv, Linköping/Malmen	
161231	Sikorsky UH-60M Black Hawk (Hkp.16A) [06]	Hkpflj 2.HkpSkv, Linköping/Malmen	
161232	Sikorsky UH-60M Black Hawk (Hkp.16A) [07]	Hkpflj 2.HkpSkv, Linköping/Malmen	
161233	Sikorsky UH-60M Black Hawk (Hkp.16A) [08]	Hkpflj 2.HkpSkv, Linköping/Malmen	
161234	Sikorsky UH-60M Black Hawk (Hkp.16A) [09]	Hkpflj 2.HkpSkv, Linköping/Malmen	
161235	Sikorsky UH-60M Black Hawk (Hkp.16A) [10]	Hkpflj 2.HkpSkv, Linköping/Malmen	
161236	Sikorsky UH-60M Black Hawk (Hkp.16A) [11]	Hkpflj 2.HkpSkv, Linköping/Malmen	
161237	Sikorsky UH-60M Black Hawk (Hkp.16A) [12]	Hkpflj 2.HkpSkv, Linköping/Malmen	
161238	Sikorsky UH-60M Black Hawk (Hkp.16A) [13]	Hkpflj 2.HkpSkv, Linköping/Malmen	
161239	Sikorsky UH-60M Black Hawk (Hkp.16A) [14]	Hkpflj 2.HkpSkv, Linköping/Malmen	
161240	Sikorsky UH-60M Black Hawk (Hkp.16A) [15]	Hkpflj 2.HkpSkv, Linköping/Malmen	

Kustbevakning/Swedish Coast Guard

Serial	Type (code/other identity)	Owner/operator, location or fate	Notes
SE-MAA	Bombardier DHC-8Q-311 [501]	Kustbevakning, Nykoping	
SE-MAB	Bombardier DHC-8Q-311 [502]	Kustbevakning, Nykoping	
SE-MAC	Bombardier DHC-8Q-311 [503]	Kustbevakning, Nykoping	

SWITZERLAND

Schweizer Luftwaffe/Swiss Air Force

(Most aircraft are pooled centrally. Some carry unit badges but these rarely indicate actual operators.)

Serial	Type (code/other identity)	Owner/operator, location or fate	Notes
A-101	Pilatus PC-21	Swiss AF Pilotenschule, Emmen	
A-102	Pilatus PC-21	Swiss AF Pilotenschule, Emmen	
A-103	Pilatus PC-21	Swiss AF Pilotenschule, Emmen	
A-104	Pilatus PC-21	Swiss AF Pilotenschule, Emmen	
A-105	Pilatus PC-21	Swiss AF Pilotenschule, Emmen	
A-106	Pilatus PC-21	Swiss AF Pilotenschule, Emmen	
A-107	Pilatus PC-21	Swiss AF Pilotenschule, Emmen	
A-108	Pilatus PC-21	Swiss AF Pilotenschule, Emmen	
A-912	Pilatus NCPC-7 Turbo Trainer	Swiss AF Instrumentenflugstaffel 14, Emmen	
A-913	Pilatus NCPC-7 Turbo Trainer	Swiss AF Instrumentenflugstaffel 14, Emmen	
A-914	Pilatus NCPC-7 Turbo Trainer	Swiss AF Instrumentenflugstaffel 14, Emmen	
A-915	Pilatus NCPC-7 Turbo Trainer	Swiss AF Instrumentenflugstaffel 14, Emmen	
A-916	Pilatus NCPC-7 Turbo Trainer	Swiss AF Instrumentenflugstaffel 14, Emmen	
A-917	Pilatus NCPC-7 Turbo Trainer	Swiss AF Instrumentenflugstaffel 14, Emmen	
A-918	Pilatus NCPC-7 Turbo Trainer	Swiss AF Instrumentenflugstaffel 14, Emmen	
A-919	Pilatus NCPC-7 Turbo Trainer	Swiss AF Instrumentenflugstaffel 14, Emmen	
A-922	Pilatus NCPC-7 Turbo Trainer	Swiss AF Instrumentenflugstaffel 14, Emmen	
A-923	Pilatus NCPC-7 Turbo Trainer	Swiss AF Instrumentenflugstaffel 14, Emmen	
A-924	Pilatus NCPC-7 Turbo Trainer	Swiss AF Instrumentenflugstaffel 14, Emmen	
A-925	Pilatus NCPC-7 Turbo Trainer	Swiss AF Instrumentenflugstaffel 14, Emmen	

Notes	Serial	Type (code/other identity)	Owner/operator, location or fate
	A-926	Pilatus NCPC-7 Turbo Trainer	Swiss AF Instrumentenflugstaffel 14, Emmen
	A-927	Pilatus NCPC-7 Turbo Trainer	Swiss AF Instrumentenflugstaffel 14, Emmen
	A-928	Pilatus NCPC-7 Turbo Trainer	Swiss AF Instrumentenflugstaffel 14, Emmen
	A-929	Pilatus NCPC-7 Turbo Trainer	Swiss AF Instrumentenflugstaffel 14, Emmen
	A-930	Pilatus NCPC-7 Turbo Trainer	Swiss AF Instrumentenflugstaffel 14, Emmen
	A-931	Pilatus NCPC-7 Turbo Trainer	Swiss AF Instrumentenflugstaffel 14, Emmen
	A-932	Pilatus NCPC-7 Turbo Trainer	Swiss AF Instrumentenflugstaffel 14, Emmen
	A-933	Pilatus NCPC-7 Turbo Trainer	Swiss AF Instrumentenflugstaffel 14, Emmen
	A-934	Pilatus NCPC-7 Turbo Trainer	Swiss AF Instrumentenflugstaffel 14, Emmen
	A-935	Pilatus NCPC-7 Turbo Trainer	Swiss AF Instrumentenflugstaffel 14, Emmen
	A-936	Pilatus NCPC-7 Turbo Trainer	Swiss AF Instrumentenflugstaffel 14, Emmen
	A-938	Pilatus NCPC-7 Turbo Trainer	Swiss AF Instrumentenflugstaffel 14, Emmen
	A-939	Pilatus NCPC-7 Turbo Trainer	Swiss AF Instrumentenflugstaffel 14, Emmen
	A-940	Pilatus NCPC-7 Turbo Trainer	Swiss AF Instrumentenflugstaffel 14, Emmen
	A-941	Pilatus NCPC-7 Turbo Trainer	Swiss AF Instrumentenflugstaffel 14, Emmen
	C-405	Pilatus PC-9	Swiss AF Zielflugstaffel 12, Emmen
	C-406	Pilatus PC-9	Swiss AF Zielflugstaffel 12, Emmen
	C-407	Pilatus PC-9	Swiss AF Zielflugstaffel 12, Emmen
	C-408	Pilatus PC-9	Swiss AF Zielflugstaffel 12, Emmen
	C-409	Pilatus PC-9	Swiss AF Zielflugstaffel 12, Emmen
	C-411	Pilatus PC-9	Swiss AF Zielflugstaffel 12, Emmen
	C-412	Pilatus PC-9	Swiss AF Zielflugstaffel 12, Emmen
	J-3015	Northrop F-5E Tiger II	Swiss AF FlSt 6 & 19, Payerne
	J-3030	Northrop F-5E Tiger II	Swiss AF FlSt 6 & 19, Payerne
	J-3033	Northrop F-5E Tiger II $	Swiss AF FlSt 6 & 19, Payerne
	J-3036	Northrop F-5E Tiger II $	Swiss AF, stored Sion
	J-3038	Northrop F-5E Tiger II $	Swiss AF FlSt 6 & 19, Payerne
	J-3041	Northrop F-5E Tiger II	Swiss AF, stored Sion
	J-3044	Northrop F-5E Tiger II	Swiss AF, stored Emmen
	J-3062	Northrop F-5E Tiger II	Swiss AF, stored Sion
	J-3063	Northrop F-5E Tiger II	Swiss AF, stored Sion
	J-3065	Northrop F-5E Tiger II	Swiss AF FlSt 6 & 19, Payerne
	J-3067	Northrop F-5E Tiger II	Swiss AF FlSt 6 & 19, Payerne
	J-3068	Northrop F-5E Tiger II	Swiss AF FlSt 6 & 19, Payerne
	J-3070	Northrop F-5E Tiger II	Swiss AF FlSt 6 & 19, Payerne
	J-3072	Northrop F-5E Tiger II	Swiss AF FlSt 6 & 19, Payerne
	J-3073	Northrop F-5E Tiger II $	Swiss AF FlSt 6 & 19, Payerne
	J-3074	Northrop F-5E Tiger II $	Swiss AF FlSt 6 & 19, Payerne
	J-3076	Northrop F-5E Tiger II	RUAG, stored Emmen
	J-3077	Northrop F-5E Tiger II	Swiss AF FlSt 6 & 19, Payerne
	J-3079	Northrop F-5E Tiger II	Swiss AF, stored Sion
	J-3080	Northrop F-5E Tiger II	RUAG, Emmen
	J-3081	Northrop F-5E Tiger II	Swiss AF *Patrouille Suisse*, Emmen
	J-3082	Northrop F-5E Tiger II	Swiss AF *Patrouille Suisse*, Emmen
	J-3083	Northrop F-5E Tiger II	Swiss AF *Patrouille Suisse*, Emmen
	J-3084	Northrop F-5E Tiger II	Swiss AF *Patrouille Suisse*, Emmen
	J-3085	Northrop F-5E Tiger II	Swiss AF *Patrouille Suisse*, Emmen
	J-3087	Northrop F-5E Tiger II	Swiss AF *Patrouille Suisse*, Emmen
	J-3088	Northrop F-5E Tiger II	Swiss AF *Patrouille Suisse*, Emmen
	J-3089	Northrop F-5E Tiger II	Swiss AF *Patrouille Suisse*, Emmen
	J-3090	Northrop F-5E Tiger II	Swiss AF *Patrouille Suisse*, Emmen
	J-3091	Northrop F-5E Tiger II	Swiss AF *Patrouille Suisse*, Emmen
	J-3092	Northrop F-5E Tiger II	Swiss AF FlSt 6 & 19, Payerne
	J-3093	Northrop F-5E Tiger II	Swiss AF FlSt 6 & 19, Payerne
	J-3094	Northrop F-5E Tiger II	Swiss AF FlSt 6 & 19, Payerne
	J-3095	Northrop F-5E Tiger II	Swiss AF FlSt 6 & 19, Payerne
	J-3097	Northrop F-5E Tiger II	Swiss AF FlSt 6 & 19, Payerne
	J-3201	Northrop F-5F Tiger II	Swiss AF, stored Emmen
	J-3203	Northrop F-5F Tiger II	Swiss AF FlSt 6 & 19, Payerne
	J-3204	Northrop F-5F Tiger II	Swiss AF FlSt 6 & 19, Payerne
	J-3206	Northrop F-5F Tiger II	Swiss AF, stored Emmen
	J-3210	Northrop F-5F Tiger II	Swiss AF FlSt 6 & 19, Payerne

Serial	Type (code/other identity)	Owner/operator, location or fate	Notes
J-3211	Northrop F-5F Tiger II	Swiss AF FlSt 6 & 19, Payerne	
J-3212	Northrop F-5F Tiger II	Swiss AF FlSt 6 & 19, Payerne	
J-5001	McDonnell Douglas F/A-18C Hornet	Swiss AF FlSt 11, Meiringen/FlSt 17 & 18 Payerne	
J-5002	McDonnell Douglas F/A-18C Hornet	Swiss AF FlSt 11, Meiringen/FlSt 17 & 18 Payerne	
J-5003	McDonnell Douglas F/A-18C Hornet	Swiss AF FlSt 11, Meiringen/FlSt 17 & 18 Payerne	
J-5004	McDonnell Douglas F/A-18C Hornet	Swiss AF FlSt 11, Meiringen/FlSt 17 & 18 Payerne	
J-5005	McDonnell Douglas F/A-18C Hornet	Swiss AF FlSt 11, Meiringen/FlSt 17 & 18 Payerne	
J-5006	McDonnell Douglas F/A-18C Hornet	Swiss AF FlSt 11, Meiringen/FlSt 17 & 18 Payerne	
J-5007	McDonnell Douglas F/A-18C Hornet	Swiss AF FlSt 11, Meiringen/FlSt 17 & 18 Payerne	
J-5008	McDonnell Douglas F/A-18C Hornet	Swiss AF FlSt 11, Meiringen/FlSt 17 & 18 Payerne	
J-5009	McDonnell Douglas F/A-18C Hornet	Swiss AF FlSt 11, Meiringen/FlSt 17 & 18 Payerne	
J-5010	McDonnell Douglas F/A-18C Hornet	Swiss AF FlSt 11, Meiringen/FlSt 17 & 18 Payerne	
J-5011	McDonnell Douglas F/A-18C Hornet $	Swiss AF FlSt 11, Meiringen/FlSt 17 & 18 Payerne	
J-5012	McDonnell Douglas F/A-18C Hornet	Swiss AF FlSt 11, Meiringen/FlSt 17 & 18 Payerne	
J-5013	McDonnell Douglas F/A-18C Hornet	Swiss AF FlSt 11, Meiringen/FlSt 17 & 18 Payerne	
J-5014	McDonnell Douglas F/A-18C Hornet	Swiss AF FlSt 11, Meiringen/FlSt 17 & 18 Payerne	
J-5015	McDonnell Douglas F/A-18C Hornet	Swiss AF FlSt 11, Meiringen/FlSt 17 & 18 Payerne	
J-5016	McDonnell Douglas F/A-18C Hornet	Swiss AF FlSt 11, Meiringen/FlSt 17 & 18 Payerne	
J-5017	McDonnell Douglas F/A-18C Hornet $	Swiss AF FlSt 11, Meiringen/FlSt 17 & 18 Payerne	
J-5018	McDonnell Douglas F/A-18C Hornet $	Swiss AF FlSt 11, Meiringen/FlSt 17 & 18 Payerne	
J-5019	McDonnell Douglas F/A-18C Hornet	Swiss AF FlSt 11, Meiringen/FlSt 17 & 18 Payerne	
J-5020	McDonnell Douglas F/A-18C Hornet	Swiss AF FlSt 11, Meiringen/FlSt 17 & 18 Payerne	
J-5021	McDonnell Douglas F/A-18C Hornet	Swiss AF FlSt 11, Meiringen/FlSt 17 & 18 Payerne	
J-5023	McDonnell Douglas F/A-18C Hornet	Swiss AF FlSt 11, Meiringen/FlSt 17 & 18 Payerne	
J-5024	McDonnell Douglas F/A-18C Hornet	Swiss AF FlSt 11, Meiringen/FlSt 17 & 18 Payerne	
J-5025	McDonnell Douglas F/A-18C Hornet	Swiss AF FlSt 11, Meiringen/FlSt 17 & 18 Payerne	
J-5026	McDonnell Douglas F/A-18C Hornet	Swiss AF FlSt 11, Meiringen/FlSt 17 & 18 Payerne	
J-5232	McDonnell Douglas F/A-18D Hornet	Swiss AF FlSt 11, Meiringen/FlSt 17 & 18 Payerne	
J-5233	McDonnell Douglas F/A-18D Hornet	Swiss AF FlSt 11, Meiringen/FlSt 17 & 18 Payerne	
J-5234	McDonnell Douglas F/A-18D Hornet	Swiss AF FlSt 11, Meiringen/FlSt 17 & 18 Payerne	
J-5236	McDonnell Douglas F/A-18D Hornet	Swiss AF FlSt 11, Meiringen/FlSt 17 & 18 Payerne	
J-5238	McDonnell Douglas F/A-18D Hornet	Swiss AF FlSt 11, Meiringen/FlSt 17 & 18 Payerne	
R-711	Aurora Flight Services Centaur OPA	Armasuisse, Emmen	
T-311	Aérospatiale AS.332M-1 Super Puma (TH 89)	Swiss AF LtSt 6 & 8, Alpnach/ LtSt 3 & 4, Dübendorf/LtSt 1 & 5, Payerne	
T-312	Aérospatiale AS.332M-1 Super Puma (TH 89)	Swiss AF LtSt 6 & 8, Alpnach/ LtSt 3 & 4, Dübendorf/LtSt 1 & 5, Payerne	
T-313	Aérospatiale AS.332M-1 Super Puma (TH 89)	Swiss AF LtSt 6 & 8, Alpnach/ LtSt 3 & 4, Dübendorf/LtSt 1 & 5, Payerne	
T-314	Aérospatiale AS.332M-1 Super Puma (TH 89)	Swiss AF LtSt 6 & 8, Alpnach/ LtSt 3 & 4, Dübendorf/LtSt 1 & 5, Payerne	
T-315	Aérospatiale AS.332M-1 Super Puma (TH 89)	Swiss AF LtSt 6 & 8, Alpnach/ LtSt 3 & 4, Dübendorf/LtSt 1 & 5, Payerne	
T-316	Aérospatiale AS.332M-1 Super Puma (TH 89) $	Swiss AF LtSt 6 & 8, Alpnach/ LtSt 3 & 4, Dübendorf/LtSt 1 & 5, Payerne	
T-317	Aérospatiale AS.332M-1 Super Puma (TH 89)	Swiss AF LtSt 6 & 8, Alpnach/ LtSt 3 & 4, Dübendorf/LtSt 1 & 5, Payerne	
T-318	Aérospatiale AS.332M-1 Super Puma (TH 89)	Swiss AF LtSt 6 & 8, Alpnach/ LtSt 3 & 4, Dübendorf/LtSt 1 & 5, Payerne	
T-319	Aérospatiale AS.332M-1 Super Puma (TH 89)	Swiss AF LtSt 6 & 8, Alpnach/ LtSt 3 & 4, Dübendorf/LtSt 1 & 5, Payerne	
T-320	Aérospatiale AS.332M-1 Super Puma (TH 89)	Swiss AF LtSt 6 & 8, Alpnach/ LtSt 3 & 4, Dübendorf/LtSt 1 & 5, Payerne	
T-321	Aérospatiale AS.332M-1 Super Puma (TH 89)	Swiss AF LtSt 6 & 8, Alpnach/ LtSt 3 & 4, Dübendorf/LtSt 1 & 5, Payerne	
T-322	Aérospatiale AS.332M-1 Super Puma (TH 89)	Swiss AF LtSt 6 & 8, Alpnach/ LtSt 3 & 4, Dübendorf/LtSt 1 & 5, Payerne	
T-323	Aérospatiale AS.332M-1 Super Puma (TH 89)	Swiss AF LtSt 6 & 8, Alpnach/ LtSt 3 & 4, Dübendorf/LtSt 1 & 5, Payerne	
T-324	Aérospatiale AS.332M-1 Super Puma (TH 89)	Swiss AF LtSt 6 & 8, Alpnach/ LtSt 3 & 4, Dübendorf/LtSt 1 & 5, Payerne	

Notes	Serial	Type (code/other identity)	Owner/operator, location or fate
	T-325	Aérospatiale AS.332M-1 Super Puma (TH 89)	Swiss AF LtSt 6 & 8, Alpnach/ LtSt 3 & 4, Dübendorf/LtSt 1 & 5, Payerne
	T-331	Aérospatiale AS.532UL Super Puma (TH 98)	Swiss AF LtSt 6 & 8, Alpnach/ LtSt 3 & 4, Dübendorf/LtSt 1 & 5, Payerne
	T-332	Aérospatiale AS.532UL Super Puma (TH 98)	Swiss AF LtSt 6 & 8, Alpnach/ LtSt 3 & 4, Dübendorf/LtSt 1 & 5, Payerne
	T-333	Aérospatiale AS.532UL Super Puma (TH 98)	Swiss AF LtSt 6 & 8, Alpnach/ LtSt 3 & 4, Dübendorf/LtSt 1 & 5, Payerne
	T-334	Aérospatiale AS.532UL Super Puma (TH 98)	Swiss AF LtSt 6 & 8, Alpnach/ LtSt 3 & 4, Dübendorf/LtSt 1 & 5, Payerne
	T-335	Aérospatiale AS.532UL Super Puma (TH 98)	Swiss AF LtSt 6 & 8, Alpnach/ LtSt 3 & 4, Dübendorf/LtSt 1 & 5, Payerne
	T-336	Aérospatiale AS.532UL Super Puma (TH 98)	Swiss AF LtSt 6 & 8, Alpnach/ LtSt 3 & 4, Dübendorf/LtSt 1 & 5, Payerne
	T-337	Aérospatiale AS.532UL Super Puma (TH 98)	Swiss AF LtSt 6 & 8, Alpnach/ LtSt 3 & 4, Dübendorf/LtSt 1 & 5, Payerne
	T-339	Aérospatiale AS.532UL Super Puma (TH 98)	Swiss AF LtSt 6 & 8, Alpnach/ LtSt 3 & 4, Dübendorf/LtSt 1 & 5, Payerne
	T-340	Aérospatiale AS.532UL Super Puma (TH 98)	Swiss AF LtSt 6 & 8, Alpnach/ LtSt 3 & 4, Dübendorf/LtSt 1 & 5, Payerne
	T-342	Aérospatiale AS.532UL Super Puma (TH 98)	Swiss AF LtSt 6 & 8, Alpnach/ LtSt 3 & 4, Dübendorf/LtSt 1 & 5, Payerne
	T-351	Eurocopter EC.135P-2	Swiss AF LTDB, Dübendorf
	T-352	Eurocopter EC.135P-2	Swiss AF LTDB, Dübendorf
	T-353	Eurocopter EC.635P-2	Swiss AF LtSt 6 & 8, Alpnach/ LtSt 3 & 4, Dübendorf/LtSt 1 & 5, Payerne
	T-354	Eurocopter EC.635P-2	Swiss AF LtSt 6 & 8, Alpnach/ LtSt 3 & 4, Dübendorf/LtSt 1 & 5, Payerne
	T-355	Eurocopter EC.635P-2	Swiss AF LtSt 6 & 8, Alpnach/ LtSt 3 & 4, Dübendorf/LtSt 1 & 5, Payerne
	T-356	Eurocopter EC.635P-2	Swiss AF LtSt 6 & 8, Alpnach/ LtSt 3 & 4, Dübendorf/LtSt 1 & 5, Payerne
	T-357	Eurocopter EC.635P-2	Swiss AF LtSt 6 & 8, Alpnach/ LtSt 3 & 4, Dübendorf/LtSt 1 & 5, Payerne
	T-358	Eurocopter EC.635P-2	Swiss AF LtSt 6 & 8, Alpnach/ LtSt 3 & 4, Dübendorf/LtSt 1 & 5, Payerne
	T-359	Eurocopter EC.635P-2	Swiss AF LtSt 6 & 8, Alpnach/ LtSt 3 & 4, Dübendorf/LtSt 1 & 5, Payerne
	T-360	Eurocopter EC.635P-2	Swiss AF LtSt 6 & 8, Alpnach/ LtSt 3 & 4, Dübendorf/LtSt 1 & 5, Payerne
	T-361	Eurocopter EC.635P-2	Swiss AF LtSt 6 & 8, Alpnach/ LtSt 3 & 4, Dübendorf/LtSt 1 & 5, Payerne
	T-362	Eurocopter EC.635P-2	Swiss AF LtSt 6 & 8, Alpnach/ LtSt 3 & 4, Dübendorf/LtSt 1 & 5, Payerne
	T-363	Eurocopter EC.635P-2	Swiss AF LtSt 6 & 8, Alpnach/ LtSt 3 & 4, Dübendorf/LtSt 1 & 5, Payerne
	T-364	Eurocopter EC.635P-2	Swiss AF LtSt 6 & 8, Alpnach/ LtSt 3 & 4, Dübendorf/LtSt 1 & 5, Payerne
	T-365	Eurocopter EC.635P-2	Swiss AF LtSt 6 & 8, Alpnach/ LtSt 3 & 4, Dübendorf/LtSt 1 & 5, Payerne
	T-366	Eurocopter EC.635P-2	Swiss AF LtSt 6 & 8, Alpnach/ LtSt 3 & 4, Dübendorf/LtSt 1 & 5, Payerne
	T-367	Eurocopter EC.635P-2	Swiss AF LtSt 6 & 8, Alpnach/ LtSt 3 & 4, Dübendorf/LtSt 1 & 5, Payerne
	T-368	Eurocopter EC.635P-2	Swiss AF LtSt 6 & 8, Alpnach/ LtSt 3 & 4, Dübendorf/LtSt 1 & 5, Payerne
	T-369	Eurocopter EC.635P-2	Swiss AF LtSt 6 & 8, Alpnach/ LtSt 3 & 4, Dübendorf/LtSt 1 & 5, Payerne
	T-370	Eurocopter EC.635P-2	Swiss AF LtSt 6 & 8, Alpnach/ LtSt 3 & 4, Dübendorf/LtSt 1 & 5, Payerne
	T-721	Beech King Air 350C	Swiss AF LTDB, Dübendorf
	T-729	Beech 1900D	Swiss AF LTDB, Dübendorf

Serial	Type (code/other identity)	Owner/operator, location or fate	Notes
T-751	Bombardier Challenger 604 (HB-JRB)	Swiss AF LTDB, Dübendorf	
T-752	Bombardier Challenger 604 (HB-JRC)	Swiss AF LTDB, Dübendorf	
T-784	Cessna 560XL Citation Excel	Swiss AF LTDB, Bern/Belp	
T-785	Dassault Falcon 900EX EASy II	Swiss AF LTDB, Bern/Belp	
T-786	Pilatus PC-24	Swiss AF LTDB, Bern/Belp	
V-612	Pilatus PC-6B/B2-H2 Turbo Porter	Swiss AF LtSt 7, Emmen	
V-613	Pilatus PC-6B/B2-H2 Turbo Porter	Swiss AF LtSt 7, Emmen	
V-614	Pilatus PC-6B/B2-H2 Turbo Porter	Swiss AF LtSt 7, Emmen	
V-616	Pilatus PC-6B/B2-H2 Turbo Porter	Swiss AF LtSt 7, Emmen	
V-617	Pilatus PC-6B/B2-H2 Turbo Porter	Swiss AF LtSt 7, Emmen	
V-618	Pilatus PC-6B/B2-H2 Turbo Porter	Swiss AF LtSt 7, Emmen	
V-619	Pilatus PC-6B/B2-H2 Turbo Porter	Swiss AF LtSt 7, Emmen	
V-620	Pilatus PC-6B/B2-H2 Turbo Porter	Swiss AF LtSt 7, Emmen	
V-622	Pilatus PC-6B/B2-H2 Turbo Porter $	Swiss AF LtSt 7, Emmen	
V-623	Pilatus PC-6B/B2-H2 Turbo Porter	Swiss AF LtSt 7, Emmen	
V-631	Pilatus PC-6B/B2-H2 Turbo Porter	Swiss AF LtSt 7, Emmen	
V-632	Pilatus PC-6B/B2-H2 Turbo Porter	Swiss AF LtSt 7, Emmen	
V-633	Pilatus PC-6B/B2-H2 Turbo Porter	Swiss AF LtSt 7, Emmen	
V-634	Pilatus PC-6B/B2-H2 Turbo Porter	Swiss AF LtSt 7, Emmen	
V-635	Pilatus PC-6B/B2-H2 Turbo Porter	Swiss AF LtSt 7, Emmen	
Swiss Government			
HB-FOG	Pilatus PC-12/45	Armasuisse, Emmen	
SYRIA			
YK-ASC	Dassault Falcon 900	Government of Syria, Damascus	
TANZANIA			
5H-ONE	Gulfstream Aerospace G.550	Tanzanian Government, Dar-es-Salaam	
THAILAND			
B.L18-1/59	Sukhoi SSJ100-95LR Superjet [60206]	Royal Thai AF 602 Sqn/6 Wing, Bangkok/ Don Muang	
B.L18-2/60	Sukhoi SSJ100-95LR Superjet [60207]	Royal Thai AF 602 Sqn/6 Wing, Bangkok/ Don Muang	
B.L18-3/61	Sukhoi SSJ100-95LR Superjet [60208]	Royal Thai AF 602 Sqn/6 Wing, Bangkok/ Don Muang	
HS-CMV	Boeing 737-4Z6 (L11Kh.MWK-01/38) [11-111, 90401]	Royal Thai AF 904 Sqn/6 Wing, Bangkok/ Don Muang	
HS-HRH	Boeing 737-448 (L11Kh.MWK-02/47) [99-999, 90409]	Royal Thai AF 904 Sqn/6 Wing, Bangkok/ Don Muang	
HS-MVS	Boeing 737-8Z6 (L11Kh2-1/50) [99-904, 90411]	Royal Thai AF 904 Sqn/6 Wing, Bangkok/ Don Muang	
HS-TYR	Airbus A.319CJ-133 (B.L15-1/47) [60202]	Royal Thai AF 602 Sqn/6 Wing, Bangkok/ Don Muang	
HS-TYT	Airbus A.320CJ-214 (L15K-1/58) [60203]	Royal Thai AF 602 Sqn/6 Wing, Bangkok/ Don Muang	
HS-TYV	Airbus A.340-541 (L19-1/59) [60204]	Royal Thai AF 602 Sqn/6 Wing, Bangkok/ Don Muang	
HS-TY.	Airbus A.320CJ-214X (F-WWIC) [60205]	Royal Thai (on order)	
TUNISIA			
Tunisian Air Force/Al Quwwat al-Jawwiya al-Jamahiriyah At'Tunisia & Tunisian Government			
Z21012	Lockheed C-130H Hercules (TS-MTB)	Tunisian AF 21 Sqn, Bizerte/Sidi Ahmed	
Z21121	Lockheed C-130J-30 Hercules II (TS-MTK)	Tunisian AF 21 Sqn, Bizerte/Sidi Ahmed	
Z21122	Lockheed C-130J-30 Hercules II (TS-MTL)	Tunisian AF 21 Sqn, Bizerte/Sidi Ahmed	
TS-IOO	Boeing 737-7HJ	Government of Tunisia, Tunis	
TURKEY			
Türk Hava Kuvvetleri (THK)/Turkish Air Force & Turkish Government			
004	Cessna 650 Citation VII	THK 212 Filo/11 HUAÜK, Ankara/Etimesgut	
3004	Canadair NF-5A-2000 Freedom Fighter [3]	THK 134 Filo, Turkish Stars/3 AJEÜ, Konya	
3023	Canadair NF-5A-2000 Freedom Fighter [2]	THK 134 Filo, Turkish Stars/3 AJEÜ, Konya	

Notes	Serial	Type (code/other identity)	Owner/operator, location or fate
	3025	Canadair NF-5A-2000 Freedom Fighter [5]	THK 134 Filo, *Turkish Stars*/3 AJEÜ, Konya
	3027	Canadair NF-5A-2000 Freedom Fighter	*Withdrawn from use*
	3032	Canadair NF-5A-2000 Freedom Fighter [6]	THK 134 Filo, *Turkish Stars*/3 AJEÜ, Konya
	3036	Canadair NF-5A-2000 Freedom Fighter	THK 134 Filo, *Turkish Stars*/3 AJEÜ, Konya
	3039	Canadair NF-5A-2000 Freedom Fighter	THK 134 Filo, *Turkish Stars*/3 AJEÜ, Konya
	3046	Canadair NF-5A-2000 Freedom Fighter [5]	THK 134 Filo, *Turkish Stars*/3 AJEÜ, Konya
	3048	Canadair NF-5A-2000 Freedom Fighter	THK 134 Filo, *Turkish Stars*/3 AJEÜ, Konya
	3049	Canadair NF-5A-2000 Freedom Fighter [6]	THK 134 Filo, *Turkish Stars*/3 AJEÜ, Konya
	3052	Canadair NF-5A-2000 Freedom Fighter [2]	THK 134 Filo, *Turkish Stars*/3 AJEÜ, Konya
	3058	Canadair NF-5A-2000 Freedom Fighter [6]	THK 134 Filo, *Turkish Stars*/3 AJEÜ, Konya
	3066	Canadair NF-5A-2000 Freedom Fighter	*Withdrawn from use*
	3072	Canadair NF-5A-2000 Freedom Fighter [2]	THK 134 Filo, *Turkish Stars*/3 AJEÜ, Konya
	4001	Canadair NF-5B-2000 Freedom Fighter [4]	THK 134 Filo, *Turkish Stars*/3 AJEÜ, Konya
	4005	Canadair NF-5B-2000 Freedom Fighter	THK 134 Filo, *Turkish Stars*/3 AJEÜ, Konya
	4009	Canadair NF-5B-2000 Freedom Fighter [4]	THK 134 Filo, *Turkish Stars*/3 AJEÜ, Konya
	4013	Canadair NF-5B-2000 Freedom Fighter [4]	THK 134 Filo, *Turkish Stars*/3 AJEÜ, Konya
	4020	Canadair NF-5B-2000 Freedom Fighter	THK 134 Filo, *Turkish Stars*/3 AJEÜ, Konya
	4021	Canadair NF-5B-2000 Freedom Fighter [1]	THK 134 Filo, *Turkish Stars*/3 AJEÜ, Konya
	4026	Canadair NF-5B-2000 Freedom Fighter [1]	THK 134 Filo, *Turkish Stars*/3 AJEÜ, Konya
	57-2609	Boeing KC-135R Stratotanker	THK 101 Filo/10 TÜK, Incirlik
	58-0110	Boeing KC-135R Stratotanker	THK 101 Filo/10 TÜK, Incirlik
	60-0325	Boeing KC-135R Stratotanker	THK 101 Filo/10 TÜK, Incirlik
	60-0326	Boeing KC-135R Stratotanker	THK 101 Filo/10 TÜK, Incirlik
	62-3539	Boeing KC-135R Stratotanker	THK 101 Filo/10 TÜK, Incirlik
	62-3563	Boeing KC-135R Stratotanker	THK 101 Filo/10 TÜK, Incirlik
	62-3567	Boeing KC-135R Stratotanker	THK 101 Filo/10 TÜK, Incirlik
	63-13186	Lockheed C-130E Hercules	THK 222 Filo/12 HUAÜ, Erkilet
	63-13187	Lockheed C-130E Hercules $	THK 222 Filo/12 HUAÜ, Erkilet
	63-13188	Lockheed C-130E Hercules	THK 222 Filo/12 HUAÜ, Erkilet
	63-13189	Lockheed C-130E Hercules $	THK 222 Filo/12 HUAÜ, Erkilet
	65-0451	Lockheed C-130E Hercules	*Withdrawn from use at Erkilet, 2019*
	67-0455	Lockheed C-130E Hercules	THK 222 Filo/12 HUAÜ, Erkilet
	68-020	Transall C-160D	*Withdrawn from use at Erkilet, 2019*
	68-023	Transall C-160D	THK 221 Filo/12 HUAÜ, Erkilet
	68-01606	Lockheed C-130E Hercules	THK 222 Filo/12 HUAÜ, Erkilet
	68-01608	Lockheed C-130E Hercules	THK 222 Filo/12 HUAÜ, Erkilet
	68-01609	Lockheed C-130E Hercules	THK 222 Filo/12 HUAÜ, Erkilet
	69-019	Transall C-160D	*Withdrawn from use at Erkilet, 2019*
	69-021	Transall C-160D	*Withdrawn from use at Erkilet, 2019*
	69-024	Transall C-160D	*Withdrawn from use at Erkilet, 2019*
	69-026	Transall C-160D	*Withdrawn from use at Erkilet, 2019*
	69-027	Transall C-160D	*Withdrawn from use at Erkilet, 2019*
	69-029	Transall C-160D	THK 221 Filo/12 HUAÜ, Erkilet
	69-031	Transall C-160D	THK 221 Filo/12 HUAÜ, Erkilet
	69-032	Transall C-160D	*Withdrawn from use*
	69-033	Transall C-160D $	*Withdrawn from use at Erkilet, 2019*
	69-034	Transall C-160D	*Withdrawn from use at Erkilet, 2019*
	69-036	Transall C-160D	THK 221 Filo/12 HUAÜ, Erkilet
	69-040	Transall C-160D $	*Withdrawn from use at Erkilet, 2019*
	70-01610	Lockheed C-130E Hercules	THK 222 Filo/12 HUAÜ, Erkilet
	70-01947	Lockheed C-130E Hercules	THK 222 Filo/12 HUAÜ, Erkilet
	71-01468	Lockheed C-130E Hercules	THK 222 Filo/12 HUAÜ, Erkilet
	73-0991	Lockheed C-130E Hercules $	THK 222 Filo/12 HUAÜ, Erkilet
	86-0066	TUSAS (GD) F-16C-30 Fighting Falcon	THK 132 Filo/3 AJEÜ, Konya
	86-0068	TUSAS (GD) F-16C-30 Fighting Falcon	THK 132 Filo/3 AJEÜ, Konya
	86-0069	TUSAS (GD) F-16C-30 Fighting Falcon	THK 132 Filo/3 AJEÜ, Konya
	86-0070	TUSAS (GD) F-16C-30 Fighting Falcon	THK 152 Filo/10 TÜK, Incirlik
	86-0071	TUSAS (GD) F-16C-30 Fighting Falcon	THK 132 Filo/3 AJEÜ, Konya
	86-0072	TUSAS (GD) F-16C-30 Fighting Falcon	THK 132 Filo/3 AJEÜ, Konya
	86-0192	TUSAS (GD) F-16D-30 Fighting Falcon	THK 132 Filo/3 AJEÜ, Konya
	86-0193	TUSAS (GD) F-16D-30 Fighting Falcon	THK 132 Filo/3 AJEÜ, Konya
	86-0194	TUSAS (GD) F-16D-30 Fighting Falcon	THK 132 Filo/3 AJEÜ, Konya

Serial	Type (code/other identity)	Owner/operator, location or fate	Notes
86-0195	TUSAS (GD) F-16D-30 Fighting Falcon	THK 132 Filo/3 AJEÜ, Konya	
86-0196	TUSAS (GD) F-16D-30 Fighting Falcon	THK 132 Filo/3 AJEÜ, Konya	
87-0002	TUSAS (GD) F-16D-30 Fighting Falcon	THK 113 Filo/1 AJÜ, Eskisehir	
87-0003	TUSAS (GD) F-16D-30 Fighting Falcon	THK 401 Filo/1 AJÜ, Eskisehir	
87-0009	TUSAS (GD) F-16C-30 Fighting Falcon	THK 113 Filo/1 AJÜ, Eskisehir	
87-0010	TUSAS (GD) F-16C-30 Fighting Falcon	THK 132 Filo/3 AJEÜ, Konya	
87-0011	TUSAS (GD) F-16C-30 Fighting Falcon	THK 132 Filo/3 AJEÜ, Konya	
87-0013	TUSAS (GD) F-16C-30 Fighting Falcon	THK 132 Filo/3 AJEÜ, Konya	
87-0014	TUSAS (GD) F-16C-30 Fighting Falcon	THK 113 Filo/1 AJÜ, Eskisehir	
87-0015	TUSAS (GD) F-16C-30 Fighting Falcon	THK 113 Filo/1 AJÜ, Eskisehir	
87-0016	TUSAS (GD) F-16C-30 Fighting Falcon	THK 132 Filo/3 AJEÜ, Konya	
87-0017	TUSAS (GD) F-16C-30 Fighting Falcon	*Crashed 1 December 2014*	
87-0018	TUSAS (GD) F-16C-30 Fighting Falcon	THK 152 Filo/10 TÜK, Incirlik	
87-0019	TUSAS (GD) F-16C-30 Fighting Falcon	THK 132 Filo/3 AJEÜ, Konya	
87-0020	TUSAS (GD) F-16C-30 Fighting Falcon	THK 152 Filo/10 TÜK, Incirlik	
87-0021	TUSAS (GD) F-16C-30 Fighting Falcon	THK 132 Filo/3 AJEÜ, Konya	
88-0013	TUSAS (GD) F-16D-30 Fighting Falcon	THK 152 Filo/10 TÜK, Incirlik	
88-0014	TUSAS (GD) F-16D-40 Fighting Falcon	THK 192 Filo/9 AJÜ, Balikesir	
88-0015	TUSAS (GD) F-16D-40 Fighting Falcon	THK 192 Filo/9 AJÜ, Balikesir	
88-0019	TUSAS (GD) F-16C-30 Fighting Falcon	THK 132 Filo/3 AJEÜ, Konya	
88-0020	TUSAS (GD) F-16C-30 Fighting Falcon	THK 132 Filo/3 AJEÜ, Konya	
88-0021	TUSAS (GD) F-16C-30 Fighting Falcon	THK 152 Filo/10 TÜK, Incirlik	
88-0024	TUSAS (GD) F-16C-30 Fighting Falcon	THK 152 Filo/10 TÜK, Incirlik	
88-0025	TUSAS (GD) F-16C-30 Fighting Falcon	THK 151 Filo/5 AJÜ, Merzifon	
88-0026	TUSAS (GD) F-16C-30 Fighting Falcon	THK 152 Filo/10 TÜK, Incirlik	
88-0027	TUSAS (GD) F-16C-30 Fighting Falcon	THK 152 Filo/10 TÜK, Incirlik	
88-0028	TUSAS (GD) F-16C-30 Fighting Falcon	THK 192 Filo/9 AJÜ, Balikesir	
88-0029	TUSAS (GD) F-16C-30 Fighting Falcon $	THK 132 Filo/3 AJEÜ, Konya	
88-0030	TUSAS (GD) F-16C-30 Fighting Falcon	THK 152 Filo/10 TÜK, Incirlik	
88-0031	TUSAS (GD) F-16C-30 Fighting Falcon	THK 401 Filo/1 AJÜ, Eskisehir	
88-0032	TUSAS (GD) F-16C-30 Fighting Falcon $	THK 132 Filo/3 AJEÜ, Konya	
88-0033	TUSAS (GD) F-16C-40 Fighting Falcon	THK 152 Filo/10 TÜK, Incirlik	
88-0034	TUSAS (GD) F-16C-40 Fighting Falcon	THK 192 Filo/9 AJÜ, Balikesir	
88-0035	TUSAS (GD) F-16C-40 Fighting Falcon	THK 152 Filo/10 TÜK, Incirlik	
88-0036	TUSAS (GD) F-16C-40 Fighting Falcon	THK 192 Filo/9 AJÜ, Balikesir	
88-0037	TUSAS (GD) F-16C-40 Fighting Falcon	THK 132 Filo/3 AJEÜ, Konya	
89-0022	TUSAS (GD) F-16C-40 Fighting Falcon	THK	
89-0023	TUSAS (GD) F-16C-40 Fighting Falcon	THK 192 Filo/9 AJÜ, Balikesir	
89-0024	TUSAS (GD) F-16C-40 Fighting Falcon	THK 192 Filo/9 AJÜ, Balikesir	
89-0025	TUSAS (GD) F-16C-40 Fighting Falcon	THK 192 Filo/9 AJÜ, Balikesir	
89-0026	TUSAS (GD) F-16C-40 Fighting Falcon	THK	
89-0027	TUSAS (GD) F-16C-40 Fighting Falcon	THK	
89-0028	TUSAS (GD) F-16C-40 Fighting Falcon	THK	
89-0030	TUSAS (GD) F-16C-40 Fighting Falcon	THK	
89-0034	TUSAS (GD) F-16C-40 Fighting Falcon	THK 161 Filo/6 AJÜ, Bandirma	
89-0035	TUSAS (GD) F-16C-40 Fighting Falcon	THK 152 Filo/10 TÜK, Incirlik	
89-0036	TUSAS (GD) F-16C-40 Fighting Falcon	THK 161 Filo/6 AJÜ, Bandirma	
89-0037	TUSAS (GD) F-16C-40 Fighting Falcon	THK 161 Filo/6 AJÜ, Bandirma	
89-0038	TUSAS (GD) F-16C-40 Fighting Falcon	THK 161 Filo/6 AJÜ, Bandirma	
89-0039	TUSAS (GD) F-16C-40 Fighting Falcon	THK 152 Filo/10 TÜK, Incirlik	
89-0040	TUSAS (GD) F-16C-40 Fighting Falcon	THK 192 Filo/9 AJÜ, Balikesir	
89-0041	TUSAS (GD) F-16C-40 Fighting Falcon	THK 152 Filo/10 TÜK, Incirlik	
89-0042	TUSAS (GD) F-16D-40 Fighting Falcon	THK 192 Filo/9 AJÜ, Balikesir	
89-0043	TUSAS (GD) F-16D-40 Fighting Falcon	THK 151 Filo/5 AJÜ, Merzifon	
89-0044	TUSAS (GD) F-16D-40 Fighting Falcon	THK 132 Filo/3 AJEÜ, Konya	
89-0045	TUSAS (GD) F-16D-40 Fighting Falcon	THK 152 Filo/10 TÜK, Incirlik	
90-0004	TUSAS (GD) F-16C-40 Fighting Falcon	THK 152 Filo/10 TÜK, Incirlik	
90-0005	TUSAS (GD) F-16C-40 Fighting Falcon	THK 192 Filo/9 AJÜ, Balikesir	
90-0006	TUSAS (GD) F-16C-40 Fighting Falcon	THK 182 Filo/8 AJÜ, Diyarbakir	
90-0007	TUSAS (GD) F-16C-40 Fighting Falcon	THK 132 Filo/3 AJEÜ, Konya	
90-0008	TUSAS (GD) F-16C-40 Fighting Falcon	THK 161 Filo/6 AJÜ, Bandirma	
90-0009	TUSAS (GD) F-16C-40 Fighting Falcon	THK 152 Filo/10 TÜK, Incirlik	

Notes	Serial	Type (code/other identity)	Owner/operator, location or fate
	90-0010	TUSAS (GD) F-16C-40 Fighting Falcon	THK 132 Filo/3 AJEÜ, Konya
	90-0011	TUSAS (GD) F-16C-40 Fighting Falcon $	THK
	90-0012	TUSAS (GD) F-16C-40 Fighting Falcon	THK 192 Filo/9 AJÜ, Balikesir
	90-0013	TUSAS (GD) F-16C-40 Fighting Falcon	THK 182 Filo/8 AJÜ, Diyarbakir
	90-0014	TUSAS (GD) F-16C-40 Fighting Falcon	THK 161 Filo/6 AJÜ, Bandirma
	90-0016	TUSAS (GD) F-16C-40 Fighting Falcon	THK 182 Filo/8 AJÜ, Diyarbakir
	90-0017	TUSAS (GD) F-16C-40 Fighting Falcon	THK 192 Filo/9 AJÜ, Balikesir
	90-0018	TUSAS (GD) F-16C-40 Fighting Falcon	THK 161 Filo/6 AJÜ, Bandirma
	90-0019	TUSAS (GD) F-16C-40 Fighting Falcon	THK 161 Filo/6 AJÜ, Bandirma
	90-0020	TUSAS (GD) F-16C-40 Fighting Falcon	THK 161 Filo/6 AJÜ, Bandirma
	90-0021	TUSAS (GD) F-16C-40 Fighting Falcon	THK 161 Filo/6 AJÜ, Bandirma
	90-0022	TUSAS (GD) F-16D-40 Fighting Falcon	THK 182 Filo/8 AJÜ, Diyarbakir
	90-0023	TUSAS (GD) F-16D-40 Fighting Falcon	THK 152 Filo/10 TÜK, Incirlik
	90-0024	TUSAS (GD) F-16D-40 Fighting Falcon	THK 182 Filo/8 AJÜ, Diyarbakir
	91-003	Grumman G.1159C Gulfstream IV	THK 212 Filo/11 HUAÜK, Ankara/Etimesgut
	91-0001	TUSAS (GD) F-16C-40 Fighting Falcon	THK 161 Filo/6 AJÜ, Bandirma
	91-0002	TUSAS (GD) F-16C-40 Fighting Falcon	THK 401 Filo/1 AJÜ, Eskisehir
	91-0003	TUSAS (GD) F-16C-40 Fighting Falcon	THK 182 Filo/8 AJÜ, Diyarbakir
	91-0004	TUSAS (GD) F-16C-40 Fighting Falcon	THK 161 Filo/6 AJÜ, Bandirma
	91-0005	TUSAS (GD) F-16C-40 Fighting Falcon	THK 182 Filo/8 AJÜ, Diyarbakir
	91-0006	TUSAS (GD) F-16C-40 Fighting Falcon	THK 161 Filo/6 AJÜ, Bandirma
	91-0007	TUSAS (GD) F-16C-40 Fighting Falcon	THK 161 Filo/6 AJÜ, Bandirma
	91-0008	TUSAS (GD) F-16C-40 Fighting Falcon	THK 192 Filo/9 AJÜ, Balikesir
	91-0010	TUSAS (GD) F-16C-40 Fighting Falcon	THK 161 Filo/6 AJÜ, Bandirma
	91-0011	TUSAS (GD) F-16C-40 Fighting Falcon $	THK
	91-0012	TUSAS (GD) F-16C-40 Fighting Falcon	THK
	91-0013	TUSAS (GD) F-16C-40 Fighting Falcon	THK 192 Filo/9 AJÜ, Balikesir
	91-0014	TUSAS (GD) F-16C-40 Fighting Falcon	THK
	91-0015	TUSAS (GD) F-16C-40 Fighting Falcon	THK 401 Filo/1 AJÜ, Eskisehir
	91-0016	TUSAS (GD) F-16C-40 Fighting Falcon	THK 182 Filo/8 AJÜ, Diyarbakir
	91-0017	TUSAS (GD) F-16C-40 Fighting Falcon	THK 182 Filo/8 AJÜ, Diyarbakir
	91-0018	TUSAS (GD) F-16C-40 Fighting Falcon	THK 192 Filo/9 AJÜ, Balikesir
	91-0020	TUSAS (GD) F-16C-40 Fighting Falcon	THK 161 Filo/6 AJÜ, Bandirma
	91-0022	TUSAS (GD) F-16D-40 Fighting Falcon	THK 192 Filo/9 AJÜ, Balikesir
	91-0024	TUSAS (GD) F-16D-40 Fighting Falcon	THK 132 Filo/3 AJEÜ, Konya
	92-0001	TUSAS (GD) F-16C-40 Fighting Falcon	THK 132 Filo/3 AJEÜ, Konya
	92-0002	TUSAS (GD) F-16C-40 Fighting Falcon	THK 182 Filo/8 AJÜ, Diyarbakir
	92-0003	TUSAS (GD) F-16C-40 Fighting Falcon	THK 192 Filo/9 AJÜ, Balikesir
	92-0004	TUSAS (GD) F-16C-40 Fighting Falcon	THK 161 Filo/6 AJÜ, Bandirma
	92-0005	TUSAS (GD) F-16C-40 Fighting Falcon	THK 192 Filo/9 AJÜ, Balikesir
	92-0006	TUSAS (GD) F-16C-40 Fighting Falcon	THK 182 Filo/8 AJÜ, Diyarbakir
	92-0007	TUSAS (GD) F-16C-40 Fighting Falcon	THK 192 Filo/9 AJÜ, Balikesir
	92-0008	TUSAS (GD) F-16C-40 Fighting Falcon	THK 152 Filo/10 TÜK, Incirlik
	92-0009	TUSAS (GD) F-16C-40 Fighting Falcon	THK 192 Filo/9 AJÜ, Balikesir
	92-0010	TUSAS (GD) F-16C-40 Fighting Falcon	THK 192 Filo/9 AJÜ, Balikesir
	92-0011	TUSAS (GD) F-16C-40 Fighting Falcon	THK 182 Filo/8 AJÜ, Diyarbakir
	92-0012	TUSAS (GD) F-16C-40 Fighting Falcon	THK 182 Filo/8 AJÜ, Diyarbakir
	92-0013	TUSAS (GD) F-16C-40 Fighting Falcon	THK 132 Filo/3 AJEÜ, Konya
	92-0014	TUSAS (GD) F-16C-40 Fighting Falcon $	THK 192 Filo/9 AJÜ, Balikesir
	92-0015	TUSAS (GD) F-16C-40 Fighting Falcon	THK 161 Filo/6 AJÜ, Bandirma
	92-0016	TUSAS (GD) F-16C-40 Fighting Falcon	THK 161 Filo/6 AJÜ, Bandirma
	92-0017	TUSAS (GD) F-16C-40 Fighting Falcon	THK 152 Filo/10 TÜK, Incirlik
	92-0018	TUSAS (GD) F-16C-40 Fighting Falcon	THK 161 Filo/6 AJÜ, Bandirma
	92-0019	TUSAS (GD) F-16C-40 Fighting Falcon	THK 181 Filo/8 AJÜ, Diyarbakir
	92-0020	TUSAS (GD) F-16C-40 Fighting Falcon	THK 181 Filo/8 AJÜ, Diyarbakir
	92-0021	TUSAS (GD) F-16C-40 Fighting Falcon	THK 192 Filo/9 AJÜ, Balikesir
	92-0022	TUSAS (GD) F-16D-40 Fighting Falcon	THK 161 Filo/6 AJÜ, Bandirma
	92-0023	TUSAS (GD) F-16D-40 Fighting Falcon	THK 132 Filo/3 AJEÜ, Konya
	92-0024	TUSAS (GD) F-16D-40 Fighting Falcon	THK 192 Filo/9 AJÜ, Balikesir
	93-005	Cessna 650 Citation VII	THK 212 Filo/11 HUAÜK, Ankara/Etimesgut
	93-0001	TUSAS (GD) F-16C-40 Fighting Falcon	THK 401 Filo/1 AJÜ, Eskisehir
	93-0003	TUSAS (GD) F-16C-40 Fighting Falcon	THK 192 Filo/9 AJÜ, Balikesir

Serial	Type (code/other identity)	Owner/operator, location or fate	Notes
93-0004	TUSAS (GD) F-16C-40 Fighting Falcon	THK 181 Filo/8 AJÜ, Diyarbakir	
93-0005	TUSAS (GD) F-16C-40 Fighting Falcon	THK 181 Filo/8 AJÜ, Diyarbakir	
93-0006	TUSAS (GD) F-16C-40 Fighting Falcon	THK 181 Filo/8 AJÜ, Diyarbakir	
93-0007	TUSAS (GD) F-16C-40 Fighting Falcon	THK 182 Filo/8 AJÜ, Diyarbakir	
93-0008	TUSAS (GD) F-16C-40 Fighting Falcon	THK 181 Filo/8 AJÜ, Diyarbakir	
93-0009	TUSAS (GD) F-16C-40 Fighting Falcon	THK 182 Filo/8 AJÜ, Diyarbakir	
93-0010	TUSAS (GD) F-16C-40 Fighting Falcon	THK 132 Filo/3 AJEÜ, Konya	
93-0011	TUSAS (GD) F-16C-40 Fighting Falcon	THK 181 Filo/8 AJÜ, Diyarbakir	
93-0012	TUSAS (GD) F-16C-40 Fighting Falcon	THK 181 Filo/8 AJÜ, Diyarbakir	
93-0013	TUSAS (GD) F-16C-40 Fighting Falcon	THK 181 Filo/3 AJÜ, Diyarbakir	
93-0658	TUSAS (GD) F-16C-50 Fighting Falcon	THK 132 Filo/3 AJEÜ, Konya	
93-0659	TUSAS (GD) F-16C-50 Fighting Falcon	THK 192 Filo/9 AJÜ, Balikesir	
93-0660	TUSAS (GD) F-16C-50 Fighting Falcon	THK 152 Filo/10 TÜK, Incirlik	
93-0661	TUSAS (GD) F-16C-50 Fighting Falcon	THK 132 Filo/3 AJEÜ, Konya	
93-0663	TUSAS (GD) F-16C-50 Fighting Falcon	THK 132 Filo/3 AJEÜ, Konya	
93-0664	TUSAS (GD) F-16C-50 Fighting Falcon	THK 132 Filo/3 AJEÜ, Konya	
93-0665	TUSAS (GD) F-16C-50 Fighting Falcon	THK 192 Filo/9 AJÜ, Balikesir	
93-0667	TUSAS (GD) F-16C-50 Fighting Falcon	THK 151 Filo/5 AJÜ, Merzifon	
93-0668	TUSAS (GD) F-16C-50 Fighting Falcon	THK	
93-0669	TUSAS (GD) F-16C-50 Fighting Falcon	THK 151 Filo/5 AJÜ, Merzifon	
93-0670	TUSAS (GD) F-16C-50 Fighting Falcon	THK 192 Filo/9 AJÜ, Balikesir	
93-0671	TUSAS (GD) F-16C-50 Fighting Falcon	THK	
93-0672	TUSAS (GD) F-16C-50 Fighting Falcon	THK 132 Filo/3 AJEÜ, Konya	
93-0673	TUSAS (GD) F-16C-50 Fighting Falcon	THK 132 Filo/3 AJEÜ, Konya	
93-0674	TUSAS (GD) F-16C-50 Fighting Falcon	THK 132 Filo/3 AJEÜ, Konya	
93-0675	TUSAS (GD) F-16C-50 Fighting Falcon	THK 192 Filo/9 AJÜ, Balikesir	
93-0676	TUSAS (GD) F-16C-50 Fighting Falcon	THK 192 Filo/9 AJÜ, Balikesir	
93-0677	TUSAS (GD) F-16C-50 Fighting Falcon $	THK	
93-0678	TUSAS (GD) F-16C-50 Fighting Falcon	THK 193 Filo/9 AJÜ, Balikesir	
93-0679	TUSAS (GD) F-16C-50 Fighting Falcon	THK 192 Filo/9 AJÜ, Balikesir	
93-0680	TUSAS (GD) F-16C-50 Fighting Falcon $	THK 192 Filo/9 AJÜ, Balikesir	
93-0681	TUSAS (GD) F-16C-50 Fighting Falcon	THK 192 Filo/9 AJÜ, Balikesir	
93-0682	TUSAS (GD) F-16C-50 Fighting Falcon $	THK 192 Filo/9 AJÜ, Balikesir	
93-0683	TUSAS (GD) F-16C-50 Fighting Falcon	THK 193 Filo/9 AJÜ, Balikesir	
93-0684	TUSAS (GD) F-16C-50 Fighting Falcon	THK	
93-0685	TUSAS (GD) F-16C-50 Fighting Falcon	THK	
93-0687	TUSAS (GD) F-16C-50 Fighting Falcon	THK 132 Filo/3 AJEÜ, Konya	
93-0688	TUSAS (GD) F-16C-50 Fighting Falcon	THK 151 Filo/5 AJÜ, Merzifon	
93-0689	TUSAS (GD) F-16C-50 Fighting Falcon	THK 192 Filo/9 AJÜ, Balikesir	
93-0690	TUSAS (GD) F-16C-50 Fighting Falcon	THK	
93-0691	TUSAS (GD) F-16D-50 Fighting Falcon $	THK 192 Filo/9 AJÜ, Balikesir	
93-0692	TUSAS (GD) F-16D-50 Fighting Falcon	THK 151 Filo/5 AJÜ, Merzifon	
93-0693	TUSAS (GD) F-16D-50 Fighting Falcon	THK 152 Filo/10 TÜK, Incirlik	
93-0694	TUSAS (GD) F-16D-50 Fighting Falcon	THK 151 Filo/5 AJÜ, Merzifon	
93-0695	TUSAS (GD) F-16D-50 Fighting Falcon	THK	
93-0696	TUSAS (GD) F-16D-50 Fighting Falcon $	THK 151 Filo/5 AJÜ, Merzifon	
94-0071	TUSAS (GD) F-16C-50 Fighting Falcon	THK 192 Filo/9 AJÜ, Balikesir	
94-0072	TUSAS (GD) F-16C-50 Fighting Falcon	THK 151 Filo/5 AJÜ, Merzifon	
94-0073	TUSAS (GD) F-16C-50 Fighting Falcon	THK 151 Filo/5 AJÜ, Merzifon	
94-0074	TUSAS (GD) F-16C-50 Fighting Falcon	THK 192 Filo/9 AJÜ, Balikesir	
94-0075	TUSAS (GD) F-16C-50 Fighting Falcon	THK 151 Filo/5 AJÜ, Merzifon	
94-0076	TUSAS (GD) F-16C-50 Fighting Falcon	THK 151 Filo/5 AJÜ, Merzifon	
94-0077	TUSAS (GD) F-16C-50 Fighting Falcon	THK 193 Filo/9 AJÜ, Balikesir	
94-0078	TUSAS (GD) F-16C-50 Fighting Falcon	THK 113 Filo/1 AJÜ, Eskisehir	
94-0079	TUSAS (GD) F-16C-50 Fighting Falcon	THK 192 Filo/9 AJÜ, Balikesir	
94-0080	TUSAS (GD) F-16C-50 Fighting Falcon	THK 192 Filo/9 AJÜ, Balikesir	
94-0082	TUSAS (GD) F-16C-50 Fighting Falcon	THK 151 Filo/5 AJÜ, Merzifon	
94-0083	TUSAS (GD) F-16C-50 Fighting Falcon	THK 151 Filo/5 AJÜ, Merzifon	
94-0084	TUSAS (GD) F-16C-50 Fighting Falcon	THK	
94-0085	TUSAS (GD) F-16C-50 Fighting Falcon	THK 192 Filo/9 AJÜ, Balikesir	
94-0086	TUSAS (GD) F-16C-50 Fighting Falcon	THK 192 Filo/9 AJÜ, Balikesir	
94-0088	TUSAS (GD) F-16C-50 Fighting Falcon	THK 151 Filo/5 AJÜ, Merzifon	

Notes	Serial	Type (code/other identity)	Owner/operator, location or fate
	94-0089	TUSAS (GD) F-16C-50 Fighting Falcon	THK 152 Filo/10 TÜK, Incirlik
	94-0090	TUSAS (GD) F-16C-50 Fighting Falcon $	THK 192 Filo/9 AJÜ, Balikesir
	94-0091	TUSAS (GD) F-16C-50 Fighting Falcon	THK 132 Filo/3 AJEÜ, Konya
	94-0092	TUSAS (GD) F-16C-50 Fighting Falcon	THK 132 Filo/3 AJEÜ, Konya
	94-0093	TUSAS (GD) F-16C-50 Fighting Falcon	THK 113 Filo/1 AJÜ, Eskisehir
	94-0094	TUSAS (GD) F-16C-50 Fighting Falcon	THK
	94-0095	TUSAS (GD) F-16C-50 Fighting Falcon	THK 192 Filo/9 AJÜ, Balikesir
	94-0096	TUSAS (GD) F-16C-50 Fighting Falcon	THK 193 Filo/9 AJÜ, Balikesir
	94-0105	TUSAS (GD) F-16D-50 Fighting Falcon	THK
	94-0106	TUSAS (GD) F-16D-50 Fighting Falcon	THK 401 Filo/1 AJÜ, Eskisehir
	94-0108	TUSAS (GD) F-16D-50 Fighting Falcon	THK 192 Filo/9 AJÜ, Balikesir
	94-0109	TUSAS (GD) F-16D-50 Fighting Falcon	THK 132 Filo/3 AJEÜ, Konya
	94-0110	TUSAS (GD) F-16D-50 Fighting Falcon	THK 193 Filo/9 AJÜ, Balikesir
	94-1557	TUSAS (GD) F-16D-50 Fighting Falcon	THK 152 Filo/10 TÜK, Incirlik
	94-1558	TUSAS (GD) F-16D-50 Fighting Falcon	THK 132 Filo/3 AJEÜ, Konya
	94-1559	TUSAS (GD) F-16D-50 Fighting Falcon	THK 152 Filo/10 TÜK, Incirlik
	94-1560	TUSAS (GD) F-16D-50 Fighting Falcon	THK 113 Filo/1 AJÜ, Eskisehir
	94-1561	TUSAS (GD) F-16D-50 Fighting Falcon	THK 192 Filo/9 AJÜ, Balikesir
	94-1562	TUSAS (GD) F-16D-50 Fighting Falcon	THK 192 Filo/9 AJÜ, Balikesir
	94-1563	TUSAS (GD) F-16D-50 Fighting Falcon	THK 192 Filo/9 AJÜ, Balikesir
	94-1564	TUSAS (GD) F-16D-50 Fighting Falcon	THK 192 Filo/9 AJÜ, Balikesir
	07-1001	TUSAS (GD) F-16C-50 Fighting Falcon	THK 161 Filo/6 AJÜ, Bandirma
	07-1002	TUSAS (GD) F-16C-50 Fighting Falcon	THK 181 Filo/8 AJÜ, Diyarbakir
	07-1003	TUSAS (GD) F-16C-50 Fighting Falcon	THK 181 Filo/8 AJÜ, Diyarbakir
	07-1004	TUSAS (GD) F-16C-50 Fighting Falcon	THK 161 Filo/6 AJÜ, Bandirma
	07-1005	TUSAS (GD) F-16C-50 Fighting Falcon	THK 181 Filo/8 AJÜ, Diyarbakir
	07-1006	TUSAS (GD) F-16C-50 Fighting Falcon	THK 181 Filo/8 AJÜ, Diyarbakir
	07-1007	TUSAS (GD) F-16C-50 Fighting Falcon	THK 161 Filo/6 AJÜ, Bandirma
	07-1008	TUSAS (GD) F-16C-50 Fighting Falcon	THK
	07-1009	TUSAS (GD) F-16C-50 Fighting Falcon	THK 152 Filo/10 TÜK, Incirlik
	07-1010	TUSAS (GD) F-16C-50 Fighting Falcon	THK 152 Filo/10 TÜK, Incirlik
	07-1011	TUSAS (GD) F-16C-50 Fighting Falcon	THK
	07-1012	TUSAS (GD) F-16C-50 Fighting Falcon	THK 161 Filo/6 AJÜ, Bandirma
	07-1013	TUSAS (GD) F-16C-50 Fighting Falcon	THK 181 Filo/8 AJÜ, Diyarbakir
	07-1014	TUSAS (GD) F-16C-50 Fighting Falcon	THK 161 Filo/6 AJÜ, Bandirma
	07-1015	TUSAS (GD) F-16D-50 Fighting Falcon	THK 161 Filo/6 AJÜ, Bandirma
	07-1016	TUSAS (GD) F-16D-50 Fighting Falcon	THK 181 Filo/8 AJÜ, Diyarbakir
	07-1017	TUSAS (GD) F-16D-50 Fighting Falcon	THK 181 Filo/8 AJÜ, Diyarbakir
	07-1018	TUSAS (GD) F-16D-50 Fighting Falcon	THK 181 Filo/8 AJÜ, Diyarbakir
	07-1019	TUSAS (GD) F-16D-50 Fighting Falcon	THK 161 Filo/6 AJÜ, Bandirma
	07-1020	TUSAS (GD) F-16D-50 Fighting Falcon	THK 182 Filo/8 AJÜ, Diyarbakir
	07-1021	TUSAS (GD) F-16D-50 Fighting Falcon	THK 181 Filo/8 AJÜ, Diyarbakir
	07-1022	TUSAS (GD) F-16D-50 Fighting Falcon	THK 181 Filo/8 AJÜ, Diyarbakir
	07-1023	TUSAS (GD) F-16D-50 Fighting Falcon	THK 161 Filo/6 AJÜ, Bandirma
	07-1024	TUSAS (GD) F-16D-50 Fighting Falcon	THK 181 Filo/8 AJÜ, Diyarbakir
	07-1025	TUSAS (GD) F-16D-50 Fighting Falcon	THK 181 Filo/8 AJÜ, Diyarbakir
	07-1026	TUSAS (GD) F-16D-50 Fighting Falcon	THK 181 Filo/8 AJÜ, Diyarbakir
	07-1027	TUSAS (GD) F-16D-50 Fighting Falcon	THK 161 Filo/6 AJÜ, Bandirma
	07-1028	TUSAS (GD) F-16D-50 Fighting Falcon	THK 161 Filo/6 AJÜ, Bandirma
	07-1029	TUSAS (GD) F-16D-50 Fighting Falcon	THK 161 Filo/6 AJÜ, Bandirma
	07-1030	TUSAS (GD) F-16D-50 Fighting Falcon	THK
	09-001	Gulfstream Aerospace G.550	THK 212 Filo/11 HUAÜK, Ankara/Etimesgut
	13-001	Boeing 737-7FS AEW&C (E-7T)	THK 131 Filo/3 AJEÜ, Konya
	13-002	Boeing 737-7FS AEW&C (E-7T)	THK 131 Filo/3 AJEÜ, Konya
	13-003	Boeing 737-7FS AEW&C (E-7T)	THK 131 Filo/3 AJEÜ, Konya
	13-0009	Airbus Military A.400M	THK 221 Filo/12 HUAÜ, Erkilet
	13-004	Boeing 737-7FS AEW&C (E-7T)	THK 131 Filo/3 AJEÜ, Konya
	14-0013	Airbus Military A.400M	THK 221 Filo/12 HUAÜ, Erkilet
	14-0028	Airbus Military A.400M	THK 221 Filo/12 HUAÜ, Erkilet
	15-0051	Airbus Military A.400M	THK 221 Filo/12 HUAÜ, Erkilet
	16-0055	Airbus Military A.400M	THK 221 Filo/12 HUAÜ, Erkilet
	17-0075	Airbus Military A.400M	THK 221 Filo/12 HUAÜ, Erkilet

Serial	Type (code/other identity)	Owner/operator, location or fate	Notes
17-0078	Airbus Military A.400M	THK 221 Filo/12 HUAÜ, Erkilet	
17-0080	Airbus Military A.400M	THK 221 Filo/12 HUAÜ, Erkilet	
18-0093	Airbus Military A.400M (17-0095)	THK 221 Filo/12 HUAÜ, Erkilet	
18-0094	Airbus Military A.400M (17-0096)	THK (on order)	
TC-ANA	Airbus A.319CJ-115X	*To the Albanian Government, February 2020*	
TC-ANK	Airbus A.318-112 (VQ-BDD)	Turkish Government, Istanbul/Ataturk	
TC-ATA	Gulfstream Aerospace G.550	Turkish Government, Ankara	
TC-CAN	Airbus A.340-541 (TC-TRK)	Turkish Government, Istanbul/Ataturk	
TC-CBK	Gulfstream Aerospace G.550	THK 212 Filo/11 HUAÜK, Ankara/Etimesgut	
TC-DAP	Gulfstream Aerospace G.550	Turkish Government, Ankara	
TC-GVA	Grumman G.1159C Gulfstream IV (TC-ATA/91-002)	Turkish Government, Ankara	
TC-GVB	Gulfstream Aerospace G.450 (TC-GAP)	Turkish Government, Ankara	
TC-IST	Airbus A.319CJ-133	Turkish Government, Istanbul/Ataturk	
TC-TRK	Boeing 747-8ZV (VQ-BSK)	Turkish Government, Istanbul/Ataturk	
TC-TUR	Airbus A.330-243	Turkish Government, Istanbul/Ataturk	

TURKMENISTAN

EZ-A777	Boeing 777-22KLR	Government of Turkmenistan, Ashkhabad	
EZ-B021	BAe 1000B	Government of Turkmenistan, Ashkhabad	
EZ-B024	Canadair Challenger 870CS	Government of Turkmenistan, Ashkhabad	

UGANDA

5X-UGF	Gulfstream Aerospace G.550	Government of Uganda, Entebbe	

UKRAINE
Ukrainian Air Force

81 y	Antonov An-30	Ukrainian AF 15 Tr AB, Kiev/Boryspil	
76321	Ilyushin Il-76MD	Ukrainian AF 25 Tr AB, Melitopol	
76322	Ilyushin Il-76MD	Ukrainian AF 25 Tr AB, Melitopol	
76323	Ilyushin Il-76MD	Ukrainian AF 25 Tr AB, Melitopol	
76413	Ilyushin Il-76MD	Ukrainian AF 25 Tr AB, Melitopol	
76423	Ilyushin Il-76MD	Ukrainian AF 25 Tr AB, Melitopol	
76531	Ilyushin Il-76MD	Ukrainian AF 25 Tr AB, Melitopol	
76559	Ilyushin Il-76MD	Ukrainian AF 25 Tr AB, Melitopol	
76564	Ilyushin Il-76MD	Ukrainian AF 25 Tr AB, Melitopol	
76566	Ilyushin Il-76MD	Ukrainian AF 25 Tr AB, Melitopol	
76585	Ilyushin Il-76MD	Ukrainian AF 25 Tr AB, Melitopol	
76631	Ilyushin Il-76MD	Ukrainian AF 25 Tr AB, Melitopol	
76637	Ilyushin Il-76MD	Ukrainian AF 25 Tr AB, Melitopol	
76645	Ilyushin Il-76MD	Ukrainian AF 25 Tr AB, Melitopol	
76647	Ilyushin Il-76MD	Ukrainian AF 25 Tr AB, Melitopol	
76654	Ilyushin Il-76MD	Ukrainian AF 25 Tr AB, Melitopol	
76660	Ilyushin Il-76MD	Ukrainian AF 25 Tr AB, Melitopol	
76661	Ilyushin Il-76MD	Ukrainian AF 25 Tr AB, Melitopol	
76680	Ilyushin Il-76MD	Ukrainian AF 25 Tr AB, Melitopol	
76683	Ilyushin Il-76MD	Ukrainian AF 25 Tr AB, Melitopol	
76697	Ilyushin Il-76MD	Ukrainian AF 25 Tr AB, Melitopol	
76698	Ilyushin Il-76MD	Ukrainian AF 25 Tr AB, Melitopol	
76699	Ilyushin Il-76MD	Ukrainian AF 25 Tr AB, Melitopol	
76732	Ilyushin Il-76MD	Ukrainian AF 25 Tr AB, Melitopol	
78820	Ilyushin Il-76MD	Ukrainian AF 25 Tr AB, Melitopol	
86915	Ilyushin Il-76MD	Ukrainian AF 25 Tr AB, Melitopol	
86922	Ilyushin Il-76MD	Ukrainian AF 25 Tr AB, Melitopol	

Government of Ukraine

UR-ABA	Airbus A.319CJ-115X	Government of Ukraine, Kiev/Boryspil	

UNITED ARAB EMIRATES
United Arab Emirates Air Force (UAEAF)

311	Lockheed L.100-30 Hercules (A6-QFY)	UAEAF 4 Sqn/Transport Wing, Abu Dhabi	
312	Lockheed C-130H-30 Hercules	UAEAF 4 Sqn/Transport Wing, Abu Dhabi	
430	Aermacchi MB339NAT	UAEAF *Al Fursan*, Dubai/Minhad	
431	Aermacchi MB339NAT	UAEAF *Al Fursan*, Dubai/Minhad	

Notes	Serial	Type (code/other identity)	Owner/operator, location or fate
	432	Aermacchi MB339NAT	UAEAF *Al Fursan*, Dubai/Minhad
	433	Aermacchi MB339NAT	UAEAF *Al Fursan*, Dubai/Minhad
	434	Aermacchi MB339NAT	UAEAF *Al Fursan*, Dubai/Minhad
	435	Aermacchi MB339NAT	UAEAF *Al Fursan*, Dubai/Minhad
	436	Aermacchi MB339NAT	UAEAF *Al Fursan*, Dubai/Minhad
	437	Aermacchi MB339NAT	UAEAF *Al Fursan*, Dubai/Minhad
	438	Aermacchi MB339NAT	UAEAF *Al Fursan*, Dubai/Minhad
	439	Aermacchi MB339NAT	UAEAF *Al Fursan*, Dubai/Minhad
	440	Aermacchi MB339NAT	UAEAF *Al Fursan*, Dubai/Minhad
	441	Aermacchi MB339NAT	UAEAF *Al Fursan*, Dubai/Minhad
	442	Aermacchi MB339NAT	UAEAF *Al Fursan*, Dubai/Minhad
	1211	Lockheed C-130H Hercules	UAEAF 4 Sqn/Transport Wing, Abu Dhabi
	1212	Lockheed C-130H Hercules	UAEAF 4 Sqn/Transport Wing, Abu Dhabi
	1213	Lockheed C-130H Hercules	UAEAF 4 Sqn/Transport Wing, Abu Dhabi
	1214	Lockheed C-130H Hercules	UAEAF 4 Sqn/Transport Wing, Abu Dhabi
	1215	Lockheed L.100-30 Hercules	UAEAF 4 Sqn/Transport Wing, Abu Dhabi
	1216	Lockheed L.100-30 Hercules	UAEAF 4 Sqn/Transport Wing, Abu Dhabi
	1217	Lockheed L.100-30 Hercules	UAEAF 4 Sqn/Transport Wing, Abu Dhabi
	1223	Boeing C-17A Globemaster III (10-0401)	UAEAF Heavy Transport Sqn, Abu Dhabi
	1224	Boeing C-17A Globemaster III (10-0402)	UAEAF Heavy Transport Sqn, Abu Dhabi
	1225	Boeing C-17A Globemaster III (10-0403)	UAEAF Heavy Transport Sqn, Abu Dhabi
	1226	Boeing C-17A Globemaster III (10-0404)	UAEAF Heavy Transport Sqn, Abu Dhabi
	1227	Boeing C-17A Globemaster III (10-0405)	UAEAF Heavy Transport Sqn, Abu Dhabi
	1228	Boeing C-17A Globemaster III (10-0406)	UAEAF Heavy Transport Sqn, Abu Dhabi
	1229	Boeing C-17A Globemaster III (14-0007)	UAEAF Heavy Transport Sqn, Abu Dhabi
	1230	Boeing C-17A Globemaster III (14-0008)	UAEAF Heavy Transport Sqn, Abu Dhabi
	1300	Airbus A.330-243 MRTT (EC-339)	UAEAF MRTT Sqn, Al Ain
	1301	Airbus A.330-243 MRTT (EC-334)	UAEAF MRTT Sqn, Al Ain
	1302	Airbus A.330-243 MRTT (EC-332)	UAEAF MRTT Sqn, Al Ain
	1303	Airbus A.330-243 MRTT	UAEAF (on order)
	1304	Airbus A.330-243 MRTT	UAEAF (on order)
	1305	Airbus A.330-243 MRTT	UAEAF (on order)
	1325	Bombardier Global 6000	UAEAF, Dubai/Minhad
	1326	Bombardier Global 6000	UAEAF, Dubai/Minhad
UAE Government			
	A6-ALN	Boeing 777-2ANER	Amiri Flight, Abu Dhabi
	A6-AUH	Boeing 737-8EX	Amiri Flight, Abu Dhabi
	A6-COM	Boeing 747-433	Dubai Air Wing
	A6-DAW	Boeing 747-48E	Dubai Air Wing
	A6-DFR	Boeing 737-7BC	Amiri Flight, Abu Dhabi
	A6-DLM	Airbus A.320-232	Amiri Flight, Abu Dhabi
	A6-ESH	Airbus A.319-113X	Amiri Flight, Abu Dhabi
	A6-FZZ	Boeing 737-8KN	Dubai Air Wing
	A6-GGP	Boeing 747-412F	Dubai Air Wing
	A6-HEH	Boeing 737-8AJ	Dubai Air Wing
	A6-HHH	Gulfstream Aerospace G.650	Dubai Air Wing
	A6-HMS	Airbus A.320-232	Dubai Air Wing
	A6-HRM	Boeing 747-422	Dubai Air Wing
	A6-HRS	Boeing 737-7F0	Dubai Air Wing
	A6-MMM	Boeing 747-422	Dubai Air Wing
	A6-MRM	Boeing 737-8EC	Dubai Air Wing
	A6-MRS	Boeing 737-8EO	Dubai Air Wing
	A6-PFC	Boeing 787-8	Amiri Flight, Abu Dhabi
	A6-PFE	Boeing 787-9	Amiri Flight, Abu Dhabi
	A6-PFG	Boeing 787-9	Amiri Flight, Abu Dhabi
	A6-RJ1	BAE RJ.85	Dubai Air Wing
	A6-RJ2	BAE RJ.85	Dubai Air Wing
	A6-SHJ	Airbus A.320-232X	Ruler of Sharjah Air Wing
	A6-SIL	Boeing 777-35RER	Amiri Flight, Abu Dhabi
	DU-141	AgustaWestland AW.139	Dubai Air Wing, Fairoaks, UK (Summer)
	DU-142	AgustaWestland AW.139	Dubai Air Wing, Fairoaks, UK (Summer)

With the retirement of the type from RAF service in 2019, the Panavia Tornado is a rare sight in the UK now. This Luftwaffe example, Tornado IDS 43+25, belongs to TLG 51 *Immelmann*, based at Schleswig/Jagel and wears special markings. The type is expected to remain in German service for another five years or so.

GBE is the code for this French Army Aerospatiale SA.342M Gazelle, 4053, operated by 3 Régiment d'Helicoptères de Combat at Etain.

54+28 is an Airbus Military A.400M of the Luftwaffe's LTG 62, based at Wunstorf. The rapid acquisition of these machines is also signalling the end for the Transall C-160D, which it is replacing.

This section lists the codes worn by some overseas air forces and, alongside, the serial of the aircraft currently wearing this code. This list will be updated occasionally and those with Internet access can download the latest version via the 'Military Aircraft Markings' Web Site, www.militaryaircraftmarkings.co.uk and via the MAM2009 Yahoo! Group.

FRANCE
FRENCH AIR FORCE
D-BD Alpha Jet

Code	Serial	Code	Serial	Code	Serial	Code	Serial
0 [PDF]	E68	705-AO	E112	2-EL	58	3-XL	603
1 [PDF]	E44	705-FJ	E33	2-EM	63	3-XM	680
3 [PDF]	E139	705-LC	E87	2-EN	46	3-XN	652
4 [PDF]	E20	705-LG	E120	2-EO	66	3-XO	629
5 [PDF]	E127	705-LJ	E137	2-EP	47	3-XP	645
6 [PDF]	E129	705-LK	E125	2-EQ	44	3-XT	648
7 [PDF]	E46	705-LP	E129	2-ET	57	3-XV	672
8 [PDF]	E113	705-LU	E148	2-EU	55	3-XY	649
9 [PDF]	E87	705-MA	E173	2-EV	59	3-XZ	685
8-AE	E75	705-MF	E98	2-EW	48	30-ID	654
8-AF	E108	705-MR	E115	2-EX	40	30-IR	674
8-AG	E109	705-ND	E26	2-EY	42	30-IS	617
8-AK	E144	705-NL	E37	2-EZ	54	30-JO	627
8-AL	E154	705-NP	E155	2-FZ	41	30-XG	625
8-FD	E151	705-RB	E163	2-ME	61	30-XQ	637
8-FM	E105	705-RF	E158	2-MG	65	30-XR	659
8-FN	E116	705-RH	E94	2-MH	67	115-AM	525
8-FO	E81	705-RI	E117	2-MK	74	115-KC	120
8-FP	E168	705-RK	E31	3-AG	681	115-KD	123
8-LH	E38	705-RM	E134	3-AS	635	115-KE	101
8-LN	E118	705-RR	E114	3-AU	653	115-KF	111
8-LO	E142	705-RT	E152	3-IA	650	115-KI	96
8-LS	E22	705-RU	E153	3-IC	626	115-KJ	523
8-LT	E147	705-RW	E166	3-IE	642	115-KL	106
8-LW	E82	705-RY	E170	3-IF	609	115-KN	121
8-MB	E176	705-RZ	E171	3-IG	668	115-KR	102
8-NA	E79	705-TA	E42	3-IH	631	115-KS	528
8-MH	E48	705-TB	E67	3-IJ	638	115-LB	87
8-NF	E141	705-TM	E128	3-IL	622	115-LC	108
8-RJ	E162	705-TU	E7	3-IN	640	115-LE	79
8-RM	E123	705-TZ	E83	3-IO	647	115-LJ	105
8-RN	E124	705-UD	E107	3-IP	604	115-OA	524
8-RO	E131	F-TELC	E87	3-IT	624	115-OC	529
8-RP	E130	F-TELP	E129	3-IU	620	115-OL	530
8-RQ	E138	F-TEMF	E98	3-IV	683	115-OR	527
8-RS	E149	F-TEMO	E68	3-JC	606	115-YA	93
8-RX	E135	F-TEMS	E20	3-JD	643	115-YB	99
8-TG	E104	F-TENE	E73	3-JF	660	115-YC	85
8-TH	E90	F-TERI	E117	3-JG	601	115-YD	107
8-TJ	E25	F-TERK	E31	3-JI	675	115-YE	122
8-TX	E93	F-TERN	E46	3-JJ	639	115-YF	100
8-UB	E11	F-TETD	E113	3-JM	657	115-YG	118
8-UC	E157	F-TETF	E45	3-JN	658	115-YH	109
8-UH	E160	F-UGFC	E139	3-JP	611	115-YL	82
102-FA	E140	F-UGFE	E119	3-JR	682	115-YO	113
102-FI	E32	F-UHRE	E44	3-JT	677	115-YT	124
102-LI	E53	F-UHRF	E46	3-JU	614	133-AL	669
102-NA	E79	F-UHRR	E146	3-JW	641	133-IQ	666
102-NB	E29	F-UHRT	E152	3-JX	679	133-IW	664
102-RJ	E76			3-JY	615	133-JB	678
120-FM	E105	**Dassault Mirage 2000**		3-LH	655	133-JE	634
120-RV	E164	2-AX	77	3-MO	613	133-JH	686
120-TT	E101	2-EA	49	3-MQ	646	133-JL	628
705-AB	E28	2-EC	78	3-XA	662	133-JV	636
705-AD	E51	2-ED	62	3-XC	618	133-LF	605
705-AH	E110	2-EF	45	3-XD	630	133-MP	623
		2-EG	56	3-XF	670	133-XE	632
		2-EH	52	3-XJ	602	133-XI	661
		2-EJ	43	3-XK	671	133-XX	610

Code	No.
188-XJ	602
188-YR	91

Dassault Rafale

Code	No.
4-EA	303
4-EC	305
4-FF	339
4-FG	340
4-FH	341
4-FI	342
4-FJ	343
4-FK	344
4-FL	345
4-FM	346
4-FN	347
4-FO	348
4-FP	349
4-FR	351
4-FS	352
4-FT	353
4-FU	354
4-FV	355
4-FW	356
4-FX	357
4-FY	358
4-GA	122
4-GH	129
4-GJ	131
4-GL	133
4-HA	308
4-HB	309
4-HC	310
4-HD	311
4-HF	312
4-HI	313
4-HM	318
4-HN	319
4-HP	314
4-HQ	321
4-HT	323
4-HU	322
4-HV	320
4-HX	325
4-HZ	327
4-IA	307
4-IC	328
4-IE	330
4-IG	332
4-IH	333
4-II	334
4-IJ	335
4-IK	336
4-IL	337
4-IM	109
4-IO	338
7-GD	125
7-GI	130
7-GY	146
30-EB	304
30-EF	102
30-GB	123
30-GC	124
30-GE	126

Code	No.
30-GF	127
30-GG	128
30-GK	132
30-GM	134
30-GN	135
30-GP	137
30-GQ	138
30-GR	139
30-GS	140
30-GU	142
30-GV	143
30-GW	144
30-GX	145
30-GZ	147
30-HE	105
30-HH	104
30-HK	315
30-HO	317
30-HR	103
30-HS	108
30-HW	324
30-IB	306
30-ID	329
30-IF	331
30-IN	110
30-IP	111
30-IQ	112
30-IR	113
30-IS	114
30-IT	115
30-IU	116
30-IV	117
30-IW	118
30-IX	119
30-IY	120
30-VA	148
104-GI	130
104-GO	136
113-FQ	350
113-HG	106
113-HJ	107
113-HY	326
113-IZ	121
118-FQ	350

Pilatus PC-21
(NB: So far none have been seen with a hyphen in the code)

Code	No.
709 FC	01
709 FD	02
709 FE	03
709 FF	04
709 FG	05
709 FH	06
709 FI	07
709 FJ	08
709 FK	09
709 FL	10
709 FM	11
709 FN	12
709 FO	13
709 FP	14

Code	No.
709 FQ	15
709 FR	16
709 FS	17

FRENCH ARMY
SA.330 Puma

Code	No.
DAA	1006
DAB	1020
DAC	1036
DAD	1037
DAE	1049
DAF	1055
DAG	1069
DAH	1078
DAI	1092
DAJ	1100
DAK	1102
DAL	1107
DAM	1109
DAN	1128
DAO	1143
DAP	1149
DAQ	1156
DAR	1173
DAS	1176
DAU	1197
DAV	1204
DAW	1211
DAX	1214
DAY	1217
DAZ	1219
DBA	1232
DBB	1243
DBC	1248
DBD	1262
DBE	1277
DBF	1417
DBG	1438
DBH	1451
DBI	1507
DBJ	1510
DBK	1512
DBL	1519
DBM	1617
DBN	1632
DBO	1634
DBP	1654
DBQ	1663
DBR	5682
DCA	1005
DCB	1052
DCC	1056
DCD	1057
DCE	1071
DCF	1073
DCG	1093
DCH	1114
DCI	1122
DCJ	1122
DCK	1130
DCM	1136
DCN	1142
DCO	1145

Code	No.
DCP	1150
DCQ	1155
DCR	1163
DCS	1164
DCT	1165
DCU	1171
DCV	1172
DCW	1177
DCX	1179
DCY	1182
DCZ	1186
DDA	1190
DDB	1192
DDC	1196
DDD	1198
DDF	1213
DDG	1222
DDH	1223
DDI	1228
DDK	1231
DDM	1236
DDN	1239
DDO	1244
DDP	1252
DDQ	1255
DDR	1256
DDS	1260
DDT	1269
DDW	1447
DDX	1662

SA.342 Gazelle

Code	No.
GAA	3459
GAB	3476
GAC	3512
GAD	3530
GAE	3548
GAF	3664
GAG	3848
GAH	3849
GAI	3850
GAJ	3856
GAK	3859
GAL	3862
GAM	3863
GAN	3865
GAO	3868
GAP	3911
GAQ	3921
GAR	3938
GAS	3947
GAT	3948
GAU	3957
GAV	3964
GAW	3996
GAX	4018
GAY	4019
GAZ	4020
GBA	4026
GBB	4034
GBC	4039
GBD	4048
GBE	4053

GBF	4059	GJC	3511	CAE	2633	BIH	2040
GBG	4061	GJF	3546	CAF	2638	BII	2041
GBH	4066	GJI	3851	CAG	2640	BIJ	2042
GBI	4072	GJJ	3855	CAH	2642	BIK	2043
GBJ	4084	GJK	3857	CGA	2252	BIL	2044
GBL	4095	GJL	3864	CGB	2266	BIM	2045
GBM	4108	GJM	3867	CGC	2267	BIN	2046
GBN	4109	GJN	3929	CGD	2271	BIO	2047
GBO	4114	GJO	3965	CGE	2272	BIP	2048
GBP	4115	GJP	4014	CGF	2273	BIQ	2049
GBQ	4119	GJQ	4022	CGG	2282	BIR	2050
GBR	4120	GJR	4038	CGH	2285	BIS	2051
GBS	4124	GJS	4047	CGI	2290	BIT	2052
GBT	4136	GJU	4067	CGJ	2292	BJA	6001
GBU	4140	GJV	4078	CGK	2299	BJB	6002
GBV	4141	GJW	4102	CGL	2300	BJC	6003
GBW	4142	GJX	4103	CGM	2301	BJD	6004
GBX	4144	GJY	4123	CGN	2303	BJE	6005
GBY	4145	GJZ	4166	CGO	2316	BJF	6006
GBZ	4151	GKA	4176	CGQ	2323	BJG	6007
GCA	4155	GKB	4177	CGR	2324	BJH	6008
GCC	4160	GKC	4182	CGS	2325	BJI	6009
GCD	4161	GKD	4185	CGT	2327	BJJ	6010
GCE	4162	GMA	3567	CGU	2331	BJK	6011
GCF	4164	GMB	4042	CGV	2336	BJL	6012
GCG	4168	GMC	4079	CGW	2443	BJM	6013
GCH	4172	GMD	4194	CGX	2446	BJN	6014
GCI	4175	GME	3870	CHA	2342	BJO	6015
GCJ	4179	GMH	4023	CHB	2369	BJP	6016
GCK	4180	GMI	4171	CHC	2375	BJQ	6017
GCL	4181	GMJ	4190			BJR	6018
GCM	4186	GMK	4201	**EC.665 Tigre**		BJS	6019
GCN	4189	GNA	3458	BHA	2010	BJT	6020
GCO	4191	GNB	3513	BHB	2009	BJU	6021
GCP	4195	GNC	3549	BHC	2013	BJV	6022
GCQ	4198	GND	3617	BHD	2015	BJW	6023
GEA	4204	GNE	3852	BHE	2018	BJX	6024
GEB	4206	GNF	3853	BHF	2019	BJY	6025
GEC	4207	GNJ	3896	BHG	2022	BJZ	6026
GED	4208	GNK	3956	BHH	2001	BKA	6027
GEF	4210	GNM	3992	BHI	2002	BKB	6028
GEG	4211	GNO	4032	BHJ	2003	BKC	6029
GEI	4214	GNP	4049	BHK	2004	BKD	6030
GEJ	4215	GNQ	4060	BHL	2006	BKE	6031
GEK	4216	GNR	4065	BHM	2011		
GEL	4217	GNS	4071	BHN	2021	**NH.90-TTH**	
GEM	4218	GNT	4083	BHO	2024	EAA	1239
GEN	4219	GNU	4096	BHP	2023	EAB	1256
GEO	4220	GNV	4118	BHQ	2025	EAC	1271
GEP	4221	GNW	4135	BHR	2026	EAD	1273
GEQ	4222	GNX	4143	BHS	2027	EAE	1290
GER	4223	GNY	4146	BHT	2012	EAF	1291
GES	4224	GNZ	4159	BHU	2028	EAG	1292
GET	4225	GOA	4178	BHV	2029	EAH	1293
GEU	4226	GOB	4183	BHW	2030	EAI	1294
GEV	4227	GOC	4184	BHX	2031	EAJ	1295
GEW	4228	GOD	4192	BHZ	2033	EAK	1306
GEX	4229			BIA	2016	EAL	1307
GEY	4230	**AS.532UL/EC.725AP Cougar**		BIB	2034	EAM	1308
GEZ	4231	CAA	2611	BIC	2035	EAN	1309
GFA	4231	CAB	2628	BIE	2037	EAO	1310
GFB	4233	CAC	2630	BIF	2038	EAP	1311
GJA	1732	CAD	2631	BIG	2039	EAQ	1312

EAR	1313	51-62	MM7182	61-143	MM55075	4-37	MM55168
EAS	1332	51-65	MM7184	61-144	MM55076	4-41	MM7299
EAT	1333	51-66	MM7169	61-145	MM55077	4-43	MM7317
EAU	1334	51-70	MM7192	61-146	MM55078	4-44	MM7300
EAV	1335	51-71	MM7189	61-147	MM55079	4-46	MM7326
EAW	1336	51-72	MM7163	61-150	MM55080	4-47	MM7327
EAX	1337	51-80	MM55037	61-151	MM55081	4-50	MM7306
EAY	1338	51-81	MM55043	61-152	MM55082	4-51	MM7295
EAZ	1386	51-82	MM55044	61-154	MM55084	4-52	MM7294
EBA	1390	51-83	MM55049	61-155	MM55085	4-55	MM7311
EBB	1391	51-84	MM55051	61-156	MM55086	4-56	MM7330
EBC	1387	RS-14	MM7177	61-157	MM55087	4-57	MM7238
EBD	1392	RS-20	MM55034	61-160	MM55088	4-60	MM7338
EBE	1401			61-162	MM55090	4-61	MM7339
EBF	1402	**Aermacchi MB339**		61-241	MM54468	4-62	MM7344
EBG	1403	0 [FT]	MM55053	RS-32	MM55091	4-64	MM7340
EBH	1404	1 [FT]	MM54551	RS-33	MM55068	36-02	MM7286
EBI	1405	2 [FT]	MM54518			36-03	MM7281
EBJ	1432	3 [FT]	MM54517	**Aermacchi T-346A Master**		36-05	MM7276
EBK	1427	4 [FT]	MM54534	61-01	MM55154	36-10	MM7341
EBL	1428	5 [FT]	MM55059	61-02	MM55144	36-12	MM7318
EBM	1429	6 [FT]	MM55052	61-04	MM55155	36-14	MM7277
EBN	1433	7 [FT]	MM54510	61-05	MM55153	36-21	MM7292
EBO	1430	8 [FT]	MM54539	61-06	MM55213	36-22	MM7296
EBP	1431	9 [FT]	MM54505	61-07	MM55214	36-23	MM7297
EBQ	14..	11 [FT]	MM55058	61-10	MM55215	36-24	MM7298
EBR	1441	32-161	MM55089	61-11	MT55152	36-25	MM7302
EBS	14..	36-06	MM55074	61-12	MM55216	36-30	MM7280
EBT	14..	61-11	MM54457	61-13	MM55217	36-31	MM7308
EBU	14..	61-15	MM55054	61-14	MM55218	36-32	MM7310
		61-20	MM55055	61-15	MM55221	36-34	MM7312
ITALIA		61-21	MM54465	61-16	MM55220	36-35	MM7313
Aeritalia-EMB AMX		61-26	MM55059	61-20	MT55219	36-40	MM7322
32-47	MM55046	61-32	MM54488	61-21	MT55222	36-41	MM7324
32-51	MM55036	61-36	MM54492	61-22	MT55223	36-42	MM7288
32-53	MM55047	61-37	MM54493	61-23	MM55224	36-44	MM7325
32-56	MM55042	61-42	MM54496			36-46	MM7315
51-10	MM7159	61-45	MM54499	**Eurofighter Typhoon**		36-50	MM7341
51-26	MM7149	61-52	MM54504	4-1	MM7270	36-51	MM7342
51-27	MM7114	61-55	MM54507	4-2	MM7303	36-53	MM7347
51-30	MM7170	61-57	MM54509	4-3	MM7287	36-54	MM7349
51-31	MM7161	61-60	MM54510	4-4	MM7274	36-55	MM7352
51-32	MM7166	61-61	MM54511	4-5	MM7289	36-56	MM7353
51-33	MM7162	61-62	MM54512	4-6	MM7323	36-60	MM55094
51-34	MM7191	61-64	MM54514	4-7	MM7290	36-62	MM55092
51-35	MM7196	61-65	MM54515	4-8	MM7282	36-64	MM55128
51-36	MM7185	61-66	MM54516	4-9	MM7351	36-65	MM55095
51-40	MM7164	61-70	MM54518	4-11	MM7291	37-01	MM7307
51-41	MM7183	61-72	MM54533	4-12	MM7284	37-05	MM7319
51-42	MM7177	61-74	MM54535	4-13	MM7235	37-11	MM7294
51-43	MM7178	61-106	MM54548	4-15	MM7271	37-12	MM7321
51-44	MM7198	61-107	MM54549	4-18	MM7272	37-15	MM7329
51-45	MM7175	61-121	MM54458	4-19	MM7275	37-16	MM7331
51-46	MM7197	61-126	MM55062	4-20	MM7279	37-22	MM7293
51-50	MM7186	61-127	MM55063	4-21	MM7304	37-24	MM7348
51-51	MM7151	61-130	MM55064	4-22	MM7309	37-33	MM54133
51-52	MM7171	61-131	MM55065	4-24	MM55097	37-37	MM7346
51-53	MM7180	61-132	MM55066	4-30	MM55096	37-45	MM7345
51-55	MM7168	61-133	MM55067	4-31	MM55093	37-54	MM7354
51-56	MM7167	61-135	MM55069	4-32	MM55129	51-01	MM7316
51-57	MM7190	61-136	MM55070	4-33	MM55130	51-02	MM7320
51-60	MM7174	61-140	MM55072	4-34	MM55131	51-03	MM7314
51-61	MM7126	61-141	MM55073	4-35	MM55132	RMV-01	MMX603

RS-01	MMX602	6-65	MM7055	79-24	E.25-24	11-52	C.16-52
RS-11	MM7343	6-66	MM7059	79-25	E.25-25	11-53	C.16-53
RS-22	MM7350	6-67	MM7068	79-27	E.25-27	11-54	C.16-54
		6-71	MM7070	79-28	E.25-28	11-55	C.16-55
Lockheed Martin F-35A/		6-72	MM7051	79-29	E.25-87	11-57	C.16-57
F-35B Lightning II		6-73	MM7030	79-31	E.25-31	11-63	C.16-63
4-01	MM7451	6-74	MM7062	79-32	E.25-86	11-70	CE.16-01
4-02	MM7452	6-75	MM7013	79-33	E.25-50	11-71	CE.16-02
4-03	MM7453	6-76	MM7044	79-34	E.25-52	11-72	CE.16-03
32-01	MM7332	6-77	MM7020	79-35	E.25-54	11-73	CE.16-04
32-02	MM7333	6-100	MM7054	79-37	E.25-37	11-74	CE.16-05
32-03	MM7334	6-101	MM7053	79-38	E.25-38	11-76	CE.16-07
32-04	MM7335	36-50	CSX7085	79-39	E.25-79	11-78	CE.16-09
32-05	MM7336	50-01	MM7021	79-40	E.25-40	11-79	CE.16-10
32-07	MM7357	50-04	MM7030	79-44	E.25-44	11-91	C.16-20
32-08	MM7358	50-53	MM7008	79-49	E.25-49	14-01	C.16-31
32-09	MM7359	50-57	MM7067	79-97	E.25-69	14-03	C.16-36
32-10	MM7360	RS-01	CSX7041	79-98	E.25-73	14-04	C.16-37
32-11	MM7361	RS-05	CSX7047	741-68	E.25-68	14-06	C.16-39
32-13	MM7337			793-57	E.25-57	14-07	C.16-41
		SPAIN				14-09	C.16-44
Panavia Tornado		**CASA 101EB Aviojet**		**CASA 212 Aviocar**		14-10	C.16-45
6-01	MM7007	54-20	E.25-35	47-12	TM.12D-72	14-11	C.16-47
6-02	MM7019	54-21	E.25-55	47-14	T.12D-75	14-12	C.16-48
6-03	MM7084	54-22	E.25-61	54-11	T.12D-74	14-13	C.16-49
6-04	MM7057	74-02	E.25-33	72-11	T.12B-65	14-14	C.16-50
6-05	MM7025	74-07	E.25-51	72-12	T.12B-67	14-17	C.16-58
6-06	MM7036	74-09	E.25-53	72-13	T.12B-13	14-18	C.16-59
6-07	MM7075	74-11	E.25-56	72-17	T.12B-70	14-19	C.16-60
6-10	MM7088	74-13	E.25-59	72-21	TR.12D-76	14-20	C.16-61
6-11	MM7058	74-17	E.25-63	72-22	TR.12D-77	14-21	C.16-62
6-12	MM7071	74-20	E.25-66	72-24	TR.12D-81	14-22	C.16-64
6-13	MM7014	74-21	E.25-67	72-49	T.12B-49	14-23	C.16-65
6-15	MM55006	74-25	E.25-71	72-62	T.12B-62	14-24	C.16-66
6-20	MM7021	74-26	E.25-72	72-63	T.12B-63	14-25	C.16-67
6-21	MM7040	74-28	E.25-74	72-66	T.12B-66	14-26	C.16-68
6-22	MM7029	74-30	E.25-76	72-69	T.12B-69	14-28	C.16-70
6-25	MM7043	74-34	E.25-81	72-71	T.12B-71	14-29	C.16-71
6-26	MM7063	74-35	E.25-83			14-30	C.16-72
6-27	MM7035	74-39	E.25-88	**Eurofighter Tifón**		14-31	C.16-73
6-30	MM7072	74-40	E.25-17	11-02	C.16-22	14-32	C.16-74
6-31	MM7006	74-41	E.25-41	11-03	C.16-23	14-33	C.16-75
6-32	MM7015	74-42	E.25-18	11-04	C.16-24	14-34	C.16-76
6-33	MM7039	74-43	E.25-43	11-05	C.16-25	14-35	C.16-77
6-34	MM7073	74-44	E.25-34	11-06	CE.16-06	14-36	C.16-78
6-35	MM7026	74-45	E.25-29	11-07	C.16-27	14-70	CE.16-11
6-37	MM7038	79-02	E.25-78	11-08	C.16-28	14-71	CE.16-12
6-41	MM7067	79-03	E.25-80	11-09	C.16-29		
6-42	MM55010	79-04	E.25-84	11-10	C.16-30		
6-43	MM7066	79-05	E.25-05	11-11	C.16-32		
6-44	MM55009	79-06	E.25-06	11-13	CE.16-13		
6-45	MM55008	79-08	E.25-08	11-14	CE.16-14		
6-50	MM7024	79-09	E.25-09	11-16	C.16-40		
6-51	MM55007	79-11	E.25-11	11-17	C.16-41		
6-52	MM55001	79-12	E.25-12	11-21	C.16-21		
6-53	MM55004	79-13	E.25-13	11-26	C.16-26		
6-55	MM7004	79-14	E.25-14	11-33	C.16-33		
6-57	MM7081	79-15	E.25-15	11-35	C.16-35		
6-60	MM7086	79-16	E.25-16	11-38	C.16-38		
6-61	MM7047	79-17	E.25-62	11-42	C.16-42		
6-62	MM7082	79-21	E.25-21	11-43	C.16-43		
6-63	MM7023	79-22	E.25-22	11-46	C.16-46		
6-64	MM7052	79-23	E.25-23	11-51	C.16-51		

All USAF and US Army aircraft have been allocated a fiscal year (FY) number since 1921. Individual aircraft are given a serial according to the fiscal year in which they are ordered. The numbers commence at 0001 and are prefixed with the year of allocation. For example F-15C Eagle 84-0001 was the first aircraft ordered in 1984. The fiscal year (FY) serial is carried on the technical data block which is usually stencilled on the left-hand side of the aircraft just below the cockpit. The number displayed on the fin is a corruption of the FY serial. Most tactical aircraft carry the fiscal year in small figures followed by the last three or four digits of the serial in large figures. Large transport and tanker aircraft such as C-130s and KC-135s sometimes display a five-figure number commencing with the last digit of the appropriate fiscal year and four figures of the production number. An example of this is Boeing KC-135R Stratotanker 58-0128 which displays 80128 on its fin.

US Army serials have been allocated in a similar way to USAF serials although in recent years an additional zero has been added so that all US Army serials now have the two-figure fiscal year part followed by five digits. This means that, for example C-20E 70140 is officially 87-00140 although as yet this has not led to any alterations to serials painted on aircraft.

USN and USMC serials follow a straightforward numerical sequence which commenced, for the present series, with the allocation of 00001 to an SB2C Helldiver by the Bureau of Aeronautics in 1940. Numbers in the 168000 series are presently being issued. They are usually carried in full on the rear fuselage of the aircraft.

US Coast Guard serials began with the allocation of the serial 1 to a Loening OL-5 in 1927.

UK-BASED USAF AIRCRAFT

The following aircraft are normally based in the UK. They are listed in numerical order of type with individual aircraft in serial number order, as depicted on the aircraft. The number in brackets is either the alternative presentation of the five-figure number commencing with the last digit of the fiscal year, or the fiscal year where a five-figure serial is presented on the aircraft. Where it is possible to identify the allocation of aircraft to individual squadrons by means of colours carried on fin or cockpit edge, this is also provided.

Serial	Type (code/other identity)	Owner/operator, location or fate	Notes
McDonnell Douglas F-15C Eagle/F-15D Eagle/F-15E Strike Eagle			
84-0001	McD F-15C Eagle [LN] *bk/y*	USAF 493rd FS/48th FW, Lakenheath	
84-0010	McD F-15C Eagle [LN] *bk/y* $	USAF 493rd FS/48th FW, Lakenheath	
84-0015	McD F-15C Eagle [LN] *bk/y* [493 FS]	USAF 493rd FS/48th FW, Lakenheath	
84-0019	McD F-15C Eagle [LN] *bk/y*	USAF 493rd FS/48th FW, Lakenheath	
84-0027	McD F-15C Eagle [LN] *bk/y*	USAF 493rd FS/48th FW, Lakenheath	
84-0044	McD F-15D Eagle [LN] *bk/y*	USAF 493rd FS/48th FW, Lakenheath	
84-0046	McD F-15D Eagle [LN] *bk/y*	USAF 493rd FS/48th FW, Lakenheath	
86-0154	McD F-15C Eagle [LN] *bk/y*	USAF 493rd FS/48th FW, Lakenheath	
86-0156	McD F-15C Eagle [LN] *bk/y*	USAF 493rd FS/48th FW, Lakenheath	
86-0159	McD F-15C Eagle [LN] *m* [48 OG]	USAF 493rd FS/48th FW, Lakenheath	
86-0160	McD F-15C Eagle [LN] *bk/y*	USAF 493rd FS/48th FW, Lakenheath	
86-0163	McD F-15C Eagle [LN] *bk/y*	USAF 493rd FS/48th FW, Lakenheath	
86-0164	McD F-15C Eagle [LN] *bk/y*	USAF 493rd FS/48th FW, Lakenheath	
86-0165	McD F-15C Eagle [LN] *bk/y*	USAF 493rd FS/48th FW, Lakenheath	
86-0166	McD F-15C Eagle [LN] *bk/y*	USAF 493rd FS/48th FW, Lakenheath	
86-0171	McD F-15C Eagle [LN] *bk/y*	USAF 493rd FS/48th FW, Lakenheath	
86-0172	McD F-15C Eagle [LN] *bk/y*	USAF 493rd FS/48th FW, Lakenheath	
86-0174	McD F-15C Eagle [LN] *bk/y*	USAF 493rd FS/48th FW, Lakenheath	
86-0175	McD F-15C Eagle [LN] *bk/y*	USAF 493rd FS/48th FW, Lakenheath	
86-0176	McD F-15C Eagle [LN] *bk/y*	USAF 493rd FS/48th FW, Lakenheath	
86-0178	McD F-15C Eagle [LN] *bk/y*	USAF 493rd FS/48th FW, Lakenheath	
91-0301	McD F-15E Strike Eagle [LN] *bl/w*	USAF 492nd FS/48th FW, Lakenheath	
91-0302	McD F-15E Strike Eagle [LN] *bl/w*	USAF 492nd FS/48th FW, Lakenheath	
91-0303	McD F-15E Strike Eagle [LN] *bl/w*	USAF 492nd FS/48th FW, Lakenheath	
91-0306	McD F-15E Strike Eagle [LN] *bl/w*	USAF 492nd FS/48th FW, Lakenheath	
91-0307	McD F-15E Strike Eagle [LN] *bl/w*	USAF 492nd FS/48th FW, Lakenheath	
91-0308	McD F-15E Strike Eagle [LN] *bl/w*	USAF 492nd FS/48th FW, Lakenheath	
91-0309	McD F-15E Strike Eagle [LN] *r/w*	USAF 494th FS/48th FW, Lakenheath	
91-0310	McD F-15E Strike Eagle [LN] *r/w*	USAF 494th FS/48th FW, Lakenheath	
91-0311	McD F-15E Strike Eagle [LN] *m* [48 FW]	USAF 494th FS/48th FW, Lakenheath	
91-0312	McD F-15E Strike Eagle [LN]	USAF 492nd FS/48th FW, Lakenheath	
91-0313	McD F-15E Strike Eagle [LN] *r/w*	USAF 494th FS/48th FW, Lakenheath	
91-0314	McD F-15E Strike Eagle [LN] *r/w* [494 FS]	USAF 494th FS/48th FW, Lakenheath	
91-0315	McD F-15E Strike Eagle [LN] *bl/w*	USAF 492nd FS/48th FW, Lakenheath	
91-0316	McD F-15E Strike Eagle [LN] *bl/w*	USAF 492nd FS/48th FW, Lakenheath	

Notes	Serial	Type (code/other identity)	Owner/operator, location or fate
	91-0317	McD F-15E Strike Eagle [LN] bl/w	USAF 492nd FS/48th FW, Lakenheath
	91-0318	McD F-15E Strike Eagle [LN] bl/w	USAF 492nd FS/48th FW, Lakenheath
	91-0320	McD F-15E Strike Eagle [LN] r/w	USAF 494th FS/48th FW, Lakenheath
	91-0321	McD F-15E Strike Eagle [LN] bl/w	USAF 492nd FS/48th FW, Lakenheath
	91-0324	McD F-15E Strike Eagle [LN] r/w	USAF 494th FS/48th FW, Lakenheath
	91-0326	McD F-15E Strike Eagle [LN] r/w	USAF 494th FS/48th FW, Lakenheath
	91-0327	McD F-15E Strike Eagle [LN] bl/w	USAF 492nd FS/48th FW, Lakenheath
	91-0329	McD F-15E Strike Eagle [LN] r/w	USAF 494th FS/48th FW, Lakenheath
	91-0331	McD F-15E Strike Eagle [LN] bl/w	USAF 492nd FS/48th FW, Lakenheath
	91-0332	McD F-15E Strike Eagle [LN] bl/w	USAF 492nd FS/48th FW, Lakenheath
	91-0334	McD F-15E Strike Eagle [LN]	USAF 494th FS/48th FW, Lakenheath
	91-0335	McD F-15E Strike Eagle [LN] r/w	USAF 494th FS/48th FW, Lakenheath
	91-0602	McD F-15E Strike Eagle [LN] r/w	USAF 494th FS/48th FW, Lakenheath
	91-0603	McD F-15E Strike Eagle [LN] r/w	USAF 494th FS/48th FW, Lakenheath
	91-0604	McD F-15E Strike Eagle [LN] r/w	USAF 494th FS/48th FW, Lakenheath
	91-0605	McD F-15E Strike Eagle [LN] bl/w	USAF 492nd FS/48th FW, Lakenheath
	92-0364	McD F-15E Strike Eagle [LN] r/w	USAF 494th FS/48th FW, Lakenheath
	96-0201	McD F-15E Strike Eagle [LN] r/w	USAF 494th FS/48th FW, Lakenheath
	96-0202	McD F-15E Strike Eagle [LN] bl/w	USAF 492nd FS/48th FW, Lakenheath
	96-0204	McD F-15E Strike Eagle [LN]	USAF 494th FS/48th FW, Lakenheath
	96-0205	McD F-15E Strike Eagle [LN] bl/w	USAF 492nd FS/48th FW, Lakenheath
	97-0218	McD F-15E Strike Eagle [LN]	USAF 492nd FS/48th FW, Lakenheath
	97-0219	McD F-15E Strike Eagle [LN] bl/w $	USAF 492nd FS/48th FW, Lakenheath
	97-0220	McD F-15E Strike Eagle [LN] bl/w	USAF 492nd FS/48th FW, Lakenheath
	97-0221	McD F-15E Strike Eagle [LN] bl/w [492 FS]	USAF 492nd FS/48th FW, Lakenheath
	97-0222	McD F-15E Strike Eagle [LN] bl/w	USAF 492nd FS/48th FW, Lakenheath
	98-0131	McD F-15E Strike Eagle [LN] bl/w	USAF 492nd FS/48th FW, Lakenheath
	98-0133	McD F-15E Strike Eagle [LN] bl/w	USAF 492nd FS/48th FW, Lakenheath
	98-0134	McD F-15E Strike Eagle [LN] bl/w	USAF 492nd FS/48th FW, Lakenheath
	98-0135	McD F-15E Strike Eagle [LN] bl/w	USAF 492nd FS/48th FW, Lakenheath
	00-3000	McD F-15E Strike Eagle [LN] r/w	USAF 494th FS/48th FW, Lakenheath
	00-3001	McD F-15E Strike Eagle [LN] r/w	USAF 494th FS/48th FW, Lakenheath
	00-3002	McD F-15E Strike Eagle [LN] r/w	USAF 494th FS/48th FW, Lakenheath
	00-3003	McD F-15E Strike Eagle [LN] r/w	USAF 494th FS/48th FW, Lakenheath
	00-3004	McD F-15E Strike Eagle [LN] r/w	USAF 494th FS/48th FW, Lakenheath
	01-2000	McD F-15E Strike Eagle [LN] r/w	USAF 494th FS/48th FW, Lakenheath
	01-2001	McD F-15E Strike Eagle [LN] r/w	USAF 494th FS/48th FW, Lakenheath
	01-2002	McD F-15E Strike Eagle [LN] r/w	USAF 494th FS/48th FW, Lakenheath
	01-2003	McD F-15E Strike Eagle [LN] r/w	USAF 494th FS/48th FW, Lakenheath
	01-2004	McD F-15E Strike Eagle [LN] r/w	USAF 494th FS/48th FW, Lakenheath

Bell-Boeing CV-22B Osprey

Notes	Serial	Type (code/other identity)	Owner/operator, location or fate
	0033	Bell-Boeing CV-22B Osprey (07-0033)	USAF 7th SOS/352nd SOW, Mildenhall
	0042	Bell-Boeing CV-22B Osprey (09-0042)	USAF 7th SOS/352nd SOW, Mildenhall
	0047	Bell-Boeing CV-22B Osprey (08-0047)	USAF 7th SOS/352nd SOW, Mildenhall
	0050	Bell-Boeing CV-22B Osprey (08-0050) $	USAF 7th SOS/352nd SOW, Mildenhall
	0051	Bell-Boeing CV-22B Osprey (08-0051)	USAF 7th SOS/352nd SOW, Mildenhall
	0052	Bell-Boeing CV-22B Osprey (10-0052)	USAF 7th SOS/352nd SOW, Mildenhall
	0059	Bell-Boeing CV-22B Osprey (11-0059)	USAF 7th SOS/352nd SOW, Mildenhall
	0060	Bell-Boeing CV-22B Osprey (11-0060)	USAF 7th SOS/352nd SOW, Mildenhall
	0063	Bell-Boeing CV-22B Osprey (12-0063)	USAF 7th SOS/352nd SOW, Mildenhall
	0064	Bell-Boeing CV-22B Osprey (12-0064)	USAF 7th SOS/352nd SOW, Mildenhall
	0065	Bell-Boeing CV-22B Osprey (12-0065) $	USAF 7th SOS/352nd SOW, Mildenhall

Lockheed MC-130J Commando II

Notes	Serial	Type (code/other identity)	Owner/operator, location or fate
	05714	Lockheed MC-130J Commando II (10-5714)	*Returned to the USA, 31 January 2020*
	15731	Lockheed MC-130J Commando II (11-5731)	USAF 67th SOS/352nd SOW, RAF Mildenhall
	15737	Lockheed MC-130J Commando II (11-5737)	USAF 67th SOS/352nd SOW, RAF Mildenhall
	25757	Lockheed MC-130J Commando II (12-5757)	*Returned to the USA, 17 December 2019*
	25759	Lockheed MC-130J Commando II (12-5759)	*Returned to the USA, 30 March 2019*
	25760	Lockheed MC-130J Commando II (12-5760)	USAF 67th SOS/352nd SOW, RAF Mildenhall
	35778	Lockheed MC-130J Commando II (13-5778)	USAF 67th SOS/352nd SOW, RAF Mildenhall

Serial	Type (code/other identity)	Owner/operator, location or fate	Notes
35786	Lockheed MC-130J Commando II (13-5786)	USAF 67th SOS/352nd SOW, RAF Mildenhall	
86205	Lockheed MC-130J Commando II (08-6205)	USAF 67th SOS/352nd SOW, RAF Mildenhall	
95713	Lockheed MC-130J Commando II (09-5713)	USAF 67th SOS/352nd SOW, RAF Mildenhall	
96207	Lockheed MC-130J Commando II (09-6207)	USAF 67th SOS/352nd SOW, RAF Mildenhall	
	Boeing KC-135R Stratotanker/Boeing KC-135T Stratotanker		
00324	Boeing KC-135R Stratotanker (60-0324) [D] *r/w/bl*	USAF 351st ARS/100th ARW, RAF Mildenhall	
00344	Boeing KC-135T Stratotanker (60-0344) [D] *r/w/bl*	*Returned to the USA, 24 September 2019*	
00355	Boeing KC-135R Stratotanker (60-0355) [D] *r/w/bl*	USAF 351st ARS/100th ARW, RAF Mildenhall	
10288	Boeing KC-135R Stratotanker (61-0288) [D] *r/w/bl*	*Returned to the USA, 22 October 2019*	
10292	Boeing KC-135R Stratotanker (61-0292) [D] *r/w/bl*	USAF 351st ARS/100th ARW, RAF Mildenhall	
23540	Boeing KC-135R Stratotanker (62-3540) [D] *r/w/bl*	USAF 351st ARS/100th ARW, RAF Mildenhall	
23551	Boeing KC-135R Stratotanker (62-3551) [D] *r/w/bl* [EP-B]	USAF 351st ARS/100th ARW, RAF Mildenhall	
37999	Boeing KC-135R Stratotanker (63-7999) [D] *r/w/bl*	*Returned to the USA, 6 November 2019*	
38878	Boeing KC-135R Stratotanker (63-8878) [D] *r/w/bl*	USAF 351st ARS/100th ARW, RAF Mildenhall	
71440	Boeing KC-135R Stratotanker (57-1440) [D] *r/w/bl*	USAF 351st ARS/100th ARW, RAF Mildenhall	
71474	Boeing KC-135R Stratotanker (57-1474) [D] *r/w/bl*	USAF 351st ARS/100th ARW, RAF Mildenhall	
71493	Boeing KC-135R Stratotanker (57-1493) [D] *r/w/bl*	USAF 351st ARS/100th ARW, RAF Mildenhall	
72605	Boeing KC-135R Stratotanker (57-2605) [D] *r/w/bl*	*Returned to the USA, 31 October 2019*	
80001	Boeing KC-135T Stratotanker (58-0001) [D] *r/w/bl*	USAF 351st ARS/100th ARW, RAF Mildenhall	
80036	Boeing KC-135R Stratotanker (58-0036) [D] *r/w/bl*	USAF 351st ARS/100th ARW, RAF Mildenhall	
80100	Boeing KC-135R Stratotanker (58-0100) [D] *r/w/bl* [EP-A]	USAF 351st ARS/100th ARW, RAF Mildenhall	
80113	Boeing KC-135R Stratotanker (58-0113) [D] *r/w/bl*	USAF 351st ARS/100th ARW, RAF Mildenhall	
91513	Boeing KC-135T Stratotanker (59-1513) [D] *r/w/bl*	USAF 351st ARS/100th ARW, RAF Mildenhall	

F-15C Eagle 86-0159 is operated by the 493rd Fighter Squadron of the 48th Fighter Wing at RAF Lakenheath. It wears special markings for the 48th Operations Group (48 OG).

These aircraft are normally based in Western Europe with the USAFE. They are shown in numerical order of type designation, with individual aircraft in serial number order as carried on the aircraft. Fiscal year (FY) details are also provided if necessary. The unit allocation and operating bases are given for most aircraft.

Notes	Serial	Type (code/other identity)	Owner/operator, location or fate
	Beech C-12 Huron		
	30499	Beech C-12D Huron (83-0499)	USAF US Embassy Flight, Taszár, Hungary
	31217	Beech C-12C Huron (73-1217)	USAF US Embassy Flight, Taszár, Hungary
	Lockheed (GD) F-16CM/F-16DM Fighting Falcon		
	87-0350	Lockheed (GD) F-16CM-40 Fighting Falcon [AV] gn/y	USAF 555th FS/31st FW, Aviano, Italy
	87-0351	Lockheed (GD) F-16CM-40 Fighting Falcon [AV] gn/y	USAF 555th FS/31st FW, Aviano, Italy
	87-0355	Lockheed (GD) F-16CM-40 Fighting Falcon [AV] pr/w	USAF 510th FS/31st FW, Aviano, Italy
	87-0359	Lockheed (GD) F-16CM-40 Fighting Falcon [AV] gn/y	USAF 555th FS/31st FW, Aviano, Italy
	88-0413	Lockheed (GD) F-16CM-40 Fighting Falcon [AV] pr/w	USAF 510th FS/31st FW, Aviano, Italy
	88-0425	Lockheed (GD) F-16CM-40 Fighting Falcon [AV] gn/y	USAF 555th FS/31st FW, Aviano, Italy
	88-0435	Lockheed (GD) F-16CM-40 Fighting Falcon [AV] gn/y	USAF 555th FS/31st FW, Aviano, Italy
	88-0443	Lockheed (GD) F-16CM-40 Fighting Falcon [AV] pr/w	USAF 510th FS/31st FW, Aviano, Italy
	88-0444	Lockheed (GD) F-16CM-40 Fighting Falcon [AV] pr/w	USAF 510th FS/31st FW, Aviano, Italy
	88-0446	Lockheed (GD) F-16CM-40 Fighting Falcon [AV] gn/y	USAF 555th FS/31st FW, Aviano, Italy
	88-0460	Lockheed (GD) F-16CM-40 Fighting Falcon [AV] pr/w	USAF 510th FS/31st FW, Aviano, Italy
	88-0462	Lockheed (GD) F-16CM-40 Fighting Falcon [AV] pr/w	USAF 510th FS/31st FW, Aviano, Italy
	88-0491	Lockheed (GD) F-16CM-40 Fighting Falcon [AV] pr/w	USAF 510th FS/31st FW, Aviano, Italy
	88-0516	Lockheed (GD) F-16CM-40 Fighting Falcon [AV] pr/w	USAF 510th FS/31st FW, Aviano, Italy
	88-0521	Lockheed (GD) F-16CM-40 Fighting Falcon [AV] pr/w	USAF 510th FS/31st FW, Aviano, Italy
	88-0525	Lockheed (GD) F-16CM-40 Fighting Falcon [AV] pr/w	USAF 510th FS/31st FW, Aviano, Italy
	88-0526	Lockheed (GD) F-16CM-40 Fighting Falcon [AV] gn/y	USAF 555th FS/31st FW, Aviano, Italy
	88-0532	Lockheed (GD) F-16CM-40 Fighting Falcon [AV] gn/y	USAF 555th FS/31st FW, Aviano, Italy
	88-0535	Lockheed (GD) F-16CM-40 Fighting Falcon [AV] gn/y	USAF 555th FS/31st FW, Aviano, Italy
	88-0541	Lockheed (GD) F-16CM-40 Fighting Falcon [AV] pr/w	USAF 510th FS/31st FW, Aviano, Italy
	89-2001	Lockheed (GD) F-16CM-40 Fighting Falcon [AV] m [31 FW]	USAF 31st FW, Aviano, Italy
	89-2008	Lockheed (GD) F-16CM-40 Fighting Falcon [AV] pr/w	USAF 510th FS/31st FW, Aviano, Italy
	89-2009	Lockheed (GD) F-16CM-40 Fighting Falcon [AV] pr/w	USAF 510th FS/31st FW, Aviano, Italy
	89-2011	Lockheed (GD) F-16CM-40 Fighting Falcon [AV] pr/w	USAF 510th FS/31st FW, Aviano, Italy
	89-2016	Lockheed (GD) F-16CM-40 Fighting Falcon [AV] gn/y	USAF 555th FS/31st FW, Aviano, Italy
	89-2018	Lockheed (GD) F-16CM-40 Fighting Falcon [AV] gn/y	USAF 555th FS/31st FW, Aviano, Italy
	89-2023	Lockheed (GD) F-16CM-40 Fighting Falcon [AV] gn/y	USAF 555th FS/31st FW, Aviano, Italy
	89-2024	Lockheed (GD) F-16CM-40 Fighting Falcon [AV] gn/y	USAF 555th FS/31st FW, Aviano, Italy
	89-2026	Lockheed (GD) F-16CM-40 Fighting Falcon [AV] pr/w	USAF 510th FS/31st FW, Aviano, Italy
	89-2029	Lockheed (GD) F-16CM-40 Fighting Falcon [AV] pr/w	USAF 510th FS/31st FW, Aviano, Italy
	89-2030	Lockheed (GD) F-16CM-40 Fighting Falcon [AV] pr/w [510 FS]	USAF 510th FS/31st FW, Aviano, Italy
	89-2035	Lockheed (GD) F-16CM-40 Fighting Falcon [AV] gn/y [555 FS]	USAF 555th FS/31st FW, Aviano, Italy
	89-2038	Lockheed (GD) F-16CM-40 Fighting Falcon [AV] pr/w	USAF 510th FS/31st FW, Aviano, Italy
	89-2039	Lockheed (GD) F-16CM-40 Fighting Falcon [AV] gn/y	USAF 555th FS/31st FW, Aviano, Italy
	89-2041	Lockheed (GD) F-16CM-40 Fighting Falcon [AV] gn/y	USAF 555th FS/31st FW, Aviano, Italy
	89-2044	Lockheed (GD) F-16CM-40 Fighting Falcon [AV] gn/y	USAF 555th FS/31st FW, Aviano, Italy
	89-2046	Lockheed (GD) F-16CM-40 Fighting Falcon [AV] pr/w	USAF 510th FS/31st FW, Aviano, Italy
	89-2047	Lockheed (GD) F-16CM-40 Fighting Falcon [AV] pr/w	USAF 510th FS/31st FW, Aviano, Italy
	89-2049	Lockheed (GD) F-16CM-40 Fighting Falcon [AV] pr/w [USAFE]	USAF 510th FS/31st FW, Aviano, Italy
	89-2057	Lockheed (GD) F-16CM-40 Fighting Falcon [AV] pr/w	USAF 510th FS/31st FW, Aviano, Italy
	89-2068	Lockheed (GD) F-16CM-40 Fighting Falcon [AV] gn/y	USAF 555th FS/31st FW, Aviano, Italy
	89-2096	Lockheed (GD) F-16CM-40 Fighting Falcon [AV] pr/w	USAF 510th FS/31st FW, Aviano, Italy
	89-2102	Lockheed (GD) F-16CM-40 Fighting Falcon [AV] pr/w	USAF 510th FS/31st FW, Aviano, Italy
	89-2118	Lockheed (GD) F-16CM-40 Fighting Falcon [AV] gn/y	USAF 555th FS/31st FW, Aviano, Italy
	89-2137	Lockheed (GD) F-16CM-40 Fighting Falcon [AV] m [31 OG]	USAF 510th FS/31st FW, Aviano, Italy
	89-2152	Lockheed (GD) F-16CM-40 Fighting Falcon [AV] gn/y	USAF 555th FS/31st FW, Aviano, Italy
	89-2178	Lockheed (GD) F-16DM-40 Fighting Falcon [AV] gn/y	USAF 555th FS/31st FW, Aviano, Italy
	90-0709	Lockheed (GD) F-16CM-40 Fighting Falcon [AV] pr/w	USAF 510th FS/31st FW, Aviano, Italy

Serial	Type (code/other identity)	Owner/operator, location or fate	Notes
90-0772	Lockheed (GD) F-16CM-40 Fighting Falcon [AV] *gn/y*	USAF 555th FS/31st FW, Aviano, Italy	
90-0773	Lockheed (GD) F-16CM-40 Fighting Falcon [AV] *gn/y*	USAF 555th FS/31st FW, Aviano, Italy	
90-0777	Lockheed (GD) F-16DM-40 Fighting Falcon [AV] *pr/w*	USAF 510th FS/31st FW, Aviano, Italy	
90-0795	Lockheed (GD) F-16DM-40 Fighting Falcon [AV] *gn/y*	USAF 555th FS/31st FW, Aviano, Italy	
90-0796	Lockheed (GD) F-16DM-40 Fighting Falcon [AV] *gn/y*	USAF 555th FS/31st FW, Aviano, Italy	
90-0800	Lockheed (GD) F-16DM-40 Fighting Falcon [AV] *gn/y*	USAF 555th FS/31st FW, Aviano, Italy	
90-0813	Lockheed (GD) F-16CM-50 Fighting Falcon [SP] *r/w*	USAF 480th FS/52nd FW, Spangdahlem, Germany	
90-0818	Lockheed (GD) F-16CM-50 Fighting Falcon [SP] *r/w*	USAF 480th FS/52nd FW, Spangdahlem, Germany	
90-0827	Lockheed (GD) F-16CM-50 Fighting Falcon [SP] *r/w*	USAF 480th FS/52nd FW, Spangdahlem, Germany	
90-0828	Lockheed (GD) F-16CM-50 Fighting Falcon [SP] *r/w*	USAF 480th FS/52nd FW, Spangdahlem, Germany	
90-0829	Lockheed (GD) F-16CM-50 Fighting Falcon [SP] *r/w* [52 OG]	USAF 480th FS/52nd FW, Spangdahlem, Germany	
90-0833	Lockheed (GD) F-16CM-50 Fighting Falcon [SP] *r/w*	USAF 480th FS/52nd FW, Spangdahlem, Germany	
91-0338	Lockheed (GD) F-16CM-50 Fighting Falcon [SP] *r/w*	USAF 480th FS/52nd FW, Spangdahlem, Germany	
91-0340	Lockheed (GD) F-16CM-50 Fighting Falcon [SP] *r/w*	*Crashed 8 October 2019, Zemmer, Germany*	
91-0342	Lockheed (GD) F-16CM-50 Fighting Falcon [SP] *r/w*	USAF 480th FS/52nd FW, Spangdahlem, Germany	
91-0343	Lockheed (GD) F-16CM-50 Fighting Falcon [SP] *r/w*	USAF 480th FS/52nd FW, Spangdahlem, Germany	
91-0344	Lockheed (GD) F-16CM-50 Fighting Falcon [SP] *r/w*	USAF 480th FS/52nd FW, Spangdahlem, Germany	
91-0351	Lockheed (GD) F-16CM-50 Fighting Falcon [SP] *r/w*	USAF 480th FS/52nd FW, Spangdahlem, Germany	
91-0352	Lockheed (GD) F-16CM-50 Fighting Falcon [SP] *m* [52 FW]	USAF 480th FS/52nd FW, Spangdahlem, Germany	
91-0358	Lockheed (GD) F-16CM-50 Fighting Falcon [SP] *r/w*	USAF 480th FS/52nd FW, Spangdahlem, Germany	
91-0360	Lockheed (GD) F-16CM-50 Fighting Falcon [SP] *r/w*	USAF 480th FS/52nd FW, Spangdahlem, Germany	
91-0361	Lockheed (GD) F-16CM-50 Fighting Falcon [SP] *r/w*	USAF 480th FS/52nd FW, Spangdahlem, Germany	
91-0368	Lockheed (GD) F-16CM-50 Fighting Falcon [SP]	USAF 480th FS/52nd FW, Spangdahlem, Germany	
91-0402	Lockheed (GD) F-16CM-50 Fighting Falcon [SP] *r/w*	USAF 480th FS/52nd FW, Spangdahlem, Germany	
91-0403	Lockheed (GD) F-16CM-50 Fighting Falcon [SP] *r/w*	USAF 480th FS/52nd FW, Spangdahlem, Germany	
91-0407	Lockheed (GD) F-16CM-50 Fighting Falcon [SP] *r/w*	USAF 480th FS/52nd FW, Spangdahlem, Germany	
91-0412	Lockheed (GD) F-16CM-50 Fighting Falcon [SP] *r/w*	USAF 480th FS/52nd FW, Spangdahlem, Germany	
91-0416	Lockheed (GD) F-16CM-50 Fighting Falcon [SP] *r/w*	USAF 480th FS/52nd FW, Spangdahlem, Germany	
91-0417	Lockheed (GD) F-16CM-50 Fighting Falcon [SP] *r/w*	USAF 480th FS/52nd FW, Spangdahlem, Germany	
91-0418	Lockheed (GD) F-16CM-50 Fighting Falcon [SP] *r/w*	USAF 480th FS/52nd FW, Spangdahlem, Germany	
91-0472	Lockheed (GD) F-16DM-50 Fighting Falcon [SP] *r/w*	USAF 480th FS/52nd FW, Spangdahlem, Germany	
91-0481	Lockheed (GD) F-16DM-50 Fighting Falcon [SP] *r/w*	USAF 480th FS/52nd FW, Spangdahlem, Germany	
92-3918	Lockheed (GD) F-16CM-50 Fighting Falcon [SP] *r/w*	USAF 480th FS/52nd FW, Spangdahlem, Germany	
96-0080	Lockheed (GD) F-16CM-50 Fighting Falcon [SP] *r/w* [480 FS]	USAF 480th FS/52nd FW, Spangdahlem, Germany	
96-0083	Lockheed (GD) F-16CM-50 Fighting Falcon [SP] *r/w*	USAF 480th FS/52nd FW, Spangdahlem, Germany	

Gates C-21A

Serial	Type (code/other identity)	Owner/operator, location or fate	Notes
40083	Gates C-21A (84-0083)	USAF 76th AS/86th AW, Ramstein, Germany	
40085	Gates C-21A (84-0085)	USAF 76th AS/86th AW, Ramstein, Germany	
40087	Gates C-21A (84-0087)	USAF 76th AS/86th AW, Ramstein, Germany	
40096	Gates C-21A (84-0096)	USAF 76th AS/86th AW, Ramstein, Germany	
40126	Gates C-21A (84-0126)	USAF 76th AS/86th AW, Ramstein, Germany	

Gulfstream Aerospace C-37A Gulfstream V

Serial	Type (code/other identity)	Owner/operator, location or fate	Notes
10029	Gulfstream Aerospace C-37A Gulfstream V (01-0029)	USAF 309th AS/86th AW, Chièvres, Belgium	
10030	Gulfstream Aerospace C-37A Gulfstream V (01-0030)	USAF 76th AS/86th AW, Ramstein, Germany	
10076	Gulfstream Aerospace C-37A Gulfstream V (01-0076)	USAF 76th AS/86th AW, Ramstein, Germany	
90402	Gulfstream Aerospace C-37A Gulfstream V (99-0402)	*Returned to the USA, May 2019*	

Boeing C-40B

Serial	Type (code/other identity)	Owner/operator, location or fate	Notes
20042	Boeing C-40B (02-0042)	*Returned to the USA, 2019*	

Sikorsky HH-60G Pave Hawk

Serial	Type (code/other identity)	Owner/operator, location or fate	Notes
26205	Sikorsky HH-60G Pave Hawk (89-26205) [AV]	USAF 56th RQS/31st FW, Aviano, Italy	
26206	Sikorsky HH-60G Pave Hawk (89-26206) [AV]	USAF 56th RQS/31st FW, Aviano, Italy	
26208	Sikorsky HH-60G Pave Hawk (89-26208) [AV]	USAF 56th RQS/31st FW, Aviano, Italy	
26212	Sikorsky HH-60G Pave Hawk (89-26212) [AV]	USAF 56th RQS/31st FW, Aviano, Italy	
26353	Sikorsky HH-60G Pave Hawk (91-26353) [AV]	USAF 56th RQS/31st FW, Aviano, Italy	

EUROPEAN-BASED USAF AIRCRAFT

Notes	Serial	Type (code/other identity)	Owner/operator, location or fate
	Lockheed C-130J-30 Hercules II		
	15736	Lockheed C-130J-30 Hercules II (11-5736)[RS] bl/w $	USAF 37th AS/86th AW, Ramstein, Germany
	43142	Lockheed C-130J-30 Hercules II (04-3142)[RS] bl/w	USAF 37th AS/86th AW, Ramstein, Germany
	55822	Lockheed C-130J-30 Hercules II (15-5822)[RS] bl/w	USAF 37th AS/86th AW, Ramstein, Germany
	55831	Lockheed C-130J-30 Hercules II (15-5831)[RS] bl/w	USAF 37th AS/86th AW, Ramstein, Germany
	65840	Lockheed C-130J-30 Hercules II (16-5840)[RS] bl/w $	USAF 37th AS/86th AW, Ramstein, Germany
	68611	Lockheed C-130J-30 Hercules II (06-8611)[RS] bl/w	USAF 37th AS/86th AW, Ramstein, Germany
	74635	Lockheed C-130J-30 Hercules II (07-4635)[RS] bl/w $	USAF 37th AS/86th AW, Ramstein, Germany
	78608	Lockheed C-130J-30 Hercules II (07-8608)[RS] bl/w $	USAF 37th AS/86th AW, Ramstein, Germany
	78609	Lockheed C-130J-30 Hercules II (07-8609)[RS] bl/w	USAF 37th AS/86th AW, Ramstein, Germany
	78614	Lockheed C-130J-30 Hercules II (07-8614)[RS] bl/w	USAF 37th AS/86th AW, Ramstein, Germany
	83176	Lockheed C-130J-30 Hercules II (08-3176)[RS] bl/w	USAF 37th AS/86th AW, Ramstein, Germany
	88601	Lockheed C-130J-30 Hercules II (08-8601)[RS] bl/w [86 AW]	USAF 37th AS/86th AW, Ramstein, Germany
	88602	Lockheed C-130J-30 Hercules II (08-8602)[RS] bl/w [86 OG]	USAF 37th AS/86th AW, Ramstein, Germany
	88603	Lockheed C-130J-30 Hercules II (08-8603)[RS] bl/w [37 AS]	USAF 37th AS/86th AW, Ramstein, Germany

EUROPEAN-BASED US NAVY AIRCRAFT

Notes	Serial	Type (code/other identity)	Owner/operator, location or fate
	Fairchild C-26D		
	900528	Fairchild C-26D	USN NAF Sigonella, Italy
	900530	Fairchild C-26D	USN NAF Sigonella, Italy
	900531	Fairchild C-26D	USN NAF Naples, Italy
	910502	Fairchild C-26D	USN NAF Naples, Italy

In connection with the 75th Anniversary of D-Day, this Lockheed Martin MC-130J Commando II, 10-5714, of the 67th Special Operations Squadron/352nd Special Operations Wing based at RAF Mildenhall received special markings on the tail and under the wings.

Serial	Type (code/other identity)	Owner/operator, location or fate	Notes
Beech C-12 Huron			
40156	Beech C-12U-3 Huron (84-00156)	US Army E/1-214th AVN, Wiesbaden, Germany	
40157	Beech C-12U-3 Huron (84-00157)	US Army E/1-214th AVN, Wiesbaden, Germany	
40160	Beech C-12U-3 Huron (84-00160)	*Returned to the USA, 2019*	
40162	Beech C-12U-3 Huron (84-00162)	US Army E/1-214th AVN, Wiesbaden, Germany	
40165	Beech C-12U-3 Huron (84-00165)	US Army E/1-214th AVN, Wiesbaden, Germany	
40173	Beech C-12U-3 Huron (84-00173)	US Army E/1-214th AVN, Wiesbaden, Germany	
Cessna UC-35A Citation V			
50123	Cessna UC-35A Citation V (95-00123)	US Army E/1-214th AVN, Wiesbaden, Germany	
70102	Cessna UC-35A Citation V (97-00102)	US Army E/1-214th AVN, Wiesbaden, Germany	
70105	Cessna UC-35A Citation V (97-00105)	US Army E/1-214th AVN, Wiesbaden, Germany	
90102	Cessna UC-35A Citation V (99-00102)	*Returned to the USA, 2019*	
Boeing-Vertol CH-47F Chinook			
13-08132	Boeing-Vertol CH-47F Chinook	US Army B/1-214th AVN, Ansbach, Germany	
13-08133	Boeing-Vertol CH-47F Chinook	US Army B/1-214th AVN, Ansbach, Germany	
13-08134	Boeing-Vertol CH-47F Chinook	US Army B/1-214th AVN, Ansbach, Germany	
13-08135	Boeing-Vertol CH-47F Chinook	US Army B/1-214th AVN, Ansbach, Germany	
13-08432	Boeing-Vertol CH-47F Chinook	US Army B/1-214th AVN, Ansbach, Germany	
13-08434	Boeing-Vertol CH-47F Chinook	US Army B/1-214th AVN, Ansbach, Germany	
13-08435	Boeing-Vertol CH-47F Chinook	US Army B/1-214th AVN, Ansbach, Germany	
13-08436	Boeing-Vertol CH-47F Chinook	US Army B/1-214th AVN, Ansbach, Germany	
13-08437	Boeing-Vertol CH-47F Chinook	US Army B/1-214th AVN, Ansbach, Germany	
15-08176	Boeing-Vertol CH-47F Chinook	US Army B/1-214th AVN, Ansbach, Germany	
15-08178	Boeing-Vertol CH-47F Chinook	US Army B/1-214th AVN, Ansbach, Germany	
Sikorsky H-60 Black Hawk			
23936	Sikorsky UH-60A+ Black Hawk (84-23936)	US Army C/1-214th AVN, Grafenwöhr, Germany	
24397	Sikorsky UH-60A+ Black Hawk (85-24397)	US Army C/1-214th AVN, Grafenwöhr, Germany	
24437	Sikorsky UH-60A+ Black Hawk (85-24437)	US Army C/1-214th AVN, Grafenwöhr, Germany	
24446	Sikorsky UH-60A+ Black Hawk (85-24446)	US Army C/1-214th AVN, Grafenwöhr, Germany	
24614	Sikorsky UH-60A+ Black Hawk (87-24614)	US Army C/1-214th AVN, Grafenwöhr, Germany	
26004	Sikorsky UH-60A+ Black Hawk (87-26004)	US Army C/1-214th AVN, Grafenwöhr, Germany	
26163	Sikorsky UH-60A+ Black Hawk (89-26163)	US Army C/1-214th AVN, Grafenwöhr, Germany	
20245	Sikorsky UH-60L Black Hawk (10-20245)	US Army A/1-214th AVN, Wiesbaden, Germany	
20272	Sikorsky UH-60L Black Hawk (10-20272)	US Army A/1-214th AVN, Wiesbaden, Germany	
20276	Sikorsky UH-60L Black Hawk (10-20276)	US Army A/1-214th AVN, Wiesbaden, Germany	
20311	Sikorsky UH-60L Black Hawk (10-20311)	US Army A/1-214th AVN, Wiesbaden, Germany	
20314	Sikorsky UH-60L Black Hawk (15-20314)	US Army A/1-214th AVN, Wiesbaden, Germany	
20741	Sikorsky UH-60L Black Hawk (15-20741)	US Army A/1-214th AVN, Wiesbaden, Germany	
20742	Sikorsky UH-60L Black Hawk (15-20742)	US Army A/1-214th AVN, Wiesbaden, Germany	
20743	Sikorsky UH-60L Black Hawk (15-20743)	US Army A/1-214th AVN, Wiesbaden, Germany	
20744	Sikorsky UH-60L Black Hawk (15-20744)	US Army A/1-214th AVN, Wiesbaden, Germany	
20745	Sikorsky UH-60L Black Hawk (15-20745)	US Army A/1-214th AVN, Wiesbaden, Germany	
20754	Sikorsky UH-60L Black Hawk (15-20754)	US Army A/1-214th AVN, Wiesbaden, Germany	
MDH AH-64D Apache			
05620	MDH AH-64D Apache (10-05620)	US Army 1-3rd AVN, Ansbach, Germany	
25316	MDH AH-64D Apache (02-05316)	US Army 1-3rd AVN, Ansbach, Germany	
25321	MDH AH-64D Apache (02-05321)	US Army 1-3rd AVN, Ansbach, Germany	
25327	MDH AH-64D Apache (02-05327)	US Army 1-3rd AVN, Ansbach, Germany	
35381	MDH AH-64D Apache (03-05381)	US Army 1-3rd AVN, Ansbach, Germany	
35384	MDH AH-64D Apache (03-05384)	US Army 1-3rd AVN, Ansbach, Germany	
45419	MDH AH-64D Apache (04-05419)	US Army 1-3rd AVN, Ansbach, Germany	
45426	MDH AH-64D Apache (04-05426)	US Army 1-3rd AVN, Ansbach, Germany	
45429	MDH AH-64D Apache (04-05429)	US Army 1-3rd AVN, Ansbach, Germany	
45431	MDH AH-64D Apache (04-05431)	US Army 1-3rd AVN, Ansbach, Germany	
45437	MDH AH-64D Apache (04-05437)	US Army 1-3rd AVN, Ansbach, Germany	
45439	MDH AH-64D Apache (04-05439)	US Army 1-3rd AVN, Ansbach, Germany	
45444	MDH AH-64D Apache (04-05444)	US Army 1-3rd AVN, Ansbach, Germany	
45453	MDH AH-64D Apache (04-05453)	US Army 1-3rd AVN, Ansbach, Germany	

Notes	Serial	Type (code/other identity)	Owner/operator, location or fate
	45467	MDH AH-64D Apache (04-05467)	US Army 1-3rd AVN, Ansbach, Germany
	57010	MDH AH-64D Apache (05-07010)	US Army 1-3rd AVN, Ansbach, Germany
	67014	MDH AH-64D Apache (06-07014)	US Army 1-3rd AVN, Ansbach, Germany
	75535	MDH AH-64D Apache (07-05535)	US Army 1-3rd AVN, Ansbach, Germany
	77037	MDH AH-64D Apache (07-07037)	US Army 1-3rd AVN, Ansbach, Germany
	77038	MDH AH-64D Apache (07-07038)	US Army 1-3rd AVN, Ansbach, Germany
	85543	MDH AH-64D Apache (08-05543)	US Army 1-3rd AVN, Ansbach, Germany
	85550	MDH AH-64D Apache (08-05550)	US Army 1-3rd AVN, Ansbach, Germany
	95580	MDH AH-64D Apache (09-05580)	US Army 1-3rd AVN, Ansbach, Germany
	95581	MDH AH-64D Apache (09-05581)	US Army 1-3rd AVN, Ansbach, Germany
	95582	MDH AH-64D Apache (09-05582)	US Army 1-3rd AVN, Ansbach, Germany
	95587	MDH AH-64D Apache (09-05587)	US Army 1-3rd AVN, Ansbach, Germany
	95589	MDH AH-64D Apache (09-05589)	US Army 1-3rd AVN, Ansbach, Germany

Eurocopter UH-72A Lakota

Notes	Serial	Type (code/other identity)	Owner/operator, location or fate
	72097	Eurocopter UH-72A Lakota (09-72097)	US Army JMRC, Hohenfels
	72098	Eurocopter UH-72A Lakota (09-72098)	US Army JMRC, Hohenfels
	72100	Eurocopter UH-72A Lakota (09-72100)	US Army JMRC, Hohenfels
	72105	Eurocopter UH-72A Lakota (09-72105)	US Army JMRC, Hohenfels
	72106	Eurocopter UH-72A Lakota (09-72106)	US Army JMRC, Hohenfels
	72107	Eurocopter UH-72A Lakota (09-72107)	US Army JMRC, Hohenfels
	72108	Eurocopter UH-72A Lakota (09-72108)	US Army JMRC, Hohenfels

The following aircraft are normally based in the USA but are likely to be seen visiting the UK from time to time. The presentation is in numerical order of the type, commencing with the B-**1B** and concluding with the C-**135**. The aircraft are listed in numerical progression by the serial actually carried externally. Fiscal year information is provided, together with details of mark variations and in some cases operating units. Where base-code letter information is carried on the aircrafts' tails, this is detailed with the squadron/base data; for example the 7th Wing's B-1B 60105 carries the letters DY on its tail, thus identifying the Wing's home base as Dyess AFB, Texas.

Serial	Type (code/other identity)	Owner/operator, location or fate	Notes
Rockwell B-1B Lancer			
50059	Rockwell B-1B Lancer (85-0059) [DY] *bk/w* $	USAF 9th BS/7th BW, Dyess AFB, TX	
50060	Rockwell B-1B Lancer (85-0060) [EL] *bk/r*	USAF 34th BS/28th BW, Ellsworth AFB, SD	
50061	Rockwell B-1B Lancer (85-0061) [OT] *bk/gy*	USAF 337th TES/53rd Wg, Dyess AFB, TX	
50064	Rockwell B-1B Lancer (85-0064) [OT] *bk/gy*	USAF 337th TES/53rd Wg, Dyess AFB, TX	
50066	Rockwell B-1B Lancer (85-0066) [EL] *bk/y* $	USAF 37th BS/28th BW, Ellsworth AFB, SD	
50068	Rockwell B-1B Lancer (85-0068) [ED]	USAF 419th FLTS/412th TW, Edwards AFB	
50069	Rockwell B-1B Lancer (85-0069) [EL] *bk/r*	USAF 34th BS/28th BW, Ellsworth AFB, SD	
50072	Rockwell B-1B Lancer (85-0072) [EL] *bk/r*	USAF 34th BS/28th BW, Ellsworth AFB, SD	
50073	Rockwell B-1B Lancer (85-0073) [DY] *bl/w* [7 OG]	USAF 28th BS/7th BW, Dyess AFB, TX	
50074	Rockwell B-1B Lancer (85-0074) [DY] *bk/w*	USAF 9th BS/7th BW, Dyess AFB, TX	
50075	Rockwell B-1B Lancer (85-0075) [ED]	USAF 419th FLTS/412th TW, Edwards AFB	
50077	Rockwell B-1B Lancer (85-0077) [WA] *y/bk* [77 WPS]	USAF 77th WPS/57th Wg, Dyess AFB, TX	
50079	Rockwell B-1B Lancer (85-0079) [EL] *bk/r*	USAF 34th BS/28th BW, Ellsworth AFB, SD	
50080	Rockwell B-1B Lancer (85-0080) [DY] *bk/w*	USAF 9th BS/7th BW, Dyess AFB, TX	
50081	Rockwell B-1B Lancer (85-0081) [EL] *bk/r*	USAF 34th BS/28th BW, Ellsworth AFB, SD	
50083	Rockwell B-1B Lancer (85-0083) [EL] *bk/r*	USAF 34th BS/28th BW, Ellsworth AFB, SD	
50084	Rockwell B-1B Lancer (85-0084) [EL] *bk/r*	USAF 34th BS/28th BW, Ellsworth AFB, SD	
50085	Rockwell B-1B Lancer (85-0085) [EL] *bk/y*	USAF 37th BS/28th BW, Ellsworth AFB, SD	
50087	Rockwell B-1B Lancer (85-0087) [DY] *bk/w*	USAF 9th BS/7th BW, Dyess AFB, TX	
50088	Rockwell B-1B Lancer (85-0088) [DY] *bk/w*	USAF 9th BS/7th BW, Dyess AFB, TX	
50089	Rockwell B-1B Lancer (85-0089) [DY] *bk/w*	USAF 9th BS/7th BW, Dyess AFB, TX	
50090	Rockwell B-1B Lancer (85-0090) [DY] *bl/w*	USAF 28th BS/7th BW, Dyess AFB, TX	
60093	Rockwell B-1B Lancer (86-0093) [EL] *bk/y*	USAF 37th BS/28th BW, Ellsworth AFB, SD	
60094	Rockwell B-1B Lancer (86-0094) [EL] *bk/y* $	USAF 37th BS/28th BW, Ellsworth AFB, SD	
60095	Rockwell B-1B Lancer (86-0095) [EL] *bk/r*	USAF 34th BS/28th BW, Ellsworth AFB, SD	
60097	Rockwell B-1B Lancer (86-0097) [DY] *bk/w*	USAF 9th BS/7th BW, Dyess AFB, TX	
60098	Rockwell B-1B Lancer (86-0098) [DY] *bl/w*	USAF 28th BS/7th BW, Dyess AFB, TX	
60099	Rockwell B-1B Lancer (86-0099) [EL] *bk/y* [28 OG]	USAF 37th BS/28th BW, Ellsworth AFB, SD	
60101	Rockwell B-1B Lancer (86-0101) [DY] *bl/w*	USAF 28th BS/7th BW, Dyess AFB, TX	
60102	Rockwell B-1B Lancer (86-0102) [EL] *bk/y*	USAF 37th BS/28th BW, Ellsworth AFB, SD	
60103	Rockwell B-1B Lancer (86-0103) [DY] *bl/w*	USAF 28th BS/7th BW, Dyess AFB, TX	
60104	Rockwell B-1B Lancer (86-0104) [EL] *bk/y*	USAF 37th BS/28th BW, Ellsworth AFB, SD	
60105	Rockwell B-1B Lancer (86-0105) [DY] *bl/w*	USAF 28th BS/7th BW, Dyess AFB, TX	
60107	Rockwell B-1B Lancer (86-0107) [DY] *bk/w*	USAF 9th BS/7th BW, Dyess AFB, TX	
60108	Rockwell B-1B Lancer (86-0108) [EL] *bk/y*	USAF 37th BS/28th BW, Ellsworth AFB, SD	
60109	Rockwell B-1B Lancer (86-0109) [DY] *bl/w*	USAF 289th BS/7th BW, Dyess AFB, TX	
60110	Rockwell B-1B Lancer (86-0110) [DY] *bl/w*	USAF 28th BS/7th BW, Dyess AFB, TX	
60111	Rockwell B-1B Lancer (86-0111) [EL] *bk/r*	USAF 34th BS/28th BW, Ellsworth AFB, SD	
60112	Rockwell B-1B Lancer (86-0112) [DY] *bl/w*	USAF 28th BS/7th BW, Dyess AFB, TX	
60113	Rockwell B-1B Lancer (86-0113) [EL] *bk/y*	USAF 37th BS/28th BW, Ellsworth AFB, SD	
60115	Rockwell B-1B Lancer (86-0115) [EL] *bk/r*	USAF 34th BS/28th BW, Ellsworth AFB, SD	
60117	Rockwell B-1B Lancer (86-0117) [WA] *y/bk*	USAF 77th WPS/57th Wg, Dyess AFB, TX	
60118	Rockwell B-1B Lancer (86-0118) [EL] *bk/y*	USAF 37th BS/28th BW, Ellsworth AFB, SD	
60119	Rockwell B-1B Lancer (86-0119) [DY] *bl/w*	USAF 28th BS/7th BW, Dyess AFB, TX	
60120	Rockwell B-1B Lancer (86-0120) [EL] *bk/y*	USAF 37th BS/28th BW, Ellsworth AFB, SD	
60121	Rockwell B-1B Lancer (86-0121) [EL] *bk/y*	USAF 37th BS/28th BW, Ellsworth AFB, SD	
60122	Rockwell B-1B Lancer (86-0122) [DY] *bk/w*	USAF 9th BS/7th BW, Dyess AFB, TX	
60123	Rockwell B-1B Lancer (86-0123) [DY] *bk/w*	USAF 9th BS/7th BW, Dyess AFB, TX	
60124	Rockwell B-1B Lancer (86-0124) [DY] *bk/w*	USAF 9th BS/7th BW, Dyess AFB, TX	
60125	Rockwell B-1B Lancer (86-0125) [DY] *bk/w*	USAF 9th BS/7th BW, Dyess AFB, TX	
60126	Rockwell B-1B Lancer (86-0126) [DY] *bl/w*	USAF 28th BS/7th BW, Dyess AFB, TX	
60127	Rockwell B-1B Lancer (86-0127) [DY] *bk/w*	USAF 9th BS/7th BW, Dyess AFB, TX	
60129	Rockwell B-1B Lancer (86-0129) [EL] *bk/r*	USAF 34th BS/28th BW, Ellsworth AFB, SD	
60132	Rockwell B-1B Lancer (86-0132) [DY] *bl/w*	USAF 28th BS/7th BW, Dyess AFB, TX	

Notes	Serial	Type (code/other identity)	Owner/operator, location or fate
	60133	Rockwell B-1B Lancer (86-0133) [DY] bl/w	USAF 28th BS/7th BW, Dyess AFB, TX
	60134	Rockwell B-1B Lancer (86-0134) [EL] bk/r [34 BS]	USAF 34th BS/28th BW, Ellsworth AFB, SD
	60135	Rockwell B-1B Lancer (86-0135) [DY] bl/w	USAF 28th BS/7th BW, Dyess AFB, TX
	60136	Rockwell B-1B Lancer (86-0136) [DY] bl/w	USAF 28th BS/7th BW, Dyess AFB, TX
	60137	Rockwell B-1B Lancer (86-0137) [EL] bk/y [37 BS]	USAF 37th BS/28th BW, Ellsworth AFB, SD
	60138	Rockwell B-1B Lancer (86-0138) [EL] bk/y	USAF 37th BS/28th BW, Ellsworth AFB, SD
	60139	Rockwell B-1B Lancer (86-0139) [EL] bl/y [34 BS]	USAF 34th BS/28th BW, Ellsworth AFB, SD
	60140	Rockwell B-1B Lancer (86-0140) [DY] bk/r [345 BS]	USAF 28th BS/7th BW, Dyess AFB, TX

Northrop B-2 Spirit
(Names are given where known. Each begins Spirit of ...)

	Serial	Type	Owner/operator
	00040	Northrop B-2 Spirit (90-0040) [WM] Alaska	USAF 509th BW, Whiteman AFB, MO
	00041	Northrop B-2 Spirit (90-0041) [WM] Hawaii	USAF 509th BW, Whiteman AFB, MO
	20700	Northrop B-2 Spirit (92-0700) [WM] Florida	USAF 509th BW, Whiteman AFB, MO
	21066	Northrop B-2 Spirit (82-1066) [WM] America	USAF 509th BW, Whiteman AFB, MO
	21067	Northrop B-2 Spirit (82-1067) [WM] Arizona	USAF 509th BW, Whiteman AFB, MO
	21068	Northrop B-2 Spirit (82-1068) [WM] New York	USAF 509th BW, Whiteman AFB, MO
	21069	Northrop B-2 Spirit (82-1069) [WM] Indiana	USAF 509th BW, Whiteman AFB, MO
	21070	Northrop B-2 Spirit (82-1070) [WM] Ohio	USAF 509th BW, Whiteman AFB, MO
	21071	Northrop B-2 Spirit (82-1071) [WM] Mississippi	USAF 509th BW, Whiteman AFB, MO
	31085	Northrop B-2 Spirit (93-1085) [ED] Oklahoma	USAF 419th FLTS/412th TW, Edwards AFB,CA
	31086	Northrop B-2 Spirit (93-1086) [WM] Kitty Hawk	USAF 509th BW, Whiteman AFB, MO
	31087	Northrop B-2 Spirit (93-1087) [WM] Pennsylvania	USAF 509th BW, Whiteman AFB, MO
	31088	Northrop B-2 Spirit (93-1088) [WM] Louisiana	USAF 509th BW, Whiteman AFB, MO
	80328	Northrop B-2 Spirit (88-0328) [WM] Texas	USAF 509th BW, Whiteman AFB, MO
	80329	Northrop B-2 Spirit (88-0329) [WM] Missouri	USAF 509th BW, Whiteman AFB, MO
	80330	Northrop B-2 Spirit (88-0330) [WM] California	USAF 509th BW, Whiteman AFB, MO
	80331	Northrop B-2 Spirit (88-0331) [WM] South Carolina	USAF 509th BW, Whiteman AFB, MO
	80332	Northrop B-2 Spirit (88-0332) [WM] Washington	USAF 509th BW, Whiteman AFB, MO
	90128	Northrop B-2 Spirit (89-0128) [WM] Nebraska	USAF 509th BW, Whiteman AFB, MO
	90129	Northrop B-2 Spirit (89-0129) [WM] Georgia	USAF 509th BW, Whiteman AFB, MO

Lockheed U-2

	Serial	Type	Owner/operator
	68-10329	Lockheed U-2S [BB]	USAF 9th RW, Beale AFB, CA
	68-10331	Lockheed U-2S [BB]	USAF 9th RW, Beale AFB, CA
	68-10336	Lockheed U-2S [BB]	USAF 9th RW, Beale AFB, CA
	68-10337	Lockheed U-2S [BB] [9 OG]	USAF 9th RW, Beale AFB, CA
	80-1064	Lockheed TU-2S [BB]	USAF 9th RW, Beale AFB, CA
	80-1065	Lockheed TU-2S [BB]	USAF 9th RW, Beale AFB, CA
	80-1066	Lockheed U-2S [BB]	USAF 9th RW, Beale AFB, CA
	80-1067	Lockheed U-2S [BB]	USAF 9th RW, Beale AFB, CA
	80-1069	Lockheed U-2S [BB]	USAF 9th RW, Beale AFB, CA
	80-1070	Lockheed U-2S [BB]	USAF 9th RW, Beale AFB, CA
	80-1071	Lockheed U-2S [BB]	USAF 9th RW, Beale AFB, CA
	80-1073	Lockheed U-2S [BB]	USAF 9th RW, Beale AFB, CA
	80-1074	Lockheed U-2S [BB]	USAF 9th RW, Beale AFB, CA
	80-1076	Lockheed U-2S [BB]	USAF 9th RW, Beale AFB, CA
	80-1077	Lockheed U-2S [BB]	USAF 9th RW, Beale AFB, CA
	80-1078	Lockheed TU-2S [BB]	USAF 9th RW, Beale AFB, CA
	80-1079	Lockheed U-2S [BB]	USAF 9th RW, Beale AFB, CA
	80-1080	Lockheed U-2S [BB]	USAF 9th RW, Beale AFB, CA
	80-1081	Lockheed U-2S [BB]	USAF 9th RW, Beale AFB, CA
	80-1083	Lockheed U-2S [BB]	USAF 9th RW, Beale AFB, CA
	80-1084	Lockheed U-2S [BB]	USAF 9th RW, Beale AFB, CA
	80-1085	Lockheed U-2S [BB]	USAF 9th RW, Beale AFB, CA
	80-1086	Lockheed U-2S [BB]	USAF 9th RW, Beale AFB, CA
	80-1087	Lockheed U-2S [BB]	USAF 9th RW, Beale AFB, CA
	80-1089	Lockheed U-2S [BB]	USAF 9th RW, Beale AFB, CA
	80-1090	Lockheed U-2S [BB]	USAF 9th RW, Beale AFB, CA
	80-1091	Lockheed TU-2S [BB]	USAF 9th RW, Beale AFB, CA
	80-1092	Lockheed U-2S [BB]	USAF 9th RW, Beale AFB, CA
	80-1093	Lockheed U-2S [BB]	USAF 9th RW, Beale AFB, CA

Serial	Type (code/other identity)	Owner/operator, location or fate	Notes
80-1094	Lockheed U-2S [BB]	USAF 9th RW, Beale AFB, CA	
80-1096	Lockheed U-2S [BB]	USAF 9th RW, Beale AFB, CA	
80-1099	Lockheed U-2S [BB]	USAF 9th RW, Beale AFB, CA	

Boeing E-3 Sentry

00137	Boeing E-3B(mod) Sentry (80-0137) [OK] w	USAF 960th AACS/552nd ACW, Tinker AFB, OK	
00138	Boeing E-3G Sentry (80-0138) [OK] r	USAF 964th AACS/552nd ACW, Tinker AFB, OK	
00139	Boeing E-3G Sentry (80-0139) [OK] w	USAF 960th AACS/552nd ACW, Tinker AFB, OK	
10004	Boeing E-3C Sentry (81-0004) [AK] gn	USAF 962nd AACS/3rd Wg, Elmendorf, AK	
10005	Boeing E-3G Sentry (81-0005) [OK] w	USAF 963rd ACCS/552nd ACW, Tinker AFB, OK	
11407	Boeing E-3B Sentry (71-1407) [ZZ] or	USAF 961st AACS/18th Wg, Kadena AB, Japan	
11408	Boeing E-3B Sentry (71-1408) [AK] gn	USAF 962nd AACS/3rd Wg, Elmendorf, AK	
20006	Boeing E-3G Sentry (82-0006) [OK] r	USAF 964th AACS/552nd ACW, Tinker AFB, OK	
20007	Boeing E-3G Sentry (82-0007) [OK]	USAF 960th AACS/552nd ACW, Tinker AFB, OK	
30009	Boeing E-3G Sentry (83-0009) [OK]	USAF 960th AACS/552nd ACW, Tinker AFB, OK	
31675	Boeing E-3G Sentry (73-1675) [OK] r	USAF 964th AACS/552nd ACW, Tinker AFB, OK	
50556	Boeing E-3G Sentry (75-0556) [OK] w	USAF 960th AACS/552nd ACW, Tinker AFB, OK	
50557	Boeing E-3B Sentry (75-0557) [OK] r	USAF 964th AACS/552nd ACW, Tinker AFB, OK	
50558	Boeing E-3G Sentry (75-0558) [OK]	USAF 965th AACS/552nd ACW, Tinker AFB, OK	
50559	Boeing E-3G Sentry (75-0559) [OK] w	USAF 960th AACS/552nd ACW, Tinker AFB, OK	
50560	Boeing E-3G Sentry (75-0560) [AK] gn	USAF 962nd AACS/3rd Wg, Elmendorf, AK	
61604	Boeing E-3G Sentry (76-1604) [OK] w	USAF 963rd ACCS/552nd ACW, Tinker AFB, OK	
61605	Boeing E-3G Sentry (76-1605) [OK] r/w	USAF 960th AACS/552nd ACW, Tinker AFB, OK	
61606	Boeing E-3B Sentry (76-1606) [OK] w	USAF 960th AACS/552nd ACW, Tinker AFB, OK	
61607	Boeing E-3G Sentry (76-1607) [OK] w	USAF 960th AACS/552nd ACW, Tinker AFB, OK	
70351	Boeing E-3G Sentry (77-0351) [OK] r	USAF 964th AACS/552nd ACW, Tinker AFB, OK	
70352	Boeing E-3B Sentry (77-0352) [OK] w	USAF 960th AACS/552nd ACW, Tinker AFB, OK	
70353	Boeing E-3G Sentry (77-0353) [OK] r	USAF 964th AACS/552nd ACW, Tinker AFB, OK	
70355	Boeing E-3B Sentry (77-0355) ZZ] or	USAF 961st AACS/18th Wg, Kadena AB, Japan	
70356	Boeing E-3G Sentry (77-0356) [OK] r	USAF 960th AACS/552nd ACW, Tinker AFB, OK	
80576	Boeing E-3G Sentry (78-0576) [OK] r	USAF 964th AACS/552nd ACW, Tinker AFB, OK	
80577	Boeing E-3G Sentry (78-0577) [OK] r	USAF 964th AACS/552nd ACW, Tinker AFB, OK	
80578	Boeing E-3G Sentry (78-0578) [OK] w	USAF 960th AACS/552nd ACW, Tinker AFB, OK	
90001	Boeing E-3G Sentry (79-0001) [OK] m	USAF 964th AACS/552nd ACW, Tinker AFB, OK	
90002	Boeing E-3G Sentry (79-0002) [OK] r	USAF 964th AACS/552nd ACW, Tinker AFB, OK	
90003	Boeing E-3B Sentry (79-0003) [OK] m	USAF 552nd ACW, Tinker AFB, OK	

Boeing E-4B

31676	Boeing E-4B (73-1676)	USAF 1st ACCS/595th CACG, Offutt AFB, NE	
31677	Boeing E-4B (73-1677)	USAF 1st ACCS/595th CACG, Offutt AFB, NE	
40787	Boeing E-4B (74-0787)	USAF 1st ACCS/595th CACG, Offutt AFB, NE	
50125	Boeing E-4B (75-0125)	USAF 1st ACCS/595th CACG, Offutt AFB, NE	

Lockheed C-5M Super Galaxy

31285	Lockheed C-5M Super Galaxy (83-1285) bl/y	USAF 9th AS/436th AW, Dover AFB, DE	
40060	Lockheed C-5M Super Galaxy (84-0060) w/bk	USAF 22nd AS/60th AMW, Travis AFB, CA	
40061	Lockheed C-5M Super Galaxy (84-0061) bl/y	USAF 9th AS/436th AW, Dover AFB, DE	
40062	Lockheed C-5M Super Galaxy (84-0062) w/bk	USAF 22nd AS/60th AMW, Travis AFB, CA	
50001	Lockheed C-5M Super Galaxy (85-0001) bl/y	USAF 9th AS/436th AW, Dover AFB, DE	
50002	Lockheed C-5M Super Galaxy (85-0002) bl/y	USAF 9th AS/436th AW, Dover AFB, DE	
50003	Lockheed C-5M Super Galaxy (85-0003) bl/y	USAF 9th AS/436th AW, Dover AFB, DE	
50004	Lockheed C-5M Super Galaxy (85-0004) bl/y	USAF 9th AS/436th AW, Dover AFB, DE	
50005	Lockheed C-5M Super Galaxy (85-0005) bl/y	USAF 9th AS/436th AW, Dover AFB, DE	
50006	Lockheed C-5M Super Galaxy (85-0006)	USAF 68th AS/433rd AW Kelly AFB, TX	
50007	Lockheed C-5M Super Galaxy (85-0007) bl/y	USAF 9th AS/436th AW, Dover AFB, DE	
50008	Lockheed C-5M Super Galaxy (85-0008) bl/y	USAF 9th AS/436th AW, Dover AFB, DE	
50009	Lockheed C-5M Super Galaxy (85-0009)	USAF 68th AS/433rd AW Kelly AFB, TX	
50010	Lockheed C-5M Super Galaxy (85-0010) w/bk	USAF 22nd AS/60th AMW, Travis AFB, CA	
60011	Lockheed C-5M Super Galaxy (86-0011) w/bk	USAF 22nd AS/60th AMW, Travis AFB, CA	
60012	Lockheed C-5M Super Galaxy (86-0012) bl/r	USAF 337th AS/439th AW, Westover ARB, MA	
60013	Lockheed C-5M Super Galaxy (86-0013) bl/y	USAF 9th AS/436th AW, Dover AFB, DE	
60014	Lockheed C-5M Super Galaxy (86-0014) bl/r	USAF 337th AS/439th AW, Westover ARB, MA	

253

Notes	Serial	Type (code/other identity)	Owner/operator, location or fate
	60015	Lockheed C-5M Super Galaxy (86-0015)	USAF 68th AS/433rd AW Kelly AFB, TX
	60016	Lockheed C-5M Super Galaxy (86-0016) w/bk	USAF 22nd AS/60th AMW, Travis AFB, CA
	60017	Lockheed C-5M Super Galaxy (86-0017) bl/y	USAF 9th AS/436th AW, Dover AFB, DE
	60018	Lockheed C-5M Super Galaxy (86-0018) bl/r	USAF 337th AS/439th AW, Westover ARB, MA
	60019	Lockheed C-5M Super Galaxy (86-0019)	USAF 68th AS/433rd AW Kelly AFB, TX
	60020	Lockheed C-5M Super Galaxy (86-0020) bl/y	USAF 9th AS/436th AW, Dover AFB, DE
	60021	Lockheed C-5M Super Galaxy (86-0021)	USAF 68th AS/433rd AW Kelly AFB, TX
	60022	Lockheed C-5M Super Galaxy (86-0022) w/bk	USAF 22nd AS/60th AMW, Travis AFB, CA
	60023	Lockheed C-5M Super Galaxy (86-0023) w/bk	USAF 22nd AS/60th AMW, Travis AFB, CA
	60024	Lockheed C-5M Super Galaxy (86-0024) w/bk	USAF 22nd AS/60th AMW, Travis AFB, CA
	60025	Lockheed C-5M Super Galaxy (86-0025) bl/y	USAF 9th AS/436th AW, Dover AFB, DE
	60026	Lockheed C-5M Super Galaxy (86-0026) w/bk	USAF 22nd AS/60th AMW, Travis AFB, CA
	70027	Lockheed C-5M Super Galaxy (87-0027)	USAF 68th AS/433rd AW Kelly AFB, TX
	70028	Lockheed C-5M Super Galaxy (87-0028) w/bk	USAF 22nd AS/60th AMW, Travis AFB, CA
	70029	Lockheed C-5M Super Galaxy (87-0029) w/bk	USAF 22nd AS/60th AMW, Travis AFB, CA
	70030	Lockheed C-5M Super Galaxy (87-0030) w/bk	USAF 22nd AS/60th AMW, Travis AFB, CA
	70031	Lockheed C-5M Super Galaxy (87-0031) bl/r	USAF 337th AS/439th AW, Westover ARB, MA
	70032	Lockheed C-5M Super Galaxy (87-0032) w/bk	USAF 22nd AS/60th AMW, Travis AFB, CA
	70033	Lockheed C-5M Super Galaxy (87-0033)	USAF 68th AS/433rd AW Kelly AFB, TX
	70034	Lockheed C-5M Super Galaxy (87-0034) bl/y	USAF 9th AS/436th AW, Dover AFB, DE
	70035	Lockheed C-5M Super Galaxy (87-0035) bl/y	USAF 9th AS/436th AW, Dover AFB, DE
	70036	Lockheed C-5M Super Galaxy (87-0036) bl/y	USAF 9th AS/436th AW, Dover AFB, DE
	70037	Lockheed C-5M Super Galaxy (87-0037) bl/r	USAF 337th AS/439th AW, Westover ARB, MA
	70038	Lockheed C-5M Super Galaxy (87-0038)	USAF 68th AS/433rd AW Kelly AFB, TX
	70039	Lockheed C-5M Super Galaxy (87-0039) bl/r	USAF 337th AS/439th AW, Westover ARB, MA
	70040	Lockheed C-5M Super Galaxy (87-0040) bl/y	USAF 9th AS/436th AW, Dover AFB, DE
	70041	Lockheed C-5M Super Galaxy (87-0041) bl/r	USAF 337th AS/439th AW, Westover ARB, MA
	70042	Lockheed C-5M Super Galaxy (87-0042) w/bk	USAF 22nd AS/60th AMW, Travis AFB, CA
	70043	Lockheed C-5M Super Galaxy (87-0043) bl/r	USAF 337th AS/439th AW, Westover ARB, MA
	70044	Lockheed C-5M Super Galaxy (87-0044) w/bk	USAF 22nd AS/60th AMW, Travis AFB, CA
	70045	Lockheed C-5M Super Galaxy (87-0045) bl/y	USAF 9th AS/436th AW, Dover AFB, DE
	80213	Lockheed C-5M Super Galaxy (68-0213) w/bk	USAF 22nd AS/60th AMW, Travis AFB, CA
	80216	Lockheed C-5M Super Galaxy (68-0216) w/bk	USAF 22nd AS/60th AMW, Travis AFB, CA
	90024	Lockheed C-5M Super Galaxy (69-0024) bl/y	USAF 9th AS/436th AW, Dover AFB, DE

Boeing E-8C J-STARS

	02000	Boeing E-8C J-STARS (00-2000) [GA] r/bk	USAF 116th ACW GA ANG, Robins AFB
	12005	Boeing E-8C J-STARS (01-2005) [GA] r/bk	USAF 116th ACW GA ANG, Robins AFB
	29111	Boeing E-8C J-STARS (02-9111) [GA] r/bk	USAF 116th ACW GA ANG, Robins AFB
	23289	Boeing E-8C J-STARS (92-3289) [GA] r/bk	USAF 116th ACW GA ANG, Robins AFB
	23290	Boeing E-8C J-STARS (92-3290) [GA] r/bk	USAF 116th ACW GA ANG, Robins AFB
	31097	Boeing E-8C J-STARS (93-1097) [GA] r/bk	USAF 116th ACW GA ANG, Robins AFB
	40284	Boeing E-8C J-STARS (94-0284) [GA] r/bk	USAF 116th ACW GA ANG, Robins AFB
	40285	Boeing E-8C J-STARS (94-0285) [GA] r/bk	USAF 116th ACW GA ANG, Robins AFB
	50121	Boeing E-8C J-STARS (95-0121) [GA] r/bk	USAF 116th ACW GA ANG, Robins AFB
	50122	Boeing E-8C J-STARS (95-0122) [GA] r/bk	USAF 116th ACW GA ANG, Robins AFB
	60042	Boeing E-8C J-STARS (96-0042) [GA] r/bk	USAF 116th ACW GA ANG, Robins AFB
	60043	Boeing E-8C J-STARS (96-0043) [GA] r/bk	USAF 116th ACW GA ANG, Robins AFB
	70100	Boeing E-8C J-STARS (97-0100) [GA] r/bk	USAF 116th ACW GA ANG, Robins AFB
	70200	Boeing E-8C J-STARS (97-0200) [GA] r/bk	USAF 116th ACW GA ANG, Robins AFB
	70201	Boeing E-8C J-STARS (97-0201) [GA] r/bk	USAF 116th ACW GA ANG, Robins AFB
	90006	Boeing E-8C J-STARS (99-0006) [GA] r/bk	USAF 116th ACW GA ANG, Robins AFB

McDonnell Douglas KC-10A Extender

	20191	McDonnell Douglas KC-10A Extender (82-0191) w/bk	USAF 60th AMW, Travis AFB, CA
	20192	McDonnell Douglas KC-10A Extender (82-0192) w/bk	USAF 60th AMW, Travis AFB, CA
	20193	McDonnell Douglas KC-10A Extender (82-0193) w/bk	USAF 60th AMW, Travis AFB, CA
	30075	McDonnell Douglas KC-10A Extender (83-0075) w/bk	USAF 60th AMW, Travis AFB, CA
	30076	McDonnell Douglas KC-10A Extender (83-0076) w/bk	USAF 60th AMW, Travis AFB, CA
	30077	McDonnell Douglas KC-10A Extender (83-0077) w/bk	USAF 60th AMW, Travis AFB, CA
	30078	McDonnell Douglas KC-10A Extender (83-0078) w/bk	USAF 60th AMW, Travis AFB, CA
	30079	McDonnell Douglas KC-10A Extender (83-0079) bl	USAF 305th AMW, McGuire AFB, NJ

Serial	Type (code/other identity)	Owner/operator, location or fate	Notes
30080	McDonnell Douglas KC-10A Extender (83-0080) *w/bk*	USAF 60th AMW, Travis AFB, CA	
30081	McDonnell Douglas KC-10A Extender (83-0081) *bl*	USAF 305th AMW, McGuire AFB, NJ	
30082	McDonnell Douglas KC-10A Extender (83-0082) *bl*	USAF 305th AMW, McGuire AFB, NJ	
40185	McDonnell Douglas KC-10A Extender (84-0185) *w/bk*	USAF 60th AMW, Travis AFB, CA	
40186	McDonnell Douglas KC-10A Extender (84-0186) *bl*	USAF 305th AMW, McGuire AFB, NJ	
40187	McDonnell Douglas KC-10A Extender (84-0187) *w/bk*	USAF 60th AMW, Travis AFB, CA	
40188	McDonnell Douglas KC-10A Extender (84-0188) *bl*	USAF 305th AMW, McGuire AFB, NJ	
40189	McDonnell Douglas KC-10A Extender (84-0189) *bl*	USAF 305th AMW, McGuire AFB, NJ	
40190	McDonnell Douglas KC-10A Extender (84-0190) *bl*	USAF 305th AMW, McGuire AFB, NJ	
40191	McDonnell Douglas KC-10A Extender (84-0191) *w/bk*	USAF 60th AMW, Travis AFB, CA	
40192	McDonnell Douglas KC-10A Extender (84-0192) *bl*	USAF 305th AMW, McGuire AFB, NJ	
50027	McDonnell Douglas KC-10A Extender (85-0027) *bl*	USAF 305th AMW, McGuire AFB, NJ	
50028	McDonnell Douglas KC-10A Extender (85-0028) *bl*	USAF 305th AMW, McGuire AFB, NJ	
50029	McDonnell Douglas KC-10A Extender (85-0029) *w/bk*	USAF 60th AMW, Travis AFB, CA	
50030	McDonnell Douglas KC-10A Extender (85-0030) *bl*	USAF 305th AMW, McGuire AFB, NJ	
50031	McDonnell Douglas KC-10A Extender (85-0031) *bl*	USAF 305th AMW, McGuire AFB, NJ	
50032	McDonnell Douglas KC-10A Extender (85-0032) *bl*	USAF 305th AMW, McGuire AFB, NJ	
50033	McDonnell Douglas KC-10A Extender (85-0033) *w/bk*	USAF 60th AMW, Travis AFB, CA	
50034	McDonnell Douglas KC-10A Extender (85-0034) *bl*	USAF 305th AMW, McGuire AFB, NJ	
60027	McDonnell Douglas KC-10A Extender (86-0027) *bl*	USAF 305th AMW, McGuire AFB, NJ	
60028	McDonnell Douglas KC-10A Extender (86-0028) *bl*	USAF 305th AMW, McGuire AFB, NJ	
60029	McDonnell Douglas KC-10A Extender (86-0029) *w/bk*	USAF 60th AMW, Travis AFB, CA	
60030	McDonnell Douglas KC-10A Extender (86-0030) *bl*	USAF 305th AMW, McGuire AFB, NJ	
60031	McDonnell Douglas KC-10A Extender (86-0031) *w/bk*	USAF 60th AMW, Travis AFB, CA	
60032	McDonnell Douglas KC-10A Extender (86-0032) *bl*	USAF 305th AMW, McGuire AFB, NJ	
60033	McDonnell Douglas KC-10A Extender (86-0033) *w/bk*	USAF 60th AMW, Travis AFB, CA	
60034	McDonnell Douglas KC-10A Extender (86-0034) *w/bk*	USAF 60th AMW, Travis AFB, CA	
60035	McDonnell Douglas KC-10A Extender (86-0035) *bl*	USAF 305th AMW, McGuire AFB, NJ	
60036	McDonnell Douglas KC-10A Extender (86-0036) *bl*	USAF 305th AMW, McGuire AFB, NJ	
60037	McDonnell Douglas KC-10A Extender (86-0037) *w/bk*	USAF 60th AMW, Travis AFB, CA	
60038	McDonnell Douglas KC-10A Extender (86-0038) *w/bk*	USAF 60th AMW, Travis AFB, CA	
70117	McDonnell Douglas KC-10A Extender (87-0117) *w/bk*	USAF 60th AMW, Travis AFB, CA	
70118	McDonnell Douglas KC-10A Extender (87-0118) *bl*	USAF 305th AMW, McGuire AFB, NJ	
70119	McDonnell Douglas KC-10A Extender (87-0119) *w/bk*	USAF 60th AMW, Travis AFB, CA	
70120	McDonnell Douglas KC-10A Extender (87-0120) *bl*	USAF 305th AMW, McGuire AFB, NJ	
70121	McDonnell Douglas KC-10A Extender (87-0121) *bl*	USAF 305th AMW, McGuire AFB, NJ	
70122	McDonnell Douglas KC-10A Extender (87-0122) *bl*	USAF 305th AMW, McGuire AFB, NJ	
70123	McDonnell Douglas KC-10A Extender (87-0123) *w/bk*	USAF 60th AMW, Travis AFB, CA	
70124	McDonnell Douglas KC-10A Extender (87-0124) *bl*	USAF 305th AMW, McGuire AFB, NJ	
90433	McDonnell Douglas KC-10A Extender (79-0433) *bl*	USAF 305th AMW, McGuire AFB, NJ	
90434	McDonnell Douglas KC-10A Extender (79-0434) *bl*	USAF 305th AMW, McGuire AFB, NJ	
91710	McDonnell Douglas KC-10A Extender (79-1710) *bl*	USAF 305th AMW, McGuire AFB, NJ	
91711	McDonnell Douglas KC-10A Extender (79-1711) *bl*	USAF 305th AMW, McGuire AFB, NJ	
91712	McDonnell Douglas KC-10A Extender (79-1712) *bl*	USAF 305th AMW, McGuire AFB, NJ	
91713	McDonnell Douglas KC-10A Extender (79-1713) *w/bk*	USAF 60th AMW, Travis AFB, CA	
91946	McDonnell Douglas KC-10A Extender (79-1946) *w/bk*	USAF 60th AMW, Travis AFB, CA	
91947	McDonnell Douglas KC-10A Extender (79-1947) *bl*	USAF 305th AMW, McGuire AFB, NJ	
91948	McDonnell Douglas KC-10A Extender (79-1948) *w/bk*	USAF 60th AMW, Travis AFB, CA	
91949	McDonnell Douglas KC-10A Extender (79-1949) *bl*	USAF 305th AMW, McGuire AFB, NJ	
91950	McDonnell Douglas KC-10A Extender (79-1950) *w/bk*	USAF 60th AMW, Travis AFB, CA	
91951	McDonnell Douglas KC-10A Extender (79-1951) *w/bk*	USAF 60th AMW, Travis AFB, CA	

Bombardier E-11A Global Express

19001	Bombardier E-11A Global Express (11-9001)	USAF 430th EECS/653rd ELSG, Hanscom MA	
19355	Bombardier E-11A Global Express (11-9355)	USAF 430th EECS/653rd ELSG, Hanscom MA	
19358	Bombardier E-11A Global Express (11-9358)	*Crashed 27 January 2020, near Herat, Afghanistan*	
29506	Bombardier E-11A Global Express (12-9506)	USAF 430th EECS/653rd ELSG, Hanscom MA	

Boeing C-17A Globemaster III

00171	Boeing C-17A Globemaster III (00-0171) [AK] *bl/y*	USAF 144th AS/176th Wg, Elmendorf AFB, AK ANG	

Notes	Serial	Type (code/other identity)	Owner/operator, location or fate
	00172	Boeing C-17A Globemaster III (00-0172) *bk*	USAF 156th AS/145th AW, Charlotte-Douglas, NC ANG
	00174	Boeing C-17A Globemaster III (00-0174) [AK] *bl/y*	USAF 144th AS/176th Wg, Elmendorf AFB, AK ANG
	00175	Boeing C-17A Globemaster III (00-0175) *bl*	USAF 6th AS/305th AMW, McGuire AFB, NJ
	00176	Boeing C-17A Globemaster III (00-0176) *r/w*	USAF 155th AS/164th AW, Memphis, TN ANG
	00177	Boeing C-17A Globemaster III (00-0177) *bl*	USAF 137th AS/105th AW, Stewart AFB, NY ANG
	00178	Boeing C-17A Globemaster III (00-0178) *r/w*	USAF 89th AS/445th AW AFRC, Wright-Patterson AFB, OH
	00179	Boeing C-17A Globemaster III (00-0179) *r/y*	USAF 58th AS/97th AMW, Altus AFB, OK
	00180	Boeing C-17A Globemaster III (00-0180) *gn*	USAF 62nd AW, McChord AFB, WA
	00181	Boeing C-17A Globemaster III (00-0181) *r/w*	USAF 167th AS/167th AW, Martinsburg, WV ANG
	00182	Boeing C-17A Globemaster III (00-0182) *r/w*	USAF 167th AS/167th AW, Martinsburg, WV ANG
	00183	Boeing C-17A Globemaster III (00-0183) *bk*	USAF 156th AS/145th AW, Charlotte-Douglas, NC ANG
	00184	Boeing C-17A Globemaster III (00-0184) *bk/y*	USAF 758th AS/911th AMW AFRC, Greater Pittsburgh, PA
	00185	Boeing C-17A Globemaster III (00-0185) [AK] *bl/y*	USAF 144th AS/176th Wg, Elmendorf AFB, AK ANG
	00213	Boeing C-17A Globemaster III (10-0213) *y/bl*	USAF 437th AW, Charleston AFB, SC
	00214	Boeing C-17A Globemaster III (10-0214) *y/bl*	USAF 437th AW, Charleston AFB, SC
	00215	Boeing C-17A Globemaster III (10-0215) *y/bl*	USAF 437th AW, Charleston AFB, SC
	00216	Boeing C-17A Globemaster III (10-0216) *gn*	USAF 62nd AW, McChord AFB, WA
	00217	Boeing C-17A Globemaster III (10-0217) *gn*	USAF 62nd AW, McChord AFB, WA
	00218	Boeing C-17A Globemaster III (10-0218) *gn*	USAF 62nd AW, McChord AFB, WA
	00219	Boeing C-17A Globemaster III (10-0219) *gn*	USAF 62nd AW, McChord AFB, WA
	00220	Boeing C-17A Globemaster III (10-0220) *gn*	USAF 62nd AW, McChord AFB, WA
	00221	Boeing C-17A Globemaster III (10-0221) *y/bl*	USAF 437th AW, Charleston AFB, SC
	00222	Boeing C-17A Globemaster III (10-0222) *y/bl*	USAF 437th AW, Charleston AFB, SC
	00223	Boeing C-17A Globemaster III (10-0223) *y/bl*	USAF 437th AW, Charleston AFB, SC
	00532	Boeing C-17A Globemaster III (90-0532) *bk*	USAF 156th AS/145th AW, Charlotte-Douglas, NC ANG
	00533	Boeing C-17A Globemaster III (90-0533) [HH] *r/y*	USAF 535th AS/15th Wg, Hickam AFB, HI
	00534	Boeing C-17A Globemaster III (90-0534) *y/bl*	USAF 437th AW, Charleston AFB, SC
	00535	Boeing C-17A Globemaster III (90-0535) *r/w*	USAF 89th AS/445th AW AFRC, Wright-Patterson AFB, OH
	10186	Boeing C-17A Globemaster III (01-0186) *bl/y*	USAF 3rd AS/436th AW, Dover AFB, DE
	10187	Boeing C-17A Globemaster III (01-0187) *gn*	USAF 62nd AW, McChord AFB, WA
	10188	Boeing C-17A Globemaster III (01-0188) *bl*	USAF 137th AS/105th AW, Stewart AFB, NY ANG
	10189	Boeing C-17A Globemaster III (01-0189) *r/w*	USAF 155th AS/164th AW, Memphis, TN ANG
	10190	Boeing C-17A Globemaster III (01-0190) *r/y*	USAF 58th AS/97th AMW, Altus AFB, OK
	10191	Boeing C-17A Globemaster III (01-0191) *bl/y*	USAF 3rd AS/436th AW, Dover AFB, DE
	10192	Boeing C-17A Globemaster III (01-0192) *bl*	USAF 137th AS/105th AW, Stewart AFB, NY ANG
	10193	Boeing C-17A Globemaster III (01-0193) *y/bl*	USAF 437th AW, Charleston AFB, SC
	10194	Boeing C-17A Globemaster III (01-0194) *r/w*	USAF 89th AS/445th AW AFRC, Wright-Patterson AFB, OH
	10195	Boeing C-17A Globemaster III (01-0195) *r/y*	USAF 58th AS/97th AMW, Altus AFB, OK
	10196	Boeing C-17A Globemaster III (01-0196) *r/w*	USAF 167th AS/167th AW, Martinsburg, WV ANG
	10197	Boeing C-17A Globemaster III (01-0197) *bk*	USAF 156th AS/145th AW, Charlotte-Douglas, NC ANG
	21098	Boeing C-17A Globemaster III (02-1098) *bl*	USAF 6th AS/305th AMW, McGuire AFB, NJ
	21099	Boeing C-17A Globemaster III (02-1099) *bk/y*	USAF 758th AS/911th AMW AFRC, Greater Pittsburgh, PA
	21100	Boeing C-17A Globemaster III (02-1100) *r/w*	USAF 155th AS/164th AW, Memphis, TN ANG
	21101	Boeing C-17A Globemaster III (02-1101) *bk/y*	USAF 758th AS/911th AMW AFRC, Greater Pittsburgh, PA
	21102	Boeing C-17A Globemaster III (02-1102) *r/y*	USAF 58th AS/97th AMW, Altus AFB, OK
	21103	Boeing C-17A Globemaster III (02-1103) *r/y*	USAF 58th AS/97th AMW, Altus AFB, OK
	21104	Boeing C-17A Globemaster III (02-1104) *r/y* [97 OG]	USAF 58th AS/97th AMW, Altus AFB, OK
	21105	Boeing C-17A Globemaster III (02-1105) *gn*	USAF 62nd AW, McChord AFB, WA
	21106	Boeing C-17A Globemaster III (02-1106) *gn*	USAF 62nd AW, McChord AFB, WA

Serial	Type (code/other identity)	Owner/operator, location or fate	Notes
21107	Boeing C-17A Globemaster III (02-1107) *bk*	USAF 156th AS/145th AW, Charlotte-Douglas, NC ANG	
21108	Boeing C-17A Globemaster III (02-1108) *gn*	USAF 62nd AW, McChord AFB, WA	
21109	Boeing C-17A Globemaster III (02-1109) *gn*	USAF 62nd AW, McChord AFB, WA	
21110	Boeing C-17A Globemaster III (02-1110) *r/w*	USAF 155th AS/164th AW, Memphis, TN ANG	
21111	Boeing C-17A Globemaster III (02-1111) *gn*	USAF 62nd AW, McChord AFB, WA	
21112	Boeing C-17A Globemaster III (02-1112) *bl/gd*	USAF 183rd AS/172nd AW, Jackson Int'l Airport, MS ANG	
23291	Boeing C-17A Globemaster III (92-3291) *r/w*	USAF 155th AS/164th AW, Memphis, TN ANG	
23292	Boeing C-17A Globemaster III (92-3292) *bk/y*	USAF 758th AS/911th AMW AFRC, Greater Pittsburgh, PA	
23293	Boeing C-17A Globemaster III (92-3293) *y/bl*	USAF 437th AW, Charleston AFB, SC	
23294	Boeing C-17A Globemaster III (92-3294) *bk*	USAF 156th AS/145th AW, Charlotte-Douglas, NC ANG	
30599	Boeing C-17A Globemaster III (93-0599) [AK] *bl/y*	USAF 144th AS/176th Wg, Elmendorf AFB, AK ANG	
30600	Boeing C-17A Globemaster III (93-0600) *r/w*	USAF 155th AS/164th AW, Memphis, TN ANG	
30601	Boeing C-17A Globemaster III (93-0601) *bk/y*	USAF 758th AS/911th AMW AFRC, Greater Pittsburgh, PA	
30602	Boeing C-17A Globemaster III (93-0602) *bk $*	USAF 156th AS/145th AW, Charlotte-Douglas, NC ANG	
30603	Boeing C-17A Globemaster III (93-0603) *r/w*	USAF 89th AS/445th AW AFRC, Wright-Patterson AFB, OH	
30604	Boeing C-17A Globemaster III (93-0604) *r/w*	USAF 89th AS/445th AW AFRC, Wright-Patterson AFB, OH	
33113	Boeing C-17A Globemaster III (03-3113) *bl/gd*	USAF 183rd AS/172nd AW, Jackson Int'l Airport, MS ANG	
33114	Boeing C-17A Globemaster III (03-3114) *bl/gd*	USAF 183rd AS/172nd AW, Jackson Int'l Airport, MS ANG	
33115	Boeing C-17A Globemaster III (03-3115) *bl/gd*	USAF 183rd AS/172nd AW, Jackson Int'l Airport, MS ANG	
33116	Boeing C-17A Globemaster III (03-3116) *bl/gd*	USAF 183rd AS/172nd AW, Jackson Int'l Airport, MS ANG	
33117	Boeing C-17A Globemaster III (03-3117) *bl/gd*	USAF 183rd AS/172nd AW, Jackson Int'l Airport, MS ANG	
33118	Boeing C-17A Globemaster III (03-3118) *bl/gd*	USAF 183rd AS/172nd AW, Jackson Int'l Airport, MS ANG	
33119	Boeing C-17A Globemaster III (03-3119) *bl/gd*	USAF 183rd AS/172nd AW, Jackson Int'l Airport, MS ANG	
33120	Boeing C-17A Globemaster III (03-3120) *gn*	USAF 62nd AW, McChord AFB, WA	
33121	Boeing C-17A Globemaster III (03-3121) [ED]	USAF 418th FLTS/412th TW, Edwards AFB, CA	
33122	Boeing C-17A Globemaster III (03-3122) *r/y*	USAF 58th AS/97th AMW, Altus AFB, OK	
33123	Boeing C-17A Globemaster III (03-3123) *r/w*	USAF 167th AS/167th AW, Martinsburg, WV ANG	
33124	Boeing C-17A Globemaster III (03-3124) *y/bl*	USAF 437th AW, Charleston AFB, SC	
33125	Boeing C-17A Globemaster III (03-3125) *bl*	USAF 6th AS/305th AMW, McGuire AFB, NJ	
33126	Boeing C-17A Globemaster III (03-3126) *bl*	USAF 6th AS/305th AMW, McGuire AFB, NJ	
33127	Boeing C-17A Globemaster III (03-3127) *gn*	USAF 62nd AW, McChord AFB, WA	
40065	Boeing C-17A Globemaster III (94-0065) *r/w*	USAF 155th AS/164th AW, Memphis, TN ANG	
40066	Boeing C-17A Globemaster III (94-0066) *gn*	USAF 62nd AW, McChord AFB, WA	
40067	Boeing C-17A Globemaster III (94-0067) *bl*	USAF 137th AS/105th AW, Stewart AFB, NY ANG	
40068	Boeing C-17A Globemaster III (94-0068) *or/y*	USAF 729th AS/452nd AMW AFRC, March ARB, CA	
40069	Boeing C-17A Globemaster III (94-0069) *r/w*	USAF 167th AS/167th AW, Martinsburg, WV ANG	
40070	Boeing C-17A Globemaster III (94-0070) *r/w*	USAF 167th AS/167th AW, Martinsburg, WV ANG	
44128	Boeing C-17A Globemaster III (04-4128) *bl*	USAF 6th AS/305th AMW, McGuire AFB, NJ	
44129	Boeing C-17A Globemaster III (04-4129) *r/y*	USAF 58th AS/97th AMW, Altus AFB, OK	
44130	Boeing C-17A Globemaster III (04-4130) *bl*	USAF 6th AS/305th AMW, McGuire AFB, NJ	
44131	Boeing C-17A Globemaster III (04-4131) *bl*	USAF 6th AS/305th AMW, McGuire AFB, NJ	
44132	Boeing C-17A Globemaster III (04-4132) *bl*	USAF 6th AS/305th AMW, McGuire AFB, NJ	
44133	Boeing C-17A Globemaster III (04-4133) *bl*	USAF 6th AS/305th AMW, McGuire AFB, NJ	
44134	Boeing C-17A Globemaster III (04-4134) *bl*	USAF 6th AS/305th AMW, McGuire AFB, NJ	
44135	Boeing C-17A Globemaster III (04-4135) *r/y*	USAF 58th AS/97th AMW, Altus AFB, OK	

Notes	Serial	Type (code/other identity)	Owner/operator, location or fate
	44136	Boeing C-17A Globemaster III (04-4136) *bl*	USAF 6th AS/305th AMW, McGuire AFB, NJ
	44137	Boeing C-17A Globemaster III (04-4137) *bl*	USAF 6th AS/305th AMW, McGuire AFB, NJ
	44138	Boeing C-17A Globemaster III (04-4138) *or/y*	USAF 729th AS/452nd AMW AFRC, March ARB, CA
	50102	Boeing C-17A Globemaster III (95-0102) *y/bl*	USAF 437th AW, Charleston AFB, SC
	50103	Boeing C-17A Globemaster III (95-0103) *gn*	USAF 62nd AW, McChord AFB, WA
	50104	Boeing C-17A Globemaster III (95-0104) *r/w*	USAF 155th AS/164th AW, Memphis, TN ANG
	50105	Boeing C-17A Globemaster III (95-0105) *bl*	USAF 137th AS/105th AW, Stewart AFB, NY ANG
	50106	Boeing C-17A Globemaster III (95-0106) *gn*	USAF 62nd AW, McChord AFB, WA
	50107	Boeing C-17A Globemaster III (95-0107) *y/bl*	USAF 437th AW, Charleston AFB, SC
	55139	Boeing C-17A Globemaster III (05-5139) *or/y*	USAF 729th AS/452nd AMW AFRC, March ARB, CA
	55140	Boeing C-17A Globemaster III (05-5140) *or/y*	USAF 729th AS/452nd AMW AFRC, March ARB, CA
	55141	Boeing C-17A Globemaster III (05-5141) *or/y*	USAF 729th AS/452nd AMW AFRC, March ARB, CA
	55142	Boeing C-17A Globemaster III (05-5142) *or/y*	USAF 729th AS/452nd AMW AFRC, March ARB, CA
	55143	Boeing C-17A Globemaster III (05-5143) *r/w*	USAF 89th AS/445th AW AFRC, Wright-Patterson AFB, OH
	55144	Boeing C-17A Globemaster III (05-5144) *or/y*	USAF 729th AS/452nd AMW AFRC, March ARB, CA
	55145	Boeing C-17A Globemaster III (05-5145) *or/y*	USAF 729th AS/452nd AMW AFRC, March ARB, CA
	55146	Boeing C-17A Globemaster III (05-5146) [HH] *r/y*	USAF 535th AS/15th Wg, Hickam AFB, HI
	55147	Boeing C-17A Globemaster III (05-5147) [HH] *r/y*	USAF 535th AS/15th Wg, Hickam AFB, HI
	55148	Boeing C-17A Globemaster III (05-5148) [HH] *r/y*	USAF 535th AS/15th Wg, Hickam AFB, HI
	55149	Boeing C-17A Globemaster III (05-5149) [HH] *r/y*	USAF 535th AS/15th Wg, Hickam AFB, HI
	55150	Boeing C-17A Globemaster III (05-5150) [HH] *r/y*	USAF 535th AS/15th Wg, Hickam AFB, HI
	55151	Boeing C-17A Globemaster III (05-5151) [HH] *r/y*	USAF 535th AS/15th Wg, Hickam AFB, HI
	55152	Boeing C-17A Globemaster III (05-5152) [HH] *r/y*	USAF 535th AS/15th Wg, Hickam AFB, HI
	55153	Boeing C-17A Globemaster III (05-5153) [HH] *r/y]*	USAF 535th AS/15th Wg, Hickam AFB, HI
	60001	Boeing C-17A Globemaster III (96-0001) *bk/y*	USAF 758th AS/911th AMW AFRC, Greater Pittsburgh, PA
	60002	Boeing C-17A Globemaster III (96-0002) *y/bl*	USAF 437th AW, Charleston AFB, SC
	60003	Boeing C-17A Globemaster III (96-0003) *gn*	USAF 62nd AW, McChord AFB, WA
	60004	Boeing C-17A Globemaster III (96-0004) *gn*	USAF 62nd AW, McChord AFB, WA
	60005	Boeing C-17A Globemaster III (96-0005) *bl*	USAF 137th AS/105th AW, Stewart AFB, NY ANG
	60006	Boeing C-17A Globemaster III (96-0006) *r/w*	USAF 167th AS/167th AW, Martinsburg, WV ANG
	60007	Boeing C-17A Globemaster III (96-0007) *bl/gd*	USAF 183rd AS/172nd AW, Jackson Int'l Airport, MS ANG
	60008	Boeing C-17A Globemaster III (96-0008) *r/y*	USAF 58th AS/97th AMW, Altus AFB, OK
	66154	Boeing C-17A Globemaster III (06-6154) *w/bk*	USAF 21st AS/60th AMW, Travis AFB, CA
	66155	Boeing C-17A Globemaster III (06-6155) *w/bk*	USAF 21st AS/60th AMW, Travis AFB, CA
	66156	Boeing C-17A Globemaster III (06-6156) *w/bk*	USAF 21st AS/60th AMW, Travis AFB, CA
	66157	Boeing C-17A Globemaster III (06-6157) *w/bk*	USAF 21st AS/60th AMW, Travis AFB, CA
	66158	Boeing C-17A Globemaster III (06-6158) *w/bk*	USAF 21st AS/60th AMW, Travis AFB, CA
	66159	Boeing C-17A Globemaster III (06-6159) *w/bk*	USAF 21st AS/60th AMW, Travis AFB, CA
	66160	Boeing C-17A Globemaster III (06-6160) *w/bk*	USAF 21st AS/60th AMW, Travis AFB, CA
	66161	Boeing C-17A Globemaster III (06-6161) *w/bk*	USAF 21st AS/60th AMW, Travis AFB, CA
	66162	Boeing C-17A Globemaster III (06-6162) *w/bk*	USAF 21st AS/60th AMW, Travis AFB, CA
	66163	Boeing C-17A Globemaster III (06-6163) *w/bk*	USAF 21st AS/60th AMW, Travis AFB, CA
	66164	Boeing C-17A Globemaster III (06-6164) *w/bk*	USAF 21st AS/60th AMW, Travis AFB, CA
	66165	Boeing C-17A Globemaster III (06-6165) *bl/y*	USAF 3rd AS/436th AW, Dover AFB, DE
	66166	Boeing C-17A Globemaster III (06-6166) *bl/y*	USAF 3rd AS/436th AW, Dover AFB, DE
	66167	Boeing C-17A Globemaster III (06-6167) *bl/y*	USAF 3rd AS/436th AW, Dover AFB, DE
	66168	Boeing C-17A Globemaster III (06-6168) *bl/y*	USAF 3rd AS/436th AW, Dover AFB, DE
	70041	Boeing C-17A Globemaster III (97-0041) *y/bl*	USAF 437th AW, Charleston AFB, SC
	70042	Boeing C-17A Globemaster III (97-0042) *r/w*	USAF 155th AS/164th AW, Memphis, TN ANG
	70043	Boeing C-17A Globemaster III (97-0043) *or/y*	USAF 729th AS/452nd AMW AFRC, March ARB, CA

Serial	Type (code/other identity)	Owner/operator, location or fate	Notes
70044	Boeing C-17A Globemaster III (97-0044) *r/w*	USAF 89th AS/445th AW AFRC, Wright-Patterson AFB, OH	
70045	Boeing C-17A Globemaster III (97-0045) *bl*	USAF 137th AS/105th AW, Stewart AFB, NY ANG	
70046	Boeing C-17A Globemaster III (97-0046) *y/bl*	USAF 437th AW, Charleston AFB, SC	
70047	Boeing C-17A Globemaster III (97-0047) *y/bl*	USAF 437th AW, Charleston AFB, SC	
70048	Boeing C-17A Globemaster III (97-0048) *r/w*	USAF 89th AS/445th AW AFRC, Wright-Patterson AFB, OH	
77169	Boeing C-17A Globemaster III (07-7169) *bl*	USAF 3rd AS/436th AW, Dover AFB, DE	
77170	Boeing C-17A Globemaster III (07-7170) *bl/y*	USAF 3rd AS/436th AW, Dover AFB, DE	
77171	Boeing C-17A Globemaster III (07-7171) *bl*	USAF 6th AS/305th AMW, McGuire AFB, NJ	
77172	Boeing C-17A Globemaster III (07-7172) *w/bk*	USAF 21st AS/60th AMW, Travis AFB, CA	
77173	Boeing C-17A Globemaster III (07-7173) *bl/y*	USAF 3rd AS/436th AW, Dover AFB, DE	
77174	Boeing C-17A Globemaster III (07-7174) *bl/y*	USAF 3rd AS/436th AW, Dover AFB, DE	
77175	Boeing C-17A Globemaster III (07-7175) *bl/y*	USAF 3rd AS/436th AW, Dover AFB, DE	
77176	Boeing C-17A Globemaster III (07-7176) *bl/y*	USAF 3rd AS/436th AW, Dover AFB, DE	
77177	Boeing C-17A Globemaster III (07-7177) *bl/y*	USAF 3rd AS/436th AW, Dover AFB, DE	
77178	Boeing C-17A Globemaster III (07-7178) *bl*	USAF 6th AS/305th AMW, McGuire AFB, NJ	
77179	Boeing C-17A Globemaster III (07-7179) *w/bk*	USAF 21st AS/60th AMW, Travis AFB, CA	
77180	Boeing C-17A Globemaster III (07-7180) *y/bl*	USAF 437th AW, Charleston AFB, SC	
77181	Boeing C-17A Globemaster III (07-7181) *y/bl*	USAF 437th AW, Charleston AFB, SC	
77182	Boeing C-17A Globemaster III (07-7182) *y/bl*	USAF 437th AW, Charleston AFB, SC	
77183	Boeing C-17A Globemaster III (07-7183) *y/bl*	USAF 437th AW, Charleston AFB, SC	
77184	Boeing C-17A Globemaster III (07-7184) *y/bl*	USAF 437th AW, Charleston AFB, SC	
77185	Boeing C-17A Globemaster III (07-7185) *y/bl*	USAF 437th AW, Charleston AFB, SC	
77186	Boeing C-17A Globemaster III (07-7186) *y/bl*	USAF 437th AW, Charleston AFB, SC	
77187	Boeing C-17A Globemaster III (07-7187) *y/bl*	USAF 437th AW, Charleston AFB, SC	
77188	Boeing C-17A Globemaster III (07-7188) *y/bl*	USAF 437th AW, Charleston AFB, SC	
77189	Boeing C-17A Globemaster III (07-7189) *y/bl*	USAF 437th AW, Charleston AFB, SC	
80049	Boeing C-17A Globemaster III (98-0049) *r/y*	USAF 58th AS/97th AMW, Altus AFB, OK	
80050	Boeing C-17A Globemaster III (98-0050) *r/y*	USAF 58th AS/97th AMW, Altus AFB, OK	
80051	Boeing C-17A Globemaster III (98-0051) [AK] *bl/y* [517 AS]	USAF 144th AS/176th Wg, Elmendorf AFB, AK ANG	
80052	Boeing C-17A Globemaster III (98-0052) *gn*	USAF 62nd AW, McChord AFB, WA	
80053	Boeing C-17A Globemaster III (98-0053) *gn*	USAF 62nd AW, McChord AFB, WA	
80054	Boeing C-17A Globemaster III (98-0054) *y/bl*	USAF 437th AW, Charleston AFB, SC	
80055	Boeing C-17A Globemaster III (98-0055) *r/y* [58 AS]	USAF 58th AS/97th AMW, Altus AFB, OK	
80056	Boeing C-17A Globemaster III (98-0056) [AK] *bl/y*	USAF 144th AS/176th Wg, Elmendorf AFB, AK ANG	
80057	Boeing C-17A Globemaster III (98-0057) *bl*	USAF 137th AS/105th AW, Stewart AFB, NY ANG	
80265	Boeing C-17A Globemaster III (88-0265) *gn*	USAF 62nd AW, McChord AFB, WA	
80266	Boeing C-17A Globemaster III (88-0266) *y/bl*	USAF 437th AW, Charleston AFB, SC	
88190	Boeing C-17A Globemaster III (08-8190) *y/bl*	USAF 437th AW, Charleston AFB, SC	
88191	Boeing C-17A Globemaster III (08-8191) *y/bl*	USAF 437th AW, Charleston AFB, SC	
88192	Boeing C-17A Globemaster III (08-8192) *gn*	USAF 62nd AW, McChord AFB, WA	
88193	Boeing C-17A Globemaster III (08-8193) *gn*	USAF 62nd AW, McChord AFB, WA	
88194	Boeing C-17A Globemaster III (08-8194) *gn*	USAF 62nd AW, McChord AFB, WA	
88195	Boeing C-17A Globemaster III (08-8195) *gn*	USAF 62nd AW, McChord AFB, WA	
88196	Boeing C-17A Globemaster III (08-8196) *gn*	USAF 62nd AW, McChord AFB, WA	
88197	Boeing C-17A Globemaster III (08-8197) *gn*	USAF 62nd AW, McChord AFB, WA	
88198	Boeing C-17A Globemaster III (08-8198) *y/bl*	USAF 437th AW, Charleston AFB, SC	
88199	Boeing C-17A Globemaster III (08-8199) *gn*	USAF 62nd AW, McChord AFB, WA	
88200	Boeing C-17A Globemaster III (08-8200) *gn*	USAF 62nd AW, McChord AFB, WA	
88201	Boeing C-17A Globemaster III (08-8201) *gn*	USAF 62nd AW, McChord AFB, WA	
88202	Boeing C-17A Globemaster III (08-8202) *gn*	USAF 62nd AW, McChord AFB, WA	
88203	Boeing C-17A Globemaster III (08-8203) *gn*	USAF 62nd AW, McChord AFB, WA	
88204	Boeing C-17A Globemaster III (08-8204) *y/bl*	USAF 437th AW, Charleston AFB, SC	
90058	Boeing C-17A Globemaster III (99-0058) *gn*	USAF 62nd AW, McChord AFB, WA	
90059	Boeing C-17A Globemaster III (99-0059) *gn*	USAF 62nd AW, McChord AFB, WA	
90060	Boeing C-17A Globemaster III (99-0060) *gn*	USAF 62nd AW, McChord AFB, WA	
90061	Boeing C-17A Globemaster III (99-0061) *r/y*	USAF 58th AS/97th AMW, Altus AFB, OK	
90062	Boeing C-17A Globemaster III (99-0062) *y/bl*	USAF 437th AW, Charleston AFB, SC	
90063	Boeing C-17A Globemaster III (99-0063) *r/y*	USAF 58th AS/97th AMW, Altus AFB, OK	
90064	Boeing C-17A Globemaster III (99-0064) *r/y*	USAF 58th AS/97th AMW, Altus AFB, OK	

US-BASED USAF AIRCRAFT

Notes	Serial	Type (code/other identity)	Owner/operator, location or fate
	90165	Boeing C-17A Globemaster III (99-0165) r/w	USAF 89th AS/445th AW AFRC, Wright-Patterson AFB, OH
	90166	Boeing C-17A Globemaster III (99-0166) gn	USAF 62nd AW, McChord AFB, WA
	90167	Boeing C-17A Globemaster III (99-0167) [AK] bl/y	USAF 144th AS/176th Wg, Elmendorf AFB, AK ANG
	90168	Boeing C-17A Globemaster III (99-0168) [AK] bl/y	USAF 144th AS/176th Wg, Elmendorf AFB, AK ANG
	90169	Boeing C-17A Globemaster III (99-0169) y/bl	USAF 437th AW, Charleston AFB, SC
	90170	Boeing C-17A Globemaster III (99-0170) r/y	USAF 58th AS/97th AMW, Altus AFB, OK
	91189	Boeing C-17A Globemaster III (89-1189) bk/y	USAF 758th AS/911th AMW AFRC, Greater Pittsburgh, PA
	91190	Boeing C-17A Globemaster III (89-1190) r/w	USAF 167th AS/167th AW, Martinsburg, WV ANG
	91191	Boeing C-17A Globemaster III (89-1191) bl	USAF 137th AS/105th AW, Stewart AFB, NY ANG
	91192	Boeing C-17A Globemaster III (89-1192) y/bl	USAF 437th AW, Charleston AFB, SC
	99205	Boeing C-17A Globemaster III (09-9205) y/bl	USAF 437th AW, Charleston AFB, SC
	99206	Boeing C-17A Globemaster III (09-9206) y/bl	USAF 437th AW, Charleston AFB, SC
	99207	Boeing C-17A Globemaster III (09-9207) y/bl	USAF 437th AW, Charleston AFB, SC
	99208	Boeing C-17A Globemaster III (09-9208) y/bl	USAF 437th AW, Charleston AFB, SC
	99209	Boeing C-17A Globemaster III (09-9209) gn	USAF 62nd AW, McChord AFB, WA
	99210	Boeing C-17A Globemaster III (09-9210) gn	USAF 62nd AW, McChord AFB, WA
	99211	Boeing C-17A Globemaster III (09-9211) gn	USAF 62nd AW, McChord AFB, WA
	99212	Boeing C-17A Globemaster III (09-9212) y/bl	USAF 437th AW, Charleston AFB, SC
		Lockheed Martin F-22A Raptor	
	91-4004	Lockheed Martin F-22A Raptor [ED]	USAF 411th FLTS/412th TW, Edwards AFB, CA
	91-4006	Lockheed Martin F-22A Raptor [ED]	USAF 411th FLTS/412th TW, Edwards AFB, CA
	91-4007	Lockheed Martin F-22A Raptor [ED] [412 TW]	USAF 411th FLTS/412th TW, Edwards AFB, CA
	91-4009	Lockheed Martin F-22A Raptor [ED]	USAF 411th FLTS/412th TW, Edwards AFB, CA
	99-4010	Lockheed Martin F-22A Raptor [OT] [422 TES]	USAF 422nd TES/53rd Wg, Nellis AFB, NV
	99-4011	Lockheed Martin F-22A Raptor [WA]	USAF 433rd WPS/57th Wg, Nellis AFB, NV
	00-4012	Lockheed Martin F-22A Raptor [TY]	USAF 43rd FS/325th FW, Eglin AFB, FL
	00-4015	Lockheed Martin F-22A Raptor [TY]	USAF 43rd FS/325th FW, Eglin AFB, FL
	00-4016	Lockheed Martin F-22A Raptor [TY] [325 FW]	USAF 1st FW, Langley AFB, VA
	00-4017	Lockheed Martin F-22A Raptor [TY]	USAF 43rd FS/325th FW, Eglin AFB, FL
	01-4018	Lockheed Martin F-22A Raptor [TY]	USAF 43rd FS/325th FW, Eglin AFB, FL
	01-4019	Lockheed Martin F-22A Raptor [TY]	USAF 1st FW, Langley AFB, VA
	01-4020	Lockheed Martin F-22A Raptor [TY]	USAF 43rd FS/325th FW, Eglin AFB, FL
	01-4021	Lockheed Martin F-22A Raptor [TY]	USAF 1st FW, Langley AFB, VA
	01-4022	Lockheed Martin F-22A Raptor [TY]	USAF 1st FW, Langley AFB, VA
	01-4023	Lockheed Martin F-22A Raptor [TY]	USAF 43rd FS/325th FW, Eglin AFB, FL
	01-4024	Lockheed Martin F-22A Raptor [TY]	USAF 1st FW, Langley AFB, VA
	01-4025	Lockheed Martin F-22A Raptor [TY]	USAF 43rd FS/325th FW, Eglin AFB, FL
	01-4026	Lockheed Martin F-22A Raptor [TY]	USAF 43rd FS/325th FW, Eglin AFB, FL
	01-4027	Lockheed Martin F-22A Raptor [TY]	USAF 1st FW, Langley AFB, VA
	02-4028	Lockheed Martin F-22A Raptor [TY]	USAF 1st FW, Langley AFB, VA
	02-4029	Lockheed Martin F-22A Raptor [TY]	USAF 43rd FS/325th FW, Eglin AFB, FL
	02-4030	Lockheed Martin F-22A Raptor [TY]	USAF 43rd FS/325th FW, Eglin AFB, FL
	02-4031	Lockheed Martin F-22A Raptor [TY]	USAF 1st FW, Langley AFB, VA
	02-4032	Lockheed Martin F-22A Raptor [TY]	USAF 43rd FS/325th FW, Eglin AFB, FL
	02-4033	Lockheed Martin F-22A Raptor [TY]	USAF 43rd FS/325th FW, Eglin AFB, FL
	02-4034	Lockheed Martin F-22A Raptor [TY]	USAF 43rd FS/325th FW, Eglin AFB, FL
	02-4035	Lockheed Martin F-22A Raptor [TY] [325 OG]	USAF 43rd FS/325th FW, Eglin AFB, FL
	02-4036	Lockheed Martin F-22A Raptor [TY]	USAF 1st FW, Langley AFB, VA
	02-4037	Lockheed Martin F-22A Raptor	USAF
	02-4038	Lockheed Martin F-22A Raptor [TY]	USAF 43rd FS/325th FW, Eglin AFB, FL
	02-4039	Lockheed Martin F-22A Raptor [TY]	USAF 43rd FS/325th FW, Eglin AFB, FL
	02-4040	Lockheed Martin F-22A Raptor [TY] [325 FW]	USAF 1st FW, Langley AFB, VA
	03-4041	Lockheed Martin F-22A Raptor [TY]	USAF 43rd FS/325th FW, Eglin AFB, FL
	03-4042	Lockheed Martin F-22A Raptor [TY]	USAF 1st FW, Langley AFB, VA
	03-4043	Lockheed Martin F-22A Raptor [TY] [43 FS]	USAF 43rd FS/325th FW, Eglin AFB, FL
	03-4044	Lockheed Martin F-22A Raptor [TY]	USAF 1st FW, Langley AFB, VA
	03-4045	Lockheed Martin F-22A Raptor [HH]	USAF 199th FS/154th Wg, Hickam AFB, HI ANG

Serial	Type (code/other identity)	Owner/operator, location or fate	Notes
03-4046	Lockheed Martin F-22A Raptor [HH] [199 FS]	USAF 199th FS/154th Wg, Hickam AFB, HI ANG	
03-4047	Lockheed Martin F-22A Raptor [HH]	USAF 199th FS/154th Wg, Hickam AFB, HI ANG	
03-4048	Lockheed Martin F-22A Raptor [HH]	USAF 199th FS/154th Wg, Hickam AFB, HI ANG	
03-4049	Lockheed Martin F-22A Raptor [HH]	USAF 199th FS/154th Wg, Hickam AFB, HI ANG	
03-4050	Lockheed Martin F-22A Raptor [HH]	USAF 199th FS/154th Wg, Hickam AFB, HI ANG	
03-4051	Lockheed Martin F-22A Raptor [HH]	USAF 199th FS/154th Wg, Hickam AFB, HI ANG	
03-4052	Lockheed Martin F-22A Raptor [HH]	USAF 199th FS/154th Wg, Hickam AFB, HI ANG	
03-4053	Lockheed Martin F-22A Raptor [HH]	USAF 199th FS/154th Wg, Hickam AFB, HI ANG	
03-4054	Lockheed Martin F-22A Raptor [HH] [154 Wg]	USAF 199th FS/154th Wg, Hickam AFB, HI ANG	
03-4055	Lockheed Martin F-22A Raptor [HH]	USAF 199th FS/154th Wg, Hickam AFB, HI ANG	
03-4056	Lockheed Martin F-22A Raptor [HH]	USAF 199th FS/154th Wg, Hickam AFB, HI ANG	
03-4057	Lockheed Martin F-22A Raptor [HH]	USAF 199th FS/154th Wg, Hickam AFB, HI ANG	
03-4058	Lockheed Martin F-22A Raptor [HH]	USAF 199th FS/154th Wg, Hickam AFB, HI ANG	
03-4059	Lockheed Martin F-22A Raptor [HH]	USAF 199th FS/154th Wg, Hickam AFB, HI ANG	
03-4060	Lockheed Martin F-22A Raptor [HH]	USAF 199th FS/154th Wg, Hickam AFB, HI ANG	
03-4061	Lockheed Martin F-22A Raptor [HH]	USAF 199th FS/154th Wg, Hickam AFB, HI ANG	
04-4062	Lockheed Martin F-22A Raptor [HH]	USAF 199th FS/154th Wg, Hickam AFB, HI ANG	
04-4063	Lockheed Martin F-22A Raptor [HH]	USAF 199th FS/154th Wg, Hickam AFB, HI ANG	
04-4064	Lockheed Martin F-22A Raptor [HH]	USAF 199th FS/154th Wg, Hickam AFB, HI ANG	
04-4065	Lockheed Martin F-22A Raptor [FF]	USAF 94th FS/1st FW, Langley AFB, VA	
04-4066	Lockheed Martin F-22A Raptor [OT]	USAF 422nd TES/53rd Wg, Nellis AFB, NV	
04-4067	Lockheed Martin F-22A Raptor [FF]	USAF 94th FS/1st FW, Langley AFB, VA	
04-4068	Lockheed Martin F-22A Raptor [OT]	USAF 422nd TES/53rd Wg, Nellis AFB, NV	
04-4069	Lockheed Martin F-22A Raptor [OT]	USAF 422nd TES/53rd Wg, Nellis AFB, NV	
04-4070	Lockheed Martin F-22A Raptor [FF]	USAF 27th FS/1st FW, Langley AFB, VA	
04-4071	Lockheed Martin F-22A Raptor [WA]	USAF 433rd WPS/57th Wg, Nellis AFB, NV	
04-4072	Lockheed Martin F-22A Raptor [TY]	USAF 1st FW, Langley AFB, VA	
04-4073	Lockheed Martin F-22A Raptor [FF]	USAF 27th FS/1st FW, Langley AFB, VA	
04-4074	Lockheed Martin F-22A Raptor [AK]	USAF 90th FS/3rd Wg, Elmendorf AFB, AK	
04-4075	Lockheed Martin F-22A Raptor [AK]	USAF 90th FS/3rd Wg, Elmendorf AFB, AK	
04-4076	Lockheed Martin F-22A Raptor [TY]	USAF 1st FW, Langley AFB, VA	
04-4077	Lockheed Martin F-22A Raptor [AK]	USAF 525th FS/3rd Wg, Elmendorf AFB, AK	
04-4078	Lockheed Martin F-22A Raptor [TY]	USAF 1st FW, Langley AFB, VA	
04-4079	Lockheed Martin F-22A Raptor [TY]	USAF 1st FW, Langley AFB, VA	
04-4080	Lockheed Martin F-22A Raptor [HH]	USAF 199th FS/154th Wg, Hickam AFB, HI ANG	
04-4082	Lockheed Martin F-22A Raptor [FF] [149 FS]	USAF 149th FS/192nd FW/1st FW, Langley AFB, VA ANG	
04-4083	Lockheed Martin F-22A Raptor [TY] [301 FS]	USAF 301st FS/44th FG AFRES/325th FW, Eglin AFB, FL	
05-4081	Lockheed Martin F-22A Raptor (04-4081) [TY]	USAF 1st FW, Langley AFB, VA	
05-4084	Lockheed Martin F-22A Raptor [HH]	USAF 199th FS/154th Wg, Hickam AFB, HI ANG	
05-4085	Lockheed Martin F-22A Raptor [FF]	USAF 94th FS/1st FW, Langley AFB, VA	
05-4086	Lockheed Martin F-22A Raptor [AK]	USAF 90th FS/3rd Wg, Elmendorf AFB, AK	
05-4087	Lockheed Martin F-22A Raptor [AK]	USAF 90th FS/3rd Wg, Elmendorf AFB, AK	
05-4088	Lockheed Martin F-22A Raptor [AK]	USAF 90th FS/3rd Wg, Elmendorf AFB, AK	
05-4089	Lockheed Martin F-22A Raptor [TY]	USAF 1st FW, Langley AFB, VA	
05-4090	Lockheed Martin F-22A Raptor [AK]	USAF 90th FS/3rd Wg, Elmendorf AFB, AK	
05-4091	Lockheed Martin F-22A Raptor [TY]	USAF 1st FW, Langley AFB, VA	
05-4092	Lockheed Martin F-22A Raptor [AK]	USAF 525th FS/3rd Wg, Elmendorf AFB, AK	
05-4093	Lockheed Martin F-22A Raptor [HH]	USAF 199th FS/154th Wg, Hickam AFB, HI ANG	
05-4094	Lockheed Martin F-22A Raptor [AK]	USAF 525th FS/3rd Wg, Elmendorf AFB, AK	
05-4095	Lockheed Martin F-22A Raptor [TY] [95 FS]	USAF 1st FW, Langley AFB, VA	
05-4096	Lockheed Martin F-22A Raptor [WA]	USAF 433rd WPS/57th Wg, Nellis AFB, NV	
05-4097	Lockheed Martin F-22A Raptor [TY]	USAF 1st FW, Langley AFB, VA	
05-4098	Lockheed Martin F-22A Raptor [TY]	USAF 1st FW, Langley AFB, VA	
05-4099	Lockheed Martin F-22A Raptor [TY]	USAF 1st FW, Langley AFB, VA	
05-4100	Lockheed Martin F-22A Raptor [TY]	USAF 1st FW, Langley AFB, VA	
05-4101	Lockheed Martin F-22A Raptor [TY]	USAF 1st FW, Langley AFB, VA	
05-4102	Lockheed Martin F-22A Raptor [AK] [302 FS]	USAF 302nd FS/477th FG AFRES/3rd Wg, Elmendorf AFB, AK	
05-4103	Lockheed Martin F-22A Raptor [AK] [3 Wg]	USAF 90th FS/3rd Wg, Elmendorf AFB, AK	
05-4104	Lockheed Martin F-22A Raptor [TY]	USAF 1st FW, Langley AFB, VA	

Notes	Serial	Type (code/other identity)	Owner/operator, location or fate
	05-4105	Lockheed Martin F-22A Raptor [TY] [44 FG]	USAF 1st FW, Langley AFB, VA
	05-4106	Lockheed Martin F-22A Raptor [TY]	USAF 1st FW, Langley AFB, VA
	05-4107	Lockheed Martin F-22A Raptor [TY]	USAF 1st FW, Langley AFB, VA
	06-4108	Lockheed Martin F-22A Raptor [AK]	USAF 525th FS/3rd Wg, Elmendorf AFB, AK
	06-4109	Lockheed Martin F-22A Raptor [WA]	USAF 433rd WPS/57th Wg, Nellis AFB, NV
	06-4110	Lockheed Martin F-22A Raptor [AK] [11 AF]	USAF 525th FS/3rd Wg, Elmendorf AFB, AK
	06-4111	Lockheed Martin F-22A Raptor [OT]	USAF 422nd TES/53rd Wg, Nellis AFB, NV
	06-4112	Lockheed Martin F-22A Raptor [AK]	USAF 525th FS/3rd Wg, Elmendorf AFB, AK
	06-4113	Lockheed Martin F-22A Raptor [AK] [3 OG]	USAF 525th FS/3rd Wg, Elmendorf AFB, AK
	06-4114	Lockheed Martin F-22A Raptor [AK]	USAF 525th FS/3rd Wg, Elmendorf AFB, AK
	06-4115	Lockheed Martin F-22A Raptor [AK] [525 FS]	USAF 525th FS/3rd Wg, Elmendorf AFB, AK
	06-4116	Lockheed Martin F-22A Raptor [WA] [433 WPS]	USAF 433rd WPS/57th Wg, Nellis AFB, NV
	06-4117	Lockheed Martin F-22A Raptor [AK]	USAF 525th FS/3rd Wg, Elmendorf AFB, AK
	06-4118	Lockheed Martin F-22A Raptor [AK]	USAF 525th FS/3rd Wg, Elmendorf AFB, AK
	06-4119	Lockheed Martin F-22A Raptor [AK]	USAF 525th FS/3rd Wg, Elmendorf AFB, AK
	06-4120	Lockheed Martin F-22A Raptor [OT]	USAF 422nd TES/53rd Wg, Nellis AFB, NV
	06-4121	Lockheed Martin F-22A Raptor [AK]	USAF 525th FS/3rd Wg, Elmendorf AFB, AK
	06-4122	Lockheed Martin F-22A Raptor [AK]	USAF 525th FS/3rd Wg, Elmendorf AFB, AK
	06-4123	Lockheed Martin F-22A Raptor [AK]	USAF 525th FS/3rd Wg, Elmendorf AFB, AK
	06-4124	Lockheed Martin F-22A Raptor [OT]	USAF 422nd TES/53rd Wg, Nellis AFB, NV
	06-4126	Lockheed Martin F-22A Raptor [AK]	USAF 525th FS/3rd Wg, Elmendorf AFB, AK
	06-4127	Lockheed Martin F-22A Raptor [AK]	USAF 525th FS/3rd Wg, Elmendorf AFB, AK
	06-4128	Lockheed Martin F-22A Raptor [OT]	USAF 422nd TES/53rd Wg, Nellis AFB, NV
	06-4129	Lockheed Martin F-22A Raptor [AK]	USAF 525th FS/3rd Wg, Elmendorf AFB, AK
	06-4130	Lockheed Martin F-22A Raptor [AK]	USAF 525th FS/3rd Wg, Elmendorf AFB, AK
	07-4131	Lockheed Martin F-22A Raptor [AK]	USAF 525th FS/3rd Wg, Elmendorf AFB, AK
	07-4132	Lockheed Martin F-22A Raptor [ED] [411 FLTS]	USAF 411th FLTS/412th TW, Edwards AFB, CA
	07-4133	Lockheed Martin F-22A Raptor [AK]	USAF 525th FS/3rd Wg, Elmendorf AFB, AK
	07-4134	Lockheed Martin F-22A Raptor [AK]	USAF 525th FS/3rd Wg, Elmendorf AFB, AK
	07-4135	Lockheed Martin F-22A Raptor [AK]	USAF 90th FS/3rd Wg, Elmendorf AFB, AK
	07-4136	Lockheed Martin F-22A Raptor [AK]	USAF 90th FS/3rd Wg, Elmendorf AFB, AK
	07-4137	Lockheed Martin F-22A Raptor [AK]	USAF 90th FS/3rd Wg, Elmendorf AFB, AK
	07-4138	Lockheed Martin F-22A Raptor [AK]	USAF 90th FS/3rd Wg, Elmendorf AFB, AK
	07-4139	Lockheed Martin F-22A Raptor [AK]	USAF 90th FS/3rd Wg, Elmendorf AFB, AK
	07-4140	Lockheed Martin F-22A Raptor [AK]	USAF 90th FS/3rd Wg, Elmendorf AFB, AK
	07-4141	Lockheed Martin F-22A Raptor [AK]	USAF 90th FS/3rd Wg, Elmendorf AFB, AK
	07-4142	Lockheed Martin F-22A Raptor [AK]	USAF 90th FS/3rd Wg, Elmendorf AFB, AK
	07-4143	Lockheed Martin F-22A Raptor [AK]	USAF 90th FS/3rd Wg, Elmendorf AFB, AK
	07-4144	Lockheed Martin F-22A Raptor [AK]	USAF 90th FS/3rd Wg, Elmendorf AFB, AK
	07-4145	Lockheed Martin F-22A Raptor [AK]	USAF 90th FS/3rd Wg, Elmendorf AFB, AK
	07-4147	Lockheed Martin F-22A Raptor [AK] [477 FG]	USAF 90th FS/3rd Wg, Elmendorf AFB, AK
	07-4148	Lockheed Martin F-22A Raptor [AK]	USAF 90th FS/3rd Wg, Elmendorf AFB, AK
	07-4149	Lockheed Martin F-22A Raptor [AK]	USAF 90th FS/3rd Wg, Elmendorf AFB, AK
	07-4150	Lockheed Martin F-22A Raptor [AK]	USAF 90th FS/3rd Wg, Elmendorf AFB, AK
	07-4151	Lockheed Martin F-22A Raptor [AK]	USAF 90th FS/3rd Wg, Elmendorf AFB, AK
	08-4152	Lockheed Martin F-22A Raptor [FF]	USAF 94th FS/1st FW, Langley AFB, VA
	08-4153	Lockheed Martin F-22A Raptor [FF]	USAF 27th FS/1st FW, Langley AFB, VA
	08-4154	Lockheed Martin F-22A Raptor [FF]	USAF 94th FS/1st FW, Langley AFB, VA
	08-4155	Lockheed Martin F-22A Raptor [FF]	USAF 27th FS/1st FW, Langley AFB, VA
	08-4156	Lockheed Martin F-22A Raptor [FF]	USAF 94th FS/1st FW, Langley AFB, VA
	08-4157	Lockheed Martin F-22A Raptor [FF]	USAF 27th FS/1st FW, Langley AFB, VA
	08-4158	Lockheed Martin F-22A Raptor [FF]	USAF 27th FS/1st FW, Langley AFB, VA
	08-4159	Lockheed Martin F-22A Raptor [FF]	USAF 27th FS/1st FW, Langley AFB, VA
	08-4160	Lockheed Martin F-22A Raptor [FF]	USAF 94th FS/1st FW, Langley AFB, VA
	08-4161	Lockheed Martin F-22A Raptor [FF]	USAF 27th FS/1st FW, Langley AFB, VA
	08-4162	Lockheed Martin F-22A Raptor [FF] [1 FW]	USAF 94th FS/1st FW, Langley AFB, VA
	08-4163	Lockheed Martin F-22A Raptor [FF]	USAF 27th FS/1st FW, Langley AFB, VA
	08-4164	Lockheed Martin F-22A Raptor [FF]	USAF 94th FS/1st FW, Langley AFB, VA
	08-4165	Lockheed Martin F-22A Raptor [FF]	USAF 27th FS/1st FW, Langley AFB, VA
	08-4166	Lockheed Martin F-22A Raptor [FF]	USAF 94th FS/1st FW, Langley AFB, VA
	08-4167	Lockheed Martin F-22A Raptor [FF]	USAF 27th FS/1st FW, Langley AFB, VA
	08-4168	Lockheed Martin F-22A Raptor [FF]	USAF 94th FS/1st FW, Langley AFB, VA

Serial	Type (code/other identity)	Owner/operator, location or fate	Notes
08-4169	Lockheed Martin F-22A Raptor [FF]	USAF 27th FS/1st FW, Langley AFB, VA	
08-4170	Lockheed Martin F-22A Raptor [FF]	USAF 27th FS/1st FW, Langley AFB, VA	
08-4171	Lockheed Martin F-22A Raptor [FF]	USAF 27th FS/1st FW, Langley AFB, VA	
09-4172	Lockheed Martin F-22A Raptor [FF] [27 FS]	USAF 27th FS/1st FW, Langley AFB, VA	
09-4173	Lockheed Martin F-22A Raptor [FF]	USAF 27th FS/1st FW, Langley AFB, VA	
09-4174	Lockheed Martin F-22A Raptor [FF]	USAF 27th FS/1st FW, Langley AFB, VA	
09-4175	Lockheed Martin F-22A Raptor [FF]	USAF 94th FS/1st FW, Langley AFB, VA	
09-4176	Lockheed Martin F-22A Raptor [FF]	USAF 27th FS/1st FW, Langley AFB, VA	
09-4177	Lockheed Martin F-22A Raptor [FF]	USAF 27th FS/1st FW, Langley AFB, VA	
09-4178	Lockheed Martin F-22A Raptor [FF]	USAF 27th FS/1st FW, Langley AFB, VA	
09-4179	Lockheed Martin F-22A Raptor [FF]	USAF 94th FS/1st FW, Langley AFB, VA	
09-4180	Lockheed Martin F-22A Raptor [FF]	USAF 27th FS/1st FW, Langley AFB, VA	
09-4181	Lockheed Martin F-22A Raptor [FF]	USAF 94th FS/1st FW, Langley AFB, VA	
09-4182	Lockheed Martin F-22A Raptor [FF]	USAF 27th FS/1st FW, Langley AFB, VA	
09-4183	Lockheed Martin F-22A Raptor [FF]	USAF 94th FS/1st FW, Langley AFB, VA	
09-4184	Lockheed Martin F-22A Raptor [FF]	USAF 27th FS/1st FW, Langley AFB, VA	
09-4185	Lockheed Martin F-22A Raptor [FF] [1 OG]	USAF 27th FS/1st FW, Langley AFB, VA	
09-4186	Lockheed Martin F-22A Raptor [FF]	USAF 27th FS/1st FW, Langley AFB, VA	
09-4187	Lockheed Martin F-22A Raptor [FF]	USAF 94th FS/1st FW, Langley AFB, VA	
09-4188	Lockheed Martin F-22A Raptor [OT]	USAF 422nd TES/53rd Wg, Nellis AFB, NV	
09-4189	Lockheed Martin F-22A Raptor [FF]	USAF 27th FS/1st FW, Langley AFB, VA	
09-4190	Lockheed Martin F-22A Raptor [AK] [90 FS]	USAF 90th FS/3rd Wg, Elmendorf AFB, AK	
09-4191	Lockheed Martin F-22A Raptor [FF]	USAF 94th FS/1st FW, Langley AFB, VA	
10-4192	Lockheed Martin F-22A Raptor [FF] [192 FW]	USAF 149th FS/192nd FW/1st FW, Langley AFB, VA ANG	
10-4193	Lockheed Martin F-22A Raptor [AK] [3 Wg]	USAF 525th FS/3rd Wg, Elmendorf AFB, AK	
10-4194	Lockheed Martin F-22A Raptor [FF] [94 FS]	USAF 94th FS/1st FW, Langley AFB, VA	
10-4195	Lockheed Martin F-22A Raptor [AK] [525 FS]	USAF 525th FS/3rd Wg, Elmendorf AFB, AK	

Boeing VC-25A/VC-25B

28000	Boeing VC-25A (82-8000)	USAF PAS/89th AW, Andrews AFB, MD	
29000	Boeing VC-25A (92-9000)	USAF PAS/89th AW, Andrews AFB, MD	
N894BA	Boeing VC-25B	USAF (on order)	
N895BA	Boeing VC-25B	USAF (on order)	

Pilatus U-28A Draco

10415	Pilatus U-28A Draco(N415PB/01-0415)	USAF 318th SOS/27th SOW, Cannon AFB, NM	
40688	Pilatus U-28A Draco (N707KH/04-0688)	USAF 318th SOS/27th SOW, Cannon AFB, NM	
50409	Pilatus U-28A Draco (N922RG/05-0409)	USAF 319th SOS/1st SOW, Hurlburt Field, FL	
50419	Pilatus U-28A Draco (N419WA/05-0419)	USAF 319th SOS/1st SOW, Hurlburt Field, FL	
50424	Pilatus U-28A Draco (N424PB/05-0424)	USAF 318th SOS/27th SOW, Cannon AFB, NM	
50446	Pilatus U-28A Draco (N131JN/05-0446)	USAF 318th SOS/27th SOW, Cannon AFB, NM	
50447	Pilatus U-28A Draco (N447PC/05-0447)	USAF 319th SOS/1st SOW, Hurlburt Field, FL	
50482	Pilatus U-28A Draco (N482WA/05-0482)	USAF 319th SOS/1st SOW, Hurlburt Field, FL	
50556	Pilatus U-28A Draco (N556HL/05-0556)	USAF 318th SOS/27th SOW, Cannon AFB, NM	
50573	Pilatus U-28A Draco (N666GT/05-0573)	USAF 319th SOS/1st SOW, Hurlburt Field, FL	
50597	Pilatus U-28A Draco (N597CH/05-0597)	USAF 318th SOS/27th SOW, Cannon AFB, NM	
60692	Pilatus U-28A Draco (N692BC/06-0692)	USAF 318th SOS/27th SOW, Cannon AFB, NM	
60740	Pilatus U-28A Draco (N740AF/06-0740)	USAF 318th SOS/27th SOW, Cannon AFB, NM	
70488	Pilatus U-28A Draco (N56EZ/07-0488)	USAF 319th SOS/1st SOW, Hurlburt Field, FL	
70691	Pilatus U-28A Draco (N691PC/07-0691)	USAF 319th SOS/1st SOW, Hurlburt Field, FL	
70711	Pilatus U-28A Draco (N711PN/07-0711)	USAF 319th SOS/1st SOW, Hurlburt Field, FL	
70712	Pilatus U-28A Draco (N609TW/07-0712)	USAF 319th SOS/1st SOW, Hurlburt Field, FL	
70777	Pilatus U-28A Draco (N72DZ/07-0777)	USAF 318th SOS/27th SOW, Cannon AFB, NM	
70779	Pilatus U-28A Draco (N779PC/07-0779)	USAF 319th SOS/1st SOW, Hurlburt Field, FL	
70793	Pilatus U-28A Draco (N96MV/07-0793)	USAF 319th SOS/1st SOW, Hurlburt Field, FL	
70808	Pilatus U-28A Draco (N531MP/07-0808)	USAF 318th SOS/27th SOW, Cannon AFB, NM	
70821	Pilatus U-28A Draco (N821PE/07-0821)	USAF 319th SOS/1st SOW, Hurlburt Field, FL	
70829	Pilatus U-28A Draco (N829PE/07-0829)	USAF 319th SOS/1st SOW, Hurlburt Field, FL	
70838	Pilatus U-28A Draco (N838PE/07-0838)	USAF 319th SOS/1st SOW, Hurlburt Field, FL	
70840	Pilatus U-28A Draco (N840PE/07-0840)	USAF 319th SOS/1st SOW, Hurlburt Field, FL	
80519	Pilatus U-28A Draco (N519PC/08-0519)	USAF 319th SOS/1st SOW, Hurlburt Field, FL	

Notes	Serial	Type (code/other identity)	Owner/operator, location or fate
	80581	Pilatus U-28A Draco (N581PC/08-0581)	USAF 319th SOS/1st SOW, Hurlburt Field, FL
	80646	Pilatus U-28A Draco (N875RJ/08-0646)	USAF 319th SOS/1st SOW, Hurlburt Field, FL
	80700	Pilatus U-28A Draco (N600KP/08-0700)	USAF 319th SOS/1st SOW, Hurlburt Field, FL
	80718	Pilatus U-28A Draco (N824BK/08-0718)	USAF 319th SOS/1st SOW, Hurlburt Field, FL
	80790	Pilatus U-28A Draco (N757ED/08-0790)	USAF 319th SOS/1st SOW, Hurlburt Field, FL
	80809	Pilatus U-28A Draco (N36EG/08-0809)	USAF 319th SOS/1st SOW, Hurlburt Field, FL
	80822	Pilatus U-28A Draco (N822BM/08-0822)	USAF 319th SOS/1st SOW, Hurlburt Field, FL
	80835	Pilatus U-28A Draco (N100MS/08-0835)	USAF 318th SOS/27th SOW, Cannon AFB, NM
	80850	Pilatus U-28A Draco (N850CB/08-0850)	USAF 319th SOS/1st SOW, Hurlburt Field, FL

Boeing C-32

* Please note that there is evidence to suggest that the serials 25001, 86001, 86006 and 96143 are used by more than one airframe.

	09001	Boeing C-32B (00-9001)	USAF 150th SOS/108th Wg, McGuire AFB, NJ
	24452	Boeing C-32B (02-4452)	USAF 150th SOS/108th Wg, McGuire AFB, NJ
	25001	Boeing C-32B (N226G or N610G/02-5001)*	USAF 486th FLTS/46th TW, Eglin AFB, FL
	80001	Boeing C-32A (98-0001)	USAF 1st AS/89th AW, Andrews AFB, MD
	80002	Boeing C-32A (98-0002)	USAF 1st AS/89th AW, Andrews AFB, MD
	86006	Boeing C-32B (N226G or N610G/98-6006)*	USAF 486th FLTS/46th TW, Eglin AFB, FL
	90003	Boeing C-32A (99-0003)	USAF 1st AS/89th AW, Andrews AFB, MD
	90004	Boeing C-32A (99-0004)	USAF 1st AS/89th AW, Andrews AFB, MD
	90015	Boeing C-32A (09-0015)	USAF 1st AS/89th AW, Andrews AFB, MD
	90016	Boeing C-32A (09-0016)	USAF 1st AS/89th AW, Andrews AFB, MD
	90017	Boeing C-32A (09-0017)	USAF 1st AS/89th AW, Andrews AFB, MD
	90018	Boeing C-32A (19-0018)	USAF 1st AS/89th AW, Andrews AFB, MD
	96143	Boeing C-32B (N226G or N610G/99-6143)*	USAF 486th FLTS/46th TW, Eglin AFB, FL

Gulfstream Aerospace C-37 Gulfstream V

	1778	Gulfstream Aerospace C-37A Gulfstream V (04-01778)	US Army OSAC/PAT, Andrews AFB, MD
	1863	Gulfstream Aerospace C-37A Gulfstream V (02-01863)	US Army OSAC/PAT, Andrews AFB, MD
	1942	Gulfstream Aerospace C-37B Gulfstream V (18-1942)	USAF 99th AS/89th AW, Andrews AFB, MD
	1944	Gulfstream Aerospace C-37A Gulfstream V (97-01944)	US Army OSAC/PAT, Andrews AFB, MD
	1947	Gulfstream Aerospace C-37B Gulfstream V (18-1947)	USAF 99th AS/89th AW, Andrews AFB, MD
	10028	Gulfstream Aerospace C-37A Gulfstream V (01-0028)	USAF 65th AS/15th Wg, Hickam AFB, HI
	10065	Gulfstream Aerospace C-37A Gulfstream V (01-0065)	USAF 65th AS/15th Wg, Hickam AFB, HI
	10550	Gulfstream Aerospace C-37B Gulfstream V (11-0550)	USAF 99th AS/89th AW, Andrews AFB, MD
	60500	Gulfstream Aerospace C-37B Gulfstream V (06-0500)	USAF 99th AS/89th AW, Andrews AFB, MD
	70400	Gulfstream Aerospace C-37A Gulfstream V (97-0400)	USAF 99th AS/89th AW, Andrews AFB, MD
	70401	Gulfstream Aerospace C-37A Gulfstream V (97-0401)	USAF 99th AS/89th AW, Andrews AFB, MD
	90402	Gulfstream Aerospace C-37A Gulfstream V (99-0402)	USAF 99th AS/89th AW, Andrews AFB, MD
	90404	Gulfstream Aerospace C-37A Gulfstream V (99-0404)	USAF 99th AS/89th AW, Andrews AFB, MD
	90525	Gulfstream Aerospace C-37B Gulfstream V (09-0525)	USAF 99th AS/89th AW, Andrews AFB, MD

Boeing C-40

	10015	Boeing C-40B (N378BJ/01-0015)	USAF 1st AS/89th AW, Andrews AFB, MD
	10040	Boeing C-40B (N371BJ/01-0040)	USAF 1st AS/89th AW, Andrews AFB, MD
	10041	Boeing C-40B (N374BC/01-0041)	USAF 1st AS/89th AW, Andrews AFB, MD
	20042	Boeing C-40C (N237BA/02-0042)	USAF 1st AS/89th AW, Andrews AFB, MD
	20201	Boeing C-40C (N752BC/02-0201)	USAF 201st AS/113th FW DC ANG, Andrews AFB, MD
	20202	Boeing C-40C (N754BC/02-0202)	USAF 201st AS/113th FW DC ANG, Andrews AFB, MD
	20203	Boeing C-40C (N236BA/02-0203)	USAF 201st AS/113th FW DC ANG, Andrews AFB, MD
	50730	Boeing C-40C (N365BJ/05-0730)	USAF 73rd AS/932nd AW AFRC, Scott AFB, IL
	50932	Boeing C-40C (N366BJ/05-0932)	USAF 73rd AS/932nd AW AFRC, Scott AFB, IL
	54613	Boeing C-40C (N368BJ/05-4613)	USAF 73rd AS/932nd AW AFRC, Scott AFB, IL
	90540	Boeing C-40C (N736JS/09-0540)	USAF 73rd AS/932nd AW AFRC, Scott AFB, IL

Boeing 767-2C/KC-46A Pegasus

	16001	Boeing 767-2LKC (N461FT/11-46001)	Boeing, Everett, for USAF
	16002	Boeing KC-46A Pegasus (N462KC/11-46002)	Boeing, Seattle, for USAF

Serial	Type (code/other identity)	Owner/operator, location or fate	Notes
16003	Boeing 767-2LKC (N463FT/11-46003)	Boeing, Everett, for USAF	
16004	Boeing KC-46A Pegasus (N464KC/11-46004)	Boeing, Seattle, for USAF	
56005	Boeing KC-46A Pegasus (N842BA/15-46005)	USAF 418th FLTS/412th TW, Edwards AFB, CA	
56006	Boeing 767-2LKC (N884BA/15-46006)	Boeing, Everett, for USAF	
56007	Boeing KC-46A Pegasus (15-46007)	Boeing, Everett, for USAF	
56008	Boeing KC-46A Pegasus (15-46008)	Boeing, Everett, for USAF	
56009	Boeing KC-46A Pegasus (N50217/15-46009)	USAF 344th ARW/22nd ARW, McConnell AFB, KS	
56010	Boeing KC-46A Pegasus (15-46010)	Boeing, Everett, for USAF	
56011	Boeing KC-46A Pegasus (N6009F/15-46011)	Boeing, Seattle, for USAF	
66012	Boeing KC-46A Pegasus (16-46012)	Boeing, Everett, for USAF	
66013	Boeing KC-46A Pegasus (16-46013)	Boeing, Everett, for USAF	
66014	Boeing KC-46A Pegasus (N5573S/16-46014)	Boeing, Everett, for USAF	
66015	Boeing KC-46A Pegasus (N6009F/16-46015)	Boeing, Seattle, for USAF	
66016	Boeing KC-46A Pegasus (N6018N/16-46016)	USAF 344th ARW/22nd ARW, McConnell AFB, KS	
66017	Boeing KC-46A Pegasus (N5573S/16-46017)	USAF 344th ARW/22nd ARW, McConnell AFB, KS	
66018	Boeing KC-46A Pegasus (N5514J/16-46018)	USAF 133rd ARS/157th ARW, Pease ANGB, NH ANG	
66019	Boeing KC-46A Pegasus (N5514K/16-46019)	USAF 133rd ARS/157th ARW, Pease ANGB, NH ANG	
66020	Boeing KC-46A Pegasus (N5514V/16-46020)	Boeing, Everett, for USAF	
66021	Boeing KC-46A Pegasus (N5514X/16-46021)	Boeing, Everett, for USAF	
66022	Boeing KC-46A Pegasus (N5573S/16-46022)	USAF 344th ARW/22nd ARW, McConnell AFB, KS	
66023	Boeing KC-46A Pegasus (N6018N/16-46023)	USAF 344th ARW/22nd ARW, McConnell AFB, KS	
76024	Boeing KC-46A Pegasus (N5514J/17-46024)	Boeing, Everett, for USAF	
76025	Boeing KC-46A Pegasus (17-46025)	Boeing, Seattle, for USAF	
76026	Boeing KC-46A Pegasus (N6018N/17-46026)	USAF 344th ARW/22nd ARW, McConnell AFB, KS	
76027	Boeing KC-46A Pegasus (17-46027)	USAF 56th ARS/97th AMW, Altus AFB, OK	
76028	Boeing KC-46A Pegasus (N55141/17-46028)	USAF 56th ARS/97th AMW, Altus AFB, OK	
76029	Boeing KC-46A Pegasus (N55141/17-46029)	USAF 133rd ARS/157th ARW, Pease ANGB, NH ANG	
76030	Boeing KC-46A Pegasus (N6009F/17-46030)	USAF 344th ARW/22nd ARW, McConnell AFB, KS	
76031	Boeing KC-46A Pegasus (N5513X/17-46031)	USAF 344th ARW/22nd ARW, McConnell AFB, KS	
76032	Boeing KC-46A Pegasus (N5016R/17-46032)	USAF 56th ARS/97th AMW, Altus AFB, OK	
76033	Boeing KC-46A Pegasus (17-46033)	USAF 56th ARS/97th AMW, Altus AFB, OK	
76034	Boeing KC-46A Pegasus (17-46034)	USAF 133rd ARS/157th ARW, Pease ANGB, NH ANG	
76035	Boeing KC-46A Pegasus (17-46035)	USAF 344th ARW/22nd ARW, McConnell AFB, KS	
76036	Boeing KC-46A Pegasus (17-46036)	USAF 344th ARW/22nd ARW, McConnell AFB, KS	
76037	Boeing KC-46A Pegasus (17-46037)	USAF 344th ARW/22nd ARW, McConnell AFB, KS	
76038	Boeing KC-46A Pegasus (N5020K/17-46038)	USAF 344th ARW/22nd ARW, McConnell AFB, KS	
86039	Boeing KC-46A Pegasus (N1785B/18-46039)	USAF 344th ARW/22nd ARW, McConnell AFB, KS	
86040	Boeing KC-46A Pegasus (18-46040)	USAF 344th ARW/22nd ARW, McConnell AFB, KS	
86041	Boeing KC-46A Pegasus (N50217/18-46041)	Boeing, Everett, for USAF	
86042	Boeing KC-46A Pegasus (N5512A/18-46042)	USAF 344th ARW/22nd ARW, McConnell AFB, KS	
86043	Boeing KC-46A Pegasus (N1785B/18-46043)	USAF 344th ARW/22nd ARW, McConnell AFB, KS	
86044	Boeing KC-46A Pegasus (18-46044)	Boeing, Seattle, for USAF	
86045	Boeing KC-46A Pegasus (N1794B/18-46045)	Boeing, Seattle, for USAF	
86046	Boeing KC-46A Pegasus (N55077/18-46046)	Boeing, Seattle, for USAF	
86047	Boeing KC-46A Pegasus (N5016R/18-46047)	Boeing, Seattle, for USAF	
86048	Boeing KC-46A Pegasus (N1794B/18-46048)	USAF 344th ARW/22nd ARW, McConnell AFB, KS	
86049	Boeing KC-46A Pegasus (N5510E/18-46049)	Boeing, Seattle, for USAF	
86050	Boeing KC-46A Pegasus (N5511Z/18-46050)	Boeing, Seattle, for USAF	
86051	Boeing KC-46A Pegasus (N6018N/18-46051)	Boeing, Everett, for USAF	
86052	Boeing KC-46A Pegasus (N55077/18-46052)	Boeing, Everett, for USAF	
86053	Boeing KC-46A Pegasus (18-46053)	Boeing, Everett, for USAF	
96054	Boeing KC-46A Pegasus (19-46054)	Boeing, Everett, for USAF	
96055	Boeing KC-46A Pegasus (19-46055)	Boeing, Everett, for USAF	
96056	Boeing KC-46A Pegasus (19-46056)	USAF (on order)	
96057	Boeing KC-46A Pegasus (19-46057)	USAF (on order)	
96058	Boeing KC-46A Pegasus (19-46058)	USAF (on order)	
96059	Boeing KC-46A Pegasus (19-46059)	USAF (on order)	
96060	Boeing KC-46A Pegasus (19-46060)	USAF (on order)	

US-BASED USAF AIRCRAFT

Notes	Serial	Type (code/other identity)	Owner/operator, location or fate
	96061	Boeing KC-46A Pegasus (19-46061)	USAF (on order)
	96062	Boeing KC-46A Pegasus (19-46062)	USAF (on order)
	96063	Boeing KC-46A Pegasus (19-46063)	USAF (on order)
	96064	Boeing KC-46A Pegasus (19-46064)	USAF (on order)
	96065	Boeing KC-46A Pegasus (19-46065)	USAF (on order)
	96066	Boeing KC-46A Pegasus (19-46066)	USAF (on order)
	96067	Boeing KC-46A Pegasus (19-46067)	USAF (on order)
	96068	Boeing KC-46A Pegasus (19-46068)	USAF (on order)
	Boeing B-52H Stratofortress		
	00001	Boeing B-52H Stratofortress (60-0001) [LA] *r*	USAF 96th BS/2nd BW, Barksdale AFB, LA
	00002	Boeing B-52H Stratofortress (60-0002) [LA] *gn* [2 BW]	USAF 96th BS/2nd BW, Barksdale AFB, LA
	00003	Boeing B-52H Stratofortress (60-0003) [BD] *or/bl*	USAF 93rd BS/307th BW AFRC, Barksdale AFB, LA
	00004	Boeing B-52H Stratofortress (60-0004) [MT] *r/y*	USAF 23rd BS/5th BW, Minot AFB, ND
	00005	Boeing B-52H Stratofortress (60-0005) [MT] *r/y* [5 BW]	USAF 23rd BS/5th BW, Minot AFB, ND
	00007	Boeing B-52H Stratofortress (60-0007) [MT] *r/y*	USAF 23rd BS/5th BW, Minot AFB, ND
	00008	Boeing B-52H Stratofortress (60-0008) [LA] *bl* [8th AF]	USAF 20th BS/2nd BW, Barksdale AFB, LA
	00009	Boeing B-52H Stratofortress (60-0009) [MT] *y/bk* [69 BS]	USAF 69th BS/5th BW, Minot AFB, ND
	00011	Boeing B-52H Stratofortress (60-0011) [BD] *or/bl* [11 BS]	USAF 93rd BS/307th BW AFRC, Barksdale AFB, LA
	00012	Boeing B-52H Stratofortress (60-0012) [MT] *y/bk*	USAF 69th BS/5th BW, Minot AFB, ND
	00013	Boeing B-52H Stratofortress (60-0013) [LA] *bl*	USAF 20th BS/2nd BW, Barksdale AFB, LA
	00015	Boeing B-52H Stratofortress (60-0015) [BD] *or/bl*	USAF 93rd BS/307th BW AFRC, Barksdale AFB, LA
	00017	Boeing B-52H Stratofortress (60-0017) [MT] *y/bk*	USAF 69th BS/5th BW, Minot AFB, ND
	00018	Boeing B-52H Stratofortress (60-0018) [MT] *y/bk*	USAF 69th BS/5th BW, Minot AFB, ND
	00021	Boeing B-52H Stratofortress (60-0021) [LA] *r*	USAF 96th BS/2nd BW, Barksdale AFB, LA
	00022	Boeing B-52H Stratofortress (60-0022) [LA] *r*	USAF 96th BS/2nd BW, Barksdale AFB, LA
	00023	Boeing B-52H Stratofortress (60-0023) [MT] *y/bk*	USAF 69th BS/5th BW, Minot AFB, ND
	00024	Boeing B-52H Stratofortress (60-0024) [LA] *bl*	USAF 20th BS/2nd BW, Barksdale AFB, LA
	00025	Boeing B-52H Stratofortress (60-0025) [LA] *bl*	USAF 20th BS/2nd BW, Barksdale AFB, LA
	00026	Boeing B-52H Stratofortress (60-0026) [MT] *r/y*	USAF 23rd BS/5th BW, Minot AFB, ND
	00028	Boeing B-52H Stratofortress (60-0028) [LA] *r*	USAF 96th BS/2nd BW, Barksdale AFB, LA
	00029	Boeing B-52H Stratofortress (60-0029) [MT] *r/y* [93 BS]	USAF 23rd BS/5th BW, Minot AFB, ND AFB, LA
	00031	Boeing B-52H Stratofortress (60-0031) [OT] *or/w*	USAF 49th TES/53rd TEG, Barksdale AFB, LA
	00032	Boeing B-52H Stratofortress (60-0032) [MT] *y/bk*	USAF 69th BS/5th BW, Minot AFB, ND
	00033	Boeing B-52H Stratofortress (60-0033) [MT] *r/y*	USAF 23rd BS/5th BW, Minot AFB, ND
	00034	Boeing B-52H Stratofortress (60-0034) [BD] *or/bl*	USAF 93rd BS/307th BW AFRC, Barksdale AFB, LA
	00035	Boeing B-52H Stratofortress (60-0035) [BD] *or/bl*	USAF 93rd BS/307th BW AFRC, Barksdale AFB, LA
	00036	Boeing B-52H Stratofortress (60-0036) [ED]	USAF 419th FLTS/412th TW, Edwards AFB, CA
	00037	Boeing B-52H Stratofortress (60-0037) [MT] *r/y*	USAF 23rd BS/5th BW, Minot AFB, ND
	00038	Boeing B-52H Stratofortress (60-0038) [BD] *or/bl*	USAF 93rd BS/307th BW AFRC, Barksdale AFB, LA
	00041	Boeing B-52H Stratofortress (60-0041) [BD] *or/bl*	USAF 93rd BS/307th BW AFRC, Barksdale AFB, LA
	00042	Boeing B-52H Stratofortress (60-0042) [BD] *or/bl*	USAF 93rd BS/307th BW AFRC, Barksdale AFB, LA
	00044	Boeing B-52H Stratofortress (60-0044) [MT] *r/y*	USAF 23rd BS/5th BW, Minot AFB, ND
	00045	Boeing B-52H Stratofortress (60-0045) [BD] *or/bl* [307 OG]	USAF 93rd BS/307th BW AFRC, Barksdale AFB, LA
	00048	Boeing B-52H Stratofortress (60-0048) [LA] *bl*	USAF 20th BS/2nd BW, Barksdale AFB, LA
	00050	Boeing B-52H Stratofortress (60-0050) [ED]	USAF 419th FLTS/412th TW, Edwards AFB, CA
	00051	Boeing B-52H Stratofortress (60-0051) [OT] *or/w* [49 TES]	USAF 49th TES/53rd TEG, Barksdale AFB, LA

Serial	Type (code/other identity)	Owner/operator, location or fate	Notes
00052	Boeing B-52H Stratofortress (60-0052) [LA] *bl*	USAF 20th BS/2nd BW, Barksdale AFB, LA	
00054	Boeing B-52H Stratofortress (60-0054) [LA] *bl*	USAF 20th BS/2nd BW, Barksdale AFB, LA	
00055	Boeing B-52H Stratofortress (60-0055) [MT] *r/y* [5 OG]	USAF 23rd BS/5th BW, Minot AFB, ND	
00056	Boeing B-52H Stratofortress (60-0056) [MT] *r/y*	USAF 23rd BS/5th BW, Minot AFB, ND	
00057	Boeing B-52H Stratofortress (60-0057) [BD] *or/bl* [340 WPS]	USAF 93rd BS/307th BW AFRC, Barksdale AFB, LA	
00058	Boeing B-52H Stratofortress (60-0058) [LA] *bl*	USAF 20th BS/2nd BW, Barksdale AFB, LA	
00059	Boeing B-52H Stratofortress (60-0059) [LA] *r* [96 BS]	USAF 96th BS/2nd BW, Barksdale AFB, LA	
00060	Boeing B-52H Stratofortress (60-0060) [MT] *r/y*	USAF 23rd BS/5th BW, Minot AFB, ND	
00061	Boeing B-52H Stratofortress (60-0061) [BD] *or/bl* [307 BW]	USAF 93rd BS/307th BW AFRC, Barksdale AFB, LA	
00062	Boeing B-52H Stratofortress (60-0062) [LA] *bl*	USAF 20th BS/2nd BW, Barksdale AFB, LA	
10001	Boeing B-52H Stratofortress (61-0001) [MT] *y/bk*	USAF 69th BS/5th BW, Minot AFB, ND	
10002	Boeing B-52H Stratofortress (61-0002) [LA] *gn* [2D OG]	USAF 96th BS/2nd BW, Barksdale AFB, LA	
10003	Boeing B-52H Stratofortress (61-0003) [MT] *y/bk*	USAF 69th BS/5th BW, Minot AFB, ND	
10004	Boeing B-52H Stratofortress (61-0004) [LA] *r*	USAF 96th BS/2nd BW, Barksdale AFB, LA	
10005	Boeing B-52H Stratofortress (61-0005) [MT] *y/bk*	USAF 69th BS/5th BW, Minot AFB, ND	
10006	Boeing B-52H Stratofortress (61-0006) [LA] *r*	USAF 96th BS/2nd BW, Barksdale AFB, LA	
10007	Boeing B-52H Stratofortress (61-0007) [MT] *y/bk*	USAF 69th BS/5th BW, Minot AFB, ND	
10008	Boeing B-52H Stratofortress (61-0008) [BD] *or/bl*	USAF 93rd BS/307th BW AFRC, Barksdale AFB, LA	
10010	Boeing B-52H Stratofortress (61-0010) [LA] *or/bl* [343 BS]	USAF 93rd BS/307th BW AFRC, Barksdale AFB, LA	
10011	Boeing B-52H Stratofortress (61-0011) [BD] *or/bl*	USAF 93rd BS/307th BW AFRC, Barksdale AFB, LA	
10012	Boeing B-52H Stratofortress (61-0012) [LA] *r*	USAF 96th BS/2nd BW, Barksdale AFB, LA	
10013	Boeing B-52H Stratofortress (61-0013) [LA] *bl*	USAF 20th BS/2nd BW, Barksdale AFB, LA	
10014	Boeing B-52H Stratofortress (61-0014) [MT] *y/bk*	USAF 69th BS/5th BW, Minot AFB, ND	
10015	Boeing B-52H Stratofortress (61-0015) [LA] *r*	USAF 96th BS/2nd BW, Barksdale AFB, LA	
10016	Boeing B-52H Stratofortress (61-0016) [LA] *r*	USAF 96th BS/2nd BW, Barksdale AFB, LA	
10017	Boeing B-52H Stratofortress (61-0017) [BD] *or/bl*	USAF 93rd BS/307th BW AFRC, Barksdale AFB, LA	
10018	Boeing B-52H Stratofortress (61-0018) [MT] *y/bk*	USAF 69th BS/5th BW, Minot AFB, ND	
10019	Boeing B-52H Stratofortress (61-0019) [LA] *bl*	USAF 20th BS/2nd BW, Barksdale AFB, LA	
10020	Boeing B-52H Stratofortress (61-0020) [LA] *bl* [20 BS]	USAF 20th BS/2nd BW, Barksdale AFB, LA	
10021	Boeing B-52H Stratofortress (61-0021) [BD] *or/bl*	USAF 93rd BS/307th BW AFRC, Barksdale AFB, LA	
10028	Boeing B-52H Stratofortress (61-0028) [OT] *y/w* [49 TES]	USAF 49th TES/53rd TEG, Barksdale AFB, LA	
10029	Boeing B-52H Stratofortress (61-0029) [BD] *or/bl* [93 BS]	USAF 93rd BS/307th BW AFRC, Barksdale AFB, LA	
10031	Boeing B-52H Stratofortress (61-0031) [BD] *or/bl*	USAF 93rd BS/307th BW AFRC, Barksdale AFB, LA	
10032	Boeing B-52H Stratofortress (61-0032) [MT] *r/y*	USAF 23rd BS/5th BW, Minot AFB, ND	
10034	Boeing B-52H Stratofortress (61-0034) [MT] *r/y*	USAF 23rd BS/5th BW, Minot AFB, ND	
10035	Boeing B-52H Stratofortress (61-0035) [MT] *r/y*	USAF 23rd BS/5th BW, Minot AFB, ND	
10036	Boeing B-52H Stratofortress (61-0036) [LA] *r*	USAF 96th BS/2nd BW, Barksdale AFB, LA	
10038	Boeing B-52H Stratofortress (61-0038) [BD] *or/bl*	USAF 93rd BS/307th BW AFRC, Barksdale AFB, LA	
10039	Boeing B-52H Stratofortress (61-0039) [MT] *y/bk*	USAF 69th BS/5th BW, Minot AFB, ND	
10040	Boeing B-52H Stratofortress (61-0040) [MT] *r/y*	USAF 23rd BS/5th BW, Minot AFB, ND	

Lockheed C-130

Serial	Type (code/other identity)	Owner/operator, location or fate	Notes
00162	Lockheed MC-130H Combat Talon II (90-0162)	USAF 15th SOS/1st SOW, Hurlburt Field, FL	
00164	Lockheed AC-130U Spooky (90-0164)	USAF 4th SOS/1st SOW, Hurlburt Field, FL	
00165	Lockheed AC-130U Spooky (90-0165)	USAF 4th SOS/1st SOW, Hurlburt Field, FL	
00166	Lockheed AC-130U Spooky (90-0166)	*To 309th AMARG, September 2019*	
00167	Lockheed AC-130U Spooky (90-0167)	*To 309th AMARG, December 2019*	

Notes	Serial	Type (code/other identity)	Owner/operator, location or fate
	00322	Lockheed C-130H-2 Hercules (80-0322) y/bk	USAF 118th AS/103rd AW, Bradley ANGB, CT ANG
	00324	Lockheed C-130H-2 Hercules (80-0324)	USAF 186th AS/120th AW, Great Falls, MT ANG
	00326	Lockheed C-130H-2 Hercules (80-0326) y/bk	USAF 118th AS/103rd AW, Bradley ANGB, CT ANG
	01057	Lockheed C-130H-2 Hercules (90-1057) bl	USAF 142nd AS/166th AW, New Castle County, DE ANG
	01058	Lockheed AC-130W Stinger II (90-1058)	USAF 16th SOS/27th SOW, Cannon AFB, NM
	01791	Lockheed C-130H-2 Hercules (90-1791)	USAF 180th AS/139th AW, Rosencrans Memorial, MO ANG
	01792	Lockheed C-130H-2 Hercules (90-1792)	USAF 180th AS/139th AW, Rosencrans Memorial, MO ANG
	01793	Lockheed C-130H-2 Hercules (90-1793)	USAF 180th AS/139th AW, Rosencrans Memorial, MO ANG
	01794	Lockheed C-130H-2 Hercules (90-1794)	USAF 180th AS/139th AW, Rosencrans Memorial, MO ANG
	01795	Lockheed C-130H-2 Hercules (90-1795)	USAF 180th AS/139th AW, Rosencrans Memorial, MO ANG
	01796	Lockheed C-130H-2 Hercules (90-1796)	USAF 180th AS/139th AW, Rosencrans Memorial, MO ANG
	01797	Lockheed C-130H-2 Hercules (90-1797)	USAF 180th AS/139th AW, Rosencrans Memorial, MO ANG
	01798	Lockheed C-130H-2 Hercules (90-1798)	USAF 180th AS/139th AW, Rosencrans Memorial, MO ANG
	01934	Lockheed EC-130J Commando Solo III (00-1934)	USAF 193rd SOS/193rd SOW, Harrisburg, PA ANG
	02103	Lockheed HC-130N Combat King (90-2103)	*To 309th AMARG, December 2019*
	05700	Lockheed C-130J-30 Hercules II (10-5700) w/bk	USAF 61st AS/19th AW Little Rock AFB, AR
	05701	Lockheed C-130J-30 Hercules II (10-5701) r [317 AG]	USAF 39th AS/317th AW, Dyess AFB, TX
	05714	Lockheed MC-130J Commando II (10-5714)	USAF 17th SOS/353rd SOG, Kadena AB, Japan
	05716	Lockheed HC-130J Combat King II (10-5716) [DM]	USAF 79th RQS/355th Wg, Davis-Monthan AFB, AZ
	05717	Lockheed HC-130J Combat King II (10-5717) [FT]	USAF 71st RQS/347th RQG, Moody AFB, GA
	05728	Lockheed C-130J-30 Hercules II (10-5728)	USAF 62nd AS/314th AW, Little Rock AFB, AR
	05771	Lockheed C-130J-30 Hercules II (10-5771) w/bk	USAF 61st AS/19th AW Little Rock AFB, AR
	09107	Lockheed C-130H-2 Hercules (90-9107) bl/r	USAF 757th AS/910th AW AFRC, Youngstown ARS, OH
	09108	Lockheed C-130H-2 Hercules (90-9108) bl/r	USAF 757th AS/910th AW AFRC, Youngstown ARS, OH
	10626	Lockheed C-130H-2 Hercules (81-0626) r	USAF 164th AS/179th AW, Mansfield, OH ANG
	10629	Lockheed C-130H-2 Hercules (81-0629) r $	USAF 154th TS/189th AW, Little Rock, AR ANG
	11231	Lockheed C-130H-2 Hercules (91-1231) w/bk	USAF 165th AS/123rd AW, Standiford Field, KY ANG
	11232	Lockheed C-130H-2 Hercules (91-1232) w/bk	USAF 165th AS/123rd AW, Standiford Field, KY ANG
	11233	Lockheed C-130H-2 Hercules (91-1233) w/bk	USAF 165th AS/123rd AW, StandifordField, KY ANG
	11234	Lockheed C-130H-2 Hercules (91-1234) w/bk	USAF 165th AS/123rd AW, Standiford Field, KY ANG
	11235	Lockheed C-130H-2 Hercules (91-1235) w/bk	USAF 165th AS/123rd AW, Standiford Field, KY ANG
	11236	Lockheed C-130H-2 Hercules (91-1236) w/bk	USAF 165th AS/123rd AW, Standiford Field, KY ANG
	11237	Lockheed C-130H-2 Hercules (91-1237) w/bk	USAF 165th AS/123rd AW, Standiford Field, KY ANG
	11238	Lockheed C-130H-2 Hercules (91-1238) w/bk $	USAF 165th AS/123rd AW, Standiford Field, KY ANG
	11461	Lockheed C-130J-30 Hercules II (01-1461) gn	USAF 115th AS/146th AW, Channel Island ANGS, CA ANG
	11462	Lockheed C-130J-30 Hercules II (01-1462) gn	USAF 115th AS/146th AW, Channel Island ANGS, CA ANG
	11652	Lockheed C-130H-2 Hercules (91-1652)	USAF 180th AS/139th AW, Rosencrans Memorial, MO ANG

Serial	Type (code/other identity)	Owner/operator, location or fate	Notes
11653	Lockheed C-130H-2 Hercules (91-1653)	USAF 180th AS/139th AW, Rosencrans Memorial, MO ANG	
11935	Lockheed EC-130J Commando Solo III (01-1935)	USAF 193rd SOS/193rd SOW, Harrisburg, PA ANG	
14862	Lockheed EC-130H Compass Call (64-14862) [DM]	To 309th AMARG, August 2019	
14866	Lockheed C-130H Hercules (64-14866)	Withdrawn from use, Fort Benning, 2019	
15719	Lockheed HC-130J Combat King II (11-5719) [DM]	USAF 79th RQS/355th Wg, Davis-Monthan AFB, AZ	
15725	Lockheed HC-130J Combat King II (11-5725) [FT]	USAF 71st RQS/347th RQG, Moody AFB, GA	
15727	Lockheed HC-130J Combat King II (11-5727) [FT]	USAF 71st RQS/347th RQG, Moody AFB, GA	
15729	Lockheed MC-130J Commando II (11-5729)	USAF 522nd SOS/27th SOW, Cannon AFB, NM	
15731	Lockheed MC-130J Commando II (11-5731)	USAF 67th SOS/352nd SOG, RAF Mildenhall, UK	
15732	Lockheed C-130J-30 Hercules II (11-5732)	USAF 317th AW, Dyess AFB, TX	
15733	Lockheed MC-130J Commando II (11-5733)	LMTAS, Marietta, GA	
15734	Lockheed C-130J-30 Hercules II (11-5734) w/bk	USAF 61st AS/19th AW Little Rock AFB, AR	
15735	Lockheed MC-130J Commando II (11-5735)	USAF 522nd SOS/27th SOW, Cannon AFB, NM	
15736	Lockheed C-130J-30 Hercules II (11-5736) [RS] bl/w $	USAF 37th AS/86th AW, Ramstein AB, Germany	
15737	Lockheed MC-130J Commando II (11-5737)	USAF 67th SOS/352nd SOG, RAF Mildenhall, UK	
15738	Lockheed C-130J-30 Hercules II (11-5738) w/bk	USAF 41st AS/19th AW Little Rock AFB, AR	
15740	Lockheed C-130J-30 Hercules II (11-5740)	USAF 317th AW, Dyess AFB, TX	
15745	Lockheed C-130J-30 Hercules II (11-5745) w/bk	USAF 41st AS/19th AW Little Rock AFB, AR	
15748	Lockheed C-130J-30 Hercules II (11-5748) w/bk	USAF 61st AS/19th AW Little Rock AFB, AR	
15752	Lockheed C-130J-30 Hercules II (11-5752) w/bk	USAF 61st AS/19th AW Little Rock AFB, AR	
15765	Lockheed HC-130J Combat King II (11-5765) [FT]	USAF 71st RQS/347th RQG, Moody AFB, GA	
19141	Lockheed C-130H-2 Hercules (91-9141) bl/w	USAF 357th AS/908th AW AFRC, Maxwell AFB, AL	
19142	Lockheed C-130H-2 Hercules (91-9142) bl/w	USAF 357th AS/908th AW AFRC, Maxwell AFB, AL	
19143	Lockheed C-130H-2 Hercules (91-9143) bl/w	USAF 357th AS/908th AW AFRC, Maxwell AFB, AL	
19144	Lockheed C-130H-2 Hercules (91-9144) bl/w	USAF 357th AS/908th AW AFRC, Maxwell AFB, AL	
20055	Lockheed C-130H-2 Hercules (82-0055) r	Withdrawn from use, 2019	
20056	Lockheed C-130H-2 Hercules (82-0056)	USAF 16th SOS/27th SOW, Cannon AFB, NM	
20061	Lockheed C-130H-2 Hercules (82-0061)	Withdrawn from use, July 2019	
20314	Lockheed C-130J-30 Hercules II (02-0314)	USAF 41st AS/19th AW Little Rock AFB, AR	
20547	Lockheed C-130H-2 Hercules (92-0547) bl/w	USAF 192nd AS/152nd AW, Reno, NV ANG	
20548	Lockheed C-130H-2 Hercules (92-0548) bl/w	USAF 192nd AS/152nd AW, Reno, NV ANG	
20549	Lockheed C-130H-2 Hercules (92-0549) bl/w	USAF 192nd AS/152nd AW, Reno, NV ANG	
20550	Lockheed C-130H-2 Hercules (92-0550) bl	USAF 700th AS/94th AW AFRC, Dobbins ARB, GA	
20551	Lockheed C-130H-2 Hercules (92-0551) bl	USAF 700th AS/94th AW AFRC, Dobbins ARB, GA	
20552	Lockheed C-130H-2 Hercules (92-0552) bl	USAF 700th AS/94th AW AFRC, Dobbins ARB, GA	
20553	Lockheed C-130H-2 Hercules (92-0553) bl/w	USAF 192nd AS/152nd AW, Reno, NV ANG	
20554	Lockheed C-130H-2 Hercules (92-0554) bl/w	USAF 192nd AS/152nd AW, Reno, NV ANG	
21094	Lockheed LC-130H Hercules (92-1094)	USAF 139th AS/109th AW, Schenectady, NY ANG	
21095	Lockheed LC-130H Hercules (92-1095)	USAF 139th AS/109th AW, Schenectady, NY ANG	
21434	Lockheed C-130J-30 Hercules II (02-1434) r	USAF 143rd AS/143rd AW, Quonset, RI ANG	
21451	Lockheed C-130H-3 Hercules (92-1451) or/bk	USAF 169th AS/182nd AW, Peoria, IL ANG	
21452	Lockheed C-130H-3 Hercules (92-1452) or/bk	USAF 169th AS/182nd AW, Peoria, IL ANG	
21453	Lockheed C-130H-3 Hercules (92-1453) bl/bk	USAF 181st AS/136th AW, NAS Dallas, TX ANG	
21454	Lockheed C-130H-3 Hercules (92-1454) bl/bk	USAF 181st AS/136th AW, NAS Dallas, TX ANG	
21463	Lockheed C-130J Hercules II (02-1463) gn	USAF 115th AS/146th AW, Channel Island ANGS, CA ANG	
21464	Lockheed C-130J Hercules II (02-1464) gn	USAF 115th AS/146th AW, Channel Island ANGS, CA ANG	
21531	Lockheed C-130H-3 Hercules (92-1531) y/bk	USAF 187th AS/153rd AW, Cheyenne, WY ANG	
21532	Lockheed C-130H-3 Hercules (92-1532) y/bk	USAF 187th AS/153rd AW, Cheyenne, WY ANG	
21533	Lockheed C-130H-3 Hercules (92-1533) y/bk	USAF 187th AS/153rd AW, Cheyenne, WY ANG	
21534	Lockheed C-130H-3 Hercules (92-1534) y/bk	USAF 187th AS/153rd AW, Cheyenne, WY ANG	
21535	Lockheed C-130H-3 Hercules (92-1535) y/bk	USAF 187th AS/153rd AW, Cheyenne, WY ANG	
21536	Lockheed C-130H-3 Hercules (92-1536) y/bk	USAF 187th AS/153rd AW, Cheyenne, WY ANG	
21537	Lockheed C-130H-3 Hercules (92-1537) y/bk	USAF 187th AS/153rd AW, Cheyenne, WY ANG	
21538	Lockheed C-130H-3 Hercules (92-1538) y/bk	USAF 187th AS/153rd AW, Cheyenne, WY ANG	
22104	Lockheed HC-130N Combat King (92-2104)	USAF 39th RQS/920th RQW AFRC, PatrickSFB, FL	

Notes	Serial	Type (code/other identity)	Owner/operator, location or fate
	23021	Lockheed C-130H-2 Hercules (92-3021) *bl/r*	USAF 757th AS/910th AW AFRC, Youngstown ARS, OH
	23022	Lockheed C-130H-2 Hercules (92-3022) *bl/r*	USAF 757th AS/910th AW AFRC, Youngstown ARS, OH
	23023	Lockheed C-130H-2 Hercules (92-3023) *bl/r*	USAF 757th AS/910th AW AFRC, Youngstown ARS, OH
	23024	Lockheed C-130H-2 Hercules (92-3024) *bl/r*	USAF 757th AS/910th AW AFRC, Youngstown ARS, OH
	23281	Lockheed C-130H-3 Hercules (92-3281) *pr/w*	USAF 96th AS/934th AW AFRC, Minneapolis/ St Paul, MN
	23282	Lockheed C-130H-3 Hercules (92-3282) *pr/w*	USAF 96th AS/934th AW AFRC, Minneapolis/ St Paul, MN
	23283	Lockheed C-130H-3 Hercules (92-3283) *pr/w*	USAF 96th AS/934th AW AFRC, Minneapolis/ St Paul, MN
	23284	Lockheed C-130H-3 Hercules (92-3284) *pr/w* $	USAF 96th AS/934th AW AFRC, Minneapolis/ St Paul, MN
	23285	Lockheed C-130H-3 Hercules (92-3285) *pr/w*	USAF 96th AS/934th AW AFRC, Minneapolis/ St Paul, MN
	23286	Lockheed C-130H-3 Hercules (92-3286) *pr/w*	USAF 96th AS/934th AW AFRC, Minneapolis/ St Paul, MN
	23287	Lockheed C-130H-3 Hercules (92-3287) *pr/w*	USAF 96th AS/934th AW AFRC, Minneapolis/ St Paul, MN
	23288	Lockheed C-130H-3 Hercules (92-3288) *pr/w*	USAF 96th AS/934th AW AFRC, Minneapolis/ St Paul, MN
	25753	Lockheed AC-130J Ghostrider (12-5753)	USAF 73rd SOS/1st SOW, Hurlburt Field, FL
	25754	Lockheed AC-130J Ghostrider (12-5754)	LMTAS, Marietta, GA
	25755	Lockheed HC-130J Combat King II (12-5755)	USAF 415th SOS/58th SOW, Kirtland AFB, NM
	25756	Lockheed C-130J-30 Hercules (12-5756) *w/bk*	USAF 61st AS/19th AW Little Rock AFB, AR
	25757	Lockheed MC-130J Commando II (12-5757)	USAF
	25759	Lockheed MC-130J Commando II (12-5759)	USAF
	25760	Lockheed MC-130J Commando II (12-5760)	USAF 67th SOS/352nd SOG, RAF Mildenhall, UK
	25761	Lockheed MC-130J Commando II (12-5761)	USAF 17th SOS/353rd SOG, Kadena AB, Japan
	25762	Lockheed MC-130J Commando II (12-5762)	USAF 17th SOS/353rd SOG, Kadena AB, Japan
	25763	Lockheed MC-130J Commando II (12-5763)	USAF 17th SOS/353rd SOG, Kadena AB, Japan
	25768	Lockheed HC-130J Combat King II (12-5768) [FT]	USAF 71st RQS/347th RQG, Moody AFB, GA
	25769	Lockheed HC-130J Combat King II (12-5769) [FT]	USAF 71st RQS/347th RQG, Moody AFB, GA
	25772	Lockheed AC-130J Ghostrider (12-5772)	USAF 73rd SOS/1st SOW, Hurlburt Field, FL
	25773	Lockheed HC-130J Combat King II (12-5773) [FT]	USAF 71st RQS/347th RQG, Moody AFB, GA
	28155	Lockheed C-130J-30 Hercules (02-8155) *r*	USAF 815th AS/403rd AW AFRC, Keesler AFB, MO
	30487	Lockheed C-130H-2 Hercules (83-0487)	USAF 139th AS/109th AW, Schenectady, NY ANG
	30489	Lockheed C-130H-2 Hercules (83-0489)	USAF 139th AS/109th AW, Schenectady, NY ANG
	30490	Lockheed LC-130H Hercules (83-0490)	USAF 139th AS/109th AW, Schenectady, NY ANG
	30491	Lockheed LC-130H Hercules (83-0491)	USAF 139th AS/109th AW, Schenectady, NY ANG
	30492	Lockheed LC-130H Hercules (83-0492)	USAF 139th AS/109th AW, Schenectady, NY ANG
	30493	Lockheed LC-130H Hercules (83-0493)	USAF 139th AS/109th AW, Schenectady, NY ANG
	31036	Lockheed C-130H-3 Hercules (93-1036) *bl*	USAF 700th AS/94th AW AFRC, Dobbins ARB, GA
	31037	Lockheed C-130H-3 Hercules (93-1037) *bl*	USAF 700th AS/94th AW AFRC, Dobbins ARB, GA
	31038	Lockheed C-130H-3 Hercules (93-1038) *bl*	USAF 700th AS/94th AW AFRC, Dobbins ARB, GA
	31039	Lockheed C-130H-3 Hercules (93-1039) *bl*	USAF 700th AS/94th AW AFRC, Dobbins ARB, GA
	31040	Lockheed C-130H-3 Hercules (93-1040) *bl*	USAF 700th AS/94th AW AFRC, Dobbins ARB, GA
	31041	Lockheed C-130H-3 Hercules (93-1041) *pr/w*	USAF 731st AS/302nd AW AFRC, Peterson AFB, CO
	31096	Lockheed LC-130H Hercules (93-1096)	USAF 139th AS/109th AW, Schenectady, NY ANG
	31455	Lockheed C-130H-3 Hercules (93-1455) *bl/bk*	USAF 181st AS/136th AW, NAS Dallas, TX ANG
	31456	Lockheed C-130H-3 Hercules (93-1456) *bl/bk*	USAF 181st AS/136th AW, NAS Dallas, TX ANG
	31457	Lockheed C-130H-3 Hercules (93-1457) *bl/bk*	USAF 181st AS/136th AW, NAS Dallas, TX ANG
	31459	Lockheed C-130H-3 Hercules (93-1459) *bl/bk*	USAF 181st AS/136th AW, NAS Dallas, TX ANG
	31561	Lockheed C-130H-3 Hercules (93-1561) *r/bk*	USAF 158th AS/165th AW, Savannah, GA ANG
	31562	Lockheed C-130H-3 Hercules (93-1562) *r/bk*	USAF 158th AS/165th AW, Savannah, GA ANG
	31563	Lockheed C-130H-3 Hercules (93-1563) *r/bk*	USAF 158th AS/165th AW, Savannah, GA ANG

Serial	Type (code/other identity)	Owner/operator, location or fate	Notes
31580	Lockheed EC-130H Compass Call (73-1580) [DM]	USAF 43rd ECS/55th ECG, Davis-Monthan AFB, AZ	
31581	Lockheed EC-130H Compass Call (73-1581) [DM] $	USAF 43rd ECS/55th ECG, Davis-Monthan AFB, AZ	
31583	Lockheed EC-130H Compass Call (73-1583) [DM] r	USAF 43rd ECS/55th ECG, Davis-Monthan AFB, AZ	
31584	Lockheed EC-130H Compass Call (73-1584) [DM]	USAF 43rd ECS/55th ECG, Davis-Monthan AFB, AZ	
31585	Lockheed EC-130H Compass Call (73-1585) [DM]	USAF 43rd ECS/55th ECG, Davis-Monthan AFB, AZ	
31586	Lockheed EC-130H Compass Call (73-1586) [DM] bl	USAF 43rd ECS/55th ECG, Davis-Monthan AFB, AZ	
31587	Lockheed EC-130H Compass Call (73-1587) [DM]	*Withdrawn from use, February 2020*	
31588	Lockheed EC-130H Compass Call (73-1588) [DM]	USAF 43rd ECS/55th ECG, Davis-Monthan AFB, AZ	
31590	Lockheed EC-130H Compass Call (73-1590) [DM]	USAF 43rd ECS/55th ECG, Davis-Monthan AFB, AZ	
31592	Lockheed EC-130H Compass Call (73-1592) [DM] bl	*Withdrawn from use, September 2018*	
31594	Lockheed EC-130H Compass Call (73-1594) [DM]	USAF 41st ECS/55th ECG, Davis-Monthan AFB, AZ	
31595	Lockheed EC-130H Compass Call (73-1595) [DM]	USAF 43rd ECS/55th ECG, Davis-Monthan AFB, AZ	
32041	Lockheed C-130H-3 Hercules (93-2041) or/bk	USAF 169th AS/182nd AW, Peoria, IL ANG	
32042	Lockheed C-130H-3 Hercules (93-2042) or/bk	USAF 169th AS/182nd AW, Peoria, IL ANG	
32105	Lockheed HC-130N Combat King (93-2105)	*To 309th AMARG, December 2019*	
32106	Lockheed HC-130N Combat King (93-2106)	USAF 39th RQS/920th RQW AFRC, Patrick SFB, FL	
33300	Lockheed LC-130H Hercules (73-3300)	USAF 139th AS/109th AW, Schenectady, NY ANG	
35770	Lockheed MC-130J Commando II (13-5770)	USAF 9th SOS/27th SOW, Cannon AFB, NM	
35775	Lockheed MC-130J Commando II (13-5775)	USAF 17th SOS/353rd SOG, Kadena AB, Japan	
35776	Lockheed MC-130J Commando II (13-5776)	USAF 17th SOS/353rd SOG, Kadena AB, Japan	
35777	Lockheed MC-130J Commando II (13-5777)	USAF 17th SOS/353rd SOG, Kadena AB, Japan	
35778	Lockheed MC-130J Commando II (13-5778)	USAF 67th SOS/352nd SOG, RAF Mildenhall, UK	
35782	Lockheed HC-130J Combat King II (13-5782) [FT]	USAF 71st RQS/347th RQG, Moody AFB, GA	
35783	Lockheed AC-130J Ghostrider (13-5783)	USAF 73rd SOS/1st SOW, Hurlburt Field, FL	
35784	Lockheed C-130J-30 Hercules II (13-5784) w/bk	USAF 61st AS/19th AW Little Rock AFB, AR	
35785	Lockheed HC-130J Combat King II (13-5785) [FT]	USAF 71st RQS/347th RQG, Moody AFB, GA	
35786	Lockheed MC-130J Commando II (13-5786)	USAF 67th SOS/352nd SOG, RAF Mildenhall, UK	
35790	Lockheed HC-130J Combat King II (13-5790) [FT]	USAF 71st RQS/347th RQG, Moody AFB, GA	
37311	Lockheed C-130H-3 Hercules (93-7311) bl/w	USAF 192nd AS/152nd AW, Reno, NV ANG	
37312	Lockheed C-130H-3 Hercules (93-7312) or/bk	USAF 169th AS/182nd AW, Peoria, IL ANG	
37313	Lockheed C-130H-3 Hercules (93-7313) bl/w	USAF 192nd AS/152nd AW, Reno, NV ANG	
37314	Lockheed C-130H-3 Hercules (93-7314) bl/w	USAF 192nd AS/152nd AW, Reno, NV ANG	
38154	Lockheed C-130J-30 Hercules II (03-8154) r	USAF 815th AS/403rd AW AFRC, Keesler AFB, MO	
40206	Lockheed C-130H-2 Hercules (84-0206) bl	USAF 142nd AS/166th AW, New Castle County, DE ANG	
40207	Lockheed C-130H-2 Hercules (84-0207) bl	USAF 142nd AS/166th AW, New Castle County, DE ANG	
40208	Lockheed C-130H-2 Hercules (84-0208) bl	USAF 142nd AS/166th AW, New Castle County, DE ANG	
40209	Lockheed C-130H-2 Hercules (84-0209) bl	USAF 142nd AS/166th AW, New Castle County, DE ANG	
40210	Lockheed C-130H-2 Hercules (84-0210) bl	USAF 142nd AS/166th AW, New Castle County, DE ANG	
40212	Lockheed C-130H-2 Hercules (84-0212) bl	USAF 142nd AS/166th AW, New Castle County, DE ANG	
40213	Lockheed C-130H-2 Hercules (84-0213) bl	USAF 142nd AS/166th AW, New Castle County, DE ANG	
41659	Lockheed C-130H Hercules (74-1659) y/bk	USAF 118th AS/103rd AW, Bradley ANGB, CT ANG	
41660	Lockheed C-130H Hercules (74-1660) r	*Withdrawn from use, September 2019*	
41661	Lockheed C-130H Hercules (74-1661)	USAF 186th AS/120th AW, Great Falls, MT ANG	
41663	Lockheed C-130H Hercules (74-1663) r	*To Ramstein for BDRT, April 2019*	

Notes	Serial	Type (code/other identity)	Owner/operator, location or fate
	41664	Lockheed C-130H Hercules (74-1664) y/bk	USAF 118th AS/103rd AW, Bradley ANGB, CT ANG
	41666	Lockheed C-130H Hercules (74-1666) r	USAF 164th AS/179th AW, Mansfield, OH ANG
	41669	Lockheed C-130H Hercules (74-1669) y/bk	USAF 118th AS/103rd AW, Bradley ANGB, CT ANG
	41670	Lockheed C-130H Hercules (74-1670)	USAF 186th AS/120th AW, Great Falls, MT ANG
	41671	Lockheed C-130H Hercules (74-1671)	USAF 186th AS/120th AW, Great Falls, MT ANG
	41674	Lockheed C-130H Hercules (74-1674) r	USAF 164th AS/179th AW, Mansfield, OH ANG
	41679	Lockheed C-130H Hercules (74-1679)	USAF 186th AS/120th AW, Great Falls, MT ANG
	41680	Lockheed C-130H Hercules (74-1680) y/bk	USAF 118th AS/103rd AW, Bradley ANGB, CT ANG
	41682	Lockheed C-130H Hercules (74-1682) y/bk	USAF 118th AS/103rd AW, Bradley ANGB, CT ANG
	41685	Lockheed C-130H Hercules (74-1685) y/bk	USAF 118th AS/103rd AW, Bradley ANGB, CT ANG
	41687	Lockheed C-130H Hercules (74-1687) y/bk	USAF 118th AS/103rd AW, Bradley ANGB, CT ANG
	41688	Lockheed C-130H Hercules (74-1688)	USAF 186th AS/120th AW, Great Falls, MT ANG
	41691	Lockheed C-130H Hercules (74-1691)	USAF 186th AS/120th AW, Great Falls, MT ANG
	41692	Lockheed C-130H Hercules (74-1692) r	USAF 164th AS/179th AW, Mansfield, OH ANG
	42061	Lockheed C-130H Hercules (74-2061) r	USAF 164th AS/179th AW, Mansfield, ANG
	42065	Lockheed C-130H Hercules (74-2065)	USAF 186th AS/120th AW, Great Falls, MT ANG
	42067	Lockheed C-130H Hercules (74-2067) r	USAF 164th AS/179th AW, Mansfield, OH ANG
	42069	Lockheed C-130H Hercules (74-2069) y/bk	USAF 118th AS/103rd AW, Bradley ANGB, CT ANG
	42132	Lockheed C-130H Hercules (74-2132)	USAF 186th AS/120th AW, Great Falls, MT ANG
	42134	Lockheed C-130H Hercules (74-2134) y/bk	USAF 118th AS/103rd AW, Bradley ANGB, CT ANG
	43142	Lockheed C-130J-30 Hercules II (04-3142) [RS] bl/w	USAF 37th AS/86th AW, Ramstein AB, Germany
	43143	Lockheed C-130J-30 Hercules II (04-3143) r	USAF 39th AS/317th AW, Dyess AFB, TX
	45787	Lockheed AC-130J Ghostrider (14-5787)	USAF 73rd SOS/1st SOW, Hurlburt Field, FL
	45788	Lockheed C-130J-30 Hercules II (14-5788) w/bk	USAF 61st AS/19th AW Little Rock AFB, AR
	45789	Lockheed AC-130J Ghostrider (14-5789)	USAF 15th SOS/1st SOW, Hurlburt Field, FL
	45791	Lockheed C-130J-30 Hercules II (14-5791) w/bk	USAF 61st AS/19th AW Little Rock AFB, AR
	45793	Lockheed MC-130J Commando II (14-5793)	USAF 17th SOS/353rd SOG, Kadena AB, Japan
	45795	Lockheed MC-130J Commando II (14-5795)	USAF 9th SOS/27th SOW, Cannon AFB, NM
	45796	Lockheed C-130J-30 Hercules II (14-5796) w/bk	USAF 61st AS/19th AW Little Rock AFB, AR
	45797	Lockheed AC-130J Ghostrider (14-5797)	USAF 73rd SOS/1st SOW, Hurlburt Field, FL
	45800	Lockheed MC-130J Commando II (14-5800)	USAF 9th SOS/27th SOW, Cannon AFB, NM
	45802	Lockheed C-130J-30 Hercules II (14-5802) $	USAF 62nd AS/314th AW, Little Rock AFB, AR
	45803	Lockheed AC-130J Ghostrider (14-5803)	USAF 415th SOS/58th SOW, Kirtland AFB, NM
	45804	Lockheed C-130J-30 Hercules II (14-5804) y	USAF 48th AS/314th AW, Little Rock AFB, AR
	45805	Lockheed MC-130J Commando II (14-5805)	USAF 9th SOS/27th SOW, Cannon AFB, NM
	45807	Lockheed C-130J-30 Hercules II (14-5807) [YJ] r [374 AW]	USAF 36th AS/374th AW, Yokota AB, Japan
	45809	Lockheed AC-130J Ghostrider (14-5809)	USAF 73rd SOS/1st SOW, Hurlburt Field, FL
	45815	Lockheed HC-130J Combat King II (14-5815) [AK]	USAF 211th RQS/176th Wg, Elmendorf AFB, AK ANG
	45864	Lockheed MC-130J Commando II (14-5864)	LMTAS, Marietta, GA
	46701	Lockheed C-130H-3 Hercules (94-6701) or/bk	USAF 169th AS/182nd AW, Peoria, IL ANG
	46702	Lockheed C-130H-3 Hercules (94-6702) or/bk	USAF 169th AS/182nd AW, Peoria, IL ANG
	46703	Lockheed C-130H-3 Hercules (94-6703) or/bk	USAF 169th AS/182nd AW, Peoria, IL ANG
	46705	Lockheed C-130H-3 Hercules (94-6705) r/bk	USAF 158th AS/165th AW, Savannah, GA ANG
	46706	Lockheed C-130H-3 Hercules (94-6706) r/bk	USAF 158th AS/165th AW, Savannah, GA ANG
	46707	Lockheed C-130H-3 Hercules (94-6707) r/bk	USAF 158th AS/165th AW, Savannah, GA ANG
	46708	Lockheed C-130H-3 Hercules (94-6708) r/bk	USAF 158th AS/165th AW, Savannah, GA ANG
	47310	Lockheed C-130H-3 Hercules (94-7310) pr/w	USAF 731st AS/302nd AW AFRC, Peterson AFB, CO
	47315	Lockheed C-130H-3 Hercules (94-7315) pr/w	USAF 731st AS/302nd AW AFRC, Peterson AFB, CO
	47316	Lockheed C-130H-3 Hercules (94-7316) pr/w	USAF 731st AS/302nd AW AFRC, Peterson AFB, CO
	47317	Lockheed C-130H-3 Hercules (94-7317) pr/w	USAF 731st AS/302nd AW AFRC, Peterson AFB, CO
	47318	Lockheed C-130H-3 Hercules (94-7318) pr/w	USAF 731st AS/302nd AW AFRC, Peterson AFB, CO
	47319	Lockheed C-130H-3 Hercules (94-7319) pr/w	USAF 731st AS/302nd AW AFRC, Peterson AFB, CO

Serial	Type (code/other identity)	Owner/operator, location or fate	Notes
47320	Lockheed C-130H-3 Hercules (94-7320) pr/w	USAF 731st AS/302nd AW AFRC, Peterson AFB, CO	
47321	Lockheed C-130H-3 Hercules (94-7321) r/bk	USAF 158th AS/165th AW, Savannah, GA ANG	
48151	Lockheed C-130J Hercules II (94-8151) r	USAF 815th AS/403rd AW AFRC, Keesler AFB, MO	
48152	Lockheed C-130J Hercules II (94-8152) r	USAF 815th AS/403rd AW AFRC, Keesler AFB, MO	
48153	Lockheed C-130J-30 Hercules II (04-8153) r	USAF 815th AS/403rd AW AFRC, Keesler AFB, MO	
50011	Lockheed MC-130H Combat Talon II (85-0011)	USAF 15th SOS/1st SOW, Hurlburt Field, FL	
50963	Lockheed C-130H Hercules (65-0963)	Withdrawn from use, 2019	
50966	Lockheed C-130H Hercules (65-0966)	Withdrawn from use, 2019	
50967	Lockheed EC-130H Compass Call (65-0967) [DM]	USAF 43rd ECS/55th ECG, Davis-Monthan AFB, AZ	
50974	Lockheed HC-130P Combat King (65-0974)	USAF 102nd RQS/106th RQW, Suffolk Field, NY ANG	
50978	Lockheed HC-130P Combat King (65-0978)	USAF 102nd RQS/106th RQW, Suffolk Field, NY ANG	
50980	Lockheed WC-130H Hercules (65-0980)	Withdrawn from use, 2019	
50984	Lockheed WC-130H Hercules (65-0984)	Scrapped at Savannnah, April 2019	
50985	Lockheed WC-130H Hercules (65-0985)	Withdrawn from use, 2018	
51001	Lockheed C-130H-3 Hercules (95-1001) pr/bk	USAF 109th AS/133rd AW, Minneapolis, MN ANG	
51002	Lockheed C-130H-3 Hercules (95-1002) pr/bk	USAF 109th AS/133rd AW, Minneapolis, MN ANG	
51363	Lockheed C-130H-2 Hercules (85-1363) bl/bk	USAF 181st AS/136th AW, NAS Dallas, TX ANG	
51364	Lockheed C-130H-2 Hercules (85-1364) bl/bk	USAF 181st AS/136th AW, NAS Dallas, TX ANG	
51365	Lockheed C-130H-2 Hercules (85-1365) bl/bk	USAF 181st AS/136th AW, NAS Dallas, TX ANG	
51366	Lockheed C-130H-2 Hercules (85-1366) bl/bk	USAF 181st AS/136th AW, NAS Dallas, TX ANG	
51367	Lockheed C-130H-2 Hercules (85-1367) r	USAF 154th TS/189th AW, Little Rock, AR ANG	
51435	Lockheed C-130J-30 Hercules II (05-1435) r	USAF 143rd AS/143rd AW, Quonset, RI ANG	
51436	Lockheed C-130J-30 Hercules II (05-1436) r	USAF 143rd AS/143rd AW, Quonset, RI ANG	
51465	Lockheed C-130J-30 Hercules II (05-1465) gn	USAF 115th AS/146th AW, Channel Island ANGS, CA ANG	
51466	Lockheed C-130J-30 Hercules II (05-1466) gn	USAF 115th AS/146th AW, Channel IslandANGS, CA ANG	
53145	Lockheed C-130J-30 Hercules II (05-3145) w/bk	USAF 53rd AS/19th AW Little Rock AFB, AR	
53146	Lockheed C-130J-30 Hercules II (05-3146) w/bk	USAF 53rd AS/19th AW Little Rock AFB, AR	
53147	Lockheed C-130J-30 Hercules II (05-3147) gn	USAF 41st AS/19th AW Little Rock AFB, AR	
55810	Lockheed C-130J-30 Hercules II (15-5810) [YJ] r [374 OG]	USAF 36th AS/374th AW, Yokota AB, Japan	
55811	Lockheed AC-130J Ghostrider (15-5811)	USAF 73rd SOS/1st SOW, Hurlburt Field, FL	
55813	Lockheed C-130J-30 Hercules II (15-5813) [YJ] r [36 AS]	USAF 36th AS/374th AW, Yokota AB, Japan	
55817	Lockheed C-130J-30 Hercules II (15-5817) [YJ] r	USAF 36th AS/374th AW, Yokota AB, Japan	
55822	Lockheed C-130J-30 Hercules II (15-5822) [RS] bl/w	USAF 37th AS/86th AW, Ramstein AB, Germany	
55825	Lockheed MC-130J Commando II (15-5825)	USAF 15th SOS/1st SOW, Hurlburt Field, FL	
55826	Lockheed C-130J-30 Hercules II (15-5826)	USAF 40th AS/317th AW, Dyess AFB, TX	
55827	Lockheed HC-130J Combat King II (15-5827) [AK]	USAF 211th RQS/176th Wg, Elmendorf AFB, AK ANG	
55828	Lockheed C-130J-30 Hercules II (15-5828) gn/bk	USAF 41st AS/19th AW Little Rock AFB, AR	
55829	Lockheed HC-130J Combat King II (15-5829) [AK]	USAF 211th RQS/176th Wg, Elmendorf AFB, AK ANG	
55831	Lockheed C-130J-30 Hercules II (15-5831) [RS] bl/w	USAF 37th AS/86th AW, Ramstein AB, Germany	
55832	Lockheed HC-130J Combat King II (15-5832) [AK]	USAF 211th RQS/176th Wg, Elmendorf AFB, AK ANG	
55842	Lockheed HC-130J Combat King II (15-5842) [CA]	USAF 130th RQS/129th RQW, Moffett Field CA ANG	
56709	Lockheed C-130H-3 Hercules (95-6709) pr/y	USAF 130th AS/130th AW, Yeager Int'l, Charleston, WV ANG	
56710	Lockheed C-130H-3 Hercules (95-6710) pr/y	USAF 130th AS/130th AW, Yeager Int'l, Charleston, WV ANG	
56711	Lockheed C-130H-3 Hercules (95-6711) pr/y	USAF 130th AS/130th AW, Yeager Int'l, Charleston, WV ANG	

Notes	Serial	Type (code/other identity)	Owner/operator, location or fate
	56712	Lockheed C-130H-3 Hercules (95-6712) pr/y	USAF 130th AS/130th AW, Yeager Int'l, Charleston, WV ANG
	58152	Lockheed C-130J-30 Hercules II (05-8152) r	USAF 815th AS/403rd AW AFRC, Keesler AFB, MO
	58156	Lockheed C-130J-30 Hercules II (05-8156) r	USAF 815th AS/403rd AW AFRC, Keesler AFB, MO
	58157	Lockheed C-130J-30 Hercules II (05-8157) r	USAF 815th AS/403rd AW AFRC, Keesler AFB, MO
	58158	Lockheed C-130J-30 Hercules II (05-8158) r	USAF 815th AS/403rd AW AFRC, Keesler AFB, MO
	60212	Lockheed MC-130P Combat Shadow (66-0212) bl	Preserved at Castle AFB, September 2019
	60222	Lockheed HC-130P Combat King (66-0222)	USAF 102nd RQS/106th RQW, Suffolk Field, NY ANG
	60411	Lockheed C-130H-2 Hercules (86-0411)	Withdrawn from use at Sheppard AFB, 2019
	60418	Lockheed C-130H-2 Hercules (86-0418)	USAF 186th AS/120th AW, Great Falls, MT ANG
	60419	Lockheed C-130H-2 Hercules (86-0419) r	USAF 164th AS/179th AW, Mansfield, OH ANG
	61003	Lockheed C-130H-3 Hercules (96-1003) pr/bk	USAF 109th AS/133rd AW, Minneapolis, MN ANG
	61004	Lockheed C-130H-3 Hercules (96-1004) pr/bk	USAF 109th AS/133rd AW, Minneapolis, MN ANG
	61005	Lockheed C-130H-3 Hercules (96-1005) pr/bk	USAF 109th AS/133rd AW, Minneapolis, MN ANG
	61006	Lockheed C-130H-3 Hercules (96-1006) pr/bk	USAF 109th AS/133rd AW, Minneapolis, MN ANG
	61007	Lockheed C-130H-3 Hercules (96-1007) pr/bk	USAF 109th AS/133rd AW, Minneapolis, MN ANG
	61008	Lockheed C-130H-3 Hercules (96-1008) pr/bk	USAF 109th AS/133rd AW, Minneapolis, MN ANG
	61437	Lockheed C-130J-30 Hercules II (06-1437) r	USAF 143rd AS/143rd AW, Quonset, RI ANG
	61438	Lockheed C-130J-30 Hercules II (06-1438) r	USAF 143rd AS/143rd AW, Quonset, RI ANG
	61467	Lockheed C-130J-30 Hercules II (06-1467) gn	USAF 115th AS/146th AW, Channel Island ANGS, CA ANG
	61699	Lockheed MC-130H Combat Talon II (86-1699)	USAF 15th SOS/1st SOW, Hurlburt Field, FL
	63171	Lockheed C-130J-30 Hercules II (06-3171) bl	USAF 40th AS/317th AW, Dyess AFB, TX
	63301	Lockheed LC-130H Hercules (76-3301)	USAF 139th AS/109th AW, Schenectady, NY ANG
	63302	Lockheed LC-130H Hercules (76-3302)	USAF 139th AS/109th AW, Schenectady, NY ANG
	64631	Lockheed C-130J-30 Hercules II (06-4631) w/bk	USAF 41st AS/19th AW Little Rock AFB, AR
	64632	Lockheed C-130J-30 Hercules II (06-4632) y/bk	USAF 41st AS/19th AW Little Rock AFB, AR
	64633	Lockheed C-130J-30 Hercules II (06-4633) [YJ] r	USAF 36th AS/374th AW, Yokota AB, Japan
	64634	Lockheed C-130J-30 Hercules II (06-4634) w/bk	USAF 41st AS/19th AW Little Rock AFB, AR
	65300	Lockheed WC-130J Hercules II (96-5300)	USAF 53rd WRS/403rd AW AFRC, Keesler AFB, MO
	65301	Lockheed WC-130J Hercules II (96-5301)	USAF 53rd WRS/403rd AW AFRC, KeeslerAFB, MO
	65302	Lockheed WC-130J Hercules II (96-5302)	USAF 53rd WRS/403rd AW AFRC, KeeslerAFB, MO
	65833	Lockheed C-130J-30 Hercules II (16-5833) [YJ] r [5 AF]	USAF 36th AS/374th AW, Yokota AB, Japan
	65834	Lockheed C-130J-30 Hercules II (16-5834)	USAF 40th AS/317th AW, Dyess AFB, TX
	65835	Lockheed AC-130J Ghostrider (16-5835)	USAF 73rd SOS/1st SOW, Hurlburt Field, FL
	65837	Lockheed AC-130J Ghostrider (16-5837)	USAF 4th SOS/1st SOW, Hurlburt Field, FL
	65638	Lockheed C-130J-30 Hercules II (16-5858) [YJ] r	USAF 36th AS/374th AW, Yokota AB, Japan
	65839	Lockheed MC-130J Commando II (16-5839)	USAF 415th SOS/58th SOW, Kirtland AFB, NM
	65840	Lockheed C-130J-30 Hercules II (16-5840) [RS] bl/w $	USAF 37th AS/86th AW, Ramstein AB, Germany
	65641	Lockheed C-130J-30 Hercules II (16-5841) [YJ] r	USAF 36th AS/374th AW, Yokota AB, Japan
	65843	Lockheed C-130J-30 Hercules II (16-5843) [YJ] r	USAF 36th AS/374th AW, Yokota AB, Japan
	65844	Lockheed AC-130J Ghostrider (16-5844)	LMTAS, Marietta, GA
	65846	Lockheed HC-130J Combat King II (16-5846)	LMTAS, Marietta, GA
	65849	Lockheed C-130J-30 Hercules II (16-5849)	USAF 39th AS/317th AW, Dyess AFB, TX
	65850	Lockheed MC-130J Commando II (16-5850)	USAF 9th SOS/27th SOW, Cannon AFB, NM
	65851	Lockheed C-130J-30 Hercules II (16-5851) gn/bk	USAF 41st AS/19th AW Little Rock AFB, AR
	65853	Lockheed C-130J-30 Hercules II (16-5853)	USAF 40th AS/317th AW, Dyess AFB, TX
	65855	Lockheed C-130J-30 Hercules II (16-5855) w/bk	USAF 53rd AS/19th AW Little Rock AFB, AR
	65856	Lockheed C-130J-30 Hercules II (16-5856) r	USAF 39th AS/317th AW, Dyess AFB, TX
	65857	Lockheed HC-130J Combat King II (16-5857) [CA]	USAF 130th RQS/129th RQW, Moffett Field CA ANG
	65858	Lockheed HC-130J Combat King II (16-5858) [CA]	USAF 130th RQS/129th RQW, Moffett Field CA ANG
	65859	Lockheed C-130J-30 Hercules II (05-3146) gn/bk	USAF 41st AS/19th AW Little Rock AFB, AR
	65861	Lockheed AC-130J Ghostrider (16-5861)	LMTAS, Crestview, FL

Serial	Type (code/other identity)	Owner/operator, location or fate	Notes
65862	Lockheed HC-130J Combat King II (16-5862) [CA]	USAF 130th RQS/129th RQW, Moffett Field CA ANG	
65863	Lockheed HC-130J Combat King II (16-5863) [LI]	USAF 102nd RQS/106th RQW, Suffolk Field, NY ANG	
67322	Lockheed C-130H-3 Hercules (96-7322) *pr/y*	USAF 130th AS/130th AW, Yeager Int'l, Charleston, WV ANG	
67323	Lockheed C-130H-3 Hercules (96-7323) *pr/y*	USAF 130th AS/130th AW, Yeager Int'l, Charleston, WV ANG	
67324	Lockheed C-130H-3 Hercules (96-7324) *pr/y*	USAF 130th AS/130th AW, Yeager Int'l, Charleston, WV ANG	
67325	Lockheed C-130H-3 Hercules (96-7325) *pr/w*	USAF 731st AS/302nd AW AFRC, Peterson AFB, CO	
68153	Lockheed EC-130J Commando Solo III (96-8153)	USAF 193rd SOS/193rd SOW, Harrisburg, PA ANG	
68154	Lockheed EC-130J Commando Solo III (96-8154)	USAF 193rd SOS/193rd SOW, Harrisburg, PA ANG	
68159	Lockheed C-130J Hercules II (06-8159) *r*	USAF 815th AS/403rd AW AFRC, Keesler AFB, MO	
68610	Lockheed C-130J-30 Hercules II (06-8610)[YJ] *r*	USAF 36th AS/374th AW, Yokota AB, Japan	
68611	Lockheed C-130J-30 Hercules II (06-8611) [RS] *bl/w*	USAF 37th AS/86th AW, Ramstein AB, Germany	
68612	Lockheed C-130J-30 Hercules II (06-8612) *w/bk*	USAF 61st AS/19th AW Little Rock AFB, AR	
70023	Lockheed MC-130H Combat Talon II (87-0023)	USAF 15th SOS/1st SOW, Hurlburt Field, FL	
70024	Lockheed MC-130H Combat Talon II (87-0024)	USAF 15th SOS/1st SOW, Hurlburt Field, FL	
70125	Lockheed MC-130H Combat Talon II (87-0125)	USAF 15th SOS/1st SOW, Hurlburt Field, FL	
70126	Lockheed MC-130H Combat Talon II (87-0126)	USAF 15th SOS/1st SOW, Hurlburt Field, FL	
70128	Lockheed AC-130U Spooky (87-0128)	USAF 4th SOS/1st SOW, Hurlburt Field, FL	
71351	Lockheed C-130J Hercules II (97-1351)	USAF 62nd AS/314th AW, Little Rock AFB, AR	
71352	Lockheed C-130J Hercules II (97-1352)	USAF 19th AW Little Rock AFB, AR	
71353	Lockheed C-130J Hercules II (97-1353) *r*	USAF 815th AS/403rd AW AFRC, Keesler AFB, MO	
71354	Lockheed C-130J Hercules II (97-1354)	USAF 62nd AS/314th AW, Little Rock AFB, AR	
71468	Lockheed C-130J-30 Hercules II (07-1468) *gn*	USAF 115th AS/146th AW, Channel Island ANGS, CA ANG	
71931	Lockheed EC-130J Commando Solo III (97-1931)	USAF 193rd SOS/193rd SOW, Harrisburg, PA ANG	
73170	Lockheed C-130J-30 Hercules II (07-3170) *bl*	USAF 40th AS/317th AW, Dyess AFB, TX	
74635	Lockheed C-130J-30 Hercules II (07-4635) [RS] *bl/w* $	USAF 37th AS/86th AW, Ramstein AB, Germany	
74636	Lockheed C-130J-30 Hercules II (07-4636) *w/bk*	USAF 41st AS/19th AW Little Rock AFB, AR	
74637	Lockheed C-130J-30 Hercules II (07-4637) *w/bk*	USAF 41st AS/19th AW Little Rock AFB, AR	
74638	Lockheed C-130J-30 Hercules II (07-4638)	USAF 317th AW, Dyess AFB, TX	
74639	Lockheed C-130J-30 Hercules II (07-4639) *w/bk*	USAF 41st AS/19th AW Little Rock AFB, AR	
746310	Lockheed C-130J-30 Hercules II (07-46310) *w/bk*	USAF 41st AS/19th AW Little Rock AFB, AR	
746311	Lockheed C-130J-30 Hercules II (07-46311) *w/bk*	USAF 41st AS/19th AW Little Rock AFB, AR	
746312	Lockheed C-130J-30 Hercules II (07-46312) *w/bk*	USAF 41st AS/19th AW Little Rock AFB, AR	
75303	Lockheed WC-130J Hercules II (97-5303)	USAF 53rd WRS/403rd AW AFRC, Keesler AFB, MO	
75304	Lockheed WC-130J Hercules II (97-5304)	USAF 53rd WRS/403rd AW AFRC, Keesler AFB, MO	
75305	Lockheed WC-130J Hercules II (97-5305)	USAF 53rd WRS/403rd AW AFRC, Keesler AFB, MO	
75306	Lockheed WC-130J Hercules II (97-5306)	USAF 53rd WRS/403rd AW AFRC, Keesler AFB, MO	
75865	Lockheed C-130J-30 Hercules II (17-5865)	USAF 39th AS/317th AW, Dyess AFB, TX	
75867	Lockheed C-130J-30 Hercules II (17-5867)	USAF 61st AS/19th AW Little Rock AFB, AR	
75869	Lockheed MC-130J Commando II (17-5869)	LMTAS, Marietta, GA	
75873	Lockheed HC-130J Combat King II (17-5873) [LI]	USAF 102nd RQS/106th RQW, Suffolk Field, NY ANG	
75876	Lockheed MC-130J Commando II (17-5876)	USAF 9th SOS/27th SOW, Cannon AFB, NM	
75877	Lockheed MC-130J Commando II (17-5877)	LMTAS, Marietta, GA	
75878	Lockheed HC-130J Combat King II (17-5878) [LI]	USAF 102nd RQS/106th RQW, Suffolk Field, NY ANG	
78608	Lockheed C-130J-30 Hercules II (07-8608) [RS] *bl/w* $	USAF 37th AS/86th AW, Ramstein AB, Germany	

Notes	Serial	Type (code/other identity)	Owner/operator, location or fate
	78609	Lockheed C-130J-30 Hercules II (07-8609) [RS] bl/w	USAF 37th AS/86th AW, Ramstein AB, Germany
	78613	Lockheed C-130J-30 Hercules II (07-8613) w/bk	USAF 41st AS/19th AW Little Rock AFB, AR
	78614	Lockheed C-130J-30 Hercules II (07-8614) [RS] bl/w	USAF 37th AS/86th AW, Ramstein AB, Germany
	79281	Lockheed C-130H-2 Hercules (87-9281)	USAF
	79282	Lockheed C-130H-2 Hercules (87-9282)	Withdrawn from use, 2019
	79283	Lockheed C-130H-2 Hercules (87-9283) r	USAF 164th AS/179th AW, Mansfield, OH ANG
	79285	Lockheed C-130H-2 Hercules (87-9285) r	USAF 164th AS/179th AW, Mansfield, OH ANG
	79286	Lockheed AC-130W Stinger II (87-9286)	USAF 16th SOS/27th SOW, Cannon AFB, NM
	79287	Lockheed C-130H-2 Hercules (87-9287) r	USAF 164th AS/179th AW, Mansfield, OH ANG
	79288	Lockheed AC-130W Stinger II (87-9288)	USAF 16th SOS/27th SOW, Cannon AFB, NM
	80191	Lockheed MC-130H Combat Talon II (88-0191)	USAF 15th SOS/1st SOW, Hurlburt Field, FL
	80193	Lockheed MC-130H Combat Talon II (88-0193)	USAF 15th SOS/1st SOW, Hurlburt Field, FL
	80194	Lockheed MC-130H Combat Talon II (88-0194)	USAF 15th SOS/1st SOW, Hurlburt Field, FL
	80195	Lockheed MC-130H Combat Talon II (88-0195)	USAF 15th SOS/1st SOW, Hurlburt Field, FL
	80264	Lockheed MC-130H Combat Talon II (88-0264)	USAF 15th SOS/1st SOW, Hurlburt Field, FL
	81301	Lockheed AC-130W Stinger II (88-1301)	USAF 16th SOS/27th SOW, Cannon AFB, NM
	81302	Lockheed AC-130W Stinger II (88-1302)	USAF 16th SOS/27th SOW, Cannon AFB, NM
	81303	Lockheed AC-130W Stinger II (88-1303)	USAF 16th SOS/27th SOW, Cannon AFB, NM
	81304	Lockheed AC-130W Stinger II (88-1304)	USAF 16th SOS/27th SOW, Cannon AFB, NM
	81305	Lockheed AC-130W Stinger II (88-1305)	USAF 16th SOS/27th SOW, Cannon AFB, NM
	81306	Lockheed MC-130H Combat Talon II (88-1306)	USAF
	81307	Lockheed AC-130W Stinger II (88-1307)	USAF 16th SOS/27th SOW, Cannon AFB, NM
	81308	Lockheed AC-130W Stinger II (88-1308)	USAF 16th SOS/27th SOW, Cannon AFB, NM
	81355	Lockheed C-130J Hercules II (98-1355)	USAF 62nd AS/314th AW, Little Rock AFB, AR
	81356	Lockheed C-130J Hercules II (98-1356)	USAF 62nd AS/314th AW, Little Rock AFB, AR
	81357	Lockheed C-130J Hercules II (98-1357)	USAF 62nd AS/314th AW, Little Rock AFB, AR
	81358	Lockheed C-130J Hercules II (98-1358)	USAF 62nd AS/314th AW, Little Rock AFB, AR
	81803	Lockheed MC-130H Combat Talon II (88-1803)	USAF 15th SOS/1st SOW, Hurlburt Field, FL
	81932	Lockheed EC-130J Commando Solo III (98-1932)	USAF 193rd SOS/193rd SOW, Harrisburg, PA ANG
	83172	Lockheed C-130J-30 Hercules II (08-3172) bl	USAF 40th AS/317th AW, Dyess AFB, TX
	83173	Lockheed C-130J-30 Hercules II (08-3173) bl	USAF 40th AS/317th AW, Dyess AFB, TX
	83175	Lockheed C-130J-30 Hercules II (08-3175) bl	USAF 40th AS/317th AW, Dyess AFB, TX
	83176	Lockheed C-130J-30 Hercules II (08-3176) [RS] bl/w	USAF 37th AS/86th AW, Ramstein AB, Germany
	83177	Lockheed C-130J-30 Hercules II (08-3177) [YJ] r	USAF 36th AS/374th AW, Yokota AB, Japan
	83178	Lockheed C-130J-30 Hercules II (08-3178)	USAF 317th AW, Dyess AFB, TX
	83179	Lockheed C-130J-30 Hercules II (08-3179)	USAF 39th AS/317th AW, Dyess AFB, TX
	84401	Lockheed C-130H-2 Hercules (88-4401) r	USAF 164th AS/179th AW, Mansfield, OH ANG
	84402	Lockheed C-130H-2 Hercules (88-4402) r	USAF 154th TS/189th AW, Little Rock, AR ANG
	84403	Lockheed C-130H-2 Hercules (88-4403)	Withdrawn from use at Sheppard AFB, 2019
	84405	Lockheed C-130H-2 Hercules (88-4405) r	USAF 164th AS/179th AW, Mansfield, OH ANG
	84406	Lockheed C-130H-2 Hercules (88-4406) bl/w	USAF 357th AS/908th AW AFRC, Maxwell AFB, AL
	85307	Lockheed WC-130J Hercules II (98-5307)	USAF 53rd WRS/403rd AW AFRC, Keesler AFB, MO
	85308	Lockheed WC-130J Hercules II (98-5308)	USAF 53rd WRS/403rd AW AFRC, Keesler AFB, MO
	85675	Lockheed C-130J-30 Hercules II (08-5675)	USAF 317th AW, Dyess AFB, TX
	85678	Lockheed C-130J-30 Hercules II (08-5678)	USAF 317th AW, Dyess AFB, TX
	85679	Lockheed C-130J-30 Hercules II (08-5679)	USAF 62nd AS/314th AW, Little Rock AFB, AR
	85683	Lockheed C-130J-30 Hercules II (08-5683)	USAF 317th AW, Dyess AFB, TX
	85684	Lockheed C-130J-30 Hercules II (08-5684)	USAF 317th AW, Dyess AFB, TX
	85685	Lockheed C-130J-30 Hercules II (08-5685) r	USAF 39th AS/317th AW, Dyess AFB, TX
	85686	Lockheed C-130J-30 Hercules II (08-5686)	USAF 317th AW, Dyess AFB, TX
	85691	Lockheed C-130J-30 Hercules II (08-5691) r	USAF 39th AS/317th AW, Dyess AFB, TX
	85692	Lockheed C-130J-30 Hercules II (08-5692) [YJ] r	USAF 36th AS/374th AW, Yokota AB, Japan
	85693	Lockheed C-130J-30 Hercules II (08-5693) r	USAF 39th AS/317th AW, Dyess AFB, TX
	85697	Lockheed MC-130J Commando II (08-5697)	USAF 522nd SOS/27th SOW, Cannon AFB, NM
	85705	Lockheed C-130J-30 Hercules II (08-5705) r	USAF 39th AS/317th AW, Dyess AFB, TX
	85712	Lockheed C-130J-30 Hercules II (08-5712)	USAF 39th AS/317th AW, Dyess AFB, TX
	85715	Lockheed C-130J-30 Hercules II (08-5715)	USAF 317th AW, Dyess AFB, TX

Serial	Type (code/other identity)	Owner/operator, location or fate	Notes
85724	Lockheed C-130J-30 Hercules II (08-5724) *r*	USAF 39th AS/317th AW, Dyess AFB, TX	
85726	Lockheed C-130J-30 Hercules II (08-5726)	USAF 317th AW, Dyess AFB, TX	
85879	Lockheed MC-130J Commando II (18-5879)	LMTAS, Marietta, GA	
85882	Lockheed AC-130J Ghostrider (18-5882)	LMTAS, Crestview, FL	
85884	Lockheed MC-130J Commando II (18-5884)	USAF 9th SOS/27th SOW, Cannon AFB, NM	
85886	Lockheed AC-130J Ghostrider (18-5886)	LMTAS, Crestview, FL	
85888	Lockheed MC-130J Commando II (18-5888)	LMTAS, Marietta, GA	
86201	Lockheed MC-130J Commando II (08-6201)	USAF 9th SOS/27th SOW, Cannon AFB, NM	
86202	Lockheed MC-130J Commando II (08-6202)	USAF 17th SOS/353rd SOG, Kadena AB, Japan	
86203	Lockheed MC-130J Commando II (08-6203)	USAF 9th SOS/27th SOW, Cannon AFB, NM	
86204	Lockheed MC-130J Commando II (08-6204)	USAF 522nd SOS/27th SOW, Cannon AFB, NM	
86205	Lockheed MC-130J Commando II (08-6205)	USAF 67th SOS/352nd SOG, RAF Mildenhall, UK	
86206	Lockheed MC-130J Commando II (08-6206)	USAF 415th SOS/58th SOW, Kirtland AFB, NM	
88601	Lockheed C-130J-30 Hercules II (08-8601) [RS] *bl/w* [86 AW]	USAF 37th AS/86th AW, Ramstein AB, Germany	
88602	Lockheed C-130J-30 Hercules II (08-8602) [RS] *bl/w* [86 OG]	USAF 37th AS/86th AW, Ramstein AB, Germany	
88603	Lockheed C-130J-30 Hercules II (08-8603) [RS] *bl/w* [37 AS]	USAF 37th AS/86th AW, Ramstein AB, Germany	
88604	Lockheed C-130J-30 Hercules II (08-8604) [YJ] *r*	USAF 36th AS/374th AW, Yokota AB, Japan	
88605	Lockheed C-130J-30 Hercules II (08-8605) [YJ] *r*	USAF 36th AS/374th AW, Yokota AB, Japan	
88606	Lockheed C-130J-30 Hercules II (08-8606) *w/bk*	USAF 41st AS/19th AW Little Rock AFB, AR	
88607	Lockheed C-130J-30 Hercules II (08-8607) *r*	USAF 39th AS/317th AW, Dyess AFB, TX	
90108	Lockheed HC-130J Combat King II (09-0108) [OT]	USAF 85th TES/53rd Wg, Eglin AFB, FL	
90109	Lockheed HC-130J Combat King II (09-0109) [FT]	USAF 79th RQS/355th Wg, Davis-Monthan AFB, AZ	
90280	Lockheed MC-130H Combat Talon II (89-0280)	USAF 15th SOS/1st SOW, Hurlburt Field, FL	
90282	Lockheed MC-130H Combat Talon II (89-0282)	USAF 15th SOS/1st SOW, Hurlburt Field, FL	
90283	Lockheed MC-130H Combat Talon II (89-0283)	USAF 15th SOS/1st SOW, Hurlburt Field, FL	
90510	Lockheed AC-130U Spooky (89-0510)	USAF 4th SOS/1st SOW, Hurlburt Field, FL	
90513	Lockheed AC-130U Spooky (89-0513)	*To 309th AMARG, August 2019*	
91051	Lockheed AC-130W Stinger II (89-1051)	USAF 16th SOS/27th SOW, Cannon AFB, NM	
91052	Lockheed AC-130U Spooky (89-1052)	*To 309th AMARG, June 2019*	
91053	Lockheed AC-130U Spooky (89-1053)	USAF 4th SOS/1st SOW, Hurlburt Field, FL	
91054	Lockheed AC-130U Spooky (89-1054)	USAF 4th SOS/1st SOW, Hurlburt Field, FL	
91055	Lockheed C-130H-2 Hercules (89-1055) *bl/w*	USAF 357th AS/908th AW AFRC, Maxwell AFB, AL	
91056	Lockheed AC-130U Spooky (89-1056)	USAF 4th SOS/1st SOW, Hurlburt Field, FL	
91181	Lockheed C-130H-2 Hercules (89-1181) *r/bk*	USAF 158th AS/165th AW, Savannah, GA ANG	
91182	Lockheed C-130H-2 Hercules (89-1182) *bl/bk*	USAF 181st AS/136th AW, NAS Dallas, TX ANG	
91183	Lockheed C-130H-2 Hercules (89-1183) *r*	USAF 154th TS/189th AW, Little Rock, AR ANG	
91184	Lockheed C-130H-2 Hercules (89-1184) *r* $	USAF 154th TS/189th AW, Little Rock, AR ANG	
91185	Lockheed C-130H-2 Hercules (89-1185) *bl/bk*	USAF 181st AS/136th AW, NAS Dallas, TX ANG	
91186	Lockheed C-130H-2 Hercules (89-1186) *r*	USAF 154th TS/189th AW, Little Rock, AR ANG	
91187	Lockheed C-130H-2 Hercules (89-1187) *bl/w*	USAF 357th AS/908th AW AFRC, Maxwell AFB, AL	
91188	Lockheed C-130H-2 Hercules (89-1188) *bl/w*	USAF 357th AS/908th AW AFRC, Maxwell AFB, AL	
91431	Lockheed C-130J-30 Hercules II (99-1431) *r*	USAF 143rd AS/143rd AW, Quonset, RI ANG	
91432	Lockheed C-130J-30 Hercules II (99-1432) *r*	USAF 143rd AS/143rd AW, Quonset, RI ANG	
91433	Lockheed C-130J-30 Hercules II (99-1433) *r*	USAF 143rd AS/143rd AW, Quonset, RI ANG	
91933	Lockheed EC-130J Commando Solo III (99-1933)	USAF 193rd SOS/193rd SOW, Harrisburg, PA ANG	
95309	Lockheed WC-130J Hercules II (95-5309)	USAF 53rd WRS/403rd AW AFRC, Keesler AFB, MO	
95706	Lockheed HC-130J Combat King II (09-5706)	USAF 415th SOS/58th SOW, Kirtland AFB, NM	
95707	Lockheed HC-130J Combat King II (09-5707) [FT]	USAF 71st RQS/347th RQG, Moody AFB, GA	
95708	Lockheed HC-130J Combat King II (09-5708) [FT]	USAF 79th RQS/355th Wg, Davis-Monthan AFB, AZ	
95709	Lockheed HC-130J Combat King II (09-5709) [FT]	USAF 79th RQS/355th Wg, Davis-Monthan AFB, AZ	
95711	Lockheed MC-130J Commando II (09-5711)	USAF 9th SOS/27th SOW, Cannon AFB, NM	
95713	Lockheed MC-130J Commando II (09-5713)	USAF 67th SOS/352nd SOG, RAF Mildenhall, UK	
95829	Lockheed HC-130N Combat King (69-5829)	USAF 39th RQS/920th RQW AFRC, Patrick SFB, FL	
96207	Lockheed MC-130J Commando II (09-6207)	USAF 67th SOS/352nd SOG, RAF Mildenhall, UK	

Notes	Serial	Type (code/other identity)	Owner/operator, location or fate
	96208	Lockheed MC-130J Commando II (09-6208)	USAF 415th SOS/58th SOW, Kirtland AFB, NM
	96209	Lockheed MC-130J Commando II (09-6209) [58 SOW]	USAF 415th SOS/58th SOW, Kirtland AFB, NM
	96210	Lockheed MC-130J Commando II (09-6210)	USAF 15th SOS/1st SOW, Hurlburt Field, FL
	99102	Lockheed C-130H-2 Hercules (89-9102) *r*	USAF 154th TS/189th AW, Little Rock, AR ANG
	99103	Lockheed C-130H-2 Hercules (89-9103) *bl/w*	USAF 357th AS/908th AW AFRC, Maxwell AFB, AL
	99104	Lockheed C-130H-2 Hercules (89-9104) *bl/r*	USAF 757th AS/910th AW AFRC, Youngstown ARS, OH
	99105	Lockheed C-130H-2 Hercules (89-9105) *bl/r*	USAF 757th AS/910th AW AFRC, Youngstown ARS, OH
	99106	Lockheed C-130H-2 Hercules (89-9106) *bl/r*	USAF 757th AS/910th AW AFRC, Youngstown ARS, OH
	Boeing C-135		
	00313	Boeing KC-135R Stratotanker (60-0313)	USAF 22nd ARW, McConnell AFB, KS
	00314	Boeing KC-135R Stratotanker (60-0314) *r/w*	USAF 74th ARS/434th ARW AFRC, Grissom AFB, IN
	00315	Boeing KC-135R Stratotanker (60-0315) *w/bl*	USAF 126th ARS/128th ARW, Mitchell Field, WI ANG
	00316	Boeing KC-135R Stratotanker (60-0316) *bl/bk*	USAF 191st ARS/151st ARW, Salt Lake City, UT ANG
	00318	Boeing KC-135R Stratotanker (60-0318)	USAF 314th ARS/940th ARW, Beale AFB, CA
	00320	Boeing KC-135R Stratotanker (60-0320) *y/bl*	USAF 6th ARW, MacDill AFB, FL
	00322	Boeing KC-135R Stratotanker (60-0322) *bl*	USAF 72nd ARS/434th ARW AFRC, Grissom AFB, IN
	00323	Boeing KC-135R Stratotanker (60-0323)	USAF 314th ARS/940th ARW, Beale AFB, CA
	00324	Boeing KC-135R Stratotanker (60-0324) [D] *r/w/bl*	USAF 351st ARS/100th ARW, RAF Mildenhall, UK
	00328	Boeing KC-135R Stratotanker (60-0328) *y/r*	USAF 54th ARS/97th AMW, Altus AFB, OK
	00329	Boeing KC-135R Stratotanker (60-0329) [HH] *y/bk*	USAF 203rd ARS/15th Wg, Hickam AFB, HI ANG
	00331	Boeing KC-135R Stratotanker (60-0331)	USAF 314th ARS/940th ARW, Beale AFB, CA
	00332	Boeing KC-135R Stratotanker (60-0332) [AK] *bl/y*	USAF 168th ARS/168th ARW, Eielson AFB, AK ANG
	00333	Boeing KC-135R Stratotanker (60-0333)	USAF 92nd ARW, Fairchild AFB, WA
	00334	Boeing KC-135R Stratotanker (60-0334) [AK] *bl/y*	USAF 168th ARS/168th ARW, Eielson AFB, AK ANG
	00335	Boeing KC-135T Stratotanker (60-0335)	USAF 92nd ARW, Fairchild AFB, WA
	00336	Boeing KC-135T Stratotanker (60-0336) *y/bl*	USAF 6th ARW, MacDill AFB, FL
	00337	Boeing KC-135T Stratotanker (60-0337) *y/bl*	USAF 6th ARW, MacDill AFB, FL
	00339	Boeing KC-135T Stratotanker (60-0339)	USAF 92nd ARW, Fairchild AFB, WA
	00341	Boeing KC-135R Stratotanker (60-0341)	USAF 153rd ARS/186th AW, Meridian, MS ANG
	00342	Boeing KC-135T Stratotanker (60-0342) *y/bl*	USAF 6th ARW, MacDill AFB, FL
	00343	Boeing KC-135T Stratotanker (60-0343)	USAF 22nd ARW, McConnell AFB, KS
	00344	Boeing KC-135T Stratotanker (60-0344)	USAF
	00345	Boeing KC-135T Stratotanker (60-0345) *bk/y* $	USAF 171st ARS/127th Wg, Selfridge ANGB, MI ANG
	00346	Boeing KC-135T Stratotanker (60-0346) *bk/y*	USAF 171st ARS/127th Wg, Selfridge ANGB, MI ANG
	00347	Boeing KC-135R Stratotanker (60-0347) *r/w*	USAF 166th ARS/121st ARW, Rickenbacker ANGB, OH ANG
	00348	Boeing KC-135R Stratotanker (60-0348) *y/r*	USAF 54th ARS/97th AMW, Altus AFB, OK
	00349	Boeing KC-135R Stratotanker (60-0349)	USAF
	00350	Boeing KC-135R Stratotanker (60-0350) *y/r*	USAF 54th ARS/97th AMW, Altus AFB, OK
	00351	Boeing KC-135R Stratotanker (60-0351) *y/r*	USAF 54th ARS/97th AMW, Altus AFB, OK
	00353	Boeing KC-135R Stratotanker (60-0353)	USAF 92nd ARW, Fairchild AFB, WA
	00355	Boeing KC-135R Stratotanker (60-0355) [D] *r/w/bl*	USAF 351st ARS/100th ARW, RAF Mildenhall, UK
	00356	Boeing KC-135R(RT) Stratotanker (60-0356)	USAF 22nd ARW, McConnell AFB, KS
	00357	Boeing KC-135R(RT) Stratotanker (60-0357)	USAF 22nd ARW, McConnell AFB, KS
	00358	Boeing KC-135R Stratotanker (60-0358) *w/bl*	USAF 108th ARS/126th ARW, Scott AFB, IL ANG
	00359	Boeing KC-135R Stratotanker (60-0359) *r/w*	USAF 74th ARS/434th ARW AFRC, Grissom AFB, IN
	00360	Boeing KC-135R Stratotanker (60-0360)	USAF 92nd ARW, Fairchild AFB, WA
	00362	Boeing KC-135R(RT) Stratotanker (60-0362)	USAF 22nd ARW, McConnell AFB, KS

Serial	Type (code/other identity)	Owner/operator, location or fate	Notes
00363	Boeing KC-135R Stratotanker (60-0363) *bl*	USAF 72nd ARS/434th ARW AFRC, Grissom AFB, IN	
00364	Boeing KC-135R Stratotanker (60-0364) *r/w*	USAF 74th ARS/434th ARW AFRC, Grissom AFB, IN	
00365	Boeing KC-135R Stratotanker (60-0365) *bl/y*	USAF 117th ARS/190th ARW, Forbes Field, KS ANG	
00366	Boeing KC-135R Stratotanker (60-0366) *r*	USAF 141st ARS/108th ARW, McGuire AFB, NJ ANG	
00367	Boeing KC-135R Stratotanker (60-0367) *r/w*	USAF 166th ARS/121st ARW, Rickenbacker ANGB, OH ANG	
10264	Boeing KC-135R Stratotanker (61-0264) *r/w*	USAF 166th ARS/121st ARW, Rickenbacker ANGB, OH ANG	
10266	Boeing KC-135R Stratotanker (61-0266) *bl/y*	USAF 117th ARS/190th ARW, Forbes Field, KS ANG	
10267	Boeing KC-135R Stratotanker (61-0267)	USAF 92nd ARW, Fairchild AFB, WA	
10272	Boeing KC-135R Stratotanker (61-0272) *r/w*	USAF 74th ARS/434th ARW AFRC, Grissom AFB, IN	
10275	Boeing KC-135R Stratotanker (61-0275) *bl/bk*	USAF 191st ARS/151st ARW, Salt Lake City, UT ANG	
10276	Boeing KC-135R Stratotanker (61-0276) *r/w*	USAF 173rd ARS/155th ARW, Lincoln, NE ANG	
10277	Boeing KC-135R Stratotanker (61-0277) *bl/y*	USAF 117th ARS/190th ARW, Forbes Field, KS ANG	
10280	Boeing KC-135R Stratotanker (61-0280) *or/y*	USAF 336th ARS/452nd AMW AFRC, March ARB, CA	
10284	Boeing KC-135R Stratotanker (61-0284)	USAF 197th ARS/161st ARW, Phoenix, AZ ANG	
10288	Boeing KC-135R Stratotanker (61-0288)	USAF Ugden ALC, UT	
10290	Boeing KC-135R Stratotanker (61-0290) [HH] *y/bk*	USAF 203rd ARS/15th Wg, Hickam AFB, HI ANG	
10292	Boeing KC-135R Stratotanker (61-0292) [D] *r/w/bl*	USAF 351st ARS/100th ARW, RAF Mildenhall, UK	
10293	Boeing KC-135R(RT) Stratotanker (61-0293)	USAF 22nd ARW, McConnell AFB, KS	
10294	Boeing KC-135R Stratotanker (61-0294)	USAF 328th ARS/914th ARW AFRC, Niagara Falls NY	
10295	Boeing KC-135R Stratotanker (61-0295) *y/r*	USAF 54th ARS/97th AMW, Altus AFB, OK	
10298	Boeing KC-135R Stratotanker (61-0298) *w/bl*	USAF 126th ARS/128th ARW, Mitchell Field, WI ANG	
10299	Boeing KC-135R Stratotanker (61-0299) *or/y*	USAF 336th ARS/452nd AMW AFRC, March ARB, CA	
10300	Boeing KC-135R Stratotanker (61-0300) *w/bl*	USAF 126th ARS/128th ARW, Mitchell Field, WI ANG	
10305	Boeing KC-135R Stratotanker (61-0305) *y/r*	USAF 54th ARS/97th AMW, Altus AFB, OK	
10307	Boeing KC-135R Stratotanker (61-0307) *y/bk*	USAF 756th ARS/459th ARW AFRC, Andrews AFB, MD	
10308	Boeing KC-135R Stratotanker (61-0308) *y/bl*	USAF 6th ARW, MacDill AFB, FL	
10309	Boeing KC-135R Stratotanker (61-0309) *w/bl*	USAF 126th ARS/128th ARW, Mitchell Field, WI ANG	
10310	Boeing KC-135R Stratotanker (61-0310) *w/bl*	USAF 126th ARS/128th ARW, Mitchell Field, WI ANG	
10311	Boeing KC-135R Stratotanker (61-0311)	USAF 92nd ARW, Fairchild AFB, WA	
10313	Boeing KC-135R Stratotanker (61-0313) [ZZ] *or/bk*	USAF 909th ARS/18th Wg, Kadena AB, Japan	
10314	Boeing KC-135R Stratotanker (61-0314)	USAF 92nd ARW, Fairchild AFB, WA	
10315	Boeing KC-135R Stratotanker (61-0315)	USAF 22nd ARW, McConnell AFB, KS	
10317	Boeing KC-135R Stratotanker (61-0317)	USAF 197th ARS/161st ARW, Phoenix, AZ ANG	
10318	Boeing KC-135R Stratotanker (61-0318) *w/r*	USAF 106th ARS/117th ARW, Birmingham, AL ANG	
10320	Boeing KC-135NK Stratotanker (61-0320) [ED]	USAF 418th FLTS/412th TW, Edwards AFB, CA	
10321	Boeing KC-135R Stratotanker (61-0321)	USAF 22nd ARW, McConnell AFB, KS	
10323	Boeing KC-135R Stratotanker (61-0323) *y/bl*	USAF 6th ARW, MacDill AFB, FL	
10324	Boeing KC-135R Stratotanker (61-0324) *or/y*	USAF 336th ARS/452nd AMW AFRC, March ARB, CA	
12662	Boeing RC-135S Cobra Ball (61-2662) [OF] *bk*	USAF 45th RS/55th Wg, Offutt AFB, NE	
12663	Boeing RC-135S Cobra Ball (61-2663) [OF] *bk*	USAF 45th RS/55th Wg, Offutt AFB, NE	
12666	Boeing NC-135W (61-2666)	USAF 645th Materiel Sqn, Greenville, TX	
12667	Boeing WC-135W Constant Phoenix (61-2667) [OF] *bk*	USAF 45th RS/55th Wg, Offutt AFB, NE	

Notes	Serial	Type (code/other identity)	Owner/operator, location or fate
	12670	Boeing OC-135B Open Skies (61-2670) [OF] bk	USAF 45th RS/55th Wg, Offutt AFB, NE
	12672	Boeing OC-135B Open Skies (61-2672) [OF] bk	USAF 45th RS/55th Wg, Offutt AFB, NE
	14828	Boeing KC-135R Stratotanker (64-14828) bl/bk	USAF 191st ARS/151st ARW, Salt Lake City, UT ANG
	14829	Boeing KC-135R Stratotanker (64-14829)	USAF 197th ARS/161st ARW, Phoenix, AZ ANG
	14830	Boeing KC-135R Stratotanker (64-14830)	USAF
	14831	Boeing KC-135R Stratotanker (64-14831)	USAF 197th ARS/161st ARW, Phoenix, AZ ANG
	14832	Boeing KC-135R Stratotanker (64-14832) w/or	USAF 151st ARS/134th ARW, Knoxville, TN ANG
	14834	Boeing KC-135R Stratotanker (64-14834) r/w	USAF 74th ARS/434th ARW AFRC, Grissom AFB, IN
	14835	Boeing KC-135R Stratotanker (64-14835) or/y	USAF 336th ARS/452nd AMW AFRC, March ARB, CA
	14836	Boeing KC-135R Stratotanker (64-14836)	USAF
	14837	Boeing KC-135R Stratotanker (64-14837)	USAF 92nd ARW, Fairchild AFB, WA
	14839	Boeing KC-135R Stratotanker (64-14839) w/bl	USAF 108th ARS/126th ARW, Scott AFB, IL ANG
	14840	Boeing KC-135R Stratotanker (64-14840) r/w	USAF 166th ARS/121st ARW, Rickenbacker ANGB, OH ANG
	14841	Boeing RC-135V Rivet Joint (64-14841) [OF] gn	USAF 38th RS/55th Wg, Offutt AFB, NE
	14842	Boeing RC-135V Rivet Joint (64-14842) r	USAF 38th RS/55th Wg, Offutt AFB, NE
	14843	Boeing RC-135V Rivet Joint (64-14843) gn	USAF 38th RS/55th Wg, Offutt AFB, NE
	14844	Boeing RC-135V Rivet Joint (64-14844) [OF] gn	USAF 38th RS/55th Wg, Offutt AFB, NE
	14845	Boeing RC-135V Rivet Joint (64-14845) [OF] m $ [55 Wg]	USAF 38th RS/55th Wg, Offutt AFB, NE
	14846	Boeing RC-135V Rivet Joint (64-14846) [OF] bk	USAF 45th RS/55th Wg, Offutt AFB, NE
	14847	Boeing RC-135U Combat Sent (64-14847) [OF] bk	USAF 45th RS/55th Wg, Offutt AFB, NE
	14848	Boeing RC-135V Rivet Joint (64-14848) [OF] gn	USAF 38th RS/55th Wg, Offutt AFB, NE
	14849	Boeing RC-135U Combat Sent (64-14849) [OF] bk	USAF 45th RS/55th Wg, Offutt AFB, NE
	23498	Boeing KC-135R Stratotanker (62-3498) [ZZ] or/bk	USAF 909th ARS/18th Wg, Kadena AB, Japan
	23499	Boeing KC-135R Stratotanker (62-3499)	USAF 92nd ARW, Fairchild AFB, WA
	23500	Boeing KC-135R Stratotanker (62-3500)	USAF
	23502	Boeing KC-135R Stratotanker (62-3502) y/bl	USAF 6th ARW, MacDill AFB, FL
	23503	Boeing KC-135R Stratotanker (62-3503) bl/y	USAF 465th ARS/507th ARW AFRC, Tinker AFB, OK
	23505	Boeing KC-135R Stratotanker (62-3505) y/r	USAF 54th ARS/97th AMW, Altus AFB, OK
	23506	Boeing KC-135R Stratotanker (62-3506) bl/y	USAF 117th ARS/190th ARW, Forbes Field, KS ANG
	23507	Boeing KC-135R Stratotanker (62-3507) or/y	USAF 336th ARS/452nd AMW AFRC, March ARB, CA
	23508	Boeing KC-135R Stratotanker (62-3508) r $	USAF 141st ARS/108th ARW, McGuire AFB, NJ ANG
	23509	Boeing KC-135R Stratotanker (62-3509) bl/y	USAF 465th ARS/507th ARW AFRC, Tinker AFB, OK
	23510	Boeing KC-135R Stratotanker (62-3510) r/w	USAF 74th ARS/434th ARW AFRC, Grissom AFB, IN
	23511	Boeing KC-135R Stratotanker (62-3511) r/w	USAF 166th ARS/121st ARW, Rickenbacker ANGB, OH ANG
	23512	Boeing KC-135R Stratotanker (62-3512) w/bl	USAF 126th ARS/128th ARW, Mitchell Field, WI ANG
	23513	Boeing KC-135R Stratotanker (62-3513) w/gn	USAF 132nd ARS/101st ARW, Bangor, MN ANG
	23514	Boeing KC-135R Stratotanker (62-3514) r	USAF 141st ARS/108th ARW, McGuire AFB, NJ ANG
	23515	Boeing KC-135R Stratotanker (62-3515) w/bl	USAF 108th ARS/126th ARW, Scott AFB, IL ANG
	23516	Boeing KC-135R Stratotanker (62-3516) $	USAF 197th ARS/161st ARW, Phoenix, AZ ANG
	23517	Boeing KC-135R Stratotanker (62-3517) y/bl	USAF 6th ARW, MacDill AFB, FL
	23518	Boeing KC-135R Stratotanker (62-3518) bl	USAF 72nd ARS/434th ARW AFRC, Grissom AFB, IN
	23519	Boeing KC-135R Stratotanker (62-3519)	USAF 92nd ARW, Fairchild AFB, WA
	23521	Boeing KC-135R Stratotanker (62-3521) bl	USAF 72nd ARS/434th ARW AFRC, Grissom AFB, IN
	23523	Boeing KC-135R Stratotanker (62-3523)	USAF 22nd ARW, McConnell AFB, KS
	23524	Boeing KC-135R Stratotanker (62-3524) [AK] bl/y	USAF 168th ARS/168th ARW, Eielson AFB, AK ANG

Serial	Type (code/other identity)	Owner/operator, location or fate	Notes
23526	Boeing KC-135R Stratotanker (62-3526) r/w	USAF 173rd ARS/155th ARW, Lincoln, NE ANG	
23528	Boeing KC-135R Stratotanker (62-3528)	USAF 92nd ARW, Fairchild AFB, WA	
23529	Boeing KC-135R Stratotanker (62-3529)	USAF 314th ARS/940th ARW, Beale AFB, CA	
23530	Boeing KC-135R Stratotanker (62-3530) bl	USAF 72nd ARS/434th ARW AFRC, Grissom AFB, IN	
23531	Boeing KC-135R Stratotanker (62-3531) r/w	USAF 166th ARS/121st ARW, Rickenbacker ANGB, OH ANG	
23533	Boeing KC-135R Stratotanker (62-3533)	USAF 328th ARS/914th ARW AFRC, Niagara Falls NY	
23534	Boeing KC-135R Stratotanker (62-3534)	USAF 22nd ARW, McConnell AFB, KS	
23537	Boeing KC-135R Stratotanker (62-3537)	USAF 92nd ARW, Fairchild AFB, WA	
23538	Boeing KC-135R Stratotanker (62-3538) y/r	USAF 54th ARS/97th AMW, Altus AFB, OK	
23540	Boeing KC-135R Stratotanker (62-3540) [D] r/w/bl	USAF 351st ARS/100th ARW, RAF Mildenhall, UK	
23541	Boeing KC-135R Stratotanker (62-3541)	USAF 92nd ARW, Fairchild AFB, WA	
23542	Boeing KC-135R Stratotanker (62-3542)	USAF	
23543	Boeing KC-135R Stratotanker (62-3543) y/bk	USAF 756th ARS/459th ARW AFRC, Andrews AFB, MD	
23544	Boeing KC-135R Stratotanker (62-3544) r $	USAF 141st ARS/108th ARW, McGuire AFB, NJ ANG	
23545	Boeing KC-135R Stratotanker (62-3545)	USAF 22nd ARW, McConnell AFB, KS	
23547	Boeing KC-135R Stratotanker (62-3547) bl/y	USAF 117th ARS/190th ARW, Forbes Field, KS ANG	
23549	Boeing KC-135R Stratotanker (62-3549) y/r	USAF 54th ARS/97th AMW, Altus AFB, OK	
23550	Boeing KC-135R Stratotanker (62-3550)	USAF 197th ARS/161st ARW, Phoenix, AZ ANG	
23551	Boeing KC-135R Stratotanker (62-3551) [D] r/w/bl	USAF 351st ARS/100th ARW, RAF Mildenhall, UK	
23552	Boeing KC-135R Stratotanker (62-3552)	USAF 22nd ARW, McConnell AFB, KS	
23553	Boeing KC-135R Stratotanker (62-3553) y/bl	USAF 6th ARW, MacDill AFB, FL	
23554	Boeing KC-135R Stratotanker (62-3554)	USAF 22nd ARW, McConnell AFB, KS	
23556	Boeing KC-135R Stratotanker (62-3556) y/bk	USAF 756th ARS/459th ARW AFRC, Andrews AFB, MD	
23557	Boeing KC-135R Stratotanker (62-3557)	USAF 328th ARS/914th ARW AFRC, Niagara Falls NY	
23558	Boeing KC-135R Stratotanker (62-3558) or/y	USAF 336th ARS/452nd AMW AFRC, March ARB, CA	
23559	Boeing KC-135R Stratotanker (62-3559)	USAF 92nd ARW, Fairchild AFB, WA	
23561	Boeing KC-135R Stratotanker (62-3561) [ZZ] or/bk	USAF 909th ARS/18th Wg, Kadena AB, Japan	
23562	Boeing KC-135R Stratotanker (62-3562) y/r	USAF 54th ARS/97th AMW, Altus AFB, OK	
23564	Boeing KC-135R Stratotanker (62-3564)	USAF 92nd ARW, Fairchild AFB, WA	
23565	Boeing KC-135R Stratotanker (62-3565) [ZZ] or/bk	USAF 909th ARS/18th Wg, Kadena AB, Japan	
23566	Boeing KC-135R Stratotanker (62-3566) y/bk	USAF 174th ARS/185th ARW, Sioux City, IA ANG	
23568	Boeing KC-135R Stratotanker (62-3568) y/bl	USAF 6th ARW, MacDill AFB, FL	
23569	Boeing KC-135R Stratotanker (62-3569)	USAF 22nd ARW, McConnell AFB, KS	
23571	Boeing KC-135R Stratotanker (62-3571) [AK] bl/y	USAF 168th ARS/168th ARW, Eielson AFB, AK ANG	
23572	Boeing KC-135R Stratotanker (62-3572) bl/y	USAF 117th ARS/190th ARW, Forbes Field, KS ANG	
23573	Boeing KC-135R Stratotanker (62-3573)	USAF 22nd ARW, McConnell AFB, KS	
23575	Boeing KC-135R Stratotanker (62-3575)	USAF 92nd ARW, Fairchild AFB, WA	
23576	Boeing KC-135R Stratotanker (62-3576) w/bl	USAF 108th ARS/126th ARW, Scott AFB, IL ANG	
23577	Boeing KC-135R Stratotanker (62-3577)	USAF 92nd ARW, Fairchild AFB, WA	
23578	Boeing KC-135R Stratotanker (62-3578) r	USAF 141st ARS/108th ARW, McGuire AFB, NJ ANG	
23580	Boeing KC-135R Stratotanker (62-3580)	USAF 328th ARS/914th ARW AFRC, Niagara Falls NY	
23582	Boeing WC-135C Constant Phoenix (62-3582) [OF] bk	USAF 45th RS/55th Wg, Offutt AFB, NE	
24125	Boeing RC-135W Rivet Joint (62-4125) [OF] bl	USAF 343rd RS/55th Wg, Offutt AFB, NE	
24126	Boeing RC-135W Rivet Joint (62-4126) [OF] bl	USAF 343rd RS/55th Wg, Offutt AFB, NE	
24127	Boeing TC-135W (62-4127) [OF] bl	USAF 343rd RS/55th Wg, Offutt AFB, NE	
24128	Boeing RC-135S Cobra Ball (62-4128) [OF] bk	USAF 45th RS/55th Wg, Offutt AFB, NE	
24129	Boeing TC-135W (62-4129) [OF] bl	USAF 343rd RS/55th Wg, Offutt AFB, NE	
24130	Boeing RC-135W Rivet Joint (62-4130) gn	USAF 38th RS/55th Wg, Offutt AFB, NE	
24131	Boeing RC-135W Rivet Joint (62-4131) [OF] bl	USAF 343rd RS/55th Wg, Offutt AFB, NE	

Notes	Serial	Type (code/other identity)	Owner/operator, location or fate
	24132	Boeing RC-135W Rivet Joint (62-4132) *gn*	USAF 38th RS/55th Wg, Offutt AFB, NE
	24133	Boeing TC-135W (62-4133) [OF] *bk*	USAF 45th RS/55th Wg, Offutt AFB, NE
	24134	Boeing RC-135W Rivet Joint (62-4134) *bl*	USAF 343rd RS/55th Wg, Offutt AFB, NE
	24135	Boeing RC-135W Rivet Joint (62-4135) [OF] *gn*	USAF 38th RS/55th Wg, Offutt AFB, NE
	24138	Boeing RC-135W Rivet Joint (62-4138) *bl*	USAF 343rd RS/55th Wg, Offutt AFB, NE
	24139	Boeing RC-135W Rivet Joint (62-4139) *gn*	USAF 38th RS/55th Wg, Offutt AFB, NE
	37976	Boeing KC-135R Stratotanker (63-7976) *y/r*	USAF 54th ARS/97th AMW, Altus AFB, OK
	37977	Boeing KC-135R Stratotanker (63-7977) *y/r*	USAF 54th ARS/97th AMW, Altus AFB, OK
	37978	Boeing KC-135R Stratotanker (63-7978)	USAF 92nd ARW, Fairchild AFB, WA
	37979	Boeing KC-135R Stratotanker (63-7979) *y/bl*	USAF 6th ARW, MacDill AFB, FL
	37980	Boeing KC-135R Stratotanker (63-7980) [ED]	*To 309th AMARG, December 2018*
	37981	Boeing KC-135R Stratotanker (63-7981) *w/bl*	USAF 108th ARS/126th ARW, Scott AFB, IL ANG
	37982	Boeing KC-135R Stratotanker (63-7982)	USAF 92nd ARW, Fairchild AFB, WA
	37984	Boeing KC-135R Stratotanker (63-7984) *w/r*	USAF 106th ARS/117th ARW, Birmingham, AL ANG
	37985	Boeing KC-135R Stratotanker (63-7985) *bl/y*	USAF 465th ARS/507th ARW AFRC, Tinker AFB, OK
	37987	Boeing KC-135R Stratotanker (63-7987) *y/r*	USAF 54th ARS/97th AMW, Altus AFB, OK
	37988	Boeing KC-135R Stratotanker (63-7988) *r/w*	USAF 173rd ARS/155th ARW, Lincoln, NE ANG
	37991	Boeing KC-135R Stratotanker (63-7991) *r/w*	USAF 173rd ARS/155th ARW, Lincoln, NE ANG
	37992	Boeing KC-135R Stratotanker (63-7992)	USAF 153rd ARS/186th ARW, Meridian, MS ANG
	37993	Boeing KC-135R Stratotanker (63-7993) *m*	USAF 166th ARS/121st ARW, Rickenbacker ANGB, OH ANG
	37995	Boeing KC-135R Stratotanker (63-7995)	USAF 22nd ARW, McConnell AFB, KS
	37996	Boeing KC-135R Stratotanker (63-7996) *bl*	USAF 72nd ARS/434th ARW AFRC, Grissom AFB, IN
	37997	Boeing KC-135R Stratotanker (63-7997) *y/r*	USAF 54th ARS/97th AMW, Altus AFB, OK
	37999	Boeing KC-135R Stratotanker (63-7999)	USAF
	38000	Boeing KC-135R Stratotanker (63-8000)	USAF 92nd ARW, Fairchild AFB, WA
	38002	Boeing KC-135R Stratotanker (63-8002)	USAF 22nd ARW, McConnell AFB, KS
	38003	Boeing KC-135R Stratotanker (63-8003) *r*	USAF 141st ARS/108th ARW, McGuire AFB, NJ ANG
	38004	Boeing KC-135R Stratotanker (63-8004) *bl/y*	USAF 117th ARS/190th ARW, Forbes Field, KS ANG
	38006	Boeing KC-135R Stratotanker (63-8006) *y/r*	USAF 54th ARS/97th AMW, Altus AFB, OK
	38007	Boeing KC-135R Stratotanker (63-8007) *w/r*	USAF 106th ARS/117th ARW, Birmingham, AL ANG
	38008	Boeing KC-135R Stratotanker (63-8008)	USAF 92nd ARW, Fairchild AFB, WA
	38011	Boeing KC-135R Stratotanker (63-8011) *y/r*	USAF 54th ARS/97th AMW, Altus AFB, OK
	38012	Boeing KC-135R Stratotanker (63-8012)	USAF 314th ARS/940th ARW, Beale AFB, CA
	38013	Boeing KC-135R Stratotanker (63-8013) *r/w*	USAF 166th ARS/121st ARW, Rickenbacker ANGB, OH ANG
	38014	Boeing KC-135R Stratotanker (63-8014)	USAF 92nd ARW, Fairchild AFB, WA
	38015	Boeing KC-135R Stratotanker (63-8015) [AK] *bl/y*	USAF 168th ARS/168th ARW, Eielson AFB, AK ANG
	38017	Boeing KC-135R Stratotanker (63-8017)	USAF 328th ARS/914th ARW AFRC, Niagara Falls NY
	38018	Boeing KC-135R Stratotanker (63-8018) *r/w*	USAF 173rd ARS/155th ARW, Lincoln, NE ANG
	38019	Boeing KC-135R Stratotanker (63-8019) *y/bl*	USAF 6th ARW, MacDill AFB, FL
	38020	Boeing KC-135R Stratotanker (63-8020)	USAF 22nd ARW, McConnell AFB, KS
	38021	Boeing KC-135R Stratotanker (63-8021) [ZZ] *or/bk*	USAF 909th ARS/18th Wg, Kadena AB, Japan
	38022	Boeing KC-135R Stratotanker (63-8022)	USAF 92nd ARW, Fairchild AFB, WA
	38023	Boeing KC-135R Stratotanker (63-8023) *w/bl*	USAF 126th ARS/128th ARW, Mitchell Field, WI ANG
	38024	Boeing KC-135R Stratotanker (63-8024) *or/y*	USAF 336th ARS/452nd AMW AFRC, March ARB, CA
	38025	Boeing KC-135R Stratotanker (63-8025)	USAF 92nd ARW, Fairchild AFB, WA
	38026	Boeing KC-135R Stratotanker (63-8026) *bl/bk*	USAF 191st ARS/151st ARW, Salt Lake City, UT ANG
	38027	Boeing KC-135R Stratotanker (63-8027) *y/bl*	USAF 6th ARW, MacDill AFB, FL
	38028	Boeing KC-135R Stratotanker (63-8028) [AK] *bl/y*	USAF 168th ARS/168th ARW, Eielson AFB, AK ANG

Serial	Type (code/other identity)	Owner/operator, location or fate	Notes
38029	Boeing KC-135R Stratotanker (63-8029) *r*	USAF 141st ARS/108th ARW, McGuire AFB, NJ ANG	
38030	Boeing KC-135R Stratotanker (63-8030) [HH] *y/bk*	USAF 203rd ARS/15th Wg, Hickam AFB, HI ANG	
38031	Boeing KC-135R Stratotanker (63-8031)	USAF 92nd ARW, Fairchild AFB, WA	
38032	Boeing KC-135R Stratotanker (63-8032) *bl*	USAF 72nd ARS/434th ARW AFRC, Grissom AFB, IN	
38033	Boeing KC-135R Stratotanker (63-8033) *y/r*	USAF 54th ARS/97th AMW, Altus AFB, OK	
38034	Boeing KC-135R Stratotanker (63-8034)	USAF 92nd ARW, Fairchild AFB, WA	
38035	Boeing KC-135R Stratotanker (63-8035) *w/r*	USAF 106th ARS/117th ARW, Birmingham, AL ANG	
38036	Boeing KC-135R Stratotanker (63-8036)	USAF 197th ARS/161st ARW, Phoenix, AZ ANG	
38038	Boeing KC-135R Stratotanker (63-8038) [HH] *y/bk*	USAF 203rd ARS/15th Wg, Hickam AFB, HI ANG	
38039	Boeing KC-135R Stratotanker (63-8039) *bl/y*	USAF 465th ARS/507th ARW AFRC, Tinker AFB, OK	
38040	Boeing KC-135R Stratotanker (63-8040) *r*	USAF 141st ARS/108th ARW, McGuire AFB, NJ ANG	
38041	Boeing KC-135R Stratotanker (63-8041) *bl*	USAF 72nd ARS/434th ARW AFRC, Grissom AFB, IN	
38043	Boeing KC-135R Stratotanker (63-8043) [AK] *bl/y*	USAF 168th ARS/168th ARW, Eielson AFB, AK ANG	
38044	Boeing KC-135R Stratotanker (63-8044)	USAF 328th ARS/914th ARW AFRC, Niagara Falls NY	
38045	Boeing KC-135R Stratotanker (63-8045)	USAF 92nd ARW, Fairchild AFB, WA	
38871	Boeing KC-135R Stratotanker (63-8871)	USAF 92nd ARW, Fairchild AFB, WA	
38872	Boeing KC-135R Stratotanker (63-8872) *w/gn*	USAF 132nd ARS/101st ARW, Bangor, MN ANG	
38873	Boeing KC-135R Stratotanker (63-8873) *w/gn*	USAF 132nd ARS/101st ARW, Bangor, MN ANG	
38874	Boeing KC-135R Stratotanker (63-8874)	USAF 92nd ARW, Fairchild AFB, WA	
38875	Boeing KC-135R Stratotanker (63-8875) *bl/y*	USAF 117th ARS/190th ARW, Forbes Field, KS ANG	
38876	Boeing KC-135R Stratotanker (63-8876) [AK] *bl/y*	USAF 168th ARS/168th ARW, Eielson AFB, AK ANG	
38878	Boeing KC-135R Stratotanker (63-8878) [D] *r/w/bl*	USAF 351st ARS/100th ARW, RAF Mildenhall, UK	
38879	Boeing KC-135R Stratotanker (63-8879)	USAF 314th ARS/940th ARW, Beale AFB, CA	
38880	Boeing KC-135R Stratotanker (63-8880) [HH] *y/bk*	USAF 203rd ARS/15th Wg, Hickam AFB, HI ANG	
38881	Boeing KC-135R Stratotanker (63-8881) *bl/bk*	USAF 191st ARS/151st ARW, Salt Lake City, UT ANG	
38883	Boeing KC-135R Stratotanker (63-8883) *y/bl*	USAF 6th ARW, MacDill AFB, FL	
38884	Boeing KC-135R Stratotanker (63-8884) *y/r*	USAF 54th ARS/97th AMW, Altus AFB, OK	
38885	Boeing KC-135R Stratotanker (63-8885) *y/bl*	USAF 6th ARW, MacDill AFB, FL	
38887	Boeing KC-135R Stratotanker (63-8887) *y/bl*	USAF 6th ARW, MacDill AFB, FL	
38888	Boeing KC-135R Stratotanker (63-8888) [ZZ] *or/bk*	USAF 909th ARS/18th Wg, Kadena AB, Japan	
39792	Boeing RC-135V Rivet Joint (63-9792) [OF] *bl*	USAF 343rd RS/55th Wg, Offutt AFB, NE	
71419	Boeing KC-135R Stratotanker (57-1419)	USAF 197th ARS/161st ARW, Phoenix, AZ ANG	
71427	Boeing KC-135R Stratotanker (57-1427) *bl/y*	USAF 117th ARS/190th ARW, Forbes Field, KS ANG	
71428	Boeing KC-135R Stratotanker (57-1428) *w/or*	USAF 151st ARS/134th ARW, Knoxville, TN ANG	
71430	Boeing KC-135R Stratotanker (57-1430) *bk/y*	USAF 171st ARS/127th Wg, Selfridge ANGB, MI ANG	
71432	Boeing KC-135R Stratotanker (57-1432) *bl/bk*	USAF 191st ARS/151st ARW, Salt Lake City, UT ANG	
71435	Boeing KC-135R Stratotanker (57-1435) *bl/bk*	USAF 191st ARS/151st ARW, Salt Lake City, UT ANG	
71436	Boeing KC-135R Stratotanker (57-1436) *w/or*	USAF 151st ARS/134th ARW, Knoxville, TN ANG	
71437	Boeing KC-135R Stratotanker (57-1437)	USAF 92nd ARW, Fairchild AFB, WA	
71438	Boeing KC-135R Stratotanker (57-1438) *or/y*	USAF 336th ARS/452nd AMW AFRC, March ARB, CA	
71439	Boeing KC-135R Stratotanker (57-1439) [ZZ] *or/bk*	USAF 909th ARS/18th Wg, Kadena AB, Japan	
71440	Boeing KC-135R Stratotanker (57-1440) [D] *r/w/bl*	USAF 351st ARS/100th ARW, RAF Mildenhall, UK	
71441	Boeing KC-135R Stratotanker (57-1441) *y/bk*	USAF 174th ARS/185th ARW, Sioux City, IA ANG	
71451	Boeing KC-135R Stratotanker (57-1451) *w/or*	USAF 151st ARS/134th ARW, Knoxville, TN ANG	
71453	Boeing KC-135R Stratotanker (57-1453) *w/r*	USAF 106th ARS/117th ARW, Birmingham, AL ANG	

Notes	Serial	Type (code/other identity)	Owner/operator, location or fate
	71454	Boeing KC-135R Stratotanker (57-1454) [ZZ] or/bk	USAF 909th ARS/18th Wg, Kadena AB, Japan
	71456	Boeing KC-135R Stratotanker (57-1456)	USAF 314th ARS/940th ARW, Beale AFB, CA
	71459	Boeing KC-135R Stratotanker (57-1459) or/y	USAF 336th ARS/452nd AMW AFRC, March ARB, CA
	71461	Boeing KC-135R Stratotanker (57-1461) r/w	USAF 173rd ARS/155th ARW, Lincoln, NE ANG
	71462	Boeing KC-135R Stratotanker (57-1462)	USAF 153rd ARS/186th ARW, Meridian, MS ANG
	71468	Boeing KC-135R Stratotanker (57-1468) or/y	USAF 336th ARS/452nd AMW AFRC, March ARB, CA
	71469	Boeing KC-135R Stratotanker (57-1469) $	USAF 197th ARS/161st ARW, Phoenix, AZ ANG
	71472	Boeing KC-135R Stratotanker (57-1472) bl	USAF 72nd ARS/434th ARW AFRC, Grissom AFB, IN
	71473	Boeing KC-135R Stratotanker (57-1473) w/r	USAF 106th ARS/117th ARW, Birmingham, AL ANG
	71474	Boeing KC-135R Stratotanker (57-1474) [D] r/w/bl	USAF 351st ARS/100th ARW, RAF Mildenhall, UK
	71479	Boeing KC-135R Stratotanker (57-1479) y/bk	USAF 756th ARS/459th ARW AFRC, Andrews AFB, MD
	71483	Boeing KC-135R Stratotanker (57-1483)	USAF 92nd ARW, Fairchild AFB, WA
	71486	Boeing KC-135R Stratotanker (57-1486)	USAF 153rd ARS/186th ARW, Meridian, MS ANG
	71487	Boeing KC-135R Stratotanker (57-1487) y/bk	USAF 756th ARS/459th ARW AFRC, Andrews AFB, MD
	71488	Boeing KC-135R Stratotanker (57-1488) y/r	USAF 54th ARS/97th AMW, Altus AFB, OK
	71493	Boeing KC-135R Stratotanker (57-1493) [D] r/w/bl	USAF 351st ARS/100th ARW, RAF Mildenhall, UK
	71499	Boeing KC-135R Stratotanker (57-1499) bl/bk	USAF 191st ARS/151st ARW, Salt Lake City, UT ANG
	71502	Boeing KC-135R Stratotanker (57-1502)	USAF 92nd ARW, Fairchild AFB, WA
	71506	Boeing KC-135R Stratotanker (57-1506) y/r	USAF 54th ARS/97th AMW, Altus AFB, OK
	71508	Boeing KC-135R Stratotanker (57-1508)	USAF 314th ARS/940th ARW, Beale AFB, CA
	71512	Boeing KC-135R Stratotanker (57-1512) y/bk	USAF 756th ARS/459th ARW AFRC, Andrews AFB, MD
	71514	Boeing KC-135R Stratotanker (57-1514) w/bl	USAF 126th ARS/128th ARW, Mitchell Field, WI ANG
	72597	Boeing KC-135R Stratotanker (57-2597) w/or	USAF 151st ARS/134th ARW, Knoxville, TN ANG
	72598	Boeing KC-135R Stratotanker (57-2598) or/y	USAF 336th ARS/452nd AMW AFRC, March ARB, CA
	72599	Boeing KC-135R Stratotanker (57-2599)	USAF 92nd ARW, Fairchild AFB, WA
	72603	Boeing KC-135R Stratotanker (57-2603) or/y	USAF 336th ARS/452nd AMW AFRC, March ARB, CA
	72605	Boeing KC-135R Stratotanker (57-2605)	USAF
	72606	Boeing KC-135R Stratotanker (57-2606) y/bk	USAF 174th ARS/185th ARW, Sioux City, IA ANG
	80001	Boeing KC-135R Stratotanker (58-0001) [D] r/w/bl	USAF 351st ARS/100th ARW, RAF Mildenhall, UK
	80004	Boeing KC-135R Stratotanker (58-0004) w/r	USAF 106th ARS/117th ARW, Birmingham, AL ANG
	80009	Boeing KC-135R Stratotanker (58-0009) w/bl	USAF 126th ARS/128th ARW, Mitchell Field, WI ANG
	80010	Boeing KC-135R Stratotanker (58-0010) r	USAF 141st ARS/108th ARW, McGuire AFB, NJ ANG
	80011	Boeing KC-135R(RT) Stratotanker (58-0011)	USAF 22nd ARW, McConnell AFB, KS
	80015	Boeing KC-135R Stratotanker (58-0015) bl/y	USAF 465th ARS/507th ARW AFRC, Tinker AFB, OK
	80016	Boeing KC-135R Stratotanker (58-0016)	USAF 92nd ARW, Fairchild AFB, WA
	80018	Boeing KC-135R(RT) Stratotanker (58-0018)	USAF 22nd ARW, McConnell AFB, KS
	80021	Boeing KC-135R Stratotanker (58-0021) w/gn	USAF 132nd ARS/101st ARW, Bangor, MN ANG
	80023	Boeing KC-135R Stratotanker (58-0023) bl/bk	USAF 191st ARS/151st ARW, Salt Lake City, UT ANG
	80027	Boeing KC-135R Stratotanker (58-0027) bl/bk	USAF 191st ARS/151st ARW, Salt Lake City, UT ANG
	80030	Boeing KC-135R Stratotanker (58-0030) w/gn	USAF 132nd ARS/101st ARW, Bangor, MN ANG
	80034	Boeing KC-135R Stratotanker (58-0034) y/r	USAF 54th ARS/97th AMW, Altus AFB, OK
	80035	Boeing KC-135R Stratotanker (58-0035)	USAF 92nd ARW, Fairchild AFB, WA
	80036	Boeing KC-135R Stratotanker (58-0036) [D] r/w/bl	USAF 351st ARS/100th ARW, RAF Mildenhall, UK
	80038	Boeing KC-135R Stratotanker (58-0038)	USAF 328th ARS/914th ARW AFRC, Niagara Falls NY

Serial	Type (code/other identity)	Owner/operator, location or fate	Notes
80042	Boeing KC-135T Stratotanker (58-0042)	USAF 22nd ARW, McConnell AFB, KS	
80045	Boeing KC-135T Stratotanker (58-0045)	USAF 171st ARW, Greater Pittsburgh, PA ANG	
80046	Boeing KC-135T Stratotanker (58-0046) y/bl	USAF 6th ARW, MacDill AFB, FL	
80047	Boeing KC-135T Stratotanker (58-0047)	USAF 22nd ARW, McConnell AFB, KS	
80049	Boeing KC-135T Stratotanker (58-0049) bk/y	USAF 171st ARS/127th Wg, Selfridge ANGB, MI ANG	
80050	Boeing KC-135T Stratotanker (58-0050) y/bl	USAF 6th ARW, MacDill AFB, FL	
80051	Boeing KC-135R Stratotanker (58-0051) bl/y	USAF 465th ARS/507th ARW AFRC, Tinker AFB, OK	
80052	Boeing KC-135R Stratotanker (58-0052) or/y	USAF 336th ARS/452nd AMW AFRC, March ARB, CA	
80054	Boeing KC-135T Stratotanker (58-0054) y/bk	USAF 171st ARW, Greater Pittsburgh, PA ANG	
80055	Boeing KC-135T Stratotanker (58-0055) [ZZ] or/bk	USAF 909th ARS/18th Wg, Kadena AB, Japan	
80056	Boeing KC-135R Stratotanker (58-0056) [HH] y/bk	USAF 203rd ARS/15th Wg, Hickam AFB, HI ANG	
80057	Boeing KC-135R Stratotanker (58-0057) y/bk	USAF 174th ARS/185th ARW, Sioux City, IA ANG	
80058	Boeing KC-135R Stratotanker (58-0058) bl/y	USAF 465th ARS/507th ARW AFRC, Tinker AFB, OK	
80059	Boeing KC-135R Stratotanker (58-0059) bl/y	USAF 117th ARS/190th ARW, Forbes Field, KS ANG	
80060	Boeing KC-135T Stratotanker (58-0060) y/bk	USAF 171st ARW, Greater Pittsburgh, PA ANG	
80061	Boeing KC-135T Stratotanker (58-0061)	USAF 22nd ARW, McConnell AFB, KS	
80062	Boeing KC-135T Stratotanker (58-0062) bk/y	USAF 171st ARS/127th Wg, Selfridge ANGB, MI ANG	
80063	Boeing KC-135R Stratotanker (58-0063)	USAF 328th ARS/914th ARW AFRC, Niagara Falls NY	
80065	Boeing KC-135T Stratotanker (58-0065)	USAF 22nd ARW, McConnell AFB, KS	
80066	Boeing KC-135R Stratotanker (58-0066) w/r	USAF 106th ARS/117th ARW, Birmingham, AL ANG	
80067	Boeing KC-135R Stratotanker (58-0067) y/bk	USAF 174th ARS/185th ARW, Sioux City, IA ANG	
80069	Boeing KC-135T Stratotanker (58-0069)	USAF 92nd ARW, Fairchild AFB, WA	
80071	Boeing KC-135T Stratotanker (58-0071) y/bl	USAF 6th ARW, MacDill AFB, FL	
80072	Boeing KC-135T Stratotanker (58-0072) y/bk	USAF 171st ARW, Greater Pittsburgh, PA ANG	
80073	Boeing KC-135R Stratotanker (58-0073) w/r	USAF 106th ARS/117th ARW, Birmingham, AL ANG	
80074	Boeing KC-135T Stratotanker (58-0074) y/bk	USAF 171st ARW, Greater Pittsburgh, PA ANG	
80075	Boeing KC-135R Stratotanker (58-0075) y/bk	USAF 756th ARS/459th ARW AFRC, Andrews AFB, MD	
80076	Boeing KC-135R Stratotanker (58-0076) r/w	USAF 74th ARS/434th ARW AFRC, Grissom AFB, IN	
80077	Boeing KC-135T Stratotanker (58-0077) y/bk	USAF 171st ARW, Greater Pittsburgh, PA ANG	
80079	Boeing KC-135R Stratotanker (58-0079)	USAF 153rd ARS/186th ARW, Meridian, MS ANG	
80083	Boeing KC-135R Stratotanker (58-0083) r/w	USAF 166th ARS/121st ARW, Rickenbacker ANGB, OH ANG	
80084	Boeing KC-135T Stratotanker (58-0084) y/bk	USAF 171st ARW, Greater Pittsburgh, PA ANG	
80085	Boeing KC-135R Stratotanker (58-0085) or/y	USAF 336th ARS/452nd AMW AFRC, March ARB, CA	
80086	Boeing KC-135T Stratotanker (58-0086) [ZZ] or/bk	USAF 909th ARS/18th Wg, Kadena AB, Japan	
80088	Boeing KC-135T Stratotanker (58-0088) bk/y	USAF 171st ARS/127th Wg, Selfridge ANGB, MI ANG	
80089	Boeing KC-135T Stratotanker (58-0089) y/bl	USAF 6th ARW, MacDill AFB, FL	
80092	Boeing KC-135R Stratotanker (58-0092)	USAF 92nd ARW, Fairchild AFB, WA	
80093	Boeing KC-135R Stratotanker (58-0093) [ZZ] or/bk	USAF 909th ARS/18th Wg, Kadena AB, Japan	
80094	Boeing KC-135T Stratotanker (58-0094)	USAF 22nd ARW, McConnell AFB, KS	
80095	Boeing KC-135T Stratotanker (58-0095) [ZZ] or/bk	USAF 909th ARS/18th Wg, Kadena AB, Japan	
80098	Boeing KC-135R Stratotanker (58-0098) w/gn	USAF 132nd ARS/101st ARW, Bangor, MN ANG	
80099	Boeing KC-135T Stratotanker (58-0099) y/bk	USAF 171st ARW, Greater Pittsburgh, PA ANG	
80100	Boeing KC-135R Stratotanker (58-0100) [D] r/w/bl [EP-A]	USAF 351st ARS/100th ARW, RAF Mildenhall, UK	
80102	Boeing KC-135R Stratotanker (58-0102) bl/y	USAF 465th ARS/507th ARW AFRC, Tinker AFB, OK	
80103	Boeing KC-135T Stratotanker (58-0103) y/bl	USAF 6th ARW, MacDill AFB, FL	
80104	Boeing KC-135R Stratotanker (58-0104) w/bl	USAF 108th ARS/126th ARW, Scott AFB, IL ANG	

Notes	Serial	Type (code/other identity)	Owner/operator, location or fate
	80106	Boeing KC-135R Stratotanker (58-0106) w/r	USAF 106th ARS/117th ARW, Birmingham, AL ANG
	80107	Boeing KC-135R Stratotanker (58-0107) w/gn	USAF 132nd ARS/101st ARW, Bangor, MN ANG
	80109	Boeing KC-135R Stratotanker (58-0109) y/bk	USAF 174th ARS/185th ARW, Sioux City, IA ANG
	80112	Boeing KC-135T Stratotanker (58-0112) y/bk	USAF 171st ARW, Greater Pittsburgh, PA ANG
	80113	Boeing KC-135R Stratotanker (58-0113) [D] r/w/bl	USAF 351st ARS/100th ARW, RAF Mildenhall, UK
	80117	Boeing KC-135T Stratotanker (58-0117)	USAF 171st ARW, Greater Pittsburgh, PA ANG
	80118	Boeing KC-135R Stratotanker (58-0118)	USAF 92nd ARW, Fairchild AFB, WA
	80119	Boeing KC-135R Stratotanker (58-0119) w/or	USAF 151st ARS/134th ARW, Knoxville, TN ANG
	80120	Boeing KC-135R Stratotanker (58-0120)	USAF 153rd ARS/186th ARW, Meridian, MS ANG
	80121	Boeing KC-135R Stratotanker (58-0121) bl/y	USAF 465th ARS/507th ARW AFRC, Tinker AFB, OK
	80122	Boeing KC-135R Stratotanker (58-0122) bl/y	USAF 117th ARS/190th ARW, Forbes Field, KS ANG
	80123	Boeing KC-135R Stratotanker (58-0123) y/r	USAF 54th ARS/97th AMW, Altus AFB, OK
	80124	Boeing KC-135R(RT) Stratotanker (58-0124)	USAF 22nd ARW, McConnell AFB, KS
	80125	Boeing KC-135T Stratotanker (58-0125) y/bl	USAF 6th ARW, MacDill AFB, FL
	80126	Boeing KC-135R(RT) Stratotanker (58-0126)	USAF 22nd ARW, McConnell AFB, KS
	80128	Boeing KC-135R Stratotanker (58-0128) y/r	USAF 54th ARS/97th AMW, Altus AFB, OK
	80129	Boeing KC-135T Stratotanker (58-0129) bk/y	USAF 171st ARS/127th Wg, Selfridge ANGB, MI ANG
	91444	Boeing KC-135R Stratotanker (59-1444) r/w	USAF 166th ARS/121st ARW, Rickenbacker ANGB, OH ANG
	91446	Boeing KC-135R Stratotanker (59-1446) w/gn	USAF 132nd ARS/101st ARW, Bangor, MN ANG
	91448	Boeing KC-135R Stratotanker (59-1448)	USAF 153rd ARS/186th ARW, Meridian, MS ANG
	91450	Boeing KC-135R Stratotanker (59-1450)	USAF 197th ARS/161st ARW, Phoenix, AZ ANG
	91453	Boeing KC-135R Stratotanker (59-1453)	USAF 153rd ARS/186th ARW, Meridian, MS ANG
	91455	Boeing KC-135R Stratotanker (59-1455) [HH] y/bk	USAF 203rd ARS/15th Wg, Hickam AFB, HI ANG
	91458	Boeing KC-135R Stratotanker (59-1458) r/w	USAF 166th ARS/121st ARW, Rickenbacker ANGB, OH ANG
	91459	Boeing KC-135R Stratotanker (59-1459) [ZZ] or/bk	USAF 909th ARS/18th Wg, Kadena AB, Japan
	91460	Boeing KC-135T Stratotanker (59-1460) y/bk	USAF 171st ARW, Greater Pittsburgh, PA ANG
	91461	Boeing KC-135R Stratotanker (59-1461) w/bl	USAF 126th ARS/128th ARW, Mitchell Field, WI ANG
	91462	Boeing KC-135T Stratotanker (59-1462)	USAF 22nd ARW, McConnell AFB, KS
	91463	Boeing KC-135R Stratotanker (59-1463) r/w	USAF 173rd ARS/155th ARW, Lincoln, NE ANG
	91464	Boeing KC-135T Stratotanker (59-1464)	USAF 92nd ARW, Fairchild AFB, WA
	91466	Boeing KC-135R Stratotanker (59-1466) w/bl	USAF 108th ARS/126th ARW, Scott AFB, IL ANG
	91467	Boeing KC-135T Stratotanker (59-1467) w/r	USAF 106th ARS/117th ARW, Birmingham, AL ANG
	91468	Boeing KC-135T Stratotanker (59-1468) y/bk	USAF 171st ARW, Greater Pittsburgh, PA ANG
	91469	Boeing KC-135R Stratotanker (59-1469) y/bk	USAF 756th ARS/459th ARW AFRC, Andrews AFB, MD
	91470	Boeing KC-135T Stratotanker (59-1470) y/bl	USAF 6th ARW, MacDill AFB, FL
	91471	Boeing KC-135T Stratotanker (59-1471)	USAF 92nd ARW, Fairchild AFB, WA
	91472	Boeing KC-135R Stratotanker (59-1472)	USAF 314th ARS/940th ARW, Beale AFB, CA
	91474	Boeing KC-135T Stratotanker (59-1474) bk/y	USAF 171st ARS/127th Wg, Selfridge ANGB, MI ANG
	91475	Boeing KC-135R Stratotanker (59-1475)	USAF 92nd ARW, Fairchild AFB, WA
	91476	Boeing KC-135R Stratotanker (59-1476)	USAF 92nd ARW, Fairchild AFB, WA
	91478	Boeing KC-135R Stratotanker (59-1478) w/or	USAF 151st ARS/134th ARW, Knoxville, TN ANG
	91480	Boeing KC-135T Stratotanker (59-1480)	USAF 92nd ARW, Fairchild AFB, WA
	91482	Boeing KC-135R Stratotanker (59-1482)	USAF 328th ARS/914th ARW AFRC, Niagara Falls NY
	91483	Boeing KC-135R Stratotanker (59-1483) r/w	USAF 166th ARS/121st ARW, Rickenbacker ANGB, OH ANG
	91486	Boeing KC-135R Stratotanker (59-1486)	USAF 92nd ARW, Fairchild AFB, WA
	91488	Boeing KC-135R Stratotanker (59-1488) w/gn	USAF 132nd ARS/101st ARW, Bangor, MN ANG
	91490	Boeing KC-135T Stratotanker (59-1490) y/bk	USAF 171st ARW, Greater Pittsburgh, PA ANG
	91492	Boeing KC-135R Stratotanker (59-1492) [ZZ] or/bk	USAF 909th ARS/18th Wg, Kadena AB, Japan
	91495	Boeing KC-135R Stratotanker (59-1495) r/w	USAF 173rd ARS/155th ARW, Lincoln, NE ANG
	91498	Boeing KC-135R Stratotanker (59-1498) w/gn	USAF 132nd ARS/101st ARW, Bangor, MN ANG

Serial	Type (code/other identity)	Owner/operator, location or fate
91499	Boeing KC-135R Stratotanker (59-1499) [HH] *y/bk*	USAF 203rd ARS/15th Wg, Hickam AFB, HI ANG
91500	Boeing KC-135R Stratotanker (59-1500) *w/bl*	USAF 108th ARS/126th ARW, Scott AFB, IL ANG
91501	Boeing KC-135R Stratotanker (59-1501)	USAF 92nd ARW, Fairchild AFB, WA
91502	Boeing KC-135R Stratotanker (59-1502)	USAF 22nd ARW, McConnell AFB, KS
91504	Boeing KC-135T Stratotanker (59-1504) *w/r*	USAF 106th ARS/117th ARW, Birmingham, AL ANG
91505	Boeing KC-135R Stratotanker (59-1505) *w/or*	USAF 151st ARS/134th ARW, Knoxville, TN ANG
91506	Boeing KC-135R Stratotanker (59-1506) *y/bk*	USAF 174th ARS/185th ARW, Sioux City, IA ANG
91507	Boeing KC-135R Stratotanker (59-1507) *bl/y*	USAF 117th ARS/190th ARW, Forbes Field, KS ANG
91508	Boeing KC-135R Stratotanker (59-1508)	USAF 92nd ARW, Fairchild AFB, WA
91509	Boeing KC-135R Stratotanker (59-1509) *w/or*	USAF 151st ARS/134th ARW, Knoxville, TN ANG
91510	Boeing KC-135T Stratotanker (59-1510)	USAF 92nd ARW, Fairchild AFB, WA
91511	Boeing KC-135R Stratotanker (59-1511)	USAF 92nd ARW, Fairchild AFB, WA
91512	Boeing KC-135T Stratotanker (59-1512) *bk/y*	USAF 171st ARS/127th Wg, Selfridge ANGB, MI ANG
91513	Boeing KC-135T Stratotanker (59-1513) [D] *r/w/bl*	USAF 351st ARS/100th ARW, RAF Mildenhall, UK
91515	Boeing KC-135R Stratotanker (59-1515)	USAF 92nd ARW, Fairchild AFB, WA
91516	Boeing KC-135R Stratotanker (59-1516) *w/bl*	USAF 126th ARS/128th ARW, Mitchell Field, WI ANG
91517	Boeing KC-135R Stratotanker (59-1517) *w/or*	USAF 151st ARS/134th ARW, Knoxville, TN ANG
91519	Boeing KC-135R Stratotanker (59-1519) *y/bk*	USAF 174th ARS/185th ARW, Sioux City, IA ANG
91520	Boeing KC-135T Stratotanker (59-1520) [ZZ] *or/bk*	USAF 909th ARS/18th Wg, Kadena AB, Japan
91521	Boeing KC-135R Stratotanker (59-1521) [AK] *bl/y*	USAF 168th ARS/168th ARW, Eielson AFB, AK ANG
91522	Boeing KC-135R Stratotanker (59-1522) *w/bl*	USAF 108th ARS/126th ARW, Scott AFB, IL ANG
91523	Boeing KC-135T Stratotanker (59-1523) *y/bk*	USAF 171st ARW, Greater Pittsburgh, PA ANG

PZL-Mielec C-145A Combat Coyote

Serial	Type (code/other identity)	Owner/operator, location or fate
20331	PZL-Mielec C-145A Combat Coyote (N331MF/12-0331)	USAF 6th SOS/919th SOW, Duke Field, FL
20335	PZL-Mielec C-145A Combat Coyote (N335RH/12-0335)	USAF 6th SOS/919th SOW, Duke Field, FL
20336	PZL-Mielec C-145A Combat Coyote (N336MJ/12-0336)	USAF 6th SOS/919th SOW, Duke Field, FL
20337	PZL-Mielec C-145A Combat Coyote (N337GU/12-0337)	USAF 6th SOS/919th SOW, Duke Field, FL
20338	PZL-Mielec C-145A Combat Coyote (N338CH/12-0338)	USAF 6th SOS/919th SOW, Duke Field, FL

Dornier C-146A Wolfhound

Serial	Type (code/other identity)	Owner/operator, location or fate
03026	Dornier C-146A Wolfhound (N929EF/10-3026)	USAF 524th SOS/27th SOW, Cannon AFB, NM
03068	Dornier C-146A Wolfhound (N565EF/10-3068)	USAF 524th SOS/27th SOW, Cannon AFB, NM
03077	Dornier C-146A Wolfhound (N577EF/10-3077)	USAF 524th SOS/27th SOW, Cannon AFB, NM
13013	Dornier C-146A Wolfhound (N645HM/11-3013)	USAF
13016	Dornier C-146A Wolfhound (N941EF/11-3016)	USAF 524th SOS/27th SOW, Cannon AFB, NM
13031	Dornier C-146A Wolfhound (N975EF/11-3031)	USAF 524th SOS/27th SOW, Cannon AFB, NM
13075	Dornier C-146A Wolfhound (N953EF/11-3075)	USAF 524th SOS/27th SOW, Cannon AFB, NM
13097	Dornier C-146A Wolfhound (N307EF/11-3097)	USAF 524th SOS/27th SOW, Cannon AFB, NM
13104	Dornier C-146A Wolfhound (N907EF/11-3104)	USAF 524th SOS/27th SOW, Cannon AFB, NM
23040	Dornier C-146A Wolfhound (N340LS/12-3040)	USAF 524th SOS/27th SOW, Cannon AFB, NM
23047	Dornier C-146A Wolfhound (N347EF/12-3047)	USAF 524th SOS/27th SOW, Cannon AFB, NM
23050	Dornier C-146A Wolfhound (N355EF/12-3050)	USAF 524th SOS/27th SOW, Cannon AFB, NM
23060	Dornier C-146A Wolfhound (N360EF/12-3060)	USAF 524th SOS/27th SOW, Cannon AFB, NM
23085	Dornier C-146A Wolfhound (N385EF/12-3085)	USAF 49th SOS/919th SOW, Duke Field, FL
53058	Dornier C-146A Wolfhound (N570EF/95-3058)	USAF 524th SOS/27th SOW, Cannon AFB, NM
53086	Dornier C-146A Wolfhound (N328ST/15-3086)	USAF 524th SOS/27th SOW, Cannon AFB, NM
63020	Dornier C-146A Wolfhound (N524AW/16-3020)	USAF 49th SOS/919th SOW, Duke Field, FL
63025	Dornier C-146A Wolfhound (N250BG/16-3025)	USAF 859th SOS/919th SOW, Duke Field, FL
73091	Dornier C-146A Wolfhound (N391EF/97-3091)	USAF 524th SOS/27th SOW, Cannon AFB, NM
73093	Dornier C-146A Wolfhound (N545EF/97-3093)	USAF 859th SOS/919th SOW, Duke Field, FL
93106	Dornier C-146A Wolfhound (N525EF/99-3106)	USAF 524th SOS/27th SOW, Cannon AFB, NM

Notes	Serial	Type (code/other identity)	Owner/operator, location or fate
	150521	Lockheed NP-3D Orion [341]	USN VX-30, NAS Point Mugu, CA
	156511	Lockheed EP-3E ARIES II [511]	USN VQ-1, NAS Whidbey Island, WA
	156517	Lockheed EP-3E ARIES II [517]	USN VQ-1, NAS Whidbey Island, WA
	156528	Lockheed EP-3E ARIES II [528]	USN VQ-1, NAS Whidbey Island, WA
	156529	Lockheed EP-3E ARIES II [529]	USN VQ-1, NAS Whidbey Island, WA
	157316	Lockheed EP-3E ARIES II [316]	USN VQ-1, NAS Whidbey Island, WA
	157318	Lockheed EP-3E ARIES II [318]	USN VQ-1, NAS Whidbey Island, WA
	157325	Lockheed EP-3E ARIES II [325]	USN VQ-1, NAS Whidbey Island, WA
	157326	Lockheed EP-3E ARIES II [326]	USN VQ-1, NAS Whidbey Island, WA
	158210	Lockheed P-3C AIP+ Orion [PJ-210]	*To 309th AMARG, February 2019*
	158222	Lockheed P-3C AIP+ Orion [222]	*To 309th AMARG, October 2019*
	158224	Lockheed P-3C AIP+ Orion [224]	*To 309th AMARG, August 2019*
	158564	Lockheed P-3C AIP+ Orion [564]	*To 309th AMARG, October 2019*
	158570	Lockheed P-3C-IIIR Orion [RL-570]	USN VXS-1, Patuxent River, MD
	158574	Lockheed P-3C-IIIR Orion	USN BUPERS SDC, Dallas/Love Field, TX
	158912	Lockheed NP-3C Orion [RL-912]	USN VXS-1, Patuxent River, MD
	158934	Lockheed P-3C AIP+ Orion [302]	USN VX-30, NAS Point Mugu, CA
	159326	Lockheed P-3C AIP+ Orion [326]	USN VQ-1, NAS Whidbey Island, WA
	159504	Lockheed P-3CSPA Orion	*To 309th AMARG, September 2019*
	159887	Lockheed EP-3E ARIES II [887]	USN VQ-1, NAS Whidbey Island, WA
	159893	Lockheed EP-3E ARIES II [893]	USN VQ-1, NAS Whidbey Island, WA
	160287	Lockheed P-3C AIP+ Orion [287]	*To 309th AMARG, October 2019*
	160290	Lockheed P-3CSPA Orion [LL-290]	USN VPU-2, NAS Whidbey Island, WA
	160292	Lockheed P-3CSPA Orion [292]	USN VPU-2, NAS Whidbey Island, WA
	160293	Lockheed P-3C BMUP Orion [LL-293]	USN VP-30, NAS Jacksonville, FL
	160610	Lockheed P-3C AIP+ Orion [610]	USN VQ-1, NAS Whidbey Island, WA
	160627	Lockheed KC-130R Hercules [627]	USN VX-20, Patuxent River, MD
	160764	Lockheed EP-3E ARIES II [764]	USN VQ-1, NAS Whidbey Island, WA
	161012	Lockheed P-3C AIP+ Orion [012]	*To 309th AMARG, April 2019*
	161121	Lockheed P-3C BMUP+ Orion [121]	USN VP-62, NAS Jacksonville, FL
	161122	Lockheed P-3CSPA Orion [226]	USN VPU-2, NAS Whidbey Island, WA
	161127	Lockheed P-3C BMUP Orion [127]	*To 309th AMARG, February 2019*
	161129	Lockheed P-3C BMUP Orion [129]	USN VXS-1, Patuxent River, MD
	161132	Lockheed P-3C BMUP+ Orion [132]	USN VP-30, NAS Jacksonville, FL
	161337	Lockheed P-3C-II½ Orion [RL-337]	USN VXS-1, Patuxent River, MD
	161339	Lockheed P-3C BMUP Orion [339]	USN VP-69, NAS Whidbey Island, WA
	161404	Lockheed P-3C BMUP+ Orion [404]	USN VP-62, NAS Jacksonville, FL
	161405	Lockheed P-3C BMUP+ Orion [405]	USN VP-69, NAS Whidbey Island, WA
	161406	Lockheed P-3C AIP+ Orion [RC-406]	*Scrapped at Whidbey Island*
	161407	Lockheed P-3C AIP+ Orion [407]	*Scrapped at Whidbey Island*
	161408	Lockheed P-3C BMUP+ Orion [408]	USN VP-62, NAS Jacksonville, FL
	161410	Lockheed EP-3E ARIES II [410]	USN VQ-1, NAS Whidbey Island, WA
	161411	Lockheed P-3C BMUP+ Orion [411]	USN VP-69, NAS Whidbey Island, WA
	161413	Lockheed P-3C AIP+ Orion [413]	*To 309th AMARG, March 2019*
	161414	Lockheed P-3C BMUP+ Orion [414]	USN VP-69, NAS Whidbey Island, WA
	161415	Lockheed P-3C BMUP+ Orion [415]	USN VP-62, NAS Jacksonville, FL
	161586	Lockheed P-3C BMUP+ Orion [586]	USN VP-62, NAS Jacksonville, FL
	161587	Lockheed P-3C BMUP+ Orion [587]	USN VP-69, NAS Whidbey Island, WA
	161588	Lockheed P-3C BMUP+ Orion [588]	USN VP-69, NAS Whidbey Island, WA
	161589	Lockheed P-3C BMUP+ Orion [589]	USN VP-30, NAS Jacksonville, FL
	161590	Lockheed P-3C BMUP+ Orion [590]	USN VP-62, NAS Jacksonville, FL
	161593	Lockheed P-3C BMUP+ Orion [593]	USN VP-69, NAS Whidbey Island, WA
	161596	Lockheed P-3C BMUP+ Orion [596]	*To 309th AMARG, October 2019*
	162308	Lockheed KC-130T Hercules [WB-407]	USN VX-30, NAS Point Mugu, CA
	162309	Lockheed KC-130T Hercules [309]	USN VX-20, Patuxent River, MD
	162310	Lockheed KC-130T Hercules [310]	USN VX-20, Patuxent River, MD
	162311	Lockheed KC-130T Hercules [405]	USN VX-30, NAS Point Mugu, CA
	162317	Lockheed P-3C AIP+ Orion [317]	*Withdrawn from use at Greenville, 2019*
	162318	Lockheed P-3C AIP+ Orion [318]	USN
	162770	Lockheed P-3C AIP+ Orion [770]	USN VP-30, NAS Jacksonville, FL
	162772	Lockheed P-3C AIP+ Orion [772]	USN VPU-2, NAS Whidbey Island, WA
	162773	Lockheed P-3C AIP+ Orion [773]	*To 309th AMARG, October 2019*

Serial	Type (code/other identity)	Owner/operator, location or fate	Notes
162776	Lockheed P-3C AIP+ Orion [776]	*Withdrawn from use at Pensacola, October 2019*	
162777	Lockheed P-3C AIP+ Orion [777]	USN VQ-1, NAS Whidbey Island, WA	
162778	Lockheed P-3C AIP+ Orion [304]	USN VX-30, NAS Point Mugu, CA	
162782	Boeing E-6B Mercury	USN VQ-3/SCW-1, Tinker AFB, OK	
162783	Boeing E-6B Mercury	USN VQ-3/SCW-1, Tinker AFB, OK	
162784	Boeing E-6B Mercury	USN VQ-4/SCW-1, Tinker AFB, OK	
162998	Lockheed P-3C AIP+ Orion [998]	USN VQ-1, NAS Whidbey Island, WA	
162999	Lockheed P-3C AIP+ Orion [999]	USN VX-30, NAS Point Mugu, CA	
163000	Lockheed P-3C AIP+ Orion [000]	*Sold to NASA, 2019*	
163001	Lockheed P-3C AIP+ Orion [001]	USN VPU-2, NAS Whidbey Island, WA	
163004	Lockheed P-3C AIP+ Orion [004]	*To 309th AMARG, April 2019*	
163023	Lockheed KC-130T Hercules [404]	USN VX-30, NAS Point Mugu, CA	
163290	Lockheed P-3C AIP+ Orion [LL-290]	USN VP-30, NAS Jacksonville, FL	
163291	Lockheed P-3C AIP+ Orion [291]	USN VXS-1, Patuxent River, MD	
163293	Lockheed P-3C AIP+ Orion [LL-293]	*Sold to NASA, 2019*	
163294	Lockheed P-3C AIP+ Orion [303]	USN VX-30, NAS Point Mugu, CA	
163295	Lockheed P-3C AIP+ Orion [295]	USN VP-30, NAS Jacksonville, FL	
163310	Lockheed KC-130T Hercules [WB-310]	USN VX-20, Patuxent River, MD	
163311	Lockheed KC-130T Hercules [RU-311]	USN VR-55, NAS Point Mugu, CA	
163591	Lockheed KC-130T Hercules [RU-591]	USN VR-55, NAS Point Mugu, CA	
163691	Grumman C-20D Gulfstream III	USN VR-1, NAF Washington, MD	
163692	Grumman C-20D Gulfstream III	USN VR-1, NAF Washington, MD	
163918	Boeing E-6B Mercury	USN VQ-3/SCW-1, Tinker AFB, OK	
163919	Boeing E-6B Mercury	USN VQ-3/SCW-1, Tinker AFB, OK	
163920	Boeing E-6B Mercury	USN VQ-3/SCW-1, Tinker AFB, OK	
164105	Lockheed KC-130T Hercules [NY-105]	USMC VMGR-452, Stewart Field, NY	
164106	Lockheed KC-130T Hercules [RU-106]	USN VR-55, NAS Point Mugu, CA	
164180	Lockheed KC-130T Hercules [NY-180]	USMC VMGR-452, Stewart Field, NY	
164181	Lockheed KC-130T Hercules [NY-181]	*To 309th AMARG, August 2019*	
164386	Boeing E-6B Mercury	USN VQ-4/SCW-1, Tinker AFB, OK	
164387	Boeing E-6B Mercury	USN VQ-3/SCW-1, Tinker AFB, OK	
164388	Boeing E-6B Mercury	USN VQ-4/SCW-1, Tinker AFB, OK	
164404	Boeing E-6B Mercury	USN VQ-4/SCW-1, Tinker AFB, OK	
164405	Boeing E-6B Mercury	USN VQ-4/SCW-1, Tinker AFB, OK	
164406	Boeing E-6B Mercury	USN VQ-3/SCW-1, Tinker AFB, OK	
164407	Boeing E-6B Mercury	USN VQ-4/SCW-1, Tinker AFB, OK	
164408	Boeing E-6B Mercury	USN VQ-4/SCW-1, Tinker AFB, OK	
164409	Boeing E-6B Mercury	USN VQ-4/SCW-1, Tinker AFB, OK	
164410	Boeing E-6B Mercury	USN VQ-4/SCW-1, Tinker AFB, OK	
164441	Lockheed KC-130T Hercules [NY-441]	USN, stored Patuxent River, MD	
164442	Lockheed KC-130T Hercules [NY-442]	USMC VMGR-452, Stewart Field, NY	
164597	Lockheed KC-130T-30 Hercules [RU-597]	USN VR-55, NAS Point Mugu, CA	
164598	Lockheed KC-130T-30 Hercules [AX-598]	USN VR-53, NAF Washington, MD	
164762	Lockheed C-130T Hercules [CW-762]	USN VR-54, NAS New Orleans, LA	
164763	Lockheed C-130T Hercules	*Withdrawn from use, May 2019*	
164993	Lockheed C-130T Hercules [BD-993]	USN VR-64, NAS Willow Grove, PA	
164994	Lockheed C-130T Hercules [CW-994]	USN VR-54, NAS New Orleans, LA	
164995	Lockheed C-130T Hercules [AX-995]	USN VR-53, NAF Washington, MD	
164996	Lockheed C-130T Hercules [BD-996]	USN VR-64, NAS Willow Grove, PA	
164997	Lockheed C-130T Hercules [AX-997]	USN, stored Patuxent River, MD	
164998	Lockheed C-130T Hercules [BD-998]	USN VR-64, NAS Willow Grove, PA	
164999	Lockheed KC-130T Hercules [NY-999]	USMC VMGR-452, Stewart Field, NY	
165094	Grumman C-20G Gulfstream IV	USN VX-30, NAS Point Mugu, CA	
165151	Grumman C-20G Gulfstream IV	USN CFLSW Det., Sigonella, Italy	
165152	Grumman C-20G Gulfstream IV	USMC VMR-Det, MCBH Kaneohe Bay, HI	
165153	Grumman C-20G Gulfstream IV	USMC VMR-Det, MCBH Kaneohe Bay, HI	
165158	Lockheed C-130T Hercules [CW-158]	USN VR-54, NAS New Orleans, LA	
165159	Lockheed C-130T Hercules [CW-159]	USN VR-54, NAS New Orleans, LA	
165160	Lockheed C-130T Hercules [CW-160]	USN VR-54, NAS New Orleans, LA	
165161	Lockheed C-130T Hercules [BD-161]	USN VR-64, NAS Willow Grove, PA	
165162	Lockheed KC-130T Hercules [NY-162]	*To 309th AMARG, April 2019*	
165163	Lockheed KC-130T Hercules [NY-163]	USMC VMGR-452, Stewart Field, NY	

Notes	Serial	Type (code/other identity)	Owner/operator, location or fate
	165313	Lockheed C-130T Hercules [JW-313]	USN VR-62, NAS Jacksonville, FL
	165314	Lockheed C-130T Hercules [JW-314]	USN VR-62, NAS Jacksonville, FL
	165315	Lockheed KC-130T Hercules [NY-315]	USMC VMGR-452, Stewart Field, NY
	165316	Lockheed KC-130T Hercules [NY-316]	USMC VMGR-452, Stewart Field, NY
	165348	Lockheed C-130T Hercules [AX-348]	USN VR-53, NAF Washington, MD
	165349	Lockheed C-130T Hercules [JW-349]	USN VR-62, NAS Jacksonville, FL
	165350	Lockheed C-130T Hercules [350]	USN VX-20, Patuxent River, MD
	165351	Lockheed C-130T Hercules [AX-351]	USN VR-53, NAF Washington, MD
	165352	Lockheed KC-130T Hercules [NY-352]	USMC VMGR-452, Stewart Field, NY
	165353	Lockheed KC-130T Hercules [NY-353]	USMC VMGR-452, Stewart Field, NY
	165378	Lockheed C-130T Hercules [JW-378]	USN VR-62, NAS Jacksonville, FL
	165379	Lockheed C-130T Hercules [BD-379]	USN VR-64, NAS Willow Grove, PA
	165735	Lockheed KC-130J Hercules II [QB-735]	USMC VMGR-352, Miramar MCAS, CA
	165736	Lockheed KC-130J Hercules II [QB-736]	USMC VMGR-352, Miramar MCAS, CA
	165737	Lockheed KC-130J Hercules II [BH-737]	USMC VMGR-252, Cherry Point MCAS, NC
	165738	Lockheed KC-130J Hercules II [BH-738]	USMC VMGR-252, Cherry Point MCAS, NC
	165739	Lockheed KC-130J Hercules II [QH-739]	USMC VMGR-234, Fort Worth JRB, TX
	165740	Cessna UC-35C Citation V [EZ]	USMC MWHS-4, NAS New Orleans, LA
	165741	Cessna UC-35C Citation V [EZ]	USMC MWHS-4, NAS New Orleans, LA
	165809	Lockheed KC-130J Hercules II [BH-809]	USMC VMGR-252, Cherry Point MCAS, NC
	165810	Lockheed KC-130J Hercules II [BH-810]	USMC VMGR-252, Cherry Point MCAS, NC
	165829	Boeing C-40A Clipper (N1003N) [829]	USN VR-58, NAS Jacksonville, FL
	165830	Boeing C-40A Clipper (N1003M) [830]	USN VR-59, Fort Worth JRB, TX
	165831	Boeing C-40A Clipper (N1786B) [831]	USN VR-59, Fort Worth JRB, TX
	165832	Boeing C-40A Clipper (N1787B) [832]	USN VR-61, Fort Worth JRB, TX
	165833	Boeing C-40A Clipper [833]	USN VR-59, Fort Worth JRB, TX
	165834	Boeing C-40A Clipper [834]	USN VR-61, Fort Worth JRB, TX
	165835	Boeing C-40A Clipper (N543BA) [835]	USN VR-57, NAS North Island, CA
	165836	Boeing C-40A Clipper [836]	USN VR-57, NAS North Island, CA
	165939	Cessna UC-35D Citation V	USMC MAW-4, Miramar MCAS, CA
	165957	Lockheed KC-130J Hercules II [QD-957] $	USMC VMGR-152, Iwakuni MCAS, Japan
	166374	Cessna UC-35D Citation V	USMC VMR-2, NAF Washington, MD
	166375	Gulfstream Aerospace C-37A Gulfstream V [365]	USN CFLSW Det, MCBH Kaneohe Bay, HI
	166376	Gulfstream Aerospace C-37B Gulfstream V [376]	USN VR-1, NAF Washington, MD
	166377	Gulfstream Aerospace C-37B Gulfstream V [377]	USN VR-1, NAF Washington, MD
	166378	Gulfstream Aerospace C-37B Gulfstream V [378]	USN VR-1, NAF Washington, MD
	166379	Gulfstream Aerospace NC-37B Gulfstream V [BH-100]	USN VX-30, NAS Point Mugu, CA
	166380	Lockheed KC-130J Hercules II [BH-380]	USMC VMGR-252, Cherry Point MCAS, NC
	166381	Lockheed KC-130J Hercules II [BH-381]	USMC VMGR-252, Cherry Point MCAS, NC
	166382	Lockheed KC-130J Hercules II [QB-382]	USMC VMGR-352, Miramar MCAS, CA
	166472	Lockheed KC-130J Hercules II [BH-472]	USMC VMGR-252, Cherry Point MCAS, NC
	166473	Lockheed KC-130J Hercules II [QH-473]	USMC VMGR-234, Fort Worth JRB, TX
	166474	Cessna UC-35D Citation V	USMC MAW-4, Miramar MCAS, CA
	166500	Cessna UC-35D Citation V	USMC MAW-4, Miramar MCAS, CA
	166511	Lockheed KC-130J Hercules II [511]	USN VX-20, Patuxent River, MD
	166512	Lockheed KC-130J Hercules II [QB-512]	USMC VMGR-352, Miramar MCAS, CA
	166513	Lockheed KC-130J Hercules II [BH-513]	USMC VMGR-252, Cherry Point MCAS, NC
	166514	Lockheed KC-130J Hercules II [BH-514]	USMC VMGR-252, Cherry Point MCAS, NC
	166693	Boeing C-40A Clipper [693]	USN VR-51, MCBH Kaneohe Bay, Hawaii
	166694	Boeing C-40A Clipper [694]	USN VR-56, NAS Oceana, VA
	166695	Boeing C-40A Clipper (N1787B) [695]	USN VR-61, Fort Worth JRB, TX
	166696	Boeing C-40A Clipper [696]	USN VR-56, NAS Oceana, VA
	166712	Cessna UC-35D Citation V	USMC MWHS-1, Futenma MCAS, Japan
	166713	Cessna UC-35D Citation V	USMC MWHS-1, Futenma MCAS, Japan
	166714	Cessna UC-35D Citation V [VM]	USMC VMR-2, NAF Washington, MD
	166715	Cessna UC-35D Citation V	USMC VMR-1, Fort Worth JRB, TX
	166762	Lockheed KC-130J Hercules II [BH-762]	USMC VMGR-252, Cherry Point MCAS, NC
	166763	Lockheed KC-130J Hercules II [QD-763]	USMC VMGR-152, Iwakuni MCAS, Japan
	166764	Lockheed KC-130J Hercules II [BH-764]	USMC VMGR-252, Cherry Point MCAS, NC
	166765	Lockheed KC-130J Hercules II [QB-765]	USMC VMGR-352, Miramar MCAS, CA
	166766	Cessna UC-35D Citation V	USMC MWHS-1, Futenma MCAS, Japan
	166767	Cessna UC-35D Citation V [VM]	USMC VMR-2, NAF Washington, MD

Serial	Type (code/other identity)	Owner/operator, location or fate	Notes
167108	Lockheed KC-130J Hercules II [QB-108]	USMC VMGR-352, Miramar MCAS, CA	
167109	Lockheed KC-130J Hercules II [QD-109]	USN VX-20, Patuxent River, MD	
167110	Lockheed KC-130J Hercules II [QB-110]	USMC VMGR-352, Miramar MCAS, CA	
167111	Lockheed KC-130J Hercules II [QH-111]	USMC VMGR-234, Fort Worth JRB, TX	
167112	Lockheed KC-130J Hercules II [BH-112]	USMC VMGR-252, Cherry Point MCAS, NC	
167923	Lockheed KC-130J Hercules II [QD-923]	USMC VMGR-152, Iwakuni MCAS, Japan	
167924	Lockheed KC-130J Hercules II [QB-924]	USMC VMGR-352, Miramar MCAS, CA	
167925	Lockheed KC-130J Hercules II [QD-925]	USMC VMGR-152, Iwakuni MCAS, Japan	
167926	Lockheed KC-130J Hercules II [QD-926]	USMC VMGR-152, Iwakuni MCAS, Japan	
167927	Lockheed KC-130J Hercules II [QD-927]	USMC VMGR-152, Iwakuni MCAS, Japan	
167951	Boeing P-8A Poseidon (N541BA) [951]	USN VX-20, Patuxent River, MD	
167952	Boeing P-8A Poseidon (N398DS) [952]	USN BUPERS SDC, Dallas/Love Field, TX	
167953	Boeing P-8A Poseidon (N441BA) [953]	USN VX-20, Patuxent River, MD	
167954	Boeing P-8A Poseidon (N397DS)	USN VX-20, Patuxent River, MD	
167955	Boeing P-8A Poseidon (N328DS) [JA-955]	USN VX-1, NAS Patuxent River, MD	
167956	Boeing P-8A Poseidon (N391DS) [JA-956]	USN VX-1, NAS Patuxent River, MD	
167982	Lockheed KC-130J Hercules II [QD-982]	USMC VMGR-152, Iwakuni MCAS, Japan	
167983	Lockheed KC-130J Hercules II [QD-983]	USMC VMGR-152, Iwakuni MCAS, Japan	
167984	Lockheed KC-130J Hercules II [QB-984]	USMC VMGR-352, Miramar MCAS, CA	
167985	Lockheed KC-130J Hercules II [QB-985]	USMC VMGR-352, Miramar MCAS, CA	
168065	Lockheed KC-130J Hercules II [QD-065]	USMC VMGR-152, Iwakuni MCAS, Japan	
168066	Lockheed KC-130J Hercules II [QD-066]	USMC VMGR-152, Iwakuni MCAS, Japan	
168067	Lockheed KC-130J Hercules II [QB-067]	USMC VMGR-352, Miramar MCAS, CA	
168068	Lockheed KC-130J Hercules II [QB-068]	USMC VMGR-352, Miramar MCAS, CA	
168069	Lockheed KC-130J Hercules II [BH-069]	USMC VMGR-252, Cherry Point MCAS, NC	
168070	Lockheed KC-130J Hercules II [BH-070]	USMC VMGR-252, Cherry Point MCAS, NC	
168071	Lockheed KC-130J Hercules II [BH-071]	USMC VMGR-252, Cherry Point MCAS, NC	
168072	Lockheed KC-130J Hercules II [QB-072]	USMC VMGR-352, Miramar MCAS, CA	
168073	Lockheed KC-130J Hercules II [QH-073]	USMC VMGR-234, Fort Worth JRB, TX	
168074	Lockheed KC-130J Hercules II [QD-074]	USMC VMGR-152, Iwakuni MCAS, Japan	
168075	Lockheed KC-130J Hercules II [QD-075]	USMC VMGR-152, Iwakuni MCAS, Japan	
168428	Boeing P-8A Poseidon (N392DS) [LA-428]	USN VP-5, NAS Jacksonville, FL	
168429	Boeing P-8A Poseidon (N397DS) [LN-429]	USN VP-45, NAS Jacksonville, FL	
168430	Boeing P-8A Poseidon (N398DS) [LD-430]	USN VP-10, NAS Jacksonville, FL	
168431	Boeing P-8A Poseidon (N507DS) [LD-431]	USN VP-10, NAS Jacksonville, FL	
168432	Boeing P-8A Poseidon (N516DS) [LK-432]	USN VP-26, NAS Jacksonville, FL	
168433	Boeing P-8A Poseidon (N530DS) [LK-433]	USN VP-26, NAS Jacksonville, FL	
168434	Boeing P-8A Poseidon (N532DS) [LN-434]	USN VP-45, NAS Jacksonville, FL	
168435	Boeing P-8A Poseidon (N533DS) [435]	USN VP-45, NAS Jacksonville, FL	
168436	Boeing P-8A Poseidon (N536DS) [LF-436]	USN VP-16, NAS Jacksonville, FL	
168437	Boeing P-8A Poseidon (N537DS) [LF-437]	USN VP-16, NAS Jacksonville, FL	
168438	Boeing P-8A Poseidon (N327DS) [LK-438]	USN VP-26, NAS Jacksonville, FL	
168439	Boeing P-8A Poseidon (N539DS) [LA-439]	USN VP-5, NAS Jacksonville, FL	
168440	Boeing P-8A Poseidon (N708DS) [440]	USN VP-26, NAS Jacksonville, FL	
168754	Boeing P-8A Poseidon (N736DS) [LC-754]	USN VP-8, NAS Jacksonville, FL	
168755	Boeing P-8A Poseidon (N740DS) [YD-755]	USN VP-4, NAS Whidbey Island, WA	
168756	Boeing P-8A Poseidon (N753DS) [LN-756]	USN VP-45, NAS Jacksonville, FL	
168757	Boeing P-8A Poseidon (N755DS) [YD-757]	USN VP-4, NAS Whidbey Island, WA	
168758	Boeing P-8A Poseidon (N758DS) [RD-758]	USN VP-47, NAS Whidbey Island, WA	
168759	Boeing P-8A Poseidon (N762DS) [LF-759]	USN VP-16, NAS Jacksonville, FL	
168760	Boeing P-8A Poseidon (N768DS) [RD-760]	USN VP-47, NAS Whidbey Island, WA	
168761	Boeing P-8A Poseidon (N771DS) [LN-761]	USN VP-45, NAS Jacksonville, FL	
168762	Boeing P-8A Poseidon (N780DS) [LF-762]	USN VP-16, NAS Jacksonville, FL	
168763	Boeing P-8A Poseidon (N781DS) [LK-763]	USN VP-26, NAS Jacksonville, FL	
168764	Boeing P-8A Poseidon (N783DS) [LN-764]	USN VP-45, NAS Jacksonville, FL	
168848	Boeing P-8A Poseidon (N784DS) [LK-848]	USN VP-26, NAS Jacksonville, FL	
168849	Boeing P-8A Poseidon (N785DS) [YB-849]	USN VP-1, NAS Whidbey Island, WA	
168850	Boeing P-8A Poseidon (N789DS) [YD-850]	USN VP-4, NAS Whidbey Island, WA	
168851	Boeing P-8A Poseidon (N790DS) [YD-851]	USN VP-4, NAS Whidbey Island, WA	
168852	Boeing P-8A Poseidon (N715DS) [852]	USN VP-30, NAS Jacksonville, FL	
168853	Boeing P-8A Poseidon (N717DS) [RD-853]	USN VP-47, NAS Whidbey Island, WA	
168854	Boeing P-8A Poseidon (N722DS) [LC-854]	USN VP-8, NAS Jacksonville, FL	

Notes	Serial	Type (code/other identity)	Owner/operator, location or fate
	168855	Boeing P-8A Poseidon (N729DS) [855]	USN VP-45, NAS Jacksonville, FL
	168856	Boeing P-8A Poseidon (N805DS) [856]	USN VP-30, NAS Jacksonville, FL
	168857	Boeing P-8A Poseidon (N590DS) [LK-857]	USN VP-26, NAS Jacksonville, FL
	168858	Boeing P-8A Poseidon (N591DS) [LD-858]	USN VP-10, NAS Jacksonville, FL
	168859	Boeing P-8A Poseidon (N592DS) [LD-859]	USN VP-10, NAS Jacksonville, FL
	168860	Boeing P-8A Poseidon (N593DS) [LF-860]	USN VP-16, NAS Jacksonville, FL
	168980	Boeing C-40A Clipper (N513NV) [980]	USN VR-61, Fort Worth JRB, TX
	168981	Boeing C-40A Clipper (N514NV) [981]	USN VR-61, Fort Worth JRB, TX
	168996	Boeing P-8A Poseidon (N595DS) [996]	USN NASC-FS, NAS Jacksonville, FL
	168997	Boeing P-8A Poseidon (N597DS) [PD-997]	USN VP-9, NAS Whidbey Island, WA
	168998	Boeing P-8A Poseidon (N598DS) [LD-998]	USN VP-10, NAS Jacksonville, FL
	168999	Boeing P-8A Poseidon (N910DS) [999]	USN VP-30, NAS Jacksonville, FL
	169000	Boeing P-8A Poseidon (N914DS) [LF-000]	USN VP-16, NAS Jacksonville, FL
	169001	Boeing P-8A Poseidon (N931DS) [001]	USN VP-30, NAS Jacksonville, FL
	169002	Boeing P-8A Poseidon (N934DS) [PD-002]	USN VP-9, NAS Whidbey Island, WA
	169003	Boeing P-8A Poseidon (N935DS) [LK-003]	USN VP-26, NAS Jacksonville, FL
	169004	Boeing P-8A Poseidon (N936DS) [004]	USN VP-9, NAS Whidbey Island, WA
	169005	Boeing P-8A Poseidon (N941DS) [LL-005]	USN VP-30, NAS Jacksonville, FL
	169006	Boeing P-8A Poseidon (N942DS) [LN-006]	USN VP-45, NAS Jacksonville, FL
	169007	Boeing C-40A Clipper (N943DS) [007]	USN BUPERS SDC, Dallas/Love Field, TX
	169008	Boeing P-8A Poseidon (N944DS) [YD-008]	USN VP-4, NAS Whidbey Island, WA
	169009	Boeing P-8A Poseidon (N949DS) [YD-009]	USN VP-4, NAS Whidbey Island, WA
	169010	Boeing P-8A Poseidon (N957DS) [010]	USN BUPERS SDC, Dallas/Love Field, TX
	169011	Boeing P-8A Poseidon (N958DS) [LA-011]	USN VP-5, NAS Jacksonville, FL
	169018	Lockheed KC-130J Hercules II [QH-018]	USMC VMGR-234, Fort Worth JRB, TX
	169036	Boeing C-40A Clipper (N515NV) [036]	USN VR-61, Fort Worth JRB, TX
	169225	Lockheed KC-130J Hercules II [BH-225]	USMC VMGR-252, Cherry Point MCAS, NC
	169226	Lockheed KC-130J Hercules II [QB-226]	USMC VMGR-352, Miramar MCAS, CA
	169227	Lockheed KC-130J Hercules II [QD-227]	USMC VMGR-152, Iwakuni MCAS, Japan
	169228	Lockheed KC-130J Hercules II [QH-228]	USMC VMGR-234, Fort Worth JRB, TX
	169229	Lockheed KC-130J Hercules II [QH-229]	USMC VMGR-234, Fort Worth JRB, TX
	169230	Lockheed KC-130J Hercules II [QB-230]	USMC VMGR-352, Miramar MCAS, CA
	169324	Boeing P-8A Poseidon (N960DS) [LK-324]	USN VP-26, NAS Jacksonville, FL
	169325	Boeing P-8A Poseidon (N962DS) [YD-325]	USN VP-4, NAS Whidbey Island, WA
	169326	Boeing P-8A Poseidon (N969DS) [326]	USN VP-30, NAS Jacksonville, FL
	169327	Boeing P-8A Poseidon (N963DS) [RD-327]	USN VP-47, NAS Whidbey Island, WA
	169328	Boeing P-8A Poseidon (N964DS) [PD-328]	USN VP-9, NAS Whidbey Island, WA
	169329	Boeing P-8A Poseidon (N968DS) [PD-329]	USN VP-9, NAS Whidbey Island, WA
	169330	Boeing P-8A Poseidon (N843DS) [330]	USN VP-30, NAS Jacksonville, FL
	169331	Boeing P-8A Poseidon (N852DS) [RD-331]	USN VP-47, NAS Whidbey Island, WA
	169332	Boeing P-8A Poseidon (N848DS) [PD-332]	USN VP-9, NAS Whidbey Island, WA
	169333	Boeing P-8A Poseidon (N838DS) [333]	USN VX-1/VX-20, NAS Patuxent River, MD
	169334	Boeing P-8A Poseidon (N839DS) [LC-334]	USN VP-8, NAS Jacksonville, FL
	169335	Boeing P-8A Poseidon (N854DS) [335]	USN BUPERS SDC, Dallas/Love Field, TX
	169336	Boeing P-8A Poseidon (N857DS) [LC-336]	USN VP-8, NAS Jacksonville, FL
	169337	Boeing P-8A Poseidon (N858DS) [LA-337]	USN VP-5, NAS Jacksonville, FL
	169338	Boeing P-8A Poseidon (N860DS) [338]	USN VP-30, NAS Jacksonville, FL
	169339	Boeing P-8A Poseidon (N863DS) [RC-339]	USN VP-46, NAS Whidbey Island, WA
	169340	Boeing P-8A Poseidon (N864DS) [LA-340]	USN VP-5, NAS Jacksonville, FL
	169341	Boeing P-8A Poseidon (N869DS) [LC-341]	USN VP-8, NAS Jacksonville, FL
	169342	Boeing P-8A Poseidon (N874DS) [LC-342]	USN VP-8, NAS Jacksonville, FL
	169343	Boeing P-8A Poseidon (N873DS) [YB-343]	USN VP-1, NAS Whidbey Island, WA
	169344	Boeing P-8A Poseidon (N304DS) [RC-344]	USN VP-46, NAS Whidbey Island, WA
	169345	Boeing P-8A Poseidon (N308DS) [YB-345]	USN VP-1, NAS Whidbey Island, WA
	169346	Boeing P-8A Poseidon (N318DS) [RC-346]	USN VP-46, NAS Whidbey Island, WA
	169347	Boeing P-8A Poseidon (N322DS) [YB-347]	USN VP-1, NAS Whidbey Island, WA
	169348	Boeing P-8A Poseidon (N323DS) [348]	USN VP-46, NAS Whidbey Island, WA
	169349	Boeing P-8A Poseidon (N328DS) [349]	USN VP-10, NAS Jacksonville, FL
	169426	Boeing P-8A Poseidon (N332DS) [YD-426]	USN VP-4, NAS Whidbey Island, WA
	169532	Lockheed KC-130J Hercules II [QD-532]	USMC VMGR-152, Iwakuni MCAS, Japan
	169533	Lockheed KC-130J Hercules II [BH-533]	USMC VMGR-252, Cherry Point MCAS, NC
	169534	Lockheed KC-130J Hercules II [BH-534]	USMC VMGR-252, Cherry Point MCAS, NC

Serial	Type (code/other identity)	Owner/operator, location or fate	Notes
169535	Lockheed KC-130J Hercules II [QD-227]	USMC VMGR-152, Iwakuni MCAS, Japan	
169542	Boeing P-8A Poseidon (N348DS) [542]	USN VX-1/VX-20, NAS Patuxent River, MD	
169543	Boeing P-8A Poseidon (N347DS) [543]	USN VP-30, NAS Jacksonville, FL	
169544	Boeing P-8A Poseidon (N360DS) [544]	USN VP-47, NAS Whidbey Island, WA	
169545	Boeing P-8A Poseidon (N364DS) [545]	USN VP-30, NAS Jacksonville, FL	
169546	Boeing P-8A Poseidon (N368DS) [546]	USN VP-47, NAS Whidbey Island, WA	
169547	Boeing P-8A Poseidon (N374DS) [547]	USN VP-30, NAS Jacksonville, FL	
169548	Boeing P-8A Poseidon (N383DS) [548]	USN VP-1, NAS Whidbey Island, WA	
169549	Boeing P-8A Poseidon (N392DS) [549]	USN VP-30, NAS Jacksonville, FL	
169550	Boeing P-8A Poseidon (N410DS/169573) [550]	USN (on order)	
169551	Boeing P-8A Poseidon (N438DS) [551]	USN VP-30, NAS Jacksonville, FL	
169552	Boeing P-8A Poseidon (N459DS) [552]	USN VP-30, NAS Jacksonville, FL	
169553	Boeing P-8A Poseidon (N486DS) [553]	USN (on order)	
169554	Boeing P-8A Poseidon (N489DS) [554]	USN (on order)	
169555	Boeing P-8A Poseidon (N508DS) [555]	USN (on order)	
169556	Boeing P-8A Poseidon (N512DS) [556]	USN (on order)	
169557	Boeing P-8A Poseidon [557]	USN (on order)	
169558	Boeing P-8A Poseidon (N516DS) [558]	USN (on order)	
169559	Boeing P-8A Poseidon (N532DS) [559]	USN (on order)	
169573	Boeing P-8A Poseidon (N410DS) [573]	*Re-registered as 169550, October 2019*	
169792	Boeing C-40A Clipper (N1799B) [792]	USN VR-51, MCBH Kaneohe Bay, Hawaii	
169793	Boeing C-40A Clipper (N517NV) [793]	USN VR-57, NAS North Island, CA	
169...	Boeing P-8A Poseidon	USN (on order)	
169...	Boeing P-8A Poseidon	USN (on order)	
169...	Boeing P-8A Poseidon	USN (on order)	

US-BASED US COAST GUARD AIRCRAFT

Notes	Serial	Type (code/other identity)	Owner/operator, location or fate
	01	Gulfstream Aerospace C-37A Gulfstream V (N527GA)	USCG, Commandants Flt, Washington DC
	02	Gulfstream Aerospace C-37B Gulfstream V (N640W)	USCG, Commandants Flt, Washington DC
	1503	Lockheed HC-130H Hercules	*Withdrawn from use, 2019*
	1701	Lockheed HC-130H Hercules	*Withdrawn from use, 2019*
	1702	Lockheed HC-130H Hercules	USCG, USCGS Kodiak, AK
	1703	Lockheed HC-130H Hercules	USCG, USCGS Barbers Point, HI
	1704	Lockheed HC-130H Hercules	USCG, USCGS Sacramento, CA
	1706	Lockheed HC-130H Hercules	USCG, USCGS Barbers Point, HI
	1707	Lockheed HC-130H Hercules	USCG, USCGS Elizabeth City, NC
	1709	Lockheed HC-130H Hercules	USCG, USCGS Kodiak, AK
	1711	Lockheed HC-130H Hercules	USCG, USCGS Clearwater, FL
	1712	Lockheed HC-130H Hercules	USCG, USCGS Clearwater, FL
	1715	Lockheed HC-130H Hercules	USCG, USCGS Clearwater, FL
	1716	Lockheed HC-130H Hercules	USCG, USCGS Barbers Point, HI
	1718	Lockheed HC-130H Hercules	USCG, USCGS Clearwater, FL
	1720	Lockheed HC-130H Hercules	USCG, USCGS Barbers Point, HI
	1790	Lockheed HC-130H Hercules	*Withdrawn from use, 2019*
	2001	Lockheed HC-130J Hercules II	USCG, USCGS Elizabeth City, NC
	2002	Lockheed HC-130J Hercules II	USCG, USCGS Elizabeth City, NC
	2003	Lockheed HC-130J Hercules II	USCG, USCGS Elizabeth City, NC
	2004	Lockheed HC-130J Hercules II	USCG, USCGS Elizabeth City, NC
	2005	Lockheed HC-130J Hercules II	USCG, USCGS Elizabeth City, NC
	2006	Lockheed HC-130J Hercules II	USCG, USCGS Kodiak, AK
	2007	Lockheed HC-130J Hercules II	USCG, USCGS Elizabeth City, NC
	2008	Lockheed HC-130J Hercules II	USCG, USCGS Elizabeth City, NC
	2009	Lockheed HC-130J Hercules II	USCG, USCGS Kodiak, AK
	2010	Lockheed HC-130J Hercules II	USCG, USCGS Elizabeth City, NC
	2011	Lockheed HC-130J Hercules II	USCG, USCGS Kodiak, AK
	2012	Lockheed HC-130J Hercules II	USCG, Waco, TX
	2013	Lockheed HC-130J Hercules II	USCG, Waco, TX
	2014	Lockheed HC-130J Hercules II	USCG (on order)

Aircraft in US Government or Military Service with Civil Registrations

Notes	Serial	Type (code/other identity)	Owner/operator, location or fate
	N85	Canadair CL.601 Challenger	Federal Aviation Administration, OKlahoma City, OK
	N86	Canadair CL.601 Challenger	Federal Aviation Administration, Oklahoma City, OK
	N87	Canadair CL.601 Challenger	Federal Aviation Administration, Oklahoma City, OK
	N88	Canadair CL.604 Challenger	Federal Aviation Administration, Oklahoma City, OK
	N89	Canadair CL.605 Challenger	Federal Aviation Administration, Oklahoma City, OK
	N90	Canadair CL.605 Challenger	Federal Aviation Administration, Oklahoma City, OK

The list below is not intended to be a complete list of military aviation sites on the Internet. The sites listed cover Museums, Locations, Air Forces, Companies and Organisations that are mentioned elsewhere in 'Military Aircraft Markings'. Sites listed are in English or contain sufficient English to be reasonably easily understood. Each site address was correct at the time of going to press. Additions are welcome, via the usual address found at the front of the book, or via e-mail to admin@aviation-links.co.uk. An up to date copy of this list is to be found at The 'Military Aircraft Markings' Web Site, http://www.militaryaircraftmarkings.co.uk/.

Name of Site	Web Address All prefixed 'http://')
MILITARY SITES-UK	
No 1 Sqn	www.raf.mod.uk/our-organisation/squadrons/1-f-squadron/
No 2 Sqn	www.raf.mod.uk/our-organisation/squadrons/ii-ac-squadron/
No 3 Sqn	www.raf.mod.uk/our-organisation/squadrons/3-f-squadron/
No 4 Sqn	www.raf.mod.uk/our-organisation/squadrons/iv-squadron/
No 5 Sqn	www.raf.mod.uk/our-organisation/squadrons/v-ac-squadron/
No 6 Sqn	www.raf.mod.uk/our-organisation/squadrons/6-squadron/
No 7 Sqn	www.raf.mod.uk/our-organisation/squadrons/7-squadron/
No 8 Sqn	www.raf.mod.uk/our-organisation/squadrons/8-squadron/
No 9 Sqn	www.raf.mod.uk/our-organisation/squadrons/ix-b-squadron/
No 10 Sqn	www.raf.mod.uk/our-organisation/squadrons/10-squadron/
No 11 Sqn	www.raf.mod.uk/our-organisation/squadrons/xi-f-squadron/
No 12 Sqn	www.raf.mod.uk/our-organisation/squadrons/12-squadron/
No 13 Sqn	www.raf.mod.uk/our-organisation/squadrons/13-squadron/
No 14 Sqn	www.raf.mod.uk/our-organisation/squadrons/14-squadron/
No 16 Sqn	www.raf.mod.uk/our-organisation/squadrons/16-squadron/
No 17 Sqn	www.raf.mod.uk/our-organisation/squadrons/17-squadron/
No 18 Sqn	www.raf.mod.uk/our-organisation/squadrons/18-squadron/
No 24 Sqn	www.raf.mod.uk/our-organisation/squadrons/xxiv-squadron/
No 25 Sqn	www.raf.mod.uk/our-organisation/squadrons/xxv-f-squadron/
No 27 Sqn	www.raf.mod.uk/our-organisation/squadrons/27-squadron/
No 28 Sqn	www.raf.mod.uk/our-organisation/squadrons/28-squadron/
No 29 Sqn	www.raf.mod.uk/our-organisation/squadrons/29-squadron/
No 32(The Royal) Sqn	www.raf.mod.uk/our-organisation/squadrons/32-squadron/
No 33 Sqn	www.raf.mod.uk/our-organisation/squadrons/33-squadron/
No 39 Sqn	www.raf.mod.uk/our-organisation/squadrons/39-squadron/
No 41 Sqn	www.raf.mod.uk/our-organisation/squadrons/41-squadron/
No 45 Sqn	www.raf.mod.uk/our-organisation/squadrons/45-squadron/
No 47 Sqn	www.raf.mod.uk/our-organisation/squadrons/47-squadron/
No 51 Sqn	www.raf.mod.uk/our-organisation/squadrons/51-squadron/
No 54 Sqn	www.raf.mod.uk/our-organisation/squadrons/54-squadron/
No 56 Sqn	www.raf.mod.uk/our-organisation/squadrons/56-squadron/
No 57 Sqn	www.raf.mod.uk/our-organisation/squadrons/lvii-squadron/
No 60 Sqn	www.raf.mod.uk/our-organisation/squadrons/60-squadron/
No 70 Sqn	www.raf.mod.uk/our-organisation/squadrons/lxx-squadron/
No 72 Sqn	www.raf.mod.uk/our-organisation/squadrons/72-squadron/
No 84 Sqn	www.raf.mod.uk/our-organisation/squadrons/84-squadron/
No 92 Sqn	www.raf.mod.uk/our-organisation/squadrons/92-squadron/
No 99 Sqn	www.raf.mod.uk/our-organisation/squadrons/99-squadron/
No 100 Sqn	www.raf.mod.uk/our-organisation/squadrons/100-squadron/
No 101 Sqn	www.raf.mod.uk/our-organisation/squadrons/101-squadron/
No 115 Sqn	www.raf.mod.uk/our-organisation/squadrons/115-squadron/
No 120 Sqn	www.raf.mod.uk/our-organisation/squadrons/120-squadron/
No 202 Sqn	www.raf.mod.uk/our-organisation/squadrons/202-squadron/
No 206 Sqn	www.raf.mod.uk/our-organisation/squadrons/206-squadron/
No 230 Sqn	www.raf.mod.uk/our-organisation/squadrons/230-squadron/
No 617 Sqn	www.raf.mod.uk/our-organisation/squadrons/617-squadron/
No 700X NAS	www.royalnavy.mod.uk/our-organisation/the-fighting-arms/fleet-air-arm/support-and-training/700x-naval-air-squadron
No 703 NAS	www.royalnavy.mod.uk/our-organisation/the-fighting-arms/fleet-air-arm/support-and-training/703-naval-air-squadron
No 705 NAS	www.royalnavy.mod.uk/our-organisation/the-fighting-arms/fleet-air-arm/support-and-training/705-naval-air-squadron

Name of Site	Web Address All prefixed 'http://')
No 727 NAS	www.royalnavy.mod.uk/our-organisation/the-fighting-arms/fleet-air-arm/support-and-training/727-naval-air-squadron
No 736 NAS	www.royalnavy.mod.uk/our-organisation/the-fighting-arms/fleet-air-arm/hawk-jets/736-naval-air-squadron
No 750 NAS	www.royalnavy.mod.uk/our-organisation/the-fighting-arms/fleet-air-arm/support-and-training/750-naval-air-squadron
No 809 NAS	www.royalnavy.mod.uk/our-organisation/the-fighting-arms/fleet-air-arm/future-aircraft/809-naval-air-squadron
No 814 NAS	www.royalnavy.mod.uk/our-organisation/the-fighting-arms/fleet-air-arm/helicopter-squadrons/merlin-mk2/814-naval-air-squadron
No 815 NAS	www.royalnavy.mod.uk/our-organisation/the-fighting-arms/fleet-air-arm/helicopter-squadrons/wildcat/815-naval-air-squadron
No 820 NAS	www.royalnavy.mod.uk/our-organisation/the-fighting-arms/fleet-air-arm/helicopter-squadrons/merlin-mk2/820-naval-air-squadron
No 824 NAS	www.royalnavy.mod.uk/our-organisation/the-fighting-arms/fleet-air-arm/helicopter-squadrons/merlin-mk2/824-naval-air-squadron
No 825 NAS	www.royalnavy.mod.uk/our-organisation/the-fighting-arms/fleet-air-arm/helicopter-squadrons/wildcat/825-naval-air-squadron
No 845 NAS	www.royalnavy.mod.uk/our-organisation/the-fighting-arms/fleet-air-arm/helicopter-squadrons/merlin-mk-3/845-naval-air-squadron
No 846 NAS	www.royalnavy.mod.uk/our-organisation/the-fighting-arms/fleet-air-arm/helicopter-squadrons/merlin-mk-3/846-naval-air-squadron
No 847 NAS	www.royalnavy.mod.uk/our-organisation/the-fighting-arms/fleet-air-arm/helicopter-squadrons/wildcat/847-naval-air-squadron
The Army Air Corps	www.army.mod.uk/who-we-are/corps-regiments-and-units/army-air-corps/
Fleet Air Arm	www.royalnavy.mod.uk/our-organisation/the-fighting-arms/fleet-air-arm
Ministry of Defence	www.gov.uk/government/organisations/ministry-of-defence
QinetiQ	www.qinetiq.com/
RAF Akrotiri	www.raf.mod.uk/our-organisation/stations/raf-akrotiri/
RAF Benson	www.raf.mod.uk/our-organisation/stations/raf-benson/
RAF Brize Norton	www.raf.mod.uk/our-organisation/stations/raf-brize-norton/
RAF College Cranwell	www.raf.mod.uk/our-organisation/stations/raf-college-cranwell/
RAF Coningsby	www.raf.mod.uk/our-organisation/stations/raf-coningsby/
Coningsby Aviation Site (unofficial)	milky01.co.uk/
RAF Cosford	www.raf.mod.uk/our-organisation/stations/raf-cosford/
RAF Leeming	www.raf.mod.uk/our-organisation/stations/raf-leeming/
RAF Linton-on-Ouse	www.raf.mod.uk/our-organisation/stations/raf-linton-on-ouse/
RAF Lossiemouth	www.raf.mod.uk/our-organisation/stations/raf-lossiemouth/
RAF Marham	www.raf.mod.uk/our-organisation/stations/raf-marham/
RAF Mount Pleasant	www.raf.mod.uk/our-organisation/stations/raf-mount-pleasant/
RAF Northolt	www.raf.mod.uk/our-organisation/stations/raf-northolt/
RAF Odiham	www.raf.mod.uk/our-organisation/stations/raf-odiham/
RAF Scampton	www.raf.mod.uk/our-organisation/stations/raf-scampton/
RAF Shawbury	www.raf.mod.uk/our-organisation/stations/raf-shawbury/
RAF Syerston	www.raf.mod.uk/our-organisation/stations/raf-syerston/
RAF Valley	www.raf.mod.uk/our-organisation/stations/raf-valley/
RAF Waddington	www.raf.mod.uk/our-organisation/stations/raf-waddington/
RAF Wittering	www.raf.mod.uk/our-organisation/stations/raf-wittering/
RAF Woodvale	www.raf.mod.uk/our-organisation/stations/raf-woodvale/
RAF Wyton	www.raf.mod.uk/our-organisation/stations/raf-wyton/
Red Arrows	www.raf.mod.uk/display-teams/red-arrows/
Royal Air Force	www.raf.mod.uk/
University Air Squadrons	www.raf.mod.uk/our-organisation/university-air-squadrons/

MILITARY SITES-US

Air Combat Command	www.acc.af.mil/
Air Force Reserve Command	www.afrc.af.mil/
Air National Guard	www.ang.af.mil/
Aviano Air Base	www.aviano.af.mil/
Liberty Wing Home Page (48th FW)	www.lakenheath.af.mil/
NASA	www.nasa.gov/
Mildenhall	www.mildenhall.af.mil/

Name of Site	Web Address All prefixed 'http://')
Ramstein Air Base	www.ramstein.af.mil/
Spangdahlem Air Base	www.spangdahlem.af.mil/
USAF	www.af.mil/
USAF Europe	www.usafe.af.mil/
USAF World Wide Web Sites	www.af.mil/AF-Sites/
US Army	www.army.mil/
US Marine Corps	www.marines.mil/
US Navy	www.navy.mil/
US Navy Patrol Squadrons (unofficial)	www.vpnavy.com/
MILITARY SITES-ELSEWHERE	
Armée de l'Air	www.defense.gouv.fr/air/
Aeronautica Militare	www.aeronautica.difesa.it
Austrian Armed Forces (in German)	www.bundesheer.at/
Finnish Defence Force	puolustusvoimat.fi/en/frontpage
Forca Aerea Portuguesa	www.emfa.pt/
German Marine	www.marine.de
Greek Air Force	www.haf.gr/en/
Irish Air Corps	www.military.ie/en/who-we-are/air-corps/
Luftforsvaret	forsvaret.no/en/
Luftwaffe	www.luftwaffe.de
NATO	www.nato.int/
Royal Australian Air Force	www.airforce.gov.au/
Royal Canadian Air Force	www.airforce.forces.gc.ca/
Royal Danish Air Force (in Danish)	www2.forsvaret.dk/Pages/forside.aspx
Royal Netherlands AF	www.defensie.nl/organisatie/luchtmacht
Royal New Zealand AF	www.airforce.mil.nz/
Singapore Air Force	www.mindef.gov.sg/web/portal/rsaf/home/
South African AF Site (unofficial)	www.saairforce.co.za/
Swedish Air Force	www.forsvarsmakten.se/sv/var-verksamhet/verksamhetsomraden/flygvapnet/
Turkish Air Force	www.hvkk.tsk.tr/Portal/Page/HvkkEN
AIRCRAFT & AERO ENGINE MANUFACTURERS	
Airbus Defence & Security	www.airbus.com/defence.html
BAE Systems	www.baesystems.com/
Beechcraft	beechcraft.txtav.com/
Bell	www.bellflight.com/
Boeing	www.boeing.com/
Bombardier	www.bombardier.com/
Britten-Norman	www.britten-norman.com/
Dassault	www.dassault-aviation.com/
Embraer	www.embraer.com/
General Electric	www.ge.com/
Grob Aircraft AG	grob-aircraft.com/en/
Gulfstream Aerospace	www.gulfstream.com/
Kaman Aerospace	www.kaman.com/
Leonardo	www.leonardocompany.com/
Lockheed Martin	www.lockheedmartin.com/
Rolls-Royce	www.rolls-royce.com/
Sikorsky	www.lockheedmartin.com/en-us/capabilities/sikorsky.html
UK AVIATION MUSEUMS	
Boscombe Down Aviation Collection, Old Sarum	www.boscombedownaviationcollection.co.uk/
Bournemouth Aviation Museum	www.bamhurn.org/
Brooklands Museum	www.brooklandsmuseum.com/
City of Norwich Aviation Museum	www.cnam.org.uk/
de Havilland Aircraft Museum	www.dehavillandmuseum.co.uk/
Dumfries & Galloway Aviation Museum	www.dumfriesaviationmuseum.com/
Fleet Air Arm Museum	www.fleetairarm.com/
Gatwick Aviation Museum	gatwick-aviation-museum.co.uk/
IWM, Duxford	www.iwm.org.uk/visits/iwm-duxford
Imperial War Museum, Duxford (unofficial)	abetheaviator.wixsite.com/website/about

Name of Site	Web Address All prefixed 'http://')
The Jet Age Museum	jetagemuseum.org/
Lincs Aviation Heritage Centre	www.lincsaviation.co.uk/
Midland Air Museum	www.midlandairmuseum.co.uk/
Museum of Army Flying	www.armyflying.com/
Museum of Berkshire Aviation	www.museumofberkshireaviation.co.uk/
Museum of Science & Industry, Manchester	www.scienceandindustrymuseum.org.uk/
National Museum of Flight, East Fortune	www.nms.ac.uk/national-museum-of-flight?item_id=
Newark Air Museum	www.newarkairmuseum.org/
North East Land, Sea & Air Museums	www.nelsam.org.uk/
RAF Museum, Cosford & Hendon	www.rafmuseum.org.uk/
Science Museum, South Kensington	www.sciencemuseum.org.uk/
South Yorkshire Aircraft Museum	www.southyorkshireaircraftmuseum.org.uk/
Yorkshire Air Museum, Elvington	www.yorkshireairmuseum.org/

AVIATION SOCIETIES

Air Britain	www.air-britain.com/
Air Yorkshire	www.airyorkshire.org.uk/
Aviation Heritage UK (was BAPC)	aviationheritageuk.org/
LAAS International	www.laasdata.com/
Military Aviation Review	militaryaviationreview.com/
Royal Aeronautical Society	www.aerosociety.com/
Scramble (Dutch Aviation Society)	www.scramble.nl/
Solent Aviation Society	www.solent-aviation-society.co.uk/
Spitfire Society	www.spitfiresociety.org/
The Aviation Society Manchester	www.tasmanchester.com/
Ulster Aviation Society	www.ulsteraviationsociety.org/
Wolverhampton Aviation Group	www.wolverhamptonaviationgroup.co.uk/

OPERATORS OF HISTORIC AIRCRAFT

The Aircraft Restoration Company	www.aircraftrestorationcompany.com/
Battle of Britain Memorial Flight	www.raf.mod.uk/display-teams/battle-of-britain-memorial-flight/
The Catalina Society	www.catalina.org.uk/
Hangar 11 Collection	www.hangar11.co.uk/
Historic Helicopters	www.historichelicopters.com/
Horizon Aircraft Services	www.horizonaircraftservices.com/
Navy Wings	www.navywings.org.uk/
The Fighter Collection	www.fighter-collection.com/
The Real Aeroplane Company	www.realaero.com/
The Shuttleworth Collection	www.shuttleworth.org/

SITES RELATING TO SPECIFIC TYPES OF MILITARY AIRCRAFT

The 655 Maintenance & Preservation Society	www.xm655.com/
B-24 Liberator	www.b24bestweb.com/
C-130 Hercules	www.c-130hercules.net/
EE Canberra	www.bywat.co.uk/
English Electric Lightning - Vertical Reality	www.aviation-picture-hangar.co.uk/Lightning.html
The Eurofighter site	www.eurofighter.com/
The ex FRADU Canberra Site	www.fradu-canberras.co.uk/
The ex FRADU Hunter Site	www.fradu-hunters.co.uk/
F-4 Phantom II Society	www.f4phantom.com/
F-16: The Complete Reference	www.f-16.net/
The Gripen	saab.com/gripen/
Jet Provost Heaven	www.jetprovosts.com
K5083 - Home Page (Hawker Hurricane)	www.k5083.mistral.co.uk/
Lockheed SR-71 Blackbird	www.wvi.com/~lelandh/sr-71~1.htm
The MiG-21 Page	www.topedge.com/panels/aircraft/sites/kraft/mig.htm
P-3 Orion Research Group	www.p3orion.nl/
Thunder & Lightnings (Postwar British Aircraft)	www.thunder-and-lightnings.co.uk/
UK Apache Resource Centre	www.ukapache.com/

Name of Site	Web Address All prefixed 'http://')
MISCELLANEOUS	
Aerodata Software Ltd.	www.aerodata.org/
AeroResource	www.aeroresource.co.uk/
The AirNet Web Site	www.aviation-links.co.uk/
Aviation Databases	www.aviationdatabases.com/
Delta Reflex	www.deltareflex.com/forum
Demobbed - Out of Service British Military Aircraft	demobbed.org.uk/
Euro Demobbed	www.eurodemobbed.org.uk/
Fighter Control	fightercontrol.co.uk/
Freebird Aviation Database	www.freebirddb.com/
Iconic Aircraft	www.iconicaircraft.co.uk/
Joseph F. Baugher's US Military Serials Site	www.joebaugher.com/
The 'Military Aircraft Markings' Web Site	www.militaryaircraftmarkings.co.uk/
Pacific Aviation Database Organisation	www.gfiapac.com/
PlaneBaseNG	www.planebase.biz/
Thunder & Lightnings: Airfield Viewing Guides	www.thunder-and-lightnings.co.uk/spotting/
UK Airshow Review	www.airshows.co.uk/
UK Military Aircraft Serials Resource Centre	www.ukserials.com/

While most of the fleet of RAF Typhoon FGR4s have had squadron markings removed, this one, ZK366, still wears the bars and tail badge of No 11 Squadron, based at RAF Coningsby.

ZJ130/O is a Merlin HC3i of 846 NAS, based at RNAS Yeovilton. The 'i' in its designation denotes the interim nature of this conversion, used as the Navy transitioned from the HC3 inherited from the RAF to the HC4, which is the full, navalised variant.

Serial	Type	Operator

Serial	Type	Operator

NEW MILITARY SERIALS LOG

Serial	Type	Operator